THE
ALASKA
WILDERNESS
GUIDE

8TH EDITION

A PUBLICATION OF THE MAGAZINE DIVISION
OF MORRIS COMMUNICATIONS CORPORATION

Cover photo by © Tom Bol

Managing Editor, Kris Valencia Graef
Communities Editor, Carol A. Phillips
Attractions Editor, Leah Burke
Design and Production, David L. Ranta
Advertising Sales, Nyla Simmons
Advertising Traffic, Sheryl Granger
General Manager, David C. Foster
Advertising Sales Director, Lea Cockerham
Circulation Director, Connie Cotner
Circulation Fulfillment, Fran Jarriel
Manufacturing Director, Kevin Miller

Publisher, William S. Morris III

Thanks: The Alaska Wilderness Guide wishes to thank the chambers of commerce, visitors bureaus, Native corporations and hundreds of individuals who provided information for this new edition. We also appreciate the tremendous assistance of the many state and federal government agencies who contributed their expertise to this edition, in particular the Alaska Dept. of Fish and Game, the Alaska Dept. of Natural Resources, the Alaska Dept. of Community and Economic Development, the U.S. Forest Service, the Bureau of Land Management, the U.S. Fish and Wildlife Service and the National Park Service.

To order copies of *The ALASKA WILDERNESS GUIDE* and related books, phone 1-800-726-4707; e-mail: books@themilepost.com; or visit our book catalog at www.themilepost.com.

The *ALASKA WILDERNESS GUIDE* is a publication of Morris Communications Corporation, 735 Broad Street, Augusta, GA 30901.

Editoral and Advertising Sales office: 619 E. Ship Creek, Suite 329, Anchorage, AK 99501; phone (907) 272-6070; fax (907) 258-5360.

ISBN 1-892154-09-9 ISSN 1070-003X
Key title: The Alaska Wilderness Guide
Printed in U.S.A.

First Edition (1986)
The Alaska Wilderness MILEPOST

Second Edition (1987)
The Alaska Wilderness MILEPOST

Third Edition (1988)
The Alaska Wilderness MILEPOST

Fourth Edition (1989)
The Alaska Wilderness MILEPOST

Fifth Edition (1990)
The Alaska Wilderness MILEPOST

Sixth Edition (1991)
The Alaska Wilderness MILEPOST

Seventh Edition (1993)
The Alaska Wilderness Guide

 A PUBLICATION OF THE MAGAZINE DIVISION OF MORRIS COMMUNICATIONS CORPORATION

CONTENTS

INTRODUCTION

Welcome to Alaska's wilderness. Welcome to "The Bush." A word originally used to describe large expanses of wilderness inhabited by trappers and miners, today "the Bush" is any part of Alaska inaccessible by road, but accessible on foot, by dog team, snow machine, bush plane or boat. Humorist and former *ALASKA Magazine* columnist Mike Doogan defined The Bush as "an area of small towns and smaller villages surrounded by lots and lots of nothing."

For those people eager to see backcountry Alaska, whether it's a Bush village hundreds of miles from any major population center, or a wilderness lake a few hour's hike from the highway, The Alaska Wilderness Guide offers some very basic guidance on where to go.

The Alaska Wilderness Guide will help you plan your trip to Alaska's remote bush communities, parks and wildlife refuges; point you in the direction of hiking trails and floatable rivers; and (we hope) answer any questions you may have on the many aspects of wilderness travel and recreation in Alaska's Bush.

Information in this guide is organized by geographic region (see map), beginning with Southeast, the most southerly region; moving northward to Southcentral; then down through Southwestern; over to Western Alaska; around through Arctic; and finally ending with the Interior. Each region begins with a Communities section, an alphabetical listing of bush communities within that region. The community descriptions include basic information on population, transportation, climate, emergency services, airstrips and visitor facilities, as well as details of geography, history and lifestyle of the people.

Following the region's community descriptions is the region's Attractions section. Here you will find helpful information about national and state parks, national forests and wildlife refuges, river running, fishing, recreation cabins, hiking trails and special features such as lighthouses, hot springs, and geographical and historical sites. The introduction to each region's Attractions section includes an index of destinations by activity. For information on regional providers of goods and services for recreational wilderness travel, check the Travel Directory for that region. (Keep in mind that Travel Directory listings are by no means comprehensive, and we urge readers to thoroughly research the categories of interest to them when planning a trip.)

We have made a sincere effort to supply complete, accurate and current information to help you plan a successful wilderness trip. The publisher cannot be responsible for changes which may have taken place between the time our research was done and the date of your trip.

SOUTHEAST

A lush northern rain forest of incomparable beauty, Alaska's Southeast is a land where eagles soar, whales flourish and brown bears roam at will. Dramatic tidewater glaciers, spectacular fjords, massive ice fields and rugged mountains bear the imprint of the last ice age. A rich cultural mix of Natives, Russians and gold prospectors enlivens the history of the region.

Southeast's mighty Indian cultures ruled the region when the first white men, the Russians, came on the scene. After several skirmishes, the Russians won a foothold in the area and made Sitka, known as Nova Arkhangelsk or New Archangel, the capital of Russian America. After the United States purchase of Alaska from Russia in 1867, mining, fishing and timber provided the economic base.

Southeast remained Alaska's dominant region until WWII, when military activity and construction of the Alaska Highway shifted the focus to Anchorage and Fairbanks.

Today fishing, government, tourism and timber fuel Southeast's economy. Seven population centers and hundreds of small settlements dot the region's shoreline. About 20 percent of Southeast's population is Native, predominantly Tlingit, Haida and Tsimshian. Most of the Haidas live near Hydaburg and the Tsimshians make their home at Metlakatla.

Amid the breathtaking beauty and the rich history of Southeast, opportunities for outdoor adventure are endless. The protected waterways offer a lifetime of bays, fjords and channels to explore and some of the finest fishing in Alaska. Whale watching, river rafting, hiking and hunting, skiing the ice fields or retreating to a snug lodge in a secluded cove are other popular pursuits.

Location: Southeast Alaska stretches 560 miles from Dixon Entrance at the U.S.-Canada border south of Ketchikan to Icy Bay northwest of Yakutat.

Geography: Geological activity has sculpted more than a thousand islands in Southeast, including Prince of Wales, the country's third largest (after Hawaii and Kodiak) at 2,231 square miles. The region's narrow strip of mainland is isolated from the rest of North America by the St. Elias and Coast mountains. The St. Elias, topping out at 18,008 feet at the summit of Mount St. Elias, is the highest coastal range in the world. Numerous rivers drain this steep, wet land. Among the more important are the Stikine and the Taku, which breach the mountain barrier and provide some access into the Interior.

Heavy rainfall and a mild climate encourage timber growth. Three-quarters of Southeast is covered with dense forests, primarily western hemlock and Sitka spruce, interspersed with red cedar and Alaska yellow cedar. Ground cover is luxuriant and includes devil's club, blueberries, huckleberries, mosses and ferns. Tongass National Forest, largest national forest in the United States, encompasses 16.9 million acres, or more than 73 percent of the land in southeastern Alaska.

Climate: Warmed by ocean currents, Southeast enjoys mild, warm temperatures averaging around 60°F in the summer. Winters are cool, alternating snow, rain and sunshine; January temperatures average 20°F to 40°F. Subzero winter temperatures are uncommon.

The region experiences considerable annual rainfall, from 80 to more than 200 inches, with the heaviest rains in late fall and the lightest in summer. Populated areas receive from 30 to 200 inches of snow annually; the high mountains get more than 400 inches a year.

Wildlife: Southeast has prime habitat for Sitka blacktail deer, bears and wolves. Brown bears inhabit Admiralty, Baranof and Chichagof island and portions of the mainland. Black bears roam on other forested islands and the mainland. Moose browse in scattered populations, and mountain goats scale the steep cliffs of Glacier Bay and other mountainous areas.

Furbearers and nongame species in Southeast include lynx, wolverine, coyote, fox, mink, beaver, muskrat, river otter, marten, porcupine, an occasional fisher and an assortment of small mammals.

Marine mammals abound in the region. Humpback and killer whales, sea lions and seals are often seen in season in many waterways.

Southeast boasts the largest bald eagle population in the world. Thousands congregate each fall at the Alaska Chilkat Bald Eagle Preserve near Haines. Waterfowl pass through the area during migration, with huge flocks congregating on the Stikine Flats and near other estuaries.

Salmon, halibut, black cod, shellfish, herring, steelhead, trout, grayling— Southeast has some of the world's finest fishing, both sport and commercial.

Angoon

GPS: N57°30' W134°35'

Located on the west coast of Admiralty Island on Chatham Strait, at the mouth of Kootznahoo Inlet, 55 miles southwest of Juneau, 41 miles northeast of Sitka. **Transportation:** Scheduled ferry service via Alaska Marine Highway; scheduled seaplane service from Juneau. **Population:** 616 (82 percent Native). **Zip code:** 99820. **Emergency Services:** Police, Volunteer Fire Department, phone (907) 788-3631; EMS/Ambulance/Angoon Health Clinic, phone (907) 788-3411.

Elevation: Sea level. **Climate:** Moderate maritime weather, with monthly mean temperatures of 28°F in January and 55°F in July. Annual rainfall is 40 inches.

Private Aircraft: Angoon seaplane base; 0.9 mile southeast.

Private Boats: Fuel service (gas and diesel) and transient moorage are available at boat harbor. Port Official: Paul Thomas, phone (907) 788-3653, fax (907) 788-3821.

NOTE: Angoon prohibits the possession of alcoholic beverages.

Visitor Facilities: Accommodations are available at Favorite Bay Inn/Whalers Cove Sports Fishing Lodge, (907) 788-3125; and Kootznahoo Inlet Lodge, (907) 788-3501. Groceries and supplies are available at Angoon Trading Co., (907) 788-3111. Angoon Community Assoc. operates a laundry. No banking services. Fishing/hunting licenses may be purchased locally. Charter fishing boats and canoes are available; no other rental transportation.

Angoon is a long-established Tlingit Indian settlement at the entrance to Kootznahoo Inlet (pronounced Hu-che-nu). It is the only permanent community on Admiralty Island. On Killisnoo Island, across the harbor from the state ferry landing at Angoon, a community of summer homes has grown along the island beaches. The lifestyle of this primarily Tlingit town is heavily subsistence: fish, shellfish, seaweed, berries, geese, deer and bears. Commercial fishing, mostly hand trolling for king and coho salmon, is the principal industry. Unemployment in Angoon is high throughout the year.

The scenery of Admiralty Island draws many visitors to Angoon. The island boasts the largest nesting population of eagles anywhere. Angoon and vicinity offer exceptional feeding areas for killer and humpback whales and excellent saltwater and freshwater fishing. All but the northern portion of the island is a national monument, managed by the U.S. Forest Service.

Kootznahoo Inlet and Mitchell Bay near Angoon offer a network of small wooded islands, reefs and channels for kayaking. Wildlife includes many Sitka blacktail deer and brown bears (Admiralty Island's Indian name Kootznoowoo means "Fortress of Bears").

Ask local residents for directions to the interesting old Killisnoo graveyards, located both on Killisnoo Island and on the Angoon shore of the old Killisnoo settlement, once one of the larger communities in southeastern Alaska.

Community Services: Communications include phones in most households (and CB radios for local communication), daily mail service by plane, good radio reception and TV via satellite and cable. There are churches and a school with grades kindergarten through 12 with enrollment of 154. Community electric power, water and sewage systems are available. Freight comes in by barge and ferry. Government address: City of Angoon, P.O. Box 189, Angoon, AK

99820, phone (907) 788-3653, fax (907) 788-3821. Village corporation: Kootznoowoo Inc., 8585 Old Dairy Road #201, Juneau, AK 99801, phone (907) 790-2992, fax (907) 790-2995. Village council: Angoon Community Assoc., P.O. Box 188, Angoon, AK 99820, phone (907) 788-3411, fax (907) 788-3412, e-mail: Angoon@aitc.org.

Coffman Cove

GPS: N56°01' W132°50'

Located on the northeast coast of Prince of Wales Island, 53 miles north of Klawock, 42 miles southeast of Wrangell, and 73 miles northeast of Ketchikan. **Transportation**: Accessible via Prince of Wales Island road system and by boat; daily floatplane service from Ketchikan; weekly service from Wrangell. **Population**: 200. **Zip code**: 99918. **Emergency Services**: Alaska State Troopers in Klawock, phone (907) 755-2955; Coffman Cove Fire/EMS, phone (907) 329-2209/2213/2302; Prince of Wales Island Area EMS, phone (907) 826-2367/3330.

Elevation: 10 feet. **Climate**: Cool and rainy, with average temperatures of 32°F in winter, 55°F in summer.

Private Aircraft: Floatplane landings only. Nearest airstrip is in Klawock.

Private Boats: Diesel and regular gas and propane are available, as is skiff rental. There is a state dock.

Visitor Facilities: Overnight lodging is offered at Coffman Cove Cabins, (907) 329-2251; and Rain Country B&B, (907) 329-2274. Oceanview RV Park/Campground, (907) 329-2015, has a bunkhouse and RV hookups. Groceries and supplies are available at the Riggin' Shack, (907) 329-2213. No banking services. Arts and crafts and gift items, including wood carvings, paintings, Indian beadwork, leather work and jewelry made by local artists, may be purchased. Fishing/ hunting licenses and fishing charters are available. Tire repair and car rental are available.

Coffman Cove was a family logging community, one of the largest independent camps in Southeast. Formerly owned and operated by Mike and Leta Valentine, the camp was in operation in this area for about 23 years. Housing consists of mobile homes and stick-built structures. Outdoor recreation includes hunting (deer and bear), good fishing in area lakes and streams, boating, hiking, and photography.

Coffman Cove has fresh air, clean water and other advantages, but residents also know the disadvantages of seasonal work, a faltering timber industry and a lack of some conveniences taken for granted by people in larger communities.

Coffman Cove is now incorporated. Communications include phones, mail plane, radio and TV. There is a Roman Catholic church and 2 Protestant churches here, all served by itinerant clergy. Coffman Cove's school has grades 1 through 12 with enrollment of 31. The community has electrical power, water and sewage systems. Freight arrives by cargo plane, barge, ship and by road from Craig. Government address: City of Coffman Cove, P.O. Box 18135, Coffman Cove, AK 99918, phone (907) 329-2233, fax (907) 329-2212; e-mail: coffman@coveconnect.com; Web: http://www.coffmancove.org/.

Visitor Information: Prince of Wales Chamber of Commerce, P.O. Box 497, Craig, AK 99921, phone (907) 826-3870, fax (907) 826-5467, e-mail: powcc@aptaaska.net; Web: http://www.princeofwalescoc.org.

Craig

GPS: N55°28' W133°09'

Located on the west side of Prince of Wales Island, 31 road miles west of Hollis, 60 air miles west of Ketchikan, at the south end of Klawock Inlet across from Fish Egg Island. **Transportation**: Air taxi service from Ketchikan; ferry from Ketchikan to Hollis and by road from Hollis to Craig. **Population**: 2,124. **Zip code**: 99921. **Emergency Services**: Police, Fire Department, phone 911; Public Health Nurse, phone (907) 826-3433, or Seaview Medical Center, phone (907) 826-3257; Craig EMS, phone (907) 826-2367/3330. Dentist and chiropractor available. Pharmacy, phone (907) 826-5646.

Elevation: 10 feet. **Climate:** Maritime with cool, moist, cloudy weather. Average temperature in January is 34°F; in July it is 56°F. Mean monthly precipitation ranges from 3.62 inches in June to 14.88 inches in October. Annual precipitation is 120 inches, including 40 inches of snow.

Private Aircraft: Seaplane base adjacent north; fuel 80. Airstrip located 7 miles north at Klawock; fuel 80, Av gas; transportation to Craig provided by airlines.

Private Boats: Marine repair, marine gas, diesel, propane, regular and unleaded gasoline also available. Transient moorage at the city harbor. Harbormaster: Michael Kampnich, phone (907) 826-3404, fax (907) 826-3278.

Visitor Facilities: A full range of goods and services is available in Craig including overnight accommodations, restaurants and bars, a supermarket, a general store, liquor store, gift shops, a laundromat, clothing and hardware stores, gas stations and beauty salons. Lodgings include Haida Way Lodge, (907) 347-4625; Dreamcatcher bed and breakfast, (888) 897-8167; and Sunnahae Lodge, (907) 826-4000. Waterfront lodging is available at Alaska Best Fishing, Inc., (888) 826-8500. Rain Country RV offers full hookups, (907) 826-3632. You'll find fishing, hunting and camping supplies at Log Cabin Sporting Goods, (888) 265-0375. Banking services available. Fishing and hunting trips can be arranged locally. Major repair services available in town. Rental transportation is available at TLC, (907) 826-2966; it is also possible to arrange for rental cars to be delivered to Craig via Wilderness Car Rental in Klawock, (907) 755-2691.

Craig was once a temporary fish camp for the Tlingit and Haida people of this region. In 1907, with the help of local Haidas, Craig Millar established a saltery at Fish Egg Island. A permanent saltery and cold storage facility and about 2 dozen homes were built between 1908 and 1911 at the city's present location, and the settlement was named for its

founder. In 1912, the year the post office was established, E.M. Streeter opened a sawmill, and Craig constructed a salmon cannery, both of which peaked during WWI. Craig was incorporated in 1922, and continued to grow throughout the 1930s, with some families from the Dust Bowl relocating to this Prince of Wales Island community.

Although the salmon industry has both prospered and foundered over the years, fishing still accounts for about half of the employment in Craig today. Timber harvesting on the island contributed jobs in logging and timber processing in past years, but the timber industry has been severely impacted recently and is comparatively small now. There is employment in government, construction and tourism.

Craig has become a service center for Prince of Wales Island, which is drawing an increasing number of visitors each year for its sportfishing and wildlife, both made more accessible by the extensive island road system.

Fishing on the island includes steelhead in spring and midwinter; rainbow, Dolly Varden and cutthroat trout from spring through fall; pink salmon, July through August; silver and chum salmon, August to October; king salmon, May to October; and rockfish, halibut and cod all season. A salmon derby runs April through July 1, with prizes including trips to Hawaii and Europe.

Wildlife, particularly black bear and deer, is abundant on Prince of Wales Island. Crab Bay, within the Craig city limits, is one of the major resting and feeding areas for migratory waterfowl and shorebirds in southeastern Alaska. At low tide, visitors can hike around Cemetery Island, beachcomb and explore tide pools.

Prince of Wales Island's road system provides good access to remote locations for fishing, hiking, berry picking and hunting.

Communications in Craig include phones, mail plane, radio and TV. The community has 3 churches; a school district (elementary and high school) with enrollment of 527; a library; and public electric power, water and sewage systems. Freight arrives by cargo plane, barge and by ferry to and from Hollis. Government address: City of Craig, P.O. Box 725, Craig, AK 99921; phone (907) 826-3275, fax (907) 826-3278, e-mail: tbriggs@aptalaska.net. Village corporation: Shaan-Seet Inc., P.O. Box 690, Craig, AK 99921, phone (907) 826-3251, fax (907) 826-3980, e-mail: ssinc@ptialaska.net. Prince of Wales Chamber of Commerce, P.O. Box 497, Craig, AK 99921, phone (907) 826-3870, fax (907) 826-5467, e-mail: powcvc@aptalaska.net, Web: http://princeofwalescoc.org.

Cube Cove

GPS: N57°56' W134°45'

Located on Cube Cove, on northwest coast of Admiralty Island, 20 miles southwest of Juneau. **Transportation:** Boat or seaplane. **Population:** 139. **Emergency Services:** Alaska State Troopers in Juneau; logging camp EMT.

Elevation: Sea level.

Private Aircraft: Floatplane landings only.

Visitor Facilities: A privately operated logging camp. Formerly known as Eight Fathom Bight. No accommodations or visitor services. Telephone available.

Community Services: There is one school with enrollment of 20.

Dolomi

GPS: N55°08' W132°03'

Located in Port Johnson on the southeast side of Prince of Wales Island, 20 miles from Metlakatla, 27 miles from Ketchikan, due east of Hydaburg. **Transportation:** Charter seaplane from Metlakatla or Ketchikan; by boat. **Population:** 200. **Zip code:** 99926. **Emergency Services:** Alaska State Troopers and hospital in Ketchikan; emergency aid available at Camp Dolomi.

Elevation: Sea level. **Climate:** Typical Southeast weather, cool and rainy.

Private Aircraft: Floatplane landings on Port Johnson.

Private Boats: Emergency accommo-

dations only; diesel fuel may be available.

Visitor Facilities: Originally a mining town established around the turn of the century, Dolomi is now a floating logging camp owned by Long Island Development, which provides a bunkhouse and cookhouse for residents. There are no visitor accommodations or services. Emergency accommodations and meals may be available. Supplies are obtained in Ketchikan. There are no tourist attractions, but excellent fishing and deer hunting in the area are reported. Communications at the camp are provided by mail plane and radio. There is a school with grades 1 through 8.

Dora Bay

GPS: N55°13' W132°14'

Located on Moira Sound, southeast side of Prince of Wales Island, 40 miles southeast of Craig. **Transportation:** Charter plane or private boat. **Population:** 10. **Zip code:** via Ketchikan. **Emergency Services:** Police in Ketchikan, phone (907) 225-6631; hospital in Ketchikan, (907) 225-5171; Emergency only for police and medical personnel: phone 911.

Elevation: Sea level. **Climate:** Typical Southeast, cool and rainy.

Private Aircraft: Floatplane landings only.

Visitor Facilities: This floating logging camp, previously located at Neets Bay, is operated by J.R. Gildersleeve Logging Co. The camp has no visitor facilities except for a radiophone.

Edna Bay

GPS: N55°57' W133°40'

Located on Edna Bay at the southeast end of Kosciusko Island off the northwest coast of Prince of Wales Island, 45 miles north of Craig, 90 miles northwest of Ketchikan. **Transportation:** By boat or floatplane. **Population:** 55. **Zip code:** 99825. **Emergency Services:** For medical emergencies, contact the U.S. Coast Guard, VHF radio channel 16; Alaska State Troopers in Ketchikan, contact by VHF radio; Edna Bay Health Clinic; Edna Bay EMS, phone (907) 594-6335; Prince of Wales Island Area EMS/Ambulance, phone (907) 826-2367/3330.

Elevation: Sea level. **Climate**: Cool and wet.

Private Aircraft: Floatplane landings only.

Visitor Facilities: Edna Bay is primarily a fishing community with no visitor facilities or services. (A fish buyer is located in the bay in the summer.) Supplies are brought in by cargo plane or boat from Craig, Ketchikan or Petersburg, and supplies and groceries are available at the Cedar Bite Trading Post. Many logging roads can be used for hunting. Communications are by mail plane, radio and community phone, (907) 594-9001.

Eight Fathom Bight

(See Cube Cove)

Elfin Cove

GPS: N58°11' W136°20'

Located at the northern tip of Chichagof Island, 70 miles west of Juneau, 33 miles northwest of Hoonah and in sight of Cape Spencer. **Transportation**: By seaplane or boat. **Population**: 10 in winter, 250 in summer. **Zip code**: 99825. **Emergency Services**: Elfin Cove EMT Shirley phone (907) 239-2246; Bartlett Regional Hospital in Juneau, phone (907) 586-2611; Alaska State Troopers in Juneau, phone (907) 465-4000, and in Hoonah, phone (907) 945-3655; Coast Guard, phone 1-800-478-5555. No emergency 911 available in Elfin Cove.

Elevation: 20 feet. **Climate**: Cool and wet in summer, with a mean monthly temperature in July of 54°F and 4.98 inches of precipitation. Precipitation averages 9.54 inches in January, with low temperatures to 28°F.

Private Aircraft: Floatplane dock and small seadrome, used by scheduled and commercial aircraft. Fuel available emergency only. Private moorage available. *CAUTION: Westerly swells and downdrafts on approach.*

Private Boats: Marine fuels and propane available at fuel dock. Public

floats are all transient, and private moorage is available. Marine repairs available in Pelican.

Visitor Facilities: Many services in Elfin Cove are seasonal. Lodging is available at The Hobbit Hole Guesthouse, offering commodious housing, summer and winter, (907) 723-8514 or (907) 697-2580; South Pass Lodging: Sandy Craig offers sightseeing and wildlife charters, (907) 239-2255; Gull Cove Lodge: Paul Johnson, a professional guide, offers custom bear photography tours, summer, (907) 697-2720; winter, (907) 789-0944. South Pass Outfitters: Dennis Montgomery rents cabins and boats, (907) 697-2507. Sportfishing packages are available at: Elfin Cove Sport Fishing Lodge, summer, (907) 239-2212; anytime, 1-800-422-2824; Cross Sound Lodge, summer, (907) 239-2210; winter, (907) 766-3104; Fishmaster's Inn, (907) 239-2209; Tanaku Lodge, summer, (907) 239-2205; winter, 1-800-482-6258; Inner Harbor Lodge, summer, (907) 239-2245; winter, (541) 742-4031; Eagle Charters, summer, (907) 239-2242; winter, (360) 750-1336; Cove Lodge, summer, (907) 239-2221; anytime, 1-800-382-3847; Shearwater Lodge, (907) 239-2223; Angler's Choice, (907) 789-0051; Northern Star Lodge, summer, (907) 239-2250; winter, 1-888-809-2626. Web pages for most of the above can be found on the Internet. Elfin General Supply has groceries, package store, laundromat, showers and sauna, (907) 239-2236. Coho's Bar & Grill has overnight accommodations, (907) 239-2246. Jim's Hardware & Bait, (907) 239-2240; Patti's Salmon Smoker, (907) 239-2244; Elfin Cove Oysters, (907) 239-2222, provide a variety of goods. Post office, public telephone, gift shops and a notary public, fishing gear, boat electronics and marine hardware are available. No banking services, no public TV, and radio reception is poor, although cell phones work. Fishing/hunting licenses are available. Good fresh water is available on floats. There is a picnic area with fire pit and volleyball court, a monument of Ernie Swanson, founder of Elfin Cove, and a children's playground area. Tongass

National Forest is within walking distance; however, there is no developed campground site or garbage dump.

Elfin Cove is uniquely situated on Cross Sound, known for good fishing. The cove is protected from wide-open ocean by several islands of historical interest from World War II. There is spectacular scenery with a view of the Fairweather Range and Brady Glacier looming above Cross Sound waters. Elfin Cove's protected, flask-shaped harbor was originally called "Gunkhole," meaning safe, quiet anchorage, by fishermen anchoring here. With its proximity to the fishing grounds, it became a natural spot for fish buyers and a supply point for fishermen. Ernie Swanson began buying fish here in the late 1920s and recruited people with necessary skills to build a town. When his wife Ruth applied for a post office in 1936, she gave it the new name of Elfin Cove, saying that at times the inner harbor was so still and misty that one could imagine little elves running around. (According to legend, the Tlingits who visited the harbor would not winter over because of "evil spirits" there.) John Lowell, another fish buyer, arrived in the 1940s and built a second dock, a warehouse, store and restaurant.

Boardwalks and trails connect everything at Elfin Cove. Most structures are multilevel due to the scarcity of private land, and many structures are built on pilings over the water. The community becomes active during the summer when local businesses serve the commercial fishing fleet and guests fill the sportfishing lodges. While most local people are fishermen or depend on the commercial fishing industry for a living, the area's scenery, sportfishing and other recreation are drawing an increasing number of tourists. There is year-round bottom fish and halibut fishing. Clamming has declined due to competition from sea otters, which returned to the area in the mid-1980s. There is also salmon fishing in season. Local activities besides fishing include hiking, berry picking, rock climbing, mushrooming, scuba diving, exploring, beach combing, kayaking,

photography, scenery, wildlife and sea life. Glacier Bay National Park is an hour's skiff ride, and within 20 minutes by skiff are the Port Althorp Bear Preserve, the Port Althorp Cannery site and the WWII cannon emplacement on George's Island.

Communications at Elfin Cove, which is unincorporated, include phones, mail plane and VHF radio. Messages may be phoned in to Elfin Cove Travel, (907) 239-2202. There is community water and power but no public sewer system. Freight comes in by plane or by boat. Community nonprofit: Elfin Cove Community Council, P.O. Box 1, Elfin Cove, AK 99825, phone (907) 239-2222, fax (907) 239-2224.

Excursion Inlet

GPS: N58°23' W135°26'

Located 38 miles northwest of Juneau, due east of Gustavus, at the mouth of Excursion Inlet off Icy Strait. **Transportation:** By boat or plane. **Population:** 350 in summer, 3 or 4 in winter. **Zip code:** 99850. **Emergency Services:** Hospital and Alaska State Troopers in Juneau.

Elevation: Sea level.

Climate: Cool and wet.

Private Aircraft: Seaplane base. Dirt road near cannery serves as airstrip. Use caution in strong SE winds.

Private Boats: Marine gas, diesel, propane and regular gasoline available in summer. Boats may be tied to SPB dock/float ramp. Transient moorage available at Excursion Inlet Dock; fuel available at Excursion Inlet Cannery dock.

Visitor Facilities: Excursion Inlet Packing Co. camp, phone (907) 945-3203, operates here in summer, and the company store (also known as Coho Mercantile) stocks clothing, first-aid supplies, hardware, film and sporting goods. Fishing/hunting licenses may be purchased. No overnight accommodations or food service for visitors. Communications in summer include phones, mail plane, radio and TV. Freight comes in by barge and ship.

Funter Bay

GPS: N58°26' W134°53'

Located 19 miles southwest of Juneau at the north end of Admiralty Island.

Transportation: By boat or plane. **Population:** 10 to 20. **Zip code:** 99850. **Emergency Services:** Hospital and Alaska State Troopers in Juneau.

Elevation: Sea level. **Climate:** Cool and wet.

Private Aircraft: Floatplane landings only with dock.

Private Boats: 2 public dock facilities and 2 coves in the bay for anchoring small boats.

Visitor Facilities: Joe and Karey Giefer, 4 Crab Cove, Funter Bay, AK 99850, phone (907) 789-4786, rent their guest house with meals or on a housekeeping basis. Boat charters are available with an emphasis on whales, eagles and brown bears. Advance reservations are required. Fishing licenses may be purchased in Funter Bay. Service is seasonal.

Funter Bay is an important anchorage and the site of an abandoned cannery, gold mine and World War II Aleut relocation camp. The cemetery provides interesting glimpses of the lives and deaths of some of those Aleuts. This area is the site of a state marine park. There are some summer cabins at Funter Bay. Most of the permanent residents are commercial fishermen. Funter Bay is not just a remarkable place to visit; it's a wonderful place to live and raise a family, says Joe Giefer. Excellent area fishing for salmon and halibut. There is a 3-mile trail to Bear Creek and about a 7-mile trail to Mount Robert Barron; both are unmaintained. Residents provide their own power, water and sewage disposal. Communications include radio and a weekly mail plane. Freight comes in by cargo plane and private boat.

Gustavus

GPS: N58°24' W135°44'

Located near the entrance to Glacier Bay, 48 miles northwest of Juneau and 10 miles from Bartlett Cove, headquarters of Glacier Bay National Park. **Transportation:** Year-round air taxi serv-ice to/from Haines, Hoonah, Juneau and Skagway. Charter boat, jet service, foot ferry available between Gustavus and Juneau mid-May to mid-September. Local ground transportation in Gustavus either by TLC Taxi, (907) 697-2239; or Bud's Rental Car, (907) 697-2403. Private boat, private aircraft. **Population:** 300 in winter, and up to 750 in summer. **Zip code:** 99826. **Emergency Services:** Volunteer Emergency Response, phone 911; Alaska State Troopers in Hoonah; Gustavus Community Clinic, (907) 697-3008.

Elevation: 20 feet and rising as the land rebounds almost an inch per year due to the retreat of the adjacent glaciers. **Climate:** Cool and rainy with average temperatures in January of 27°F and in July of 55°F. Mean precipitation ranges from 7.66 inches in October to 2.40 inches in June.

Private Aircraft: Gustavus airport 0.5 mile northeast; elev. 36 feet; length 6,700 feet; asphalt. Tie-downs available, aviation gas, Jet-A fuel and av-lubes/oils. Contact (907) 697-2217/2517 for attendant. Four year-round passenger terminals and ticket counters; seasonal jet terminal; coffee shop, air taxi offices, travel center and taxi; arts and crafts shop, fish products shop and bus service. Contact (907) 697-2239 for permitted taxi service with gate access to transient area for pick-up (prior to arrival) and drop-off. Aircraft repair, contact Flight Engineering Inc., (907) 697-2454 (day) or 2517 (night).

Private Boats: Marine fuel may be purchased at Hoonah or Elfin Cove prior to arrival at Bartlett Cove in Glacier Bay. Summer transient moorage at Bartlett Cove by permit only. Contact Glacier Bay National Park for permit information, (907) 697-2230. Anchorage available at least 1/4 mile from Gustavus dock and temporary tie-up floats (no facilities: water, fuel, waste disposal or more than 3-hour tie-up). Pay phone at head of dock. Marine repair: Panhandle Diesel, (907) 697-3034 (day) or 2424 (night).

Visitor Facilities: As the gateway to Glacier Bay National Park and Preserve, Gustavus offers most visitor services, including several lodges, inns, cabin rentals and bed and breakfasts. Most accommodations can book day boat tours and ferry/whale watching. Meals available at Annie Mae Lodge, (907) 697-2346; Glacier Bay Country Inn and Whalesong Lodge, (800) 628-0912; and Gustavus Inn, (800) 697-5220. Lunch and dinner also available at Bear's Nest Café, (907) 697-2440; dinner only at Bear Track Inn, (907) 697-3017; lunch only at Puffin Inn, (907) 697-2716; and coffee and sandwiches at Wings of Alaska passenger terminal at the airport. (Except for Wings of Alaska, these restaurants are open in summer only.) One lodge, a campground and dormitory, open in summer only, are located within the park at Bartlett Cove, approximately 10 road miles from Gustavus. There is a par 36, 9-hole golf course. Groceries, hardware, building supplies, fishing licenses and some fishing supplies are available. Gift shops and art galleries are located in Gustavus and Bartlett Cove. Glacier Bay Travel, (907) 697-2474 or www.glacierbaytravel.com, can arrange 1- and 2-day adventures. Spirit Walker Expeditions, Alaska Discovery, Gustavus Marine Charters, Seawolf Wilderness Adventures, Wild Alaska and many other businesses offer package or custom 1-2 day or longer trips. Year-round taxi and summer bus service are available, as well as air taxis and flightseeing. Boats and planes may be chartered for sightseeing, photography or fishing trips. Day tours aboard the Spirit of Adventure; whale and wildlife tours aboard the *Auk Nu*. Kayak rentals and guided trips may be arranged. Propane and white gas availalble for campers. Camping (no user fee) at campground on north shore of Bartlett Cove in Glacier Bay National Park, 10 miles from Gustavus airport or dock, (907) 697-2627/2230.

Surrounded on three sides by the snow-covered peaks of the Chilkat Range and the Fairweather Mountains, Gustavus offers miles of level land with expansive sandy beaches, farmland and forest. Homesteaded in 1914 as a small agricultural community, the area was once named Strawberry Point because it produced abundant wild strawberries along the beach and in the meadows. Today, local residents and visitors still enjoy huckleberries, blueberries, nagoonberries, strawberries and other berries, flowers and a variety of animals and birds. Most residents maintain gardens and make their living by fishing, processing fish, supplying services, creating arts and crafts and working for the school or the National Park Service. Gustavus caters to fishermen, sightseers and park visitors. Local residents recommend fishing for salmon, halibut and trout as well as beachcombing, hiking, kayaking, bird watching and photography. The commu-

Some of the world's most impressive tidewater glaciers are found in Glacier Bay, making it one of the top five visitor attractions in Alaska. The area is experiencing the most rapid retreat of glaciers since the Ice Age. Near the northern end of the Alaska Panhandle, Glacier Bay is bordered by Icy Strait and Cross Sound on the south, the Gulf of Alaska on the west and Canada on the north. Glacier Bay was made a national park and preserve in 1980.
— From *Alaska A to Z*

nity enjoys an old-fashioned Fourth of July celebration with a parade, art auction, community events and annual 3-mile run.

The Nature Conservancy is in the process of purchasing approximately 2,000 acres of beach, forest and wetlands in Gustavus. These lands will form an almost continuous chain of undeveloped habitats and open space linking the two arms of Glacier Bay National Park that surround Gustavus. No public facilities are planned. Moose, black bears, coyotes, wolves, eagles, hawks, martens, river otters, waterfowl and shorebirds frequent the area. In the spring and fall, thousands of lesser sandhill cranes stop in this area during their migrations. Beach hiking, camping, photography, berry picking, hunting and fishing opportunities are abundant. For more information, contact The Nature Conservancy in Juneau, (907) 586-8621.

Communications include phones, mail plane, Internet, radio and TV. The community has a church, fire station, library, community park and a school for grades kindergarten through 12 with enrollment of 48. Heavy freight arrives by barge. For more information write: Gustavus Community Assoc., P.O. Box 62, Gustavus, AK 99826, phone and fax (907) 697-2451, e-mail: president@gca.gustavus.ak.us, Web: http://gca.gustavus.ak.us/. Gustavus Visitors Assoc., P.O. Box 167, Gustavus, AK 99827.

Haines

GPS: N59°14' W135°26'

Located on Portage Cove, Chilkoot Inlet, on the upper arm of Lynn Canal, 80 air miles northwest of Juneau, 13 nautical miles southwest of Skagway, 155 road miles south of Haines Junction, YT. **Transportation:** Scheduled air service from Juneau, Skagway and Gustavus; mainline port on the Alaska Marine Highway; connected to the Alaska Highway by the Haines Highway. **Population:** 2,516. **Zip code:** 99827. **Emergency Services:** City Police, phone (907) 766-2121; Alaska State Troopers,

Fire Department and Ambulance, emergency only phone 911; Doctor, phone (907) 766-2521.

Elevation: Sea level. **Climate:** Average daily maximum temperature in July 66°F; average daily minimum in January, 17°F. Average annual precipitation 61 inches. Snow on ground usually from October through April.

Private Aircraft: Haines airport, 3.5 miles west, elev. 16 feet; length 4,000 feet; asphalt/gravel; unattended; fuel 100. Passenger terminal with restroom and pay phone. Commercial airlines provide transportation to and from motels and some motels offer courtesy car pickup.

Private Boats: Marine repairs available. Propane, diesel, regular gasoline and marine gas are available Transient moorage at the city small boat harbor 1 block from city center. Port Official: David Gross, phone (907) 766-2448, fax (907) 766-3010.

Visitor Facilities: Haines has all visitor facilities. There are 6 hotels/motels, 10 bed-and-breakfast accommodations, a hostel, a lodge and 4 public campgrounds, 4 private camper parks and bunk-style accommodations. All supplies are available from local hardware and grocery stores. Fishing/ hunting licenses may be purchased in Haines; there are registered hunting guides, and local charter boat operators offer fishing trips. There are restaurants and cafes, taverns, laundromats, a bank, car rental, automotive repair and gas stations.

"Haines is the Alaska of your dreams," states Michelle Glass, director of conventions and tourism for the City of Haines. "It is a small community steeped in all the traditional aspects of Alaska, with an amazing cultural and historical heritage where spectacular art abounds. There are magnificent snow-capped mountains and pristine rivers, wildlife in the water and on the shore. Haines is the natural choice."

Tlingit Indians, who jealously guarded fur-trading routes from the coast into the Interior, first inhabited the Chilkat Valley. A Presbyterian missionary named S. Hall Young established a mission at the present site of Haines in 1881. By 1884 there was a post office here, and as placer gold mining began in the Porcupine District, about 36 miles upriver from Haines, the town became an important outlet. The Klondike gold rush of 1898 brought an influx of gold seekers, who opened up the Chilkat mountain pass to the Interior. In 1904, the U.S. government established Fort William H. Seward. Renamed Chilkoot Barracks in 1922 and deactivated in 1946, the fort is a popular tourist attraction today. Haines was incorporated in 1910.

As a mainline port on the state ferry system and 1 of 3 Southeast communities connected to the Alaska Highway (the others are Hyder and Skagway), Haines remains an important route to the Interior for today's travelers. The Haines Highway, which connects the port of Haines with the Alaska Highway at Haines Junction, YT, is open year-round. The majority of employment in Haines is in service trades, including tourism, followed by fishing, timber, government and construction. Fishing was one of the initial industries in Haines' early days, and remains a commercial industry and a visitor attraction. A sawmill owned by Chilkoot Lumber Co. began operation in November 1987, at the site of an earlier sawmill along Lutak Inlet.

Visitors may explore the town's early history at the Sheldon Museum and Fort Seward. The Sheldon Museum, located on the corner of Front and Main streets, displays the art, history, ethnology and geology of the Haines area; it features special exhibits, guided tours, workshops and films. The Bald Eagle Foundation offers a diorama of animals from the area and an informative presentation on the bald eagle. Both of these museums are open from 1-5 P.M. daily during the summer, plus many evenings also. Winter hours vary. Another attraction is the Alaska Indian Arts, Inc. arts center and gallery located in Building 23 on Fort Seward Drive, featuring the arts and crafts of southeastern Alaska; year-round hours are 9 A.M. to 5 P.M. A small business incubation center is located at the fairgrounds in

Dalton City, an 1890s-style gold-rush town recreated from the movie set of *White Fang*. The Southeast Alaska State Fair is held in August. The fair phone is (907) 766-2476, and fair administrator is Judy Murphy.

The world's greatest concentration of American bald eagles comes together near Haines annually from October through December. At least 4,000 eagles gather in the Chilkat Valley to feed on the late run of chum salmon in the Chilkat River. The 48,000-acre Alaska Chilkat Bald Eagle Preserve was established in 1982. Several custom and group tour operators offer trips to the preserve, including trips on snow machines, snowshoes, cross-country skis and jet boats, and photographic blinds for serious wildlife photographers. There are also opportunities to bike, hike, flightsee, raft, and take a sled-dog ride or a kayaking excursion. Water taxis provide daily fast ferry service between Haines, Skagway and Juneau.

Communications include phones and two local newspapers, *Chilkat Valley News* and *The Eagle Eye*. KHNS radio station operates through the Public Broadcasting System, servicing the upper Lynn Canal. Television is available through cable and satellite dish. There are 13 churches, a preschool and elementary and secondary schools with total enrollment of 425. There is an excellent library that participates in the interlibrary loan system accessing library materials throughout the country. The city operates water and sewage systems. Private utilities provide electricity, phone, Internet services, and garbage collection and treatment. Freight arrives by ship, barge, plane or truck. Government address: City of Haines, P.O. Box 1049, Haines, AK 99827, phone (907) 766-2231, fax (907) 766-3179, Web: http://www.haines.ak.us. Visitors Bureau, Box 530, Haines, AK 99827, phone (907) 766-2234 or 1-800-458-3579, fax (907) 766-3155; e-mail: Hcvb@haines.ak.us, Web: http://www.haines.ak.us.

For more information, see *The MILE-POST®*, a complete guide to communities on Alaska's road and marine highway systems.

Hobart Bay

GPS: N57°24' W133°28'

Located 70 miles south of Juneau and 40 miles north of Petersburg on the east shore of Stephens Passage. **Transportation**: Boat or seaplane. Population: 48. **Zip code**: 99850. **Emergency Services**: None available.

Elevation: Sea level.

Private Aircraft: No facilities.

Private Boats: There is a public dock.

Visitor Facilities: Lodging is available at Goldbelt Guest House, (907) 673-2247/2282, and food is available at the bunkhouse. No supplies are available.

Hobart Bay is a logging camp owned by Goldbelt, Inc., the Juneau-based Native corporation which owns nearly 23,000 acres in the area. Ninety percent of the logging is done by helicopter. Hobart Bay is a beautiful spot with great fishing.

Hollis

GPS: N55°29' W132°40'

Located on the east coast of Prince of Wales Island on Twelvemile Arm, 25 road miles east of Klawock, 35 miles west of Ketchikan. **Transportation**: By ferry from Ketchikan; on the Prince of Wales Island road system. Daily air service. **Population**: 111. **Zip code**: 99950. **Emergency Services**: Hollis Community Council Fire/EMS, (907) 530-7006; Prince of Wales Island Area EMS, phone (907) 826-2367/3330; Craig Family Medical Clinic or Klawock Clinic; Hospital in Ketchikan. Emergency medical service can be contacted by using CB Channel 14 or "phone through just about anyone who lives here," says Johnnie Laird.

Elevation: 20 feet. **Climate**: Mean monthly temperature in January is 32°F and in July 58°F. Mean monthly precipitation ranges from 3.28 inches in July to 18.14 inches in October.

Private Aircraft: Seaplane base with new aircraft float and sheltered anchorage.

Private Boats: Boat ramp, docks and floats for moorage. No facilities.

Visitor Facilities: There is a store and a library, but no restaurants, gas stations or other visitor facilities here. The ferry from Ketchikan that serves Prince of Wales Island docks at Hollis. Ferry terminal, (907) 530-7115; public phones are located at the ferry terminal, floatplane dock and harbor.

Hollis was a mining town with a population of 1,000 from about 1900 to 1915. In the 1950s, Hollis became the site of Ketchikan Pulp Co.'s logging camp and served as the base for timber operations on Prince of Wales Island until 1962, when the camp was moved to Thorne Bay. State land sales spurred the growth of a small residential community here, the subdivisions built in thick second-growth timber. A school with grades 1 through 12 with enrollment of 14, the ferry terminal and U.S. Forest Service buildings are located here.

Hollis has public utilities, including electricity and phone service. There is a phone, (907) 530-7112, at the public library. Government address: Hollis Community Council, P.O. Box 706, Hollis, AK 99950, phone (907) 530-7043, fax (907) 530-7030. Visitor information: Prince of Wales Chamber of Commerce, P.O. Box 497, Craig, AK 99921, phone (907) 826-3870, fax (907) 826-5467, e-mail: powcc@aptalaska.net, Web: www.princeofwalescoc.org.

Hoonah

GPS: N58°06' W135°26'

Located on the northeast shore of Chichagof Island, about 40 miles west of Juneau and 20 miles south across Icy Strait from the entrance to Glacier Bay. **Transportation**: Scheduled and charter air service from Juneau; twice weekly state ferry service in summer. **Population**: 880. **Zip code**: 99829. **Emergency Services**: Alaska State Troopers and city police, phone (907) 945-3655; Hoonah Volunteer EMS, phone (907) 945-3631/3540; Hoonah Medical Clinic, phone (907) 945-3235; emergencies, phone 911.

Elevation: 30 feet. **Climate**: Typical southeastern Alaska climate, with considerable rainfall (100 inches annually). Summer temperatures in the 50s; winter lows to 14°F in February.

Private Aircraft: Hoonah airport, adjacent southeast; elev. 30 feet; length 2,997 feet; asphalt; unattended, prior visual inspection recommended. Seaplane base with sheltered anchorage and dock.

Private Boats: Marine fuel docks. Major marine repair and marine gas, diesel and regular gasoline are available. Transient moorage available at the city harbor; the marina, which has showers and a laundromat, is a popular layover for boaters awaiting permits to enter Glacier Bay. Harbormaster: Paul Dybdahl, phone (907) 945-3670, fax (907) 945-3445.

Visitor Facilities: Food and lodging are available at Icy Straits Lodge, (907) 945-3636. Lodging is also available at local bed and breakfasts. There are 3 restaurants, 1 deli, 2 grocery stores, an ice cream parlor, video shop, a local Native craft shop, a fishing tackle supply store, a bank, a gas pump and 2 flying services. Two taxi companies. Guided hunting and fishing trips may be arranged locally. Historical artifacts and photos at the Hoonah Indian Assoc., Russian Orthodox church and Presbyterian church.

Hoonah is a small coastal community with a quiet harbor for the seining and trolling fleets. The most prominent structures are a cold storage facility, the lodge, bank, post office and public school. The village has been occupied since prehistory by the Tlingit people. In the late 1800s, missionaries settled here. Canneries established in the area in the early 1900s spurred the growth of commercial fishing, which remains the mainstay of Hoonah's economy. During the summer fishing season, residents work for nearby Excursion Inlet Packing Co. or Hoonah Cold Storage in town. Halibut season begins in May and salmon season opens in midsummer and runs through September. Some logging also contributes to the economy. Subsistence hunting and fishing remain an important lifestyle here, and many families gather food in the traditional way: catching salmon and halibut in summer, shellfish and bottom fish year-round; hunting deer, geese and ducks; and berry-picking in late summer and fall.

Communications include phones in most households (residents also use CB radios for local communication), Hoonah Net Internet services, mail plane, radio and TV via satellite and cable. There are several churches and an elementary school and high school with total combined enrollment of 226. There are community water and sewage systems, and electricity is provided by a public utility. Freight arrives by plane or barge. Government address: City of Hoonah, P.O. Box 360, Hoonah, AK 99829, phone (907) 945-3663, fax (907) 945-3445. Village corporation address: Huna Totem Corp., 9301 Glacier Highway, #A-103, Juneau, AK 99801, phone (907) 789-1773, fax (907) 789-1896. Village council: Hoonah Indian Assoc., P.O. Box 602, Hoonah, AK 99829, phone (907) 945-3545, fax (907) 945-3703, e-mail: Hoonah@aitc.org.

Hydaburg

GPS: N55°12' W132°49'

Located on the southwest coast of Prince of Wales Island, 36 road miles from Hollis, 45 road miles from Craig, 50 air miles west of Ketchikan. **Transportation**: Scheduled air service from Ketchikan; state ferry service to Hollis; private boat. **Population**: 369. **Zip code**: 99922. **Emergency Services**: State Troopers in Klawock, phone (907) 755-2918; Village Public Safety Officer, phone (907) 285-3321; Hydaburg Health Clinic, phone (907) 285-3462; Prince of Wales Island Area EMS, phone (907) 826-2367/3330; Volunteer Fire Department, phone (907) 285-3333.

Elevation: 30 feet. **Climate**: Cool, moist maritime climate with complete cloud cover about 60 percent of the time. Summer temperatures from 46°F to 70°F. June and July are the driest months with an average of 5 inches of precipitation. Mild winter temperatures, range from 32°F to the low 40s. October and November are the wettest months with up to 18 inches of precipitation. Annual average precipitation is 160 inches.

Private Aircraft: Seaplane base with sheltered anchorage and dock; watch for boat traffic.

Private Boats: Marine machine shop and fuel available at harbor. Diesel and regular gasoline available in town. Moorage at city floats, 0.5 mile north of town; phone (907) 285-3761, fax (907) 285-3760.

NOTE: No alcoholic beverages are sold in Hydaburg.

Visitor Facilities: Bed-and-breakfast accommodations are available at Fran Sanderson's, (907) 285-3139; and at Marlene Edenshaw's, (907) 285-3254. Hyda Market, (907) 285-3311, offers foodstuffs; and Dot's Dry Goods and Hardware, (907) 285-3375, has household items for sale. Crafts, such as Haida Indian carvings and baskets, may be purchased from residents. There are no public laundry facilities, banking services or rental transportation. Fishing/hunting licenses and guide services are available at the local hardware store.

Hydaburg was founded in 1911 and combined the populations of 3 Haida villages: Sukkwan, Howkan and Klinkwan. President William Howard Taft established an Indian reservation on the surrounding land in 1912, but, at the residents' request, most of the land was restored to its former status as part of Tongass National Forest in 1926. Hydaburg was incorporated in 1927, 3 years after its people had become U.S. citizens.

Most of the residents are commercial fishermen, although there are some jobs in construction and the timber industry. Subsistence is also a traditional and necessary part of life here. Hydaburg has an excellent collection of restored Haida totems. The totem park was developed in the 1930s by the Civilian Conservation Corps. There is good salmon fishing here in the fall. According to former resident Frank Alby, "Hydaburg retains its small-town quality— lots of fishing, shrimping, hunting, hiking... things to do that don't take money."

Communications include phones and cable TV. There are Assembly of God and Presbyterian churches here. Hydaburg has an elementary and a high school with combined enrollment of 89. There are community water, sewage and electrical power systems. Freight arrives by plane, barge and truck. Government address: City of Hydaburg, P.O. Box 49, Hydaburg, AK 99922, phone (907) 285-3761, fax (907) 285-3760. Village corporation address: Haida Corp., P.O. Box 89, Hydaburg, AK 99922, phone (907) 285-3721, fax (907) 285-3944, e-mail: coehaida@excite.com. Village council: Hydaburg Cooperative Assoc., P.O. Box 349, Hydaburg, AK 99922, phone (907) 285-3666, fax (907) 285-3667, e-mail: Haidanatio@aol.com. Visitor information: Prince of Wales Chamber of Commerce, P.O,. Box 497, Craig, AK 99921, phone (907) 826-3870, fax (907) 826-5467, e-mail: powcc@aptalaska.net, Web: www.princeofwalescoc.org.

Hyder

GPS: N55°55' W130°30'

Located at the head of Portland Canal, 2 miles west of Stewart, BC. **Transportation:** By road via a spur of the Cassiar Highway; charter air service and mail plane. **Population:** 126. Zip code: 99923. **Emergency Services:** Hyder Health Clinic; Hyder Emergency Services, phone (250) 636-6809/2722; Stewart General Hospital in Stewart, BC.

Elevation: Sea level. **Climate:** Maritime, with warm winters and cool, rainy summers. Slightly less summer rain than other southeastern communities, but heavy snowfall in winter. Summer temperatures range from 57°F to 80°F; winter temperatures range from 25°F to 43°F.

Private Aircraft: Seaplane base at Hyder; airstrip at Stewart.

Private Boats: Small boat harbor operated by the state offers open moorage, a launching ramp and a deep-draft dock. No repair facilities in Hyder.

Visitor Facilities: Lodging is available at Sealaska Inn, (888) 393-1199; and Grandview Inn, (250) 636-9174, in Hyder; and at King Edward Hotel, (250) 636-2244, in nearby Stewart. Food is available at Sealaska Restaurant, (250) 636-9001, in Hyder; and at King Edward Hotel and Fong's Garden, (250) 636-9074, in Stewart.

Groceries are available at Ghosttown Grocery, (250) 636-2422, in Hyder.

Hyder has gift shops, a gallery featuring local art, a post office, 1 cafe, 3 bars, 2 bed and breakfasts and 2 inns, 1 of which offers a cocktail lounge and restaurant. A small-boat harbor operated by the state offers open moorage and a launching ramp. Hardware and sporting goods available. Stewart has 3 hotels/motels, 3 restaurants, 2 grocery stores, service stations, a bank, liquor store and other shops. Stewart has shops and a repair service.

Hyder and Stewart, on either side of the U.S.-Canada border, share commerce and history. Captain D.D. Gaillard explored Portland Canal in 1896 for the U.S. Army Corps of Engineers. In the late 1890s, gold and silver were discovered in the hills near Hyder, attracting prospectors. With the discovery in 1917 and 1918 of rich silver veins in the upper Salmon River basin, Hyder boomed. Few of the structures from this boom period survive, although many of the pilings which supported the buildings are still visible on the tidal flats. Hyder became an access and supply point for the mines, while Stewart served as the center for Canadian mining activity. Mining ceased in 1956, with the exception of the Granduc copper mine, which operated until 1984.

Today's economy is based on local trade and tourism. Some Hyder residents supplement their incomes by fishing, hunting and gardening. A water bottling facility opened in Fall 2001.

Attractions in the Hyder/Stewart area include the stone storehouse built by Capt. D.D. Gaillard in 1896; it is the oldest masonry building in Alaska. Sightseeing tours of Salmon Glacier are available out of Stewart, and charter small-boat trips on Portland Canal are available at the Hyder marina. Five species of Pacific salmon are found in waters near Hyder, with Salmon River and Fish Creek supporting one of Southeast's largest chum salmon runs. A new viewing platform on Fish Creek provides safe views of the chum salmon spawning area and the many black and brown bears that come to feed each summer.

The U.S. Forest Service operates a visitor information center for Misty Fiords National Monument during the summer months (July to Labor Day). The office is located in the Hyder community building and fire hall.

Communications include phones, mail plane, radio and TV. Hyder has a public school. The community has electricity provided by a public utility. Wood, propane and diesel are used to heat most homes. Residents rely on individual wells for water and septic tanks for sewage waste disposal. Freight arrives by barge, plane or truck.

Government address: Hyder Community Assoc. Inc., Box 149, Hyder, AK 99923-0149, phone (250) 636-9148, fax (250) 636-2518.

Icy Bay

GPS: N59°58' W141°39'

Located 66 miles northwest of Yakutat, 150 miles southeast of Cordova, at the terminus of Guyot and Malaspina glaciers on the Gulf of Alaska coast. **Transportation:** Charter plane. **Population:** Varies. **Zip code:** 99850. **Emergency Services:** Alaska State Troopers in Cordova; medical facilities in Cordova and Yakutat.

Elevation: 50 feet. **Climate:** Cool and rainy in summer, with rain and snow in winter. Some below-zero days in winter.

Private Aircraft: Airstrip 0.3 miles; elev. 50 feet; length 3,430 feet; gravel; unattended and unmaintained.

Private Boats: No facilities or services.

Visitor Facilities: This is a privately operated logging camp; there are no visitor facilities or services here. The camp obtains supplies from Cordova, and freight arrives by cargo plane or barge. Communications include mail plane, radio and TV. Icy Bay school has grades kindergarten through 12.

Juneau

GPS: N58°18' W134°24'

Located on Gastineau Channel opposite Douglas Island, 91 nautical miles south of Haines, 577 air miles southeast of Anchorage, 900 air miles north of Seattle, WA. **Transportation**: Daily scheduled jet service from Seattle and from Alaska communities; commuter air service from Haines, Skagway and other Southeast points; year-round state ferry service. **Population**: 31,262. **Zip codes**: 99801, 99802, 99803, 99811. **Emergency Services**: Alaska State Troopers, Police, Fire Department and Ambulance, phone 911; Bartlett Regional Hospital, phone (907) 586-2611; Capital City Fire/Rescue/Medevac, phone (907) 586-5322/789-7554; Juneau Quick Response Dive Team; Juneau Mountain Rescue Group, phone (907) 789-2161; Airlift Northwest/Air Ambulance, phone (907) 790-4944; U.S. Coast Guard Rescue Coordination Center, phone (907) 463-2000.

Elevation: Sea level. **Climate**: Mild and wet. Average daily maximum temperature in July is 64°F; daily minimum in January is 16.1°F. Record high was 90°F in July of 1975; record low, -22°F in January 1972. Average annual precipitation 91.98 inches downtown and 53.15 inches at the airport. Snow on ground intermittently from mid-November to mid-April.

Private Aircraft: Juneau International Airport, 9 miles northwest of downtown; elev. 24 feet; length 8,456 feet; asphalt; fuel 100, jet A. Full-service passenger terminal. Bus service to downtown. Juneau International Seaplane Basin, 9 miles northwest of downtown, dock and ramp available for public use. Juneau Harbor Seaplane, adjacent north; unattended; watch for harbor boat traffic; fuel 80, 100 and Al. Juneau AF55, (907) 789-7351.

Private Boats: Transient moorage available at Harris Harbor, 1 mile from city center; at Douglas Boat Harbor, across the channel from Juneau; and at the Auke Bay float facilities, 12 miles north of Juneau. Marine fuel is available. Harbormaster, phone (907) 586-5255, fax (907) 586-2507.

Visitor Facilities: As capital of Alaska and the largest city in Southeast, Juneau has all services. This includes 12 hotels/motels, approximately 20 bed and breakfasts, a hostel, dozens of restaurants and gift shops, a few major shopping centers, laundries, banks, major repair service and rental transportation. Many fishing charter services operate out of Juneau and hunting/fishing licenses may be purchased at numerous outlets. All types of fuel are available. The City and Borough of Juneau operates harbors. Juneau is a gateway for fly/boat tours to Glacier Bay. For information on the Pack Creek Bear Preserve on Admiralty Island, contact the U.S. Forest Service at (907) 586-8751.

The area was originally the home of the Alaska Native Tlingit people. When gold was discovered in 1880 by Joe Juneau and Dick Harris, the gold rush boom town of Juneau came to be and prospered due to its location on the water route to Skagway and the Klondike. By 1900, after the Russians left Sitka, and Sitka's whaling and fur trade fell off, it was decided to move Alaska's capital to Juneau. Transfer of government functions occurred in 1906. Today, government (federal, state and local) comprises an estimated half of the total basic industry, with tourism, construction, mining, retail trade and services making up the total. Despite being a regional supply and service center for Southeast Alaska, Juneau has been able to preserve its special charm and character because of its isolation from other communities.

Dubbed "a little San Francisco," Juneau is a picturesque city, backed by the steep slopes of Mount Juneau (elev. 3,576 feet) and Mount Roberts (elev. 3,819 feet) and looking out over Gastineau Channel. The city has an attractive waterfront park, a good spot to watch the floatplanes and ships in the channel. Juneau's skyline is dominated by several government buildings, including the Federal Building, the massive State Office Building, and the older brick and marble-columned Capitol Building.

The city and surrounding area offer a number of attractions. Boat, plane and helicopter operators offer charter sightseeing and fishing. A rustic 9-hole par 3 golf course puts golfers amid fields of wildflowers in full view of the Mendenhall Glacier. There is downtown shopping and self-guided walking tours to see the government buildings and Governor's Mansion. The Alaska State Museum, located just off Egan Drive at 395 Whittier St., features the archaeology, art, botany, history, ethnology, geology and paleontology of the state. The museum offers special exhibits, guided tours, workshops, lectures, film presentations and demonstrations. More than 150 exhibits depict wildlife and habitats, Native culture, Russian America, pioneer days and industrial history. Summer hours are 8:30 A.M. to 5:30 P.M. daily. Hours from October through mid-May are 10 A.M. to 4 P.M. Tuesday through Saturday. Admission is $5 in summer, $4 in winter. A $15 pass, good for the calendar year, can also be purchased. Another popular attraction is the Juneau-Douglas City Museum, 114 W. 4th, which features Juneau's mining history from a personal viewpoint. Persons visiting the museum receive specialized historical walking tour maps. Summer hours are 9 A.M. to 5 P.M. Monday through Friday and 10 A.M. to 5 P.M. Saturday and Sunday. Open during the winter at reduced hours. Admission $3 summer; $2 winter; 18 and under free. The Macaulay Salmon Hatchery, 3 miles from downtown, offers tours for a small charge (daily tours in summer, reduced hours in winter).

There are several hiking trails accessible from downtown: Perseverance trail, 3.5 miles, begins at the end of Basin Road and leads to the old Perseverance Mine; Mount Juneau trail, steep and rugged, begins 0.5 mile up Perseverance trail; Granite Creek Basin trail begins about 1.8 miles up Perseverance trail and leads 1.5 miles along Granite Creek to a scenic basin; Mount Roberts trail begins at the top of Starr Hill (the east end of 6th Street) and leads 3.7 miles to Mount Roberts.

For bicyclists, there are intermittent bike paths to Douglas and to Mendenhall Glacier. The glacier bike path begins at the intersection of 12th Street and Glacier Avenue and leads 13 miles north to Mendenhall Glacier. This magnificent glacier is about 13 miles by car from downtown Juneau. The U.S. Forest Service visitor center at the glacier has audiovisual displays, daily slide and film programs and guided hikes from early June through Labor Day; on weekends during the winter months. On Douglas Island, west of Juneau and connected by bridge, Eaglecrest ski area has downhill and cross-country skiing in winter.

Juneau has all the amenities of city life. There are churches of many denominations. Juneau Borough Schools enroll 5,463 students in 13 elementary, middle and high schools. The University of Alaska Southeast, Juneau branch, enrolls 2,000 students. Four Native corporations have offices in Juneau. Freight arrives by cargo plane or water. Government address: City and Borough of Juneau, City and Borough Manager, 155 S. Seward St., Juneau, AK 99801, phone (907) 586-5240, fax (907) 586-5385. Visitor Information Center, Centennial Hall, 101 Egan Drive, Juneau, AK 99801, phone (907) 586-2201 or toll free (888) 581-2201, e-mail: info@traveljuneau.com, Web: www.traveljuneau.com

For more information, see *The MILEPOST®* a complete guide to communities on Alaska's road and marine highway systems.

Kake

GPS: N56°58' W133°56'

Located on the northwest coast of Kupreanof Island, 40 air miles and 65 nautical miles northwest of Petersburg, 95 air miles southwest of Juneau. **Transportation:** Scheduled airline from Petersburg or Juneau; state ferry from Petersburg and Sitka. **Population:** 702. **Zip code:** 99830. **Emergency Services:** Police, phone (907) 785-3393; Kake Health Center, phone (907) 785-3333; Kake EMS, phone (907) 785-3333/3500; Volunteer Fire Department, phone (907) 785-3464.

Elevation: 10 feet. **Climate:** Temperate, with summer temperatures in the 50s, occasional highs in the 80s. Moderate rainfall most months, very little snow in winter.

Private Aircraft: Seaplane base southwest of town with dock. Airstrip 1 mile west of town; elev. 148 feet; length 5,000 feet; paved; unattended, prior visual inspection recommended.

Private Boats: Marine, diesel, propane, unleaded and regular gas are available. Public moorage at city floats. Harbormaster: Oscar Demmert, phone (907) 785-3804, fax (907) 785-4815.

Visitor Facilities: Accommodations and meals available. There is also a coffee shop. Some hardware, clothing and other supplies are available at local grocery stores. Fishing/hunting licenses are sold locally. No banking services. Laundromat available. There is a car mechanic, and all types of fuel are available.

The town is a permanent village of the Kake tribe of the Tlingit Indians. The Tlingits from Kake had a reputation for aggression in the 18th and 19th centuries. In 1869, the Kakes murdered 2 Sitka traders in revenge for the shooting of a Native by a Sitka sentry. Reprisals by the U.S. government resulted in the shelling and destruction of 3 Kake villages. The tribe eventually settled at the present-day site of Kake, where the government established a school in 1891. Today, Kake is noted for its friendliness and is very hospitable to visitors.

Residents have historically drawn ample subsistence from the sea. However, with the advent of a cash economy, the community has come to depend on commercial fishing, fish processing (there is a cannery) and logging. The post office was established in 1904, and the city was incorporated in 1952. The city's claim to fame is its totem, reputedly the world's tallest, at 132 feet, 6 inches. It was carved for the 1967 Alaska Purchase Centennial Celebration.

Kake has phones, radio, TV and mail plane service. Church groups include Baptist, Salvation Army, Presbyterian, Assembly of God and Kake Evangelistic Outreach. Schools include an elementary school and a high school, with combined enrollment of 165. Community electrical power, water and sewage systems are available. Freight comes in on the airlines or by barge. Government address: City of Kake, P.O. Box 500, Kake, AK 9983, phone (907) 785-3804, fax (907) 785-4815; e-mail: krisa@seaknet.alaska.edu; Web: http://www.seaknet.alaska.edu/~clerkake. Village corporation: Kake Tribal Corp., P.O. Box 263, Kake, AK 99830, phone (907) 785-3221, fax (907) 785-6407, e-mail: ktribal@ptialaska.net. Village council: Organized Village of Kake, P.O. Box 316, Kake, AK 99830-0316, phone (907) 785-6471, fax (907) 785-4902, e-mail: ovkgovt@seaknet.alaska.edu.

Kasaan

GPS: N56°58' W133°56'

Located on the east side of Prince of Wales Island, southeast of Thorne Bay, on Kasaan Bay on the Kasaan Peninsula. **Transportation**: Road connects to Prince of Wales Island road system. Charter plane or private boat. **Population**: 44. **Zip code**: 99950-0340. **Emergency Services**: Alaska State Troopers and hospital in Ketchikan; Kasaan Health Clinic; Kasaan EMS, phone (907) 542-2207; Volunteer Fire Department.

Elevation: Sea level. Climate: Typical Southeast, cool and rainy, with average temperatures of 55°F in summer. Precipitation ranges from 3.89 inches in June to 11.30 inches in November.

Private Aircraft: Seaplane base, dock.

Private Boats: Propane, diesel and regular gasoline are available at the public floats and dock.

Visitor Facilities: Lodging and a cafe are available at Country and Lace bed and breakfast, (907) 542-2210. Overnight accommodations with cooking and laundry facilities are maintained by Kavilco Inc., the local Native corporation, in remodeled buildings that were originally used as bunkhouses by the salmon cannery until 1953. Groceries and supplies are available from Capella's General Store; other supplies are flown in from Ketchikan, or drive to Craig or Thorne Bay. There is a post office.

Kasaan is a beautiful, secluded village situated along the beachfront in Kasaan Bay. Nestled against the forest, Kasaan is one of the few places in Southeast Alaska that still reflects an older, simpler, yet fulfilling lifestyle.

Kasaan was founded by a group of businessmen from Outside as a copper mine site. A sawmill and general store were established around 1900 and a salmon cannery was built in 1902. Members of the tribe of Haidas living at Old Kasaan, located south of Kasaan on Skowl Arm, eventually relocated at New Kasaan, site of the mine and cannery. The copper mining company went bankrupt after 4 years, but the cannery continued to operate sporadically with a half-dozen different owners until 1953. Kasaan incorporated in 1976 under the Alaska Native Claims Settlement Act.

The community was revitalized with the incorporation, but jobs are still scarce. Residents depend heavily on a subsistence lifestyle: fishing for salmon, halibut and bottom fish; hunting for deer; trapping for mink and marten; harvesting black seaweed in April and May; and gathering clams, shrimp and Dungeness crab. The valuable timberland owned by Kavilco holds promise for economic improvement. There are a few jobs with the city and the power plant, but as one resident states, "most people fish or are retired."

A 1,300-foot boardwalk leads from the harbor to a gravel footpath, which leads another half-mile through the village to a totem park. The Kasaan Totem Park, part of a government-sponsored totem restoration program begun in 1937, contains a number of totems from Old Kasaan. Kasaan is only a few miles away from the Karta River, a favorite of sportsmen. The village corporation, however, does not allow camping on its land for fear of forest fires. Residents also fish in front of the village and watch for killer whales going up the bay and for the great numbers of eagles that often soar overhead. The village has a community house and hosts a number of community dinners.

Communications include phones, mail plane, radio and TV. Kasaan's one-room schoolhouse has a kindergarten through grade 12 curriculum with enrollment of 11. The community has electric power and water systems; sewage system is individual septic tanks. Freight is brought in by barge or cargo plane. Government address: City of Kasaan, P.O. Box KXA, Kasaan, AK 99950-0340, phone (907) 542-2212, fax (907) 542-2223. Village corporation address: Kavilco Inc., P.O. Box KXA, Kasaan, AK 99950-0340, phone (907) 542-2214. Village council: Organized Village of Kasaan, One Coppercrest Dr., Kasaan, AK 99924, phone (907) 542-2230, fax (907) 542-2223, e-mail: Kasaan@aitc.org. Visitor information: Prince of Wales Chamber of Commerce, P.O. Box 497, Craig, AK 99921, phone (907) 826-3870, fax (907) 826-5467, e-mail: powcc@aptalaska.net, Web: www/princeofwalescoc.org.

Ketchikan

GPS: N55°20' W131°38'

Located on the southwest side of Revillagigedo Island on Tongass Narrows opposite Gravina Island, 235 miles south of Juneau, 90 miles north of Prince Rupert, BC. **Transportation:** Scheduled jet service, commuter and charter flights; state ferry service. **Population:** 8,295 (City), approximately 14,800 (Borough). **Zip code:** 99901. **Emergency Services:** Alaska State Troopers, phone (907) 225-5118; Police, phone (907) 225-6631; Ketchikan General Hospital, phone (907) 225-5171; SEARHC Clinic, phone (907) 225-4156; Ketchikan Fire/EMS Division, phone (907) 225-9611/9616; Emergency only for police, fire or ambulance, phone 911.

Elevation: Sea level. **Climate:** Rainy. Average yearly rainfall 162 inches and snowfall of 32 inches, with June the driest month and October the wettest. July high temperatures average 65°F, minimum 51°F. Daily maximum in January 39°F; minimum 29°F.

Private Aircraft: Ketchikan International Airport on Gravina Island; elev. 88 feet; length 7,497 feet; asphalt; fuel 80, 100, jet A. All facilities at airport. Ketchikan Harbor seaplane base downtown; fuel 80, 100.

Private Boats: Transient moorage is available at Thomas Basin, Ryus Float and the City Float downtown, and at Bar Harbor north of downtown. Port Director: Lori Kolanko, phone (907) 228-5632, fax (907) 247-3610. Contact in advance for moorage. Rental boats are also available.

Visitor Facilities: Ketchikan has 8 hotels/motels. There is a hostel (open Memorial Day through Labor Day) and numerous bed-and-breakfast accommodations. There are 5 area lodges, 4 resorts and 3 marinas. A full-service community, Ketchikan offers all the amenities of a medium-sized city: restaurants, laundromats, banks, 2 shopping centers, gift shops and all types of fuel. Fishing/hunting licenses are available. There are 2 registered hunting guides (deer and bear hunting seasons begin in August), and more than 80 charter boat operators offer fishing and sightseeing trips. Rental cars are available at the airport and downtown.

Ketchikan's colorful history is highlighted in several local attractions, including Creek Street, a former red-light district; Dolly's House, which was the brothel of the street's most famous madam; First City Players' weekly performance of *The Fish Pirate's Daughter*; Totem Heritage Center; Tongass Historical Museum; Totem Bight State Park, 10 miles north of town; and Saxman Totem Park, 2.5 miles south of town.

Ketchikan hosts a Mayfest celebration, several summer fishing derbies and a Blueberry Festival in August. The July 4th celebration includes Ketchikan's famous Logging Carnival. The Festival of the North in February includes music, Native arts and culture.

Ketchikan is the gateway to Misty Fiords National Monument located 30 miles east of town and accessible only by boat or floatplane. A number of tour operators in Ketchikan offer a variety of trips into this scenic area.

The area supports 4 public elementary schools, a junior high school and 2 high schools with a total combined enrollment of 2,511; a branch campus of the University of Alaska, and several churches. Freight arrives by cargo plane and barge. Government addresses: Ketchikan Gateway Borough, 344 Front St., Ketchikan, AK 99901, phone (907) 228-6625, fax (907) 247-0483; e-mail: boroclerk@borough.ketchikan.ak.us, web: http://www.borough.ketchikan.ak.us; City of Ketchikan, 334 Front St., Ketchikan, AK 99901, phone (907) 225-3111, fax (907) 225-5075, web: http://www.ketchikan.ak.us. Parks and Recreation, phone (907) 228-5608. Visitors Bureau, 131 Front St., Ketchikan, AK 99901, phone (907) 225-6166, fax (907) 225-4250, e-mail: kvb@ktn.net; web: http://www.visit-ketchikan.com/.

For more information, see *The MILE-POST®*, a complete guide to communities on Alaska's road and marine highway systems.

Klawock

GPS: N55°33' W133°05'

Located on the west coast of Prince of Wales Island on Klawock Inlet, 24 road miles west of Hollis, 7 road miles north of Craig, 55 air miles west of Ketchikan. **Transportation**: Scheduled air service from Ketchikan; private boat; state ferry to Hollis. **Population**: 750. **Zip code**: 99925. **Emergency Services**: Alaska State Troopers, phone (907) 755-2918; Police, phone (907) 755-2261; Alicia Roberts Medical Center, phone (907) 755-4800; Klawock Volunteer Fire/EMS, phone (907) 755-2341/2626; Prince of Wales Island Area EMS, phone (907) 826-2367/3330.

Elevation: Sea level. **Climate**: Maritime with cool, moist, cloudy weather; mild winters. Average temperature in January is 34°F; in July it is 56°F. Mean monthly precipitation ranges from 3.62 inches in June to 14.88 inches in October. Annual precipitation is 120 inches, including 40 inches of snow.

Private Aircraft: Klawock airstrip, 2 miles northeast; elev. 50 feet; length 5,000 feet; paved; fuel 80; unattended; air service provides courtesy bus to town. Klawock seaplane base, sheltered anchorage, dock, fuel 80.

Private Boats: Marine engines and boats may be repaired in nearby Craig. Boats may be rented in Klawock. All types of fuel are available. Transient moorage at public floats and public dock.

Visitor Facilities: Columbine Inn, (907) 755-2287; Log Cabin Resort, (800) 544-2205; Southeast Retreat, (907) 755-2994; and Trophy Inn, (907) 755-2209, offer lodging. Meals are available at Dave's Diner, (907) 755-2986; and at Prince of Wales Island. Groceries and supplies are available locally. Log Cabin RV Park & Resort also has RV spaces. Gas, ATM, laundromat, film, first-aid supplies, sporting goods, clothing and some Native arts and crafts are available. Fishing/hunting licenses may be purchased locally. Guided hunting and fishing trips and equipment available. Major repair services include cars; automobiles may be rented at Wilderness Car Rental, (907) 755-2691.

Klawock originally was a Tlingit Indian summer fishing village; a trading post and salmon saltery were established here in 1868. Ten years later, a salmon cannery was built—the first cannery in Alaska and the first of several cannery operations in the area. Over the years, the population of Klawock, like other Southeast communities, grew and then declined with the salmon harvest. The local economy is still dependent on fishing and cannery operations, along with timber cutting and sawmilling. A nonprofit fish hatchery is located on Klawock Lake, very near the site of a salmon hatchery that operated from 1897 until 1917. The Prince of Wales Hatchery Association, (907) 755-2231, offers tours, an aquarium and a gift shop August through October, with a self-walking tour available anytime. Klawock Lake offers good canoeing and boating. Recreation includes good fishing for trout and salmon in Klawock River, salmon and halibut fishing in Big Salt Lake and surrounding salt water, and deer and bear hunting. Klawock's totem park contains 21 totems (both replicas and originals) from the abandoned Indian village of Tuxekan.

Klawock is a first-class city, incorporated in 1929. Communications include phones, mail plane, radio and cable TV. Churches include Roman Catholic, Baha'i and Assembly of God. Schools, with a total enrollment of 190, include an elementary, junior high and high school. Public electric power, water and sewage systems are available. Freight arrives by cargo plane, barge and truck. Government address: City of Klawock, P.O. Box 469, Klawock, AK 99925, phone (907) 755-2261, fax (907) 755-2403. Village corporation address: Klawock Heenya Corp., P.O. Box 129, Klawock, AK 99925, phone (907) 755-2270, fax (907) 755-2966. Village council: Klawock Cooperative Assoc., P.O. Box 411, Klawock, AK 99925, phone (907) 755-2265, fax (907) 755-8800, e-mail: Klawock@aitc.org. Visitor information:

Prince of Wales Chamber of Commerce, P.O. Box 497, Craig, AK 99921, phone (907) 826-3870, fax (907) 826-5467, e-mail: powcc@aptalaska.net, Web: www.princeofwalescoc.org.

Klukwan

GPS: N59°24' W135°53'

Located along the Haines Highway, 21 miles north of Haines, on the north shore of the Chilkat River and near the junction of the Klehini and Tsirku rivers, 22 miles west of Skagway and 100 miles northeast of Juneau. **Transportation**: Road from Haines. **Population**: 110. **Zip code**: 99827. **Emergency Services**: Alaska State Troopers and Clinic in Haines; Fire Department, phone (907) 767-5555; Klukwan Village Safety Officer, phone (907) 767-5588; Klukwan Health Aide, phone (907) 767-5505.

Elevation: Less than 500 feet above sea level.

Private Aircraft: No facilities. (See Haines, this section.)

Visitor Facilities: No visitor accommodations or services. Virtually all facilities are available in nearby Haines.

Klukwan is the only surviving village of 4 Tlingit villages in the Chilkat Valley. A survey in the late 1800s showed a population of more than 500 people in Klukwan. It is the only inland settlement in southeastern Alaska. Klukwan has a strong sense of identity. Although the town has electricity, phone service and a modern school with grades kindergarten through 12, many residents continue a lifestyle based, in part, on subsistence activities. They fish for salmon and eulachon in the Chilkat River and use berries, trees and animals of the Tongass National Forest. The area also borders the Alaska Chilkat Bald Eagle Preserve.

For more information, see *The MILE-POST®*, a complete guide to communities on Alaska's road and marine highway system.

Kupreanof

GPS: N56°45' W133°30'

Located on Lindenberg Peninsula, on the northeast shore of Kupreanof Island,

across from Petersburg. **Transportation**: Primarily by small boat from Petersburg. **Population**: 24, plus, according to one resident: "about 40 cats, 20 dogs, 1 goat, 1 pig, 2 geese and 1 ferret." **Zip code**: 99833. **Emergency Services**: Alaska State Troopers and hospital in Petersburg; Volunteer Fire Department.

Elevation: Sea level. **Climate**: Summer temperatures range from 40°F to 76°F, winter temperatures from 5°F to 43°F. Average annual precipitation 105 inches, with mean monthly snowfall in winter from 0.9 to 29.2 inches.

Private Aircraft: Floatplane landings only, public dock.

Private Boats: No facilities or services.

Visitor Facilities: There are no facilities or services here for visitors. Residents obtain services and supplies in Petersburg, which is accessible by skiff and kayak.

Formerly known as West Petersburg, Kupreanof incorporated as a second-class city in 1975, mostly to avoid annexation by the City of Petersburg and preserve its independent, rustic lifestyle.

A small sawmill was started here in 1911 by the Knudsen brothers, and in the 1920s, the Yukon Fur Farm began raising foxes, then mink; both the mill and fur farm operated into the 1960s. Today, Kupreanof has no industrial base or commercial activities. Most residents are self-employed or work outside the community. Subsistence activities also contribute to each household.

Boardwalks and trails connect some of Kupreanof, although locals use skiffs to travel around the community. Kupreanof is adjacent to Petersburg Creek-Duncan Salt Chuck Wilderness Area. A planked trail runs behind private property toward the Petersburg Mountain Trail and another trail which leads 1 mile to Petersburg Creek.

Communications include radio, and 3 households have phones. Mail is received in Petersburg, as Kupreanof has no post office. Children also attend school in Petersburg. About half the residents have electricity, supplied by individual diesel or gasoline-powered generators. Most homes use wood stoves for heating. Residents also provide their own water (from wells or creeks) and sewage systems (septic tanks or privies). Freight is transported by private skiff from Petersburg to Kupreanof. Government address: City of Kupreanof, P.O. Box 50, Petersburg, AK 99833, phone (907) 772-2400, fax (907) 772-2401.

Loring

GPS: N55°36' W131°38'

Located on Revillagigedo Island, 20 miles north of Ketchikan, at the northeast corner of Naha Bay on the east side of Behm Canal. **Transportation**: Accessible by boat or floatplane only.

Private Boats: Open moorage available at state float; no services.

Visitor Facilities: Open moorage available at state float; no other services or facilities here. There is a village phone, reached through the Ratz Mountain marine operator.

A small group of residents lives at this former cannery site. Established in 1885, the cannery closed in 1930, and the post office was discontinued in 1936.

In 1889, the side-paddle steamer *Ancon*, which carried mail, freight and passengers between the U.S. west coast and southeastern Alaska, was wrecked at Loring. A cannery hand had cast off the lines as the ship prepared to depart, when no one was in control of the vessel. The ship drifted onto a reef, a rock punctured the hull and the ship sank (no lives were lost). Today, pieces of the *Ancon*'s rusted boiler can be seen at Loring at low tide.

Metlakatla

GPS: N55°07' W131°34'

Located on the west coast of Annette Island, 15 miles south of Ketchikan. **Transportation**: Charter air service; state ferry from Ketchikan. **Population**: 2,026. Zip code: 99926. **Emergency Services**: Police, phone (907) 886-6721; Annette Island Family Medical Center, phone (907) 886-4744; Metlakatla Volunteer Fire/EMS/Ambulance, phone (907) 886-7922; Emergency only, phone 911.

Elevation: Sea level. **Climate**: Mild and moist. Summer temperatures range from 36°F to 65°F, winter from 28°F to 44°F. Average annual precipitation is 115 inches; October is the wettest month with a maximum of 35 inches of rainfall. Annual snowfall averages 61 inches.

Private Aircraft: Floatplane landings only at seaplane base. Annette Island airstrip, length 7,493 feet, asphalt. Request permission to land from Metlakatla Indian Community.

Private Boats: Transient moorage available at Metlakatla boat harbor; marine gas at UnAnnette Island Gas EDA dock; marine repairs available at cannery in season. An enclosed bay is popular with kayakers. Port Director: Bruce W. Guthrie Sr., phone (907) 886-4646, fax (907) 886-7997.

Visitor Facilities: Permit required for long-term visits to Metlakatla; contact the tourism department, phone (907) 886-8687. Overnight accommodations, including several bed and breakfasts, and restaurant service are available; phone (907) 886-4441 for information. Groceries and other supplies and banking services are available.

Metlakatla was founded in 1887 by William Duncan, a Scottish-born lay minister, who moved here with several hundred Tsimshian Indians from a settlement in British Columbia after a falling-out with church authorities. Congress granted reservation status and title to the entire island in 1891, and the new settlement prospered under Duncan, who built a salmon cannery and sawmill. Today, fishing and lumber continue to be the main economic base of Metlakatla. As the community and island retained the status of a federal Indian reservation, the use of fish traps is permitted here.

This planned community has a town hall, a recreation center with an Olympic-size swimming pool, well-maintained woodframe homes, a post office, the mill and cannery. The Metlakatla Indian Community is the largest employer in town, with retail and service trades the second largest. Many residents also are commercial fishermen. Subsistence activities remain an important source of food for residents, who harvest seaweed, salmon, halibut, cod, clams, waterfowl and a variety of berries.

Attractions include the Duncan Cottage, the original cottage occupied by Father Duncan until his death in 1918. A replica of the turn-of-the-century William Duncan Memorial Church, built after the original was destroyed by fire in 1948, is also open to the public. Several traditional Native dancers perform at the community Long House. Metlakatla has a very active tourism program that offers a Salmon Bake with traditional Native dance; phone (907) 886-8687 for schedule.

Communications include phones, daily mail plane from Ketchikan, radio and TV. There are several churches, and elementary and high schools with enrollment of 325. The City of Metlakatla provides electric power, water and sewage systems. Freight arrives by barge. Government address: Metlakatla Indian Community, P.O. Box 008, Metlakatla, AK 99926, phone (907) 886-4441, fax (907) 886-7997, e-mail: Metlakatla@aitc.org.

Meyers Chuck

GPS: N55°44' W132°15'

Located on the northwest tip of Cleveland Peninsula off Clarence Strait, 40 miles northwest of Ketchikan. **Transportation**: Floatplane or private boat. **Population**: 30. **Zip code**: 99903. **Emergency Services**: Meyers Chuck EMS, phone (907) 946-8309; Police and Hospital in Ketchikan and the Coast Guard.

Elevation: Sea level. **Climate**: No official records exist for Meyers Chuck. Residents say it's cool and rainy, with temperatures usually ranging from 20°F to 40°F, with a few weeks of 0°F to 20°F weather in winter.

Private Aircraft: Seaplane base with sheltered anchorage and dock.

Private Boats: Open moorage available at the community dock. The harbor offers excellent shelter from storms. There is a state boat grid available for repairs.

Visitor Facilities: Accommodations at local lodge, or visitors may arrange for food and lodging in private homes. Fishing/hunting licenses may be purchased at the post office. Fuel, groceries,

banking services, laundromat and rental transportation are not available.

The early history of Meyers Chuck is a bit hazy, although records suggest that white settlers began living here in the late 1800s, and the community was probably named after one of these early residents. (The name, too, is somewhat in question: there has been some argument whether it was Meyer, Myer, Myers or Meyers. Longtime resident Leo C. "Lone Wolf" Smith favored Myers Chuck. "Chuck" is a Chinook jargon word, usually applied to a saltwater body that fills at high tide.)

The natural harbor and the large Union Bay cannery nearby (which operated from 1916 to 1945) attracted fishermen to the townsite in the 1920s, and postal service began in 1922. Today, most residents make their living fishing and supplement their income by working outside the community or depend on subsistence. Several retired people also make their homes here. Traditional tourist attractions are few here, except for the surrounding natural beauty. Chief attractions, according to Robert Meyer, are "lovely sunsets and scenery."

Communications include phones, mail plane, radio and TV (via satellite dish). The Meyers Chuck school, which also serves as a community center, has no students enrolled at the present time. Most households have their own electrical generators and heat with wood. There is a community water system but no public sewage disposal. Freight comes in by ship or plane. The village phone, (907) 946-1234, is situated outdoors on a community pathway, where it is answered by postmaster Mary Ann Glenz or anyone who happens by.

Pelican

GPS: N57°57' W136°13'

Located on Lisianski Inlet on the northwest coast of Chichagof Island, 70 miles west of Juneau, 80 miles north of Sitka. **Transportation**: Scheduled air service from Juneau; charter air service available from other points; state ferry service monthly in winter, bimonthly in summer. **Population**: 135. **Zip code**: 99832.

Emergency Services: Fire or health emergencies, phone 911; Public Safety Officer, phone (907) 735-2213; Pelican Health Clinic, phone (907) 735-2250; Fire Department and EMS, phone (907) 735-2245/2243/2313.

Elevation: Sea level. **Climate:** Winter temperatures range from 21°F to 39°F, summer temperatures from 51°F to 62°F. Total average annual precipitation is 127 inches, with 120 inches of snow.

Private Aircraft: Seaplane base with sheltered anchorage and dock; fuel 80, 100.

Private Boats: Small boat harbor, marine repair and a fuel dock. Marine gas, diesel, propane and regular gas are available. Transient moorage is available at the Pelican City Harbor, and repairs at Terry's Marine Repair and at Svensson's Boatworks. Harbormaster: David Duffey, phone (907) 735-2212, fax (907) 735-2258.

Visitor Facilities: Pelican has 2 bar-and-grills (1 with 4 rooms for rent) and a café. Accommodations also available at Lisianski Inlet Lodge, (907) 735-2266; The Whale's Tale Lodge; The Paddle House; and Big Mick's Little Inn. There is also a bed and breakfast. There are a grocery and dry goods store, laundromat and 2 liquor stores. Pelican Seafoods Inc., (907) 735-2204, provides groceries, hardware, first-aid supplies, film, and fishing gear at the General Store; also marine gas, diesel, propane, and regular gasoline.

Established in 1938 by Katie (Charley) Raataikainen, and named for his fish packer, *The Pelican*, Pelican relies on commercial fishing and seafood processing for its economic base. The cold storage plant processes salmon, halibut, crab, herring and black cod, and is the primary year-round employer. Pelican has dubbed itself "closest to the fish," a reference to its proximity to the rich Fairweather salmon grounds. Nonresident fishermen swell the population during the fishing season, from about May to mid-October. Pelican was incorporated in 1943. Most of Pelican is built on pilings over tidelands. A wooden boardwalk extends the length of the community, and there are about 2 miles of gravel road.

Local recreation includes kayaking, hiking, fishing and watching birds and marine mammals. The Boardwalk Boogie is an annual mid-May music festival. According to a local wag, other notable events include the arrival and departure of the state ferry, the tide change, sunny days and a woman in a dress.

Chichagof Island boasts several attractions, such as abandoned mines and White Sulphur Hot Springs, where there is a Forest Service cabin. Across Lisianski Inlet from Pelican is the West Chichagof-Yakobi Wilderness of Tongass National Forest, a 265,000-acre area encompassing a 65-mile stretch of rugged Pacific Ocean coastline, a paradise for powerboat, sailboat and kayak enthusiasts. Denny Corbin from Lizianski Inlet Lodge and Howard Charters Outfitters & Guide, both holding permits from the U.S. Forest Service, guide hikers on trails to spectacular alpine lakes and scenic viewpoints.

Communications include phones, mail plane, radio courtesy of Raven Radio, Sitka 91-AM and TV. There is 1 church and a public school system serving kindergarten through 12th grade with enrollment of 23. Public electric power and water and sewage systems are available. Freight arrives by barge or on the state ferry. Government address: City of Pelican, P.O. Box 737, Pelican, AK 99832, phone (907) 735-2202, fax (907) 735-2258, e-mail: pelican@ptialaska.net, Web: http://www.pelican.net/.

Petersburg

GPS: N56°48' W132°58'

Located on the northwest tip of Mitkof Island at the northern end of Wrangell Narrows, midway between Juneau and Ketchikan. **Transportation:** Daily scheduled jet service from major Southeast cities: Juneau, Ketchikan and Wrangell; local flights and charter air service; scheduled state ferry service. **Population:** 3,387. **Zip code:** 99833. **Emergency Services:** Alaska State Troopers, phone (907) 772-3100; City Police, Ambulance, phone (907) 772-3838; Petersburg Medical Center, phone

(907) 722-4291; Petersburg Volunteer Fire Department, phone (907) 772-3355/3830.

Elevation: Sea level. **Climate**: Maritime, wet and cool.

Private Aircraft: Petersburg airport, 1 mile southeast; elev. 107 feet; length 6,000 feet; asphalt; fuel 100, jet A; ticket counter and waiting room. Petersburg seaplane base has sheltered anchorage, dock, and fuel 80, 100.

Private Boats: Major engine repair and all types of fuel are available. Boat rentals. Transient moorage available at city harbor. Harbormaster: Jim Stromdahl, phone (907) 772-4688, fax (907) 772-4687.

Visitor Facilities: Accommodations are available at Scandia House, (907) 772-5006; Tides Inn, (907) 772-4288; and several bed and breakfasts and guest houses. There are several restaurants. Groceries, hardware and fishing supplies are available. Petersburg also has a bakery, a community gym and a public swimming pool, 2 banks, drugstores, gas stations and gift shops. Fishing/hunting licenses are sold at several outlets and charter fishing trips are available locally. There are car rental agencies and air charters. There are a number of public and private campgrounds and RV facilities. Many opportunities exist for recreation, including fishing, hunting, boating, kayaking, hiking and bicycling.

Petersburg's attractions include the Sons of Norway Hall, built in 1912 and listed on the National Register of Historic Places; Clausen Memorial Museum, with its collection of local historical items; its busy waterfront, Scandinavian decorations, neatly laid-out streets and spectacular scenery. The big event of the year is the Little Norway Festival, usually held on the weekend closest to Norwegian Independence Day (May 17), when residents and visitors celebrate the community's heritage with costumes, dancing, contests and a big fish bake.

The community has all communications and public utilities. There are more than a dozen churches in Petersburg. The elementary and high schools have a combined total enrollment of 657. Freight arrives by barge, ferry or cargo plane. Government address: City of Petersburg, P.O. Box 329, Petersburg, AK 99833, phone (907) 772-4519, fax (907) 772-3759, e-mail: kathyo@ci.petersburg.ak.us, Web: http://www.petersburg.org.

For more information, see *The MILE-POST®*, a complete guide to communities on Alaska's road and marine highway systems.

Point Baker

GPS: N56°21' W133°37'

Located at the northwest tip of Prince of Wales Island, 50 miles west of Wrangell. **Transportation**: Private boat or charter plane. **Population**: 51. **Zip code**: 99927. **Emergency Services**: Alaska State Troopers in Petersburg; Hospital in Wrangell; Point Baker EMS, phone (907) 559-2218/2212; Prince of Wales Island Area EMS, phone (907) 826-2367/3330.

Elevation: Sea level. **Climate**: Like other Prince of Wales Island communities, a maritime climate with cool, wet, cloudy weather.

Private Aircraft: Seaplane float in harbor.

Private Boats: Transient moorage with power is available at the state-operated floats. Gas, diesel and propane are available.

Visitor Facilities: No accommodations and limited services for visitors. There are a bar, restaurant, showers and laundry. Groceries, liquor, ice, gas, diesel, propane and aviation fuel, fishing/hunting licenses and bait are available at the trading post, (907) 559-2204. The community building on the dock contains the post office, and there are pay phones at both ends of the dock.

Point Baker was named by Capt. George Vancouver in 1793 for the second lieutenant on his ship *Discovery*. Fish buyers operated here from about 1919 through the 1930s. The Forest Service opened the area for homesites, then in 1955 withdrew the townsite from Tongass National Forest. Most of Point Baker's year-round residents are fishermen, and the population increases in summer with visiting fishermen. Halibut and salmon fishing is excellent in the area, and residents also hunt for deer. Humpback whales pass by Point Baker, and the bird life here includes eagles and blue herons.

Communications include mail plane, radio and TV. Residents take care of their own electric power and sewage, and get their water either from collecting rain water or from streams, although there is a freshwater hose at the dock. Freight arrives by plane or barge. Community nonprofit: Point Baker Community, Box 31, Point Baker, AK 99927, phone (907) 559-2204, fax (907) 559-2224.

Port Alexander

GPS: N56°15' W133°38'

Located on the south end of Baranof Island, 5 miles northeast of Cape Ommaney on the west side of Chatham Strait, 65 miles south of Sitka, 90 miles west of Wrangell. **Transportation**: Private boat or charter plane and scheduled air taxi service from Sitka. **Population**: 90. **Zip code**: 99836. **Emergency Services**: Alaska State Troopers and Hospital in Sitka; Port Alexander EMS, phone (907) 568-2210.

Elevation: 20 feet. **Climate**: Average summer temperatures range from 41°F to 55°F; winter temperatures from 32°F to 45°F. Record high was 80°F in June 1958; record low 4°F in January 1953. Average annual precipitation is 172 inches, with October the wettest month.

Private Aircraft: Seaplane base. Sheltered anchorage and dock.

Private Boats: Public moorage at state floats (inner and outer harbors).

NOTE: *Port Alexander prohibits the sale of alcoholic beverages.*

Visitor Facilities: Limited groceries are available at Puget Sound Fisherman's Service (locals call it "Bud's Store"), phone (907) 568-2206. Several lodges and bed and breakfasts offer lodging and meals.

Port Alexander evolved into a year-round fishing community in the 1920s, settled by fishermen who trolled the Chatham Strait fishing grounds. In its heyday, Port Alexander's protected harbor was filled with up to 1,000 fishing boats at a time. The community prospered until the late 1930s, when the decline in salmon and herring stocks and the outbreak of WWII knocked the bottom out of fish buying, packing and processing at Port Alexander. Today, the majority of residents are commercial fishermen who choose to live here for the independent and subsistence lifestyle the area offers. Port Alexander was incorporated in 1974.

Communications include phones, and a mail boat twice a week. Port Alexander has a community water system, but electrical power and sewage systems are provided by individual households. The school, located next to Bear Hall community center, has grades kindergarten through 12 with enrollment of 18. Freight arrives by plane or barge. Government address: City of Port Alexander P.O. Box 8068, Port Alexander, AK 99836, phone (907) 568-2211, fax (907) 568-2207; e-mail: ddwall2000@yahoo.com.

Port Protection

GPS: N56°19' W133°36'

Located at the northwest tip of Prince of Wales Island near Point Baker, 50 miles west of Wrangell and southwest of Petersburg. **Transportation**: Private boat or charter plane. **Population**: 50. **Zip code**: 99950. **Emergency Services**: Alaska State Troopers in Petersburg; Hospital in Wrangell; Port Protection EMS, phone (907) 489-2220; Prince of Wales Island Area EMS, phone (907) 826-2367/3330.

Elevation: Sea level. **Climate**: Like other Prince of Wales Island communities, a maritime climate with cool, wet, cloudy weather. According to one resident, "the summers are nice and the winters are not."

Private Aircraft: Floatplane landings only.

Private Boats: Limited boat repair and state-owned grid are available. Transient moorage at public float. Gas and diesel available; no propane.

Visitor Facilities: Food and lodging available in a private home, (907) 489-2212. Groceries, hardware, film, bait, ice, gas and diesel are available. Aviation fuel is available upon request, for emergency purposes only. No propane is available. No banking services. Laundromat, public showers are available. Limited boat repair and state-owned grid are available. Fishing/hunting licenses are available. Guide service may be arranged. Transient moorage at public float.

Like its neighbor Point Baker, Port Protection was used as a fish-buying station and later settled by fishermen who had long used the cove for shelter from southeast storms. Credit for its "discovery" is given to a man named Johnson, who came ashore in the early 1900s to replace a wooden wheel lost off his boat and gave the spot its first name: Wooden Wheel Cove. In the late 1940s, Laurel "Buckshot" Woolery established a trading post and fish-buying station. Although the original trading post burned several years ago, a new store was erected, and the post still functions as a fish-buying station. The residents are either fishermen or retirees. Each household has at least one small boat, in addition to fishing vessels, to travel between homes in Port Protection and to Point Baker to pick up mail.

Excellent fishing in the immediate area in summer for salmon, halibut and rockfish. Boaters, kayakers and canoeists can make Port Protection their starting point for circumnavigating Prince of Wales Island. The trading post sponsors an end-of-fishing-season barbecue.

Communications include phones; CB radios are used by most households. A public phone for collect or credit card calls is available at the trading post. Port Protection also has radio and TV reception. A school housed in the community building offers grades kindergarten through 12 for 27 students. Residents have their own generators for power or use kerosene for lighting. Wood-burning stoves provide heat. A community water system provides fresh water to all homes, the trading post float and for fire hydrants. No water is available at the state float. Sewage system is outdoor privies or outfall pipes into the cove. Freight comes in by chartered boat or floatplane. Community nonprofit: Port Protection Community

Assoc., P.O. Box PPV, Port Protection, Ketchikan, AK 99950-0180, phone (907) 489-2214, fax (907) 489-2255. Visitor information: Prince of Wales Chamber of Commerce, P.O. Box 497, Craig, AK 99921, phone (907) 826-3870, fax (907) 826-5467, e-mail: powcc@altalaska.net, Web: www.princeofwalescoc.org.

Saxman

GPS: N55°19' W131°35'

Located 2 miles south of Ketchikan. **Transportation**: Road and biking/walking trail from Ketchikan. **Population**: 370. **Zip code**: 99901. **Emergency Services**: Alaska State Troopers and hospital in Ketchikan; Fire Department, phone (907) 225-1981; Saxman EMS, phone (907) 225-9616.

Elevation: Sea level.

Visitor Facilities: Virtually all facilities are available in nearby Ketchikan. Saxman has seasonal gift shops and a gas station with snack bar. There is no public boat dock or boat gas; no seaplane dock. There is a city-owned seaport. Harbormaster: Tom Fitzgerald, phone (907) 225-9040, fax (907) 8225-4706.

The town's major attraction is Saxman Totem Park, which contains the largest collection of totem poles in the world. Saxman is also home to the Beaver Clan House, which is the only clan house built in Alaska for many years. Constructed of hand-adzed cedar, it features artwork by Tlingit artist Nathan Jackson. A Native Artist Co-op is located in the City Hall, featuring only local, handmade Native items. The park is open year-round. Admission is charged to tour groups. Also in summer, Native artists can usually be seen in various parts of Saxman, carving totems, weaving spruce baskets or doing beadwork. Government address: City of Saxman, Route 2, Box 1, Saxman, AK 99901, phone (907) 225-4166, fax (907) 225-6450, e-mail: saxcity@ptialaska.net.

Sitka

GPS: N57°03' W135°20'

Located on the west side of Baranof Island, 95 miles southwest of Juneau. Unlike many Southeast Alaska towns,

Sitka faces the open ocean. **Transportation**: Scheduled jet service, commuter and charter flights; state ferry service. **Population**: 8,788. **Zip code**: 99835. **Emergency Services**: Alaska State Troopers, Police, Ambulance and Fire Department, phone 9911; SEARHC Mt. Edgecumbe Hospital, phone (907) 966-2411; Sitka Community Hospital, phone (907) 747-3241.

Elevation: Sea level. **Climate**: Maritime, with cool summers (55°F daily temperature in July) and mild winters (33°F in January). Annual precipitation, 96 inches.

Private Aircraft: Sitka airport on Japonski Island; elev. 21 feet; length 6,500 feet; asphalt; fuel 80, 100, jet A-50. Sitka seaplane base adjacent; fuel 80, 100. Passenger terminal at airport.

Private Boats: All types of fuel, repair available. Transient moorage available at Thomsen Harbor, Katlian Street, 0.6 miles from city center. Harbormaster: Roy Majeski, phone (907) 747-3439, fax (907) 747-6278, or Channel 16 VHS.

Visitor Facilities: Overnight accommodations available at several hotels/motels, most with adjacent restaurants; a hostel, and several bed and breakfasts, including Alaska Ocean View bed and breakfast, (907) 747-8310. The U.S. Forest Service maintains 2 campgrounds: Starrigavan at Milepost 7.8 Halibut Point Road and Sawmill Creek at Milepost 5.4 Sawmill Creek Road. The downtown area has an array of businesses, including restaurants, bookstore, biking/camping store, library, laundromats, banks, drugstore, clothing and grocery stores and gift shops. Fishing/hunting licenses are sold at several outlets. Taxi service and car rentals are available. Local charter operators offer sportfishing trips. Major engine repair, rental transportation and all types of fuel available. Sitka National Historical Park preserves the community's Tlingit and Russian heritage. Here a fine collection of totem poles is set among majestic spruce and hemlocks on a trail to the Russian fort site. In mid- and late summer, blueberries and huckleberries ripen along this trail. One visitor reflected, "The Native presence in the stand of totems adds such a powerful reminder of the history of the area." Sitka's Tlingit and Russian past is the major attraction for visitors. Replicas of the old Russian Blockhouse and St. Michael's Cathedral (rebuilt from original plans after a fire in 1966), and the original Russian Bishop's House (built in 1842), are open to the public. Museums in town include the Sheldon Jackson Museum on the campus of Sheldon Jackson College and the Isabel Miller Museum located in the Centennial Building.

The city has all communications and public utilities. There are more than a dozen churches, a school district with enrollment of 1,945 students in 3 elementary schools, a junior high school and 2 high schools (including a boarding school with 329 students), and 2 colleges: Sheldon Jackson College and University of Alaska Southeast, Sitka branch. Freight comes in by barge and cargo plane. For visitor information contact: Sitka Convention and Visitors Bureau, P.O. Box 1226, Sitka, AK 99835; phone (907) 747-5940, fax (907) 747-3739, e-mail: scvb@sitka.org, Web: http://www.sitka.org. Government address: City and Borough of Sitka, 100 Lincoln Street, Sitka, AK 99835, phone (907) 747-1812, fax (907) 747-7403, e-mail: colleen@cityofsitka.com, Web: http://www.cityofsitka.com. Native corporation address: Shee Atika, Inc., 201 Katlian Street, Sitka, AK 99835, phone (907) 747-3534, fax (907) 747-5727. Village council: Sitka Tribe of Alaska, 456 Katlian St. #200, Sitka, AK 99835, phone (907) 747-3207, fax (907) 747-4915, e-mail: Sitka@aitc.org.

For more information, see *The MILE-POST®*, a complete guide to communities on Alaska's road and marine highway systems.

Skagway

GPS: N59°27' W135°18'

Located at the north end of Taiya Inlet on Lynn Canal, 90 air miles northwest of Juneau, 13 nautical miles from Haines, 100 road miles from the Alaska Highway. **Transportation**: Daily scheduled flights from Juneau and Haines via local commuter services; charter air service; scheduled state ferry service; connected to the Alaska Highway by Klondike Highway 2. **Population**: 880. **Zip code**: 99840. **Emergency Services**: Police, phone (907) 983-2301; Skagway Medical Clinic, phone (907) 983-2255/2418; Skagway Volunteer Fire Department/EMS, phone (907) 983-2300/2450, or 911.

Elevation: Sea level. **Climate**: A maritime climate with cool summers and mild winters. Average summer temperatures range from 45° to 67°; winter temperatures average 18° to 37°. Within the shadow of the mountains, Skagway receives less rain than is typical of Southeast Alaska, averaging 26 inches of precipitation per year, and 39 inches of snow.

Private Aircraft: Skagway airport adjacent west; elev. 44 feet; length 3,750 feet; asphalt, fuel 80, 100. Due to downdrafts and winds in the area, landing a small plane can be tricky. Also, the airport approach is different from the norm.

Private Boats: Transient boat moorage available at the city harbor. Propane and marine gas are available, also major repair services. Harbormaster: Ken Russo, phone (907) 983-2628, fax (907) 983-2151.

Visitor Facilities: Hotels and other lodging include Westmark Inn, (907) 983-6000; Gold Rush Lodge, (907) 983-2831; At the White House, (907) 983-9000; the Historic Skagway Inn, (907) 983-2289; Cindy's Place, (907) 831-8095; and Wind Valley Lodge, (907) 983-2236. There are several bed and breakfasts, a hostel, a dozen or so restaurants, cafes and bars; grocery, hardware and clothing stores; a laundromat; a bank; and many gift and novelty shops. RV parks include Mountain View RV Park, (888) 778-7700; Pullen Creek RV Park next to the Alaska State Ferry dock, (800) 936-3731; and Garden City RV Park, (907) 983-2378. Rental cars are available. Propane, marine and automobile gas are available, as are major repair services.

A 6-block area of downtown Skagway is included in Klondike Gold Rush National Historical Park. The main street, Broadway, is lined with false-fronted buildings and boardwalks. The city is easy to get around by foot, and Park Service rangers lead walks through downtown.

Films and slide shows are offered at the visitor center. The Trail of '98 Museum, owned and operated by the citizens of Skagway, has an interesting collection of gold rush memorabilia. Also included in the historical park is the 33-mile-long Chilkoot Trail, the old gold rush route over the mountains to Lake Bennett, where early gold seekers built boats to take them down the Yukon River to the Klondike. The Chilkoot Trail attracts more than 3,500 hardy souls each summer.

The historic White Pass & Yukon Route railroad provided train service between Skagway and Whitehorse until 1982, when it shut down operations. In the spring of 1988, it renewed operation as an excursion train to the summit of White Pass and back. The 3-hour trip departs daily from Skagway May to September. There is a scheduled switch-thru service from Skagway to Whitehorse, YT, with a bus shuttling passengers between the border and Whitehorse. There is a hikers' service into Lake Bennett (see Chilkoot Trail under Special Features in Attractions section).

Special events in the community include the annual Windfest held the third weekend in March; the Buckwheat Ski Classic, cross-country skiing on a groomed trail in scenic White Pass; a large Fourth of July celebration; the Dyea Dash, a 3.5-mile race held the last Saturday in August; and the Klondike Trail of '98 Road Relay from Skagway to Whitehorse, held the third weekend in September.

Communications include phones, mail plane, radio and TV. There are 4 churches and an elementary school and a high school with combined enrollment of 132. There are community electric power, water and sewage systems. Freight arrives by ferry or barge and by road. Government address: City of Skagway, P.O. Box 415, Skagway, AK 99840, phone (907) 983-2297, fax (907) 983-2151, e-mail: bwardmgr@aptalaska.net, Web: http://www.skagway.net. Village council: Skagway Traditional Council, Box 149, Skagway, AK 99840, phone (907) 983-2121, fax (907) 983-3068, e-mail: Skagway@aitc.org.

For more information, see *The MILE-POST®*, a complete guide to communities on Alaska's road and marine highway systems.

Tenakee Springs

GPS: N57°46' W135°13'

Located on the north shore of Tenakee Inlet on the east side of Chichagof Island, 50 miles northeast of Sitka. **Transportation**: Scheduled and charter air service; state ferry service. **Population**: 105. **Zip code**: 99841. **Emergency Services**: Alaska State Troopers in Juneau; Volunteer Fire Department; Tenakee Springs Volunteer Fire/EMS, phone (907) 736-2211; Genevieve Soboleff Health Clinic, phone (907) 736-2347.

Elevation: Sea level. **Climate**: Maritime, with cool summers (45°F to 65°F) and mild winters (24°F to 39°F). Total precipitation averages 69 inches a year.

Private Aircraft: Seaplane base with dock.

Private Boats: Public moorage available at city-operated floats. Marine gas, diesel and propane are available. There is a boat mechanic in town.

Visitor Facilities: Lodging is available at Snyder's Mercantile, (907) 736-2205; and Tenakee Hot Springs Lodge, (907) 736-2400, which also supplies custom sportfishing packages. Groceries, first-aid supplies, hardware, film, sporting goods and fishing/hunting licenses available. No banking services. Supplies, charter boat information and rental cabins available through Snyder's Mercantile. Tenakee Springs has one street, Tenakee Avenue, which is about 2 miles long and 4 to 12 feet wide. There are only 2 vehicles in town. People walk or use bicycles or 3-/4-wheel ATVs for transportation.

Tenakee's natural hot springs first drew early prospectors and miners, and by 1895, the springs were enlarged to accommodate the increasing number of visitors. Ed Snyder built a general store here in 1899, and a post office was established in 1903. Three canneries operated at various times at Tenakee from 1916 to the 1960s. Some residents still make their living fishing commercially, although most year-round residents are retirees. The community also sees an influx of summer visitors: tourists, commercial fishermen and pleasure boaters, and Juneau and Sitka residents who have summer homes here. Tenakee Springs was incorporated as a second-class city in 1971.

Tenakee's major attractions are its quiet isolation and its hot springs. The bathhouse is located on the waterfront and has posted times for use by men and women. There is a U.S. Forest Service trail that runs east 7.8 miles from Tenakee Springs along the shoreline of Tenakee Inlet to Coffee Cove. The area also offers beachcombing, hunting and fishing. Communications include phones, daily mail plane, radio and TV. A new school offers grades kindergarten through 12 with enrollment of 11. A large generator plant provides electrical service to most households. There are no water or sewage systems. Residents haul water from streams, and households have their own

Alaska has many natural hot springs. The U.S. Geological Survey identifies 79 thermal springs in Alaska, about half of which are found along volcanic Alaska Peninsula and Aleutian chain. Many communities near springs were populated around the turn of the century when miners were exploring Alaska's creeks in search of gold.

—From Alaska A to Z

privies. Freight comes in by seaplane, ferry and barge. Government address: City of Tenakee Springs, P.O. Box 52, Tenakee Springs, AK 99841, phone and fax (907) 736-2207.

Thorne Bay

GPS: N55°41' W132°32'

Located on the east coast of Prince of Wales Island, in the heart of the scenic Tongass National Forest, 47 air miles northwest of Ketchikan, 42 road miles east of Craig. **Transportation:** Scheduled air service from Ketchikan; 60 road miles from Hollis (ferry port); private boat. **Population:** 582. **Zip code:** 99919. **Emergency Services:** Village Public Safety Officer, phone (907) 828-3905; Alaska State Troopers in Klawock; Thorne Bay Health Clinic, phone (907) 828-3906; doctor in Craig; Thorne Bay Volunteer Rescue Squad/EMS, phone (907) 828-3313; Prince of Wales Island Area EMS, phone (907) 826-2367/3330.

Elevation: Sea level. **Climate:** Maritime, with cool, moist weather and mild temperatures.

Private Aircraft: Seaplane base with sheltered anchorage and dock.

Private Boats: Concrete boat launch ramp. Boat repair and marine fuel available. Dock serves private boats and commercial fishing vessels. Fish cleaning station available.

Visitor Facilities: Accommodations available at McFarland's Floatel, (907) 828-3335; Boardwalk Wilderness Lodge, (907) 828-3918; Adventure Alaska Southwest, (907) 828-3907; The Landing at Otter Cove, (360) 278-3528; South Haven Guest House, (907) 828-2471; and Welcome Inn bed and breakfast, (888) 828-3940. Stores and services include a restaurant; auto and boat repair; grocery, liquor, sporting goods, gift and hardware stores; and fuel supply outlets (marine gas, diesel, propane, unleaded and regular gasoline available). Gifts include pine needle raffia baskets made locally. No banking services. Fishing/hunting licenses and charter trips available.

Thorne Bay was incorporated in 1982, making it one of Alaska's newest cities.

The settlement began as a logging camp in 1962, when Ketchikan Pulp Co. moved its operations from Hollis. Thorne Bay was connected to the island road system in 1974. Camp residents created the community and gained city status from the state as private ownership of the land was made possible under the Alaska Statehood Act. Employment here depends mainly on the U.S. Forest Service, with assorted jobs in local trades and services. Thorne Bay was home to one of the area's largest log sort yards. The area has good access to hunting, camping and saltwater and freshwater sportfishing.

Communications include phones, regular mail service, radio and cable TV. There are 3 churches and a school with grades kindergarten through 12 with enrollment of 94. The community has electrical power, water and sewage systems. Freight comes in by plane, barge, ship and truck. Government address: City of Thorne Bay, P.O. Box 19110, Thorne Bay, AK 99919, phone (907) 828-3380, fax (907) 828-3374; e-mail: tbclerk@thornebay.net. Visitor information: Prince of Wales Chamber of Commerce, P.O. Box 497, Craig, AK 99921, phone (907) 826-3870, fax (07) 826-5467, e-mail: powcc@aptalaska.net, Web: www.princeofwalescoc.org.

Tokeen

GPS: N55°56' W133°19'

Located on the west coast of El Capitan Island off Sea Otter Sound, 60 miles southwest of Wrangell, 30 miles northwest of Craig, 80 miles northwest of Ketchikan. **Transportation:** Charter air service or private boat. Ketchikan Air Service provides daily mail flights. **Population:** 3. **Zip code:** 99950. **Emergency Services:** Alaska State Troopers in Klawock; hospital in Ketchikan.

Private Aircraft: Seaplane base, unattended.

Private Boats: Public moorage at float. Limited emergency fuel available.

Visitor Facilities: A store here carries some groceries, first-aid supplies, hardware, film, sporting goods and liquor. Limited emergency fuel available includes marine gas, diesel and regular gasoline. Tokeen Lodge, P.O. Box TKI, Ketchikan, AK 99950-0230, provides rental camping units, skiffs, kayaks and canoes. Contact the lodge through the marine operator (Tokeen 1, WYW8107).

Tokeen, which once had a mink farm and a cold storage plant, is now privately owned and operated. It is a stop for commercial fishermen. The settlement likely was established by the former residents of Old Tokeen in the late 1930s or early 1940s.

Old Tokeen, located on the northwest end of Marble Island, 7 miles to the northwest, once had Alaska's largest marble quarry. Nearly $2 million worth of marble was taken out between 1905 and 1932. Tokeen marble was used in the Federal Building in Fairbanks, the Capitol Building in Juneau, Washington's state capitol in Olympia, WA, and in various other buildings around the country. Little remains of the mining operation except piles of waste marble.

Whale Pass

GPS: N56°06' W133°10'

Located on the northeast coast of Prince of Wales Island on Whale Passage, 64 road miles north of Klawock. **Transportation:** By road from other Prince of Wales Island communities; floatplane or private boat. **Population:** 62. **Zip code:** 99950. **Emergency Services:** Whale Pass Volunteer EMS, phone (907) 846-5315; Prince of Wales Island Area EMS, phone (907) 826-2367/3330.

Elevation: Sea level. **Climate:** Maritime, with cool, moist weather and mild temperatures.

Private Aircraft: Floatplane landings only.

Private Boats: Transient moorage available. No fuel (nearest fuel at Coffman Cove).

Visitor Facilities: Lodging is available at Northend Cabin, (907) 846-5315. Snacks, fuel, propane, showers and laundromat are available at Whale Pass Gas and Grocery, (907) 846-5205. There are 2 pay phones.

Whale Pass was the site of a floating logging camp. The camp moved out in the early 1980s, but new residents moved in after a state land sale. The community was connected to the Prince of Wales Island road system in 1981, and private phones were installed in 1992.

Whale Pass is nestled in the scenic Tongass National Forest along the inside coastline. Many birds rest here on their migrations. It is not uncommon to see wolves, otter, marten and mink. There are many natural caves and pits in the surrounding area. A nonprofit fish station is located at Neck Lake outlet. Sitka blacktail deer and black bear hunting are popular, as well as fishing for salmon, halibut, steelhead, trout, etc. Whale Pass has retained its rustic, rural atmosphere, and the people are friendly and helpful.

Community nonprofit: Whale Pass Homeowners Assoc., Box WWP, Whale Pass, Ketchikan, AK 99950, phone or fax (907) 846-5221. Visitor information: Prince of Wales Chamber of Commerce, P.O. Box 497, Craig, AK 99921, phone (907) 826-3870, fax (907) 826-5467, e-mail: powcc@aptalaska.net, Web: www.princeofwalescoc.org.

Wrangell

GPS: N56°28' W132°22'

Located at the northwest tip of Wrangell Island on Zimovia Strait near the Stikine River delta, 154 miles south of Juneau and 90 miles north of Ketchikan. **Transportation:** Daily scheduled jet service from major Southeast cities and Seattle; daily commuter service to Ketchikan and Petersburg; air charter services; state ferry service. **Population:** 2,569. **Zip code:** 99929. **Emergency Services:** Alaska State Trooper, phone (907) 874-3215; Police, phone (907) 874-3304; Wrangell Medical Center, phone (907) 874-7000; Wrangell Volunteer Fire Dept./Rescue, phone (907) 874-3223.

Elevation: Sea level. **Climate:** Mild and moist with slightly less rain than other Southeast communities. Mean annual precipitation is 79.16 inches, with 63.9 inches of snow. Average daily maximum temperature in July is 61°F; daily

SOUTHEAST • COMMUNITIES

minimum in January is 21°F.

Private Aircraft: Wrangell airport adjacent northeast; elev. 44 feet; length 6,000 feet; lighted asphalt runway; fuel 80, 100, A. Seaplane base adjacent south.

Private Boats: Transient moorage is available at the city harbor downtown and at Shoemaker Bay, 4.5 miles south of the city. Repair service and fuel are available. Harbormaster: David Mork, phone (907) 874-3736, fax (907) 874-3952.

Visitor Facilities: There are several motels and bed and breakfasts, a hostel, a municipal campground and RV park; restaurants, fast-food outlets, gas stations, hardware, drugstore, grocery, clothing and sporting goods stores, gift shops, banks and a laundromat. Car rental, major repair service and all types of fuel are available. Fishing/hunting licenses may be purchased locally, and there are several charter operations for fishing and hunting, Stikine River trips and glacier flightseeing. A visitor information center, located in the A-frame building next to city hall, is open during the summer. Visitor information is also available from Wrangell Museum, (907) 874-3770. The museum also has information on digging for garnets at Garnet Ledge, a garnet schist ledge located 8 miles from Wrangell by boat.

Wrangell's history is featured at 3 local museums: Our Collections, Tribal House of the Bear on Chief Shakes Island and Wrangell Museum. The Wrangell Museum is housed in the oldest building in Wrangell, and, according to a local source, its collection is second only to the state museum in Juneau for its age and quality.

Wrangell is the home of Wrangell Forest Products, and the mill is open for tours each Friday during the summer season.

Celebrations and events include a salmon derby, held mid-May to early June; a big Fourth of July celebration; annual Coho and Halibut Derby on Labor Day weekend; and Tent City Days, the first weekend in February, which commemorates Wrangell's 3 gold rushes.

A variety of U.S. Forest Service roads (excellent for mountain biking) lead to hiking trails, trout and steelhead streams and scenic overlooks. There are 22 Forest

Service cabins available for public use by reservation in the Wrangell area. The most popular, the Anan cabin, has plank trails to excellent black and brown bear observation posts during the pink salmon run from July through August.

See Tongass National Forest Cabins this section or contact the Wrangell District Rangers office for information on Forest Service lands. The Forest Service has a courtesy phone at the Alaska Marine Highway ferry terminal to help facilitate visitor inquiries. The entire area has excellent salmon and halibut fishing, a large bald eagle population and outstanding scenery.

Wrangell has all communications and public utilities. There are a dozen churches; the elementary and high school have a total combined enrollment of 491. Freight arrives by ship, barge, ferry and cargo plane. Government address: City of Wrangell, P.O. Box 531, Wrangell, AK 99929; phone (907) 874-2381, fax (907) 874-3952, e-mail: ctyclerk@seapac.net, Web: http://www.wrangell.com. Chamber of Commerce: Wrangell Chamber of Commerce, P.O. Box 49, Wrangell, AK 99929, phone (907) 874-3902, fax (907) 874-3905, e-mail: chamber@seapac.net, Web: www.wrangell.com.

For more information, see *The MILE-POST®*, a complete guide to communities on Alaska's road and marine highway systems.

Yakutat
GPS: N59°33' W139°44'

Located on Yakutat Bay on the Gulf of Alaska coast, where southeastern Alaska joins the major body of Alaska to the west; 225 miles northwest of Juneau, 220 miles southeast of Cordova. **Transportation**: Daily scheduled jet service; air charter; private boat. **Population**: 744. **Zip code**: 99689. **Emergency Services**: Police or Fire Department, phone 911; Yakutat Community Health Center, phone (907) 784-3275; Yakutat Volunteer EMS/Rescue, phone (907) 784-3206.

Elevation: Sea level. **Climate**: Maritime, with mild rainy weather.

Average summer temperatures 42°F to 60°F, with a record high of 86°F. Average winter temperatures 17°F to 39°F, with a record low of -24°F. "Cloudiness is abundant," says one resident.

Private Aircraft: Yakutat airport, 3 miles southeast; elev. 33 feet; length 7,800 feet; asphalt; fuel 80, 100, Al+. Passenger and freight terminals; transportation to town available. Seaplane base 1 mile northwest; sheltered anchorage and dock.

Private Boats: Transient moorage at borough harbor. Marine gas is available. Harbormaster: Fred Henry, phone (907) 784-3323, fax (907) 784-3281.

Visitor Facilities: Meals and lodging available at Glacier Bear Lodge, (907) 784-3202; Harlequin Lodge, (907) 784-3341; and Yakutat Lodge, (907) 784-3232. Lodging is available at the Silvertip Guest House, (907) 784-3533, and the Blue Heron Inn, (907) 784-3287. Cabins with kitchens for rent at Leonard's Landing Lodge, (907) 784-3245. The Light House Café, (907) 784-3238, serves meals, and there are 3 bars in town. All supplies are available at local businesses. There is a bank, but no public laundry. Fishing/hunting licenses may be purchased locally. Fishing guide services are available through local lodges, and there are 5 registered hunting guides. Rental cars and charter aircraft are available. Marine gas, diesel, unleaded and regular gasoline are sold locally.

Yakutat Bay is one of the few refuges for vessels along this long stretch of coast in the Gulf of Alaska. The site was originally the principal winter village of the local Tlingit Indian tribe. Sea otter pelts brought Russians to the area in the 19th century. Fur traders were followed by gold seekers, who came to work the black sand beaches. Commercial salmon fishing developed in this century and the first cannery was built here in 1904. Today's economy is based primarily on fishing and fish processing. Salmon, black cod, halibut and crab make up the fishery. Government and local businesses employ most people. Subsistence activities are primarily fishing (salmon and shellfish), hunting (moose, bear, goats, ducks and small game) and gathering sea-weed and berries. The soil is not suitable for agriculture, and a vegetable garden requires a great deal of preparation to produce even small quantities.

The Yakutat School District's information sheet for teacher applicants describes Yakutat's primary attraction as outdoor recreation: "If you enjoy the outdoors, there is plenty for you to do, including cross-country skiing, snowmobiling, hunting, fishing, hiking, biking and berry-picking in the late summer and early fall." Hunting and fishing in particular draw visitors. Steelhead fishing is considered among the finest anywhere, and king and silver salmon run in abundance in Yakutat area salt water, rivers and streams May through September. The Situk River, 12 miles south of Yakutat by road, is one of Alaska's top fishing spots.

The surrounding scenery is also spectacular. Some Lower 48 travelers flying to Anchorage pick a flight with a Yakutat stop, hoping for a clear day and a clear view from the air of Malaspina Glacier northwest of town. Some cruise ships include Hubbard Glacier and Yakutat Bay in their itineraries. Nearer to town, Cannon Beach has good beachcombing and a picnic area. Surfing fanatics from as far away as Fairbanks and Sitka make an annual pilgrimage to ride the waves which pound Yakutat's beaches.

Communications include phones in most households, a local radio station and 1 TV channel via satellite. Mail and newspapers are delivered daily by plane. There are 4 churches. School enrollment (an elementary school and a high school) totals 167. Freight comes in by cargo plane or barge. Government address: City and Borough of Yakutat, P.O. Box 160, Yakutat, AK 99689, phone (907) 784-3323, fax (907) 784-3281, e-mail: bmanager@pti/pwescott@pti. Native corporation address: Yak-tat Kwaan, Inc., P.O. Box 416, Yakutat, AK 99689, phone (907) 784-3335, fax (907) 784-3622. Village council: Yakutat Tlingit Tribe, P.O. Box 418, Yakutat, AK 99689, phone (907) 784-3238, fax (907) 784-3595, e-mail: Yakutat@aitc. org.

SOUTHEAST • ATTRACTIONS

Opportunities for outdoor adventure abound in scenic Southeast Alaska. Sea kayaking and fishing are the most popular activities in Southeast, although there are many close seconds. Watching whales, rafting rivers, hiking lush rainforest trails, hunting, flying over ice fields and staying in luxurious wilderness lodges or rustic cabins are some of the other popular recreational pursuits in this region.

Index of Southeast Attractions

Alaska State Parks
See Chilkat State Park; Point Bridget State Park

Bear Viewing
See Anan Observatory; Fish Creek Wildlife Observation Site; Pack Creek

Bird Watching
See Alaska Chilkat Bald Eagle Preserve; Alaska Maritime National Wildlife Refuge; Dude Creek Critical Habitat Area

Cabins
Alaska State Parks Cabins
Tongass National Forest Cabins

Fishing
Admiralty Island Area
Haines-Skagway Area
Juneau Area
Ketchikan Area
Petersburg Area
Sitka Area
Wrangell Area
Yakutat Area

Glaciers
See Glacier Bay National Park; Mendenhall Glacier; Russell Fiord Wilderness Area (Hubbard Glacier)

Hiking Trails
(See also Chilkoot Trail)
Craig Area
Haines Area
Juneau Area
Ketchikan Area
Petersburg Area
Sitka Area
Skagway Area
Wrangell Area
Yakutat Area

Hot Springs

Lighthouses

Marine Parks

Mountaineering

National Forests
See Tongass National Forest

National Parks and Monuments

See Admiralty Island National Monument; Glacier Bay National Park and Preserve; Klondike Gold Rush National Historical Park; Misty Fiords National Monument

 River Running

See also Stikine River; Tatshenshini-Alsek Wilderness Park

 Sea Kayaking

See also Glacier Bay National Park; Misty Fiords National Monument; Russell Fiord Wilderness Area; Tebenkof Bay and Kuiu Island wilderness areas; Tracy Arm-Fords Terror Wilderness Area

 Special Features

See Basket Bay; Chilkoot Trail; Juneau Icefield; New Eddystone Rock; Stikine Icefield; Stikine River

 State Game Refuges

Dude Creek Critical Habitat Area
Mendenhall Wetlands

 Whale Watching

See Glacier Bay National Park; Point Adolphus

Wilderness Areas

See Chuck River; Coronation Island, Warren Island, Maurelle Islands; Endicott River; Karta River; Petersburg Creek-Duncan Salt Chuck; Pleasant-Lemesurier-Inian Islands; Russell Fiord; South Baranof; South Etolin Island; South Prince of Wales; Stikine-LeConte; Tebenkof Bay and Kuiu; Tracy Arm-Fords Terror; West Chichagof-Yakobi

 Wildlife Refuges

See Alaska Maritime NWR

⛰ Admiralty Island National Monument (Kootznoowoo Wilderness)

Located about 15 miles west of Juneau, this monument encompasses 955,567 acres, over 90 percent of Admiralty Island. The island is bounded on the east and north by Stephens Passage, on the west by Chatham Strait and on the south by Frederick Sound.

The predominantly Tlingit village of Angoon lies at the mouth of Mitchell Bay on the west side of Admiralty Island, adjacent to the wilderness. Excluded from the monument are mining interests at the north end of the island. The predominate terrain of the island is gentle and rolling with spruce/hemlock forest interspersed with small areas of muskeg. Tree line is generally at 1,500 to 2,000 feet. Above timberline, the forest changes to alpine-tundra with rock outcrops and ice fields.

Climate: Annual precipitation is 100 inches over most of the island. Angoon, in the rain shadow of Baranof Island, is drier.

Wildlife: The island boasts the densest population of brown bears in the world, averaging 1 per square mile. (The Tlingit referred to the area as the "Fortress of Bears.") Other wildlife includes Sitka blacktail deer, bald eagles, harbor seals, whales and sea lions. Because it is isolated from the mainland, some species occurring elsewhere in Southeast are not found on the island.

Outstanding areas are the numerous bays and inlets. Seymour Canal, the major inlet on the east side of the island supports one of the largest concentrations of bald eagles in southeastern Alaska.

Activities: Kayaking and canoeing around the island are popular, as are hunting, fishing, bird watching, nature study and photography. Mitchell Bay and Admiralty Lakes Recreational Area are the 2 major recreational attractions within the monument. A 25-mile trail system links the 8 major lakes on the island. This system is part of the Cross-Admiralty canoe trail, which consists of a series of lakes, streams and portages across the island from Mole Harbor on the east to Mitchell Bay. Guided trips and canoe rentals are available in Juneau for the Cross-Admiralty trail. The trail is a popular winter traverse when the lakes are frozen.

The other 2 attractions within the monument are Pack Creek, for bear viewing, and Seymour Canal, for sea kayaking. (See Pack Creek and Sea Kayaking.)

Accommodations: There are overnight accommodations at Angoon. Facilities in the monument include 1 commercial lodge on Thayer Lake and scattered shelters and 18 recreation cabins maintained by the Forest Service. (See Cabins this section.)

Access: Primary access to the monument is by boat from Juneau or Angoon or by floatplane from Juneau.

For more information: Contact Admiralty Island National Monument, 8461 Old Dairy Road, Juneau, AK 99801; phone (907) 586-8800, fax (907) 586-8808; www.fs.fed.us/r10/tongass/districts/admiralty. Or the Alaska Department of Fish and Game, Wildlife Division, P.O. Box 240020 (804 3rd St.), Douglas, AK 99824; phone (907) 465-4265. USGS maps: Juneau, Sitka, Sumdum.

🏛 Alaska Chilkat Bald Eagle Preserve

This 48,000-acre state park is located in the Chilkat River valley northwest of Haines. It was created in 1982 to protect the largest known congregation of bald eagles in North America. (Alaska has more bald eagles than all of the other states combined.) Each year, thousands of bald eagles come to this 5-mile stretch of the Chilkat River to feed on spawned-out chum salmon.

An upwelling of warm water usually prevents the Chilkat River from freezing over at its confluence with the Tsirku River near the village of Klukwan. The open water and the late salmon run draw eagles from all over southeastern Alaska and provide abundant food when other sources are low. As many as 3,900 eagles have gathered at the preserve during peak times in November, and hundreds stay into January. Extremely cold weather, which will freeze the open water, may force the eagles to leave at any time.

Bald eagles develop their characteristic white head and tail between 4 and 6 years of age. Immature bald eagles are mottled brown and white and are occasionally confused with golden eagles. Wingspan of these birds is 5 1/2 to 8 feet; average weight is 12 1/2 pounds, with females slightly larger than males.

Bald eagles can fly at 30 mph and dive at 100 mph. They can see fish in the water at a distance of more than half a mile. Their basic diet consists of fish although they do feed on waterfowl, small mammals and carrion when food is in short supply. Preferred habitat for these birds is in old-growth stands of timber along coastal shorelines. It is easy to spot their white heads as they perch high in trees, sit on beach rocks or soar on the winds.

The gathering of eagles takes place within sight of the Haines Highway, which parallels the river. The heaviest concentration of eagles occurs between Mileposts 17 and 22 on the highway. This core area was set aside in 1972 as the Chilkat River Critical Habitat Area, 10 years before the protective area was enlarged and the larger area designated a preserve.

Other wildlife in the area includes brown and black bears, moose, Sitka blacktail deer, coyote, red fox, lynx, wolverine, wolves, mink, weasel, land otters and other small mammals.

Activities permitted within the preserve include hunting, fishing, trapping, berry picking and picnicking as long as the eagles are not disturbed. The eagles have adjusted to the noise along the highway, but they become greatly agitated and will take flight if approached too closely. State land surrounding the preserve is part of the Haines State Forest Resource Management Area, in which logging, mining and other development is permitted. In the vicinity of Klukwan, much of the easily accessible land is Native-owned and should be treated as private property.

There are limited visitor facilities in the preserve. Vehicle pullouts, parking and a handicap-accessible trail are available in the prime eagle viewing area of the council grounds. The park office provides a list of commercial guides for permitted activities in the area, including river raft trips, photography and natural history tours. Rental cars, bus transportation and all other visitor facilities and guide services are available in Haines. There are pullouts along the highway from which to view and photograph eagles (telephoto lenses are recommended; best light is between 10 A.M. and 2 P.M.); heavy truck traffic makes it unsafe to park or walk along the roadway. Visitors should also avoid walking out on the mud flats for their own safety and to avoid disturbing the eagles. Visitors should note that weather during the peak gathering times can be rainy, windy and/or snowy. Permits are required for building temporary blinds and for certain other activities in the preserve.

Access: Haines is accessible via the Haines Highway from Haines Junction; the Alaska Marine Highway System; and scheduled air service from Juneau.

For more information: Contact: Alaska State Parks, 400 Willoughby Ave., Juneau, AK 99801; phone (907) 465-4563, fax (907) 465-5330; www.dnr.state.ak.us/parks/units/eagle prv.htm.

Alaska Maritime National Wildlife Refuge

This wildlife refuge includes more than 2,400 parcels of land on islands, islets, rocks, spires, reefs and headlands of Alaska coastal waters from Point Franklin in the Arctic Ocean to Forrester Island in southern Southeast Alaska. Most of this refuge is managed to protect wildlife and the coastal ecosystem. The refuge has the most diverse wildlife species of all the refuges in Alaska, including thousands of sea lions, seals, walrus and sea otters.

Alaska Maritime is synonymous with seabirds—millions of them. They congregate in colonies along the coast. Each species has a specialized nesting site, be it rock ledge, crevice, boulder rubble, pinnacle or burrow. (This adaptation allows many birds to use a small area of land.) Of the 50 million seabirds that nest in Alaska, 80 percent of them nest on the refuge.

Alaska Maritime, like most refuge lands, is wild and lonely, extremely rugged and virtually inaccessible. Some portions are classified as wilderness. Swift tides, rough seas, high winds, rocky shorelines and poor anchorages hamper efforts to view wildlife.

Alaska Maritime totals about 3.5 million acres and is divided into 5 management units. Southeast Alaska islands included in the Gulf of Alaska Unit are: 5-mile-long Forrester Island, located 10 miles west of Dall Island; the Hazy Islands, a group of small islands extending 2.7 miles in Christian Sound, 9 miles west of Coronation Island; and St. Lazaria Island, located at the entrance to Sitka Sound, approximately 15 miles southwest of Sitka.

St. Lazaria Island is host to one of the largest seabird colonies in Southeast. This 65-acre, volcanic island has been set aside as a wildlife refuge since 1909. A half million seabirds of 11 different species breed here. Burrowing seabirds on the island include tufted puffins, rhinoceros auklets, ancient murrelets and storm-petrels, both Leach's and fork-tailed. Common and thick-billed murres, pelagic cormorants, glaucous-winged gulls, pigeon guillemots and others inhabit the sea cliffs while song and fox sparrows and hermit thrushes flit through the lush growth.

A nearly impenetrable mass of salmonberry bushes, growing up to 6 feet high, hinders foot travel on the island. St. Lazaria was uninhabited and apparently seldom visited until a military outpost was established there during WWII. Remains of the outpost are overgrown and difficult to find; the metal is corroding, and the wood is rotting rapidly in the mild, wet climate.

Since seabirds are sensitive to disturbance, and foot traffic crushes the closely spaced burrows of ground nesting birds, one should not land on the island. Small boats can land on the island only at high tide (with great difficulty) because of constant swells from the open ocean. The seabirds can be seen easily from boats which can circle the island. Binoculars and spotting scopes are recommended to view wildlife from a distance. May through June is the best time to visit. Visitors should be prepared for wet and windy weather. Charter boats, lodging and campgrounds are available in Sitka.

For more information: Contact Refuge Manager, Alaska Maritime National Wildlife Refuge, 451 Sterling Highway #2, Homer, AK 99603; phone (907) 235-6961, fax (907) 235-7469, www.r7.fws.gov/nwr/akmnwr/akmnwr.html.

Anan Wildlife Observatory

Managed by the U.S. Forest Service, Anan (pronounced an-an) Wildlife Observatory is located 35 miles southeast of Wrangell. It is accessible by boat or plane only. During July, August and early September, visitors can watch black and brown bears catch pink salmon headed for spawning grounds. Bald eagles and seals may also be seen feeding on the fish.

The only facilities at the observatory are a large, wooden deck with a small observation building and a public-use recreation cabin nearby. A ranger is on duty in July and August, the peak viewing season. Check with the Wrangell Visitors Bureau about local tours to Anan Wildlife Observatory available from Wrangell. There are flightseeing tours out of Ketchikan. Call the Ketchikan Visitor's Bureau or floatplane service providers.Charter service to the observatory may be arranged, but there is no scheduled tour boat service.

For more information: Contact Wrangell Ranger District office, P.O. Box 51 Wrangell, AK 99929; phone (907) 874-2323, fax (907) 874-7595, www.fs.fed.us/r10/tongass/recreation/wildlife_viewing/ananobservatory.html.

Basket Bay

Basket Bay is located on Chichagof Island on the west side of Chatham Strait, northwest of Angoon, 8 miles south of the mouth of Tenakee Inlet. The bay is exposed to the southeast and has a rocky bottom with depths of 12 to 40 fathoms. According to the United States Coast Pilot, the bay is not recommended as an anchorage. The mid-channel course up the bay is clear. This is a scenic spot for sightseeing or fishing. Many silver salmon enter this bay in August; use herring or spoons. A flat extends about 400 yards into the head of the bay from the mouth of Kook Creek, a large stream that enters the bay through a limestone cliff. The stream goes underground 3 times between the bay and Kook Lake, which has fishing for cutthroat and Dolly Varden. There is an old, unmaintained trail between Basket Bay and Kook Lake; the trail does not extend to the Forest Service cabin at the west end of the lake. USGS map: Sitka C-4.

 Cabins

Alaska State Park Cabins

Alaska State Parks maintains 4 public-use cabins in Southeast. The state public-use cabins may be rented for $25 to $35 per night. Maximum stay is 3 nights, and reservations are required. Reservations are confirmed when the full amount is paid. This can be done in person or by mail. Credit cards are not accepted. Reservations can be made up to 180 days in advance. Cabins are equipped with wooden sleeping platforms, wood and propane stoves, chairs, benches, tables and latrines. Treat all stream water before use.

Contact Alaska State Parks office in Juneau, 400 Willoughby Ave., 99801; phone (907) 465-4563; or in Ketchikan, 9883 North Tongass Highway, 99901; phone (907) 247-8574. Go to www.dnr.state.ak.us/parks/index.htm and click on recreation cabins.

Blue Mussel Cabin. Located in Point Bridget State Park, 39 miles north of Juneau by highway. Access via 3.4-mile trail. Also accessible by boat in summer. Winter access by snowshoes or skis. Sleeps 8. Excellent salmon runs in fall off Berner's Bay. Activities include beachcombing, wildlife viewing, hiking and boating. Bears in the area.

Cowee Meadow Cabin. Located in Point Bridget State Park, 39 miles north of Juneau by highway. Access via 2.5-mile trail. Also accessible by boat in summer. Winter access by snowshoes or skis. Sleeps 8. Water supply from creek. Excellent salmon runs in Cowee Creek.

Grindall Island Cabin. Located at Grindall Island State Marine Park, 18 miles from Ketchikan and 40 air miles from Craig. Summer and winter access by air or boat from Ketchikan. Sleeps 6. Saltwater fishing and beachcombing are the main attractions, and the island is known for its king salmon fishing. Bring your own water.

Seymour Canal Cabin. Located at Oliver Inlet State Marine Park on tip of Seymour Canal on Admiralty Island, 23 miles south of Juneau. Summer and winter access by float-plane or boat from Juneau. Tramway from Oliver Inlet to access the cabin. Sleeps 6. Activities include hiking, hunting and boating. Area has one of the largest brown bear populations in Southeast. Seals, sea lions, whales, trumpeter and whistling swans and other waterfowl inhabit the area. Freshwater streams near cabin for water.

Tongass National Forest Cabins

The more than 150 Tongass National Forest recreational cabins are among the best lodging bargains in the state. Current cost is $25 to $45 per night for these rustic but comfortable cabins, accessible by road, boat, floatplane, helicopter or hiking trail. Use is limited to 7 consecutive days between April 1 and September 30 and 10 consecutive days between October 1 and March 31. A few cabins have a less-than-7-night limit. A reservation day begins and ends at noon.

Reservations for use of the cabins are issued on a first-come, first-served basis through www.reserveusa.com or at (800) 444-6777. Reservations are accepted up to 180 days in advance of intended use. Fees are payable by check or credit card. Anyone who is at least 18 years of age may reserve a cabin. Guides or outfitters may not reserve cabins for commercial purposes.

Cabins have tables, benches, bunks (without mattresses), wood or oil stoves, brooms and pit toilets. You must bring your own bedding and cooking utensils. An ax or maul is provided at cabins with wood stoves, but bring a small ax or hatchet in case the tools are not there. The Forest Service does not provide stove oil. Five to ten gallons of diesel oil per week are required, depending on weather conditions. Check with the Forest Service about stove and fuel types (call or go to www.fs.fed.us/r10/tongass). It is advisable to bring a gas camp stove for cooking. Most cabins located on lakes have skiffs with oars. You must bring your own life preservers and motor. Be sure to pull the boat above the high-water mark and tie it. Also, turn it over, so it does not fill with rain water. Bring good rain gear, waterproof boots and plenty of warm clothing. Also bring extra food and other supplies in case bad weather prolongs your stay. Insect repellent is a must during the summer. Treat all stream water before use. Those traveling in bear country may want to carry a .30-06 or larger caliber rifle as a safety precaution if you know how to use the firearm. Pack out all garbage to avoid attracting bears. Resist the temptation to leave unused food for the next campers. The Forest Service cautions that you are "on your own" at these remote cabins. Be prepared to be self-sufficient, and bring emergency equipment such as maps, a compass, waterproof matches, a strong knife, a first-aid kit and a space blanket. A detailed list of suggested items to take along is available from the Forest Service on request. Also, note that cabin conditions and facilities change frequently; please contact the Forest Service for current cabin information before making reservations.

Keep in mind that trail access is often required in addition to plane or boat access. (See Hiking Trails this section for details on trails to cabins.)

Obtain additional cabin information from the Tongass National Forest website at www.fs.fed.us/r10/tongass/recreation/cabin_info/cabin_info.html, or from anyof the ranger district offices listed below.

Hoonah area: Hoonah Ranger District, P.O. Box 135, Hoonah, AK 99829; phone (907) 945-3631, fax (907) 945-3385.

Juneau area (including Admiralty Island): Juneau Ranger District, 8465 Old Dairy Road, Juneau, AK 99801; phone (907) 586-8800, fax (907) 586-8088.

Ketchikan area (including Misty Fiords): Ketchikan-Misty Fiords Ranger District, 3031 Tongass Avenue, Ketchikan, AK 99901; phone (907) 225-2148, fax (907) 225-8738. or Southeast Alaska Discovery Center, 50 Main Street, Ketchikan, AK 99901; phone (907) 228-6220, fax (907) 228-6234.

Petersburg area: Petersburg Ranger District, P.O. Box 1328, Petersburg, AK 99833; phone (907) 772-3871.

Prince of Wales Island area: Thorne Bay Ranger District, P.O. Box 19001, Thorne Bay, AK 99919; phone (907) 828-3304, fax (907) 828-3309.

Sitka area: Sitka Ranger District, 204 Siginaka Way, Sitka, AK 99835; phone (907) 747-4220, fax (907) 747-4331.

Wrangell area: Wrangell Ranger District, P.O. Box 51, Wrangell, AK 99929; phone (907) 874-2323.

Yakutat area: Yakutat Ranger District, Box 327, Yakutat, AK 99689; phone (907) 784-3359, fax (907) 874-7595.

Admiralty Island USFS Cabins

Admiralty Cove Cabin. Located on northern tip of island, 1/4-mile up trail from tide flat. Floatplane and boat accessible; 15-minute flight from Juneau; requires +13-foot tide. Civilian Conservation Corps shelter at cabin. Cabin has 2 single and 2 double bunks and an oil stove (uses #2 diesel). Sleeps 4 to 6. Brown bears frequent area; salmon runs July through August. Cabin is on beach overlooking Admiralty Creek and tidal meadow.

Big Shaheen Cabin. Located in center of island on Hasselborg Lake. Lake is part of the Cross Admiralty Canoe trail. Floatplane accessible, 45 minutes from Juneau. Lake is ice free mid-May through November. Cabin contains 4 double bunks, a wood stove and a boat. Sleeps 4 to 8. Cabin is in bear country.

Church Bight Cabin. Located on small bight in Gambier Bay. Boat accessible and 1 hour floatplane flight from Juneau. Accessible all year. Cabin has 4 single bunks, a loft, a wood stove and a boat. Sleeps 8. Stream nearby with intermittent water; boat is necessary to get water from other drainages. Bay provides good boat anchorage, no mooring facility and large tidal flats. Cabin is popular for hunting. Cabin is in bear country.

Distin Shelter Cabin. Located in central part of island on north side of Distin Lake. Accessible by floatplane, 45 minutes from Juneau. Lake is ice free mid-May through November. Cabin is enclosed Adirondack shelter with 4 single bunks, a wood stove and a boat. Sleeps 4. Lake is part of Cross Admiralty Canoe route with two short portage trails. Cabin has a 3-mile trail to Thayer Lake. Cabin is in bear country.

East Florence Cabin. Located on northwest side of island on east end of Lake Florence. Accessible by floatplane, 30 minutes from Juneau. Lake is ice free early May through November. Cabin located on nice beach with 3 single bunks, a loft, a boat and an oil stove (uses #1 diesel). Sleeps 7 to 8. Area surrounded by Shee Atika Native Corporation lands; access with permit only. Clearcuts, roads and equipment are visible. One-mile trail to salt water begins on north side of outlet stream at west end of lake. Cabin is in bear country.

Hasselborg Creek Cabin. Located in central part of island on Hasselborg Lake. Accessible by floatplane, 45 minutes from Juneau. Lake is ice free mid-May through November. Cabin is a small, enclosed Adirondack shelter with a concrete floor, fireplace, wood stove, 2 single bunks and a boat. Cabin has trails to Hasselborg River, Guerin Lake and a shelter. Lake is part of the Cross Admiralty Canoe route. Cabin is in bear country.

Jim's Lake Cabin. Located on central part of island at north end of Jim's Lake near the outlet stream. Accessible by floatplane, 50 minutes from Juneau. Lake is ice free mid-May to November. Cabin has nice overlook of lake and is adjacent to beach. Cabin contains 2 single and 2 double bunks, a wood stove and a boat. Sleeps 4 to 6. Cabin has most soltitude on the island and is in bear country.

Lake Alexander Cabin. Located in center of island on west end of Lake Alexander near outlet stream. Accessible by floatplane, 45 minutes from Juneau. Lake is ice free mid-May through November. Cabin has nice overlook of lake and a beach. There are 2 single and 2 double bunks, a wood stove and a boat. Sleeps 4 to 6. A 2 3/4-mile trail to salt water heads at shelter on opposite end of lake. Lake is on Cross Admiralty Canoe route and is in bear country.

Lake Kathleen Cabin. Located on west side of island within Shee Atika Native lands; access by permit only. Accessible by floatplane, 30 minutes from Juneau. Lake is ice free mid-May through November. Cabin is near beach in a small, timbered area. Adjacent land has been logged. Cabin has 2 single bunks and a loft, a wood stove and a boat. Sleeps 4 to 5. Lake is surrounded by an active road system.Cabin is in bear country

Little Shaheen Cabin. Located in center of island on Hasselborg Lake. Accessible by floatplane, 45 minutes from Juneau. Lake is ice free mid-May through November. Cabin has 2 single and 2 double bunks, a wood stove and a boat. Sleeps 4 to 6. A 100-yard trail leads to Big Shaheen cabin. Area has four boat-accessible trails, and lake is part of the Cross Admiralty Canoe trail. Cabin is in bear country.

North Young Lake Cabin. Located on north end of island at north end of Young Lake. Accessible by floatplane, 20 minutes from Juneau. There is a 4 3/4-mile, flat trail to Admiralty Cove at cabin. Admiralty Cove Cabin is 4 1/2 miles down trail. Lake is ice free mid-May through November. South Young Lake Cabin is 1 mile down trail along shore. Cabin is on small beach under tree canopy. There are 2 single and 2 double bunks, a wood stove and a boat. Sleeps 4 to 6. Cabin is in bear country with substantial plane traffic.

Pybus Cabin. Located on north side of Donkey Bay in protected cove in Pybus Bay. Year-round access by floatplane, 1 1/4 hours from Juneau and by boat. High tide is recommended for access. Cabin contains 4 single bunks, a loft and an oil stove (uses #2 stove oil). Sleeps 7. There is a small stream nearby and a game trail to Donkey Bay at high tide. No mooring facility. Seasonal commercial fishing, hunting and large tide flats in Plybus Bay. Cabin is in bear country.

South Young Lake Cabin. Located on north end of island at south end of Young Lake. Accessible by floatplane, 20 minutes from Juneau. North Young Lake Cabin is 1 mile up trail along shore. Cabin is in large, open area on a flat beach. There are 2 single and 2 double bunks, a wood stove and a boat. Sleeps 4 to 6. Cabin is in bear country with substantial plane traffic.

Sportsmen Cabin. Located in center of island on north side of Distin Lake. Accessible by floatplane, 45 minutes from Juneau. Lake is ice free mid-May through November. Small cabin is under tree canopy near beach. There are 2 single bunks, a loft, a wood stove and a boat. Sleeps 5 to 6. Lake is part of Cross Admiralty Canoe route. There are 2 short portage trails, Thayer Lake and Davidson. Trail is 3 miles to Thayer Lake.

Hoonah Area USFS Cabins

Greentop Harbor Cabin. Located in West Chichagof-Yakobi Wilderness at Greentop Harbor on southwest tip of Yakobi Island. Safe anchorage for boats provided. Accessible by floatplane or boat. Cabin has wood stove. Sleeps 6. Popular with kayakers. USGS map: Sitka D-8.

Salt Lake Bay Cabin. Located at south end of Port Frederick, 14 miles from Hoonah. Accessible by boat or floatplane. Sleeps 4. Logging in area; log transfer facility across bay. Popular with kayakers between Hoonah and Tenakee Springs. Port Frederick-Tenakee Inlet portage is 6 miles west of cabin. USGS maps: Sitka D-5, D-6.

Juneau Area USFS Cabins

Berner's Bay Cabin. Located on salt water, 8 miles north of Echo Cove boat ramp. Road is not maintained year-round. Cabin has 3 single and 1 double bunk and a wood stove. Excellent views of river deltas and mountains. USGS map: Juneau D-3.

Dan Moller Cabin. Located in alpine environment on Douglas Island across from downtown Juneau. Accessible by 3-mile trail on local road system. Cabin has 2 double and 2 single bunks, a large loft and a wood stove. Sleeps 16. Activities are hiking, wildlife viewing, cross-country skiing and snow machining. Two-night maximum stay. USGS map: Juneau B-2.

Denver Caboose. Retired railroad caboose located 5.5 miles north of Skagway near White Pass and Yukon Railroad. Accessible by railroad in summer and from Skagway along railroad tracks in off-season. Excellent views of Skagway River and Sawtooth Mountains. Cabin has 4 single and 1 double bunk and an oil stove (use #1 stove oil). USGS map: Skagway C-1.

Eagle Glacier Memorial Cabin. Located on south side of lake in front of Eagle Glacier. Accessible by 5.5-mile trail at mile 27.5 on Glacier Highway. Cabin has 1 single and 1 double bunk, a large loft, a wood stove (no wood provided) and a propane wall furnace (propane supplied). Sleeps 12. Excellent views of lake, Eagle Glacier and surrounding mountains. Two-night maximum stay. USGS map: Juneau C-3.

East Turner Lake Cabin. Located 20 miles east of Juneau. Accessible by floatplane 40 minutes from Juneau. Cabin has 2 double and 2 single bunks, an oil stove (use #1 stove oil) and a skiff. Fishing for cutthroat, Dolly Varden and Kokanee in lake. Opportunities for wildlife viewing and mountain and lake scenery. USGS map: Taku River B-6.

John Muir Cabin. Located in a subalpine meadow above Mendenhall Valley, 13 miles north of Juneau near Auke Bay. Accessible by hiking, cross-country skiing or snowshoeing from Glacier Highway on the 3-mile Auke Nu Trail. Cabin has 3 double and 2 single bunks and a large loft. Sleeps 16 people. There is a wood stove (no wood provided) and a propane wall furnace (propane supplied). Two-night maximum stay. USGS map: Juneau B-2.

Laughton Glacier Cabin. Located in alpine/subalpine area 14 miles northeast of Skagway near Skagway River. Accessible to mile 12 by White Pass and Yukon Railroad and up 2-mile Forest Service trail in summer. Cabin has 2 double and 2 single bunks and an oil stove (use #1 stove oil). Activities include glacier and wildlife viewing. USGS map: Skagway C-1.

Peterson Lake Cabin. Located in muskeg, coastal forest on west side of Peterson Lake, 24 miles north of Juneau. Accessible by 4.3-mile trail between miles 24 and 25 on Glacier Highway. Cabin has 2 double and 2 single bunks, a wood stove (no wood provided) and a propane wall furnace (propane provided). Fishing for steelhead, trout, coho and pink salmon in creek below falls and Dolly Varden and cutthroat trout in lake. Hiking, cross-country skiing and snowshoeing are area activities. Two-night maximum stay. USGS map: Juneau B-3.

Taku Glacier Cabin. Located 26 miles northeast of Juneau on Taku Inlet across from Taku Glacier. Handicap-accessible boardwalk, outhouse, decking and cabin facilities. Accessible by floatplane or boat with 12-foot tide recommended (sandbars nearby). Mooring buoy is available. Cabin has 2 single and 2 double bunks and an oil stove (use #1 stove oil). Opportunities for glacier and wildlife viewing, fishing and hunting. USGS map: Juneau B-1.

West Turner Lake Cabin. Located 18 miles east of Juneau near cliffs and waterfalls. Accessible by floatplane 35 minutes from Juneau or by boat at high tide and 0.8-mile hike from Taku Inlet. Cabin has 2 double and 2 single bunks, a skiff and an oil stove (use #1 stove oil). Fishing for cutthroat, Dolly Varden, and kokanee in lake and pink salmon in Turner River and Taku Inlet. USGS map: Taku River B-6.

Windfall Lake Cabin. Located on east side of Windfall Lake. Accessible by flat, 3.3-mile Windfall Lake Trail to Montana Creek Trail at end of Herbert River Road, Mile 26 on Glacier Highway. Also accessible by floatplane, snow machine, cross-country skis or snowshoes. Undeveloped trail near cabin provides access to Spaulding Meadows. Cabin has 2 single and 2 double bunks, a wood stove (no wood provided) and a propane wall furnace (propane supplied). USGS map: Juneau C-3.

Ketchikan Area USFS Cabins

Fees for Ketchikan cabins are $25 per night October to April and $25-$35 per night May to September. Cabins have 2 single and 2 double bunks, axes, mauls and wedges; sleep 4 to 6 people and have untreated water available (exceptions are Deer Mountain and Heckman Lake cabins). All trails and buoys are noted on the Forest Service Misty Fiords National Monument map available from the Southeast Alaska Discovery Center for $4.

Anchor Pass Cabin. Located on salt water, 50 air miles north of Ketchikan near boundary of Misty Fiords National Monument. Accessible by floatplane or boat. Cabin has wood stove and mooring buoy. Fishing for king salmon in Unuk River and salmon, halibut, red snapper and shrimp in area. Spectacular mountain views.

Blind Pass Cabin. Located 40 air miles north of Ketchikan on salt water in sheltered cove. Accessible by floatplane or boat. Cabin has wood stove and mooring buoy. Area provides bay and inlet exploration near northern Behm Canal. King salmon fishing in Unuk River and fishing for other salmon species, halibut, red snapper and shrimp. Freshwater lake for trout fishing 1/2 mile upstream. No trail to lake.

Deer Mountain Cabin. Located above timberline on Deer Mountain. Accessible by helicopter or 2.5-mile hike up Deer Mountain National Recreation Trail located 4 miles from downtown Ketchikan. Cabin well-insulated but has no stove; backpacking stove is recommended. Sleeps 4. Cabin offers dramatic alpine scenery.

Fish Creek Cabin. Located on salt water, 20 air miles east of Ketchikan. Accessible by floatplane or boat. Cabin offers oil stove (use #1 stove oil) and a mooring buoy. Cabin accesses 2 trails: Low Lake Trail, follows Low Lake, Fish Creek and ends at Big Lake in Misty Fiords National Monument; Gokachin Lake Trail, leads to Star Lake and Fish Creek. Fishing in Fish Creek for salmon, steelhead and trout. Saltwater fishing for halibut, salmon and crab.

Heckman Lake Cabin. Located 15 air miles north of Ketchikan. Accessible by floatplane or by 6-mile trail from Naha Bay. Trail follows Naha River through old-growth Sitka Spruce and Western Hemlock rainforest. Cabin has wood stove and skiff with oars. Fishing in Naha River for steelhead, salmon, trout and Dolly Varden.

Helm Bay Cabin. Located on saltwater in old-growth Sitka Spruce and Western Hemlock rainforest, near tidal flat, 25 air miles northwest of Ketchikan. Accessible by floatplane or boat. Cabin provides wood stove and floating dock. Area has crab, salmon, halibut and red snapper.

Helm Creek Cabin. Located on beach near tidal flat, 24 air miles northwest of Ketchikan. Accessible by floatplane or boat. Cabin provides wood stove and mooring buoy. Beach allows skiff landings. Area offers crab, salmon, halibut and red snapper. Fishing for trout and Dolly Varden in Helm Lake. No trail to lake.

Jordan Lake Cabin. Located 15 air miles north of Ketchikan. Accessible by trail only. Floatplane access 4 miles from Naha Bay or 2 miles from Heckman Lake. Cabin accessible upstream and downstream by Naha Trail. Cabin provides wood stove and skiff with oars. Fishing in Naha River for steelhead, salmon, trout and Dolly Varden.

McDonald Lake Cabin. Located in old-growth cedar, Sitka Spruce and Western Hemlock rainforest, 50 air miles north of Ketchikan. Accessible by floatplane or 1.5-mile trail from Yes Bay. Cabin provides wood stove and skiff with oars; no mooring buoy at trailhead. Trail accesses Wolverine Creek and a shelter. Fishing for steelhead and salmon in Wolverine Creek and trout and Dolly Varden in lake.

Phocena Bay Cabin. Located 15 air miles southwest of Ketchikan. Accessible by float-plane or boat during high tide. Cabin provides wood stove, mooring buoy, mountain views, tide pools and large tidal flat for hiking. Fishing outside bay for ling cod, red snapper, halibut and salmon.

Patching Lake Cabin. Located in old-growth cedar, Sitka Spruce and Western Hemlock rainforest, 20 air miles north of Ketchikan. Accessible only by floatplane. Cabin provides wood stove and a skiff with oars. Fishing for cutthroat trout in Patching and Chamberlain Lakes. No trail to Chamberlain Lake.

Plenty Cutthroat Cabin. Located on Orchard Lake 35 miles north of Ketchikan. Accessible by floatplane or boat and 1-mile trail from Shrimp Bay. Cabin provides oil stove (use #1 stove oil) and skiff with oars. Mooring buoy in Klu Bay. Lake outlet, saltwater and waterfall accessible by Orchard Lake trail. Fishing for cutthroat trout and kokanee in Orchard Lake.

Rainbow Lake Cabin. Located 27 air miles northwest of Ketchikan. Accessible by float-plane. Cabin has wood stove and views of muskeg and peaks across lake. Fishing for rainbow trout in lake.

Reflection Lake Cabin. Located 50 air miles north of Ketchikan. Accessible by floatplane or boat and a 2-mile hike from Short Bay. No bridge across Short Creek. Cabin has wood stove and a skiff with oars. Excellent views of mountains and clinging ice fields. Fishing for salmon and steelhead in Short Creek and trout and Dolly Varden in lake.

Misty Fiords Area USFS Cabins

Fees for Misty Fiords cabins are $25/night October-April and $25-$35/night May-September. Cabins have 2 single and 2 double bunks, axes, mauls and wedges; sleep 4 to 6 people and have untreated water available. All trails and buoys are noted on the Forest Service Misty Fiords National Monument map available from the Southeast Alaska Discovery Center for $4.

Alava Bay Cabin. Located on salt water, 20 miles southeast of Ketchikan on Revillagigedo Island. Accessible by floatplane or boat. Cabin includes mooring buoy and wood stove (firewood provided). Area offers saltwater fishing, sightseeing, hiking, hunting for Sitka blacktail deer and black bear and beachcombing. Alava Bay provides safe boat anchorage. USGS map: Ketchikan A-4.

Bakewell Lake Cabin. Located 40 air miles east of Ketchikan on the mainland south of Bakewell Arm of Smeaton Bay. Accessible by floatplane or canoe. Cabin offers oil stove (use #1 stove oil or kerosene), outhouse and skiff with oars. Cabin provides sandy beach; fishing for Dolly Varden, cutthroat trout, sockeye, pink, chum and coho salmon and steelhead; hunting and wildlife including wolves, Sitka blacktail deer, beavers, otters, eagles, loons and other birds. USGS map: Ketchikan B-2.

Beaver Camp Cabin. Located 28 air miles northeast of Ketchikan on Revillagigedo Island on the southern arm of Manzanita Lake. Accessible by floatplane or canoe. Cabin provides wood stove (firewood provided), outhouse, wood shed and skiff with oars. Cabin offers mountain views; old-growth forest; fishing for cutthroat trout, Dolly Varden and kokanee; hunting for Sitka blacktail deer and black bears; and wildlife, including beaver, mink and marten. USGS map: Ketchikan C-4.

Checats Lake Cabin. Located 45 air miles northeast of Ketchikan on mainland east of Rudyerd Bay. Accessible by floatplane. Cabin may be inaccessible in fall, winter and spring due to ice on lake. Cabin offers wood stove (firewood provided), outhouse and skiff with oars. Checats Lake is glacial with rocky cliff faces. Cabin is at outlet of lake and provides stream and lake fishing for rainbow trout. Other attractions are scenery and photography and hunting for mountain goat, Sitka blacktail deer, and black and brown bears. USGS map: Ketchikan B-3.

Ella Narrows Cabin. Located 24 air miles northeast of Ketchikan on Revillagigedo Island on north end of Ella Lake. Accessible by floatplane or canoe. Cabin provides wood stove (firewood provided), outhouse and skiff with oars. Cabin also offers cobble beach with sand beach nearby; old-growth forest; fishing for cutthroat, Dolly Varden and kokanee; hunting for Sitka blacktail deer and black bear and wildlife including beaver, mink, marten and birds. USGS map: Ketchikan C-4, B-4.

Hugh Smith Cabin. Located on point of land on Hugh Smith Lake, 55 air miles southeast of Ketchikan on mainland south of Martin Arm. Accessible by floatplane. May be inaccessible in fall, winter and spring due to ice on lake. Cabin includes wood stove (firewood provided), outhouse and skiff with oars. Area features Southeast Alaska Historic abandoned cannery on east end of lake, trail to salt water, working fish weir, fishing for cutthroat and Dolly Varden and salmon and hunting for Sitka blacktail deer and black bears. USGS map: Ketchikan A-3.

Humpback Lake Cabin. Located 48 air miles southeast of Ketchikan on mainland east of Mink Bay. Accessible by floatplane. May be inaccessible in fall, winter and spring due to ice on lake. Cabin provides oil stove (use #1 stove oil or kerosene), outhouse and skiff with oars. Area features views of alpine peaks with granite walls, solitude, commercial lodging and hiking. Humpback Creek Trail is located on west end of lake and offers views of Humpback Falls; trailhead located behind log jam at end of lake. Fishing is excellent for Dolly Varden and cutthroat. Area also provides hunting for Sitka blacktail deer, black and brown bears and mountain goats. USGS map: Ketchikan A-2.

Manzanita Lake Cabin. Located 28 air miles northeast of Ketchikan on Revillagigedo Island on northwest arm of Manzanita Lake. Accessible by floatplane or canoe. May be inaccessible in fall, winter and spring due to ice on lake. Cabin provides oil stove (use #1 diesel), outhouse and skiff with oars. Cabin is 100 yards from lake near series of cascading waterfalls with views of granite walls, glacial valley and snow-capped peaks. Area also provides old-growth forest; fishing for cutthroat, Dolly Varden and kokanee; hunting for Sitka blacktail deer and black bears; and wildlife, including beaver, mink and marten. USGS map: Ketchikan C-4.

Red Alders Cabin. Located 24 air miles northeast of Ketchikan on Revillagigedo Island on north end of Ella Lake. Accessible by floatplane or canoe. May be inaccessible in fall, winter and spring due to ice on lake. Cabin provides wood stove (firewood provided), outhouse and skiff with oars. Area offers old-growth forest; cobblestone beach; sandy beach; open muskeg; deer; excellent fishing for cutthroat, Dolly Varden and kokanee; hunting for Sitka blacktail deer and black bears; and wildlife, including beaver, mink, marten, and birds. USGS map: Ketchikan B-4.

Wilson Narrows Cabin. Located 44 air miles east of Ketchikan on mainland north of Wilson Arm at south end of Wilson Lake. Accessible by floatplane. May be inaccessible in fall, winter and spring due to ice on lake. Cabin provides wood stove (firewood provided), outhouse and skiff with oars. Area offers glacial lake, rugged terrain and hunting for mountain goats, Sitka blacktail deer and black bears and brown bears. Big Goat Lake is above cabin and to the north. Outlet of Wilson Lake provides excellent fishing for cutthroat, Dolly Varden and kokanee. USGS map: Ketchikan B-2, C-2.

Wilson View Cabin. Located 44 air miles east of Ketchikan on mainland north of Wilson Arm at north end of glacial Wilson Lake. Accessible by floatplane. May be inaccessible in fall, winter and spring due to ice on lake. Cabin provides oil stove (use #1 stove oil or kerosene), outhouse and skiff with oars. Area offers rugged terrain, fishing, wildlife viewing and hunting for mountain goats, Sitka blacktail deer and black and brown bears. USGS map: Ketchikan B-2, C-2.

Winstanley Island Cabin. Located on salt water, 30 air miles or 45 water miles east of Ketchikan on the east of Behm Canal, between Rudyerd and Smeaton Bays. Accessible by floatplane or boat. Cabin includes wood stove (firewood provided), outhouse and a mooring buoy. Scenic attractions include Rudyerd Bay, east Behm Canal, Walker Cove, Chickamin River and Smeaton Bay. Winstanley Lake, Checats, Ella, Manzanita and Nooya Lake Trails provide access to freshwater streams and lakes and hunting areas (accessible by boat). Area also offers saltwater fishing, wilderness exploration, hiking, hunting and beachcombing. USGS map: Ketchikan B-3.

Winstanley Lake Cabin. Located 33 air miles northeast of Ketchikan on mainland, east of Winstanley Island. Accessible by floatplane or canoe. May be inaccessible in fall, winter and spring due to ice on lake. Canoe access requires 2.5-mile hike from salt water and 2.5-mile paddle to the cabin. Mooring buoy at trailhead. Cabin provides wood stove (firewood provided), outhouse and skiff with oars. Area offers scenic views, fishing, hunting, solitude and relaxation. A paddle to the outlet brings you to Winstanley Lake Shelter and a hike to salt water on the Winstanley Lake Trail. Fishing includes cutthroat and kokanee. The area also offers hunting for mountain goats, Sitka blacktail deer and black and brown bears. Wildlife includes mink, marten, beaver and otter. USGS map: Ketchikan B-3.

Petersburg Area USFS Cabins

Beecher Pass Cabin. Located on Woewodski Island, in Duncan Canal, on south side of Beecher Pass, 17 air miles and 20 water miles from Petersburg. Accessible in any tide with good boat anchorage in front of cabin. Strong north winds can make anchoring difficult. Cabin is on a gravel beach and includes 4 single bunks, wood stove and outhouse. Sleeps 4. Water available from creek. Area offers wildlife viewing, including martens, eagles, herons, deer, beavers and sea mammals. Waterfowl hunting and fishing for salmon and halibut are also popular in Duncan Canal. Fee is $35/night May 1- September 30, $25/night rest of year. USGS maps: Petersburg C-4, C-3.

Big John Bay Cabin. Located on tidal flat at north end of Big John Bay, in Rocky Pass of Keku Strait, on west side of Kupreanof Island, 18 water miles or a 16-mile drive and 1.75-mile hike from Kake, 28 air miles from Petersburg. Accessible by boat or plane with 15-foot required tide. Cabin provides oil stove (use #1 heating oil), outhouse and 4 single bunks. Sleeps 4. Water available from stream 1/4 mile from cabin. Area offers hunting for bears, grouse and waterfowl and fishing for trout and pink and coho salmon in Hamilton and Big John Creeks. The 1.75-mile Big John Bay Trail provides access from Kake but is difficult to follow. The trail follows the tide flats along a small creek to a logging road. Other hiking includes Hamilton Bay, Goose Lake and Cathedral Falls trails. Fee is $35/night May 1 to September 30, $25/night rest of year. USGS maps: Petersburg D-6, C-6, D-5.

Breiland Slough Cabin. Located near old barite mine on west side of Duncan Canal, near Castle Island. Cabin is 15 air miles or 25 water miles from Petersburg and located on gravel beach. Cabin offers oil stove, 2 double bunks and outhouse. Water from small stream south of cabin. Area offers dungeness crab, shrimp, coho salmon and waterfowl hunting. Sleeps 6. Fee is $35/night May 1- September 30, $25/night rest of year. USGS maps: Petersburg C-3, D-4.

Cascade Creek Cabin. Located on edge of mud flats of Castle River on west side of Duncan Canal, 16 air miles or 30 water miles from Petersburg. Cabin in old-growth forest, muskeg and riparian area. Cabin has oil heater (use #1 stove oil), wood stove, outhouse, covered porch and rowboat with oars. Sleeps 4. Water available from stream west of cabin. Area offers steelhead and coho salmon fishing and waterfowl, grouse and bear hunting. Fee is $35/night May 1 to September 30, $25/night rest of year. USGS maps: Petersburg C-4, C-3, D-4.

Castle River Cabin. Located at mouth of Castle River on west side of Duncan Canal, 16 air miles or 30 water miles from Petersburg; 16-foot tide required for direct access. Cabin offers wood stove, outhouse, sleeping loft, 2 double bunks and rowboat 1/2 mile upstream. Sleeps 6. Exceptional steelhead, coho and trout fishing and bear, waterfowl and grouse hunting. Fee is $35/night May 1- September 30, $25/night rest of year. USGS maps: Petersburg C-4, C-3, D-4.

DeBoer Lake Cabin. Located on west end of DeBoer Lake, 3 miles northwest of Thomas Bay, 20 air miles from Petersburg. Area is mountainous and located in alpine valley. Cabin offers oil stove (use #1 stove oil), outhouse, sleeping loft, 4 single bunks and rowboat with oars. Sleeps 6. Area offers spectacular views of Jefferson, Fulton, Hancock and Hamilton mountains, hiking, and rainbow trout fishing. Wildlife viewing and photography, mountain goats, ptarmigan and wildflowers in area. Fog and high winds can prevent scheduled travel. Fee is $25/night. USGS map: Sumdum A-3.

Devil's Elbow Cabin. Located in Rocky Pass in Keku Strait, on east side of Kuiu Island, 40 air miles or 66 water miles from Petersburg. 16-foot tide required for plane access. Cabin offers oil heater (use #1 stove oil), outhouse, sleeping loft and 2 double bunks. Sleeps 6. Water from creek south of cabin. Area offers waterfowl resting area, waterfowl hunting, geese, grouse, seals, bears, kayaking, canoeing and fishing for coho salmon. Fee is $25/night. USGS maps: Petersburg C-6, D-6.

Harvey Lake Cabin. Located near a sandy beach and swimming area on Woewodski Island, near Duncan Canal, 18 air miles or 21 water miles from Petersburg. The cabin is on the west end of the lake, 1/2-mile hike from saltwater. Trail is marked with white diamond. Cabin offers large deck, wood stove, outhouse, sleeping loft, 2 single bunks, rowboat and swimming/ picnic area. Water available from lake or creek. Sleeps 6. Wildlife includes deer, moose, ducks and loons. Fishing for cutthroat in lake and coho near mouth of Harvey Creek. Island has long histroy of mining. Fee is $35/night May 1- September 30, $25/night rest of year. USGS maps: Petersburg C-4, C-3.

Kadake Bay Cabin. Located on northeast side of Kuiu Island at mouth of Kadake Creek, 39 air miles from Petersburg or 13 water miles from Kake. Accessible by boat or plane with 18-foot tide. Cabin offers oil heater (use #1 stove oil), wood stove, outhouse and 2 double and 2 single bunks. Sleeps 6. Water available from creek. Area offers scenery, bear and waterfowl hunting and fishing for steelhead, coho and pink salmon, Dolly Varden and cutthroat in Kadake Creek. Fee is $35/night May 1- September 30, $25/night rest of year. USGS maps: Petersburg D-6, C-6; Port Alexander D-1.

Kah Sheets Bay Cabin. Located at mouth of Kah Sheets (Tlingit meaning "by the fisheries") Creek on south end of Kupreanof Island, 24 air or water miles from Petersburg. 14-foot tide required to reach cabin. Cabin has oil heater (use #1 stove oil), wood stove, outhouse and 4 single bunks. Sleeps 4. Excellent fishing for steelhead, trout and sockeye, coho and pink salmon. Bear, grouse and waterfowl hunting in area. Area offers hiking on old logging roads and trails and viewing of spring bird migrations. Fee is $35/night May 1- September 30, $25/night rest of year. USGS maps: Petersburg C-4, C-3.

Kah Sheets Lake Cabin. Located on south end of Kupreanof Island above Kah Sheets Bay on southeast end of lake, 22 air miles or 24 water miles (plus 2.75-mile hike) from Petersburg. Handicap-accessible boat/floatplane dock and connecting trails. Cabin offers oil heater (use #1 stove oil), covered deck, dock, outhouse, sleeping loft, 2 single bunks and 2 rowboats. Fishing for steelhead, Dolly Varden, cutthroat trout and coho, sockeye and pink salmon in lake and stream. Area offers berries, wildflowers and bear and waterfowl viewing. Fee is $35/night May 1- September 30, $25/night rest of year. USGS maps: Petersburg C-4, C-3.

Petersburg Lake Cabin. Located on southeast end of lake within Petersburg Creek/Duncan Salt Chuck Wilderness on Kupreanof Island. Distance from Petersburg is 9 air miles and 4 water miles (15-foot tide required) plus 6.5-mile hike or 1/2 mile across Wrangell Narrows to Kupreanof State Dock with 10.3-mile hike. Lake is ice free April through November. Cabin offers oil heater (use #1 stove oil), wood stove, outhouse, 4 single bunks, small oven and rowboat. Sleeps 4. Water from stream or lake. Fishing for steelhead, cutthroat trout and coho and sockeye salmon. Area offers wildlife viewing for black bears and eagles, wildflowers and hiking. Fee is $35/night May 1- September 30, $25/night rest of year. USGS map: Petersburg D-4, D-3.

Portage Bay Cabin. Hunter-style cabin on eastern shore of Portage Bay on Kupreanof Island due east of Stop Island. Distance from Petersburg is 15 air miles o 25 water miles. Cabin offers oil heater (use #1 stove oil), outhouse and 4 single bunks. Sleeps 4. Water from creek 100 feet south of cabin. Fishing for halibut in mouth of Portage Bay and coho and pink salmon, steelhead and trout in Portage Creek. Popular site for black bear, waterfowl and grouse hunting. Hiking on 10.5-mile Portage Mountain Trail. Fee is $25/night. Related USGS maps: Petersburg D-4, D-3; Sumdum A-4.

Ravens Roost Cabin. Located atop mountain behind Petersburg airport, 3 air miles by helicopter or 4 hiking miles from water towers behind airport. Cabin offers propane heater, deck, outhouse and sleeping loft. Sleeps 6. Water from muskeg pools. Activities include cross-country and telemark skiing and snowshoeing. Area offers wildflowers and wild berries. Fee is $35/night. USGS maps: Petersburg D-3, C-3.

Salt Chuck East Cabin. Located on Kupreanof Island on east side of Duncan Canal in Petersburg Creek/ Duncan Salt Chuck Wilderness Area. Distance from Petersburg is 15 air miles or 40 water miles. Access requires 14-foot tide, and rapids south of Salt Chuck are navigable only at high slack tide. Cabin includes wood stove, outhouse, 2 single bunks and rowboat. Sleeps 7. Water from stream. Fishing for steelhead and coho salmon and hunting for bears, grouse and waterfowl in area. Fee is $35/night May 1- September 30, $25/night rest of year. USGS maps: Petersburg D-3, D-4, D-5, C-3, C-4.

Spurt Cove Cabin. Located on north side of Thomas Bay, 16 air miles or 18 water miles from Petersburg. Cabin includes oil heater (use #1 stove oil), wood stove, outhouse and 2 single and 1 double bunk. Sleeps 4. Water from small stream. Fishing for halibut and king salmon near cove and trout in beaver ponds. Wildlife includes Orca whales and porpoises. Spurt Lake is located to northeast by 1.1-mile, moderate trail. Destinations include Thomas Bay, the Baird, Muddy and Patterson Glaciers, Scenery Cove and the Cosmos Mountain Range. Kayaking in Thomas Bay. Fee is $25/night. USGS map: Sumdum A-3.

Swan Lake Cabin. Located on alpine lake east of Thomas Bay, 18 air miles from Petersburg. Fog and high winds can prevent scheduled travel. Facilities include oil heater (use #1 stove oil), 2 rowboats, outhouse, sleeping loft and 2 single bunks. Sleeps 5. Water from lake and stream. Fishing for rainbow trout in lake. Mountain goats in area, and alpine flowers are abundant. Hiking in area on Cascade Creek Trail to Falls Lake, and rock, ice and glacier climbing in area. Fee is $35/night. USGS maps: Sumdum A-3, A-2.

Towers Arm Cabin. Located on west side of Towers are at Duncan Canal, 16 air miles and 38 water miles from Petersburg; 15-foot tide required for access. Cabin includes wood stove, outhouse and 4 single bunks. Sleeps 4. Water from stream north of cabin. Area offers waterfowl viewing or hunting for bears, deer, waterfowl and grouse and fishing for steelhead and coho salmon. Fee is $25/night. USGS maps: Petersburg D-3, D-4, D-5, C-3, C-4.

West Point Cabin. Handicap-accessible cabin with wooden access walkway and outhouse located on Kupreanof Island at mouth of Portage Bay, 18 air miles or 24 water miles from Petersburg. Strong tidal currents near cabin. Cabin includes oil stove (use #1 stove oil), cooking counter, benches, outhouse, sleeping loft, 2 bunks and mooring buoy. Water from stream west of cabin. Activities include beach hiking, hunting, saltwater fishing for king and coho salmon and halibut and wildlife viewing. Black bears and waterfowl abundant. Humpback whales frequent area. Fee is $35/night May 1-September 30. $25/night rest of year. USGS maps: Sumdum A-4, A-5; Petersburg D-5, D-4.

Northern Prince of Wales Island USFS Cabins

Barnes Lake Cabin. Located on saltwater lagoon 70 air miles northwest of Kethchikan on northeast Prince of Wales Island. Accessible by boat or floatplane. Use caution in Indian Creek Rapids, Lake Bay Creek and Gold and Galligan Lagoon. Cabin has wood stove and skiff with oars. Sleeps 4 to 6. Wildlife includes waterfowl, Sitka blacktail deer and black bears. Fishing for silver salmon in Barnes Lake mid-August to late September.

Control Lake Cabin. Located on central Prince of Wales Island. Accessible by car and small boat. Cabin has wood stove, and Forest Service maintains skiff with oars at dock. Sleeps 8. Fishing for cutthroat, Dolly Varden and coho.

Honker Lake Cabin. Located 54 air miles northwest of Ketchikan on Honker Lake along Honker Divide Canoe Route, which runs from Hatchery Creek Bridge to Thorne Bay. Accessible by floatplane or canoe. Cabin has wood stove and skiff and oars. Sleeps 4 to 6. Wildlife includes Sitka blacktail deer, black bears and wolves. Fishing for cutthroat and rainbow trout, Dolly Varden, sockeye and coho.

Karta Lake Cabin. Located 34 air miles northwest of Ketchikan. Accessible by floatplane or boat and 1.5-mile trail from Karta Bay. Cabin provides oil stove. Lake and river in Karta Wilderness Area. Sleeps 4 to 6. Fishing for winter and spring steelhead runs, cutthroat and rainbow trout, Dolly Varden and 4 salmon species. Wildlife includes Sitka blacktail deer, wolves, black bears, otters, mink and marten.

Karta River Cabin. Located 34 air miles northwest of Ketchikan at mouth of Karta River. Accessible by boat or floatplane. Cabin has oil stove. Sleeps 4 to 6. Mooring buoy in bay. Lake and river in Karta Wilderness Area. Attractions include winter and spring steelhead runs and fishing for cutthroat and rainbow trout, Dolly Varden and 4 salmon species. Wildlife includes Sitka blacktail deer, wolves, black bears, otters, mink and marten.

Red Bay Lake Cabin. Located 84 air miles northwest of Ketchikan on Red Bay Lake. Access by floatplane or 3/4-mile hike on road #20 and 1-mile row in provided skiff. Cabin provides wood stove and 2 skiffs with oars. Sleeps 4. Fishing for steelhead, cutthroat and rainbow trout, Dolly Varden and coho, pink, chum and sockeye salmon. Wildlife includes Sitka blacktail deer and black bears.

Salmon Bay Lake Cabin. Located 84 air miles northwest of Ketchikan on Salmon Bay Lake. Access by floatplane or trail from Salmon Bay. Trail is high in intertidal flat and is muddy with bad footing. Boat access only possible during highest tides. Cabin includes wood stove and 2 skiffs with oars. Sleeps 4 to 6. Sandy beach at cabin for swimming. Popular fishing area for cutthroat, Dolly Varden, steelhead and coho, pink, chum and sockeye salmon. Wildlife includes mink, marten, otters, Sitka blacktail deer and black bears.

Salmon Lake Cabin. Historic cabin located 36 air miles west of Ketchikan on Salmon Lake in Karta Wilderness Area. Access by floatplane or 5-mile trail from Karta Bay. Cabin provides wood stove and sandy beach. Sleeps 4 to 6. Fishing is popular for cutthroat and rainbow trout, Dolly Varden and pink, coho and sockeye salmon. Wildlife includes Sitka blacktail deer and black bears.

Sarkar Lake Cabin. Located 76 air miles northwest of Ketchikan on Sarkar Lake near start of Sarkar Lake Canoe Route. Accessible by floatplane or road and canoe or boat from Sarkar Trailhead on the #20 road. Cabin has wood stove and skiff with oars. Sleeps 4 to 6. Fishing for cutthroat trout, Dolly Varden and coho, pink, chum and sockeye salmon. Wildlife includes Sitka blacktail deer, black bears, otters, minks and martens. Waterfowl includes geese, ducks, swans and loons.

Shipley Bay Cabin. Located on salt water, 85 air miles northwest of Ketchikan. Accessible by floatplane or boat. Cabin has wood stove and skiff with oars at outlet of lake. Sleeps 4 to 6. 3/4-mile trail to Shipley Lake. Fishing in stream and lake for cutthroat and rainbow trout, Dolly Varden, steelhead and 3 salmon species. Wildlife includes black bears, Sitka blacktail deer, geese and ducks.

Staney Creek Cabin. Located 68 air miles northwest of Ketchikan. Accessible by floatplane or boat at high tide or by vehicle to trailhead on road #2054-300 and 1/2-mile trail. Cabin has propane heater. Sleeps 4 to 6. Fishing for cutthroat and rainbow trout, Dolly Varden and 4 salmon species. Wildlife includes Sitka blacktail deer, wolves, black bears, geese and ducks.

Sweetwater Lake Cabin. Located 63 air miles northwest of Ketchikan. Accessible by floatplane or road #3030 and short trail to lake with skiff. Cabin has wood stove. Sleeps 4 to 6. Fishing for trout and coho salmon. Wildlife includes geese, Sitka blacktail deer, black bears, martens, minks, otters, beavers and seals in lake.

South Prince of Wales Island USFS Cabins

Black Bear Lake Cabin. Located 50 air miles west of Ketchikan on Black Bear Lake. Accessible by floatplane. Cabin has wood stove and skiff with oars. Sleeps 4 to 6. Lake is ice free mid- to late June. Attractions include scenic mountain cliffs and photography, hiking, fishing for rainbow trout and black bear and deer hunting.

Essowah Lake Cabin. Located 65 air miles southwest of Ketchikan on Essowah Lake on southwest end of Dall Island. Accessible by floatplane. Cabin provides wood stove and skiff with oars. Sleeps 4 to 6. Remote setting. Abundant fishing for cutthroat, Dolly Varden, steel-head and pink, chum, coho and sockeye salmon.

Josephine Lake Cabin. Located 38 miles west of Ketchikan. Accessible by floatplane. Cabin has oil stove and skiff with oars. Sleeps 4 to 6. Lake is ice free mid- to late June. Attractions include hunting, hiking, photography, mountain scenery, wildflowers, deer and black bears. No fish in Josephine Lake.

Kegan Cove Cabin. Located 30 air miles southwest of Ketchikan, on salt water at Moira Sound. Accessible by boat or floatplane. Cabin has wood stove and mooring buoy. Sleeps 4 to 6. Activities include hiking, fishing and wildlife viewing for bears, deer and eagles. Cabin is located at trailhead of Kegan Lake Trail.

Kegan Creek Cabin. Located 30 air miles southwest of Ketchikan, 1/2 mile from salt-water at Moira Sound on Kegan Lake Trail. Accessible by floatplane to Kegan Lake or by boat to Kegan Cove and 1/2-mile hike. Cabin has wood stove and skiff with oars. Sleeps 4 to 6. Activities include hiking, fishing and wildlife viewing of bears, deer and eagles.

Point Amargura Cabin. Located 70 air miles west of Ketchikan, 8 water miles west of Craig on salt water on southern tip of San Fernando Island. Accessible by floatplane or boat from Craig. Cabin has wood stove. Sleeps 6. Saltwater fishing for halibut and bottom fish and pink, chum, coho and king salmon. Hunting and beachcombing are also popular.

Troller's Cove Cabin. Located 38 air miles southwest of Ketchikan near sal twater in Troller's Cove. Accessible by floatplane or boat from Ketchikan or the boat ramp at Hollis. Cabin provides wood stove and mooring buoy at Troller's Cove. Sleeps 4 to 6. Saltwater fishing for bottom fish, and trolling for salmon at 20 Fathom Bank. Attractions include small lakes and waterfalls in area.

Sitka Area USFS Cabins

Allan Point Cabin. Located on Halleck Island, 16 miles north of Sitka. Accessible by floatplane or boat. Sleeps 15. Area offers hunting, fishing and beachcombing. Cabin has oil stove (use #1 stove oil) and mooring buoy. Water from small stream. Activities include salt-water fishing and deer hunting. Brown bear frequent area.

Appleton Cove Cabin. Located 50 water miles north of Sitka. Accessible by boat or floatplane. Cabin provides mooring buoy and oil stove (use #1 stove oil). Water from small stream. Sleeps 5. Activities include deer hunting, wildlife viewing and fishing for rainbow trout and pink and coho salmon. Brown bear frequent area.

Avoss Lake Cabin. Located 30 miles southeast of Sitka within wilderness area. Accessible by floatplane. Cabin provides oil stove (use #1 stove oil) and skiff with oars. Water from inlet stream. Sleeps 8. Activities include fishing for Dolly Varden and rain-bow trout and hunting for deer and moun-tain goats. Brown bears frequent area.

Baranof Lake Cabin. Located 20 miles east of Sitka. Accessible by floatplane. Cabin has wood stove and skiff with oars. Sleeps 6. Water from inlet stream. Fishing for cutthroat and rainbow trout and Dolly Varden. Brown bears frequent area.

Brent's Beach Cabin. Located 15 miles northwest of Sitka. Accessible by boat or helicopter. Cabin provides mooring buoy and wood stove. Water from stream. Sleeps 4 to 6. Activities include deer hunting, beachcombing and hiking. Attractions include lava domes and brown bears.

Davidof Lake Cabin. Located 40 miles southeast of Sitka within wilderness area. Accessible by floatplane. Cabin has wood stove and skiff with oars. Sleeps 8 to 10. Water from lake. Fishing for Dolly Varden, coho salmon and rainbow trout. Deer hunting in season. A 1.2-mile trail to Plotnikof Lake at south end of lake. Brown bears frequent area.

Fred's Creek Cabin. Located 10 miles west of Sitka. Accessible by boat or helicopter. Difficult to approach at low slack tide. No protected anchorage. Cabin provides wood stove. Water from creek. Sleeps 4 to 6. Activities include beachcombing and 6.7-mile trail to Mt. Edgecumbe.

Goulding Lake Cabin. Located 60 miles northwest of Sitka within wilderness area. Accessible by floatplane. Cabin has wood stove and skiff with oars. Sleeps 6 to 8. Fishing for cutthroat, steelhead and coho salmon. Hunting for deer in season. Brown bears frequent area.

Kanga Bay Cabin. Located 12 miles south of Sitka overlooking saltwater bay. Accessible by floatplane or boat. Provides safe boat anchorage. Cabin provides wood stove. Water from stream. Sleeps 6. Attractions include Goddard Hot Springs (20-minute boat ride), deer hunting, brown bears and sockeye and coho salmon fishing.

Kook Lake Cabin. Located 45 miles northwest of Sitka. Accessible by floatplane. Cabin provides wood stove and skiff with oars. Sleeps 8. Water from stream. Fishing for cutthroat, Dolly Varden and coho salmon. Bear hunting in season. Hiking on logging roads. Brown bears frequent area.

Lake Eva Cabin. Located 27 miles northeast of Sitka. Accessible by floatplane. Handicap-accessible dock, outhouse and deck at cabin. Cabin has oil stove (use #1 stove oil), deck with fire pit (wood not provided, charcoal suggested), fishing platform, floatplane dock and skiff with oars. Water from stream. Sleeps 6. Fishing for cutthroat, Dolly Varden, steelhead and coho and sockeye salmon. Brown bears frequent the area.

Moser Island Cabin. Located on small island 48 miles north of Sitka. Accessible by boat or floatplane. Good anchorage with easy access. Cabin has wood stove. Water from stream. Sleeps 6. Fishing for coho, pink and chum salmon. Brown bears frequent area.

North Beach Cabin. Located 20 miles northwest of Sitka. Accessible by helicopter or boat and 7.5-mile ATV trail from Mud Bay. Cabin has wood stove and sandy beach. Water from creek crossing. Sleeps 8. Area provides trails to Iris Meadows and Mud Bay. Fishing for Dolly Varden and coho and pink salmon. Brown bears frequent area.

Piper Island Cabin. Located 30 miles north of Sitka within Fish Bay. Accessible by boat or floatplane. Cabin includes sleeping loft and oil stove (use #1 stove oil). Sleeps 6. No water source on island. Activities include fishing, hunting and wildlife viewing. Brown bears frequent area.

Plotnikof Lake Cabin. Located 45 miles southeast of Sitka within designated wilderness area. Accessible by floatplane. Cabin provides oil stove (use #1 stove oil) and skiff with oars. Sleeps 4 to 6. Water from stream or lake. A 1.2-mile trail to Davidof Lake behind cabin (not maintained). Fishing for steelhead, coho salmon and rainbow trout. Deer hunting in season. Brown bears frequent area.

Redoubt Lake Cabin. Located 10 miles south of Sitka. Accessible by floatplane or boat and trail. Cabin provides wood stove and skiff with oars. Water from stream. Sleeps 8. Salmon Lake- Redoubt Lake Trail (6 miles) leads from Silver Bay to cabin. Fishing for Dolly Varden and sockeye and coho salmon. Deer hunting in season.

Salmon Lake Cabin. Located 11 miles south of Sitka. Accessible by boat and trail or by air. Cabin has wood stove and skiff with oars. Water from lake. Sleeps 6. Salmon Lake- Redoubt Lake Trail leads from Silver Bay to cabin. Fishing for cutthroat, Dolly Varden and pink and coho salmon. Deer hunting in season. Brown bears frequent area.

Samsing Cove Cabin. Located 5.5 miles south of Sitka. Accessible by boat. Cabin has oil stove (use #1 stove oil). Water from spring. Sleeps 15. Cabin offers ocean view and saltwater fishing. Brown bears frequent area.

Sevenfathom Bay Cabin. Located 22 miles south of Sitka. Accessible by boat. Cabin includes wood stove and ocean bay view. Water from stream or lake. Sleeps 8. Deer hunting in season. Brown bears frequent area.

Shelikof Cabin. Located 20 miles northwest of Sitka. Accessible by helicopter or boat and 6.8-mile trail from Mud Bay. Cabin provides wood stove. Water from spring. Sleeps 8. Area provides trails to Iris Meadows and Mud Bay. Activities include beachcombing and fishing for Dolly Varden and coho salmon. Brown bears frequent area.

Sitkoh Lake East Cabin. Located 30 miles northeast of Sitka. Accessible by floatplane or boat and 4.3-mile trail from Sitkoh Bay. Cabin includes wood stove and skiff with oars. Water from stream. Sleeps 6. Hiking on logging roads. Fishing for Dolly Varden, cutthroat, steelhead and pink and coho salmon. Deer and bear hunting in season. Brown bears frequent area.

Sitkoh Lake West Cabin. Located 30 miles northeast of Sitka. Accessible by floatplane. Cabin includes wood stove and skiff with oars. Water from stream. Sleeps 4 to 6. Hiking on logging roads. Deer and bear hunting in season. Fishing for Dolly Varden, cutthroat trout, steelhead and pink and coho salmon. Brown bears frequent area.

Suloia Lake Cabin. Located 30 miles northwest of Sitka. Accessible by floatplane. Cabin provides wood stove and skiff with oars. Water from stream. Sleeps 6. Deer hunting in season. Fishing for Dolly Varden and rainbow trout. Brown bears frequent area.

White Sulphur Springs Cabin. Located 65 miles northwest of Sitka in wilderness area. Accessible by boat and trail. Cabin provides wood stove. Water from rainwater collection barrel. Activities include hot springs pool, easy hikes and coho salmon and cutthroat trout fishing in creek. NOTE: Bathhouse is open to any visitor and is used by commercial fishermen, kayakers and campers. No overnight camping is allowed, and only cabin can be reserved.

Wrangell Area USFS Cabins

Anan Bay Cabin. Located on Cleveland Peninsula at Anan Bay, across Ernest Sound from southeast corner of Wrangell Island, 31 miles southeast of Wrangell. Accessible by boat or floatplane. Trail to Anan Lake is not maintained and is closed June 15 to September 15. Cabin provides 25-foot mooring buoy, sleeping loft, 2 single bunks, outdoor privy, oil stove (use #1 stove oil) and outdoor cooking grill. Sleeps 7. Water from seasonal creek behind cabin. Bear activity in area. Wildlife includes black and brown bears, harbor seals and bald eagles. Fishing for cutthroat, Dolly Varden and pink salmon. Attractions include the Anan Wildlife Observatory where Forest Service interpreters are on duty at trailhead. USGS map: Bradfield A-6.

Anan Lake Cabin. Located on Cleveland Peninsula above Anan Bay at south end of Anan Lake, 31 air miles from Wrangell. Accessible by floatplane. Cabin provides 2 single and 2 double bunks, outdoor privy, oil stove (use #1 stove oil) and skiff with oars. Fishing for cutthroat, silver and pink salmon and steelhead. Wildlife includes brown and black bears, deer and waterfowl. Other attractions include Boulder Lake, 0.3 mile from cabin along unmaintained trail. USGS map: Bradfield A-6.

Berg Bay Cabin. Overlooks Berg Bay and Blake Channel. Located on shore of Berg Bay on east side of Blake Channel near mouth of Aaron creek, 22 miles southeast of Wrangell. Accessible by boat or floatplane.A 25-foot mooring buoy in bay. Cabin provides sleeping loft, wooden cooler box, 2 single bunks, fire grill, outdoor privy and oil stove (use #1 stove oil). Water from stream. Sleeps 7. Hiking in area includes Aaron Creek Trail and Berg Creek Trail. Wildlife includes brown and black bears, moose, mountain goats, waterfowl, grouse and ptarmigan. Fishing for pink, silver and chum salmon and steelhead. Crabbing in Berg Bay and Aaron Creek tidal flats. Wildflowers on Aaron Creek grass flats.

Binkley Slough Cabin. Located in Stikine-LeConte Wilderness, adjacent to Binkley Slough on southwest side of Farm Island on Stikine River tidal flats, 12 miles from Wrangell, 9 miles from Banana Point boat ramp on Mitkof Island. Accessible by shallow draft boat; 16-foot tide required. Cabin includes 2 single and 2 double bunks, outdoor privy, wooden cooler box and oil stove (use #1 stove oil). Water from catchment. Sleeps 6. Activities include waterfowl hunting and bird viewing in spring and fall. Wildlife includes shorebirds, owls, hawks, bald eagles and moose. Wildflowers prominent. USGS maps: Petersburg B-1, B-6.

Eagle Lake Cabin. Located on east shore of Eagle Lake above Bradfield Canal, 44 air miles south of Wrangell. Accessible by floatplane. Cabin includes covered front porch, wooden cooler box, 2 double and 2 single bunks, wood stove, wood shed, outdoor privy and skiff with oars. Water from stream. Sleeps 6. Cabin offers scenic views of Eagle Lake. Wildlife includes brown and black bears and mountain goats. Fishing for cutthroat trout. USGS map: Bradfield A-5.

Frosty Bay Cabin. Located in Frosty Bay on Cleveland Peninsula, 36 miles south of Wrangell. Accessible by boat and floatplane. A 25-foot mooring float in bay. Wood-planked trail to 10-mile Forest Service road system. Cabin provides half-loft, small deck, wooden cooler box, 2 single and 2 double bunks, oil stove (use #1 stove oil) and outdoor privy. Cabin overlooks Frosty Bay and Deer Island. Water from stream. Sleeps 6. Wildlife includes brown and black bears, moose and Sitka blacktail deer. Fishing for king, pink and silver salmon. Crab and halibut in salt water.

Garnet Ledge Cabin. Located near Garnet Ledge at mouth of Stikine River, south of Point Rothsay, 8 miles northeast of Wrangell, 14 miles east of Banana Point boat ramp on Mitkoff Island. 15-foot tide required for access. Cabin has sleeping loft, wooden cooler box 2 single bunks, wood stove, wood shed, splitting maul and outdoor privy. Water from stream. Sleeps 7. Attractions include garnet outcropping, fishing for Hooligan in Stikine River and wildlife including bald eagles, sea lions, harbor seals, brown and black bears and moose. Cabin overlooks Stikine River tidal flats.

Gut Island #1 Cabin. Located in Stikine-LeConte Wilderness, 12 miles from Wrangell and 7 miles from Banana Point boat ramp on Mitkof Island. Accessible by floatplane or shallow draft boat. 17-foot tide required for plane, 15-foot for boat. Cabin has deck, loft, 2 single and 2 double bunks, an oil stove (use #1 stove oil), wooden cooler box and outdoor privy. Water from catchment. Sleeps 6. Area offers bird viewing during spring and fall migrations and waterfowl hunting. Wildlife includes waterfowl, shorebirds, bald eagles, owls and hawks. USGS map: Petersburg C-2.

Gut Island #2 Cabin. Located on Gut Island on Stikine River tidal flats, in Stikine-LeConte Wilderness, 12 miles from Wrangell, 7 miles from Banana Point boat ramp on Mitkof Island. Accessible by shallow draft boat or floatplane; 17-foot tide required for plane, 15-foot tide for boat. Cabin provides 2 single and 2 double bunks, oil stove (use #1 stove oil), outdoor privy and wooden cooler box. Water from catchment. Sleeps 4. Good bird viewing during spring and summer migrations and waterfowl hunting in fall. Birds include waterfowl, shorebirds, bald eagles, owls and hawks. USGS map: Petersburg C-2.

Harding River Cabin. Located at the mouth of the Harding River overlooking Bradfield Canal, 40 water miles or 31 air miles southeast of Wrangell. Cabin provides wooden cooler box, easy boat anchorage, 2 single and 2 double bunks, oil stove (use #1 stove oil), outdoor privy and mooring float. Water from Harding River. Sleeps 6. Wildlife includes brown and black bears, harbor seals, bald eagles and waterfowl. Fishing for silver and chum salmon in Harding River and in Eagle River. Crabbing in Bradfield Canal. USGS map: Bradfield A-5.

Koknuk Cabin. Located in Stikine-LeConte Wilderness, on west side of Sergief Island on Stikine River, 10 miles from Wrangell, 8 miles from Banana Point boat ramp on Mitkof Island. Accessible by shallow draft boat; requires 16-foot tide. Cabin includes 2 single and 2 double bunks, oil stove (use #1 stove oil), outdoor privy and wooden cooler box. Water from catchment. Sleeps 4. Area offers bird viewing during spring and fall migrations, waterfowl hunting in fall and wildlife viewing including shorebirds, bald eagles, owls, hawks and moose. USGS map: Petersburg C-2.

Little Dry Island Cabin. Located in Stikine-LeConte Wilderness on south side of Little Dry Island on Stikine River tidal flats, 12 miles from Wrangell and 7 miles from Banana Point boat ramp on Mitkof Island. Accessible by shallow draft boat or floatplane; 17-foot tide required for plane, 15-foot tide for boat. Cabin provides wooden coller box, 2 single bunks, loft, wood stove, wood shed and outdoor privy. Water from catchment. Sleeps 7. Good bird viewing during fall and spring migrations, waterfowl hunting in fall, and wildlife viewing including waterfowl, shore-birds, bald eagles, owls and hawks. USGS map: Petersburg C-2.

Mallard Slough Cabin. Located in Stikine-LeConte Wilderness between LeConte Bay and North Arm of Stikine River, 22 miles from Wrangell, 20 miles from Petersburg. Accessible by shallow draft boat or floatplane. 16-foot tide required for plane, 14-foot tide for boat. Cabin offers 2 single bunks, loft, wooden cooler box, wood stove, wood shed (wood provided) and outdoor privy. Water from catchment. Sleeps 7. Good bird viewing during spring and fall migrations. Waterfowl and moose hunting in fall. Waterfowl, shorebirds, bald eagles, owls, hawks, moose and brown and black bears inhabit area. Wildflowers prominent in May and June. LeConte Bay and LeConte Glacier within boating distance; icebergs in LeConte Bay and along Horn Cliffs. USGS map: Petersburg B-1.

Marten Lake Cabin. Located at upper end of Marten Lake above Blake Channel and Bradfield Canal, 25 air miles southeast of Wrangell. Accessible by floatplane. Cabin provides wooden cooler box, 2 single and 2 double bunks, wood stove, wood shed, splitting maul and skiff with oars. Water from stream. Sleeps 4. Wildlife includes brown and black bears, and mountain goats. Fishing for cutthroat trout and Dolly Varden in Marten and Clay lakes and steelhead in Marten Creek. Sand beach in front of cabin. NOTE: Cabin floor may flood after periods of heavy rainfall. Related USGS map: Bradfield B-6.

Mount Flemer Cabin. Located in Stikine-LeConte Wilderness near confluence of Clearwater Slough and the Stikine River, 2 miles downriver from the Canadian border, 32 miles northeast of Wrangell. Accessible by shallow draft boat; requires a 14-foot tide. Cabin has wooden cooler box, boardwalk trail to cabin, 2 single bunks and oil stove (use #1 stove oil). Water from stream. Sleeps 7. Wildlife includes brown and black bears, moose and mountain goats. Fishing for cutthroat and Dolly Varden. USGS map: Bradfield C-6.

Mount Rynda Cabin. Located on south side of Stikine River at the Andrew Creek-Andrew Slough confluence, 18 miles northeast of Wrangell. Accessible by shallow draft boat; requires 14-foot tide. Cabin offers wooden cooler box, 2 single bunks, loft, oil stove (use #1 stove oil) and outdoor privy. Water from creek. Sleeps 7. Wildlife includes brown and black bears, moose harbor seals and bald eagles. Fishing for pink silver and king salmon, cutthroat trout and Dolly Varden. Other activities include kayaking and canoeing up Andrew Creek. USGS map: Petersburg C-1.

Sergief Island Cabin. Located in Stikine-LeConte Wilderness on northwest side of Sergief Island on Stikine River tidal flats, 10 miles from Wrangell and 10 miles from Banana Point boat ramp on Mitkof Island. Accessible by shallow draft boat or float plane. 17-foot tide required for plane; 16-foot tide for boat. Cabin has wooden cooler box, 2 single and 2 double bunks, outdoor privy, covered deck and oil stove (use #1 stove oil). Water from catchment. Sleeps 4. Good bird viewing during spring and fall migrations. Waterfowl hunting in fall. Waterfowl, shorebirds, bald eagles, owls, hawks and moose inhabit area. Wildflowers prominent in May and June. USGS map: Petersburg C-2.

Shakes Slough #1 Cabin. Located in Stikine-LeConte Wilderness on north side of Stikine River at mouth of Shakes Slough, 25 miles northeast of Wrangell. Accessible by shallow draft boat or floatplane; 14-foot tide required for access. Cabin overlooks Shakes Slough and offers spectacular views of Popof Glacier, Mt. Basargin and surrounding mountains. Cabin provides wooden cooler box, 2 single and 2 double bunks, oil stove (use #1 stove oil) and outdoor privy. No water available near cabin. Sleeps 4. Wildlife includes brown and black bears, moose and mountain goats. Fishing for cutthroat and Dolly Varden. Attractions include Chief Shakes Hot Springs, 4 miles upriver on Kitili Slough and Shakes Lake and Glacier, 3 miles north of cabin. USGS map: Petersburg C-1.

Shakes Slough #2 Cabin. Located in Stikine-LeConte Wilderness on north side of Stikine River at mouth of Shakes Slough, 25 miles northeast of Wrangell. Accessible by shallow draft boat or floatplane. 14-foot tide required for access. Cabin offers spectacular views of Popof Glacier, Mt. Basargin and surrounding mountains and overlooks Shakes Slough. Cabin has wooden cooler box, 2 single bunks, oil stove (use #1 stove oil) and outdoor privy. No water available near cabin. Sleeps 7. Wildlife includes brown and black bears, moose and mountain goats. Fishing for cutthroat and Dolly Varden. Attractions include Chief Shakes Hot Springs, 4 miles upriver on Kitili Slough and Shakes Lake and Glacier, 3 miles north of cabin. USGS map: Petersburg C-1.

Steamer Bay Cabin. Located on northwest Etolin Island on east shore of Steamer Bay, 27 water miles and 25 air miles west of Wrangell. Accessible by boat and floatplane; no docking or mooring facilities, gravel beach at cabin. Cabin provides loft, wooden cooler box, 2 single bunks, wood shed, wood stove, outdoor privy and fire grill. Water from stream. Sleeps 7. Fishing for king, silver and pink salmon, Dolly Varden and halibut in saltwater and Porcupine Creek; clam digging and crabbing in Steamer Bay. Wildlife includes brown and black bears, elk, porcupine, deer and waterfowl. Beachcombing is also popular. USGS map: Petersburg A-1.

Twin Lakes Cabin. Located in Stikine-LeConte Wilderness overlooking Limb Island and Hooligan Slough. Cabin is at the mouth of Twin Lakes, 18 miles northeast of Wrangell. Accessible by shallow draft boat; requires 14-foot tide. Cabin has loft, sand beach, 2 single bunks, oil stove (use #1 stove oil) and outdoor privy. Water from lake or slough. Sleeps 7. Wildlife includes brown and black bears, moose and mountain goats. Activities include swimming, paddling, water-skiing and fishing for pink, chum and silver salmon and cutthroat. USGS map: Petersburg C-1.

Virginia Lake Cabin. Handicap-accessible cabin located on east end of Virginia Lake, 10 miles east of Wrangell. Accessible by floatplane or by 9-mile boat trip from Wrangell and 0.9-mile Mill Creek Trail to cabin. Cabin provides deck, outdoor privy, floating dock, sand beach, 2 single bunks with trundles and 3 single bunks, wood stove, fire ring, wood shed, dock and skiff with oars. Water from stream. Sleeps 6. Wildlife includes brown and black bears and moose. Activities include hiking on Mill Creek Trail and fishing for cutthroat, Dolly Varden and sockeye salmon. USGS map: Petersburg B-1.

Yakutat Area USFS Cabins

Alsek River Cabin. Located on Yakutat Forelands near Alsek River, 55 miles south of Yakutat. Accessible by wheel plane; no trails to cabin; airstrip at cabin. Wet terrain; hip boots recommended for hiking. Cabin provides 4 single bunks, oil heater (use #1 stove oil), meat shed and outhouse. Sleeps 4. Excellent moose hunting in area and mountain goat hunting in Brabazon Range. Brown and black bears common in area. Sandhill cranes in area during spring and fall migrations. Strawberries on airstrip.

Eagle Cabin (Formerly Middle Situk North). Located on east bank of Situk River, 8 air miles from Yakutat. Accessible by trail, boat or wheel plane. Trail is 3 miles from Nine Mile Bridge on Forest Highway 10. Cabin provides Forest Service airstrip, 3 single and 1 double bunk, oil heater (use #1 stove oil), fire ring, outhouse and meat shed. Water from river. Outstanding fishing for rainbow trout, Dolly Varden, steelhead and sockeye, pink, king and silver salmon. Hunting for moose in area. Other wildlife includes brown bears and bald eagles.

Harlequin Lake North and South Cabin. Double A-frame cabin located in Russell Fiord Wilderness Area, 30 miles southeast of Yakutat on east side of Dangerous River, 0.25 mile south of Forest Highway 10 Dangerous River Bridge. Parking available at end of road, and maintained trail leaves from east side of bridge. Cabin provides airstrip, 4 single bunks, oil heater (use #1 stove oil), loft, meat shed and outhouse. Sleeps 4 plus. Lake accessible by 1-mile trail. Attractions include Yakutat Glacier, floating icebergs, Brabazon mountain range and the Dangerous River. Good moose hunting in area. Wildlife includes brown and black bears and sandhill cranes.

Italio River Cabin. Located on west bank of Old Italio River, 1/2 mile from Gulf of Alaska, 30 air miles from Yakutat. Accessible by wheel plane. *NOTE: Airstrip may flood at high tide or after heavy rains. Area is flat and wet; hip boots recommended.* Cabin provides Forest Service airstrip, 2 single bunks, oil heater (use #1 stove oil), loft, meat shed and outhouse. Water from lake and river. Sleeps 2+. Outstanding fishing for rainbow trout, Dolly Varden, steelhead and sockeye, pink, king and silver salmon in Old Italio, New Italio and Akwe River systems. Good moose hunting in area. Other wildlife includes brown bears and bald eagles.

Lower Dangerous Cabin. Located on Yakutat Forelands near the Dangerous River, 17 miles east of Yakutat. Accessible by wheel plane. Area is flat and wet; hip boots recommended. Cabin provides 4 single bunks, oil heater (use #1 stove oil), outhouse, meat shed and airstrip. Sleeps 4. Excellent moose hunting in area. Other wildlife includes brown and black bears and sandhill cranes. Excellent strawberry picking.

Middle Dangerous Cabin. Located on east bank of Dangerous River, 30 miles southeast of Yakutat. Accessible by 4-mile trail from Dangerous River Bridge at end of Forest Highway 10 or by boat. Dangerous River is a large, glacial river with logjams, sandbars and floating ice. Jet boats are recommended. Cabin provides 4 single bunks, oil heater (use #1 stove oil), outhouse and meat shed. Sleeps 4. Excellent moose hunting in area. Other wildlife includes brown and black bears, sandhill cranes and geese. Cabin provides spectacular view of Dangerous River and gull nesting colonies.

Raven Cabin. Located 8 air miles from Yakutat on east bank of Situk River. Accessible by trail, boat or wheel plane. Trail is 3 miles from Nine Mile Bridge 10. Cabin has Forest Service airstrip, 3 single and 1 double bunk, oil heater (use #1 stove oil), fire ring, outhouse and meat shed. Water from Situk River. Sleeps 5. Outstanding fishing for rainbow trout, Dolly Varden, steelhead and sockeye, pink, king and silver salmon. Good moose hunting in area. Brown bears and bald eagles abundant in area.

Situk Lake Cabin. Located in Russell Fiord Wilderness Area, 14 miles northeast of Yakutat on southeast shore of Situk Lake. Accessible by floatplane or by 2 trails. Unmaintained, 6-mile trail starts at Forest Highway 10 Nine Mile Bridge, and 3-mile trail starts at end of Eastgate Road. Both trails can be wet with standing water 12 inches deep. Cabin includes 4 single bunks, wood stove (wood provided), skiff with oars and outhouse. Water from lake. Sleeps 4. Outstanding fishing for king, sockeye, coho and pink salmon, steelhead, rainbow trout and Dolly Varden. Wildlife includes moose, brown and black bears, bald eagles, trumpeter swans and waterfowl.

Square Lake. Located 40 miles southeast of Yakutat on southeast shore of Square Lake. Accessible by floatplane. Area is flat and wet; hip boots recommended. Cabin provides 4 single bunks, oil heater (use #1 stove oil), skiff with oars and outhouse. Water from lake. Sleeps 4. Fishing for cutthroat and coho and hunting for moose and brown bears in area. Excellent waterfowl hunting in fall. Trumpeter swans nest at head of lake in summer.

Tanis Mesa North and South Cabin. Double A-frame cabin 50 miles southeast of Yakutat between Tanis Mesa and Brabazon Range. Accessible by wheel plane; airstrip at cabin. Each side includes 4 single bunks, oil heater (use #1 stove oil), loft, meat shed and outhouse. Sleeps 4+. Attractions include Brabazon Mountain Range to east, Tanis Mesa to west and Tanis Lake to north with Fassett Glacier cascading into lake at northeast end. Excellent mountain goat hunting in Brabazon Range, and excellent moose and brown bear hunting near cabin.

Chilkat State Park

Located south of Haines on the Chilkat Peninsula, Chilkat State Park offers spectacular beach and mountain views and excellent recreational opportunities. The 6,045-acre park consists of 2 sections. The northern unit, about 3,000 acres, includes Battery Point, which was known as the Battery Point State Recreation Area until 1975 when the legislature added the 3,090-acre southern part and changed the name to Chilkat State Park.

Climate: In general, area weather is clearer and drier than in other areas of Southeast with warmer summers and colder winters. Average annual precipitation at Haines is 53 inches compared to 91 inches in downtown Juneau. The coldest winter temperature recorded in Haines was -17°F, but on sunny, summer days, it is not uncommon for temperatures to rise to 80°F.

Wildlife: Within the park boundaries, animal populations include black and brown bears, moose, eagles, grouse, coyotes and wolverine. Sitka blacktail deer have also been spotted. In the waters surrounding the park, visitors are likely to see humpback whales, seals, sea lions, porpoises, and occasionally killer whales. There is also an abundance of waterfowl, and anglers will find 5 species of salmon and Dolly Varden, char and cutthroat trout.

Activities: The park offers camping, beachcombing, fishing, boating and a hiking trail to Seduction Point (see detailed description in Hiking Trails, Haines Area, this section). Cross-country skiing and snowshoeing are popular in winter.

Accommodations: Chilkat has 32 campsites for RVs or tent campers, 3 tent sites on the beach and day-use only picnic sites. There is a 2-week camping limit. A $5-per-night camping fee is charged. Toilets with handicap access, water and a shelter are also found in the park. There is a small dock and a concrete boat launch.

Access: Chilkat State Park is located 6.7 miles south of Haines via Mud Bay Road. *NOTE: Gravel access road with grades to 11 percent.*

For more information: Contact Alaska Division of Parks and Outdoor Recreation, Southeast Region, 400 Willoughby, Juneau, AK 99801; phone (907) 465-4563, fax (907) 465-5330; Haines District Office, Box 430, Haines, AK 99827; phone (907) 766-2292, www.dnr.state.ak.us/parks/units/haines.htm.

Chilkoot Trail

(see also Klondike Gold Rush National Historical Park)

The discovery of gold in a tributary of the Klondike River in the upper Yukon River valley in August of 1896 lured thousands of souls to the unforgiving, northern wilderness in frantic pursuit of riches. Most of them made their way to the gold fields during the winter of 1897-98 by way of the torturous Chilkoot Trail, hiking from tidewater at Dyea (pronounced dai-yee), over the Chilkoot Pass to Lake Bennett, then rafting down the Yukon River to Dawson City.

Today, the 33-mile Chilkoot Trail is managed as a historic backcountry trail. It is marked and has designated campsites and several day-use shelters. The hike is still arduous, usually taking 3 to 5 days. This is not a trail that offers wilderness solitude. An average of 3,500 hikers make the trip each year. Peak season is mid-July to mid-August.

The trail begins at a bridge over the Taiya River across from the Dyea townsite, about 9.5 miles from Skagway. Little is left of Dyea, which once rivaled Skagway as the largest town in Alaska, except some foundation ruins and several rows of piling stubs, remains of a nearly 2-mile-long wharf that once extended to salt water. Most of the buildings were torn down and the lumber used elsewhere. Of interest is the Slide Cemetery where some 60 victims of an avalanche in April 1898 lie buried, poignant reminders of the hardships and tragedies of the gold rush.

Along the fabled Chilkoot Trail, tragedy, irony and comedy traveled together through events of superhuman bravery and endurance, incredible lunacy and the unspeakable suffering of hapless animals and human beings alike. This legacy survives in landmarks, artifacts, historical records and the indelible impressions of those who have been there. The Chilkoot Trail has been called "the longest museum in the world." Many modern-day Chilkoot hikers, suffering their own torments of exhaustion beneath 40-pound backpacks, experience a dramatic sense of history as they ascend the Pass.

Serious hikers and outdoor enthusiasts express the belief that their repertoire of activities is incomplete until they've "done the Chilkoot." Many who have achieved that goal agree it was the high point of their hiking careers. And a few, no doubt reliving some of the awesome challenges of the route, add wryly, "But I'll never do it again!"

The Park Service cautions that hikers must be properly equipped and prepared to be self-sufficient on this trail. Weather conditions can change rapidly from hour to hour, especially in the summit area. You must be prepared for cold temperatures, snow, rain, fog and wind. An inch of rain in 24 hours is not uncommon. Trail conditions below tree line are often rough, with deep mud, standing water, slick rocks and roots making footing tricky. Conditions along the 8 miles of trail above tree line are even more severe. High winds, driving rain, low temperatures, heavy fog and rocky terrain may make hiking this section extremely difficult. The Park Service recommends that hiking gear include a tent with waterproof rain fly, sturdy hiking boots, rain gear, wool or pile clothing, sunglasses, sunblock and a small stove with adequate fuel (there is no wood in the summit area, and campfires are not allowed on the trail). Camping gear and supplies are available in Skagway (Skagway Sports Emporium). Camping is permitted only in designated areas. If you bring a dog, it must be on a leash.

The Chilkoot Trail is administered by the U.S. National Park Service and Parks Canada as part of Klondike Gold Rush National Historical Park. A permit is required to hike both the U.S. and Canadian portions of the Chilkoot Trail. At our press time, the U.S permit was free, and Canadian permits cost $35 (Canadian funds) for adults and $17.50 for children 6 to 15.

Reservations are recommended for the Canadian portion of the trail, since Parks Canada limits use of the Canadian side of the Chilkoot Trail to 50 hikers per day. Permit reservations can be made in advance ($10 per hiker Canadian funds). Eight permits per day are held for hikers without reservations.

Information on permits and fees, customs requirements, regulations, camping, weather, equipment and trail conditions are available from the Chilkoot Trail Center in Skagway. The center is open 8 A.M. to 4 P.M. daily, late May through mid-September; phone (907) 983-9234.

The White Pass & Yukon Route railroad offers daily service for Chilkoot Trail hikers from Lake Bennett to the customs office at Fraser, BC, in summer. From Fraser, hikers can travel the 28 miles back to Skagway on the regular train. For a current train schedule, phone (800) 343-7373 or (907) 983-2217. Tour operators in Skagway offer transportation to the trailhead and from the highway/railroad intersection at Log Cabin.

USGS maps for Dyea to Chilkoot Pass: Skagway B-1 and C-1. Related Canadian topographic maps for Chilkoot Pass to Lake Bennett: White Pass 104M/11 East, Homan Lake 104M/14 East. An illustrated map of the Chilkoot Trail is available from the park.

For more information: Contact Klondike Gold Rush National Historical Park, Box 517, Skagway, AK 99840; phone (907) 983-2921. On the Internet, visit www.nps.gov/klgo/chilkoot.htm. From this site, you may link to the Parks Canada web site for current Chilkoot Trail fees and permit information. For Parks Canada fees and reservations, phone (867) 667-3910 in Whitehorse, or from Canada and the U.S. mainland, phone toll-free (800) 661-0486.

Historic highlights along the Chilkoot Trail

Mile 4.9 Finnegan's Point. This is reputed to be the site of a bridge across a creek built by Pat Finnegan and his 2 sons. The Finnegans charged a toll for use of the bridge until they were overwhelmed by the hordes of gold seekers. A restaurant operated intermittently at the site.

Mile 7.8 Canyon City. In 1897 and 1898, this was the fourth largest settlement along the trail after Dyea, Lindeman and Sheep Camp. A year later, it was gone.

Mile 10.5 Pleasant Camp. This was the site of a toll bridge (long since washed out) and a restaurant in 1897. As the best level spot north of Canyon City, it was a popular campsite.

Mile 13 Sheep Camp. In the summer and fall of 1897, some stampeders cached their goods here before ascending the final leg over the pass. A half-dozen businesses served the transient population.

Mile 16 The Scales. This was a weighing place for goods hoisted or packed over the pass. It is said that packers reweighed their loads here and charged a higher rate for the steep climb over the summit. Restaurants, saloons and bunkhouses served the stampeders, who cached or discarded their goods here for the final push across the pass.

Mile 16 to 16.5 The "Golden Stairs." This was the name by which the 45-degree climb from The Scales to the 3,739-foot summit became known. In the winter, steps were chopped into the snow; in late summer the snow melted and the route crossed large boulders. It took the stampeders approximately an hour per trip; some took as many as 30 trips to get their outfits across the pass.

At Chilkoot Summit (Mile 16.5), hikers cross the border into Canada. In February 1898 the Royal Northwest Mounted Police established a customs station near here. They levied a

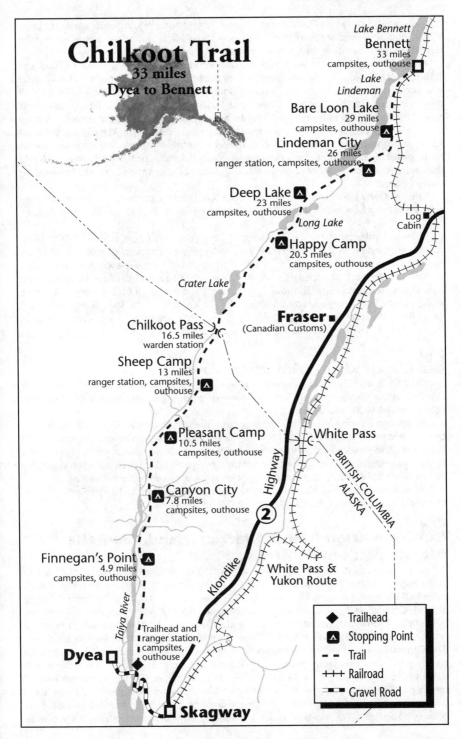

Chilkoot Trail
33 miles
Dyea to Bennett

Lake Bennett

Bennett
33 miles
campsites, outhouse

Lake Lindeman

Bare Loon Lake
29 miles
campsites, outhouse

Lindeman City
26 miles
ranger station, campsites, outhouse

Deep Lake
23 miles
campsites, outhouse

Log Cabin

Long Lake

Happy Camp
20.5 miles
campsites, outhouse

Crater Lake

Fraser ■
(Canadian Customs)

Chilkoot Pass
16.5 miles
warden station

Sheep Camp
13 miles
ranger station, campsites, outhouse

Pleasant Camp
10.5 miles
campsites, outhouse

White Pass

Canyon City
7.8 miles
campsites, outhouse

Highway

BRITISH COLUMBIA

ALASKA

(2)

Finnegan's Point
4.9 miles
campsites, outhouse

White Pass & Yukon Route

Klondike

Taiya River

Trailhead and ranger station, campsites, outhouse

Dyea □

Skagway

◆ Trailhead
▲ Stopping Point
- - - Trail
+++ Railroad
▬▬ Gravel Road

duty on goods going into Canada and enforced a new rule requiring each person to carry a year's supply of food and equipment—the so-called "ton of goods"—into the Yukon. The rule later prevented many stampeders from starving once they reached Dawson.

Mile 17 Stone Crib. The remains of the northern terminus of the Chilkoot Railroad and Transportation Company's aerial tramway are just above the shores of Crater Lake. When it was completed in May 1898, this tramway looped 45 miles of metal cables along the 9 miles between Canyon City and Crater Lake, enabling stampeders to have their goods hauled for 7¢ per pound from Dyea to Lindeman City via wagon road and tramway. Within a year after its completion, the tram system was purchased by the White Pass & Yukon Route and dismantled to avoid competition with the new railroad. The tramway towers have collapsed, and their remains can be seen along the trail. The stone crib that anchored the end of the cable continues to crumble. Sections of the wagon road are followed by today's hikers.

Mile 23 Deep Lake. This was the site of a major freight transfer point. Goods were ferried across Long Lake in the summer, then transferred to horses at Deep Lake for the trip to Lindeman City.

Mile 26 Lindeman City. By the spring of 1898, this was a tent city of 10,000. Here, stampeders built boats and prepared for their water journey across Lake Lindeman and Lake Bennett and down to Dawson. In a cemetery on a hillside, 11 stampeders are buried.

Mile 33 Bennett. Stampeders from both the White Pass and Chilkoot trails gathered here during the gold rush. The town's population swelled to 20,000 as they built boats along the shore of Lake Bennett and waited for the ice to leave the lake. There isn't much left at Bennett except some cabin sites and the shell of St. Andrews Presbyterian Church on the hill. The church was built during the winter and spring of 1899.

Chuck River Wilderness Area

The 72,503-acre Chuck River area was designated a wilderness area in 1990. The area is adjacent to the Tracy Arm-Fords Terror Wilderness on the south and abuts areas of logging activity on the south and southeast.

Fishing and hunting are popular activities in this wilderness area, which is accessible by boat or floatplane from Juneau. The Chuck River boasts the largest pink salmon run in Southeast. All 5 species of salmon are found in Windham Bay. According to rangers, much of the trail system shown on topographic maps is overgrown. There is a trail from Windham Bay to Taylor Lake. Watch for private land holdings at the head of Windham Bay.

For more information: Contact Tongass National Forest, Juneau Ranger District, 8465 Old Dairy Road, Juneau, AK 99801; phone (907) 586-8800.

Coronation Island, Warren Island, Maurelle Islands Wilderness Areas

All 3 of these island wilderness areas are located off the northwest coast of Prince of Wales Island, south of Kuiu Island and north of Noyes Island. By air from Ketchikan, it is 73 miles to the Maurelle Islands, 75 miles to Warren Island, and 110 miles to Coronation Island.

The Coronation Island Wilderness encompasses 19,232 acres; the Maurelle Islands Wilderness, 4,937 acres; and the Warren Island Wilderness, 11,181 acres. Warren Peak is a prominent feature of the Warren Island Wilderness, rising abruptly from sea level to 2,329 feet. The Coronation Island Wilderness includes the Spanish Island group as well as Coronation Island, which has numerous peaks rising sharply to nearly 2,000 feet. Maurelle Islands Wilderness is a group of nearly 30 small islands rising less than 400 feet above sea level. A number of islets, pinnacles and rocky Shoals are found in surrounding waters. These island wildernesses have rocky, windswept beaches with steep cliffs. Trees near the shoreline are often wind-sculpted. Tall stands of spruce are found in more sheltered portions of the islands.

Wildlife: Wolves, black bears, Sitka blacktail deer, bald eagles, whales, seals, sea lions and sea otters are present in these areas. The cliffs and rocks are important seabird nesting and perching areas. Some streams contain trout and salmon.

Activities: Kayaking among the Maurelle Islands is possible but rugged. On the 2 larger islands, principal activities are beachcombing, wildlife observation and photography. There is a protected harbor at Hole-in-the-wall in the San Lorenzo Islands, which form the southern point of the Maurelle group. Access to these islands is by boat or floatplane from Ketchikan, Craig or Klawock.

Access to many of the islands is difficult as there is a lack of boat anchorage and plane landing sites, and the islands are exposed to the winds and surf of the Pacific Ocean. Warren Island is so exposed to the prevailing southeast winds that it is inaccessible much of the year. The leeward sides of some of the islands do have some protected coves and beaches. There are no facilities on any of these islands.

For more information: Contact Tongass National Forest, Thorne Bay Ranger District, Recreation and Lands Dept., P.O. Box 19001, Thorne Bay, AK 99919; phone (907) 828-3304, fax (907) 828-3309. USGS map: Craig.

Dude Creek Critical Habitat

The Dude Creek Critical Habitat is located in northern Southeast Alaska adjacent to Gustavus and Glacier Bay National Park. At 4,083 acres, it is the largest undisturbed wet meadow in the region.

The large population of migrating lesser sandhill cranes is the main attraction to Dude Creek in the fall. Thousands of these birds stop to rest and feed in these wet meadows before migrating south for winter. Smaller numbers of cranes also stop to feed at Dude Creek during the spring migration north. The people of Gustavus take great pride in the resident crane populations; in the fall, the favorite pasttime seems to be waiting for the first crane call and discussing the different sounds.

A high water table and flat, wide-open terrain has produced low-growing shrubs, sedges, mosses and horsetail with willow thicket and scrub forest. Since cranes are shy birds, this habitat provides the perfect setting for feeding and resting during migration.

Though the sandhills are the most popular attraction, Dude Creek Critical Habitat is also host to many other species of wildlife. Canada geese forage in the meadows during spring and fall migrations, and flocks as large as 300 have been spotted in the area. Other waterfowl and birds include mergansers, mallards, snipe, least sandpipers, savannah sparrows, songbirds, marsh hawks, short-eared owls, ravens, magpies and bald eagles. Long-tailed voles, coyotes, wolves, short-tailed weasels, moose, black bears, marten, porcupines, red squirrels and river otters also frequent the meadows and surrounding areas.

Access to Dude Creek is via scheduled flight from Juneau to Gustavus and then by Good River Road to the critical habitat boundary. There are no public use facilities in the Dude Creek area.

Endicott River Wilderness Area

The Endicott River Wilderness is located on the Chilkat Peninsula, on the west side of Lynn Canal, 45 miles northwest of Juneau and 30 miles south of Haines. The western alpine portion of this 98,729-acre wilderness area abuts Glacier Bay National Park for about 40 miles. This area is rugged, extending from sea level to elevations up to 5,280 feet. The Endicott River is the central feature of this wilderness area. It heads in broad, brush-covered flats within the Chilkat Mountains and flows easterly through a deep, glacially-carved canyon. Glaciers cover the highlands of the upper valley. The vegetation is typical southeastern Alaska spruce and hemlock rain forest at lower elevations and brush, small trees and alpine plants higher up. Average annual precipitation is 92 inches, highest in the fall and lowest April through June.

Wildlife includes black and brown bears, mountain goats and a limited number of moose and deer. Hundreds of bald eagles may be seen along the river during salmon runs; a large number of eagles nest here also. Fish in the Endicott River include chum, coho and pink salmon.

Access is primarily by boat from Juneau or Haines to the confluence of the Endicott River and Lynn Canal, then by foot 2.5 miles through dense alder and thick brush to the eastern boundary of the wilderness. According to the Forest Service, it is another 2- to 3-day hike through extremely difficult terrain to reach the plateau. The plateau can be reached from Adams Inlet on the Glacier Bay National Park side, but this route is also considered extremely difficult as it crosses many glacier-fed streams, and there is heavy brush.

Boat access is best in spring and summer. There is limited wheel plane access near the headwaters of the Endicott River. There are no facilities in this wilderness.

For more information: Contact Tongass National Forest, 8465 Old Dairy Road, Juneau, AK 99801-8041; phone (907) 586-8800. USGS map: Juneau.

Fish Creek Wildlife Observation Site

Located 6 miles north of Hyder, Fish Creek flows south 4.5 miles to the Salmon River. According to the Alaska Dictionary of Place Names, there are about 40 streams in Alaska named Fish Creek, but only one offers formal bear viewing. The Fish Creek Wildlife Observation Site is a day-use recreation area operated by the U.S. Forest Service and accessed via the Salmon River Road out of Stewart, BC. It is the only formal bear viewing area in Alaska accessible by road. Between mid-July and early September each year, visitors from all over the world come to observe and photograph brown/grizzly and black bears fishing for chum and pink salmon in the shallow waters of Fish Creek and Marx Creek.

The site is open from 6 A.M. to 10 P.M. daily, and Forest Service personnel are on site to provide information about the bears and enforce site rules. Facilities include a small parking area and elevated viewing platform set in the trees along Fish Creek. Bears can also be seen from the shoulders of the Salmon River Road and from a dike that separates Fish Creek and Marx Creek.

Fishing

About fishing in Southeast Alaska, the Dept. of Fish and Game has stated: "The wide range of species and availability is overwhelming and beyond the capability of most anglers to visit and test the waters." Fishermen are advised to identify whether they wish to fish fresh water or salt water and their desired species.

A variety of species are available in Southeast. Salmon are the most popular sport fish; during the summer, several communities sponsor derbies that offer prizes for the largest salmon caught.

The sheltered marine waters of Southeast are perhaps the best place in Alaska to fish for king salmon. These fish range from 10 to 50 pounds (trophy size) and can reach 90 to 100 pounds. Kings are present in southeastern Alaska marine waters all year. The best period for big fish, however, is from mid-April to mid-June when mature fish are moving through. "Feeders" or smaller kings up to 25 pounds are available throughout the remainder of the year. Preferred bait is trolled or drifted herring. Try the edges of reefs where they drop off into deep water.

Silver (coho) salmon are available from July through September; the best month is August. Herring or large spoons are used for bait, and flashers are often used for attraction. These flashy fighters usually run shallow but do not necessarily follow shorelines. Silvers average 12 pounds but can exceed 20 pounds.

Fishing for pink salmon is good during July and August. Pinks often follow the beach in schools as they swim toward their spawning streams. These fish are best if caught fresh from the sea. Use small, bright spoons (most fishermen use spinning gear), and keep the spoon or spinner moving and lively. These salmon average 3 or 4 pounds but occasionally reach 10 pounds.

Chum and red (sockeye) salmon do not take bait in salt water nearly as well as other species of salmon. In freshwater streams, reds can be taken on small flies drifted slowly or on small spinning lures. Chum salmon are available in Southeast waters from July to September. They range from 2 to 15 pounds, but commercially caught chums have weighed in at 35 pounds. Red salmon are available in June and July. These are small salmon, commonly weighing 2 to 7 pounds (trophy size is anything over 10 pounds).

Other fish found in Southeast include halibut, which can weigh more than 300 pounds; rainbow trout and steelhead, which may tip the scales at 10 pounds and occasionally reach 20 pounds; Dolly Varden, which usually weigh 1 to 3 pounds (world's record is 8.07 pounds); cutthroat from 1 to 3 pounds, may reach 7 pounds; arctic grayling up to 2 pounds; and brook trout from 1 to 5 pounds. An isolated population of northern pike is found in the Pike Lakes system near Yakutat.

Since the majority of southeastern Alaska's best fish locations are accessible only by plane or boat, the availability and cost of a charter must also be considered. A charter flight can range in cost from $180 to $450 per hour, depending on the size of the plane. Charter planes are available in the larger communites, such as Ketchikan, Juneau, Sitka, etc. Bare-boat charters are generally not available, but there are dozens of skippered boat fish charters to choose from in most Southeast communities.

In narrowing down their choices, fishermen might also consider whether or not a public-use cabin is available. Many of the Tongass National Forest cabins are located on fishing lakes.

For more information: Consult the current sportfishing regulations, or contact Alaska Deparment of Fish and Game, Sport Fish Division, P.O. Box 25526, Juneau, AK 99802-5526; phone (907) 465-4100, www.state.ak.us/adfg/adfghome.htm

Regional offices of the Alaska Department of Fish and Game in Southeast are as follows:

For Juneau-Yakutat area (including Admiralty Island, Haines and Skagway): Area Management Biologist, Sport Fish Division, P.O. Box 240020 (802 3ed St.), Douglas, AK 99824; phone (907) 465-4180.

For Ketchikan-Petersburg-Wrangell area: Area Management Biologist, Sport Fish Division, 2030 Sea Level Dr., Suite 205, Ketchikan, AK 99901; phone (907) 225-2859, fax (907) 225-0497.

For Sitka area: Area Management Biologist, Sport Fish Division, 304 Lake St., Room 103, Sitka, AK 99835-0510; phone (907) 747-5828.

Following are sport-fishing destinations in Southeast arranged alphabetically within areas and by areas. The areas are (in alphabetical order): Admiralty Island; Haines-Skagway; Juneau; Ketchikan; Petersburg; Sitka; Wrangell; Yakutat.

Admiralty Island Fishing

Barlow Cove. A 4-mile-long cove located on the north end of the Mansfield Peninsula, 19 miles northwest of Juneau. Accessible by boat. Fish available: king salmon all year but best for large fish May to June, use herring or spoons; silver salmon best in August, use herring or spoons; pink salmon July to August, use small spoons; chum salmon July to September, use spoons; halibut available all year, best in summer, use bait or jigs; rockfish occasional all year, use smaller bait or jigs.

Chatham Strait. Located on the west side of Admiralty Island. Accessible by boat. Fish available: king salmon all year but best for large fish May to June, use herring or spoons; silver salmon best in August, use herring or spoons; pink salmon July to August, use small spoons; chum salmon, best July to September, use herring or spoons; halibut best in summer, use bait; rockfish all year, use smaller baits or jigs.

Doty Cove. Located on the northeast coast of the Glass Peninsula on the east side of Admiralty Island, 16 miles southeast of Juneau. Accessible by boat. Fish available: king salmon all year but best for large fish May to June, use herring or plugs; silver salmon best in August, use herring or spoons; pink salmon July to August, use small spoons; chum salmon July to September, use spoons; Dolly Varden May to October, use spoons, spinners, flies; halibut best in summer, use bait.

Gambier Bay. Located on the southeast coast of Admiralty Island, 70 boat miles south of Juneau, 57 miles east of Sitka. Forest Service cabin available. Fish available: king salmon all year but best for large fish May to June, use herring or plugs; silver salmon best in August, use herring or spoons; pink salmon July to August, use small spoons; Dolly Varden May to October, use small spoons, spinners, flies; halibut best in summer, use bait.

Hasselborg Lake. An 8.5-mile-long lake located on central Admiralty Island, 17 miles northeast of Angoon, 37 air miles south of Juneau. Forest Service cabin and boat available. Accessible by floatplane. Fish available: cutthroat best May to September, use small spoons, spinners, flies; Dolly Varden best May to October, use small spoons, spinners, flies; kokanee best May to September, use spinners, small flies.

Jims, Davidson, Distin and Guerin lakes. Group of small lakes located on central Admiralty Island, 45 air miles south of Juneau. Forest Service cabins and boats available. Accessible by floatplane. Fish available: cutthroat best May to September, use small spoons, spinners, flies; Dolly Varden best May to October, use spoons, spinners, flies; kokanee best May to September, use spinners, flies.

Lake Florence. A 4-mile-long lake located on the west coast of Admiralty Island, 21 miles north of Angoon, 33 air miles southwest of Juneau. Forest Service cabin and boat available. Accessible by floatplane. Fish available: cutthroat best May to September, use bait, spinners, flies; Dolly Varden best May to October, use bait, spinners, flies.

Lake Kathleen. A 1.7-mile-long lake located on the west coast of Admiralty Island, 28 miles north of Angoon, 28 air miles southwest of Juneau. Forest Service cabin and boat available. Accessible by floatplane. Fish available: Dolly Varden best May to September, use spoons, spinners, flies; Kokanee best May to October, use spinners or flies.

Mitchell Bay. A 3.5-mile-wide bay located on west-central Admiralty Island, 7 miles northeast of Angoon, 49 air miles South of Juneau. Accessible by floatplane from Juneau or boat from Angoon. Excellent spring sea-run cutthroat fishing, use spoons, spinners, flies. Other fish: Dolly Varden May to October, use flies or spinners; king salmon all year but best for large fish May to June, use herring or plugs; silver salmon best in August, use herring or spoons; pink salmon July to August, use small spoons.

Mole Harbor. A 1.3-mile-wide bay located on Seymour Canal on the southeast side of Admiralty Island, 24 air miles northeast of Angoon, and 45 air miles or 70 boat miles south of Juneau. Accessible by floatplane or boat. Fish available: king salmon all year but best for large fish May to June, use herring or plugs; silver salmon best in August, use herring or spoons; pink salmon July to August, use small spoons; chum salmon July to September, use spoons; Dolly Varden May to October, use small spoons, spinners, flies; cutthroat best mid- to late summer, use small spoons, spinners or flies; steelhead April to June, use spoons, flies.

Piling Point. Located on Stephens Passage on the northeast coast of the Mansfield Peninsula on Admiralty Island, 14 miles west of Juneau. Accessible by boat. Fish available: king salmon all year but best for large fish May to June, use herring or plugs; silver salmon best in August, use herring or spoons; pink salmon July to August, use small spoons; chum salmon July to September, use spoons; Dolly Varden May to October, use spoons, spinners, flies; halibut in summer, use bait or jigs.

Pleasant Bay Creek. Located on Admiralty Island on the west shore of Seymour Canal, 2 miles southeast of Mole Harbor, 50 air miles and 65 boat miles south of Juneau. Popular for steelhead, April to June, use spoons, flies. Other fish: silver salmon best in August, use flies or spoons; pink salmon July to August, use small spoons; Dolly Varden May to October, use spoons, spinners, flies; cutthroat best mid- to late summer, use spoons, spinners or flies.

Point Arden. Located on Admiralty Island in Stephens Passage on the north coast of Glass Peninsula, 13 miles southeast of Juneau. Accessible by boat. Fish available: king salmon all year but best for large fish May to June, use herring or plugs; silver salmon best in August, use herring or spoons; pink salmon July to August, use small spoons; chum salmon July to September, use spoons; Dolly Varden May to October, use spoons, spinners, flies; halibut in summer, use bait or jigs.

Point Retreat. Located on the north tip of the Mansfield Peninsula on Admiralty Island, 20 miles northwest of Juneau. Accessible by boat. Lighthouse on point. Fish available: king salmon all year but best for large fish May to June, use herring or plugs; silver salmon best in August, use herring or spoons; pink salmon July to August, use small spoons; chum salmon July to September, use spoons; Dolly Varden May to October, use spinners or small spoons; halibut all year, season closed in January, best in summer, use bait.

Pybus Bay. A 4-mile-wide bay located on the east coast of Admiralty Island, 53 miles east of Sitka, 80 boat miles south of Juneau. Accessible by boat. Good summer fishing for large king salmon (smaller kings available all year), use herring or plugs. Other fish: silver salmon best in August, use herring or spoons; pink salmon July to August, use small spoons; Dolly Varden May to October, use spoons, spinners, flies; halibut in summer, use bait.

Thayer Lake. A 7-mile-long lake located on west-central Admiralty Island, 10 miles northeast of Angoon, 42 air miles south of Juneau. Lodge with all facilities on lake. Fish available: cutthroat trout year-round, best May to September, use spoons, spinners, flies; Dolly Varden best May to October, use spoons, spinners, flies.

Young Lake. A 6-mile-long lake located on the northeastern end of Admiralty Island, 15 miles south of Juneau by boat or plane. Forest Service cabins with boats available. Fish available: cutthroat trout best May to September, use spoons, spinners, flies; Dolly Varden best May to October, use spoons, spinners, flies; silver salmon, best August to September use spoons or flies.

Haines-Skagway Area Fishing

Chilkat Inlet. Inlet extends 16 miles south from the mouth of the Chilkat River, 1 mile southwest of Haines, to Lynn Canal. Accessible by boat; beach access from Mud Bay Road (get directions locally). Chilkat State Park provides camping sites, picnic areas, boat launch, small dock and trails and is a good access point for the inlet. Fish available: king salmon best early summer, use herring or plugs; silver salmon September to October, use herring or spoons; pink salmon July to August, use small spoons; Dolly Varden May to October, use spoons, spinners, flies.

Chilkat Lake. A 6-mile-long lake located 3 miles south of Klukwan and about 15 miles northwest of Haines. Accessible by boat or air from Haines or Skagway. Fish available: cutthroat best May to September, use flies or spoons; Dolly Varden May to October, use spoons, spinners, flies; silver salmon September to October, use spoons; red salmon June, use spoons or flies.

Chilkat River. Flows into Chilkat Inlet 1 mile southwest of Haines. Accessible by boat from Haines or from the Haines Highway, which parallels the river at intervals. Fish available: silver salmon September to October, use spinners or spoons; chum salmon September to October, use spoons; red salmon best in June, use spoons or flies; Dolly Varden May to October, use spoons, spinners, flies; cutthroat best mid- to late summer, use spoons, spinners, flies.

Chilkoot Inlet. Extends 20 miles to Lynn Canal about 5 miles north of Haines, 32 miles south of Skagway. Accessible by boat from Haines or Skagway; beach access from Lutak Road from Haines. Fish available: king salmon best early summer; use herring or plugs; silver salmon September to October, use herring or spoons; pink salmon July to August, use small spoons; Dolly Varden May to October, use spoons, spinners, flies.

Chilkoot Lake. A 3.6-mile-long lake near the mouth of the Chilkoot River, 12 miles southwest of Skagway. Accessible by boat or from the end of Lutak Road north of Haines. Fish available: silver salmon September to October, use spoons or flies; pink salmon best July to August, use small spoons; chum salmon September to October, use spoons; red salmon best June to August, use spoons or flies; Dolly Varden May to October, use spoons, spinners, flies. A 32-unit camping site, located on the southern shore of the lake, is part of the Chilkoot Lake State Recreation Area.

Chilkoot River. Flows into Lutak Inlet at the head of Chilkoot Inlet, 12 miles southwest of Skagway. Accessible by boat from Haines or Skagway or from the end of Lutak Road from Haines. Fish available: silver salmon September to October, use spoons or flies; pink salmon best July to August, use small spoons; chum salmon September to October, use spoons; red salmon best in June, use spoons or flies; Dolly Varden May to October, use bait, spinners, flies; cutthroat best mid- to late summer, use bait, spinners, flies.

Dewey Lakes. Lower Dewey Lake, 0.8 mile long, located 2 miles southeast of Skagway. Upper Dewey Lake, 0.4 mile long, located 1.4 miles east of Lower Dewey Lake. Lower lake accessible by 0.8-mile trail from the end of 4th Street in Skagway; trail continues to upper lake. Fish available: brook trout 8 to 14 inches, June to September, use salmon eggs, small spinners, flies; Dolly Varden May to October, use bait, spinners, flies.

Herman Lake. A 0.3-mile-long lake located on Herman Creek, southwest of Haines. Accessible via trail from Porcupine Road (get directions locally). Fish available: grayling best July to September, use flies.

Letnikof Cove. Located on the southwest coast of the Chilkat Peninsula in Chilkat Inlet south of Haines. Accessible by boat or from Mile 5 Mud Bay Road (get directions locally). Fish available: king salmon best early summer, use herring or spoons; silver salmon September to October, use herring or plugs; pink salmon July to August, use small spoons; chum salmon 8 to 17 pounds, September to early November, fish from banks with flashing lures; Dolly Varden May to October, use spoons, spinners, flies.

Lutak Inlet. Located north of Haines on Lutak Road. Chilkoot River empties into head of Lutak Inlet. Accessible by boat or from Lutak Road, which parallels the inlet. Fish available: pink salmon July and early August, use small spoons; red salmon June to August, use spoons or flies; ocean run Dolly Varden June through November, use spoons, spinners, flies; king salmon best early summer, use herring or spoons; silver salmon September to October, use herring or spoons.

Lynn Canal. A 60-mile-long channel that extends south from Chilkat Island near Haines to Chatham Strait, 22 miles west of Juneau. Accessible by boat. Weather and water conditions should be watched closely in this large, open waterway. Fish available: king salmon best early summer, use herring or spoons; silver salmon August to October, use herring or spoons; pink salmon July to August, use small spoons; Dolly Varden June to November, use spoons or spinners; halibut in summer, use bait or jigs.

Skagway Harbor. Located in front of the city of Skagway. Accessible from shore or by boat. Windy weather often dangerous for small boats. Fish available: Dolly Varden 18 to 20 inches, May to June, use spoons, good fishing from shore; king salmon 8 to 30 pounds all summer, use herring. Windy weather often dangerous for small boats.

Taiya Inlet. Extends 13 miles south from the mouth of the Taiya River to Chilkoot Inlet, 12 miles south of Skagway. Accessible by boat or from shore in Skagway. Fish available: king salmon best early summer, use herring or spoons; silver salmon September to October, use herring or spoons; pink salmon July to August, use small spoons; Dolly Varden 18 to 20 inches, May to June, use spoons, good fishing from shore.

Taiya River. Enters Taiya Inlet 1 mile north of Dyea Point, 2 miles northwest of Skagway. Accessible by boat or from the bridge on Dyea Road. Fish available: silver salmon September to October, use spoons; pink salmon July to August, use small spoons; chum salmon September to October, use spoons; Dolly Varden 18 to 20 inches, May to June, use spoons, spinners, flies.

Juneau Area Fishing

Aaron Island. A 0.4-mile-long island located in Favorite Channel, 17 miles northwest of Juneau. Accessible by boat. Fish available: king salmon best May to June, use herring or spoons; silver salmon best in August, use herring or spoons; pink salmon July to August, use small spoons; chum salmon July to September, use spoons; Dolly Varden May to October, use spoons or spinners; halibut in summer, use bait or jigs.

Antler Lake. Located on the mainland 11 miles east of Berners Bay, 39 air miles northwest of Juneau. Accessible by floatplane. No facilities. Grayling to 18 inches, best July to September, use flies. Lake is very high with limited accessibility.

Auke Bay. Located 11.8 miles north of Juneau on the Glacier Highway. Fishing primarily accessible by boat. Fish available: king salmon all year but best for large fish May to July, use herring or spoons; silver salmon best in August, use herring or spoons; pink salmon July to August, use small spoons; chum salmon July to September, use spoons; Dolly Varden May to October, use spoons, spinners, flies; halibut in summer, use bait or jigs.

Benjamin Island. A 1.5-mile-long island located on the east shore of Favorite Channel, 25 miles northwest of Juneau. Accessible by boat. Fish available: king salmon all year but best for large fish May to June, use herring or spoons; silver salmon best in August, use herring or spoons; pink salmon July to August, use small spoons; Dolly Varden June to July, use spoons, spinners, flies; halibut in summer, use bait or jigs.

Berners Bay. A 3-mile-wide bay located on the east shore of Lynn Canal, 34 miles northwest of Juneau. Accessible by boat or from the end of the Glacier Highway (39.6 miles north of Juneau). Fish available: king salmon all year, best for large fish May to June, use herring or spoons; silver salmon best in August, use herring or spoons; pink salmon July to August, use small spoons; chum salmon July to September, use spoons; Dolly Varden May to October, use spoons, spinners, flies; cutthroat best mid- to late summer, use spoons, spinners or flies; halibut in summer, use bait.

The Breadline. A 1.2-mile-long stretch of cliffs on the east shore of Favorite Channel, just north of Tee Harbor, 17 miles northwest of Juneau. Accessible by boat. Fish available: king salmon all year, best for large fish May to June, use herring or spoons; silver salmon best in August, use herring or spoons; pink salmon July to August, use small spoons; chum salmon July to September, use spoons; Dolly Varden May to October, use small spoons, spinners, flies; cutthroat trout best mid- to late summer, use small spoons, spinners, flies; halibut in summer, use bait.

Dupont. Located on the northeast shore of Gastineau Channel, 7.5 miles southeast of Juneau. Accessible by boat or by trail 1.5 miles from the end of Thane Road. Fish available: king salmon all year, best for large fish May to June, use herring or spoons; silver salmon best in August, use herring or spoons; pink salmon July to August, use small spoons; chum salmon July to September, use spoons; Dolly Varden May to October, use small spoons, spinners, flies; halibut in summer, use bait or jigs.

Echo Cove. A 1.8-mile-long cove located on the south shore of Berners Bay, 34 miles northwest of Juneau. Accessible by boat or from the end of the Glacier Highway (39.6 miles north of Juneau). Fish available: king salmon all year, best for large fish May to June, use herring or spoons; silver salmon best in August, use herring or spoons; pink salmon July to August, use small spoons; chum salmon July to September, use spoons; Dolly Varden May to October, use small spoons, spinners, flies; cutthroat trout best mid- to late summer, use small spoons, spinners, flies; halibut in summer, use bait or jigs.

Favorite Reef. Located off the southwest coast of Shelter Island, about 28 miles north of Juneau. Accessible by boat. Fish available: king salmon all year, best for large fish May to June, use herring or spoons; silver salmon best in August, use herring or spoons; pink salmon July to August, use small spoons; chum salmon July to September, use spoons; halibut in summer, use bait or jigs; rockfish occasional, use smaller baits or jigs.

Gastineau Channel. A 19-mile-long channel that lies between Juneau on the mainland and Douglas Island. Accessible by boat from Juneau or Douglas or from access points along area roads to shorelines. Fish available: king salmon all year, best for large fish May to June and July near hatchery, use herring or spoons; silver salmon best in August and September, use herring or spoons; pink salmon July to August, use small spoons; chum salmon July to September, use spoons; Dolly Varden May to October, use small spoons, spinners, flies; halibut occasional in summer, use bait or jigs.

Hand Trollers Cove. Located on the northeast side of Shelter Island north of Juneau. Accessible by boat. Fish available: king salmon all year, best for large fish May to June, use herring or spoons; silver salmon best in August, use herring or spoons; pink salmon July to August, use small spoons; halibut in summer, use bait or jigs; rockfish occasional, use smaller baits or jigs.

Icy Point. Located on the south shore of Douglas Island, 9 miles south-southwest of Juneau. Accessible by boat. Fish available: king salmon all year, best for large fish May to June, use herring or spoons; silver salmon best in August, use herring or spoons; pink salmon July to August, use small spoons; chum salmon July to Septemher, use spoons; Dolly

Varden May to October, use small spoons, spinners, flies; halibut in summer, use bait.

Lena Point. Located at the south entrance to Lena Cove on Favorite Channel, 14 miles northwest of Juneau. Accessible by boat. Wreck of Princess Kathleen down below. Fish available: king salmon all year, best for large fish in May, use herring or spoons; silver salmon best in August, use herring or spoons; pink salmon July to August, use small spoons; chum salmon July to September, use spoons; Dolly Varden May to October, use small spoons, spinners, flies; halibut in summer, use bait or jigs; rockfish occasional year-round, use smaller baits or jigs.

Lincoln Island. A 4.7-mile-long island located in Lynn Canal, 24 miles northwest of Juneau. Accessible by boat. Fish available: king salmon all year, best for large fish May to June, use herring or spoons; silver salmon best in August, use herring or spoons; pink salmon July to August, use small spoons; halibut in summer, use bait or jigs; rockfish occasional year-round, use smaller baits or jigs.

Marmion Island. A 0.2-mile-wide island located southeast of Douglas Island at the south end of Gastineau Channel, 9 miles southeast of Juneau. Accessible by boat. Fish available: king salmon all year, best for large fish May to June, use herring or spoons; silver salmon best in August, use herring or spoons; pink salmon July to August, use small spoons; chum salmon July to September, use spoons; Dolly Varden May to October, use small spoons, spinners, flies; halibut in summer, use bait or jigs; rockfish occasional year-round, use smaller baits or jigs.

Middle Point. Located in Stephens Passage on the west coast of Douglas Island, 9 miles southwest of Juneau. Accessible by boat. Fish available: king salmon all year, best for large fish May to June, use herring or spoons; silver salmon best in August, use herring or spoons; pink salmon July to August, use small spoons; chum salmon July to September, use spoons; Dolly Varden May to October, use small spoons, spinners, flies; halibut in summer, use bait or jigs.

North Pass. A passage between Lincoln Island and the north end of Shelter Island, 22 miles northwest of Juneau. Accessible by boat. Fish available: king salmon all year, best for large fish May to June, use herring or spoons; silver salmon best in August, use herring or spoons; pink salmon July to August, use small spoons; chum salmon July to September, use spoons; halibut in summer, use bait or jigs.

Outer Point. Located on the west tip of Douglas Island in Stephens Passage, 4 miles northwest of Middle Point, 10 miles west of Juneau. Accessible by boat or by trail from end of North Douglas Highway. Fish available: king salmon all year, best for large fish May to June, use herring or spoons; silver salmon best in August, use herring or spoons; pink salmon July to August, use small spoons; chum salmon July to September, use spoons; Dolly Varden May to October, use small spoons, spinners, flies; halibut in summer, use bait or jigs.

Point Bishop. Located at the south end of Taku Inlet on Stephens Passage, 4.8 miles southeast of Dupont, 12 miles southeast of Juneau. Accessible by boat or by trail 8 miles from the end of Thane Road. Fish available: king salmon all year, best for large fish May to June, use herring or spoons; silver salmon best in August, use herring or spoons; pink salmon July to August, use small spoons; chum salmon July to September, use spoons; Dolly Varden May to October, use small spoons, spinners, flies; halibut in summer, use bait or jigs; rockfish occasional year-round, use smaller baits or jigs.

Point Hilda. Located in Stephens Passage on the south shore of Douglas Island, 7 miles southwest of Juneau. Accessible by boat. Fish available: king salmon all year, best for large fish May to June, use herring or spoons; silver salmon best in August, use herring or spoons; pink salmon July to August, use small spoons; chum salmon July to September, use spoons; Dolly Varden May to October, use small spoons, spinners, flies; halibut in summer, use bait or jigs; rockfish occasional year-round, use smaller baits or jigs.

Point Louisa. Located on the east shore of Stephens Passage, west of Auke Bay, 12 miles northwest of Juneau. Accessible by boat or short trail from Forest Service campground. This is a favorite spot to fish from shore. Fish available from shore: silver salmon best in late August, use spoons; pink salmon July to August, use small spoons; chum salmon July to September, use spoons; Dolly Varden May to October, use spoons, spinners, flies.

Point Salisbury. Located on Stephens Passage at the south end of Gastineau Channel, 2.5 miles west of Point Bishop, 10 miles southwest of Juneau. Accessible by boat or the Dupont-Point Bishop trail from the end of Thane Road. Fish available: king salmon all year, best for large fish May to June, use herring or spoons; silver salmon best in August, use herring or spoons; pink salmon July to August, use small spoons; chum salmon July to September, use spoons; Dolly Varden May to October, use bait, spinners, flies; halibut available all year, season closed in January, best in summer, use bait or jigs; rockfish all year, best May to September, use smaller baits or jigs.

Salmon Creek and Reservoir. Reservoir located 3 miles up trail beginning at Mile 2.3 on the Old Glacier Highway north of Juneau. Trail follows creek. Fish available in creek below waterfall: pink and chum salmon July to August, use small spoons; Dolly Varden May to October, use small spoons, spinners, flies. Fish available in reservoir: eastern brook trout year-round, use eggs, spinners, flies.

Shrine of St. Therese. Located on Favorite Channel, 18 miles north of Juneau. Accessible by boat or from Mile 23.3 on the Glacier Highway. This is a favorite spot to fish from shore. Fish available from shore: silver salmon best in late August and early September, use herring or spoons; pink salmon July to August, use small spoons; Dolly Varden May to October, use spoons, spinners, flies; cutthroat best mid- to late summer, use spoons, spinners, flies.

South Shelter Island. South end of 9-mile-long island located between Favorite and Saginaw Channels, 15 miles northwest of Juneau. Accessible by boat. Fish available: king salmon all year, best for large fish May to June, use herring or spoons; silver salmon best in August, use herring or spoons; pink salmon July to August, use small spoons; chum salmon July to September, use spoons; halibut in summer, use bait or jigs.

Stephens Passage. Located along the west side of Douglas Island, about 11 miles west of Juneau. Accessible by boat. Fish available: king salmon all year, best in late May and early June, use herring or spoons; silver salmon best in August, use herring or spoons; pink salmon July to August, use small spoons; Dolly Varden May to October, use spoons, spinners, flies; halibut in summer, use bait or jigs; rockfish occasional year-round, use smaller baits or jigs.

Tee Harbor. A 1.5-mile-long, T-shaped bay on the east shore of Favorite Channel, 0.4 mile north of Lena Cove, 15 miles northwest of Juneau. Accessible by boat or from 18.5 Mile Glacier Highway north of Juneau. Fish available: king salmon in late April and May, use herring or plugs; silver salmon best in August and early September, use herring or spoons; pink salmon July to August, use small spoons; Dolly Varden May to October, use spoons, spinners, flies; cutthroat occasional in summer, use spoons, spinners, flies; halibut in summer, use bait or jigs.

Turner Lake. A 9-mile-long lake located 1 mile east of Taku Inlet, 25 air miles east of Juneau. Accessible by boat and trail from salt water or by floatplane. Two Forest Service cabins and boats available. Fish available: cutthroat May to September, catch-and-release only, use spoons, spinners, flies; Dolly Varden May to October, use spoons, spinners, flies; kokanee, May to September, use spinners or flies.

White Marker. Located on the west coast of Douglas Island, south of Middle Point. Accessible by boat. Fish available: king salmon all year, best for large fish May to June, use herring or plugs; silver salmon best in August, use herring or spoons; pink salmon July to August, use spoons; chum salmon July to September, use herring or spoons; Dolly Varden May to October, use spoons, spinners, flies; halibut in summer, use bait or jigs.

Windfall Lake. A 0.8-mile-long lake located south of the terminus of Herbert Glacier, 18 miles northwest of Juneau. Accessible by 4-mile trail from the end of Windfall Lake Road (no sign) at Mile 27.4 of the Glacier Highway north of Juneau. U.S. Forest Service cabin available. Fish available: silver salmon September to October, use spoons, spinners, flies; Dolly Varden year-round, use spoons, spinners, flies; cutthroat year-round, use spoons, spinners, flies.

Ketchikan Area Fishing

Bakewell Lake. A 4.3-mile-long lake located on the mainland east of East Behm Canal, 39 air miles southeast of Ketchikan. Accessible by floatplane or boat to Smeaton Bay, then a 0.8-mile hike to the lake. Fish available: silver salmon late August to early September, use flies, spoons, spinners; cutthroat best May to September, use bait, spinners, flies; Dolly Varden best May to October, use bait, spinners, flies.

Bell Island. An 8.7-mile-long island located north of Revillagigedo Island in North Behm Canal, 45 miles north of Ketchikan. Accessible by boat or floatplane. Private resort (not open to the public) at hot springs on southwest end of island. Area considered a "hot spot" for king salmon, best mid-May to mid-June, use herring or spoons. Other fish: silver salmon best in August, use herring or spoons; pink salmon July to August, use small spoons; chum salmon July to September, use spoons; Dolly Varden May to October, use bait, spinners, flies; cutthroat trout best mid- to late summer, use bait, spinners, flies; steelhead April to June and October to November, use spoons, eggs; halibut all year, season closed in January, best in summer, use bait; rockfish all year, best May to September, use smaller baits or jigs.

Big Goat Lake. A 2.4-mile-long lake located 38 air miles northeast of Ketchikan. Accessible by floatplane. Recreation cabin and skiff available. Fish available: grayling up to 2 pounds, use small flies, shrimp, spinners.

Blank Inlet. Extends northwest 3.3 miles off Nichols Passage on the east coast of Gravina Island, 7 miles south of Ketchikan by boat. Fish available: king salmon best May to June, use herring or spoons; silver salmon best in August, use herring or spoons; pink salmon July to August, use small spoons; chum salmon July to September, use spoons; halibut available all year, season closed in January, best in summer, use bait; rockfish all year, best May to September, use smaller baits or jigs; lingcod all year, best in summer, use herring.

Caamano Point. Located at the south tip of the Cleveland Peninsula between Behm Canal and Clarence Strait, 18 miles northwest of Ketchikan by boat. Use of guide recommended. Fish available: king salmon best May to June, use herring or spoons; silver salmon best in August, use herring or spoons; pink salmon July to August, use small spoons; chum salmon July to September, use spoons; halibut available all year, season closed in January, best in summer, use bait; rockfish all year, best May to September, use smaller baits or jigs; lingcod all year, best in summer, use herring.

Chasina Point. Located on the east coast of Prince of Wales Island between Cholmondeley Sound and Clarence Strait, 22 miles southwest of Ketchikan by boat. Use of guide recommended. Fish available: king salmon best May to June, use herring or spoons; silver salmon best in August, use herring or spoons; pink salmon July to August, use small spoons; chum salmon July to September, use spoons; halibut available all year, season closed in January, best in summer, use bait; rockfish all year, best May to September, use smaller baits or jigs; lingcod all year, best in summer, use herring.

Clover Pass. Located at Potter Point on Revillagigedo Island, 11 miles northwest of Ketchikan by road or boat. Commercial lodges and marina available. Fish available: king salmon best May to June, use herring or spoons; silver salmon best in August, use herring or spoons; pink salmon July to August, use small spoons; chum salmon July to September, use spoons; halibut all year, season closed in January, best in summer, use bait; rockfish all year, best May to September, use smaller baits or jigs; lingcod all year, best in summer, use herring.

Ella Lake. A 5-mile-long lake located on Revillagigedo Island, 24 air miles northeast of Ketchikan. Accessible by floatplane. Forest Service cabin and skiff on lake. Fishing for cutthroat May to September and Dolly Varden May to October, use bait, spinners, flies.

Fish Creek. Located at the head of Thorne Arm, 21 miles east of Ketchikan by boat, or 18 miles by floatplane. Forest Service cabin available. Fish available: silver salmon best in August, use herring or spoons; pink salmon July to August, use small spoons; red salmon June, use spoons; Dolly Varden May to October, use bait, spinners, flies; cutthroat best mid- to late summer, use bait, spinners, flies; steelhead April to June and October to November, use spoons, eggs; rainbow trout May to September, use flies, lures, bait.

Grace Lake. Located inland from the east coast of Revillagigedo Island, 30 air miles from Ketchikan. Accessible by floatplane. Fishing for eastern brook trout, May to September, use eggs or spinners.

Grindall Island. A 1.5-mile-long island located between Clarence Strait and Kasaan Bay on the east coast of Prince of Wales Island, 20 miles northwest of Ketchikan by boat. Use of guide recommended. Fish available: king salmon best May to June, use herring or spoons; silver salmon best in August, use herring or spoons; pink salmon July to August, use small spoons; chum salmon July to September, use spoons; halibut all year, season closed in January, best in summer, use bait; rockfish all year, best May to September, use smaller baits or jigs; lingcod all year, best in summer, use herring.

Humpback Lake. A 6.3-mile long lake located above Mink Bay in Boca de Quadra, 48 miles southeast of Ketchikan. Forest Service cabin, skiff and commercial lodge available. Fish available: cutthroat best May to September, use bait, spinners, flies; Dolly Varden best May to October, use bait, spinners, flies; grayling use small flies, shrimp, spinners.

Karta River. Located above Karta Bay on Prince of Wales Island, 42 air miles northwest of Ketchikan. Accessible by boat or floatplane. Forest Service cabins available. Excellent for steelhead April to June, use spoons or eggs. Other fish available: silver salmon best in July and August, use flies or spoons; pink salmon July to August, use small spoons; red salmon in June and July, use spoons; chum salmon July to September, use spoons; Dolly Varden May to October, use bait, spinners, flies; cutthroat best mid- to late summer, use bait, spinners, flies; excellent for steelhead April to June, use spoons, eggs; rainbow trout May to September, use flies, lures, bait.

Klawock Creek. Heads in Klawock Lake on the west coast of Prince of Wales Island. Accessible by boat, state ferry or floatplane. Excellent spring run of steelhead, use spoons or eggs, also good October to November. Excellent silver salmon late August to September, use flies, spinners, spoons. Closed to red salmon fishing.

LeDuc Lake. A 2.5-mile-long lake located above the Chickamin River, 49 air miles northeast of Ketchikan. Accessible by float-plane. Fishing for rainbow trout May to September, use flies, lures, bait.

Manzanita Lake. Located above Manzanita Bay, 28 air miles northeast of Ketchikan. Forest Service cabin and skiff available. Fish available: cutthroat best May to September, use bait, spinners, flies; Dolly Varden best May to October, use bait, spinners, flies; kokanee best May to September, use spinners or eggs.

Manzoni Lake. A 2.4-mile-long lake located on the mainland, south of Walker Cove at the head of Granite Creek. Accessible by floatplane. Fishing for grayling up to 2 pounds, use small flies, shrimp, spinners.

McDonald Lake. Located 45 air miles north of Ketchikan above Yes Bay. Accessible by floatplane or boat and trail. Forest Service cabin and skiff available. Excellent for steelhead April to June, use spoons or eggs; Other fish available: silver salmon best in September, use flies or spoons; red salmon August, use flies or spoons; Dolly Varden May to October, use bait, spinners, flies; cutthroat best mid- to late summer, use bait, spinners, flies; excellent for steelhead April to June, use spoons, eggs; rainbow trout May to September, use flies, lures, bait.

Naha River. Located on Revillagigedo Island, 21 miles north of Ketchikan by boat. Also accessible by floatplane. Forest Service cabins and skiffs available; trail follows river. Fish available: silver salmon best in September, use flies or spoons; pink salmon July to August, use small spoons; red salmon June, use flies or spoons; chum salmon July to September, use spoons; Dolly Varden May to October, use bait, spinners, flies; cutthroat best mid- to late summer, use bait, spinners, flies; steelhead April to June and October to November, use spoons, eggs; rainbow trout May to September, use flies, lures, bait.

Orchard Lake. A 3.5-mile-long lake located on the northwest coast of Revillagigedo Island above Shrimp Bay, 32 air miles north of Ketchikan. Forest Service cabin available. Fish available: cutthroat best May to September, use bait, spinners, flies; Dolly Varden best May to October, use bait, spinners, flies.

Patching Lake. A 3.3-mile-long lake located in the course of the Naha River, 6 miles east of Loring, 19 air miles north of Ketchikan. Accessible by floatplane. Forest Service cabin available. Fish available: cutthroat best May to September, use bait, spinners, flies; Dolly Varden best May to October, use bait, spinners, flies.

Point Alava. Located on the south tip of Revillagigedo Island, 20 miles southeast of Ketchikan. Accessible by boat. Fish available: king salmon best May to June, use herring or spoons; silver salmon best in August, use herring or spoons; pink salmon July to August, use small spoons; chum salmon July to September, use spoons; halibut season closed in January, best in summer, use bait; rockfish all year, best May to September, use smaller baits or jigs; lingcod all year, best in summer, use herring.

Point Sykes. Located at the east point of the entrance to Behm Canal, 25 miles southeast of Ketchikan. Accessible by boat. Use of guide recommended. Fish available: king salmon best May to June, use herring or spoons; silver salmon best in August, use herring or spoons; pink salmon July to August, use small spoons; chum salmon July to September, use spoons; halibut season closed in January, best in summer, use bait; rockfish all year, best May to September, use smaller baits or jigs; lingcod all year, best in summer, use herring.

Reflection Lake. A 4.5-mile-long lake located above Short Bay on the Cleveland Peninsula, 46 air miles north of Ketchikan. Forest Service cabin and skiff available. Fish available: silver salmon best in July and August, use flies or spoons; cutthroat best mid- to late summer, use bait, spinners, flies.

Salt Lagoon Creek. Located at the head of George Inlet, 22 miles north of Ketchikan. Accessible by boat. Fish available: silver salmon best in July and August, use flies or spoons; pink salmon July to August, use small spoons; Dolly Varden May to October, use bait, spinners, flies; cutthroat best mid- to late summer, use bait, spinners, flies.

Silvis Lake. Located 1.5 miles from the end of the Tongass Highway, north of Ketchikan. Accessible by trail. Fish available: rainbow trout May to September, use flies, lures, bait.

Snow Lake. A 0.9-mile-long lake located on Revillagigedo Island near the head of the Naha River, 7 miles northeast of Loring. Accessible by floatplane. Fish available: grayling up to 2 pounds, use small flies, shrimp, spinners.

Unuk River. Located at the head of Burroughs Bay, 50 miles north of Ketchikan. Accessible by floatplane or boat. Fish available: silver salmon best in August and September, use flies or spoons; pink salmon July to August, use small spoons; chum salmon July to September, use spoons; Dolly Varden May to October, use bait, spinners, flies; cutthroat best mid- to late summer, use bait, spinners, flies.

Vallenar Point. Located at the north tip of Gravina Island, 11 miles northwest of Ketchikan. Accessible by boat. Fish available: king salmon best May to June, use herring or spoons; silver salmon best in August, use herring or spoons; pink salmon July to August, use small spoons; chum salmon July to September, use spoons; halibut season closed in January, best in summer, use bait; rockfish all year, best May to September, use smaller baits or jigs; lingcod all year, best in summer, use herring.

Walker Lake. Located on the mainland 3.5 miles east of Walker Cove in Misty Fiords National Monument; drains southwest into Rudyerd Bay. Accessible by floatplane. Fishing for rainbow trout May to September, use flies, lures, bait.

Wilson Lake. A 5-mile-long lake located on the mainland; drained by the Wilson River into Wilson Arm. Accessible by floatplane. Has 2 Forest Service cabins and skiffs. Fishing for Dolly Varden May to October, use bait, spinners, flies; cutthroat best mid- to late summer.

Yes Bay. Located in North Behm Canal, 44 miles north of Ketchikan by boat. Also accessible by floatplane. Commercial resort available. Fish available: king salmon best May to June, use herring or spoons; silver salmon best in August and September, use herring or spoons; pink salmon July to August, use small spoons; chum salmon July to September, use spoons; halibut season closed in January, best in summer, use bait; rockfish all year, best May to September, use smaller baits or jigs; lingcod all year, best in summer, use herring.

Petersburg Area Fishing

Cape Strait. Located off the Kupreanof Island shoreline, 12 miles north of Petersburg. Accessible by boat. Fish available: king salmon best May to June, use herring or spoons; silver salmon best in August, use herring or spoons; halibut season closed in January, best in summer, use bait; rockfish all year, best May to September, use smaller baits or jigs.

Castle River. Located on the west shore of Duncan Canal, 22 miles southwest of Petersburg. Accessible by floatplane or boat. Fish available: silver salmon best in August, use flies, bait or spoons; pink salmon July to August, use small spoons; chum salmon July to September, use spoons; Dolly Varden May to October, use bait, spinners, flies; cutthroat best mid- to late summer, use bait, spinners, flies; steelhead April to June and October to November, use spoons, eggs; rainbow trout May to September, use flies, lures, bait.

DeBoer Lake. A 1.5-mile-long lake located 20 air miles north of Petersburg. Accessible by floatplane. Fishing for rainbow trout midsummer to September, use flies, lures, bait.

Duncan Salt Chuck. Located at the head of Duncan Canal, 28 miles by boat west of Petersburg. Fish available: silver salmon best in August, use bait, flies, spoons; Dolly Varden May to October, use bait, spinners, flies; cutthroat best mid- to late summer, use bait, spinners, flies; steelhead April to June and October to November, use spoons or eggs; rainbow trout May to September, use flies, lures, bait.

Frederick Sound. Located northeast of Petersburg. Accessible by boat. Fish available: king salmon best May to June, use herring or spoons; silver salmon best in August, use herring or spoons; halibut season closed in January, use bait; rockfish all year, use smaller baits or jigs.

Kadake Creek. Located on Kuiu Island, 60 miles by boat or 20 minutes by floatplane west of Petersburg. Forest Service cabin available. Excellent spring cutthroat fishery. Other fish: silver salmon best in August, use bait, flies or spoons; pink salmon July to August, use small spoons; chum salmon July to September, use spoons; Dolly Varden May to October, use bait, spinners, flies; steelhead April to June and October to November, use spoons or eggs; rainbow trout May to September, use flies, lures, bait.

Kah Sheets Creek. Located on Kupreanof Island 21 miles southwest of Petersburg by boat. Also accessible by floatplane. Forest Service cabin on Kah Sheets Lake and on the bay. Fish available: silver salmon best in August, use bait, flies, spoons; pink salmon July to August, use small spoons; chum salmon July to September, use spoons; red salmon best in July, use flies and small spoons; Dolly Varden May to October, use bait, spinners, flies; steelhead April to June, use spoons or eggs; cutthroat best mid- to late summer, use bait, spinners, flies.

Petersburg Creek. Located across Wrangell Narrows from Petersburg by boat. Boats and accommodations available in Petersburg. Fish available: silver salmon best in August, use bait, flies, spoons; pink salmon July to August, use small spoons; chum salmon July to September, use spoons; red salmon best in June and July, use flies and small spoons; Dolly Varden May to October, use bait, spinners, flies; steelhead April to June and October to November, use spoons or eggs; cutthroat best mid- to late summer, use bait, spinners, flies; rainbow trout May to September, use flies, lures, bait.

Petersburg Lake. Located 4.5 miles by trail up Petersburg Creek (see above). Forest Service cabin and boat available. Fish available: silver salmon best in August, use bait, flies, spoons; Dolly Varden May to October, use bait, spinners, flies; cutthroat trout best mid- to late summer, use bait, spinners, flies.

Security Bay. Located on the north coast of Kuiu Island, 60 miles west of Petersburg by boat. Fish available: king salmon best May to June, use herring or spoons; silver salmon best in August, use herring or spoons; halibut season closed in January, best in summer, use bait; rockfish all year, best May to September, use smaller baits or jigs; lingcod all year, best in summer, use herring.

Swan Lake. Located on the mainland above Thomas Bay, 18 air miles north of Petersburg. Forest Service cabin and boat available. Excellent fall fishery for rainbow trout.

Thomas Bay. Located 15 miles north of Petersburg on mainland. Two Forest Service cabins. Accessible by boat or plane. Fish available: king salmon best May to June, use herring or spoons; halibut season closed in January, best in summer, use bait.

Towers Lake. Located on Kupreanof Island 20 air miles west of Petersburg. Accessible by floatplane. Fish available: Dolly Varden May to October, use bait, spinners, flies; cutthroat best mid- to late summer, use bait, spinners, flies.

Sitka Area Fishing

Avoss Lake. A 1.7-mile-long lake located on central Baranof Island, 29 air miles southeast of Sitka. Accessible by floatplane. Forest Service cabin available. Good fishery for rainbow trout May to September, use flies, lures, bait.

Baranof Lake. A 2.5-mile-long lake located on the east coast of Baranof Island, 18 miles west of Sitka. Accessible by floatplane and road. Forest Service cabin available. Fishing for cutthroat trout best mid- to late summer, use spinners or flies.

Davidof Lake. A 1.7-mile-long lake located on southcentral Baranof Island, 35 air miles southeast of Sitka. Accessible by floatplane. Forest Service cabin available. Good fishery for rainbow trout May to September, use flies, lures, bait.

Gar Lake. Located on Baranof Island, 39 air miles southeast of Sitka. Accessible by floatplane. Good fishing for rainbow trout May to September, use flies, lures, bait.

Goulding Lakes. Located on Chichagof Island, 61.3 air miles north of Sitka. Accessible by floatplane. Forest Service cabin available. Fish available: Dolly Varden May to October, use bait, spinners, flies; cutthroat best mid- to late summer, use spinners or flies.

Green Lake. A 2-mile-long lake located near the head of Silver Bay, 10 miles southeast of Sitka. Accessible by floatplane or boat and short hike. Fish available: brook trout best May to September, use eggs or spinners.

Heart Lake. A 0.1-mile-wide lake located 3.5 miles east of Sitka. Accessible by trail from Blue Lake Road. Fishing for brook trout best May to September, use eggs or spinners.

Katlian River. Located on the west coast of Baranof Island, 11 miles northeast of Sitka. Accessible by boat. Fish available: silver salmon best in August, use herring or spoons; pink salmon July to August, use small spoons; chum salmon July to September, use spoons; Dolly Varden May to October, use bait, spinners, flies.

Khvostof Lake. A 1.4-mile-long lake located on southcentral Baranof Island, 39 air miles southeast of Sitka. Accessible by floatplane. Fishing for rainbow trout May to September, use flies, lures, bait.

Lake Eva. A 1.7-mile-long lake located on the north coast of Baranof Island, 20 air miles northeast of Sitka. Forest Service cabin and boat available; cabin equipped for the handicapped. Accessible by floatplane. Excellent fishing for Dolly Varden May to October, use spinners or flies; cutthroat best mid- to late summer, use spinners or flies. Lake also has silver and red salmon and steelhead.

Lake Plotnikof. A 4-mile-long lake located on southcentral Baranof Island, 38 air miles southeast of Sitka. Accessible by floatplane. Forest Service cabin and boat available. Good fishing for rainbow trout May to September, use flies, lures, bait.

Little Lake Eva. Located on the north coast of Baranof Island, 20 air miles northeast of Sitka. Accessible by trail from Lake Eva. Excellent fishing for cutthroat best mid- to late summer, use spinners or flies.

Nakwasina River. Located 15 miles north of Sitka. Accessible by boat. Excellent sea-run Dolly Varden fishing in July and August, use spinners or flies. Other fish available: silver salmon best in August, use herring or spoons; pink salmon July to August, use small spoons; chum salmon July to September, use spoons.

Pass Lake. Located on southeastern Baranof Island, 33 air miles southeast of Sitka. Accessible by floatplane. Fishing for rainbow trout May to September, use flies, lures, bait.

Port Banks. Located on the west coast of Baranof Island, 35 air miles southeast of Sitka. Accessible by boat or floatplane. No facilities. Excellent fishery for silver salmon late July and August, use herring or spoons.

Redoubt Lake. A 9.5-mile-long lake located at the head of Redoubt Bay on the west coast of Baranof Island, 12 miles south of Sitka. Accessible by floatplane or boat. Forest

Service cabin available. Fish available: silver salmon best in August, use herring or spoons; pink salmon July to August, use small spoons; chum salmon July to September, use spoons; red salmon best in June, use spoons; Dolly Varden May to October, use bait, spinners, flies.

Rezanof Lake. A 3-mile-long lake located on southcentral Baranof Island, 40 air miles southeast of Sitka. Accessible by floatplane. Forest Service cabins and skiff available. Fishing for rainbow trout May to September, use flies, lures, bait.

Salmon Lake. A 1-mile-long lake located at the southeast end of Silver Bay, 11 miles by boat south of Sitka. Accessible by boat and 1-mile hike to lake. Skiff available. Fish available: silver salmon best in August, use herring or spoons; pink salmon July to August, use small spoons; chum salmon July to September, use spoons; red salmon best in June, use spoons; Dolly Varden May to October, use spinners or flies; steelhead April to June, use spoons; cutthroat best mid- to late summer, use spinners or flies.

Sitka Sound. Located in front of the city of Sitka. Accessible by boat. Boats, tackle and guides available in Sitka. Good fishing for king salmon best May to June, use herring or spoons; silver salmon best in September, use herring or spoons; pink salmon July to August, use small spoons; Dolly Varden May to October, use bait, spinners, flies; halibut all year, season closed in January, best in summer, use bait; rockfish all year, best May to September, use smaller baits or jigs; lingcod all year, best in summer, use herring.

Sitkoh Lake Creek. Located on the southeast end of Chichagof Island. Accessible by floatplane to lake (see below). Good steelhead fishing in April and May, use spoons or eggs. Other fish available: silver salmon best in August, use herring or spoons; Dolly Varden May to October, use spinners, flies; cutthroat best mid- to late summer, use spinners or flies.

Sitkoh Lake. A 2.5-mile-long lake located on the southeast tip of Chichagof Island, 30 air miles northeast of Sitka. Forest Service cabin and boat available. Excellent fishery for silver salmon best in August, use spoons; cutthroat best mid- to late summer, use spinners or flies; Dolly Varden all year.

Thimbleberry Lake. A 0.2-mile-wide lake located 3 miles east of Sitka. Accessible by trail from Blue Lake Road. Fishing for brook trout best May to September, use eggs or spinners.

Wrangell Area Fishing

Anan Creek. Located 40 miles south of Wrangell by boat or floatplane. Forest Service cabin available. Fish available: silver salmon best in August, use bait, flies, spoons; pink salmon July to August, use small spoons; chum salmon July to September, use spoons; Dolly Varden May to October, use bait, spinners, flies; steelhead April to June, use spoons or eggs; cutthroat best mid- to late summer, use bait, spinners, flies; rainbow trout May to September, use flies, lures, bait.

Anan Lake. A 2.5-mile-long lake located 30 air miles southeast of Wrangell. Accessible by floatplane. Forest Service cabin available. Fishing for silver and pink salmon, rainbow trout and Dolly Varden.

Greys Pass. Located 8 miles northwest of Wrangell by boat. Fish available: king salmon best before April 15, use herring or spoons, closed to salmon fishing from April 16 to June 15; halibut available all year, season closed in January, best in summer, use bait.

Harding River. Located in Bradfield Canal 35 air miles southeast of Wrangell. Accessible by boat or plane. Forest Service cabin available. Fish available: silver salmon best in August; chum salmon (possible record-size chum in this system) best in late June and July; Dolly Varden May to October; steelhead in spring; cutthroat mid- to late summer.

Kunk Lake. A 1.5-mile-long lake located on the northeast coast of Etolin Island, 14 miles south of Wrangell. Accessible by boat and short hike or by floatplane. Forest Service cabin and boat available. Fish available: silver salmon best in August, use bait, flies, spoons; Dolly Varden May to October, use bait, spinners, flies; steelhead April to June, use spoons or eggs; cutthroat trout best mid- to late summer, use bait, spinners, flies.

Luck Lake. Located inland from Luck Point on Prince of Wales Island, 35 miles southwest of Wrangell. Accessible by floatplane or road from Coffman Cove. Fish available: silver salmon best in August, use bait, flies, spoons; pink salmon July to August, use small spoons;

chum salmon July to September, use spoons; red salmon best in June and July, use flies and small spoons; Dolly Varden May to October, use bait, spinners, flies; steelhead April to June and October to November, use spoons or eggs; cutthroat best mid- to late summer, use bait, spinners, flies; rainbow trout May to September, use flies, lures, bait.

Marten Lake. Located 2 miles north of Bradfield Canal, 25 air miles southeast of Wrangell. Accessible by floatplane. Forest Service cabin and boat available. Fish available: Dolly Varden May to October, use bait, spinners, flies; cutthroat best mid- to late summer, use bait, spinners, flies; kokanee May to September, use spinners or eggs; steelhead available below lake toward mouth of Martin River, April to late May; coho available below lake toward mouth of Martin River, August and September.

Salmon Bay Lake. A 3-mile-long lake located on the north coast of Prince of Wales Island, 40 miles west of Wrangell. Accessible by floatplane. Forest Service cabin available. Fish available: silver salmon best in August, use bait, flies, spoons; pink salmon July to August, use small spoons; chum salmon July to September, use spoons; red salmon best in June, use spoons and flies; Dolly Varden May to October, use bait, spinners, flies; steelhead April to June and October to November, use spoons or eggs; cutthroat best mid- to late summer, use bait, spinners, flies; rainbow trout May to September, use flies, lures, bait.

Stikine River. Located north of Wrangell. Accessible by boat or floatplane. Use of guide recommended. Forest Service cabins available. Excellent fishery. Fish available: silver salmon best in August, use bait, flies, spoons; pink salmon July to August, use small spoons; chum salmon July to September, use spoons; Dolly Varden May to October, use bait, spinners, flies; steelhead April to June and October to November, use spoons or eggs; cutthroat best mid- to late summer, use bait, spinners, flies; whitefish all year, use flies or eggs. Fishery is closed to king salmon all year.

Thoms Lake. A 1.5-mile-long lake located on the southwest coast of Wrangell Island, 18 miles south-southeast of Wrangell. Accessible by boat and 2-mile hike, road and 0.5-mile hike, or by floatplane. Forest Service cabin available. Fish available: silver salmon best in August, use bait, flies, spoons; red salmon best in June, use flies or spoons; steelhead April to June, use spoons, eggs; cutthroat best mid- to late summer, use bait, spinners, flies.

Virginia Lake. A 2-mile-long lake located 8 miles east of Wrangell. Accessible by boat and short hike or floatplane. Forest Service cabin and boat available. Fish available: red salmon best in June, use spoons or flies; Dolly Varden May to October, use bait, spinners, flies; cutthroat best mid- to late summer, use bait, spinners, flies.

Wrangell Harbor. Located in front of the city of Wrangell. Accessible by skiff. Fish available: king salmon best April to June, use herring or spoons; silver salmon best in August, use herring or spoons; halibut available all year, season closed in January, best in summer, use bait; rockfish all year, best May to September, use smaller baits or jigs.

Zimovia Strait. Located west of Wrangell; separates Wrangell Island from Etolin and Woronkofski islands. A "hot spot" for king salmon best mid-May to mid-June, use trolled or drifted herring or spoons.

Yakutat Area Fishing

Akwe River. Heads at Akwe Lake and flows southwest 20 miles to the Gulf of Alaska, 32 air miles southeast of Yakutat. Private airstrip. Excellent fishing at fork with Ustay River in fall. Fish available: king salmon best early summer, use spoons or flies; silver salmon mid-August, use spoons; red salmon best in June, use small spoons; Dolly Varden May to October, use spoons, spinners, flies; cutthroat best mid- to late summer, use spoons, spinners, flies.

Ankau Lagoon. An estuary system located 2.6 miles west of Yakutat. Accessible by boat or from bridge at Mile 4 Ocean Cape Road. Fish available: silver salmon September to October, use spoons; red salmon best in June, use small spoons; Dolly Varden May to October, use spoons, spinners, flies; cutthroat trout best mid- to late summer, use spoons, spinners, flies.

Coast Guard Lake. Located about 4 miles southwest of Yakutat. Accessible from Beach Road or by canoe or trail from Kardy Lake (see Kardy Lake entry). Fish available: silver salmon September to October, use spoons; pink salmon July to August, use small spoons; red salmon best in June, use small spoons; Dolly Varden May to October, use spoons, spinners, flies; cutthroat best mid- to late summer, use spoons, spinners, flies.

Gulf of Alaska. Coastline located southeast of Yakutat. Accessible by boat, plane to beaches or via Ocean Cape, Cannon Beach and Lost River roads. Fish available: king salmon all year but best for large fish in late spring, use herring or spoons; silver salmon best August to September, use herring or spoons; pink salmon July to August, use small spoons; Dolly Varden May to October, use spoons, spinners, flies; cutthroat trout best mid- to late summer, use spoons, spinners, flies; halibut available all year, season closed in January, best in summer, use bait or jigs; rockfish all year, best May to September, use smaller baits or jigs.

Italio River. Heads 3 miles southeast of Harlequin Lake and flows west 20 miles to the Gulf of Alaska, 28 miles southeast of Yakutat. Accessible by boat or floatplane. Fish available: silver salmon September to October, use lures; Dolly Varden May to October, use spoons, spinners, flies; cutthroat best mid- to late summer, use spoons, spinners, flies. Smelt run in this river.

Kardy Lake. A 1-mile-long lake located on the Phipps Peninsula, 1.1 miles southeast of Ocean Cape and 3.4 miles southwest of Yakutat. Accessible by boat through the Ankau Lagoon system. Fish available: silver salmon September to October, use spoons; red salmon best in June, use small spoons; Dolly Varden May to October, use bait, spinners, flies; cutthroat best mid- to late summer, use bait, spinners, flies. The upper lake is closed to sport fishing from August 15 to September 30.

Monti Bay. A 3.5-mile-long bay located on the southeast shore of Yakutat Bay west of Yakutat. Accessible primarily by boat or from shorelines. Fish available: king salmon all year, best for large fish in late spring, use herring or spoons; silver salmon best September to October, use herring or spoons; pink salmon July to August, use small spoons; Dolly Varden May to October, use bait, spinners, flies; cutthroat best mid- to late summer, use bait, spinners, flies; halibut available all year, season closed in January, best in summer, use bait or jigs; rockfish all year, best May to September, use smaller baits or jigs.

Ocean Cape. Located on the Gulf of Alaska at the west end of Phipps Peninsula, 4.6 miles west of Yakutat. Accessible by boat. Fish available: king salmon all year, best for large fish in early summer, use herring or spoons; silver salmon best September to October, use herring or spoons; pink salmon July to August, use small spoons; Dolly Varden May to October, use bait, spinners, flies; cutthroat best mid- to late summer, use bait, spinners, flies; halibut all year, season closed in January, best in summer, use bait; rockfish all year, best May to September, use smaller baits or jigs.

Situk River. Heads at Situk Lake and flows southwest 18 miles to the Gulf of Alaska, 11 miles southeast of Yakutat. Accessible by boat, floatplane or Forest Highway 10. One of the top fishing spots in Alaska, spring, summer and fall. Excellent runs of steelhead April to May and October to November, use flies or artificial lures; bait is prohibited; outstanding for silver salmon mid-August to October, use spoons and spinners; Other fish available: king salmon best early summer, use spoons; pink salmon July to August, use small spoons; red salmon late June through August, use spoons or flies; Dolly Varden May to October, use spinners or flies; cutthroat best mid- to late summer, use spinners or flies; Smelt run in this river.

Summit Lake. A 0.8-mile-long lake located on the Phipps Peninsula, 2.8 miles southwest of Yakutat. Accessible by canoe or trail from Kardy Lake (see above). Fish available: silver salmon September to October, use spoons; red salmon best in June, use small spoons; pink salmon July to August, use small spoons; Dolly Varden May to October, use spinners or flies; cutthroat trout best mid- to late summer, use spinners or flies.

Yakutat Bay. Located west of Yakutat. Accessible primarily by boat. Fish available: king salmon all year, best for large fish in late spring, use herring or spoons; silver salmon late August through September, use herring or spoons; pink salmon August, use small spoons; Dolly Varden May to October, use bait, spinners, flies; cutthroat best mid- to late summer, use bait, spinners, flies; halibut all year, season closed in January, best in summer, use bait or jigs; rockfish all year, best May to September, use smaller baits or jigs.

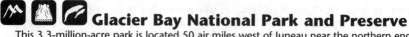# Glacier Bay National Park and Preserve

This 3.3-million-acre park is located 50 air miles west of Juneau near the northern end of the Alaska Panhandle. It is bordered by Icy Strait and Cross Sound on the south, the Pacific Ocean on the west and Canada on the north. The park contains some of the world's most impressive examples of tidewater glaciers. Other major attractions are the bay itself, whales and other wildlife, the massive Fairweather Range and the vast, unspoiled outer coast.

Glacier Bay is the ancestral home of the Chookenaidi and Wukitan clans of the Native Tlingit people, whose descendants now reside primarily in Hoonah. The clans hunted and fished and gathered berries, eggs and intertidal food along the shores of Glacier Bay before the glaciers advanced. Captain James Cook sighted and named 15,300-foot Mount Fairweather in 1778. Jean Francois de la Perouse, a French explorer, made the first record-ed landing in what is now the park at Lituya Bay on the outer coast in 1786.

Russians and Aleuts pursuing sea otters and prospectors looking for gold were the only visitors to the vast wilderness until the late 19th century. In 1879, naturalist John Muir, with a group of Indian guides and interpreters, paddled a canoe into Glacier Bay from Wrangell. Muir returned in 1880 and again in 1890 when he built a cabin at what is now called Muir Point. Other scientists followed, and a few settlers homesteaded on the expanse of the gla-cial alluvial outwash at nearby Gustavus.

In 1794, when Captain George Vancouver sailed through Icy Strait, he charted but did not enter Glacier Bay. The bay was then just a slight indentation in a 4,000-foot-thick wall of ice which marked the terminus of a massive glacier flowing down 100 miles from the St. Elias Range. Almost 100 years later, when Muir built his cabin at Muir Point just north of Mount Wright, the terminus of Muir Glacier was just to the north, 35 miles from where Vancouver had seen it.

In what is the most rapid retreat of glaciers documented since the Ice Age, the Muir Glacier terminus has retreated more than 25 additional miles, leaving a broad bay and a long, narrow inlet.

Glacier Bay is an invaluable outdoor laboratory for scientists seeking to understand the dynamics of glaciers. It is possible to travel from the "little ice age" across 2 centuries of plant succession, seeing how ice-scoured land evolves by stages into mature, coastal forest.

For summer visitors, the boat excursion from park headquarters at Bartlett Cove up Glacier Bay to calving Margerie Glacier is like watching a time-lapse movie which condens-es the centuries of glaciation and plant succession into a day. Leaving the dock, passengers watch vegetation along the shoreline change from moss-laden coastal hemlock forests to spruce forests as the boat chugs along. Spruce trees give way to thickets of willow and alder in Muir Inlet, which is often full of floating pan ice and icebergs. Here and there, the stumps of huge trees, buried by moraines that were exposed by erosion centuries ago, stick out along a barren beach.

Glacier Bay National Park and Preserve encompasses 16 active, tidewater glaciers, including several on the remote and seldom visited western edge of the park along the Gulf of Alaska and Lituya Bay. Icebergs calved off the glaciers float in the waters of the bay.

Season: The national park is open year-round, but most visitor facilities and transporta-tion operate from May to early September.

Climate: Gray and rainy days are typical. May and June usually have the most sunshine. Rainfall generally increases as the summer progresses. Summer temperatures average 50°F but can vary to extremes. Visitors should bring clothing for possible below-freezing tem-peratures no matter what the month. Also bring full rain gear. Layer clothing, with shirts and sweaters worn under a windproof, rainproof parka or jacket, so you can withstand a range of temperatures when outdoors. Alaska's infamous biting insects are very much in evi-dence at Glacier Bay; gnats and flies are generally worse than mosquitoes. Bring plenty of insect repellent.

Wildlife: A trip by water into the park's many fjords offers sightings of marine mammals.

Whales in Glacier Bay include humpback, minke and killer (orca) whales. Humpbacks spend spring, summer and fall in Alaska, migrating in winter to the Hawaiian Islands and south as far as Mexico. During late spring, hundreds of hair seals haul out on floating ice to give birth to their pups.

A decline in the number of humpback whales using Glacier Bay for feeding and calf-rearing led the National Park Service to limit the number of boats visiting the bay between June and September. These regulations apply to all commercial fishing boats, private craft, cruise ships and excursion boats. Check with the National Park Service office for current regulations. *NOTE: The whales come to Glacier Bay for only one reason: to eat enough to store the fat needed to see them through the winter. They do not feed year-round. Do not disturb them.*

Along gravel beaches, brown/grizzly, black and occasionally rare glacier bears (the bluish color phase of the black bear) forage for food. On high, rocky ledges, mountain goats are often sited. *CAUTION: Wildlife in the park is protected, and hunting is not allowed. Firearms are prohibited within the park. Backcountry users should be careful to avoid encounters with bears.*

More than 225 bird species have been reported in the park. Among the more common are black oystercatchers, cormorants, guillemots, puffins, gulls and terns.

Activities: Exploring the park by boat or on foot and watching wildlife are the main activities in Glacier Bay National Park.

Two nature trails radiate from Bartlett Cove. One section of trail is handicap accessible, leading 0.2 mile through the rain forest to Blackwater Pond. Park naturalists lead hikes daily and are available at the visitor center at the lodge to answer questions. Films and slide-illustrated talks are also scheduled daily at Glacier Bay Lodge. In summer, rangers are stationed up the bay and elsewhere in the park.

Glacier Bay Tours and Cruises offers a day cruise up the West Arm of the bay. The cruises, included in the Glacier Bay Lodge package, depart from Bartlett Cove aboard the high-speed catamaran Spirit of Adventure. The cruise is narrated by a National Park Service ranger and includes lunch.

Kayaking is very popular in Glacier Bay. Guided full-day kayaking excursions and independent kayak rentals are available at Glacier Bay Lodge and in Gustavus and Juneau. Independent kayakers should check with the private ferry services about transporting their kayaks to the park. The nearest state ferry service is to Hoonah, on the northeast shore of Chichagof Island. From Hoonah, it is a 20-mile paddle across Icy Strait to the entrance of Glacier Bay.

First time visitors are often surprised to find that upper reaches of the bay are not forested (because they so recently lay under glacial ice). Most motorized vessels head up the bay's longer west arm to Tarr and John Hopkins inlets. Caution is advised for boaters in Glacier Bay because storms are sudden, and floating ice can overturn or fracture off without warning.

Certain areas of the park offer excellent cross-country hiking and backpacking possibilities. Many peaks more than 10,000 feet-high challenge the experienced mountaineer. There are no established trails, but camping and hiking are generally permitted throughout the park. (Some areas may have camping restrictions because of bear, bird and seal activity. Be sure to check for safe areas with park service personnel.)

Kayaker and camper drop-off and pickup service is available from the tour boat at Bartlett Cove; contact Glacier Bay Lodge for details.

Fishing for silver and king salmon, Dolly Varden, cutthroat and halibut is excellent in the bay. An Alaska fishing license is required; charter fishing trips are available in Gustavus.

Accommodations: Meals and lodging are available by advance reservation at Glacier Bay Lodge at Bartlett Cove, the only accommodation within the national park; phone (800) 451-5952. Meals and lodging for park visitors are also available in Gustavus, located 10 miles by road from Bartlett Cove, just outside the park boundary.

A campground with 35 sites is located near the lodge and park headquarters at Bartlett Cove. The campground has a 2-week limit; it is free, and no reservations are required.

Private Boats: Gasoline and diesel fuel may be purchased at Bartlett Cove, where a good anchorage is available. There are no other public facilities for boats within the park;

Gustavus has a dock and a high-tide, small-boat harbor. *CAUTION: Do not attempt to navigate Glacier Bay without appropriate charts, tide tables and local knowledge.*

Access: There is no state ferry service to Glacier Bay. There is daily, round-trip, private ferry passenger service between Juneau and Gustavus via Auk Nu Tours; phone (800) 820-2628. Day and overnight cruises to Glacier Bay are available from Juneau, Haines and Skagway via Glacier Bay Tours and Cruises; phone (800) 451-5952. The bay is accessible by scheduled airline or air charter from Juneau, Haines or Skagway to the airport at Gustavus, then by road from Gustavus to Bartlett Cove (10 miles, bus and taxi services available). It is also accessible by private boat or charter boat. Several cruise lines include Glacier Bay in their itineraries.

For more information: Visitor center at Bartlett Cove, open mid-May to mid-September; phone (907) 697-2230. Or write Glacier Bay National Park and Preserve, P.O. Box 140 Gustavus, AK 99826-0140; fax (907) 697-2654, website: www.nps.gov/glba. USGS maps: Mount Fairweather, Skagway and Yakutat.

 Hiking Trails

Following is a list of some of Southeast Alaska's more popular hiking trails, most maintained by the U.S. Forest Service. For more information on U.S. Forest Service trails, contact the Forest Service, P.O. Box 21628 (709 W. 9th St.), Juneau, AK 99802-1628; www.fs.fed.us/r10/tongass/recreation/rec_facilities.

Most trails in Southeast are more difficult than trails with similar ratings in the Lower 48. Seasonal and daily variations in rainfall can drastically alter trail conditions. Maintenance may be sporadic. Waterproof footwear such as knee-high, rubber boots with good traction soles are often the best choice. Check with the local Forest Service or Alaska State Parks office for current trail conditions.

Craig Area Trails

Kegan Lake Trail. This easy, 0.5-mile trail begins at Kegan Cove cabin and ends at the lake, where steelhead, sockeye and coho runs are internationally acclaimed. The lake has a native rainbow trout population and excellent fishing, which has been featured in fishing magazines. Recommended season, July to September. The Kegan Cove and Kegan Creek Forest Service cabins are so popular that they are on a lottery system and must be reserved well in advance. The trail is an easy, pleasant walk through an old-growth forest with very little undergrowth. USGS map: Craig A-1.

One Duck Trail. This more difficult, 1-mile trail begins 1.5 miles south of Harris River bridge on Hydaburg Road and climbs 700 feet to a large, alpine area with easy walking, good hunting for deer and bear and good cross-country skiing in winter and spring. Although the trail is unfinished, it is passable and easy to find. It has been brushed, and basic treadwork has been done. USGS map: Craig B-3.

Haines Area Trails

Trails here are found on USGS Topographic maps Skagway A-1, A-2 and B-2. Only the Mount Riley, Seduction Point and Battery Point trails are maintained by state parks on a regular basis. The others receive periodic volunteer maintenance, so check at the Haines Visitor Center before you hike.

Battery Point Trail. The trail starts 2 miles east of Port Chilkoot and 1 mile beyond Portage Cove at the end of the road. This is a fairly level walk of about 2 miles with a primitive campsite behind Kelgaya Point. The last 3/4 mile of the trail is along pebble beaches and across Kelgaya Point with excellent views of Lynn Canal. Allow 2 hours for a round-trip.

Mount Riley Trails. There are 3 routes to the 1,760-foot summit of Mount Riley: Mud Bay Road, via Port Chilkoot and from Portage Cove.

Mud Bay Road: This route is the steepest and most direct. Take the Mud Bay Road from

Port Chilkoot, heading southward on the west side of the Chilkat Peninsula, to the top of the second steep hill a few yards short of the Mile 3 marker. The marked path starts on the left side of the road and heads for the ridge in a southeasterly direction. Distance to the summit is 2.1 miles. Estimated roundtrip time is 3.5 hours.

Via Port Chilkoot: This route connects with the Mud Bay Road trail. Take the FAA Road behind Officers Row in Port Chilkoot and follow it to its end, about 1 mile. Walk along the city of Haines water supply access route about 2 miles then take the spur trail which branches to the right to connect with the route from Mud Bay Road. Estimated round-trip time, 4.5 hours.

From Portage Cove: This route is recommended for snowshoe travel in winter. Follow the Battery Point trail almost 2 miles to a junction then take the right fork which climbs steeply at first through thick undergrowth and tall spruce forests. The trail becomes less steep and continues through small muskeg meadows over Half Dome before the final climb to the summit.

It is also possible to traverse Mount Riley from Portage Cove to the Mud Bay Road. This trip is about 7.6 miles and takes about 4 hours.

Mount Ripinsky Summit. The trail starts north of Haines toward Lutak Inlet at the top of Young Road and along the pipeline right-of-way. The pipeline road rises gradually through wooded hillside, then descends steeply after about a mile. At this point, the tank farm is visible. The trail takes off to the left a few yards down the hill and ascends through hemlock and spruce forest to alpine meadows above Johnson Creek, elevation 2,500 feet. From the ridge on clear days, you can see snowcapped mountain peaks from Haines all the way to Admiralty Island. At the summit there are views of Lutak Inlet, Taiya Inlet and a panorama of peaks and ice fields. This is a strenuous, all-day hike or overnight camp. It is possible to descend the summit and continue west-northwest along a ridge to Peak 3,920 and down to 7 Mile Saddle to the Haines Highway. This traverse is about 10 miles, and overall elevation gain is about 5,100 feet. The trail is steep in places and easily lost. Until late June, water or snowmelt is found on the ridge. After that it is necessary to carry water beyond Johnson Creek where the last water is found. NOTE: No untreated water is recommended for drinking. USGS maps: Skagway A-2, B-2.

Seduction Point. Drive the Mud Bay Road to the Chilkat State Park and park at the bend of the steep hill at the cul-de-sac. The trail alternates between inland forest trail and beach walking with excellent views of the Davidson Glacier. Estimated roundtrip time for the 13.5-mile hike is 9 to 10 hours. Seasonal water supplies at Twin and David's coves (not recommended unless treated). Campsites along the way and at the cove east of Seduction Point. Hikers should check the tides before leaving and plan to do the last long beach stretch after David's Cove at low or mid-tide.

7 Mile Saddle. The trailhead is located 0.2 mile east of Milepost 7. The trail climbs steeply at first through a small, pine forest then more gradually through spruce and hemlock until open slopes are reached at about 2,000 feet. Water is available all year in streams found in the forested sections (should be treated) but water should be carried after passing through those areas. It is possible to continue east toward Mount Ripinsky and reverse the traverse described above.

Juneau Area Trails

Hikers in the Juneau area rely on 2 excellent trail guides, Juneau Trails and 90 Short Walks in Juneau. Both are available from Alaska Natural History Association, Juneau Ranger Station, 8465 Old Dairy Road, Juneau, AK 99801, and from Juneau bookstores.

Amalga (Eagle Glacier) Trail. Trailhead is in the parking lot on the left at Mile 28.4 from Juneau on the Juneau Veterans' Memorial Highway. Trail extends 4 miles to the old Amalga mine site and another 3.5 miles to the front of Eagle Glacier. Usable spring, summer and fall. First 5.5. miles rated more difficult, last 2 miles most difficult. Elevation gain is 500 feet. Estimated round-trip time is10 to 12 hours. Rubber boots recommended. Bring mosquito repellent in summer. Amalga was a settlement between 1902 and 1927; the mine site is now difficult to find. Wildlife includes bears and beavers. Black and brown bears use this trail intensely. Impressive views of Eagle Glacier. This trail was extended in 1990 to provide access to the Juneau Icefield via Eagle Glacier. USGS map: Juneau C-3.

Auke Nu Trail. This Forest Service trail is reached from the Spaulding trail, which begins at a parking area just off the Juneau Veterans' Memorial Highway at Mile 12.3 (just past the post office.) The Auke Nu trailhead is 0.5 mile up the Spaulding trail, on the left. Trail then extends 2.5 miles to the John Muir Cabin. Usable all year; crosscountry skiing in winter. Rated moderate. Elevation gain 1,552 feet. Estimated roundtrip time 5 to 6 hours.

First part of trail runs through forested area and contains some sections of an old corduroy road. Middle part also is forested. The last section of trail goes through muskeg meadows. The majority of the trail is planked to protect the fragile plants. Rubber boots are recommended. Blueberries and huckleberries are found in season. Be alert for bears. This trail features views of the Chilkat Mountains, Admiralty Island, Gastineau Channel and Mounts Stroller White and McGinnis. An unmarked crosscountry route leads to Peterson Lake. Map, compass and a good sense of direction are essential. USGS map: Juneau B-3.

Blackerby Ridge Trail. From Egan Drive, take the Salmon Creek exit and drive about 0.1 mile. Walk up short road to the right. Trail begins to the left just before the end of the road and extends 3.6 miles to Cairn Peak. Trail crosses state, private and Forest Service lands. Usable summer and fall. Rated most difficult; it's steep and strenuous. The trail is not maintained and reportedly in poor condition. Elevation gain 4,505 feet. No switchbacks. Estimated round-trip time 8 to 10 hours. Waterproof hiking boots recommended; carry your own water. Above timberline carpets of alpine flowers bloom in season. Salmonberries and blueberries are found in season. Views of Salmon Creek Reservoir and Stephens Passage from the ridge; views of Lemon and Ptarmigan glaciers from Cairn Peak. USGS map: Juneau B-2.

Dan Moller Trail. Located on Douglas Island. Cross Juneau-Douglas bridge, turn left on Douglas Highway and take first right on Cordova Street. Turn left on Pioneer Avenue, and the trail starts past the fifth or sixth house on the right. Trailhead is marked and there is a small parking area. This Forest Service trail extends 3 miles to the Dan Moller cabin in an alpine meadow. (This is a public warming cabin from 10 A.M. to 5 P.M. but can be rented for overnight use through the Forest Service; see Cabins this section.) Usable all year. Open to snowmobiles (12 inches of snow required) and crosscountry skiing in winter. Rated easy. Boardwalk section over muskeg may be slippery when wet or frosty. Elevation gain 1,800 feet. Waterproof hiking boots recommended. Sneakers are fine on the boardwalks. Estimated round-trip time 5 to 6 hours. Trail offers excellent wildflowers in season, wildlife and scenery. Climb from bowl to ridge for view of Stephens Passage and Admiralty Island. This area is avalanche prone. Contact the Weather Service at 586-SNOW for avalanche conditions before skiing or hiking this trail. USGS map: Juneau B-2.

Heintzleman Ridge Route. Trailheads off Mendenhall Loop Road behind Glacier Valley Elementary School at the end of Jennifer Drive or at Mile 7 Old Glacier Highway just past Department of Transportation maintenance facility. This undeveloped Forest Service trail extends 9.5 miles to the top of Heintzleman Ridge. Usable in summer only. Extreme avalanche danger in winter or early spring. Rated most difficult. Should be attempted only by those in excellent physical condition. Estimated round-trip time 10 to 12 hours, so start early in the morning or plan to camp overnight. Trail is sparsely marked and extremely steep with no switch-backs and many false side trails. Elevation gain 3,000 to 4,000 feet. Mountain goats may be seen; many alpine wildflowers in season. The top of Steep Creek Bowl offers an excellent view of Mendenhall Glacier. Ridge continues toward Nugget Glacier and Nugget Mountain. It is possible to hike to the Mendenhall Glacier visitor center on the Nugget Creek trail from the ridge. USGS map: Juneau B-2.

Herbert Glacier Trail. Trailhead is just past the Herbert River bridge, 28 miles from Juneau on the Juneau Veterans' Memorial Highway. A small gravel parking lot is located to the right of the trailhead. Trail extends 4.6 miles to the moraine about 0.5 mile from Herbert Glacier. Usable all year. Rated easy. Elevation gain 300 feet. Estimated round-trip time is 5 to 6 hours. Trail relatively flat, but wet in places. Trail offers opportunity to view wildflowers in season, wildlife and a good view of the glacier. Notice the plant succession as you hike up the valley through large Sitka spruce to pioneering alder and bare rock, Cross-country skiing possible in winter. Do not cross the branching streams to approach the glacier. It is possible to climb over the rocks to the left of the glacier for a good view of the glacier and a spectacular waterfall. *CAUTION: Do not approach the face of the glacier. Ice falls are dangerous.* Also, this is bear country; keep a clean camp, and make noise while hiking. USGS map: Juneau C-3.

Montana Creek Trail. From Mendenhall Loop Road, take the Montana Creek Road about 3 miles to the end at the rifle range. Forest Service trail leads northwest 9.5 miles to Windfall Lake, where it connects with the Windfall Lake trail. This is part of a trail system established in 1907-09 by the Territory of Alaska to serve mining sites. Trail usable for hiking from late spring through fall and for cross-country skiing in winter. Rated moderate. Elevation gain 800 feet. Estimated 8 to 10 hours ending at Windfall Lake trailhead (where you should leave a car). There are high concentrations of bears on this trail, especially during late summer when salmon are spawning. USGS maps: Juneau B-2, B-3.

Mount Bradley (Mount Jumbo) Trail. Trail begins in Douglas at a vacant lot behind the 300 section of 5th Street. The trail extends 2.6 miles to the summit of Mount Bradley and crosses state and private lands. Usable spring, summer and fall. Rated most difficult. Elevation gain 3,337 feet. Estimated round-trip time 10 to 12 hours. Both rubber boots and hiking boots recommended. The mountain was originally named after the Jumbo Mine at its base but was renamed in 1939 to honor a former president of the American Mining Institute. Trail is muddy with windblown trees and is not maintained. Trail crosses Paris Creek, then the Treadwell Ditch. The muskeg meadows are boardwalked. In the alpine, the trail is difficult to follow, so observe your route to the summit carefully. There are dangerous dropoffs near the top, and the trail becomes quite slippery when wet. An ice ax will be helpful during ascents in late spring. The trail offers scenery, wildflowers in season and spectacular views of Gastineau Channel and Juneau from the summit. USGS maps: Juneau A-2 and B-2.

Mount McGinnis Trail. Trailhead is at the end of the West Glacier trail but is difficult to find. Look for survey flagging and rock cairns. This unmaintained Forest Service trail extends 2 miles to the summit of Mount McGinnis; steep and sparsely marked. Usable in summer and fall; best hiked from mid-July on. Rated most difficult. Elevation gain 4,228 feet. Estimated round-trip time 8 hours. Carry map and compass. Lower section of trail passes through thick brush; watch for markers. Trail ascends through dense forest then continues to the top above timberline. The top part is generally covered with snow; carry an ice ax. Exercise extreme care in sliding on snow patches. Avalanche danger may continue until late spring. From the summit, there is a remarkable view of Auke Bay and Mendenhall Valley. USGS map: Juneau B-2.

Perserverance Trail. This easy, 3-mile trail to the ruins of the old Perserverance Mine is the most popular in the Juneau area. The mine, located in Silverbow Basin, operated between 1885 and 1895 when a snowslide destroyed the mill and camp buildings. From downtown Juneau, take Gold Street to Basin Road past the slide on the left above the city's main water supply lines. After crossing Gold Creek, take the lefthand fork. The trail follows a gentle grade around the horn of Mount Juneau. There is extreme danger of snowslide during winter and early spring. Old mining ruins are scattered throughout the area, so use caution while exploring. Athletic shoes or light boots are recommended. Estimated roundtrip time is 4 to 5 hours; elevation gain 1,000 feet. USGS map: Juneau B-2.

Peterson Lake Trail. Trailhead is at Mile 24.5 on the Juneau Veterans' Memorial Highway. Parking is limited; be sure not to park on private property. Forest Service trail extends 4.3 miles to Peterson Lake cabin. (This is a public warming cabin from 10 A.M. to 5 P.M.but can be rented for overnight use through the Forest Service; see Cabins this section.) Trail usable all year. Rated more difficult, but it is muddy in some places. Waterproof footwear recommended. Elevation gain 700 feet. Estimated round-trip time 5 to 7 hours. Trail named for John Peterson, a prospector who had a claim in the area during 1899. Trail starts out on steps but soon joins an old tramway. Narrow rails are still in place in some sections; planks have been placed alongside the old rails. About 0.7 mile from the trailhead, a spur trail to the left leads to a good fishing spot below some steep waterfalls. Keep right on this spur to avoid a portion of the lower trail that is subject to landslides. Main trail continues through forest and muskeg areas. (All of the muskeg areas have been planked.) Trail turns right in the last muskeg and continues through dense forest to Peterson Lake, which has Dolly Varden fishing. USGS map: Juneau B-3.

Point Bishop/Dupont Trail. Trailhead is at the end of Thane Road, 5.5 miles South of downtown Juneau. This is a Forest Service trail except for the start, which passes over state and private lands. It's 1.5 miles to the Dupont dock and 8 miles to Point Bishop. Usable spring, summer and fall. Rated easy, but tiring due to many roots, windfalls and other obstacles. Elevation gain 200 feet. Estimated round-trip time to Dupont is 2 hours, 12 hours to Point Bishop, longer if heavy windfalls from 1991 have not been cleared. Point Bishop was named in 1794 by Captain George Vancouver for the Bishop of Salisbury. Dupont was named after the Dupont Powder Co., which built the powder magazine there in 1914 to supply local mines. Trail is fairly level, but quite muddy. Waterproof boots recommended. About 1 mile from the trailhead, a branch to the right leads to Dupont, where there is good saltwater Dolly Varden fishing in the spring. Main trail runs above Dupont to Point Salisbury then to Point Bishop. USGS maps: Juneau A-1, B-1.

Salmon Creek Trail. Drive north from Juneau, then turn right just past the cement abutment at mile 2.5 of Egan Drive. Turnoff is located just before the Salmon Creek exit. Trail begins behind the new Salmon Creek powerhouse. It extends 3.5 miles to Salmon Creek dam. Usable spring, summer and early fall. Rated moderate. Condition good; trail was replaced with a road in 1984. Elevation gain 1,100 feet. Estimated round-trip time 5 to 6 hours. Hiking boots recommended. The first part of the trail follows the route of the old tramline and consists of a roadbed up a long, steep slope. (Many berries along the road in season.) At the top, the trail continues to the right and eventually branches. The right branch leads to a dam (a sign marks the intersection). The dam was built in 1914 by the Alaska-Gastineau Mining Company. It is the world's first true constant-angle arch dam and is still the largest of its kind. Just before the dam, the trail goes up a steep slope to the reservoir. There is fishing for eastern brook trout in the reservoir. The trail is on BLM lands and is maintained by Alaska Electric Light & Power Company; watch for occasional company vehicles using the road. USGS map: Juneau B-2.

Sheep Creek Trail. Trailhead is located on Thane Road, 4 miles south of downtown Juneau. Trail extends 3 miles to alpine ridge. Usable late spring, summer and fall. Winter travel not recommended due to avalanche danger. Rated moderate. Elevation gain 700 in valley, 3,500 feet to ridge. Estimated round-trip time 2 hours to valley, 5 to 8 hours to ridge. Waterproof hiking or rubber boots recommended. Joe Juneau and Richard Harris named Sheep Creek in 1880 after mistaking mountain goats for sheep. Gold mining in the valley began in 1881. This is a scenic trail with historical mining ruins. Slope is switchbacked and brushy. Trail begins through moss-covered forest with dense brush then rises abruptly and drops into Sheep Creek valley. A profusion of songbirds make this the ultimate early morning bird walk. Marmot, porcupine and black bear are frequently encountered. Old mining buildings are barely standing and should not be disturbed. Trail is relatively level through the valley, then scrambles up a forested hillside until it reaches the alpine zone. If trail is hard to find above timberline, follow the power line, but stay a safe distance from the lines. Carry an ice ax; snow sometimes persists on the ridge through the summer. A Canadian company is attempting to reopen the A-J gold mine and proposes to use Sheep Camp valley as a tailings disposal site. Check with Alaska State Parks for trail status. Active exploration is ongoing in the Portal Camp area, and a dirt road leads into the valley. USGS map: Juneau B-1.

Spaulding Trail. Trailhead located at Milepost 12.6 from Juneau on the Juneau Veterans' Memorial Highway, just past the Auke Bay post office. Trail extends 3 miles to Spaulding Meadows. Usable all year though largely unmaintained above the Auke Nu turnoff. Rated moderate. Elevation gain 1,800 feet. Estimated round-trip time 5 to 6 hours. This trail is extremely muddy during the warm seasons (waterproof footwear is a must) but is an important cross-country ski route in winter. Trail starts on an old road that leads to the first muskeg meadow, then continues about 1 mile through a wooded area to a second meadow. After another stand of trees, the trail ends in the last muskeg meadow. Provides access via Auke Nu Trail to John Muir cabin. In winter, the rolling hills of Auke Mountain and Spaulding Meadows offer excellent cross-country skiing with views of the Chilkat Mountains, upper Mendenhall Glacier, Lynn Canal and Auke Bay. USGS maps: Juneau B-2, B-3.

Treadwell Ditch Trail. Trail may be reached by hiking about 1 mile from the beginning of the Dan Moller trail or from the Eaglecrest ski area on North Douglas Island. Trail extends 12 miles from Eaglecrest to the Dan Moller trail. Usable all year. Rated easy. Elevation gain/drop 700 feet. Estimated time 10 hours one way. The 18-mile-long Treadwell Ditch once carried water from Cropley Lake and Fish Creek to the Treadwell Mine and other mines at the south end of Douglas. The ditch was built between 1882 and 1889. Remains of the ditch project are historic artifacts and should not be disturbed. Trail features porcupines, deer, muskeg meadows and a view of Gastineau Channel. The trail was developed as a hiking and cross-country ski trail, but skiing is often marginal because heavy forest prevents sufficient snow cover in some areas. This is a good sheltered hike for dreary days. The trail was brushed from Eaglecrest all the way to Douglas in 1981; the section between the Dan Moller trail and downtown Douglas (accessible just above D Street in Douglas) is on City and Borough of Juneau land and is not maintained. Trail is flat and wide but slopes in some places. Stay on the trail during the warmer months; delicate muskeg vegetation deteriorates rapidly with constant foot traffic. Be prepared to encounter windfalls and bridges out. USGS map: Juneau B-2.

West Glacier Trail. Turn off the Mendenhall Loop Road onto Montana Creek Road and take the first right. Follow this road past the campground entrance and the remains of Skaters Cabin to the parking area at the end of the road. This Forest Service trail begins on the north side of the parking lot. It extends 3.4 miles to a rock outcrop above Mendenhall Glacier. Usable in spring and summer. Rated moderate. Elevation gain 1,300 feet. Estimated round-trip time 5 to 6 hours. Athletic shoes or waterproof hiking boots recommended, depending on the weather. Most of this trail is below the glacier trimline and passes through willow and alder trees. In a few places, the trail skirts spruce and hemlock forest which the glacier did not reach on its most recent advances. The trail seems to end at a scenic overlook and then curves back toward the glacier; be alert for cairns that mark the route. The trail ends at the top of a rock outcrop and offers spectacular views of Mendenhall Glacier, ice falls and other glacial features. This trail is also used for access onto the glacier by experienced and properly equipped climbers; this is not recommended for inexperienced hikers. On most summer days there is significant tour-related helicopter and small plane traffic overhead. USGS map: Juneau B-2.

Windfall Lake Trail. Turn right off the Juneau Veterans' Memorial Highway at Milepost 27 from Juneau, just before the Herbert River. This 0.2-mile road ends in a parking lot; trailhead is to the right. Forest Service trail extends 3.5 miles to Windfall Lake. Usable all year. Rated easy. Elevation gain 100 feet. Estimated round-trip time 4 hours. Waterproof boots recommended in summer. Used for cross-country skiing in winter. Trail follows the Herbert River through Sitka spruce and western hemlock forest. Trail muddy in summer, but some of the worst spots have been planked over. A spur trail once led to Herbert Glacier, but flooding from beaver dams has made this impassable. When the river is safely frozen, many people ski 5 miles from the parking lot to the glacier. The Windfall Lake trail connects with the Montana Creek trail at Windfall Lake. There is a small rowboat for fishing at the lake; fishing is good for sea-run cutthroat trout, and Dolly Varden. Pink, chum, red and silver salmon spawn in the area. Other features are highbush cranberries, blue heron, swans and geese and a healthy mosquito population. Bears frequent the area. USGS map: Juneau C-3.

Ketchikan Area Trails

Bakewell Lake Trail. Trailhead located on the east side of Bakewell Creek, south side of

Bakewell Arm about 40 miles east of Ketchikan in Misty Fiords National Monument. This trail extends 1 mile to Bakewell Lake; does not provide access to Bakewell Lake Forest Service recreation cabin. Accessible by boat or floatplane. Rated moderate. Elevation gain 200 feet. Estimated round-trip time 2 hours. Rubber boots recommended. The first half mile of this trail follows an overgrown, abandoned road. At the midpoint there is a waterfall and fish ladder overlook. The remaining half mile leads through timber and wet muskeg. Fishing in Bakewell Lake for Dolly Varden, cutthroat; fishing near the lake outlet for red, pink, chum and silver salmon and some steelhead. (See Sportfishing, Ketchikan Area, in this section.) USGS map: Ketchikan B-2.

Black Mountain Trail. Trailhead is in Ice House Cove off Carroll Point 7 miles southeast of Ketchikan. Forest Service trail extends 2.5 miles to Snag and Hidden lakes. Accessible by boat, but watch for submerged rocks. The first 0.5-mile traverses moderate slopes with grades of more than 20 percent. The rest of the trail is on rolling muskeg and scrub timberland. The tread is in poor shape with many wet spots and rough stretches. Primarily used for hiking and fishing access to the lakes. No developed facilities on this trail system. USGS map: Ketchikan B-5.

Checats Cove Trail. Trailhead is on the east side of Checats Creek in Checats Cove, about 35 miles northeast of Ketchikan in Misty Fiords National Monument. Forest Service trail extends 1.1 miles to Lower Checats Lake. Does not provide access to Forest Service recreation cabin on Upper Checats Lake. Trail accessible by boat or floatplane; cove large enough for safe anchorage. Trail usable late spring through early fall. Rated moderate; elevation gain 100 feet. Estimated round-trip time is 2 1/2 hours. The trail begins in spruce-hemlock forest; tread is level, but low boggy areas will be encountered. At the 0.5-mile mark, the trail enters a large blowdown area. The point where the lake becomes visible is a good camping spot. After this point, the trail has a steep incline then levels off when it returns to the creek's edge. At the logjam, there is another good camping spot. The trail continues along the lake for another quarter mile then ends by a small rock island. No developed facilities. Brown bears frequent this area. Good fishing in the lake. USGS map: Ketchikan B-3.

Deer Mountain/John Mountain Trail. This most difficult, 9.9-mile trails begins at the junction of Granite Basin and Ketchikan Dump roads and gains 3,000 feet before ending at Lower Silvis Lake. Spectacular views of Ketchikan and Tongass Narrows make the long climb worthwhile. Experienced hikers can continue past the summit. There is a Forest Service cabin just below and north of the summit and a remote shelter 2.3 miles farther above timberline at Blue Lake. The shelter is not maintained and may be in poor repair. USGS map: Ketchikan B-5.

Ella Lake Trail. Trailhead is at the mouth of Ella Creek on Ella Bay on East Behm Canal, 24 miles northeast of Ketchikan in Misty Fiords National Monument. Access is by boat or floatplane. Forest Service trail extends 2.5 miles to Lower Ella Lake. Trail does not reach Forest Service cabin at Ella Narrows. Trail usable spring to fall. Rated moderate. Elevation gain 250 feet. Estimated round-trip time 5 1/2 hours. Rubber boots recommended. There is a beach marker sign at the trailhead which is visible from Ella Bay. The first 0.25 mile runs through old second-growth timber. The next 1.5 miles cross wet muskeg and marsh with tall grass. The last 0.8 mile leads through timber with a slight incline that levels off at the lake outlet. There is excellent trout and salmon fishing in Ella Creek. The area also features beaver, wildflowers and berries. Near the trailhead are soda springs ringed with concrete foundations built by the Civilian Conservation Corps in the 1930s. USGS maps: Ketchikan B-3, B-4, C-4.

Humpback Lake Trail. Trailhead at the mouth of Humpback Creek in Mink Bay off Boca de Quadra, about 60 miles southeast of Ketchikan. Trail extends 3 miles to Humpback Lake. Accessible by boat or floatplane; Forest Service buoy in Mink Bay. Usable late spring through fall. Rated moderate. Elevation gain 270 feet. Rubber boots recommended. Trail is in fair condition. Fairly level for the first 2 miles. After passing small waterfall on the right, the trail begins a steep climb for approximately 500 feet with a grade increase of 50 to 70 percent. At the top of the ridge, the trail levels off and leads through muskeg for 0.5 mile. No boardwalk. Trail is hard to follow. After the muskeg, the trail enters timber area where recent slides have buried the trail. Trail ends where a 3-sided shelter stood until it was demolished by a landslide.

Excellent trout fishing at the outlet of Humpback Lake. Brown bear very abundant on this trail. USGS maps: Ketchikan A-2, A-3; Prince Rupert D-2, D-3.

Low Lake Trail. Trailhead located at mouth of Fish Creek in the northeast corner of Thorne Arm on Revillagigedo Island in Misty Fiords National Monument. Accessible by float-plane or boat; Forest Service buoy in Fish Creek Cove for small boat moorage. Trail extends 2.1 miles to Big Lake. Usable late spring through fall. Rated moderate. Elevation gain 290 feet. Estimated round-trip time 3 1/2, hours. The first 0.5 mile of the trail is partly board-walk with split log and drainage structures in wet areas. The trail proceeds without tread improvement to the lake. Short stretches traverse sections of steep, rocky ground, some with a 20 percent grade. Fish Creek supports a run of steelhead, Dolly Varden, salmon and cutthroat. (See Sportfishing, Ketchikan Area, in this section.) Also, black bears, wildflowers and berries in the area. USGS map: Ketchikan A-4.

Manzanita Lake Trail. Trailhead located on the west side of Manzanita Bay on East Behm Canal about 28 miles northeast of Ketchikan in Misty Fiords National Monument. Forest Service trail extends 3.5 miles to Manzanita Lake; does not provide access to the 2 Forest Service cabins on the lake. Accessible by floatplane or boat. Usable late spring through fall. Rated moderate. Elevation gain 250 feet. Estimated round-trip time 9 hours. There is a float-ing dock and mooring buoy within sight of the trailhead sign. The first mile of trail is largely muskeg, after which it closely parallels the creek, eventually climbing away from the creek. The trail crosses the creek on a puncheon bridge in the last half mile and ends at the lake. There are no developed facilities on the trail. The tread is mostly natural, with wet and muddy foot-ing in places. Large rocks and steep dropoffs along the last third of the trail may be hazardous. Trail's primary use is hiking, sightseeing and access to fishing in Manzanita Lake. (See Sportfishing, Ketchikan Area, in this section.) USGS maps: Ketchikan C-3 and C-4.

Naha River Trail. From Naha Bay (accessible by boat or floatplane), this 5.4-mile trail ends at Heckman Lake. The trail features excellent salmon and trout fishing, one of the best steel-head runs in Southeast, and the scenic, interesting salt chuck at the outlet of Roosevelt Lagoon. Jordan Lake and Heckman Lake cabins are located on this trail. Small boat tram at outlet to Roosevelt Lagoon. Picnic shelters at outlet of Roosevelt Lagoon and on Naha River. Beginning on boardwalk, the trail does have some wet and muddy spots farther in, but is generally in good condition. Allow 5 hours one-way walking time. USGS map: Ketchikan C-5.

Nooya Lake Trail. Trailhead located in a small bight on the west shore of the North Arm of Rudyerd Bay in Misty Fiords National Monument. Trail extends 1.1 miles to Nooya Lake. Access is by boat or floatplane. Usable late spring through fall. Rated moderate. Elevation gain 400 feet. Estimated round-trip time 2 to 3 hours. Access to the trail is fair; anchorage at the mouth of Nooya Creek is poor. The first quarter-mile leads through wet, boggy areas; the next half-mile gently increases in grade, and wet areas are less common. At the 0.8-mile point, the trail turns left away from the creek and starts a steep, 35 to 45 percent grade. The trail is wet but solid. There is a 3-sided Civilian Conservation Corps shelter at the outlet of Nooya Lake. Black and brown bears are common along this trail. USGS map: Ketchikan C-3.

Punchbowl Lake Trail. Trailhead located at the south end of Punchbowl Cove in the Rudyerd Bay area of Misty Fiords National Monument. Forest Service trail extends 0.7 mile to Punchbowl Lake. Accessible by floatplane or boat; moorage buoy in cove. Trail usable late spring through fall. Rated moderate. Elevation gain 600 feet. Estimated round-trip time 3 1/2 hours. This is a fairly steep trail with switchbacks, but its condition is good. Trail is very scenic. At the 0.5-mile point, there is an overlook of Punchbowl Creek waterfall. Within 500 feet of this point is another vista overlooking Punchbowl Cove. Here, the trail runs along a 2-foot-wide rock ledge with a 300-foot drop. Near the lake, the trail runs along Punchbowl Creek where rock walls rise approximately 250 feet. Trail ends at a new 3-sided shelter on Punchbowl Lake. Activities include fishing in the lake. (See Sportfishing, Ketchikan Area, in this section.) USGS map: Ketchikan C-3.

Shelokum Lake Trail. Trailhead is approximately 90 miles north of Ketchikan on Bailey Bay, 0.5 mile south of Shelokum Creek. The trail climbs 2.2 miles to Shelokum Lake at an elevation of 348 feet. Rated most difficult. Estimated round-trip hiking time 4 hours. This trail is perhaps the most scenic trail in the Ketchikan area. Special features include the largest waterfall in the area, an undeveloped hot springs, views of extremely scenic mountains and cliffs and developed boat access. Hikers must ford Maude Creek before reaching Shelokum Lake. It is impassable during high water. A 3-sided shelter is located at the inlet of Lake Shelokum, near Shelokum Hot Springs. USGS map: Ketchikan D-5.

Winstanley Lake Trail. Trailhead located in Misty Fiords National Monument on the south side of Winstanley Creek, across from the southern tip of Winstanley Island in East Behm Canal. Trail extends 2.3 miles to Winstanley Lake. Accessible by floatplane or boat. Usable late spring through fall. Rated moderate. Elevation gain 400 feet. Estimated round-trip time 4 to 5 hours.

The trail begins 30 feet to the right of the south bank of Winstanley Creek. There is a beach marker and mooring buoy. The first mile of trail leads through dense spruce and hemlock forest. The trail crosses over a handmade bridge to the north side of the creek at the 1-mile marker. There is a scenic view of Winstanley Creek and Falls. The trail continues on the north side of Lower Winstanley Lake, crossing over to the south side of Winstanley Creek at the lake's inlet. The remaining 0.5-mile of trail goes through 2 small muskegs before it ends at a 3-sided Civilian Conservation Corps shelter on Winstanley Lake. There are no other facilities on the trail. USGS map: Ketchikan B-3.

Wolf Lake Trail. This more difficult 2.6-mile trail leads from salt water in Moser Bay, 19 miles from Ketchikan, through muskegs and river bottomland and past 2 small unnamed ponds and Lower Wolf Lake, terminating at the Upper Wolf Lake shelter. Rubber boots are a must because of the wet tread. There are deer, black bears, and a large population of wolves, especially evident in winter. Cutthroats can be caught in Upper Wolf Lake. This is a year-round trail, good for skiing or snowshoeing in winter. USGS map: Ketchikan C-5.

Petersburg Area Trails

Big John Bay Trail. Trail extends 1 3/4 miles from Forest Road 6314, 16 miles from Kake, to the Big John Bay cabin. Trailhead accessible by auto from Kake. No access to cabin by trail at high tide. Rated moderate. Elevation loss 100 feet. Estimated round-trip time 2 hours. Usable spring, summer and fall. Trail marked with blue diamonds with blazes and pink flagging. Provides access to excellent waterfowl, grouse and black bear hunting. USGS maps: Petersburg D-5, D-6.

Cascade Creek Trail. Trail extends 4 miles to Swan Lake from the Forest Service cabin at Cascade Creek, 16 air miles northeast of Petersburg on Thomas Bay. Accessible by floatplane or boat. Rated most difficult. The upper portion of the trail is currently closed due to safety hazards. Requires good hiking skills; use caution. Elevation gain 1,514 feet. Provides access to mouth of Cascade Creek at 1 mile, Falls Lake at 3 miles and Swan Lake at 5 miles. Follows edge of Thomas Bay and north side of creek. There is rainbow trout fishing in Falls and Swan Lakes. There is also outstanding scenery and photo opportunities and an overnight Adirondack shelter (no fee, reservation only). There is an exit from Swan Lake to salt water. USGS maps: Petersburg D-3; Sumdum A-3.

Cathedral Falls Trail. Trail extends 0.25 mile to Cathedral Falls from Forest Road 6312, about 9 miles from Kake. Usable spring, summer and fall. Rated moderate. Elevation loss 100 feet. Estimated round-trip time 30 minutes. Provides access to trout and salmon fishing and photo opportunities at the falls. USGS maps: Petersburg D-5, D-6.

Colp Lake Trail. Trail extends 2.5 miles from the mouth of Five Mile Creek on Frederick Sound to Colp Lake, 5 miles northwest of Petersburg. Accessible by boat or floatplane. Usable spring, summer and fall. Rated moderate. Elevation gain 588 feet. Estimated round-trip time 2 1/2 hours. Provides access to cutthroat fishing, hiking, swimming, camping and cross-country skiing. Excellent views of Del Monte Peak and surrounding alpine terrain. USGS maps: Petersburg D-3, D-4.

Goose Lake Trail. This easy, 3.5-mile round-trip hike begins from road #6312. Trail provides access to trout fishing, waterfowl hunting and cross-country skiing. A small boat is provided. USGS map:s: Petersburg D-5, D-6.

Green Rocks Trail. This 2-mile round-trip trail provides boat access, trout fishing and waterfowl hunting. Rated easiest. Trail is flat and marshy; boots recommended. USGS map: C-3.

Hamilton Creek Trail. Trail is 2 miles round-trip, 13 miles up road #6314. Rated easiest. Trail accesses Hamilton Bay tidal flats and provides fishing for trout, char and salmon and waterfowl hunting. Black bears in area. USGS maps: Petersburg D-5, D-6.

Harvey Lake Trail. This 1-mile round-trip trail is rate easiest and accessible by boat or floatplane. Area provides trout fishing, swimming and picnicking. Cabin on lake provides rowboat; permit needed. USGS map: Petersburg C-4.

Hooter and Castle River Trails. Trails are 2.2 miles round-trip combined. Rated easiest. Accessible by boat or floatplane. Area provides silver salmon and steelhead fishing. Boat is provided. Trails join at Castle River Cabin; permit needed for cabin use. USGS map: Petersburg C-4.

Ideal Cove Trail. This 3-mile round-trip, more difficult trail parallels Hill Creek. Trail extends through muskeg, timber and beach terrain. Provides excellent views of Frederick Sound. Trail is muddy in some spots. USGS map: Petersburg C-3.

Kah Sheets Lake Trail. This easy, 5-mile round-trip trail is accessible by boat or floatplane. Trail accesses small waterfalls and fishing for sockeye salmon on the lake and steelhead fishing in the creek. Trail is handicap-accessible and extends to a cabin with outhouse, mooring float and ramp. Permit required for cabin use. USGS map: Petersburg C-4.

Ohmer Creek Trail. Easy to more difficult, 2-mile round-trip trail runs through muskeg and timber and from bridge at Snake River Road. Trail is muddy in spots. Trail has interpretive signs and provides access to trout and king salmon fishing. USGS map: Petersburg D-3.

Petersburg Lake Trail. This trail extends 6.5 miles from Petersburg Creek to Petersburg Lake cabin, 9 miles northwest of Petersburg. Rated easy. Tide of 15 feet is best for reaching trailhead, which is approximately 4 miles up Petersburg Creek from Wrangell Narrows. (Or hikers can walk 10 miles on a partial boardwalk from the public dock just across Wrangell Narrows from Petersburg.) The trail follows Petersburg Creek most of the way. There is fishing for salmon and trout and wildflower meadows and photo opportunities. USGS maps: Petersburg D-3, D-4.

Petersburg Mountain Trail. Trail extends 2.5 miles from Wrangell Narrows to the top of Petersburg Mountain. Located within Petersburg Creek-Duncan Salt Chuck Wilderness. Primarily accessible by boat. Trail rated difficult. High tide access is behind Sasby Island. Low tide access is from the Kupreanof public dock. Trail offers outstanding views and photo opportunities of Petersburg, coastal mountains and glaciers, Wrangell Narrows and part of the wilderness area. USGS map: Petersburg D-3.

Portage Mountain Loop Trail. Trail begins at the junction of the Petersburg Creek trail and the spur trail to Petersburg Lake recreation cabin and extends 10.2 miles to the Salt Chuck East cabin. Usable summer and fall for hiking; winter for cross-country skiing and snowshoeing. Rated moderately difficult. Elevation gain 150 feet. Round-trip hiking time 12 hours. Trailhead accessible by floatplane via the Petersburg Lake cabin drop-off point or by boat and foot to the Petersburg Creek trail. Portions of this trail were blazed by the Civilian Conservation Corps in the 1930s. Efforts to reestablish the trail began in 1978. The trail extends from near the Petersburg Lake cabin to Goose Cove, to Salt Chuck East cabin, around the base of Portage Mountain and back to the existing trail at Petersburg Lake. Trail passes through areas of muskeg and heavy timber and crosses numerous streams. Trail offers spectacular views of Portage Mountain and the Duncan Canal Salt Chuck. Moose, deer, black bear, waterfowl and other birds may be seen. USGS map: Petersburg D-4.

Raven Trail. Trail extends 4 miles from behind the Petersburg airport to Ravens Roost Forest Service cabin. Drive to end of the airport road past the red and white water tower, and watch for trail marker. Trail rated more difficult. About half the trail is boardwalk, but some very steep (70 percent slope) and muddy sections require good hiking skills. Trail offers outstanding views of Petersburg, Frederick Sound and Wrangell Narrows, as well as access to upland bird hunting and winter cross-country skiing and snowshoeing. USGS map: Petersburg D-3.

Spurt Lake Trail. Trail extends 1.5 miles from Thomas Bay to Spurt Lake. Trailhead on bay south of Wind Point. Accessible by boat or floatplane. Trail usable spring, summer and fall. Rated easy, elevation gain 450 feet. Estimated round-trip time 1 1/2 hours. This trail provides access to Spurt Lake, which was the original location of the Spurt Cove cabin. Lake has fair fishing for cutthroat; small boat provided. USGS map: Sumdum A-3.

Three Lakes Trail. This 4.5-mile one way trail accesses Sand, Crane, Shelter and Hill lakes. Rated easiest with boardwalk. Some steep sections. Picnic tables, fire rings and rowboats on all but Shelter Lake where there is an Adirondack shelter. Wildlife includes beavers, bears, deer, eagles and cranes. Area provides trout fishing. USGS map: Petersburg D-3.

Twin Ridge Ski Trail. Trail begins at Milepost 3.4 on Twin Creeks Road and extends 4.9 miles to Ravens Roost cabin. Usable November to April for cross-country skiing June to October for hiking. Rated moderately difficult. Elevation gain 1,200 feet. Estimated round-trip time 8 hours. Trailhead at Raven's Roost cabin can be reached via the 3.8-mile Raven Trail from town. Intermediate skiing skills required at this end. Trailhead on Twin Creeks Road can be reached by driving or skiing 3.4 miles up the road, which is very steep and narrow. Road is dangerous when it is covered with snow; at those times, park at beginning of road, and ski to trailhead in a small muskeg clearing on the left-hand side of the road. Trail marked with pink flagging and blue diamond markers, which may become covered with snow at times. Trail follows ridge. Advanced skiing skills or snowshoes required to traverse the steeper slopes. Trail offers spectacular views of Wrangell Narrows, LeConte Bay and the mainland. Moose, deer and black bear may be seen. USGS maps: Petersburg C-3, D-3.

Upper Twin Ski Trail. This 3.2-mile loop trail connects to Twin Creeks Road at Miles 3.3 and 4. Usable November to April for intermediate and advanced cross-country skiing, June to October for hiking. Rated moderately difficult. Elevation gain 600 feet. Estimated loop time 3 hours. Trailhead on Twin Creeks Road can be reached by driving or skiing up the road, which is very steep and narrow. Road is very dangerous when it is covered with snow; at those times, park at beginning of road and ski to trailheads on the righthand side of the road. Trail marked with pink flagging and blue diamond markers, which may become covered with snow at times. Entire length of trail is good for intermediate skiers, except for one steep, 0.3-mile slope about 0.5 mile in from the western trailhead. Skiers of intermediate skill may want to start from the eastern trailhead, then walk down the steep slope. Advanced skiers should have no trouble. This trail offers spectacular views of Wrangell Narrows. Moose, deer and black bear may be seen. USGS map: Petersburg C-3.

Sitka Area Trails

Contact the Tongass National Forest, Sitka Ranger District, 204 Siginaka Way, Sitka, AK 99835, for an up-to-date guide to Sitka trails. There will be a small fee.

Beaver Lake Trail. Begins at Sawmill Creek Campground about 5 air miles east of Sitka. Trail extends 1 mile to Beaver Lake. From Sawmill Creek Road, turn left onto Blue Lake Road which leads 1.5 miles to the campground. Usable all year. Rated moderate. Elevation gain, 250 feet. Round-trip hiking time 1 to 2 hours. This is a popular, maintained trail suited to family outings. It offers good views of nearby mountains and a nice walk over muskegs, along marshes and through stunted forests. The trail begins across the bridge over Sawmill Creek on the south side of a small clearing. At the beginning, a series of switchbacks and stairs lead through a forest of hemlock, Sitka spruce and yellow cedar up 200 feet. After the climb, the planked boardwalk portion of the trail begins as it breaks out onto sloping, stunted forests. The boardwalk runs through open forest and parallels the Beaver Lake outlet stream and marshes. Trail continues to several fishing plaforms along southern edge of lake. Boat available. There are plans to extend the trail around the lake. The trail ends with a dilapidated pier in a small muskeg at the western edge of Beaver Lake which was stocked with grayling in 1986, 1987 and 1988. Bears may be present; use caution. USGS map: Sitka A-4.

Gavan Hill and Harbor Mountain Trail. Trail starts just past the house at 508 Baranof Street, within walking distance of downtown Sitka. Trail extends 3 miles to the 2,505-foot summit of Gavan Hill and connects with the Harbor Mountain Ridge Trail. Rated moderate. Elevation gain 2,500 feet. Estimated round-trip time 6 to 8 hours. Trail usable midspring to late fall. First built in 1937 to provide access to recreationists and hunters, this maintained trail continues to offer access to alpine country for exploring and camping. The first 0.5 mile of the trail follows the path of an old pipeline and heads northeast across gently sloping muskegs and scrubby forests before entering the forests and beginning the climb up Gavan Hill. About 0.75 mile up the hill, the Cross Trail, which skirts Sitka, branches off to the left while the Gavan Hill Trail continues looping up east and north along a low ridge. Once on the Gavan Hill Ridge, about elevation 500 feet, the trail runs through a forest of stunted trees which gives way to subalpine meadows after a 0.25 mile. The first peak at 2,100 feet is reached after 0.5 mile and includes a steep, 200-foot climb. The trail continues another 0.25 mile northwest along the ridge to the second, higher peak. Bears may be present. USGS map: Sitka A-4.

Goulding Lake Trail. Trailhead is located at the head of Goulding Harbor on West Chichagof Island about 65 miles northwest of Sitka. Accessible by floatplane. Trail extends 1 mile to the outlet of the lowest Goulding Lake. Trail is located within West Chichagof-Yakobi Wilderness Area; it does not extend to the Forest Service's Goulding Lakes cabin. Trail usable all year. Rated moderate. Elevation gain 200 feet. This trail is wet and muddy; rubber boots highly recommended. Estimated round-trip time 2 hours. Trail generally follows the lower part of an abandoned mining tramway. Some of the old mining machinery, structures and a railroad engine remain. Do not disturb them. The trail begins on the north side of the inlet stream at the head of the harbor. Sections of the trail pass through spruce-hemlock forest, muskeg and marsh. The point where the trail meets the Goulding River is a good viewpoint for a large waterfall just upstream. Above the viewpoint, the trail crosses a tributary and continues a short distance to the lowest Goulding Lake. Steelhead and small cutthroat fishing is good. USGS map: Sitka D-7.

Harbor Mountain Ridge Trail. Trailhead is 9 miles from Sitka at the end of the Harbor Mountain Road. The trail extends 2 miles where it joins the Gavan Hill Trail at a peak with an elevation of 2,505 feet. Usable spring through fall. Rated moderate. Elevation gain 500 feet. This is the only subalpine area in southeastern Alaska that is accessible by road. It offers wonderful views of Sitka Sound, Sitka Mount Edgecumbe and numerous other mountains and islands. The trailhead is marked by a bulletin board and handrailings. It proceeds 300 feet up the hillside in a series of switchbacks. At the ridge, a short spur trail leads to the left to an overlook. The main trail turns to the right and follows the ridge toward the summit of a knob where WWII lookout ruins are located. As the trail continues along the ridge toward the peaks, it forks to the right and skirts the hillside, circling around to join the Gavin Hill Trail. The last section of the trail is little more than a deer path and is difficult to locate at times. The other fork of the trail continues up the steep shoulder slope of the peaks and ends as it reaches the steep, rocky alpine at about 2,500 feet. USGS maps: Sitka A-4, A-5.

Indian River Trail. Trailhead is located within walking distance from Sitka. Trail extends 4.3 miles to the base of Indian River Falls, usable year-round. Rated easy. Elevation gain 700 feet. Estimated round-trip time 8 hours. The trail offers views of the Sisters Mountains and is a relaxing walk through northwest, coastal rain forest. To find the trailhead, follow Sawmill Creek road a short distance to Indian River Road, an unmarked road east of the Troopers Academy driveway. Walk around the road gate. The trail begins on the left of the pumphouse. The trail follows Indian River up a wide valley, meandering from the trailhead. Good picnic spots can be found in numerous places along the trail. Birds and animals are common in the forest and along the river. Deer are seen frequently, and bears may be present. USGS map: Sitka A-4.

Lake Eva-Hanus Bay Trail. Trailhead is at Hanus Bay on the northeast coast of Baranot Island about 27 miles northeast of Sitka. Accessible by floatplane or boat. Trail extends 2.9 miles to an old Civilian Conservation Corps shelter on the southwest shore of Lake Eva.

Usable all year. Rated moderate. Elevation gain 50 feet. Estimated round-trip time 4 to 8 hours. Rubber boots recommended. Trail begins on the west side of the bay on the east side of the Lake Eva outlet stream. Trail heads west along the south side of the estuary then winds along the south side of the Lake Eva outlet stream through dense spruce-hemlock forest that offers fine vistas and good fishing for spring-run steelhead, fall coho salmon and year-round cutthroat and Dolly Varden. (See Sportfishing, Sitka Area, in this section.) Lake is accessed at Mile 1.1 from salt water. The trail follows the south shore of Lake Eva through old-growth forest and ends at the shelter, which is in poor condition. The last 1.5 miles of the trail are not maintained and difficult to find due to windfall and landslides. The trail does not lead to the Forest Service Lake Eva cabin, which is on the northwest side of the lake. USGS map: Sitka B-4.

Mount Edgecumbe Trail. Trailhead is behind the Freds Creek recreation cabin on the southeast shore of Kruzof Island about 10 miles west of Sitka. Accessible by floatplane or half-hour boat ride from Sitka. Trail extends 7 miles to the summit crater of Mount Edgecumbe, a dormant volcano. Usable spring through late fall. Rated moderate. Elevation gain 3,000 feet. Estimated round-trip time 8 to 12 hours. Rubber boots recommended. The trail starts on flat, forested land then gradually rises while running through several miles of muskeg alternating with forest. About 3 miles up the trail at an elevation of 700 feet, a spur leads to a trail shelter. About 1 mile beyond the shelter turnoff, the trail steepens considerably. Timberline is at about 2,000 feet, where the trail ends. Above this, the ground is covered with red volcanic ash and fragile vegetation. To reach the crater rim, continue straight up the mountain. The summit offers spectacular views on clear days. If you use any flagging or marking, be sure to remove it all. Also, pack out all garbage. USGS maps: Sitka A-5, A-6.

Mount Verstovia Trail. Trail begins a mile east of Sitka along Sawmill Creek Road, near the Orka Bay Bar & Grill and extends 2.5 miles to the summit of Mount Verstovia. Usable year-round. Rated difficult. Elevation gain 2,550 feet to Verstovia and 3,300 feet to Arrowhead. Estimated round-trip hiking time 6 hours. The lower hillside was logged by the Russians in 1860, and charcoal pits are still somewhat visible about 0.25 mile up the trail. The trail was built in the 1930s for recreational purposes. The view from Verstovia is spectacular, and the trail progresses through thickets of salmonberry and alder to western hemlock-spruce forest into brushy meadows, across snowfields, through grassy meadows and finally into a rocky alpine area with stunted, twisted plants. At about 2,000 feet, the trail reaches a gentle ridge which it follows east to the summit of Verstovia. Arrowhead Peak can be climbed by heading northeast along the rocky alpine ridge. The last part of the climb is quite steep and exposed. Bears may be present. USGS map: Sitka A-4.

Salmon Lake-Redoubt Lake Trail. Trailhead located at the southwest end of Silver Bay about 10 miles southeast of Sitka. Accessible by boat or floatplane. Trail extends 2 miles to the Salmon Lake Forest Service cabin and 5.9 miles to the cabin on Redoubt Lake. Usable all year. Rated moderate. Elevation gain 600 feet. Estimated round-trip time 8 to 10 hours. Rubber boots recommended. Trail begins on the east side of the mouth of the Salmon Lake stream, which is the westernmost inlet stream at the head of Silver Bay. Trail passes through Sitka spruce, hemlock and cedar forest for the first 3 miles and follows the eastern shore of Salmon Lake for about a mile. The trail crosses several creeks and streams that must be forded. At about 3 miles, the trail travels through muskegs and meadows. There are trail forks in this area; stay on the main (southwestern) trail as the forks are unmaintained trails leading up to the Lucky Chance Mountain mining areas. The trail then reenters the forest and climbs 500 feet up a narrow saddle to the pass that separates the Salmon Lake and Redoubt Lake drainages. The tread is rough in areas, planking is often slick, and there are muddy areas. The pass is about 1 mile from Redoubt Lake; the downhill slope can be slippery and muddy. The trail follows the lakeshore for about half a mile, then turns southwest a short distance to the cabin. There is fishing for cutthroat and rainbow trout and Dolly Varden along this trail. USGS map: Port Alexander D-4.

Sashin Lake Trail. Trailhead is at the head of Little Port Walter on the eastern side of

Baranof Island about 55 miles southeast of Sitka. Accessible by boat or floatplane. Trail extends 1.7 miles to Sashin Lake. Usable all year. Rated moderate but not maintained. Elevation gain 400 feet. Rubber boots recommended. Trail was built and planked by the Civilian Conservation Corps in the 1930s. Planking is collapsed and dangerous in places. Go ashore at the dock in front of the fisheries research station (a large white brick house) in Little Port Walter. The trail heads southwest along the western shore of Little Port Walter for a quarter-mile, past various research station buildings and then past the king salmon holding pens, which are quite interesting. The bridge is out above the fish weir, and the Forest Service recommends using hip-boots to make the crossing. The trail then meanders southwest up Sashin Creek through open forests and meadows. Just northeast of Sashin Lake, the trail goes over a low shoulder and enters a heavy forest; stay on the north side of the lake. The trail ends at the remains of a Civilian Conservation Corps shelter. About 1.3 miles from the trailhead, another branch leads north to Round Lake. Round Lake trail is not maintained and difficult to follow. There is good trout fishing in Sashin Lake. This is bear country, so exercise caution. USGS maps: Port Alexander B-2, B-3, B-4.

Sea Lion Cove Trail. Trailhead at Kalinin Bay on the north side of Kruzof Island, about 25 miles northwest of Sitka. Access is by boat or floatplane. Trail extends 2.5 miles to Sea Lion Cove, a beautiful mile-long white sand beach. Usable all year. Rated moderate. Elevation gain 250 feet. Estimated round-trip time 4 hours. Rubber boots recommended; trail is muddy and rough in places. Some sections are planked. Bridges are slippery and unsafe. Hikers should be aware that bears frequent this area. Trail begins at the southern end of Kalinin Bay on the upper beach just west of the high-water island where there is a red, diamond-shaped trail marker on a tree. The trail runs south along the western side of the estuary for about half a mile. This stretch is inundated during high tides. The trail then turns west up into the forest at the next trail sign. At the top of the hill, it cuts through muskeg, reenters the forest and follows the north shore of an unnamed lake. The trail becomes rougher and begins to drop into the Sea Lion Cove drainage just past the lake. For the last mile, it winds west on low flat ground through forest and muskeg. The trail breaks out on the northern end of Sea Lion Cove. This beach is wonderful for beachcombing, exploring, camping, watching sea lions and viewing surf and the open Pacific Ocean. Camping is also possible at Kalinin Bay. During the summer, there is usually a fishbuying scow anchored in the bay from which groceries and showers may be purchased. USGS map: Sitka B-6.

Sitkoh Lake Trail. Trailhead at Sitkoh Bay on the southeast part of Chichagof Island about 35 miles northeast of Sitka. Accessible by floatplane and boat. Trail extends 4.3 miles to the Forest Service recreation cabin on Sitkoh Lake. Trail usable spring through fall. Rated moderate. Elevation gain 200 feet. Estimated round-trip time 6 to 8 hours. Rubber boots recommended. Trail begins on the north side of the mouth of Sitkoh Creek (about 0.5 mile northwest of the abandoned Chatham Cannery, which is on the western shore of Sitkoh Bay). The trail marker is just above the beach. The trail is easy to follow, but portions have been washed away by Sitkoh Creek. Some sections are planked, and some have stairs that are in poor condition. Near the lake, the trail crosses some muskeg, and in some areas, it is muddy and/or under water. At the cabin, a spur trail leads northwest about 0.5 mile to an old logging road. Bears are numerous in the area. There is good fishing in Sitkoh Creek and Lake. The creek has a good run of pink salmon from July to mid-August, red salmon from mid-July to mid-August and silver salmon from late August through September. The creek reportedly has the best spring steelhead run in the Sitka Ranger District, generally starting in late April. The lake has an over-wintering population of cutthroat and Dolly Varden. (See Sportfishing, Sitka Area, in this section.) Deer hunting is good in the area. USGS maps: Sitka C-3, C-4.

Warm Springs Bay Trail. Located 20 miles east of Sitka on the east shore of Baranof Island. Accessible by boat or floatplane. Trail extends 0.5 mile from Baranof Warm Springs to Baranof Lake where a Forest Service cabin is located (see Cabins this section). Trail does not extend to cabin. Rated easy with no elevation gain. Round-trip hiking time 1 hour. Usable all year. Hot springs, pools and streamlets are common interruptions of the mossy forest floor. Generally, the trail is on boardwalk over areas with hot springs. The trail terminates by fading out near the north side of the lake's outlet. Several short, unmaintained spur trails radiate from this area; these go along the lakeshore, along the river, into the muskeg, and one leads to Sadie Lake. USGS map: Sitka A-3.

Skagway Area Trails

A.B. Mountain Trail. Trail is 10 miles round-trip and rated difficult. Elevation gain is 5,000 feet. Trail extends through spruce/hemlock forest with views of Skagway. Some spots thick with brush; trail not visible. Trail offers alpine meadows and panoramic views. Trail is dangerous above treeline.

Denver Glacier Trail. Four- to 6-mile round-trip trail accesses Forest Service cabin. Rated moderate. Elevation gain is 900 feet. Trail follows East Fork Skagway River through spruce and hemlock. Two miles up, trail turns south up glacier outwash; brushy and slippery.

Devil's Punchbowl Trail. Trail is 2 hours from Upper Dewey Lake, 2 1/2 miles round-trip. Rated moderate. Elevation gain 600 feet. Trail follows alpine ridge to overlook of Punchbowl Lake.

Dewey Lakes Trail. This steep trail takes off near the east end of 4th Avenue. The hike to Lower Dewey Lake is 1/2- to 1-hour. Upper Dewey Lake is a steep, 3-mile, 2- to 4-hour hike to above tree line. Elevation gain 3,000 feet. Both lakes were stocked with Colorado brook trout in the 1920s.

Gold Rush Cemetery and Reid Falls Trail. Trail is 4 miles round-trip. Hiking time is 2 hours. Rated easy. Elevation gain 50 feet.

Icy Lake and Upper Reid Falls Trails. Seven-mile round-trip trail leaves from Lower Dewey Lake. Hiking time is 3 to 4 hours. Rated steep to moderate. Elevation gain 850 feet. Trail is muddy near lake.

Laughton Glacier Trail. Trail is 3 to 5 miles round trip from railroad stop and accesses cabin. Rated moderate. Elevation gain is 200 to 600 feet. Trail follows Skagway River upstream and south along glacier outwash.

Lost Lake Trail. Two-mile trail is 3 to 4 hours from Dyea Slide Cemetery. Rated strenuous. Elevation gain 1,500 feet. Trail is seldom used and follows gully to right (not straight up). Area offers blueberry picking. Ridge overlooks lake.

Sturgill's Landing Trail. Seven-mile round-trip trail leaves from south end of Lower Dewey Lake. Hiking time is 4 to 5 hours. Rated moderate. Elevation gain 500 feet. Trail extends through sawmill ruins and spruce, hemlock and lodgepole. Area offers picnic tables, toilets and a beach. Boggy areas may be muddy.

Yakutania Point Trail. One- to 2-mile round-trip trail provides picnic tables and toilets. Hiking time is 1 to 2 hours. Rated easy. Elevation gain 100 feet.

Wrangell Area Trails

Aaron Creek Trail. Trail extends 4 miles from the Berg Bay cabin, located 15 miles southeast of Wrangell, to the mouth of Berg Creek. Accessible by floatplane or boat. Rated easy. The Berg Creek trail continues 5 miles up Berg Creek into the mountains. Former mining activity in this area. Trail provides access to waterfowl, moose and bear hunting on tideflats and goat hunting in the mountains.

Anan Creek Trail. Trail extends 1 mile from the mouth of Anan Creek to Anan Fishpass and Bear Observatory, a wood-frame shelter. Accessible by floatplane or boat 34 miles south of Wrangell on the mainland. Rated easy; elevation gain 100 feet. Estimated round-trip time 1 1/2 hours. Trail begins at marker just above beach adjacent to Anan Bay cabin. Most of trail follows easy grade through spruce-hemlock forest. Trail is unsurfaced except for occasional staircases and bridges used for abrupt elevation changes or wet spots. Provides access to fishpass and bear viewing station at falls. Wildlife viewing/photography and pink salmon fishing available. Bears also use this trail heavily, so make your presence known. USGS map: Bradfield A-6.

Kunk Lake Trail. Trail extends 1.3 miles from Zimovia Strait to Kunk Lake on the northeast coast of Etolin Island about 13 miles south of Wrangell. Accessible by boat or floatplane. Rated difficult; estimated roundtrip time about 2 hours. Trail covers varied terrain with grades ranging from easy to steep and with much wet ground. Waterproof boots highly recommended. Provides access to trout fishing and picnicking areas. USGS map: Petersburg B-2.

Mill Creek Trail. Trail extends 0.8 mile from Eastern Passage to the Virginia Lake outlet about 10 miles east of Wrangell. Accessible by boat or floatplane. Rated easy. Elevation gain 100 feet. Estimated round-trip time 1 1/2 hours. Provides portage from salt water to the lake. Abandoned sawmill site at the head of the trail. A portion of the trail lies atop an old corduroy truck road. Evidence of old mining activity in the area. Activities include trout fishing and picnicking. The trail also provides snowmobile access to ice fishing in winter. USGS map: Petersburg B-1.

Rainbow Falls and Institute Creek trails. Rainbow Falls Trail begins at Mile 4.6 Zimovia Highway directly across from the Shoemaker Bay Recreation Area and Boat Harbor. It extends 0.8 mile to Rainbow Falls and leads to picnicking and scenic views at 2 modest observation sites. Midway between the 2 sites is the junction with Institute Creek Trail, which leads 3.5 miles (1,100-foot elevation gain) to Shoemaker Overlook Recreation Site. Here are excellent vistas and cross-country skiing opportunities, also access to grouse and deer hunting in season. At trail's end are a 3-sided shelter, picnic table, fire grill and outdoor privy. Although trail was recently surfaced, conditions can range from excellent to poor. Allow 1 1/2 hours round-trip hiking time for the Rainbow Falls portion and 6 hours (round-trip) for the Institute Creek hike. These 2 trails are the most popular on Wrangell Island. USGS map: Petersburg B-2.

Yakutat Area Trails

Esker Stream to Turner Glacier. A 1-mile bike (allow 3 days round trip) from the airstrip at Esker Stream to the face of Turner Glacier on the Malaspina Forelands Coast in Wrangell-St. Elias National Park. Access is by air charter to the beach airstrip at Esker Stream. It is also possible to land a boat near Turner Glacier. There are approximately 10 miles of coastal beach hiking. The last mile is bushwhacking through alder to Turner Glacier. There are 5 knee-deep streams to cross. Allow at least 1 hour on either side of low tide when going around Bancas Point. Plenty of campsites; do not camp too close to tidal zone. Beached icebergs at low tide. According to the Park Service, this is a good trip for the beginning- level hiker who has a good working knowledge of southeastern Alaska tides. USGS map: Yakutat D-5.

Grotto Glacier. A 3- to 4-day roundtrip hike. Hiking to Tsaa Fiord to see Grotto Glacier is partly a beach hike and also involves going over bluffs and walking along a valley floor. It is a very scenic hike, and you will often be able to see the icebergs beached at low tide. (Use caution walking around large beached icebergs; these can break or roll over in a moment's notice.) Fly-in to Icy Bay logging camp airstrip or Independence Creek Beach airstrip at low tide. From the Icy Bay logging camp, it is 5 miles via logging road to the jetty. Then, it is a 3-mile hike (at low tide) from the jetty to Independence Creek. From Independence Creek to Grotto Glacier is approximately 10-12 miles of beach hiking. This hike between the jetty and Independence Creek requires going over the headwall at Kichyat Point. Going over the headwall is tricky due to the steep trail and having to bushwhack through alder. Stay away from the edge of the steep cliff. USGS maps: Bering Glacier A-2; Icy Bay D-2, D-3.

Sudden Stream to Point Manby. A 12-mile beach hike (allow 2 days) between Sudden Stream beach airstrip to Point Manby on the Malaspina Forelands Coast in Wrangell-St. Elias National Park. Fly-in to either Sudden Stream beach airstrip or Point Manby. According to the Park Service, there are 12 miles of wide, sandy coastal beaches, and 2 miles north of Point Manby is a beached Navy barge. Campsites are available along the way; carry water. Bear, moose and coyote travel the beach. Local fishermen travel the beach on their ATVs between Sudden Stream, Manby Stream and Spoon River. USGS map: Yakutat D-5.

 **Hot Springs**

Hot springs are scattered throughout Southeast. The soothing springs are often a destination for wilderness travelers, but in many cases, they are simply an added treat. The town of Tenakee Springs actually grew up around the hot springs which are still a major attraction for this community. (See Communities this section.) Following are a few of the springs found in Southeast Alaska.

Baranof Warm Springs. Located 20 miles east of Sitka on the east shore of Baranof Island. A private hot springs bath is located on Warm Springs Bay (status unknown). Accessible by boat or floatplane. A Forest Service trail extends a half mile from the hot springs to Baranof Lake where a cabin is located. Cabin access is by floatplane. It is not possible to hike from the springs to the cabin.

Chief Shakes Hot Springs. Located off Ketili River, a slough of the Stikine River, approximately 12 miles upriver. The Hot Springs Slough Route is one of several established Canoe/Kayak Routes along the Stikine. Two hot tubs, 1 enclosed in a screened structure, provide a good place to soak. The open-air tub has a wooden deck around it, and both tubs have changing areas. There are also a picnic table, fire ring, benches and an outdoor privy. The area is used heavily during evenings and weekends, according to the Forest Service. Paddlers should also be aware that use of the Stikine and the slough by powerboats is especially high during evenings and weekends. The Forest Service maintains 2 cabins just upriver.

Goddard Hot Springs. Located on the outer coast of Baranof Island on Hot Springs Bay off of Sitka Sound, 16 miles south of Sitka. This may have been the earliest Alaska mineral springs known to the Europeans, and before their arrival, Natives came from many miles away to benefit from the healing waters. In the mid-1800s, there were 3 cottages at Goddard that were used to house invalids from Sitka. In the late 1880s, a Sitka company erected frame buildings for people seeking the water's benefits. By the 1920s, a 3-story hotel was built to provide more sophisticated accommodations. The building was purchased in 1939 by the Territorial Legislature as an overflow home for the Sitka Pioneers' Home. After 1946, the building fell into disuse and was torn down. Today, the city of Sitka owns the property and maintains 2 modern cedar bathhouses for recreational use. A few people live year-round on nearby private land.

There are open shelters over the hot tubs, which feature natural hot springs water and cold water. The springs are very popular with area residents. The area has outhouses. Boardwalks provide easy walking. Boaters can anchor in the bay and go ashore in skiffs. This is not a place to take a boat without a chart; there are many rocks and shoals, especially around the hot springs. There are protected routes to Sitka and a fascinating series of coves and channels just north of the hot springs. At the springs, there are campsites in a grassy, meadow-like area and on higher ground. Biting black flies (whitesox) are plentiful in the summer months.

Shelokum Hot Springs. Located approximately 90 miles north of Ketchikan in the Tongass National Forest on the Cleveland Peninsula. A 2.2-mile trail begins at Bailey Bay just south of Shelokum Creek and leads to Lake Shelokum. A 3-sided shelter stands at the inlet to the lake. The hot springs are completely undisturbed and support a healthy population of unique algal plant life.

Trocadero Soda Springs. These seldom-visited, carbonated "soda" springs are located on the west coast of Prince of Wales Island about 12 miles southeast of Craig. Access is by boat. Rubber boots are advised for hike. This is bear country; exercise caution, particularly when salmon are spawning. The springs are reached by walking up a nameless creek that has its outlet in a small inlet on the south shore of the bay. The springs flow into the creek about a mile upstream. The first sign of the springs are 2 giant, golden steps. These are banks of yellow tufa formed by the constant runoff from the springs. Tufa is a geological term referring to a concretionary sediment of silica or calcium carbonate deposited near the mouth of a mineral spring or geyser. The 4- to 5-acre area around the bubbling, hissing springs features lunar-like mounds and craters, splashed with colors ranging from subtle yellow to iron red. The springs originate in muskeg. Then, the mineralized water meanders about 100 feet, forming a deep crust of tufa in which there are hundreds of small vents with escaping gas and bubbling water. The highly carbonated water is described as having "a sharp, pleasant taste" and has no unpleasant odors. Although water from other carbonated springs in Southeast has been bottled and sold in the past, Trocadero water has never been commercially marketed.

White Sulphur Hot Springs. Located within the West Chichagof-Yakobi Wilderness area, some 65 miles northwest of Sitka. Many visitors fly in to a small lake nearby and hike to the cabin or boat to Mirror Harbor and walk the easy, year-round, 0.8-mile trail to the hot springs. Various log bathhouses have been built over the principal springs, and in earlier years, occasional hunters and trappers camped here. At that time, the pools were called Hoonah Warm Springs, but years ago, they were renamed for a dentist, Dr. White. In 1916, the U.S. Forest Service built its first cabin and bathhouse here. This cabin has been modernized in recent years, so bathers can pull back a translucent fiberglass screen and admire the view of the often turbulent Pacific Ocean while soaking in the hot water. This is a popular bathing spot for commercial fishing and charter boat guests and a destination for kayakers (primarily paddling from Pelican).

Juneau Icefield

This is the world's largest glacial accumulation outside of Greenland and Antarctica. The ice cap is 15 miles wide, 70 miles long and covers 1,500 square miles. Located in the Coast Mountains 25 miles north of Juneau, it extends over the border into Canada and north nearly to Skagway. The glaciers of southeastern Alaska are born in the high mountains that rise out of the sea and tower more than 13,000 feet within a few miles of the coast. The Juneau Icefield's annual snowfall of more than 100 feet does not melt during the summer and thus accumulates over the years until the weight of the snow compacts it into ice which then deforms and begins to flow down the valleys and into the sea. When the rate of ice buildup is greater than the amount lost annually to melting or calving of icebergs at the terminus, the glacier will gain ground or advance. If the reverse happens, and the ice melts faster than new ice accumulates, the glacier will lose ground or retreat.

More than 30 glaciers, including the most visited glacier in Alaska—Mendenhall—begin in this ice field. Mendenhall Glacier is about 12 miles long and 1.5 miles across at its face. It is retreating slowly, fewer than 100 feet per year. The glacier has melted back more than 2 miles in the last 200 years. The Mendenhall is only 13 miles from downtown Juneau by road, and there's an excellent view of it even from the parking lot. The Forest Service main-

tains a visitor center and several trails in the area.

CAUTION: Do not approach the face of this or any glacier. The glacier can 'calve' (break off) at any time and crush anyone too close under tons of ice.

Other glaciers emanating from the Juneau Icefield that can be seen from the highway north of Juneau or from the water include Lemon Creek Glacier, Herbert Glacier and Eagle Glacier. None of these descends to tidewater; all are retreating. One glacier that is definitely advancing at a steady rate is the Taku Glacier on the north side of Taku Inlet, 13 miles southeast of Juneau. Extending about 30 miles, this glacier is the largest from the Juneau Icefield. If it keeps advancing, perhaps one day, ice bergs will float again in Juneau Harbor as they did in the 1890s. Today, the bergs melt before they reach Juneau. Taku Glacier can be accessed by charter boat and plane.

Since 1946, scientists have been studying the ice field each summer, searching for secrets about weather patterns, the ice age and about the plants and wildlife that survive some of the world's worst weather. The Coast Range is located in the path of storms that sweep eastward from the Pacific Ocean. Studying dust and other deposits laid down by storms going back hundreds of years can help scientists predict weather patterns of the future as well as the behavior of glaciers. There are at least 6 main research camps and 20 or so lesser camps on the ice field, where winds frequently reach 80 mph, and the summer temperature drops into the 20s.

Several companies in Juneau and Skagway offer small plane or helicopter tours that may include the opportunity to walk on the ice field.

 # Karta River Wilderness Area

This 39,889-acre area is located on Prince of Wales Island, about 5 miles from Hollis. The main attraction of the wilderness area is the Karta River.

A 5-mile trail runs the length of the river system, offering good hiking and access to excellent stream fishing for steelhead and trout. The Karta River area contains high- value habitat for coho salmon. The 2 major lakes, Salmon Lake and Karta Lake, are important spawning sites for sockeye salmon. Wildlife in the area includes black bears, Sitka black-tailed deer and wolves. There are no brown bears on Prince of Wales Island.

Karta Lake is a popular site for photographers who fly in to capture mirror images on the lake. The 4 Forest Service cabins in the wilderness area are in such high demand that reservations are managed using a lottery system (see Tongass National Forest Cabins this section for details).

For more information: Tongass National Forest, Thorne Bay Ranger District, Recreation and Lands Department, P.O. Box 19001, Thorne Bay, AK 99919; phone (907) 828-3304, fax (907) 828-3309. USGS map: Craig.

 # Klondike Gold Rush National Historical Park

(see also Chilkoot Trail)

In August 1896, George Washington Carmack and 3 Native companions, Skookum Jim Klondike Kate and Tagish Charlie, found gold in a tributary creek of the Thron'duck (Klondike) River in the upper Yukon valley, setting off one of the greatest gold rushes in history. Although most of the good claims were already staked by the time the rush got under way, that didn't stop a horde of gold seekers, disheartened and out of work because of a severe, nationwide economic depression, from streaming to Seattle and other West Coast ports to book passage North.

A small percentage succeeded; most did not. A sobering number died, some by their own hands when reality overwhelmed them. The majority of the gold seekers saw their dreams of glory savaged by the brutal conditions, the criminal element and their own delusions. It is doubtful if any similarly brief (less than 2 years) period in our history has witnessed a more flagrant example of concentrated insanity than that of the Klondike Gold Rush. As described by Pierre Berton in his definitive history, *The Klondike Fever:* "It was the last and most frenzied of the great international gold rushes."

The first boatloads of stampeders landed at Skagway and nearby Dyea in July 1897, and more arrived in the months that followed. The population of Skagway ballooned from a handful of homesteaders to approximately 15,000. The stampeders each spent an average of 3 months hauling their year's supply of goods over either the Chilkoot Trail or the longer White Pass Trail to Lake Bennett, where they built boats to float the remaining 560 miles downriver to the boom town of Dawson City in the Klondike. The frenzied parade lasted until the newly built White Pass & Yukon Route reached Lake Bennett in the summer of 1899, supplanting the Chilkoot Trail. But by then, the gold rush was over. The Chilkoot Trail was all but abandoned. Dyea became a ghost town; its post office closed in 1902, and its population in 1903 consisted of 2 or 3 settlers. Skagway's population plummeted to 1,000 by 1905.

Klondike Gold Rush National Historical Park was authorized in 1976 by the United States to commemorate the Klondike Gold Rush of 1897-98. In 1998, it became the nation's only International Historical Park, with units in Seattle, Skagway, British Columbia and the Yukon Territory.

The U.S. portion of the park, managed by the National Park Service, consists of 4 units: A 6-block historical district in Skagway's business area; a 1-mile-wide, 17-mile-long corridor of land comprising the Chilkoot Trail (managed in conjunction with Parks Canada; see Chilkoot Trail this section); a 1-mile-wide, 5-mile-long corridor of land comprising the White Pass Trail; and a visitor center in Seattle, WA. The Skagway unit is the most-visited national park in Alaska. The National Park Service offers a variety of free programs in Skagway during the summer. There are daily, guided walking tours of the downtown Skagway historic district and ranger talks on a variety of topics. The original Moore cabin and the restored J. Bernard Moore House at 5th Avenue and Spring Street provide insights into the Alaska pioneer lifestyle during Skagway's early years.

An interpretive center for the Klondike (117 S. Main St., Seattle, WA 98104) has been established in Pioneer Square. This unit of the park explains Seattle's role in the Klondike gold rush and has exhibits of supplies sold to stampeders and newspaper stories of the day. In Skagway, a mannequin surrounded by food and equipment depicts the "ton of goods" each stampeder was required to have before he was allowed to enter Canada. (The so-called "ton of goods" actually amounted to roughly 1,150 pounds of food and about 400 pounds of other necessities for survival.) The trail center across the street also has information to help in planning a trip on the Chilkoot Trail, including lists of recommended equipment and maps. For more about the Chilkoot Trail, see Chilkoot Trail in this section.

For more information: Park Service Visitor Center located in the restored railroad depot on 2nd Avenue and Broadway. Visitor center summer hours are 8 A.M. to 6 P.M. from May to September, 8 A.M. to 8 P.M. from June to August. Check here for schedules of guided walks and ranger talks. Films are also shown. Or write: Klondike Gold Rush National Historical Park, Box 517, Skagway, AK 99840; phone (907) 983-2921, fax (907) 983-9249, www.nps.gov/klgo.

Lighthouses

Southeastern Alaska has 9 historic light stations (see alphabetical list following) owned and managed by the U.S. Coast Guard; 8 are still active navigation aids. These lighthouses appear as familiar sights to those who navigate the Inside Passage. From south to north, they are: Tree Point, Mary Island, Guard Islands, Cape Decision, Five Finger Islands, Cape Spencer, Point Retreat, Sentinel Island and Eldred Rock. An inventory of historic light stations is kept by the National Park Service. For more details on Alaska's historic light stations, go to www.cr.nps.gov/maritime/light/ak.htm.

Cape Decision Light. Located at the south tip of Kuiu Island between Sumner and Chatham straits, 26 miles southeast of Port Alexander. This was the last lighthouse to be completed in Alaska, at a cost of $158,000. It began operation March 15, 1932 and was automated in 1974.

The original Fresnel lens is at the Clausen Museum in Petersburg. Active navigation aid.

Cape Spencer Light. Located at the north side of the entrance to Cross Sound/Icy Strait, 30 miles west of Gustavus, 45 miles northwest of Hoonah. The station was established in 1913, with an acetylene beacon placed above the water. The tower was built in 1925, lit on December 11 of that year. A radio beacon established in 1926 was the first in Alaska. It was automated in 1974. Present optic is solar powered The original Fresnel lens is in the Alaska State Museum in Juneau. Active navigation aid.

Eldred Rock Light. Located in Lynn Canal, 55 miles northwest of Juneau and 20 miles southeast of Haines. This was the last major station commissioned in Alaska during the surge of lighthouse construction between 1902-06. It was established and lit in 1905 and automated in 1973. Present optic is solar powered. The original Fresnel lens was moved to the Sheldon Museum in Haines in 1978. Active navigation aid.

Five Finger Islands Light. Located in Frederick Sound at the south entrance to Stephens Passage, 5 miles northwest of Whitney Island, 67 miles east of Sitka and 45 miles northwest of Petersburg. Established in 1902, this was the first Alaska lighthouse built by the Lighthouse Service. It was first lit in 1935 and automated in 1984, making it the last manned lighthouse in Alaska. Present optic is solar powered. Active navigation aid and weather forecasting center.

Guard Islands Light. Located about 8 miles from downtown Ketchikan, this light marks the easterly entrance to Tongass Narrows/Clarence Strait. It was established in 1904. The early station featured a fog bell. It was first lit in 1924 and automated in 1969. Present optic is solar powered. Active navigation aid.

Mary Island Light. This is the second lighthouse encountered by mariners entering Alaska's Inside Passage from the south. It is located on a 198-acre lighthouse reservation on a 5-mile-long island located between Felice Strait and Revillagigedo Channel, 30 miles southeast of Ketchikan. It was established in 1903, first lit in 1937 and automated in 1969. Active navigation aid.

Point Retreat Light. Located on the northerly tip of the Mansfield Peninsula on Admiralty Island in Lynn Canal, 20 miles northwest of Juneau. This was one of 4 minor light stations established in 1904. It was first lit in 1923, then automated in 1973. Presdent optic is solar powered. Active navigation aid.

Sentinel Island Light. Located on a small island in Auke Bay at the entrance to Lynn Canal, approximately 25 miles northwest of Juneau. This is one of the earliest lighthouses in Alaska. Constructed by George James of Juneau at a cost of $21,000, the station began operation on March 1, 1902. The tower was first lit in 1935 and automated in 1966. The present optic is solar powered. It is leased to Gastineau Channel Historical Society and open to the public by appointment only. Active navigation aid.

North of Sentinel Island is Vanderbilt Reef, where the SS *Princess Sophia* ran aground on Oct. 24, 1918. The ship's 288 passengers and 61 crew perished when a combination of stormy seas and a high tide forced the Princess Sophia off the reef, and she sank early in the evening of Oct. 25. Vanderbilt Reef is now marked by a navigation light.

Tree Point Light. This is the first light mariners see upon entering Alaska's Inside Passage from the south. It is located on a point extending to the southwest from the east shore of Revillagigedo Channel and marks the entrance to the channel near the U.S.-Canada border. It was built on a 1,207-acre lighthouse reservation. The light station was established in 1903. It was first lit in 1935 and deactivated in 1969.

⚓ Marine Parks

The state of Alaska has established 34 marine parks as part of an international system of shoreline parks and recreation areas stretching from near Olympia, WA, up through British Columbia, Canada, and as far north as Prince William Sound. The majority of these parks have no developed facilities.

Following is a list of the 15 marine parks located in Southeast, listed in order of geographical location, starting with the farthest south park and ending with the farthest north park. For more nformation, contact Alaska Division of Parks, Southeast Region, 400 Willoughby Ave., Juneau, AK 99801; phone (907) 465-4563, fax (907) 465-5330.

Dall Bay. Located 12 miles south of Ketchikan. The 850-acre marine park provides boaters a protected anchorage before venturing out of Nichols Passage into Clarence Strait.

Grindall Island. Located 18 miles northwest of Ketchikan. This is a protected holdover spot for small boats venturing across Clarence Strait in stormy weather. Mooring buoy. State public-use cabin available (see Cabins this section).

Thoms Place. Located in a cove 22 miles south of Wrangell, off Zimovia Strait. A trail leads from the 1,400-acre marine park to Thoms Lake.

Beecher Pass. Located 15 miles south of Petersburg at the junction of Duncan Canal and Wrangell Narrows. The 740-acre marine park is filled with inlets and reefs.

Joe Mace Island. Located near the community of Point Baker on the northern tip of Prince of Wales Island. Activities at the 62-acre marine park (surrounded by old-growth forest) include boating and fishing.

Security Bay. Located on Kuiu Island, 20 miles southwest of Kake, near the junction of Chatham Strait and Frederick Sound. This is an island-filled bay which offers protected anchorage.

Magoun Islands. This small group of islands 10 miles north of Sitka in Krestof Sound offers protected anchorage for through boaters as well as day use for nearby residents.

Big Bear/Baby Bear. These 2 bays in the middle of Peril Straits offer the only protected anchorage for boaters traveling this waterway. About 25 miles north of Sitka on Baranof Island, this is a well-used anchorage for both recreational and commercial fishing vessels.

Taku Harbor. Located 19 miles south of Juneau. The 700-acre park provides a well-protected anchorage and is a popular weekend boating destination.

Oliver Inlet. Located 12 miles south of Juneau on Admiralty Island between Seymour Canal and Stephens Passage. Good protected moorages are available in both Oliver Inlet and Seymour Canal. Oliver Inlet is one end of an overland portage route for boaters entering Seymour Canal from Juneau, and it provides access to Admiralty Island National Monument. The area has a State Parks Division recreation cabin (see State Park Cabins this section for details), a 1-mile narrow-gauge tramway and a registration/ information station for the monument. Recreational activities include hunting, fishing, boating, kayaking, beachcombing and wildlife viewing and photography. Humpback and killer whales, seals, sea lions, porpoise, salmon, halibut, rock fish, Sitka blacktail deer and brown bear inhabit this area.

Funter Bay. Located 30 miles from Juneau on the west side of Admiralty Island. The park offers one of the best protected anchorages in the area and is popular for hunting and fishing.

Shelter Island. Located 6 miles west of Tee Harbor and approximately 20 miles northwest of downtown Juneau. The park, located on the northcentral portion of the island, offers kayaking, boating, fishing, diving, beachcombing, picnicking, hiking and fall hunting for Sitka blacktail deer.

St. James Bay. Located on the west side of Lynn Canal, 12 miles northwest of Tee Harbor (Juneau) and approximately 42 miles south of Haines. This bay is a recreational destination as well as an overnight stop for boaters traveling between Haines and Juneau. There are many protected beaches and tidal flats. Activities include boating, kayaking, fishing, beachcombing, hiking, camping and picnicking. The Alaska Deptartment of Fish and Game has identified this bay as the best waterfowl habitat and hunting area on Lynn Canal. Black and brown bear and mountain goats are found in the area.

Sullivan Island. Located in Lynn Canal approximately 19 miles south of Haines and 6 miles south of the Chilkat Islands. The park is on a 3-mile-long peninsula at the southern tip of the island. There is protected moorage within the area. Recreational activities include salmon and halibut fishing, picnicking, beachcombing and camping. The area also is popular for deer hunting.

Chilkat Islands. Located 13 miles south of Haines, directly off the tip of the Chilkat

Peninsula, which is part of Chilkat State Park. This 503-acre marine park includes 4 small, forested islands with several reasonably well-protected anchorages. The islands offer excellent kayaking, boating, fishing, beachcombing and camping.

 # Mendenhall Glacier

Mendenhall Glacier is located about 13 miles from downtown Juneau at the end of the Mendenhall Glacier Spur Road. The 12-mile-long glacier heads in the Juneau Icefield and ends in Mendenhall Lake, a 200-foot-deep freshwater reservoir formed in the early part of this century, which continues to enlarge as the glacier retreats. The glacier was named for Thomas Corwin Mendenhall (1841-1924), a former superintendent of the U.S. Coast and Geodetic Survey. It is one of the few road-accessible glaciers in Alaska and one of the most visited sights in the state.

There is a large parking area adjacent Mendenhall Lake. Trails lead down to the edge of the lake (a sign warns visitors to stay back; falling ice can create huge waves). The U.S. Forest Service operates the Mendenhall Glacier Visitor Center. The center features an exhibit area with a model of a glacier and displays on glacial processes, an observatory for viewing the glacier and lake and a 100-seat theatre. Programs and guided hikes with Forest Service interpreters are offered in summer. A 0.5-mile nature trail starts behind the visitor center. Trailheads for 2 longer trails—East Glacier and Nugget Creek—are a short walk from the visitor center. Phone (907) 789-0097 for more information. There is a $3 entrance fee for the visitor center only; no charge for access to the lake, trail and parking lot. The visitor center is open 8 A.M. to 6 P.M. daily in summer, 9 A.M. to 4 P.M. Thursday through Sunday in winter.

 # Mendenhall Wetlands State Game Refuge

This 4,000-acre refuge located along the coastline adjacent to the Juneau road system provides excellent opportunities to view a variety of migrating birds, including geese, ducks, swans, shorebirds and a variety of overwintering birds. The refuge encompasses estuaries created by numerous streams which flow into Gastineau Channel from the surrounding mountains. As the tides ebb and flow, much of the refuge alternately becomes a pasture, then a shallow sea. During the year, the wetlands host about 200 species of birds, 18 species of mammals, over 40 fish species and a variety of other marine life.

Spring bird migrations peak in April and May, and by June, most of the waterfowl and shorebirds have moved on to breeding grounds farther north. Relatively few species of birds nest in the Mendenhall Refuge, but it remains important through the summer as a feeding station. After the breeding season, birds traveling south to wintering grounds stop at the refuge. Shorebirds arrive first, feeding on mollusks and other invertebrates in late July. Waterfowl begin arriving in late August and September, feeding on the seeds of sedges, grasses and other plants. Species of waterfowl and shorebirds found along the edge of the sedge meadow include mallards, pintails, green-winged teals, northern shovelers, American wigeons and several species of sandpipers.

A number of waterfowl species winter in the ice-free marine waters of the refuge. Species include mallards, goldeneyes, scaup, scoters, bufflehead and harlequin ducks.

Beach rye grass, which grows in sandy soils beyond the reach of most high tides, provides shelter for American kestrels, marsh hawks, semipalmated sandpipers, western sandpipers, least sandpipers, arctic terns, short-eared owls and savannah sparrows. A spruce-hemlock forest rims most of the refuge, providing a year-round home for bald eagles, common ravens and northwestern crows, as well as habitat for migratory songbirds, including American robins, hermit thrush, ruby-crowned kinglet and warblers.

In the tidal mudflats and open salt water of the channel, goldeneye, bufflehead, scoters, pigeon guillemots, loons, grebes, scaup, mergansers and marbled murrelet may be found. The most visible waterfowl in the refuge are Vancouver Canada geese, 400 to 600 of which form a resident population that overwinters on open water near the mouth of the

Mendenhall River and some creeks. Other geese found in the refuge include cackling Canada geese, lesser Canada geese, white-fronted geese and snow geese.

Mammals found in the refuge include harbor seals, Sitka blacktail deer, black bears, muskrats, land otter, mink, shorttailed weasels, snowshoe hares, porcupines, little brown bats and long-tailed voles.

Recreational activities allowed in the refuge include hiking, wildlife viewing and photography, boating, fishing and waterfowl hunting in season. Boats are the only motorized vehicles permitted. Visitors walking in the refuge should wear waterproof footwear. Always consult a tide book; much of the land is submerged at high tide.

The refuge is accessible by road from several points along Egan Drive or off Berners Avenue, just west of the airport. A raised dike trail, accessible from the Berners Avenue access point, has been developed as an interpretive trail with educational signs to aid visitors.

For more information: Alaska Department of Fish and Game, Wildlife Division, P.O. Box 240020 (802 3rd St.), Douglas, AK 99824; phone (907) 465-4180, fax (907) 465-2034. Or the Juneau Audubon Society, P.O. Box 021725, Juneau, AK 99802-1725; website: www.juneau.com/audubon/audubon1.htm.

Misty Fiords National Monument

Located at the southern end of the national forest adjacent to the Canadian border on the east and south, extending northward from Dixon Entrance to beyond the Unuk River. Its western boundary is about 22 air miles east of Ketchikan.

Misty Fiords National Monument encompasses 2.3 million acres (of which only 142,757 acres is nonwilderness), making it the largest wilderness in Alaska's national forests and the second largest in the nation. In the nonwilderness portion at Quartz Hill, U.S. Borax and Chemical Corp. has attempted (so far unsuccessfully) to acquire permits to develop and mine a deposit of molybdenum estimated to be one of the largest in the world. Fort Tongass, occupied from 1868 to 1870 as Alaska's first U.S. Army post, was located within this monument.

Taking its name from the almost constant precipitation characteristic of the area, Misty Fiords is covered with thick forests which grow on nearly vertical slopes from sea level to mountaintops. Dramatic waterfalls plunge into the salt water through narrow clefts or course over great rounded granite shoulders, fed by lakes and streams which absorb the annual rainfall of more than 14 feet. The major waterway cutting through the monument, Behm Canal, is more than 100 miles long and extraordinary among natural canals for its length and depth. Active glaciers along the Canadian border are remnants of massive ice sheets that covered the region as recently as 10,000 years ago. Periodic lava flows have occurred for the last several thousand years in an area near the Blue River in the eastern portion of the wilderness. The latest of these flows was in the early 1900s and is an attractive and unusual geologic feature.

Forested areas consist of Sitka spruce, western hemlock and cedar. Some Pacific silver fir, subalpine fir and black cottonwood are found. Beneath these trees grow huckleberry, alder, willow and other brush creating impenetrable thickets.

Few areas of the United States contain as many unusual wildlife species: mountain goats, brown bears, black bears, moose, martens, wolves, wolverines, river otters, sea lions, harbor seals, killer whales and Dail porpoises. A large number of birds, ranging from hummingbirds and trumpeter swans to herons and bald eagles, are found in the area. Misty Fiords is a major producer of coho, sockeye, pink and chum salmon and is especially important for king salmon. Numerous other saltwater and freshwater fish and shellfish also inhabit the area.

This monument offers magnificent scenery. Inlets, bays, arms and coves-some long and narrow, some short and broad-are variations on the fjords for which the area is named. The highlands are dotted with thousands of lakes, large and small, and innumerable streams. The Walker Cove-Rudyerd Bay Scenic Area, with its vertical granite cliffs topped by snowy peaks, has been protected for many years and is now part of the monument.

Activities: A sheltered circle route out of Ketchikan makes this national monument popular with kayakers. Paddling is easy to moderate difficulty. Camping is difficult. Tides of up to 18 feet may be encountered; often the only safe campsite is up among the trees above high tide line. Firewood is plentiful, but usually wet. Forest Service wilderness rangers patrol Misty Fiords by kayak. Two rangers are stationed in the Rudyerd Bay area. A sea kayaking brochure, with paddling and camping information, is available from the Forest Service. Kayak rentals, guided kayak excursions, and drop-off and pickup service for kayakers are available in Ketchikan. Natural hot springs, Bell Island and Bailey Bay, make appealing stops near the scenic fjords.

Accommodations: There are 3 wilderness lodges in or near the monument: Yes Bay Lodge, Salmon Falls Resort and Mink Bay Lodge. The Forest Service maintains 14 cabins in the Misty Fiords area, both on freshwater lakes and on salt water, as well as several saltwater mooring buoys and some 20 miles of trails. (See Tongass National Forest Cabins this section.)

Access: The most comfortable way to visit Misty Fiords is by cabin cruiser or some other sleep-aboard boat. Good moorages can be found; fresh water is plentiful ashore. The monument is also readily accessible by floatplane from Ketchikan or any other Southeast community. Tours are available on charter boats out of Ketchikan. Some large cruise ships include the deep waters of Behm Canal and Rudyerd Bay in their itineraries.

For more information: Southeast Alaska Discovery Center, 50 Main St., Ketchikan, AK 99901; phone (907) 228-6220, fax (907) 228-6234; www.fs.fed.us/r10/ketchikan. Misty Fiords National Monument, 3031 Tongass Ave., Ketchikan, AK 99901-5743; phone (907) 225-2148, fax (907) 225-8738, email r10_ketchikan_alaska_info@fs.fed.us. USGS maps: Prince Rupert, Ketchikan, Bradfield Canal.

Mountaineering

The coastal mountains in the St. Elias Range of Wrangell-St. Elias National Park and Preserve, topped by 18,008-foot Mount St. Elias on the Alaska-Canada border, 67 miles northwest of Yakutat, are among the least-visited mountains of their elevation in North America. According to the Park Service, mountaineering is made especially challenging by a stormy weather pattern including an excess of 100 inches of precipitation a year. Unpredictable storms frequently cause delays in transportation to base camp and often force "hunkering down" for several days or abandoning summit attempts. Many climbs involve as much as 4 weeks of time for a serious attempt. Many mountains in the range are unnamed, and only limited information is available on most routes.

The best time of year for climbing activity is April through June. The most popular peak for expeditions within the park in Southeast is Mount St. Elias, first summited on July 31, 1897, by the Duke of Abruzzi and his party. Many other peaks are equally challenging, and some have never been climbed. There is limited weather data available on the St. Elias range. It can snow any month of the year at higher elevations and as low as 6,000 feet during the summer. The month of May can be more wintry than spring-like. Overcast days and rain are typical in summer, and July and August are characterized by slushy conditions and high avalanche danger. Severe storms and heavy snowfall as early as September may signal the arrival of winter. Most climbing routes are accessed via charter boat or float plane out of Yakutat or Canada. A partial list of air taxi operators offering service in the park is available from the Park Service. Fixed wing aircraft landings are allowed in the park, but helicopter landings and airdrops are prohibited. Wrangell-St. Elias National Park and Preserve does not have a high alititude rescue team. Climbing parties should arrange and plan their own backup. It is recommended that climbers leave a trip itinerary at the ranger station in Yakutat.

All climbing expeditions that enter Kluane National Park, Canada, must secure a permit in advance from the Superintendent, Kluane National Park, P.O. Box 5495, Haines Junction, YT, Canada YB 1 LO; phone (403) 634-7279.

For more information: Contact the Yakutat District Ranger, Wrangell-St. Elias National Park/Preserve, P.O. Box 137, Yakutat, AK 99689 (907) 784-3295. Or the Wrangell-St. Elias, Chief Ranger at park headquarters, P.O. Box 439, Copper Center, AK 99573; phone (907) 822-5234, fax (907) 822-7216. Or visit www.nps.gov/wrst/cabins.htm. Or e-mail wrst_interpretation@nps.gov.

New Eddystone Rock

A spectacular, picturesque landmark located east of Revillgigedo Island in East Behm Canal, 35 miles northeast of Ketchikan and 3 miles north of Winstanley Island. It is within Misty Fiords National Monument. This 234-foot shaft of rock, called a "stack" by geologists, was named in 1793 by Captain George Vancouver of the Royal Navy because of its resemblance to the lighthouse rock off Plymouth, England. A popular subject for photographers, the rock rises from a low, sandy island in the middle of the canal, with deep water surrounding it. It may be passed on either side, keeping at least 1/2-mile away to avoid the sand shoal.

Pack Creek

The Stan Price State Wildlife Sanctuary at the mouth of Pack Creek, on the east side of Admiralty Island within the monument, is an excellent location for viewing and photographing brown bears. Pack Creek flows east 8 miles to Seymour Canal at the mouth of Windfall Harbor, 28 air miles south of Juneau. Visitors may see brown bears fishing for spawning pink, chum and silver salmon. The photography is especially good during the summer and fall salmon runs. The "peak bear-viewing season" is July 5 to August 25. Seymour Canal is also known for its numerous humpback whales. Bald eagles, deer, and gulls also are numerous in the area. Best access is by charter floatplane or boat from Sitka or Juneau. Check locally for guided tours to Pack Creek.

Visitors must obtain a permit from the U.S. Forest Service in Juneau between June 1 and September 10 before departing for Pack Creek. Regulations restrict access to portions of the area, limit visiting time and prohibit possession of food in the area. During peak season, only 24 visitors per day are permitted. Camping is not allowed within the bear viewing area but is allowed on nearby islands. Camping is not recommended on Admiralty Island within 2 miles of Pack Creek. Hunting of brown bears is not allowed.

For more information: Contact the Tongass National Forest, phone (907) 586-8800, fax (907) 586-8808, www.fs.fed.us/r10/chatham/anm or www.fs.fed.us/r10/tongass.

Petersburg Creek-Duncan Salt Chuck Wilderness Area

This 46,777-acre area is located on the northeast portion of Kupreanof Island. The eastern boundary is near the unincorporated community of Kupreanof, directly across Wrangell Narrows from the city of Petersburg. The area continues west through the Petersburg Creek drainage to the salt chuck at the north end of Duncan Canal.

The Petersburg Creek drainage is a typical, U-shaped, glacier-carved valley. Its walls are steep in some areas, with visible rock out-croppings. The valley sides are forested with spruce and hemlock; muskeg bogs are common below.

Wildlife includes black bears, Sitka blacktail deer, wolves, numerous furbearers and a variety of waterfowl. All species of salmon (except kings), Dolly Varden and cutthroat are found in Petersburg Creek and Petersburg Lake and its tributaries.

Recreational activities include hiking, backpacking, kayaking, fishing, wildlife observation and photography, as well as hunting in season. The wilderness area is reached primarily by boat at high tide from Petersburg to Petersburg Creek or to Duncan Canal and Duncan Salt Chuck. Floatplanes can land in Duncan Canal, on the Salt Chuck at high tide, and on Petersburg Lake. Petersburg Lake National Recreation Trail leads from salt water to Petersburg

Lake. The Forest Service maintains 2 cabins in the area, located at Petersburg Lake, and in the vicinity of Duncan Canal and Salt Chuck. (See Cabins in this section.)

For more information: Tongass National Forest, Petersburg Ranger District, P.O. Box 1328, Petersburg, AK 99833; phone (907) 772-3871, fax (907) 772-5995, www.peters burg.org. USGS map: Petersburg.

Pleasant-Lemesurier-Inian Islands Wilderness Area

This 23,154-acre area consists of islands located in Icy Strait between Chichagof Island and Glacier Bay National Park. Pleasant Island is just offshore of the community of Gustavus. The Inian Islands are close to Elfin Cove. This area was designated wilderness in 1990.

Wildlife on Pleasant Island includes Sitka black-tailed deer and black bears. On Lemesurier and Inian islands are deer and brown bears which may have swum from the mainland to the islands. Cliffy areas of the Inian Islands provide opportunities for observing cliff-nesting shore-birds. Sea otters, porpoise, seals, sea lions and whales inhabit the waters of Icy Strait.

There are no facilities within the wilderness area. Guided sea kayaking trips to Pleasant Island are available out of Gustavus. Charter boats may be hired in Elfin Cove for sightsee-ing the Inian Islands. Currents in the Inian Islands area are treacherou,s and boaters should exercise extreme caution and consult with locals before navigating the area.

For more information: Tongass National Forest, Hoonah Ranger District, Resource Officer, P.O. Box 135, Hoonah, AK 99829; phone (907) 945-3631, fax (907) 945-3385. USGS maps: Mount Fairweather, Juneau.

Point Adolphus

A point of land at the north end of Chichagof Island, in Icy Strait, this is the premier place for whale-watching at any time during the summer. It's not uncommon to see humpbacks feeding cooperatively with their unique bubble-net technique. Orcas and minke whales also frequent the rich feeding grounds. Easy paddling along the north shore of Chichagof Island. Paddlers access via Alaska state ferry to Hoonah. Or visitors may charter out of Gustavus.

Point Bridget State Park

Located 38 miles north of Juneau, this 2,850-acre park stretches from Juneau Veterans' Memorial Highway west to Lynn Canal and Berners Bay. The park encompasses meadow-land, open forest, rocky beaches and ocean cliffs. Point Bridget State Park was created in 1988, largely through local efforts to acquire a state park for the state capital.

The major activity in the park is hiking. In summer, be ready for rain and wet ground; carry extra dry clothes. The park is open for skiing and showshoeing in winter.

The main trail is the 3.5-mile-long Point Bridget Trail, which leads from the trailhead at Milepost 39 on the highway (watch for turnout 1 mile north of North Bridget Cove sign) to Point Bridget. The panoramic view of Lynn Canal and the Chilkat Mountains from the point is highly recommended. Hiking time is 7 hours round-trip. Meadowlands along the trail sup-port wildflowers (mid- and late May through June) and a variety of birdlife. The rocky beach-es at Point Bridget offer prime viewing of sea lions and humpback whales (April through September). In the spring, thousands of white-winged and surf scoters feed on blue mussels in Lynn Canal. Tidepooling is possible with minus 1-foot tides (check local tide tables).

At Upper Cowee Meadow, 1/2 mile from the trailhead, watch for black bear feeding in the meadows or fishing in Cowee Creek. Also, please respect private property boundaries of Echo Bible Camp to the northeast across Cowee Creek.

The Point Bridget Trail junctions with the Cedar Lake Trail approximately 2.5 miles from the Glacier Highway trailhead. Cedar Lake Trail begins about 500 feet east of Echoeing Creek just above the Intertidal Meadow and leads 2.1 miles southwest to Camping Cove on

Lynn Canal. Cedar Lake itself lies at about 400 feet elevation, 1.5 miles from Camping Cove. From the Camping Cove trailhead, a popular picnic site for hikers and boaters, it is 1.5 miles to Akiyatna Bight to the east, and 1 mile out Trappers Trail to the west. Trappers Trail goes up and down along the outer coast; it is difficult to get to the water along much of this trail. From Akiyama Bight, the McMurchie Cat Road leads 1.2 miles north to Upper Cowee Meadow on the Point Bridget Trail. The Raleigh Trailhead at Milepost 38.6 on Juneau Veterans' Memorial Highway connects with the McMurchie Cat Road (1/2 mile). The North Bridget Cove beach access trail, just before Milepost 38 on Juneau Veterans' Memorial Highway, is a Juneau City/Borough trail that leads to Akiyama Bight.

There are no established campgrounds in the park, but wilderness camping is allowed. There are 2 public-use cabins; see Cabins this section for details on cost and reservations.

For more information: Alaska Division of Parks and Outdoor Recreation, 400 Willoughby Ave., Juneau, AK 99801; phone (907) 465-4563, fax (907) 465-5330. USGS map: Juneau C-3.

 River Running

Following area several Southeast rivers suitable for floating. See also descriptions of 2 major destinations for river ruuners in Southeast Alaska: the Stikine River and Alsek-Tatshenshini (known to river runners as "the Tat") Wilderness Park in this section.

Chickamin-LeDuc-South Fork Rivers. This river system, which offers excellent scenery and river running, is located 45 miles northeast of Ketchikan within Misty Fiords National Monument. The Chickamin River heads at Chickamin Glacier and flows southwest 40 miles to Behm Canal. The LeDuc heads at a glacier in British Columbia and flows southwest 30 miles to the Chickamin. The South Fork Chickamin River heads at a glacier and flows west 18 miles to the Chickamin. Since these rivers are fed by alpine glaciers, they are silty. Boaters should be alert for sweepers, logs and high water. Brown bears inhabit this drainage. Fish include rainbow trout and several species of salmon. Access is by riverboat, floatplane or helicopter from Ketchikan.

Chilkat-Klehini-Tsirku Rivers. The 42-mile-long Klehini and the 25-mile-long Tsirku are tributaries to the Chilkat River, which enters salt water near Haines. These are swift rivers, but have no white water. The Chilkat and Tsirku rivers flow through the Chilkat Bald Eagle Preserve. Many Haines residents use airboats on the rivers in summer. Rafts are recommended. The trip down the Klehini-Chilkat takes 4 to 6 hours. The trip down the Tsirku-Chilkat takes 1 to 2 days, allowing time to explore glaciers. Rafts are recommended.

Access to the Chilkat River is by car to Milepost 19 from Haines on the Haines Highway. Access to the Klehini River is by car to Milepost 26 on the Haines Highway. Access to the lower Tsirku is from a turnoff at Milepost 25 on the Haines Highway. Access to the Tsirku headwaters is by plane to LeBlondeau Glacier.

Taku River. This river heads in Canada and flows southwest 54 miles into Taku Inlet, 20 miles northeast of Juneau. This silty river is rated moderately difficult for riverrunning. Usable in summer. Rafts and canoes used most often. Access is by boat or small plane from Juneau. Most float trips start at Canoe Corner in Canada.

Floaters should be alert for numerous jet and motorboats and numerous sweepers. This river offers excellent wildlife viewing, fishing, hunting and climbing areas.

Unuk River. This silty river heads in Canada on the east side of Mount Stoeckl and flows southwest 28 miles to the head of Burroughs Bay, 50 miles northeast of Ketchikan. The river is located within Misty Fiords National Monument. It can be floated in 1 to 2 days. Many old mining claims line the river and its small tributaries.

Access is by riverboat upriver or by floatplane to Border Lake in Canada or to other points on the river itself. One turn about one-third of the way down the river from the Canadian border may need to be portaged. The Unuk becomes braided near its outlet. Floaters should be alert for sweepers and logs. Huge and numerous brown bears inhabit this area. Fish in the river include rainbow, cutthroat and steelhead trout and pink, king, silver and chum salmon.

Russell Fiord Wilderness Area

Located 25 miles northeast of Yakutat between the rugged Saint Elias Range and the Brabazon Range. The most dramatic features of this 348,701-acre area are the heavily glaciated Russell Fiord, which extends more than 30 miles inland from Disenchantment Bay, and Nunatak Fiord, a narrow, 15-mile channel off Russell Fiord to the east. Situk Lake and the headwaters of the Situk River are within the wilderness area.

Also located within Russell Fiord Wilderness Area is Hubbard Glacier, which heads in an icefield in Canada and trends some 80 miles to tidewater, about 34 miles northeast of Yakutat. Hubbard Glacier is tucked into the corner of the Alaska coastline as it curves around the Gulf of Alaska between the panhandle and the main body of Alaska. In recent years, Hubbard Glacier has become a popular port of call with cruise ships crossing the Gulf of Alaska. Framed by snow-covered mountains, Hubbard Glacier rolls toward the sea like a breaking wave. The glacier made headlines in June 1986, when it surged, damming Russell Fiord. The ice dam eventually weakened and broke, but scientists predict the glacier will close off the fjord again.

Vegetation in the wilderness area ranges from heavily forested river channels to alpine meadows. Wildlife includes mountain goats, wolves, moose, numerous furbearers, harbor seals, sea lions, shorebirds, songbirds, waterfowl, bald eagles and brown, black and glacier bears. Fisheries are fairly limited, with the exception of lower Russell Fiord and the head-waters of the Ahrnklin River.

Access: By floatplane from Juneau, 200 miles to the southeast, or by plane or boat from Yakutat, which has overnight accommodations and scheduled commercial jet air service. There is also logging road access from Yakutat to a 3/4-mile portage to the head of Russell Fiord.

Activities: Sea kayakers fly into Yakutat, then paddle up Yakutat Bay to Disenchantment Bay and enter Russell Fiord at the neck of the fiord (a long paddle; inquire about hazardous sections). Guided sea kayaking trips of Russell Fiord are available.

Accommodations: There is 1 Forest Service cabin within the wilderness area at Situk Lake. A second cabin is located just outside the park boundary at Harlequin Lake. (See Tongass National Forest Cabins this section.)

For more information: Contact Tongass National Forest, Box 327, Yakutat, AK 99689; phone (907) 784-3359. USGS maps: Yakutat, Mount St. Elias.

Sea Kayaking

The hundreds of miles of sheltered waterways in Southeast are ideal for sea kayaking. There are endless choices of routes for paddling, but the favorite put-in places described here are: Gastineau Channel, Outer Chichagof Island, Point Adolphus, Seymour Canal, Sitka Sound and Yakutat Bay. Other popular sea kayaking destinations in Southeast include Glacier Bay, Misty Fiords, Point Adolphus, Russell Fjord, Tebenkof Bay and Kuiu Island, Tracy Arm and Fords Terror (see individual descriptions this section).

Visitors seldom paddle in Southeast without seeing whales, porpoises, eagles and ravens. The distinctive beauty, solitude, rich wildlife and breathtaking scenery compensate for the wet, rainy weather is characteristic of the area. The kayak's covered deck makes it the pad-dlecraft of choice here.

Boats can be carried aboard ferries of the Alaska State Ferry System which serves Southeast's communities. Tour operators offer drop-off services for kayakers, and charter boats are also available for drop-offs and pickups. Flying into remote spots by charter air-craft is suitable for paddlers with folding boats only.

Hypothermia is the resident hazard to be reckoned with, more of a threat than the local bears. Water temperatures in the 40s quickly sap the energy of anyone who goes for a swim.

It's important to have a quick, reliable self-rescue system and an extra set of dry clothes that may be necessary for comfort and survival here. Stormy weather and the area's remoteness demand that kayakers be skilled, well-equipped and prepared to wait out hazardous conditions.

Gastineau Channel. Day-tripping sea kayakers enjoy paddling the northern portion of this channel from Auke Bay to downtown Juneau, with glaciers and mountains as a backdrop to the Mendenhall Wetlands State Game Refuge and the busy harbor scene. (The 19-mile-long water passage extends from Auke Bay south to Stephens Passage.) Kayak rentals and drop-off service are available locally. State ferries dock at Auke Bay, so if you have brought your own kayak, you can put in at the terminal and head down the channel for town. Remember that much of the shallow channel goes dry at low tide; it's easy to find yourself high-and-dry and red-faced. North of Auke Bay, you'll find a series of beautiful coves, popular with local kayakers for day trips and weekend outings. Berner's Bay, 34 miles northwest of Juneau on the east shore of Lynn Canal, is the northernmost of these coves. Easy paddling. Juneau is accessible by air and via the Alaska State Ferry.

Outer Chichagof Island. Spectacular sunsets, beaches open to the ocean swells and protected paddling in beautiful coves make this one of Southeast's great places for kayaking. At White Sulphur Springs, you'll find a natural hot spring (attractively roofed by the Forest Service) where you can soak as the sun sinks into the open Pacific. Kayak rentals are available in Sitka. This trip is not for novices, as exposed stretches of water can challenge the best. Access via Alaska Airlines, smaller air services and Alaska State Ferry to Sitka; via smaller air services and Alaska state ferry (twice monthly in summer) to Pelican. (See also Hot Springs and West Chichagof-Yakobi Wilderness Area this section.)

Seymour Canal. An estuary on the east coast of Admiralty Island, this 40-mile-long canal offers fishing and wildlife viewing within Admiralty Island National Monument. The north end of the canal is a day's paddle south of Juneau via Oliver Inlet and a manually operated tram that makes for an easy portage of less than a mile. Easy paddling except for one exposed crossing between Juneau and Oliver Inlet. Drop-off and pickup service available in Juneau. (See also Admiralty Island National Monument this section.)

Sitka Sound. A beautiful scattering of islands and semi-protected water draws daytrippers and overnighters from Sitka. Goddard Hot Springs to the south is a popular destination, as is Brent's Beach on the sound's western shore. Other attractions include beachcombing and a bird refuge (San Lazario Island). Kayak rentals are available in Sitka. Easy to moderate difficulty, depending on wind and ocean swells. Access via Alaska Airlines, smaller air services and Alaska State Ferry to Sitka.

Yakutat Bay. Wildlife abounds in this beautiful bay ringed with islands. Yakutat Bay is 18 miles across, extending southwest from Disenchantment Bay to the Gulf of Alaska, southeast of Malaspina Glacier. It is one of the few refuges for vessels along this stretch of coast. At its upper reaches, it accesses Russell Fiord and Nunatak Fiord. The community of Yakutat is situated on Monti Bay on the southeast shore of Yakutat Bay. Yakutat Bay offers easy to moderate difficulty. Access via Alaska Airlines and smaller air carriers.

South Baranof Wilderness Area

This 319,568-acre wilderness is located on the southern portion of Baranof Island, bounded by the open Gulf of Alaska on the west and Chatham Strait on the east. It is 50 miles south of Sitka and 20 miles north of Port Alexander.

High mountains rise sharply from sea level to more than 4,000 feet in less than 2 miles from the beach. Much of the higher areas have permanent ice fields and numerous active glaciers. Many valleys are U-shaped, carved by recent glacial activity with amphitheater-like cirques at their sources, hanging valleys along their walls and dramatic waterfalls. Most of the valleys empty into long, deep fjords. Rainfall in portions of this area is among the highest in Southeast; recording up to 200 inches a year at Little Port Walter, just south of the wilderness. Storms from September through December can generate winds exceeding 100 mph.

Wildlife in the area includes Sitka blacktailed deer, brown bears, hair seals, mink, marten, land otters, bald eagles and a variety of other birds. There are major steelhead-producing lakes and streams in this wilderness; other fish available include coho, red, pink and chum salmon, cutthroat and rainbow trout and Dolly Varden. Marine species include Dungeness and tanner crab, shrimp, herring and halibut.

Recreational activities include boating, kayaking, fishing and hunting. Access is primarily by floatplane or boat from Sitka, which has commercial air service and is on the Alaska Marine Highway System route. Many sheltered bays and fjords provide safe anchorage and sheltered floatplane landings. The Forest Service maintains 3 cabins, located at Avoss, Davidof and Plotnikof lakes. (See Tongass National Forest Cabins in this section.)

For more information: Tongass National Forest, 201 Katlian Street, Suite 109, Sitka, AK 99835; phone (907) 747-4220. USGS map: Port Alexander.

 ## South Etolin Island Wilderness Area

Located about midway between Ketchikan and Wrangell, and about 15 miles north of Thorne Bay, this wilderness area comprises 83,642 acres on the south end of Etolin Island.

Elk were introduced on the island in 1987, prior to its designation as wilderness. The state traded 15 mountain goats for 33 Roosevelt elk from Oregon, then obtained 17 Rocky Mountain elk in exchange for some river otters. Other wildlife includes wolves, black bears, brown bears, Sitka blacktail deer and bald eagles.

The multitude of small islands and passages provide numerous anchorages for recreational activities and opportunities for small-boat travel. The area has also been studied for potential mariculture activity sites, but mariculture is not currently allowed in designated wilderness. Wrangell residents use this area for subsistence harvests.

For more information: Tongass National Forest, Wrangell Ranger District, P.O. Box 51, Wrangell, AK 99929; phone (907) 874-2323, fax (907) 874-7595. USGS map: Craig.

 ## South Prince of Wales Wilderness Area

This 90,996-acre wilderness is located at the southern tip of Prince of Wales Island, about 40 miles southwest of Ketchikan and approximately 15 miles south of Hydaburg. The area fronts on Dixon Entrance and on Cordova Bay, extending north to take in all of Klakas Inlet.

One of the first Haida villages in southeastern Alaska, Klinkwan, is within the South Prince of Wales Wilderness. This historic village site was established in the 19th century and abandoned in 1911.

The coast of Prince of Wales Island is deeply indented with numerous bays and inlets. The Barrier Islands, a collection of more than 75 islets ranging in size from a few acres up to 500 acres, jut out into Cordova Bay. They are exposed to fierce ocean storms, and their trees are stunted and sculpted by the wind. Topography on Prince of Wales Island ranges from lowlands containing many streams, lakes and wetlands to the sheer, 2,000-foot rock walls of Klakas Inlet, which extends 12 miles inland from Cordova Bay.

Precipitation usually exceeds 100 inches per year, and vegetation includes dense stands of large, old-growth Sitka spruce, western hemlock, Alaska cedar and western red cedar, as well as numerous shrubs, wildflowers and grasses.

Wildlife includes black bears, wolves, Sitka black-tailed deer, small furbearers, land and shorebirds and bald eagles. This is one of the better sea otter habitats in southeastern Alaska. Many species of waterfowl migrate along the coastline. Coho, red, pink and chum salmon, cutthroat, rainbow trout and Dolly Varden trout inhabit waters of this area. Dungeness and tanner crab, shrimp, herring, halibut, abalone, giant barnacles, clams, mussels, octopus, sea urchins, sea anemones and starfish are also present in this wilderness area.

Access to this area is by floatplane or boat. Small boats can negotiate the area during the summer; however, Dixon Entrance is exposed to the ocean and can be extremely stormy and rough during other seasons. There are no facilities in this wilderness area.

For more information: Tongass National Forest, Craig Ranger District, P.O. Box 500, Craig, AK 99921; phone (907) 826-3271, fax (907) 826-2972. USGS maps: Dixon Entrance, Craig.

❊ Stikine Icefield

Naturalist-explorer John Muir ventured up one of the glaciers of the Stikine Icefield in 1879 and wrote with awe about what he saw. Adventurers today ski, climb and hike this icy wilderness, braving crevasses, avalanches, rock slides and the notoriously harsh weather.

The Stikine Icefield lies in Southeast's Coast Range along the British Columbia border. It covers 2,900 square miles and encompasses at least 4 peaks reaching higher than 10,000 feet; this is quite spectacular with sea level being only a few miles away. Much of the ice field lies within the Stikine-LeConte Wilderness. Mountain climbers are attracted by the 9,077-foot Devil's Thumb, and glacier ski touring and hiking parties are drawn by the area's spectacular scenery.

The weather does its best to keep human intrusions to a minimum. Wet and windy, it can pin parties in their tents for days. The unprepared or inexperienced had best stay home.

Petersburg or Wrangell serve as staging areas for ice field trips. Generally, Wrangell is used to enter the ice field via the Stikine River drainage. Petersburg is the better choice for access via the Thomas Bay drainages. If you plan to hire a helicopter, you'll have to be dropped off outside the wilderness boundaries, for no helicopters are allowed to operate within, except under emergency circumstances.

Good cross-country skiing opportunities abound for either day touring or extended excursions into the heart of the ice field. The most popular practice for day skiers is to wait for good weather then helicopter onto the Horn Mountain-Thunder Mountain ridgeline. A variety of terrain for touring and telemarking awaits skiers there. Day touring season lasts from January into June. Even on short outings, the party should carry safety and survival equipment in case the weather makes a return pickup impossible.

Extended ski touring is best between April and late June. Dozens of sites are suitable for base camps. Waxless skis best suit the variable snow conditions. Absolute necessities include very good rain gear and a completely waterproof, domed tent. Pack out everything you pack in, and bring plenty of extra food in case you get weathered in for several days.

❊ 🛖 Stikine River

The Stikine has headwaters in British Columbia and flows 400 miles through 2 Provincial parks and the Coast Range to salt water near Wrangell. The lower 130 miles of the river, from Telegraph Creek, BC, to Alaska tidewater, are used by many canoeists, motorboaters, kayakers and rafters. A 60-mile section above Telegraph Creek flows through the Grand Canyon of the Stikine and is considered unnavigable and dangerous.

The Stikine is multi-channeled in the lower reaches and is heavily laden with silt throughout. Glaciers cover the mountains along the route and descend down to river level in some points along the side channels. Fish available in the Stikine include several species of trout and salmon.

The river's name is derived from a Tlingit name meaning "Great River." For centuries, the river has been a highway for the coastal Natives to travel inland to fish or trade. Stern-wheel steamers ferried gold seekers to and from Alaska and Canada until 1916 along this route. Only one town, Telegraph Creek, is found along the entire river.

Access is from Wrangell, Petersburg or Telegraph Creek. Boaters can drive to Telegraph Creek via the all-weather Cassiar Highway, then the 75-mile Telegraph Creek Road. (The latter is not designed for large vehicles, has many hairpin turns and steep slopes, but offers spectacular scenery.) Other boaters use air charter services from Wrangell, Petersburg or Telegraph Creek for transportation to upstream put-in sites. Charter boats and aircraft from Wrangell also deliver some river runners. The river can also be accessed from Petersburg (Mile 35.5 of the Mitkof Highway) or from the Wrangell waterfront. Many rafters arrange for pickup from the Stikine flats by boat or plane.

The water level can change considerably in the Stikine, varying from 10 to 25 feet. During rainfall events, the river can rise several feet in 1 day, so camping areas should be planned carefully. The river is runnable from May through October. Usually, snow is off the ground by mid-May. The mosquitoes do not usually become bothersome until mid-June.

From Telegraph Creek, the river can be floated or paddled in four days. However, a trip of 7 to 10 days will allow river enthusiasts time to explore the sloughs, many of which lead to glaciers or fine fishing areas, and to soak in Chief Shakes Hot Springs. Several Forest Service cabins along the river are available on a reservation basis (see Cabins in this section). No public-use cabins are located on the Canadian side.

Although the river flow is swift at various points, it is considered easy Class I or II. The Stikine drops 8 feet per mile. Boaters should, however, be alert for logjams along some of the side routes and sweepers and floating logs throughout. The water is extremely cold. Black and brown bears are common along the river. Deer, moose, wolves, beavers, mountain goats and bald eagles may also be seen.

The U.S. Forest Service has a $4 booklet, *Stikine River Canoe–Kayak Trails*, which shows the main and secondary river routes in the lower river where it divides into numerous channels. It shows tent spots, logjams and which routes are best at the varying water stages. The guide shows 3 routes for canoers and kayakers who wish to go upstream following eddies, tides and side sloughs to the Canadian border, about 35 miles from tidewater. But the guide also points out that lining will be necessary (for those going upriver) in several places where the water is too shallow or too swift. The booklet is available from the Forest Service in Wrangell, P.O. Box 51, Wrangell, AK 99929 or Petersburg, P.O. Box 1328, Petersburg, AK 99833. The British Columbia Ministry of Forests also has a map of the Stikine River for $2.95 +tax (Canadian). The map is titled Lower Stikine River Recreation Map and covers Telegraph Creek to the U.S.-Canada border. The map is available from Canadian Cartographics Limited, 576 Clipper St. Coquilam, B.C. Canada, by email at canmap@canmap.com, or at www.canmap.com.

Stikine-LeConte Wilderness Area

Located on the mainland of southeastern Alaska, 6 miles east of Petersburg and 7 miles north of Wrangell, this wilderness area extends from Frederick Sound on the west to the Alaska-Canada border on the east.

The most prominent feature of this 448,841-acre wilderness area is the powerful Stikine River. The river valley is narrow, surrounded by steep, rugged peaks, many of them glaciated. The river is heavily laden with silt from numerous glaciers. The delta at the mouth of the river is 17 miles wide, formed from numerous, slow-moving, braided channels (3 of which are navigable). One hot and 2 warm springs are found along the river. The vicinity of LeConte Glacier—southernmost glacier in North America to empty directly into salt water—is mountainous, with numerous ice fields that extend into Canada. Alpine vegetation, including mosses, lichens and other small plants, grows above 2,000 feet. The lower slopes near salt water support typical Southeast spruce-hemlock rain forest. In the east, rainfall decreases, and cottonwoods appear.

This is an important fish and wildlife area. Moose, mountain goats, brown and black bears, Sitka black-tailed deer and wolves inhabit the area. The delta of the Stikine is a major resting area for migratory birds. The lower Stikine has the second largest seasonal concentration of bald eagles in southeastern Alaska when the birds gather to feed on hooligan (also called eulachon or smelt) runs in April. Several varieties of salmon, including kings, are found in the area.

Recreational activities include fishing and hunting in season, as well as power boat, kayak, canoe and raft trips down the Stikine. Thick brush along the river makes hiking difficult. Access is primarily by small boat from Wrangell. Charter boat tours to the Stikine River and LeConte Bay are available from Wrangell and Petersburg. Air taxis in both communities also offer flight-seeing trips. There is limited access to the wilderness by floatplane. There are no commercial lodges. The Forest Service maintains a number of cabins in the area and 2 bathhouses at Chief Shakes Hot Springs. (See Tongass National Forest Cabins and Hot Springs this section.)

For more information: Tongass National Forest, Wrangell Ranger District, P.O. Box 51, Wrangell, AK 99929; phone (907) 874-2323, fax (907) 874-7595. USGS maps: Petersburg, Bradfield Canal, Sumdum.

Tatshenshini-Alsek Wilderness Park

Created in 1993, this park protects the magnificent Tatshenshini and Alsek rivers area in Canada. These 2 spectacular rivers join together in Canada and flow (as the Alsek) to the Gulf of Alaska at Dry Bay, about 50 miles east of Yakutat and 110 miles northwest of Gustavus. The Tatshenshini is famous for its whitewater rafting, stunning scenery and wildlife. Part of the river flows through Glacier Bay National Park and is under the jurisdiction of the National Park Service. Due to a dramatic increase in river traffic in recent years, permits are required from the park agencies. Check with the National Park Service, B.C. Parks or Parks Canada for details on permits for commercially guided trips and private tour groups.

Portions of the upper Alsek are considered dangerous, even for seasoned river runners. The entire Alsek River has been traveled by only a few parties. There is a 10-mile portage of Tweedsmuir Glacier, which crosses the river, approximately 140 miles downstream from the access point on the Dezedeash River near Haines junction, YT. The entire Alsek River is 230 miles in length.

The section above Tweedsmuir Glacier is difficult, Class IV white water, with high water volume and velocity. High winds and brown bears are other hazards. After the long, diffi-cult portage, the river still demands respect but becomes broader and moves more slowly. This trip is a major undertaking not to be embarked upon lightly.

The Tatshenshini is floated each year by numerous raft and kayak parties, including many commercial groups. The best months are July and August. Access to the Tatshenshini is at the abandoned Dalton Post (turnoff at Milepost 104.2 from Haines on the Haines Highway), which once served as a way point on the famed Dalton Trail. Those running the river should have advanced to expert river skills and also be well- versed in wilderness and survival skills, as the distances from the nearest communities are considerable. For pickup, arrangements should be made in advance with charter plane operators from Yakutat, Gustavus, Juneau or Whitehorse since communication from Dry Bay is limited.

The Tatshenshini route winds through 120 miles of rugged wilderness, judged by many to be some of the best in the area. (This wilderness is 70% Canadian.) The trip can take 11 to 12 days. Allow time for exploring the river-level glaciers and pristine country. Use cau-tion as this is bear country.

Below Dalton Cache, there are several rapids rated Class III and IV. From there to near the confluence with the Alsek, the Tatshenshini winds through numerous valleys where high winds can sometimes stall boat movement. There are some Class IV rapids in the lower reaches. In the lower river, standing waves of 4 to 12 feet may be encountered. *CAUTION: At Gateway Knob, boaters should scout downriver for icebergs floating at the entrance of Alsek Lake.* The Tatshenshini joins the Alsek below Tweedsmuir Glacier. This area is used by many river runners in the summer, and campers should be courteous. Leave campsites in their primitive state. Camping regulations are explained in the information package that is mailed with the permit. Contact Glacier Bay National Park Service for permits.

For more information: Contact BC Parks, Tatshenshini Office, Box 5544, Haines Junction, YT Y0B 1L0; phone (867) 634-7043, fax (867) 634-7208.

Tebenkof Bay and Kuiu Wilderness Areas

Both of these wilderness areas are located on Kuiu (pronounced CUE-you) Island, 50 miles southwest of Petersburg and 35 miles south of Kake. Tebenkof Bay Wilderness Area includes 66,839 acres on the west side of Kuiu Island. Kuiu Wilderness Area, designated in 1990, spans from Kuiu south of Tebenkof Bay.

This expansive and complex system of bays includes many small islands, islets and coves. Kayaking is excellent in the protected waters of Tebenkof Bay. The area has spruce-hemlock forest up to about the 2,000-foot elevation, where alpine plants take over. There is some muskeg and many small lakes and creeks.

Wildlife on the island includes small furbearers, wolves and black bears, 1.2 per square mile according to the Alaska Department of Fish Game. (That estimate is based on the results of a hunter survey and tetracycline baiting program sponsored by the ADF&G.) Marine mammals are abundant. The area is on the migration route of many waterfowl. Trumpeter swans and bald eagles also nest here. The area is rich in fish and shellfish, including coho, red, pink and chum salmon, rainbow and steelhead trout, Dolly Varden, Dungeness and tanner crab, shrimp and halibut. The remains of Tlingit villages and camps as well as fur farms may also be seen.

Recreational activities include kayaking and exploring the many streams, bays and coves. Access is by boat or floatplane from Petersburg or Wrangell. Many coves provide good anchorage. Chatham Strait can be hazardous at times because of swells and strong winds from the Pacific Ocean. There are 3 kayak portage trails (descriptions follow) which provide access to Tebenkof Bay Wilderness Area. The trailheads, marked by large, red and white portage diamonds, are reached by water from the town of Kake, a ferry stop on the Alaska Marine Highway System. Portage trails are marked with blue diamond markers. Canoers and kayakers are advised to pay attention to changing weather and water conditions for their safety.

Affleck Canal Portage Trail. (In wilderness) Trail begins on the beach at the north end of Affleck Canal and extends 1.5 miles to the beach at Petrof Bay. Usable June to September. Rated difficult due to blown down trees along trail. Elevation gain 50 feet. Estimated time across 3 hours. Trail offers spectacular views and access to beachcombing. Shore and land birds, wolves and black bear may be seen. Bears are especially common in summer along the creek that parallels the trail as they feed on spawning salmon. Make plenty of noise to avoid an encounter with a bear, and hang food in a tree at night. USGS map: Port Alexander B-1.

Bay of Pillars Portage Trail. (Outside wilderness) Trail begins on the beach at the east end of Bay of Pillars on Kuiu Island and extends 1 3/4 miles to the beach at Port Camden. Usable May to September. Rated moderate. Elevation gain 100 feet. Estimated time across 1 1/2 hours. During the summer, black bears will be on or near the portage trail; make plenty of noise to let them know you're coming. Always hang food in a tree at night. USGS map: Port Alexander C-1.

Threemile Arm Portage Trail. (Outside wilderness) Trail begins on the beach at the northwest end of Threemile Arm on Kuiu Island and extends 2 miles to the beach at the southeast end of Port Camden. Usable June to September. Rated difficult; elevation gain 100 feet. Estimated time across 4 hours. This trail follows a creek for the first 1,500 feet; the portager can put in and paddle the deeper sections and line the shallower areas. A beaver pond can also be paddled for about 1,300 feet. Much of the portage is over road. This trail offers spectacular views and fishing. During the summer, there are plenty of black bears on or near the trail; make noise to let them know you are there. Always hang food in a tree at night. USGS map: Petersburg C-6.

For more information: Tongass National Forest, Stikine Area, P.O. Box 309, Petersburg, AK 99833; phone (907) 772-3841. USGS maps: Port Alexander.

▲ Tongass National Forest

This national forest encompasses 16.9 million acres, more than 73 percent of the land in southeastern Alaska. Created in 1907 by President Theodore Roosevelt to protect the timber resources, wildlife and fisheries of Southeast, this is the largest national forest in the United States. Its name comes from the Tongass clan of Tlingit Indians, who lived on an island at the southern end of the forest.

The forest lies west of the U.S.-Canada border and stretches from Ketchikan north to Cross Sound and up the eastern side of Lynn Canal. Excluded from the forest are Glacier Bay National Park and the general area around Haines and Skagway. Another section of the forest surrounds Yakutat. Like all national forests, this is managed as a working forest, with logging and mining activities taking place along with recreational pursuits and fishery management.

Tree line usually extends from sea level to about 3,000 feet in the southern part of the forest and to 1,800 feet farther north around Icy Strait. In the south, the forests are primarily western hemlock and Sitka spruce, with scattered red cedar and Alaska yellow cedar. In the north, the percentage of spruce increases, and mountain hemlock becomes more abundant. Red cedar extends only to the northern shore of Frederick Sound, and Alaska yellow cedar is often found as a small tree in swamps or muskeg. Other common species are red alder, black cottonwood and lodgepole pine.

Beneath the towering conifers are young evergreens and shrubs such as devil's club, blueberry and huckleberry. Moss and ferns cover the ground, and lichens drape many trees. The dense forest is broken by muskeg bogs, glacial outwash plains and marshlands in river valleys and deltas. Wildflowers splash color against a variegated green background.

Timber harvest has taken place in this region since before the Tongass National Forest was established. All but a small percentage has occurred since 1950. Out of the 16.9 million acres encompassed by the national forest, about 5 million acres have been identified as commercial forest, with about 2 million acres of that considered available for harvesting. Another 5.6 million acres has been set aside as wilderness in 2 national monuments and 17 designated wilderness areas, most of which are remote and accessible only by boat or aircraft.

Wilderness areas within Tongass National Forest were established by President Jimmy Carter on Dec. 2, 1980, under the Alaska National Interest Lands Conservation Act, which set aside nearly 103 million acres throughout the state as national parks, wildlife refuges, wilderness areas, wild and scenic rivers and other conservation areas. Additional wilderness was added in 1990 by the Tongass Timber Reform Act.

Wilderness classification directs that these areas be managed to retain their natural qualities, unmarked by man. However, there are some exceptions because of Alaska's terrain: Motorized vehicles such as airplanes, boats and snow machines may be used for access to and within some of the wilderness areas. Also, because of the climate, existing shelter cabins were allowed to remain, and others may be built for public safety. Fishing, hunting and trapping are allowed, subject to state regulations. Check with the local Forest Service office for the most up-to-date regulations.

The 19 wilderness areas within the Tongass National Forest, from south to north, are: South Prince of Wales Wilderness Area; Misty Fiords National Monument; Karta River Wilderness Area; South Etolin Island Wilderness Area; Coronation Island, Warren Island and Maurelle Islands Wilderness Areas; Tebenkof Bay and Kuiu Wilderness Areas; Stikine-LeConte Wilderness Area; Petersburg Creek-Duncan Salt Chuck Wilderness Area; South Baranof Wilderness Area; Chuck River Wilderness Area; Tracy Arm–Fords Terror Wilderness Area; Admiralty Island National Monument (Kootznoowoo Wilderness Area); Pleasant-Lemesurier-Inian Islands Wilderness Area; West ChichagofYakobi Wilderness Area; Endicott River Wilderness Area; and Russell Fiord Wilderness Area. See descriptions of each in this section.

Wildlife: Sitka blacktail deer and its 2 main predators, the wolf and the bear, are found in the forest. Wolves and black bears range throughout the mainland and most islands, except Baranof, Chichagof and Admiralty. These 3 islands, plus the mainland, are home to enormous brown/grizzly bears. The blue, or glacier, bear (a color phase of the black bear) is seen occasionally near Yakutat and in the coastal mountain range as far south as Juneau. It is legal to carry firearms in the national forest for bear protection; rifles with a caliber larger than .30-06 are recommended.

Mountain goats have been transplanted to Baranof and Revillagigedo islands, but their natural range is the alpine area of the mainland. Some moose inhabit the larger river drainages and the Yakutat area. A limited number of lynx, wolverines, foxes, mink and land otters range widely through the area. The forest is also home for smaller mammals, including shrews, red squirrels, brown bats, flying squirrels, deer mice, red-backed voles, porcupines and pine marten.

Blue grouse, great horned owls, woodpeckers, Steller's jays and thrushes are some of the common birds in the forests. Robins, fox sparrows, hummingbirds and swallows can be seen along the forest edge. More bald eagles live in this region than in any other place in the world. Large numbers of waterfowl, such as diving ducks, mallards, mergansers and Canada geese, and more than 50 species of seabirds, including terns, gulls, kittiwakes, auklets and murres can be seen here.

Marine mammals found along the shores of the forest include Dall and harbor porpoises, hair seals and humpback, minke, sei and Pacific killer whales. Gray whales and northern fur seals pass by during migrations, and an occasional elephant seal has been spotted. Sea otters have been successfully reintroduced and are expanding their range in western Southeast Alaska. Waters of the region teem with fish, including halibut and 5 species of salmon. Also present are Dungeness, tanner and king crab, shrimp and butter clams.

Activities: Tongass National Forest has almost 600 miles of hiking trails, dozens of campgrounds, more than 150 public-use cabins and thousands of acres of wilderness areas known for their recreational opportunities: hunting (check state regulations), fishing, sea kayaking and wildlife viewing, to name just a few. See descriptions of Fishing, Hiking Trails and Cabins this section. See also individual descriptions of Tongass National Forest wilderness areas in this section. Tongass National Forest also operates the visitor center at Mendenhall Glacier near Juneau.

Gathering forest resources is also a recreational activity. Opportunities for obtaining berries, firewood, Christmas trees, and other forest resources are found throughout Tongass National Forest. You should know edible plants well before picking. There are at least 2 poisonous plants in Southeast (baneberry and poison hemlock), and visitors gather wild plants at their own risk. Permits are not required for Forest Service managed lands, but visitors should exercise discretion in gathering plants. Fragile alpine and meadow areas may harbor rare and possibly endangered species. A general rule of thumb is to leave 6 plants for every 1 plant picked, and pick plants 100 feet or more from all roadways or trails.

The local Forest Service office should be contacted prior to cutting live trees to learn the areas where this activity is permitted.

Accommodations: Camping is permitted anywhere in the national forest unless it is a day-use area, or there is a sign specifically prohibiting it. No permits or fees are required for wilderness camping. Fees are charged for some developed campgrounds. Contact any Forest Service office for information.

The U.S. Forest Service maintains some 150 cabins (see Tongass National Forest Cabins this section) in Southeast which are available by advance reservation. The current fee is $20 to $35 per party per night. Many Southeast communities have Forest Service offices which will provide information on local places to camp and hike. The Forest Service operates road-accessible campgrounds for tents and trailers at Juneau, Ketchikan, Sitka and Petersburg. (For more information on road-accessible attractions within Tongass National Forest, see *The MILEPOST®*, a complete guide to communities and attractions on Alaska's road and marine highway system.)

For more information: Tongass National Forest, Regional Office, P.O. Box 21628 (709 W. 9th St.), Juneau, AK 99802; phone (907) 586-8806, www.fs.fed.us/r10/tongass/. A Tongass National Forest map detailing cabins and campgrounds is available for $4.

Tracy Arm-Fords Terror Wilderness Area

Located 50 miles southeast of Juneau and 70 miles north of Petersburg adjacent to Stephens Passage and bordered on the east by Canada.

Tracy and Endicott arms are the major features of this 653,179-acre wilderness area. Both are long, deep, narrow fjords that extend more than 30 miles into the heavily glaciated Coast Mountain Range. At the head of these fjords are active tidewater glaciers, which continually calve icebergs into the fjords. During the summer, both fjords have quantities of floating ice ranging from the size of a 3-story building to handsized chunks, often obstructing small-boat travel. Fords Terror, off of Endicott Arm, is an area of sheer rock walls enclosing a narrow entrance into a small fjord. The fjord was named for a crew member of a naval vessel who rowed into the narrow canyon at slack tide in 1889 and was caught in turbulent, iceberg-laden currents for 6 "terrifying" hours when the tide changed. Most of the area is rugged snow- and glacier-covered mountains with steeply walled valleys dotted with high, cascading waterfalls. The lower slopes are covered with early successional spruce-hemlock rain forest; tree line is about 1,500 feet elevation. There are a few muskeg bogs with sedges, grass and sphagnum moss.

Wildlife includes mountain goats, wolverines, brown and black bears, numerous furbearers, a few Sitka blacktail deer, bald eagles, shorebirds, sea lions, whales and harbor seals.

Activities: This dramatic wilderness area is increasingly popular with kayakers. Moderate to easy paddling; main hazards are wind, strong tidal currents and limited haul-out sites. Drop-off and pickup service available in Juneau.

Accommodations: There are no facilities available in these areas. Camping is limited due to the steep terrain; beware of areas with rockfalls A boat with sleeping accommodations is a comfortable means of visiting this wilderness.

Access: Primarily by boat or floatplane from Juneau. Large cruise ships and small charter boats include Tracy Arm and Endicott Arm on their itineraries.

For more information: Tongass National Forest, P.O. Box 2097, Juneau, AK 99803; phone (907) 586-8800.

West Chichagof-Yakobi Wilderness Area

This 264,747-acre wilderness occupies the western portions of Chichagof and Yakobi islands in the extreme northwest portion of the Alexander Archipelago of southeastern Alaska. It is a few miles west of Pelican and 30 miles north of Sitka.

The most dramatic feature of this wilderness area is the 65-mile-long stretch of rugged Pacific coastline with exposed offshore islands and rocky highlands. Behind the barrier islands, rocks and reefs of the outer coast lie the quiet waters of a scenic inside passage, honeycombed with bays, inlets and lagoons. There are quiet tidal meadows and estuaries and steep mountains with peaks to 3,600 feet that rise out of the ocean. Western hemlock and Sitka spruce forests cover about one-third of the area, and there are scattered lodgepole pines and cedar. Offshore islands support glades under open spruce cover, and there are scattered alpine terrain, muskeg and estuaries. Hiking can be difficult in upland meadows because of downed logs, holes and hidden streams.

Wildlife includes Sitka blacktail deer, brown bear, numerous furbearers, sea otters, sea lions and seals. The area is wonderful for boaters and kayakers. Strong winds off the Pacific Ocean can be dangerous in exposed stretches.

Access is by charter boat from Pelican or Sitka or chartered floatplane from Sitka or Juneau. The coastal area has excellent moorage and landing sites for boats and planes. There are Forest Service cabins on West Chichagof at Goulding Lake, Greentop Harbor on Yakobi Island, Lake Suloia and White Sulphur Springs, which also has a bathhouse overlooking Bertha Bay. (See Tongass National Forest Cabins in this section.)

For more information: Tongass National Forest, 201 Katlian Street, Suite 109, Sitka, AK 99835; phone 747-4220. USGS maps: Sitka, Mount Fairweather.

SOUTHCENTRAL

Sooner or later, every visitor hears the old saying that Alaska is just 20 minutes from Anchorage. As with most proverbs, there is some truth to that statement, both about Anchorage and about Southcentral Alaska.

Southcentral is Alaska's most populated region, with Anchorage accounting for a huge chunk of the state's populace. Anchorage has skyscrapers, shopping malls, "big-box" stores, modern airports and freeways. But drive north or south from the city for 20 minutes and you can hike off the road into the kind of wild country and solitude that is the true Alaska. Fly a small plane 20 minutes in any direction and you'll be over roadless wilderness. You can't even entirely categorize Anchorage as an urban area: moose often wander through backyards and along streets, sled dog races are held downtown in winter, and occasionally a bicyclist or hiker runs into a grizzly bear.

Southcentral is an incredibly diverse region, both geographically and historically. History and geography help to define it more closely into 4 distinct subregions: Copper River/Wrangell-St. Elias; Prince William Sound; Anchorage/Mat-Su Valley; and the Kenai Peninsula. (West Cook Inlet destinations, popular with bush planes from Anchorage, are included in the WESTERN section; the Kodiak archipelago, which extends southwest from the Kenai Peninsula, is included in the SOUTHWESTERN section.)

Location: The Southcentral region curves north and west from Yakutat in southeastern Alaska around the Gulf Coast to the Kenai Peninsula. It extends inland to the south flank of the Alaska Range, encompassing the Chugach and Wrangell-St. Elias mountains.

Geography: Southcentral's mainland has a roller-coaster topography of high mountains and broad river valleys. At the eastern edge of the region lies 13.2-million acre Wrangell-St. Elias National Park and Preserve, largest unit in the national park system. The area is famous for trophy Dall sheep hunting. The coast from Icy Bay to the Copper River Delta is primarily flatlands flanked by the Robinson Mountains and the large glaciers that flow from the Bagley Icefield in the Chugach and Mount St. Elias mountains.

The Copper River, historic gateway to rich copper deposits in the Wrangell Mountains, drains into the Gulf of Alaska east of Cordova. The mud flats of the Copper River Delta are a major landfall for migrating shorebirds and waterfowl. River rafting, bird watching (trumpeter swans nest here), and witnessing the calving of icebergs from Childs Glacier are popular activities.

At Hinchinbrook Entrance, the Gulf of Alaska merges with Prince William Sound, a 15,000-square-mile maze of water, ice and islands. The Sound is the site of important salmon, crab and shrimp fisheries. Tour boats and charter flightseeing services from Valdez and

Whittier take visitors to view Columbia Glacier, a major visitor attraction. Sportfishing, boating and blue-water kayaking rate as principal recreational activities in the Sound.

The Susitna River, flowing from the south slopes of the Alaska Range, and the Matanuska River, which heads in the Chugach Mountains, have carved out the Mat-Su Valley area north of Anchorage and bounded by the Talkeetna Mountains. The Matanuska River flows through Alaska's agricultural heartland. A 120-day growing season, with up to 19 hours of summer sunlight, nourishes the giant vegetables for which the Matanuska Valley is noted. River rafting, hunting, fishing, hiking and winter sports are among the many favored activities.

The Susitna River winds through prime moose habitat into the silty upper reaches of Cook Inlet. The Iditarod Trail follows portions of an old mail and freight route from the Cook Inlet area to Nome on the Bering Sea coast of Western Alaska. The state's major long-distance sled dog race, the Iditarod Trail Sled Dog Race from Anchorage to Nome, runs along much of the trail. Anchorage, home to nearly half of Alaska's population, stands at the head of 220-mile-long Cook Inlet, which extends between the Kenai Peninsula and the Aleutian Range. Sportfishing, jet boating, flightseeing and hunting are popular here.

The Kenai Peninsula, famous for its sportfishing in the Kenai, Russian, Anchor and Kasilof rivers, is heavily used along portions of its road system, but sees little visitation in more remote areas. Kenai Fjords National Park, Chugach National Forest, Kenai National Wildlife Refuge, Kachemak Bay State Park and Kachemak Bay State Wilderness Park offer a wide range of recreational opportunities. The Kenai Peninsula and Resurrection Pass trail systems and the Swan Lake and Swanson River canoe trails should not be overlooked. Major access points include Seward, Kenai, Soldotna, Homer and Seldovia. Offshore, halibut fishing generally offers liberal reward. Homer and Kenai are major access points for flights across Cook Inlet, especially to McNeil River State Game Sanctuary.

Variable terrain and climate provide suitable habitat for an assortment of plants. The moisture-demanding vegetation of Southeast continues along the coast to the Kenai Peninsula. Sitka spruce and western hemlock dominate coastal forests. Inland, birch, alder and aspen are the primary species. At higher elevations, forests give way to subalpine brush thickets, fields of wildflowers, berries and alpine meadows. Major river valleys have stands of black cottonwood. Chugach National Forest (the nation's second largest) encompasses 5.8 million acres of Southcentral.

Climate: Southcentral's climate is primarily maritime, with rain and fog and mild temperature fluctuations. Nearer the mountains, the climate becomes transitional; temperature changes are greater and the climate is generally harsher. In Anchorage, January temperatures average 13°F and July temperatures average 57°F. Protected by the Chugach and Kenai mountains from the moisture-laden clouds from the gulf, Anchorage averages only about 15 inches of precipitation annually. However, at Whittier, on the coast side, average annual precipitation is 174 inches.

Wildlife: Grizzly and brown bears are found in the coastal forests of Prince William Sound and portions of the Matanuska and Susitna valleys. Mountain goats roam the sheer cliffs of the Chugach and Wrangell mountains. Moose thrive on the Kenai Peninsula, where the nearly 2-million-acre Kenai National Wildlife Refuge provides habitat for these giants. Moose occur throughout the rest of Southcentral, except on the islands of Prince William Sound. Dall sheep are found in the Talkeetna, Wrangell and Chugach mountains, on the slopes of the Alaska Range and on inland peaks of the Kenai Mountains. Sitka blacktail deer inhabit the coastal forests of Prince William Sound. Wolves live on the Kenai Peninsula, in the Nelchina basin, the Copper River valley, the Eagle River valley near Anchorage and

in the rolling country northwest of Cook Inlet.

Smaller nongame and fur-bearing mammals include lynx, martens, weasels, beavers, muskrats, minks, red foxes, land otters, porcupines, wolverines, snowshoe hares, shrews, voles and lemmings.

Southcentral has congregations of bald and golden eagles, hawks and falcons and overwhelming numbers of shorebirds and waterfowl. The world's population of dusky Canada geese summers on the Copper River flats, and rare trumpeter swans nest on the Kenai Peninsula and near the Copper River. The mud flats of the river's delta are a major landfall for migrating shorebirds and waterfowl.

Rich Gulf Coast waters support crab, shrimp and clams. Salmon, herring, cod, Dolly Varden and cutthroat trout abound and nourish, in turn, harbor and Dall porpoises, sea lions, sea otters and killer whales. Largest marine mammals in the area are the baleen whales (humpbacks, fins and minkes) that feed on the krill and other marine invertebrates that thrive in the nutrient-rich waters.

you'll miss it — glaciers are on search has taught us more about than we've ever known before.

Alexander Creek

GPS: N61°25' W150°35'

Located in the Mat-Su Valley area near the mouth of Alexander Creek in the Susitna River delta 27 miles northwest of Anchorage. **Transportation**: Boats; charter floatplane service from Anchorage. **Population**: 39. **Zip code**: 99695. **Emergency Services**: Alaska State Troopers, Anchorage; hospitals and clinics in Anchorage.

Visitor Facilities: Accommodations available at several lodges, including Alexander Creek Lodge, (907) 733-1556; meals available at two of the lodges. No public laundry facilities. No stores; supplies are obtained from Anchorage. Marine engine and boat repair available. Boats and motors available for rent, and river-taxi service available. Guide services available. Hunting/fishing licenses and public moorage facilities available. Fuel available: regular gasoline.

Alexander Creek is a scattered, unincorporated community located on or near the former site of a small Indian village reported by U.S. Geological Survey geologist George Homans Eldridge in 1898.

Some residents of the area are commercial fishermen; others are retired.

Sportfishing is excellent for king salmon from May 20 to July 6; silver, pink, red and chum salmon from July 16 to September; rainbow trout in May and September; and grayling from July to September.

Area hunting is for moose, black bear and ducks.

Communications include mail plane, commercial radio and TV. There are no schools or churches. Electricity is from individual generators; water is from wells. Sewage system is flush toilets. Freight arrives by charter plane. Village corpora-

tion address: Alexander Creek Inc., 8126 Wisteria, Anchorage, AK 99502, phone (907) 243-5323, fax (907) 243-5428.

Anchorage

GPS: N61°13' W149°53'

Located on Knik Arm, Cook Inlet, 1,445 air miles north of Seattle, 578 air miles northwest of Juneau, 263 air miles (364 road miles) south of Fairbanks. **Transportation**: By vehicle via the Glenn, Parks and Seward highways; daily jet service by domestic and international airlines; Alaska Railroad from Fairbanks, Whittier or Seward. **Population**: 260,283. **Emergency Services**: Police, Fire Department, Ambulance and Search & Rescue, emergencies only, phone 911. Police, non-emergency, phone (907) 786-8500. Alaska State Troopers, phone (907) 269-5511. **Hospitals**: Alaska Regional Hospital, phone (907) 276-1131; Alaska Native Medical Center, phone (907) 562-2262; Providence Medical Center, phone (907) 562-2211; Elmendorf Air Force Base emergency room, phone (907) 552-5555. **Elevation**: 38 to 120 feet.

Private Aircraft: Anchorage is home to 2 of the busiest small plane bases in the nation: Lake Hood Seaplane Facility, located just north of the Ted Stevens International Airport, and Merrill Field, located 1 mile east of downtown, which has tiedowns for 1,422 planes. See the Alaska Supplement for details on Ted Stevens International Airport, Merrill Field, Birchwood, Campbell Airstrip and Lake Hood seaplane base.

Private Boats: Small boat launch site only; no moorage, no facilities or fuel.

Visitor Facilities: All services are available in Anchorage. There are more than 70 motels and hotels in the Anchorage area; numerous bed and breakfasts; 4 hostels; and some 600 restaurants. There are 5 shopping malls (Dimond, 5th Avenue Mall, Northway Mall, Sears Mall and University Center).

Anchorage is Alaska's largest city and the center of commerce and distribution for much of the state. In addition to offering a long list of visitor attractions and special events in the city, Anchorage is also the jumping-off point for many bush destinations. Tour operators, guides and outfitters in Anchorage offer every kind of wilderness experience, from package tours to remote communities to fishing, hunting, hiking, mountaineering, ski touring, river rafting, canoeing, sea kayaking, wildlife viewing and dog sled trips (guided or unguided, with everything you need or with you supplying your own equipment).

A good first stop for visitors planning to head into the backcountry is the Alaska Public Lands Information Center in the historic Old Federal Building, 605 W. 4th Ave., Anchorage, AK 99501, phone (907) 271-2737. Films, brochures and knowledgeable staffers provide information on every kind of outdoor activity and will help you plan your trip.

See also Chugach National Forest and Chugach State Park in Southcentral Attractions section for details on these wilderness areas surrounding Anchorage, as well as other destinations accessible from Anchorage.

Anchorage, a unified home-rule municipality first incorporated in 1920, has all the amenities of big-city life, a daily newspaper, and many radio and TV stations, 96 schools with enrollment of 49,212, and 2 universities (University of Alaska Anchorage and Alaska Pacific University).

Government address: Municipality of Anchorage, Pouch 6-650, Anchorage, AK 99502-0650, phone (907) 264-4431/4432.

Visitor information: Anchorage Convention and Visitors Bureau, 524 W. 4th Ave., Anchorage, AK 99501, phone (907) 274-3531, www.anchorage.net.

For more information on Anchorage see also The MILEPOST®, a complete guide to communities on Alaska's road and marine highway systems.

Cape Yakataga
GPS: N60°04' W142°29'

Located on the Gulf of Alaska, 35 miles west of Icy Bay, 106 miles west of Yakutat, 109 miles east of Cordova, 265 miles southeast of Anchorage. **Transportation**: Scheduled or charter air service. Gulf Air Taxi flies 3 scheduled flights a week from Yakutat to Cape Yakataga and Icy Bay. Gulf Air flies 3 days a week in the summer from Yakutat to Icy Bay to Cape Yakataga to Cordova and back. Charter flights available. **Population**: 4 to 8. **Zip Code**: 99574. Emergency Services: Alaska State Troopers, Cordova, phone (907) 424-7331.

Elevation: 12 feet at airport. Climate: Mild in the summer with temperatures in the 60s and rainy in the winter, with temperatures dropping to the middle teens to 35°F, according to one resident. Mean annual precipitation is 102 inches.

Private Aircraft: Airstrip 2 miles from homes; elev. 12 feet; length 4,350 feet; gravel; no fuel; unattended. Mountains north through northeast to east; 2,258-foot hill 3 nautical miles east. Runway not maintained. Contact Cordova radio for latest field conditions. Water stands on runway; soft spots rutted when dry.

Visitor Facilities: Don and Lahoma Leishman, Box 387, Yakutat, AK 99689, run a bunkhouse-type lodge and provide meals. There are no other services available.

The Indian name Yakataga is said to mean "canoe road," referring to 2 reefs that form a canoe passage to the village. The name was reported in 1904 by C.G. Martin of the U.S. Geological Survey. At that time there was placer mining in the area. Cape Yakataga is the site of a Federal Aviation Administration aero-beacon. Some residents mine and also trap.

Activities in the area include beachcombing and hunting for moose, mountain goat, black and brown bear, according to one resident. Also, a large number of birds pass through the area during migrations.

Chenega Bay
GPS: N60°06' W147°57'

Located at Crab Bay on Evans Island in Prince William Sound, 50 miles east of Seward. **Transportation**: Boat or charter floatplane from Anchorage, Cordova, Seward or Valdez. Population: 69. **Zip code**: 99574. Emergency Services: Village Public Safety Officer; Alaska State Troopers, Seward, phone (907) 224-3346; Chenega Bay Health Clinic/EMS, phone (907) 573-5129.

NOTE: *Some lands near Chenega Bay are owned by the local village corporation, which should be contacted regarding the location of its lands and authorization for use.*

Climate: Moderately rainy, with daytime temperatures in the mid-50s, according to one resident. Winters mild with average snowfall accumulation of 4 to 5 feet. Daytime winter temperatures from the mid-20s to the 30s.

Private Aircraft: Runway unattended; length 3,000 feet.

Visitor Facilities: Room with cooking facilities available in the community building. Laundry facilities available; no banking services. Limited supplies available. No arts and crafts available for purchase at present. Fishing/hunting licenses available; no guide services. Fuel is not available. The community has a dock and a floatplane landing area.

The original community of Chenega, located on the south tip of Chenega Island north of Evans Island, was destroyed by the tsunami that followed the 1964 Good Friday earthquake. Chenega Bay was dedicated on the 20th anniversary of that quake, the culmination of years of effort to provide a new village for former residents of Chenega.

Most of the buildings were constructed in the summer of 1984. The new village consists of 21 homes, an office building, a school with enrollment of 13, a community store, a church, community hall and 2 school faculty houses.

The primary occupations in Chenega Bay are subsistence and commercial fishing and other seasonal employment.

Chenega Bay is built on the site of the former Crab Bay herring saltery. At nearby Sawmill Bay between Chenega Bay and Port San Juan are the ruins of Port Ashton, another abandoned herring saltery, which is accessible by boat, floatplane or by foot along the beach at low tide.

The Port San Juan Hatchery, operated by the Prince William Sound Aquaculture Assoc., is located about 2 miles across Sawmill Bay by boat from Chenega Bay. The hatchery, which is open to visitors, grows pink and chum salmon and reportedly is one of the largest of its kind in the world in terms of number of fry released.

Latouche Island, site of an abandoned copper mining community, is located about 4 miles from Chenega Bay across Elrington Passage. Today there is a private airstrip on the island and a few homes.

The historic site of old Chenega is accessible by private air or boat charter.

Recreational activities at Chenega Bay include rockhounding, bottle collecting, beachcombing, hiking or backpacking. Cross-country skiing is good in winter. Whales and sea lions may be seen nearby. Bird watching is possible year-round. Fishing in nearby waters is good in season for salmon, trout, halibut and rockfish. Hunting is primarily for deer and black bear on Evans and neighboring islands.

Communications at Chenega Bay, which is unincorporated, include phones, twice-weekly mail plane, radio and TV. There are community electric, water and sewer systems. Freight arrives by barge or mail plane. Government address: Native Village of Chenega, P.O. Box 8079, Chenega Bay, AK 99574, phone (907) 573-5132, fax (907) 573-5120, e-mail: Chenega@aitc.org. Village corporation: Chenega Corp., 4000 Old Seward Hwy., Suite 101, Anchorage AK 99503, phone (907) 573-5118, fax (907) 573-5134.

Chisana
GPS: N62°04' W142°02'

(Pronounced Shoe-SHAN-na) Located in the Wrangell Mountains on the Chisana River near its headwaters, 30 miles southeast of Nabesna and about 60 miles south of Northway. Transportation: Charter air service from Northway, Glennallen or Tok. Population: 6 to 20, depending on the season. Zip code: 99780. Emergency Services: Alaska State Troopers, Glennallen, phone (907) 822-3263; Tok Health Clinic, phone (907) 883-5855, or Crossroads Medical Center,

Glennallen, phone (907) 822-3203.

Elevation: 3,170 feet. Climate: Mean temperature in July 51°F; mean temperature in January -14°F, with lows to -30°F. According to resident Ray McNutt, 1991 saw the thermometer dip to -50°F twice in January. Mean annual precipitation 11.4 inches, with 61 inches of snow.

Private Aircraft: Airstrip adjacent north; elev. 3,318 feet; length 3,000 feet; turf and gravel; unattended. Runway has loose rocks up to 3 inches. Airport active for hunting from the end of August to mid-September.

Visitor Facilities: Accommodations and meals available by advance reservation at 2 local lodges: Wrangell R Ranch , P.O. Box 222475, Anchorage, AK 99522, radiophone 345-1160, call sign WHV 34; and Pioneer Outfitters, P.O. Box CZN, Tok, AK 99780. There are no other facilities. Guide services are available locally.

This community, located within Wrangell-St. Elias National Park and Preserve, was settled during the Chisana gold rush of 1913. At one time the area had a population of more than 1,000. The gold rush was short-lived and Chisana quickly became a ghost town. It now serves as the base of operations for a few hunting guides and recreationists.

Anthony Dimond, Alaska's territorial delegate to Congress from 1932-45, was the town's U.S. Commissioner. His courtroom, cabin, women's jail and several other historic structures, built of logs during the town's peak years (1913 to 1920), were restored by the National Park Service in 1988.

Hunting, horseback trips, hiking and history are the primary visitor attractions.

A regular mail plane serves Chisana, which is unincorporated. There are no phones, schools or churches. Electricity is from individual generators, water is from wells or the river. There is no community sewage system. Freight arrives by plane.

Chitina

GPS: N61°31' W144°26'

(CHIT-na) Located in the Copper River/Wrangell-St. Elias area on the Edgerton Highway at the confluence of the Copper and Chitina rivers, 116 miles northeast of Valdez. **Transportation**: Edgerton Highway, 33 miles from its junction with the Richardson Highway; air charter service from Gulkana. **Population**: 103. **Zip code**: 99566. **Emergency Services**: Chitina Health Clinic; Chitina First Responders/Copper River EMS, phone (907) 822-3671; Chitina Volunteer Fire Dept., phone (907) 823-2263/2250; Alaska State Troopers at Glennallen, phone 911.

Elevation: 556 feet. **Climate**: Summers warm (by Alaska standards), windy and sunny; winters cold, dark and snowy.

Private Aircraft: Airstrip adjacent; elev. 556 feet; length 2,850 feet; gravel; unattended. Runway conditions not monitored; visual inspection recommended prior to use. Aircraft at one end cannot see aircraft at other end because of downward slopes. Brush first 1,000 feet.

Visitor Facilities: Chitina has a post office, general store and grocery, gas stations, a tavern, at least 3 places to eat, rental cabins, a couple of tire repair services and a public phone. Spirit Mountain Artworks, offering Alaska arts and crafts, is housed in the original tinsmith building, which is included on the National Register of Historic Places.

A big attraction in Chitina is the seasonal run of Copper River salmon, which draws hundreds of dip-netters. It's a fine opportunity to see fish wheels and dip nets in action. Check with Fish and Game regarding subsistence fishery dates. *NOTE: The fishery is open only to Alaska residents with permits specific to this fishery.*

A bridge crossing the Copper River at Chitina gives access to the 58-mile McCarthy Road, which leads deep into the Wrangell-St. Elias National Park and Preserve. The Chitina Ranger Station, located in the historic Ed S. Orr Cabin, provides information about the park and McCarthy Road during the summer months. Chitina, as one of the gateway communities to the Wrangell-St. Elias, serves as jumping-off point for a number of wilderness trips that originate along the McCarthy Road. Horseback tours of the area are available in Chitina.

Community Nonprofit: Community Improvement Assoc. of Chitina, P.O. Box 2, Chitina, AK 99566, phone (907) 823-2222, fax (907) 823-2233. Village corporation: Chitina Native Corporation, P.O. Box 3, Chitina, AK 99566, phone (907) 823-2223, fax (907) 823-2202, e-mail: jhart@ahtna-inc.com. Village council: Chitina Traditional Village Council, P.O. Box 31, Chitina, AK 99566, phone (907) 823-2215, fax (907) 823-2202, e-mail: Chitina@aitc.org.

For more about Chitina, see *The MILEPOST®*, a complete guide to communities on Alaska's road and marine highway systems.

Copper Center

GPS: N61°59' W145°21'

Located in the Copper River/Wrangell-St. Elias area on the Klutina River, 1 mile west of its junction with the Copper River, 104.8 miles northeast of Valdez via the Richardson Highway. **Transportation**: By vehicle via the Richardson Highway, 104.8 miles from Valdez, about 15 miles south of Glennallen; an inner loop road leads through Copper Center and rejoins the Richardson Highway at Mile 101.1. Charter air service. **Population**: 362. **Zip code**: 99573. **Emergency Services**: State Troopers and ambulance in Glennallen; Copper Center Health Clinic; Copper Center EMS, phone (907) 822-3671.

Elevation: 1,000 feet.

Private Aircraft: Copper Center NR 2 airstrip, 1 S; elev. 1,150 feet; length 2,200 feet; gravel; unattended.

Visitor Facilities: Lodging and meals at the historic Copper Center Lodge, phone (907) 822-5035; this lodge is on the National Register of Historic Places. There are also several private campgrounds. Groceries and supplies at the Copper River Cash Store. Fishing charters, tackle, riverboat services and guides available locally for fishing the Klutina River for kings and red salmon.

Copper River has community electricity. Most homes have individudal wells and septic tanks, and 75 percent of the homes are fully plumbed. There is one school with enrollment of 52.

Village council: Native Village of Kluti-Kaah, P.O. Box 68, Copper Center, AK 99573, phone (907) 882-5541, fax (907) 882-5130, e-mail: Kluti-Kaah@aitc.org. Regional health corporation: Copper River Native Assoc., P.O. Drawer H, Copper Center, AK 99573, phone (907) 822-5241. fax (907) 822-5247. e-mail: mododds 2000@yahoo.com.

For more information on Copper Center, see *The MILEPOST®*, a complete guide to communities on Alaska's road and marine highway systems.

Cordova

GPS: N60°33' W145°45'

Located on Orca Inlet on the southeast shore of Prince William Sound at the entrance to the Copper River valley, 147 miles southeast of Anchorage. **Transportation**: Daily jet service from Anchorage; Alaska Marine Highway from Valdez, Whittier and Seward. **Population**: 3,184. **Zip code**: 99574. **Emergency Services**: Alaska State Troopers, phone (907) 424-7331, emergency phone 911; Police, Cordova Community Medical Center, phone (907) 424-8000; Cordova Volunteer Fire Department/EMS/Search & Rescue, phone (907) 424-6117/6100; Ambulance, emergency phone 911; police department business calls, phone (907) 424-6100.

Elevation: Sea level to 400 feet. **Climate**: Average temperature in July 54°F, in January 21°F. Average annual precipitation 167 inches. Prevailing winds easterly at about 5 mph.

Private Aircraft: Cordova Municipal (city airfield), 0.9 mile east; elev. 12 feet; length 1,840 feet; gravel; fuel 100, 100LL; unattended. Merle K. "Mudhole" Smith Airport, Mile 12.1 Copper River Highway; elev. 42 feet; length 7,499 feet; asphalt; attended. Eyak Lake seaplane base, 0.9 mile east.

Private Boats: Transient moorage at Small Boat Harbor; water and fuel available; Harbormaster phone (907) 424-6400, fax (907) 424-6000, Web: www.ptialaska.net/~cordharb.

Visitor Facilities: Lodging at the

Prince William Motel, (888) 796-6835; The Northern Nights Inn, (907) 424-5356; Cordova Rose Lodge, (907) 424-7673; The King's Chamber Bed & Breakfast, (907) 424-3373; Enchanted Garden Lodging, (907) 424-5445; and Orca Adventure Lodge, (866) 424-6722. Cordova has several eating spots, a laundromat, a supermarket, a bookstore and other shops. There are 2 banks in town. Local merchants prefer cash and checks to credit cards.

The name Cordova probably is derived from the original Spanish name Puerto Cordova (Port Cordova), given to the area by the Spanish naval explorer Fidalgo, who sailed into Orca Inlet in 1790. Modern-day Cordova owes its origins to Michael J. Heney, builder of the Copper River & Northwestern Railway. The town was the railroad terminus and ocean shipping port for copper ore from the Kennecott mines near Kennicott and McCarthy, 112 air miles northeast of Cordova in the Wrangell Mountains. The railroad and the town prospered until 1938 when the mine was closed. Following the end of copper mining, fishing became the area's major economic base. One of the first producing oil fields in Alaska was located in Katalla, some 47 miles southeast of Cordova on the Gulf of Alaska. The discovery was made in 1902, and the field produced small amounts of oil until 1933 when part of the plant burned.

Supporting the area's economy today are the Prince William Sound fishery and fish processing plants. The fishing and canning season for salmon runs from about May to September, with red, king and silver salmon taken from the Copper River area, and chum, king and pink salmon from Prince William Sound. The season for Dungeness crab is March to June and August to December; tanner crab is caught in January; king crab season opens in October and continues until the quota is caught.

Surrounded by Chugach National Forest and the waters of Prince William Sound, Cordova is a prime staging area for wilderness adventures such as sea kayaking, hiking, fishing, canoeing, rafting, bird watching and cross-country skiing. Numerous guides and outfitters operate from Cordova.

Wildlife watchers can observe moose, bears, waterfowl, sea otters and shorebirds in and around Cordova. Each year, millions of shorebirds pass through the Copper River Delta during their spring migration. This annual migration is the focus of the Copper River Delta Shorebird Festival, timed to coincide (it is hoped) with the peak of the migration. Two favorite bird-watching areas are: Hartney Bay and Alaganik Slough.

The Cordova Ranger District of Chugach National Forest maintains miles of trails, public-use cabins and recreation areas around Cordova. The district office is located at 612 2nd Street in Cordova; phone (907) 424-7661.

The 48-mile Copper River Highway, which leads east from Cordova through the Copper River Delta to the historic Million Dollar Bridge, provides access to several Forest Service trails and recreation areas.

Cordova, a home-rule city, has all the amenities of a medium-sized city, including a radio station (KLAM-AM), cable TV and a weekly newspaper, *The Cordova Times*. There are 2 schools with enrollment of 465. Government address: City of Cordova, P.O. Box 1210, Cordova, AK 99574, phone (907) 424-6200, fax (907) 424-6000, e-mail: cicdv@ctcak.net, web: http://www.ptialaska/~cchamber/. Visitor information: Cordova Chamber of Commerce, P.O. Box 99, 404 1st St., Cordova, AK 99574, phone (907) 424-7260, e-mail: cchamber@ptialaska.net; Web: www.ptialaska.net/~cchamber.

For additional information on Cordova see *The MILEPOST®*, a complete guide to communities on Alaska's road and marine highway system.

Ellamar

Located on the east shore of Virgin Bay in Tatitlek Narrows on Prince William Sound, 180 miles east-southeast of Anchorage, 40 miles northwest of Cordova, 24 miles southwest of Valdez, 2 miles northeast of Tatitlek. **Transportation**: Boat; charter air service from Anchorage, Cordova or Valdez direct or via Tatitlek. **Population**: About 10 year-round. **Zip code**: 99695. **Emergency Services**: Alaska State Troopers, Valdez, phone (907) 822-3263; Health Aide, Tatitlek Clinic, phone (907) 835-2235; Valdez Community Hospital, phone (907) 835-2249.

Private Aircraft: Floatplane landings only at Ellamar. Airstrip located at Tatitlek.

Private Boats: Transient moorage available.

Visitor Facilities: Arrangements for cabin rental may be made through Ellamar Properties Inc., P.O. Box 203113, Anchorage, AK 99520, phone (907) 278-1311, e-mail: cjgroh@alaska.net. No laundromat. No stores or supplies available. Boat, aircraft may be chartered. Guide services available. No major repair services or fuel. Fishing/ hunting licenses not available. Roads and dock facilities have been developed for those who purchase lots.

Ellamar, a historic copper mining town, is now a summer and weekend recreational community developed by Ellamar Properties.

Copper was discovered at Ellamar in 1897. By 1902 Ellamar was a bustling town of 700 residents, complete with stores, shops, 3 bars and an opera house. Mines throughout Prince William Sound started closing in 1919 and by the end of the 1920s Ellamar Mining was closed.

The economy was revitalized for a time when 2 cannery operations, attracted by the dock and labor force from Tatitlek, opened at Ellamar. The first cannery burned down in the 1940s; the second quit operating in the 1950s.

Recreational activities in the area include fishing for salmon and halibut, boating, hunting, cross-country skiing and photography. Whales, sea otters and sea lions frequent the area. Behind Ellamar, 3,051-foot Ellamar Mountain offers good views of waterfalls. Columbia Glacier is 12 miles to the northwest.

Communications at Ellamar are by cell phone or by a public phone located at Tatitlek. There are no community electric, sewer or water systems. Water is available from 3 creeks. The nearest church and school are at Tatitlek. Freight arrives at Ellamar by barge or floatplane.

English Bay

(See Nanwalek)

Glennallen

GPS: N62°07' W145°33'

Located near the junction of the Glenn and Richardson highways, in the Copper River valley. **Transportation**: Via the Glenn and Richardson highways. **Population**: 554. **Zip code**: 99588. **Emergency Services**: Alaska State Troopers, phone (907) 822-3263; Fire Department emergency, phone 911; Crossroads Medical Center, phone (907) 822-3203; Glennallen Ambulance/ Copper River EMS, phone (907) 822-3671; Cross Road Air Ambulance, phone (907) 822-3203.

Elevation: 1,460 feet.

Private Aircraft: Gulkana airstrip, 4.3 miles northeast of Glennallen; elev. 1,579 feet; length 2,070 feet; asphalt; fuel 100LL.

Visitor Facilities: Accommodations are available the New Caribou Hotel, (907) 822-3302. There are restaurants, also stores providing automobile parts, groceries, gifts, clothing, sporting goods and other supplies. Fuel and major car repairs are available.

Glennallen is a staging area for trips into Wrangell-St. Elias National Park and the Copper River Basin. An Alaska Dept. of Fish and Game office is located in Glennallen, phone (907) 822-3309. Flying services, wilderness guides and outfitters, and hunting/fishing licenses are available locally.

Glennallen has community electricity. Most homes have private wells and more than 90 percent of homes are fully plumbed. Most residences have individual septic tank systems. There are 4 schools with enrollment of 489. Visitor information: Greater Copper Valley Chamber of Commerce, P.O. Box 469, Glennallen, AK 99588, phone (907) 822-5555, fax (907) 822-5558.

For more information on Glennallen, see *The MILEPOST®*, a complete guide to communities on Alaska's road and marine highway systems.

Halibut Cove

GPS: N59°37' W151°14'

Located on the Kenai Peninsula, 7 miles southeast of Homer on the east shore of Kachemak Bay. **Transportation**: Floatplane; private Kachemak Bay Ferry, M/V *Danny J*, departs from Homer daily in summer for the 45-minute ride to Halibut Cove, phone (907) 235-7847. **Population**: 35; greater number in summer. **Zip code**: 99603. **Emergency Services**: Alaska State Troopers in Homer, phone (907) 235-8239; South Peninsula Hospital in Homer, phone (907) 235-8101.

Elevation: 10 feet. **Climate**: Average daily temperature in July, the warmest month, is 54°F; average daily temperature in January, the coldest month, is 19°F. Mean annual precipitation is 18 inches, including 26 inches of snow.

Private Aircraft: No airstrip.

Private Boats: Public moorage available.

Visitor Facilities: Accommodations are available at Halibut Cove Cabins, (907) 296-2214; and Quiet Place Lodge, (907) 296-2212. Meals are served at The Saltry restaurant. Banking, laundromat and groceries are not available. Supplies are obtained from Homer. Arts and crafts available for purchase at several galleries include octopus-ink paintings, oil paintings, fish prints, pottery, batiks and silkscreen prints. Fishing/hunting licenses not available. No major repair services or fuel available.

Between 1911 and 1928, Halibut Cove had 42 herring salteries and a population of about 1,000. From 1928 to 1975 the population stayed around 40, mostly fishermen. Today, the community of Halibut Cove is made up of self-employed artists, commercial fishermen and craftsmen. There are no schools here.

There are no roads in Halibut Cove, but some 12 blocks of boardwalk run along the water's edge and provide access to galleries displaying the work of local artists, such as Diana Tillion, famous for her octopus-ink and watercolor paintings.

Bird watching in the area is excellent. The ferry ride from Homer to Halibut Cover includes Gull Island bird sanctuary.

Kachemak Bay State Park hiking trails are accessible from Halibut Cove. China Poot Lake Trail begins at Halibut Cove Lagoon. Phone the Alaska State Parks district office at (907) 235-7024 for current information on the state park trails. (See also Kachemak Bay State Park in Southcentral Attractions section.)

The bay shoreline offers excellent kayaking, clamming, tide-pooling and beachcombing opportunties. Keep in mind that Kachemak Bay tidal fluctuations are substantial. Carry a tide book.

Kachemak Bay is also one of Alaska's most popular spots for halibut fishing, with catches often weighing 100 to 200 pounds. Halibut up to 350 pounds are fished from June through September. Inquire locally or in Homer about fishing guides.

Communications in unincorporated Halibut Cove include phones, mail plane, radio and TV. There is a community electric system; water is from creeks or wells. Sewage system is septic tanks or honey buckets. Freight arrives by charter or private boat.

Homer

GPS: N59°38' W151°28'

Located on the southwestern edge of the Kenai Peninsula on the north shore of Kachemak Bay at the easterly side of the mouth of Cook Inlet, about 173 road miles southwest of Seward and 226 miles via the Sterling and Seward highways from Anchorage. **Transportation**: A 4-plus hour drive from Anchorage; scheduled air service from Anchorage (40 minutes by jet); and on the Southcentral/Southwest system of the Alaska Marine Highway. **Population**: 3,946. **Zip code**: 99603. **Emergency Services**: Phone 911 for all emergency services. City Police, phone (907) 235-3150; Alaska State Troopers, phone (907) 235-8239; Homer Volunteer Fire Department/EMS, phone (907) 235-3155/3150; Coast Guard, phone Zenith 5555; South Peninsula Hospital, phone (907) 235-8101; Veterinary Clinic, phone (907) 235-8960.

Private Aircraft: Airport 1.7 miles east; elev. 78 feet; length 6,701 feet; asphalt; fuel 100LL, jet A. Attended. Terminal building.

Private Boats: Small Boat Harbor; water and fuel available; Port Director; phone (907) 235-3160, fax (907) 235-3152.

Visitor Facilities: Homer has many hotels and motels, bed and breakfasts, 2 hostels, campgrounds, dozens of restaurants, a post office, library, museum, laundromats, gas stations with propane and dump stations, many churches, 2 banks and a hospital. There are many boat and aircraft charter operators, boat repair and storage facilities, marine fuel at Homer marina, bait, tackle and sporting goods stores, and grocery stores.

Homer's picturesque setting, mild climate and great fishing attract thousands of visitors each year. Homer is also the jumping-off point for Kachemak Bay State Park—one of Alaska's most popular

parks for sea kayaking, hiking, fishing and beachcombing—accessible by floatplane or private water taxi; for McNeil River State Game Sanctuary on the west side of Cook Inlet, and Katmai National Park, both accessible by floatplane; and for flights to Kodiak Island for hunting, fishing, or bear viewing. Several booking agencies for guides, accommodations and charters operate in Homer.

There is access to Fox River Flats Critical Habitat Area via a steep switchback trail that leads down to the flats from East End Road in Homer.

The Kachemak Bay Shorebird Festival takes place in Homer in early May. This annual event celebrates the arrival of 100,000 migrating shorebirds to the tidal flats of Kachemak Bay.

The U.S. Fish and Wildlife Alaska Maritime National Wildlife Refuge visitor center, 451 Sterling Highway, phone (907) 235-6961, is open 9 A.M. to 6 P.M. daily in summer. Pratt Museum, 3779 Bartlett St., is open daily from 10 A.M. to 6 P.M., May through September; and noon to 5 P.M. Tuesday through Sunday from October through April; closed in January, phone (907) 235-8635.

Homer is a first-class city (incorporated in 1964) with a mayor, city manager and city council. It has all modern amenities. There are 8 schools with a total enrollment of 1,481. Communications include radio stations, TV and 2 weekly newspapers, the *Homer News* and *Homer Tribune*. Government address: City of Homer, 491 E. Pioneer Ave., Homer, AK 99603, phone (907) 235-8121. Visitor information: Homer Chamber of Commerce, P.O. Box 541, Homer, AK 99603, phone (907) 235-7740/5300, fax (907) 235-8766.

For more information see *The MILE-POST®*, a complete guide to communities on Alaska's road and marine highway systems.

Lake Creek

Located in the Mat-Su Valley area on the Yentna River at Lake Creek, 70 miles northwest of Anchorage, 18 miles east of Skwentna. **Transportation**: Boat; charter air service or private plane. **Population**: 41 year-round. **Zip code**: 99667 (Skwentna). **Emergency Services**: Alaska State Troopers, Anchorage; Anchorage clinics and hospitals; Riversong Lodge is the first EMS responder station. Several local residents are trained as emergency medical technicians.

Climate: Summer temperatures can reach as high as 70°F to 80°F, according to one resident, while -50°F for periods of time during the winter is not uncommon.

Private Aircraft: No airstrip. Planes land on the river or on a gravel bar. A winter ski plane landing strip is maintained by 2 local lodges, including Cottonwood Lodge, (907) 733-2716.

Visitor Facilities: Accommodations at King Point Lodge, (907) 248-7447; Lake Creek Lodge, (907) 248-3530; Northwoods Lodge, (907) 694-1951; Riversong Lodge, (907) 696-2290; and Wilderness Place Lodge, (907) 248-4337. No stores; most supplies are obtained from Anchorage, although a few grocery items, film and sporting goods may be purchased at the lodges. Raw furs may be purchased from local trappers. Native furs and crafts from the Kuskokwim Delta area are available at Riversong Lodge. Local crafts are available at Northwoods Lodge. Fishing/hunting licenses are available at lodges. Boats may be rented. Guide services can be arranged, as well as natural history tours.

At the turn of the century a trading post was established on the Yentna River near Lake Creek to serve the trappers and gold miners in the area, writes one resident. Ruined cabins remain, as does the hulk of a paddle-wheeled steamboat once used for transportation.

Today, 11 families live year-round in the area. Residents guide fishermen and hunters, and provide lodging for recreationists. Residents travel 18 miles to Skwentna to pick up mail and some children attend school there, traveling by snow machine in winter.

There are cross-country ski trails in winter. Lake Creek is a checkpoint for the 200-mile Iditasport. The Iditarod Trail Sled Dog Race also passes by Lake Creek. Northwoods Lodge at Fish Lakes Creek, 3 miles above

Lake Creek, welcomes winter guests.

Locally there is excellent fishing for 5 species of salmon, some up to 65 pounds, as well as for trout, northern pike and grayling. Wildlife that may be seen in the area includes eagles, ducks, moose, bears and beavers.

Lake Creek is a clear stream that flows about 50 miles south from near Mount McKinley through scenic countryside. (Both Mount McKinley and Mount Foraker can be seen from Lake Creek.) It provides white-water excitement for river floaters, as well as good fishing. Guided raft trips are also available.

Radio is the main form of communication at unincorporated Lake Creek, which does have private telephones. There is no church or school. Electricity is from individual generators; water is from private wells. Sewage is managed by septic tanks and outhouses. Freight arrives by barge or charter plane.

May Creek

GPS: N61°20' W142°41'

Located in the Copper River/ Wrangell-St. Elias area on the Nizina River, 12 miles from McCarthy, 65 miles from Chitina. **Transportation**: Mail plane from Gulkana; charter air service from Gulkana, McCarthy. **Population**: 10-12. **Zip code**: 99588. **Emergency Services**: Alaska State Troopers, Glennallen, phone (907) 822-3263; Copper River EMS at Glennallen, phone (907) 822-3203; Cross Road Medical Center, Glennallen, phone (907) 822-3203.

Private Aircraft: Airstrip 1 mile south; elev. 1,650 feet; length 2,700 feet; gravel and dirt; no fuel; unattended. Runway condition not monitored; visual inspection recommended prior to using. Wind cone in 30-foot trees. Road adjacent to east side of runway.

Visitor Facilities: No hotel, restaurant, store or other facilities.

The May Creek area had a roadhouse during the early 1900s gold rush when the Nizina District was booming, according to one resident. Mining was the main reason for the development as well as the eventual decline of the entire area. The

May Creek airstrip was developed by the Alaska Road Commission in territorial days and was used by the entire region from McCarthy to Dan Creek before local strips were built. May Creek is located within Wrangell-St. Elias National Park and Preserve. A National Park Service Operations Center in May Creek is staffed only during the summer.

Area residents rely primarily on subsistence hunting, fishing and gathering, although there is some gold panning.

The biggest attraction in the area is superb hiking and beautiful scenery. Hiking opportunities range from easy rambles in meadows to more strenuous mountain and glacier treks. Roads and trails remaining from the early mining days make it fairly easy to get around, although some areas are wet. There are many beaver dams and swampy areas across or near the roads.

The area is rich in wildlife, particularly black and grizzly bears, beavers and other water mammals. Trumpeter swans migrate to this area in summer and nest in the lakes.

May Creek, which is unincorporated, has no phones or TV; KCAM radio from Glennallen is received. There are no churches, schools or community electric, water or sewer systems. Freight arrives on the weekly mail plane.

McCarthy/Kennicott

GPS: N61°26' W142°54'

Located in the Copper River/ Wrangell-St. Elias area on the east side of the Kennicott River, 61 miles east of Chitina via the Edgerton Highway and McCarthy Road. Transportation: Via the McCarthy Road to road end, then across the Kennicott River via pedestrian bridge; air service from Gulkana, Chitina and Anchorage; bus service from Valdez and Glennallen; shuttle service available between McCarthy and Kennicott. Population: 25. Zip code: 99588. Emergency Services: Copper River EMS at Glennallen, phone (907) 822-3203; Alaska State Troopers at Glennallen, phone (907) 822-3263.

Elevation: 1,531 feet at McCarthy; Kennicott considerably higher. Climate: Summers bring cool, cloudy, often rainy weather, though hot, sunny days are not uncommon. Winters are cold, dark and usually clear, with temperatures dropping well below zero for long periods.

Private Aircraft: Airstrip adjacent; elev. 1,531 feet; length 3,500 feet; turf and gravel; no fuel; unattended. Runway conditions not monitored; visual inspection recommended prior to using.

Visitor Facilities: Accommodations and meals at McCarthy Lodge, (907) 554-4402; at Kennicott Glacier Lodge, (800) 582-5128; and Historic Kennicott Bed & Breakfast (907) 554-4469. Hostel accommodations at Kennicott River Hostel, (907) 479-6822. McCarthy has a pizza place and espresso bar

McCarthy and neighboring Kennicott lie in a beautiful area of glaciers and mountains in the heart of the Wrangell-St. Elias Park and Preserve. The Kennicott River flows by on the west side of the town and joins the Nizina River that flows into the Chitina River.

The McCarthy–Kennicott Museum, located in the old railway depot, has historical photos and artifacts from the early mining days.

Kennicott, which lies about 5 miles up the mountain from McCarthy, is a National Historic Landmark. The town was built by Kennecott Copper Corp. between 1910 and 1920 at the site of the richest copper mine in the world. (An early-day misspelling made the mining company Kennecott, while the region, river and settlement are Kennicott.) When economic conditions forced the mine to shut down abruptly in 1938, the town was left virtually intact: eating utensils still in kitchen drawers; maps, charts and records still in offices; surgical instruments in the infirmary.

The distinctive red mill buildings perched on the side of the mountain were locked up and left as they were. The National Park Service is currently restoring some of the mill buildings. There are also private land holdings in the area; do not trespass. National park interpretive programs are held in the Jurik Building in

Kennicott during the summer.

Visitors to Kennicott and McCarthy have their choice of river rafting, mountaineering, glacier travel, backpacking, day hiking, bicycling, flightseeing, grayling fishing, taking nature walks, or simply relaxing in the rustic, historic accommodations. Contact St. Elias Alpine Guides, (907) 554-4445, or Kennicott–McCarthy Wilderness Guides, (907) 554-4444, for trip itineraries. Wrangell Mountain Air, phone (800) 478-1160, offers flight tours, fly-in wilderness hiking and scheduled service.

McCarthy and Kennicott have no phones, radio, TV or school. A mail plane comes in twice a week. The communities are unincorporated.

For more information on McCarthy and Kennicott see *The MILEPOST®*, a complete guide to communities on Alaska's road and marine highway system.

Nanwalek (English Bay)

GPS: N59°21′ W151°55′

Located at the south entrance to Port Graham on the Kenai Peninsula, 10 miles southwest of Seldovia, 3 miles from Port Graham. **Transportation**: Boat; scheduled and charter air service from Homer. **Population**: 170. **Zip code**: 99603. **Emergency Services**: Village Public Safety Officer, phone (907) 281-2218; Alaska State Troopers, Homer, phone (907) 235-8573; Nanwalek Health Clinic and Nanwalek First Responders, phone (907) 281-2250.

NOTE: Traditional Native village.

Private Aircraft: Airstrip adjacent southwest; elev. 27 feet; length 1,850 feet; fuel jet A-1; unattended. Runway not regularly maintained, visual inspection recommended prior to using. Approach to one end of runway restricted by village on hillside; approach to other end restricted by abrupt mountain face.

Visitor Facilities: Visitors with official business may be able to sleep on the floor of the school, (907) 281-2210, or in private homes. Village leaders ask that other visitors request permission from the village council before coming to Nanwalek. The store, (907) 281-2228, sells limited

groceries; no fuel, no hunting/fishing licenses. No bank or laundromat.

The Russians applied the name Bukhta Anglitskaya (English Bay) to what is now called Port Graham, probably because the area was mapped by the English explorer Nathaniel Portlock in 1789. Portlock, however, called the bay "Grahams Harbour" or Port Graham, and English Bay later was reapplied to a small cove in the bay. In 1991, English Bay was renamed Nanwalek, allegedly its original name meaning "place by lagoon."

This Native community is unincorporated. Its Russian Orthodox church, built about 1930 to replace the original 1870 structure, is a national historic site.

Nanwalek has community electric, water and sewer systems. Communications include phones, TV and CB radios. The village has a school with grades kindergarten through 12 with enrollment of 48. Freight arrives by commercial air service and barge. Government address: Nanwalek IRA Council, P.O. Box 8028, Nanwalek, AK 99603, phone (907) 281-2274, fax (907) 281-2252, e-mail: Nanwalek@aitc.org. Village corporation: English Bay Corp., P.O. Box KEB, Homer, AK 9960, phone and fax (907) 281-2252.

Port Graham

GPS: N59°21′ W151°49′

Located on the south side of Port Graham Bay at the southern end of the Kenai Peninsula, 4 miles from Nanwalek and 28 air miles from Homer. **Transportation**: Boat, and air charter service from Homer and Anchorage; 4-mile trail from Nanwalek. **Population**: 178. **Zip code**: 99603 (via Homer). **Emergency Services**: Village Public Safety Officer, phone (907) 284-2234; Alaska State Troopers, Homer, phone (907) 235-8573; Port Graham Health Clinic, phone (907) 284-2241; Port Graham EMS/Ambulance, phone (907) 284-2227/2262; Fire Department, phone (907) 284-2224.

Private Aircraft: Airstrip adjacent west; elev. 93 feet; length 1,975 feet; gravel; maintained. Visual inspection recommended before landing. Orange highway cones mark the runway.

Private Boats: Visiting boats under 25 feet may be anchored in Port Graham Bay for short periods of time.

Visitor Facilities: Accommodations and meals by advance reservation at Fedora's Bed-N-Breakfast-N-Skiffs, (907) 284-2239. Accommodations may also be available in private homes, on the school floor and at the cannery. Supplies available at 2 stores, one operates a snack bar. Gas and diesel fuel available. A limited number of skiffs are available for use by visitors.

The sportfisherman will find waters teeming with salmon, halibut, rock bass and cod. Wildlife enthusiasts can watch eagles, sea otters, land otters, bears and goats, even the occasional whale and sea lion.

The earliest known settlers in Port Graham were Russians who had established a trading post at Nanwalek. In 1850 the Russian-American Co. established a coal mine at Port Graham but this operation only lasted a few years because it was not economically successful.

The Aleuts who make up the majority of the current population came from Nanwalek and settled in Port Graham in 1911. The Fidalgo Island Packing Co. established a cannery in 1911 that provided the economic base of the community until it burned in 1960. Whitney/Fidalgo rebuilt the cannery in 1968 and sold it to the village corporation in 1983. The cannery continues to be the main economic force in the community. Most of the workers in the cannery are from Port Graham and Nanwalek. Residents also rely on local fish and game for food.

Communications in Port Graham include phones, radio and TV. The community is served by 2 churches, a school with grades kindergarten through 12 with enrollment of 29, and a preschool. There are community electric, water and sewage systems. Government address: Port Graham Village Council, P.O. Box 5510, Port Graham, AK 99603, phone (907) 284-2227, fax (907) 284-2222, e-mail: Port Graham@aitc.org. Village corporation: Port Graham Corp., P.O. Box 5569, Port Graham, AK 99603, phone (907) 284-2212, fax (907) 284-2219.

Seldovia

GPS: N59°26' W151°42'

Located on the east shore of Seldovia Bay on the Kenai Peninsula, 16 miles southwest of Homer. **Transportation**: Boat; scheduled and charter air service from Homer; Alaska Marine Highway ferry from Homer or Kodiak. **Population**: 284. **Zip code**: 99663. **Emergency Services**: City Police, Ambulance, Fire and Rescue, phone 911; Alaska State Troopers, in Homer, phone (907) 235-8239; Seldovia Medical Clinic, phone (907) 234-7825.

Elevation: Sea level to 300 feet. **Climate**: Average daytime temperatures from 21°F in January to 57°F in July. Average annual precipitation 34.5 inches. Prevailing wind is from the north at 10 to 15 mph.

Private Aircraft: Seldovia airport, 1 E; elev. 29 feet; length 1,845 feet; gravel; no fuel; unattended. Runway condition not monitored, visual inspection recommended prior to using. Turbulence southeast and southwest due to winds. Wind shear on approach to runway 16. A short walk to town. Seldovia seaplane base, adjacent south in boat harbor; unattended.

Private Boats: Transient moorage available at the Small Boat Harbor; water and fuel available; Harbormaster, phone (907) 234-7886, fax (907) 234-7430.

Visitor Facilities: Accommodations at Seldovia Bayview Suites, (907) 234-7631; Seldovia Rowing Club B&B, (907) 234-7614; Seldovia Seaport Cottages, (907) 234-7483; Gerry's Place B&B, (907) 234-7471; Seldovia Boardwalk Hotel, (907) 234-7816; and the Seldovia Harbor Inn, (907) 234-1414. Dining at The Buzz Coffee House and The Mad Fish Restaurant. There are a grocery/deli, a general store, and a variety of shops.

Fishing guide services available. Fishing/hunting licenses available. Fuel available: marine gas, diesel, propane, unleaded and regular gasoline.

Because Seldovia is not connected to the road system, it has retained much of its old Alaska charm. Among activities enjoyed by residents and visitors are halibut, trout and salmon fishing, clam digging at low tides, kayaking and kayaking lessons, picnicking, hiking, cross-country skiing, bicycling (rentals available) and berry picking. These attractions, along with the town's proximity to population centers, make Seldovia a convenient, relaxing getaway destination.

Local special events include the Fourth of July celebration, Fishing Derby, Blueberry Festival and Winter Carnival.

Seldovia has phones, regular mail service, commercial radio reception from Anchorage and Homer, and TV. The community is served by 5 churches and a school with grades kindergarten through 12. There are community electric, water and sewer systems. Freight arrives by barge, airlines and ferry. Government address: City of Seldovia, P.O. Drawer B, Seldovia, AK 99663, phone (907) 234-7643. Visitor information: Chamber of Commerce, P.O. Drawer F, Seldovia, AK 99663. Village corporation address: Seldovia Native Assoc. Inc., P.O. Drawer L, Seldovia, AK 99663, phone (907) 234-7625, fax (9070 234-7637, e-mail: snai@snai.com. Tribal government: Seldovia Village Tribe, P.O. Drawer L., Seldovia, AK 99663, phone (907) 234-7898.

For more information on Seldovia see *The MILEPOST®*, a complete guide to communities on Alaska's road and marine highway systems.

Seward

GPS: N60°07' W149°26'

Located on Resurrection Bay on the east coast of the Kenai Peninsula, 127 miles south of Anchorage by road. **Transportation:** Daily scheduled air service; auto or bus via the Seward Highway from Anchorage; Alaska Marine Highway System from Kodiak, Homer, Cordova or Valdez; Alaska Railroad from Anchorage. **Population:** 2,830. **Zip code:** 99664. **Emergency Services:** Police, Fire Department and Ambulance, emergency only, phone 911; Providence Seward Medical Center, phone (907) 224-5205; Bear Creek Volunteer Fire & EMS, Inc., phone (907) 224-3345/3338; Seward Volunteer Ambulance Corps, phone (907) 224-3987; Coast Guard Search and Rescue, phone (800) 478-5555.

Elevation: Sea level. **Climate:** Average daily maximum temperature in July 63°F; average daily minimum in January 18°F. Average annual precipitation 60 inches; average snowfall 80 inches.

Private Aircraft: Seward airport 2 NE; elev. 22 feet; length 4,240 feet, asphalt; and 2,279 feet, asphalt; fuel 100LL, Jet. Taxi service to town available. Automated weather telephone, (907) 224-2440.

Private Boats: Transient moorage available at the small boat harbor; water and fuel available; Port Director, phone (907) 224-3138, fax (907) 224-7187.

Visitor Facilities: Seward has all visitor facilities, including hotels, motels, bed and breakfasts, many cafes and restaurants, post office, grocery stores, drugstores, travel agencies, gift shops, gas stations, bars and laundromats.

Seward is the gateway to Kenai Fjords National Park, which includes coastal mountains and fjords on the southeastern side of the Kenai Peninsula, the 300-square-mile Harding Icefield and Exit Glacier. Several tour operators in Seward offer day cruises to view the park's scenic coastline and to see the substantial populations of marine mammals that inhabit the park's coastal waters. Exit Glacier in Kenai Fjords National Park is accessible by road from Milepost S 3.7 on the Seward Highway. Harding Icefield is reached via a strenuous 3- to 4-hour hike from the base of Exit Glacier or by charter flightseeing trip out of Seward.

Resurrection Bay is a year-round ice-free harbor, making Seward an important cargo and fishing port. Resurrection Bay is also a popular fishing and boating destination, especially for kayakers. More than 100 charter boats operate out of Seward's Small Boat Harbor, offering fishing, kayaking, sailing and sightseeing trips on Resurrection Bay, as well as out to Kenai Fjords National Park and Chiswell Islands National Wildlife Refuge (see Southcentral Attractions section).

Caines Head State Recreation Area, 6 miles south of Seward, has several WWII bunkers and gun emplacements that once guarded the entrance to Resurrection Bay. It is accessible by boat or via a 4.5-mile beach trail (low tide only).

The annual Fourth of July celebration draws thousands of people to Seward. The event includes a parade and the Mount Marathon Race.

Seward, a home-rule city, has all the amenities of a medium-sized city, including radio stations, TV and a weekly newspaper, the *Seward Phoenix Log*. There are 3 schools with enrollment of 854. Government address: City of Seward, P.O. Box 167, Seward, AK 99664-0167, phone (907) 224-3331, fax (907) 224-4038, e-mail: clerk@arctic.net. Visitor information: Chamber of Commerce, Box 749, Seward, AK 99664, phone (907) 224-8051, fax (907) 224-5353, e-mail: chamber@seward.net, web: www.seward.net/chamber.

For additional information see *The MILEPOST®*, a complete guide to communities on Alaska's road and marine highway systems.

Skwentna

GPS: N61°57' W151°10'

Located in the Mat-Su Valley area in the Yentna River valley on the Skwentna River at its junction with Eightmile Creek, 62 miles north of Tyonek, 70 miles northwest of Anchorage. **Transportation:** Riverboat; daily commuter service or air charter service from Anchorage. **Population:** About 20 locally; 200 more in the surrounding area. **Zip code:** 99667. **Emergency Services:** Alaska State Troopers, Talkeetna; Lake Creek/Skwentna First Responders, phone (907) 373-8800/745-4811; Anchorage clinics and hospitals. Several local residents have been trained as emergency medical technicians.

Climate: Mean temperature for July, the warmest month, is 58°F; mean temperature for January, the coldest month, is 5°F. Mean annual precipitation is 28 inches, including 119 inches of snow.

Private Aircraft: Airstrip adjacent northwest; elev. 148 feet; length 3,400 feet; gravel; fuel 80, 100 (available from Skwentna Roadhouse in 5-gallon cans only); unattended. Runway condition not monitored, visual inspection recom-

mended prior to using. Runway soft during spring thaw. Ski strip west of west threshold.

Visitor Facilities: Accommodations and meals at area lodges, including those at nearby Lake Creek. Lodging at Skwentna includes Hewitt Lake Lodge, (907) 345-7291; Shell Lake Lodge, (907) 733-2817; Whiskey Lake Lodge, cell phone (907) 441-2702 or (907) 333-0305; and Skwentna Roadhouse, (907) 733-2722. Groceries and laundry facilities available. Snow machines, boats, outboard motors, all-terrain vehicles, generators and parts are available locally. Arts and crafts available for purchase include carved wood burl spoons, fur mitts and hats, raw furs. Fishing/hunting licenses, guided and unguided fishing and hunting trips available locally. Snow machines, off-road vehicles and boats may be rented. Snow machine, marine engine, boat and aircraft repair services available. Fuel available: marine gas, diesel, unleaded and regular gasoline. Moorage facilities available.

Skwentna was founded in 1923 when Max and Belle Shellabarger homesteaded and started a guide service, and later a flying service and weather station. After WWII Morrison-Knudson built an airstrip and in 1950 the Army established a radar station at Skwentna and a recreation camp at Shell Lake, 15 air miles from Skwentna. The Shell Lake area remains a popular year-round outdoor recreation site. The airfield was turned over to the Federal Aviation Administration, who maintained it until the early 1970s when it was abandoned. The community grew up around the airstrip, which the state started maintaining in 1981.

Only a few families live in this unincorporated community; many more people receive their mail at the post office, but live up to 30 miles away. There are several fishing lodges in the area, most located on the Talachulitna River, Lake Creek and Fish Creek.

Most area residents make their living in Anchorage, on the North Slope or through their own fishing lodges. According to one resident, "There is no work and not everybody can live off of trapping as people think they can when they show up."

Skwentna is an official checkpoint on the annual Iditarod Trail Sled Dog Race from Anchorage to Nome each March, as well as a gas stop for the Anchorage-to-Nome Gold Rush Classic snow machine race in February. It also is the turnaround point for the 200-mile Iditasport (combines skiing, mountain biking and snowshoeing). The area is a popular spot for weekend snowmobilers and cross-country skiers.

Hunting is good along area rivers for moose and grizzly and black bear. Fly-out hunts for Dall sheep and caribou are available. There also is hunting in the area for grouse and ptarmigan.

The area drained by the Skwentna and Yentna rivers has many lakes and small streams. Five species of salmon are found here in season, as well as rainbow trout, Dolly Varden, grayling, whitefish and pike.

Communications in Skwentna include bush phone service, twice-weekly mail

plane, radio and satellite TV. The community has a school with grades 1 through 12 with enrollment of 14. There is no church. Electricity is from private generators; water from the river or wells. Sewage systems vary from flush toilets to outhouses. Freight arrives via periodic barge service or plane.

Community nonprofit: Skwentna Community Council, General Delivery, Skwentna, AK 99667.

Talkeetna

GPS: N62°19' W150°06'

Located at the junction of the Talkeetna and Susitna rivers, 113 driving miles north of Anchorage via the Parks Highway and Talkeetna Spur Road. **Transportation**: By highway; boat; charter air service; and via the Alaska Railroad. **Population**: 772. **Zip code**: 99676. **Emergency Services**: Alaska State Troopers, Talkeetna Ambulance Service, phone (907) 376-8800 or (907) 745-4811; Fire Department and Ambulance, phone 911; Sunshine Community Medical Center, 4.4 miles Spur Road, phone (907) 733-2273.

Visitor Facilities: Lodging at 5 motels/hotels, a hostel, and several bed and breakfasts. Talkeetna also has several good restaurants, gift shops and shopping for outdoor gear and crafts.

Talkeetna is the jumping-off point for riverboat travel on the Susitna, Talkeetna and Chulitna rivers, and is the staging area for climbing assaults on Mount McKinley and other peaks of the central Alaska Range. Numerous air taxis take visitors to Kahiltna Glacier Base Camp. Local flying services include Doug Geeting Aviation, (800) 770-2366; K2 Aviation, (800) 764-2291; Mt. McKinley Air Service, (800) 564-1765; Talkeetna Air Taxi, (800) 533-2219; and Talkeetna Aero Services, (800) 660-2688. All climbers must register for climbs of Mount McKinley and Mount Foraker. Mountaineering information may be obtained from Talkeetna Ranger Station, P.O. Box 588, Talkeetna, AK 99676; phone (907) 733-2231.

As in the early years, Talkeetna's location near the junction of the Talkeetna,

Chulitna and Susitna rivers acts as a magnet for adventurers and for adventure travel companies offering trips on the Chulitna, Tokositna and other rivers flowing from the southern slopes of the Alaska Range. Riverboat service and float trips are available from: Denali Floats, (907) 733-2384; Talkeetna River Guides, (800) 353-2677; Mahay's Riverboat Service (800) 736-2210; and Talkeetna Riverboat Service (907) 733-3336. Guided fishing from Denali Anglers, (907) 733-1505.

Visitor information: Talkeetna Chamber of Commerce, P.O. Box 334, Talkeetna, AK 99676-0334, phone (907) 733-2330, fax (907) 733-3940.

For more information on Talkeetna, see *The MILEPOST®*, a complete guide to communities on Alaska's road and marine highways systems.

Tatitlek

GPS: N60°52' W146°41'

Located on the northeast shore of Tatitlek Narrows on Prince William Sound, 2 miles southeast of Ellamar, 25 miles southwest of Valdez, 40 miles northwest of Cordova. **Transportation:** Boat; scheduled and charter air service from Valdez. **Population:** 107. **Zip code:** 99677. **Emergency Services:** Village Public Safety Officer, phone (907) 325-2248; Tatitlek Health Clinic, phone (907) 325-2235; Tatitlek EMS, phone (907) 325-2235/2301/2313; Fire Department, phone (907) 325-2248/2311.

Climate: Rain frequent summer and winter. High winds possible in fall. January temperatures in Prince William Sound average 16°F to 30°F; July temperatures range from 48°F to 62°F. Temperatures are seldom below zero or above 75°F.

NOTE: *The village prohibits the sale and importation of alcoholic beverages.*

Private Aircraft: Airstrip adjacent northwest; elev. 25 feet; length 3,700 feet; gravel; no fuel. Runway condition monitored daily, phone (907) 325-2311. Visual inspection recommended prior to using. Use caution—dogs and children on runway at times.

Private Boats: Moorage facilities available. Fuel available; diesel.

Visitor Facilities: Accommodations at apartment operated by Tatitlek Village Council, or arrangements may be made to stay at private homes. Laundry facilities available. No banking services or hunting/fishing licenses. Some groceries may be available at private stores. One charter boat service may be available: Old Mid's Charters, (907) 325-2310).

No major repair services available. Air charter services available through Cordova or Valdez; boats may be available locally for rent.

An Indian village in Gladhaugh Bay was reported as "Tatikhlek" by Ivan Petroff in the 1880 census. Around the turn of the century the village was moved to its present location in the shadow of 3,858-foot Copper Mountain.

Many residents of the ruined village of Chenega moved to Tatitlek following the 1964 Good Friday earthquake and tsunami.

The dominant feature in Tatitlek is the blue-domed Russian Orthodox church.

Residents of this Native village make their living primarily by fishing. Tatitlek's traditional subsistence lifestyle was severely disrupted by the oil spill in Prince William Sound in the spring of 1989. In response to Tatitlek's plight, several Native villages on the shores of nearby Cook Inlet shared their own catch, which volunteers airlifted into Tatitiek.

Bird watching and wildlife viewing opportunities in the area are good. Seabirds, bald eagles, sea otters, bears and mountain goats are seen frequently.

Communications in unincorporated Tatitlek include phones, mail plane, radio and TV. The community is served by 2 churches and a school with grades kindergarten through 12 with enrollment of 22. There is also a community college extension program. There are community electric, water and sewer systems. Freight arrives by boat and cargo plane. Government address: Native Village of Tatitlek, P.O. Box 171, Tatitlek, AK 99677, phone (907) 325-2311, e-mail: Tatitlek@aitc.org. Village corporation: Tatitlek Corp., P.O. Box 650, Cordova, AK 99574, phone (907) 424-3777, fax (907) 424-3773.

Tutka Bay

GPS: N59°28' W151°28'

Located on the Kenai Peninsula on Tutka Bay 9 miles across Kachemak Bay south of Homer. **Transportation**: 45-minute boat ride or 10-minute floatplane or helicopter trip from Homer; water taxi service available from Homer. **Population**: About 30 year-round. **Zip code**: 99603 (via Homer). **Emergency Services**: Alaska State Troopers, Homer, phone (907) 235-8239; South Peninsula Hospital, Homer, phone (907) 235-8101.

Climate: Weather similar to Homer's. Winter temperatures occasionally fall below zero, but seldom colder. Highest temperature recorded in the area 81°F; average annual precipitation 28 inches.

Private Aircraft: No airstrip; helicopter or floatplane landings only.

Private Boats: Free transient moorage at state-owned float at Jakolof Bay, 1 mile west of Tutka Bay.

Visitor Facilities: Accommodations and meals by advance reservation at Tutka Bay Lodge, (907) 235-3905. Water taxi service and fishing and hunting licenses are available at the lodge. There are no stores or other visitor facilities.

Residents of this tiny community are scattered about the coves, bights and lagoons of Tutka Bay, the largest bay adjoining Kachemak Bay. Much of the bay is within Kachemak Bay State Park, and there is a state fish hatchery in Tutka Lagoon.

Residents earn their livings by boat building, fishing, working for the Alaska Dept. of Fish and Game, and producing cottage crafts. One resident reports that what she likes best about Tutka Bay is living close to nature, scheduling activities according to the tides, weather and seasonal abundance of fish, crab, clams, berries and mushrooms.

Tutka Bay has secluded bays, virgin forests and tide pools teeming with marine life. Wildlife that may be seen includes orca and minke whales, sea lions, sea otters, land otters, black bear, seals, porpoises, bald eagles and a wide variety of birds including puffins, cormorants, mallards, oldsquaws, pintails, mergansers, buffleheads, goldeneyes, loons and common murres.

Recreational activities include fishing for salmon, halibut and Dolly Varden, harvesting shrimp and crab, clam digging, photography, berry picking, beachcombing, sea kayaking, hiking and hunting for bear and ducks.

Communications: Call Tutka Bay Lodge, phone (907) 235-3905.

Tyonek

GPS: N61°04' W151°08'

Located on the northwest shore of Cook Inlet on the Cook Inlet Lowland, 43 miles southwest of Anchorage. **Transportation**: Boat; scheduled and charter air service from Anchorage. **Population**: 162. **Zip code**: 99682. **Emergency Services**: Village Public Safety Officer; Tyonek Health Clinic, phone (907) 583-2461; Volunteer Fire Department/Rescue Squad, phone (907) 583-2271.

NOTE: Traditional Native village.

Elevation: 80 feet. **Climate**: Maritime climate characterized by moderate precipitation, generally cool summers and warm winters. Lowest recorded temperature -27°F; recorded high 91°F. Average annual precipitation 23 inches.

Private Aircraft: Airstrip 0.3 mile northeast; elev. 110 feet; length 4.100 feet; gravel; no fuel. Pilots must obtain prior permission from the village before landing. Unicom radio is manned from 8 A.M. to 5 P.M. Monday through Friday. Pilots report turbulence when the wind blows from the east.

Private Boats: No public moorage facilities.

Visitor Facilities: Tyonek Lodge, new in 1997, offers lodging, meals and 2- to 6-day fishing packages on the Chuitna River; for information and reservations phone (800) 557-7087, fax (530) 527-3246. Accommodations at guest house, contact Native Village of Tyonek, (907) 583-2201. No laundry facilities. Groceries available. No major repair services or rental transportation. Fuel available: regular gasoline.

Prehistory of the upper Cook Inlet

region is practically unknown. Earliest written descriptions of the Cook Inlet Athabascans are found in Captain Cook's journal. Cook explored the inlet that bears his name some 37 years after Vitus Bering discovered Alaska in 1741. Cook found that the Natives had iron knives and glass beads, which led him to conclude they were trading indirectly with the Russians. Russian fur-trading posts proliferated in Alaska, and trading settlements were established at Tuiunuk (one of the various past spellings of Tyonek) and Iliamna. These 2 outposts were destroyed in the 1790s due to dissension between the Natives and Russians. After the sale of Alaska to the United States in 1867, the American Alaska Commercial Co. (ACC) replaced the Russian-American Co. as the dominant trading company in Alaska.

ACC's major outpost in upper Cook Inlet was Tyonek. Records show that this post operated from at least 1875. Following the discovery of gold at Resurrection Creek near Turnagain Arm in the 1880s, Tyonek became a major disembarking point for goods and people. The population of Tyonek decreased when Anchorage was founded, but it still is the main settlement on the western shore of Cook Inlet.

In 1965 the Tyonek Indians won a landmark decision when the federal court ruled that the Bureau of Indian Affairs had no right to lease Tyonek Reservation land for oil development without permission of the Indians themselves. The tribe subsequently sold rights to drill for oil and gas beneath the reservation to a group of oil companies for $12.9 million, which has been invested for the benefit of Tyonek residents.

Employment opportunities at Tyonek are limited. Many residents are commercial fishermen or have jobs with the school, store, post office, village administration and other government agencies.

Tyonek residents continue to follow a subsistence lifestyle resembling that of their ancestors. They fish for king, pink and red salmon, hooligan, rainbow trout, Dolly Varden and whitefish. Hunting is for moose, ducks, geese, spruce hens, porcupines, beluga whales and seals. There is some trapping for marten, mink, red fox and beaver. Highbush and lowbush cranberries, blueberries, raspberries and salmonberries are gathered in late summer and early fall.

Accessible by road from Tyonek is Trading Bay State Game Refuge, established to protect waterfowl nesting, feeding and migration wetlands; moose calving areas; and salmon spawning and rearing habitats. Tyonek residents hunt, fish, trap and gather plants and berries on the refuge. A number of commercial set-net fishing sites are operated along the coast of Trading Bay in the summer. Trapping is done in winter.

NOTE: *Much of the land along the Chuitna River is owned by the Tyonek Native Corp., and fishermen must have a guide from Tyonek. Land on the north side of the Chuitna River mouth is public land.*

Communications at Tyonek include phones, daily mail service, radio and TV. The community is served by a Russian Orthodox church and a school with grades kindergarten through 12 with enrollment of 44. There are community electric and water systems. Sewage is managed by septic tanks. Freight arrives by cargo plane and barge. Government address: Native Village of Tyonek, P.O. Box 82009, Tyonek, AK 99682, phone (907) 583-2201, e-mail: tyonek@aitc.org. Village corporation: Tyonek Native Corp., 1689 C St., #219, Anchorage, AK 99503, phone (907) 272-0707, fax (907) 274-7125.

Valdez

GPS: N61°07′ W146°16′

(Val-DEEZ) Located on the Richardson Highway, near the east end of Port Valdez on Valdez Arm in Prince William Sound. **Transportation**: By vehicle via the Richardson Highway; daily scheduled jet service; Alaska Marine Highway ferry to Cordova, Whittier and Seward. **Population**: 4,036. **Zip code**: 99686. **Emergency Services**: Alaska State Troopers, phone (907) 822-3263; City Police, Fire Department and Ambulance, phone (907) 835-4560 or, emergency only, phone 911; Valdez Community Hospital, phone (907) 835-2249. To report oil spills to Dept. of Environmental Conservation, dial operator and ask for Zenith 9300, toll free. For Coast Guard Search and Rescue, dial operator and ask for Zenith 5555, toll free.

Elevation: Sea level. **Climate:** Normal daily maximum in January 30°F; daily minimum 21°F. Normal daily maximum in July 61°F; daily minimum 46°F. Snow from October to April. Winds up to 40 mph common in late fall.

Private Aircraft: Valdez airport, 3 miles east; elev. 120 feet; length 6,500 feet; asphalt; fuel 100LL, jet B.

Private Boats: Transient moorage at Small Boat Harbor; water and fuel available; Harbormaster, phone (907) 835-4981, fax (907) 835-2958.

Visitor Facilities: Valdez has several hotels, motels and bed and breakfasts; a hostel; restaurants and bars; grocery stores, sporting goods stores, drugstore, gift shops, hardware store; public library, museum, post office; and numerous churches.

Valdez is a jumping-off point for wilderness travel in and around Prince William Sound. There are several tour boat operators at the small-boat harbor that offer tours to Columbia Glacier and Prince William Sound, as well as charter boat operators offering fishing trips, sightseeing trips and drop-off service for hikers and kayakers. Kayak rentals and kayak tours of Prince William Sound available from local outfitters. Raft trips of Keystone Canyon are also available.

Valdez, a home-rule city incorporated in 1901, has all the amenities of a medium-sized city, including 2 radio stations, TV and a weekly newspaper, the *Valdez Vanguard*, elementary, junior and senior high schools with total combined enrollment of 965, and Prince William Sound Community College. The college sponsors an annual, nationally recognized theatre conference in June and Elderhostel programs in July and August. Government address: City of Valdez, P.O. Box 307, Valdez, AK 99686, phone (907) 835-4313. Visitor information: Valdez Convention and Visitors Bureau, Box 1603, Valdez, AK 99686, phone (907) 835-2984, e-mail valdezak@alaska.net.

For more information on Valdez, see *The MILEPOST®*, a complete guide to communities on Alaska's road and marine highway systems.

Whittier

GPS: N60°46' W148°41'

Located on the Kenai Peninsula at the head of Passage Canal on Prince William Sound, 60 miles southeast of Anchorage. **Transportation:** By vehicle via the Seward Highway and Whittier Access Road; Alaska Railroad from Anchorage; Alaska Marine Highway from Valdez and Cordova. **Population:** 182. **Zip code:** 99693. **Emergency Services:** Whittier Health Clinic, phone (907) 472-2303; Whittier Volunteer Ambulance Corps, phone clinic (907) 472-2303 or (907) 472-2340; Police, Fire and Medical emergencies, phone (907) 472-2340.

Elevation: 30 feet. **Climate:** Moderate; normal daily temperature for July 56°F; for January, 25°F. Recorded maximum 88°F; minimum -29°F. Mean annual precipitation 174 inches, with 263.5 inches of snow. Winter winds can reach 85 mph.

Private Aircraft: Airstrip adjacent northwest; elev. 30 feet; length 1,480 feet; gravel; no fuel; unattended. Birds in airport area. Runway condition not monitored, visual inspection recommended prior to landing. No winter maintenance; closed from first snowfall until after breakup.

Private Boats: Transient moorage at Small Boat Harbor; water and fuel available; oil disposal system and marine pumpout available; Harbormaster, phone (907) 472-2330, fax (907) 472-2472.

Visitor Facilities: Accommodations available at the Anchor Inn, (907) 472-2534; June's B&B Condo Suites, (888) 472-2396; and Soundview Getaway, (907) 262-4958. Food at Varly's Swiftwater Cafe and at the Anchor Inn. Food is also available from several vendors operating seasonally. Laundry facilities available. No banking services. Fuel available: diesel, unleaded, regular and supreme gasoline and marine gas.

Named after poet John Greenleaf Whittier, the town is nestled at the base of mountains that line Passage Canal, a fjord that extends into Prince William Sound. The passage was, at one time, the quickest route from the Sound to Cook Inlet and interior regions. Originally it was used as part of a portage route for the Chugach Indians traveling Turnagain Arm in search of fish. The surrounding peaks are snowcapped much of the year, and a glacier hangs above the town to the west. Just across from Passage Canal from Whittier is Kittiwake Rookery, largest of its kind in the world. Whittier is also a berry-picker's paradise: blueberries and salmonberries grow in abundance at the edge of town.

Whittier was created by the U.S. government during WWII as a port and petroleum delivery center tied to bases farther north by the Alaska Railroad and later a pipeline. Between 1942 and 1943, the military constructed the 12.4-mile-long Whittier Cutoff, a railway line connecting Whittier with the Seward Highway. The Whittier Cutoff included 2 railroad tunnels: the Anton Anderson Memorial Tunnel, 13,200 feet long, and a second tunnel 4,910 feet long. The railway line remained Whittier's only land link with the rest of Alaska until the Whittier Access Road opened in June 2000. The access road was built by the State of Alaska and took 3 years to complete. The project included construction of a new 430-foot-long vehicle tunnel under Begich Peak, and modification of the 2.5-mile-long Anton Anderson Memorial Tunnel to handle both railroad and vehicle traffic.

Whittier consists largely of 2 massive structures built by the U.S. Army as housing for port workers. The 14-story Begich Towers, formerly the Hodge Building, contains 198 apartments and houses more than half Whittier's population as well as the post office, library and a video-rental store. The Buckner Building, completed in 1953, was once the largest build-ing in Alaska and was called a "city under one roof." Now vacant, it is privately owned and is to be renovated.

A third structure, Whittier Manor, was built in the early 1950s by private developers as rental units for civilian employees and soldiers who were ineligible for family housing elsewhere. In early 1964, the building was bought by another group of developers and became a condominium, which now houses the remainder of Whittier's population.

Since military and government activities ceased, the economy of Whittier rests largely on the fishing industry, charter boat and rental operations, guiding, tourism and the port.

As the gateway to Prince William Sound, Whittier's 332-slip small boat harbor is a busy place. Many Anchorage residents keep pleasure boats here, and there are charter boats available for fishing and hiker/kayaker drop-off service. Kayak rentals and guided trips are available from a local outfitter. Fishing is for silver, pink, chum and king salmon, halibut, red snapper, cutthroat trout, Dolly Varden, crab or shrimp.

There is a hiking trail to Shotgun Cove, and the 2-mile-long Portage Pass Trail to Divide Lake.

Communications at Whittier, a second-class city incorporated in 1969, include phones, radio (CB Channel 11 and Channel 16 VHF) and TV. The community has a school with grades preschool through 12 with enrollment of 24. There are no churches, but services are held locally. There are community electric, water and sewer systems. Freight arrives by barge or rail. Government address: City of Whittier, P.O. Box 608, Whittier, AK 99693, phone (907) 472-2337, fax (907) 472-2404, e-mail: admin@ci.whittier.ak.us, web: www.ci.whittier.ak.us/. Visitor information: Greater Whittier Chamber of Commerce, P.O. Box 607, Whittier, AK 99693, phone (907) 472-3340, fax (907) 472-2491.

For more information on Whittier see *The MILEPOST®*, a complete guide to communities on Alaska's road and marine highway systems.

I n Southcentral Alaska, with its large population (relatively speaking) and extensive high-way system, most wilderness recreation is accessible by road. But it doesn't take long to get off the road and into the bush.

Index of Southcentral Attractions

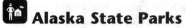
Alaska State Parks
See Anchor River State Recreation Area (SRA); Caines Head SRA; Captain Cook SRA; Chugach State Park; Denali State Park; Independence Mine State Historical Park; Kachemak Bay State Park; Nancy Lake SRA

Bird watching
See Alaska Maritime NWR; Anchorage Coastal Wildlife Refuge (Potter Marsh); Copper River Delta; Gull Island

Cabins
Alaska State Parks
Chugach National Forest
Kenai Fjords National Park
Wrangell-St. Elias National Park

Canoeing
See Kenai National Wildlife Refuge; Nancy Lake Recreation Area

Fishing
Anchorage/Mat-Su Area
Copper River/Wrangell-St.Elias
Kenai Peninsula
Prince William Sound

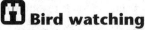
Hiking Trails
Anchorage/Mat-Su Area
Copper River/Wrangell-St. Elias Area
Kenai Peninsula Area
See also Iditarod National Historic Trail

Lighthouses
Cape Hinchinbrook
Cape St. Elias

Marine Parks
Western Prince William Sound
Eastern Prince William Sound
Resurrection Bay

Mountain Biking

Mountaineering

National Forests
Chugach National Forest

National Parks and Monuments
See Kenai Fjords National Park;
Wrangell-St. Elias National Park

Recreational Mining

 Riverrunning
Anchorage/Mat-Su Area
Copper River/Wrangell-St. Elias Area
Kenai Peninsula Area

 Sea Kayaking

 Special Features
See Columbia Glacier; Katalla;
Kayak Island; Prince William Sound

 State Game Refuges
See Goose Bay Refuge; Palmer Hay Flats
Refuge; Susitna Flats Refuge; Trading Bay
Refuge

 Whale Watching
See Alaska Maritime National Wildlife
Refuge; Kenai Fjords National Park;
Kachemak Bay State Park; Prince William
Sound

 Wildlife Refuges
See Alaska Maritime National Wildlife
Refuge; Anchorage Coastal Wildlife
Refuge (Potter Marsh); Kenai National
Wildlife Refuge; Tetlin National Wildlife
Refuge

 Winter Activities
See Hatcher Pass Public Use Area

*Photographing shorebirds at
Hartney Bay near Cordova, during
the Copper River Delta Shorebird
Festival. (© Kris Graef, staff)*

Alaska Maritime National Wildlife Refuge

This wildlife refuge includes more than 2,400 parcels of land on islands, islets, rocks, spires, reefs and headlands of Alaska coastal waters from Point Franklin in the Arctic Ocean to Forrester Island in southeastern Alaska. The refuge totals about 3.5 million acres. In Southcentral, the Duck and Chisik islands in Cook Inlet and the Barren, Pye and Chiswell islands off the Kenai Peninsula are part of this refuge.

Most of this refuge is managed to protect wildlife and the coastal ecosystem. The refuge has the most diverse wildlife species of all the refuges in Alaska. About 75 percent of Alaska's marine birds (40 to 60 million birds among 38 species) use the refuge, congregating in colonies along the coast. Each species has a specialized nesting site, be it rock ledge, crevice, boulder rubble, pinnacle or burrow. This adaptation allows many birds to use a small area of land.

Wildlife: It is estimated that nearly 60 percent of the 105,000 nesting seabirds on the south side of the Kenai Peninsula use the dozen islands of the Chiswell group. Reportedly the largest seabird colony in Cook Inlet, some 80,000 birds, mostly black-legged kittiwakes and common murres, is on 5,700-acre Chisik Island and tiny nearby Duck Island. Other birds that may be seen throughout this area include cormorants, puffins, parakeet auklets, pigeon guillemots, gulls, kittiwakes and fork-tailed storm petrels.

The Chiswells and the Pye Island group harbor Steller sea lion rookeries. Other marine mammals that may be seen in this area are sea otters, seals, porpoises and several species of whales. Land mammals in some areas include black bears and land otters.

The Barren Islands, so named by Captain James Cook in May 1778 because of "their very naked appearance," are anything but barren when seabirds and sea mammals by the thousands arrive annually to give birth and rear their young. The 7 islands (Ishagat, West and East Amatuli, Sugarloaf, Nord, Sud and Carl) total more than 10,000 acres and are geologic remnants of the Kenai Mountains. Some 18 bird species with an estimated population of 500,000 feed in the productive waters around the islands, as do sea lions, harbor seals and whales.

Activities and Access: Most lands of the refuge are virtually inaccessible. Swift tides, rough seas, high winds, rocky shorelines and poor anchorages hamper efforts to view wildlife. However, the Chiswell Islands, 35 miles southwest of Seward, and the Pye Islands, 30 miles west of the Chiswells, are accessible by boat from Seward. Several of Seward's cruise tour operators offering wildlife and glacier cruises of Kenai Fjords National Park include the Chiswell Islands in their itineraries. Charter boats are also available in Seward for viewing the Chiswell and Pye island groups.

On the west side of Cook Inlet, 55 miles southwest of Kenai, Chisik and Duck islands can be reached by charter boat from Kenai or Homer. The Barren Islands, located between the Kenai Peninsula and the Kodiak Island group, are accessible by boat or air charter from Homer.

Visitors who boat near most of the islands may view seabirds and marine mammals. Although permits for landing on the islands are required only for commercial activities, visitors are urged to view wildlife from boats whenever possible to reduce disturbance. Regulations to protect sea lions, however, prohibit boating within a 3-nautical-mile radius of sea lion colonies. Similarly, no person is allowed to approach on land closer than one-half mile or within sight of a listed Steller sea lion rookery. Binoculars and spotting scopes are recommended to view wildlife from a distance. Visitors should be prepared for wet and windy weather.

The refuge operates a visitor center, located on the Sterling Highway in Homer, which offers wildlife exhibits, films and information. The center is open daily from 10 A.M. to 6 P.M., Memorial Day to Labor Day.

For more information: Contact Refuge Manager, Alaska Maritime National Wildlife Refuge, 2355 Kachemak Bay Dr., Suite 101, Homer, AK 99603-8001; phone (907) 235-6546, fax (907) 235-7783.

📌 Anchor River State Recreation Area

Located on the Kenai Peninsula, 16 miles north of Homer and 62 miles south of Soldotna via the Sterling Highway, Anchor River is known for its popular fishing holes.

Activities: The main attraction at Anchor River State Recreation Area is fishing, notably for seasonal king and silver salmon, steelhead and rainbow. The Anchor River is Alaska's only major steelhead stream accessible by road. Steelhead run from late August to November; there is excellent fishing for sea-run Dollies in July and late summer; silvers run in August. Fishing holes are located along a 2-mile segment of the river between the Sterling Highway at Anchor Point and Cook Inlet. Access is from the 1.6-mile Anchor River Road west of the Old Sterling Highway.

Accommodations: There are 5 state campgrounds with a total of 116 campsites along Anchor River Road. All campsites offer picnic and tent sites and, with the exception of Halibut, day-use parking areas. Silver King Campground has 37 campsites; Coho has 28; Steelhead has 32; Slidehole has 17. Halibut Campground has 24 campsites and offers a scenic view of the Aleutian Range. Overnight camping and parking fees are charged.

Access: Turn off Sterling Highway at Milepost 156.9 onto Old Sterling Highway and continue over the Anchor River Bridge, also known as the Erector Set Bridge. Take the first right onto Anchor River (Beach) Road.

For more information: Contact Alaska Department of Natural Resources Public Information Center, 550 W. 7th Ave., Suite 1260, Anchorage, AK 99501-3557; phone, (907) 269-8400, fax (907) 269-8901, TDD (907) 269-8411, email pic@dnr.state.ak.us. Or contact Kenai Area State Parks, P.O. Box 1247, Soldotna, AK 99669; phone (907) 262-5581.

For details on access and accommodations, see *The MILEPOST®*, a complete guide to Alaska's road system.

🦢 Anchorage Coastal Wildlife Refuge (Potter Marsh)

The Anchorage Coastal Wildlife Refuge extends 16 miles south along the coast from Point Woronzof at Anchorage to Potter Creek. The 32,476-acre refuge, established in 1988, includes extensive tidal flats, marsh and alder-bog forest. According to the Alaska Department of Fish and Game, at least 130 bird species have been sighted in the refuge. The best known feature of this coastal refuge is Potter Marsh, a popular bird-viewing area south of Anchorage.

Potter Marsh was created in 1917 when a small creek was dammed during construction of the Alaska Railroad embankment. The resulting marsh is now a favorite nesting area for the lesser Canada goose, mallards, northern pintails, northern shovelers, American wigeons, canvasbacks, red-necked grebes, horned grebes, yellowlegs, northern phalaropes, arctic terns and mew gulls.

Peak concentrations of migrating birds can be viewed from late April through mid-May, when waterbirds stop here on their way to breeding grounds in the north and from late July through August, when shorebirds flock up before setting off to overwinter in more southern climates.

An extensive elevated boardwalk through Potter Marsh offers great bird viewing.

For waterfowl hunting areas within Anchorage Coastal Wildlife Refuge, check with the Alaska Department of Fish and Game.

Access: South 9.6 miles via the Seward Highway from Anchorage. Take Boardwalk Wildlife Viewing (Potter Marsh) exit at Mile S 117.4. Bicyclists, joggers and walkers may use the 11-mile Tony Knowles Coastal Trail from Elderberry Park in Anchorage around Point Woronzof to Point Campbell.

🏚 Cabins

For a reasonable rate, the public can enjoy the wilderness from the cozy confines of a recreation cabin, also referred to as public-use cabins. These cabins are scattered around the Southcentral region of Alaska. Some are located on inland lakes; others are found along the coast. The cabins are used by a variety of outdoor recreationists, everyone from kayakers and canoeists to hikers and hunters, who arrive by boat, by plane, on foot or by snowmachine. Three government agencies operate these backcountry retreats in Southcentral: Alaska State Parks, the U.S. Forest Service (Chugach National Forest) and the National Park Service (see Kenai Fjords and Wrangell-St. Elias). The Alaska State Parks and U.S. Forest Service cabins must be reserved (and paid for) in advance. Details follow.

Keep in mind that poor weather can result in extended cabin stays; therefore, cabin users should come prepared with extra food, fuel and clothing. Most cabins are open year-round.

Alaska State Parks Cabins

Alaska State Parks maintains 28 cabins for public-use in the Southcentral region. Following are brief descriptions of Alaska State Parks public-use cabins in the Anchorage, Kenai, Mat-Su and Prince William Sound areas. Full descriptions (with photos) and current information on cabin availability may be found online at www.alaskastateparks.org.

Cabins sleep 3 to 8 persons and are equipped with wooden sleeping platforms, a wood or oil stove for heating only, a table, chairs or benches and a nearby latrine. A water source is usually nearby, but water should be purified before drinking. See list of cabin essentials on facing page. Visitors should be prepared to gather firewood (dead and down wood only) for heat.

A permit is required to use these cabins, and cabins must be reserved in advance. When a cabin reservation is accepted, a combined receipt and permit to the use cabin is issued. The permit-day begins at noon on the assigned day and ends at noon on the following day. Full payment must accompany reservations. Fees range from $25 to $65 per night, depending on the cabin. Cabin reservations may NOT be made online. The application form is available on the website, and you may use your MasterCard or Visa and fax your cabin request to the Anchorage Public Information Center at (907) 269-8901 or to the Fairbanks Public Information Center at (907) 451-2706. Cabins can be reserved up to 6 months in advance of the first day of intended use.

Cabin reservations may be made by mail or in person to the following offices: Department of Natural Resources Public Information Center, 550 W. 7th Ave., Suite 1260, Anchorage, AK 99501-3557; phone (907) 269-8400; fax (907) 269-8901; TDD (907) 269-8411. Or 3700 Airport Way, Fairbanks, AK 99709-4699; phone (907) 451-2705; fax (907) 451-2706; TDD (907) 451-2770.

Kenai Area Office, Alaska State Parks, Morgan's Landing, P.O. Box 1247, Soldotna, AK 99669; phone (907) 262-5581. (Does not accept credit cards.)

Mat-Su Area Office, Alaska State Parks, Mile 0.7 Bogard Road, HC 32, Box 6706, Wasilla, AK 99654-9719; phone (907) 745-3975. (Does not accept credit cards.)

Anchorage Area State Park Cabins

Eagle River Nature Center Cabin. Sleeps 8; 7-night maximum; fee $45/day. Access: year-round by foot; 1 1/4 miles from Nature Center on Iditarod Trail. Operated by Friends of Eagle River Nature Center, a non-profit organization that manages the Chugach State Park interpretive center at Mile 12 Eagle River Road outside Eagle River. Contact Eagle River Nature Center, 32750 Eagle River Road, Eagle River, AK 99577; phone (907) 694-2108; web site www.ernc.org/.

Eagle River Nature Center Yurt. Sleeps 4; 7-night maximum; fee $45/day. Access: year-round by foot; 2 miles from Nature Center on Albert Loop Trail. A second yurt is located near Rapid Camp on the Crow Pass Trail. It is a 3-mile hike. See Eagle River Nature Center Cabin above for reservation information.

Serenity Falls Hut. Alpine-style hut located 12 miles via Eklutna Lakeside Trail by hike, bike, non-motorized boat or ATV. There are 3 bays with single and double bunks available for rent. Reservations must be made in person at the Anchorage Department of Natural Resources Public Information Center, 550 W. 7th Ave., Ste. 1260, Anchorage, AK 99501. Bunk rentals are $10 and $15 per night. A bay rents for $25-$45 per night. The entire hut may be rented for 2 consecutive nights from Sunday to Thursday for $115 per night. Only one full hut rental is allowed per week.

Yuditnu Creek Cabin. Located at the mouth of Yuditnu Creek on Eklutna Lake in Chugach State Park. Sleeps 6-8; 3-night maximum. Summer access: for Eklutna Lake Cabin is 3 miles via Eklutna Lakeside Trail (hike, bike or ATV), or by non-motorized boat. Winter access via snowshoe, dog sled or snow machine. ATVs are only allowed Sunday through Wednesday.

Kenai Peninsula Area State Park Cabins

Calisto Canyon Cabin. Located in Caines Head State Recreation Area. Sleeps 8; 7-night maximum. Access via Caines Head trail system.

China Poot Lake Cabin. Located in Kachemak Bay State Park on the shores of China Poot (Leisure) Lake. Sleeps 6; 7-night maximum. Access is 2.4 trail miles from Halibut Cove Lagoon trailhead or 13 air miles from Homer. Air taxis can land on lake, but there is no dock at cabin.

Derby Cove Cabin. Located in Caines Head State Recreation Area in forest behind gravel beach. Sleeps 8; 7-night maximum. Cabin is 1/4 mile from ranger station at head of Caines Head trail system.

Halibut Cove Lagoon Overlook Cabin. Located in Kachemak Bay State Park on a rocky point overlooking lagoon. Sleeps 8; 7-night maximum. Access from Halibut Cove Lagoon Public Dock. Ranger station nearby.

Halibut Cove Lagoon East Cabin. Located in Kachemak Bay State Park on a rock bluff overlooking lagoon. Sleeps 6; 7-night maximum. Access from Halibut Cove Lagoon Public Dock. Ranger station nearby.

Halibut Cove Lagoon West Cabin. Located in Kachemak Bay State Park on a rock bluff overlooking lagoon. Sleeps 6; 7-night maximum. Access from Halibut Cove Lagoon Trailhead or by boat.

Porcupine Glacier Cabin. Located in Thumb Cove State Marine Park, 7.5 miles from Seward on east side of Resurrection Bay. Sleeps 8; 7-night maximum. Accessible by boat from Seward.

Sea Star Cove Cabin. Located at the western edge of Kachemak Bay State Park on the south shore of Tutka Bay. Sleeps 6; 7-night maximum. Access is by boat, 14 miles from Homer Harbor. Public buoy at cabin. Boaters are cautioned to stay in middle of bay on approach from Eldred Passage because of underwater rocks and spires along shoreline. Use beach to right of cabin on approach, and watch for rocks. View of Eldred Passage and Cook Inlet from cabin; hiking trail to fish hatchery in Tutka Lagoon.

Spruce Glacier Cabin. Located in Thumb Cove State Marine Park, 7.5 miles from Seward on east side of Resurrection Bay. Sleeps 8; 7-night maximum. Access by boat from Seward. Water source not accessible to all users. Handicap-accessible boardwalk from beach to cabin, approximately 300 feet; assistance necessary from beach landing to boardwalk.

Mat-Su Area State Park Cabins

Bald Lake Cabin. Located in Nancy Lake State Recreation Area on Bald Lake. Sleeps 6; 5-night maximum. Access year-round via

Cabin Essentials You Must Bring

- Lantern
- Portable camp stove and fuel*
- Matches in waterproof container
- Cookware and eating utensils
- Water bottle
- Toilet paper
- Sleeping bag
- Air mattresss or pad
- Towels
- First aid kit
- Insect repellent
- Food*

Always bring extra food, clothing and fuel in case weather conditions prevent you from departing as planned.

well-marked 1/4-mile trail from trailhead at Mile 2.5 Nancy Lake Parkway.

Byers Lake Cabins #1 and #2. Located in Denali State Park on Byers Lake. Sleeps 6; 5-night maximum. Cabin #1 is a traditional, sod-roofed log cabin with summer access via gravel access road to Byers Lake. Summer access to Cabin #2 is via gravel access road to campground, then 1/2 mile walk or via gravel access road to boat launch and 1/2 mile canoe paddle. Both cabins are accessible in winter by snowmachine, skis, dogsled or snowshoes.

James Lake Cabin. Located in Nancy Lake State Recreation Area on James Lake. Sleeps 6; 5-night maximum. The most isolated cabin in the recreation area. Summer access via canoe trail system. Winter access by snowmachine, skis, snowshoes or dogsled using winter trail.

Lynx Lake Cabins #1 #2 and #3. Located in Nancy Lake State Recreation Area on Lynx Lake. Sleeps 4-6; 5-night maximum. Summer access via canoe trail system involving 3 to 4 miles of portages and canoeing across several lakes. Winter access by snowmachine, skis, snowshoes or dogsled using winter trail. Accessible by floatplane except during freeze-up and breakup.

Nancy Lake Cabins #1 #2 #3 and #4. Located in Nancy Lake State Recreation Area on Nancy Lake. Sleep 6-8; 5-night maximum. Summer access to Cabins 1, 2 and 4 via 1/2-mile walking trail from trailhead at Mile 1.8 Nancy Lake Parkway, or via boat or floatplane. Winter access via 1-mile winter trail on lake or summer trail if snow has been packed, by snowmachine, skis, snowshoes or dogsled. Skiplane access if lake ice is thick enough. Cabin 3 access is by boat or floatplane ONLY in summer; cabin is surrounded by private property. In winter, use 2-mile lake trail.

Red Shirt Lake Cabins #1, #2, #3 and #4. Located in Nancy Lake State Recreation Area on Red Shirt Lake. Sleep 6-8; 5-night maximum. Summer access by floatplane or 3-mile hike to lake followed by canoeing across lake to cabin. Carry canoe to Red Shirt, or arrange for canoe with Tippecanoe Rentals (907/495-6688) prior to departure. Winter access by plane or via 8-mile winter trail using snowmachine, skis, snowshoes or dogsled. Not accessible during freeze-up or breakup.

Prince William Sound Area State Park Cabins

Kittiwake Cabin. Located in Shoup Bay State Marine Park, 8.5 miles from Valdez, on east side of inner lagoon. Sleeps 8; 7-night maximum. Oil stove (use #1 stove oil). Access by boat or floatplane from Valdez or by 12-mile trail (foot traffic only) from Valdez.

McAllister Creek Cabin. Located in Shoup Bay State Marine Park, 8.5 miles from Valdez, at mouth of creek on west side of outer bay. Sleeps 8; 7-night maximum. Oil stove (use #1 stove oil). Access by boat or floatplane from Valdez.

Moraine Cabin. Located in Shoup Bay State Marine Park, 8.5 miles from Valdez on east side of inner lagoon, northwest of Uno Creek. Sleeps 8; 7-night maximum. Oil stove (use #1 stove oil). Access by boat or floatplane from Valdez or by 12-mile trail (foot traffic only) from Valdez. This cabin is unavailable to the public between May 15 and September 1.

Chugach National Forest Cabins

There are 42 public-use cabins within Chugach National Forest. Occupany is by permit only, and reservations may be made up to 180 days in advance. Cabins are reserved on a first-come, first-served basis to anyone 18 years in age or older. Cost ranges from $25 to $45 per night per party, depending on cabin. Cabin reservations are made through the National Recreation Reservation Center; phone (877) 444-6777; overseas phone (518) 885-3639; web site http://www.ReserveUSA.com/.

Cabins are available year-round. Frozen lakes may make some fly-in cabins inaccessible in the fall, winter and early spring because floatplanes cannot land. Snow and ice conditions may make winter access difficult at some hike-in cabins. Motorized vehicles and horse/packstock access may be restricted; check with district ranger. Maximum stay is 3 consecutive nights for hike-in cabins from May 15 through August 31; 7 nights from September 1 through May 14. Fly-in and boat-in cabins have a maximum stay of 7 consecutive nights year-round, unless otherwise noted.

The cabin designs include log, A-frame or frame construction, and most are furnished with a table, benches, oil or wood stove and wooden bunks for 4 to 8 people. Many cabins are also equipped with boats and other equipment, such as saws, splitting mauls and brooms. See "Cabins Essentials You Must Bring" on page 155.

Brief descriptions of Chugach National Forest public-use cabins on the Kenai Peninsula and in Prince William Sound are listed below. For more detailed information, contact the U.S. Forest Service, 3301 C St., Suite 300, Anchorage, AK 99503, phone (907) 271-2500. Or contact one of the ranger district offices: Cordova Ranger District, P.O. Box 280, Cordova, AK 99574-0280; phone (907) 424-7661; Seward Ranger District, P.O. Box 390, Seward, AK 99664-0390; phone (907) 224-3374; or Glacier Ranger District, P.O. Box 129, Girdwood, AK 99587; phone (907) 783-3242. Details on individual Chugach National Forest Cabins are also available on the Internet at http://www.fs.fed.us/r10/chugach/.

(See also Hiking Trails and Chugach National Forest this section.)

Kenai Peninsula Area USFS Cabins

Aspen Flats Cabin. Located on the Russian Lakes Trail between Lower and Upper Russian Lakes on the Russian River. Hike-in 9 miles from Russian River Campground trailhead or 12 miles from Cooper Lake trailhead. Sleeps 6.

Barber Cabin. Located on the Russian Lake Trail on the eastern shore of Lower Russian Lake. Easy access via 4-mile hike from Russian River Campground. Also accessible via floatplane from Seward or Cooper Landing (25 minutes). Sleeps 6.

Caribou Cabin. Located on the Resurrection Pass Trail, 7 miles south of north trailhead. Popular for hiking and cross-country skiing. Snowmobile access December 1 to February 15. Trail is relatively flat. Sleeps 6.

Crescent Cabin. Located at the end of Crescent Creek Trail on northwest end of Crescent Lake. Hike in 6.5 miles from trailhead, or fly in from Moose Pass (15 minutes) or Cooper Landing (20 minutes) via floatplane. Sleeps 6.

Crescent Saddle Cabin. Located on the south shore of Crescent Lake. Hike in 11 miles from Crescent Creek trailhead or 7.5 miles via Carter Lake trail. Crescent Lake is very popular for trophy-sized grayling. Sleeps 6.

Crow Pass Cabin. Located in the Chugach Mountains on Crow Creek Trail, 3 miles from Crow Pass trailhead. Alpine setting; elevation is 3,400 feet. Cabin is available June 1 through September 30 only due to winter avalanche hazard. Sleeps 8.

Dale Clemens Memorial Cabin. Located above treeline in the Lost Lake area overlooking Seward and Resurrection Bay. Access is by summer hiking trail (4.5 miles) from Lost Lake subdivision at Mile 5 Seward Highway. Also accessible from Primrose Campground via Primrose Trail (13 miles from trailhead). Winter access route is 2.5 miles. Lost Lake is very popular for rainbow trout fishing. Sleeps 4.

Devil's Pass Cabin. Located at the junction of Devil's Pass and Resurrection Pass trails; 10 miles from Devil's Pass trailhead and 18 miles from south trailhead of Resurrection Pass Trail. Sleeps 6.

East Creek Cabin. Located on the Resurrection Pass Trail, 14.5 miles from north trailhead. Sleeps 6.

Fox Creek Cabin. Located on the Resurrection Pass Trail, 11.5 miles from north trailhead. Sleeps 6.

Juneau Lake Cabin. Located on the Resurrection Pass Trail, 9.5 miles from the south trailhead. Accessible by floatplane from Cooper Landing (10 minutes) or Moose Pass (20 minutes). Sleeps 6.

Lower Paradise Cabin. Located on Lower Paradise Lake in the Paradise Valley, a 15-minute flight southeast of Moose Pass, 20-minute flight northeast of Seward; accessible by floatplane. Hikers may bushwhack their way to Paradise Valley from the Ptarmigan Creek Trail via Snow River Pass. Very scenic and remote area; good fishing for grayling. Sleeps 6.

Resurrection River Cabin. Located on the Resurrection River Trail, approximately 6 miles from trailhead on Exit Glacier Road. Cabin overlooks small pond. Sleeps 6.

Romig Cabin. Located on Resurrection Pass Trail, 9 miles from south trailhead, on south shore of Juneau Lake. Also accessible by floatplane via 10-minute flight from Cooper Landing or 20-minute flight from Moose Pass. Cabin elevation is 1,300 feet. Sleeps 6.

Swan Lake Cabin. Located on Resurrection Pass Trail, 13 miles from south trailhead, on southeast corner of Swan Lake. Also accessible by floatplane via 15-minute flight from Cooper Landing or 30-minute flight from Moose Pass. Fishing for rainbow trout, Dolly Varden and sockeye salmon. Sleeps 6.

Trout Lake Cabin. Located off the Resurrection Pass Trail, 7 miles from south trailhead and 1/2 mile from main trail, on east shore of Trout Lake. Also accessible by floatplane via 10-minute flight from Cooper Landing or 20-minute flight from Moose Pass. Fishing for rainbow trout and whitefish in Trout Lake. Fishing for Dolly Varden, rainbow and grayling in Juneau Creek. Sleeps 6.

Upper Paradise Cabin. Located on Upper Paradise Lake in the Paradise Valley, a 15-minute flight southeast of Moose Pass, 20-minute flight northeast of Seward; accessible by floatplane. Hikers may bushwhack their way to Paradise Valley from the Ptarmigan Creek Trail via Snow River Pass. Very scenic and remote area; good fishing for grayling. Popular with hunters in the fall. Wildlife include moose, black and brown bears and mountain goats. Sleeps 6.

Upper Russian Lake Cabin. Located on Russian Lakes trail on the north shore of Upper Russian Lake, 12 miles from Russian River campground trailhead and 9 miles from Cooper Lake trailhead. Also accessible by floatplane via 20-minute flight from Seward. Sleeps 4.

West Swan Lake Cabin. Located on west side of Swan Lake, 15 minutes north of Cooper Landing by floatplane. No maintained hiking trail to this cabin; Swan lake Cabin at southeast end of lake is accessible via the Resurrection Pass Trail. Secluded cabin; good fishing for rainbow trout, Dolly Varden and sockeye salmon. Sleeps 6.

Prince William Sound USFS Cabins

Beach River Cabin. Located 40 minutes southwest of Cordova by wheel plane (accessible only at low tide) on the east side of Montague Island. Sleeps 6.

Double Bay Cabin. Located on the north side of Hinchinbrook Island, 20 minutes from Cordova by floatplane or 35 miles by boat. Sleeps 6.

Green Island Cabin. Located on the northwest end of Green Island, 40 minutes from Cordova by floatplane or 75 miles from Cordova by boat. Cabin is handicap-accessible. Sleeps 6.

Hook Point Cabin. Located on the southeast side of Hinchinbrook Island, 25 miles southwest of Cordova by wheel plane (accessible at low tide only). Sleeps 10.

Jack Bay Cabin. Located at the east end of Jack Bay off of Valdez Narrows, 15 minutes from Valdez or 40 minutes from Cordova by floatplane, 20 miles from Valdez or 70 miles from Cordvoa by boat. Sleeps 6.

Log Jam Bay Cabin. Located on Stump lake on the northeast side of Montague Island, 45 minutes from either Cordova or Seward by floatplane or wheel plane. Sleeps 4.

Martin Lake Cabin. Located 42 miles east of Cordova at the mouth of Martin Lake; accessible via 30-minute flight by floatplane. Sleeps 4.

Martin Lake Cabin. Located 30 minutes from Cordova by floatplane; sleeps 6. High-use period late August through late September; limit one reservation per person.

McKinley Lake Cabin. Accessible via 2-mile McKinley Lake trail from Mile 21 Copper River Highway; 10 minutes from Cordova via floatplane; or by 2-mile boat or canoe trip up Alaganik Slough. Sleeps 6.

McKinley Trail Cabin. Located at Mile 22 Copper River Highway adjacent McKinley Lake trailhead. Sleeps 6.

Nellie Martin River Cabin. Located 80 miles southwest of Cordova on the southeast side of Montague Island off Patton Bay; 45 minutes by air from either Cordova or Seward (wheel plane access at low tide only). Cabin is located 3/4 mile from beach landing area on the north side of the Nellie Martin River. Sleeps 6.

Pete Dahl Cabin. Located 10 minutes from Cordova by floatplane (accessible at high tide) or 6 miles from Alaganik Slough boat ramp by boat; sleeps 6.

Pigot Bay Cabin. Located on the southwest shore near the head of Pigot Bay, 18 miles northeast of Whittier by boat, 40 minutes from Anchorage by floatplane. Limited hiking in area due to rugged topography. Best situated for exploring by boat. Sleeps 10.

Port Chalmers Cabin. Located on the northwest side of Montague Island at the south end of Port Chalmers. Accessible via floatplane, 40 minutes from Cordova, 60 minutes from Seward; or by boat, 65 miles from Cordova, 70 miles from Whittier, 100 miles from Seward. Sleeps 6.

Power Creek Cabin. Located on the Power Creek trail near Cordova. Spectacular views. Sleeps 6-8.

San Juan Bay Cabin. Located 90 miles southwest of Cordova on the southwest end of Montague Island; access is via wheel plane (50 minutes from Cordova, 40 minutes from Seward). Cabin is 1/2 mile from beach landing area. Sleeps 4.

Shelter Bay Cabin. Located on the west coast of Hinchinbrook Island on the southwest shore of Shelter Bay. Accessible via 20-minute flight from Cordova by floatplane (at high tide) or wheel plane (low tide); 50 miles from Cordova by boat.

Softuk Bar Cabin. Located 45 miles southeast of Cordova on the Gulf of Alaska. Access via wheel plane only at low tide (25 minutes from Cordova). Sleeps 6.

Tiedeman Slough. Located on the Copper River flats; accessible via 10-minute flight from Cordova by floatplane (high tide only) or 7-mile boat trip from Alaganik Slough boat ramp at Mile 17 Copper River Highway. Sleeps 6.

Kenai Fjords National Park Cabins

Occupancy of the Kenai Fjords National Park cabins is by permit only and costs $35 per night. Reservations are accepted, beginning January 2, for May 22 through September 20. Information and reservations are available by phone (907/224-3175), mail or in person at the Seward Visitor Center. Reservations are limited to 3 nights maximum within a calendar year for Aialik Bay and Holgate Arm cabins and 9 nights maximum within a calendar year for North Arm Cabin.

Aialik Bay Cabin. Located on Port Graham Corporation land on upper end of Aialik Bay. Accessible by 4 1/2-hour boat ride or 30-minute flight from Seward. Cabin includes 2 twin bunks, couch, oil stove (oil provided), informational bulletin board and pit toilet with boardwalk. Handicap-accessible. Sleeps 4. Activities in area include kayaking, boating, fishing, hiking, wildlife viewing and tidepooling. Area accesses Aialik and Pedersen glaciers and Pedersen Lagoon. Wildlife includes black and brown bears, bald eagles, salmon, sea otters, sea birds, humpback whales and other marine mammals. Tour boats frequent this area. There are numerous bugs in the area; headnets are highly recommended in July and August. USGS map: Blying Sound D-8.

Holgate Arm Cabin. Located on northeastern shore of Holgate Arm in Aialik Bay. Accessible by 4-hour boat trip or 35-minute flight from Seward. Cabin includes 6 bunks, diesel oil stove (fuel provided), informational bulletin board and a pit toilet. Sleeps 6. Activities in area include kayaking, boating, wildlife viewing, photography and hiking. Area offers spectacular views and sounds of calving ice from Holgate Glacier. Limited fishing opportunities for halibut, rockfish, Dolly Varden and red and silver salmon. Boat is required to access fishing areas in saltwater and Pedersen Lagoon. Blueberries are abundant in late August. Wildlife includes black and brown bears, mountain goats, humpback whales, sea otters, salmon, sea birds and other marine mammals. Tour boats frequent area. Heavy ice pack in Holgate Arm make boating, kayaking and beach landings difficult at times. There are numerous bugs in the area; headnets are highly recommended in July and August. USGS map: Blying Sound D-8.

North Arm Cabin. Located on eastern shore of North Arm in Nuka Bay. Accessible by 40-minute flight from Homer or 60-minute flight from Seward. Cabin includes 6 bunks, oil stove (oil provided), informational bulletin board and pit toilet. Sleeps 6. Cabin offers superb view of a spectacular, 900-foot waterfall tumbling off Storm Mountain across the bay. Activities in area include kayaking, boating, tidepooling, fishing for halibut, rockfish and pink salmon in season and wildlife viewing. Wildlife includes black and brown bears, bald eagles, sea birds and various marine mammals. Low tides make boat anchoring difficult. USGS map: Seldovia C-2.

Wrangell-St. Elias National Park and Preserve Cabins

There are 10 cabins available for public use within Wrangell-St. Elias National Park and Preserve. The cabins are available on a first-come, first-served basis. Wrangell-St. Elias does not have a cabin reservation system at this time.

Users should not expect amenities or furnishings of any kind. All cabins have woodstoves and bunkbeds. The Park Service asks that users replenish firewood supplies and leave the cabins clean and ready for emergency use. Also, be aware of any safety precautions, including bear avoidance.

For more information on cabins within Wrangell St. Elias National Park and Preserve, contact the visitor center at P.O. Box 439, Copper Center, AK 99573, phone (907) 822-5234, fax (907) 822-7216; the Chitina Ranger Station, phone (907) 823-2205; or the Slana Ranger Station on Nabesna Road, phone (907) 822-5238, fax (907) 822-5248, web site www.nps.gov/wrst/cabins.htm, email wrst_interpretation@nps.gov.

Nugget Creek Cabin. 15x19 feet. Located on the north side of Nugget Creek at elevation 3,000 feet. Accessible by ATV, foot, horse, or mountain bike via a 23-mile trail or by small airplane at a short airstrip approximately 200 yards from the cabin. Sleeps 4.

Chelle Lake Cabin. 24x36 feet. Located on the shore of Chelle Lake on the west slope of Mt. Drum at 3,200 feet elevation. Access by air. Sleeps 4.

Glacier Creek Cabin. 8x10 feet. Located 18 miles east of McCarthy, about 1 mile south of the Chitistone River, in an extremely scenic area surrounded by towering cliffs and glaciers. Access by wheel plane. Sleeps 2.

Huberts Landing Cabin. 15x16 feet. Located on a gravel bar at the east end of the Chitina River Valley. Access by wheel plane. Sleeps 2.

Jake's Bar Cabins 1 and 2. 9x13 feet and 6x9 feet. Located on the north shore of the Chitina River about 15 miles south of McCarthy, at elevation 1,000 feet. Access by wheel plane; no summer hiking trail. Each sleeps 2.

Peavine Cabin. 20x24 feet. Situated 14 miles east of McCarthy, on a gravel bar of the Chitistone River surrounded by towering cliffs. It is usually accessed by air, as it offers only limited opportunities for hiking. Sleeps 6.

Solo Mountain Cabin. 10x12 feet. Situated at the base of Solo Mountain about 15 miles southeast of Chisana. Accessible by trail from Chisana or fly in to a short airstrip near the mouth of Solo Creek on the White River, about 8 miles south. Sleeps 1-2.

Too Much Johnson Cabin. 11x15 feet. Located in the historic mining settlement of Chisana. Hike along the Chisana River or to the Gold Hill historic mining district, 10 miles northeast. Access by wheel plane. Sleeps 2.

Upper Gold Run Cabin. 10x16 feet. Located above timberline near the center of the Gold Hill historic mining district, 10 miles north of Chisana. Accessible by foot from Chisana or by air via a short airstrip on Chicken Creek. Sleeps 2.

Caines Head State Recreation Area

This 5,961-acre park is located on Caines Head, a headland that juts into the west side of Resurrection Bay 8 nautical miles south of Seward. To the west, the terrain rises sharply to an elevation of 3,200 feet, from which Harding Icefield in Kenai Fiords National Park can be seen to the west, and Bear Glacier is visible to the south. To the southeast, across Resurrection Bay, lie Renard (Fox) Island and others that form the gateway to Blying Sound and the Pacific Ocean. This area has the abandoned Fort McGilvray and several WWII ammunition storage bunkers and gun emplacements that were used to guard the entrance to Resurrection Bay and the Port of Seward when the territory of Alaska was attacked and occupied by imperial Japanese ground forces.

Facilities include a latrine, fireplaces, campsites and 2 picnic/camping shelters at North Beach. Campsites and a latrine are also located at South Beach. Approximately 4.5 miles of trail allow hikers to explore the WWII fort and the area's natural attractions, including scenic views of the mountains, glaciers and the bay.

North Beach is marked by the remains of an Army dock built in 1941. The land on which the dock was built dropped 5 feet after the 1964 earthquake, and waves eventually destroyed the dock, leaving the pier to stand alone. The pier is no longer safe. Visitors are advised to stay away from it and not to attempt to tie up to its pilings. A public mooring buoy is available nearby for boats up to 30 feet in length.

Fort McGilvray is perched on a 650-foot rocky cliff with beautiful views of Resurrection Bay. Its two firing platforms are intact. The fort is open to explore, but visitors are advised to carry a flashlight as they explore the maze of underground passages and rooms, and to stay away from the cliffs, which are dangerous.

South Beach is a garrison ghost town with remains of the utility buildings and barracks that were home for the 500 soldiers stationed here from July 1941 to May 1943. Visitors are advised not to disturb the remaining structures, as they are unsafe.

Accommodations: Seward has all visitor facilities. There are 2 public-use cabins within the recreation area, Derby Cove Cabin and Calisto Canyon Cabin (see Cabins this section). Open fires are permitted only on ocean beaches or in provided fire rings. Drinking water is scarce; all water must be purified before use.

Access: Primarily by boat from Seward. Charter boats in Seward provide shuttle services to and from the park and cabins. Private boaters note: a mooring buoy exists at North Beach, but there is no mooring buoy at cabins, anchor at your own risk. Pull skiffs, kayaks or inflatables ashore, and secure against high tides and rough surf. Adventurous hikers may hike the 4.5 miles from Lowell Point near Seward to Caines Head. Two miles of the trail are on the beach and must be crossed at low tide.

For more information: Contact Alaska Department of Natural Resources Public Information Center, 550 W. 7th Ave., Suite 1260, Anchorage, AK 99501-3557; phone (907) 269-8400, fax (907) 269-8901, TDD (907) 269-8411, email pic@dnr.state.ak.us. Or contact Kenai Area State Parks, P.O. Box 1247, Soldotna, AK 99669; phone (907) 262-5581.

For details on highway access and accommodations in Seward, see The MILEPOST®, a complete guide to Alaska's road system.

Captain Cook State Recreation Area

Virtually undiscovered by most visitors to the Kenai Peninsula, Captain Cook State Recreation Area offers a peaceful setting of forests, lakes, streams and saltwater beaches.

The recreation area is named for Captain James Cook, the English mariner, who in 1778, explored what is now known as Cook Inlet. At that time, the area was occupied by Denaina Indians, who harvested seasonal runs of salmon and other wild foods. Remains of Denaina barabaras, or housepits, are evidence of the Indians' earlier presence. In recent years, this area has been used for commercial fishing with beach set-nets.

Wildlife: Animals you may see during your visit include moose, bears, coyotes, wolves, beavers and muskrats. In the waters of the inlet are beluga whales and harbor seals, and in the salt-free waters of Swanson River and Stormy Lake, sportsmen will find rainbow trout, silver salmon and arctic char. Birds include bald eagles, sandhill cranes, trumpeter swans, pacific and common loons, golden-eye ducks, mergansers, thrushes, warblers and jays.

Activities: Visitors to the recreation area enjoy canoeing and boating on Stormy Lake, beachcombing the inlet's tide-swept shores, birdwatching, berry picking, riding ATVs (in restricted areas only), bow hunting, hiking nature trails, swimming and searching for agate along the beaches. Visitors are warned to be careful while exploring the mud flats because the tide comes in quickly-it can move in faster than you can run. In winter, ice fishing, riding snow machines and cross-country skiing are popular.

Accommodations: Discovery Campground at the end of the Kenai Spur Highway has 52 campsites. Food, gas and lodging available in Kenai/Soldotna.

Access: From Kenai, drive north 25 miles on the North Kenai Spur Highway to Milepost 36.

For more information: Contact Alaska State Parks Public Information Center, 550 W. 7th Ave., Suite 1260, Anchorage, AK 99501-3557; phone (907) 269-8400, fax (907) 269-8901, TDD (907) 269-8411, email pic@dnr.state.ak.us. Or contact Kenai Area State Parks Box 1247, Soldotna, AK 99669; phone (907) 262-5581.

For details on access and accommodations, see *The MILEPOST®*, a complete guide to Alaska's road system.

Chugach National Forest

This national forest ranks second in size only to Tongass National Forest in southeastern Alaska. Chugach totals 5.8 million acres—about the size of the state of New Hampshire. It stretches from the Kenai Peninsula east across Prince William Sound to encompass the Gulf Coast surrounding the Copper River Delta, then east from there as far as Bering Glacier. Special features of Chugach National Forest are Kayak Island, site of the first documented landing of Europeans in Alaska; Columbia Glacier, one of the largest tidewater glaciers in the world; the wetlands of the Copper River Delta, which serve as nesting, staging and feeding habitat for millions of birds each year; and Portage Glacier and the Begich, Boggs Visitor Center, one of the most visited recreational facilities in Alaska. (See Columbia Glacier, Copper River Delta and Kayak Island this section.)

The 127-mile Seward Highway connecting Anchorage and Seward was designated a National Forest Scenic Byway in 1990. The scenic byways program is designed to alert motorists to areas of unique interest and inform them of the history, geology and biology of national forest lands along our nation's highways.

The Begich, Boggs Visitor Center on Portage Lake is located off the Whittier Access Road, 53 miles south of Anchorage via the Seward Highway. Renovated in 2001, the visitor center features displays on the history of Portage Valley, with information about Chugach National Forest resources. The visitor center is open daily in summer; phone (907) 783-2326 or 783-3242 for current hours.

Portage Glacier has retreated dramatically in recent years. In the 1970s, the glacier extended across the lake to within a mile of the visitor center. By summer 2000, Portage Glacier had retreated around the corner of Byron Peak's northeast ridge. Best views of Portage Glacier are from the sightseeing boat or from the Byron Glacier trail. From the visitor center's lakefront parking lot, it is 1.2 miles to Byron Glacier trailhead and 1.5 miles to M/V Ptarmigan sightseeing boat cruise dock and passenger waiting area.

Wildlife: Chugach National Forest is home to a wide variety of birds, mammals and fish. Black and brown bear inhabit most of the forest, foraging on open tundra slopes and in intertidal zones. In late summer, bears may be seen feeding on spawned-out salmon along streams and rivers. Black bears inhabit most areas, with the exception of some of the islands. Brown bears are found along the eastern shore of Prince William Sound, on the Copper River Delta and occasionally on the Kenai Peninsula.

Record-size moose (some with antler spreads of more than 6 feet) also inhabit the Kenai Peninsula; moose have been transplanted to the Copper River Delta. Sitka black-tailed deer have been transplanted to many islands in Prince William Sound, and caribou have been transplanted to the Kenai Peninsula. Dall sheep can be seen on Kenai Peninsula mountainsides; mountain goats are found on steep hillsides along Prince William Sound, the Copper River Delta and occasionally above Portage Valley. Smaller mammals found within the Chugach include coyotes, lynx, red foxes, wolverines, wolves, porcupines, red squirrels, beavers, land otters, parka squirrels, pikas and hoary marmots.

More than 214 species of resident and migratory birds occupy Chugach National Forest. Seabirds, such as black-legged kittiwakes, nest in seacliff colonies by the thousands. Ptarmigan scurry over alpine tundra, and bald eagles perch on shoreline snags. The tangled rain forest undergrowth hosts Steller's jays, named in 1741 by naturalist Georg Wilhelm Steller, the first European to set foot on Alaskan soil. The Copper River Delta protects one of the largest known concentrations of nesting trumpeter swans in North America. The total population of dusky Canada geese on the delta ranges from 7,500 to 13,500; the delta is the only nesting area of this subspecies. Nesting waterfowl are joined in spring and fall by thousands of migrating shorebirds. (See the checklist of birds found in the Copper River Delta on page 167.)

Saltwater fish available include halibut, red snapper and 5 species of salmon. Razor clams can be dug near Cordova, and shrimp and 3 species of crab may be harvested. Lakes on the Kenai Peninsula contain land-locked Dolly Varden, and many larger lakes and streams are migratory routes for Dolly Varden, rainbow trout and salmon. Other freshwater fish include arctic grayling, hooligan, burbot, lake trout and cutthroat trout.

Boaters in Prince William Sound may see Dall porpoises, harbor seals, sea otters, sea lions and killer and humpback whales.

Activities: Some 200 miles of hiking trails lead to backcountry cabins, ski areas and popular fishing and hunting spots within the Chugach National Forest. Resurrection Pass, Johnson Pass, Russian Lakes, Resurrection River, Lost Lake, Primrose, Ptarmigan Creek, Crescent Lake and Carter Lake trails are located on the Kenai Peninsula. The Cordova Ranger District maintains 13 hiking trails in the Copper River Delta, ranging from the 900-foot boardwalk at Alagnik Slough to the 6-mile Ridge Route Intertie/Alice Smith Cutoff/Ridge. (See Hiking Trails this section for details.)

Backcountry camping is allowed through Chugach National Forest. There are 14 developed campgrounds within Chugach National Forest; see description below under Accommodations.

Boating, fishing and kayaking are popular in Chugach National Forest. Outfitters under permit from the Forest Service offer river-running trips on several rivers and creeks within the national forest.

Chugach National Forest Campgrounds

Bertha Creek (Milepost S 65.5 Seward Highway) 12 tent sites. Near Sixmile Creek raft/kayak put in.

Black Bear (Mile 3.7 Whittier Access Road) 13 tent sites.

Coeur d'Alene (Mile 6.4 Palmer Creek Road) 6 tent sites.

Cooper Creek (Milepost S 50.5 Sterling Highway) 23 sites at South; 7 sites at North.

Crescent Creek (Mile 2.6 Quartz Creek Road off Sterling Highway) 9 sites. Crescent Creek Trail trailhead nearby.

Granite Creek (Milepost S 63 Seward Highway) 19 sites. Near Sixmile Creek raft/kayak put in

Porcupine (Mile 17.8 Hope Highway) 24 sites. Gull Rock Trail trailhead.

Primrose (Milepost S 17 Seward Highway) 10 sites overlooking Kenai Lake. Primrose Trail trailhead.

Ptarmigan Creek (Milepost S 23.3 Seward Highway) 16 sites. Ptarmigan Creek Trail trailhead.

Quartz Creek (Mile 0.5 Quartz Creek Road) 45 sites overlooking Kenai Lake. Fishing in Quartz Creek.

Russian River (Milepost S 52.6 Sterling Highway) 84 sites. Russian Lakes Trail trailhead; fishing in Russian River.

Tenderfoot (Milepost S 46 Seward Highway) 27 sites.

Trail River (Milepost S 24.2 Seward Highway) 64 sites on Kenai Lake.

Williwaw (Mile 4.3 Whittier Access Road) 60 sites. View of Explorer Glacier.

Recreational streams on the Kenai Peninsula include the Kenai River and Sixmile Creek. Sixmile Creek has some Class V whitewater opportunities.

Hunting is permitted within Chugach National Forest, subject to Alaska Department of Fish and Game regulations. Recreational gold panning is also permitted in several areas. *NOTE: Avoid trespassing on private mining claims.*

Popular winter destinations in Chugach National Forest offer cross-country skiing, alpine mountaineering, snowshoeing and snowmobiling. These areas include: Summit Lake/Manitoba Mountain, accessible from Milepost 48 on the Seward Highway; Muskeg Meander Ski Trail, the only cross-country ski trail in the Cordova Ranger District, beginning at Milepost 18.6 Copper River Highway; and Turnagain Pass, 60 miles southeast of Anchorage, open from December 1 to February 15 (and later if snow cover is adequate) for snowmobiling on the west side of the highway and snowshoeing and cross-country skiing on the east side of the highway.

Accommodations: There are 42 Chugach National Forest recreational cabins available to rent; (see Cabins this section for details.) There are 14 Forest Service campgrounds located along the Southcentral road system (see list on page 163). Campground facilities include picnic tables, fire rings, dumpsters, toilets and water pumps. There are no RV hookups. There is a 14-day limit at all campgrounds except Russian River Campground, which has a 3-day limit. A camping fee is charged at all campgrounds. The campgrounds are generally open from Memorial Day through Labor Day. Campsites are available on a first-come, first-served basis at all campgrounds except Cooper Creek South, Ptarmigan Creek, Russian River, Trail River and Williwaw, which are on the National Recreation Reservation Service (as are all of the recreation cabins in Chugach National Forest). For campsite reservations, phone (877) 444-6777; overseas phone (518) 885-3639; or check the web site http://www.ReserveUSA.com/.

For more information: U.S. Forest Service, 3301 C St., Suite 300 Anchorage, AK 99503; phone (907) 271-2500; web site http://www.fs.fed.us/r10/chugach/. Or contact one of the ranger district offices: Cordova Ranger District, P.O. Box 280, Cordova, AK 99574-0280; phone (907) 424-7661; Seward Ranger District, P.O. Box 390, Seward, AK 99664-0390; phone (907) 224-3374; or Glacier Ranger District, P.O. Box 129, Girdwood, AK 99587; phone (907) 783-3242.

For details on access and accommodations, see *The MILEPOST®*, a complete guide to Alaska's road system.

Chugach State Park

Although located on the doorstep of Anchorage, Alaska's largest city, this mountainous park offers excellent wilderness experiences, summer or winter. Chugach State Park is one of the nation's largest state parks, with nearly 495,000 acres.

Several thousand years ago, massive glaciers covered this area. This park's beautiful mountain lakes, sharp ridges and broad, U-shaped valleys were all glacially carved. Ice fields and glaciers still remain in the park, and a few such as Eklutna Glacier can be viewed on a day's hike.

Although the spectacular alpine scenery is the park's predominant feature, it offers other natural phenomena such as the bore tide in Turnagain Arm. Twice each day, a wall of water up to 6 feet high races up the channel as the tide comes in. Spectators say the bore tides come in at a speed of 10 to 15 mph, and larger ones sound like trains. A good place to watch the event is from Beluga Point viewpoint at Milepost S 110.4 on the Seward Highway.

Wildlife: Chugach State Park's abundant wildlife ranges from the popular bald eagles and whales to the less popular mosquitoes (27 varieties inhabit the park). Viewing areas at Eklutna Lake and Eagle River valley afford excellent opportunities to see Dall sheep and moose. The adventurous can see more elusive species that live in remote areas of the park, such as mountain goats, wolves and sharp-shinned hawks. Brown/grizzly and black bears roam throughout the park. Do not leave open food around campsites, and make noise while hiking through the bush to avoid bear encounters.

The elevation change in the park, from sea level to 8,000 feet, supports a variety of vegetation from dense forests to alpine tundra, mosses, mushrooms, trees, berries and lichens.. Summer wildflowers range from common fireweed to orchids.

Activities: Chugach State Park provides a variety of recreational opportunities for all seasons. Hiking, back-country camping, wildlife viewing, berry picking and cross-country skiing are among the many wilderness activities available. Snowmobiling and mountain biking in season are allowed within the state park on designated trails.

Chugach State Park has several road accessible campgrounds and picnic areas on the Glenn and Seward Highways; see The MILEPOST® for details.

There are several access points by highway to centers of activity in Chugach State Park since the park flanks Anchorage to the north, east and south. North from Anchorage on the Glenn Highway, take the Eklutna Road exit (Milepost A 26.3), and drive in 10 miles to reach Eklutna Lake Recreation Area. Eklutna Lake is 7 miles long, the largest lake in Chugach State Park. It is open to watercraft although there is no boat ramp. Watersports include windsurfing, canoeing, kayaking, fishing, sailing and motorboating. The recreation area has a 50-site campground and picnic area. It has several popular hiking trails, including the Lakeside Trail, Bold Ridge Trail, East Fork Trail and Eklutna Glacier Trail. Lakeside Trail is popular with mountain bikers in the summer and snowmobilers in the winter. There are free remote campsites located along the Lakeside Trail at Mile 8, 11 and 12. There is a public-use cabin at Yuditnu Creek and a communal shelter (Serenity Falls Hut) at Mile 12.5 on the Lakeside Trail (see Cabins this section). Good mountain biking, horseback riding and climbing area. Cross-country skiing and snowmobiling in winter.

Eagle River Road, accessed from the Eagle River Loop Road or Eagle River exit off the Glenn Highway, leads 12.3 miles east to Eagle River Nature Center in Chugach State Park. This beautifully situated nature center, with its views of the Chugach Mountains, has viewing telescopes and offers educational and interpretive programs throughout the year. Two self-guiding natural trails are accessed from the Nature Center: the 2/3-mile Rodak Nature Trail loop and the 3-mile Albert Loop Trail. Both are easy walks along gravel paths. The trails are usually packed for winter walkers. The trailhead for the Old Iditarod-Crow Pass trail is also located at Eagle River Nature Center. A public-use cabin and two yurts are available for rent (see Cabins this section). Cross-country skiing and snowshoeing in winter. For more information contact: Eagle River Nature Center, 32750 Eagle River Road, Eagle River, AK 99577; phone (907) 694-2108, or (907) 694-6391 for recorded message, web site www.ernc.org/.

River running within the park is confined to the Eagle River. Kayaks, rafts and canoes can put in at Mile 7.4 Eagle River Road at the North Fork Eagle River access/day-use area. Additional river access at Mile 9 Moose Pond Put In for nonmotorized craft. The Eagle River offers class II, III and IV float trips. Be sure to read the information posted at the trailhead before heading downriver. Check with Chugach State Park rangers for current river conditions; phone (907) 345-5014.

Chugach State Park's Hillside Trail System in Anchorage has several hiking trails including Flattop, the most popular in the state, Williwaw Lakes and Powerline. The Hillside Trail system is accessed from either the Glen Alps or Prospect Heights trailheads. Both are reached by driving south from downtown Anchorage via the Seward Highway to the O'Malley Road exit, then driving east on O'Malley Road 3.7 miles to Hillside Drive. For Glen Alps trailhead, turn right and follow signs 5.5 miles to parking lot. For Prospect Heights trailhead, keep left at Hillside intersection and continue on Upper O'Malley for about 2 miles; follow signs. Parking fee is $5 per day at both trailheads.

The Seward Highway south from Anchorage gives access to several Chugach State Park campgrounds, picnic areas, viewpoints and hiking trails. Turnagain Arm Trail is a popular hike, with trailheads at Potter Creek Viewpoint, McHugh Creek Picnic Area, Rainbow and Windy Corner. The Crow Pass (Old Iditarod Trail) is accessed from Crow Creek Road off the Alyeska Highway. An endurance race is run over the Crow Pass Trail in summer. Other trails include the Indian Valley trail and the Bird Ridge trail, the first snow-free spring hike in Chugach State Park, according to park rangers.

Beluga Point scenic viewpoint at Milepost S 110.4 is a good place to see the all-white beluga whales and boretides. (Beluga Point is also accessible from the Turnagain Arm Trail.) The best time to see belugas is at high tide from mid-July through August when salmon make their spawning runs.

A bore tide is a wall of water coming in with the tide. It is created by a wide range between high and low tides (more than 35 feet in Cook Inlet) and by the narrow, shallow, gently sloping shape of the arm. Bore tides in Turnagain Arm range from a half-foot to 6 feet high and travel between 10 and 15 mph. Minus tides, new or full moons and high winds contribute to a large bore tide, which may sound like a train. The bore tide generally occurs about 45 minutes after the predicted Anchorage low tide.

Beluga Point also has the earliest evidence of humans along Turnagain Arm. It was the lookout of choice for prehistoric hunters in search of beluga whales and Dall sheep.

For more information: Contact Alaska Department of Natural Resources Public Information Center, 550 W. 7th Ave., Suite 1260, Anchorage, AK 99501-3557; phone (907) 269-8400, fax (907) 269-8901, TDD (907) 269-8411, email pic@dnr.state.ak.us. Or contact Chugach State Park, HC 52, Box 8999, Indian, AK 99540; phone (907) 345-5014; email Chugach_State_Park@dnr.state.ak.us. The Chugach State Park office is located in the Potter Section House on the Seward Highway, 11.8 miles south of downtown Anchorage. The office has maps showing access to the park's recreation areas.

(See also Cabins, Hiking Trails and River Running this section.)

Copper River Delta

The 20-mile-wide mouth of the glacier-fed Copper River is noted for its annual waterfowl and shorebird migrations. The 400-square-miles of habitat ranges from open meadows, small ponds and sloughs to hemlock and spruce forest to remote islands and marine waters.

The Copper River Delta lies within Chugach National Forest. The Cordova Ranger District maintains a number of hiking trails and interpetive sites along the Copper River Highway, which leads east from the community of Cordova to dead end near Childs Glacier. There are also several U.S. Forest Service recreation cabins in the Copper River Delta area, accessible by boat, trail or floatplane. (See Cabins and Hiking Trails this section.)

The 2 best bird watching areas in the Copper River Delta are Hartney Bay for shorebirds and Alaganik Slough for wetland birds. Alaganik Slough Chugach National Forest Recreation Area is located 16.8 miles east of Cordova via the Copper River Highway, then 3.2 miles south via a gravel road. Alaganik Slough is the best place to see the largest and most conspicuous of waterfowl, the trumpeter swan, with its 6- to 8-foot wingspan. Once an endangered species, the greatest concentration of trumpeter swans in North America now breeds along the Copper River and its tributaries in summer. The Copper-Bering river deltas and adjacent areas also provide nesting grounds for dusky Canada geese. Alaganik Slough has a 1,000-foot wetland boardwalk with interpretive information, viewing blinds and a tower for bird watchers. The recreation area also has picnic tables, firepits, toilets and a boat launch.

Hartney Bay, about 6 miles from downtown Cordova via Whitshed Road, is a popular bird watching spot for the spring shorebird migration. Flocks of western and dunlin sandpipers occur in late April and early May. Densities of more than 250,000 shorebirds per square mile have been observed feeding on the delta. Cordova hosts an annual Copper River Delta Shorebird Festival in May, with 5 days of birding along the tidal mutflats and wetlands of the Copper River Delta.

Migratory waterfowl in the delta include white-fronted geese, snow geese, teals, wigeons, shovellers, scaups and goldeneyes. The most abundant duck is the pintail. Hundreds of thousands pass through in the spring, and many remain to breed and nest.

Thousands of sandhill cranes stop to rest and feed on the flats on their way north to nest. Pelagic birds in marine waters off the Copper River Delta area include pigeon guillemots, marbled murrelets, pelagic and red-faced cormornats, white-winged and surf scoters,

BIRDS OF THE COPPER RIVER DELTA

American Dipper
American Robin
American Wigeon
Arctic Tern
Baird's Sandpiper
Bald Eagle
Bar-tailed Godwit
Barrow's Goldeneye
Belted Kingfisher
Black Oystercatcher
Black Turnstone
Black-bellied Plover
Black-billed Magpie
Black-legged Kittiwake
Brown Creeper
Bufflehead
Canada Goose
Chestnut-backed Chickadee
Common Goldeneye
Common Merganser
Common Murre
Common Raven
Common Redpoll
Common Snipe
Downy Woodpecker
Dunlin
Fox Sparrow
Gadwall
Glaucous-winged Gull
Golden-crowned Kinglet
Golden-crowned Sparrow
Gray-cheeked Thrush
Great Blue Heron
Great White-fronted Goose
Greater Scaup
Greater Yellowlegs
Green-winged Teal
Hairy Woodpecker
Horned Grebe
Least Sandpiper
Lesser Golden Polover
Lesser Scaup

Lesser Yellowlegs
MallardMew Gull
Northern Flicker
Northern Goshawk
Northern Harrier
Northern Pintail
Northern Shoveler
Northwestern Crow
Orange-crowned Warbler
Parasitic Jaeger
Pectoral Sandpiper
Pine Grosbeak
Pine Siskin
Red Crossbill
Red Knot
Red-breasted Merganser
Red-breasted Nuthatch
Red-necked Phalarope
Red-throated Loon
Rock Sandpiper
Ruddy Turnstone
Rufous Hummingbird
Sanderling
Savannah Sparrow
Semipalmated Plover
Semipalmated Sandpiper
Sharp-shinned Hawk
Short-billed Dowitcher
Short-eared owls
Song Sparrow
Steller's Jay
Surfbird
Tree Swallow
Tumpeter Swan
Varied Thrush
Wandering tattler
Western Sandpiper
Whimbrel
Wilson's Warbler
Winter Wren

Bonaparte's gulls and harlequin ducks. Charter boats for pelagic bird watching are available in Cordova. (See "Birds of the Copper River Delta" below.)

Mammals that may be seen in the Copper River Delta include black-tailed deer, moose, beaver, muskrat, mink and otter. Black and brown bears leave their dens in spring to feed on grasses in the Delta meadows, and return in late summer and fall to feed on spawning salmon. The Delta moose herd, which thrives on the abundant supply of willow in the area, was first introduced in 1949. The overlook at the end of Haystack Trail, a short 0.8-mile hike from Mile 19.1 Copper River Highway through a lush spruce-hemlock forest, is a good place to see moose, bears and the delta. Several glaciers in the Chugach Mountains surrounding the Copper River Delta can be seen from the Copper River Highway: Scott Glacier, Sheridan Glacier, Sherman Glacier and Goodwin Glacier. Sheridan and Saddlebag glaciers are accessible by hiking trail. Childs Glacier is accessible via the Copper River Highway to Childs Glacier Recreation Area at Mile 48. The USFS site has picnic tables, toilets, short trails (gravel, handicap-accessible) and a handicap-accessible viewing platform to see the 300-foot-high glacier face located 1,000 feet across the Copper River. The longer 1.2-mile Childs Glacier Trail (also handicap accessible) begins at the Million Dollar Bridge viewing platform and follows the Copper River to an excellent viewpoint of Childs Glacier. This is an active glacier, and calving ice may cause waves to break over the beach and into the viewing area. Be prepared to run to higher ground.

Other safety concerns in the Copper River Delta area are bears and tides. Always watch for bears on hiking trails. When traveling on the mudflats, pay attention to tide tables; tidewaters come in quickly, and it's easy to become stranded by tidal sloughs and softening mud.

Access to the delta is by floatplane or boat from Cordova (see Communities this section) or via the Copper River Highway. *NOTE: Snow may prevent access to many points along the Copper River Highway well into spring.* For a detailed log of the 48-mile-long Copper River Highway, see *The MILEPOST®*, a complete guide to Alaska's road and marine highway systems.

For more information: Chugach National Forest, Cordova Ranger District, P.O. Box 280, Cordova, AK 99574; phone (907) 424-7661.

(See also Cabins, Hiking Trails and Marine Parks this section.)

Denali State Park

Located adjacent to the southern border of Denali National Park (listed under Attractions in the INTERIOR regional section), this 324,420-acre park offers a spectacular view of nearby Mount McKinley/Denali and surrounding peaks and glaciers. The park is located between the Talkeetna Mountains and the Alaska Range and straddles the Parks Highway, the main route between Anchorage and Fairbanks. Denali State Park's landscape is dominated by Curry and Kesugi ridges, which form a rugged, 30-mile spine down the length of the park. Small lakes dot these rock- and tundra-covered ridges; high points up to 4,600 feet overlook the heart of the Alaska Range. Mount McKinley's 20,320-foot summit, the highest in North America, rises just 40 miles from Curry Ridge. The mountain and its companions, known as the McKinley Group, are accented by a year-round mantle of snow above 8,000 feet, with spectacular glaciers and deep gorges. Other prominent peaks seen from Denali State Park viewpoints are Mounts Hunter and Silverthrone, the Moose's Tooth and the spires of the Tokosha Mountains. Valley glaciers, including Ruth, Buckskin and Eldridge, flow from these high peaks and feed the wide, braided Chulitna River.

The park is a relatively untouched wilderness: wildlife undisturbed by contact with man; a summer explosion of tundra plantlife; and constantly shifting channels of wide, glacierfed streams.

The landscape is dominated by upland spruce-hardwood forests, especially along the highway and by fragile alpine tundra above tree line at about 2,000 feet. Moist tundra occurs in some poorly drained areas, and patches of dense birch, alder and willow thickets grow on hillsides. Black spruce grows in muskeg areas, and large, black cottonwoods inhabit riverbanks, particularly west of the Chulitna River. In late summer and early fall, berry pickers are rewarded with blueberries, highbush and lowbush cranberries, currants, watermelon berries, crowberries and cloud-berries.

Climate: Weather in the park is moderated by coastal waters 100 miles to the south near Anchorage. The Alaska Range shields the park from the extreme cold of the Interior to the north. Snow accumulations, beginning in October, build to 5 or 6 feet by March. Snow usually melts during April and May although snow patches above 2,500 feet often last into July. Summer temperatures average 44°F to 68°F, with rare highs above 80°F. Midsummer brings more than 20 hours of daylight. In winter, average temperatures range from zero to 40°F, although extreme lows can drop to -40°F and lower.

Wildlife: Brown/grizzly and black bears are common throughout the park above and below tree line. Other large mammals found in the park are moose, wolves and very rarely caribou in the northern section. Smaller mammals include red fox, wolverine, lynx, marten, mink, weasel, beaver, snowshoe hare and red squirrel. A large number of resident and migratory birds, including ravens, ptarmigan, golden and bald eagles, peregrine falcons and many songbirds can be seen in the throughout the park.

Fish in the Susitna and Chulitna rivers include Dolly Varden, arctic grayling, rainbow trout and chum, pink, king, red and silver salmon. Small numbers of lake trout occur in Byers, Spink and Lucy lakes and rainbow trout, grayling and Dolly Varden are found in Byers Lake and Troublesome and Little Coal creeks.

Activities: One of the focuses of Denali State Park is to provide hiking opportunities. There is access to the park's alpine areas and spectacular views from the Troublesome Creek Trail, Ermine Hill Trail and Little Coal Creek Trail, and an easy hike around Byers Lake via Byers Lake Loop Trail; see Hiking Trails this section for details. Hikers should plan for a variety of conditions, including gravel bars, woodland, heavy brush and soggy tundra. No fires are permitted in the backcountry; use camp stoves.

Canoe and kayak rentals are available from Susitna Expeditions, located on the Byers Lake Campground access road. A boat launch is located on the campground access road as well. Gas-powered motors are not allowed on Byers Lake.

Cross-country skiing is outstanding during March, April and often into May. No trails are maintained in the park in winter. Snow depths may reach 6 feet, covering most brush and rocks. Skiers who travel up Curry or Kesugi ridges should take care to avoid potential avalanche slopes, especially above timberline. Snowmobiles and other off-road vehicles are permitted in the park only when the snow is deep enough to protect vegetation (about 16 inches).

Accommodations: The main recreational development at the park is Byers Lake Campground at Milepost A 147 on the Parks Highway. Overnight camping fee is charged. Byers Lake has 66 campsites, picnic areas, fishing and boating. Fires must be confined to developed fire rings. Denali View North Campground, Milepost 162.5, provides fee-camping with spectacular views of Denali and the Alaska Range. There is ample RV parking.

Access: Denali State Park is accessible from the Parks Highway, 147 miles north of Anchorage and 215 miles south of Fairbanks. The seldom-used east side of the park offers excellent wilderness recreation opportunities and is accessible via the Alaska Railroad. The best place to get off the train is just after the railroad crosses the Susitna River past Gold Creek.

For more information: Contact Alaska Department of Natural Resources Public Information Center, 550 W. 7th Ave., Suite 1260, Anchorage, AK 99501-3557; phone (907) 269-8400, fax (907) 269-8901, TDD (907) 269-8411, email pic@dnr.state.ak.us. Or contact Mat-Su Area State Parks, HC32, Box 6706, Wasilla, AK 99654-9719; phone (907) 745-3975.

For details on access and accommodations, see *The MILEPOST®*, a complete guide to Alaska's road system.

Fishing

Home to the renowned Kenai River and other major fisheries, Southcentral offers many excellent sportfishing opportunities for halibut, Dolly Varden and a variety of salmon and trout species. Salmon are the most popular species of sport fish in Southcentral. For more information on fishing in Southcentral Alaska, contact the Alaska Department of Fish and Game, 333 Raspberry Road, Anchorage, AK 99518-1599; phone (907) 746-6300, fax (907) 746-6305, web site http://www.state.ak.us/adfg/adfghome.htm.

Anchorage/Mat-Su Area Sportfishing

Alexander Creek. Heads in Alexander Lake and flows southeast 35 miles to the Susitna River, 27 miles northwest of Anchorage. One of the best fishing streams in southcentral Alaska. Numerous lodges in the area. Primary access by floatplane from Anchorage. Fish available: king salmon excellent from late May through June, use egg clusters, spinners, spoons; silver salmon mid-July to September, use spinners or egg clusters; pink salmon in even-numbered years, mid-July through mid-August, use small spoons; rainbow trout excellent late May through September 1, use flies or spinning-type lures; grayling in late May and early June, use flies and small spinners.

Deshka River. Located about 60 miles northwest of Anchorage. One of the best fishing streams in southcentral Alaska. Primary access by floatplane from Anchorage or riverboat from Susitna Landing. Numerous lodges in the area. Fish available: excellent fishing for king salmon, 20 to 25 pounds and up, late May to early July, use egg clusters, spinners, spoons; silver salmon, 4 to 6 pounds, mid-July through September, use spinners or egg clusters; pink salmon in even-numbered years, mid-July to mid-August, use small spoons; rainbow trout excellent late May through September, use flies or spinning-type lures; grayling, 10 to 16 inches, best late May and early June, use flies and small spinners; northern pike June through September, use bait.

High Lake. A 1-mile-wide lake at the 3,006-foot elevation in the Chugach Mountains southwest of Glennallen, 5.2 miles southeast of Tazlina Lake. Accessible by floatplane from Glennallen. Lake trout to 22 inches, June and early July with small spoons; some rainbow fly-fishing. Cabins, boats and motors available.

Jan Lakes. Fly-in lakes located 5 miles from Lake Louise or 12 miles from Tolsona Lake at Milepost 160 on the Glenn Highway. Accessible by floatplane from Lake Louise, Lee's Lake or Tolsona Lake. North Jan Lake has good rainbow trout fishery. South Jan Lake has land-locked silver salmon and king salmon.

Judd Lake. Lake 0.9 mile across located on the Talachulitna River, about 65 miles northwest of Anchorage. Primary access by floatplane from Anchorage. Lodge on lake. Fish available: silver salmon average 6 to 8 pounds, best in August; red salmon average 7 to 8 pounds, best mid-July to early August; chum salmon average 10 to 12 pounds, best mid-July to early August; pink salmon in even-numbered years, average 3 to 4 pounds, best mid-to late July; grayling and Dolly Varden mid-June through September, best early and late.

Lake Creek. Flows from the foothills of Mount McKinley, about 70 miles northwest of Anchorage. One of the best fishing streams in southcentral Alaska. Primary access by float-plane from Anchorage. Numerous lodges in the area. Fish available: king salmon excellent late May through early July, use egg clusters, spinners, spoons; silver and chum salmon mid-July through August, use spinners or egg clusters; pink salmon in even-numbered years, mid-July through mid-August, use small spoons; rainbow trout and grayling excellent just after breakup and just before freezeup, use flies or spinning-type lures for rainbows, flies for grayling.

Lewis River. Heads on Mount Susitna and flows 30 miles to Cook Inlet, 30 miles west of Anchorage. Accessible by small wheel plane from Anchorage. Fish available: king salmon late May through June, use egg clusters, spinners, spoons; silver salmon July to September, use egg clusters, spinners, spoons; pink salmon July and August, use small spoons; rainbow trout year-round, use flies or lures.

Little Susitna River. Heads at Mint Glacier in the Talkeetna Mountains and flows 110 miles southwest to Cook Inlet. Tremendous king salmon run and one of the largest silver salmon runs in Southcentral. Access from Milepost A 57 Parks Highway; riverboat charters available. Fish available: king salmon to 30 pounds, late May and June, use large red spinners or salmon eggs; silver salmon to 15 pounds, biggest run in late July, use small weighted spoons or fresh salmon roe; red salmon to 10 pounds, mid-July, use coho flies or salmon eggs.

Lucy Lake. Fly-in lake 1.6 miles long located within Denali State Park near Eldridge Glacier terminus, 40 miles north of Talkeetna. Fish available: lake trout to 20 pounds, June and July, use spinner and spoons; grayling, use flies.

Portage Creek. A 1.5-mile-long tributary to the Susitna River, located 2.5 miles southwest of Curry and 18 miles northeast of Talkeetna. Fish available: rainbow trout, grayling, salmon July, August and September, use spoons, spinners, flies.

Shell Lake. A 5-mile-long lake located 85 miles northwest of Anchorage, 15 miles from Skwentna. Primary access by floatplane in summer, skiplane in winter. Fish available: red and silver salmon late July through September; large lake and rainbow trout; some grayling. Winter ice fishing for burbot. Also wildlife watching and photography, cross-country skiing and dog mushing.

Spink Lake. A 1.3-mile-long, fly-in lake located in Denali State Park, 31 miles north of Talkeetna. Fish available: rainbow trout to 8 pounds; a few Dolly Varden July, August and September, use spinners and spoons.

Susitna River. This major Southcentral river heads at Susitna Glacier in the Alaska Range and flows southwest 260 miles to Cook Inlet. Access to fishing spots by boat or fly-in. Road access at Willow Creek Parkway, Milepost A 70.8 Parks Highway. Fish available: king, sockeye, coho, pink and chum salmon; Dolly Varden; rainbow trout, lake trout, northern pike, burbot. grayling and whitefish.

Talachulitna River. Located about 65 miles northwest of Anchorage. Primary access by floatplane from Anchorage. One of the best fishing streams in southcentral Alaska. Lodges in the area. Fish available: king salmon, 25 to 50 pounds, best mid-June through early July, use big spoons and spinners; silver salmon average 6 to 8 pounds, best August through early September, use flies or lures; red salmon average 7 to 8 pounds, best mid-July to mid-August; chum salmon average 10 to 12 pounds, best mid-June through mid-July; pink salmon in even-numbered years averaging 3 to 4 pounds, best mid- to late July; rainbow trout average 1 to 3 pounds; grayling average 1 to 2 pounds; Dolly Varden average 2 to 4 pounds, mid-June through September, best early and late. NOTE: Single hook, artificial lures only, release rainbow trout.

Talkeetna River. Heads at Talkeetna Glacier in the Talkeetna Mountains and flows 85 miles southwest to the Susitna River near the community of Talkeetna. Access by riverboat from Talkeetna to fishing streams. Fish available: 5 species of Pacific salmon, rainbow trout and lake trout.

Theodore River. This river flows southeast 35 miles to Cook Inlet, 32 miles west of Anchorage. Accessible by small wheel plane from Anchorage. Fish available: king salmon late May through June, use egg clusters, spinners, spoons; silver salmon July to September, use egg clusters, spinners, spoons; pink salmon July and August, use small spoons; rainbow trout year-round, use flies or lures.

Yentna River. Located about 50 miles (35 minutes by small plane) northwest of Anchorage. Primary access by floatplane from Anchorage. Excellent fishery. Lodges on river. Fish available: king salmon late May to early July, use spoons; red salmon mid-June to late July, use spoons or flies; silver, chum and pink salmon mid-July through August, use spoons; rainbow trout and grayling year-round in season, best late August through September.

Copper River/Wrangell-St. Elias Area Sportfishing

Copper Lake. A 5.5-mile-long, fly-in lake located within Wrangell-St. Elias National Park and Preserve, west of Tanada Lake. Accessible via Nabesna Road, which leaves the Tok Cutoff at Milepost GJ 59.8. Fish available: lake trout 10 to 12 pounds, mid-June to September, use red and white spoons; kokanee 10 to 12 inches, mid-June to July, use small spinner; grayling 12 to 20 inches, July through September, use flies; burbot, use bait.

Crosswind Lake. An 8-mile-long, fly-in lake located northwest of Lake Louise, 23 miles northwest of Glennallen. Accessible by floatplane from Glennallen. Deep, clear lake offers excellent fishing. Open water from early June through October. Best fishing early June to early July. Fish available: lake trout, use spoons or plugs; whitefish, use flies or eggs; grayling, use flies.

Deep Lake. A 1.8-mile-long, fly-in lake at the head of Dog Creek in the Copper River Basin, 30 miles north-northwest of Glennallen. Accessible by floatplane from Glennallen. Good fishing all summer for take trout to 30 inches.

Gulkana River. Located near the community of Gulkana. Public access at Gulkana River bridge, Sailor's Pit and Popular Grove on the Richardson Highway. Excellent king salmon fishery. Fly-fishing only below highway bridge. Above bridge, use bright lures and/or salmon eggs. Also good fly-fishing for red salmon. River guides for float fishing available. NOTE: Check for current restrictions on bait and tackle. Rainbow/steelhead trout may not be possessed or retained in the Gulkana River drainage.

Hanagita Lake. A 1-mile-long, fly-in lake located in the Chugach Mountains, 32 miles southwest of McCarthy. Accessible by small plane from Glennallen. Excellent grayling fishing all summer; lake trout and steelhead in September.

Klutina Lake. A 16-mile-long lake, 27 miles from the Copper Center bridge via extremely bad road. Excellent grayling and Dolly Varden fishing.

Klutina River. Located at Milepost 100.7 from Valdez on the Richardson Highway. Foot and vehicle access; river guides available for float fishing. King salmon in June and July, with peak in August, use bright lures and/or salmon eggs; red salmon, use streamer flies; Dolly Varden also available.

Lake Louise. An 8.5-mile-long lake located in the Copper River Basin, 32 miles northwest of Glennallen. Accessible by floatplane or skiplane from Anchorage, Glennallen and other communities. Access also via Lake Louise Road from the Glenn Highway turnoff at Milepost A 159.8. Lodges on lake. Excellent grayling and lake trout fishing. Lake trout average 10 pounds, up to 20 to 30 pounds, good year-round, best spring through July, late September, early season use herring or whitefish bait, cast from boat, later (warmer water) troll with #16 red and white spoons, silver Alaskan plug, large silver flatfish; grayling, 10 to 12 inches, cast flies or small spinners, June, July and August; burbot (freshwater lingcod) average 5 pounds, still fish from boat using hook with herring, dangle on bottom, in winter set lines with herring-baited hook through ice holes, or jig for lake trout. Lake can be rough; small, underpowered boats not recommended.

Susitna Lake. A 10-mile-long lake located just northwest of Lake Louise in the Copper River Basin, 42 miles northwest of Glennallen. Accessible by boat across Lake Louise or by small floatplane or skiplane from Anchorage, Glennallen or other communities. Excellent fishing for lake trout, use spoons or plugs; grayling, use flies. Lake can be rough; underpowered boat is not recommended.

Tanada Lake. A 5.7-mile-long, 1-mile-wide, fly-in or hike-in lake located within Wrangell-St. Elias National Park and Preserve. Accessible via Nabesna Road, which leaves the Tok Cutoff at Milepost GJ 59.8. Tanada Lake trailhead at Mile 24 Nabesna Road. Considered one of the top lake trout fisheries in the state. Fish available: lake trout 3 to 10 pounds, occasionally up to 30 pounds, excellent last week of June and first 2 weeks of July, use large lures; grayling 14 to 16 inches, best last of June and first 2 weeks of July, use flies; whitefish and burbot available.

Tebay Lakes. Located in a line 7 miles long trending northeast in the Chugach Mountains southwest of McCarthy and 68 miles east of Valdez. Accessible by small plane from Glennallen. Excellent fishing for rainbow trout 12 to 15 inches, all summer, use small spinners.

Kenai Peninsula Area Sportfishing

Anchor River. The entire Anchor River drainage is closed to all fishing from January 1 to May 25. Unbaited single-hook artificial lures only from September 1 to December 31. King salmon fishing permitted only on 5 consecutive weekends beginning Memorial Day weekend; check current limits. Steelhead from late August to November; check current regulations for catch and release dates and seasonal limits. Excellent fishing for 12- to 24-inch sea-run Dollies in July and late summer. Also saltwater trolling for king salmon to 80 pounds, halibut to 200 pounds. Access from Anchor River Beach Road; turn off Sterling Highway at Milepost S 156.9 near Anchor Point. Fishing guides and charters available locally.

Bench Lake. A 1-mile-long lake located on the Kenai Peninsula in Chugach National Forest at the head of Bench Creek, 0.5 mile from Johnson Lake and 22 miles southeast of Sunrise. Lake is about halfway in on the 23-mile-long Johnson Pass trail. Arctic grayling available, best June to September, use flies or small spinners. Lake is above tree line.

Cook Inlet. From Kachemak Bay at Homer north to the waters between Deep Creek and Ninilchik, Cook Inlet is known for its fishing. Fish available include: king salmon to 76 pounds year-round, best May through July; halibut, up to 350 pounds, from June through October; pink salmon 4 to 5 pounds, July and August; silver salmon to 15 pounds, August and September; red salmon to 4 pounds, July and August; Dolly Varden June through September; rainbow trout taken from nearby streams from April to October. Fishing guides and charters available locally.

Crescent Lake. A 6-mile-long lake on the west side of Madsen Mountain on the Kenai Peninsula in Chugach National Forest. Fish available: grayling best July to September, use flies or small spinners. Check ADF&G regulations for restrictive seasons and bag limits. Accessible by 15-minute floatplane flight from Moose Pass or via the 6.2-mile Crescent Lake trail. (See Cabins and Hiking Trails this section.)

Crooked Creek. Open season August 1 to December 31. Unbaited single-hook artificial lures only Septmber 1 to Dcember 31. Fishing for coho salmon, peaks in mid-August; steelhead from August 1, catch and release only. Fishing access to confluence of Crooked Creek and Kasilof River is through the state recreation site on Coho Loop Road. Fishing access to Crooked Creek frontage above confluence is through a private RV park on Coho Loop Road; fee charged.

Deep Creek. Closed to all fishing January 1 to last weekend in May. King salmon; check current regulations for season and limits. Freshwater fishing for king salmon to 40 pounds, Last weekend May and first 2 weekends in June, use spinners with bead lures; Dolly Varden in July and August; silver salmon to 15 pounds, August and September; steelhead to 15 pounds, late September through October, use large, red spinners. No bait fishing permitted September 1 to December 31. Access to mouth of Deep Creek is from Deep Creek State Recreation Area at Milepost S 137.3 Sterling Highway. Salt water south of the mouth of Deep Creek is known for producing top king salmon fishing in late May, June and July, with kings to 50 pounds.

Fuller Lakes. Located in Kenai National Wildlife Refuge. Accessible by the 4.8-mile-long Fuller Lakes trail from the Sterling Highway. Spring, summer and fall fishery for grayling in South Fuller Lake, use flies; Dolly Varden available year-round in North Fuller Lake, use bait, spinners, flies.

Grayling Lake. This 0.3-mile-long lake is located on the Kenai Peninsula 4.5 miles south of Kenai Lake and 10 miles north of Seward. Accessible by the Forest Service's 1.6-mile-long Grayling Lake trail, which leaves the Seward Highway at Milepost 13.2 from Seward. Fish available: 10- to 20-inch grayling, May to October, use flies.

Hidden Lake. Access from Hidden Lake Campground on the Skilak Lake Loop Road. Fish available: lake trout average 16 inches and kokanee 9 inches, year-round, best from mid-May to July 1, use spoons, red and white or weighted, by trolling, casting and jigging. This lake is a favorite with local ice fishermen from late December through March.

Johnson Lake. A 0.8-mile-long lake located within Chugach National Forest on the Kenai Peninsula, at the head of Johnson Creek, 0.5 mile from Bench Lake, 22 miles southeast of Sunrise. Lake is about halfway in on the 23-mile-long Johnson Pass trail. Fish available: rainbow trout, use flies, lures, bait. Lake is above tree line. (See Hiking Trails this section.)

Juneau Lake. A 1-mile-long lake located within Chugach National Forest on the Kenai Peninsula, 25 miles southwest of Hope. Accessible via the Resurrection Pass Trail from the

Sterling Highway at Milepost S 53.1 (see Hiking Trails this section). Lake located 6 miles up trail. Summer fishery for rainbow trout, use flies, lures, bait; lake trout, use spoons or plugs; whitefish, use flies or eggs.

Kasilof River. Unbaited single-hook artificial lures only September 1 to May 15. King salmon, late May through July, best in mid-June, open season January 1 to July 31; coho salmon, mid-August to September, use salmon egg clusters, wet flies, assorted spoons, spinners; steelhead in May and September, catch-and-release only from mouth upstream to Sterling Highway bridge.

Kenai Lake. Lake trout, mid-May to September 30; Dolly Varden and rainbow trout, May to September. Kenai Lake and tributaries are closed to salmon fishing.

Kenai River. Check current regulations for seasonal and daily closures, legal tackle, limits and for waters closed to fishing from boats. Upper Kenai River (from Kenai Lake to Skilak Lake): closed for king samon 20 inches or more in length;. silver salmon 5 to 15 pounds, August through October; pink salmon 3 to 7 pounds, July and August; red salmon 3 to 12 pounds, late May through mid-August; Dolly Varden, April to November.

Lower Kenai River (from Skilak Lake to Cook Inlet): King salmon 20 to 80 pounds, excellent fishing June and July; red (sockeye) salmon 6 to 12 pounds, best July 15 to August 10; pink salmon 4 to 8 pounds, August 1 to September 1 in even years; silver (coho) salmon 6 to 15 pounds, mid-August to November; rainbow trout, Dolly Varden 15 to 20 inches, June through September.

Lost Lake. A 1.5-mile-long lake located at the head of Lost Creek on the Kenai Peninsula within Chugach National Forest, 10 miles north of Seward. Accessible via the 7-mile-long Lost Lake Trail from the Seward Highway at Milepost 5.2 from Seward. Obtain permission from landowner to hike in from the south or hike from the north via Primrose Trail. (See Hiking Trails this section.) Rainbow trout available, use flies, lures, bait.

Moose River. From Moose River bridge at Milepost 82.1 on the Sterling Highway to confluence with Kenai River, there is fishing for sockeyes in June. Big summer run of reds follows into August; silvers into October. Dolly Varden, rainbow trout and salmon (red, king, pink and silver) available at confluence of Kenai and Moose rivers, but check regulations for closures and restrictions.

Resurrection Bay. Seward has all facilities for fishermen, including marine supplies, fuel, guides, charter boats and a small-boat harbor. Inquire locally for best fishing locations. Fish available include the following: silver salmon to 20 pounds, use herring, troll or cast, July to October (Silver Salmon Derby with more than $100,000 in prizes takes place in August); bottom fish includes flounder, halibut to 200 pounds and cod, year-round, jig with large lures and bait.

Russian Lakes. Accessible via the 21-mile-long Russian Lakes trail from the Sterling Highway at Milepost S 52.8 (see Hiking Trails this section). Rainbow trout available at Lower Russian Lake (Mile 2.6) and Upper Russian Lake (Mile 12). Check regulations for seasonal closures and limits.

Russian River. Closed to all fishing April 15 through May 30. No bait area. Check regulations for limits and other restrictions. Red salmon run starts during first half of June, lasts 2 to 3 weeks. A second run of larger fish in July lasts about 3 weeks, must use flies only (streamer or coho). Silver salmon to 15 pounds, run begins mid-August, flies only; rainbow trout (catch-and-release only) average 15 inches. Accessible from Russian River Campground at Milepost S 52.8 Sterling Highway.

Seldovia Area. The community of Seldovia is located 20 miles across Kachemak Bay from Homer. Accessible by boat, scheduled and charter air service from Homer and Alaska Marine Highway System from Homer or Kodiak. Area fishing includes the following: Seldovia Bay, king, silver and red salmon June 20 through September, use small spinners; halibut, average size, June 20 to September, use herring. Excellent bottom fishing. Fishing guides and skiffs available in Seldovia, which has food and lodging facilities. Outside Beach, 1.9 miles from Seldovia, has great fishing, casting from beach into surf for silver salmon, July 1 to 30, use any shiny lure. Silver and chum salmon and trout fishing available in Rocky

River, 17 miles southeast of Seldovia during August, use red spinning lures. *NOTE: Rocky River is on Native-owned lands, and a fee for fishing is required. Contact Port Graham Corporation, Port Graham, via Homer, AK 99603, for details.*

Skilak Lake. Fish available: salmon (sockeye, coho, pink), Dolly Varden, rainbow trout, lake trout and whitefish. Red (sockeye) salmon enter lake in mid-July. Access from Skilak Lake Campground on Skilak Lake Loop Road, or boat in. The lake is cold, and winds are fierce and unpredictable.

Swan Lake. A 2-mile-long lake near the head of the Chickaloon River on the Kenai Peninsula within Chugach National Forest, 22 miles southwest of Hope. Accessible via the Resurrection Pass trail from the Sterling Highway at Milepost 53.1 from Seward. Lake located 9 miles up trail. Summer fishery for rainbow trout, use flies, lures, bait; lake trout, use spoons or plugs; Dolly Varden, use bait, spinners, flies; and red salmon, use spoons or flies. Campground at lake.

Swanson River. Access via Swanson River Road or via canoe route from Paddle Lake on Swan Lake Road. The river has a significant Dolly Varden and rainbow trout fishery; closed to all fishing April 15 to June 14.

Tustumena Lake. Located 6.4 miles from the Sterling Highway, this huge lake is 6 miles wide and 25 miles long, subject to severe winds. Fish available: coho salmon, Dolly Varden, rainbow trout, brook trout and sheefish. Boat launch on the Kasilof River.

Prince William Sound Sportfishing

Flying services and charter boat operators in Prince William Sound know some of the best fishing locations, and several have cabins and tents near hot spots. Winter fishing for king salmon (up to 30 pounds) can prove to be the fishing trip of a lifetime. Other species available are halibut, pollock, Dolly Varden, cutthroat trout, and pink, sockeye and chum salmon.

Cordova Area. Cordova has all facilities for fishermen, including marine supplies, fuel, guides, charter boats and a small-boat harbor. Inquire locally for best fishing locations. Fish available in nearby waters include the following: silver salmon late July through mid-September, best in August and September, use herring or spoons (Silver Salmon Derby with top prize of $5,000 takes place mid-August to September 1); pink and chum salmon good in July and August, use large red spinner or small spoons; halibut and other bottom fish, best fishing in small bays, jig with large lures and bait. Dungeness, king and tanner crab available in nearby bays or coves. Steamer clams common on gravel/mud beaches, razor clams in Orca Inlet and south of the Copper River Delta.

Valdez Area. Valdez has all facilities for fishermen, including marine supplies, fuel, guides, charter boats and a small-boat harbor. Inquire locally for good fishing locations. Fish available include the following: silver salmon late July through mid-September, excellent in August, use herring or spoons (Silver Salmon Derby with $10,000 top prize takes place the month of August); pink salmon during the summer, use large, red spinners or small spoons; king salmon best late winter and early spring, use herring or large trolling lures; halibut, red snapper and shrimp available all summer, generally in small bays, jig with large lures and bait. Littleneck clams on most gravel/mud beaches in protected bays at half-tide level in Valdez Arm. Tanner, King and Dungeness crab also available in bays or coves.

Whittier Area. Whittier has all facilities for fishermen, including marine supplies, fuel, guides, charter boats and a small-boat harbor. Inquire locally for good fishing locations. Fish available in area waters include the following: silver salmon in August, use large, red spinners and spoons, herring and large trolling spoons; pink and chum salmon late summer, use large, red spinners and spoons; king salmon June and early July, use herring, large trolling lures, spoons, spinners; red snapper in Passage Canal and Dungeness crab in Shotgun Cove.

🐦 Goose Bay State Game Refuge

Located on the west side of Knik Arm, this 10,880-acre refuge encompasses the Goose

Bay wetlands complex drained by Goose Creek. It was established in 1975. The inland boundary is shrub habitat. The shoreline is subject to the extreme tides of Knik Arm, and safety precautions are advised as "essential" by the Alaska Department of Fish and Game.

The wetlands are a spring and fall stopover for migrating waterfowl. More than 20,000 geese stop at the refuge between mid-April and mid-May, and again in the fall on their way south. Canada geese are most numerous, followed by snow geese. Trumpeter and tundra swans may also be observed in the area in spring and fall. Other species observed include bald eagles, sandhill cranes, mallards, green-winged teal, pintails, northern shovelers, snipe and yellowlegs.

The refuge offers good waterfowl hunting in the fall. Offroad use of motorized vehicles is restricted. Excellent spring bird watching opportunities with waterfowl and raptor numbers peaking between April 25 and May 5.

There are no developed public access points or public-use facilities in the refuge. Nearby Knik has a liquor store, gas station and private campground.

From Wasilla, follow Knik-Goose Bay Road south approximately 18.5 miles. Point Mackenzie Road intersects with the Knik-Goose Bay Road and provides access to the refuge at several points. Also accessible from Big Lake Road via the Burma Road.

For more information contact the Alaska Department of Fish and Game, 1800 Glenn Highway, Suite 4, Palmer, AK 99645-6736; phone (907) 745-5015, fax (907) 745-7362.

Gull Island

Distinguished for its bird colonies, if not for its name (there are 17 Gull Islands listed in the Dictionary of Alaska Place Name), Gull Island in Kachemak Bay is a popular destination for bird watchers. The island is owned by Seldovia Native Association and is not open to the public, but bird watchers can approach by boat.

The 0.1-mile-long island is located 8 miles southeast of Homer. The private Kachemak Bay Ferry, M/V *Danny J*, cruises around Gull Island on its daily summer trip between Homer and Halibut Cove. Gull Island is also a favorite destination for charter boat operators.

Bird watchers can also get a close-up look at Gull Island's sea bird colonies at the Pratt Museum in Homer. The museum has a remote cam on Gull island, which transmits live images of the the sea birds between May and September. Pratt Museum is located on Bartlett Street in Homer; phone (907) 235-8635, web site www.prattmuseum.org

Hatcher Pass Public Use Area

Created by the state legislature in 1986, Hatcher Pass Public Use Area encompasses land along the Little Susitna River and Hatcher Pass Road in the Talkeetna Mountains. It is managed by the Department of Natural Resources divisions of Parks and Outdoor Recreation and Mining, Land and Water. The Alaska Department of Fish and Game manages fish and game resources within the Hatcher Pass area. Hatcher Pass Public Use Area is open to a variety of recreational activities, including hiking and recreational mining in summer and cross-country skiing and snowmobiling in winter.

Hiking trails begin at the Gold Mint Trailhead across from the Motherlode Lodge at Mile 13.8 Hatcher Pass Road, and at the Fishhook Trailhead at Mile 16.4. There are also hiking trails at Hatcher Pass Summit (elev. 3,886 feet) at Mile 19.2. Parasailers launch from a spot known as "Nixon's Nose" in the vicinity of the summit.

Skiers and snowmobilers can usually count on good snow conditions at Hatcher Pass, even when other places in Southcentral may be suffering from a lack of snow, which is one reason for the area's popularity with winter recreationists. The $1000 Run on the north side of Bald Mountain Ridge is managed as a ski-only area and reserved for backcountry and telemark skiing. Snowmobiles may use the marked and groomed trails from the Fishhook and Gold Mint parking lots to reach the Willow Creek drainage on the west side of the pass, where snowmobiling is encouraged and not restricted. On the east side of Hatcher Pass, Marmot Mountain above Fishhook parking lot is open to snowmobiling. Snowmobiling is prohibited within the 271-acre Independence Mine State Historical Park.

Access to the Hatcher Pass area is via the 49-mile-long Hatcher Pass Road from either Palmer or Willow. From Palmer, take the Palmer-Fishhook Road turnoff at Milepost 49.5 Glenn Highway. From Willow, take the Fishhook-Willow Road from Milepost A 71.2 Parks Highway. Hatcher Pass Public Use Area begins on the Palmer side at approximately Mile 7.8 on Hatcher Pass Road. The turnoff for Independence Mine State Historical Park is at Mile 17. In winter, the road is open from the Glenn Highway to the park. It is closed over the pass to within about 14 miles of the Parks Highway from the first snow in late September until late June. For details on access and accommodations, see *The MILEPOST®*, a complete guide to Alaska's road system.

(See also Independence Mine State Historical Park and Recreational Mining this section)

🥾 Hiking Trails

Hiking in Southcentral ranges from short, easy day hikes on trails not that far from downtown Anchorage, such as the ever-popular Flattop, to multi-day backpacking trips along established trails like the 38-mile Resurrection Pass Trail on the Kenai Peninsula, to strenuous scrambles across the glaciers and steep scree slopes of the Wrangell Mountains with topo map in hand.

Most hiking trails in Southcentral are either on Chugach National Forest (U.S. Forest Service) land or they are located on Alaska State Parks land. Southcentral's Chugach State Park has the most extensive hiking trail system of any state park unit in the state. There are also more than a dozen hiking routes over unmaintained trails in Wrangell-St. Elias National Park and Preserve that fall under the management of the National Park Service. The few trails located within Kenai National Wildlife Refuge come under the auspices of the U.S. Fish and Wildlife Service. And finally, there are many public rights-of-way (RS 2477) managed as trails by the state's Division of Mining, Land and Water. Although detailed information on these trails is sketchy, brief descriptions of RS 2477 trails is available by clicking on the appropriate map quads at http://www.dnr.state.ak.us/land/q/index.html.

Wherever you hike, always go prepared for sudden changes in the weather. Purify water before drinking. And remember to pack out your trash.

Potential hazards exist on all wilderness trails, although some have a higher hazard factor than others. In Wrangell-St. Elias National Park, for example, there are few maintained trails, and hiking destinations are in an area famous for its remoteness. Bears may be present anywhere along the routes. Streams are swift and cold and noted for sudden, dramatic changes in volume and velocity due to heavy rain or snowmelt. Also, rescue and medical evacuation services may take several days longer in the Wrangells than they would on the Kenai.

It is important to obtain current trail conditions, as well as more detailed information on the trails than is given here, from the appropriate government agency. For details on Chugach National Forest hiking trails, that would be one of the ranger district offices, depending upon the location of the trail: Cordova Ranger District, P.O. Box 280, Cordova, AK 99574-0280; phone (907) 424-7661; Seward Ranger District, P.O. Box 390, Seward, AK 99664-0390; phone (907) 224-3374; Glacier Ranger District, P.O. Box 129, Girdwood, AK 99587; phone (907) 783-3242; or the USFS office in Anchorage at 3301 C St., Suite 300, Anchorage, AK 99503; phone (907) 271-2500. See also http://www.fs.fed.us/r10/chugach. Note that most Chugach National Forest trails are closed to motorized vehicles from mid-February to late November and to saddle/packstock from April through June.

For Alaska State Park hiking trails, contact the Alaska Department of Natural Resources Public Information Center, 550 W. 7th Ave., Suite 1260, Anchorage, AK 99501-3557; phone (907) 269-8400, fax (907) 269-8901, TDD (907) 269-8411, email pic@dnr.state.ak.us. The office has maps showing access to the park's recreation areas.

For hiking in Wrangell St. Elias National Park and Preserve, it is critical hikers consult with park rangers beforehand for detailed route information. Contact Park headquarters at P.O. Box 439, Copper Center, AK 99573; phone (907) 822-5234, fax (907) 822-7216; the Chitina Ranger Station in Chitina, phone (907) 823-2205; or the Slana Ranger Station (Nabesna District) on Nabesna Road, phone (907) 822-5238, fax (907) 822-5248. Or visit www.nps.gov/wrst/home.html. Or e-mail wrst_interpretation@nps.gov.

For information on hiking trails in Kenai National Wildlife Refuge, contact the Refuge Manager, P.O. Box 2139, Soldotna, AK 99669-2139; phone (907) 262-7021. Or stop by the U.S. Fish and Wildlife Service information cabin, located at Milepost S 58 Sterling Highway, or the Kenai National Wildlife Refuge Visitor Center, located just off the Sterling Highway on Ski Hill Road south of Soldotna.

For hiking trails on BLM land, contact the Bureau of Land Management, 222 W. 7th Avenue, #13, Anchorage, AK 99513-7599; phone (907) 271-5960. The BLM Public Information Center is located in Room 148 on the first floor of the New Federal Building-U.S. Courthouse in downtown Anchorage. Or contact the BLM's Glennallen Field office at Box 147, Glennallen, AK 99588; phone (907) 822-3217, web site http://www.ak.blm.gov/gdo.

Anchorage Area Trails

Bird Creek Trail. Trailhead at end of Konikson Road, turnoff at Milepost S 100.6 Seward Highway. First 5.2 miles of trail is on an unmaintained road, suitable for ATVs and bikes. Unmaintained and unmarked trail beyond leads to Bird Pass; elevation gain 2,000 feet. Also access to Penguin Creek trail at Mile 0.7; access to Penguin Peak (4,305 feet)

Bird Ridge Trail. From traihead it is 2.5 miles to Bird Ridge Point (3,505 feet) at crest of ridge, or 5 miles to Bird Ridge Overlook (4,055 feet). There is a steep scramble to above treeline from trailhead at Milepost S 102.1 Seward highway. This is the first snow-free spring hike in Chugach State Park, according to park rangers. The elevation gain to the ridge offers good views of Turnagain Arm.

Bold Ridge Trail. This 3.5-mile-long trail begins at Mile 5 of the Lakeside Trail in the Eklutna Lake Recreation Area in Chugach State Park and climbs steeply to the alpine tundra. Hikers in good condition allow about one hour, 45 minutes to hike in, one hour to hike out. This trail provides excellent views of the Eklutna Valley and Glacier and the Knik Arm of Cook Inlet. The maintained trail ends at the base of the snowcapped Bold Peak. Experienced climbers may continue on to the summit of this 7,552-foot mountain. Hunters and other hikers use the Bold Ridge Trail to reach the Hunter Creek drainage. This trail is considered moderate to difficult.

Crow Pass (Old Iditarod) Trail. This trail is about 27 miles long. Four miles are within Chugach National Forest; the rest of the trail is in Chugach State Park. The south trailhead is 7 miles up Crow Creek Road, accessed via the Seward Highway south from Anchorage 37 miles, then 1.9 miles east on the Alyeska Highway to junction with Crow Creek Road. The Crow Pass Trail climbs steeply to ruins of an old gold mine and a public-use cabin; 2,000 feet in altitude is gained between trailhead and the cabin at Mile 3 at Crow Pass near Raven Glacier. Hiking time to the pass is approximately 2-1/2 hours. Trail offers outstanding alpine scenery and access to several glaciers and peaks. From Crow Pass, the Old Iditarod trail extends 22.5 miles down Raven Creek drainage to the the north trailhead at Eagle River Nature Center at the end of Eagle River road. This trailhead is accessed via the Glenn Highway from Anchorage to the Eagle River/Eagle River Road exit, then 12.3 miles to the Nature Center. All of the hiking trail, from Crow Creek trailhead to the Eagle River Nature Center, is part of the Iditarod National Historic Trail. Trail is closed to motorized vehicles; horses prohibited. Winter travel not recommended due to extreme avalanche danger. Trail usually free of snow by mid-June. Most hikers start at the Girdwood end of the trail and hike to the Eagle River Nature Center. Cabin located in alpine area without firewood; camp stove recommended. Water available from glacial stream. USGS map: Anchorage A-6.

East Fork Trail. This trail begins at Mile 10.5 of the Lakeside Trail in the Eklutna Lake Recreation Area in Chugach State Park, paralleling the East Fork of Eklutna River to a glacial lake that reflects the surrounding peaks and glacier. Bashful, the tallest peak in Chugach State Park, at 8,005 feet, and its neighbors, Bold and Baleful, tower above the river to the northeast, while the Mitre forms the west wall of the valley. Wildflowers display in summer. Berry picking in season. Watch for Dall sheep, mountain goats and moose on mountain slopes. Also watch for the ouzel, a small water bird that bobs in the water and feeds along the river bottom. Tulchina Falls at Mile 2 is a pretty spot for a rest stop. This trail is considered easy to moderate in difficulty.

Eklutna Glacier Trail. This trail begins 3/4 mile from Mile 13 of the Lakeside Trail in the Eklutna Lake Recreation Area in Chugach State Park. It is considered easy to moderate in difficulty. It begins where the Lakeside Trail ends and leads to a view of the Eklutna Glacier. Notice the change in vegetation as you hike along. The glacier has quickly retreated in the last few years, and you can witness the birth of a new landscape here.

The trail is well-marked, but sections bordering the swiftly flowing Eklutna River require care. Rocks falling from the steep canyon walls present a hazard to hikers. For your safety, remain on the trail, and do not approach the glacier. Because it is rapidly receding, the glacier's snout is unstable and dangerous. Glaciers and peaks in this area are popular with climbers. A traverse beginning at the end of this trail crosses the Eklutna, Whiteout, Eagle and Raven Glaciers and ends 31 miles away at Crow Pass near Girdwood. Three huts along the route are maintained by the Mountaineering Club of Alaska. Only those who are trained and properly equipped should venture onto the glacier.

Falls Creek Trail. Trailhead at Milepost S 105.7 Seward Highway. A moderate 1.5-mile hike along creek through lush woods to treeline in Chugach State Park. Access to Suicide Peaks (technical climb).

Flattop Trail. This hike up Flattop Mountain is the most popular trail in the state, due both to its proximity to Anchorage and its stunning views. The Flattop trail begins at the Glen Alps trailhead parking area. (Two other popular hikes in Chugach State Park start from the Glen Alps trailhead; see also Powerline and Williwaw Lakes trails this section.) Total elevation gain is 1,550 feet. Distance is 3.5 miles roundtrip; hiking time is estimated at 3 to 5 hours. The trail is well-marked and well-traveled with beautiful views of Anchorage and the Alaska Range on clear days. Snow is usually gone by early July.

Indian Valley Trail. A 6-mile, moderately steep hike to Indian Pass in Chugach State Park from trailhead on Bore Tide Road off the Seward Highway. Elevation gain is 1,900 feet. In winter, this is part of "Arctic to Indian" ski traverse.

Lakeside Trail. Located in Eklutna Lake Valley in Chugach State Park. To reach the trailhead, take Glenn Highway to Milepost A 26, and follow park signs 10 miles to Eklutna Lake. From the trailhead parking lot, this scenic trail follows the north edge of the lake for 8 miles then on to glacial gravel bars for 5.5 miles to junction with Eklutna Glacier Trail. Berry picking in season. This trail is very popular with mountain bikers. It is also popular with hikers, joggers, and horseback riders in summer and skiers and snowmobilers in winter. Each mile is marked for easy reference. It is considered a relatively easy trail, and typical travel time for the 13-mile trail is 6 hours one-way. The trail is usually open to ATVs Sunday through Wednesday. For information, call the ranger station or Chugach State Park Headquarters.

McHugh and Rabbit Lakes Trail. A 7-mile, moderate hike to very scenic Rabbitt and McHugh lakes. From trailhead at McHugh Creek Picnic Area at Milepost S 111.9 Seward Highway, hike 1/2 mile on Turnagain Arm Trail to McHugh Lake Trail through McHugh Creek Valley. Elevation gain is 2,750 feet; rated moderate. Extremely scenic alpine lakes framed by Suicide Peaks. Loop trip is possible for experienced hikers using Ptarmigan Pass to Powerline Trail, according to Alaska State Park rangers.

Middle Fork Trail. This trail begins at Mile 1.3 of the Near Point Trail and leads 6.5 miles to the largest of Williwaw Lakes in Chugach State Park. Bicycles are allowed the first 3 miles. It is considered easy to moderate.

Near Point Trail. A 4-mile hike to Near Point from Prospect Heights trailhead in Chugach State Park. The first 3 miles is open to mountain bikes in summer and popular with cross-country skiers in winter. The last mile to Near Point is steep and narrow. Views of Anchorage and Alaska Range. Two other popular hikes in Chugach State Park start from the Prospect Heights trailhead; see also Wolverine Peak and Middle Fork trails this section.

Peters Creek Trail. A 5-mile hike along an abandoned roadbed through wooded valley. Unmarked and unmaintained trail continues up valley 11 miles to open tundra. Moderate difficulty. No trailhead parking; private property first 1/4 mile of trail. Open to bicycles first 5 miles. Excellent cross-country skiing in winter. Accesss from Peters Creek exit on Glenn Highway, and follow city map uphill to Malcolm Drive.

Powerline. This popular trail starts at the Glen Alps trailhead parking lot in Chugach State Park. Total length of trail is 11 miles with an elevation gain of 1,300 feet. Trail ends at Indian near Milepost 103 Seward Highway. It is a short, easy walk to reach alpine terrain; berry picking in summer. Bicycles are allowed on the trail in summer, snow machine use on part of trail in winter. Steep descent into Indian from Powerline Pass.

South Fork Valley Trail. A 12-mile-round-trip hike across open tundra to Symphony and Eagle lakes in Chugach State Park. Rated easy, with an elevation gain of 400 feet. Boardwalk over some muddy areas. Trail begins at Mile 7.5 on Hiland Drive, accessible from Milepost A 11.6 Glenn Highway.

Thunderbird Falls Trail. Popular 2-mile-round-trip hike to view Thunderbird Falls, this Chugach State Park trail is rated easy. Trailhead is accessible from the Glenn Highway, Milepost A 26.3 (Eklutna exit) for southbound access; Milepost A 25.2 northbound.

Turnagain Arm Trail. This 9.4-mile trail in Chugach State Park parallels the coastline and the Seward Highway from Potter Creek to Windy Corner. The trail leads hikers through spruce forests, birch and alder groves, and flower-filled meadows. Scenic overlooks provide views of the Chugach Mountains to the north and the Kenai Mountains across Turnagain Arm.

Formerly known as the Old Johnson Trail, the trail emerged in the 19th century as the vegetation was downtrodden by miners, trappers and prospectors. The U.S. government improved the trail during construction of the Alaska Railroad in 1915. Remnants of the railroad construction camps can still be seen along the trail. The trail was also used to deliver mail, and in 1917, telegraph lines were installed.

There are 4 trailheads on the Seward Highway for the Turnagain Arm Trail: at Potter Creek Viewpoint, Milepost 115.1, across from Chugach State Park Headquarters at Potter Section House; at McHugh Creek Picnic Area, Milepost 111.9; Rainbow trailhead at Milepost 108.4; and Windy Corner trailhead at Milepost 106.7.

From Potter Creek Viewpoint, it is 3.3 miles (1-1/2 hour hike) to the McHugh Creek trailhead; this is considered a good choice for a family hike. Turnagain Arm Trail then continues to Rainbow (7.5 miles from Potter Creek) and to Windy Corner (9.4 miles from Potter Creek). Between McHugh Creek and Rainbow, there is a side trail to Beluga Point, a good place to watch the bore tide come in if your timing's right. Windy Corner is popular with the local Dall sheep population. While it is not uncommon to see several ewes and lambs gathered there, the rams prefer higher ground.

Twin Peaks Trail. Located in Eklutna Lake Valley in Chugach State Park. To reach the trailhead, take Glenn Highway to Milepost 26, and follow park signs 10 miles to Eklutna Lake. The 3.5-mile trail begins at the parking lot, crosses the Twin Peaks Creek Bridge and continues to the alpine tundra. It is rated moderate to difficult due to its steepness in places. Hiking time for those in good condition is about two hours going up and one hour down. It is well maintained and offers good views of the valley.

About halfway up, there is a good spot to rest, have a picnic and enjoy views of the valley and lake. The trail continues around the west side of the mountain, where dozens of sheep are often seen grazing in the Goat Mountain bowl. Careful observers may spot ptarmigan roosting in the vegetation or a golden eagle in flight.

Hikers who reach the end of the maintained trail are rewarded with a panoramic view of the Eklutna Valley and Knik Arm. From here, hikers may choose their own route across the tundra. Berry picking is very good along the upper part of the trail and beyond.

Climbers use this trail to reach East and West Twin Peaks and Goat Mountain.

Williwaw Lakes. Hike Powerline Trail from Glen Alps trailhead 3/4 mile to Middle Fork Loop Trail. It is 6 miles to the jewel-like alpine lakes in the Williwaw Valley. Round-trip is 13 miles with a 742-foot elevation gain. Berry picking in season.

Wolverine Peak. This trail begins at Mile 2 of the Near Point Trail and leads 5.2 miles to the summit of Wolverine Peak. Elevation gain is 3,380 feet; rated easy to moderate.

Copper River Delta Area Trails

All of these trails are within the Cordova Ranger District. Their office is located on the second floor of the old federal building at 612 Second Street in Cordova. There is a natural history display, as well as brochures on hiking, wildlife viewing and other activities on national forest lands. Staff members are also available to answer questions. The office is open weekdays from 8 A.M. to 5 P.M.

Crater Lake Trail. This 2.4-mile hike climbs steeply from a 40-foot elevation at Eyak Lake to 1,500 feet at Crater Lake. Rated as difficult, it begins at Mile 1.8 Power Creek Road near Cordova, climbs a steep grade through mature spruce and hemlock forest and ends at the picturesque alpine lake. Crater Lake trail provides day hikers with magnificent views of Copper River Delta, Chugach Mountains and Prince William Sound. From Crater Lake, hikers can follow a ridge route marked by rock cairns to the top of Eyak peak. Or the hike can be extended to 12 miles by using the 6-mile Ridge Route Intertie Trail (see description this section) that connects the 2.4-mile Crater Lake trail to the Power Creek trail. USGS map: Cordova C-5.

Eyak River Trail. This 2.2-mile trail follows the west bank of the Eyak River south to Mountain Slough. Access from the trailhead at Milepost 5.7 Copper River Highway or from the boat ramp at Milepost 5.9. Trail habitat ranges from delta alder and grasses to mature timber and muskeg meadows. Used by fishermen during sockeye and coho salmon runs in July and August to mid-September. Rated easy. Boardwalk on most of trail, but rubber boots are recommended. USGS map: Cordova C-5.

Heney Ridge Trail. Trailhead at Mile 5.1 Whitshed Road. This 3.5-mile trail climbs from Hartney Bay through spruce-hemlock forest to the ridge above treeline. Spectacular views of Prince William Sound, Copper River Delta and Kayak Island on a clear day. Trail can be muddy and wet in places; rubber boots recommended. Beware of bears in area. First section of trail follows contours of Hartney Bay and offers views of wetlands and excellent bird watching. Next 2 miles are a moderate climb through spruce-hemlock forest. Last mile is a steep climb to ridge. Rated difficult. Elevation gain from trailhead to ridge is 1,800 feet. USGS maps: Cordova B-5, C-5.

McKinley Lake Trail. Easy 2.4-mile hike provides access to public-use cabin at McKinley Lake from trailhead at Milepost 21.6 Copper River Highway. (There is also a public-use cabin located 100 yards beyond the trailhead sign.) Access at midway point to Pipeline Lake Trail. Provides access to fishing in McKinleky Lake and big game hunting in the Chugach Mountains. USGS map: Cordova B-4.

Pipeline Lakes Trail. Moderate, 1.8-mile-long trail through dense spruce-hemlock forest to muskeg meadows and picturesque lakes (several stocked with grayling) with impressive views of the Chugach Mountains. Also cutthroat trout fishing and blueberry picking in season. Junctions with McKinley Lake trail. Trailhead at Milepost 21.4 Copper River Highway. No elevation gain. Boardwalk planking through muskeg meadows, but trail is wet in places with muddy spots and quagmires. Rubber boots are recommended. USGS map: Cordova B-4.

Power Creek Trail. Begins at Mile 6.9 Power Creek Road near Cordova and ends in Power Creek Basin at the Power Creek public-use cabin (see Cabins this section). Ridge Route Intertie Trail/Alice Smith Cutoff (see description this section) junctions with Power Creek Trail 3 miles from trailhead and connects with Crater Lake Trail. It is 5 miles from the Power Creek trailhead to the Power Creek cabin. It is 9 miles from the Power Creek trailhead to Crater Lake using the Ridge Route Intertie and 12 miles to do the loop from Power Creek trailhead to Crater Lake trailhead using the intertie route. Rated moderate to Power Creek Basin; most difficult on Ridge Route. This popular trail is also heavily used by bears during berry season. Trail can be mucky in places; rubber boots are recommended. Extraordinary panoramic views of surrounding mountains from cabin. USGS map: Cordova C-5.

Ridge Route Intertie Trail/Alice Smith Cutoff. This 6-mile-long trail connects the Crater Lake Trail with the Power Creek Trail. The 4.5-mile section along the ridge (marked by rock cairns and rated difficult) offers spectacular views of Prince William Sound, Eyak Lake, Copper River Delta and Chugach Mountains. Small shelter located at halfway mark on ridge. Trail heavily used by bears during berry season. USGS map: Cordova C-5.

Saddlebag Glacier Trail. Easy, 3-mile trail through cottonwood and spruce trees to outlet of Saddlebag Lake with incredible view of Saddlebag Glacier. Look for mountain goats on cliffs above lake. Recommended as the best trail in district for mountain biking because it is flat and "relatively dry." Also popular for cross-country skiing in winter. Access to trailhead via gravel side road from Mile 24.8 Copper River Highway. USGS map: Cordova B-3.

Sheridan Mountain Trail. A 2.9-mile hike from road to picturesque alpine basin. Rated as difficult. Spectacular views of Sheridan and Sherman glaciers and the Copper River Delta. Used by hunters and hikers. Boardwalk covers most wet sections, but rubber boots are still recommended. Trailhead on Sheridan Glacier Road, 3 miles from turnoff at Milepost 13 Copper River Highway. USGS map: Cordova C-4.

Kenai Peninsula Area Trails

Alpine Ridge Trail. This steep, 2.5-mile hike in Kachemak Bay State Park, rated moderate to difficult, begins at the high point on the Saddle Trail and follows a ridge up through spruce and alder to alpine tundra and its many wildflowers. Views of Grewingk Glacier on one side and a deep glacial valley on the other are spectacular. Pick out some landmarks to help find the end of the trail for the trip back down. Hiking time is 2 hours to get above timberline.

Bear Creek Trail. Trailhead on north shore Tustumena Lake in Kenai National Wildlife Refuge; no road access. Length 16.5 miles round-trip; elevation range 100 to 2,100 feet; rated moderate; minimum maintenance.

Bear Mountain Trail. Trailhead at Mile 6.2 Skilak Lake Loop Road off the Sterling Highway in Kenai National Wildlife Refuge. Length 1.5 miles round-trip; elevation range 900 to 1,400 feet; rated moderate to strenuous.

Carter Lake Trail. This popular, 3.3-mile Chugach National Forest trail along an old jeep road has a 955-foot elevation gain. It is 2 hours one way to Carter Lake from trailhead at Mile 33.1 Seward Highway. Trail provides access to alpine country after the first 1.5 miles. Trail steep in places; rated difficult. Dall sheep and goats may be seen. Carter Lake is stocked with rainbow trout. Good winter access. Carter Lake Trail connects with Crescent Lake Trail. USGS maps: Seward B-7, C-7.

China Poot Lake Trail. This 2.6-mile trail, rated easy to moderate, begins at Halibut Cove Lagoon and passes 3 lakes beneath China Poot Peak in Kachemak Bay State Park. About 15 minutes of hiking uphill brings you to the first lake. The trail crosses the lake outlet stream and continues through forest and bog for 30 minutes to Two Loon Lake. China Poot Lake is another 30 minutes away through more spruce and muskeg. Hiking time is 1 hour, 30 minutes.

Coalition Loop Trail. Moderate, 5.5-mile trail accessed by China Poot Bay Trailhead and at 0.2 mile and 1.8 mile China Poot Lake Trail. Elevation gain 400 feet; hiking time 3 hours for loop. Trail connects Halibut Cove with China Poot Bay, dedicated to Kachemak Bay Citizen's Coalition. Trail opens to views of China Poot Bay and passes along China Poot Creek to views of China Poot Lake. Bald eagles over bluffs.

Coastal Trail. Located at Caines Head State Recreation Area near Seward on the eastern edge of the Kenai Peninsula, this 7-mile trail leads to the abandoned Fort McGilvray and garrison ghost town. To reach the trail, take Lowell Point Road south 2 miles from Seward. Park at Lowell Point State Recreation Site Trailhead parking lot, and begin the hike south. After 1 1/2 miles, the trail drops down to Tonsina Creek and Tonsina Point. The 3-mile stretch of beach between this point and the next area of interest, North Beach, can only be hiked during very low tide. Leave Seward at least 2 hours before low tide to avoid being stranded. The trip takes the average hiker 2 to 3 hours. Most hikers stay overnight at North Beach.

North Beach is marked by the remains of an army dock built in 1941. A ranger station, anchorage, camping shelter and campsites, latrine and picnic area are located near the beach. The abandoned Fort Mcgilvray is two miles further south. To reach the fort and sweeping vistas of the bay, hike the old roadbed until it forks, one mile south of the North Beach trailhead. Follow the left fork another 1 1/4 miles to the fort. Along the way, explore the remains of old ammunition magazines and bog meadows.

In WWII, Fort McGilvray was the strategic command center for protecting the port of Seward from imperial Japanese forces. It is perched on a 650-foot, rocky cliff. The fort is open to explore, but take a flashlight to find your way through the maze of underground passages and rooms.

To reach South Beach, travel back up the old road to the fork, this time choosing the southwestern branch. Follow this branch of the road 1 1/2 miles to the South Beach ghost town. The town includes the remains of utility buildings and barracks that were home to the 500 soldiers stationed here from July 1941 to May 1943. These structures are not safe to enter or walk on.

Cottonwood Creek Trail. Length 5 miles round-trip; elevation range 300 to 2,400 feet; steep, rated moderate to strenuous. Trailhead on the south side of Skilak Lake in Kenai National Wildlife Refuge. No road access to trail; boat ramps at campgrounds on lake.

Crescent Lake Trail. This 6.4-mile Chugach National Forest trail ends at Crescent Lake (3 to 4 hours one way); public-use cabin at lake. Lake has grayling. The trail, which has a gain of 864 feet, is in excellent condition. Winter use is hazardous because of avalanche danger. Trailhead is 3.5 miles south of Milepost S 44.9 Sterling Highway on Quartz Creek Road. USGS maps: Seward B-7, C-7, C-8.

Devil's Pass Trail. This 10-mile Chugach National Forest trail begins at Milepost 39.4 on the Seward Highway and ends at Devil's Pass, elevation 2,400 feet, where it connects with the Resurrection Pass trail. Campsite at Beaver Pond (2 miles from trailhead). Recreation cabin at Devil's Pass. Hiking time for this trail is 5 to 6 hours one way. Winter travel not recommended due to avalanche hazard. USGS maps: Seward C-7, C-8.

Drake and Skookum Lakes Trail. Trailhead at Mile 13.3 Swanson River Road in Kenai National Wildlife Refuge. Length 2 miles round-trip; rainbow trout and arctic char fishing.

Emerald Lake Trail. This 6.4-mile, moderate to difficult trail is accessed from the Grewingk Glacier Trail and theHumpy Creek Trail. Elevation gain 1650 feet. Hiking time 2 hours to Emerald Lake, 5 hours to Humpy Creek. Trail follows glacial moraine into forest, bridges Upper Humpy Creek, and climbs to treeline. Fantastic views of Kachemak Bay from Portlock Plateau. Bears and mountain goats on high ridges. Upper trail marked with rock cairns and orange posts. Trail ends at Humpy Lake Creek Trail junction.

Fuller Lakes Trail. Trailhead at Milepost S 57.1 Sterling Highway in Kenai National Wildlife Refuge. It is 1.5 miles to the first lake; elevation range 400 to 1,500 feet; rated strenuous. Grayling in South Fuller Lake. This is bear country.

Funny River Horse Trail. Access is reached via the Funny River Road, which branches off the Soldotna Airport Road near the airport. Also for hiking. Trail is 40 miles long round-trip; elevation range 250 to 2,200 feet; rated moderate. Provides access to alpine benchlands. Minimum maintenance.

Glacier Lake Trail. Access to this 2.2-mile, easy trail is by Grewingk and Glacier Lake trails. Popular, 80-minute family loop. Trail ends on open beaches of Grewingk Glacier Lake.

Goat Rope Spur Trail. This short, steep trail, extending 1.5 miles and rated difficult, begins at the highest point on Lagoon Trail in Kachemak Bay State Park. It leads hikers up through a "notch" to alpine areas, where the trail ends. Be sure to bring along your camera to record the views. Hiking time is 1 hour 30 minutes.

Grace Ridge Trail. Moderate to difficult, 8.2-mile trail. Hiking time 1.5 hours to first alpine knob, 2.5 hours to summer, 6 to 8 hours entire trail. Elevation gain at summit 3,145 feet. Marine access at north end at Kayak Beach Campsite or at south end by Grace

Trailhead. Trail follows old, aldered road and climbs through Sitka spruce forest to excellent view of Sadie Knob. Huge falls below. Stunning views of Eldred Passage, Sadie Peak and Cook Inlet volcanoes. Mountain goats, black bears, golden and bald eagles in area. Good spring skiing in bowls. Trail ends at Tutka Bay.

Grayling Lake Trail. This easy, 2-mile, family trail in Chugach National Forest begins at Milepost 13.3 Seward Highway and climbs gradually through spruce forests and open meadows to Grayling Lake; fishing for grayling. Access to Meridian and Leech lakes for fishing. USGS map: Seward B-7.

Grewingk Glacier Trail. This 6.5-mile trail, rated easy, covers flat terrain through stands of spruce and cottonwood and across the outwash of Grewingk Glacier in Kachemak Bay State Park. It offers superb views of the glacier and surrounding area. There is a small campground about 10 minutes from the trailhead and another at Right Beach, a favorite water taxi drop-off point. Rock cairns mark the trail across the outwash of the glacier. Access to the glacial ice is difficult and hazardous. There is a stream near the junction of this trail and the Saddle Trail. Hiking time is 2 to 3 hours.

Gull Rock Trail. A popular, 5.1-mile Chugach National Forest trail that starts from trailhead at Porcupine Campground at the end of the Hope Highway and ends at Gull Rock (which is on Kenai Naitonal Wildlife Refuge land) overlooking Turnagain Arm. Parking and restrooms at trailhead. The trail is relatively flat and leads through lush vegetation. Rated easy; 2- to 3-hour hike one way. Mountain bikers use this trail, but there are lots of tree roots and some muddy spots. USGS map: Seward D-8.

Hidden Creek Trail. Trailhead at Mile 4.6 Skilak Lake Loop Road in Kenai National Wildlife Refuge. It is 1.3 miles to Skilak Lake; elevation range 500 to 300 feet; rated easy.

Hope Point Trail. Strenuous, 2.5-mile day hike. This Chugach National Forest trail starts near the emtrance to Porcupine Creek campground at the end of the Hope Highway and climbs 3,630 feet to above timberline. Impressive view of Turnagain Arm, Cook Inlet, Fire Island and Chugach Mountains. Winter travel is unsafe due to avalanche danger. USGS map: Seward D-8.

Humpy Creek Trail. Easy to moderate, 5.2-mile trail. Hiking time 2 to 3 hours; elevation gain 300 feet. Trail connects to Grewingk Creek with Mallard Bay. Also accesses north end of Emerald Lake Trail. Bears frequent mouth of Humpy Creek in July and August. Trail continues south over Kachemak Bay tidal flats to campsite.

Johnson Pass Trail. This 23-mile Chugach National Forest trail offers spectacular scenery with few extreme elevation changes (elevation gain: 1,000 feet). Extremely popular mountain bike trail, especially on weekends. Johnson Pass trail has 2 trailheads on the Seward Highway: the north trailhead at Milepost 63.7 and the south trailhead at Milepost 32.6. Fishing for grayling in Bench Lake and rainbow trout in Johnson Lake. Watch for black bears. Not recommended for winter use due to avalanche danger. USGS maps: Seward C-6, C-7.

Kenai River Trail. Trailheads at Mile 0.6 and 2.3 Skilak Lake Loop Road in Kenai National Wildlife Refuge. It is approximately 2 miles to trail's end; elevation range 600 to 300 feet; rated moderate.

Lagoon Trail. This 6.2-mile trail, rated moderate to difficult, winds along Halibut Cove and passes through a boggy area to Halibut Creek Trailhead and delta in Kachemak Bay State Park. Continue on by walking upstream on the south side about 200 yards, or walk around the delta on the tide flats. A series of steep switchbacks then leads through a spruce forest up to where the trail intersects Goat Rope Spur Trail at 1,200 feet. The trail continues downhill and south, across Falls Creek and on to the end of the lagoon and the ranger station. Here, you may take the stairs down to the stream where a sign directs hikers to the China Poot Lake Trail. Hiking time for Lagoon Trail is 5 to 7 hours.

Lake Emma Trail. Trailhead on north shore Tustumena Lake in Kenai National Wildlife Refuge; no road access. Length 9.2 miles round-trip; elevation range 100 to 2,500 feet; rated strenuous.

Lost Lake Trail. This scenic, 7-mile Chugach National Forest trail offers spectacular views and access to high alpine terrain. Elevation gain: 1,820 feet. For trailhead, turn off Seward Highway at Milepost 5.2 onto Scout Way; drive up hill, and turn left; take next right (Hayden Berlin Road) 1/4 mile to trailhead parking.

Trail ends at Lost Lake (above treeline); fishing for rainbow trout. Salmonberry patches between Mile 4 and 5 in August. Access to Dale Clemens Memorial Cabin from Mile 4. Popular area for snowmobiling in winter (snowmachine trail leaves summer trail at Mile 1.5). The upper part of Lost Lake trail is not free of snow until mid-July. Brown and black bear in the spring. This trail connects with the Primrose Trail at Lost Lake. USGS map: Seward A-7, B-7.

Mallard Bay Trail. This 1-mile, easy to moderate trail heads at Mallard Bay and crosses ridge to Portlock Glacier and Kenai National Wildlife Refuge. Also accesses Humpy Creek Trail. Elevation gain 250 feet; hiking time 30 minutes.

Moose Creek Trail. Trailhead on north shore Tustumena Lake in Kenai National Wildlife Refuge; no road access. Length 14.5 miles round-trip; elevation range 100 to 2,700 feet; rated moderate.

Moose Valley Trail. This moderate, 6.7-mile trail begins at China Poot Lake Trail junction and passes along shore of Two-Loon Lake. Ascends through forested ridges and valleys and opens into Moose Valley's cottonwood meadows. Eleevation gain 2,000 feet. Wildflowers and cow parsnip abundant in summer; goats on mountain ridges.

Poot Peak Trail. This steep, slick, unmaintained 4.6-mile route, rated difficult, begins across the China Pool Lake inlet stream bridge and heads up to timberline in Kachemak Bay State Park. CLimbing the 2,100-foot peak is hazardous because of shifting scree and rotten rock. Superb views of Wosnesenski Glacier and Kachemak bay. Hiking time is 3 to 4 hours.

Primrose Trail. This 8-mile Chugach National Forest trail connects with Lost Lake Trail. Trailhead is at Primrose Campground at Milepost 17 Seward Highway. Access to Porcupine Creek Falls at Mile 3 (recommended family day hike) on Primrose Trail. Backcountry campsites at Lost Lake; fishing for rainbow trout. Climbers can summit Mount Ascension (5,710 feet), which forms the west border of lake. Excellent area for skiing and snowmobiling in winter. USGS map: Seward B-7.

Ptarmigan Creek/Falls Creek Trail. This 7.5-mile Chugach National Forest trail offers a good chance to see sheep and goats on mountain slopes. Trailhead at Ptarmian Creek Campground at Milepost 23.1 Seward Highway. Trail climbs through spruce forest to alpine terrain surrounding Ptarmigan Lake at Mile 3.5. Trail continues 4 miles to east end of lake. Access to Andy Simons Mountain south of Ptarmigan Lake for mountaineering. Fishing for Dolly Varden and rainbow trout in Ptarmigan Creek, grayling in Ptarmigan Lake. Sockeye salmon spawn in creek late July to early August. Not recommended for winter use due to avalanche danger. USGS maps: Seward B-6, B-7.

Resurrection Pass Trail. This 38.5-mile Chugach National Forest trail is a National Recreation Trail that follows a route originally established in the late 1800s by miners along gold-bearing Resurrection Creek. Beautiful scenery, fairly easy backpacking and good fishing in summer. Popular for cross-country skiing in winter, with snowmobile access between December 1 and February 15. Eight public-use cabins are located along the trail (see Cabins this section).

The Forest Service divides the trail into 2 sections: Resurrection Pass Trail North and Resurrection Pass Trail South. Resurrection Pass Trail North follows Resurrection Creek from the north trailhead, located 4 miles south of Milepost 16.2 Hope Highway on Resurrection Creek Road, south 19.25 miles to 2,600-foot-high Resurrection Pass. Recreation cabins are located at Mile 7, 11.5 and 14.5 (see Caribou Creek, Fox Creek and East Creek cabins under Cabins this section).

Resurrection Pass Trail South begins at the south trailhead at Milepost 53 Sterling Highway near Cooper Landing and follows Juneau Creek north 19.3 miles to junction with the north half of the trail at Resurrection Pass. Recreation cabins are located at Mile 7, 9, 9.5, 13 and 18 (see Trout Lake, Romig, Juneau Lake, Swan Lake and Devil's Pass cabins under Cabins this section). Day hike to Juneau Creek Falls is 4.5 miles from south trailhead.

Fishing in Juneau Creek, Trout Lake, Juneau Lake and Swan Lake. Resurrection Pass Trail South connects with Devil's Pass Trail for a 28-mile hike to Devil's Pass trailhead.

Both the north and south sections of the Resurrection Pass Trail are rated easy with level path, gradual grade and some steep grades with switchbacks. This is a well-maintained trail although it may be muddy in places. Several designated campsites are located along the Resurrection Pass Trail. Popular cross-country skiing and snowmobiling area; heavy snow in Resurrection Pass persists into late spring. Hikers can extend their trip at the south end of the Resurrection Pass Trail by continuing on the 21-mile Russian Lakes Trail from the Russian River campground. USGS map: Seward B-8, C-8, D-8.

Resurrection River Trail. This 16-mile Chugach National Forest trail begins at Mile 7.1 Exit Glacier Road and connects with the Russian Lakes Trail. The trail parallels the Resurrection River through spruce and hardwood forests. Relatively high bear density. Trail may be wet, boggy in places with poor drainage. Difficult to walk on when raining. Recreation cabin located 6.5 miles from trailhead (see Cabins this section). The Resurrection River, Russian Lakes and Resurrection Pass trails connect to form a 72-mile trek between Seward and Hope. USGS maps: Seward A-7, A-8, B-8.

Russian Lakes Trail. This 21-mile Chugach National Forest trail is a popular summer hike and offers easy hiking for a family outing. Trail access from either the north trailhead at Russian River Campground, Milepost 52.8 Sterling Highway or from the east trailhead on Cooper Lake Road, 12 miles south of Milepost 48 Sterling Highway. Russian River Falls at Mile 2 and Lower Russian Lake at Mile 3 from Russian River Campground. First 3 miles from north trailhead are heavily used by fishermen. Excellent rainbow trout fishing at Lower Lake, Aspen Flats and Upper Lake. The Russian River provides the largest sport fishery in Alaska for sockeye salmon, starting mid-June and mid-July. There are 3 recreation cabins along this trail (Barber, Aspen Flats and Upper Russian Lake) as well as designated campsites at Lower and Upper Russian Lakes. USGS maps: Seward B-8, Kenai B-1.

Saddle Trail. This 1-mile hike leads over the saddle between Halibut Cove and Grewingk Glacier in Kachemak Bay State Park. The trail, rated moderate, accesses the Alpine Ridge and Lagoon trails as well as the Grewingk Glacier Trail. It is steep on the Halibut Cove side. There is no transportation available from the trailhead to Glacier Spit or Halibut Cove unless you've made prior arrangements. Hiking the beach from the trailhead to Right Beach isn't possible because of steep cliffs. The Saddle Trail trailhead is a popular spot to land boats during bad weather. Please respect private property near this trail. Hiking time is 25 minutes.

Sadie Knob Trail. Moderate to difficult, 6.3-mile trail accesses alpine ridge between Sadie Cove and Kachemak Bay. Access from north end of beach, north of Anisom Point or south end by north side of Sadie Cove Inlet. Elevation gain 2100 feet; hiking time 3 hours to Sadie Knob. Sadie Knob offers 360-degree vies of Kachemak Bay, Sadie Peak, Sadie Cove, Eldred Passage and Cook Inlet volcanoes. Mountain goats, black bears and eagles in area.

Seven Lakes Trail. Length 8.8 miles round-trip; relatively level; wet in some places; rated easy. Starts at Engineer Lake Campground parking lot; turn off on short side road at Mile 9.5 Skilak Lake Loop Road. This trail links Engineer Lake with Hidden, Kelly, Petersen and other smaller lakes in Kenai National Wildlife Refuge.

Silver Lake Trail. Trailhead at Mile 9.1 Swanson River Road in Kenai National Wildlife Refuge. Length 1 mile round-trip; rainbow trout and arctic char fishing.

Skilak Lookout Trail. Trailhead at Mile 5.4 Skilak Lake Loop Road off the Sterling Highway in Kenai National Wildllife Refuge. Length 4 miles round-trip; elevation range 600 to 1,450 feet; rated moderate. Trail offers glimpses of Skilak Lake and climbs to a knob that provides panoramic view of the lake and surrounding area. Round-trip is 4 to 5 hours.

Skyline Trail. Trailhead at Milepost S 61.4 Sterling Highway in Kenai National Wildlife Refuge. It is 3 miles round-trip; elevation gain 1,800 feet; rated very strenuous. The trail provides quick access into the Mystery Hills, beginning in forest and emerging above tree line in about 1/4 mile; it gradually disappears about 1 1/4 mile from the trailhead in a beautiful alpine area. Spectacular views; berry picking. Winter travel not recommended due to avalanche hazard. USGS map: Kenai C-1.

Surprise Creek Trail. Trailhead on Skilak Lake Loop Road off the Sterling Highway in Kenai National Wildlife Refuge. Length 4.2 miles; elevation range 300 to 2,500 feet; steep, rated strenuous; minimum maintenance. A river crossing is necessary to reach the trailhead.

Tutka/Jakolof Trail. This 2-mile, easy to moderate trail is accessed by Tutka Bay Lagoon and Jakolof Road Trailhead. Campsite at Tutka trailhead. Trail joins Tutka Bay Lagoon and Rocky River road. Much of trail is on Seldovia Native Association property; please stay on main trail. Elevation gain 250 feet; hiking time 1 hour.

Tutka Lake Trail. Moderate, 2.9-mile trail accessed by Tutka Lake Trailhead and at Sea Star Cove Public-use Cabin. Trail climbs from trailhead and intersects trail to cabin. Trail continues along Tutka Lake and intersects trail to Tutka Bay Lagoon Fish Hatchery. Follows above Tutka Creek and ends near Kachemak Bay State Wilderness Park boundary with views of Tutka Creek waterfalls.

Victor Creek Trail. This 2-mile Chugach National Forest trail is rated strenuous with an elevation gain of 1,100 feet; recommended for summer hiking only. Trailhead at Milepost 19.5 Seward Highway. Mountain goats may be seen along slopes at upper end of trail. USGS map: Seward B-7.

Wosnesenski Trail. This 2-mile trail, rated easy to moderate, begins from the China Poot Peak Trail, about 10 minutes after crossing the inlet stream bridge at China Poot Lake in Kachemak Bay State Park. It winds along the shoreline of 3 lakes formed by a geologic fault. After about 25 minutes on the trail, you will find a good camping area in a stand of cottonwoods by the lake. After another 25 minutes of hiking, the trail climbs over a low saddle and drops down into the valley. Crossing the glacial rivers in the valley can be hazardous. Hiking time is 1 hour 15 minutes.

Wosnesenski River Trail. This 11.3-mile, easy to moderate trail is 10 hours from Haystack Trailhead to China Poot Lake; elevation gain 300 feet. Trail begins along Poot Peak Trail and winds along shores of 3 lakes. Drops into Wosnesenski River Valley with spectacular 600-foot waterfall. Trail intersects with small utility access road. Highly scenic trail with mountain and glacier views.

Mat-Su Area Trails

Byers Lake Loop Trail. Trailhead at Byers Lake Campground in Denali State Park at Milepost A 147 George Parks Highway. This 4.8-mile trail offers an easy hike around Byers Lake. The trail connects with the 7-mile Cascade route at the northeast end of the lake and climbs Curry Ridge to Tarn Point, a 1,900-foot elevation change. Byers Lake Loop trail also accesses the longer Troublesome Creek and Little Coal Creek trails. Trail is regularly maintained. USGS maps: Talkeetna C-1, C-2, D-1; Talkeetna Mountains C-6, D-6.

Ermine Hill Trail. Trailhead is at Milepost 158.5 Parks Highway. A 3.3-mile trail with low-angle switchbacks; elevation gain 900 feet. Connects with Kesugi Ridge Trail. From Ermine Hill Trailhead, it is about 17 miles to Little Coal Creek Trailhead or Byers Lake Campground.

King River Trail. This multi-use trail, popular with ATVers, begins at Milepost S 66.3 Glenn Highway. The 6.5-mile-long trail heads north along the southwest side of Castle Mountain, following the King River. It connects with the Chickaloon-Knik-Nelchina trail system. USGS maps: Anchorage D-4, D-5.

Little Coal Creek Trail. This Denali State Park trailhead is located at Milepost A 163.8 George Parks Highway. According to park rangers, this trailhead offers easy access to alpine country (1 1/2-hour hike) and to Indian Mountain (a day-long, 9-mile-round-trip hike, elevation gain 3,300 feet, outstanding view). It is 27.4 miles from the Little Coal Creek trailhead to Byers Lake Campground via the Kesugi Ridge route. It is 36.2 miles from Little Coal Creek trailhead to the Troublesome Creek trailhead via the Kesugi Ridge route. Marked by rock cairns, the Kesugi Ridge route is rated difficult. USGS map: Talkeetna C-1, C-2, D-1; Talkeetna Mountains C-6, D-6.

Red Shirt Lake Trail. Located in the Nancy Lake Recreation Area, this 3-mile (one-way) route bridges the gap between the Nancy Lake Parkway and Red Shirt Lake. To find the trail-head, turn west onto the Nancy Lake Parkway at Mile 67.3 of the Parks Highway. The trail leaves the parkway at mile 5.7. The route stays primarily on high ground and occasionally affords a view of the area's lakes with the Chugach Mountains on the distant horizon. There are lakeshore campsites at the end of the trail. Just 1-1/2 miles south of the parkway, there is a 2-1/2-mile one-way trail that winds its way eastward between Big Noluck Lake and Chicken Lake, and Frazer and Little Frazer lakes.

Troublesome Creek Trail. This Denali State Park trail has 2 trailheads: the upper trail-head is at Milepost A 137.6 Parks Highway; the lower trailhead is at Lower Troublesome Creek Campground at Milepost A 137.3 Parks Highway. It is a 15.2-mile hike from the Upper Troublesome Creek trailhead to Byers Lake. Rated moderate. The trailhead and trail to Mile 5.5 is closed from mid-July through the end of August due to the high concentra-tion of bears feeding on spawning salmon. Exercise extreme caution from the Chulitna River upstream to Ultima Poole. (Ultima Poole is reached via a 500-yard-long side trail at Mile 4.5 of Troublesome Creek trail; it is a deep pool at the base of a small falls on the creek and a pleasant place for a rest or a bracing swim.) Salmon cannot get beyond the falls, and the bear danger beyond Ultima Poole is not as great. From Troublesome Creek trailhead to the Little Coal Creek trailhead via the Kesugi Ridge route, it is 36.2 miles and rated difficult. Rock cairns mark trail. USGS maps: Talkeetna C-1, C-2, D-1; Talkeetna Mountains C-6, D-6.

Wrangell-St. Elias Area Hiking Trails

Baultoff Creek Area. Fly-in from Tok, Gulkana or Nabesna to Baultoff airstrip in Wrangell-St. Elias National Park for a variety of day and overnight hikes. The Nabesba Ranger District recommends hikes to East Fork Snag Creek, Four Mile Creek, Gravel Creek and up Baultoff Creek. Most routes follow creeks and may involve traversing steep scree slopes. All trips are strenuous. Travel in this remote area should be done only by experienced parties in good physical condition. USGS map: Nabesna A-1.

Chelle Lake. Fly-in to Chelle Lake NPS airstrip, located 20-minutes flying time east-southeast from Gulkana airstrip at the foot of Mount Drum. Spectacular views of the moun-tain. Public-use cabin at Chelle Lake. Although topographical maps indicate one lake, dry land exists between what are presently 2 lakes. In the vicinity of the lakes, ground moisture makes for spongy, wet hiking. At higher elevations, around 4,500 feet, the ground becomes hard, with low alpine tundra. Hiking is easy, and the small peaks surrounding Mount Drum are easily reached during a day hike. Strong downdrafts from Mount Drum should be con-sidered when choosing a campsite. In hot weather, large cumulonimbus clouds around the mountain dissipate in the form of strong rain or hale. Watch for crevassed ice when cross-ing glaciers at higher elevations. Chelle Lake and adjacent 40 acres of land are located on Wrangell-St. Elias National Preserve land; surrounding land is owned primarily by Ahtna Corporation. USGS map: Gulkana A-2

Copper River Trail. This BLM trail is 7 miles round trip and recommended as a good trail for bird watchers. Access is from the trailhead at Milepost R 12.5 Edgerton Highway. The trail is fairly flat and marshy, winding around several small lakes and through dense veg-etation. It ends at the entrance to a small ravine that leads down to the Copper River. Use caution along Copper River: it is very swift and cold.

Dixie Pass. A 24-mile round trip hike is one of the only backcountry hikes in Wrangell-St. Elias National Park that can be accessed by road. Allow 3 to 4 days. Access to the trail-head is from Milepost 13.5 McCarthy Road via Nugget Creek/Kotsina Road. Continue past Nugget Creek trailhead on Kotsina Road for 1.3 miles to Dixie Pass trailhead. The trail goes through woods for 3 miles to Strelna Creek, then follows the creek 4 miles to a drainage leading to Dixie Pass. Continue along the Dixie Pass drainage for approximately 3 miles to a game trail that switchbacks 2 miles up to the pass. This route requires frequent creek crossings and may require frequent detours during periods of high runoff. Good campsites on sand/gravel bars along Strelna Creek and the Dixie Pass drainage. Camping in Dixie Pass is not advised due to bears. Water is accessible for most of the trip. In Dixie Pass, water may possibly be collected from snow field runoff (snowpack dependent). Use extreme caution when crossing snow fields as they may conceal drainage systems underneath. USGS maps: Valdez C-1; McCarthy C-8

Donoho Peak. A 14-mile round trip from Kennicott to the summit of 6,696-foot Donoho Peak in Wrangell-St. Elias National Park, this hike is considered strenuous and requires a glacier crossing (crampons advisable). This route starts at the north edge of town and follows the Erie Mine Trail for less than a mile before crossing Root Glacier. After exiting the glacier on the west side, an animal trail leads north along the top of the moraine to a campsite beside a small pool. Several hundred yards north of the campsite, a trail leads through the brush and around 2 lakes to the junction of the Kennicott and Gates glaciers. The adventureous can climb Donoho Peak via the gully on the south side of the mountain: bushwhack to the base of the scree slope from the trail between the first and second lakes. Remnants of the old Regal Mine and the mining trail are found on the south side of Donoho Peak. The summit of Donoho Peak offers excellent views of Mount Blackburn and, on a clear day, Mounts Logan and St. Elias to the southeast. USGS maps: McCarthy B-6, C-5, C-6.

Goodlata Peak. This is a 10 to 14 day cross-country hike through the Chugach Mountains covering approximately 35 miles between the Tana River and Goodlata Peak by way of the old Bremner Mine. Access is by charter flight to "Cross" landing strip on the west side of the Tana River south of Towhead Mountain. Scout route and location of Bremner airstrip on bush flight in. This route leads west across mountain passes, along streams and through valleys to the Bremner Mine near the West Fork of the Tana, and continues on to Goodlata Peak. It offers many small valleys to explore, mountain peaks for non-technical ascents, gold panning, panoramic views of the highest peaks in Wrangell-St. Elias National Park and one of the highest concentrations of grizzlies in North America. USGS maps: Bering Glacier D-5, D-6, D-7.

Jacksina Creek. Length of hike and travel time depends on route. The hiking varies from solid shale to spongy tundra. Access is by charter flight to Jaeger Mesa, approximately 3 miles south of Gold Hill and 8 miles south of Nabesna. Hike south along crest of mesa towards P6628' at the southern end of the mesa. The view from the mesa is spectacular. The Nutzotin Mountains and Mounts Sanford, Wrangell, Jarvis and Blackburn in the Wrangells are visible. Mount Gordon, to the south, can be climbed via a rock scramble up its southern slopes. Descend from the mesa around the east side of P6628' to a lake to the south; clear water and camping are available nearby. From the lake, hike west along the creek drainage for 2 to 3 miles before going southwest into the upper Mesa Creek drainage. From Mesa Lake, elevation 4,720 feet, there are several pleasant day hikes. Or follow game trail at south end of the lake, and desend into the Jacksina Creek drainage. Fording the Jacksina is usally impossible: the main channel is 40 feet wide and 5 feet deep. Hike along south side of the Jacksina Glacier, and cross the glacier on the lower rocky moraine. Once across the glacier, a short hike downstream leads to a creek bed which provides access to the mesa north of the glacier. Descend from the mesa off P5695', which is at the northeast end of the mesa south of Tumble Creek. Tumble Creek is swift and must be crossed early in the morning. Once across Tumble Creek, there are several ways in which to end this hike: by floatplane pickup from either Grizzly Lake or Tanada Lake (both offer fishing); or by hiking 1 of 2 routes to the Nabesna Road. For the latter, either follow the ATV trail along Tanada Lake, and intersect Nabesna Road at Mile 24.3; or cross the mesa east of Tanada Lake, and descend the creek drainage to Jack Creek bridge on Nabesna Road and walk 5.5 miles to Devil's Mountain Lodge. USGS maps: Nabesna A-5, A-6, B-4, B-5.

Lost Creek. Rangers for the Nabesna district of Wrangell-St. Elias National Park suggest this hike as a long day hike or extended multi-day hike using Trail Creek as an option for a loop route. From the trailhead at Mile 31.2 Nabesna Road, follow the ATV trail up Lost Creek to where the creek narrows, then either climb east up the hillside, and make an upstream traverse, or climb up the west hillside, and travel along a bench area for about 1 mile until the creek bed ascends to the same elevation. It is 6 miles one way to where the creek bed narrows and an additional 2.5 miles to the headwaters for a total of 8.5 miles. On warm, summer days, the creek level can be low in the early morning and rise several feet during the day. An easy morning ford may be impassable by the late afternoon. Also, the creek level can rise suddenly during and after rain storms. Bears are present in the area. USGS map: Nabesna C-5.

Lower Skolai Lake to Glacier Creek. This 25-mile route (one way) via the Chitistone Canyon and the Goat Trail can take anywhere from 5 to 8 days, depending on side trips planned and route taken. From the Lower Skolai Lake airstrip (elev. 4,500 feet), it is a 1,300-foot climb to Chitistone Pass (elev. 5,800 feet). From the pass, the route follows a highly scenic and rugged alpine valley. The Goat Trail can be picked up on the northerly side of the valley. There are 2 parallel Goat Trails: the Upper and the Lower routes. The Upper Goat Trail is the recommended route. The Upper and Lower Goat trails eventually rejoin and travel around the head of the Chitistone Canyon. The Chitistone Trail/Goat Trail then descends to the canyon floor along the north side of the Chitistone River. Cross to the south side of the Chitistone River by fording the creek which proceeds from the Chitistone Falls, and then, cross the terminus of the Chitistone Glacier. Great care should be taken when traversing the glacier. (Another option is to cross the Chitistone River if flow conditions permit.) Once across the river, the route follows the Chitistone Canyon to the southwest, crossing a rockslide area and sections of dense brush before fording Toby Creek (difficult crossing during periods of high water). From Toby Creek, it is a 4-mile hike to the Glacier Creek airstrip (elev. 2,340 feet). USGS maps: McCarthy B-4, C-3, C-4.

Nikolai Pass. This is either a 30-mile-round-trip hike or a 15-mile hike with fly-in to Nikolai Pass in Wrangell-St. Elias National Park. From the town of McCarthy, the trail starts across the log footbridge that crosses McCarthy Creek at the south edge of town. Follow dirt road (take left fork) to trail up McCarthy Creek for 7 miles to the junction with Nikolai Creek. The trail then continues 4.5 miles up to Nikolai Pass, an elevation gain of 2,100 feet. Wildlife includes Dall sheep, grizzly bears and moose. McCarthy Creek is high during the summer, making crossings difficult and dangerous. USGS maps: McCarthy B-5, C-5.

Nugget Creek Trail. A 30-mile-round-trip hike taking 2 to 4 days; rated moderate. Access is from Milepost 13.5 McCarthy Road; turn on Nugget Creek/Kotsina Road, and continue 2.5 miles to trailhead. Ford Strelna Creek, and follow trail northeast across low bench (may be wet and muddy) for several miles before gaining elevation. Several creeks must be forded on the remaining 13 miles of trail before reaching Nugget Creek at the end of the trail. Hikers are cautioned not to attempt excursions onto Kuskulana Glacier. USGS maps McCarthy C-8; Valdez C-1.

Orange Hill/Bond Creek. This mineral-rich area offers superb views of the Nabesna Glacier and surrounding snowcapped Wrangell Mountains. Fly-in to either Bond Creek or Orange Hill airstrips. The Orange Hill strip is approximately 600 feet long and subject to seasonal changes; check with park headquarters' aviation staff before trying to land at this airstrip. Bond Creek airstrip is less than 1000 feet and rocky. From Bond Creek, it is a short but steep hike to the east to point 6815. This high point affords a panoramic view of the entire area, including the Nabesna Gold Mine, Nabesna River, Nabesna Glacier and Bond Creek. Remnants of a tractor trail from Bond Creek to Orange Hill remain. Except for the first mile, which is quite bushy, the route is easy to follow, winding its way over open tundra and through spruce forest to Orange Hill. Nearby Nikonda Creek canyon offers excellent exploring opportunities. USGS maps: Nabesna A-4, B-4.

Root Glacier Trail. An easy to moderate day hike of approximately 3 miles from Kennicott to Root Glacier in Wrangell-St. Elias National Park. Also recommended for mountain bikes to a certain point. Described by the Park Service as a great day hike with views of Mount Blackburn, Regal Mountain and Donaho Peak. The terrain is relatively level with some moderate elevation gain and loss. Follow the trail north from Kennicott. The trail eventually curves to the right and comes upon another trail. Turn left onto that trail, and follow it along the lateral moraine of the Kennicott and Root glaciers. After 1/4 mile, cross Bonanza Creek on a footbridge. After about a mile, the trail curves sharply to the right and upstream to cross Jumbo Creek via a footbridge. After another 1/4 mile, the trail reaches the Root Glacier access trail. Primitive campsites with an outhouse are located here. For access to the glacier, turn left at the sign, and follow the trail as it winds down the moraine to the toe of the glacier. Use extreme caution walking on the glacier; the ice can be very slippery and dangerous. Avoid walking along the edge of Root Glacier. This hike may be extended for several miles across Amazon Creek and beyond; ask park rangers about the Kennicott to the Knoll hike. USGS maps: McCarthy B-6, C-6.

Soda Lake. Approximately 26 miles round trip; allow 3 days for hike plus additional time for exploring the lake and surrounding areas. Trailhead at Mile 31.2 Nabesna Road (Lost Creek). It is 8 miles from the trailhead to Soda Creek, 2 miles from Soda Creek to Soda Lake and 3 miles from Soda Lake to Totschunda Creek. Follow the ATV trail along Lost Creek for approximately 1 1/2-miles, then veer right to follow the Big Grayling Lake trail through spruce forest, open tundra and sedge tussocks. The area around the lake may be wet, depending on seasonal rains. Avoid private property at the northwest and southeast corners of the lake. Past Big Grayling Lake, the trail veers left and goes through spruce forest for about 1 mile, then follows Platinum Creek for about 2 1/2 miles to the confluence with Soda Creek. Follow Soda Creek for an additional 2 miles. The end of the ATV trail is located on the right bank of Soda Creek. From this point, the hiker may follow the left fork of Soda Creek into the hills for some pleasant, high-tundra walking. Or follow the right fork of the creek to Soda Lake. A horse trail past Mineral Springs also leads past Soda Lake and on to Totschunda Creek. USGS maps: Nabesna C-4, C-5.

Stairway Icefall. This 7- to 8-day hike is approximately 28 miles round trip. The terrain includes trail, scree, brush, streambed, glacial ice and morraine. It begins in Kennicott at the north edge of town and follows the trail to the Erie Mine. From the mine, the route goes across a glacier and up a brushy hillside beside a waterfall. Good views of the Stairway Icefall from knoll, elevation 3,800 feet. The route then crosses Bonanza Ridge and drops down to follow the McCarthy Creek drainage back to the town of McCarthy. It is 4.5 miles from McCarthy back to Kennicott via a gravel road. USGS maps: McCarthy B-5, B-6, C-5, C-6.

Tonsina River Trail. This well-marked, 2-mile BLM trail starts at Milepost R 12.3 Edgerton Highway and leads south through the woods to a picnic site overlooking the Tonsina River. Look for calypso orchids in the spring. Rated easy. Private property borders trail.

Upper Sanford River to Dadina Drainage. This hike is 20 miles one way and takes 4 to 8 days depending on route and side trips. Fly-in to Upper Sanford River airstrip east of Gulkana airport. From the airstrip, it is about a 3.5-mile hike along the south side of the Sanford River to Sanford Glacier in Wrangell-St. Elias National Park. From the glacier, this route heads south through thick alders, climbs through alpine tundra to 5,000 feet, then leads east approximately 2 miles to a campsite with views of the east face of Mount Drum, the southwest face of Sanford and west side of Mounts Wrangell and Zanetti. Day hiking is possible for over 5 miles in any direction from this site. The hike continues south to drop down to the Dadina River and reach a short airstrip on the southeast side of the river. USGS maps: Gulkana A-1, A-2, B-2; Valdez D-2.

Iditarod National Historic Trail

The Iditarod trail was originally surveyed in 1910 as a mail route from Seward to Nome. The mail trail was 938 miles long and was used as a major route until 1924 when the airplane came into use. It is best known today for the Iditarod Trail Sled Dog Race, which uses 2 alternate routes from Anchorage to Nome, both of which follow substantially longer routes than the original mail trail. Since the Iditarod Trail is primarily a winter trail, only a short section of the original trail is suitable for summer hiking. The best place to view the Iditarod Historic Trail is at its start in Seward, where the trail begins at the ferry terminal and follows a marked course through town as a bike path. The trail continues for hikers from a gravel parking area on the east side of Sawmill Creek at Mile 2.1 Nash Road (turn off at

Milepost S 3.2 Seward Highway) and leads north to Bear Lake (accessible via Bear Lake Road from Milepost S 6.6 Seward Highway). From the north end of Bear Lake, the trail continues to Mile 12 on the Seward Highway.

A longer hike on the Iditarod Trail is possible from the Crow Pass trailhead on Crow Creek Road south of Anchorage. This section of the trail is about 27 miles long and climbs 2,000 feet in altitude before descending the Raven Creek drainage to the the north trail-head at Eagle River Nature Center at the end of Eagle River road. The north trailhead is accessible via the Glenn Highway from Anchorage to the Eagle River/Eagle River Road Exit, then 12.3 miles to the Nature Center. All of the hiking trail, from Crow Creek trailhead to the Eagle River Nature Center, is part of the Iditarod National Historic Trail. Most of the trail is on state park land although the first 4 miles are within Chugach National Forest.

For more information about specific portions of the trail, access points and user rules, contact the following agencies: BLM, Anchorage Field Office, 6881 Abbott Loop Road, Anchorage, AK 99507, web site www.anchorage.ak.blm.gov/; Iditaord National Historic Trail Inc., P.O. Box 2323, Seward, AK 99664; Iditarod Trail Blazers, Seward Chapter, P.O. Box 1923, Seward, AK 99664; Chugach National Forest, Seward Ranger District, P.O. Box 390, Seward, AK 99664; web site www.fs.fed.us/r10/chugach/; Fish and Wildlife Service, 1011 East Tudor Road, Anchorage, AK 99503; web site www.r7.fws.gov/; Alaska Department of Natural Resources Public Information Center, 550 W. 7th Ave., Suite 1260, Anchorage, AK 99501-3557; phone (907) 269-8400, fax (907) 269-8901, TDD (907) 269-8411, email pic@dnr.state.ak.us, web site www.dnr.state.ak.us/parks/; Iditarod Trail Committee, P.O. Box 87800, Wasilla, AK 99687-0800; phone (907) 376-5155, web site www.iditarod.com/.

Independence Mine State Historical Park

Located near Hatcher Pass in the Talkeetna Mountains, the 271-acre Independence Mine State Historical Park was established in 1980, 6 years after Independence Mine was added to the National Register of Historic Places. The park includes 2 former lode gold mining sites: the Alaska Free Gold (Martin) Mine on Skyscraper Mountain, active from 1909 to 1924, and Independence Mine on Granite Mountain, which operated from 1938 to 1941 under Alaska-Pacific Consolidated Mining Company (APC). The historical park offers a fascinating look at Alaska lode mining and spectacular mountain scenery.

At its peak in 1941, APC employed 204 men, and produced 34,416 ounces of gold worth $1,204,560. In 1942, with the advent of WWII, gold mining was declared a nonessential wartime activity although Independence Mine continued to operate until 1943 by producing scheelite. The wartime ban was lifted in 1946, but gold prices were fixed at $35 per ounce, and gold mining became an unprofitable venture. In January 1951, Independence Mine was closed, and by 1958, the owners had sold the equipment and machinery. Only the buildings remained.

Since establishing the park, the state has restored the manager's house, which now serves as a visitor center and features interpretative exhibits and displays, and the assay office, which now contains a hard rock mining museum. Other buildings in the complex, including a timber shed, warehouse, collapsed mill, mess halls and bunkhouses have been preserved.

Climate: Elevations in the area range from less than 1,200 feet to more than 6,000 feet. Generally, it is warmer and drier at lower elevations. The average maximum accumulation of snow at Independence Mine (elev. 3,300 feet) is 55 inches while along the lower elevations of the Little Susitna River, it is only 42 inches. The average temperature in January ranges from 11°F to 25°F. Temperatures rise above 50°F only during the summer months. Temperature inversions are common on calm, clear nights, and as the cold air drains down valley floors, it can get windy.

Wildlife: Moose populations in the forested western and southern portions of the Hatcher Pass area are said to be among the largest in Southcentral. Other wildlife present includes occasional caribou, black and brown bears, wolves, wolverines, coyotes, beavers, foxes, martens, minks, weasels, lynx, hares, marmots and other small animals.

Nesting tundra birds live within the area as well as bald and golden eagles, sharp-shinned hawks, red-tailed hawks, merlins, kestrels, gyrfalcons, peregrine falcons, boreal owls and great horned owls. Three resident ptarmigan species are found in the area as well as spruce grouse and a variety of songbirds.

Activities: Explore the mine and surrounding area on foot on your own, or take a tour. Guided tours of the mine are offered at 1:30 P.M. and 3:30 P.M. on weekdays, with an additional 4:30 P.M. tour offered on weekends and holidays. A tour fee is charged. The visitor center is open daily, 11 A.M. to 7 P.M., from June to Labor Day; phone the visitor center at (907) 745-2827 in summer, or the Mat-Su Area State Park Office at (907) 745-3975 for current information.

The area surrounding Independence Mine State Historical Park is a favorite for summer hiking and winter recreation (See Hatcher Pass Public Use Area this section.)

Accommodations: Hatcher Pass Lodge (phone 907/745-5897) at Independence Mine State Historical Park offers meals and lodging year-round and maintains several miles of groomed cross-country ski trails in the winter. Motherlode Lodge at Mile 14 Hatcher Pass Road offers bed and breakfast accommodations year-round (phone 907/746-1464). There are no developed campgrounds in the area. Public restrooms are located at the park visitor center. Additional lodging and services are available in Palmer, Wasilla and along Palmer-Fishhook Road.

Access: Access to the Hatcher Pass area is via the 49-mile-long Hatcher Pass Road from either Palmer or Willow. From Palmer, take the Palmer-Fishhook Road turnoff at Milepost 49.5 Glenn Highway. From Willow, take the Fishhook-Willow Road from Milepost A 71.2 Parks Highway. Hatcher Pass Public Use Area begins on the Palmer side at approximately Mile 7.8 on Hatcher Pass Road. The turnoff for Independence Mine State Historical Park is at Mile 17. A parking fee is charged at the entrance to the park.

It is 68 miles from Anchorage to Independence Mine via the Glenn Highway and Hatcher Pass Road. The road is open year-round from the Glenn Highway to the park visitor center. It is closed over the pass to within about 14 miles of the Parks Highway from the first snow in late September until late June.

For more information: Contact Alaska Department of Natural Resources Public Information Center, 550 W. 7th Ave., Suite 1260, Anchorage, AK 99501-3557; phone (907) 269-8400, fax (907) 269-8901, TDD (907) 269-8411, email pic@dnr.state.ak.us. Or contact Mat-Su Area State Parks, HC32, Box 6706, Wasilla, AK 99654-9719; phone (907) 745-3975.

For details on access and accommodations, see *The MILEPOST®*, a complete guide to Alaska's road system. USGS maps: Anchorage C-6, C-7, D-6, D-7, D-8.

Kachemak Bay State Park and State Wilderness Park

Located across Kachemak Bay from Homer, Kachemak Bay State Park is one of the largest parks in the state system, encompassing 120,000 acres with 280,000 adjoining acres designated wilderness. It is Alaska's only wilderness state park. Kachemak Bay State Park was the Alaska's first state park. Largely undeveloped, the park offers wilderness experiences combining ocean, forest, mountains, glaciers and a variety of wildlife. Scenic highlights and other attractions include Grewingk Glacier, Poot Peak, Gull Island, China Poot Bay, Humpy Creek, Halibut Cove Lagoon, Tutka Bay and Sadie Cove.

Climate: Kachemak Bay is an arm of the North Pacific Ocean and is subject to severe and unpredictable weather. On clear, summer days, seas are usually calm until midmorning, when breezes begin, bringing southwest winds of 15 to 20 knots and seas of 3 to 6 feet. Conditions are often calm again in the evening.

Kachemak Bay's tides, among the largest in the world, are a primary factor affecting boating in the area. The average vertical difference between high and low tides is about 15 feet; the extreme, on large tide cycles, is 28 feet. Tidal currents are substantial, and whitewater rapids are frequently created in narrow passages. A tide book is essential. Use the tables for Seldovia, and be aware of local variations. For weather and tide information, contact the Homer harbormaster, phone (907) 235-8959.

Since the bay can be extremely rough, visitors should know the capabilities of their boats and themselves. Do not rush; wait for poor boating conditions to improve as they often do in the evenings. Fjords, bays and coves of Kachemak Bay contain navigational hazards; marine charts are available at sporting goods stores in Homer. Also, boaters should stay away from fishermen's buoys as their lines can damage outboard motors and propellers if run over, or the line may be cut. In July and August, commercial salmon seiners operate in the area, particularly at Tutka Bay. Seine nets often stretch long distances across the water, and recreational boaters must carefully maneuver around them.

Wildlife: This park offers excellent opportunities for observation and study of wildlife, including seabirds, seals, sea otters, whales, eagles and bears.

Activities: Boating, sea kayaking, beachcombing, camping, hiking and mountain climbing are the major activities. Protected waters of the park can be visited by large and small craft. Favorite destinations include Tutka Bay, which is located at the western end of the park between Jackalof Bay and Sadie Cove, and Halibut Lagoon, located 10 miles from Homer across Kachemak Bay. Intertidal zones provide an excellent setting for marine studies. Visitors are cautioned to respect tides, weather and currents of coastal Alaskan waters.

More than 85 miles of rugged hiking trails wind through the park. These include Alpine Ridge, China Poot Lake, Goat Rope Spur, Grewingk Glacier, Lagoon, Poot Peak, Saddle, and Wosnesenski. See trail description under Hiking Trails this section. For the trails listed, the hiking times given are the minimum needed by a person in good physical condition without a pack to hike the trail one way.

Above tree line, climbers and skiers will find glaciers and snowfields stretching for miles. The park is open to hunting and fishing in accordance with state regulations.

Accommodations: There are 20 developed campsites and 3 public-use cabins in the Halibut Cove Lagoon area, 1 cabin on China Poot Lake and 1 cabin on Tutka Bay (see Cabins this section). Campgrounds are located north of Rusty's Lagoon and on the south portion of Glacier Spit; restrooms, picnic tables and firepits are available. Fresh water is available from streams or springs; all drinking water obtained in the park should be boiled or treated. Open campfires are permitted only on beaches or gravel bars; portable stoves must be used elsewhere. Trash containers are not provided in the park; all litter must be packed out and human waste buried well away from sources of drinking water or trails. For more information on campsites and trails, consult the Trails Illustrated Map #763 for Kachemak State Park. Accommodations and meals are available in Homer, Seldovia and Halibut Cove.

There is a ranger station at Halibut Cove Lagoon, near the public-use cabins and at the hub of the Halibut Cove trail system. The ranger station is staffed from May 15 to September 15.

Hikers and campers should be well-equipped with wilderness gear. Boaters should be equally well-equipped since boating supplies are not available in the park or at Halibut Cove. Emergency assistance can be obtained through the U.S. Coast Guard Auxiliary (CB Channel 9, VHF Channel 16); Homer harbormaster (CB Channel 17 call number KCN 7188 Base 3, VHF Channel 16 call number WAB 958); or Alaska State Troopers, phone (907) 235-8239.

Access: This park is reached only by plane or boat. Air and water taxi services and charter boats are available in Homer. Private boats may use the Halibut Cove Lagoon Public Dock located by the ranger station. The floating dock is 80 feet long and can accommodate boats up to 26 feet. Moorage is on a first-come, first-served basis. Park staff recommends accessing the lagoon at high tide only, as the inlet channel is not navigable at mid- to low tides. Water currents entering and leaving the lagoon can be swift and treacherous at mid- to low tides. Boats over 30 feet, or with a draft of more than 4 feet generally do not enter the lagoon.

NOTE: Many of the most attractive beaches and camping sites in the park are privately owned. Respect No Trespassing signs.

For more information: Contact Alaska Department of Natural Resources Public

Information Center, 550 W. 7th Ave., Suite 1260, Anchorage, AK 99501-3557; phone (907) 269-8400, fax (907) 269-8901, TDD (907) 269-8411, email pic@dnr.state.ak.us. Or contact Alaska State Parks, P.O. Box 3248, Homer, AK 99603; phone (907) 262-5581, fax (907) 235-8386.

Katalla

Although a ghost town today, Katalla (ka-TELL-a) was once an oil and coal boom town. Katalla, located near the mouth of the Katalla River on Katalla Bay 50 miles southeast of Cordova, is near the site of one of the first oil discoveries in Alaska, made in 1896, and the state's first oil well, drilled in 1902. The town was established about 1903 as a supply point for the oil field 3.5 miles to the east. The Bering River coal fields are about 15 miles to the northeast and were once connected to Katalla by a railroad. The boom town's population may have been as high as 10,000 at one time but had dwindled to 188 by 1910 and 23 by 1940. Today, a caretaker and his family are the only residents of Katalla. The town's post office, opened in 1904, was closed in 1943.

Around 1910, the government restricted coal mining and other mineral development in Alaska, and Katalla lost much of its population practically overnight. From 1902 to 1931, a total of 36 wells were drilled in the Katalla oil field; 18 were successful. A small refinery built in 1911 produced gasoline and heating oil for local markets until part of the plant burned in 1933, and the entire operation was abandoned.

Katalla is also noteworthy as the location where the coastal steamer *Portland*, which ran from Seattle to St. Michael at the mouth of the Yukon River, was wrecked in 1910. The *Portland* gained fame when it arrived in Seattle on July 17, 1897 with 1-1/2 tons of gold from the Klondike on board and helped set off one of the biggest gold rushes in history.

The only way to get to Katalla is by charter plane or helicopter from Cordova (see description in Communities section). It is possible to get to Katalla by boat, but not usually feasible. Katalla is exposed to the full force of North Pacific storms, and waters in the area are often extremely rough. Much of the land surrounding Katalla is part of Chugach National Forest. However, visitors should be aware that some land is privately owned.

Kayak Island

Located 200 miles east-southeast of Anchorage and 62 miles southeast of Cordova in the Gulf of Alaska, this remote, narrow island is the location of the first documented landing by Europeans on North America's northwest coast. Naturalist George Wilhelm Steller and other members of an expedition led by Captain Commander Vitus Bering landed near the mouth of a creek on the leeward (west) shore of Kayak Island on July 20, 1741. They were the first Europeans to set foot on the island. Although the party was ashore just a few hours to replenish water supplies, Steller sketched and named many plants and animals in the area, including the Steller's jay. Reportedly, Steller found an empty Native camp on the island and took some goods from its absent inhabitants, leaving European goods in their place. No trace of their landing remains today, and it is theorized that the landing site became submerged in the gulf during the 1964 earthquake. The Bering Expedition Landing Site is a National Historic Landmark. This 22-mile-long, 1.5-mile-wide island is also the location of another historic site, the Cape St. Elias Light Station (see Lighthouses this section). This wild, uninhabited island offers excellent opportunities for beachcombing, hiking, camping, photography, berry picking, fishing, hunting and exploring.

Kayak Island is not easy to get to because of its remoteness and frequent rainy, windy weather. A boat trip from Cordova usually takes 12 to 16 hours one way, depending on conditions, which in this area are often extremely rough. A state marine park is located at Kayak Island (see Marine Parks, Eastern Prince William Sound, this section).

The U.S. Forest Service recommends that visitors bring extra food and other supplies since bad weather can prolong your stay for days at a time. Also, take a tide table with the Sitka-area tide data; some beaches are impassable at higher tides. Pinnacle Rock, 494 feet high, is connected to the southernmost tip of the island (Cape St. Elias) by a low, 0.2-mile ribbon of land and may not be accessible at higher tides. It's not a pleasant place to be stranded.

For more information: Chugach National Forest, Cordova Ranger District, P.O. Box 280, Cordova, AK 99574; phone (907) 424-7661.

Kenai Fjords National Park

This park of approximately 607,000 acres encompasses a coastal mountain-fjord system on the southeastern side of the Kenai Peninsula. The park is capped by the 700-square-mile Harding Icefield almost a mile above the Gulf of Alaska. It is believed to be a remnant of the last ice age, when ice masses covered half of the state of Alaska. The ice field's skyline is marked by nunataks, the tips of mountains whose lower slopes are submerged in ice.

Moist, marine air from the Gulf of Alaska dumps 700 to 1,000 inches of snow on the ice field each year. The pull of gravity and weight of the overlying new snow causes the ice to spread until it is shaped into glaciers that flow downward, carving the landscape into spectacular shapes. There are 33 named glaciers that radiate from the ice field; along the coast, tidewater glaciers calve directly into salt water.

The park was named after the long valleys once filled with glacial ice that are now deep, ocean-filled fjords. The seaward ends of mountain ridges are dipping into the water, being dragged under by the collision of 2 tectonic plates. As the land sinks into the sea, mountain peaks become wave-beaten islands, sea stacks and jagged shorelines. Glacier-carved cirques become half-moon bays.

Climate: A subarctic, maritime climate prevails in Kenai Fjords. Spring is usually the driest time of the year; fall and early winter are wettest. Storms are most common in winter, when waves up to 30 feet have been reported. Mean annual rainfall for nearby Seward is 67 inches. June normally begins the travel season, as spring storms cease and daytime temperatures climb into the 50s and 60s. Mean winter low temperatures range from 0°F to 20°F. Warm, sunny days do occur, but they are the exception rather than the rule. Visitors should be prepared for the usual overcast and/or cool days by bringing comfortable, wool clothing and good rain gear.

The Park Service cautions that the coastal fjords are rugged, remote and exposed to the stormy Gulf of Alaska. Strong currents flow past them, and few landing sites exist. Those entering the fjords without a guide should seek information from Kenai Fjords Natioal Park headquarters or the U.S. Coast Guard in Seward on mooring areas, navigational hazards and weather. Also, crevasses and foul weather pose hazards on the Harding Icefield and its glaciers. The Park Service says anyone venturing to that area should have experience, good equipment and stamina. It also is recommended that you leave an itinerary with a friend, and contact that person upon completion of your trip. The National Park Service has a free backcountry registration program; people heading into the backcountry should register.

Wildlife: Bald eagles nest in spruce and hemlock treetops along the shoreline, and mountain goats inhabit rocky slopes. Moose, black and brown bears, wolves and mountain goats are found in the park. Raucous Steller sea lions live on rocky islands at the entrance to Aialik and Nuka bays; centuries of hauling out have worn the granite rocks smooth. Harbor seals can be seen resting on icebergs. Minke, gray, fin, humpback and killer whales are found in these waters, as well as Dall porpoise, harbor seals and sea otters. Thousands of seabirds, including horned and tufted puffins, auklets, petrels, common murres and black-legged kittiwakes rear their young on the steep cliffs along the coast.

Dolly Varden and 5 species of salmon spawn in clear-water drainages within the park. Shrimp, crabs and other shellfish are found off the coast. Sportfishing for salmon and bottom fish is popular in Resurrection and Aialik bays.

Activities and Access: Several charter boat operators in Seward, gateway to Kenai Fjords

National Park, offer all-day tours to view the park's tidewater glaciers and abundant marine life. Tours are offered from mid-May through October (some run tours all winter), and usually include lunch and beverages; check at the Seward Small Boat Harbor. Kenai Fjords is also a popular destination for experienced kayakers. Kayak rentals and guided kayak trips may be arranged in Seward. The national park visitor center in Seward features exhibits and a slide show.

Exit Glacier is the most accessible of the park's glaciers and a center of activity. Turn off at Milepost 3.7 Seward Highway, and follow the 9-mile dirt and gravel Exit Glacier Road to its end at a parking lot with toilets and picnic area next to Exit Glacier ranger station. A flat and easy 0.8-mile Lower Loop trail (and steeper 0.5-mile Upper Loop trail) leads to the base of the glacier; the first 0.3 mile of the trail is paved and handicap-accessible. There is also a nature trail. A strenuous, 7-mile-round-trip trail leads to Harding Icefield from a branch off the mail trail about 1/2 mile toward Exit Glacier. Summer activities at Exit Glacier include daily ranger-led walks and hikes. The Exit Glacier area is open in winter for skiing, snowshoeing, snowmobiling and dog mushing.

Accommodations: There are overnight accommodations in Seward. For summer visitors, public-use cabins are located in Aialik Bay, Holgate Arm and North Arm for $35 per night. (See Cabins this section for details.) In the winter, visitors may use a cabin at Exit Glacier for $35 per night. The cabin is open only when the road is closed to vehicle use. Reservations may be made up to 180 days in advance and will be confirmed upon receipt of fee. For information or to reserve the cabins, contact the park headquarters.

Backcountry camping is permitted in the park; no fees or permits are required, but you should register at park headquarters and gather information. There is a 12-site walk-in campground at Exit Glacier; no fee, water available.

For more information: The park visitor center is located at 1212 4th Ave. in Seward next to the small-boat harbor. Or contact the Superintendent, Kenai Fjords National Park, P.O. Box 1727, Seward, AK 99664; phone (907) 224-3175.

USGS maps: Seward, Blying Sound, Seldovia.

For details on access and accommodations, see *The MILEPOST®*, a complete guide to Alaska's road system.

Kenai National Wildlife Refuge

This refuge was originally established in 1941 as the Kenai National Moose Range to protect habitat of these huge animals. In 1980, the refuge was renamed and expanded to encompass 2 million acres, 1.35 million of which are wilderness lands. Kenai Refuge is bounded to the northeast by Chugach National Forest, to the southeast by Kenai Fjords National Park and to the south by Kachemak Bay State Park. Most developed recreation is accessible from either Skilak Lake Loop Road or the Swanson River and Swan Lake roads, which branch off the Sterling Highway.

The refuge encompasses much of the total land area of the Kenai Peninsula. It includes the western slopes of the Kenai Mountains and forested lowlands along Cook Inlet. These lowlands feature spruce and birch forests intermingled with hundreds of lakes. The Kenai Mountains with their glaciers rise more than 6,000 feet to the southeast. The refuge includes a variety of Alaskan habitats: tundra, mountains, wetlands and forests.

Special features of the refuge include a portion of the Harding Icefield to the southeast, 1 of 4 major ice caps in the United States. Numerous lakes in the northern lowland region have been connected by portages to form the Swanson River and Swan Lake canoe trails, enjoyed annually by thousands of visitors.

Other special features are the Tustumena Skilak benchlands, a unique ecological area of mountain and glacial formations; Dall sheep and mountain goat ranges, and brown bear and timberline moose habitat; the Kenai River Special Management Area which includes the Kenai River, its tributaries and several lakes which provide vital spawning and rearing habitat for millions of salmon; the Chickaloon watershed and estuary, the major waterfowl and shorebird staging area on the peninsula; and the Skilak Lake area, a road-accessible region with abundant wildlife and scenic vistas.

Climate: Summer temperatures on the Kenai Peninsula generally range in the 60s and 70s and rarely rise above 80°F. The region receives up to 19 hours of daylight in the summer. Winter's extreme low is about -30°F, but extended periods of below 0°F are rare. Late summer and fall weather is wet; rain gear is recommended for hiking and hunting. Annual precipitation on the western side of the peninsula ranges from 19 inches at Kenai to 23 inches at Homer. On the mountainous eastern section, precipitation exceeds 40 inches annually. The first snow normally falls in October; by November, the ground is usually snow-covered. Spring breakup on low lakes occurs in April, on high lakes in May.

Wildlife: Nearly 200 species of birds and mammals live in or seasonally use the refuge. Mammals include moose, brown and black bear, caribou, Dall sheep, mountain goat, wolverine, wolf, coyote, river otter, beaver, muskrat, lemming, marten, red squirrel, shrew, lynx, porcupine, snowshoe hare, weasel, red fox and hoary marmot.

Birds found on the refuge include trumpeter swan, bald and golden eagles, peregrine falcon, northern pintails, sandhill cranes, arctic terns, gulls, lesser Canada geese, mallards, green-winged teal, woodpeckers, ptarmigan, spruce grouse, cormorant, great horned owls, snow geese, junco, Swainson's thrush, common redpoll and many more.

The Kenai River king salmon fishery is world-renowned. The river is reputed to support the largest genetic strain of king salmon anywhere. The world's record sport-caught king salmon, weighing 97 1/4 pounds, was caught here in 1985. Other fish inhabiting the refuge waters include red, pink and silver salmon, lake trout, Dolly Varden, rainbow trout, steelhead, kokanee, grayling and arctic char.

Activities: Camping, fishing, hiking, hunting and canoeing are all popular activities in the refuge. There are more than 200 miles of trails in the refuge. Most U.S. Fish and Wildlife Service trailheads and campgrounds are found along the Sterling Highway and Skilak Lake Loop Road. All of the established trails get a lot of use in the summer, but most of the refuge is undeveloped with no roads or trails. The more adventurous can travel on foot through undeveloped areas. The winter is a good time to visit; skiing and snowshoeing are excellent ways to explore the refuge. (See Hiking Trails, Kenai Peninsula Area, this section for details.)

The popular Swanson River and Swan Lake canoe trails provide excellent opportunities to see many kinds of wildlife in their natural habitat. Cow moose visit this area to give birth in late May or early June. Many species of songbirds, shorebirds and waterfowl nest along the lakeshores, marshlands and surrounding forests. Beaver inhabit many lakes and streams.

Canoe or kayak parties are limited to 15 people or less; register at the entrance to each trail. All trails and portages are well-marked. Minimum-impact camping is expected of all visitors. Life preservers must be carried. NOTE: Lakes can become dangerous during high winds. Stay close to shore, and watch the weather. Canoe rentals available in Sterling and Soldotna. (See River Running this section.)

Accommodations: The refuge has 15 road-accessible public campgrounds with tables, fireplaces, parking spurs, boat ramps, water and restrooms. Camping is restricted to 3 consecutive days at Kenai-Russian River Campground, 7 days at Hidden Lake Campground and 14 days elsewhere. Camping along refuge roads is permitted only at improved sites. Backcountry camping opportunities vary from fly-in and boat-in locations to sites accessible only by trail. There are also a few unmaintained primitive cabins available. Use minimum-impact techniques in all backcountry areas. Build fires in established fire rings if possible; use only dead and downed timber and camp stoves where firewood is scarce. Pack out all trash.

Access: The Kenai Refuge is bisected by the Sterling Highway, which enters the refuge westbound at Milepost 55. Secondary access roads are Skilak Lake Loop Road, Swanson River and Swan Lake roads and Funny River Road. The northern refuge boundary is 20 air miles from Anchorage. Airports are located at Kenai, Soldotna and Homer. The refuge is also accessible along river trails and by float- and skiplane to many lakes. However, some lakes are closed to aircraft to protect wildlife. Be sure to check with the refuge office regarding which lakes are open to aircraft landings. To reach refuge headquarters, drive south on the Sterling Highway to Soldotna, and turn left after crossing the Kenai River Bridge. Follow the signs to the office.

For more information: There is a U.S. Fish and Wildlife Service information cabin at the junction of Skilak Lake Loop Road, Milepost 58 on the Sterling Highway. The Kenai National Wildlife Refuge Visitor Center is located at the top of Ski Hill Road in Soldotna; turn off the Sterling Highway just south of the Kenai River Bridge. The modern center has dioramas containing lifelike mounts of area wildlife. Free wildlife films are shown all day Saturday and Sunday and on weekdays June through Labor Day. All films are shown on the hour beginning at noon and ending at 4 P.M. Information is available on canoeing, backcountry hiking and camping. Open weekdays, 8 A.M. to 4:30 P.M., and weekends 10 A.M. to 5 P.M. (call for summer hours). Mailing address: Refuge Manager, Kenai National Wildlife Refuge, P.O. Box 2139, Soldotna, AK 99669-2139; phone (907) 262-7021, email kenai@fws.gov, web site http://kenai.fws.gov.

For details on access and accommodations, see *The MILEPOST®*, a complete guide to Alaska's road system.

 Kenai River

Few natural treasures are as resolutely safeguarded as the habitat and use of Southcentral Alaska's Kenai River. Originating in Kenai Lake, about 100 road miles south of Anchorage, and flowing 68.2 miles west to Cook Inlet, the river sustains an astounding assortment of fish. All varieties of salmon—king or chinook, red or sockeye, silver or coho, pink or humpy, chum or dog—abound here, along with lake trout, Dolly Varden and 30 other species. The river holds International Game Fish Association's all-tackle world records for 3 of the 5 species of Pacific salmon, including the king salmon (97 1/4 -pound, caught in May 1985).

The watershed of the Kenai covers approximately 2,200 square miles or 1.4 million acres across the central region of the Kenai Peninsula. From glacier-fed Kenai Lake, the stream travels 17.3 "upper" river miles to Skilak Lake; no motors are allowed on this upper section. From Skilak Lake, a 10.5-mile course leads to Naptowne Rapids, where many large boulders extend for about a mile to the 19.5-mile "middle" stretch to the bridge near the visitor center in Soldotna. This section is faster and rock-strewn although still navigable with caution. From the bridge, 21 gentler "lower" miles wind to Cook Inlet; the final 12 miles are intertidal waters.

Based on the sustained-yield principle as required by the Alaska Department of Fish and Game, spawning escapement goals are established for early (mid-May to early July) and late (early July through July 31) king salmon runs. Daily and seasonal fishing cosures, restrictions on boating and tackle, and established catch limits, are all designed to protect the river's salmon runs.

For more information on the Kenai River (all of these agencies are located in Soldotna, AK 99669), contact: Kenai River Center, 514 Funny River Road, phone (907) 260-4882, fax (907) 260-5992, email kenairivcenter@borough.kenai.ak.us, web site http://www.borough.kenai.ak.us/KenaiRiverCenter; Alaska Department of Fish and Game, 43961 K-Beach Rd., Suite B; Kenai River Sportfishing Association, Inc., P.O. Box 1228; Kenai Watershed Forum, P.O. Box 2937; and the U.S. Fish & Wildlife Service, Kenai Fishery Resource Office, 35030 K-Beach Rd.

For details on fishing access and area accommodations and services, see *The MILEPOST®*

🗼 Lighthouses

Southcentral has 2 historic light stations: Cape St.Elias and Cape Hinchinbrook. Both are described below. For more details on these lighthouses and a National Park Service inventory of historic light stations, go to www.cr.nps.gov/maritime/light/ak.htm

Cape Hinchinbrook Light Station. This light, which stands 235 feet above the water, marks Hinchinbrook Entrance, main entrance to Prince William Sound from the east. Cape Hinchinbrook, named on May 12, 1778 by the English explorer Captain James Cook for Viscount Hinchinbroke, is located on the south tip of Hinchinbrook Island, 35 miles southwest of Cordova. Construction of the station was completed on November 15, 1910 at a cost of about $100,000. It was rebuilt after earthquakes in 1927 and 1928 for $91,000. It was first lit in 1934. The U.S. Coast Guard automated the station in 1974. The original Fresnel lens, approximately 5 feet high, is now on display at the museum in Valdez. Present optic is solar-powered.

Cape St. Elias Light Station. This light, 85 feet above the water, is located on the southernmost tip of Kayak Island on Cape St. Elias. The cape was named by Captain Commander Vitus Bering on July 20, 1741 for the saint whose day it was according to the Russian Orthodox Church calendar. This 1,665-foot-high cape forms an unmistakable landmark for mariners. The waters south of the cape were regarded as "one of the most dangerous points along the entire coast." Congress appropriated money for the project in 1913, and construction of the lighthouse was completed on September 16, 1916 at a cost of $115,000. It was automated in 1984. At one time, there were 3 lighthouse keepers in residence. Present optic is solar-powered. The original Fresnel lens is on display in the museum in Cordova. The Cape St. Elias Light Station is considered the best existing architectural example of a historic Alaska lighthouse. It is open to the public.

Marine Parks

The state of Alaska has established 36 marine parks, of which 17 are located in Southeast Alaska, 14 in Prince William Sound and 5 in and around Resurrection Bay. These parks are part of an international system of shoreline parks and recreation areas stretching from near Olympia, Washington, up through British Columbia and as far north as Prince William Sound. Eventually, there may be more than 150 of these parks, most a 1-day boat trip from each other.

For more information contact the Department of Natural Resources Public Information Center, 550 W. 7th Ave., Suite 1260, Anchorage, AK 99501-3557; phone (907) 269-8400, fax (907) 269-8901, TDD (907) 269-8411, email pic@dnr.state.ak.us, web site www.alaskastateparks.org. Or contact Kenai Area State Parks, P.O. Box 1247, Soldotna, AK 99669; phone (907) 262-5581.

Following is a list of the 19 marine parks located in Prince William Sound and Resurrection Bay.

Western Prince William Sound Marine Parks

Bettles Bay. Located on the western shore of Port Wells, approximately 20 miles from Whittier. This large, well-protected bay is a favorite of boaters exploring the Port Wells area, as it is considered one of the most scenic on the west shore. Wildlife in the area includes black bears, sea lions, whales, seals and waterfowl. Fishing includes halibut, pink and chum salmon and Dungeness crab. An abandoned mine is located approximately 1/2 mile southwest of the park.

Decision Point. Located at the eastern end of Passage Canal approximately 8 miles from Whittier. The park is generally used by kayakers and small boat users as there is no adequate anchorage. Along with forested uplands of spruce and hemlock, there are two excellent camping beaches. At the head of Squirrel Cove, a small pebble and sand beach provides room for 2 tents during all but the highest tide cycles. Drinking water is not available at this site. Just south of Decision Point is an east-facing, medium-pebble beach that provides dry, flat camping for up to 10 tents between the dead trees. The camp areas are above high tide and have 2 fire rings. A number of tent platforms, latrine and bearproof food locker have been added to expand the capacity of this popular kayaker campsite. Additionally, within

Squirrel Cove, a series of tent platforms, a bearproof food locker and latrine are linked by a boardwalk system to a public contact station seasonally staffed by Alaska State Parks volunteers. Water is available in the bight, or bend, on the coast behind the small peninsula. Bountiful intertidal life on the rocks at Decision Point may be viewed during minus tides.

Entry Cove. Located 2 miles directly east of Decision Point on the northeast corner where Passage Canal and Port Wells meet. Forested uplands of spruce and hemlock interspersed with muskeg surround a small cove and lagoon. There is good anchorage near the cove entrance on northwind days, but it is generally not used overnight because of variable winds out of Blackstone Bay. The lagoon is a good site for clamming, but the entrance is shallow and can only be accessed by small boats during full high tide. Just east of the entrance to the lagoon, above the gravel beach, are sites for about 10 tents on beach gravel between the trees. A natural arch located on the east shore of the cove and a beautiful view of Tebenkof Glacier can be seen from the camp area. During moderate and low tide cycles, some people camp on the sand spit that attaches the Pigot Point Island.

Granite Bay. Located on the northwest corner of Esther Island about 25 miles from Whittier. The park includes 2 bays, protective islands, muskeg and old-growth forest uplands. Most of the shoreline has steep granite cliffs, boulders and slabs. The surrounding hills provide excellent hiking and climbing with views in all directions. Many lakes and ponds dot the uplands. Tange Lake drains into the head of the northern arm and has been stocked with rainbow trout. Anchorage is excellent in both bays. A mooring buoy is located between the bays, behind the islands. A tent platform is located on the northernmost island at the mouth of the north bay. There are other tent sites on heather or in beach grass. Boaters should be aware of a reef that extends nearly a mile off shore, just south of the mouth of the southern bay.

Horseshoe Bay. Located on Latouche Island in southwestern Prince William Sound, about halfway between Seward and Whittier. Although somewhat exposed to southwesterly winds, Horseshoe Bay offers the most protected anchorage along the island's shoreline. The bay and island are very scenic, with nearby peaks rising to 2,000 feet. The old gold mining town of Latouche is located 2 miles to the northeast. Excellent hiking and climbing at nearby Broon Buttes. Whales, seals and sea lions frequent Latouche Passage. Except for recreational lots at the old town of Latouche and an area south of the park, Chugach Natives Limited owns most of the island. Private property; respect No Trespassing signs.

South Esther Island. Located at the confluence of Wells Passage and Port Wells in upper Prince William Sound, approximately 20 miles due east of Whittier. This is a popular base of operations for excursions in the Port Wells, Port Nellie Juan and Culross Passage areas. Anchorages are found in both Lake and Quillian bays. Lake Bay is the home of one of the world's largest fish hatcheries. The Wally H. Noerenberg Fish Hatchery offers free tours of the facility. A boardwalk and trail system connects the hatchery with the Esther Falls scenic overlook, and then to a small bight south and east where tent platforms and a latrine are available for park visitors. Esther Island is very scenic, with a number of 2,000-foot granite peaks. Whales may be observed in Port Wells; sea lions frequently haul out on nearby islands and rocks. Seabirds nest in the area, and seals and sea otters may also be seen.

Surprise Cove. Located at the entrance to Cochrane Bay approximately 15 miles east of Whittier along a major route for pleasure boats between Whittier and western Prince William Sound. The park includes 2 small embayments off Cochrane Bay and 2 freshwater lakes, and it offers a well-protected anchorage. A boardwalk and trail system links both the campsite area at the beach on the north side of the cove with the cove to the west, and then to the north lake within this state marine park. The main camping beach has three tent platforms, a latrine and a bearproof food locker in addition to the great beach gravel campsites. Mountain goats are found on nearby peaks; porpoises are often observed at Point Cochrane. A small beach near the entrance to the cove is used as a campsite by kayakers. Other sites are available on the exposed beach north of Point Cochrane and by the northern bend in the coast.

Surprise Cove is one of the most popular anchorages in the area, and on weekends, 8 or more boats may be anchored in the cove.

Zeigler Cove. Located on the northern shore of the entrance to Pigot Bay on the west side of Port Wells, approximately 14 miles east of Whittier. The cove is on a low, forested point extending into both Pigot Bay and Port Wells. It offers a small, but very well-protected anchorage suitable for 4 boats. There is good hiking in the uplands and good fishing nearby for red snapper, halibut, pink, chum and king salmon, as well as Dungeness crab. A campsite is located on the east corner of the cove above the shale pebble beach.

Eastern Prince William Sound Marine Parks

Boswell Bay. Located on the eastern tip of Hinchinbrook Island. Evidence of a geologic land lift can be seen here. In 30 years, the shoreline has expanded toward the sea by more than 1 mile. This southern edge of the park is a high-energy beach exposed to the Gulf of Alaska. Beachcombing and hunting are popular. Areas of the park are adjacent to the Copper River Delta State Critical Habitat.

Canoe Passage. Located on Hawkins Island 8 miles west of Cordova. This park encompasses the natural low pass on the island. Forested uplands and considerable wetlands line Canoe Passage. The seas are shallow to the south. The rest of Hawkins Island is private land.

Jack Bay. Located 15 miles from Valdez, southeast of Valdez Narrows. The uplands of the park consist of alder, muskeg, salt marsh and old-growth forest of spruce hemlock. The northern arm of Jack Bay within the marine park becomes shallow 0.25 mile out, and caution is recommended. Although the bay can be used as a fair-weather anchorage, it is not protected.

The best campsite is located on the island in the middle of the bay. On the southeast end of the island is a protected bight, or bend in the coast, with four campsites. The main one is immediately above the beach on beach gravel, while the others are behind in the forest and on the peninsula just north of the beach. Another site exists near the tip of the peninsula on the mainland just east of the island in a wet, boggy area. None of these campsites have water nearby. Water can be obtained on the northern shore of the bay. Developed tent platforms and a latrine are available at the island's southeast end. Within the southeast end of Jack Bay's north arm, there are additional tent platforms and a latrine. This site receives little use and can be a good alternative to the more popular campsite on the island.

Kayak Island. Located 62 miles southeast of Cordova. (See Kayak Island this section.)

Sawmill Bay. Located on the north shore of Port Valdez, approximately 14 miles west and south of Valdez. This large, well-protected bay is surrounded by 4,000-foot peaks; it offers several good anchorages for pleasure boaters and receives considerable use by boaters from Valdez. There is fishing for silver salmon and halibut; crab and clams are also available. The boreal forest consists of spruce, hemlock and muskeg. There is good hiking along Twin Falls Creek and near Devish Lake. Tent platforms, a latrine and bearproof food lockers are now located within this state marine park.

Shoup Bay. Located on the north shore of Port Valdez, 8.5 miles west of Valdez. The park encompasses most of Shoup Bay and the southern half of Shoup Lake, also known as the inner lagoon. Shoup Bay offers salmon fishing, hiking, wildlife viewing and spectacular scenery.

Ice from 17-mile-long Shoup Glacier calves into the lake. This glacier has receded dramatically in the last decade , and there is now a 2-plus-mile-long lake at the toe of the glacier that is tidally influenced but separate from the Shoup Bay inner bay by a 1/3-mile-long river. This river is best negotiated at high tide by power boats or kayaks as the current can be quite swift, and there is significant danger with icebergs floating downstream at certain tide levels. A rocky island with Prince William Sound's largest colony of Black-legged kittiwakes is inside the inner lake. Visitors are advised to stay at least 100 yards from the colony to minimize disturbance to nesting birds. Within the inner lake, all power boats are limited to 5 mph, and personal watercraft are prohibited.

An underwater moraine stretches across the mouth of the bay, creating shallow shoals off the spit. Mountain goats can be seen on the slopes above the bay, and ducks feed on the tidal flats. A black-legged kittiwake rookery can be found in the lagoon. Bald eagles, arctic terns and various waterfowl are frequently seen there. Shoup Glacier is the main tributary of the huge glacier that carved Valdez Arm thousands of years ago. During the 1964 earthquake, an undersea slide from its submerged moraine created a 170-foot-high wave (listed in the Guinness Book of World Records); reportedly, the bay emptied and refilled 3 times. A well-protected anchorage does not exist in the bay, and there is no mooring buoy at the marine park. Anchor at your own risk. Short-term or fair-weather anchorages can be found in several areas depending on wind direction. Secure small boats on shore.

Two cabins are located on the eastern end of the inner lake, with a third cabin located in Shoup Bay at the mouth of McAllister Creek, on the south side of the bay. A rugged, 12-mile-long hiking trail connects Shoup Bay and the inner lake with a trailhead in Valdez. Campsites are located along the trail at the Gold Creek bridge crossing. This trail is in primitive condition with steep climbs on several sections. The most popular section to hike is between Valdez and Gold Creek, a 4.5-mile hike, one way. Campsites are available at the eastern end of the lagoon, around the perimeter of the bay and at the base of the spit at the eastern edge of the bay.

Resurrection Bay Marine Parks

Driftwood Bay. Located along the southwest coast of Day Harbor to the east of Resurrection Bay, a 23-mile boat ride from Seward. The park's shoreline includes medium to coarse gravel beaches interspersed with steep rock cliffs. Driftwood Bay, the largest of the area's marine parks at 1,480 acres, offers excellent mountain views and wildlife viewing opportunities.

The bay is a popular anchorage for recreational boaters and offers good protection from Day Harbor's often rough seas. Fishing for saltwater fish species is popular in Driftwood Bay and Day Harbor. Fresh water is limited to runoff during wet weather.

Safety Cove. Located along the western side of Day Harbor to the east of Resurrection Bay, a 28-mile boat ride from Seward. The park's 960 acres include the cove's marine environment and an upland spruce, hemlock and alder forest. An attractive geologic feature of this park is a 3-acre freshwater lake just above a gravel storm berm at the head of the cove.

Safety Cove offers excellent beach camping as well as safe anchorage for recreational boats. Upland exploration is also an appealing activity in the park, and there are excellent views of Ellsworth Glacier, an arm of the Sargent Icefield near the cove's entrance. Fresh water can be taken from the lake at the head of the cove.

Sandspit Point. Located at the northeast tip of Fox Island (Renard Island) in Resurrection Bay, 12 miles southeast of Seward. The park includes steep, inaccessible uplands to the west and a half-mile-long spit to the east, for a total of 560 acres. The north beach of the spit is fine sand while the south beach is medium to large cobbles. Marine tide pools abound near the west end of the spit, and a low spruce forest dominates the higher east end.

Sandspit Point offers spectacular panoramic views of Resurrection Bay to the north and Eldorado Narrows to the south. The variety of marine life found in tide pools, the ease of launching and landing on the sandy northern beach and suitability for beach camping make this a popular destination for kayakers. The southern beach is not recommended for landings due to its rocky nature and the often heavy surf. There is no fresh water available in the park.

Sunny Cove. Located 14 miles south of Seward at the south end of Fox Island (Renard Island) in Resurrection Bay. The cove faces west, providing a good view of Callisto Head, Bear Glacier and Kenai Fjords National Park. The park provides a good camping beach along the south shore of the cove with fine to medium beach gravel. The park's 960 acres encompass the entire south portion of Fox Island, including an unnamed peak of 1,362 feet. With the exception of the south beach of Sunny Cove, the park's coastline is characterized by vertical rock cliffs.

Sunny Cove is popular as an anchorage for sailboats and power boats. Excellent wildlife viewing exists around the vertical cliffs, especially along the eastern shore. Numerous seabird species and marine mammals can be easily viewed from skiff or kayak. Fresh water is available seasonally in the park; during wet weather, water is generally available from small waterfalls south along the shore from the cove, but these can only be reached at low tide.

Thumb Cove. Located approximately 7.5 miles south of Seward on the east side of Resurrection Bay. The park's 720 acres include the southeast shoreline of the cove-a long beach of fine to medium sand and beach gravel; forested uplands of spruce, hemlock and alder; and most of the waters of Thumb Cove. Perhaps the most striking geologic feature in the area is Porcupine Glacier, towering above the park and providing a dramatic backdrop to this popular marine destination.

Thumb Cove is a favorite stop for Seward's recreational boaters, and camping is popular along the beaches. There are 2 mooring buoys at Thumb Cove, available on a first-come, first served basis. Anchor at your own risk. Boats 30 feet or longer beware of low tides. Secure small boats ashore. Fishing for salmon is a favorite activity during the various runs, and Thumb Cove offers good protection from the often unstable weather of Resurrection Bay. Fresh water is available from a stream flowing from Porcupine Glacier. There are 2 public-use cabins at Thumb Cove available by reservation only. (See Cabins, Kenai Area, this section.)

 # Mountain Biking

Popular mountain biking trails in Southcentral include Saddlebag Glacier (Cordova area) and Johnson Pass (Kenai Peninsula) in Chugach National Forest; and in Chugach State Park: Lakeside, Peters Creek, Near Point, Powerline, Indian Creek and Bird Creek trails. See Hiking Trails this section for more detailed descriptions.

Two Anchorage mountain biking clubs organize group rides and are sources of information on trails and events: the Arctic Bicycle Club (www.articbike.org) and the Women's Mountain Bike and Tea Society, also known as WOMBATS (visit www.wombats.org and go to "Alaska events and rides" page).

Other trails specifically recommended for mountain biking are:

Bernard Creek. This 15-mile BLM access road is recommended for mountain bikes and ATVs. Access from Milepost V 78.6 Richardson Highway; look for "Tonsina Controlled Use Area" sign. Follow the BLM road around to the right, and park at the fork. The left fork leads up a steep hill for 1 mile to the Bernard Creek trailhead. This road travels atop a mesa for some time, allowing for pleasant views of the Wrangell Mountains. The trail crosses several shallow streams, as well as many mud puddles in early season then continues gradually toward the high country and access to Kimball Pass.

Chistochina River Trail. This BLM trail is recommended for hiking, mountain bikes and ATVs. Access is from Milepost GJ 35.4 on the Tok Cutoff; turn off at the west end of Chitochina River Bridge No. 1, and drive in 1 mile for trailhead parking. Follow the road north from parking area until it becomes a trail. Easy hiking "for miles and miles" over flat terrain and rolling hills. Beautiful views above treeline of the Alaska, Wrangell and Mentasta mountain ranges. Popular trail during hunting season with heavy use by ATVs and large-track vehicles. As a consequence, the trail is well worn and may be muddy during wet weather.

Klutina Road. This 25-mile BLM access road is recommended for mountain biking and ATVs. Access from Milepost V 102 (Brenwick-Craig Road) Richardson Highway. The road is uphill for the first mile, then follows along the top of the bluff with opportunities for excellent views of the Wrangell Mountains and the Copper and Klutina drainages. Near Mile 12, the road drops back down to the river until Mile 17.5 where the road becomes steep, rocky, and well-rutted. Two-wheel drive use is not recommended beyond this point. Toward the end of the road, expect to encounter several mud holes, most of which can be avoided if travelling by foot or bike. There is public access to Klutina Lake at the end of the road. Access to the river along the Klutina Road is private.

Liberty Falls Trail. This 2.5-mile BLM trail is recommended for biking or hiking. Access from trailhead at Milepost R 23.5 on the Edgerton Highway, just west of Liberty Falls State Recreation Site. The trail is mostly dirt with a few rock outcrops, offering good views of both the Copper River and Tonsina river drainages, as well as the Wrangell Mountains. The trail rises gently and ends at a forested area near Upper Liberty Creek.

O'Brien Creek Road. This road follows a portion of the old Copper River and Northwestern Railway grade from Chitina southeast along the Copper River. It is recommended for mountain bikes, ATVs or hikers. It is possible to travel this road for up to 20 miles from Chitina to the Uranitina River, depending on the condition of the road and the desire of the traveler. O'Brien Creek Road follows the narrow Wood's Canyon, with sudden, deep drops into narrow drainages. It travels through the original CR&NW railroad tunnels. Good views of the Copper River and Spirit Mountain. O'Brien Creek Road is subject to slides and washouts; it is also very narrow with sharp curves and steep dropoffs. Keep in mind that vehicles also use this road and that it is bordered by private property. Access to the Copper River is permitted only at O'Brien Creek and Haley Creek and prohibited across private lands and elsewhere unless official signs indicate access is allowed.

Quarry Road. A 3.5-mile road recommended for mountain bikes and ATVs. Access from Milepost V 74.5 Richardson Highway. The road is in very good condition although seldom used. Turn off the highway on the west side at a pipeline access road; take a left at the first 2 forks; then, take a right at the next 2 forks. Road goes uphill for 3 miles; good view of Mount Drum. The road flattens out at an old quarry, where there are views of the Copper and Tonsina river valleys and the Wrangell Mountains. Ridge access nearby for alpine hiking.

 Mountaineering

Mountaineering in this region ranges from one day non-technical climbs to multi-day expedition-type climbs demanding a high degree of technical skill.

The Chugach Range, with 21 peaks above 7,000-feet and many more in the 5,000- to 6,000-foot range, has plenty of technical and non-technical climbing opportunities, everything from 8,290-foot Amulet Peak to 5,005-foot Suicide Peak. The Chugach Range has the added advantage of close proximity to Anchorage.

Also within easy reach of Anchorage are the Kenai Mountains, with such easy climbs as Mount Alpenglow and Mount Ascension, and the Talkeetnas, with climbs like Arkose Peak, Castle Mountain and Mount Apollo.

A helpful source of information on mountaineering these peaks is the Mountaineering Club of Alaska (MCA), P.O. Box 102037, Anchorage, AK 99510-2037, www.mcak.org. The MCA conducts hikes and climbs, loans gear to members and offers mountaineering courses. They also maintain a "peak file" at Alaska Mountaineering and Hiking, located on Spenard Road in Anchorage, that has detailed information on local climbs. Climbing trip reports are also published in the MCA newsletter, *Scree.*

MCA built and maintains 8 mountain hunts in the Chugach and Talkeetna mountains. For public use, these huts hold 8 to 10 people and are equipped with cooking stoves and lanterns. They are not heated and have no beds. Reservations are not required. All are located above treeline and 6 are next to glaciers. All of the Chugach huts require glacier travel skills to reach and only 2 of the 8 huts can be reached by fixed-wing aircraft (without special permission). Directions and maps to each hut are available on the MCA web site or from Alaska Mountaineering and Hiking.

The region's highest and most challenging mountains lie within Wrangell-St. Elias National Park. The Wrangell Mountains and St. Elias Range in Southcentral include 6 of Alaska's 15 highest peaks: Bona, 16,500 feet; Blackburn, 16,390 feet; Sanford, 16,237 feet; Churchill, 15,638 feet; Bear, 14,831 feet; and Wrangell (a volcano), 14,163 feet.

The remoteness of the Wrangell-St. Elias peaks, combined with their elevation, extreme weather conditions, potential avalanche dangers, and ice, make them particularly demanding. Access is usually by chartered aircraft. An extensive knowledge of wilderness and mountaineering survival skills is necessary. Climbers must be fully prepared and self-sufficient. For more information, contact: Wrangell-St. Elias National Park and Preserve, Park Headquarters, P.O. Box 439, Copper Center, AK 99573; phone (907) 822-5234, fax (907)

822-7216; Chitina Ranger Station in Chitina, phone (907) 823-2205; and Slana Ranger Station (Nabesna District) on Nabesna Road, phone (907) 822-5238, fax (907) 822-5248. Or visit www.nps.gov/wrst/cabins.htm. Or email wrst_interpretation@nps.gov.

The most popular Wrangell peaks for climbing expeditions are Mount Sanford (elev. 16,237 feet) and Mount Blackburn (elev. 16,390 feet). The best time of year for climbing activity is April through June. Folllowing are examples of 3 current climbing routes in the Wrangells detailed by the National Park Service. Contact park headquarters or check their web site for more complete text, other peaks and routes, and for a current list of guides authorized to lead climbs in the Park.

Mount Blackburn via North Ridge. This is currently the most used route and has an elevation gain of approximately 9,190 feet. Fly-in to the 7,200-foot level of the Nabesna Glacier. Climb to pass at 9,880 feet, and ascend North Ridge to summit. Deep snow is common at 9,800 feet and hard-packed conditions exist above 11,500 feet. Severe weather, avalanches, crevasses, and serac fall are dangers.

Mount Blackburn via Southeast Ridge. Access from Nugget Creek trail or Kennicott via Kuskulana or Kennicott Glacier to the 9,000-foot level of the Southeast Ridge. Ascend ridge to the summit. Elevation gain via these routes is approximately 13,690 feet. According to the Park Service, there are no recorded successful climbs via Mount Blackburn's southwesterly ridges. Severe weather, crevasses, avalanches, difficult snow and rock conditions, and impossible route situations have been noted as the reasons for failures.

Mount Sanford via Sheep Glacier Route. Fly-in 13 miles from Chistochina airstrip at Milepost GJ 33 Tok Cutoff to Windy Ridge airstrip at elevation 3,800 feet. It is 6 1/2 miles across tundra to the toe of the Sheep Glacier (elev. 5,300 feet), then 11 miles up the Sheep Glacier to the summit. Elevation gain is 12,437 feet. Distance is about 35 miles round-trip; allow 10 to 14 days. Crevasse fields are at the 7,000- and 15,000-foot elevations. Steep wind slab and sastrugi snow conditions are common at 10,000 feet.

⭐ Nancy Lake State Recreation Area

Located just 67 miles north of Anchorage via the Glenn and Parks highways between the Susitna River and the Talkeetna Mountains, this 22,685-acre state recreation area provides easily accessible wilderness experiences all year.

The area is dominated by lakes, streams and swamps which drain into the Susitna River or Cook Inlet. Mature spruce, birch and poplar forests surround the lake. Blueberry, raspberry and crowberry plants are plentiful and provide good berry picking in late summer and early fall. Pickers should learn to identify baneberry, which looks edible but is poisonous.

Once covered by huge glaciers, the area has been free of ice for at least 9,000 years, and state archaeologists believe that early Natives heavily used the area. Nancy Lake's Indian Bay is the site of an Indian village that was established near the turn of the century, and a few descendants of the village residents still live in the area. In 1917, the Alaska Railroad was built on the east side of the lower Susitna Valley, bringing homesteaders and fueling the growth of the towns of Wasilla, Houston and Willow. The Nancy Lake area was avoided by settlers because it was too wet.

Climate: Summer temperatures range from lows between 40°F and 50°F and highs in the 70s and 80s, reflecting the warmer and sunnier weather patterns of interior Alaska. Winter temperatures can fall to -40°F or colder and rarely rise above freezing before mid-March. The lakes freeze in late October, about the same time the first snow falls, and they are ice free by late May. Average snow accumulation is about 48 inches.

Wildlife: Beavers are found on numerous lakes throughout and are important in maintaining water levels in the area. Moose and black bears are common. Lynx, coyote, wolves and brown bears may be seen in more remote areas.

Grebes, ducks, geese and shorebirds use the lakes and ponds in the area during their migrations, and many stay to nest in the area. Green-headed loons, with their eerie laugh-

SOUTHCENTRAL • ATTRACTIONS

ing call, are one of the trademarks of the area. Loons seen ashore are frequently nesting and easily spooked, often deserting their nests. Visitors should leave them alone. Arctic terns are also summer residents. The hiker unlucky enough to stumble into a nest is likely to be repeatedly dive-bombed by screeching terns. Sandhill cranes may be seen exhibiting their courtship dance along the Nancy Lake Parkway during their spring migration. Hawks, owls, kingfishers, woodpeckers and numerous songbirds are also seen in the area.

Lake trout, rainbow trout, whitefish and Dolly Varden are found in Red Shirt, Butterfly, Lynx and Nancy lakes. Big and Little Noluck lakes were restocked with trout and silver salmon in 1975 by the Alaska Department of Fish and Game. Northern pike are found in Red Shirt, Lynx and Tanaina lakes.

Vegetation within the recreation area is dominated in drier areas by white spruce and paper birch, with some aspen interspersed. Wetter forests support stands of smaller black spruce, which give way to lowbrush bogs and muskeg swamps highlighted by cotton grass plumes. Violets, bluebells, fireweed, bog rosemary and wild iris add color. Large parts of the Nancy Lake area have been burned by forest fires in the past 100 years, resulting in thick stands of birch.

Activities: The area's summertime attraction is its canoe trail system. Visitors can spend an afternoon or a long weekend canoeing through the various chains of lakes and streams that dot the area. Two favorites are the 8-mile Lynx Lake Loop and the Little Susitna River. Canoes can be rented at a local marina and at South Rolly Campground. Other summer activities include hiking, camping and fishing.

The summer canoe and hiking trails are transformed in winter to 40 miles of trails for cross-country skiing, dog mushing, snowshoeing and snowmobiling. While most trails are open for motorized snow vehicles, 10 miles of trails are set aside for cross-country skiers only. Ice fishing is also a popular winter activity. Nancy, Lynx and Red Shirt lakes offer the best opportunities for catching winter rainbow trout. Burbot and pike are found in Red Shirt.

Accommodations: Camping at South Rolly Lake Campground (98 sites, fee), located at Mile 6.6 on the Nancy Lake Parkway. Nancy Lake State Recreation Site on the northeast shore of Nancy Lake has more than 30 sites and is reached from Milepost 66.5 of the Parks Highway. There are 13 public-use cabins in Nancy Lake State Recreation Area. (For descriptions, see Cabins, Mat-Su Area, this section.)

Access: Located 67 miles north of Anchorage via the Parks Highway. The park's hiking trails, picnic area, campground and canoe launch are found along the gravel access (Nancy Lake Parkway).

For more information: Detailed maps of the canoe and hiking trails and information on established campgrounds can be obtained from the Alaska Department of Natural Resources Public Information Center, 550 W. 7th Ave., Suite 1260, Anchorage, AK 99501-3557; phone (907) 269-8400, fax (907) 269-8901, TDD (907) 269-8411, email pic@dnr.state.ak.us. Or contact Mat-Su Area State Parks, HC32, Box 6706, Wasilla, AK 99654-9719; phone (907) 745-3975.

For details on access and accommodations, see The MILEPOST®, a complete guide to Alaska's road system.

Palmer Hay Flats State Game Refuge

This 45-square-mile refuge encompasses the forest, wetlands and tideflats at the head of Knik Arm. The 26,048-acre refuge, established in 1975 and expanded in 1985, includes the mouths of the Knik and Matanuska rivers. Palmer Flats is a major waterfowl stop during spring and fall migrations. Moose may also be seen.

Palmer Hay Flats is one of the most heavily utilized waterfowl hunting areas in Alaska, according to the Alaska Department of Fish and Game. The refuge also offers salmon fishing in Rabbit Slough and Cottonwood Creek. Moose hunters and trappers also use Palmer Hay Flats Refuge.

There are no campgrounds within the refuge, but camping, lodging and other services are readily available along the highways which form the eastern boundary of the refuge.

Boat and foot access at Rabbit Slough; exit at Milepost A 34 Glenn Highway for parking area. Boats can be launched at the Knik River Bridge. Cottonwood Creek off Knik-Goose Bay Road offers foot and canoe access to the marsh. Aircraft landings on the refuge prohibited from April 1 to November 9. Off-road vehicle use restricted to specified corridors and seasons.

For more information contact the Alaska Department of Fish and Game, 333 Raspberry Road, Anchorage, AK 99518-1599; phone (907) 746-6300.

✳ Prince William Sound

Southcentral Alaska's Prince William Sound is an area famous for its scenery and its wildlife. Dotted with islands, this 70-mile-wide gulf extends 30 miles north and west from the Gulf of Alaska to the Kenai Peninsula. It is bounded to the southeast by Montague Island and Hinchinbrook Island, which form Hinchinbrook Entrance, the 10-mile-long water passage from the Gulf of Alaska to Prince William Sound. To the north: a rugged, glaciated coastline and the Chugach Mountains. Wilderness recreation in Prince William Sound takes place both on the water and along the coastline. Sightseeing wildlife and glaciers, fishing and kayaking are probably the most popular recreational activities in Prince William Sound (see Fishing and Sea Kayaking this section for more details on those activities). Almost any foray into Prince William Sound will originate from either Whittier, Valdez or Cordova (see descriptions in Southcentral Comunities). All 3 of these port towns offer charter boats for sightseeing, fishing, and drop-off/pickup service for hikers and kayakers. Scheduled tour boats depart from Whittier and Valdez.

The big attraction for many visitors to Prince William Sound are its glaciers, and the star is, of course, Columbia Glacier. Named by the Harriman Alaska expedition in 1899 for Columbia University in New York City, the glacier's source is Mount Einstein (elev. 11,552 feet) in the Chugach Mountains.

Columbia Glacier is one of Alaska's largest tidewater glaciers (Hubbard is the largest) and also one of its fastest moving glaciers, retreating at a speed of 80 to 115 feet per day. It has receded more than 6 miles since 1982. The glacier is currently 34 miles in length, 3 miles wide and more than 3,000 feet thick in some places. Visitors can see its terminus from Columbia Bay.

Another well-known feature of Prince William Sound is College Fjord, an 18-mile-long estuary that extends northeast from Port Wells (another estuary) near Whittier. Glaciers cascade down the west side of College Fjord, and at the north end of the estuary are 2 tidewaters glaciers-Harvard and Yale. College Fjord is a popular port of call with cruise ships, as well as a destination for kayakers.

The Cordova Ranger District offers an extensive system of established hiking trails on Chugach National Forest lands (for details see Hiking Trails this section). The U.S. Forest Service also maintains public-use cabins in the Cordova area and western Prince William Sound (see Cabins this section for details). Alaska State Parks provides shoreline camping at 14 marine parks in Prince William Sound (see Marine Parks this section).

Wildlife: Prince William Sound usually rewards wildlife watchers with frequent sightings of harbor seals, sea otters, dolphins and killer whales. Also known as orcas, the distinctive black and white killer whale is a carnivorous cetacean, feeding on sea lions, porpoises and other marine animals. The Sound is also an important summer feeding ground for humpback whales, who inhabit the shallow coastal waters of Southcentral and Southeast Alaska. The abundance of fish attracts bald eagles, kittiwakes and gulls. Birders can view up to 31 different species of shorebirds in the spring as millions of birds pass through the Copper River delta during their annual migration (see Copper River Delta this section).

Access: There are 2 major overland entry points to Prince William Sound: Whittier, located 58 miles south of Anchorage via the Seward Highway and Whittier Access Road; and Valdez, 304 driving miles from Anchorage via the Glenn and Richardson highways. The Alaska State ferry MV *Bartlett* provides cross-sound service during the summer between Whittier, Valdez and Cordova.

 # Recreational Mining

Recreational gold panning, mineral prospecting or mining using light portable field equipment (e.g. hand-operated pick, shovel, pan, earth auger or backpack power drill or auger) is allowed without mining claims in 3 designated recreational mining areas managed by the Department of Natural Resources in Southcentral: Caribou Creek, Hatcher Pass and Petersville. These areas are closed to the staking of new mining claims. Suction dredging requires a permit from the Alaska Department of Fish and Game. Suction dredge must have a nozzle intake of 6 inches or less; restrictions on horsepower of dredge engine also apply; contact the Alaska Department of Fish and Game.

Caribou Creek Recreational Mining Area. Access is from a large, gravel parking area located at Milepost 106 Glenn Highway. Steep trail leads from parking area down to creek (pedestrians only, no ATVs); outhouse at parking lot. Recreational mining allowed below the ordinary high water mark of Caribou Creek, its tributaries and the Matanuska River.

Hatcher Pass Public Use Area. Access is from Palmer via the Palmer-Fishhook (Hatcher Pass) Road from Milepost 49.5 Glenn Highway. Hatcher Pass Public Use Area begins at approximately Mile 7.8 Hatcher Pass Road and includes the gold-bearing Little Susitna River. The Department of Natural Resources recommends recreational miners use the Gold Mint Trail at Mile 13.8, which follows the Little Susitna River for approximately 8 miles. Outhouse at trailhead. Mining is allowed anywhere within the boundaries of Hatcher Pass Public Use Area, except on valid (active) mining claims. Gold panning is allowed within Independence Mine State Historical Park; check with park staff first.

Petersville Recreational Mining Area. Access is from Milepost 114.9 Parks Highway via Petersville Road west 18.7 miles via gravel road to Forks Roadhouse, then 14.9 miles north via primitive road (4-wheel drive only) to downstream end of Recreational Mining Area. Peters Creek must be forded to reach upper end of mining area (do not try to cross the creek with a passenger car). The Alaska Department of Fish and Game asks that drivers follow existing trail patterns and not drive in creek because it is important king salmon rearing habitat. There are no sanitation facilities.

For more information, contact the Department of Natural Resources, Public Information Center, 550 West 7th Avenue, Suite 1260, Anchorage, AK 99501-3557; phone (907) 269-8400; fax (907) 269-8901; TDD (907) 269-8411. For dredging permits, contact Alaska Deparment of Fish & Game, Habitat Division, 333 Raspberry Road, Anchorage, AK 99518; phone (907) 267-2285.

 # River Running

Floating and whitewater paddling rivers are popular activities in Southcentral, but never underestimate these streams. Glacial rivers in particular are very cold and challenging. River levels can rise dramatically and quickly with meltwater on sunny days. Rainstorms can also quickly swell rivers.

River runners should obtain current information on river conditions from reliable local sources, such as bush pilots, park rangers and local guides. Knik Canoers and Kayakers provide information on local rivers at www.kck.org. Also contact the appropriate land manager for more detailed information on rivers listed here.

Of the 25 National Wild and Scenic Rivers in Alaska, Southcentral has 2: the Delta and Gulkana, both managed by the Bureau of Land Management (BLM). (Alaska is second only to Oregon in number of designated Wild and Scenic Rivers.) Other Southcentral rivers are managed by the Forest Service, Fish & Wildlife Service, National Park Service and Alaska State Parks.

For more information on rivers on Alaska State Parks land, contact the DNR Public Information Center, 550 W. 7th Ave., Suite 1260, Anchorage, AK 99501-3557; phone (907) 269-8400, fax (907) 269-8901, TDD (907) 269-8411.

For the BLM's National Wild and Scenic Rivers (Delta and Gulkana rivers), contact the Glennallen BLM Field Office, Box 147, Glennallen, AK 99588; phone (907) 822-3217, web site www.glenallen.ak.blm.gov. Or contact the BLM Alaska State Office, 222 W. 7th Avenue, #13, Anchorage, AK 99513-7599; phone (907) 271-5960. The BLM Public Information Center is located in Room 148 on the first floor of the New Federal Building-U.S. Courthouse in downtown Anchorage.

For information on canoe routes in Kenai National Wildlife Refuge, contact the Refuge Manager, P.O. Box 2139, Soldotna, AK 99669-2139; phone (907) 262-7021. Or stop by the Kenai National Wildlife Refuge Visitor Contact Station cabin at Milepost S 58 Sterling Highway, or the Kenai National Wildlife Refuge Visitor Center near Soldotna.

For information on rivers within Wrangell St. Elias National Park and Preserve, contact the visitor center at P.O. Box 439, Copper Center, AK 99573; phone (907) 822-5234, fax (907) 822-7216; the Chitina Ranger Station, phone (907) 823-2205; or the Slana Ranger Station on Nabesna Road, phone (907) 822-5238, fax (907) 822-5248.   Or visit www.nps.gov/wrst/float.htm, or email wrst_interpretation@nps.gov.

For information on rivers on Chugach National Forest Land, contact one of the following: Cordova Ranger District, P.O. Box 280, Cordova, AK 99574-0280; phone (907) 424-7661; Seward Ranger District, P.O. Box 390, Seward, AK 99664-0390; phone (907) 224-3374; Glacier Ranger District, P.O. Box 129, Girdwood, AK 99587; phone (907) 783-3242; or U.S. Forest Service, 201 E. 9th Ave., Anchorage, AK 99501; phone (907) 271-2500, web site www.fs.fed.us/r10/chugach.

Anchorage/Mat-Su Area River Running

Chulitna River. The Chulitna River, formed by its Middle and East Forks, flows southwest to the Susitna River. The Middle Fork is accessible from the highway bridge at Milepost A 194.5 Parks Highway, just below Broad Pass; undeveloped parking area at bridge. The East Fork can be reached from the highway bridge at Milepost A 185.1 Parks Highway, about 25 miles north of Cantwell. Traditional takeout is the Chutlitna River bridge at Milepost A 132.8 Parks Highway, about 17 miles north of Trapper Creek at the south boundary of Denali State Park, or at Talkeetna. The Chulitna is also accessible via the Alaska Railroad from Broad Pass, Colorado, East Fork bridge, Honolulu, Hurricane and Talkeetna.

Canoes, kayaks or rafts may be used on this river. The trip is 98 river miles from the bridge put in on the Middle Fork; other alternatives are shorter. Trip length is 1 to 5 days. Along this river, boaters may see eagles, black bears and other wildlife. There also are views of the Alaska Range, including Mount McKinley.

The Middle Fork of the Chulitna is clear water, generally shallow and rocky. The East Fork is clear but fast (4 to 5 mph). Below Honolulu Creek at the West Fork confluence, the Chulitna moves even faster (5 to 7 mph). Water volume can change river conditions drastically. Fallen trees and sweepers are hazards. Also watch for log jams, cross-currents and rollers at the confluence with the West Fork and Fountain rivers. Chulitna Braids below the confluence with the Fountain River.

The upper section of the Chulitna River drops 28 feet per mile and offers exciting white water (up to Class III). It is recommended that only skilled whitewater paddlers with wilderness river experience test the section north of the Chulitna River Bridge at Milepost A 132.8.

From the Parks Highway Bridge at Milepost A 132.8 to Talkeetna, its gradient is 10 feet per mile, and it is an easy river to float, although fast and very cold. Below Talkeetna, the river joins the Susitna. USGS maps: Healy A-5, A-6; Talkeetna B-1, C-1; Talkeetna Mountains D-6.

Eagle River. The Eagle River offers Class II, III and IV float trips of varying lengths to 21 miles. This river is very cold and silty with several hazards. The first put in point is on the

North Fork at Mile 7.4 Eagle River Road. The first 11 miles are Class I and II with many sweepers. Float time to Briggs Bridge averages 4 to 5 hours. According to Alaska State Parks, this section is not recommended for canoes unless very experienced. The second put in point is at Briggs Bridge for a 3.5-mile stretch of Class II and III water with many boulders and steep banks down to Eagle River Campground (adjacent the Glenn Highway) and a takeout above Campground Rapids. Scout the rapids before trying. Below the campground, Eagle River is on Fort Richardson, and a $50 paddler permit is required to float this 6-mile section to the Route Bravo Bridge; phone the Outdoor Recreation Director for Fort Richardson at (907) 384-1476 for details. This last section is rated Class III and IV, with some very hazardous spots.

Kahiltna River. This river heads at Kahiltna Glacier, 35 miles northeast of Talkeetna between Mount Foraker and Mount Hunter in the Alaska Range, and flows southeast to the Yentna River, 53 miles northwest of Anchorage. This Class II braided river flows through an immense valley. The gradient in the first 28 miles is 8 feet per mile. Just above the Peters Creek confluence, the pace quickens appreciably, the gradient increases to 15 feet per mile for the last 46 miles and huge boulders create numerous rapids. Silty and ice cold, this is considered a challenging river. Decked canoes, kayaks or rafts are suitable.

The Kahiltna is accessible by air charter from Talkeetna or Anchorage, landing a few miles from where it emerges from the glacier. Exit is by small plane from the Yentna River, or voyagers may continue down the Yentna to the Susitna River and Cook Inlet. USGS maps: Talkeetna B-3, B-2, A-2; Tyonek D-2, D-3.

Klutina River. This river heads at Stevenson Glacier in the Chugach Mountains and flows 63 miles northeast to the Copper River at Copper Center on the Richardson Highway, 66 miles northeast of Valdez. This Class III river offers excellent whitewater paddling at low water volume. It is more dangerous at high water, which is usually in mid-July to August. The usual put in point is at 16-mile-long Klutina Lake. The first 10 miles of the river from

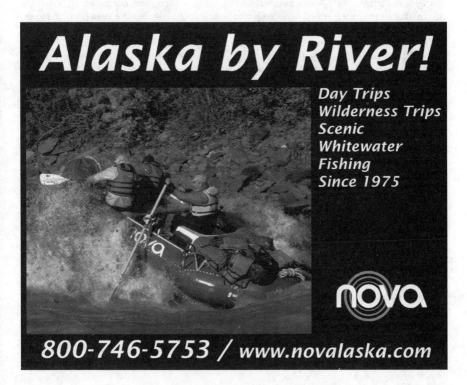

the lake have a gradient of 17 feet per mile. The pace quickens for the last 16 miles, where the gradient increases to 23 feet per mile. Kayaks or rafts are suitable for this river; canoes and riverboats only for the very experienced. The trip takes 1 day. The river offers excellent mountain scenery and fishing for king and red salmon in June and July. Dolly Varden and grayling are available in Klutina Lake.

Access to the Klutina River is possible by 4-wheel-drive vehicle over a bad road through private land from Copper Center Bridge to the outlet of Klutina Lake. Access is also by float-plane to the lake. Exit at Copper Center, or continue on the Copper River to Chitina or the Gulf of Alaska. USGS maps: Valdez C-5, C-6, D-4, D-5.

Lake Creek. This clear-water stream heads in Chelatna Lake and flows southeast 56 river miles to the Yentna River, 58 miles northwest of Anchorage. Lake Creek is rated Class I to IV for the first 48 miles. About halfway downriver is a severe Class IV canyon with huge boulders; this section should be scouted or portaged. It is possible to line the boat along the right bank. Portage is only 150 to 200 yards. It is possible to depart the river near this point via 2 portage trails. One well-marked trail leads to Shovel Lake where there is floatplane access. The other trail, marked with black ink on gray rock, leads to Martana Lake. From the canyon, the river is a rocky, challenging Class III. The last 8 miles are rated Class I. Kayaks or rafts are suitable for this river. The trip takes 3 to 4 days, depending on conditions. This river offers spectacular views of the Alaska Range and Mount McKinley to the northeast. Fair fishing for grayling and rainbow trout.

Access is by floatplane from Anchorage or Talkeetna to Chelatna Lake. Exit via floatplane or riverboat from the Yentna River. USGS maps: Talkeetna A-2, A-3, B-3; Tyonek D-3.

Little Susitna River. The "Little Su" heads at Mint Glacier in the Talkeetna Mountains and flows southwest 110 miles to Cook Inlet, 13 miles west of Anchorage. This is a fairly small river, ranging in width from 20 to 40 feet. Except for the upstream stretch, where the gradient is 20 feet per mile, it's also a slow river (2 to 4 mph) and meanders considerably as it makes its way through spruce, birch and willow forest. Be alert for sweepers, shallows, logjams, and air and jet boats.

There are 2 common put in points: at the Schrock Road bridge about 7 miles north of the Parks Highway and at the Parks Highway bridge at Milepost A 57. From the first put in, the river is rated Class III for 26 miles, after which it is flat water for about 106 river miles. Canoes, kayaks or rafts are suitable. The trip takes 1 to 3 days.

Fishing in the Little Susitna is excellent for king salmon from late May through June and for silver salmon in July and August. There are also red salmon to 10 pounds in mid-July. Other fish available include Dolly Varden and rainbow trout.

Exit from this river may be by prearranged charter flight or takeout at Burma Road, which starts 0.2 mile west of the Lake Marion turnoff on Big Lake Road. USGS maps: Anchorage C-7, C-8; Tyonek B-1, C-1.

Maclaren River. This river heads at Mactaren Glacier in the Clearwater Mountains and flows southwest 55 miles to the Susitna River. The Maclaren flows from the high tundra country into the forests of the Lake Louise basin. Wildlife that may be seen along the way includes bear, moose and caribou. From the usual access point on the Denali Highway, the river flows 52 miles with a gradient of 18 feet per mile. It is rated Class II and III and is rocky with many shallow rapids. Voyagers should take plenty of boat repair materials. Water volume can change rapidly. Canoes, kayaks and rafts are suitable.

Put in point is at the end of a state road that leaves the Denali Highway at Milepost P 43.3. Once on the Susitna River, it is possible to exit via the Tyone River to the road at Lake Louise. Or continue down the Susitna to the portage to Stephan Lake. USGS maps: Mount Hayes A-5, A-6; Gulkana D-6, D-5; Talkeetna Mountains D-1.

Portage Creek. This is a 2- to 3-hour, 6-mile float from the put in at Portage Lake to the takeout at the Seward Highway. The usually Class I water, combined with the river's proximity, to Anchorage make it a popular trip.

Skwentna River. This river heads at South Twin Glacier below Mount Spurr and flows north and east 100 miles to the Yentna River near the settlement of Skwentna, 70 miles northwest of Anchorage. The Skwentna is considered one of the most difficult and remote, but spectacular, wilderness rivers in Alaska. *CAUTION: This river is recommended only for expert paddlers who are experienced in wilderness travel.*

The Skwentna is extremely fast. It has many difficult rapids and steep-walled canyons. From its headwaters, the gradient is 40 feet per mile. The first 24 miles are rated Class IV. The next 40 miles, also with a gradient of 40 feet per mile, are rated Class II and IV. Then, the gradient changes to 17 feet per mile for 50 miles, rated Class II and III. The final 55-mile stretch is rated Class II; the gradient is 10 feet per mile. Decked, 2-man canoes or kayaks are recommended for this river. Moose, bears and an occasional wolf may be encountered along this river.

The Skwentna is not easy to get to. It is possible to reach the headwaters via a portage from Chakachamna Lake, but this route is difficult and takes at least a week. The primary means of access is by helicopter to the headwaters. Exit is at Skwentna. USGS maps: Tyonek B-8, C-8, D-8, D-7, D-6, D-5, D-4.

Susitna River. This large river heads at Susitna Glacier in the Alaska Range and flows southwest 260 miles to Cook Inlet, 24 miles west of Anchorage. The Susitna offers 2 very different trips on its upper and lower sections.

A few miles from its origin, the river emerges from the eastern Alaska Range. The mountains provide a magnificent backdrop to the swift, silty water. Wildlife includes moose, bear, caribou, wolf and beaver. The best access is at the Susitna River Bridge on the Denali Highway at Milepost P 79.5. From this point, the river has a gradient of 7 feet per mile and is rated Class III for 55 miles. Braided gravel flats alternate with a single river channel; some difficult rapids are in this section. Sparse forest growth clings to the shores along the river. Approximately 30 miles downriver from the bridge, the beautiful Maclaren River joins from the east. Then, after 10 miles of braided gravel flats, the Tyone River comes in from the east.

The Tyone River connects Lake Louise and the Susitna. The slow, meandering Tyone can be used as a connecting waterway to leave the Susitna Valley for the extensive Lake Louise plains. A small outboard motor on a canoe speeds an otherwise slow, upriver paddle; it takes about a day to get to Tyone Lake with a motor.

Below the Tyone River confluence, the Susitna has several huge oxbow bends and approximately 20 miles of swift water and rapids rated Class II. Gradient increases to 20 feet per mile.

After this stretch, the river, rated Class I to II, slows for the next 70 miles. Gradient is 10 feet per mile. This tame section ends at treacherous Devil Canyon, which should not be attempted. Look for Log Creek on the left, shortly after a sharp right bend. Pick-up may be made by floatplane at this point, or it is possible to portage 5 miles to Stephan Lake for a prearranged pickup by floatplane.

The Upper Susitna trip should be attempted only by experienced wilderness travelers. Decked canoes, kayaks, rafts or riverboats are suitable for this river.

The Lower Susitna is a Class I river that poses no technical difficulties although its many channels do test water-judging abilities. There are no rapids, but there are boils and upwellings. Some branches and sloughs may be blocked by logjams and may be hazardous. Access points are the Alaska Railroad station at Gold Creek, Talkeetna and the Susitna River bridge on the Parks Highway at Milepost A 104. Exit at Talkeetna, the Parks Highway Bridge or via floatplane pickup at the river mouth. Distance from Gold Creek to Cook Inlet is about 120 river miles. Trip takes 1 to 3 days, depending on put in point. Canoes, kayaks, rafts or riverboats are suitable. USGS maps: Healy A-1, A-2; Talkeetna Mountains D-1, D-2, D-3, D-4, D-5, D-6, C-1, C-2, C-6; Talkeetna C-1, B-1, A-1; Tyonek D-1, C-1, C-2, B-2.

Talachulitna River. This river heads on Beluga Mountain and flows south and northwest to the Skwentna River, 14 miles upriver from the settlement of Skwentna, which is 70 miles northwest of Anchorage. The upper reaches of Talachulitna Creek, which drains Judd Lake, may be shallow and have logjams. The upper river is slow and rated Class I to II. The river flows faster through a section of canyons in the lower 20 miles, rated Class II to III. Just below the Hiline Lake put in near the midpoint of the river, there is a tricky, Class III drop. Kayaks or rafts are suitable for this river. The trip takes 3 to 5 days depending on put in point. The Talachulitna offers excellent views of Beluga Mountain and the Alaska Range. Moose and black bear may be seen. Fishing is good for 5 species of salmon, grayling and rainbow trout (catch and release only).

Access is by floatplane to Judd Lake or to the Talachulitna River at midpoint just south of Hiline Lake. Exit is by floatplane from the confluence with the Skwentna River, or continue down the Skwentna River, and exit via scheduled air service at Skwentna or floatplane pickup from the Yentna River at its confluence with the Skwentna. USGS maps: Tyonek C-4, C-5, D-4.

Tazlina, Nelchina and Little Nelchina rivers. These rivers offer a variety of water conditions and trip alternatives. The Tazlina River drains Tazlina Lake and flows east 30 miles to the Copper River, 7 miles southeast of Glennallen and about 140 miles east of Anchorage. The Nelchina River heads at Nelchina Glacier and flows north and southeast 28 miles into Tazlina Lake. The Little Nelchina is a 48-mile-long tributary to the Nelchina.

Access is from the Glenn Highway via the Little Neichina River at Milepost A 137.5. Access is also by floatplane to Tazlina Lake.

From the Glenn Highway put in, the Little Nelchina is a fast, narrow and rocky clearwater stream. It is shallow during low water times. It flows 4 Class IV river miles and drops 50 feet per mile, before joining the Nelchina River. The glacial Nelchina flows 22 river miles rated Class I to II to Tazlina Lake. This section drops 20 feet per mile.

It's an 8-mile paddle on Tazlina Lake to the Tazlina River. Be alert for a whirlpool at the lake outlet. The Tazlina flows about 50 river miles to the Copper River. This stretch, with a gradient of 15 feet per mile, is rated Class II to III. Exit at the Tazlina River Bridge on the Richardson Highway at Milepost V 110.7, or continue down the Copper River.

Water volume on these rivers should be judged carefully. The rivers are generally least difficult before spring runoff in May and June, late in a dry summer or after cold weather slows glacial runoff. The Little Nelchina may have logjams. Kayaks or rafts are suitable, or canoes for the experienced. This trip takes 2 to 3 days to the Richardson Highway, depending on put in point. USGS maps: Gulkana A-3, A-4, A-5, A-6; Valdez D-7, D-8.

Tokositna River. The Tokositna River heads at Tokositna Glacier and flows 41 miles to join the Chulitna River 25 miles northwest of Talkeetna. An alternative put-in point for running the lower portion of the Chulitna River, the Tokositna can be reached in a few minutes by air charter from Talkeetna to Home Lake. Its flow is moderately swift, but it presents no special obstacles down to its confluence with the Chulitna River just above the bridge on the Parks Highway. Distance is about 26 river miles from the usual put in point to the Chulitna River. The Tokositna River is described as one of the most scenic and easy-to-run rivers in the area. It has glaciers along its course, and Mount McKinley towers above it. USGS maps: Healy A-5, A-6; Talkeetna B-1, C-1; Talkeetna Mountains D-6.

Tyone River. This river heads at Tyone Lake and flows northwest 30 miles to the Susitna River. This trip combines lake paddling with an easy river journey. About half the distance is across 3 adjoining lakes: Louise, Susitna and Tyone. Lake Louise and Susitna Lake have excellent fishing for grayling, lake trout and lingcod. The flat-water river flows slowly and meanders. This route is suitable for kayaks, paddled canoes and riverboats and canoes with small motors. This is considered a good trip for less experienced paddlers who are experienced in the wilderness. Access is via the 19.3-mile-long Lake Louise Road from Glenn Highway at Milepost A 159.8 to Lake Lousie or fly-in by floatplane. Exit is by floatplane from the Susitna River. The Tyone can also be run upstream from the Susitna by strong paddlers.

Paddlers can extend this wilderness trip by makes a series of 4 portages from the Tyone River to reach the south branch of the West Fork Gulkana River. The south branch joins the north branch to form the West Fork. From this junction, the river flows slowly for 4 miles before entering a canyon where the water speeds through riffles and around large boulders. The river then slows until it junctions with the Main Fork of the Gulkana River. The BLM suggests allowing 12 to 20 days to complete this 110-mile trip. USGS maps: Gulkana C-6;

Talkeetna Mountains C-1.

Yentna River. This river is formed by its east and west forks and flows southeast 75 miles to the Susitna River, 30 miles northwest of Anchorage. This flat-water glacial river winds in graceful sweeps through the basin south of Mount McKinley. It has a large volume; white-water problems are minimal, but boaters should be alert for sweepers, logjams and floating trees. Canoes, kayaks, rafts and riverboats are all suitable.

Moose and bears may be seen; there is good fishing on clear-water tributary streams and creeks. There are several homesteads on the Yentna, and riverboats may be encountered.

Access is by small plane to the headwaters. Exit by floatplane from the Susitna, or continue floating down the Susitna. USGS maps: Talkeetna A-3, A-4, B-4; Tyonek B-2, C-2, D-2, D-3, D-4

Copper River/Wrangell-St. Elias Area River Running

Chitina River. This silty glacial river is located in the Chugach Mountains in Wrangell-St. Elias National Park and Preserve. The river heads at Chitina Glacier and flows west-northwest 112 miles to junction with the Copper River 1.2 miles east of Chitina. This river is considered Class I to Class II from its headwaters and has a gradient of 10 feet per mile. It is a fast but not technically difficult river. At about its midpoint, the Chitina is joined by the Nizina River, which should be run only by experienced paddlers. Parks rangers suggest 2 possible floats on this river: Hubert's Landing to Chitina; and the Kennicott, Nizina and Chitina rivers float.

The trip between Hubert's Landing and Chitina covers approximately 125 miles and takes 5 to 10 days. It is recommended for rafts or kayaks. Canoes are advisable for experts only, and ballast and spray covers should be used. Fly-in to Hubert's Landing Strip near the toe of the Chitina Glacier. From Hubert's Landing Strip, it is necessary to haul boats and gear 1 mile south to the main channel of the river. The upper section of the river is fast, with numerous rapids in the Class II range. Then, the river becomes braided, and the volume increases as a multitude of tributary streams and rivers merge their flow. Navigating the deeper main channels becomes necessary to keep from beaching on gravel bars. Near the confluence with the Tana River, the river snakes through a series of bends in a singular channel, and another series of rapids is encountered. At the confluence with the Nizina River, the river again becomes braided for the final 50 miles. At a point about 2 miles upstream from the town of Chitina, there is a series of boulders and hydraulics on river-right (North bank) that should be avoided by all but the most skilled kayakers. After this point, boaters should position themselves near river-right to prepare for a takeout near the Copper River Bridge or at O'Brien Creek, which is several miles downstream along the Copper River.

The 70-mile trip to Chitina via the Kennicott, Nizina and Chitina rivers takes 3 to 5 days and is primarily Class II water. Kayaks or rafts are recommended. Put in at the Kennicott River crossing at the end of the McCarthy Road, or several hundred yards downstream of the pedestrian bridge to avoid rapids. The 5-mile stretch on the Kennicott River to the Nizina is swift and braided. It is also shallow and may need to be lined or portaged. The next 12 miles is on the Nizina River, which has less gradient and more water volume than the Kennicott. It flows through a steep canyon and is considered Class II, fairly fast with difficult rapids. The paddle through the canyon is scenic, but it is necessary to float the inside of the curves on the tight elbows to avoid strong and potentially dangerous currents and eddies along the outer canyon walls. The final 50 miles of this paddle is on the Chitina from the Nizina confluence to the highway bridge at Chitina (see description of this stretch in preceding paragraph.)

Several good camping spots exist along the Nizina, both within the canyon and at the confluence with the Chitina River, as well as along the Chitina, where tributary streams have formed small gravel deltas. Bears are common, and some tributaries should be avoided during salmon runs. Firearms or bear spray may be carried for protection. This trip passes through some rugged and remote wilderness areas, and adequate preparation is essential.

Access to the Chitina's glacial headwaters is by chartered wheel plane. The Kennicott

River is accessed by the McCarthy Road from Chitina. Air charter services are available in Chitina, at the Gulkana airport near Glennallen, as well as other Southcentral communities. USGS maps: McCarthy A-2, A-3, A-4, A-5, A-6, B-6, B-7, B-8; Valdez B-1, C-1, C-2

Copper River. This major glacial river heads on the north side of the Wrangell Mountains and flows south 250 miles to the Gulf of Alaska, just east of Cordova. The river's gradient is 7 feet per mile for about 150 river miles from Slana to Copper Center; 6 feet per mile for the next 60 miles to Chitina; and 5 feet per mile from Chitina to the gulf. The Copper forms the western boundary of Wrangell-St. Elias National Park and Preserve. The lower portion passes through Chugach National Forest. This is considered a Class II river. Canoes, rafts or kayaks are suitable. Paddlers will be treated to outstanding and abundant wildlife.

The National Park Service recommends 2 floats on the Copper River: from Tazlina to the Million Dollar Bridge and from the Gulkana River bridge to Chitina.

Copper River (Tazlina to Million Dollar Bridge). From the put-in at the Tazlina River rest area at Milepost V 110.6 Richardson Highway to the Million Dollar Bridge at the end of the Copper River Highway, this 140-mile river trip through Wrangell-St. Elias National Park and Preserve and Chugach National Forest land takes 5 to 10 days. Alternate put ins are the Klutina River confluence at Copper Center or the Copper River Bridge at Chitina.

From the Tazlina River rest area, it is 1/2 mile to the confluence with the Copper River. Watch for shallow spots and rocks along the Tazlina. The Copper River is a large glacial river with mostly Class I and II water. From the Tazlina River to the confluence with the Chitina River, the Copper meanders through a valley sided with forested bluffs. The river is braided for the most part, and navigating the main channel is necessary to keep from running aground on gravel bars. Waves and holes along various stretches make for exciting travel. Once past Chitina, the river cuts through the Chugach Mountains to Prince William Sound, and it is more than 100 river miles to the exit point at the Million Dollar Bridge. High winds along this stretch of the route can make travel difficult. It is recommended to travel in the morning, as the winds tend to come up in the afternoon, blowing dust along the gravel bars and making downstream travel almost impossible at times. Just south of Chitina, the Copper passes through Wood Canyon, a scenic section of fast water. Beyond Wood Canyon is the Haley Creek hydraulic, which can be avoided by staying river-left. Near the confluence with the Bremner River, the river braids extensively, and the main channels are usually found toward river-right. Approximately 8 miles before the Million Dollar Bridge are the Abercrombie Rapids, a series of large waves and fast water. This area can be avoided by staying on river-right although some rough water may be encountered here as well. Beyond the rapids is the slow, flat water of scenic Miles Lake. Takeout is at the other end of the lake at the Million Dollar Bridge. Arrange for pickup and transportation to Cordova.

Copper River (Gulkana to Chitina). Put in at the Gulkana River Bridge, 1.8 miles from the Gakona junction on the Tok Cutoff (Glenn Highway) and a short distance from the confluence of the Gakona and Copper rivers. The Gulkana River is moderately shallow with many exposed rocks. Stay in the main channel for unobstructed travel to the confluence with the Copper River. Swift currents and cut banks at the confluences with the Klawasi River (Mile 25) and Chetaslina River (Mile 53) make landings difficult. Good freshwater campsites and access to preserve at the Nadina River (Mile 36) and Cheshnina River (Mile 54.5). Some of the islands also provide good camping spots with lots of driftwood and relatively few mosquitos. Watch for working fish wheels along this route. Shallow water and heavily braided river near the Chitina Airfield at Mile 66 make it a challenging takeout point, according to one paddler. USGS maps: Gulkana A-3, B-3; Valdez A-3, B-2, B-3, C-2, C-3, D-3, D-4; Cordova B-3, C-2, C-3, D-2, D-3.

Delta River. The Delta River flows north out of Lower Tangle Lake through the Alaska Range and joins the Tanana River, which flows into the Yukon River. It is designated a National Wild and Scenic River, managed by the BLM. The Delta River canoe trail starts at Tangle Lakes Campground at Milepost P 21 Denali Highway and goes north across Round Tangle Lake, Long Tangle Lake and Lower Tangle Lake to the Delta River. The 3 lakes are connected by shallow channels of slow-moving water. During low-water levels, lining canoes might be required. This section of the trip covers 9 miles.

It is 20 miles from the Delta River's outlet on Lower Tangle Lake to the traditional take-out point in the Phelan Creek area around Milepost V 212.5 on the Richardson Highway. (The take-out point varies from year to year depending on the river channel, but it is marked with a large, yellow sign. It is 49 miles by road from the Tangle Lake launch point on the Denali Highway to the Phelan Creek take-out point on the Richardson Highway.

The first 1.3 miles of the Delta River are Class II water, shallow and rocky. There is a 15-foot waterfall 2 miles below the last lake. A quarter-mile portage on the right bank around the falls crosses the Denali Fault, one of the longest fault zones in Alaska. Two hundred yards after reentering the river below the falls, traverse to the left bank to run a difficult rapid, or line on the right bank. The Class II-III rapids for the next 2 miles require quick maneuvering around the rocks. NOTE: Boaters must have white-water experience. Each year, 5 or 6 canoes are damaged beyond repair along this stretch. It is a long walk out. The next 12 miles are Class I to the confluence with Eureka Creek. The last 7 miles are shallow and braided with numerous channels and gravel bars. The water is swift and generally Class II. There is a view of Rainbow Mountain to the right.

From Tangle Lakes Campground put in to the Phelan Creek takeout, the canoe trail covers 29 miles of lakes and river and takes about 2 to 3 days. The trail is suitable for canoes and kayaks. The trip can be extended 17 miles from the traditional takeout point at Phelan Creek to the Black Rapids takeout at Milepost V 227.4 Richardson Highway. This section of the Delta, rated Class III and IV, has long stretches of rapids with high, irregular waves and hidden boulders. It is not recommended for open canoes.

The Delta River can be floated between mid-June and mid-September and offers outstanding grayling fishing. Other fish available include lake trout, whitefish and burbot. Wildlife that may be seen along the Delta River includes moose, bear, Dall sheep, caribou, beaver, muskrat, golden eagles, bald eagles and many species of waterfowl. USGS maps: Mount Hayes A-4, B-4, A-5, C-5; Gulkana D-4.

Gulkana River. A river trip of nearly 300 miles is possible by using this National Wild and Scenic River managed by the BLM. The most popular paddle is the Main Fork, which starts at Paxson Lake Campground, Milepost V 175 Richardson Highway, and ends at Sourdough Campground, Milepost V 147.6. Total distance is about 50 river miles or 4 days travel. The vehicle shuttle is 62 miles round trip. Start this trip by paddling 3 miles across Paxson Lake to the river outlet in southwest corner. From the outlet to the junction with the Middle Fork, the first 3 miles of the Gulkana River are shallow and rocky with Class II-III rapids and a gradient of 38 feet per mile. Lining is required at low water levels. Whitewater experience is neccessary to navigate this section of the river. From the confluence of the Middle Fork and Main Fork, the river slows, and the next 15 miles are Class I with occasional rocks and waves. This stretch is followed by the 1/4-mile Canyon Rapids at River Mile 20. These Class III-IV rapids should be run only by experienced paddlers. Takeout signs mark the portage on the left side of the river before Canyon Rapids. It is recommended that experienced boaters portage gear prior to running the rapids. At high water, open canoes and small rafts must be portaged. Even experienced boaters have destroyed rafts and canoes here, according to the BLM. Below Canyon Rapids are 8.5 miles of Class II-III rocky and shallow rapids. Several canoes are wrecked here each year. At the first bend after the portage, there is a 1-mile side trip to Canyon Lake, which has excellent grayling fishing; trail begins on the left bank. The remainder of the trip to Sourdough is a 17-mile stretch of Class I water. There is road access at the Sourdough Campground at Milepost V 147.6 Richardson Highway.

The float can be extended beyond Sourdough Campground to the Gulkana River bridge at Milepost V 126.8 Richardson Highway, near Gulkana village, at the confluence of the Gulkana and Copper rivers. This section of river is Class I-II.

The Middle Fork Gulkana River is accessed from Tangle River campground at Milepost P 21.7 Denali Highway. The Middle Fork is generally Class I with some Class II-IV water. Paddle south through Tangle Lakes; there is a 300-foot portage between first lake and Upper Tangle Lake. At the southwest end of Upper Tangle Lake, a 0.3-mile portage leads to Lake 2865. A shallow, wadeable portage between Lake 2865 and the southernmost Tangle Lake is necessary, followed by a 1.3-mile portage to Dickey Lake. There are no trail markings, but most of the portage is low tundra brush. The Middle Fork Gulkana flows out of Dickey Lake at the extreme southeast corner. The first 3 miles of the river are shallow-less than 1 foot deep-and rocky, with a gradient of 30 feet per mile. The river then plunges into a steep canyon, and the gradient triples. Large boulders in Class III-IV rapids make maneuvering difficult. This section requires careful lining or portaging. After the canyon, riffles and rocks are common for the next 6 miles. The next 19 miles are easy Class I-II as the gradient drops from 25 feet to 1 foot per mile before joining the Main Fork. Watch for sweepers and logjams in some sections, especially between Swede Lake and Hungry Hollow Creek. Allow 6 to 7 days for the 76-mile trip from Tangle Lake to Sourdough. The Middle Fork is also accessed from the Swede Lake Trail (suitable for ATVs), which junctions with the Middle Fork 8 miles downstream from Dickey Lake. Paddlers can also charter a floatplane and fly in to Dickey Lake, subtracting 1 or 2 days from the trip.

Use canoes or kayaks on Tangle Lakes; canoes, kayaks or rafts are suitable on the rivers. Fish available include rainbow trout, whitefish, arctic grayling, red and king salmon, lake trout and burbot, depending on location and season. Wildlife includes moose, bear, wolf, fox, caribou, muskrat, beaver, eagle, hawk and waterfowl. USGS maps: Mount Hayes A-5; Gulkana B-3, B-4, C-4, D-4, D-5.

Maclaren River. This river heads at Maclaren Glacier in the Clearwater Mountains and flows southwest 55 miles to the Susitna River. The Maclaren flows from the high tundra country into the forests of the Lake Louise basin. Wildlife that may be seen along the way includes bear, moose and caribou. From the usual access point on the Denali Highway, the river flows 52 miles with a gradient of 18 feet per mile. It is rated Class II and III and is rocky with many shallow rapids. Voyagers should take plenty of boat repair materials. Water volume can change rapidly. Canoes, kayaks and rafts are suitable.

Put in point is at the end of a state road that leaves the Denali Highway at Milepost P 43.3. Once on the Susitna River, it is possible to exit via the Tyone River to the road at Lake Louise. Or continue down the Susitna to the portage to Stephan Lake. USGS maps: Mount Hayes A-5, A-6; Gulkana D-5, D-6; Talkeetna Mountains D-1.

Nabesna River. This river heads at Nabesna Glacier and flows northeast to join with the Chisana River to form the Tanana River near Northway Junction on the Alaska Highway. The river begins in Wrangell-St. Elias National Park and Preserve and flows through Tetlin National Wildlife Refuge.

The Nabesna River is a moderate-flowing, heavily braided glacial river with primarily Class I water and occasional Class II stretches. The first 10 miles are especially swift, with a gradient of 20 feet per mile and rated Class I-II. The gradient for the next 15 miles of flat water is 13 feet per mile, and the gradient for the last 40 miles is 5 feet per mile as the river slows to meander through the foothills and taiga forest east of the Wrangell Mountains. Rowing tends to be necessary along the lower half of the river, where head winds can be quite strong. For the most part, it is shallow, but heavy spring and summer rains and snowmelt can bring the volume up substantially. Canoes, kayaks or rafts are suitable. The water is also cold, and hypothermia is a potential hazard for paddlers.

For a 3 to 4 day trip, the National Park Service recommends flying in to Orange Hill airstrip. The put in point is a short distance from the airstrip. The river can also be reached by a 5-mile trail from Milepost J 40.2 on the Nabesna Road. Exit the river at Northway, 1.5 miles from Northway Airport, or at the Alaska Highway at the confluence of the Chisana River. USGS maps: Nabesna B-4, C-3, C-4, D-2, D-3; Tanacross A-2.

Tangle Lakes. The name Tangle is a descriptive term for the maze of lakes and feeder streams of the Delta and Gulkana river drainages. The system includes Long Tangle, Round Tangle, Upper Tangle and Lower Tangle Lakes, and it accesses the National Wild and Scenic

Rivers-the Delta and the Gulkana.

Upper Tangle Lakes canoe trail continues south through Tangle Lakes (portages required) to Dickey Lake, then follows the Middle Fork of the Gulkana River. Access is from Upper Tangle Lakes BLM Campground at Milepost 21.7 Denali Highway. The Lower Tangle Lakes canoe trail begins at Round Tangle Lake and follows the Tangle Lakes for 9 miles to the Delta River. The 4 lakes are connected by shallow channels of moving water. Access is from Tangle Lakes BLM Campground at Milepost 21.5 Denali Highway. See the Gulkana River and Delta River this section. USGS maps: Mount Hayes A-4, B-4, C-4.

Kenai Peninsula Area River Running

Kenai River. This river heads at Kenai Lake on the Kenai Peninsula and flows west 75 miles to Cook Inlet at Kenai. Much of this river is located in the Kenai National Wildlife Refuge. It ranges from Class II to III and features an exciting white-water canyon for the experienced paddler. This trip is suitable for kayakers, rafters or experienced canoeists. Fish available on this trip include Dolly Varden, rainbow trout and pink, king, silver and red salmon.

Access this river at turnouts near the Kenai River bridge on the Sterling Highway at Milepost S 47.8, about 100 miles from Anchorage, for the 17-mile stretch to Skilak Lake. Or put in at the bridge at Milepost S 53. Be alert for the Class III rapids at Schooner Bend below the second put in point; stay close to the right bank. The most exciting rapids on this river are just downstream from Jean Creek; the 2-mile-long canyon is rated Class II to III. This stretch should only be run by experienced paddlers; vertical walls prevent lining. The river braids before it enters Skilak Lake, and there may be sweepers or logjams.

Paddle 6 miles on the lake to the Upper Skilak Lake Campground. Strong winds on the lake may be hazardous, so stay close to shore. There are several miles of rock bluffs along this stretch, which means there is no place to take out if the winds suddenly whip up. From the upper campground, it's 7 miles of paddling to Lower Skilak Lake Campground and 2 miles farther to the Kenai River outlet. There are Class III rapids 12 miles downriver from the outlet. Exit the river at Soldotna or Kenai or at numerous other points in between. USGS maps: Seward B-8; Kenai B-1, B-2, B-3, C-2, C-3, C-4.

Swan Lake. Established canoe trail within Kenai National Wildlife Refuge, managed by U.S. Fish & Wildlife Service. This route connects 30 lakes with forks of the Moose River. Terminus of the trip is the confluence of the Moose and Kenai rivers at the Moose River bridge on the Sterling Highway at Milepost 82.1. This route can be traveled in less than a week. Longest portage is about 1 mile. Rainbow trout, Dolly Varden and silver salmon are found in most lakes, except for Birch, Teal, Mallard, Raven, Otter and Big Mink lakes. West entrance to the canoe route is at Canoe Lake on Swan Lake Road off the Swanson River Road, 21.2 miles from the Sterling Highway. East entrance is from Portage Lake, 5.8 miles beyond Canoe Lake on Swan Lake Road. Consult the canoe pamphlet described under Swanson River. USGS map: Kenai C-2.

Swanson River. This 80-mile canoe trail within Kenai National Wildlife Refuge links more than 40 lakes with 46 miles of the Swanson River. The entire route can be traveled in less than a week. Portages between lakes are generally short and cross level or slightly hilly terrain. Longest portage is about 1 mile. Rainbow trout, Dolly Varden and some red and silver salmon are found in most of the lakes, except Berry, Redpoll, Twig, Eider, Birch Tree and Olsjold lakes. The first trailhead is on the Swanson River Road at Milepost 14.9 from the junction with the Sterling Highway. Enter the Swanson River at a campground here, and float downstream 1 or 2 days to Swanson River canoe landing at Mile 38.6 on the Kenai Spur Highway within Captain Cook State Recreation Area. To make the entire 80-mile trip, take Swan Lake Road, which turns off to the east from Swanson River Road. Drive about 12 miles, and turn left at the Swanson River Route sign. Then, drive north about 1/2 mile to launch at Paddle Lake. Refer to the Fish and Wildlife Service pamphlet "Canoeing in the Kenai National Wildlife Refuge" for a map of all the routes and other details. USGS maps: Kenai C-2, C-3, D-2, D-3.

 Sea Kayaking

Some of the popular sea kayaking destinations in the Southcentral region follow. While kayakers can put in and take off from almost any Southcentral port, some of the more desirable destinations require chartering a boat for drop-off service. Charter prices depend on destination and number of persons in the party. A 4-hour charter boat trip for 6 persons and 4 kayaks, for example, may cost $500 or more, round-trip.

Aialik Bay. A 5-mile-wide bay extending 22 miles south from Aialik Glacier to the Gulf of Alaska, located 33 miles south of Seward within Kenai Fjords National Park. Kayakers can also explore Holgate Arm, a 5-mile-long estuary off Aialik Bay that ends at Holgate Glacier. The tidewater glaciers and abundant wildlife are the attractions. Kayakers can charter out to Aialik bay and paddle back to Seward on calm days, but most paddlers are dropped off and picked up. Access is by charter boat or floatplane out of Seward. Guided kayak trips and rental kayaks are available in Seward. Consult with local outfitters, charter operators and the park service for detailed information on boating conditions before departing.

There are 3 public-use cabins available in summer by reservation. The cabins are located at Holgate Arm, Aialik Bay, Delight Spit and North Arm. Kayakers and boaters can also camp on beaches but must be aware of land status; 42,000 acres of coastline are owned by Native corporations and are not available for public camping. Maps indicating land ownership are available from the park visitor center in Seward.

Kachemak Bay. An 8-mile-wide, 40-mile-long bay located on the southwest coast of the Kenai Peninsula between Seldovia and Homer. The scenery (snow-capped peaks and glaciers) and the abundant wildlife are the attractions. Because the bay can be extremely rough, preferred kayaking destinations include the protected waters along the east shore of Kachemak Bay between China Poot Bay, 9 miles southeast of Homer; Halibut Cove, 12 miles from Homer, within Kachemak Bay State Park; and Seldovia Bay, 16 miles southwest of Homer.

There are both private property and Native corporation land holdings within the park. Kayakers should check with the Kachemak Bay State Park office regarding public campsites.

The Alaska Marine Highway connects Homer and Seldovia; it is about a 2-hour ferry trip. The private Kachemak Bay Ferry connects Homer with the community of Halibut Cove in summer. Air charters and boat charters are available in Homer.

Because of a prevailing southwesterly winds on sunny, summer days, paddlers departing from Homer into Kachemak Bay should plan to return to port before 11 A.M. or after 7 P.M.

Prince William Sound. A 70-mile-wide gulf extending 30 miles north off the Gulf of Alaska. Kayaking in Prince William Sound originates out of the communities of Whittier, Valdez and Cordova. Popular destinations include the 14 marine parks that dot the area. Attractions in Prince William Sound are its tidewater glaciers, mountain scenery and abundant wildlife.

Easy access from Anchorage has drawn many paddlers to western Prince William Sound,

and in recent years, the number of ocean kayakers in the area has exploded, with most kayakers entering the western Sound from Whittier, located at the head of Passage Canal. Kayakers depart directly from Whittier or may charter out to destinations and paddle back to Whittier. Popular destinations out of Whittier include Port Wells, Port Nellie Juan and Culross Passage, as well as points along Passage Canal. Two-day trips from Whittier might include a charter out to Harriman Fjord, Bainbridge Passage or Port Nellie Juan and a paddle back to Whittier; or a paddle from Whittier along Passage Canal to Shotgun Cove and overnight at Squirrel Cove campsite at Decision Point marine park. Campsites at marine parks along Passage Canal during peak holiday weekends are often full. Kayakers can arrange for charter boat service in Whittier to drop them off in more remote areas.

Kayakers entering Prince William Sound from Valdez, located at the east end of the 13-mile-long estuary, Port Valdez, paddle through Valdez Narrows (2 miles), and connect with 15-mile-long Valdez Arm. With its numerous campsites and scenic views of Shoup Glacier Shoup Bay is a popular kayaking destination from Valdez. Marine parks are also located at Sawmill Bay on Port Valdez and at Jack Bay southeast of Valdez Narrows.

The paddle from Valdez to Whittier is growing in popularity. The trip averages about 140 miles, depending on how closely one hugs the coast and explores the fjords and bays. The Alaska Marine Highway ferry takes about 7 hours to make the trip. Charter boat service, kayak rentals and guided kayaking trips are available in Valdez.

Kayaking eastern Prince William Sound out of Cordova is becoming increasingly popular. Cordova is located on Orca Inlet, a 15-mile-long water passage, opposite Hawkins Island. Kayak rentals and guided kayaking trips are available from an outfitter located at Cordova Harbor. Charter boat service is also readily available in Cordova. Cordova is not connected to the state highway system, but it is served regularly by the Alaska Marine Highway system, and the community is accessible by air.

Changing wind direction and tidal currents can make paddling Prince William Sound a tricky business at best. Also keep in mind the weather can change abruptly. Be prepared for wind and rain.

Resurrection Bay. A 24-mile-long estuary extending from the mouth of the Resurrection River at Seward to Harding Gateway (water passage) and Blying Sound (bight). Attractions include abundant wildlife and challenging conditions. Access to Resurrection Bay is from Seward, 127 miles south of Anchorage via the Seward Highway. Rental kayaks and guided kayak trips are available in Seward. Popular kayaking destinations in Resurrection Bay include the marine park at Thumb Cove, 9 miles south of Seward on the east side of the bay; Sandspit Point marine park on Fox Island, 12 miles southeast of Seward; South Beach at Caines Head State Recreation Area, located on the west side of the bay about 8 miles south of Seward; and Bear Glacier, 15 miles south of Seward in Kenai Fjords National Park on the edge of the bay, the park's southern coastal boundary.

(See also Caines Head State Recreation Area, Kachemak Bay State Park, Kenai Fjords National Park, Marine Parks and Prince William Sound this section.)

Susitna Flats State Game Refuge

An expansive lowlands area along upper Cook Inlet, the east side of Susitna Flats is bisected by the Little Susitna River. The Ivan, Lewis, Theodore and Beluga rivers cross the west side of the refuge. The 300,800-acre refuge encompasses salt marsh, meadow, numerous lakes and bogs.

An extremely high concentration of migrating waterfowl use the refuge during spring and fall. Large numbers of mallards, pintails and Canada geese are present by mid-April. As many as 100,000 waterfowl are present in early May when peak densities are reached. About 10,000 mallards, pintails and green-winged teal remain to nest in the refuge. Other birds using the refuge include lesser sandhill cranes, swans, northern phalaropes, dowitchers, godwits, whimbrels, snipe, yellowlegs, sandpipers, plovers and dunlin.

Approximately 10 percent of the state's waterfowl harvest occurs on Susitna Flats, according to the Alaska Department of Fish and Game, with about 15,000 ducks and 500 geese taken. The Little Susitna, Theodore and Lewis rivers are popular salmon fishing streams.

Access to the refuge is by road from Wasilla. Follow Knik-Goose Bay Road 17.2 miles south, then Goose Bay-Point Mackenzie Road 12 miles west to reach the Little Susitna River Public-use Site; 83 parking spaces, 65 campsites, boat ramps, a dump station, water, tables and toilets. Boats may be launched at the Little Susitna facility. Many hunters reach the refuge by floatplane, using one of the area lakes. Extreme tides, winds and dangerous mudflats make boat access from Cook Inlet hazardous.

For more information contact the Alaska Department of Fish and Game, 333 Raspberry Road, Anchorage, AK 99518-1599; phone (907) 746-6300.

Tetlin National Wildlife Refuge

This 730,000-acre refuge is located in east-central Alaska. It is bordered on the north by the Alaska Highway, on the east by the Canadian border, on the south by Wrangell-St. Elias National Park and Preserve and on the west by the Tetlin Reserve (formerly the Tetlin Indian Reservation).

Tetlin Refuge is a showcase of natural features created by wildfires, permafrost and fluctuating river channels. The refuge features an undulating plain broken by hills, forests, ponds, lakes and extensive marshes. The glacial Chisana and Nabesna rivers dominate the valley where they meander before joining to form the Tanana River. Parabolic sand dunes, formed of windblown glacial flour, are found southeast of Northway and at Big John Hill.

Tetlin's vegetation is a good example of the benefits of wildfires. These natural phenomena help create diverse plant habitats such as grasslands or birch forests. Spruce forests are usually the dominant vegetation in a subarctic environment. When fire destroys such a forest, a series of habitats follow until once again spruce trees dominate.

Climate: Temperatures in June and July often exceed 80°F, with lows to 40°F. During these months, it is light around the clock. By mid-September, daytime temperatures of 45°F and nighttime temperatures of 25°F are common. Winter temperatures can drop to -70°F, and often stay below -40°F for a week or below 0°F for several months. Weather can change rapidly. Snow can occur as late as May or as early as August.

Wildlife: These varied habitats are home to a diverse group of animals: moose, black and brown bears, ptarmigan, wolf, lynx and red fox. Caribou winter in the refuge, and Dall sheep can be seen on mountain slopes. The refuge is a stopover for migrating birds, and its wetlands provide important summer breeding habitat. Refuge wetlands are critical when drought in Canada and the Prairie Pothole region sends birds farther north. The refuge supports a growing population of trumpeter swans, as well as the largest population of nesting osprey in Alaska. As many as 100,000 sandhill cranes pass through the refuge each fall. Other large birds found in the refuge include arctic and common loons, bald eagles and golden eagles. Birds that are rarely, if ever, seen in other parts of Alaska (because their usual range is farther south) may be seen here, including blue-winged teals, ruddy ducks, ring-necked ducks, red-winged blackbirds and mountain bluebirds. The refuge also is the western or northern limit of distribution of the American coot, rail and brown-headed cowbird.

Arctic grayling, whitefish, lake trout, burbot and northern pike inhabit lakes and streams. There are no significant salmon runs although a few chum salmon run up the Tanana and its tributaries.

Activities: Recreational activities popular on Tetlin refuge include canoeing, fishing, hunting, wildlife observation and photography. There are no maintained hiking trails within the refuge with the exception of a 1-mile trail to Hidden Lake at Milepost 1240. The Nabesna River, a glacial river with primarily Class I water, flows through the refuge (see River Running this section.) Fishing and hunting guide service is available in Tok. The refuge office is located on the Alaska Highway in Tok directly across from the Alaska Public Lands Information Center at Milepost 1314.1. Tetlin National Wildlife Refuge Visitor Center is located at Milepost 1229 Alaska Highway; open 8 A.M. to 4:30 P.M. from mid-May to mid-September. The center has an excellent scenic vista, interpretive displays, animal mounts and general information on natural resources.

Accommodations: There are 2 refuge campgrounds on the Alaska Highway: Deadman at Historic Milepost 1254 and Lakeview at Milepost 1256.7. Wilderness camping is allowed throughout the refuge. The best summer campsites are river bars and ridges where breezes reduce the insect problem. Choose sites carefully to avoid possible flooding from rainstorms or rising rivers. Dead or downed wood is usually available on river bars or in spruce stands. Bear-proof containers are recommended. Pack out all trash, and bury firepits. Human waste should be buried at least 100 yards from the water source. Camping supplies,food, gas and lodging are available in Tok.

Access: The Alaska Highway provides access along 65 miles of the refuge's northern border. Foot access is possible along the highway from the Canadian border to Gardiner Creek and at other points. The refuge is accessible by small boat from the Alaska Highway at Desper Creek and from the Northway Road at the Chisana River Bridge. Charter planes are available in Tok. There are no designated roads or trails for motorized vehicles in the refuge.

For more information: Contact Refuge Manager, Tetlin National Wildlife Refuge, P.O. Box 779, Tok, AK 99780; phone (907) 883-5312, fax (907) 883-5747, email tetlin@fws.gov, www.r7.fws.gov/nwr/tetlin/tetnwr.html.

For details on access and accommodations, see The MILEPOST®, a complete guide to Alaska's road system.

Trading Bay State Game Refuge

Located on the west side of Cook Inlet, this 160,960-acre refuge encompasses a large coastal marsh fed by the Kustatan, McArthur, Chakachatna and Middle rivers, and Chuitkilnachna and Nikolai creeks. It was established in 1976 to protect wetlands that provide critical spring feeding, summer nesting and fall staging habitat for ducks, geese, swans and cranes. Nesting ducks include mallard, pintail, greenwinged teal, widgeon, shoveler, common eider, mergansers, scoters, scaup and goldeneye. Healthy populations of moose, bears and other mammals use the refuge.

This is a popular waterfowl and moose hunting area in the fall. There is sportfishing for salmon in summer. The refuge is also used for subsistence hunting and fishing by residents of Tyonek.

There are no developed facilities within the refuge. Access is by road from the community of Tyonek, or by small plane or boat.

For more information contact the Alaska Department of Fish and Game regional office at 333 Raspberry Road, Anchorage, AK 99518-1599; phone (907) 746-6300.

Wrangell-St. Elias National Park and Preserve

Located northwest of Yakutat and northeast of Cordova and Valdez, Wrangell-St. Elias is the largest unit in the national park system, encompassing 13.2 million acres of superlative scenery, abundant wildlife and fascinating history. In conjunction with adjacent Kluane National Park in Canada, the 2 areas make up the largest parkland in North America. Here, the Wrangell, St. Elias and Chugach mountain ranges converge, forming a mountain wilderness unsurpassed in North America and comparable to all other major mountain groups in the world. The region contains the largest concentration of peaks, exceeding 14,500 feet, in North America; Wrangell-St. Elias park contains 9 of the 16 highest peaks in the United States. Mount St. Elias, at 18,008 feet, is the second tallest peak in the United States; Mount Logan, across the border in Kluane National Park, soars to a height of 19,850 feet, second only to Mount McKinley in North American summits.

This park has been shaped by both volcanoes and ice. Mount Wrangell (14,163 feet) experienced a phreatic eruption (like a geyser) as recently as 1924. Dormant volcanoes include Mount Blackburn (16,390 feet), Mount Sanford (16,237 feet) and Mount Drum (12,010 feet). There are 3 large thermal springs known as mud volcanoes on the western flank of Mount Drum.

The area also contains the largest concentration of glaciers on the continent. One of these, Malaspina Glacier, is North America's largest piedmont glacier, a type formed when 2 or more glaciers flow from confined valleys to form a broad fan- or lobe-shaped ice mass. Malaspina Glacier covers an area of about 1,500 square miles-larger than the state of Rhode Island. It has been designated a national natural landmark. Hubbard Glacier, which flows out of the St. Elias Mountains into Disenchantment Bay, is one of the largest and most active glaciers in North America. In 1986, the glacier made national headlines when it surged forward, sealing off adjacent Russell Fiord. Within 2 months, the ice dam had broken, but Hubbard Glacier continues to advance, and scientists agree the glacier will eventually close off the fjord permanently.

The Park Service says Chitistone and Nizina canyons "far exceed the scale of Yosemite Valley in California" and include an even greater variety of geological wonders. There is a spectacular, 300-foot waterfall in upper Chitistone Canyon, and the lower canyon has sheer walls rising 4,000 feet above the river.

Wrangell-St. Elias contains many prehistoric sites, such as ancient Native Alaskan and Native American villages and camps, and the historic ruins of many mines dot the landscape. Kennicott is the best preserved of these mine sites, and it is accessible via the Edgerton Highway and McCarthy Road and located about 5 miles from McCarthy (see description under attractions).

Copper mining inspired some of the early prospectors to travel to the land that is now Wrangell-St. Elias National Park and Preserve, but it was the discovery of gold in Chisana (pronounced Shooshana) that began the last great gold rush in Alaska. In 1913, thousands of stampeders made the treacherous journey through rugged country by whatever means possible to reach the newfound mining district. Chisana soon became known as "the largest log cabin town in the world." It was a short boom, lasting only a few years, but an important part of the history of this area.

Tree line in the park's interior is about 3,000 to 4,000 feet. Below tree line the forest cover is composed of white and black spruce, balsam poplar and a mixture of aspen, birch and balsam poplar where fires have transformed the forest. Streambeds contain thick underbrush, usually alder, which also grows well on steep, south-facing hillsides. Labrador tea and dwarf birch are major shrubs. Above 3,000 feet, moist sedges and grasses form open tundra meadows interlaced with blueberries and Labrador tea. The Bremner and Copper river valleys have typical coastal vegetation near their mouths: western and mountain hemlock and Sitka spruce rain forest with devil's club, blueberries and salmonberries.

Climate: Weather in most of the area is typical of interior Alaska. Summer brings cool, often cloudy and rainy weather, which can interfere with scheduled air pickups and prolong trips. Clear, hot days are not uncommon, particularly in July, which has the warmest weather. August is cooler and wetter but generally has fewer mosquitoes. Fall is excellent, but doesn't last long. Winters are cold and dark, with temperatures dropping to -50°F, but clear weather is common. Average snow cover is about 2 feet. In coastal areas, precipitation is higher (130 inches in some areas), and temperatures are relatively moderate with winter lows around 0°F and summer highs in the 70s.

The Park Service cautions that visitors to the Wrangell-St. Elias backcountry must well-equipped and self-sufficient; have wilderness travel and survival skills; and carry enough food to cover unexpected delays. Leave an itinerary with the Park Service or with a friend. The park's headquarters on the Richardson Highway is open year-round. Ranger stations are open during the summers at Slana, Chitina and Yakutat. Also, some of the land within the park/preserve is privately owned, and local residents carry on subsistence lifestyles; respect their property and privacy.

Wildlife: These diverse habitats support varied wildlife. Dall sheep and mountain goats range on higher slopes-sheep in the Wrangell Mountains and northern slopes of the Chugach Range, goats in the coastal mountains. Caribou from 3 herds forage on parklands. Moose browse throughout the lowlands and river bottoms, and 2 herds of introduced bison range along the Copper and Chitina rivers. Brown/grizzly and black bears share lower elevations with wolves, wolverines, coyotes, red foxes and a variety of small furbearers.

Marine mammals, which can be observed in Yakutat Bay where the park touches the sea, include seals, sea lions, sea otters, 2 species of dolphin and killer whales. Sport fish, such as arctic grayling, burbot and trout thrive in lakes adjacent to the Chitina River valley and on the northern slopes of the Wrangells. The Copper River supports a major salmon run utilized by both commercial and subsistence fishermen.

Bird life is not outstanding within the park/preserve, but trumpeter swans, bald and golden eagles, 3 species of ptarmigan and ruffed and spruce grouse can be seen. Just to the south of the park, the Copper River Delta is a major nesting area.

Activities: Recreational opportunities in Wrangell-St. Elias include hunting, fishing, expedition mountaineering, backpacking/hiking, cross-country skiing, rafting/kayaking and wildlife observation. Navigable rivers in the park include the Copper and Chitina rivers. It is possible to float several other streams in the park, such as the Nabesna and Kennicott rivers. Hikes follow unimproved backcountry routes consisting of mining trails, historic routes, streambeds, shorelines, game trails and open country. Several guides and outfitters offer a variety of trips in the park and preserve. Guides and outfitters are located in Kennicott and in nearby McCarthy, as well as communities like Glennallen.

For many hikers, hiring the services of a local guide will make the trip safer and more enjoyable. In general, the areas above treeline afford the easiest hiking and best views. These areas are often accessed by charter plane to one of the many "bush" landing strips in the park. Keep in mind that there are many more places to land than are shown on maps. Air taxis will often land on gravel bars or on the tundra. Ask a park ranger or pilot about some of the lesser known areas. A list of licensed air taxi operators is available from the park. Be flexible and prepared for alternative destinations. Your air taxi or the Park Service may know of high water conditions, wildlife hazards or overcrowding in an area and may encourage you to choose an alternative at the last minute. Backcountry permits are not required, but travelers are encouraged to complete a "Backcountry Itinerary" available at any park office. Also, leave your route and expected time of return with a friend or family member. If you fail to check in from a backcountry trip, rangers will not initiate a search until a specific request from a friend or family member is made. If you are flying in or out of a remote airstrip, your pilot will be your main communication link to safety. Be sure to discuss "what if" scenarios with your pilot before you are dropped off. Carry food for several extra days in case of unexpected delays. Assistance may be days or miles away, so be extraordinarily careful in this vast region.

Sport hunting is allowed only within the National Preserve. Anyone may trap in the preserve, but only local, rural residents may trap in the park. A local, rural resident is any person who has his/her primary home within the resident zone for the park as defined by federal regulation or has a subsistence permit issued by the superintendent.

A valid Alaska State license is required for all hunters age 16 or older to hunt or trap in the park and preserve. All hunting and trapping must be done in accordance with state laws and regulations. Hunters and trappers using the park and preserve should be familiar with the park and preserve boundaries and regulations concerning the use of areas. Maps can be obtained from the park upon request.

There are 17 registered hunting guides that are allowed to operate under permit in the park. Guided hunting opportunities range from private fly-in lodging facilities and hunts to basic "spike" camp operations accessible by horseback. For more information and to receive a list of registered guides, contact the park.

Aircraft may be used in the park or preserve. However, aircraft are not permitted to support subsistence hunting or trapping in the park. Permits for the use of aircraft are not required. Snowmachines may be used when there is adequate snow cover. Motoboats, horses and dogteams may also be used. Permits are not required. Off-road vehicles (ORV), including all-terrain vehicles (ATV), may be used on established routes only. Sport hunters are required to obtain ORV permits at any Ranger Station or the Park Headquaters. Subsistence hunters are encouraged to obtain ORV permits and use only established routes.

Attractions: The town of Kennicott, the major attraction for many visitors, is perched on the side of Bonanza Ridge next to Kennicott Glacier. The mill town was built by Kennecott Copper Corporation beginning in 1907. (An early day misspelling made the mining company Kennecott, while the glacier and river are Kennicott.) The Kennecott mines, including 70 miles of subterranean tunnels, are up near the ridge top and were connected to the mill by aerial trams. Still known as the richest copper mine ever discovered, Kennecott processed more than 591,535 tons of copper ore valued at $200,000 and employed some 800 workers in its heyday between 1911-1938. The place was left as a ghost town after 1938 and was resettled in the 1970s.

Today, the area is a national historic landmark. The National Park Service purchased many of the remaining structures, but several are still privately owned. At present, the NPS is working to stabilize the site and many buildings are locked. Tours into some of the buildings are available through private guide services. National Park Service interpretive programs are offered during the summer; check at the Jurik Building.

Accommodations: There are 10 cabins available for public use within Wrangell-St. Elias National Park and Preserve. The cabins are available on a first-come, first-served basis. Wrangell-St. Elias does not have a cabin reservation system at this time.

Privately operated lodges, cabins and camps are scattered throughout the park and preserve in the McCarthy/Kennicott area and along the Nabesna and McCarthy roads. Businesses in Kennicott include the Kennicott Glacier Lodge, a bed and breakfast, a flightseeing service and 2 guide services.

A camping area with bear-proof storage and a pit toilet is located 1.5 miles beyond Kennicott. There are no other designated campgrounds within the park/preserve; wilderness camping only. No permits are necessary for camping or backpacking although voluntary registration is requested. All water obtained from streams or lakes should be boiled or treated. Several BLM and state park campgrounds are located just outside the park boundaries along the Richardson Highway, Tok Cutoff and Edgerton Highway.

Access: The major road access is to the west side of the park via the Edgerton Highway to Chitina. From Chitina, the McCarthy Road extends some 60 miles to the Kennicott River just west of McCarthy. The McCarthy Road, a 3- to 4-hour drive, follows the abandoned railroad bed of the Copper River and Northwestern Railway. The road ends about a mile west of McCarthy at the 2 forks of the Kennicott River. Pedestrian bridges cross the river. It is about a 1-mile walk to McCarthy. It is about 5 miles from McCarthy to Kennicott by road; shuttle bus service is available in McCarthy.

Road access to the northern section of the park/preserve is from Slana (on the Tok Cutoff) via the 43-mile Nabesna Road. This gravel road is plowed intermittently in winter.

All other access to the park/preserve is by boat or air. There are 4,000-foot gravel airstrips at Chisana, McCarthy and May Creek. Floatplanes can land on lakes within the park/preserve. Flying services are located in McCarthy. Charter air service is also available from Anchorage, Fairbanks, Northway, Glennallen/Gulkana airport, McCarthy, Cordova, Valdez and Yakutat.

For more information: The park visitor center is located at Milepost V 105.1, just north of Copper Center on the Richardson Highway; rangers there provide briefings on the park and trip planning assistance. There are also ranger stations at Slana, Mile 0.2 Nabesna Road; Chitina, Mile 33 Edgerton Highway; and in Yakutat. Contact Wrangell St. Elias National Park and Preserve, Park Headquarters, P.O. Box 439, Copper Center, AK 99573; phone (907) 822-5234, fax (907) 822-7216; the Chitina Ranger Station, phone (907) 823-2205; Slana Ranger Station on Nabesna Road, phone (907) 822-5238, fax (907) 822-5248; Yakutat Ranger Station, phone (907) 784-3295, fax (907) 784-3535. Or visit www. nps.gov/wrst/cabins.htm. Or email wrst_interpretation@nps.gov.

(See also Cabins, Hiking Trails, Mountaineering and River Running this section.)

Leave No Trace Camping

Locate your campsite: 1 mile from the nearest airstrip; 200 feet from any water source; away from any game trail; where it will not intrude on the visual experience of others.

Avoid pitching your tent on vegetation.

Travel on durable surfaces. Avoid walking on vegetation.

Use a stove to avoid fire rings. If you do have a fire, destroy the fire ring, scatter the ashes and insure that the next camper will not observe your impact. In high-use areas, use existing fire rings.

Use only dead and downed wood; do not cut standing or living trees.

Pack out trash, including toilet paper.

Bury human waste at least 6 inches deep and 200 feet from water sources. On the coast, deposit human waste in the low tide zones.

Wash dishes and yourself 200 feet from water sources.

Minimize soap and food residues in waste water.

Minimize site alterations. Leave your campsite "naturalized" by replacing rocks, picking up bits of trash and scattering natural materials back where they were found.

Travel in small groups.

In popular areas, concentrate use. In remote areas, spread use.

Plan ahead by packaging food and selecting appropriate equipment.

Avoid contaminating water sources when cleaning fish.

Leave natural objects and cultural artifacts where you find them.

Avoid disturbing wildlife.

SOUTHWESTERN

Active volcanoes, fish-rich rivers, huge brown bears and remote storm-washed islands characterize this dramatic region of critical wildlife habitat that draws fishermen, hunters and bird-watchers from all over the world. Historically, it was the abundant marine mammal populations with their valuable furs that brought the first Russians to the Aleutians. Kodiak was Russian Alaska's first capital city. After 1867, when the United States purchased Alaska, the marine mammal populations were again hunted to near extinction. Later fox farming and fishing stirred the region's economy.

The Aleutians bore the brunt of WWII activities on Alaskan soil when the Japanese invaded Attu and Kiska islands and bombed Dutch Harbor. Kodiak Island was a prime target of the 1964 Good Friday earthquake, which measured 9.2 on the Richter scale. The land subsidence and tsunami that followed virtually destroyed downtown Kodiak.

Today most residents in the region live by fishing or seafood processing or are in the military. Kodiak is one of the largest commercial fishing ports in the United States, followed by Dutch Harbor-Unalaska. The federal government maintains bases in the Aleutians and on the Alaska Peninsula.

Access to the region is usually by air, although a state ferry regularly serves Kodiak and makes the run down the peninsula to the Aleutians about 4 times annually.

Location: This region takes in the Alaska Peninsula, which curves about 500 miles southwest from Naknek Lake to the first of the Aleutians and the 200 islands of the Kodiak Archipelago in the Gulf of Alaska. The more than 124 islands of the Aleutian chain and the Pribilof group to the north in the Bering Sea make up the rest of the region. The Aleutians, extending more than 1,000 miles from Unimak to remote Attu, separate the Bering Sea from the North Pacific in a divide known as the "birthplace of winds."

Geography: The Aleutians and Pribilofs are treeless tops of submerged volcanic mountains. Few rivers etch their steep slopes. The Aleutians sit atop the "Ring of Fire," a necklace of volcanoes around much of the Pacific Rim. Shishaldin Volcano on Unimak Island, highest point in the Aleutians, rises 9,372 feet above sea level and 32,472 feet from the ocean floor. Off the Pacific side of the region lies the Aleutian Trench, 2,000 miles long, 50 to 100 miles wide, and up to 25,000 feet deep, where continental plates meet and the Pacific plate is carried down into the earth. To the north, the Bering Sea slopes downward in a shallow underwater valley, 249 miles long and up to 10,677 feet deep.

In summer the Aleutians and Pribilofs are carpeted with thick grasses and abundant wildflowers. The islands are treeless except for a few stands, transplanted from other regions, which have survived in sheltered nooks.

The Alaska Peninsula is a slender spine, steep-sloped and topped with volcanoes on the Pacific side. Pavlof Volcano and Mount Veniaminof on the peninsula are active volcanoes, although neither has matched the huge and violent eruption of Novarupta Volcano in 1912, which created the Valley of Ten Thousand Smokes in Katmai National Park and Preserve. On the Bering Sea side, fish-clogged rivers drain from the peninsula's lakes down to the rich, coastal wetland along Bristol Bay.

Kodiak Island is known as the Emerald Island, and summers bring lush, tall green grass dotted with wildflowers. It is the largest island within the Kodiak Island group, followed in size by Afognak, Sitkalidak, Sitkinak, Raspberry, Tugidak, Shuyak, Uganik, Chirikof, Marmot and Spruce islands.

Climate: Rain is common in this region. Measurable precipitation occurs more than 200 days each year. Annual average is 33.44 inches at Cold Bay near the tip of the peninsula and 28.85 inches at Shemya in the western Aleutians. Kodiak averages 6 inches of rain a month during September, October and May, its wettest months, and planes are sometimes grounded by fierce storms off the Gulf of Alaska.

Aleutian weather has been called the worst in the world. Storm fronts generally move from west to east here. But climatic conditions on the Pacific side often differ vastly from those on the Bering side, placing the islands in the middle of a continual weather conflict.

Aleutian temperatures usually are milder than elsewhere in Alaska because of the chain's southern location and the moderating influence of surrounding waters. At Shemya summer temperatures range from 39°F to 53'F, with 28°F to 39°F in winter. Summer temperatures at Dutch Harbor in the eastern Aleutians range from 40°F to 60°F in summer and 27°F to 37°F in winter.

Wildlife: Brown/grizzly bears inhabit Unimak, easternmost of the Aleutians, but are absent from the rest of the chain and the Pribilofs. They are abundant on the peninsula, and Katmai rangers claim to have the largest unhunted brown/grizzly population in Alaska within their park's boundary. Hunters from all over the world come to Kodiak for its trophy-class brown bear.

The natural range of wolves, wolverine and most small mammals does not extend beyond Unimak Island. Only introduced mammal species inhabit the rest of the Aleutians with the possible exception of the arctic fox population in the western islands. Norway rats arrived aboard sailing ships in the mid-1800s and the Rat Islands were named for them.

Marine mammals, from the great baleen whales to sea lions, northern fur seals, true seals and sea otters, are found in numerous colonies. Seabirds, shorebirds and waterfowl by the millions throng to the peninsula, Aleutians and Pribilofs. More than 230 species have been recorded in the region.

Sockeye salmon congest the rivers of the peninsula in season; other species of salmon, grayling, arctic char, Dolly Varden and trout also fill the streams in this fishermen's paradise.

Offshore, commercial fishermen seek halibut, salmon, bottom fish, crab and shrimp.

Adak

GPS: N51°45′ W176°45′

Located on Kuluk Bay on Adak Island in the Aleutians, 1,200 miles southwest of Anchorage. Adak is a former military base currently in a period of transition as the Navy prepares to turn over the island to the Aleut Corp.

Transportation: Evergreen International Airlines carries mail, freight and passengers to Adak. **Population**: Currently 200; expected to increase to several thousand when resettled. Approximately 60 military and civilian contractors are working on the island during 2001. **Zip code**: FPO Seattle, WA 98791. **Emergency Services**: Navy Security, phone (907) 592-8051; Adak Medical Center; Aleutian Family Wellness Center, phone (907) 592-8383; Navy Branch Hospital; Adak Volunteer Fire/EMS, phone (907) 592-8400.

Elevation: 20 feet. **Climate**: The average relative humidity is 83 percent. Precipitation occurs throughout the year, including an average of 102 inches of snow during the winter months (November through March). Rain in the summer and occasional blizzards during the winter are common. Drizzle, ice, snow and fog occur at various times of the year. Adak is occasionally buffeted by intense storms which migrate east-northeastward. Average wind velocity throughout the Aleutian chain is 16 knots; however, winds in excess of 40 knots are not uncommon. The highest recorded gust is 109 knots in March 1954. Hence, Adak's well-known nickname, "birthplace of the winds."

Private Aircraft: Mitchell Field 1 mile from town; elev. 19 feet; 2 runways: length 7,790 and 7,606 feet; asphalt. No public transportation to town. *NOTE: Prior approval from the Navy required for all civilian aircraft.*

Visitor Facilities: There is no tourist or unsponsored casual visitation to Adak at this time. After the transfer of the island to the Aleut Corp., this situation is likely to change. There is a McDonald's and a Baskin-Robbins; other dining facilities are private at this time. Banking, laundromat/dry cleaning, barber/beauty shop and recreational services are available. Fishing/hunting licenses available; no guide services. Repair services available for autos. Rental cars available for island residents and authorized visitors. Available fuel limited to unleaded gasoline and JP5 (substitute for diesel). Moorage facilities available only for U.S. Navy or other military vessels, and vessels under government contract.

The former U.S. Navy base on 28-mile-long Adak Island, in the Andreanof group, was the westernmost city in the United States. Before its closure in March 1997, it was Alaska's largest naval base and "home" for the Naval Air Station, Naval Security Group Activity, Naval Facility, Marine Barracks and several other associated tenant commands and activities. Since 1986 the Navy has been involved in cleaning up hazardous ordnance left over from WWII and Cold War days. This cleanup will continue even after the transfer of the base to the Aleut Corp., which plans to develop a commercial fishing town and transportation hub on the island. In November 2000, the state granted Adak's request to incorporate as a city with authority to levy taxes, and in April 2001 a 7-member city council was elected.

There is archaeological evidence of earlier habitation, but Adak was unoccupied in 1942 when the military arrived after the outbreak of WWII. The installations on Adak are significant in the history of the Aleutian campaign because they allowed U.S. forces to mount a successful offensive against the Japanese-held islands of Kiska and Attu. Facilities from the old Adak Army base and Adak naval operating base have been nominated to the National Register of Historic Places. The Adak Community Museum houses WWII memorabilia, wildlife displays and Native artifacts.

The southern part of the island is part of Alaska Maritime National Wildlife Refuge. The U.S. Fish and Wildlife Service maintains a headquarters on the island.

Communications at Adak include phones, radio and TV. The base is served by 2 chapels and 2 schools with grades preschool through 12 with enrollment of 23. College courses are offered through the University of Alaska Extension Service. Utilities and services have been provided by the military up to this time. Government address: City of Adak, P.O. Box 1961, Adak, AK 99546-1961, phone (907) 592-4243, fax (907) 592-4140. Community non-profit: Adak Reuse Corp., P.O. Box, Adak, AK 99546, phone (907) 592-4506, fax (907) 592-4262, e-mail: srozar@ptialaska.net.

Akhiok

GPS: N56°56' W154°10'

(AH-ke-awk) Located at Alitak Bay on the south side of Kodiak Island 80 miles southwest of the city of Kodiak, 340 miles south-southwest of Anchorage. **Transportation**: Boat; scheduled or charter air service from Kodiak. **Population**: 99. **Zip code**: 99615. **Emergency Services**: Village Public Safety Officer, phone (907) 836-2213; Alaska State Troopers, Kodiak, phone (907) 486-4121; Akhiak Health Clinic, phone (907) 836-2230; Akhiok Village Response Team, at clinic, phone (907) 836-2230 (clinic) or (907) 836-2218; Volunteer Fire Department.

Elevation: 5O feet at airport. **Climate**: Strong marine influence, characterized by moderately heavy precipitation, cool temperatures, high clouds and frequent fog. Humidity generally high, temperature variation small. Little or no freezing weather. Average temperatures from 25°F

to 54°F. Annual precipitation 35 inches.

Private Aircraft: Airstrip 1 mile southwest, elev. 5O feet; length 3,320 feet; gravel; no fuel; unattended. Runway condition not monitored; visual inspection recommended prior to using. No public transportation to village.

Visitor Facilities: Arrange for accommodations at Community Building by contacting the City of Akhiok, phone (907) 836-2229. No other facilities or services available here. According to the city office there is a store at Alitak, 7 miles by skiff. Fuel available: marine gas, diesel, regular.

The name Akhiok was reported in the 1880 census. The village was renamed Alitak during WWI to avoid confusion with a village near Bethel called Akiak. The name later was changed back to Akhiok. Residents of Kaguyak relocated to Akhiok after the 1964 earthquake and tsunami washed out their village. The community was incorporated as a second-class city in 1972.

No roads connect Akhiok to any other town on Kodiak Island; a foot trail leads to the cannery.

The village is located adjacent to Kodiak National Wildlife Refuge. The community's Russian Orthodox church, Protection of the Theotokos Chapel, which was built around 1900 on the site of an earlier structure, is on the National Register of Historic Places.

The community originally was a sea otter-hunting settlement. With the decline of the sea otter industry; however, the village became oriented toward fishing, which today forms the basis of its economy. Many of the residents are commercial fishermen.

Other employers include the cannery, school, health services, the city and occasional construction jobs. Almost all of Akhiok's residents depend on subsistence fishing and hunting for various food sources, including salmon, crab, shrimp, scallop, clam, duck, seal, deer, rabbit and bear.

Communications in Akhiok include phones, shortwave radio, mail plane and TV. The community has a school with grades kindergarten through 12, with enrollment of 14. There are community electric, water and sewage systems. Freight arrives by barge or plane. Village government address: City of Akhiok, P.O. Box 5050, Akhiok, AK 99615, phone (907) 836-2229, fax (907) 836-2209. Village corporation: Akhiok/Kaguyak Inc., 1400 W. Benson Blvd., #330, Anchorage, AK 99503, phone (907) 258-0604, fax (907) 258-0608; or Ayakulik Inc., General Delivery, Akhiok, AK 99615, phone (907) 486-4349. Village council: Native Village of Akhiok, P.O. Box 5030, Akhiok, AK 99615-5030, phone (907) 836-2313, fax (907) 836-2345, e-mail: Akhiok@aitc.org.

Akutan

GPS: N54°08' W165°46'

Located on the north shore of Akutan Harbor on the east coast of Akutan Island, one of the Krenitzin Islands of the Fox Island group in the mid-Aleutian chain, 45 miles east of Unalaska, 750 miles southwest of Anchorage. **Transportation**: Boats; scheduled and charter amphibious aircraft from Dutch Harbor. **Population**: 425, plus temporary, seasonal processor workers. **Zip code**: 99553. **Emergency Services**: Police, phone (907) 698-2315; Anesia Kudrin Memorial Clinic, phone (907) 698-2208; Akutan First Responders, phone (907) 698-2208/2315; Volunteer Fire Department, phone 698-2227.

Climate: Maritime, characterized by mild winters and cool summers. High winds with gusts up to 100 mph are common in winter. Weather is frequently cloudy, and there is fog 64 percent of the days in July. The warmest month of the year is August; the coldest is February. Precipitation averages 28 inches per year.

Private Aircraft: No airstrip; amphibious or floatplane only, seaplane landing ramp.

Visitor Facilities: Accommodations available at Akutan Bayview Plaza, (907) 698-2206; meals at Grab-A-Dab Café, (907) 698-2260. There is a laundromat. Groceries, clothing, first-aid supplies, hardware, camera film and sporting goods are available in the community at Native Dockside Store, phone (907) 698-

2226, fax (907) 698-2207. No fishing/hunting licenses available; no guide service. Repair service for marine engines and boats may be available. Arrangements may be made to rent boats. Fuel available includes diesel and regular gasoline. Moorage facilities available. The village was established in 1878 as a fur storage and trading port by the Western Fur and Trading Co. The company's first resident agent helped establish a commercial cod fishing and processing business. Residents of nearby villages moved to Akutan and a church and school were built in 1878. The community was incorporated as a second-class city in 1979.

After the Japanese attacked Dutch Harbor and seized Attu and Kiska in June 1942, the U.S. government evacuated Akutan residents to the Ketchikan area. They were allowed to return in 1944, but many chose not to. Exposure to the outside world brought about many changes in the traditional lifestyle of the community. Although the Aleut language is still spoken in many homes, it is dying out; however, the community is making an effort to relearn its Native heritage through such things as traditional arts and crafts.

Librarian Doug Welch describes Akutan as "a quiet community of neighbors bridged together by a maze of boardwalks replacing roads. A place where people truly care and share."

Commercial fishing and fish processing dominate Akutan's economy. Trident Seafoods has one of the largest onshore fish processing plants in Alaska. There is also employment at the school, post office, store, tavern and clinic. Subsistence hunting and fishing also are important. Game includes seals, wild cattle, ducks and geese. Fish include salmon, pogies, black bass, cod, herring, halibut, flounder and trout. Shellfish include clams, sea urchins and "bidarkies" (chitons).

Alexander Nevsky Chapel, a Russian Orthodox church built in 1918 to replace the 1878 structure, is listed on the National Register of Historic Places.

Akutan Island is mountainous and rugged, and 4,275-foot Akutan Volcano is considered active, belching fire and smoke throughout the fall of 1978. Lava flows occasionally run into the sea on a distant side of the peak. Akutan village also is within an area affected by tsunamis. In 1946 a tsunami run-up reached 115 feet and destroyed Scotch Cap Lighthouse on the west side of Unimak Island facing Unimak Pass, less than 30 miles east of Akutan.

Communications in Akutan include phones, radio, fax, mail plane and TV. The community has a school with grades kindergarten through 12 with enrollment of 15. There are community electric, water and sewer systems. Freight arrives by ship or by air. Government address: City of Akutan, 1600 A St., Suite 103, Anchorage, AK 99501, phone (907) 274-7555, fax (907) 276-7569, e-mail: tantee@juno.com. Village corporation: Akutan Corp., Box 8, Akutan, AK 99553, phone (907) 698-2206, fax (907) 698-2207. Village council: Native Village of Akutan, P.O. Box 89, Akutan, AK 99553-0089, phone (907) 698-2228, fax (907) 698-2301, e-mail: Akutan@aitc.org.

Atka

GPS: N52°12' W174°12'

Located on Atka Island in the Andreanof Island group, 90 miles east of Adak, 1,100 miles southwest of Anchorage. **Transportation**: Scheduled aircraft from Unalaska. **Population**: 99. **Zip code**: 99547. **Emergency Services**: Village Public Safety Officer, phone (907) 839-2300; Atka Health Clinic, phone (907) 839-2232; Atka City EMS, phone (907) 839-2214; Volunteer Fire Department, (907) 839-2214.

Elevation: 40 feet. **Climate**: Atka's maritime climate is characterized by mild winters and cool summers. The wind is calm only 2.5 percent of the time. The warmest month is August; the coldest is February. Mean annual precipitation is 60 inches, including 61 inches of snow.

Private Aircraft: Airstrip 1.5 miles north; elev. 33 feet; length 3,287 feet; asphalt; unattended. Runway condition monitored by GPS/AWOS; visual inspection recommended prior to using.

Visitor Facilities: The City of Atka has 2 rooms with kitchen facilities for rent. The Atka Village Council has a 3-bedroom bed and breakfast for rent with kitchen and laundry facilities. Nazan Bay Inn, owned by APICDA Joint Venture, has 4 bedrooms with kitchen, laundry facilities and sauna. No banking services or laundromat. Groceries, first-aid supplies, hardware and film are available for purchase at Atka Native Store. There is a local Snack Bar, post office, and a processing plant: Atka Pride Seafoods. Local dock, maintained by the City of Atka. Atxam Corporation has crab pot storage. Traditional grass baskets may be sold locally. Fishing/hunting licenses available. No guide or repair services. Fuel available includes marine gas, diesel and regular gasoline. City has moorage facilities.

Atka is the most western and most isolated Native village on the Aleutian chain. The island has been occupied for at least 2,000 years and recent archaeological evidence suggests that the present village site may have had human use even earlier. The town was settled in the 1860s.

Atka residents were evacuated to the Ketchikan area after the Japanese attack on Dutch Harbor and seizure of Attu and Kiska in June 1942. The community was almost completely burned during the war by the Navy to keep the Japanese from using it. The Navy rebuilt it after the war. Many Attuans who had been held captive in Japan resettled in Atka after their release in 1945.

The community has persisted through the decades despite a lack of local jobs. After the end of the sea otter hunting era in the late 1800s, Atka had no cash economy, although it became relatively affluent during the fox farming boom in the 1920s. The economy today is based primarily on subsistence hunting and fishing and wages earned from Atka Pride Seafoods seasonal employment in the halibut fisheries around Atka.

The village is located within Alaska Maritime National Wildlife Refuge. Fish include halibut, salmon, black cod, rock bass, Pacific perch and king crab. Reindeer introduced in 1914 have multiplied and provide meat for the villagers. Foxes, seals, sea lions, fresh-water ducks and geese are also common.

Forming the northern end of the island is 4,852-foot Korovin Volcano, which has been active in recent years.

Communications in Atka, which incorporated in 1988 as a second-class city, include e-mail, phones, fax, and mail plane. The community is served by St. Nicholas Russian Orthodox Church and a school with grades kindergarten through 12 with enrollment of 19. Importation of alcohol is legal. Freight arrives at the community year-round. Government address: City of Atka, P.O. Box 47070, Atka, AK 99547, phone (907) 839-2233, fax (907) 839-2234, e-mail: atka2@arctic.net. Village corporation: Atxam Corp., P.O. Box 47001, Atka, AK 99547, phone (907) 839-2237, fax (907) 839-2217. Village council: Atka IRA Council, P.O. Box 47030, Atka, AK 99547, phone (907) 839-2229, fax (907) 839-2269, e-mail: Atka@aitc.org. Fisheries address: Atka Pride Seafoods, P.O. Box 47037, Atka, AK 99547, phone (907) 839-2221, fax (907) 839-2224.

Attu

GPS: N52°49' E173°10'

Located on Attu Island in the Aleutian chain, 1,700 miles west of Anchorage, 500 miles east of the USSR mainland. **Transportation**: Air charter or U.S. Coast Guard aircraft. **Population**: 29. **Zip code**: 99502.

Elevation: 60 feet. **Climate**: Storms and dense fog are common. Mean annual precipitation is 54 inches, including 86 inches of snow.

Private Aircraft: Airport at southeast end of island; elev. 40 feet; length 5,800 feet; asphalt. *NOTE: Civilian authorization other than emergency must be obtained from U.S. Coast Guard District 17, Juneau. No transient service or maintenance available.*

Visitor Facilities: No accommodations; camping only.

Attu Island is farthest west of the Aleutian chain and westernmost of the Near Islands. A Coast Guard loran station is located at Massacre Bay on the southeast coast of the island.

A granite memorial was dedicated at Attu in 1981 to honor American soldiers who fought and died in the Aleutians during WWII. Attu was the site of a brutal 19-day battle during May 1943 between American forces and Japanese entrenched on the island, second only to the Pacific theater's Iwo Jima in terms of troops involved. U.S. forces suffered 2,300 casualties, including 549 killed. While only 29 Japanese were captured on Attu, Americans counted 1,851 bodies and estimated 650 others had been buried in the hills. The Japanese have erected several monuments to their dead since the war. Much evidence of the battle still remains on the east end of the island. The Attu battlefield and old Army and Navy airfields have been named national historic landmarks; listed on the National Register of Historic Places is the wreckage of a P-38 fighter aircraft on the east bank of the Temnac River a mile from its mouth.

The entire island is part of Alaska Maritime National Wildlife Refuge, administered by the U.S. Fish and Wildlife Service. Arctic fox, sea otters, whales and a variety of North American and Asiatic birds can be seen on the island. Although remote, the island is popular for spring birding expeditions. For information about the refuge contact Refuge Manager, Aleutian Islands Unit, Alaska Maritime National Wildlife Refuge, PSC 486, Box 5251 (NAS), FPO, AP Adak, AK 96506-5251, phone (907) 592-2406.

Belkofski

(See King Cove)

Chignik

GPS: N56°18' W158°24'

Located on the south shore of the Alaska Peninsula at the head of Anchorage Bay, 5 miles southeast of Chignik Lagoon, 450 miles southwest of Anchorage. **Transportation**: Boat; scheduled airline and air charter from King Salmon; limited state ferry service from Kodiak in summer. **Population**: 96. **Zip code**: 99564. **Emergency Services**: Alaska State Troopers, King Salmon, phone (907) 246-3346; Chignik Bay

Subregional Clinic, phone (907) 749-2282; Emergency Care Center, Chignik Bay Fire and Rescue, phone (907) 749-2207/2282.

Elevation: 30 feet. **Climate**: Chignik's maritime climate is characterized by cool summers, relatively warm winters and rainy weather. Precipitation averages 127 inches annually with 58 inches of snow. Average temperature in January is 20°F; average in July is 65°F.

Private Aircraft: Airstrip 2 miles from village; elev. 50 feet; length 2,600 feet; gravel; no fuel; unattended. Runway condition not monitored; visual inspection recommended prior to using. Birds on and in vicinity of airfield. No airport facilities or public transportation to village.

Visitor Facilities: Accommodations available at Aleutian Dragon Fisheries guest house. Groceries and supplies at Chignik Community Store and Chignik Pride Store. Restaurant at The Bakery. There is a variety store, laundry and post office. Check with the City of Chignik about rental equipment. Fishing/hunting licenses available; no guide service. There is a 600-foot dock and boat haulout available. Marine vessel repair available. Fuel available includes marine gas, diesel, propane and regular gasoline; no avgas. Fuel is available through the fisheries.

Chignik, also called Chignik Bay, is an Aleut village established as a fishing village and cannery in the late 1800s on the site of an earlier Native village, Kaniagmuit, destroyed by the Russians in the 1700s. Chignik is a second-class city, incorporated in 1983.

Chignik's economy is based on commercial fishing for salmon, halibut, black cod and tanner crab. NorQuest Fisheries and Chignik Pride Fisheries operate year-round fishing processing plants here. During the summer, some 500 additional people come here to work in the commercial fishing and processing industry.

Most people in Chignik depend on subsistence hunting and fishing. Salmon are caught year-round. Other fish caught are rainbow trout and Dolly Varden. Dungeness, king and tanner crab, clams and octopus also are taken. Game includes moose, caribou, ptarmigan, ducks and geese.

The village is located within 3.5-million-acre Alaska Peninsula National Wildlife Refuge. During the winter, warm ocean currents keep much of the water relatively ice free and thousands of Steller's, common and king eiders, scoters, harlequins, oldsquaws and loons winter there. Brant and Canada geese fly over Chignik in the spring and fall. There are many seabird colonies along the coast and cormorants, puffins, murres, black-legged kittiwakes, gulls, terns and jaegers are occasional visitors at Chignik. Bald eagles, common along the coast, concentrate along streams during the salmon runs and along lagoons and bays in the winter. Peregrine falcons nest in the area, usually near seabird colonies.

A variety of marine mammals are present near Chignik, including harbor seals, sea otters, Steller sea lions, Dall porpoises and several species of whales.

Communications in Chignik include phones, mail plane and TV. The community is served by a church and a school with grades kindergarten through 12 with enrollment of 11. There are public water, sewer and electric systems. Freight arrives by barge. Government address: City of Chignik, P.O. Box 110, Chignik, AK 99564, phone (907) 749-2280, fax (907) 749-2300. Village corporation: Far West Inc., General Delivery, Chignik, AK 99564, phone (907) 749-2230. Village council: Chignik Bay Village Council, Box 50, Chignik, AK 99564, phone (907) 749-2445, fax (907) 749-2423. e-mail: CbayTC@aol.com.

Chignik Lagoon

GPS: N56°20' W158°29'

Located on the south shore of the Alaska Peninsula 5 miles west of Chignik, 450 miles southwest of Anchorage. **Transportation**: Boat; charter plane from King Salmon, Dillingham or Kodiak. **Population**: 68. **Zip code**: 99565. **Emergency Services**: Alaska State Troopers, King Salmon, phone (907) 246-3346; Chignik Health Clinic, phone (907) 840-2218; Chignik First Responder

Group, phone (907) 840-2248. Volunteer Fire Department.

Elevation: 50 feet. **Climate**: Maritime climate characterized by cool summers, relatively warm winters and rainy weather. Total precipitation averages 127 inches annually, with an average of 58 inches of snow. Summer temperatures range from 39°F to 60°F; winter temperatures range from 21°F to 36°F.

Private Aircraft: Airstrip adjacent southwest; elev. 50 feet; length 1,600 feet; gravel; unattended. Runway condition not monitored; visual inspection recommended prior to using. Seabirds on and near airfield. No airport facilities or transportation to village. Public domain seaplane base.

Visitor Facilities: Accommodations available at Chignik Lagoon School during school months. Eagles Roost bed and breakfast, phone (907) 840-2273. No laundromat or banking services; 1 small restaurant (fast food). Small grocery store. No arts and crafts available for purchase. Fuel available from Chignik Lagoon Council. No public moorage facilities.

Chignik Lagoon took its name from its proximity to Chignik. The area was originally populated by Kaniagmiut Eskimos. After the Russian occupation, intermarriage of Kaniags and Aleuts produced the Koniags who now reside in Chignik Lagoon. The village was a fishing village and now serves, along with Chignik, as a regional fishing center. The community is not incorporated.

Subsistence hunting and fishing are the mainstay of the local economy, with commercial fishing providing seasonal employment. Fish include pink, chum and silver salmon, cod, black bass, halibut, rainbow trout and Dolly Varden. Also taken are Dungeness, king and tanner crab, clams and octopus. Game includes moose, caribou, ptarmigan, ducks and geese. In the fall, residents pick blueberries, cranberries, raspberries and salmonberries.

Veniaminof Volcano (erupted in 1983) dominates the horizon to the west, sending up occasional puffs of steam. Wildflowers abound along the beaches and there is fossil hunting along the

north side of the lagoon. The nearby valley provides hiking opportunities, although care must be taken not to surprise brown bears. Eagles can be observed nesting and hunting in the area. There is beach recreation along Ocean Spit, which protects the lagoon from the open sea.

Communications in Chignik Lagoon include phones, mail plane, post office, radio and TV. There are church services in the summer. The school has grades kindergarten through 8 with 29 enrolled. No community electricity, but there are water and sewer systems. Freight arrives by plane, barge and ship. Government address: Native Village of Chignik, General Delivery, Chignik Lagoon, AK 99565, phone (907) 840-2206. Village corporation address: Chignik Lagoon Native Corp., General Delivery, Chignik Lagoon, AK 99565, phone (907) 840-2262.

Chignik Lake
GPS: N56°14' W158°47'

Located on Chignik Lake on the Alaska Peninsula, 15 miles southwest of Chignik, 265 miles southwest of Kodiak. **Transportation**: Scheduled airline and air charter from Anchorage. **Population**: 136. **Zip code**: 99548. **Emergency Services**: Chignik Lake Health Clinic, phone (907) 845-2236; Chignik Lake Rescue Squad, phone (907) 845-2245.

Climate: Cool summers, warm winters. Summer temperatures range from 39°F to 60°F. Average winter temperatures range from 21°F to 50°F.

Private Aircraft: Airstrip adjacent southwest; elev. 50 feet; length 2,800 feet; gravel; unattended. Runway condition not monitored; visual inspection recommended prior to using. No airport facilities or transportation to village.

Visitor Facilities: Groceries can be purchased from J&K Co., (907) 845-2228. Fuel available from local fuel company.

Established in the 1950s, the village has developed as a fishing village. During the summer, most residents move to a fish camp near the village of Chignik Lagoon.

Communications include phone, mail plane, radio and TV. There is a washeteria and community well. Electricity is purchased from the school. Sewage system is private septic tanks. There are 15 HUD homes and a sewage treatment lagoon. The community has an old and a new Russian Orthodox church. School offers preschool through grade 12 with 44 enrolled. Freight arrives by air transport and barge. Village corporation address: Chignik River Limited, P.O. Box 4, Chignik Lake, AK 99548. Government address: Chignik Lake Village Council, P.O. Box 33, Chignik Lake, AK 99548; phone (907) 845-2212, fax (907) 845-2217, e-mail: chigniklake@aitc.org.

Cold Bay

GPS: N55°12' W162°42'

Located on the west shore of Cold Bay, 40 miles from the extreme westerly tip of the Alaska Peninsula, 630 miles southwest of Anchorage. **Transportation**: 40-mile gravel road system; boat; scheduled and charter service from Anchorage and local area via PenAir; limited state ferry access in summer. **Population**: 104. **Zip code**: 99571. **Emergency Services**: Alaska State Troopers, Sand Point, phone (907) 383-3535; Anna Livingston Memorial Clinic, phone (907) 532-2000; Peter Pan Seafoods' Port Moller Medical Clinic (seasonal), phone (907) 987-2207; Volunteer Fire Department, phone (907) 532-2416; Cold Bay EMS Squad/Ambulance, phone (907) 532-2437/2447.

Elevation: 100 feet. **Climate**: The area has frequent but light rains, cool temperatures, high clouds and fog. Measurable precipitation occurs approximately 200 days per year. Mean annual precipitation is 35 inches, including 55 inches of snow.

Private Aircraft: Airport adjacent north; elev. 98 feet; length 10,420 feet; asphalt; fuel 100, jet A; attended. The paved, crosswind runway is one of the largest in the state. All facilities at airport; no public transportation to town.

Visitor Facilities: Pavlof Services, (907) 532-2437, operates a restaurant, bar and hotel and sells groceries. There is a laundromat. No banking services. Fishing/hunting licenses available. Truck rental available from Cold Bay Truck Rental, (907) 532-2404. Fuel available includes white gas, kerosene, diesel and regular gasoline. No moorage facilities. A new dock was built in 1993.

Cold Bay was near the southern edge of the Bering Land Bridge and may have played an important role in the migration of Asiatic peoples to North America. Although not yet excavated, the presence of numerous middens in the area suggests that it was inhabited by a relatively large population of Native people. Russian ships wintered nearby during the first coastal explorations by Europeans. The name Izembek was bestowed on the region in 1827 by Count Feodor Lutke when he named Izembek Lagoon after Karl Izembek, surgeon aboard the sloop *Moller*.

After the onset of WWII a large air base was built at Cold Bay. The airstrip is the third longest in Alaska and the airport now serves as the transportation and communications hub for the entire Aleutian-Pribilof islands region. An FAA office is located here. Cold Bay is used to visitors and welcomes tourists, fishermen and others coming through this isolated community.

Cold Bay is the gateway to Izembek National Wildlife Refuge and the southwestern portion of 3.5-million-acre Alaska Peninsula National Wildlife Refuge. Izembek refuge attracts 142 species of birds, but was established in 1960 primarily to benefit the brant. Izembek Lagoon has the world's largest eelgrass beds on which more than 100,000 brant, the North American continent's entire population, feed during spring and fall migrations. For more information, contact the Refuge Manager, Izembek National Wildlife Refuge, Pouch 2, Cold Bay, AK 99571, phone (907) 532-2445, fax (907) 532-2549. (See also Izembek National Wildlife Refuge in Attractions.)

Cold Bay has been called the Canada goose hunting capital of the world. Up to 70,000 Canada geese migrate through Cold Bay in the fall. Also plentiful in the area are red, blue and cross fox, brown bear and park squirrels.

The west side of the Izembek Lagoon also is the site of the wreck of the 3-masted schooner Courtney Ford in 1902. It is a good example of commercial ships used in the late 19th century and is the oldest intact hull in the state.

The land surrounding Cold Bay is rolling and treeless. Mount Frosty, a 5,785-foot-high volcano, is located 9 miles southwest of town. Two active volcanoes, Pavlof (35 miles east) and Shishaldin (60 miles west), are visible from Cold Bay when weather permits. The weather in this broad, exposed area is among the worst along the Alaska Peninsula and probably has contributed more to limiting development than any other factor.

There is good fishing in the area for Dolly Varden, salmon, steelhead, arctic char, Pacific cod, flounder and halibut. Contact the Alaska Dept. of Fish and Game, Box 127, Cold Bay, AK 99571, for more information. The City of Cold Bay and the Emergency Medical Squad sponsor a Silver Salmon Derby every Labor Day weekend. It is not unusual for 18 to 20 lb. silver salmon to be caught.

Communications in Cold Bay, a second-class city incorporated in 1982, include phones, fax, mail plane and radio. The community is served by a church and a school with grades kindergarten through 12 with enrollment of 23. Community water, sewer, electricity available. Freight arrives in the community by cargo plane and barge. Government address: City of Cold Bay, P.O. Box 10, Cold Bay, AK 99571, phone (907) 532-2401, fax (907) 532-2671, e-mail: shicks@corecom.net. Aleutians East Borough, P.O. Box 349, Sand Point, AK 99661, phone (907) 383-2699, fax (907) 383-3496, e-mail: aebclerk@aol.com, Web: http://www.aleutianseast.org/.

Danger Bay
(See Kazakof Bay)

Dutch Harbor
(See Unalaska)

Egegik
GPS: N58°13' W162°42'

(EEG-gah-gik) Located on the northwest coast of the Alaska Peninsula near the mouth of the Egegik River, 50 miles south of King Salmon and 340 miles west of Anchorage. **Transportation**: Boat; scheduled and charter plane. **Population**: 123 in winter; 1,000 to 3,000 in summer. **Zip code**: 99579. **Emergency Services**: Public Safety Officer, phone (907) 233-2202; Egegik Health Clinic, phone (907) 233-2229; Egegik First Responders, phone (907) 233-2202/2244.

Elevation: 50 feet. **Climate**: The predominantly maritime climate is characterized by cool, humid and windy weather. Average summer temperatures range from 42°F to 63°F; average winter temperatures range from -29°F to 40°F. Total precipitation averages 20 inches annually; average annual snowfall is 45 inches.

Private Aircraft: Airstrip adjacent northeast; elev. 100 feet; length 3,000 feet; gravel; fuel limited 80, 100; unattended. Runway condition not monitored; visual inspection recommended prior to using. Tie-down chain available. Transportation to village with air carrier agent.

Visitor Facilities: Accommodations in private homes. A community-owned facility has a few rooms with showers available; phone (907) 233-2211 for more information. Meals at lodge or at restaurants in town during summer. Laundromat available; no banking services. Groceries, some clothing, hardware, film and sporting goods may be purchased in the community. Arts and crafts available for purchase include carved ivory and fur hats. Fishing/hunting licenses available, as well as guide service. Marine engine and boat repair available in summer. No rental transportation. Fuel available includes marine gas, diesel, propane and regular gasoline. No moorage facilities.

This village was first reported as a fish camp called Igagik during the early U.S. administration of 1867 to 1890. In 1895, the Alaska Packers Assoc. established a salmon saltery at the mouth of the river. The town developed around a cannery in the early 1900s, that also was established at the river's mouth. Egegik is unincorporated.

The economy in Egegik is based on commercial fishing, and residents there claim one of the largest red salmon runs in the world. Several canneries in the area provide seasonal employment from May to August. Residents supplement their income with subsistence hunting and fishing.

Becharof National Wildlife Refuge is accessible by plane or skiff up the Egegik River. There is sportfishing for salmon and trout and hunting for caribou and bear. (See also Wildlife Refuges in Attractions.)

Communications in Egegik include phones, mail plane, radio and TV. The community is served by the Egegik Bible Church and a school with grades kindergarten through 12 with enrollment of 20. There is a community electrical system and public water and sewer. Freight arrives by cargo plane and barge. Government address: City of Egegik, P.O. Box 189, Egegik, AK 99578, phone (907) 233-2240, fax (907) 233-2231, e-mail: john@cityofegegik.com. Village corporation: Becharof Corp., 1577 C Street Plaza #124, Anchorage, AK 99501, phone (907) 263-9820. Village Council: Egegik Village Tribal Council, P.O. Box 29, Egegik, AK 99579, phone (907) 233-2211, fax (907) 233-2312, e-mail: Egigik@aitc.org.

False Pass

GPS: N54°51' W163°24'

Located on the east end of Unimak Island on Isanotski Strait which separates Unimak Island from the Alaska Peninsula, 35 miles southwest of Cold Bay, 646 air miles southwest of Anchorage. **Transportation**: Boat; scheduled and charter airline from Cold Bay. **Population**: 72, plus temporary processor workers. **Zip code**: 99583. **Emergency Services**: Village Public Safety Officer; False Pass Clinic, False Pass First Responders (Clinic EMT), phone (907) 548-2241. Fire Department.

Elevation: 20 feet. **Climate**: Mild winters and cool summers. The warmest month is August; the coldest is February. Average annual precipitation at Cold Bay is 33 inches, including 56 inches of snow.

Private Aircraft: Airstrip adjacent south; elev. 20 feet; length 2,100 feet; gravel; no fuel available; unattended. Runway condition not monitored; visual inspection recommended prior to using.

Surface may be soft during spring thaw and heavy rains.

Visitor Facilities: Accommodations are limited. There is one bed and breakfast, and bunkhouse rooms may be available seasonally at Bering Pacific or Peter Pan. Food available at Peter Pan Seafoods cookhouse (May through August) or at Bering Pacific Seafoods; groceries and supplies may be obtained at Peter Pan Seafoods store year-round. Fishing/hunting licenses available. No guide service. Rental transportation includes boats, charter aircraft from Cold Bay. Fuel available includes marine gas, diesel, propane and regular gas. Moorage facilities available. New (1993) deep-water city dock.

Isanotski is the Russianized Aleut word "Issanak" or "Isanax" which means The Pass. Americans whose large ships could not navigate through the narrow Isanotski Strait into the Bering Sea from the Gulf of Alaska called it False Pass. The name stuck for the village. The strait is used extensively by vessels under 150 feet and the U.S. Coast Guard has buoyed the entrance to guide the vessels.

False Pass was settled in the early 1900s by homesteader William Gardner. A cannery, established by P.E. Harris, was relocated to False Pass from Mozhovoi Bay. As the cannery grew, additional people moved to the area. An airstrip and school were built in the early 1960s, and the city was incorporated in 1990. The cannery, now Peter Pan Seafoods, is owned by the Nichiro Corp. of Japan A new processor, Bering Pacific Seafoods, started operation in June 2000.

The local economy is based on the commercial salmon, halibut, herring and cod fisheries. False Pass is also an important stop for fishing fleets enroute to Bristol Bay and the Bering Sea fishing grounds.

Subsistence hunting and fishing also play an important role in the local economy. The area has abundant geese, ducks, caribou, bear, seals, octopus, cod, halibut, salmon and a variety of berries. The Ikatan River offers sportfishing.

The village is located within Alaska Maritime National Wildlife Refuge. Bears are often seen near the village. During migrations, spectacular concentrations of waterfowl rest and feed in the freshwater and saltwater wetlands, lagoons and shoals bordering the Bering Sea side of the pass. St. Catherine's Cove is a highly recommended bird-watching spot. Shorebirds frequent the beaches, tidal flats and shallow areas. Harbor seals are abundant; sea lions are present; an occasional walrus also is observed. The once-rare sea otter reestablished itself in the area and is now abundant.

Communications in False Pass include phones, fax, mail plane, radio and TV. There are no churches. The community has a school with grades kindergarten through 12 with 13 enrolled. Freight arrives by cargo plane, barge and ship. Government address: City of False Pass, P.O. Box 50, False Pass, AK 99583, phone (907) 383-2319, fax (907) 383-2214. e-mail: cityof-falsepass@ak.net. Village corporation: Isanotski Corp., 101 Isanotski Drive, False Pass, AK 99583, phone (907) 548-2217, fax (907) 548-2214. Village council: False Pass Tribal Council, P.O. Box 29, False Pass, AK 99583, phone 548-2227, fax (907) 548-2256, e-mail: FalsePass@aitc.org.

Ivanof Bay

GPS: N55°54' W159°29'

Located on the Alaska Peninsula at the north end of Ivanof Bay on the northeast end of the Kupreanof Peninsula, 200 miles from Sand Point, 510 miles southwest of Anchorage. **Transportation**: Scheduled air service available. **Population**: 29. **Zip code**: 99695. **Emergency Services**: Alaska State Troopers, Sand Point; Ivanof Bay Health Clinic, phone (907) 669-2213; Ivanof Bay First Responders, phone (907) 669-2218.

Climate: Maritime climate characterized by cool summers, relatively warm winters and rainy weather. Total precipitation at Chignik, the nearest weather station 50 miles away, averages 127 inches annually. Average annual snowfall is 58 inches.

Private Aircraft: No public airstrip; private airstrip 0.3 mile from village; no airport facilities; no transportation to village. Approximately 10,000 feet of open water used for seaplane landing. High winds occasionally create violent turbulence.

Visitor Facilities: The local community hall accommodates 4 people in 2 rooms; kitchen and dining area. Contact Elizabeth or Archie Kalmakoff at the Ivanof Village Council, (907) 669-2207. The Kalmakoffs also run the K-Family Market. No restaurant, laundromat or banking services. No arts and crafts available. Fishing/ hunting licenses not available. No guides, major repair service, rental transportation or moorage facilities. Fuel may be available.

The bay on which this predominantly Aleut village is located was named by Lieutenant Dall of the U.S. Coast and Geodetic Survey in 1880. The village occupies the site of a former salmon cannery which operated from the 1930s to the early 1950s.

Almost all residents of Ivanof Bay fish for a living. Most families move to cabins in Chignik for the summer salmon fishing season. A few residents work for the store, school and village, and most of the men run traplines in the winter for mink, otter, red fox, wolverine, ermine and lynx. Subsistence hunting and fishing also play a big role in the economy of Ivanof Bay.

Fish include salmon, cod, black bass and halibut. Also taken are king and Dungeness crab, cockles and clams. Game includes moose, caribou, bear, ptarmigan, ducks, geese, seals, porcupine and rabbits.

Communications include phones, mail plane, radio and TV. There is no church or school. There are community electric and water systems. Freight arrives by air. Government address: Ivanof Bay Village, P.O. Box KlB, Ivanof Bay, AK 99695, phone (907) 669-2200, fax (907) 669-2207, e-mail: IvanoffBay@aitc.org.

Karluk

GPS: N57°34' W154°27'

Located on Karluk Lagoon on the west coast of Kodiak Island 75 air miles from Kodiak. **Transportation**: Boat; scheduled and charter air service from Kodiak. **Population**: 41. **Zip code**: 99608. **Emergency Services**: Village Public Safety Officer, phone (907) 241-2230; Alaska State Troopers, Kodiak, phone (907) 486-

4761; Karluk Health Clinic, Karluk Village Response Team (Clinic), phone (907) 241-2222; Kodiak Hospital, phone (907) 486-3281; Volunteer Fire Department.

Elevation: 137 feet at airport. **Climate**: Kodiak Island has a strong marine influence, characterized by moderately heavy precipitation, cool temperatures and frequent clouds and fog, with little or no freezing weather. Humidity is generally high and the temperature variation is small. Temperature at Karluk ranges from 31°F to 54°F.

Private Aircraft: Airstrip 1 mile east; elev. 137 feet; length 2,000 feet; gravel; no fuel; unattended. Runway condition not monitored; visual inspection recommended prior to using.

Visitor Facilities: No overnight accommodations or restaurant available at the village. Accommodations in summer at a private fishing lodge located across Karluk Lagoon from the village. No banking services or laundromat. Limited groceries, first-aid supplies and hardware available at small store operated by tribal council; most supplies obtained from Kodiak. No arts and crafts available for purchase. Fishing/hunting licenses and guide services available. No rental transportation, major repair services, moorage facilities or fuel available.

Prior to 1979, the village was located on both sides of the Karluk River at Karluk Lagoon. A spit and footbridge connected Old Karluk on the northeast side of the lagoon with Karluk on the southwest side. On January 7 and 8, 1978, waves driven by northeasterly winds reaching 100 mph breached the spit at the mouth of the river. Travel between the 2 settlements was disrupted and the residents decided to relocate to an entirely new site about 0.75 mile upstream on the south side of the lagoon.

Karluk has been inhabited by the Alutiiq people for more than 7,000 years. Russian hunters established a trading post in Karluk in 1786; however, the mouth of the Karluk River is thought to have been populated many hundreds of years before the Russians' arrival. In 1805, Capt. U.T. Lisianski of the Imperial Russian Navy reported the name of the settlement as "Carlook" or "Karloock." Between 1790 and 1850 many tanneries, salteries and canneries were established in the area. In 1890, Karluk was renowned for having the largest salmon cannery in the world and the river was known as the greatest red salmon stream in the world.

In the early 1900s canneries were constructed by the Alaska Packers Assoc. Overfishing of the area forced the canneries to close in the 1930s, and today the buildings stand vacant and deteriorating.

Karluk is located adjacent to the Kodiak National Wildlife Refuge. The community's Ascension of Our Lord Russian Orthodox Chapel, built in 1888, is a national historic site.

Fishing is the primary source of livelihood for Karluk residents; there are a few year-round, part-time positions. Almost all residents depend on fishing and hunting as a food source. Species found in the area include salmon, trout, steelhead, flounder, duck, seal, deer, reindeer, rabbit and ptarmigan.

NOTE: *Land along the Karluk River as well as the riverbed is owned by Koniag Inc. There is a $125/per-person fee for fishing or camping on the Karluk River. Permits may be obtained from Koniag Inc., 202 Center St., Ste. 201, Kodiak, AK 99615, phone (907) 486-2530.*

Communications in unincorporated Karluk include phones, daily mail plane, commercial radio from Kodiak and satellite TV. The community has a school with grades kindergarten through 10. There are community electric, water and sewage systems. Freight arrives by mail plane and charter planes, fishing boats and occasional barges. Government address: Native Village of Karluk, P.o. Box 22, Karluk, AK 99608, phone (907) 241-2218. fax (907) 241-2208, e-mail: Karluk@aitc.org. Village corporation, Koniag Inc., 202 Center St., Ste. 201, Kodiak, AK 99615, phone (907) 486-2530.

Kazakof Bay

Located at Kazakof (Danger) Bay on Afognak Island, approximately 20 miles north of Kodiak. **Transportation**: Boat or charter air service. **Population**: Private logging camp; size **Zip varies**. code: 99615. **Emergency Services**: EMT aide at logging camp; Alaska State Troopers, Kodiak; Kodiak Hospital, phone (907) 486-3281; Coast Guard, call operator and ask for Zenith 5555.

Climate: Summers moist and cool, with highs occasionally up to 75°F. Winters windy, wet and gray, with low temperatures reaching 0°F. Average temperature from November to the first of March is 20°F.

Private Aircraft: No airstrip. Floatplane landings only.

Visitor Facilities: Fishing and hunting cabins are available for rent from Afognak Native Corp., phone (907) 486-6014. No restaurant, laundromat or banking services. No stores; supplies are obtained from Kodiak. No rental transportation; public moorage facilities available.

Alaska's only elk herds live on Afognak and nearby Raspberry Island. Other wildlife includes Sitka black-tailed deer and Kodiak brown bear, as well as otter, fox and marten. Fishing is active from late May to mid-September for pink, red, chum and coho salmon, Dolly Varden and rainbow trout. Halibut also are available. Waters around Afognak are fished commercially for salmon, tanner and Dungeness crab, halibut, and herring. Photography, hiking and kayaking are also favorite pastimes.

Air and boat charters are available in Kodiak for the 15-minute flight or 1 1/2- to 3-hour boat trip to Kazakof Bay. Communications at the camp include daily mail planes and telephone service. The camp has its own electric, water and sewer services. Freight arrives by plane, barge or charter boats.

Much of Afognak Island is owned by the Afognak Native Corp., Box 1277, Kodiak, AK 99615, phone (907) 486-6014, fax (907) 486-2514. Contact the corporation to reserve cabins or to use private lands.

King Cove

GPS: N55°03' W162°19'

Located on the Pacific Ocean side of the Alaska Peninsula, 18 miles southeast of Cold Bay, 630 miles southwest of Anchorage. **Transportation**: Boat; scheduled and charter aircraft from Cold Bay or Sand Point. **Population**: 671; almost double that number during fishing season. **Zip code**: 99612. **Emergency Services**: Police, phone (907) 497-2211; King Cove Medical Clinic, phone (907) 497-2311; King Cove Volunteer Fire Department, phone (907) 497-2553.

Climate: King Cove's maritime climate is characterized by mild winters and cool summers. The warmest month is August; the coldest is February. Precipitation averages 33 inches per year at Cold Bay.

Private Aircraft: Airstrip 4.8 miles northeast; elev. 148 feet; length 3,360 feet; gravel; no fuel; unattended. No airport facilities. Public transportation available to town. Runway condition not monitored; visual inspection recommended prior to using.

Visitor Facilities: Accommodations at Fleets Inn, (907) 497-2312. There are 2 restaurants: Fleets Inn, and Dobsons Pizza, (907) 497-2292. A laundromat is available at the hotel for guests. No banking services. Groceries, clothing, first-aid supplies, hardware, camera film and sporting goods may be purchased at Peter Pan Seafoods, (907) 497-2234, or John Gould & Sons, (907) 497-2212. No arts and crafts are available. Fishing/hunting licenses available. There is no guide service. Auto repair service is available and arrangements may be made to rent autos. Fuel available includes marine gas, diesel, propane and regular gas. Moorage facilities are available.

King Cove, one of the larger communities in the Aleutian region, was founded in 1911 when Pacific American Fisheries built a salmon cannery. It is a first-class city, incorporated in 1947. Although the cannery burned down in 1976, it was immediately rebuilt and is now the largest cannery operation under one roof in Alaska.

The community has a fairly stable economy, dependent almost entirely on fishing and seafood processing. Other employment locally is with the store, school and city government. Subsistence activities add salmon, halibut, caribou, waterfowl, eggs of marine birds, ptarmigan and berries to local diets.

King Cove is located near the 4.3-million-acre Alaska Peninsula National Wildlife Refuge. The Alaska Peninsula has long been a major big-game hunting area, especially for huge brown/grizzly bears. Other mammals found in the refuge are caribou, wolves and wolverine.

King Cove is 20 miles east of 5,784-foot Frosty Peak, a dormant volcano. The active Pavlof Volcano complex and Cathedral Ledge are 40 miles east of King Cove.

Twelve miles southeast of King Cove lies the ghost town of Belkofski, settled in 1823 by Russians who reported the name as Selo Belkovskoe, from the word "belka," meaning squirrel. The Russians came to harvest sea otters in the Sandmand Reefs and other near-shore banks. During the height of this exploitation, Belkofski was one of the most affluent villages in the area. The near extinction of the sea otter forced residents to seek subsistence elsewhere.

An imposing Holy Resurrection Russian Orthodox Church was built in Belkofski in the 1880s, and the village became an administrative center for the church. The structure is on the National Register of Historic Places. When the last of the Belkofski residents moved to King Cove in the early 1980s, they took the church's bell and icons with them and built a new Orthodox church at King Cove. A seldom-used trail connects the former village to King Cove.

King Cove goes all out for the Fourth of July with a fishing derby, games, contests, a community barbecue and fireworks display.

Communications at King Cove include phones, mail plane and TV. Radio reception is occasional. The community has 2 churches and a school with grades kindergarten through 12. with 121 enrolled. There are community electric, water and sewer systems. Freight arrives by cargo plane, barge and ship. Government address: City of King Cove, P.O. Box 37, King Cove, AK 99612, phone (907) 497-

2340, fax (907) 497-2594. Village corporation: King Cove Corp., P.O. Box 38, King Cove, AK 99612, phone (907) 497-2312, fax (907) 497-2444. Village council: Agdaagux Tribe of King Cove, P.O. Box 38, King Cove, AK 99612, phone (907) 497-2648, fax (907) 497-2803, e-mail: Agdaagux@aitc.org. Aleutians East Borough, P.O. Box 349, Sand Point, AK 99661, phone (907) 383-2699, fax (907) 383-3496, e-mail: aeb clerk@aol.com, web: http/www.aleutianseast.org/.

King Salmon

GPS: N58°41' W156°39'

Located on the Alaska Peninsula on the Naknek River, 15 miles east of Naknek, 290 miles southwest of Anchorage. **Transportation**: Scheduled air service via PenAir from Anchorage. **Population**: 499. **Zip code**: 99613. **Emergency Services**: Police, phone (907) 246-4222; Alaska State Troopers, phone (907) 246-3346; King Salmon Health Clinic, (907) 246-3322; Camai Clinic, Naknek, phone (907) 246-6155; Volunteer Fire Department.

Elevation: 50 feet. **Climate**: Cool, humid and windy weather. Average summer temperatures range from 42°F to 63°F; average winter temperatures range from 29°F to 44°F. Total precipitation averages 20 inches annually, including an average snowfall of 48 inches. Cloud cover is present an average of 76 percent of the time year-round. Naknek River is usually ice free between May and October.

Private Aircraft: Airport adjacent southeast; elev. 57 feet; length 8,500 feet; asphalt; fuel 100, jet A; attended. Passenger and freight terminals, ticket counter, restrooms; visitor center. Traffic control tower at airport scheduled to close January 2002. Transportation available. *CAUTION: U.S. Air Force uses King Salmon for annual training exercises, although response aircraft are no longer stationed here.*

Visitor Facilities: Accommodations at Quinnat Landing Hotel, (907) 246-3000 or 1-800-770-3474; and King Ko Inn, (907) 246-3377, fax (907) 246-3357; both offer restaurants and lounges. Area lodges include Antlers Inn, (907) 246-8525 or 1-888-735-8525; Bear Trail Lodge, (907) 246-2327, fax (907) 246-7297; Eagle Bluff Lodge, (907) 246-4464; Last Frontier Lodge, (907) 246-4269; Naknek Riverine Lodge, (907) 246-4270; Ponderosa Lodge, (907) 246-3444, fax (907) 246-6898; and Prestage's Sportfishing Lodge, (907) 246-3320. Lodging and boat rental at Rainbow Bend Cabin/Boat Rental, (907) 246-3750 or 1-888-575-4249. Restaurant and lounge at Eddie's Fireplace Inn, (907) 246-3435. Groceries, and sundry items may be purchased at City Market. Banking services available. Laundromat. Arts and crafts available for purchase include carved ivory, baskets and masks. Fishing/hunting licenses available, as well as guide service. Major repair service for marine engines, boats and aircraft. Rental transportation includes autos, boats and charter aircraft. Boat rental at R&G Boat Rental, (907) 246-3353. Fuel available includes marine gas and regular gas. Moorage facilities. NOTE: Land on the south side of the Naknek River from King Salmon is owned by the Alaska Peninsula Corp. Contact the corporation for details on use and fees.

In the 1930s, an air navigation silo was built at the present site of King Salmon. At the onset of WWII an Air Force base was constructed as the major military installation in western Alaska. In 1949, the U.S. Army Corps of Engineers built the road connecting King Salmon to Naknek. The community, located in the Bristol Bay Borough, has continued to develop as a government, transportation and service center.

King Salmon is the gateway to several large lakes on the Alaska Peninsula (Naknek, Iliamna, Becharof, Ugashik) and to Katmai National Park and Preserve. A 10-mile unimproved road leads from King Salmon to the park's western boundary and there are floatplane connections from King Salmon to the lodge at Brooks River, the National Park Service ranger station and public campground on Naknek Lake. There are 3 other lodges in the park. Independent travelers must make their own arrangements for visiting Katmai, including air service to King Salmon and Brooks River. Campers can purchase meals and scenic bus tour tickets at the lodge. The visitor center at the King Salmon airport offers trip planning assistance for U.S. Fish &Wildlife Service and National Park Service lands in the area. The center is open daily in summer (May–October) from 8 A.M. to 5 P.M.; in winter (November–April) Mon.-Sat. 8 A.M. to 5 P.M. There is a staffed information desk, phone (907) 246-4250, fax (907) 246-8550.

Communications in King Salmon include phones, mail plane, radio and TV. The community is served by several churches. Children are bused to school in Naknek. There is a community electric system and sewage system; water is from individual wells. Freight arrives by air cargo or by barge to Naknek then trucked to King Salmon. Government address: Bristol Bay Borough, Box 189, Naknek, AK 99633, phone (907) 246-4224. King Salmon Visitor Center, P.O. Box 298, King Salmon, AK 99613, phone (907) 246-4250. Village corporation: Alaska Peninsula Corp., Box 104360, Anchorage, AK 99510, phone (907) 274-2433, fax (907) 274-8694. Village council: King Salmon Traditional Village Council, P.O. Box 68, King Salmon, AK 99613-0068, phone (907) 246-3553, fax (907) 246-3449, e-mail: kstvc@bristolbay.com.

Kodiak

GPS: N57°47' W152°24'

Located at the north end of Chiniak Bay near the eastern tip of Kodiak Island. **Transportation:** Commercial jet service from Anchorage; commuter air service from Anchorage; Alaska State Ferry System from Seward and Homer. **Population:** 6,836 city; 13,913 borough. **Zip code:** 99615. **Emergency Services:** Dial 911 for emergencies. Alaska State Troopers, phone (907)486-4121; City Police, phone (907) 486-8000; Fire Department, phone (907) 486-8040; Providence Kodiak Island Medical Center, phone (907) 486-3281; KANA Clinic, phone (907) 486-9825; U.S. Coast Guard Integrated Support Center/Rockmore-King Medical Clinic, phone (907) 487-5757; Kodiak Area Fire &

Rescue, phone (907) 486-8040/8000; Coast Guard emergency, dial operator and ask for Zenith 5555.

Elevation: Sea level. Climate: Average daily temperature in July 54°F; in January 32°F. Average annual precipitation 74 inches. September, October and May are the wettest months, each averaging more than 6 inches of rain.

Private Aircraft: Kodiak state airport, 7 miles southwest; 3 runways; elev. 73 feet; length 7,562, 5,400 and 5011 feet; asphalt; fuel 80, 100, jet A-1. Kodiak Municipal Airport, 2 miles northeast; elev. 139 feet; length 2,475 feet; asphalt; attended daylight hours. Kodiak (Lilly Lake) seaplane base, 1 mile northeast; elev. 130 feet. Inner Harbor seaplane base, adjacent north; unattended; docks; watch for boat traffic; no fuel.

Visitor Facilities: Accommodations at several motels/hotels and approximately 30 bed and breakfasts. There are several restaurants, sporting goods stores, gift shops, hardware stores and general merchandise stores. There are several air charter services in Kodiak for flightseeing trips, brown bear viewing, fly-in hunting and fishing or side trips to nearby points of interest. Boats can be chartered for fishing and hunting trips, sightseeing and photography. There are 3 car rental agencies, taxi cabs, several year-round van touring services and seasonal sightseeing bus tours. Kodiak has about 100 miles of road which offer beautiful scenery and access to tidewater but not to the Kodiak National Wildlife Refuge. Kodiak's world-famous brown bears are rarely seen from the roads.

Kodiak Island, home of the oldest permanent European settlement in Alaska, is about 100 miles long. Kodiak is the largest island in Alaska, and second largest in the United States, with an area of 3,670 square miles. The Kodiak Island archipelago includes some 200 islands, the largest being Kodiak.

Commercial fishing is the backbone of Kodiak's economy. Kodiak was the largest commercial fishing port in the United States in 1988 for product landed. Some 3,000 commercial fishing vessels use the harbor each year delivering salmon, shrimp, herring, halibut and whitefish, plus king, tanner and Dungeness crab to seafood processing companies in Kodiak.

Kodiak also is an important cargo port and transshipment center. Container ships stop here to transfer goods to smaller vessels bound for the Aleutians, the Alaska Peninsula and other destinations.

Kodiak, a home-rule city incorporated in 1940, has all the amenities of a medium-sized city, including schools with

enrollment of 2,181, radio stations, TV via cable and satellite and a daily newspaper, the Kodiak Daily Mirror. City government address: City of Kodiak, P.O. Box 1397, Kodiak, AK 99615, phone (907) 486-8640, fax (907) 486-8600, e-mail: mayor@cityko diak.ak.us; manager@citykodiak.ak.us; clerk@citykodiak.ak.us, web: www. city. kodiak.ak.us. Borough: Kodiak Island Borough, 710 Mill Bay Road, Kodiak, AK 99615; phone (907) 486-9310. Kodiak Area Chamber of Commerce, P.O. Box 1485, Kodiak, AK 99614, phone (907) 486-5557, fax (907) 486-7605, e-mail: cham ber@kodiak.org, web: www.kodiak.org/. Kodiak Island Convention and Visitors Bureau, 100 Marine Way, Ste, 200, Kodiak, AK 99615, phone (907) 486-4782, fax (907) 486-6545, e-mail: kicvb@ ptialaska.net, web: www.kodiak.org/. Native corporation: Kodiak Area Native Assoc., 402 Center Ave., Kodiak, AK 99615, phone (907) 486-5725, or Koniag, Incorporated, 4300 B Street #407, Anchorage, AK 99503, phone (907) 561-2668, fax (907) 562-5258, web: www.koni ag.com/.

For more information on Kodiak, see *The MILEPOST®*, a complete guide to communities on Alaska's road and marine highway systems.

Larsen Bay

GPS: N57°32' W153°58'

Located near the mouth of Larsen Bay on the west shore of Uyak Bay on the northwest coast of Kodiak Island, 62 miles west-southwest of Kodiak. **Transport-ation**: Boat; scheduled and charter air service from Kodiak. **Population**: 120. **Zip code**: 99624. **Emergency Services**: Village Public Safety Officer, phone (907) 847-2262; Alaska State Troopers, Kodiak, phone (907) 486-4761; Larsen Bay Health Clinic, Larsen Bay Village Response Team, phone (907) 847-2208; Volunteer Fire Department.

Elevation: 20 feet. **Climate**: Kodiak Island's climate is dominated by a strong marine influence, characterized by moderately heavy precipitation, cool temperatures and frequent high clouds and fog. There is little freezing weather. Humidity

is generally high and temperature variation is small. Mean maximum temperatures range from 32°F to 62°F. Larsen Bay gets approximately 23 inches of precipitation a year, with 23 inches of snow.

Private Aircraft: Airstrip adjacent southwest; elev. 77 feet; length 2,700 feet; gravel; no fuel; unattended. Runway condition not monitored; visual inspection recommended prior to using. No public transportation to town.

Visitor Facilities: No hotel or restaurant. Arrangements may be made for accommodations in private homes. Accommodations by advance reservation at area lodges, including Amook Lodge, (907) 47-2312; Bayside Inn, (907) 847-2313; Larsen Bay Lodge, (907) 847-2238; and Uyak Bay Lodge, (907) 847-2350. No laundromat or banking services. Limited groceries, clothing, first-aid supplies, film and sporting goods may be purchased at Larsen Bay Mercantile store, (907) 847-2233, during the summer months only. No arts and crafts available for purchase. Fishing/hunting licenses available. No guide or major repair services. Private boats may be rented; charter aircraft available locally. No public moorage facilities. Fuel available: marine gas, diesel, propane, regular gasoline.

Larsen Bay was named for Peter Larsen, an Unga Island furrier, hunter and guide. The Native name for the town is Uyak. The area is thought to have been inhabited for 2,000 years by the Aleut people. In the early 1800s there was a tannery in Uyak Bay. The Alaska Packers Assoc. built a cannery in the village of Larsen Bay in 1911. The cannery is now owned by Kodiak Salmon Packers Inc.

Larsen Bay is a second-class city, incorporated in 1974. It is located adjacent to Kodiak National Wildlife Refuge.

The economy is primarily based on fishing and cannery work. A large majority of the residents depend on subsistence activities for their livelihood. Species found in the area include seals, sea lions, salmon, halibut, codfish, ducks, clams, sea urchins, gumboots (chitons), crab, deer and various types of berries. There are a few local jobs with the city, the tribal council, school, post office and lodges.

The main attraction in the area is the Karluk River, located 2 to 3 miles from the head of Larsen Bay. This river is known for its excellent king salmon, silver salmon and steelhead fishing. Raft trips from Karluk Lake to Karluk Lagoon also are popular.

NOTE: *Land along the Karluk River as well as the riverbed is owned by Koniag Inc. and the village corporations or Karluk and Larsen Bay. There is a $125/per-person fee for fishing or camping on the Karluk River. Permits may be obtained from Koniag Inc., 202 Center St., Ste. 201, Kodiak, AK 99615, phone (907) 486-2530.*

Hunting in the area is good for Sitka black-tailed deer. Other wildlife includes Kodiak brown bear, fox, rabbit, ermine, otter, seal, whale, sea lion and porpoise. Bird-watchers may see eagles, gulls, petrels, kittiwakes, mallards, green-winged teals, wigeons, pintails, lesser Canada geese, puffins, loons, cormorants and more. (Approximately 120 species of birds have been recorded in the Kodiak area, although most are migratory.)

Communications in Larsen Bay include phones, mail plane, commercial and single sideband radio and satellite TV. The community is served by 1 church and a school with grades kindergarten through 12 with enrollment of 17. There are community electric, water and sewer systems. Freight arrives by cargo plane, barge, ship and charter plane. Government address: City of Larsen Bay, P.O. Box 8, Larsen Bay, AK 99624, phone (907) 847-2211, fax (907) 847-2239. Village council: Larsen Bay Tribal Council, Attn: Tribal President, P.O. Box 35, Larsen Bay, AK 99624, phone and fax (907) 847-2207. e-mail: LarsonBay@aitc.org.

Naknek

GPS: N58°43′ W157°00′

Located on the Alaska Peninsula on the Naknek River near its mouth, 15 miles west of King Salmon, 300 miles southwest of Anchorage. **Transportation**: Most passenger, freight and charter service is out of King Salmon. King Air operates primarily out of Naknek. Daily pas-senger, charter and freight service from Anchorage and Dillingham via PenAir, Alaska Airlines and Northern Air Cargo; Bristol Air, King Air Service, Windy's Mag Air and Katmai Air Service. A 15-mile paved road connects Naknek with King Salmon. **Population**: 624 (borough 1,252). **Zip code**: 99633. **Emergency Services**: Police, phone (907) 246-4222; Alaska State Troopers, King Salmon, phone (907) 246-3346; Camai Medical Center, phone (907) 246-6155; Naknek Health Clinic, phone (907) 246-4214. Bristol Bay Volunteer Rescue Squad, phone (907) 246-4224/4222.

Elevation: 50 feet. **Climate**: Cool, humid and windy weather predominates. Average summer temperatures at nearest weather station in King Salmon range from 42°F to 63°F. Average winter temper-atures range from 29°F to 44°F. Total pre-cipitation in King Salmon averages 20 inches annually, with an average snowfall of 48 inches. Portions of Kvichak Bay and the Naknek River freeze solid during the winter months.

Private Aircraft: Airstrip 1 mile north; elev. 70 feet; length 1,600 feet; gravel; fuel 80, 100; attended; adjoining runway, length 1,985 feet; gravel. Runway condi-tions monitored by Alaska Dept. of Transportation; visual inspection recom-mended prior to using. Airstrip is equipped with lights. Aircraft parking along entire length. Seaplane base adja-cent north; elev. 30 feet; fuel 80, 100.

Visitor Facilities: Accommodations at several bed and breakfasts, at Naknek Hotel, (907) 246-4430; Leader Creek Inn, (907) 246-4415; and Red Dog Inn, (907) 246-4213. There are 2 restaurants and a summer-only sandwich shop. Laundry facilities. Banking services available. Groceries, clothing, first-aid supplies, hardware, film and sporting goods may be purchased in the community. Arts and crafts available for purchase include ivory, baskets and masks. Fishing/hunting licenses available, as well as guide service. Major repair service for marine engines, boats, autos and aircraft. Rental trans-portation includes autos, boats and air-craft. Fuel available includes marine gas, diesel and regular gasoline. Moorage facilities available.

Naknek is the seat of the 531-square-mile Bristol Bay Borough, the state's oldest borough, incorporated in 1962. The region was settled more than 6,000 years ago by Yup'ik Eskimo and Athabascan Indians. The Russians built a fort near the village and fur trappers inhabited the area for some time prior to the U.S. purchase of Alaska.

By 1883, the first salmon cannery opened in Bristol Bay; in 1890, the first cannery opened on the Naknek River. By 1900, there were approximately 12 canneries in Bristol Bay.

The community was developed as a major center for commercial fishing and processing, which today form the base of the area's economy. There are 6 salmon processors on the Naknek side of the river and Naknek bustles during the summer as several thousand people arrive in June to fish and work in the canneries. Borough government also is a significant source of employment. Many residents also depend on subsistence hunting and fishing.

Hunting, fishing, camping and photography provide most of the outdoor recreation for borough residents. The Naknek River is famous for its excellent sportfishing; caribou and bear hunting are popular. There are scores of excellent fishing streams throughout the region.

The Russian Orthodox St. John the Baptist Chapel in Naknek, reportedly constructed in 1886, is on the National Register of Historic Places. Naknek also has the Bristol Bay Historical Museum, P.O. Box 43, Naknek, AK 99633. The collections of this "living history museum" feature archaeology, history and ethnology, and document Naknek's history as one of the largest commercial salmon fishing and canning headquarters in the world. Displays show the progression from the early subsistence-oriented lifestyle of the first Bristol Bay residents to the coming of the Russian fur traders on up to the oral histories and family trees of present residents. The museum building is the original Fisherman's Hall, an early meeting place for fishermen. Facilities include a gift shop, a library and parking.

Open by appointment every day. No admission fee; donations accepted.

Communications in Naknek include phones, radio and cable TV. The community is served by 4 churches and a school with grades preschool through 12 and total enrollment of 240. There is an indoor community swimming pool. There is a community electric and sewage system; water is from individual wells. Freight arrives in the community by cargo plane and barge. Government address: Bristol Bay Borough, Box 189, Naknek, AK 99633. Village corporation: Paug-Vik Incorporated, Ltd., Box 61, Naknek, AK 99633, phone (907) 246-4278. Village council: Naknek Native Village, P.O. Box 106, Naknek, AK 99633, phone (907) 246-4210, fax (907) 246-3563, e-mail: Naknek@aitc.org.

Nelson Lagoon/Port Moller

GPS: N56°00' W161°00'

Located on a narrow spit that separates Nelson Lagoon and low-lying north coastal areas of the western Alaska Peninsula from the Bering Sea, 30 miles west of Port Moller, 550 miles southwest of Anchorage. **Transportation**: Air charter from Cold Bay. **Population**: 87. **Zip code**: 99571. **Emergency Services**: Nelson Lagoon Health Clinic, Nelson Lagoon First Responders, phone (907) 989-2202; Volunteer Fire Department; Village Public Safety Officer, phone (907) 989-2232.

Climate: The area's maritime climate features mild winters and cool summers. The warmest month is August; the coldest is February. Precipitation averages 37 inches per year at Port Moller, including 99 inches of snow.

Private Aircraft: Airstrip 1 mile east; elev. 13 feet; length 4,000 feet; gravel; attended. Runway conditions monitored. Large seabirds feed along beach adjacent to runway.

The following description of Nelson Lagoon was provided several years ago by students of Nelson Lagoon School courtesy of principal Mark Massion. Our thanks to Priscilla Brandell, Valerie Johnson, Leona Nelson, Melinda Nelson and Craig Rysewyk.

Visitor Facilities: "Harold Johnson Sr. owns an apartment building called the Bering Inn. There are 5 rooms available with cable TV and phone. They all have bathrooms and some have small kitchenettes. Rates are $102 a night; $300 a week; and $800 a month. Harold's phone number is (907) 989-2209.

"We do not have a restaurant. Newcomers that stop in should bring their own food.

"Nelson Lagoon is located on a picturesque spit and is surrounded by the Bering Sea on one side. Nelson Lagoon is very small, but peaceful. In the summer, the lagoon is a professional fishing site. It attracts lots of fishermen. The winter brings high winds and lots of snow.

"Our community isn't very large, but it is growing slowly. About 90 residents live here year-round. In the summer, the population grows to about 95 to 110 people. That is because people come here to fish. Almost everyone in town is related and of Aleut descent. We hunt for caribou, geese, ducks and other land mammals.

"Our town is well-kept. Some people might think our town is boring, but there are fun things to do here. You can go out and have picnics when it is sunny. You can go for a ride on 4-wheelers down the coast to Dick's camp if you like. In the winter you go on snowmobile rides. The people in Nelson Lagoon are very friendly, kind and helpful. They enjoy visitors. There are several great cooks in town. You may even get invited to dinner."

The community derived its name from the lagoon, which was named in 1882 for Edward William Nelson of the U.S. Signal Corps, an explorer in the Yukon delta region between 1877 and 1920. The area was settled in 1906 when a salmon saltery was built there. A cannery operated between 1915 and 1917. Peter Pan Seafoods currently operates in the area. For many years Nelson Lagoon was a seasonal camp, but families began to settle there and a school was established in 1965. Nelson Lagoon is part of the Aleutians East Borough.

According to its students, Nelson Lagoon School is the first place you see upon arriving in town. The school, with an enrollment of 16, has a "great gym," used by students and community members alike. The school also has several computers and students learn several computer programs.

Nelson Lagoon has phones, mail service and a central water system. Sewage system is flush toilets and seepage pits. There is a community electric system. Freight arrives by ship or by barge via Port Moller. Government address: Native Village of Nelson Lagoon, P.O. Box 13-NLG, Nelson Lagoon, AK 99571, phone (907) 989-2234, fax (907) 989-2233, e-mail: NelsonLagoon@aitc.org. Village corporation: Nelson Lagoon Corp., General Delivery, Nelson Lagoon, AK 99571, phone (907) 989-2204, fax (907) 989-2233. Borough: Aleutians East Borough, P.O. Box 349, Sand Point, AK 99661, phone (907) 383-2699, fax (907) 383-3496, e-mail: aebclerk@aol.com, web: http://www.aleutianseast/org/.

Nikolski

GPS: N52°56' W168°51'

(Ni-KOL-ski) Located on Nikolski Bay on Umnak Island, one of the Fox Island group in the central Aleutian Chain, 110 miles from Dutch Harbor, 880 miles southwest of Anchorage. **Transportation:** Scheduled or charter flights from Dutch Harbor; rain and wind often close the dirt airstrip. **Population:** 19. **Zip code:** 99638. **Emergency Services:** Alaska State Troopers, Unalaska.

Elevation: 73 feet. **Climate:** Mild winters and cool summers characterize the climate. The warmest month is August; the coldest is February. Precipitation is 21 inches annually; snowfall averages 41 inches annually.

Visitor Facilities: Food and some necessities available at the Nikolski Native Store. Nikolski has about 25 houses, some outbuildings, a Russian Orthodox church and a school all clustered together, separated from the ocean by a wide rocky beach.

Occupied by the Russians in the mid-1700s, Nikolski's population remained constant at about 100 until World War II.

After the Japanese attacked Dutch Harbor and seized Attu and Kiska in June 1942, Nikolski residents were evacuated to the Ketchikan area until 1944.

In the mid-1950s, the Air Force built a White Alice site, later operated by RCA Alascom, but abandoned in 1977. A sheep ranch was established in Nikolski in 1926 as part of the Aleutian Livestock Co. Wild horses from the abandoned ranch roam the island.

Subsistence hunting and fishing provide a substantial part of the villagers' diets. Most families catch Dolly Varden and halibut in the bay. According to storekeeper Leonti Ermeloff, "I wouldn't trade life in Nikolski for anything. In subsistence, we generally do what Native people have done here forever. Catch fish, dry fish ... fish are our main diet."

Nikolski is one of the oldest continuously inhabited communities in the world. Ananiuliak (Anangula) Island on the north side of Nikolski Bay is the site of the earliest documented evidence of human habitation in the Aleutian Islands, dating as far back as 8,000 years. The Chaluka site in the village of Nikolski exhibits 4,000 years of virtually continuous occupation and is listed on the National Register of Historic Places. Also on the register is Nikolski's St. Nicholas Russian Orthodox Church, built in 1930.

Communications include phones and mail plane. The community has a school. There are community electric and water systems. The sewage system is septic tanks. Freight arrives by ship once or twice a year. Nikolski is unincorporated under state law but is incorporated as an IRA village under the Indian Reorganization Act. Government address: Native Village of Nikolski, General Delivery, Nikolski, AK 99638, phone (907) 576-2225, fax (907) 576-2205, e-mail: Nikolski@aitc.org. Village corporation: Chaluka Corp., General Delivery, Nikolski, AK 99638, phone (907) 576-2216.

Old Harbor

GPS: N57°13' W153°16'

Located on the southeast shore of Kodiak Island on the west shore of Sitkalidak Strait across from Sitkalidak Island, 54 milesfrom Kodiak. **Transportation**: Scheduled and charter air service from Kodiak; private boat. **Population**: 257. **Zip code**: 99643. **Emergency Services**: Village Public Safety Officer, phone (907) 286-2275; Alaska State Troopers, Kodiak, phone (907) 486-4761; Old Harbor Health Clinic, phone (907) 286-2205; Old Harbor Village Response Team, phone (907) 286-2293/2270. Volunteer Fire Department, phone (907) 286-2275.

Elevation: 20 feet. **Climate**: Kodiak Island's climate is dominated by a strong marine influence, characterized by moderately heavy precipitation, cool temperatures, frequent high clouds and fog. Humidity is generally high and temperature variation small. Average temperature at Old Harbor in January is 25°F; July temperatures average 55°F. Precipitation averages 60 inches per year, with 18.5 inches of snow.

Private Aircraft: Airstrip 2 NE; elev. 55 feet; length 2,750 feet; gravel; no fuel; unattended. Runway condition not monitored; visual inspection recommended prior to using. Vehicles may be on runway. No public transportation into town.

Visitor Facilities: Accommodations and meals at Sitkalidak Lodge, phone (907) 286-9246. No laundromat or banking services. Some groceries, clothing, first-aid supplies, hardware and film may be purchased at Tidal Wave and Gwendolook's. Most supplies are obtained from Kodiak. No arts and crafts available for purchase. Fishing/ hunting licenses not available. Guide services and charter boats can be arranged locally. No major repair services. No boat haul-out available. Diesel and regular gas available. New city tank farm under construction in 2001.

The area around Old Harbor is thought to have been inhabited for nearly 2,000 years. Grigori Shelikov, considered to be the founder of the Russian-American colonies, entered a harbor on the south coast of Kodiak Island in 1784. His flagship, the *Three Saints*, is the namesake for the harbor as well as the first Russian settlement in Alaska, Three Saints Bay. In 1788, a tsunami destroyed the settlement;

it was hit by 2 more devastating earthquakes before 1792. In 1793, Alexander Baranov, who replaced Shelikov, relocated the town to Saint Paul Harbor, now known as Kodiak. A settlement at Three Saints Harbor was reestablished in 1884. The census of 1890 designated the settlement in that area as Staruigavan, meaning "old harbor" in Russian. The town was nearly destroyed by a tsunami wave from the 1964 Good Friday earthquake; only 2 homes and the church remained standing. Old Harbor has since been rebuilt in the same location.

Visitor attractions in Old Harbor include the historic Russian Orthodox church and wildlife. Nearby Three Saints Bay, site of the first Russian settlement, has kittiwake rookeries and sea lion haulouts. Old Harbor Native Corp. is the major landowner in Old Harbor; contact them for permission to use corporation lands. Old Harbor is adjacent to Kodiak National Wildlife Refuge.

Many of Old Harbor's residents are commercial fishermen; however, most of the residents depend to some extent on subsistence activities for some food sources. Species harvested for subsistence use include salmon, halibut, cod, Dolly Varden, crab, herring, shrimp, clams, duck, seal, deer, rabbit and bear. Berries are also harvested. There are a few jobs locally with the stores, school, city and post office. Old Harbor is a second-class city, incorporated in 1966.

Communications in Old Harbor include phones, mail plane, commercial radio reception from Kodiak and satellite TV. The community is served by a Russian Orthodox church and a school with grades kindergarten through 12 with enrollment of 61. There are community electric, water and sewer systems. Freight arrives by barge, mail plane or charter boat. Government address: City of Old Harbor, P.O. Box 109, Old Harbor, AK 99643, phone (907) 286-2204, fax (907) 296-2278, e-mail: nunyuk@compuserve.com. Village corporation: Old Harbor Native Corp., P.O. Box 71, Old Harbor, AK 99643, phone (907) 286-2286, fax (907) 286-2287. Village council: Village of Old Harbor, P.O. Box 62, Old Harbor, AK 99643, phone (907) 286-2215, e-mail: OldHarbor@aitc.org.

Ouzinkie

GPS: N57°55′ W152°30′

(You-ZENK-ee) Located on the west coast of Spruce Island on Narrow Strait across from Kodiak Island, 10 miles north of the city of Kodiak. **Transportation:** Boat; scheduled or charter air service from Kodiak. **Population:** 259. **Zip code:** 99644. **Emergency Services:** Village Public Safety Officer, phone (907) 680-2259; Alaska State Troopers, Kodiak, phone (907) 486-4761; Ouzinkie Health Clinic, phone (907) 680-2265; Volunteer Fire Department, phone (907) 680-2209. Medical emergencies evacuated by air to Kodiak.

Elevation: 55 feet at airport. **Climate:** Maritime, with moderately heavy precipitation (approximately 60 inches per year), predominantly cool temperatures with little variation and frequent clouds and fog. Mean maximum temperatures 62°F in July and August, 32°F December to February. Snowfall occurs from December through March and averages 87 inches per year. Winds can become quite strong.

Private Aircraft: State airstrip adjacent north; elev. 55 feet; length 2,085 feet; gravel; no fuel. Visual inspection recommended prior to landing.

Visitor Facilities: Make arrangements for accommodations with Ouzinkie Native Corp., (907) 680-2208, and the City of Ouzinkie, (907) 680-2209/2257. No restaurant, laundromat or banking services. Groceries available at Ouzinkie Community Store. No arts or crafts available for purchase. Fishing/hunting licenses available. No guide or major repair services, rental transportation or public moorage facilities. Fuel available: diesel.

Ouzinkie is one of the oldest settlements of the Kodiak Island group. The village is nestled in a small cove among tall stands of spruce and hemlock. Spruce Island is separated from Kodiak Island by a strait named Uskiy, meaning "very narrow" in Russian. The village name is a transliteration of Uzenkiy which is derived from Uskiy.

The town was originally settled as a retirement community for the Russian-

American Co. In 1889, the Royal Packing Co. constructed a cannery at Ouzinkie. Shortly afterward, the Russian-American Packing Co. built another. In the mid-1800s, a Russian Orthodox church was built. In the early 1900s, almost all Ouzinkie residents owned cattle. Through the years, however, ranching became less popular and finally disappeared altogether.

Ouzinkie is a second-class city, incorporated in 1967. The Russian Orthodox Nativity of Our Lord Chapel, built in 1906 next to the older church, is a national historic site. The community celebrates Russian Orthodox holidays. Check with the church about guided tours of the holy sites and old gravestones at Monks Lagoon.

Other visitor activities include salmon and halibut fishing, deer hunting, birding, hiking, camping (by permission only) and taking in the view from the top of Mount St. Herman.

The fishing industry flourished through the years with new canneries replacing those that were destroyed by fire. In 1964, a tsunami wave resulting from the Good Friday earthquake destroyed the Ouzinkie Packing Co. cannery. Following that disaster, Columbia Ward bought the remains and rebuilt the store and dock, but not the cannery. In the late 1960s, the Ouzinkie Seafoods cannery was constructed. The operation, sold to Glacier Bay, burned down in 1976 shortly after the sale.

Ouzinkie's economic base is commercial fishing. Since 1976 there have been no local fish processing facilities and Ouzinkie fishermen use those in Kodiak or floating processors. There are a few other jobs locally with the store, city government, Native corporation and Ouzinkie Tribal Council, clinic and schools. There are 74 single family homes and 3 apartment buildings in Ouzinkie. The community also supports a library, school gym and community center.

Residents depend on subsistence activities for various food sources. Species harvested locally include berries, salmon, king crab, tanner crab, Dungeness crab, herring, halibut, shrimp, scallops, clams, ducks, deer and rabbits.

Zack Chichenoff, mayor of the City of Ouzinkie, says: "Ouzinkie on Spruce Island is paradise as far as I'm concerned, with an abundance of spruce trees, and access to fishing and hunting," and adds that he wouldn't want to live anywhere else.

Communications in Ouzinkie include phones, mail plane, commercial radio from Kodiak, satellite and cable TV. The community is served by Russian Orthodox and Baptist churches and a school with grades kindergarten through 12 with enrollment of 48. There are community electric, water and sewer systems. Freight is delivered by mail plane. Government address: City of Ouzinkie, P.O. Box 109, Ouzinkie, AK 99644, phone (907) 680-2209, fax (907) 680-2223. Village corporation: Ouzinkie Corp., P.O. Box 89, Ouzinkie, AK 99644, phone (907) 680-2208, fax (907) 680-2268. Village council: Ouzinkie Tribal Council, P.O. Box 130, Ouzinkie, AK 99644, phone (907) 680-2259, fax (907) 680-2214, e-mail: ouzinkietc@compuserve.com.

Perryville

GPS: N55°54' W159°09'

Located on the south coast of the Alaska Peninsula, 215 miles south-southwest of Dillingham and 285 miles southwest of Kodiak. **Transportation**: Scheduled airline, air charter from Dillingham or King Salmon. **Population**: 102. **Zip code**: 99648. **Emergency Services**: Alaska State Troopers, Sand Point or King Salmon; Perryville Health Clinic, phone (907) 853-2236; Perryville First Responders, phone (907) 853-2202; Fire Department, phone (907) 853-2206.

Elevation: 25 feet. **Climate**: Cool summers, with a fair amount of rain. Winters are relatively warm. The average snowfall is 58.5 inches. Total precipitation at Chignik, the nearest weather station (40 miles away), averages 127 inches annually.

Private Aircraft: Airstrip adjacent south; elev. 25 feet; length 2,467 feet; gravel; unattended. Runway condition not monitored; visual inspection recommended prior to use. No airport facilities or transportation to village, though private vehicles may be available.

Visitor Facilities: Limited accommodations. No restaurant, laundromat or banking services. First-aid supplies, clothing (limited), hardware, film and sporting goods may be purchased in the community. No arts and crafts available. Fishing/hunting licenses not available. No guide service, major repair service, rental transportation or public moorage facilities.

Perryville was founded in 1912 as a refuge for Native people driven away from their villages by the eruption of Mount Katmai. It was named after Captain Perry, who rescued the people with his boat and took them to Ivanof Bay, and later to the location of Perryville.

St. John the Theologian Church, a Russian Orthodox church built sometime after the 1912 founding of Perryville, is on the National Register of Historic Places.

Nearby rivers and the ocean in front of the village are used for sportfishing, and most of the residents fish commercially. There is berry picking in season and hunting for bear, moose and caribou. The village is unincorporated. *NOTE: Much of the land around Perryville is owned by the local village firm, Oceanside Corp. You will need to contact the corporation in advance for permission to enter.*

Communications include phones, mail plane, radio and TV. Public electricity and water are available. Sewage system is individual septic tanks. The community is served by the Russian Orthodox church, and a school with grades preschool through 12 with enrollment of 30. Freight arrives by cargo and mail plane. Village council address: Native Village of Perryville, P.O. Box 101, Perryville, AK 99648, phone (907) 853-2203, fax (907) 853-2230, e-mail: Perryville@aitc.org. Village corporation: Oceanside Native Corp., P.O. Box 124, Perryville, AK 99648, phone (907) 853-2300, fax (907) 853-2301.

Pilot Point

GPS: N57°33′ W157°34′

Located on the east shore of Ugashik Bay on the Alaska Peninsula, 90 miles south of King Salmon, 380 miles southwest of Anchorage. **Transportation:** Scheduled and charter air service from King Salmon. **Population:** 85. **Zip code:**

99649. **Emergency Services:** Alaska State Troopers, King Salmon, phone (907) 246-3346; Pilot Point Health Clinic, phone (907) 797-2212; Pilot Point First Responders, phone (907) 797-2200/2273; Volunteer Fire Department.

Elevation: 50 feet. **Climate:** Cool, humid and windy. Temperature and precipitation data were collected at Pilot Point from 1939 until 1945. The city installed a weather monitoring station in 1992. Low cloud cover and fog frequently limit travel into Pilot Point.

Private Aircraft: New airport on north side of village; elev. 75 feet; length 3,280 feet; gravel; fuel; some avgas available from the store; unattended. Airport capable of handling C-130 and DC-6 aircraft. Runway condition not monitored; visual inspection recommended prior to using. No airport facilities; summer taxi service to village.

Visitor Facilities: Accommodations available at Caribou Look-out Lodge, (907) 797-2216; ACE's Tundra Loon bed and breakfast, (907) 797-2207. Cabins also available; contact Aleck Griechen , (907) 797-2205. No banking services. A gift shop is open in summer. No laundromat service. Groceries, clothing, first-aid supplies, hardware, film and sporting goods may be purchased in the community. Limited arts and crafts available. Fishing/hunting licenses available; no guide service. No major repair service. Charter flights available. Fuel available includes diesel, propane and regular gasoline. Bulkhead dock at Dago Creek available for temporary tie-up, load and off-load only.

This predominantly Aleut village, which had a fish saltery in 1900, originally was known as Pilot Station, for the Ugashik River pilots who were stationed there and took boats up the river to a larger cannery at Ugashik. By 1918 the saltery had developed into a large cannery, and was forced to close in 1958 because of deterioration of the harbor. In 1933, the name of the village changed to Pilot Point. The community incorporated in 1992.

Residents depend on commercial salmon fishing for the majority of their cash income. Other jobs are found with the store, school and government.

Subsistence hunting and fishing play a major role in the economy, based primarily on salmon and caribou.

Record-sized grayling have been taken from Ugashik Lakes. Other sportfishing is for salmon and trout. Hunting is for moose, caribou and brown bear. The Kvichak River is a major migration corridor for the sandhill crane and whistling swans that nest near the village. White-fronted and emperor geese, Canada geese and loons rest in the area in the spring and fall; some stay to nest and molt. Ugashik Bay and the Ugashik, Dog Salmon and King Salmon rivers are important bald eagle feeding areas.

NOTE: The majority of the land surrounding the village, as well as the Ugashik One Airfield, is owned by the Pilot Point Native Corp. Use of this land for hunting, fishing, or recreation is forbidden without the express permission of the Pilot Point Native Corp. Board of Directors.

Communications at Pilot Point include phones, mail plane, radio and TV. A new post office will open in summer of 2001. The community is served by St. Nicholas Russian Orthodox Church, which was built circa 1912 and is on the National Register of Historic Places. There also is a school with grades kindergarten through 12 with enrollment of 23. Community electric system is available; also public water and sewage systems. Freight arrives by cargo plane and barge. Government address: City of Pilot Point, Box 430, Pilot Point, AK 99649, phone (907) 797-2200, fax (907) 797-2211, e-mail: pipclerk@aol.com. Village council: Pilot Point Traditional Council, P.O. Box 449, Pilot Point, AK 99649, phone (907) 797-2208, fax (907) 797-2258, e-mail: PilotPoint@aitc.org. Village corporation: Pilot Point Native Corp., P.O. Box 487, Pilot Point, AK 99649, phone (907) 797-8001, fax (907) 797-2255.

Pleasant Harbor

Located on Spruce Island, 3 miles east of Ouzinkie, 12 miles north of Kodiak. **Transportation**: Boat; charter air service. **Population**: 26. **Zip code**: 99644. **Emergency Services**: Village Public Safety Officer, Ouzinkie; Alaska State Troopers, Kodiak; Ouzinkie Clinic.

Climate: Winters are usually mild with very little snow, but it can snow 3 feet when you least expect it, says one resident. Winter temperatures range from 25°F to 40°F. Summers are usually sunny with occasional rain showers. Temperatures range between 60°F and 70°F.

Private Aircraft: Airstrip at Ouzinkie. Floatplane landings at Pleasant Harbor.

Visitor Facilities: Private residences only, no accommodations, meals or other visitor services available. Marine engine and boat repair services may be available. Public moorage facilities available.

Pleasant Harbor was founded in 1923 when Chris Opheim homesteaded a piece of land which included Sunny Cove and Pleasant Harbor. He and his family operated a cod saltery in Sunny Cove. Son Ed Opheim inherited the homestead and in 1947 moved his family to Pleasant Harbor where the family earned a living salting and smoking salmon. Ed Opheim later built and operated a sawmill.

The tsunami wave generated by the 1964 Good Friday earthquake washed away both the old house at Sunny Cove and the Pleasant Harbor home. The Opheims have since rebuilt on higher ground. The family sold homesites and there are now more homes in the community. Most residents earn their living by fishing. Others take seasonal jobs in Kodiak and a few work for the lodge.

Attractions include Monks Lagoon, about an hour's walk from Pleasant Harbor, where St. Herman lived and worked during the early days of Russian America. It is now a Russian Orthodox sanctuary. The chapel built over St. Herman's grave is a national historic site.

New Valaam Monastery is located at Pleasant Harbor and the monks who live there are more than willing to share their knowledge of the history of the church in Alaska with visitors.

Salmon fishing is particularly good in July and August. Halibut and Dolly Varden can be caught in May and June. There are clams nearby and tide pools where a variety of marine creatures hide. Dolphins, harbor seals and sea lions are plentiful. Deer and rabbits venture near the homes; eagles soar overhead and nest on a point overlooking the ocean. On a tiny island nearby many sea and land birds, with their nests and young, can be seen. This island is covered with wildflowers in season. Elk and deer hunting can be done on Kodiak and Afognak islands, about 2 hours by boat from Pleasant Harbor.

Communications in unincorporated Pleasant Harbor include radio and TV. Freight arrives by plane or ship.

Port Heiden

GPS: N56°55' W158°41'

(Port HI-den) Located on the Alaska Peninsula on the north shore of Port Heiden, 150 miles from King Salmon; 435 miles southwest of Anchorage. **Transportation**: Boat; scheduled airline from King Salmon. **Population**: 121. **Zip code**: 99549. **Emergency Services**: Village Public Safety Officer, phone (907) 837-2223; Port Heiden Health Clinic, phone (907) 837-2209; Port Heiden Rescue Squad, (Clinic), phone (907) 837-2209/2222; Volunteer Fire Department, phone (907) 837-2238.

Elevation: 90 feet. **Climate**: Mean annual precipitation is 15 inches, including 53 inches of snow.

Private Aircraft: 2 airstrips 6 miles northeast; elev. 86 feet; length 6,250 and 4,600 feet; gravel; fuel jet A and 100. Airport has passenger and freight terminal, ticket counter, restrooms. Taxi service to village.

Visitor Facilities: Accommodations at a boarding house. Meals at lodging facility. No laundromat or banking services. Groceries, first-aid supplies, hardware and film may be purchased in the community. Arts and crafts which may be purchased include carved ivory. Fishing/hunting licenses and guide service available. Everyone does their own marine engine, boat and auto repairs. Make arrangements with private owners to rent autos or boats. Charter aircraft available. Fuel available includes marine gas, diesel and regular gasoline. No moorage facilities.

Port Heiden was founded by a Norwegian who came to the area in the 1920s and married a Native woman. Other families moved in later. Prior to that time many Native people lived in the area, but many died during an influenza epidemic in the 1900s. Port Heiden is a second-class city, incorporated in 1972.

NOTE: Hiking, berry picking, camping and fishing are permitted on lands owned by the Alaska Peninsula Corp. upon payment of a $100/per-person fee. Hunting and woodcutting on corporation lands are not permitted. Contact the corporation for more information.

The community is the gateway to 514,000-acre Aniakchak National Monument and Preserve. Access by floatplane from King Salmon or Port Heiden to Surprise Lake inside the caldera. By foot, it's 10 miles from Port Heiden to the park boundary on a very difficult trail.

Communications in Port Heiden include phones, mail plane, radio and TV. The community is served by 2 churches and a school with grades kindergarten through 12 with enrollment of 40. There are community electric, water and sewage systems. Freight arrives in the community by cargo plane, air taxi and barge. Government address: City of Port Heiden, P.O. Box 49050, Port Heiden, AK 99549, phone (907) 837-2209, fax (907) 837-2248, e-mail: 105553.3414@compuserve.com. Village council: Native Village of Port Heiden, P.O. Box 490077, Port Heiden, AK 99549, phone (907) 837-2296, fax (907) 837-2297, e-mail: PortHeiden@aitc.org.

Port Lions

GPS: N57°52' W152°53'

Located on Settler's Cove near the mouth of Kizhuyak Bay on the north coast of Kodiak Island, 19 miles from Kodiak. **Transportation**: Boat or skiff charters and air service from Kodiak; Alaska Marine Highway System comes to Port Lions from Kodiak, Homer, Seward and the Aleutians. **Population**: 222. **Zip code**: 99550. **Emergency Services**: Village Public Safety Officer, phone (907) 454-2330, Alaska State Troopers, Kodiak, phone (907) 486-4761; Port Lions Clinic, phone (907) 454-2275.

Elevation: 52 feet at airport. **Climate**: Relatively hot summers and cold winters, moderately heavy precipitation and frequent high clouds and fog. Temperatures from 10°F to 80°F. Approximately 60 inches of precipitation per year.

Private Aircraft: Airport 2 miles northeast; elev. 52 feet; length 2,200 feet; crushed rock runway and apron; no fuel; unattended. Runway equipped with marker lights, beacon and wind direction indicator. Subject to downdrafts during northeast winds. Runway width 100 feet between edge markers.

Visitor Facilities: Accommodations and meals by advance reservation at Port Lions Lodge, (907) 454-2264; Wilderness Beach condos, (907) 454-2301; Settlers Cove bed and breakfast, (907) 454-2573; and Coho-nook Inn, (907) 454-2418. No public laundry facilities or banking services. Settlers Cove Market carries groceries, clothing, hardware, film, and has a small deli. Some arts and crafts available for purchase. Fishing/hunting licenses and guide and charter services available locally. Rak Outfitter hunting cabins/Amashook Charters, (907) 454-2333; M&L Charters, (907) 454-2467; Kodiak Sports Tour, (907) 454-2465; Whale Pass Lodge, (907) 454-2505; Heidi May Charter, (907) 454-2277; Coho-nook Charters, (907) 454-2418; Nelson Charters, (907) 454-2554. Marine engine repair available. Boats/kayaks may be rented. Fuel available: diesel, regular gasoline, Kizuyak Oils Sales, (907) 454-2424. Public moorage facilities available.

Port Lions was founded in 1964 by Lions International, the Bureau of Indian Affairs and the Public Health Service for the displaced residents of the village of Afognak, which had been partially destroyed by a tsunami in the aftermath of the March 27, 1964, earthquake. Afognak was 1 of 10 permanent settlements founded by Russian-American Co. employees between 1770 and 1799.

For many years, Port Lions was the site of the large Wakefield Cannery on Peregrebni Point. The cannery burned down in March 1975. Floating crab processors have operated there in recent years. Port Lions incorporated as a second-class city in 1966.

The economy of Port Lions is based primarily on commercial/ subsistence fishing. There are a few other jobs with the lodges, stores, boat harbor, oil company, school, city, tribal council and health clinic. All residents depend to some extent on subsistence activities. Food harvested includes salmon, halibut, crab, shrimp, scallops, clams, ducks, seals, deer, rabbits, berries and plants.

Salmon can be caught right in the Port Lions river in the heart of the community. Port Lions has excellent recreational opportunities. Boating and riding all-terrain vehicles are very popular. The surrounding area offers good hunting and fishing and an abundance of wildlife for the photographer.

Communications in Port Lions include phones, mail plane, radio, TV and Internet. The community is served by a Russian Orthodox church and Hillside Bible Chapel, Jessie Wakefield Memorial Library, and Port Lions school with grades kindergarten through 12 with enrollment of 44. Electricity is provided by Kodiak Electric Assoc. Utilities include water supply, sewer and refuse collection from the City of Port Lions. Freight arrives by air, ship and state ferry. Government address: City of Port Lions, P.O. Box 110, Port Lions, AK 99550, phone (907) 454-2332, fax (907) 454-2420. Village corporation: Afognak Native Corp., P.O. Box 1277, Kodiak, AK 99615, phone (907) 486-6014, fax (907) 486-2514. Village council: Port Lions Traditional Tribal Council, P.O. Box 69, Port Lions, AK 99550, phone (907) 454-2234, fax (907) 454-2434, e-mail: nvopl@aol.com.

Port Moller
(See Nelson Lagoon)

Port William
Located on the south shore of Shuyak Island, 45 to 50 miles north of Kodiak. **Transportation**: Boat; scheduled and chartered floatplane from Kodiak; chartered floatplane from Homer. **Population**: 10. **Zip code**: 99697. **Emergency Services**: Alaska State Troopers, Kodiak; Kodiak Island Hospital, Kodiak.

Climate: Summer temperatures are usually in the 60s and low 70s. Winters are normally mild; the temperature ranges from the upper 20s to the 30s.

Private Aircraft: Floatplane landings only.

Visitor Facilities: Accommodations and meals provided at Port William Lodge, (907) 688-2253. Laundry facilities, showers and saunas available. Fishing/hunting licenses are available. Public moorage and water available.

Port William originally was a cannery. For years it was the largest ice and cold storage plant in the Kodiak area, according to a resident. Now privately owned, the cannery is no longer operating. Port William is the only docking facility for large vessels from Kachemak Bay to Kodiak. Residents earn their livings from lodge and docking services, and commercial fishing.

Most of Shuyak Island is a wilderness. The northern end of the island is the Shuyak Island State Park, while a section along the east side has been proposed for a state game sanctuary. The middle of the island is part of the Kodiak Island Borough.

There is fishing for world-class halibut, Dolly Varden in the spring, and for silver and pink salmon in the fall. There are many birds, including bald eagles and puffins. Poor grade jade and jasper can be found on some beaches. There is hunting for deer, bear and elk (on Afognak Island just to the south). Other wildlife includes sea lions (on the Latax Rocks to the north), sea otters, land otters, beavers and whales.

Communications at Port William include mail plane and radio. There is no church or school.

Supplies are obtained from Kodiak. Freight arrives by mail plane.

Sand Point

GPS: N55°20′ W160°30′

Located on the north coast of Popof Island in the Shumagin Islands off the south coast of the Alaska Peninsula. **Transportation**: Scheduled air service from Anchorage; state ferry service in summer. **Population**: 871. **Zip code**: 99661. **Emergency Services**: Police, fire, medical, phone 911; Sand Point EMS and Sand Point Community Health Clinic, phone (907) 383-3151.

Private Aircraft: Airport 2 miles southwest; elev. 22 feet; length 4,000 feet; paved; jet A 50 fuel available; unattended. *CAUTION: 80- to 120-foot cliff on east side of runway.*

Visitor Facilities: Accommodations at a motel and a bed and breakfast. There are 3 restaurants, 2 bars and a laundry facility. Cab service available. Supplies available in the community. Fishing/hunting licenses available at the Trident office. Guide service available, also major repairs. Charter air service available, as well as diesel fuel and gasoline. Moorage facilities available. Shower facilities, 2 gyms, a teen center and an indoor swimming pool.

One of the most prosperous and modern Aleut communities, Sand Point has a cannery and a locally owned fishing fleet for crab, bottom fish and salmon. The community was founded by the Russians in the 1870s. The town became a supply center for the surrounding area after a cod-fishing station was built by the McCollam Fishing and Trading Co. In 1946 the first cold storage plant in Alaska was built there. Two quarry operations are currently active in the area. Sand Point is a first-class city, incorporated in 1966.

Sand Point's St. Nicholas Russian Orthodox Church, constructed in 1936, is on the National Register of Historic Places.

The community has 2 churches and a school with grades kindergarten through 12 with enrollment of 113. There are community electric, water and sewer systems. Freight arrives by air cargo, ship and barge.

Government address: City of Sand Point, P.O. Box 249, Sand Point, AK 9966, phone (907) 383-2696, fax (907) 383-2698, e-mail: sptcity@arctic.net. Village corporation address: Shumagin Corp., P.O. Box 189, Sand Point, AK 99661, phone (907) 383-3525, fax (907) 383-5496. Village council address: Qagun Tayagungin Tribe of Sand Point, P.O. Box 447, Sand Point, AK 99661-0447, phone (907) 383-5616, fax (907) 383-5814, e-mail: Tayagungin@aitc.org.

Shemya

GPS: N52°43′ W174°07′

(SHEAM-ee-a) Shemya Island is located near the west end of the Aleutian Chain, 1,500 miles southwest of Anchorage. *NOTE: Shemya is a military base with access strictly controlled by the U.S. Air Force. Visitors must be on official military business to go to Shemya.* The contact point for visit requests is AAC/LGX, Elmendorf AFB, AK 99506, phone (907) 552-5202. Private aircraft are not authorized access to Shemya. **Transportation:** U.S. Air Force plane or military charter plane only. **Population:** None in 2001 (Dept. of Labor estimate). **Zip code:** 98736. **Emergency Services:** Air Force Security; Air Force Medical Aid Station, phone (907) 392-3552.

Elevation: 90 feet. **Climate:** Generally winters are cloudy, windy and cold. Snow showers are numerous, but short. Considerable fog is experienced during the summer. Clear, calm days are rare. Temperatures range from an average high of 51°F in August to an average low of 28°F in February. Mean annual precipitation is 30 inches, including 65 inches of snow.

Private Aircraft: Airport adjacent south; elev. 90 feet; length 10,000 feet; asphalt. *NOTE: Official business only. Civilians must obtain prior permission to land. Contact HQ USAF/PRPJ, Washington, D.C. 20330, phone (202) 697-5967.*

Visitor Facilities: Military transient lodging and dining facilities only.

Shemya, largest in the Semichi Islands group, measures 4.5 miles long by 2.3 miles wide. The island is entirely controlled by the U.S. Air Force, which conducts operations at Shemya Air Force Base.

Black volcanic sand on the island inspired Shemya's nickname, "The Black Pearl of the Aleutians." The island also is referred to as "The Rock" because of its steep cliffs and rocky terrain. Summer brings a profusion of wildflowers, some unique to the Aleutians. Driftwood, various types of rocks and shells, and many WWII relics and ruins abound on Shemya.

Shemya's involvement in the war began in May 1943, when 2,500 Army troops landed on the island to construct runways. The plan was to use Shemya as a secret air base for the bombardment of Japan. The first bombing mission flew from Shemya on March 16, 1944; the last on Aug. 13, 1945.

Communications at Shemya include phones, mail plane, radio and TV. All utilities are provided on base.

South Naknek

GPS: N58°41' W157°00'

Located on the Alaska Peninsula on the Naknek River, 2 miles south of Naknek, 15 miles west of King Salmon and 300 miles southwest of Anchorage. **Transportation:** Scheduled airline and air taxi. **Population:** 157. **Zip code:** 99670. **Emergency Services:** Police, phone (907) 246-4222; Alaska State Troopers, King Salmon, phone (907) 246-3346; South Naknek Health Clinic, phone (907) 246-6546; Bristol Bay Volunteer Rescue Squad (Naknek), phone (907) 246-4224/4222; river crossing to Camai Medical Center; Volunteer Fire Department.

Climate: Cool, humid and windy weather. Average summer temperatures at the nearest weather station in King Salmon range from 42°F to 63°F; average winter temperatures from 4°F to 29°F. Average annual precipitation 20 inches; average snowfall 45 inches.

Private Aircraft: State airstrip 1 mile southwest; elev. 130 feet; length 3,310 feet; gravel; attended; intersecting runway, length 2,260 feet; attended. Runway condition is monitored; visual inspection recommended prior to using. The strips are lighted.

Visitor Facilities: The Pit Hotel, (907) 246-6512. There is a store, snack bar and bar. Fishing/hunting licenses and guide service available. Availability of repair service, rental transportation and fuel unknown. Borough-maintained dock.

South Naknek, located just across the river from Naknek, is part of the Bristol Bay Borough. It is a more traditional rural community than its neighbor. South Naknek is not connected by road to any other community.

Commercial fishing and salmon processing are the mainstays of South Naknek's economy. Two of the 5 canneries that line the south bank of the Naknek River are in operation and recruit 400 to

500 people from outside the village for the brief summer salmon season. Most other employment is in community service. About 75 percent of South Naknek's residents depend on subsistence hunting and fishing as a vital source of food. Hunting camps along the Naknek River date back to 3,000 to 4,000 BC. South Naknek was settled after the turn of the century as a result of salmon cannery development.

NOTE: *Hiking, berry picking, camping and fishing are permitted on lands owned by the Alaska Peninsula Corp. upon payment of a $100/per-person fee. Hunting and woodcutting on corporation lands are not permitted. Contact the corporation for more information.*

South Naknek's Russian Orthodox Elevation of the Holy Cross Church, built in the early 1900s, is listed on the National Register of Historic Places.

Communications in South Naknek include phones, radio, mail plane and satellite TV. The community is served by 2 churches and a school with grades preschool to 6 with enrollment of 24; older students are flown to Naknek daily to attend school. There is a community electric system; water is from individual wells and a community system installed in 1997. A sanitary sewage collection system is also in operation. Freight arrives by air and barge. Government address: Bristol Bay Borough, P.O. Box 189, Naknek, AK 99663, phone (907) 246-4224. Village corporation: Alaska Peninsula Corp., 800 Cordova St., Anchorage, AK 99501, phone (907) 274-2433. Village council: Native Village of South Naknek-Qinuyang, P.O. Box 70029, South Naknek, AK 99670, phone (907) 246-8614, fax (907) 246-8613, e-mail: SouthNaknek@aitc.org.

St. George

GPS: N56°36' W169°32'

Located on St. George Island, southernmost of the Pribilof Island group, 780 miles west-southwest of Anchorage. **Transportation**: Scheduled airline from Anchorage via St. Paul and twice weekly flights from Anchorage. **Population**: 125. **Zip code**: 99591-0929. **Emergency Services**: Village Public Safety Officer, phone (907) 859-2429/2263; Alaska State Troopers in Dutch Harbor; St. George Health Clinic, phone (907) 859-2254; St. George EMS First Responders, phone (907) 859-2232/2255/2204; Volunteer Fire Department.

Elevation: 100 feet. **Climate**: The climate is controlled by the cold waters of the Bering Sea; there is cool weather year-round. Temperatures ranging from a high of 63°F in summer to a low of -7°F in winter have been recorded. The warmest month is July; the coldest is March. Heavy fog is frequent from May through August. Mean annual precipitation is 30 inches, including 47 inches of snow.

Private Aircraft: Airstrip adjacent west; elev. 125 feet; length 5,000 feet; gravel; jet fuel; unattended; contact City of St. George. Avoid flying over seal rookeries May through October. Cab service available into town.

Visitor Facilities: Accommodations at the St. George Hotel (designated a national historic landmark). Hotel has cooking facilities, and meals are available there. Hotel may close during winter months. No banking services. Groceries, clothing, first-aid supplies, hardware and film are available at St. George Canteen. Arts and crafts available for purchase include seal pelts, model bidarkas (skin boats), model seals and baskets. Fishing/hunting licenses not available. Tour guide service sometimes available in summer. Repair service for marine engines, boats and autos available. Arrangements can be made to rent private autos. Fuel available includes marine gas, diesel, propane and unleaded gasoline. Moorage facilities available.

St. George Island has perhaps the largest seabird colony in the northern hemisphere: 2.5 million seabirds nest on the 1,000-foot-high cliffs each summer. In addition, an estimated 250,000 seals congregate in 4 major rookeries on the island. Because of scientific research on the island, camping is not permitted. The St. George Tanaq Corp. offers guided tour programs in the summer, which include transportation, lodging and meals. Travelers should leave itineraries loose in case weather delays flights; keep baggage to a minimum.

The treeless uplands around St. George

are inhabited by a diverse population of songbirds, blue foxes, lemmings and a few reindeer that are descendants of 3 bucks and 12 does introduced in 1911.

Communications in St. George, a second-class city incorporated in 1983, include phones, mail plane, radio and TV. The community's St. George the Great Martyr Russian Orthodox Church, built circa 1932-35 and recently restored, is on the National Register of Historic Places. There is a school with grades kindergarten through 8 with enrollment of 31. There are community electric, water and sewer systems. Freight arrives by cargo plane, barge, ship and mail. Government address: City of St. George, P.O. Box 929, St. George, AK 99591, phone (907)859-2263, fax (907) 859-2212, e-mail: mayormax@yahoo.com. Village corporation: St. George Tanaq Corp., 2600 Denali St., Ste. 300, Anchorage, AK 99503, phone (907) 272-9886. Village council address: St. George Traditional Council, P.O. Box 940, St. George, AK 99591, phone (907) 859-2205, fax (907) 859-2242, e-mail: StGeorge@aitc.org.

St. Paul

GPS: N57°07' W170°16'

Located on St. Paul Island, northernmost of the Pribilof Island group. **Transportation**: Ship; scheduled and charter plane from Anchorage via Cold Bay or Dutch Harbor. **Population**: 585. **Zip code**: 99660. **Emergency Services**: Police and Village Public Safety Officer, phone (907) 546-3132 or 911; St. Paul Health Clinic, phone (907) 546-2310; St. Paul EMS Rescue Squad, phone (907) 2477/2244; Volunteer Fire Department, VHF Channel 16.

Elevation: 20 feet. **Climate**: Cool year-round. Heavy fog is frequent May through August. Mean annual precipitation is 23 inches, including 56 inches of snow.

Private Aircraft: Airstrip 3 miles northeast; elev. 44 feet; length 6,500 feet; gravel; jet A fuel; unattended. For runway lights contact the National Weather Service on 123.6 or phone (907) 546-2215. No airport facilities. Taxi service to town available with prior arrangements.

Visitor Facilities: Accommodations at King Eider Hotel, (907) 546-2477. Laundry and shower facilities available to hotel guests. ATM available. Groceries, clothing, first-aid supplies, hardware, film and limited sporting goods available in the community. Arts and crafts including ivory jewelry, photographs of local flora and fauna, dried wildflowers and fur seal garments are available at hotel gift shop. Guide service available, as well as local tours. Vehicles available for rent. Fuel available includes diesel, propane, and unleaded gasoline.

Each summer approximately 700,000-900,000 northern fur seals gather in rookeries on the shores of the Pribilof Islands and can be observed from 2 blinds. Access is by permit or with a tour group.

More than 200 species of birds have been sighted on St. Paul Island during the summer months. Many of these birds breed and nest on the coastal cliffs west and south of the village. The U.S. Fish and Wildlife Service acquired 1,000 acres of nesting area on St. Paul and 2,000 acres on St. George as additions to Alaska Maritime National Wildlife Refuge.

The uplands around St. Paul have a diverse population of songbirds, white and blue foxes and about 450 reindeer, descendants of 4 bucks and 21 does introduced in 1911.

Tourists are encouraged to visit Black Diamond Hill, where they may find shiny crystals of augite. Crystals of olivine and rutile found on the island may reach semiprecious gem size and quality.

Communications in St. Paul, a second-class city incorporated in 1971, include phones, U.S. mail, FedEx, radio and cable TV. There are community electric, water and sewage systems. The community is served by the recently restored Saints Peter and Paul Russian Orthodox Church, which is on the National Register of Historic Places, and a school with grades kindergarten through 12 with enrollment of 113. Freight arrives by cargo plane, ship and barge. Government address: City of St. Paul, P.O. Box 901, St. Paul Island, AK 99660, phone (907) 546-2331, fax (907) 546-3188, e-mail: stpaulak@hotmail.com. Village corporation: Tanadgusix Corp., P.O. Box 88, St. Paul Island, AK 99660, phone (907) 546-2312, or Tanadgusix

Corp., 4300 B St., Anchorage, AK 99503, phone (907) 278-2311. Village council: St. Paul Tribal Government, P.O. Box 86, St. Paul Island, AK 99660, phone (907) 546-2211, e-mail: SaintPaul@aitc.org.

Uganik Bay

(You-GAN-ik) Located on Uganik Bay on the northwest side of Kodiak Island, 40 miles west of Kodiak, 270 miles south-southwest of Anchorage. **Transportation**: Charter air service from Kodiak. **Population**: 15. **Zip code**: 99615 (via Kodiak). **Emergency Services**: Alaska State Troopers, Kodiak; Kodiak Island Hospital.

Elevation: 50 feet. **Climate**: Mean daily maximum temperature in July 64°F; mean daily maximum in January 36°F. Mean annual precipitation 44 inches, with 51 inches of snow.

Private Aircraft: No airstrip; seaplane landings only.

Visitor Facilities: None.

Village Islands in Uganik Bay was the location of an Alutiiq village in the 1800s. There are a few homes at West Point and another in Mush Bay in the east arm of Uganik Bay. Fishing is the only industry, according to one resident. There were 3 canneries operating in the bay in the 1920s, and 1 operating in 2001.

Uganik Bay is located within the Kodiak Island National Wildlife Refuge. Most visitors to the area are deer or bear hunters who fly in with air charter operators from Kodiak.

Steelhead, rainbow trout and silver salmon are available at Lake Uganik.

Communications in unincorporated Uganik Bay include mail plane and short-wave radio. Electricity is from individual generators; water is from streams. Sewage systems vary from flush toilets to pit toilets. There is no school or church. Freight arrives by mail plane, barge or ship.

Village corporation address: Uganik Natives Inc., P.O. Box 2095, Kodiak, AK 99615.

Ugashik

GPS: N57°30' W157°23'

(Yoo-GA-shik) Located on the Ugashik River on the Alaska Peninsula, 90 miles south of King Salmon, 370 miles south-west of Anchorage. **Transportation**: Boat; scheduled and charter air service from King Salmon. **Population**: 13. **Zip code**: 99613. **Emergency Services**: Alaska State Troopers, King Salmon, phone (907) 246-3346; Health Aide, Pilot Point; Camai Clinic, Naknek; Kanakanak Hospital, Dillingham.

Elevation: 25 feet. **Climate**: Cool, humid and windy. Temperature and precipitation data were collected at Pilot Point from 1939 to 1945. Average summer temperatures ranged from 41°F to 60°F. Average winter temperatures ranged from 12°F to 37°F. Total precipitation averaged 19 inches annually, with an average snowfall of 38 inches.

Private Aircraft: Airstrip 1 mile north; elev. 25 feet; length 3,000 feet; gravel. No airport facilities or public transportation to village.

Visitor Facilities: Some rooms available at God's Country Outfitters, phone (907) 245-5039 for availability July to October. Most supplies are obtained from Anchorage or locally from Pilot Point.

Ivan Petroff recorded the Eskimo (Alutiiq) village of Oogashik in 1880. It was one of the largest villages in the region until the influenza epidemic of 1919 decimated the population. The village has since remained small. A cannery in the village has operated under several owners. The Ugashik Traditional Village now owns the north half of the cannery and plans on renovating it into a smoker, freezer and storage facility. Alaska Wild Salmon runs a canning operation in the village. This predominantly Aleut village is unincorporated and governed by the Ugashik Traditional Village Council.

Recreational opportunities include hunting and sportfishing at Ugashik Lakes and the surrounding area, offered by God's Country Outfitters and Ugashik River Lodge. These areas are accessible by air taxi or boat.

NOTE: Hiking, berry picking, camping and fishing are permitted on lands owned by the Alaska Peninsula Corp. upon payment of a $100/per-person fee. Hunting and woodcutting on corporation lands are not *permitted. Contact the corporation for more information.*

Communications in Ugashik are mail, phone and radio. Electricity is provided by individual generators and water from wells for each home. Sewage systems are by septic tanks and composting toilets. There is no church, school or store. Freight arrives by cargo plane or barge. Government address: Ugashik Traditional Village, 206 E. Fireweed Lane, #204, Anchorage, AK 99503, phone (907) 338-7611, fax (907) 338-7659, e-mail: Ugashik@gci.net. Village corporation: Alaska Peninsula Corp., P.O. Box 104360, Anchorage, AK 99510, phone (907) 274-2433.

Unalaska/Dutch Harbor

GPS: N53°52' W166°32'

(UN-a-las-ka) Located on the northern end of Unalaska Island, second island in the Aleutian Chain, 800 miles southwest of Anchorage; Dutch Harbor (the major port area) is located on Amaknak Island, across a bridge from Unalaska. **Transportation**: Boat; scheduled and charter airline from Anchorage; state ferry April to October. **Population**: 4,283. **Zip code**: Unalaska 99685; Dutch Harbor 99692. **Emergency Services**: For all emergencies, phone 911; Iliuliuk Family & Health Services, phone (907) 581-1202/1203; Oonalaska Wellness Center (A/PIA). Unalaska Volunteer Ambulance Service, Unalaska Search & Rescue Divers, and Volunteer Fire Department, phone (907) 581-1233.

Elevation: 20 feet. **Climate**: This is the "Cradle of the Storms," where the warm Japan Current from the south meets the colder air and water currents of the Bering Sea. This mingling creates storm centers which sweep westward, influencing weather systems over most of North America. While the temperature is moderate, there can be tremendous winds and days of almost constant rain. Mean annual precipitation is 64.5 inches.

Private Aircraft: Airport 1 mile north; elev. 22 feet; length 3,900 feet; paved; fuel 100, jet A; attended. Passenger terminal, ticket counters, restrooms, taxis.

Visitor Facilities: Accommodations at UniSea Inn, (907) 581-1325; Carl's Hotel,

(907) 581-1230; Grand Aleutian Hotel, (907) 581-3844; Eagle Inn, (907) 581-2800; and Capt's Bay Inn, (907) 581-1825; bunkhouses, operated by several seafood canneries; 8 restaurants; 2 laundromats; and banking services available. Groceries, clothing, first-aid supplies, hardware, film and sporting goods may be purchased at local stores, which include Carl's, (907) 581-1234; Alaska Commercial; Petro Mart; Aleutian Mercantile Co., (907) 581-1796; and Alaska Ship Supply, (907) 581-1284. Arts and crafts for purchase include Aleut grass baskets, woodblock prints, paintings, and wood and ivory carvings. Fishing/ hunting licenses available; no guide service. Major repair service available for ships and marine engines and equipment; limited repairs for autos; check with air carriers for aircraft mechanic or go to Cold Bay. Vehicle and boat rental available. Air and fishing boat charters available. Moorage facilities available, contact the Port Director, (907) 581-1254. Several other commercial enterprises are located in the community.

Ounalashka, or Unalaska, was the early headquarters of the Russian-American Co. and a key port for the sea otter fur trade in the 1700s. After the United States purchased Alaska, the North American Commercial Co. became manager of the seal harvest in the Pribilofs and built a station at Dutch Harbor. Unalaska became a major stop for ships heading to and from the Nome goldfields in the early part of this century. In 1939 the U.S. Army and Navy began building installations at Unalaska and Dutch Harbor. In June 1942, the area was bombed by the Japanese and almost all of the local Aleut people were evacuated to southeastern Alaska. Military relics still dot the hillsides, although there has been a major cleanup program in recent years. The Dutch Harbor Naval Base and Fort Mears on Amaknak Island have been designated national historic landmarks.

Unalaska is the major civilian port west of Kodiak and north of Hawaii and is the gateway to the Bering Sea region. It is becoming a major international transshipment port and staging area.

Unalaska/Dutch Harbor is also one of the most productive seafood processing ports in the United States and remains ice free year-round. There are several large seafood processing companies that help form the basis for the local economy.

Two local attractions are on the National Register of Historic Places. One is the Russian Orthodox Church of the Holy Ascension in Unalaska, built in 1825. The other is the Sitka Spruce Plantation in Dutch Harbor, where 6 trees which were planted by the Russians in 1805 have survived in the harsh climate of the naturally treeless Aleutians.

At the entrance of the airport is a memorial to those killed in the Aleutians in WWII; a special tribute to the Aleuts who died during their relocation to southeastern Alaska also is planned.

Hiking in the area is easy and there is no need for trails. There are no bears on Unalaska Island; however, hikers should be careful around the cliffs. Dress appropriately. Be prepared for the weather to change for the worse.

Fish include halibut; red, pink and silver salmon; and Dolly Varden. Shrimp, crab, clams and "bidarkies" (chitons) are taken, but there is no guarantee that shellfish are free of paralytic shellfish poisoning. There is no big game on Unalaska; local hunting is for ptarmigan, ducks or red fox. Contact the Alaska Dept. of Fish and Game office, (907) 581-1239, for more information.

Unalaska is a first-class city, incorporated in 1942, which encompasses Amaknak Island and Dutch Harbor, and a portion of Unalaska Island. Communications in Unalaska include phones, mail, radio and TV. There are community electric, water and sewer systems.

Government address: City of Unalaska, P.O. Box 610, Unalaska, AK 99685, phone (907) 581-1251, fax (907) 581-1417, e-mail: dmack@ci.unalaska.ak.us; web: www.unalaska.ak.us. Unalaska/Dutch Harbor Chamber of Commerce, P.O. Box 920833, Dutch Harbor, AK 99692, phone (907) 581-4242, fax (907) 581-2613, e-mail: veda @arctic.net. Village corporation: Ounalaska Corp., P.O. Box 149, Unalaska, AK 99685, phone (907) 581-1276, fax (907) 581-1496. Village council: Qawalangin Tribe of Unalaska, P.O. Box 334, Unalaska, AK 99685, phone (907) 581-2920, fax (907) 581-3644, e-mail: Qawalangin@aitc.org.

Woody Island (Leisnoi Island)

GPS: N57°46' W152°19'

Located 2.6 miles east of the city of Kodiak. **Transportation**: Private boat; charter air service. **Population**: 1 to 4 in winter; 1 to 6 in summer. **Zip code**: 99615 (via Kodiak). **Emergency Services**: Alaska State Troopers, Kodiak; Kodiak Island Hospital.

Climate: Similar to Kodiak.

Private Aircraft: No airstrip; floatplane or helicopter landings only.

Visitor Facilities: Available in nearby Kodiak.

The island was named by the Russian explorer U.T. Lisianski in 1804. Woody Island figured in the early history of Alaska as a boat-building center and a port from which the Russian American Ice Co. and Kodiak Ice Co. shipped ice to California in the early and middle 1800s. It is believed the first horses in Alaska were brought to Woody Island in 1867, and that the first road built in Alaska—2.7 miles long—was built around the island. Boat building flourished at both Kodiak and Woody Island during the late 1880s. The settlement of Woody Island gradually diminished as the population settled more steadily at Kodiak.

Woody Island has few residents. A Baptist youth camp operates here in the summer.

Communications at Woody Island include radio and satellite TV. A public electricity system is available; water is from wells and a lake; residents have flush toilets. Freight arrives by private boat. Village corporation address: Leisnoi Inc., 4300 B St., Ste. 207, Anchorage, AK 99503., phone (907) 562-1126, fax (907) 562-1128. Village council: Leisnoi Village, P.O. Box 9009, Kodiak, AK 99615, phone (907) 486-2821, fax (907) 486-2738, e-mail: twitc@ptialaska.net.

Southwestern Alaska is home to some of the most productive wildlife habitat in the world, offering visitors excellent opportunities to view bears, wolves, small land and marine mammals, and sea and shore birds. The area is renowned for its premiere fishing, hunting, bird viewing and breathtaking scenery.

Index of Southwestern Attractions

Alaska State Parks
See Shuyak Island State Park

Bear Viewing
See also McNeil River State Game Sanctuary; Katmai National Park and Preserve; Kodiak National Wildlife Refuge

Bird Watching
See Alaska Maritime National Wildlife Refuge; Alaska Peninsula National Wildlife Refuge; Aniakchak National Monument and Preserve; Katmai National Park and Preserve; Izembek National Wildlife Refuge; Kodiak National Wildlife Refuge

Cabins
Kodiak National Wildlife Refuge Cabins
Shuyak Island State Park Cabins

Fishing
Alaska Peninsula Area
Kodiak Island Area

Lighthouses
Cape Sarichef
Scotch Cap Light Station

Mountaineering

National Parks and Monuments
See Aniakchak National Monument and Preserve; Katmai National Park and Preserve

River Running

Sea Kayaking
See also Shuyak Island State Park

Special Features
See Anangula; Pribilof Islands; Unga Island Petrified Forest; World War II Military Sites

State Game Refuges
See Redoubt Bay State Critical Habitat Area

Wildlife Refuges
See Alaska Maritime National Wildlife Refuge; Alaska Peninsula National Wildlife Refuge; Becharof National Wildlife Refuge; Izembek National Wildlife Refuge; Kodiak National Wildlife Refuge

✕ ⚐ Alaska Maritime National Wildlife Refuge

This refuge contains more than 3,000 islands, islets, rock spires, reefs and headlands of Alaska coastal water from Port Franklin on the Chukchi Sea to Forrester Island in southeastern Alaska. The refuge totals about 4.5 million acres, most of which is in the Aleutian Islands.

The refuge's Aleutian Islands Unit includes nearly all of the more than 124 named islands in the Aleutian chain. The Alaska Peninsula Unit includes Simeonof and Semidi islands, the Shumagin Islands, Sutwik Island, Puale Bay islands and headlands and other lands south of the peninsula from Katmai National Park and Preserve to False Pass. (The Bering Sea Unit includes the Pribilofs, Hagemeister Island and St. Matthew Island.)

Wildlife: Alaska Maritime is synonymous with seabirds—millions of them. About 75 percent of Alaska's marine birds (40 million to 60 million birds among 38 species) use the refuge. The refuge has the most diverse wildlife species of all the refuges in Alaska, including thousands of sea lions, seals, walruses and sea otters.

Alaska Maritime is home to many Steller sea lions, which are listed as an endangered species. According to the Alaska Maritime National Wildlife Refuge, all sea lion rookeries west of 141° longitude—including the Gulf of Alaska—have a 3-nautical-mile buffer zone in which no vessels may operate. On land, the buffer zone is one half mile or within sight of a listed Steller sea lion rookery on Pye Islands, Barren Islands, Marmot Island, Semidi Islands, Shumagin Islands, Aleutian Islands and Walrus Island in the Pribilof Islands group.

Activities: Visitor activities in the refuge include wildlife observation, backpacking and photography. Bird watching is popular on Attu and Adak islands in the Aleutians where Asian birds stop on their migrations. A bird list for Adak is available at http://www.npwrc.usgs.gov/resource/othrdata/chekbird/r7/adakisle.htm. The list of 155 birds includes 34 that are "Asiatic" in origin.

The refuge provides a naturalist on board most summer sailings of the state ferry M/V *Tustumena* between Homer, Kodiak and Dutch Harbor. The naturalist presents daily programs, including slide shows, and is available to help identify seabirds and marine mammals.

The refuge operates a visitor center at 451 Sterling Highway in Homer. The center features wildlife exhibits and films. It is open 9 A.M. to 5 P.M. daily between Memorial Day and Labor Day. The center also provides bird watching and beach walks.

Access: Most of the refuge is wild and lonely, extremely rugged and virtually inaccessible. Some portions are classified as wilderness. Swift tides, rough seas, high winds, rocky shorelines and poor anchorages hamper efforts to view wildlife. Some islands within the refuge have restricted access to protect wildlife. There is scheduled air service to Dutch Harbor and Cold Bay, which have hotels, restaurants and air charter operations. Military clearance is required to visit Adak, Shemya and Attu islands. In the Pribilof Islands, St. Paul and St. George have scheduled air service from Anchorage and locally guided tours of seabird rookeries and fur seal haul-out sites.

For more information: Contact Outdoor Recreation Planner, Alaska Maritime National Wildlife Refuge, 2355 Kachemak Bay Drive, Suite 101, Homer, Alaska 99603-8021; phone (907) 235-6546, fax (907) 235-7783, email alaskamaritime@fws.gov.

✕ ⚐ Alaska Peninsula National Wildlife Refuge

This 4.3-million-acre refuge on the Pacific side of the Alaska Peninsula extends southwest from Becharof National Wildlife Refuge to False Pass. Aniakchak National Monument and Preserve splits the refuge into 2 parts.

This refuge is one of the most scenically diverse, featuring active volcanoes, lakes, rivers, tundra and a beautiful stretch of rugged, rocky Pacific Ocean coastline. The Alaska Peninsula is dominated by the spectacular Aleutian Range, part of a chain of volcanoes known as the "Ring of Fire" that encircles the Pacific Rim. Mount Veniaminof (elev. 8,225 feet) in the refuge is one of Alaska's active volcanoes and is active on an intermittent basis and last erupted from 1993 to 1995. Other special features of the refuge are the Ugashik lakes, renowned for arctic grayling fishing; Castle Cape Fjords, a famous landmark to ships with its distinctive light and dark rock layers; and the needle-pointed Aghileen Pinnacles and vertical buttresses of Cathedral Valley near recently active Pavlof Volcano.

Climate: This area is characterized by high winds, mild temperatures, cloud cover and frequent precipitation. Fog and drizzle are common in summer. Severe storms can occur year-round, often with intense winds known as williwaws. Fall is usually the wettest season, with most of the rain and fog occurring July through October. July is the warmest month, with temperatures averaging 54°F. December is the coldest month, with temperatures averaging 12°F. Summer temperatures can range from 32°F to 80°F with an average in the 50s.

Wildlife: Aside from bears, large mammals found in the refuge include moose, caribou, wolves and wolverines. The bears are especially attracted to the productive salmon streams. Large populations of sea lions, seals, sea otters and migratory whales inhabit the coastline and offshore waters. The refuge provides habitat for millions of birds—especially waterfowl—that use the area as a staging ground on their way to and from nesting grounds in the Arctic.

Activities: This refuge is renowned for big game hunting, especially for moose, caribou and brown bear. Fishing is outstanding for king and silver salmon, arctic char, lake trout, northern pike and grayling. A list of commercial guides holding permits to operate in the refuge is available from the refuge manager or the King Salmon Visitor Center.

Access: The refuge is accessible by air or by boat. There is scheduled air service from Anchorage to King Salmon, Kodiak, Sand Point and Cold Bay, where small planes may be chartered to the refuge. There are no commercial facilities, roads or trails in the refuge, wilderness camping only.

For more information: Contact Refuge Manager, Alaska Peninsula/Becharof National Wildlife Refuges, P.O. Box 277, King Salmon, AK 99613; phone (907) 246-3339. Trip planning assistance for the refuge is available at the King Salmon Visitor Center at the King Salmon airport. Jointly operated by the U.S. Fish and Wildlife Services, the National Park Service and the Bristol Bay and Lake Peninsula boroughs, the center is open daily in summer (June to September) from 8 A.M. to 5 P.M. There is a staffed information desk, bookstore, maps, posters, cultural and wildlife exhibits and an audio-visual room with videos; phone (907) 246-4250.

✳ Anangula

Dating back at least 8,000 years, Anangula is the oldest known settlement in the Aleut world. This site is located on now uninhabited Anangula (Ananiuliak) Island at the northern end of Samalga Pass off Nikolski village. Thousands of stone artifacts have been found at Anangula that link this culture to those of northern and central Asia, particularly the Kamchatka Peninsula. The fate of those who lived at Anangula is in question, however, as the site appears to have been occupied for less than a century when a heavy cover of volcanic ash rained down from Okmok Volcano, probably killing local plants and animals on which the people depended. The 4,000-year gap between settlement and evidence that man again lived in the area appears to correspond to a period of volcanism.

⛰ Aniakchak National Monument and Preserve

This 600,000-acre monument and preserve is located on the Alaska Peninsula 10 miles east of Port Heiden and 150 miles southwest of King Salmon. Its centerpiece is 6-mile-wide, 2,000-foot-deep Aniakchak caldera, which was created by the collapse of a 7,000-foot volcano some 3,500 years ago. Later activity built a 2,200-foot cone, Vent Mountain, inside the caldera.

The caldera remained hidden from the outside world until 1922 when a government geologist noticed that the taller peaks in the area formed a circle on the map he was making. Even today, few people have seen the crater; fewer still have walked upon its floor.

Some believe that the caldera at one time contained a deep lake. Eventually, the lake waters began to spill over the caldera wall, and through time, the fast-flowing Amakchak River has gouged a spectacular, 1,500-foot-deep gap in the wall called The Gates. The wild and scenic Aniakchak River heads in Surprise Lake inside the caldera, which is fed by thermal springs. The river then flows 30 miles southeastward to the Pacific Ocean.

Aniakchak last erupted in 1931, adding a "small, but impressive," explosion pit to the pocked caldera floor and scouring the caldera of vegetation. Today, the caldera chronicles a history of volcanic activity in its lava flows, cinder cones and explosion pits, as well as the beginnings of revegetation bringing life to the barren landscape.

Climate: Aniakchak is remote, difficult to reach and has "notoriously bad weather," says the National Park Service. Temperatures vary greatly. Winter's maximum may range from the low 30s to -30°F. Summer temperatures range from the mid- and upper 40s to a high of 70°F. Even when the weather is calm outside, violent windstorms in the caldera can make camping there difficult. In June and July 1973, a man's camp was destroyed twice in 6 weeks and his boat blown away. Local pilots have reported strong, turbulent winds in the caldera, particularly through the narrow Gates, which make flying conditions extremely hazardous.

Wildlife: Caribou, brown bears and eagles are found in the area. Fishing for Dolly Varden and all 5 species of Pacific salmon. Red salmon spawn up the Aniakchak River all the way to Surprise Lake (fish from here are recognizable by the flavor of soda and iron from the mineral-laden water).

Activities: Recreation in Aniakchak includes bird watching, hiking, camping, fishing, hunting and river trips. For a list of birds in the monument, go to www.npwrc.usgs.gov/resource/othrdata/chekbird/r7/akpenin.htm. Contact the National Monument's office in King Salmon for a list of hunting and fishing guides and outfitters. Guided hiking is also available; the monument has no trails. River runners may raft the Aniakchak River, whose upper reaches are termed "challenging" (see River running this section). There are 3 permitted commercial river guides operating in Aniakchak.

The Park Service recommends that anyone spending time in Aniakchak be prepared for cold, wet weather and high winds. A backcountry permit and bear-proof food canisters are required for campers and backpackers. Leave a copy of your itinerary at park headquarters in King Salmon.

Accommodations: There are accommodations at Port Heiden and in King Salmon, but nothing within the monument. The monument offers wilderness camping and there is a public-use cabin on the north side of the mouth of the Aniakchak River.

Access: Aniakchak is about 1 1/2, hours flying time from King Salmon and a 1/2 hour from Port Heiden. There are daily commercial flights from Anchorage to King Salmon. There are 6 permitted air taxi services operating within the monument. Floatplanes can land at Surprise Lake inside the caldera. Wheeled planes land on the beach at Aniakchak Bay. The park is also accessible by power boat from any of the coastal villages.

For more information: Contact Superintendent, Aniakchak National Monument and Preserve, P.O. Box 7, King Salmon, AK 99613; phone (907) 246-3305, fax (907) 246-2116, www.nps.gov/ania/. USGS maps: Sutwick Island, Chignik, Bristol Bay, Ugashik.

Bear Viewing

Bear viewing is increasingly popular in Southwestern Alaska, with viewer numbers in some locations increasing an estimated fourfold in just the last few years. This popularity has enticed many businesses to offer chartered aircraft or boat access to designated viewing areas and to areas where visitors can fish with the bears during salmon runs.

In order to preserve bear and human welfare in these close encounters, bear viewing is often limited, especially during peak seasons. Some established viewing areas, such as McNeil River, limit visitor numbers and viewing time, while more remote sites are open to viewing and photography all day. Permits or reservations are usually required for managed areas. Bear-viewing areas requiring permits either issue them on a first-come, first-served basis, or have a permit application and processing period in place. For this reason, interested parties should begin their planning early, applying for permits by January 1. The deadline for applications is usually the end of February or beginning of March. Some permits are also drawn by lottery, such as the one for McNeil River. Special arrangements must be made and trips planned in advance with concessionaires or private air or boat charters.

Managed bear viewing areas in Southwestern include Katmai National Park's Brooks River and McNeil River State Game Sanctuary. Less well known, and without—as yet—a designated viewing area or permit system, are Chinitna Bay, Hallo Bay and Wolverine Creek. Check with air taxi services in Southwestern and Southcentral regarding bear-viewing flights to these spots.

Chinitna Bay. Chinitna Bay is 100 miles north of Katmai National Park and Preserve's boundary on the fringe of Lake Clark National Park and Preserve. This 10-mile-long bay is a popular spot for bear watchers looking for unmanaged bear viewing.

Hallo Bay. This bay is located along Katmai National Park's 398-mile coast. The viewing is in the park, and access is via state lands. Floatplanes usually transport clients to state tidelands on the edge of the park. Hallo Bay is home to the Hallo Bay Wilderness Camp, an "Eco-sensitive facility" where guests can observe coastal brown bears and other wildlife in their natural habitat.

Wolverine Creek. Wolverine Creek is on the west side of Cook Inlet across from Nikiski. It is 45 minutes across the inlet from Soldotna and is a tributary of the Big River Lakes system, 20 miles inland from Redoubt Bay and Redoubt Bay State Critical Habitat Area. This area has one of the greatest densities of mainland brown bears in Alaska—approximately 750 bears. Viewing is best during the sockeye salmon runs from early June to mid-July.

(See also McNeil River State Game Sanctuary, Katmai National Park and Preserve and Kodiak National Wildlife Refuge.)

Becharof National Wildlife Refuge

This 1.2-million-acre refuge is located on the Alaska Peninsula, sandwiched between Katmai National Park and Preserve and the Alaska Peninsula National Wildlife Refuge. It is dominated by Becharof Lake, the second largest lake in Alaska, which covers a quarter of the refuge and is surrounded by low, rolling hills, tundra wetlands in the northwest and volcanic peaks to the southeast. About 30 percent or 500,000 acres of Becharof National Wildlife Refuge is federally designated wilderness.

Climate: Becharof skies are usually cloudy. Less than 20 inches of precipitation falls annually in the western lowlands while as much as 160 inches falls on the eastern side of the Aleutian Range. October is the wettest month. Fall is the wettest season, with most of the rain and fog occurring July through October. Temperatures in December, the coldest month, average 12°F. In July, the warmest month, they average 54°F. Summer temperatures can range from 32°F to 80°F with an average temperature in the 50s. Vegetation does not begin growing until late May or early June, and the first frost usually occurs in late September.

Wildlife: The salmon spawning streams attract a large concentration of brown bears, many of which make their dens on islands in Becharof Lake. Moose inhabit the refuge in moderate numbers, and about 10,000 caribou migrate through and winter in the refuge. Other mammals include wolves, wolverines, river otters, red fox and beaver. In addition, thousands of sea mammals such as sea otters, sea lions, harbor seals and migratory whales inhabit the Pacific coastline. Waterfowl are common in the wetlands and coastal estuaries while nesting eagles, peregrine falcons and thousands of seabirds inhabit the sea cliffs and islands. About 20 species of seabirds nest in 13 colonies in the refuge; 2 colonies in Puale Bay are among the largest on the Alaska Peninsula.

Activities: Becharof offers outstanding bear and caribou hunting. Sportfishing in the refuge so far has been light although trophy-sized rainbow trout, arctic char, grayling and salmon exist. Write the refuge manager for a list of commercial guides holding permits for the refuge.

Access: The refuge is accessible by air or by boat. There is scheduled air service from Anchorage to King Salmon, Kodiak, Sand Point and Cold Bay where small planes may be chartered to the refuge. There are no commercial facilities or roads in the refuge.

For more information: Contact the Refuge Manager, Alaska Peninsula/Becharof National Wildlife Refuges, P.O. Box 277, King Salmon, AK 99613; phone (907) 246-3339. Trip planning assistance for the refuge is available at the King Salmon Visitor Center at the King Salmon airport. Jointly operated by the U.S. Fish and Wildlife Services, the National Park Service and area boroughs, the center is open daily in summer (June to September) from 8 A.M. to 5 P.M. There is a staffed information desk, bookstore, maps, posters, cultural and wildlife exhibits and an audio-visual room with videos; phone (907) 246-4250.

Cabins

Kodiak National Wildlife Refuge Cabins

Kodiak National Wildlife Refuge maintains 8 public–use cabins available by advance reservation. Cabins may be reserved for up to 7 days per year. Drawings for reservations take place January 2 for April, May and June; April 1 for July, August and September; July 1 for October, November and December; and October 1 for January, February and March. Cabins not reserved during the drawing are available on a first-come, first-served basis. Mail applications with choice of dates (including second choices if desired) to the refuge office. Fee for the cabins is $10 per night, due only after successful applicants have been notified.

All cabins have oil heating stoves. You must provide oil or kerosene for oil stoves; 5 gallons is usually sufficient for 1 week in mild weather. All cabins have pit toilets. No utensils or cook stoves are provided.

For a cabin pamphlet or reservation application, contact: Refuge Manager, Kodiak National Wildlife Refuge, 1390 Buskin River Road, Kodiak, AK 99615; phone (907) 487-2600, fax (907) 487-2144, e-mail kodiak@fws.gov.

Blue Fox Bay Cabin. Accessible by floatplane or boat. Cabin is handicap-accessible. Sleeps 4. Fishing for pink salmon in late July and August; Coho salmon good in August and September. Hunting for bear, elk and deer in area. Excellent tidepooling and photography around cabin. USGS map: Afognak B-3.

Chief Cove Cabin. Accessible by floatplane or boat. Sleeps 4. Fishing for pink salmon in late July and August. Bear, deer and waterfowl hunting good in the area. Excellent area for photography.

Little River Lake Cabin. Accessible by floatplane. Sleeps 4. Sockeye salmon fishing in July; Dolly Varden good April through November; Coho salmon fair September through November; rainbow trout fair June through November. Good deer and bear hunting. Photography and wildlife viewing is excellent in area. USGS map: Kodiak D-5.

North Frazer Lake Cabin. Accessible by floatplane. Sleeps 4. Excellent fishing for Dolly Varden, April through November; rainbow trout fair June through November; sockeye salmon excellent July through August. Hunting for bears and deer in area. Area offers photography and wildlife viewing for bears, eagles, waterfowl and small game. USGS map: Karluk B-1.

South Frazer Lake Cabin. Accessible by floatplane or boat. Sleeps 5. Fishing in lake for Dolly Varden, excellent April through November. Dog Salmon Creek excellent for coho salmon August through September; sockeye excellent July through August; steelhead excellent September through November; rainbow trout good June through November. Dog Salmon Creek easily accessible by raft and motor. Hunting good for deer and bears. Excellent photography and wildlife viewing for bears, eagles, fox, otters and weasels. USGS map: Karluck A-1.

Uganik Island Cabin. Accessible by floatplane or boat. Sleeps 4. Fishing for pink salmon and Dolly Varden July through August. Deer hunting good October through December.

Bear hunting fair spring and fall. Waterfowl hunting fair. Photography and wildlife viewing in wildlife estuaries and alpine habitat. USGS map: Kodiak D-4.

Uganik Lake Cabin. Accessible by floatplane or boat. Handicap-accessible. Sleeps 4. Fishing for pink salmon good in August; rainbow trout fair June through November; Dolly Varden excellent April through November; coho salmon good August through October; sockeye salmon good June through August. Good bear and deer hunting in area. Photography and wildlife viewing for bears and eagles good in area. USGS map: Kodiak C-4.

Viekoda Bay Cabin. Accessible by floatplane or boat. Sleeps 4. Fishing for pink salmon and Dolly Varden fair July through August. Deer hunting good fall to early winter. Bear and duck hunting fair. Photography and wildlife viewing in main estuaries and alpine habitats. USGS map: Kodiak D-4.

Shuyak Island State Park Cabins

Alaska State Parks maintains 4 recreational cabins on Shuyak Island, 2 on Big Bay, 1 on Carry Inlet and 1 on Neketa Bay. All are accessible by floatplane or boat; floatplane is usually more practical.

The cabins can be rented for up to 7 days at a time. Rates are $65 per night. The cabins are 16 X 20 feet and are equipped with wood stoves, propane lights and hot plate, 4 full-sized bunks with pads, manual shower and wash area, stainless steel sink, cooking utensils and pit toilets.

Bring maps of the island, compass, first-aid kit, matches, rope, rain gear, garbage bags for packing out all garbage, sleeping bag, individual eating utensils and extra clothes and food in case bad weather prolongs your stay.

Reservations may be made up to 180 days before the requested time. Reservations are accepted on a first-come, first-served basis and must be accompanied by a check. Full descriptions (with photos) and current information on cabin availability may be found online at www.alaskastateparks.org.

Obtain additional information or make cabin reservations through Alaska State Parks, Kodiak District Office, 1400 Abercrombie Dr., Kodiak, AK 99615, phone (907) 486-6339, fax (907) 486-3320; or Department of Natural Resources, Public Information Center (PIC), 550 West 7th Ave., Suite 1260, Anchorage, AK 99501-3557, phone (907) 269-8400, fax (907) 269-8901.

Deer Haven Cabin. Sleeps 8. Cabin accesses excellent deer hunting. Good salmon streams nearby are accessible by boat. Area offers excellent beachcombing and wildlife viewing for marine mammals and sea birds.

Eagles Nest Cabin. Sleeps 8. Cabin is located between 2 excellent salmon streams which are accessible by boat.

Mulcahy View Cabin. Sleeps 8. Located on Neketa Bay. Bay offers hiking and protected sea kayaking. Wildlife viewing for marine mammals and sea birds.

Salmon Cove Cabin. Sleeps 8. Salmon Cove offers excellent fishing and hunting, accessible by 2 foot trails. Big Bay offers good kayaking and hiking.

Fishing

This region offers some of the finest sportfishing for trout, king and coho salmon and halibut in the world. Probably the most prized sport fish are the trophy-sized rainbow trout. Rainbows in this area regularly reach 10 pounds. All of Southwestern Alaska is part of the state's Wild Trout Area. Special regulations designed to perpetuate the original wild rainbow trout stocks apply here as do special management areas for catch-and-release and fly-fishing only.

Tackle-breaking king salmon are at their best from early June through early July. These fish average 20 pounds and can reach 30 pounds or more. Kodiak Island's Karluk and Ayakulik rivers have two of the best king salmon runs in the world, with kings weighing more than 40 pounds. Each river averages over 10,000 kings per year. Chums and reds show up in early June, pinks by mid-July (in even-numbered years) and silvers by mid-August. Salmon fishing is concentrated in the river systems.

Arctic char and Dolly Varden are found throughout the region and are most abundant in spring, when some migrate to the sea, or in midsummer, when large schools concentrate at river mouths to feed on out-migrating, juvenile salmon.

Cloudy skies and light rain are common here. Bring warm clothing, rain gear and hip boots. Also be sure to bring lots of insect repellent. It's recommended that you purchase your fishing license in Anchorage. Please obtain current fishing regulations and information on each area from the Alaska Department of Fish and Game.

For more information about fishing on the Alaska Peninsula, contact: Area Management Biologist, Alaska Department of Fish and Game, P.O. Box 230, Dillingham, AK 99576; phone (907) 842-2427. For the Kodiak area, contact the Alaska Department of Fish and Game, Sport Fish Division, 333 Raspberry Road, Anchorage, AK 99518, phone (907) 267-2218, or Alaska Department of Fish and Game, 211 Mission Road, Kodiak, AK 99615, phone (907) 486-4791.

Alaska Peninsula Area Fishing

Alagnak River System. Located at the top of the Alaska Peninsula partially in Katmai National Preserve. Also within the state's Wild Trout Area; check the regulation book for special rules. The Alagnak River drains Battle and Kukaklek lakes and flows into Kvichak Bay. The Nonvianuk River, a tributary of the Alagnak, drains Kulik and Nonvianuk lakes. This drainage offers excellent fishing for 5 species of salmon. Excellent rainbow trout fishery; use unbaited, single-hook, artificial flies June 8 through October 31. Also available are grayling; arctic char, use spoons; northern pike, use spoons and spinners; and lake trout, use spoons and plugs. Air charter service available from Anchorage, Kenai, Homer, King Salmon, Dillingham and Iliamna.

Egegik River System. Located approximately 40 miles south of King Salmon, partially within Becharof National Wildlife Refuge. Egegik River drains Becharof Lake and empties into Egegik Bay, as does one of the King Salmon rivers (the other is in the Ugashik system farther south). Five species of salmon are found in this drainage; sockeyes spawn in Becharof Lake. Other fish present are grayling, use flies; arctic char, use spoons and eggs; northern pike, use spoons and spinners; and lake trout, use spoons and plugs. Air charter service available in King Salmon.

Naknek River System. The Naknek system extends from the town of Naknek, adjacent to King Salmon, upstream approximately 75 miles to the east. Much of the system is in Katmai National Park and is subject to additional federal regulations. The Naknek River drains Naknek Lake, Brooks Lake, Lake Colville and Lake Grosvenor; its outlet is Kvichak Bay, a good fishing location for those operating on a restricted budget. King salmon fishing is excellent on the Naknek River at King Salmon, where boats can be rented. Naknek Lake is accessible by road from King Salmon. This drainage offers good fishing for 5 species of salmon. Excellent rainbow trout fishery. Also available are grayling, arctic char, northern pike, lake trout and whitefish. Smelt are available in winter. Outlying lakes served by charter planes from King Salmon. Several commercial fishing lodges in the area.

Ugashik System. Located approximately 80 miles south of King Salmon; Ugashik lakes are within Alaska Peninsula National Wildlife Refuge. The Ugashik River drains Upper and Lower Ugashik lakes and flows into Ugashik Bay, as does the King Salmon River, which drains Mother Goose Lake and the glacier-fed Dog Salmon River. Five species of salmon are found in this drainage; sockeyes spawn in the Ugashik lakes. The grayling fishery is closed in the Ugashik drainage due to conservation problems with that stock. Other fish present are arctic char, use spoons and eggs; northern pike, use spoons and spinners; and lake trout, use spoons and plugs. Air charter service available in King Salmon or Pilot Point.

Kodiak Island Area Fishing

Afognak Island. Located approximately 30 air miles northeast of Kodiak, Afognak Island streams offer excellent remote fishing. Accommodations at Afognak Wilderness Lodge;

phone (907) 486-6442. This is brown bear country; try to avoid bears, make noise when traveling, and carry a .30-06 or larger rifle. Part of Afognak Island is within Kodiak National Wildlife Refuge, and part is owned by Koniag Native Corporation. Afognak River and Afognak Lake provide good fishing for Dolly Varden 10 to 20 inches, abundant most of the summer; red salmon peak runs in early June; silver salmon, best August 15 through September 7; pink salmon July and August; rainbow trout 10 to 16 inches, in the upper river June 15 to September. Steelhead and rainbow trout fishery is closed April 1 to June 14. This 6-mile-long lake is 32 air miles from Kodiak.

Other fishing waters on Afognak Island are: Waterfall Lake, 40 air miles from Kodiak, excellent fishing for Dolly Varden to 20 inches; Pillar Lake, small Dolly Varden; Portage Lake, 35 air miles north of Kodiak, Malina Lake, 36 air miles northwest of Kodiak, and Laura and Pauls lakes, 40 air miles northeast of Kodiak, all yield red and silver salmon, Dolly Varden and rainbow trout. Portage, Malina and Laura lakes also yield pink salmon and steelhead.

Akalura Lake. Measures 2.5 miles across, located in the Kodiak Island National Wildlife Refuge approximately 80 air miles southwest of Kodiak, 3 miles north of Olga Bay. Accessible by floatplane from Kodiak. Fish available: rainbow trout best June 15 to September, use flies or lures, closed April 1 to June 14; Dolly Varden May to October, best May and September, use spinners or flies; silver salmon good mid-August through September, use herring or spoons; red salmon June to July, use spoons or flies; pink salmon July to August, use small spoons.

Ayakulik (Red) River. Located in Kodiak National Wildlife Refuge approximately 85 air miles southwest of Kodiak. Fish available: rainbow trout season closed April 1 to June 14, best after June 15, use flies or lures; steelhead good at lake outlet in late September and early October, use spoons or eggs; Dolly Varden May to October, best May and September, use spinners or flies; king salmon, 15 to 40 pounds, best early June at mouth to mid-July in central river areas, use herring or spoons; silver salmon September through October, use herring or spoons; red salmon June to July, use spoons or flies; pink salmon July to August, use small spoons.

Buskin River. Located a few miles south of Kodiak by road within Kodiak Island National Wildlife Refuge. The only roadside stream with a significant run of sockeye salmon in June. Coho salmon in August and September, pink salmon in August. Dolly Varden all year, best during May, September and October migrations; use spoons, spinners, eggs and flies.

Karluk Lake, River and Lagoon. Located approximately 75 air miles southwest of Kodiak. Fish available: rainbow trout season closed April 1 to June 14, use flies or lures; steelhead from 25 to 35 inches, best in October, use spoons or eggs, closed April 1 to June 14; Dolly Varden best in May and September, use spinners or flies; excellent sockeye fishing with 2 runs of red salmon running strong in June and August and tapering off by mid-September, use spoons or flies; pink salmon best in July and early August, use small spoons; silver salmon plentiful late August through October, use herring or spoons; excellent for king salmon 10 to 40 pounds, early June (Karluk and Ayakulik Rivers), peak runs mid-June to the end of June, use herring or spoons. *NOTE: Land along the Karluk River as well as the riverbed is owned by Koniag Incorporated. Some land in the Karluk Lagoon area is owned by Karluk Tribal Council. Contact the tribal council at (907) 241-2218 for permits for this area. Permits for fishing or camping on the Karluk River may be obtained from Koniag Incorporated, 202 Center Avenue, Suite 201, Kodiak, AK 99615; phone (907) 486-2530.*

Kodiak Island Salt Water. Halibut, rockfish, flounder and other marine fish are caught in Kodiak Archipelago waters throughout the year although offshore fishing is best in summer. Pacific halibut are commonly found in immediate offshore waters in late May or early June. Most halibut are taken off Long and Woody islands. Boat-caught halibut up to 300 pounds, averaging 25 pounds; use cut herring or large, shiny lures near kelp beds. Other fish: Dolly Varden along rocky beaches from June through July, use herring strips and small- to medium-sized lures; pink salmon late June to mid-August, best from mid-July on, use small spoons; chum salmon 8 to 15 pounds arrive late July through early August, use spoons; silver salmon mid-August to November, use herring or spoons.

Lake Miam. A 1-mile-long lake on the east coast of Kodiak Island, a 15- to 20-minute flight by small plane from Kodiak. Fish available: small numbers of rainbow trout, season closed April 1 to June 14, use flies or lures; small numbers of steelhead September to November, use spoons or eggs; Dolly Varden May to October, best May and September, use spinners or flies; silver salmon September through October, use herring or spoons; red salmon June to July, use spoons or flies; pink salmon July to August, use small spoons.

Pasagshak River. Accessible by road from Kodiak, this stream supports the largest road-accessible run of coho, beginning in August and continuing through September; coho average 10 to 12 pounds, use eggs, lures, flies. Sea-run Dolly Varden in mid-April, use flies or lures. King, sockeye and pink salmon also present.

Saltery Lake and River. Located 36 miles southwest of Kodiak via a 15- to 20-minute air charter from Kodiak. Fish available: rainbow trout 9 to 14 inches, present in small numbers most of the summer, use flies or lures; small numbers of steelhead, closed April 1 to June 14, October through November, use spoons or eggs; Dolly Varden 10 to 18 inches abundant in May, August and September, use spinners or flies; silver salmon excellent late August through mid-October, use spoons; red salmon abundant in July, use spoons or flies; pink salmon abundant in mid-July to August, use small spoons.

Uganik Lake and River. Located 36 air miles southwest of Kodiak in Kodiak National Wildlife Refuge. Fish available: rainbow trout, season closed April 1 to June 14, best after June 15, use flies or lures; steelhead September to November, use spoons or eggs; Dolly Varden May to October, best May and September, use spinners or flies; silver salmon September through October, use herring or spoons; red salmon June to July, use spoons or flies; pink salmon July to August, use small spoons.

Upper Station lakes. Located approximately 90 air miles southwest of Kodiak in Kodiak National Wildlife Refuge. Fish available: rainbow trout, season closed April 1 to June 14, best after June 15, use flies or lures; small numbers of steelhead September to November, use spoons or eggs; Dolly Varden May to October, best May and September, use spinners or flies; silver salmon September through October, use herring or spoons; red salmon June to July, use spoons or flies; pink salmon July to August, use small spoons.

Woody and Long Island lakes. Located 2 to 4 miles east of Kodiak. Accessible by small plane or boat. Good camping, hiking, picnicking and beachcombing. Fish available: rainbow trout year-round, best after June 15 and October, use flies or lures; Dolly Varden May to October, best May and September, use spinners or flies; silver salmon September through October, use spoons; grayling in Long Lake year-round, use flies.

Izembek National Wildlife Refuge

One of the older national refuges in the state, Izembek is located at the tip of the Alaska Peninsula just across False Pass from Unimak Island, first in the Aleutian chain. It faces the Bering Sea and abuts the Alaska Peninsula National Wildlife Refuge. The 315,000-acre Izembek Unit of the refuge encompasses the entire Izembek Lagoon watershed. (The Izembek refuge office also administers the 415,000-acre Pavlof Unit of the Alaska Peninsula National Wildlife Refuge, and the 932,000-acre Unimak Unit of the Alaska Maritime National Wildlife Refuge.)

Izembek's landscape consists primarily of low brush tundra, alder thickets, willow patches, and numerous lakes and marshes. Lowland vegetation gives way to barren scree, snowfields and glaciers. The main feature of the refuge is Izembek Lagoon, protected by barrier islands from the Bering Sea. The lagoon is managed by the state as a game refuge.

Climate: Izembek summers are characterized by fog, drizzle and cloud cover, but they can vary from year to year. Severe storms may occur year-round, often accompanied by intense winds. The average annual precipitation is about 35 inches, with most occurring in fall. Temperatures range from an average of 28°F in February to 51°F in August. Vegetation usually starts growing in late May or early June; the first frost usually occurs in October or November.

Wildlife: This lagoon, along with several smaller lagoons, hosts up to 300,000 geese, 150,000 ducks and nearly all of the world's population of black brant (120,000 to 150,000 birds) during the fall migration. These birds feed on Izembek Lagoon's 84,000-acre eelgrass bed, one of the largest in the world. Most waterfowl arrive in the refuge in late August or early September. By early November, a second wave of northern waterfowl (primarily sea ducks) arrives to winter at Izembek. The colorful Steller's eider, which nests on the Arctic coast of Alaska and Siberia, is the most common wintering duck. In addition, thousands of shorebirds feed on the bay shore at low tide. At high tide, they gather in such large flocks that in flight, they look like smoke clouds.

Other wildlife includes brown bear, caribou, ptarmigan and furbearers. Fish in the refuge include 4 species of salmon, Dolly Varden, arctic char and steelhead trout. Sea lions, sea otters, harbor seals and gray, killer and minke whales are seen in bays and lagoons. The refuge office can provide lists of mammals and fish present on the refuge.

Activities: Goose and duck hunting is at its peak from late September to late October. Popular areas, according to the refuge office, include the Izembek Lagoon shoreline and islands (especially for brant) and the wetlands within a few miles of the lagoon (for Canada geese). There are a couple of commercial guides offering waterfowl hunting trips.

A guide is required for nonresident brown bear hunters participating in the annual spring and fall Unimak Unit brown bear hunt (available through drawing permit system). Brown bear hunting is available on the Izembek and Pavlof units on an alternate spring-even-year and fall-odd-year schedule. Caribou hunting is available.

Fishing for red and pink salmon is best in June and July. Silver salmon are present from August to early October.

Hunters and fishermen can access the shorelines of Izembek Lagoon and Cold Bay, Russell Creek and the lower flanks of Frosty Peak from the Cold Bay road system. There are no designated trails, but there are unimproved trails used by hunters and wildlife observers at various locations on the Izembek Unit.

Primitive camping is allowed on the refuge at no charge. Campers must provide all of their own equipment. Trip planning assistance is available through the refuge office.

Bird watching is also popular on the refuge, with October offering the best goose and duck viewing. Other species of birds are present at various times of the year. The refuge office can provide a bird list and birding guide, or on the web go to http://www.npwrc.usgs.gov/resource/othrdata/chekbird/r7/izembek.htm.

Access: The refuge boundary is less than a mile from refuge headquarters in Cold Bay and is accessible by a road system. Vehicles may be rented in Cold Bay. Motorized travel off the roads in the refuge is prohibited. Cold Bay is reached by scheduled air service from Anchorage and has some food and lodging facilities. Private and some small, commercial aircraft are permitted to land in the refuge; check with the refuge headquarters for guidance.

The Alaska Marine Highway vessel MV *Tustumena* serves Cold Bay from Kodiak monthly between May and September. The Cold Bay–Dutch Harbor trip is recommended for its excellent seabird viewing.

For more information: Contact the Refuge Manager, Izembek National Wildlife Refuge, P.O. Box 127, Cold Bay, AK 99571; phone (907) 532-2445, fax (907) 532-2549, email r7izemwr@fws.gov.

Katmai National Park and Preserve

The original Katmai National Monument at the top of the Alaska Peninsula was created in 1918 to preserve the volcanic wonders of the Valley of Ten Thousand Smokes, formed by a cataclysmic eruption just 6 years earlier. The June 6, 1912 eruption of Novarupta Volcano, in which Mount Katmai also collapsed, was one of the most violent ever recorded, and it darkened the sky over much of the northern hemisphere for several days. Novarupta spewed 7 cubic miles of incandescent ash and pumice which buried the 40-square-mile

Ukak River valley as much as 700 feet deep.

During the 1940s, Ray Petersen of Northern Consolidated Airlines built Brooks Camp. The camp catered to fishermen who came for the salmon and rainbow trout in the Brooks River. Bears also came for the fish in increasing numbers.

Today, some 35 to 40 bears may be found in the Brooks River drainage during the peak sockeye salmon run in July, and some 80 percent of the visitors to Brooks Camp are tourists who have come to view the bears or visit the Valley of Ten Thousand Smokes.

The bears congregate at Brooks Falls, about a mile below Brooks Lake. There are 3 bear viewing platforms along the river. In July, people can be found crowding the viewing platforms to watch up to a dozen bears fishing for salmon at the falls.

The valley remains one of the prime attractions of the park, where streams have cut dramatic gorges through the volcanic debris. In the years since the eruption, the thousands of fumaroles have dwindled to a few active vents. The park has been enlarged several times and is currently 4 million acres.

Sportfishing is still a major draw at Katmai. There are fish camps at Grosvenor Lake, Kulik Lake and at several other locations. Special restrictions apply to fishing the Brooks River because of the bears. "Bears are quick learners," according to the park superintendent. "As soon as they hear that reel zinging, they come running."

Besides the salmon, Katmai's waters boast grayling, Dolly Varden, lake trout, northern pike and trophy-sized rainbow trout—all of which make the fishing here world renowned. Catch-and-release fishing is encouraged throughout the park and required on some streams for rainbows. Brooks River is fly-fishing only above the floating bridge.

Climate: Visitors to Katmai should be prepared for stormy weather as well as some sunshine. Summer daytime temperatures range from the mid-50s to the mid-60s; the average low is 44°F. Strong winds and sudden gusts frequently sweep the area. Skies are clear about 20 percent of the summer. Light rain can last for days. Bring a warm sweater, windbreaker or lightweight fiberfill jacket, footgear that provides good support, wool socks and a wool hat. Rain gear should include raincoat and pants, parka and hat. You will need insect repellent and/or a headnet.

Wildlife: Katmai is becoming best known for its world-class bear viewing. Brown bears, the coastal equivalents of grizzlies, gather at Brooks Falls for the salmon run. But bears may also be encountered on trails leading to the falls and elsewhere in the park. Visitors are required to follow park guidelines regarding bear safety.

In addition to bears, other wildlife that may be seen are moose, wolves, wolverines, river otters, martens, weasels, mink, lynx, muskrats, beavers and an occasional caribou. Harbor seals, sea lions, sea otters, and beluga, killer and gray whales can be found in the coastal waters of Shelikof Strait. A variety of birds, including bald eagles, osprey, ptarmigan, spruce grouse, swans and abundant waterfowl can be readily observed.

Activities: Recreation includes canoeing and rafting, sportfishing, wildlife viewing, day hiking and backpacking. If you aren't a backcountry hiker, Brooks Camp—where Brooks Lodge, the park visitor center and campground are located—offers the most accessible attractions within Katmai National Park. Brooks Falls, where there is a platform for viewing bears fishing for salmon, is a 1/2-mile walk from Brooks Camp. The rangers conduct guided nature walks and evening programs at Brooks Camp from June to mid-September. Also from Brooks Camp, a 4-mile trail leads up Dumpling Mountain for a view of Naknek Lake.

The same concessionaire-operated Brooks Lodge also offers bus tours out to Three Forks Overlook and the Valley of Ten Thousand Smokes. The trip takes visitors out a rough, narrow, 23-mile road to the overlook. For the hardy, a 1–1/2-mile trail leads down 800 vertical feet from the overlook to the Ukak River and the valley floor. The hike is strenuous, especially on the way back up, but it offers a closeup look at the deeply eroded ash cliffs. Cost for the round-trip tour is $79 with lunch. For overnight valley hikes, you can arrange a van drop-off and pickup with the concessionaire.

The serene Grosvenor River, the swifter Savonoski River and a series of large lakes connected by a portage form a circular waterway of about 70 miles for canoeists and kayakers.

The wild and scenic Alagnak and Nonvianuk rivers offer a good float trip to the Kvichak River, which empties into Bristol Bay. (See River Running this section.)

Katmai's rugged wilderness offers rewarding experiences providing reasonable precautions are taken. Anyone planning backcountry hiking in Katmai should stop in King Salmon to check in at the King Salmon Visitor Center before flying in to be dropped off. Cold winds and icy waters pose great hazards. Backcountry permits are required. Carry extra dry clothing. Read up on hypothermia and its treatment. Be prepared to wait out storms: carry matches, a first-aid kit, and emergency food. Rains or melting glaciers can make stream crossings impassable. You need sneakers and hiking boots. Be extremely cautious when crossing muddy waters. The Park Service also warns that firewood is limited and asks that campers use stoves. At Brooks Camp, you can arrange in advance for meals at the lodge. Otherwise, bring all food with you.

Contact the park for a list of commercial guides and outfitters operating in the park for kayak and lake touring; photography and sightseeing trips; river trips; guided walking, hiking and backpacking; sportfishing and hunting trips; and flightseeing.

Accommodations: There are hotels and restaurants in King Salmon. Within Katmai National Park, the park concessionaire, Katmailand Inc. (907/243-5448), operates Brooks Lodge, Kulik Lodge and Grosvenor Lodge. Kulik Lodge on Kulik Lake, which accommodates 15 people, specializes in fishing, as does Grosvenor Lodge on Grosvenor Lake, which can accommodate 6.

Most visitors will be visiting Brooks Camp, where Brooks Lodge, the Park Service campground, and a visitor center are located. Brooks Lodge consists of 15 4-berth cabins with hot water and private baths and a central lodge which houses the restaurant, registration, a small store and tour services. Within walking distance of the lodge is the park visitor center and auditorium, where nature talks and slide shows are presented. Books and guides are available at the visitor center. The Park Service campground is located nearby. The campground has kitchen shelters. Campsites must be reserved in advance through the national park reservation contractor at (800) 365-CAMP. There is a $10-per-person, per-day use fee at Brooks Camp. Camping is an additional $5-per-person, per-night.

Because of limited accommodations, day trips to the park have become more popular.

Access: King Salmon is the transportation gateway to the park and preserve. There is daily jet service from Anchorage to King Salmon and several scheduled floatplanes trips a day to Brooks Camp in the park between June and September. There are more than 30 air taxi services with permits to fly in the park. Air charter service is available in King Salmon, Iliamna, Kodiak and other towns for access to other areas in the park from May to October. The park and preserve is also accessible by a 10-mile road from King Salmon to Lake Camp on the western side of Naknek Lake, where there is a boat dock and ramp.

For more information: Contact the Superintendent, Katmai National Park and Preserve, P.O. Box 7, King Salmon, AK 99613; phone (907) 246-3305, fax (907) 246-2116. USGS maps: Katmai, Naknek, Iliamna.

Kodiak National Wildlife Refuge

This refuge encompasses 1.9 million acres on Kodiak, Uganik, Afognak and Ban islands—all part of the Kodiak Archipelago. The city of Kodiak is some 250 air miles from Anchorage and about 21 miles northeast of the refuge boundary. Kodiak is accessible by commercial jet and the Alaska Marine Highway System. The refuge is larger than the state of Delaware, but because of its convoluted coastline, no place on the island is more than 15 miles from the sea.

The refuge's varied landscapes include glacially carved valleys, tundra uplands, lakes, wetlands, sand and gravel beaches, salt flats, meadows and rugged mountains to 4,000 feet. Spruce forests dominate the northern part of Kodiak Island and all the Afognak Island portion of the refuge. The interior of the refuge is covered with dense vegetation in summer. Sedges and fireweed to 6 feet are often mixed with salmonberry, blueberry and rose bushes. Dense thickets of willow, alder and elderberry abound. Devil's club, with thorns that can penetrate leather, grows up to 6 feet high in the woods and on the slopes. The heath-land in the southwest portion of the refuge is covered with hummocks—small knolls of grass and soil that make walking difficult.

Climate: The climate is mild and wet. Winter temperatures average between 24°F and 36°F and rarely fall below zero. Summer days average between 48°F and 60°F. The island has an average annual precipitation of 54 inches, with 75 inches of snow. The sky is com-pletely overcast about half the time. Despite mild temperatures, the weather and winds are unpredictable and change abruptly. Climatic conditions change within short distances because of the varied terrain. The weather can make flying conditions hazardous, and flights often are delayed for days.

Visitors should be equipped with plenty of warm clothes, rain gear and appropriate footwear. Bring extra food and other supplies in case weather prolongs your stay. Use only dead or downed wood, and carry a camp stove. Trash must be packed out. Take precau-tions against unwanted encounters with bears, especially along salmon-spawning streams in midsummer. Do not leave food uncovered in camp; make noise while hiking to alert bears of your presence.

Wildlife: This refuge was originally established in 1941 to protect the habitat of the huge Kodiak brown bear and other wildlife. The brown bear remains the refuge's most well-known feature, attracting visitors from all over the world. The refuge supports the highest density of brown bears in the world. The 3 largest brown bears ever taken and 33 of the 50 largest in the Boone and Crockett North American records are from Kodiak Island. Females weigh about 650 pounds; larger males up to 1,500 pounds.

Besides the bears, there are only 5 other native land mammals in Kodiak refuge: red fox, river otter, short-tailed weasel, little brown bat and tundra vole. Several other species, including Sitka blacktail deer, elk and beaver, have been introduced. Whales, porpoises, sea otters and sea lions are found in bays.

More than 210 species of birds have been seen on the archipelago. At least 200 pairs of bald eagles nest in the refuge. An estimated 2 million seabirds winter in the refuge's bays and inlets, and at least 200,000 waterfowl also winter along shorelines.

The refuge's 11 large lakes and many rivers are major spawning grounds for king, red, silver, pink and chum salmon. The various species spawn from June through August and begin to decrease in numbers in September, although a few silver salmon continue to spawn until December. Steelhead, rainbow trout and Dolly Varden also are found in refuge waters.

Activities: Predominant activities in the refuge are hunting, fishing and trapping. Commercial hunting and fishing guides and outfitters and sportfishing lodges are available. Growing in popularity with visitors are bear-viewing and bird watching. Bear viewing trips are available from air charter services in Kodiak and in Homer. For a list of birds in the refuge, go to http://www.npwrc.usgs.gov/resource/othrdata/chekbird/r7/kodiak.htm.

Other activities include hiking, photography, beachcombing, berry picking and clamming. A visitor center located on Rezanof Road in Kodiak can provide more information for any-one traveling to the refuge. The visitor center is open year-round 8 A.M. to 4:30 P.M. Monday to Friday; weekend hours in summer.

Accommodations: There are motels and campgrounds in Kodiak. Wilderness camping is allowed throughout the refuge without advance reservations, permits or fees. There are 9 public-use cabins in the refuge which may be reserved in advance (for details see Cabins this section).

Access: Kodiak Refuge is roadless and reached most easily by chartered floatplane or boat from the city of Kodiak. Hovercraft and off-road vehicles are not permitted on refuge lands. Helicopter access is restricted to special use permit holders and is not permitted for recreational users. Recreational airboats are not permitted.

For more information: Contact Refuge Manager, Kodiak National Wildlife Refuge, 1390 Buskin River Road, Kodiak, AK 99615; phone (907) 487-2600, fax (907) 487-2144.

🏛 Lighthouses

Southwestern Alaska has 2 historic lighthouses: Cape Sarichef and Scotch Cap. The Naitonal Park Service keeps an inventory of historic light stations. For more details on Alaska's historic light stations, go to www.cr.nps.gov/maritime/light/ak.htm.

Cape Sarichef Light Station. This is the most westerly lighthouse in North America, located in the Aleutian Chain on the northwest side of Unimak Island overlooking Unimak Pass. Cape Sarichef began operating July 1, 1904. Construction crews reinforced the structures, and the station was relighted in 1950. Now automated, the station serves as a National Weather Service forecasting center.

Scotch Cap Light Station. The first to be built on the outside coast of Alaska, Scotch Cap Light Station is the second most westerly lighthouse in North America and the most southerly in Alaska. The station is also a monument to many ship disasters, before and after its establishment. It was automated in 1971. The station began operation July 18, 1903. Partly because of the hazardous duty, each of Scotch Cap's 3 keepers received a year's vacation every 4 years. On April 1, 1946, an earthquake that registered 7.4 on the Richter Scale occurred southwest of Unimak Island, generating a 100-foot tsunami that swamped Scotch Cap and killed all 5 Coastguardsmen at the station. The wave crossed the Pacific Ocean and .hit the north side of the Hawaiian Islands, killing 159 people. It then continued to Chile, rebounded and hit the southern side of Hawaii, causing what is rated as Hawaii's worst natural disaster ever because it hit with no warning.

🐃 McNeil River State Game Sanctuary

McNeil River is located approximately 200 air miles southwest of Anchorage and 100 air miles west of Homer. The river drains into Kamishak Bay in the shadow of Augustine Island, an active volcano with a history of violent eruptions, the most recent in March of 1986. McNeil River is bordered to the south and west by Katmai National Park and Preserve.

The McNeil River State Game Sanctuary draws photographers from all over the world, attracted by the large numbers of brown bears that congregate in the summer to feast on spawning chum salmon. The greatest numbers may be seen at the McNeil River falls, about 1 mile up from the river mouth. As many as 60 bears at a time have been observed fishing for chum salmon during the peak of the season.

In order to reduce disturbance of the bears and minimize the risk of human-bear encounters, the Alaska Department of Fish and Game allows visitors to the sanctuary by permit only. A special bear-viewing permit is required during the peak season June 7 through August 25. A Fish and Game employee is stationed at the camp to escort visitors to the falls each day. No more than 10 permit holders per day are allowed to visit the falls during peak season; permittees are selected by a lottery drawing held March 15. The Department of Fish and Game receives about 2,000 applications for the roughly 280 permits available. Up to 3 people may be listed on one application. An application fee of $20 per name must accompany the application. The deadline for applications is March 1. Application forms are available at Alaska Department of Fish and Game offices in Anchorage, Fairbanks, Homer, Juneau, King Salmon and Soldotna.

Winners of the computer-generated lottery must pay a user fee: $100 for Alaska residents, $250 for nonresidents. The user fee helps defray the cost of operating the sanctuary visitor program.

Access to the sanctuary is usually by floatplane from Anchorage, Kenai or Homer, landing at high tide.

Visitors to McNeil River must be self-sufficient and prepared for a wilderness experience. There are no visitor facilities. Equipment and clothing must be adequate to withstand cold, wind and rain. Bring camping gear, rain gear, hip boots (you have to wade through water over knee-deep to reach the falls) and lots of film. Carry extra food in case bad weather prolongs your stay for several days. It also is recommended that photographers bring a packboard or packsack to carry camera equipment.

For more information and application forms, contact the Alaska Department of Fish and Game, Wildlife Conservation Division, 333 Raspberry Road, Anchorage, AK 99518; phone (907) 267-2180.

 # Mountaineering

Southwestern's Aleutian Range extends 600 miles along the Alaska Peninsula to Unimak Island in the Aleutian Islands. (The Aleutian Islands are a continuation of the Aleutian Range). Climbable peaks include everything from 580-foot Artillery Hill on Attu Island to 10,197-foot Mount Redoubt. The Scree Peak Index of the The Mountaineering Club of Alaska lists 20 ascents in the Aleutians; see www.mcak.org.

While the Aleutians don't have the high elevations of the Alaska Range or the Wrangells, they certainly have the cachet of being off the beaten path. It requires a lot of energy to plan a climb in the Aleutians. And as illustrated in "Up Smoking Mountain" (see below), even seem-

Up Smoking Mountain
by Andy Hall (excerpted from ALASKA Magazine)

The strange feeling that I'm picking my way through the pumice rocks of God's own barbecue grill nags at me as I follow my friend, Ralph, up the narrow spine of a ridge that leads to the summit of Mount Peulik. The name is Aleut for "smoking mountain," and in this case refers to a small and unremarkable 4,000-foot volcano near Lake Becharof.

A few weeks earlier, Ralph and another friend had invited me to join them on a weekend climb up Mount Peulik. Ralph, a college buddy, grew up in King Salmon and, just a few years ago, took up mountaineering. He has set a goal for himself of bagging as many of southwestern Alaska's volcanoes as he can.

Alaska has more than 100 such mountains, 40 of which have erupted within the last 2 centuries. In fact, a volcano belches to life somewhere in the state almost every year. At least twice while growing up I remember gray volcanic ash raining from the sky over Anchorage.

Mindful of the explosive forces that blasted that ash hundreds of miles across Alaska, I researched Peulik before agreeing to tag along, and found that it met my most important criterion: It's dormant, and hasn't shown any signs of life since a violent outburst in 1814.

Confident that I wouldn't find myself surrounded by rivers of molten lava, I thought I'd like to see a volcano up close.

We got to within striking distance by chartering a small plane in King Salmon and heading to a makeshift landing strip on the south shore of Lake Becharof, about 5 miles from the volcano's base. We landed and set off. Three hours later we pitched our tent and collapsed.

We were up at 7 a.m. and hiked 2 hours before setting up base camp. We shed as much gear as we could and stashed our food several hundred yards away. Then, each carrying the bare necessities—food, water, ice ax and 12-gauge shotgun—we headed for the volcano. It took a couple of hours to break out of the alders into the open high country. Figuring it was unlikely we'd surprise a bear here, we stashed our shotguns.

A snow-filled gorge appeared to wind right to the top of the peak, so we started up its steep slope, keeping our ice axes handy. Caribou tracks covered the snow, and occasionally we'd spook one onto the lava flow as we ascended the couloir. When the gully became too steep, we scrambled up a rocky ridge for another hour and a half before finally collapsing at the summit.

After taking in the view, we descended to the top of the snow gully. I made a silent prayer to the volcano god asking that she clear my path of caribou, gripped my ax, and pushed off. A short time later we were at the bottom, descending in 15 minutes what had taken hours to climb.

ingly insignificant peaks can prove a strenuous climb, with the weather and wildlife offering surprises.

Pribilof Islands

In 1786, when Russians searching for fur seals first encountered this isolated island group 200 miles out in the Bering Sea, they stumbled upon some of the continent's grandest wildlife spectacles. St. Paul and St. George islands claim North America's largest northern fur seal and seabird colonies, a wildlife extravaganza that still draws visitors to this remote corner of Alaska.

Archaeological records reveal no signs of habitation of the Pribilofs prior to their occupancy by Russian fur hunters who imported Aleuts from Unalaska and Atka and founded the island group's 2 communities, St. Paul and St. George.

From 1867, when the United States purchased Alaska, to 1909, the government contracted with private companies to harvest the fur seals. From 1910, federal officials managed the sealing operations, and the residents of the Pribilof Islands were treated as wards of the government.

During WWII, the entire population of the Pribilof Islands was evacuated and restricted to an abandoned cannery and mining camp at Funter Bay in southeastern Alaska. In 1983, the Pribilof people were given full control of their islands, and in 1987, they celebrated their bicentennial.

Although the fur seal industry has dominated the islands' economy in the past, it has been replaced by a growing fisheries industry and tourism. Subsistence centers around fur seal harvesting and fishing, especially for halibut.

(For more details on St. George and St. Paul, see Communities section.)

Redoubt Bay State Critical Habitat Area

This 268-square-mile wetland and riparian habitat provides a haven for moose, fish, furbearers and hundreds of thousands of birds. It is located approximately 40 miles southwest of Anchorage on the west side of Cook Inlet.

In spring and fall, the area provides resting and feeding habitat for waterfowl on their way to and from nesting grounds in the north. In summer, the grounds sustain an important nesting area for ducks, geese, swans and many other birds. During spring, summer and early fall, the area supports the largest known concentration of Tule white-fronted geese in the world. Cackling Canada geese, Taverner's Canada geese, lesser Canada geese, snow geese and tundra and trumpeter swans also use the wetlands. In the summer, the habitat is home to several tens of thousands of breeding ducks, including pintail, mallard, green-winged teal, wigeon, shoveler, scaup, canvasback and common eider. Shorebirds in Redoubt include yellowlegs, snipe, godwits, whimbrels, sandpipers, plovers, dunlin and phalaropes. Sandhill cranes rest here during migration, and a few pairs nest occasionally. Bald eagles, ravens, gulls and passerines can also be seen in the area in the spring, summer and fall.

The riparian areas along the Big, Drift and Kustatan rivers and their tributaries serve as moose winter habitat. Brown bears are abundant mid- to late summer during salmon spawning, and black bears can also be seen but are more common farther inland in the mountains and foothills. Furbearers in the area include coyote, fox, wolf, mink, river otter, marten, muskrat, wolverine, weasel, lynx and beaver. Harbor seals haul out at the mouths of streams in the area, and beluga whales feed on the spawning salmon at river mouths in Cook Inlet.

Five species of salmon spawn in Redoubt's streams and lakes; sockeye, coho and pink salmon are the most abundant. Sockeye salmon run up the Big River from early June into August, and rainbow and Dolly Varden trout are also present.

Along with wildlife viewing, hunting and fishing are also popular in this critical habitat area. Redoubt Bay is one of the most popular non-road-accessible waterfowl hunting areas in Alaska. The area is accessible by boat or plane. There is also sport fishing on Big River Lake and the Kustatan River. Off-road use of motorized vehicles (except snow machines, boats and aircraft) is permitted in the critical habitat area only with a special area permit from the

Department of Fish and Game, Habitat and Restoration Division.

For more information: Alaska Department of Fish and Game, Division of Wildlife Conservation, 333 Raspberry Rd., Anchorage, AK 99518-1599; phone (907) 267-2182, fax (907) 267-2433.

River Running

River runners should contact the appropriate land manager for more detailed information on rivers listed here. Also obtain information on current river conditions from reliable local sources, such as bush pilots, park rangers and local guides. River levels can rise dramatically and quickly with meltwater on sunny days. Rainstorms can also quickly swell rivers.

The Southwestern region has 2 National Wild and Scenic Rivers, both managed by the National Park Service: the Alagnak River and the Aniakchak River.

Alagnak and Nonvianuk rivers. (Part of the Kvichak River watershed) The 80-mile-long Alagnak River and its 11-mile tributary, the Nonvianuk, both originate within Katmai National Preserve. The Nonvianuk and the upper 60 miles of the Alagnak were included in the National Wild and Scenic Rivers System in 1980. The Alagnak originates in Kukaklek Lake, then flows west-southwest to join the Kvichak River, which empties into Bristol Bay. Both the main branch of the Alagnak and the Nonvianuk, which drains from Nonvianuk Lake, offer excellent boating.

The Alagnak leaves Kukaklek Lake at a moderate speed (3 to 4 mph) but quickly picks up speed (7 to 8 mph) as it drops through a canyon where there are 2 sets of Class III rapids, neither of which can be easily portaged because of extremely steep canyon walls. Below the canyon, the river slows, braids and becomes a broad channel (2 to 3 mph) as it empties into the Kvichak.

The Nonvianuk River offers a leisurely float in its entirety, with some Class II rapids possible during low water periods 4 to 5 miles from its origin. High water season is typically during June and July. Inflatable rafts are recommended for the main branch; on the Nonvianuk, rafts, kayaks and canoes are all suitable. The average trip takes approximately 4 to 5 days if just floating, 5 to 6 days if floating and fishing.

These rivers offer good fishing seasonally for all 5 species of salmon (especially sockeye), Dolly Varden, rainbow and lake trout, grayling and pike in side sloughs and lakes. Floaters also have a good chance of seeing brown bears, moose, wolves, red foxes, wolverines, beavers, river otters and lynx. A variety of birds including bald eagles, osprey, ptarmigan, spruce grouse, swans and game ducks are readily observed. Hunting is allowed in the designated Alagnak Wild River Corridor and in Katmai National Park and Preserve in season.

Access to the river system is by scheduled air service from Anchorage to King Salmon, then by chartered floatplane to Kukaklek or Nonvianuk Lake, about 60 miles to the northeast. Exit is usually by floatplane from the lower 30 miles of the Alagnak before the tidal influence in the last 10 miles. Trip planning assistance and information on the Alagnak is available from the Katmai National Park office in King Salmon (P.O. Box 7, King Salmon, AK 99615; phone 907/246-3305, fax 907/246-2116). There are several commercial operators running trips on the Alagnak. USGS maps: Iliamna A-7, A-8; Dillingham A-1, A-2, A-3.

Aniakchak River. The 32-mile-long Aniakchak River is unique in that it heads in a freshwater lake inside the caldera of an active volcano, which last erupted in 1931. The river, located entirely within Aniakchak National Monument, was included in the National Wild and Scenic Rivers System in 1980.

The river starts slowly from Surprise Lake and speeds up as it flows through a narrow, 1,500-foot-high opening in the caldera wall called The Gates. The river is shallow and rocky, Class III to IV, and has low falls as it drops 70 feet per mile for the first 13 miles. Then, the river meanders slowly, Class II to I, through flatlands to Aniakchak Bay on the Pacific Ocean side of the Alaska Peninsula. Inflatable kayaks or medium-sized rafts are recommended because of numerous, closely spaced boulders. The trip from Surprise Lake to Aniakchak Bay generally takes 3 days.

The number of groups on the river is increasing, and 15 operators hold commercial use licenses for services in Aniakchak.

The caldera is scenic, featuring 2,000-foot walls, cinder cones and other volcanic wonders. There is good hiking in the monument. Fish available in the river include salmon, arctic char, Dolly Varden and rainbow trout. Wildlife that may be observed includes caribou, moose, brown bears, wolves, river otters, wolverines, sea otters, harbor seals, sea lions, bald eagles, waterfowl and shorebirds.

Weather in this area is generally miserable, with much rain, cold temperatures and high winds, especially through The Gates. (See cautionary notes in Aniakchak National Monument and Preserve this section.) Bad weather may delay put in or takeout; floaters should be equipped with extra food and supplies.

Access to Aniakchak River is by chartered floatplane from King Salmon or Port Heiden to Surprise Lake. Exit is generally by floatplane from Aniakchak Bay; the bay is often too rough for floatplanes, but small, wheeled planes can land on the beach. USGS maps: Chignik D-1, Sutwik Island D-5, D-6.

Karluk River. This river heads in Karluk Lake on the west coast of Kodiak Island and flows north and west 24 miles through Karluk Lagoon to Shelikof Strait at the village of Karluk. This is a Class I river, but a portage is necessary around a fish weir about 1 mile up from Karluk Lagoon.

This is a very popular river for king, red and silver salmon, Dolly Varden and rainbow trout in season. Canoes, kayaks, or rafts are suitable for this river. The trip takes 2 to 5 days.

NOTE: Koniag Incorporated owns the land along the Karluk River and the riverbed. There is a $125-per-person, per-year fee for fishing or camping on the Karluk River. Permits may be obtained from Koniag Incorporated, 202 Center St., Suite 201, Kodiak, AK 99615; phone (907) 486-2530, fax (907) 486-3325.

Access is by floatplane from Kodiak to Karluk Lake or to Larsen Bay, where a 2-mile trail leads to the river. Access is also by scheduled air service to Larsen Bay village. Exit is via the portage trail to Larsen Bay or from Karluk village via charter or scheduled air service. USGS maps: Karluk B-1, C-1, C-2.

Katmai Lakes. A series of large lakes and the Grosvenor and Savonoski rivers in Katmai National Park afford a circular trip of about 70 miles for kayakers and canoeists. This trip generally starts at Brooks Camp on Naknek Lake, then skirts the shore of Naknek Lake to the Bay of Islands, where there is a 1-mile portage to Grosvenor Lake. The portage begins at an old log cabin (available for public use on a first-come basis), then leads to a small lake which can either be paddled across or walked around on its eastern shore (do not take an obvious trail to the right as it will take you back to the Bay of Islands). (Cabin reservations must be made through the National Park Service headquarters at 907/246-3305.) After paddling the length of Lake Grosvenor, you'll enter the 3-mile, flat-water Grosvenor River which joins the Savonoski River, a braided, fairly slow glacial stream which will take you 12 miles to Iliuk Arm. Stay on the south shore of Iliuk Arm, as the north shore is steep with few places to pull out in case of bad weather. Iliuk Arm joins Naknek Lake just a few miles from Brooks Camp.

These are very large lakes, and easterly or westerly winds can quickly cause choppy water. Staying close to shore is highly recommended. Also, be aware that this is prime brown bear country; camping along the Savonoski River from mid-July to September is not recommended because large numbers of bears will be feeding on spawning salmon. A backcountry permit is required for this trip and can be obtained from the National Park Service in King Salmon or Brooks Camp. The trip, starting and finishing at Brooks Camp, generally takes 5 to 7 days.

This trip offers good fishing for sockeye salmon, rainbow and lake trout. Brush makes hiking difficult, except along the lake shores. Bear, moose, red fox, wolf, lynx, wolverine, river otter, mink, marten, weasel and beaver may be seen. Lake edges and marshes are nesting sites for whistling swans, ducks, loons, grebes and arctic terns.

Access to the lakes is by scheduled air service from Anchorage to King Salmon, then a scheduled flight or charter floatplane to Brooks Camp or Grosvenor Camp. Also, there is a road from King Salmon to Lake Camp at the west end of Naknek Lake. (See also Katmai National Park and Preserve this section.) USGS maps: Mount Katmai B-5, C-4, C-5, C-6.

King Salmon River. This is a slow (1 to 2 mph), silty river flowing westward about 60 miles across a soggy, tundra-covered coastal plain to Egegik Bay. (Not to be confused with the King Salmon River farther south which flows into Ugashik Bay.) This river's headwaters are in Katmai National Park, and it flows partially through Becharof National Wildlife Refuge. Raft, kayak and canoe are all suitable for this river. There can be strong upstream winds and tidal influences on the lower river. Stay in the far left channel of the King Salmon and Egegik rivers to reach the village of Egegik on Egegik Bay at low tide.

There is good scenery at the headwaters, and wildlife observation is good in season. King, sockeye and chum salmon are plentiful, and rainbow trout, Dolly Varden and grayling also are present. Brown bears and Canada geese are abundant; caribou and moose may also be seen. The area is popular for big game sport hunting.

Access is by wheeled plane or floatplane from King Salmon to a lake near the head of Gertrude Creek or to headwater gravel bars outside Katmai National Park. Exit is generally from the village of Egegik, which is served by commercial air service from King Salmon. USGS maps: Katmai A-6, Naknek A-1, A-2, A-4, A-5, B-2,B-3, B-4.

 Sea Kayaking

Kodiak Island's rocky, irregular coastline makes for miles and miles of fine sea kayaking opportunities. But precautions should be taken. The weather can change abruptly, and changing wind direction and tidal currents can make paddling a tricky business at best. Perhaps the prime area for ocean kayaking on Kodiak is Shuyak Island State Park, located on the northernmost sizable island of the Kodiak Archipelago. The inner coast, a maze of narrow, interconnected bays, inlets and passages, offers protected paddling for kayakers. Many of the bays are separated by short portages. Skiff Passage, a long, narrow channel, completely cuts through Shuyak park from north to south. Attractions include abundant wildlife and spectacular coastlines. Access is by air charter from Homer or Kodiak.

(See also Shuyak Island State Park.)

 Shuyak Island State Park

This wilderness park, created in 1984, comprises most of the Shuyak Island's 47,000 acres. Shuyak Island is the northernmost sizable island of the Kodiak Archipelago and includes a number of smaller islands, rocks, passages and beaches.

Shuyak Island is low—highest point is 660 feet—and mostly covered with a virgin forest of Sitka spruce although there are open tundra areas. On clear days, the volcanic peaks of the Alaska Peninsula across 30-mile-wide Shelikof Strait can be seen from the park.

Climate: Shuyak's climate is similar to Kodiak, where the average daily temperature in July is 54°F; in January, 30°F. Average annual precipitation at Kodiak is 54.52 inches. September, October and May are the wettest months, with each month averaging more than 6 inches of rain.

Wildlife: Seals, sea lions, brown bears, Sitka blacktail deer, land otters, beavers and large numbers of sea otters may be seen on Shuyak Island. Birds are also abundant. Species that may be seen include a large number of bald eagles, gulls, cormorants, oystercatchers, guillemots, red-breasted mergansers, harlequin ducks, common and red-throated loons, horned and tufted puffins, eider ducks, terns, kittiwakes and scoters.

Flowers are everywhere during spring and summer. Small ponds and a few isolated spruce dot the tundra. Jaegers fly overhead searching for voles; deer browse on the heath, and ducks raise their young in the ponds. Pink and silver salmon spawn in the island's many streams; fishing for silvers is particularly good in August. Other sport fish include Dolly Varden and halibut.

Activities: Alaska State Parks is developing a small network of trails on the western side of Shuyak Island. The trails give visitors access to salmon fishing, to the open capes of the outer coast and to the Big Bay ranger station/visitor center. Some of the public-use cabins are also linked by trails. Most trails wind through the old growth Sitka spruce forest. This virgin forest may be the last strand of pure Sitka spruce in Alaska; other coastal forests are generally a mixture of spruce, hemlock and sometimes cedar.

Shuyak Island's convoluted coastline of protected bays, channels and lagoons offers safe cruising by canoe or kayak. Many of the bays are separated by short portages. Skiff Passage, a long, narrow channel, completely cuts through Shuyak park from north to south.

Accommodations: Four cabins are located in the park and are available through the Division of Parks and Outdoor Recreation (see Cabins this section for details). Wilderness camping is permitted in the park. Minimum-impact camping should be practiced; all trash must be packed out. Boil or treat all drinking water.

Access: The park is easily reached by charter plane from either Kodiak or Homer, both of which have daily air service. From Kodiak, it's a 45-minute flight; Homer is a little farther away.

For more information: Contact the Alaska Dept. of Natural Resources, Division of Parks and Outdoor Recreation, 550 West 7th Ave., Suite 1260, Anchorage, AK 99501-3557; phone (907) 269-8400; www.alaskastateparks.org. Or, Division of Parks and Outdoor Recreation, Kodiak District, 1400 Abercrombie Dr., Kodiak, AK 99615; phone (907) 486-6339, fax (907) 486-3320.

✴ Unga Island Petrified Forest

Although the Aleutians are one of the most extensive treeless zones in the world, there is much evidence that trees thrived here before the ice ages. Some 150 acres of beach on the northwest coast of Unga Island, located west of Sand Point contain black, yellow and gray petrified stumps measuring 2 to 4 feet in diameter. Petrified wood is also found on Amchitka and Atka islands. Unga's forest, experts claim, rivals those of national parks in the Lower 48. The rock stumps are the remains of metasequoia trees, thought to be an ancestor of the redwood trees of the western United States. Scientists estimate the trees lived 11 million to 25 million years ago, encouraged by the warm humidity of the Miocene period. These are angiosperms rather than gymnosperms (cone-bearing evergreens), which are the trees that do well today in the Aleutians, having been transplanted to sheltered areas at Unalaska, Atka, Adak, Unga, Akutan and Squaw Harbor. Access to the Unga Island Petrified Forest is via charter plane or boat from Sand Point.

✴ World War II Military Sites

Several sites in the Aleutians relating to WWII have been designated national historic landmarks including the following:

Adak Island, Adak Army Base and Adak Naval Operating Base. The bases have been nominated to the National Register of Historic Places. Adak, one of the Andreanof Islands in the Aleutian chain, is about 1,400 air miles southwest of Anchorage.

The island was unoccupied at the outbreak of WWII. Alaska's largest and most expensive wartime base of operations was established after the Japanese bombings of Unalaska and Dutch Harbor and the invasion of Attu and Kiska islands in June 1942. The need for an advance base farther west than Unalaska and Umnak islands became urgent, and Adak was selected because of its all-weather harbor. The first airstrip was built on Adak in 12 days, and on September 14, 1942, the first Liberators flew from Adak to bomb Japanese forces on Kiska. Permanent airfields were later built, and Adak served as the command post for the invasions of Attu and Kiska in 1943. Adak continued to serve as an active base throughout the war. In 1950, the Army Air Force turned it over to the Navy. Today, Adak Naval Air Station, located on the WWII site, occupies the northern half of the island; the southern half is part of the Alaska Maritime National Wildlife Refuge. As with many of the other islands that played a major role in WWII, Adak is littered with military Quonset huts and other buildings and relics.

Formerly a restricted military installation not open to visitors, the Navy has relinquished

SOUTHWESTERN • ATTRACTIONS

Adak Island to the Aleut Corporation. So visitation policies may change. For more details, see Adak in the Communities section.

Amaknak Island, Dutch Harbor Naval Operating Base and Fort Mears. At the time of the Dec. 7, 1941, Japanese attack on Pearl Harbor in Hawaii, these, along with top secret Fort Glenn on nearby Umnak Island, were the only U.S. defense facilities in the Aleutians. Shortly after Pearl Harbor, a naval base was constructed at Unalaska. Some 60,000 men were stationed at Dutch Harbor/ Unalaska, which was the target of Japanese bombing on June 3 and 4, 1942 in conjunction with the Battle of Midway. Many of the military installations remained at Dutch Harbor and Unalaska until June 1985, when a clean-up program began. Many of the old buildings are now gone although old machine gun nests, barbed wire, trenches and bomb shelters will remain for years to come. The remains of the bombed-out ship *Northwestern*, which had been used for barracks, still lie partially submerged at the head of Captain's Bay, a short drive from town. Unalaska is accessible by commercial air service from Anchorage.

Attu Island, Attu Battlefield and the U.S. Army and Navy airfields. Site of the only WWII battle fought on the North American continent, Attu Island is at the western end of the Aleutian chain, 1,500 air miles southwest of Anchorage, 500 miles east of Russia.

The Japanese occupation of Attu and Kiska took place in June 1942, coordinated with the Battle of Midway. Attu was held for nearly a year before American troops invaded. During the bitterly fought, 19-day battle, most of the 2,500 Japanese troops were killed, many during a banzai attack out of the hills. Only 29 Japanese survived. U.S. casualties were heavy, too. Of 15,000 troops, 550 were killed, 1,500 wounded and another 1,200 disabled by Attu's harsh climate. During the remaining years of the war, the United States flew bombing raids on Japan from Attu. Today, there is much evidence of the desperate battle on Attu's eastern end: thousands of shell and bomb craters in the tundra, Japanese trenches, foxholes and gun emplacements. American ammunition magazines and dumps and spent cartridges, shrapnel and shells are found at the scenes of heavy fighting. The steel-matted runways at Atexai Field and the asphalt runways at the U.S. Naval Air Station exist, the latter still operational. Portions of deteriorating piers stand at Massacre Bay. Roads may still be traced, but only 5 miles are maintained.

The only occupants today are a few U.S. Coast Guardsmen who operate a long-range navigation (loran) station. The Aleut village of Attu, whose residents had been captured and taken to Japan, was destroyed during the battle, and no trace remains. The entire island is part of the Alaska Maritime National Wildlife Refuge, administered by the U.S. Fish and Wildlife Service. For information about Attu contact: Alaska Maritime National Wildlife Refuge, 2355 Kachemak Bay Drive, Suite 101, Homer, Alaska 99603-8021; phone (907) 235-6546, fax (907) 235-7783, e-mail alaskamaritime@fws.gov.

Kiska Island, Japanese Occupation Site. Japanese withdrew from Kiska after the United States reclaimed Attu. Kiska, one of the Rat Islands group near the western end of the Aleutian chain, is 165 miles southeast of Attu.

On June 7, 1942, a Japanese task force invaded Attu and Kiska, overrunning a U.S. weather station on Kiska and constructing coastal and antiaircraft defenses, camps, roads, an airfield, submarine base, seaplane base and other installations. The occupation marked the peak of Japan's military expansion in the Pacific and caused great alarm in North America that a Japanese invasion would be mounted through Alaska. As Allied forces prepared to invade Kiska, 5,183 Japanese were secretly evacuated in less than an hour under cover of fog on July 28, 1943. On August 15, 34,000 U.S. and Canadian troops invaded a deserted island. The Allies subsequently established their own camps. Kiska was abandoned after the war, but relics from Japanese and U.S. camps still litter the countryside.

Today, Kiska is unoccupied and is part of Alaska Maritime National Wildlife Refuge. For information about access restrictions contact: Refuge Manager, Alaska Maritime National Wildlife Refuge, 2355 Kachemak Bay Drive, Suite 101 Homer, AK 99603-8021; phone (907) 235-6546, fax (907) 235-7783, e-mail alaskamaritime@fws.gov.

WESTERN

Western Alaska encompasses fish-rich Bristol Bay, the vast watery expanse of treeless lowland known as the Yukon-Kuskokwim Delta, and the Seward Peninsula, where prehistoric nomads crossed the Bering Land Bridge from Asia. Yup'ik and Inupiat Eskimos, descendants of these ancient migrations, have dominated the culture of this region since prehistoric times.

Russian explorer Vitus Bering made the first documented sighting of the Diomede Islands in 1728, but it would be another century before the Russian-American Co. established a permanent settlement on the mainland of Western Alaska, at St. Michael in 1833. The Russians explored along the coasts and established more trading posts. And with the Russian traders came their priests, who converted many of the Eskimos to Russian Orthodoxy.

After the United States purchased Alaska from Russia in 1867, more outsiders came to this Eskimo world. Moravian missionaries established a village which they renamed Bethel in 1884, setting off a second round of conversions. A major migration occurred on the Seward Peninsula after gold was found near Nome in 1898.

But despite the influx of outsiders, the Eskimos retained their spiritual connection to the land. Respect for animals runs especially deep in the Yup'ik culture, where hunting is a way of life, and traditional festivals and dances honor the animal spirits.

Many of the traditional ways are still followed here. Subsistence hunting, fishing and trapping provide a livelihood for many, supplemented by cash incomes from seasonal fire fighting, cottage industries such as basketry and skin sewing, construction, commercial fishing, and mining. Western Alaska has led the state in gold production for several years. Near Goodnews Bay lies an important platinum deposit. The western Seward Peninsula has substantial tin deposits, while the Red Devil area near the delta contains mercury deposits. Red Dog mine near Kotzebue produces about 80 percent of the U.S. zinc.

Many visitors are drawn to the Norton Sound villages in March when Iditarod Trail Sled Dog Race teams pass through Unalakleet, Shaktoolik, Koyuk, Elim, Golovin and Solomon on their way to the finish line at Nome. The region's commercial and transportation centers are Nome, Bethel, Naknek and Dillingham.

Location: Western Alaska extends from the Arctic Circle south along the Bering Sea coast, across the top of the Alaska Peninsula to west Cook Inlet. It encompasses St. Lawrence Island, St. Matthew and Hall islands, Nunivak Island, the Yukon-Kuskokwim Delta and the Seward Peninsula.

Geography: South of the Arctic Circle, the Seward Peninsula reaches 200 miles west toward Asia. Cape Prince of Wales at the peninsula's tip points toward Little Diomede Island, about 25 miles offshore and 3 miles from the Soviet Union's Big Diomede Island. The international boundary and date line run between the islands. Norton Sound, a 125-mile finger of the Bering Sea, separates Seward Peninsula from the Yukon-Kuskokwim Delta, a wetland that stretches 250 miles south to Kuskokwim Bay and 200 miles inland.

Tundra carpets much of the region, where grasses, sedges, mosses, lichens and wildflowers grow beneath scrub willow and alder. Forests, which cover eastern Seward Peninsula and Norton Sound, give way to wetland tundra on the delta, then pick up again near Bristol Bay.

The Ahklun Mountains border the delta's flatlands on the south and separate them from Bristol Bay. The bay is renowned for its fishing, particularly the world's largest sockeye salmon run. The bay spans 200 miles from its base at Port Moller on the Alaska Peninsula to its northwest boundary at Cape Newenham, and stretches northeastward nearly the same distance to the mouths of the Nushagak and Kvichak rivers which drain its inland reaches.

The Nushagak and Kvichak are 2 of several major rivers in the region. The longest river in the region—and one of the most important—is the Yukon. These rivers, along with the Kuskokwim and Unalakleet, provide access for fish heading for spawning grounds and are the traditional route for inland travel.

Climate: The climate varies throughout the region, with temperatures ranging from the low 40s to low 60s in summer, and from -5°F to the low 20s in winter in the north. Farther south the weather moderates a bit. Highs in the 30s and lows around 0°F occur in winter; summers average from the mid-30s to mid-60s. Wind chill is an important factor in this region where few topographical features break its sweep across the land. Total annual precipitation is about 20 inches. The northern regions are drier than southern ones. North of Bristol Bay rain and snow fall more frequently on the coast than farther inland. Near the bay the opposite is true.

Wildlife: Numerous big game species make their home in mountainous areas of the region including bears, moose, caribou, wolves and Dall sheep.

Musk-oxen, once hunted to near extinction in Alaska, were reintroduced to Nunivak Island in the 1930s and now thrive there. A total of 61 musk-oxen were transplanted to the Seward Peninsula in 1970 and 1981, and their numbers have been increasing between 15 and 20 percent a year. A 1992 census found 700 musk-oxen in several small herds on the Seward Peninsula.

Reindeer, introduced from Siberia just before the 20th century, roamed much of the Bering Sea Coast region but are now confined to the Seward Peninsula and Nunivak Island. In modern times, reindeer herding has provided cash income for some Eskimo villages. (Pioneer missionary Sheldon Jackson originally introduced reindeer to the area as a new source of protein.)

The Yukon-Kuskowkim Delta lacks suitable shelter for large mammals, but small furbearers such as foxes, muskrats, beaver, otters and weasels find the area a haven. Bowhead, gray, killer and beluga whales, sea lions, fur seals, and several species of true seals pass offshore.

Akiachak

GPS: N60°54' W161°25'

(ACK-ee-a-chuck) Located on the Kuskokwim River, 15 miles northeast of Bethel, 390 miles west of Anchorage. **Transportation**: Scheduled air service from Bethel. **Population**: 560. **Zip code**: 99551. **Emergency Services**: Village Public Safety Officer, phone (907) 825-4313; Alaska State Troopers, Bethel, phone (907) 543-3494; Akiachak Health Clinic, phone (907) 825-4011; Volunteer Fire Department.

Climate: Maritime; mean summer temperature 53°F; mean winter temperature 11°F. Mean annual precipitation 17 inches with 50 inches of snow.

Private Aircraft: Airstrip adjacent southeast; elev. 25 feet; length 1,625 feet; gravel and dirt; no fuel; unattended. The runway is used year-round.

NOTE: Akiachak prohibits the sale, importation and possession of alcoholic beverages.

Visitor Facilities: Lodging available at Yupiit School District or the IRA (Indian Reorganization Act) Council offices; make arrangements through the school, phone 825-4013. Food is available at Guy J's Restaurant. Groceries/supplies are available at Akiachak Enterprises, George Enterprises and General Merchandise Store. There is a washeteria. Fishing/hunting licenses available.

Akiachak was founded in the early 1890s by former residents of another village; a population of 43 was recorded in the 1890 census. By 1895 the Moravian Church at Bethel had stationed a helper here.

Akiachak's school was established in 1930 and an airstrip was built in 1967. Akiachak is located within Yukon Delta National Wildlife Refuge. Many village residents are likely to be at their fish camps during the summer.

This Eskimo community has a Moravian church. There is a school here which offers grades kindergarten through 12 with 161 enrolled. There is a community electric system and a community water supply at the washeteria; sewage system is privies and honey buckets. Freight arrives by barge or mail plane. Government address: Akiachak Native Community, P.O. Box 70, Akiachak, AK 99551; phone (907) 825-4626, fax (907) 825-4029, e-mail: Akiachak@aitc.org. Village corporation: Akiachak Ltd., P.O. Box 51010, Akiachak, AK 99551, phone (907) 825-4328, fax (907) 825-4115.

Akiak

GPS: N60°55' W161°13'

(ACK-ee-ack) Located on the Kuskokwim River, 20 miles northeast of Bethel, 380 miles west of Anchorage. **Transportation**: Scheduled air service from Bethel. **Population**: 325. **Zip code**: 99552. **Emergency Services**: Village Public Safety Officer, phone (907) 765-7527; Alaska State Troopers, Bethel, phone (907) 543-3494; Akiak Health Clinic, phone (907) 765-7527; Volunteer Fire Department.

Climate: Maritime, summers cool, winters moderate.

Private Aircraft: Airstrip adjacent southwest; elev. 22 feet; length 3,200 feet; gravel; no fuel; unattended. Runway condition not monitored; visual inspection recommended prior to using. Southwest 1,000 feet of runway subject to flooding during breakup.

Visitor Facilities: Arrangements for accommodations may be made through the village office, phone (907) 765-74111; or at the school, P.O. Box 52227, Akiak, AK 99552, phone (907) 765-7212. No restaurant or banking. Laundry facilities are available. Supplies available in the community at Ivan Gro and Kashatok Trading

Post. Fishing/hunting licenses available.

The name Akiak reportedly means "crossing over" and refers to a trail that connected the Kuskokwim River at Akiak with the Yukon River. The earliest census including Akiak was that of 1880 when 175 people were reported living here.

An early convert to the Moravian Church, Helper Neck, who was noted for writing a syllabary of the Eskimo language, was born in Akiak and was stationed here in 1895.

A school was established at Akiak in 1911 by John H. Kilbuck, co-founder in 1885 of the Moravian Mission at Bethel, the first Protestant mission on the Kuskokwim. Kilbuck was a Bureau of Education teacher at Akiak for several years; he died here of typhoid in 1922.

In 1907, gold was discovered along the upper Tuluksak River near present-day Nyac. Akiak was a supply point for the mining operations until an airstrip was built at Nyac.

An airport was completed in 1958 and a National Guard armory in 1960. Akiak, located within Yukon Delta National Wildlife Refuge, was incorporated as a second-class city in 1970.

Visitors may view commercial fishing on the Kuskokwim River. The local Eskimo population is described as very warm and friendly.

The community is served by 2 schools with grades kindergarten through 12 with enrollment of 107. There is a community electric system. Water is from individual wells; the sewage system is septic tanks. Freight arrives by barge or mail plane. Government address: City of Akiak, P.O. Box 187, Akiak, AK 99552, phone (907) 765-7411, fax (907) 765-7512. Village corporation: Kokarmuit Corp., P.O. Box 195, Akiak, AK 99552, phone (907) 765-7228, fax (907) 765-7619. Village council: Akiak Native Community, P.O. Box 52165, Akiak, AK 99552, phone and fax (907) 765-7112, e-mail: Akiak@aitc.org.

Alakanuk

GPS: N62°41' W164°40'

(A-LUCK-a-nak) Located at the east entrance to Alakanuk Pass (the major southern channel of the Yukon River delta) 160 miles northwest of Bethel and 110 miles south of Nome. **Transportation:** Small commuter aircraft from Bethel, St. Marys and Emmonak. **Population:** 677. **Zip code:** 99554. **Emergency Services:** Police, phone (907) 238-3421; Alakanuk Health Clinic, phone (907) 238-3210; Bethel Hospital, phone (907) 543-3711; Volunteer Fire Department.

Climate: Subarctic. Temperatures from -25°F in winter to 79°F in summer. Annual average snowfall 60 inches, precipitation 19 inches.

Private Aircraft: Airport adjacent southwest; elev. 10 feet; length 2,200 feet; gravel; no fuel; unattended; 60-foot gravel turnaround midway of runway. Condition not monitored; visual inspection recommended prior to using.

NOTE: Alakanuk prohibits the sale and importation of alcoholic beverages.

Visitor Facilities: No accommodations available. Groceries, clothing, first-aid supplies, hardware, film and sporting goods can be purchased at 4 stores in the community: D.F. Jorgensen & Co., Alakanuk Native Store, Alstroms Store, and The Annex Store. Local arts and crafts available for purchase include carved ivory, grass baskets, Eskimo boots and beading. Laundromat facilities available. No banking or major repair services. Diesel fuel available at the Native store. Moorage facilities available at city dock with depth of 7 feet. Water available from the city.

Alakanuk is a Yup'ik word (Yup'ik pronunciation: A-LAR-neq) meaning "wrong way," aptly applied to a village on a maze of watercourses. The Eskimo village was first reported by G.R. Putnam of the U.S. Coast and Geodetic Survey in 1899, although it was occupied before Russians arrived in the delta region in the 1830s.

With the establishment of a school in 1959, population increased and the village became a second-class city with its incorporation in 1969. It is the longest village on the lower Yukon River, stretching for 3 miles along a slough.

One local resident describes Alakanuk as "a wonderful place to live, with friendly people and fresh, clean air." There are 2 annual potlatches, one in mid-February, the other in mid-April.

Recreation is fishing and hunting. Fish include king, coho and chum salmon, whitefish, sheefish and lush. Traveling is done by snowmobile in winter and boat in summer. Larger boats should use caution at the entrance of the Yukon. The controlling depth is 10 feet and extreme caution is advised because of shifting sandbars. Pilot services available: John Ayunerak for Grant Aviation Airlines, phone (907) 238-3212; John D. Ayunerak Sr. for Hageland Aviation Airlines, phone (907) 238-35212; Louis Chikigak for Tanana Air Service, Larry's Air, Camai Air and Alaska Transportation Service, phone (907) 238-3415.

Communications include phones, mail plane, radio and TV. The community is served by Roman Catholic and Assembly of God churches and a school with grades kindergarten through 12 with enrollment of 189. Public water and electricity are available. Sewage system is vacuum system; honey buckets also used. Freight arrives by cargo plane and barge. Government address: City of Alakanuk, P.O. Box 167, Alakanuk, AK 99554, phone (907) 238-3316, fax (907) 238-3620. Village corporation: Alakanuk Native Corp., P.O. Box 89, Alakanuk, AK 99554, phone (907) 238-3117, fax (907) 238-3773. Village council: Alakanuk Traditional Council, P.O. Box 149, Alakanuk, AK 99554, phone (907) 238-3419, fax (907) 238-3429, e-mail: Alakanuk @ aitc.org.

Aleknagik

GPS: N59°17' W158°37'

(A-LECK-nuh-gik) Located where Wood River flows out of Lake Aleknagik, 25 miles north of Dillingham, 330 miles west of Anchorage. **Transportation:** Scheduled air service, car or taxi from Dillingham. **Population:** 291. **Zip code:** 99555. **Emergency Services:** Police, phone (907) 842-2189; North Shore Health Clinic, phone (907) 842-5512; South Shore Health Clinic, phone (907) 842-2185; Aleknagik First Responders Group, phone (907) 842-5933; or Kanakanak Hospital in Dillingham; Volunteer Fire Department,

phone (907) 842-2189.

Elevation: 70 feet. **Climate:** Cloudy skies, mild temperatures and moderately heavy precipitation. Annual precipitation ranges from 20 to 35 inches, with most occurring during the summer. Two-foot snowpack on ground in winter.

Private Aircraft: Airport 1 mile east; elev. 66 feet; length 2,070 feet; gravel; unattended. Condition not monitored, visual inspection recommended prior to use. Aleknagik Mission School airstrip, private, adjacent northeast; elev. 150 feet; length 1,200 feet; silt and gravel; unattended. Unusable during winter months. Seaplane base used during winter months when river is frozen.

Visitor Facilities: No hotels or motels. School House Inn bed and breakfast, (907) 842-1629. Wilderness lodges in the area include Aleknagik Mission Lodge, (907) 842-2250. Groceries and hardware may be purchased locally. Arts and crafts for sale at ATC Store. Hunting and fishing licenses not available. Guide service available. Marine engine, boat and car repair service available. Fuel available: marine gas, diesel and regular; Moody's Marina, (907) 842-5988.

The few early settlers in Aleknagik nearly all died in the influenza epidemic of 1918-19. Resettlement occurred around 1928, when a small Seventh-Day Adventist colony was established on the shores of Lake Aleknagik near the area now known as Mosquito Point. The settlement grew as former residents who survived the epidemic started drifting back and a school, churches and a small sawmill were established. There is an influx of people during summer when families return to summer homes for the fishing season.

Residents live by subsistence hunting for moose and caribou, and commercial fishing, mainly for salmon. Grayling and Dolly Varden are also harvested. Many varieties of berries are found in the area, although a local resident blames too many 3- and 4-wheelers for a diminishing berry crop. Many women in the community still practice traditional arts and crafts, such as basket weaving and skin sewing.

A scenic, 25-mile dirt road connects Aleknagik with Dillingham. The community is also the gateway to Wood-Tikchik State Park. Fishing in the park and surrounding watersheds is excellent, with 5 species of salmon, char, grayling, northern pike, rainbow trout and Dolly Varden available.

Aleknagik is a second-class city, incorporated in 1973. Communications include phones, mail plane, radio and TV. The community is served by Seventh-Day Adventist, Russian Orthodox and Moravian churches, and a school with grades 1 through 8. with enrollment of 44. Public electricity is available. Water is obtained from private wells or hauled from Aleknagik Lake. Freight arrives by air transport, barge or truck. Government address: City of Aleknagik, P.O. Box 33, Aleknagik, AK 99555, phone (907) 842-5953, fax (907) 842-2107, e-mail: alekclrk@excite.com. Village corporation: Aleknagik Natives Ltd., P.O. Box 1630, Dillingham, AK 99576, phone (907) 842-2385, fax (907) 842-1662. Village council: Native Village of Aleknagik, P.O. Box 115, Aleknagik, AK 99555, phone (907) 842-2229, fax (907) 842-2081, e-mail: Aleknagik@aitc.org.

Andreafsky
(See St. Marys)

Aniak
GPS: N61°34' W159°31'

(AN-ee-ack) Located on the south bank of the Kuskokwim River at the head of Aniak Slough, 59 miles southwest of Russian Mission, 90 miles northeast of Bethel, 325 miles west of Anchorage. **Transportation**: Scheduled or charter air service from Bethel. **Population**: 594. **Zip code**: 99557. **Emergency Services**: Village Public Safety Officer, phone (907) 675-4326; Alaska State Trooper, phone (907) 675-4398; Aniak Subregional Health Clinic, phone (907) 675-4346/4556; Aniak Volunteer Fire Department, phone (907) 675-4343/7777.

Elevation: 80 feet. **Climate**: Maritime in the summer and continental in the winter, thus summer temperatures are higher and winter temperatures colder than along the Bering Sea coast. Annual precipitation averages 17 inches, with 85 inches of snow. Expect snow between late September and early May. Strong winds common, especially in winter.

Private Aircraft: Airport adjacent south; elev. 88 feet; length 6,000 feet; gravel; fuel 80, 100; attended Monday to Saturday. Runway condition reports and snow and ice removal available only during duty hours. Passenger terminal, ticket counter and restrooms at airport. Transportation into village available. Seaplane landings in Aniak Slough and river in front of town.

Visitor Facilities: Accommodations available at Aniak Lodge (907) 675-4317, and Benders Bed & Breakfast, (907) 675-4329. Food is available at Aniak Lodge and at Burt's Burgers. Laundry facilities available; no banking services. Groceries, clothing, first-aid supplies, hardware, film and sporting goods available in the community. Arts and crafts available for purchase include carved ivory. Fishing/hunting licenses available. Guide services available. Repair services available for marine engines, boats and airplanes. Rental transportation available. Fuel available includes marine gas, diesel, propane and regular gasoline. No moorage facilities.

Aniak is a Yup'ik Eskimo word meaning "place where it comes out," referring to the nearby mouth of the Aniak River. This river played a key role in the placer gold rush of 1900-01 when prospectors from Nome stampeded to the Kuskokwim Delta after hearing of discoveries along the "Yellow River" (later identified as the Aniak River), so-called because of its discoloration from silt. A Russian-era trader called Semen Lukin is credited with the discovery of gold near Aniak in 1832, but no 20th century settlement was started until Tom L. Johnson homesteaded the long-abandoned site of the old Eskimo village in 1914 and opened a general store. A territorial school opened in 1936. Construction of an airfield in 1939 was followed by the erection of a White Alice radar-relay station in 1956. The community started to grow as people from the surrounding area moved to Aniak to find jobs. Several businesses were started to serve the increased population and Aniak became the transportation hub for the mid-Kuskokwim region. Aniak today is the headquarters of the regional school district, as well as the regional offices of several state and federal agencies. Aniak is a second-class city, incorporated in 1972.

NOTE: Aniak is the regional hub for the Kuskokwim Corp., the major landowner in the region. Land use permits are required to use lands owned by the Kuskokwim Corp. Uses include fishing, temporary camping, seasonal campsite, land crossing and research. There is a $100 administration fee. Big game hunting fee is $400. Seasonal campsite permits $50, annual use fee $250. Permits can be obtained at Aniak, (907) 675-4275, or from the Kuskokwim Corp., 2000 W. International Airport Road, Suite C-9, Anchorage, AK 99502, phone (907) 246-2101.

Aniak has a mixed economy comprising income from private businesses and publicly funded programs. The community is closely knit and has several related families. The Yup'ik language is still commonly spoken among the elders. Subsistence lifestyles are still practiced.

Mail plane and charter service are provided to several area villages through a local air service and other independent carriers. Aniak also is a transfer point for the commercial fishing industry and a staging area for firefighting crews in the summer.

The Kuskokwim River is frozen 6 months of the year, with ice often 8 feet thick. Spring breakup is a spectacular and often disastrous event when ice moving downriver hangs up in horseshoe bends and on sandbars. These ice jams can cause flooding at Aniak.

Fish in the Aniak area include most species of salmon, trout, pike, whitefish, sheefish and lush. Game includes moose, black and brown bear, and caribou. Other wildlife common to the region are fox, rabbit, mink, eagles, ptarmigan, beaver, lynx, marten, songbirds and waterfowl.

Communications in Aniak include phones, mail plane and TV. The community is served by Roman Catholic and Assembly of God churches and the Aniak school with grades preschool through 12 with enrollment of 173. Public electricity is available. Water is from individual wells. Community sewage system to some

homes; honey buckets also used. Freight arrives by cargo plane and barge. Government address: City of Aniak, P.O. Box 189, Aniak, AK 99557, phone (907) 675-4481, fax (907) 675-4486. e-mail: cityesim@arctic.net. Village corporation: The Kuskokwim Corp., 2000 W. International Airport Road, Ste. C-9, Anchorage, AK 99502, phone (907) 276-2101, fax (907) 279-8728. Village council: Aniak Traditional Council, Box 349, Aniak, AK 99557, phone and fax (907) 675-4349, e-mail: Aniak@aitc.org.

Atmautluak
GPS: N60°51' W162°16'

(At-MAUT-loo-ack) Located on the Petmigtalek River in the Yukon-Kuskokwim Delta, 15 miles northwest of Bethel, 410 miles west of Anchorage. **Transportation**: Boat; snow machine; scheduled and charter air service from Bethel. **Population**: 296. **Zip code**: 99559. **Emergency Services**: Police, phone (907) 553-5215Atmautluak Health Clinic, phone (907) 553-5114; Fire Department.

Private Aircraft: Airstrip adjacent southwest; elev. 17 feet; length 2,000 feet; gravel; no fuel; unattended. Runway condition not monitored; visual inspection recommended prior to using. Passenger terminal, transportation into village available.

NOTE: Atmautluak prohibits the sale and importation of alcoholic beverages.

Visitor Facilities: Sleeping accommodations available at the school, (907) 553-5112. No restaurant, laundromat or banking services. Supplies available in the community. Carved ivory and beadwork available for purchase. Fishing/hunting licenses not available. No guide or major repair services. Arrangements can be made to rent boats. Marine gas, diesel and regular gasoline and moorage available.

Atmautluak, a second-class city incorporated in 1976, is located within the Yukon Delta National Wildlife Refuge.

Communications at Atmautluak include phones, mail plane and radio. The community has 2 churches and a school with grades preschool through 12 with enrollment of 87. Community water and electricity systems available. Sewage system is honey buckets. Freight arrives by cargo plane and barge. Government address: Atmautluak Limited, General Delivery, Atmautluak, AK 99559, phone (907) 553-5428, fax (907) 553-5610. Village council: Atmautluak Traditional Council, P.O. Box 6568, Atmautluak, AK 99559, phone (907) 553-5610, fax (907) 553-5216, e-mail: Atmautluak@aitc.org.

Bethel

GPS: N60°47' W161°45'

Located on the north bank of the Kuskokwim River 90 miles from its mouth, 400 miles west of Anchorage. **Transportation:** Scheduled airline from Anchorage and all villages in the delta. **Population:** 5,471. **Zip code:** 99559. **Emergency Services:** Police, Fire Department, Ambulance, phone (907) 543-2131/3998; emergency only, phone 911; Alaska State Troopers, phone (907) 543-2294; Yukon-Kuskokwim Delta Regional Hospital, phone (907) 543-6300; Bethel Family Clinic, phone (907) 543-3773; Yukon Kuskokwim Health Corp. Ambulance & Aeromed Intnl. Medivac, phone (907) 543-6416..

Elevation: 10 feet. **Climate:** Maritime; mean summer temperature 53°F, mean winter temperature 11°F. Mean annual precipitation 17 inches, with 50 inches of snow. The last day of freezing usually is May 30 and the first freeze is usually about Sept. 9.

Private Aircraft: Airport adjacent southwest; elev. 131 feet; length 6,398 feet; asphalt; fuel 80, 100 and jet A; attended. Airport facilities include passenger and freight terminals, ticket counters, restrooms and traffic control tower. Taxi service to town available.

NOTE: *Bethel prohibits the sale of alcoholic beverages.*

Visitor Facilities: There are many lodging facilities and about a dozen restaurants. Public laundry facilities and banking services. Several grocery stores, 3 shopping areas and several specialty shops. Arts and crafts available for purchase include carved ivory, grass baskets, masks, beadwork, mukluks, kuspuks, Eskimo yo-yos, and fur coats, clothing and slippers. Fishing/hunting licenses available, as well as guide service.

Repair services for marine engines, boats, autos and airplanes. Rental transportation includes autos and charter aircraft; arrangements can be made to rent boats. Also 3 taxi services in town, and bus service on weekdays. All types of fuel available. Moorage facilities at small-boat harbor.

The popular Yugtarvik Regional Museum, first opened in 1967, closed in 1992, then reopened as part of the University of Alaska Fairbanks/Kuskokwim campus cultural center.

A visitor center for the Yukon Delta National Wildlife Refuge is located across from the Bethel Regional Hospital, on the main road to town from the airport. The center features exhibits, and refuge staff present periodic programs for schools and the public.

Bethel was settled in the 1800s and originally was known as Mumtrekhlagamute. The first trading post was established in 1867. When the Moravian Church established a mission here in 1885, its missionaries christened the place Bethel, in reference to a scripture verse which directed, "Arise, go up to Bethel, and dwell there." The community celebrated its centennial in 1985.

Bethel is one of the largest towns in western Alaska. It serves as the administrative hub for the area's villages, with a district court, superior court, and Alaska Dept. of Fish and Game, U.S. Fish and Wildlife Service, and Bureau of Indian Affairs offices.

The area's commercial fishing industry provides a major portion of Bethel's economy and employment. Bethel is the transportation center for 57 villages in the Yukon-Kuskokwim Delta. Bethel's location at the head of Kuskokwim Bay provides access to the Bering Sea. The town has the only medium-draft port for ocean-going vessels in western Alaska. Bethel's airport is reported to be the third busiest in the state. Transportation and related industries contribute significantly to the town's economy.

While there are still many people living mainly by subsistence hunting and fishing in the surrounding villages, most of Bethel's residents work year-round in the growing private industries, Native corporations and government jobs.

The Kisaralik and Kwethluk rivers, 1 to 2 hours from Bethel by boat, offer good recreational fishing for grayling, Dolly Varden and rainbow trout, as well as silver and chum salmon. The Kisaralik also is used regularly in the summer for guided float trips sponsored by the City of Bethel Parks and Recreation Dept.

NOTE: Ten nearby villages lie on lands owned by the Kuskokwim Corp. Land use permits are required to use lands owned by the Kuskokwim Corp. Uses include fishing, temporary camping, seasonal campsite, land crossing and research. There is a $100

> **F**or thousands of years, the 2,300-mile-long Yukon River and 700-mile-long Kuskokwim River have deposited tons of glacial silt into the Bering Sea on Alaska's west coast. The silt has formed one of the largest coastal flood plains in the world—the Yukon-Kuskokwim Delta. In the United States, the vast alluvial plain is exceeded in size only by the Missippi River delta. The Yukon-Kuskokwim Delta stretches 250 miles along the coast from Kuskokwim Bay to Norton Sound and extends inland 200 miles to the Kuskokwim Mountains.
>
> — From *Alaska A to Z*

administration fee. Big game hunting fee is $400. Seasonal campsite permits $50, annual use fee $250. For further information, contact the Kuskokwim Corp., 2000 W. International Airport Road, Suite C-9, Anchorage, AK 99502, phone (907) 276-2101, or in Aniak phone (907) 675-4275.

Bethel is located within the 20-million-acre Yukon Delta National Wildlife Refuge, largest in the United States. Many species of waterfowl make the refuge their summer home.

There are several recreational events during the year in Bethel, including the Kuskokwim-300 Sled Dog Race, Yukon-Kuskokwim State Fair, Mink & Fox Festival, Fourth of July Fete and Eskimo dance festivals. The Kuskokwim Ice Classic in the spring is a fundraiser sponsored by Bethel Community Services. The winner is the person who predicts most closely the time the ice begins to break up.

Communications in Bethel include phones, radio, TV and 2 weekly newspapers, the *Tundra Drums* and *Delta Discovery*. The community is served by 9 churches, 3 public schools with enrollment of 1,318, a private school, a community college, 3 day-care centers and a prematernal home. There are community electricity, water and sewage systems. Freight arrives by cargo plane, barge and ship. Government address: City of Bethel, P.O. Box 388, Bethel, AK 99559, phone (907) 543-2047, fax (907) 543-4171, e-mail: cityclerk@bethel.ak.us, web: www.ci.bethel.ak.us. Village corporation: Bethel Native Corp., P.O. Box 719, Bethel, AK 99559, phone (907) 543-2124, fax (907) 543-2897. Bethel Chamber of Commerce, P.O. Box 329, Bethel, AK 99559, phone (907) 543-2911, fax (907) 543-2255, e-mail: bethelchamber2@alaska.com, web: http://home.gci.net/~chamber1/bethel.htm. Village Council: Orutsararmiut Native Council, P.O. Box 927, Bethel, AK 99559, phone (907) 543-2608, fax (907) 543-2639, e-mail: Orutsararmiut@aitc.org.

Brevig Mission

GPS: N65°19' W166°27'

Located at the mouth of Shelman Creek on the north shore of Port Clarence on the

Seward Peninsula, 6 miles northwest of Teller, 60 miles northwest of Nome, 481 miles west of Fairbanks. **Transportation:** Scheduled or charter air service from Nome. **Population:** 234. **Zip code:** 99785. **Emergency Services:** Village Public Safety Officer; Alaska State Troopers, Nome, phone (907) 443-2835; Clinic, phone (907) 642-4311; Volunteer Fire Department.

Elevation: 25 feet. **Climate:** Maritime climate, cool and damp, when the Bering Sea is ice-free from early June to mid-November. Freezing of the sea causes a change to a more continental climate, with less precipitation and colder temperatures. Annual precipitation is 11.5 inches, with an average of 50 inches of snowfall. Average winter temperatures are between –9°F and 8°F; summer temperatures are between 44°F and 57°F.

Private Aircraft: 2 intersecting airstrips adjacent east; elev. 25 feet; length 2,110 and 3,000 feet; gravel; unattended. Runway condition not monitored; recommend visual inspection prior to using. Airport has lights and freight terminal. Transportation into village sometimes available.

NOTE: Brevig Mission prohibits the sale and importation of alcoholic beverages.

Visitor Facilities: Arrangements can be made to stay in the high school during the school year by contacting the school principal, (907) 642-4021. The Washeteria building, (907) 642-4321, and the health clinic, (907) 642-4311, also offer lodging. No hotels, restaurants or banking services. Groceries, clothing, first-aid supplies, hardware, film and sporting goods available at Brevig Muit Store (907) 642-4091. Arts and crafts available for purchase include carved ivory, fur slippers, mukluks, beadwork, crocheted and knitted items. Fishing/hunting licenses available. No guide service. Marine engine and boat repair available. Arrangements can be made to rent boats. Fuel available includes white gas, propane and regular gasoline. No moorage facilities.

The "Teller Reindeer Station" was established nearby in 1892 by Sheldon Jackson, who named it after Henry Moore Teller, U.S. senator and secretary of the Interior.

The reindeer station was operated by the U.S. government from 1892 to 1900. The Norwegian Evangelical Lutheran Mission was established in 1900 at the present site of Brevig Mission and the settlement became known as Teller Mission. By 1906, the government role in reindeer herding had diminished and the mission became dominant. Brevig Mission is a second-class city, incorporated in 1969.

The Natives living around Port Clarence were Kauwerak Eskimos with no permanent settlement prior to 1892. They lived in migratory communities, pursuing fish and game. They traded furs with Siberia, Little Diomede and King Island, and alliances were formed with Wales, Little Diomede and others for protection.

Reindeer were the economic base of this community from 1892 to 1974, but their importance is now declining. Skin sewing for arts and crafts and jobs on seasonal construction projects bring in some income.

The people of Brevig Mission depend on both sea mammals and fishing for subsistence, going to seasonal hunting and fishing camps. Seal, oogruk and beluga whale are the most important subsistence mammals. Fish staples include salmon, whitefish, herring, tomcod, flounder, sculpin and smelt. Residents also rely on waterfowl, game birds, eggs, rabbits, squirrels, moose, berries and an occasional polar bear. According to one enthusiastic resident, "Fishing is great in the summer, spring hunting is even greater, and greatest of all: the community is friendly and we welcome visitors year round."

There is a winter trail to Teller used by snow machines and dogsleds.

Communications in Brevig Mission include phones, mail plane, radio and TV. The community is served by a Lutheran church and a school with grades preschool through 12. There are community electricity and water systems; sewage system is honey buckets. Freight arrives by cargo plane and barge. Government address: City of Brevig Mission, P.O. Box 85021, Brevig Mission, AK 99785, phone (907) 642-3851. Village corporation: Brevig Mission Native Corp., General Delivery, Brevig Mission, AK 99785, phone (907) 642-4091.

Buckland

GPS: N65°59' W161°08'

Located on the west bank of the Buckland River on the Seward Peninsula, 75 miles southeast of Kotzebue, 400 miles west of Fairbanks. **Transportation**: Boats; snow machine; scheduled air service from Kotzebue. **Population**: 442. **Zip code**: 99727. **Emergency Services**: Village Public Safety Officer, phone (907) 494-2162; Alaska State Troopers, Kotzebue; Buckland Health Clinic, phone (907) 494-2122; Volunteer Fire Department.

Climate: Transitional zone characterized by long, cold winters and cool summers. Temperatures in July and August average 60°F. Precipitation is light, less than 9 inches annually, with 35 to 40 inches of snow.

Private Aircraft: Airstrip 1 mile southwest from village; elev. 30 feet; length 3,200 feet; gravel. No airport facilities. Runway condition not monitored; recommend visual inspection prior to using. Subject to turbulent crosswinds during summer months. Public transportation into village available.

Visitor Facilities: No hotel, restaurant or banking service. Laundry facilities are available at the city washeteria, open daily. Groceries, clothing, first-aid supplies, hardware, film and sporting goods available at 4 stores. Fishing/hunting licenses available. No guide or major repair services. No rental transportation. Fuel available includes marine gas, propane and regular gasoline. No moorage facilities.

This village has existed at several other locations under various names in the past, including Elephant Point, so named because fossil mammoth or mastodon bones were found at the site in 1826. The presence of the fossil finds shows that this site was used by prehistoric man.

Buckland people moved repeatedly as conditions changed and the people depended at various times on reindeer or beluga whale or seal for survival. In the 1920s, they moved with their reindeer herd from Old Buckland, 1 mile downriver, to the present area. The townsite, however, was later relocated. Today, Buckland is a second-class city, incorporated in 1966.

Buckland has a primarily subsistence economy. In the fall and winter, residents hunt caribou; in spring they hunt beluga whale and seal off Elephant Point.

Some employment is provided with a locally owned reindeer herd, numbering 2,000 head. Herring, salmon, smelt, grayling, whitefish, rabbit, ptarmigan, berries and waterfowl and their eggs supplement the local diet.

Communications in Buckland include phones, mail plane and radio. The community is served by a church and 2 schools with grades preschool through 12 with total enrollment of 168. There is a community electric system. Water is hauled from the washeteria. The city has its own honey-bucket haul system. Freight arrives by barge or by air. Government address: City of Buckland, P.O. Box 49, Buckland, AK 99727, phone (907) 494-2121, fax (907) 494-2138, e-mail: dhadley@maniilaq. org. Village corporation: NANA Regional Corp., P.O. Box 49, Kotzebue, AK 99752, phone (907) 442-3301, fax (907) 442-2866, web: http://www.nana-online.com/intro.htm. Village council: Native Village of Buckland, P.O. Box 67, Buckland, AK 99727, phone (907) 494-2171. fax (907) 494-2217, e-mail: Buckland@aitc.org.

Candle

GPS: N65°54' W161°55'

Located on the Kewalik River, 90 miles southeast of Kotzebue. **Transportation**: Scheduled air service; charter plane; boat. **Population**: 4 year-round, 35 during summer mining season. **Zip code**: 99728. **Emergency Services**: Public Health Service Hospital in Kotzebue, phone (907) 442-3321; Alaska State Troopers in Kotzebue, phone (907) 442-3911.

Climate: June clear and cool, July hot and dry. In August, expect rain, then usually 2 or 3 weeks of Indian summer in September. Winters are cold, similar to Kotzebue.

Private Aircraft: Airstrip adjacent northeast; elev. 15 feet; length 3,880 feet; gravel; no fuel; unattended.

Visitor Facilities: None. Supplies are obtained from Kotzebue and Anchorage.

Candle is a mining community which started in 1904. Most of the town burned down about 20 years ago; just a few houses were left standing. There are 4 year-round residents, with the population increasing from May until freezeup or Oct. 1. Because the mining season is so short, July 4 is the only summer holiday, and residents hold a town picnic with horseshoes and a softball game.

There is an old deserted dredge about 6 miles from town. Fishing is good in the Kewalik River from July through September for salmon, grayling and trout. There are moose, caribou, reindeer and occasionally bear. Two mining operations in Candle are available for people to walk through and watch, as well as an old cemetery to view.

Chefornak

GPS: N60°13' W164°12'

(Sha-FOR-nack) Located at the junction of the Keguk and Kinia rivers in the Yukon-Kuskokwim Delta, 100 miles southwest of Bethel, 480 miles west-southwest of Anchorage. **Transportation**: Scheduled air service from Bethel; snow machines; outboards. **Population**: 408. **Zip code**: 99561. **Emergency Services**: Village Public Safety Officer, phone (907) 867-8712; Alaska State Troopers, Bethel, phone (907) 543-2294; Chefornak Health Clinic, phone (907) 867-8919; Volunteer Fire Department, phone 867-8712.

Private Aircraft: Airstrip adjacent east; elev. 40 feet; length 2,500 feet; gravel; no fuel; unattended. Runway condition not monitored; visual inspection recommended prior to using. Seaplane float. Gulls and birds in airport area.

NOTE: Chefornak prohibits the sale and importation of alcoholic beverages.

Visitor Facilities: Make arrangements for lodging at the high school, phone (907) 867-8515/8700. Groceries, clothing, first-aid supplies, hardware, film, sporting goods, vehicles and boats available. Marine engine and boat repairs available; rental boats and off-road vehicles. No bank, laundromat or fishing/hunting licenses.

This Eskimo village, located within Yukon Delta National Wildlife Refuge, was incorporated as a second-class city in 1974. Many village residents are likely to be at their fish camps during the summer.

Local recreation includes basketball games, dancing and Eskimo dancing, bingo, 2 arcades, and Sunday night gatherings for young adults.

Communications include phones, CB radio, VHF radio, radio and TV. The community is served by a Roman Catholic church and 2 schools with grades kindergarten through 12 with enrollment of 136. There is a community electric system. Water is hauled from a community watering point or rain water or ice is collected. Sewage system is honey buckets. Freight arrives by plane and barge. Government address: City of Chefornak, P.O. Box 29, Chefornak, AK 99561, phone (907) 867-8528, fax (907) 867-8704. Village corporation: Chefornamuit Inc., P.O. Box 70, Chefornak, AK 99561, phone (907) 867-8115, fax (907) 867-8895. Village council: Village of Chefornak, Box 29, Chefornak, AK 99561, phone (907) 867-8850, fax (907) 867-8429, e-mail: Chefornak@aitc.org.

Chevak

GPS: N61°31' W165°35'

(CHEE-vak) Located on the north bank of the Ninglikfak River, 17 miles east of Hooper Bay, 120 miles northwest of Bethel, 500 miles west of Anchorage. **Transportation**: Boats; snow machines; scheduled or charter air service from Bethel. **Population**: 769. **Zip code**: 99563. **Emergency Services**: Village Public Safety Officer, phone (907) 858-7012; Alaska State Troopers, Bethel; Chevak Health Clinic, phone (907) 858-7029; Volunteer Fire Department.

Climate: Maritime; temperatures range from -25'° to 79°F at nearby Cape Romanzof. Snow depth on the tundra averages between 2 1/2 and 3 feet, with an average of 60 inches of snowfall per year. Freezeup occurs at the end of October; breakup in June.

Private Aircraft: Airstrip 1 mile north; elev. 75 feet; length 2,610 feet; gravel; no fuel; unattended. Runway condition not monitored; visual inspection recommended prior to using. Strong crosswinds. No transportation to village.

Visitor Facilities: Lodging sometimes available at the school, phone (907) 858-7713. No restaurant or banking services. Laundry facilities available. Supplies available in the community at Chevak Company Corp., Lena's Store and Wayne Hill Co. Arts and crafts available include carved ivory, grass baskets, masks, beadwork and skin boots. Fishing/ hunting licenses available. No guide service or rental transportation. Marine engine repair available. Fuel available: marine gas, regular gasoline. No moorage facilities.

Chevak is also known as New Chevak because residents inhabited another village called Chevak before 1950. "Old" Chevak, on the north bank of the Keoklevik River, 9 miles east of Hooper Bay, was abandoned because of flooding from high storm tides. The name Chevak refers to "a connecting slough" on which "old" Chevak was situated. Chevak was incorporated as a second-class city in 1967.

Employment in Chevak is at its peak in the summer months, with seasonal fire fighting for the Bureau of Land Management and summer construction projects. The city also usually hires several people for city improvement projects. Other jobs exist with the city, village corporation, local stores and the school.

Income is supplemented by public assistance programs and local subsistence activities. Residents hunt seal, walrus, geese, swans, ducks and ptarmigan. Additionally, clams, salmon, whitefish, blackfish, needlefish, sheefish, pike and tomcod are taken. In the fall, families gather greens and harvest berries.

Local recreation includes basketball games, dancing and Eskimo dancing.

Chevak is located within Yukon Delta National Wildlife Refuge, which is the summer home for many thousands of migratory birds.

Communications include phones, mail plane, radio and TV. The community has a Roman Catholic church and a school with grades kindergarten through 12. with enrollment of 313. There is community electricity; water is hauled from central watering points. Sewage system is primarily honey buckets. Freight arrives by barge or mail plane. Government address: City of Chevak, P.O. Box 136, Chevak, AK 99563, phone (907) 858-7128, fax (907) 858-7245, e-mail: ctycevaq@unicom-alaska.com. Village corporation: Chevak Co. Corp., P.O. Box 5478, Chevak, AK 99563, phone (907) 858-7011, fax (907) 858-7311, e-mail: chevakcc@unicom-alaska.com. Village council: Chevak Traditional Council, Box 140, Chevak, AK 99563, phone (907) 858-7428, fax (907) 858-7812, e-mail: chevak@aitc.org.

Chuathbaluk

GPS: N61°34' W159°13'

(Chu-ATH-ba-luck) Located on the north bank of the Kuskokwim River, 10 miles east of Aniak, 100 miles east of Bethel and 310 miles west of Anchorage. **Transportation:** Charter plane from Aniak. **Population:** 127. **Zip code:** 99557. **Emergency Services:** Alaska State Troopers, Aniak, phone (907) 675-4398; Chuathbaluk Health Clinic, phone (907) 467-4114; Volunteer Fire Department.

Climate: Continental; temperatures range between -55'° and 87°F. Annual snowfall 85 inches; precipitation 17 inches.

Private Aircraft: Airstrip 5 miles northeast; elev. 300 feet; length 1,560 feet; gravel; unattended. Runway condition not monitored; recommend visual inspection prior to using. No transportation to village; no airport facilities.

Visitor Facilities: Lodging at the school, phone (907) 467-4129, or community center through the city office, phone (907) 467-4115. Laundromat available. No banking services. Groceries and general merchandise available in the community. Fishing/hunting licenses and guide service not available. No major repair service or rental transportation. There are moorage facilities; the only fuel available is marine gas.

NOTE: Land use permits are required to use lands owned by the Kuskokwim Corp. Uses include fishing, temporary camping, seasonal campsite, land crossing and research. There is a $100 administration fee. Big game hunting fee is $400. Seasonal *campsite permits $50, annual use fee $250. For further information, contact the Kuskokwim Corp., 2000 W. International Airport Road, Suite C-9, Anchorage, AK 99502, phone (907) 276-2101, or in Aniak phone (907) 675-4275.*

The community existed as a Native settlement as early as 1833. It has been known by several names, most recently as "Little Russian Mission." However, this led to confusion between this community and a village on the lower Yukon River called Russian Mission. As a result, within the last 20 years the village was renamed Chuathbaluk, Yup'ik Eskimo for "big blueberries."

For many years the village had a small population. It grew considerably when permission to live on the property was given by the Russian Orthodox Church. It became a second-class city with its incorporation in 1975. The economy depends heavily on subsistence activities, supplemented by some construction work, and cottage industries such as skin sewing and basketry.

The community is served by a Russian Orthodox church established in 1891 and on the National Register of Historic Places, and a school with grades preschool through 12. with enrollment of 39.

Communications available are phones, radio and TV. Community electricity available. Water hauled from a community well. Sewage system is honey buckets. Freight arrives by air cargo and barge. Government address: City of Chuathbaluk, P.O. Box CHU, Chuathbaluk, AK 99557, phone (907) 467-4115, fax (907) 467-4180. Village council: Chuathbaluk Traditional Council, P.O. Box CHU, Chuathbaluk, AK 99557, phone (907) 467-4313, fax (907) 467-4113, e-mail: Chuathbaluk@aitc.org.

Clark's Point

GPS: N58°50' W158°33'

Located on a spit on the northeastern shore of Nushagak Bay, 15 miles south of Dillingham and 350 miles southwest of Anchorage. **Transportation**: Scheduled air service from Dillingham. **Population**: 76. **Zip code**: 99569. **Emergency Services**. Police, phone (907) 842-5943; Clark's Point Health Clinic, phone (907)

236-1232; Clark's Point First Responders, phone clinic; Volunteer Fire Department.

Climate: Cloudy skies, mild temperatures and moderately heavy precipitation, with frequent strong surface winds. Average summer temperatures of 37°F to 66°F; winter temperatures from 4°F to 30°F. Annual precipitation from 20 to 26 inches, with most of the precipitation occurring in July and August.

Private Aircraft: Airstrip adjacent north; elev. 10 feet; length 2,600 feet; gravel; unattended. Runway condition not monitored; visual inspection recommended prior to landing. Watch for birds on runway and pedestrians and vehicles on west end. No fuel or airport facilities.

Visitor Facilities: None. Community store available with limited selection of items.

Settled in 1888, when Nushagak Packing Co. established a cannery there, the village was named for John W. Clark. He was manager of the Alaska Commercial Co. store at Nushagak, and was reputed to have operated a saltery on the spit prior to establishment of the cannery. The cannery closed and reopened several times during the years and shut down permanently in 1952. Since that time Alaska Packers Assoc. has operated the facility as a headquarters for its fishing fleet. A major flood occurred in 1929. Plagued by erosion and threat of floods, the village has since been relocated to higher ground.

The village, incorporated in 1971 as a second-class city, is a "designated anchorage" for scows, floaters and fishing boats working the bay during the summer fishing season. Commercial fishing is the primary base of the economy, and residents depend on subsistence activities for food sources.

Communications include phones, mail plane, radio, TV and Internet. The community has a Roman Catholic church and a school with grades kindergarten through 8 with enrollment of 17. Community water, sewer, electricity. Freight is transported by air transport and skiffs from Dillingham. Government address: City of Clark's Point, P.O. Box 110, Clark's Point, AK 99569, phone (907) 236-1221, fax (907) 236-1412. Village corporation: Saguyak Inc., P.O. Box 04, Clark's Point, AK 99569, phone (907) 236-1235, fax (907) 236-1450. Village council: Clark's Point Village Council, P.O. Box 90, Clark's Point, AK 99569, phone (907) 236-1427, fax (907) 236-1428, e-mail: ClarksPoint@aitc.org.

Council

GPS: N64°54' W163°42'

Located on the left bank of the Niukluk River on the Seward Peninsula, 33 miles northeast of Solomon, 74 miles northeast of Nome, 470 miles west of Fairbanks. **Transportation**: Boat, charter plane or auto from Nome. **Population**: 11 year-round, up to 50 in summer. **Zip code**: 99790. **Emergency Services**: Alaska State Troopers, Nome; Health Aide, phone (907) 675-8001.

Elevation: 100 feet. **Climate**: Continental, with long, cold winters and short, mild summers. Average annual precipitation is 14 inches, with 46 inches of snowfall. Temperatures range between -9°F and 64°F.

Private Aircraft: Melsing Creek airstrip adjacent northeast; elev. 85 feet; length 3,000 feet; gravel; no fuel; unattended. Runway subject to crosswinds, not maintained in winter; recommend visual inspection prior to using. Runway connected to section of the road, which has been widened to serve as part of the airstrip. No airport facilities. Transportation into village sometimes available. Pederson airstrip adjacent east of mining camp; elev. 95 feet; length 2,100 feet; gravel; no fuel; unattended. Prior permission for use required in writing from owner. South end of runway rough. Runway doglegs; use east side runway by road. Grass on strip; use caution.

Visitor Facilities: Accommodations and meals available in summer at Camp Bendeleben fishing lodge, (907) 443-2880. No public laundry facilities or banking services. Limited groceries and sporting goods available at a small store in a local residence; most visitors bring their own supplies. No arts and crafts available for purchase. Fishing/hunting licenses not available. Guide services available. No repair service or rental transportation.

Fuel available includes propane and regular gasoline. No moorage facilities.

Council, once one of the largest communities in Alaska, was founded in 1897 by Daniel B. Libby and his party. Libby had been 1 of 3 members of the Van Bendeleben expedition of 1896 who discovered gold in the area. Council became the site of the recording office and center of the Council Gold Mining District. By October 1897, it was a city of approximately 50 log houses and 300 people. The gold strikes at Council Creek predate major strikes at Nome, and a single claim on Ophir Creek was said to be almost the richest claim in the world, second only to a claim in the Klondike. During the summers of 1897-99, Council's population was estimated to be as high as 15,000 people, and it was said to be bigger than Nome although the actual population was never documented. "Council City" was a genuine boom town with a hotel, wooden boardwalks, a post office, a 20-bed hospital and numerous bars. At one time 13 dredges worked streams and rivers between Solomon and Council, and the town was the southern terminus of a railroad that climbed a 600-foot ridge into Ophir Creek. Many of the boomers left Council in 1900 for the gold beaches of Nome, but a sizable community remained. Council, which still had a population of 686 in 1910, was for many years the second largest community in western Alaska. The influenza epidemic of 1918, the Great Depression and WWII contributed to its decline, and by 1950 only 9 people remained. The post office was closed in 1953.

Council is primarily a summer fish camp site for Nome residents. It is one of the few villages in the region connected to Nome by a road, which originated as a trail during the gold rush. The road was constructed in 1906-07. The road terminates across from Council at the river, which can be forded at low water periods. Three roads branch out from Council: one to Ophir Creek, the second to Melsing Creek and the airstrip, and a third over a hill northeast to Mystery. Except for the Ophir Road, 4-wheel-drive vehicles are necessary.

The movie *North to Alaska* starring John Wayne was filmed in this area. Remnants of gold mining activity are everywhere. The countryside is dotted with old cabins, roads, a railroad, mines and dredges, including an operating dredge at Ophir Creek. The old post office, school, hotel and numerous other buildings in various stages of deterioration still stand among newer buildings in the settlement.

All permanent residents of Council, and many of the seasonal residents, rely in part on local hunting and fishing for food. The Niukluk River provides some of the finest fishing on the Seward Peninsula. Arctic char, grayling, pike, whitefish, and chum, pink and king salmon abound. Rabbits, ptarmigan, moose, grizzly bears and wolves all inhabit the area. Some placer gold mining currently takes place in the area, primarily at Ophir Creek.

Communications in Council include a phone in the community building, (907) 665-8001, and radios. There is a community electric system. Water is hauled from a central watering point. The sewage system is honey buckets. Freight is hauled over the Nome/Council Road for $500 per truckload. Council is unincorporated. Village corporation address: Council Native Corp., P.O. Box 1183, Nome, AK 99762, phone (907) 443-5231. Village council: Native Village of Council, P.O. Box 2050, Nome, AK 99762, phone (907) 443-7649, fax (907) 443-5965, e-mail: Council@aitc.org.

Crooked Creek

GPS: N61°52′ W158°08′

Located on the north bank of the Kuskokwim River, at its junction with Crooked Creek, in the Kilbuck-Kuskokwim Mountains, 50 miles northeast of Aniak, 145 miles northeast of Bethel, 280 miles west of Anchorage. **Transportation**: Scheduled air service from Bethel. **Population**: 137. **Zip code**: 99575. **Emergency Services**: Alaska State Troopers, Aniak, phone 675-4398; Crooked Creek Health Clinic; Volunteer Fire Department.

Elevation: 130 feet. **Climate**: Continental with low winter temperatures and high summer temperatures. Mean annual precipitation 15 inches,

with 61 inches of snow.

Private Aircraft: Airstrip 2 miles south; elev. 128 feet; length 2,000 feet; gravel; unattended. Runway condition not monitored; visual inspection recommended prior to using. No line of sight from one end of runway to the other. Some erosion of south end of runway.

Visitor Facilities: Accommodations for 12 people at local roadhouse. No banking services. Supplies, laundry and shower facilities available. Fishing/hunting licenses not available. Information on guide and repair services, rental transportation, fuel and moorage unavailable.

NOTE: Land use permits are required to use lands owned by the Kuskokwim Corp. Uses include fishing, temporary camping, seasonal campsite, land crossing and research. There is a $100 administration fee. Big game hunting fee is $400. Seasonal campsite permits $50, annual use fee $250. For further information, contact the Kuskokwim Corp., 2000 W. International Airport Rd., Ste. C-9, Anchorage, AK 99502, phone (907) 276-2101, or in Aniak phone (907) 675-4275.

The village of Crooked Creek, or "Kipchapuk," was first reported in 1844 by Russian explorer L.A. Zagoskin, who noted that the site was used as a summer camp by residents of a nearby village. Crooked Creek also has been known as Portage Village. A more permanent settlement was established at the site in 1909 following a gold strike along the nearby upper Iditarod River. An influx of people to the area in 1909-10 led to the founding of the Flat and Iditarod mining camps. Crooked Creek was a supply point for those camps, which were within easy access of the Kuskokwim River.

Crooked Creek village, which is spread out on both sides of Crooked Creek, is unincorporated.

There are few year-round employment opportunities at Crooked Creek. Government programs, the regional school district and a few support services provide the only permanent jobs. Subsistence activities supplement this income.

Crooked Creek residents hunt beaver, muskrat, game birds, hare, moose, caribou and waterfowl. Income also is obtained from trapping and the sale of marten, wolverine, lynx, fox and mink. In summer, the Kuskokwim River and Crooked Creek yield king, silver, red and chum salmon, as well as whitefish, pike, grayling, Dolly Varden, sheefish and eel. In the fall, cranberries, blueberries, raspberries, blackberries, salmonberries and currants are harvested.

Communications in Crooked Creek include 4 private phones; a pay phone is located at the post office. Two air/ground radios are available for planes. TV signals are relayed to Crooked Creek via statewide satellite. The community is served by a Russian Orthodox church and a school with grades preschool through 12 with enrollment of 38. Electricity is provided by the Middle Kuskokwim Electric Co-op, which serves 5 villages on the river. Water is hauled from the washeteria or laundromat. Sewage system is honey buckets. Freight arrives by mail plane or barge. Village corporation: The Kuskokwim Corp., 2000 W. International Airport Road, Ste. C-9, Anchorage, AK 99502, phone (907) 276-2101. Village council: Native Village of Crooked Creek, P.O. Box 69, Crooked Creek, AK 99575, phone (907) 432-2200, fax (907) 432-2201, e-mail: CrookedCreek@aitc.org.

Deering

GPS: N66°04' W162°42'

Located at the mouth of the Inmachuck River on Kotzebue Sound, 57 miles southwest of Kotzebue, 150 miles north of Nome, 440 miles west-northwest of Fairbanks. **Transportation**: Scheduled and charter air service from Kotzebue; boat; snow machine. **Population**: 155. **Zip code**: 99736. **Emergency Services**: Village Public Safety Officer; Alaska State Troopers, Kotzebue, phone (907) 442-3911; Deering Health Clinic, phone (907) 363-2137; Volunteer Fire Department.

Climate: Transitional zone; long cold winters and cool summers. Precipitation is light and averages less than 9 inches per year, with 36 inches of snow.

Private Aircraft: 2 intersecting runways 1 mile southwest; elev. 15 feet;

length 2,080 and 2,600 feet; gravel; no fuel; unattended. Visual inspection recommended prior to landing. No airport facilities; private transportation to village. *NOTE: Deering prohibits the sale and importation of alcoholic beverages.*

Visitor Facilities: Accommodation with kitchen privileges at Deering Multipurpose facility, (907) 363-2136. Laundromat available. Groceries, clothing, first-aid supplies and film available at Deering Native Store, (907) 363-2159, and Beep's Store, (907) 363-2125. Some carved ivory available for purchase. Fishing/hunting licenses available. No guide service, major repair service or rental transportation. Fuel available includes diesel, propane and regular gasoline. No moorage facilities.

Deering, described as a beautiful oceanside community by one local resident, is built on a spit approximately 300 feet wide and 1.1 miles long. The village was established in 1901 as a supply station for Seward Peninsula gold mines and located near the historic Malemiut Eskimo village of Inmachukmiut. The village name probably was taken from the 90-ton schooner *Abbey Deering*, which was in the nearby waters in 1900. Deering is a second-class city, incorporated in 1970.

The economy is based on subsistence hunting and fishing and reindeer herding. Main sources of meat are moose, seal and beluga whale; residents go to hunting camps in the spring and fall.

A 26-mile road connects Deering with the mining area of Utica to the south. Also, many trails along major streams and across the tundra are used year-round for traveling to other villages, hunting and fishing.

Communications in Deering include phones, mail plane, radio and cable TV. The community has a church and a school with grades preschool through 12 with enrollment of 40. There is community electricity. Water comes from a Public Health Service tank in summer; ice is hauled for water in winter. Sewage system is honey buckets. Freight arrives by cargo plane and barge. Government address: City of Deering, P.O. Box 36049, Deering, AK 99736, phone (907) 363-

2136, fax (907) 363-2156. Village corporation: NANA Regional Corp., P.O. Box 49, Kotzebue, AK 99752. Village council: Native Village of Deering, P.O. Box 89, Deering, AK 99736, phone (907) 363-2138, fax (907) 363-2195, e-mail: Deering@aitc.org.

Dillingham

GPS: N59°02' W158°27'

Located on the south side of Snag Point at the confluence of the Wood and Nushagak rivers at the north end of Nushagak Bay, 175 miles southeast of Bethel, 320 miles west of Anchorage. **Transportation:** Scheduled airline from Anchorage. **Population:** 2,466. **Zip Code:** 99576. **Emergency Services:** Police and fire, emergency only, phone 911; Alaska State Troopers, phone (907) 842-5641; Kanakanak Hospital, phone (907) 842-5201; Dillingham Health Center, phone (907) 842-5981; Dillingham Volunteer Fire and Rescue Squad, phone (907) 842-2288/5354; Ambulance service.

Elevation: 80 feet. **Climate:** Transitional climate zone, affected primarily by the waters of Bristol Bay, but also by the arctic climate of the Interior. Cloudy skies, mild temperatures and fairly heavy precipitation. There are often strong winds. Heavy fog occurs often in July and August. Mean annual precipitation 25 inches, with 71 inches of snow.

Private Aircraft: Airport 2 miles west; elev. 85 feet; length 6,404 feet; asphalt, grooved; fuel 80, 100 and jet A; attended Monday to Friday. Airport has passenger and freight terminals, ticket counters, restrooms and traffic control tower. Public transportation to town available.

Visitor Facilities: Hotel accommodations at The Bristol Inn, (907) 842-2240, Dillingham Hotel and Lake Rose Cottage, as well as about a dozen bed and breakfasts. Area wilderness lodges include Crystal Creek Lodge, (907) 842-2646; and Royal Coachman Lodge. Visitor center is open year-round. Several restaurants. Laundromat and banking services available. Supplies available at several grocery and general mercantile stores, as well as specialty shops. Arts and crafts available

for purchase include grass baskets, carved ivory, earrings, Eskimo dolls, masks, skin sewing and Eskimo yo-yos. Fishing/ hunting licenses available, as well as guide services. Kayak and canoe rentals. Repair services available for marine engines, boats, autos and aircraft. Fuel available includes marine gas, white gas, diesel, propane, unleaded and regular gasoline. Moorage facilities available.

The area around Dillingham was long inhabited by various Eskimo, Aleut and Athabascan groups. In 1818, Alexander Baranof, first governor of Russian America, ordered construction of a permanent post at the mouth of the Nushagak River. The post came to be known as Alexandrovski Redoubt and drew people from the Kuskokwim region, Cook Inlet and the Alaska Peninsula. The community was called Nushagak by 1837 when a Russian Orthodox mission was established there. In 1881 the U.S. Signal Corps established a meteorological station at Nushagak and in 1884 the first salmon cannery in the Bristol Bay region was constructed by the Arctic Packing Co. Two more canneries were established in the next 2 years, the second one at the present city of Dillingham, then known as Snag Point. In 1903, U.S. Sen. William Paul Dillingham of Vermont toured through Alaska with his subcommittee. Although he did not visit the Dillingham area, the town was named after him in 1904. Dillingham is a first-class city, incorporated in 1963.

Dillingham is the economic and transportation hub of the Bristol Bay region. Northbound cargo ships unload supplies for area villages at the Dillingham dock. The city-run dock handled 22 million pounds of freight in 2000. The city also maintains a harbor serving more than 600 boats. The economy is augmented by commercial fishing, the cannery, trapping and tourism. An annual event, the Beaver Roundup, occurs each March. Bristol Bay is the world's largest producer of red salmon.

The Samuel K. Fox Museum, P.O. Box 273, Dillingham, AK 99576, phone (907) 842-5610/5521, is an ethno-history museum featuring contemporary and traditional Alaskan arts, crafts and artifacts. The

Yup'ik Eskimo culture of southwestern Alaska is represented in basketry, carving, skin sewing and dolls. The museum also hosts traveling exhibits from around the state. The museum shares a building with the public library and is open year-round. Call for information on hours. No admission charge; donations accepted.

Dillingham offers some of the best sportfishing in the world, and numerous sportfishing lodges are located in the area. There is a 25-mile road connecting the town with the Eskimo village of Aleknagik, located on Lake Aleknagik near Wood-Tikchik State Park, largest state park in the United States. The park also is accessible by floatplane from Dillingham. Many air taxis offer flightseeing of the area.

In addition to salmon, trout, grayling and arctic char are the main species of fish caught in the area. There is hunting for brown bear, moose and caribou in the area and trapping for wolf, wolverine, fox, lynx, marten and beaver. Float trips down the Nushagak or Wood River systems are popular. (See River Running in the Attractions section.)

Much land in the Dillingham area is owned by the local Native corporation, Choggiung Ltd., which requires that a permit be obtained for any public use of its lands.

Communications in Dillingham include phones, radio, TV and 1 newspaper, *The Bristol Bay Times*. The community is served by 10 churches and a public library. The Dillingham City Schools have a total enrollment of 567. There is also a private school and the Bristol Bay campus of the University of Alaska Fairbanks. There are community electricity, water and sewer. Freight arrives by cargo plane, barge and ship. Government address: City of Dillingham, P.O. Box 889, Dillingham, AK 99576, phone (907) 842-5211, fax (907) 842-5691, e-mail: cofdlg@ci.dillingham.ak.us, web: http://www.ci.dillingham.ak.us. Village corporation: Choggiung Ltd., P.O. Box 330, Dillingham, AK 99576, phone (907) 842-5218, fax (907) 842-5462. Dillingham Chamber of Commerce, P.O. Box 348, Dillingham, AK 99576, phone (907) 842-5115, fax (907) 842-4097, web: www.dillinghamchamberofcommerce.com/. Village council: Curyung Tribal Council, P.O. Box 216, Dillingham, AK 99576, phone (907) 842-2384, fax (907) 842-4510, e-mail: Dillingham@aitc.org.

Diomede

GPS: N65°47' W169°00'

Located on the west coast of Little Diomede Island in Bering Strait, 80 miles northwest of Teller, 130 miles northwest of Nome, 650 miles west of Fairbanks. **Transportation**: Scheduled (in winter) and charter airplane service from Nome; helicopter. **Population**: 133. **Zip code**: 99762. **Emergency Services**: Alaska State Troopers, Nome, phone (907) 443-2835; Little Diomede Health Clinic, phone (907) 686-3311; Health Aide, phone (907) 686-3071; Diomede Volunteer Fire Department/First Responders, phone (907) 686-3071.

Climate: Maritime climate when the strait is ice-free June through November. When the strait and the Bering and Chukchi seas freeze, there is an abrupt change to a cold continental climate. Winters cold and windy, with average of 35 inches of snowfall. Annual precipitation, recorded at nearby Wales, 10 inches. Thick fog covers the island in May and June. Winter temperatures average between -10°F and 6°F. Summer temperatures average between 40°F and 50°F.

Private Aircraft: No airstrip. Helicopter landing pad. Floatplane access in summer; ski-equipped planes can land on the frozen strait in winter.

NOTE: Diomede prohibits the sale and importation of alcoholic beverages.

Visitor Facilities: A room with an efficiency kitchen is available through Diomede Native Corp., (907) 686-3221. No restaurant or banking services. Laundromat with showers available. Limited groceries and supplies at Diomede Native Store, (907) 686-3611. Arts and crafts available for purchase include carved ivory and hand-sewn skin slippers and other garments. Fishing/hunting licenses not available. No guide or major repair services.

Arrangements can be made to rent boats. Fuel available includes marine gas, diesel, propane and Blazo. No moorage facilities.

Residents of Diomede can look out their windows and see Russia's Big Diomede only 2.5 miles away. The international boundary between the United States and Russia lies between the islands. Early Eskimos on the island were great travelers to both Siberia and the Alaska mainland, conducting trade with both continents. The present village site, age unknown, was originally a spring hunting site. It gradually became a permanent settlement. The Native name for the village is Inalik, meaning "the other one" or "the one over there"; the village is commonly known as Diomede.

On Aug. 16, 1728, Captain Commander Vitus Bering named the islands in honor of St. Diomede. Explorers discovered that the Diomeders had an advanced culture with elaborate whale hunting ceremonies.

After WWII, the Soviet Union established a military base on Big Diomede. All Native residents were moved to mainland Russia and most residents of Little Diomede never saw their relatives again. During the Cold War, Little Diomede residents who strayed into Soviet waters were taken captive and held as prisoners in Siberia for a whole summer. The situation is far more relaxed today, with visitation between relatives and families on the two islands.

Isolated and remote, Diomede has been perhaps less influenced by modern times than other Native villages in Alaska. Diomeders depend almost entirely on a subsistence economy. Blue cod, bullhead, flounder and tanner crab are harvested during the summer, and walrus, whales, seals and bears during spring and fall when these animals migrate through the area. Seal hides are used for mukluks, rope, harpoon lines and mittens, and walrus hides are used for boat hulls. Salmonberries, greens and some roots are found on the island. Diomede has abundant seabirds in summer, and these migratory birds and their eggs supplement the subsistence diet.

The Diomede people are excellent ivory carvers. Many villagers market their crafts in Anchorage, Teller, Kotzebue and Nome.

Communications in Diomede, a second-class city incorporated in 1970, include phones, mail plane, radio and TV. The community has a church and a school with grades preschool through 12. with enrollment of 49. There are community electricity and water. Sewage system is honey buckets, except in the clinic and laundromat, which have flush toilets.. Freight arrives by plane in winter, barge in summer. Delivery of freight can be hampered by ice or weather conditions. Government address: City of Diomede, Diomede, AK 99762, phone (907) 686-3071, fax (907) 686-2192, e-mail: Sistug@aol.com. Village corporation: Diomede Native Corp., P.O. Box Holder, Little Diomede, AK 99762, phone (907) 686-3221, fax (907) 686-3061. Village council: Native Village of Diomede, P.O. Box 7099, Diomede, AK 99762, phone (907) 686-3021, fax (907) 686-3061, e-mail: Diomede@aitc.org.

Eek

GPS: N60°13' W162°01'

Located on the Eek River near the mouth of the Kuskokwim River on Kuskokwim Bay, 45 miles south of Bethel, 420 miles west of Anchorage. **Transportation**: Boat; snow machine; scheduled and charter air service from Bethel. **Population**: 289. **Zip code**: 99578. **Emergency Services**: Village Public Safety Officer, phone (907) 536-5328; Alaska State Troopers, Bethel, phone (907) 543-2595; Eek Health Clinic, phone (907) 536-5314.

Climate: Summers cool and rainy, winters cold, with a brisk north wind. Winter temperatures drop to -35°F to -40°F.

Private Aircraft: Airstrip 1 mile east; elev. 40 feet; length 1,400 feet; gravel; no fuel; unattended. Runway condition not monitored; visual inspection recommended prior to landing. No airport facilities or public transportation into village.

NOTE: Eek prohibits the sale and importation of alcoholic beverages.

Visitor Facilities: Arrangements can be made to stay at the school during the school year, mid-August to mid-May. Cost $20 per person/per day, linens and bedding not supplied. Make prior arrangements with the principal, Eek School, P.O. Box 50, Eek, AK 99578, phone (907) 536-5229. No restaurants or banking services. There is a laundromat with bathing facilities. Groceries, clothing, first-aid supplies, hardware, film and sporting goods available at Iqfijouaq Co. (536-5211); Billy's Trading Post , (907) 536-5212; and Carter's Store, (907) 536-5327. Arts and crafts available for purchase include Eskimo dolls, grass baskets and fur hats. Fishing/hunting licenses available, but best to purchase before arriving in Eek. Arrangements may be made for guide service with local hunters and fishermen. No major repair service or rental transportation available. Fuel available includes marine gas, diesel, propane and regular gasoline. No moorage facilities.

Eek was founded by residents who moved from an older village affected by erosion. Most Eek residents are commercial fishermen, but there also is subsistence hunting and fishing.

Eek is located within Yukon Delta National Wildlife Refuge. Traveling up the Eek River by boat is a treat, offering a real wilderness experience, according to one resident. There are birds, beavers and an occasional bear to be seen. Fish caught locally include salmon, pike, grayling, trout and smelt. Hunting is for moose, caribou, ptarmigan, rabbits and seal. Some prospecting for gold has been reported in the area.

The village corporation, Iqfijouaq Co., has established no user fees or other restrictions on its lands. Check with the corporation regarding location of private lands.

Communications in Eek, a second-class city incorporated in 1970, include phones, mail plane, radio and TV. The community is served by Moravian and Russian Orthodox churches and a school with grades preschool through 12 with enrollment of 88. There are community electricity and water systems. Sewage system is honey buckets. Freight arrives by plane and barge. Government address: City of Eek, P.O. Box 09, Eek, AK 99578, phone (907) 536-5129, fax (907) 536-5711. Village corporation: Iqfijouaq Co., P.O. Box 49, Eek, AK 99578, phone (907) 536-5211, fax (907) 536-5733. Village council: Eek Traditional Council, P.O. Box 87, Eek, AK 99578, phone (907) 536-5128, fax (907) 536-5711, e-mail: Eek@aitc.org.

Ekuk

GPS: N58°48' W158°33'

(E-kek) Located on the east shore of Nushagak Bay, 16 miles south of Dillingham and 340 miles west of Anchorage. **Transportation**: Small commercial and scheduled air service from Dillingham. **Population**: Currently unpopulated. **Zip code**: 99576. Emergency Services: Alaska State Troopers and health service at Dillingham.

Climate: Cloudy skies, mild temperatures and moderately heavy precipitation; subjected to strong surface winds, fog during winter months. Average summer temperatures from 37°F to 66°F; average winter temperatures from 4°F to 30°F. Annual precipitation from 20 to 26 inches, with most of the precipitation occurring in the summer months.

Private Aircraft: Private airstrip adjacent south; elev. 30 feet; length 1,200 feet; gravel and dirt; unattended. Runway not maintained during winter months; soft when wet. No fuel or airport facilities.

Visitor Facilities: None.

Ekuk, mentioned in Russian accounts of 1824 and 1828 (in the latter referred to as Village Ekouk and Seleniye Ikuk), was thought to be a major Eskimo village in prehistoric and early historic times. In Eskimo Ekuk means "the last village down," being the farthest village south of Nushagak Bay. St. Nicholas Chapel, a Russian Orthodox church in the village dating from 1917, is on the National Register of Historic Places. A cannery was opened in 1903 which drew many people to the area. Floods, erosion and lack of a school caused residents to leave.

Most local Ekuk residents maintain summer homes in the village for the commercial fishing season, which is the predominant activity in the village during the summer months, according to a spokesperson for Choggiung Ltd., the local Native corporation. The cannery employs and houses several hundred people during its peak activity time between May and August.

Fishing includes all species of salmon, as well as freshwater fish found nearby. The area supports a large and diverse population of small mammals and an abundance of birds.

Much of the land in the Ekuk area is owned by Choggiung Ltd., which requires that a permit be obtained for any use of its lands.

Communications in Ekuk, which is unincorporated, include phones, mail plane, radio and TV. Electricity and water supplied by individual generators and wells. Sewage system is honey buckets and outhouses. Freight arrives by air transport or barge. Village corporation: Choggiung Ltd., P.O. Box 330, Dillingham, AK 99576, phone (907) 842-5218, fax 842-5462. Village council: Native Village of Ekuk, P.O. Box 530, Dillingham, AK 99576, phone and fax (907) 842-5937, e-mail: Ekuk@aitc.org.

Ekwok

GPS: N59°22' W157°30'

(EK-wok) Located on the Nushagak River, 48 miles east of Dillingham, 290 miles west of Anchorage. **Transportation**: Boat; snow machine; scheduled and charter air service from Dillingham. **Population**: 123. **Zip code**: 99580. **Emergency Services**: Village Public Safety Officer, phone (907) 464-3326; Alaska State Troopers, phone (907) 842-5641; Ekwok Health Clinic and Ekwok First Responders, phone (907) 464-3322; Ekwok Volunteer Fire & EMS, phone (907) 464-3326.

Elevation: 130 feet. **Climate**: Transition zone primarily maritime, also influenced by colder Interior weather. Cloudy skies, mild temperatures, fairly heavy precipitation and strong winds. Average summer temperatures from 30°F to 66°F; average winter temperatures from 4°F to 30°F. Annual precipitation from 20 to 35 inches, most of which occurs during summer. Fog and low clouds also in summer.

Private Aircraft: Airstrip adjacent south, elev. 130 feet; length 2,720 feet; gravel and dirt; no fuel; unattended. Runway condition not monitored; visual inspection recommended prior to using. Runway has 240-foot overrun at each end. No airport facilities or public transportation.

Visitor Facilities: Arrangements can be made to stay at private homes. No restaurant, banking services or laundromat. Groceries, clothing, first-aid supplies and sporting goods can be purchased in the community. Fishing/hunting licenses available. Arts and crafts available for sale include beaver hats, mukluks and ulus. Guide services available. No repair service. Rental transportation includes boats, charter aircraft and off-road vehicles. Fuel available includes diesel, regular and unleaded gasoline. No moorage facilities.

Ekwok is the oldest continuously occupied village on Nushagak River. Approximately 100 years ago the settlement was first used in spring and summer as a fish camp, and then in the fall as a base for berry picking. The village was reputed to be the largest settlement along the river by 1923. In 1930 the Bureau of Indian Affairs established a school there, and mail service began the same year. Ekwok is a second-class city, incorporated in 1974.

The main source of income for the village is commercial fishing, but most residents fish for subsistence purposes. A few residents trap beaver, mink, wolverine, otter, red fox and marten. Ekwok's entire population depends heavily on subsistence. Species commonly harvested include salmon, pike, Dolly Varden, char, duck, moose and caribou. Villagers pick blackberries, blueberries, salmonberries and highbush cranberries. Residents grow vegetable gardens and exchange subsistence items with coastal communities.

A sportfishing lodge 2 miles downriver from Ekwok is owned by the village corporation and operates in summer only. It features modern accommodations and fishing for salmon, grayling, char, rainbow trout and pike. Near the lodge are the remains of several old sod houses used by previous Native residents of the area.

Communications in Ekwok include phones (village phone, [907] 464-8001), mail plane, radio and TV. The community is served by 2 churches and a school with grades kindergarten through 8 with 38 enrolled. Many residents celebrate Russian Orthodox holidays. Community electricity, water and sewer are available. Freight arrives by plane, barge and fishing boats. Government address: City of Ekwok, P.O. Box 49, Ekwok, AK 99580, phone (907) 464-3311, fax (907) 464-3328, e-mail: cityekwok@aol.com. Village corporation: Ekwok Natives Ltd., P.O. Box 1189, Dillingham, AK 99576, phone (907) 842-2385. Village council: Ekwok Village Council, P.O. Box 70, Ekwok, AK 99580, phone (907) 464-3336. fax (907) 464-3378, e-mail: Ekwok@aitc.org.

Elim

GPS: N64°37' W162°15'

(E-lim) Located on the northwest shore of Norton Bay on the Seward Peninsula, 85 miles east of Solomon and 100 miles east of Nome. **Transportation**: Scheduled or charter air service from Nome. **Population**: 316. **Zip code**: 99739. **Emergency Services**: Police phone (907) 890-3611/3081, or (907) 890-2281; Elim Health Clinic, phone (907) 890-3311; Volunteer Fire Department, phone (907) 890-3441.

Climate: Subarctic, but changes to a more continental climate with the freezing of Norton Sound. Winter cold and relatively dry, average 40 inches of snowfall. Average annual precipitation 18.9 inches.

Private Aircraft: Airstrip adjacent southwest; elev. 130 feet; length 3,000 feet; gravel; no fuel; unattended; recommend visual inspection prior to using. Cliff south, runway rutted but usable. No line of sight between runway ends. Use caution.

NOTE: Elim prohibits the sale and importation of alcoholic beverages.

Visitor Facilities: Accommodations may be arranged with the City of Elim, phone (907) 890-3441, which has 2 rooms available with 2 beds in each. Groceries, clothing and sundry items can be purchased at Elim Native Store and Eagles Cache Store. No restaurant. Fishing/hunting licenses available. Carved ivory available. No banking facilities or guide services. Boat, auto, aircraft repairs available; boats, autos and off-road vehicles available for rent. Heavy equipment can be rented from the city. Fuel includes marine gas, diesel, propane, kerosene and regular gasoline.

Formerly the Malemiut Eskimo village of Nuviakchak, Elim is located on a former federal reindeer reserve, established in 1911, but dissolved with the Alaska Native Claims Settlement Act. A mission and school which opened in the early 1900s increased the population. The village incorporated as a second-class city in 1970. Its economy is subsistence-based, supplemented by seasonal employment in construction, fish processing and timber.

The Iditarod Trail passes through Elim, serving as a trail to Nome to the west and Unalakleet to the south.

Communications include phones, mail plane, radio and TV. Internat access available at Ernest M. Nylin Memorial Library. The community has a church and a school for kindergarten through grade 12 with enrollment of 101. Public electricity, water and sewage systems available. Freight arrives by air transport and barge. Government address: City of Elim, P.O. Box 39009, Elim, AK 99739, phone (907) 890-3441, fax (907) 890-3811. Village corporation: Elim Native Corp., P.O. Box 39010, Elim, AK 99739-0010, phone (907) 890-3741, fax (907) 890-3091. Village council: Native Village of Elim, P.O. Box 70, Elim, AK 99739-0070, phone (907) 890-3737, fax (907) 890-3738, e-mail: Elim@aitc.org.

Emmonak

GPS: 62°47' W164°32'

(E-MON-nuk) Located at the mouth of the Yukon River on the north bank of Kwiguk Pass in the Yukon-Kuskokwim Delta, 175 miles northwest of Bethel, 490 miles west-northwest of Anchorage. **Transportation**: Scheduled and charter air service from Bethel or Nome. **Population**: 804. **Zip code**: 99581. Emergency Services: Village Public Safety

Officer, phone (907) 949-1728; Emmonak Health Clinic, phone (907) 949-1511; City Fire/EMS/Ambulance.

Elevation: 10 feet. **Climate**: Maritime; mean precipitation 24.5 inches per year; mean snowfall 57 inches.

Private Aircraft: Airstrip adjacent east; elev. 10 feet; length 4,400 feet; gravel; fuel jet A. Runway unattended and not monitored. Recommend visual inspection prior to using.

NOTE: Emmonak prohibits the sale and importation of alcoholic beverages.

Visitor Facilities: Accommodations and meals available. There are 2 restaurants. Food is also available from the Emmonak Tribal Government (907) 949-1720. No banking services. Groceries, laundry, clothing, first aid supplies, hardware, film and sporting goods available in the community. Arts and crafts available for purchase include carved ivory, grass baskets, fans, fur hats and spears. Fishing/hunting licenses available. No guide service. Marine engine repair available. Charter aircraft available. Fuel available includes marine gas, diesel, propane, unleaded and regular gasoline. No moorage facilities.

Emmonak was originally called Kwiguk, a Yup'ik Eskimo word meaning "big stream." Kwiguk Pass is one of the fingers of water leading from the Yukon River above its mouth to the sea. The village was first reported by G.R. Putnam of the U.S. Coast and Geodetic Survey in 1899. Later, commercial fishing became a major industry and Northern Commercial Co. built a cannery, which was washed away by floods in 1964. Heavy erosion affected the rest of the village and it was relocated in 1964-65 to a site 1.4 miles north. The new location was renamed Emmonak and is becoming a center for commercial fishing and processing on the lower Yukon River. Emmonak is a second-class city, incorporated in 1964.

Emmonak has a seasonal economy, with most activity in commercial fishing taking place in June, July and August. The Native-owned Yukon Delta Fish Marketing Cooperative operates a barge with a self-contained cannery at Emmonak. AMPAC also operates a fish-cleaning plant. Other jobs are provided by local businesses and government. Income from employment is supplemented by public assistance programs and subsistence activities. Residents hunt moose, beluga whale, seal, ptarmigan, hare and waterfowl, and fish for salmon, whitefish, blackfish, lush (burbot), sheefish and tomcod. In the fall, families travel upriver to harvest berries. Income also is derived from trapping mink, otter, lynx and red and arctic fox.

Recreational activities at Emmonak include winter potlatches and city league and high school basketball games. One local resident characterizes Emmonak as a progressive town, where everyone works together to build a better community.

Emmonak is located within Yukon Delta National Wildlife Refuge. Winter trails connect Emmonak with Kotlik, Alakanuk and Sheldon Point.

Communications include phones, mail plane, radio and TV. Emmonak is served by Roman Catholic and Assembly of God churches and a school with grades kindergarten through 12 with enrollment of 237. There are community electricity, water and sewer systems. Freight arrives by cargo plane and barge. Government address: City of Emmonak, P.O. Box 9, Emmonak, AK 99581, phone (907) 949-1227, fax (907) 949-1926. Village corporation: Emmonak Corp., P.O. Box 49, Emmonak, AK 99581, phone (907) 949-1129, fax (907) 949-1412. Village council: Emmonak Village, P.O. Box 126, Emmonak, AK 99581, phone (907) 949-1720, fax (907) 949-1384, e-mail: Emmonak@aitc.org.

Gambell

GPS: N63°47' W171°45'

Located on Northwest Cape on St. Lawrence Island in the Bering Sea, 200 miles west of Nome, 675 miles west of Fairbanks. **Transportation**: Scheduled or charter air service from Nome. **Population**: 653. **Zip code**: 99742. **Emergency Services**: Police, phone (907) 985-5333; Alaska State Troopers, Nome, phone (907) 443-2835; Gambell Health Clinic, phone (907) 985-5012; Volunteer Fire Department.

Elevation: 30 feet. **Climate**: Cool, moist maritime climate with some continental characteristics in the winter when much of the Bering Sea freezes. Winds and fog are common and precipitation occurs 300 days per year. Precipitation is usually very light rain, mist or snow, and total annual precipitation is only 15 inches. Average snowfall 80 inches, distributed evenly from November to May. Winter temperatures -2°F to 10°F. Summer temperatures 34°F to 48°F.

Private Aircraft: Airstrip adjacent south; elev. 27 feet; length 4,500 feet; asphalt; no fuel; unattended. No airport facilities or transportation into village.

NOTE: Gambell prohibits the possession of alcoholic beverages.

Visitor Facilities: Accommodations and meals available at 1 lodge. Laundry facilities available; no banking services. Groceries, clothing, first-aid supplies, hardware, film and sporting goods available in the community. Arts and crafts available for purchase include carved ivory, baleen boats and Eskimo artifacts. Fishing/hunting licenses available. Contact the City of Gambell regarding guide service. No major repair service available. Arrangements can be made to rent off-road vehicles or boats. Fuel available includes diesel, propane and regular gasoline. No moorage facilities. Group tours available from Anchorage or Nome.

NOTE: Visitors to Gambell and Savoonga who wish to leave the city limits are required to pay a one-time fee of $25. The entire island is private property; the fee helps monitor use and serves as a registration system to make sure people don't get lost. The corporation also requires that any stories or photographs involving areas outside the townsite be submitted for prepublication approval.

St. Lawrence Island has been inhabited for several thousand years. The island sits astride one of the great prehistoric migration routes—the Bering Land Bridge which linked Asia with the Americas. Evidence of Eskimo culture at Gambell dates back to 1700. Sivuqaq (Sivokak) is the Siberian Yup'ik name for the village and for St. Lawrence Island. The city was named in 1898 for Presbyterian missionaries and teachers Mr. and Mrs. Vene C. Gambell, who were lost on the schooner *Jane Grey* on their return from a leave of absence. The name was proposed by the new teacher, William F. Doty. The village was established under the Indian Reorganization Act of 1934 as the Native village of Gambell in 1939. It was incorporated as a second-class city under state law in 1963.

The economy in Gambell is largely based on subsistence hunting. Residents hunt walrus and bowhead and gray whales in spring and fall. During summer the people fish, crab, hunt birds, gather eggs and harvest seafoods, greens and berries. Seal, fish and crab are harvested throughout the winter. Arctic fox are trapped as a secondary source of cash income. Some reindeer roam the island, but most harvest activities take place out of Savoonga.

The Native people of Gambell still hunt from walrus-hide boats and follow many old customs. A whaling festival takes place in Gambell each spring when a whale is taken.

There are 5 prehistoric village sites at Gambell which had been on the National Register of Historic Places, but that designation was stripped from the sites because of extensive looting. For half a century artifacts have been dug up and sold to supplement meager village incomes on this harsh island where unemployment stays at about 25 percent.

Ivory carvings are a popular retail item, and the St. Lawrence Islanders are famous for their beautiful work.

Numerous species of birds, some of them rare Asiatic species, populate the island during summer.

Communications at Gambell include phones, mail plane, radio and TV. The community is served by Presbyterian and Seventh Day Adventist churches and a school with grades kindergarten through 12 with enrollment of 190. There is a community electric system. At least 90 percent of the village has water and sewer systems, showers and flush toilets. Freight arrives by cargo plane and barge. Government address: City of Gambell, P.O. Box 189, Gambell, AK 99742, phone (907) 985-5112, fax (907) 985-5927.

Village corporation: Sivuqaq Inc., P.O. Box 101, Gambell, AK 99742, phone (907) 985-5826, fax (907) 985-5426. Village council: Native Village of Gambell, P.O. Box 99, Gambell, AK 99742, phone (907) 985-5346, fax (907) 985-5014, e-mail: Gambell@aitc.org.

Georgetown

Located on the north bank of the upper Kuskokwim River east of the mouth of the George River, 16 miles northwest of Red Devil, 22 miles northwest of Sleetmute. **Transportation**: Charter air service from Bethel or Red Devil; riverboat; snow machine. **Population**: Currently unpopulated. **Zip code**: 99656. **Emergency Services**: Alaska State Troopers, Aniak.

Climate: Continental; mean precipitation 15 inches per year, with 61 inches of snow. Greatest snowfall, according to Sleetmute data, is in January.

Private Aircraft: No public airstrip. Heavy winds in the fall and winter sometimes make air travel difficult or impossible for days.

Visitor Facilities: None. *NOTE: Land use permits are required to use lands owned by the Kuskokwim Corp. Uses include fishing, temporary camping, seasonal campsite, land crossing and research. There is a $100 administration fee. Big game hunting fee is $400. Seasonal campsite permits $50, annual use fee $250. For further information, contact the Kuskokwim Corp., 2000 W. International Airport Road, Ste. C-9, Anchorage, AK 99502, phone (907) 276-2101, or in Aniak phone (907) 675-4275.*

When Russian explorer L.A. Zagoskin passed by the George River in 1844, he called it by the Indian name Keledzhichagat and noted that there were summer houses nearby that belonged to people from Kwigiumpainukamiut.

Gold was found along the George River in 1909. An early mining settlement, located west of the mouth of the river, and the George River itself, were named for the first 3 traders at the site: George Hoffman, George Fredericks and George Morgan. By summer 1910, about 300 prospectors were living in the vicinity. About 200 log cabins had been built when a fire swept through the settlement in July 1911, destroying all but 25 cabins along the riverbank and 2 general stores. By 1953 the only large structure that remained was the 2-story log house that belonged to George Fredericks.

In the 1950s, the present settlement of Georgetown began emerging east of the mouth of the George River opposite the earlier community. A school was established at the new site in 1965 and operated until 1970. The present community consists of 5 homes and an airplane hangar belonging to Vanderpool Flying Service of Red Devil.

Georgetown residents must travel to other communities for seasonal employment. Otherwise they depend on subsistence hunting and fishing. Moose, caribou, bear, waterfowl, game birds, rabbit and porcupine are hunted. Fishing yields salmon, whitefish, sheefish, burbot, grayling and trout. In the fall the tundra offers blueberries, blackberries and currants. Some income is obtained from trapping and selling beaver, marten, lynx, fox and mink pelts.

Communication is by radio; there are no phones. Fresh produce and other freight are shipped air freight from Anchorage to nearby Red Devil and then flown to Georgetown. There is no school or church. Electricity is from individual generators. Water from wells or the river. Sewage system is septic tanks or outhouses. Georgetown is not incorporated. Village corporation: Kuskokwim Corp., 2000 W. International Airport Road, Suite C-9, Anchorage, AK 99502, phone (907) 276-2101. Village council: Native Village of Georgetown, 1400 Virginia Court, Anchorage, AK 99501, phone (907) 274-2195, fax (907) 274-2196, e-mail: Georgetown@aitc.org.

Golovin

GPS N64°33' W163°02'

Located on a point between Golovnin Bay and Golovnin Inlet on the Seward Peninsula, 42 miles east of Solomon, 90 miles east of Nome and 450 miles west of Fairbanks. **Transportation**: Snow machine; scheduled and charter air service from Nome; boat. Population: 142. Zip code: 99762. Emergency Services: Village Public Safety Officer, phone (907) 779-3911; Golovin Health Clinic, phone (907) 779-3311; Volunteer Fire Department. **Elevation**: 25 feet. **Climate**: Marine climate when the sea is ice-free. Average annual precipitation 19 inches; average annual snowfall 40 inches. Average winter temperatures between -2°F and 19°F; average summer temperatures between 40°F and 60°F.

Private Aircraft: Airstrip 0.5 mile east; length 4,000 feet; gravel.

NOTE: Golovin prohibits the sale and importation of alcoholic beverages.

Visitor Facilities: No hotel, restaurant or banking services. Laundromat available. Groceries/supplies available at Olson and Sons. Arts and crafts available for purchase include fur hats, some ivory and woven wool mittens. Fishing/hunting licenses available. No guide service. Fuel available includes diesel, propane and regular gasoline.

The Eskimo village of Chinik, located at the present site of Golovin, was originally settled by the Kauweramiut Eskimos who later mixed with Unaligmiut Eskimos. Lieutenant L.A. Zagoskin of the Imperial Russian Navy reported the village as Ikalikguigmyut in 1842. The name Golovin was derived from the name of Golovnin Lagoon, which was named after Captain Vasili Mikkailovich Golovnin of the Russian Navy.

Around 1890, John Dexter established a trading post at Golovin that became the center for prospecting information for the entire Seward Peninsula. Gold was discovered in 1898 and Golovin became the supply point for the Council goldfields to the northwest. Golovin incorporated as a second-class city in 1971.

Golovin's economy is based on subsistence food harvest and commercial fishing. Local businesses, government and construction work provide additional employment. Residents go to summer fish camps to catch salmon, whitefish, trout, grayling, pike and herring. Subsistence hunting includes seals, beluga whales, moose, ducks, geese and ptarmigans. Bird eggs and berries are gathered from the tundra.

The Iditarod Trail passes through Golovin and is used as a winter trail.

Communications in Golovin include phones, mail plane, radio and TV. The community has a Covenant church and a school with grades kindergarten through 12 with enrollment of 47. Community electricity, water and sewage systems. Freight arrives in the community by cargo plane and barge. Government address: City of Golovin, P.O. Box 62059, Golovin, AK 99762, phone (907) 779-3211, fax (907) 779-2239. Village corporation: Golovin Native Corp., P.O. Box 62099, Golovin, AK 99762, phone (907) 779-3251, fax (907) 779-3261. Village council: Chinik Eskimo Community, General Delivery, Golovin, AK 99762, phone (907) 779-3261, fax (907) 779-2829, e-mail: Chinik@aitc.org.

Goodnews Bay

GPS: N59°07' W161°35'

Located on Goodnews Bay on the east shore of Kuskokwim Bay, 70 miles south of Bethel, 430 miles west of Anchorage. **Transportation**: Scheduled and charter air service from Bethel or Dillingham. **Population**: 235. **Zip code**: 99589. **Emergency Services**: Alaska State Troopers, Dillingham, phone (907) 842-5641, or Bethel, phone (907) 543-3781; Goodnews Bay Health Clinic, Goodnews Bay First Responders, phone (907) 967-8128; Volunteer Fire Department.

Private Aircraft: Airstrip adjacent southeast; elev. 15 feet; length 2,850 feet; gravel; no fuel; unattended. Runway condition not monitored; visual inspection recommended prior to using. No airport facilities or public transportation into village.

NOTE: Goodnews Bay prohibits the sale and importation of alcoholic beverages.

Visitor Facilities: Accommodations available through the village or the school, phone (907) 967-8213. Laundry facilities, showers. No restaurants or banking services. Clothing, first-aid supplies, hardware, film and sporting goods available in the community. Arts and crafts available for purchase include grass baskets, carved ivory, beadwork, hand-sewn skin garments and knitted goods. Fishing/ hunting licenses available. Fishing guide service available. No major repair service or rental transportation. Fuel available includes marine gas, diesel and propane. Moorage facilities available.

Originally known as Mumtrak, the vil-tage's present name comes from the bay on which it is located. The name comes from the Russian Port Dobrykh Vestey, which probably was named by members of a Russian expedition in 1818-19.

The community grew because of near-by gold mining activities in the early 1900s. Goodnews Bay is a second-class city, incorporated in 1970.

Communications at Goodnews Bay include phones, mail plane, radio and TV. The community has a church and a school with grades kindergarten through 12 with enrollment of 70. There are com-munity electricity and water systems. Sewage system is honey buckets. Freight arrives by cargo plane, barge and ship. Government address: City of Goodnews Bay, P.O. Box 139, Goodnews Bay, AK 99589, phone (907) 967-8614, fax (907) 967-8124. Village corporation: Kuitsarak Inc., P.O. Box 10, Goodnews Bay, AK 99589, phone (907) 967-8428, fax (907) 967-8226. Village council: Goodnews Bay Traditional Council, P.O. Box 138, Goodnews Bay, AK 99589, phone (907) 967-8929, fax (907) 967-8330, e-mail: GoodnewsBay@aitc.org.

Hooper Bay

GPS: N61°31' W166°05'

Located on Hooper Bay, 20 miles south of Cape Romanzof in the YukonKuskokwim Delta, 120 miles north-west of Bethel, 540 miles west of Anchorage. **Transportation:** Scheduled and charter air service from Bethel. **Population:** 1,350. **Zip code:** 99604. **Emergency Services:** Police, phone (907) 758-4615; Hooper Bay Health Clinic, phone (907) 758-4711; Volunteer Fire and Search and Rescue Department.

Elevation: 18 feet. **Climate:** Maritime. Mean annual snowfall and precipitation

are 75 inches and 16 inches, respectively. Mean annual temperature is 29°F, with temperatures ranging between -25°F and 79°F. Winter ice pack and strong winds often cause severe winter conditions.

Private Aircraft: Airstrip 2 miles southwest; elev. 18 feet; length 3,300 feet; asphalt; lighted; unattended. Runway condition not monitored; visual inspec-tion recommended prior to using.

NOTE: Hooper Bay prohibits the importa-tion, sale and possession of alcoholic bever-ages.

Visitor Facilities: Accommodations available at Qavartarvik, Sea Lion Hotel, (907) 758-4015. For groceries and general merchandise, contact Hooper Bay Native Store (Alaska Commercial Co.), (907) 758-4000; Sea Lion Store (ACCO), (907) 758-4029; ANICA Store, (907) 758-4841; Sea Lion Shop, (907) 758-4269; Hill's & Joe's Store, (907) 758-4431. Crafts available at most stores. Laundromat with showers is available. Hooper Bay is famous for the grass baskets and tote bags produced by village women. Other crafts include seal-skin boots, ivory and beaded earrings, and ulu knives. Fishing/hunting licenses available. Limited guiding services for bird watching, contact the Sea Lion Corp. Gasoline and diesel fuel are available at Yukon Fuel Co., (907) 758-4007. Limited motor repairs available.

The population of Hooper Bay is 98 percent Yup'ik Eskimo. The early Eskimo name for the community, Askinuk, refers to the mountainous area between Hooper Bay and Scammon Bay. The village was first reported in 1878 by E.W. Nelson of the U.S. Signal Service.

Hooper Bay incorporated as a second-class city in 1966. The local economy depends heavily upon subsistence activi-ties. Clams, blackberries and tomcod are abundant in season. A small commercial herring fishery at Kokechik Bay takes place each spring. Full-time employment is principally with the village corporation stores, school and local government.

Communications include telephones, cable and state satellite TV. There are Roman Catholic and Covenant churches and a school with 394 enrolled in grades kindergarten through 12. Community has electricity, and 2 public wells supply the community water. Sewage system for homes is honey buckets. Freight arrives by air and barge. Government address: City of Hooper Bay, P.O. Box 29, Hooper Bay, AK 99604, phone and fax (907) 758-4311. Village corporation: Sea Lion Corp., P.O. Box 87, Hooper Bay, AK 99604, phone (907) 748-4015, fax (907) 748-4815. Village council: Native Village of Hooper Bay, P.O. Box 69, Hooper Bay, AK 99604, phone (907) 758-4915, fax (907) 748-4066, e-mail: HooperBay@aitc.org.

Igiugig

GPS: N59°20′ W155°55′

(Ig-ee-AH-gig) Located in the Western Cook Inlet area on the south shore of the Kvichak River at the southwest end of Lake Iliamna, 50 miles southwest of Iliamna and 50 miles northeast of King Salmon. **Transportation**: Scheduled air service from King Salmon. **Population**: 62. **Zip code**: 99613. **Emergency Services**: Igiugig Health Clinic, Igiugig Village Response Team, phone (907) 533-3207 CHP).

Climate: Average summer temperatures from 42°F to 62°F; average winter temperatures from 6°F to 30°F. Total precipitation averages 26 inches annually, with an average snowfall of 64 inches.

Private Aircraft: Airstrip adjacent south; elev. 110 feet; length 3,000 feet; dirt and gravel; unattended. No airport facilities.

Visitor Facilities: Some supplies are available in the community. Accommodations available by advance reservation at several area fishing lodges, such as Igiugig Lodge , phone (907) 533-3216. Guide service for fishing; tackle is available for purchase. No other services available.

Igiugig began as a fishing village. Kiatagmuit Eskimos populated the village at the turn of the century. St. Nicholas Chapel, a Russian Orthodox church located in the village, is on the National Register of Historic Places. Igiugig is unincorporated.

Salmon fishing is the mainstay of Igiugig's economy. Some residents are employed in the community. During the red salmon season in late June and July, many leave the village to fish in Bristol Bay. In summer, sportfishing is popular in the Kvichak River-Lake Iliamna area.

NOTE: Contact Igiiigig Native Corp. regarding land use fees before hunting, fishing or cutting wood.

Communications include phones, mail plane, radio and TV. The community is served by old and new Russian Orthodox churches, and a school with grades 1 through 12 with 15 enrolled. There are community electric and water systems. Residents use privies and honey buckets. Freight arrives in the village by air transport or barge. Native corporation address: Igiugig Native Corp., P.O. Box 4009, Igiugig, AK 99613-4009, phone (907) 533-3204. Village council: Igiugig Village,, P.O. Box 4008, Igiugig, AK 99613, phone (907) 533-3211, fax (907) 533-3217, e-mail: Igiugig@aitc.org, Web: http://www.igiugig.com.

Iliamna

GPS: N59°45′ W154°55′

(Ill-ee-YAHM-nuh) Located in the Western Cook Inlet area on the north side of Lake Itiamna, 17 miles from Nondalton, 187 miles east-northeast of Dillingham, 225 miles southwest of Anchorage. **Transportation**: Boat; scheduled or charter air service from King Salmon, Dillingham and Anchorage. **Population**: 93. **Zip code**: 99606. **Emergency Services**: Alaska State Troopers, phone (907) 571-1236; Health Aide, phone (907) 571-1386; Iliamna Health Clinic, phone (907) 571-1383; Iliamna/Newhalen Rescue Squad, phone (907) 571-1248/1631; Volunteer Fire Department, phone (907) 571-1246/1376.

Elevation: 190 feet. **Climate**: Transitional zone, with strong maritime influences. Average summer temperatures from 42°F to 62°F; average winter temperatures from 6°F to 30°F. Mean annual precipitation 26 inches; mean annual snowfall 61 inches.

Private Aircraft: Airport 3 miles west; elev. 207 feet; 2 intersecting runways: length 4,800 and 5,080 feet; gravel; fuel 100, jet A; attended on request. Runway soft when wet. Airport facilities include ticket counter, restrooms and traffic control tower. Public transportation to town.

NOTE: Iliamna prohibits the sale of alcoholic beverages.

Visitor Facilities: Accommodations and meals available by advance reservation at several area wilderness lodges, such as Iliamna Lake Resort, (907) 571-1387. There is a laundromat. No banking services. Groceries, clothing, first-aid supplies, hardware, film and sporting goods available in the community. Arts and crafts available for purchase include grass baskets. Fishing/hunting licenses available, as well as guide service. Aircraft mechanic available. Rental transportation includes autos, boats, trucks and charter aircraft. Fuel available includes diesel, propane, marine gas, white gas, kerosene and regular and unleaded gasoline. No public moorage facilities.

"Old Iliamna" was located near the mouth of the Iliamna River. Around 1935, the Indian village moved to its present location, approximately 40 miles from the old site. The first of several hunting and fishing lodges opened in Iliamna in the 1930s. A few lodges stay open year-round for those interested in ice fishing and winter hiking. An 8-mile gravel road connects Iliamna to Newhalen, and there is an overland crossing from Old Iliamna to Iliamna Bay on Cook Inlet, still used for delivering freight and fishing boats.

Commercial fishing, sportfishing and hunting lodges are the major sources of income for the community. The majority of lodge employees, however, are hired from outside the village. There are several other jobs in the village with government agencies and local businesses.

Most Natives and an increasing number of non-Natives depend to varying degrees on subsistence hunting and fishing. Red and chum salmon are caught in summer. Freshwater fish, rabbit and porcupine are taken year-round. Moose, caribou, bear, ptarmigan, ducks and geese are hunted in season. Seals are taken occasionally from Lake Iliamna. In the fall, residents pick blackberries, blueberries, cranberries, salmonberries and raspberries. Wild celery, spinach and onions are gathered in spring. Iliamna is a major gateway to the world-class fishing and hunting in the Kvichak River drainage. The system, with headwaters in Lake Iliamna and Lake Clark, is historically the most important spawning and rearing habitat for sockeye or red salmon in the world and the largest contributor to the Bristol Bay fishery. King, coho, chum and humpback salmon also are present, although in fewer numbers. State sportfishing regulations designate the Kvichak River system as a trophy fish area. Some of the largest rainbow trout in the world can be found in these waters.

Lake Iliamna, 75 miles long and 20 miles wide, is the largest lake in Alaska. It is reputedly the home of a "sea monster," and residents from villages around the lake claim to have seen the creature on several occasions.

Visitors planning to hike or canoe in the area should contact the National Park Service in Anchorage; much of the land is privately owned or owned by Native corporations. *NOTE: Iliamna Natives Ltd. charges fees for camping on corporation land: $25 per person per night for 1 or 2 people; $50 per night for a group of 3 or more people. Fees are payable in advance and are nonrefundable. Hiking, berry picking and fishing also are permitted on corporation lands; hunting in general is not. Wood cutting is not permitted. These and other land-use regulations are available from the corporation office, P.O. Box 245, Iliamna, AK 99606.*

Communications in Iliamna, which is incorporated, include phones, mail plane, radio and TV. The community has 2 churches. There are community electricity, water and sewer systems. Freight arrives by cargo plane. Government address: Iliamna Village Council, General Delivery, Iliamna, AK 99606, phone 571-1246. Village corporation: Iliamna Natives Ltd., P.O. Box 267, Iliamna, AK 99606, phone (907) 571-1246, fax (907) 571-1256. Village council: Village of Iliamna, P.O. Box 286, Iliamna, AK 99606, phone (907) 571-1246, fax (907) 571-1256, e-mail: iliamna@aitc.org, web: http://www.arctic.net/~newhalen/index.html.

Kasigluk

GPS: N60°52' W162°32'

(Ka-SEEG-luk) Located 20 miles northwest of Bethel, 425 miles west of Anchorage. **Transportation**: Boat; snow machine; scheduled and charter air service from Bethel. **Population**: 528. **Zip code**: 99609. **Emergency Services**: Alaska State Troopers, Bethel; Kasigluk Health Clinic, phone (907) 477-6120; Volunteer Fire Department.

Climate: Average temperature in Kasigluk ranges from 65°F to 70°F during a dry, warm summer and 40°F to 55°F during a wet, cold summer, according to one resident.

Private Aircraft: Airstrip 2 miles south; elev. 40 feet; length 3,000 feet; gravel; fuel 80; unattended. Runway condition not monitored; visual inspection recommended prior to using. Runway badly rutted with dips and rolls. No summer or winter maintenance. Ice runway on river during winter. Watch for trucks and vehicles on runway.

NOTE: Kasigluk prohibits the sale and importation of alcoholic beverages.

Visitor Facilities: Arrangements can be made for accommodations at the school, phone (907) 477-6615; the clinic, phone (907) 477-6120; or private homes. No restaurant or banking services. Laundry facilities available. Groceries available in the community at Store #1 at Kasigluk, phone (907) 477-6126; and Store #2 at Akula Heights, phone (907) 477-6113/6114. Akula Heights is about 2 miles from Kasigluk. Arts and crafts available for purchase include Eskimo dolls, mukluks, beaver hats, Eskimo yo-yos and fur mittens. Fishing/hunting licenses available. No guide or major repair services, rental transportation or moorage facilities. Fuel available includes marine gas and propane.

The Eskimo village of Kasigluk, located on a small river, is one of a handful of tundra villages in the Yukon-Kuskokwim Delta. Most of the others are located on the seacoast or on a major river. Resident Anni Slim says, "If you visit Kasigluk in the summer, you will see a lot of green willow trees, and the tundra is filled with salmonberries, blueberries, red berries, cranberries and alive with other plants that the people gather up for the winter."

Kasigluk is situated within Yukon Delta National Wildlife Refuge.

Communications in Kasigluk, a second-class city incorporated in 1982, include phones, mail plane, radio and TV. There is a community electric system. Water is hauled from a central watering point. Sewage system is honey buckets. The community is served by 2 churches and 2 schools with grades kindergarten through 12, Akula Elitnaurvik, (907) 477-6615, and Akiuk Memorial, (907) 477-6829, with total enrollment of 180. Freight arrives by cargo plane and barge. Village council:: Kasigluk Traditional Council , Box 19, Kasigluk, AK 99609, phone (907) 477-6640, fax (907) 477-6212, e-mail: Kasignuk@aitc.org. Village corporation: Kasigluk Inc., P.O. Box 39, Kasigluk, AK 99609, phone (907) 477-6125, fax (907) 447-6129.

King Salmon

GPS: N58°41' W156°39'

Located on the Alaska Peninsula on the Naknek River, 15 miles east of Naknek, 290 miles southwest of Anchorage. **Transportation**: Scheduled air service via PenAir from Anchorage. **Population**: 499. **Zip Code**: 99613. **Emergency Services**: Police, phone (907) 246-4222; Alaska State Troopers, phone (907) 246-3346; King Salmon Health Clinic, phone (907) 246-3322; Camai Clinic, Naknek, phone (907) 246-6155; Volunteer Fire Department.

Elevation: 50 feet. **Climate**: Cool, humid and windy weather. Average summer temperatures range from 42°F to 63°F; average winter temperatures range from 29°F to 44°F. Total precipitation averages 20 inches annually, including an average snowfall of 48 inches. Cloud cover is present an average of 76 percent of the time year-round. Naknek River is usually ice-free between May and October.

Private Aircraft: Airport adjacent southeast; elev. 57 feet; length 8,500 feet; asphalt, fuel 100, jet A; attended. Passenger and freight terminals, ticket counter, restrooms; visitor center. Traffic control tower at airport scheduled to close January 2002. Transportation available. *CAUTION: U.S. Air Force uses King Salmon for annual training exercises, although response aircraft are no longer stationed here.*

Visitor Facilities: Accommodations are Quinnat Landing Hotel, (907) 246-3000 or 1-800-770-3474; and King Ko Inn, (907) 246-3377, fax (907) 246-3357; both offer restaurants and lounges. Area lodges include Antlers Inn, (907) 246-8525 or 1-888-735-8525; Bear Trail Lodge, (907) 246-2327, fax (907) 246-7297; Eagle Bluff Lodge, (907) 246-4464; Last Frontier Lodge, (907) 246-4269; Naknek Riverine Lodge, (907) 246-4270; Ponderosa Lodge, (907) 246-3444, fax (907) 246-6898' amd Prestage's Sportfishing Lodge, (907) 246-3320. Lodging and boat rental at Rainbow Bend Cabin/Boat Rental, (907) 246-3750 or 1-888-575-4249. Restaurant and lounge at Eddie's Fireplace Inn, (907) 246-3435. Groceries and sundry items may be purchased at City Market. Banking services available. Laundromat. Arts and crafts available for purchase include carved ivory, baskets and masks. Fishing/hunting licenses available, as well as guide service. Major repair service for marine engines, boats and aircraft. Rental transportation includes autos, boats and charter aircraft. Boat rental at R&G Boat Rental, (907) 246-3353. Fuel available includes marine gas and regular gas. Moorage facilities. *NOTE: Land on the south side of the Naknek River from King Salmon is owned by the Alaska Peninsula Corp. Contact the corporation for details on use and fees.*

In the 1930s, an air navigation silo was built at the present site of King Salmon. At the onset of WWII an Air Force base was constructed as the major military installation in western Alaska. In 1949, the U.S. Army Corps and Engineers built the road connecting King Salmon to Naknek. The community, located in the Bristol Bay Borough, has continued to develop as a government, transportation and service center.

King Salmon is the gateway to several large lakes on the Alaska Peninsula (Naknek, Iliamna, Becharof, Ugashik) and

to Katmai National Park and Preserve. A 10-mile unimproved road leads from King Salmon to the park's western boundary and there are floatplane connections from King Salmon to the lodge at Brooks River, the National Park Service ranger station and public campground on Naknek Lake. There are 3 other lodges in the park. Independent travelers must make their own arrangements for visiting Katmai, including air service to King Salmon and Brooks River. Campers can purchase meals and scenic bus tour tickets at the lodge. The visitor center at the King Salmon airport offers trip planning assistance for U.S. Fish & Wildlife Service and National Park Service lands in the rea. The center is open daily in summer (May-October) from 8 A.M. to 5 P.M.; in winter (November-April) Mon.to Sat. 8 A.M. to 5 P.M. There is a staffed information desk, phone (907) 246-4250, fax (907) 246-8550.

Communications in King Salmon include phones, mail plane, radio and TV. The community is served by several churches. Children are bused to school in Naknek. There is a community electric system and sewage system; water is from individual wells. Freight arrives by air cargo or by barge to Naknet then trucked to King Salmon. Government address: Bristol Bay Borough, Box 189, Naknek, AK 99633, phone (907) 246-4224. King Salmon Visitor Center, P.O. Box 298, King Salmon, AK 99613, phone (907) 246-4250. Village corporation: Alaska Peninsula Corp., Box 104360, Anchorage, AK 99510, phone (907) 274-2433, fax (907) 274-8694. Village council: King Salmon Traditional Village Council, P.O. Box 68, King Salmon, AK 99613-0068, phone (907) 246-3553, fax (907) 246-3449, e-mail: kstvc@bristolbay.com

Kipnuk
GPS: N59°56' W164°03'

Located on the Kugkaktlik River near the Bering Sea coast, 95 miles southwest of Bethel, 320 miles south of Nome, 500 miles west of Anchorage. **Transportation:** Scheduled air service from Bethel. **Population:** 573. **Zip code:** 99614.

Emergency Services: Alaska State Troopers, Bethel, phone (907) 543-3494; Kipnuk Health Clinic, phone (907) 896-5927; Volunteer Fire Department.

Private Aircraft: Airstrip adjacent southeast; elev. 20 feet; length 2,120 feet; gravel; no fuel; unattended. Runway condition not monitored; visual inspection recommended prior to using. *CAUTION: Frequent crosswinds and heavy bird activity near runway. Erosion in safety area outside the gravel runway surface.*

NOTE: Kipnuk prohibits the sale and importation of alcoholic beverages.

Visitor Facilities: Lodging can be arranged with the Kipnuk Traditional Council, Box 57, Kipnuk, AK 99614, phone (907) 896-5515. Groceries and supplies are available at Kipnuk Trading Co., Kugkaktlik Ltd. Corp. and Kashatok Bros. They offer a limited range of clothing, first-aid supplies, film and some hardware. Blazo available; no propane. No fishing/hunting licenses. Arts and crafts not available for purchase in stores, though they may be obtained from individual artisans. Local craftspeople usually sell their goods through the gift shop at the Alaska Native Service Center hospital in Anchorage or through the Alaska Native Arts and Crafts cooperative, with an outlet in Anchorage.

Kipnuk, which is not incorporated, is located within Yukon Delta National Wildlife Refuge.

The community is served by a Moravian church and 2 schools with grades kindergarten through 12 with enrollment of 205. There is a community electric system. Water is hauled from a central watering point. Sewage system is honey buckets. Freight arrives by mail plane and barge. Village council: Kipnuk Traditional Council, P.O. Box 57, Kipnuk, AK 99614, phone (907) 896-5515, fax (907) 896-5240, e-mail: Kipnuk@aitc.org. Village corporation: Kugkaktlik Limited, P.O. Box 36, Kipnuk, AK 99614, phone (907) 896-5414, fax (907) 896-5140.

Kokhanok

GPS: N59°26′ W154°45′

(KOKE-a-nok) Located in the Western Cook Inlet area on the south shore of Lake Iliamna, 25 miles south of Iliamna and 210 miles west of Anchorage. **Transportation**: Charter and air taxi service from Iliamna. **Population**: 163. **Zip code**: 99606. **Emergency Services**: Kokhanok Health Clinic, phone (907) 282-2203; Kokhanok First Responders, phone (907) 282-2207; Volunteer Fire Department.

Elevation: 50 feet. **Climate**: Average summer temperatures from 40°F to 64°F; average winter temperatures from 3°F to 30°F. Total precipitation about 32 inches annually; average annual snowfall 89.4 inches. Fierce windstorms are characteristic of the area.

Private Aircraft: Airstrip 2 miles west; elev. 100 feet; length 2,900 feet; gravel; attended irregularly.

NOTE: Kokhanok prohibits the sale and importation of alcholic beverages.

Visitor Facilities: No accommodations, except for cots in the Village Council Building, (907) 282-2202; bring own sleeping bag. Two stores are located in private homes. Groceries and supplies available at Nielson General Store, (907) 282-2239; or at Iliamna Trading Co. across Lake Iliamna, (907) 571-1225. The population of Kokhanok, also commonly called Kokhanok Bay, is primarily Aleut. Residents rely heavily on subsistence hunting and fishing for their survival. *NOTE: Hiking, berry picking, camping and fishing are permitted on lands owned by the Alaska Peninsula Corp. upon payment of a $100 per-person fee. Hunting and woodcutting on corporation lands is not permitted. Contact the corporation for more information.*

Community employment is available for some residents. The community is accessible only by air and water. In winter snow machines and trucks are used to cross the frozen lake to Iliamna and other villages. Village festivals take place in winter and sled dog racing is a popular pastime.

Communications include phones, mail plane, radio and TV. The community is served by the Saints Peter and Paul Russian Orthodox Church, which is on the National Register of Historic Places, and by a school with grades preschool through 12 with enrollment of 55.

Electric power is provided from the school, September through May. Village power throughout the summer is provided by Kokhanok Electric. Water is hauled from Lake Iliamna, and residents have privies or honey buckets. Freight is brought in by air transport or by barge. Village council: Kokhanok Village Council, P.O. Box 1007, Kokhanok, AK 99606, phone (907) 282-2202, fax (907) 282-2264, e-mail: Kokhanok@aitc.org. Village corporation: Alaska Peninsula Corp., 800 Cordova St., Anchorage, AK 99501, phone (907) 274-2433.

Koliganek

GPS: N59°48' W157°25'

(Ko-LIG-a-neck) Located on the Nushagak River, 65 miles northeast of Dillingham, 280 miles west of Anchorage. **Transportation**: Scheduled air service from Dillingham. **Population**: 205. **Zip code**: 99576. **Emergency Services**: Alaska State Troopers, Dillingham, phone (907) 842-5351; Koliganek Health Clinic; Koliganek First Responders, phone (907) 596-3434/3490; State VPSO, phone (907) 596-3418; Volunteer Fire Department.

Private Aircraft: Airstrip adjacent south; elev. 240 feet; length 3,000 feet; gravel; fuel information unavailable; unattended. Runway condition not monitored; visual inspection recommended prior to landing. Runways unusable during breakup and after heavy rainfall.

Visitor Facilities: Information about most facilities and services unavailable; however, fishing/hunting licenses may be obtained in the community.

This Eskimo village is unincorporated. Many residents go to their fish camps during the summer.

The community has a school with grades kindergarten through 12 with enrollment of 76. Electricity is obtained from private generators or from the school. There is a community water supply and a sewer system. Freight arrives by mail plane and barge. Village corporation address: Koliganek Natives Ltd., General Delivery, Koliganek, AK 99576., phone (907) 596-3430. Village council: Koliganek Village, P.O. Box 1007, Koliganek, AK 99576, phone (907) 596-3441. e-mail: Koliganek@aitc.org.

Kongiganak

GPS: N59°52' W163°02'

(Kon-GIG-a-nuck) Located on the west shore of Kuskokwim Bay, 70 miles west of Bethel, 460 miles west of Anchorage. **Transportation**: Scheduled air service from Bethel. **Population**: Approximately 359. **Zip code**: 99559. **Emergency Services**: Alaska State Troopers, Bethel, phone (907) 543-3494; Kongiganak Health Clinic; Volunteer Fire Department.

Private Aircraft: Airstrip 8 miles northeast; elev. 25 feet; length 1,880 feet; gravel; no fuel; unattended. Runway condition not monitored; visual inspection recommended prior to using. Runway rough its full length.

NOTE: Kongiganak prohibits the sale and importation of alcholic beverages.

Visitor Facilities: Lodging available at the school, phone (907) 557-5126. There is a washeteria with bathing facilities. Supplies available in the community at Qemirtalik Store, phone (907) 557-5630. Arts and crafts available for purchase. Fishing/hunting licenses not available. Information on other visitor services and facilities unavailable.

This Eskimo village, located within Yukon Delta National Wildlife Refuge, is unincorporated. Many residents work seasonally in the summer commercial fishery or go to their own fish camps.

The community has a school with grades kindergarten through 12 with enrollment of 110. There is a community electric system. Water is hauled from the washeteria. Sewage system is honey buckets. Freight arrives by plane and barge. Village corporation: Qemirtalik Coast Corp., P.O. Box 5070, Kongiganak, AK 99559, phone 557-5428. Village council: Kongiganak Native Village, P.O. Box 5069, Kongiganak, AK 99559, phone (907) 557-5226, fax (07) 557-5224, e-mail: Kongiganak@aitc.org.

Kotlik

GPS: N63°02' W163°32'

(KOT-lick) Located on the east bank of

Kotlik Slough, 35 miles northeast of Emmonak in the Yukon-Kuskokwim Delta. **Transportation**: Scheduled and charter plane service from Nome or Bethel. **Population**: 567. **Zip code**: 99620. **Emergency Services**: Police, phone (907) 899-4626; Alaska State Troopers, St. Marys, phone (907) 438-2018; Kotlik Health Clinic, phone (907) 899-4511/4414; Volunteer Fire Department.

Climate: Subarctic. Temperatures range between -50°F and 87°F. Snowfall averages 60 inches annually; annual precipitation averages 16 inches.

Private Aircraft: Airstrip 1 mile west; elev. 15 feet; length 4,400 feet; gravel; no fuel; unattended. Runway condition not monitored; visual inspection recommended prior to using. No airport facilities or public transportation into village. *CAUTION: Cleared airstrip west of town is unusable.*

NOTE: Kotlik prohibits possession of alcoholic beverages.

Visitor Facilities: No hotel. Arrangements may be made to sleep at the Kotlik Lodge, (907) 899-4313, or the local school, (907) 899-4415. No restaurant. Groceries and supplies available at ACCO and Kotlik Laufkak. Arts and crafts available for purchase include grass baskets, parkas and mukluks, and carved ivory, Fishing/hunting licenses available. Information on guide and repair services, rental transportation, fuel and moorage facilities unavailable.

Prior to 1960, only 5 or 6 families lived at Kotlik. Early in the 1960s, people from surrounding villages moved there because a school had been built and accessibility was easier to the oil and freight barges serving the delta. By 1965, Kotlik emerged as one of the larger ports and commercial centers of the lower Yukon River, a status that it retains today.

Kotlik was incorporated in October 1970 as a second-class city. It has a seasonal economy which peaks in the June through August fishing season. Most families leave for their fish camps up the Yukon River, where they set their nets for king, silver and chum salmon. People also hunt for seals, ducks and geese. During the winter months, families ice fish, trap,

hunt and hold potlatches. Traditional dances are celebrated on Christmas and Easter and other special days. February brings a village potlatch. Dog races are held each March.

Communications include phones, mail plane, radios and TV. Assembly of God and Roman Catholic churches serve the community, as well as a school with grades kindergarten through 12. with enrollment of 196. There is a community electric system and a community water supply at the washeteria. Sewage system is outdoor pit privies and honey buckets. Freight is transported by air and barge. Government address: City of Kotlik, P.O. Box 20268, Kotlik, AK 99620, phone (907) 899-4313, fax (907) 899-4826. Village corporation: Kotlik Yup'ik Corp., P.O. Box 20207, Kotlik, AK 99620, phone (907) 899-4014, fax (907) 899-4528. Village council: Kotlik Traditional Council, P.O. Box 20210, Kotlik, AK 99620, phone (907) 899-4326, fax (907) 899-4790, e-mail: Kotlik@aitc.org.

Koyuk

GPS: N64°56' W161°09'

Located at the mouth of the Koyuk River, at the northeastern end of Norton Bay on the Seward Peninsula, 132 miles east of Nome and 75 miles north of Unalakleet. **Transportation**: Scheduled air service to Nome. **Population**: 289. **Zip code**: 99753. **Emergency Services**: Police, phone (907) 963-3541; Koyuk Health Clinic, phone (907) 963-3311; Volunteer Fire Department.

Climate: Winters cold and relatively dry, with an average of 40 inches of snowfall. Summers cool, with most rainfall in July, August and September. Average annual precipitation 18.9 inches. Average winter temperatures -8°F to 8°F. Summer temperatures 46°F to 62°F.

Private Aircraft: Airstrip adjacent northeast; elev. 130 feet; length 3,000 feet; gravel; unattended. Runway condition not monitored in summer; recommend visual inspection prior to using. Turbulence on approach when wind from northwest. Caution advised.

NOTE: Koyuk prohibits the sale and

importation of alcoholic beverages.

Visitor Facilities: No hotel or restaurant. Lodging is available at the pool hall (907) 963-3661. Washeteria available. Groceries, clothing, first-aid supplies, hardware, film and sporting goods available at the Beluga Store, (907) 963-3551; and at Koyuk Native Store, (907) 963-3451. Pay phone available, (907) 963-9991. No arts and crafts available. Fishing/hunting licenses available, as well as guide service. No banking or major repair service; no moorage facilities or rental transportation. Fuel available includes marine gas, propane and unleaded gasoline.

The village known as Kuynkhakmuit was first recorded by Lt. L.A. Zagoskin of the Imperial Russian Navy in the 1840s. Prior to 1900, the village was nomadic, gradually settling around the present site where supplies could easily be lightered to shore. Located 40 miles downriver from the Norton Bay Station trading center and near a coal mine which supplied steamships and the city of Nome, Koyuk became a natural transfer point for goods and services.

The archaeological site of Ilatayak, with traces of early man 6,000 to 8,000 years old, is located south of Koyuk on Cape Denbigh.

The village was incorporated in 1970 as a second-class city. The economy is based on subsistence supplemented by part-time wage earnings. Some income is derived from reindeer herding, with hides and antlers being sold on the commercial market. Salmon, herring, grayling, beluga, seat, caribou, wildfowl, moose and berries are harvested.

Communications include phones, mail plane, radio and TV. The community has a Covenant church and a school with grades preschool to 12 with enrollment of 108. Community electricity system is available. Sewage system is honey buckets. Water from a community well is hauled from the washeteria. Freight arrives by air transport and barge. Government address: City of Koyuk, P.O. Box 53029, Koyuk, AK 99753, phone (907) 963-3441, fax (907) 963-3442. Village corporation: Koyuk Native Corp.,

P.O. Box 50, Koyuk, AK 99753, phone (907) 963-3551, fax (907) 963-3552. Village council: Native Village of Koyuk, P.O. Box 30, Koyuk, AK 99753, phone (907) 963-3651, fax (907) 963-2353, e-mail: Koyuk@aitc.org.

Kwethluk

GPS: N60°49' W161°26'

Located on the Kwethluk River near its junction with the Kuskokwim River, 10 miles east of Bethel, 385 miles west of Anchorage. **Transportation:** Boat; snow machine; dog team; scheduled or charter air service from Bethel. **Population:** 762. **Zip code:** 99621. **Emergency Services:** Village Public Safety Officer, phone (907) 757-6928; Alaska State Troopers, Bethel, phone (907) 534-2294; Kwethluk Health Clinic, phone (907) 757-6715; Volunteer Fire Department, phone (907) 757-6928.

Private Aircraft: Airstrip adjacent south; elev. 28 feet; length 1,750 feet; gravel; no fuel; unattended. Runway condition not monitored; visual inspection recommended prior to using. Freight terminal at airport. Seaplane base unattended. There is no public transportation to the village.

NOTE: Kwethluk prohibits the sale and importation of alcoholic beverages.

Visitor Facilities: No hotel. Arrangements can be made to stay in private homes or the high school through the city office (907) 757-6614, or the village corporation, (907) 757-6612. No restaurant or banking services. Laundry facility may be available. Groceries, clothing, first-aid supplies, hardware, film and sporting goods available in the community. Arts and crafts available for purchase include carved ivory, Eskimo dolls, ulus, baskets, model dogsleds, beadwork and fur garments. Fishing/hunting licenses not available. No guide services. No rental transportation or repairs. Fuel available includes marine gas, diesel and regular gasoline. Moorage facilities available.

The name Kwethluk means "bad river" in the Yup'ik Eskimo language. There is evidence that Kwethiuk was occupied by Native people in prehistoric times.

Kwethluk apparently was the only place along the Kuskokwim River where a

Moravian church worker was killed while doing missionary work. An Eskimo helper of missionary J.H. Kilbuck was assigned to Kwethluk in 1889. The following spring Kilbuck went to Kwethluk because he was told the helper might have gone insane. The men of Kwethluk became hostile and forced Kilbuck to leave. A few days later they took the lay missionary out of the village and killed him. Another helper was later assigned to the village and in 1895 a Moravian chapel was built.

Gold prospectors worked the Kwethluk River after discoveries were made on the George River and Crooked Creek in 1909. Most efforts were unsuccessful, but at Canyon Creek on the upper Kwethluk River a small placer deposit was found and mined until WWII.

A Russian Orthodox church was built in Kwethluk in 1912 and a school was built in 1924. An airfield was constructed in 1956 and the community became a second-class city in 1975.

Communications in Kwethiuk include phones, mail plane, radio and TV. There are 2 churches and 2 schools with grades kindergarten through 12 with enrollment of 215. Community electricity and water; sewage system serves some homes, though many residents still use honey buckets. Freight arrives by cargo plane and barge. Government address: City of Kwethluk, General Delivery, Kwethluk, AK 99621, phone (907) 757-6022, fax (907) 757-6497, e-mail: Kwtocity@uni com-alaska.com. Village corporation: Kwethluk Inc., Box 80, Kwethluk, AK 99621, phone (907) 757-6612, fax (907) 757-6212. Village council: Organized Village of Kwethluk, P.O. Box 129, Kwethluk, AK 99621, phone (907) 757-6714, fax (907) 757-6328, e-mail: Kwethluk@aitc.org.

Kwigillingok

GPS: N59°51' W163°08'

(Kwi-GILL-in-gock) Located on the west side of Kuskokwim Bay, 85 miles south-southwest of Bethel, 465 miles west of Anchorage. **Transportation**: Scheduled air service from Bethel. **Population**: 360. **Zip code**: 99622. **Emergency Services**:

Village Public Safety Officer; Alaska State Troopers, Bethel, phone (907) 543-3494; Kwigillinkok Health Clinic, phone (907) 588-8526; Volunteer Fire Department.

Private Aircraft: Airstrip 1 mile northwest; elev. 20 feet; length 2,500 feet; gravel; no fuel; unattended. Runway condition not monitored; visual inspection recommended prior to using. Erosion in safety area on fill outside the gravel runway surface.

NOTE: Kwigillingok prohibits the sale and importation of alcoholic beverages.

Visitor Facilities: Arrangements may be made to stay in private homes through the Native Council, (907) 588-8114. Limited groceries and other supplies available at Kwik Inc. and Chaninik Co-op, Inc. Fuel includes marine gas, regular gasoline, diesel and kerosene. Fishing/hunting licenses available. Arts and crafts available for purchase include carved ivory and grass baskets.

This Eskimo village, located within Yukon Delta National Wildlife Refuge, is unincorporated. Many residents work seasonally in the summer commercial fishery or go to their own fish camps. Resident James Atti describes Kwigillingok as "a coastal village in a flat country with very little high ground. Residents spend most of the year gathering food like waterfowl, seals, wild berries, and fishing in season. There are activities for all ages at the church. Almost every evening the men meet with their friends to gather wood for the fires for the steam bathhouses."

Communications include phones, mail plane, radio and TV. The community has 2 schools with grades kindergarten through 12 with enrollment of 109. Community electric system. Water is hauled from a central watering point. Sewage system is honey buckets. Freight arrives by plane and barge. Government address: Native Village of Kwigillingok, P.O. Box 49, Kwigillingok, AK 99622-0049, phone (907) 588-8114, fax (907) 588-8429. Village corporation: Kwik Inc., General Delivery, Kwigillingok, AK 99622, phone (907) 588-8112, fax (907) 588-8113.

Levelock

GPS: N59°07′ W156°51′

(Leev-lok) Located on the west bank of the Kvichak River, 40 miles north of Naknek, 60 miles east of Dillingham, 280 miles southwest of Anchorage. **Transportation**: Scheduled and charter air service from King Salmon. **Population**: 131. **Zip code**: 99625. **Emergency Services**: Alaska State Troopers, King Salmon; Levelock Health Clinic, phone (907) 287-3011; Levelock First Responders, phone (907) 287-3087. Volunteer Fire Department.

Elevation: 60 feet. **Climate**: Transitional zone with primarily a maritime influence. Because the village is located about 10 miles inland, however, the colder continental climate significantly affects local weather. Average summer temperatures from 30°F to 66°F; average winter temperatures from 4°F to 30°F. Annual precipitation from 20 to 35 inches. Most precipitation occurs during the summer.

Private Aircraft: Airstrip adjacent west; elev. 60 feet; 2 intersecting runways: length 1,900 and 1,800 feet; gravel; no fuel; unattended. Runway condition not monitored; visual inspection recommended prior to using. Runway surfaces soft and muddy during spring breakup or heavy rains. Sharp dropoff at west end of runway.

Visitor Facilities: Accommodations, meals and laundry facilities are available. No banking services. Groceries available at 2 stores. Arts and crafts available for purchase include carved ivory and pen-and-ink drawings. Fishing/hunting licenses available, as well as guide service. Boat and auto repair services available. Arrangements can be made to rent autos, off-road vehicles and boats. Fuel available includes marine gas, diesel, propane and regular gasoline. Moorage facilities available.

Early Russian explorers reported the existence of Levelock, which they called Kvichak. In 1908, a survey of Russian missions in the region referred to the village as Lovelock's Mission.

It is probable that Levelock was devastated by a smallpox epidemic in the region in 1837. A combination of measles and influenza in 1900 and flu in 1918-19 seriously reduced the population.

Canneries operated at Levelock in 1925-26 and again in 1928-29. In 1929-30 the first school was built. A third cannery operated briefly in the 1950s.

Nearly all residents participate in the commercial salmon fishery, with about 75 percent of the residents going to Naknek during the fishing season. The entire community relies on subsistence hunting and fishing. Species commonly harvested include red, silver, chum, dog and king salmon, lake trout, rainbow trout and Dolly Varden; moose and caribou; and lowbush cranberries, blueberries, salmonberries and blackberries.

One attraction of Levelock, besides its location in the designated sport trophy fishing area, is that Alaskan artist Ted Lambert used to live here and residents still have many of Lambert's paintings and block prints.

Communications in Levelock, which is unincorporated, include phones, mail plane, radio and TV. The community is served by Russian Orthodox and Baptist churches and a school with grades kindergarten through 12 with enrollment of 28. There are public water, electricity and sewer systems. Freight arrives by cargo plane, barge and ship. Government address: Levelock Village Council, General Delivery, Levelock, AK 99625, phone (907) 287-3030, e-mail: Levelock@aitc.org. Village corporation: Levelock Natives Ltd., General Delivery, Levelock, AK 99625, phone (907) 287-3040, fax (907) 287-3022.

Lime Village

GPS: N61°21′ W155°28′

Located on the Stony River, 90 miles south of McGrath, 85 miles northwest of Lake Clark and 190 miles west of Anchorage. **Transportation**: Scheduled or charter air service from McGrath or Aniak. **Population**: 62. **Zip code**: 99627. **Emergency Services**: Alaska State Troopers, McGrath, phone (907) 524-3222, or Aniak, phone (907) 675-4352; Lime Village Health Clinic, phone (907) 526-5113; Volunteer Fire Department.

Elevation: 552 feet. **Climate**: Continental; temperatures range from -47°F to 82°F. Precipitation averages 22 inches per year, with 85 inches of snowfall.

Private Aircraft: Airstrip adjacent north; elev. 552 feet; length 1,475 feet; gravel; no fuel; unattended. Runway condition not monitored; visual inspection recommended prior to using. Heavy winds in the fall and winter can limit air travel to the village for days at a time.

Visitor Facilities: None.

Lime Village is named for the nearby Lime Hills, composed almost entirely of limestone. The earliest recorded settlement at the site was in 1907 when Paul, Evan and Zacar Constantinoff were year-round residents. The community was first cited in the 1939 census, when it was named Hungry Village after nearby Hungry Creek, where some prospectors are said to have starved.

A Russian Orthodox chapel, Saints Constantine and Helen, was constructed in 1923 and is on the National Register of Historic Places. A state school was established in 1974.

Income in Lime Village is primarily from government programs, supplemented by subsistence activities. Lime Village residents hunt black and brown bear, moose, caribou, waterfowl and ptarmigan. Seasonal fishing is for red, king, silver and chum salmon; whitefish, pike and grayling. Trapping and selling the pelts of beaver, muskrat, marten, mink, fox, lynx and wolverine bring additional income. In the fall, blueberries, raspberries, highbush and lowbush cranberries and salmonberries are harvested.

Communication is by AM/FM radio reception, and TV signals are received. The community has a school that offers grades preschool through 8 with enrollment of 13. Electricity is from private generators. Sewage system is honey buckets. Freight arrives by mail plane once a week. Government address: Lime Village Traditional Council, P.O. Box LVD, McGrath, AK 99627. Village corporation: Lime Village Co., General Delivery, McGrath, AK 99627, phone (907) 526-5126.

Lower Kalskag

GPS: N61°32' W160°21'

Located on the Kuskokwim River, 65 miles north of Bethel and 350 miles west of Anchorage. **Transportation**: Scheduled air service from Bethel. **Population**: 297. Zip code: 99626. **Emergency Services**: Village Public Safety Officer; Lower Kalskag Health Clinic; Volunteer Fire Department.

Climate: Semiarctic with maritime influences from the Bering Sea. Annual precipitation 19 inches with 60 inches of snow.

Private Aircraft: Kalskag airport serves Lower Kalskag 2 miles downriver and Upper Kalskag 1 mile east; elev. 55 feet; length 3,200 feet; gravel; no fuel; runway condition not monitored; visual inspection recommended prior to using. Runway is maintained by the state. Kalskag also has a grader to service the runway and main road between Upper and Lower Kalskag. Transportation into village available.

Visitor Facilities: Arrangements may be made to stay at the school, (907) 471-2318. Restaurant located in the community. No laundromat or banking services. Supplies available at a general store. Fishing/hunting licenses available. No guide or repair services. No rental transportation or moorage facilities. Fuel available: marine gas, diesel.

NOTE: Land use permits are required to use lands owned by the Kuskokwim Corp. Uses include fishing, temporary camping, seasonal campsite, land crossing and research. There is a $100 administration fee. Big game hunting fee is $400. Seasonal campsite permits $50, annual use fee $250. For further information, contact the Kuskokwim Corp., 62000 W. International Airport Road, Suite C-9, Anchorage, AK 99502, phone (907) 243-2944, or in Aniak phone (907) 675-4275.

The site of this Eskimo village originally was used as a fish camp for families from Upper Kalskag. It wasn't until 1930 that people began living in Lower Kalskag year-round. The upper village was a Roman Catholic center, and because of religious differences many of its residents moved to Lower Kalskag after the Russian

Orthodox Chapel of St. Seraphim (now on the National Register of Historic Places) was built in 1940. Lower Kalskag was incorporated as a second-class city in 1969. It is located within Yukon Delta National Wildlife Refuge.

Lower Kalskag's economy is based primarily on subsistence activities. Employment is largely limited to public programs. Hunting is for moose, black bear, rabbit, game birds, porcupine and waterfowl; fishing for salmon, pike, whitefish, blackfish and eel; and trapping for muskrat, beaver, lynx, otter, wolverine and mink. In addition, the tundra yields raspberries, cranberries, blackberries, blueberries, strawberries and currants.

Communications include phones, mail plane, radio and TV. The community is served by 2 Russian Orthodox churches and 2 schools with grades 1 through 12 with enrollment of 151. There are community electric, water and sewer systems. Freight is transported by plane and barge. Government address: City of Lower Kalskag, P.O. Box 81, Lower Kalskag, AK 99626, phone (907) 471-2228, fax (907) 471-2363. Village corporation: The Kuskokwim Corp., 645 G St., Suite 305, Anchorage, AK 99501, phone (907) 276-2101. Village council: Village of Lower Kalskag, P.O. Box 27, Kalskag, AK 99626, phone and fax (907) 471-2379, e-mail: LowerKalskag@aitc.org.

Manokotak

GPS: N58°58' W159°03'

(Man-a-KOT-ak) Located on the Igushik River, 25 miles southwest of Dillingham, 370 miles west of Anchorage. Transportation: Air charter service from Dillingham. Population: 405. Zip code: 99628. Emergency Services: Village Public Safety Officer; Alaska State Troopers, Dillingham; Manokotak Health Clinic; Manokotak First Responders, phone (907) 289-1025; Volunteer Fire Department.

Climate: Transitional zone with strong maritime influence; however, it also is affected by the colder continental climate. Cloudy skies, mild temperatures and moderately heavy precipitation. Average summer temperatures from 40°F to 70°F; average winter temperatures from 4°F to 30°F. Annual precipitation from 20 to 26 inches, with most occurring from late June through August. Rain generally is accompanied by southwest winds.

Private Aircraft: Airstrip 1 mile north; elev. 107 feet; length 2,740 feet; gravel; no fuel; unattended. Runway condition not monitored; visual inspection recommended prior to using. Runway surface soft and muddy during spring breakup or heavy rains.

NOTE: Manokotak prohibits possession of alcoholic beverages.

Visitor Facilities: No hotel, restaurant or banking services. Laundry facilities available. Groceries, limited clothing, first-aid supplies, hardware, film and sporting goods available in the community. Arts and crafts available for purchase include carved ivory, grass baskets, masks, fur hats and coats. Fishing/hunting licenses available. No guide service. No repair service or rental transportation. Fuel available includes marine gas, diesel and regular gasoline. Moorage facilities available.

Manokotak is one of the newer communities in the Bristol Bay region, although it is still strongly traditional, reflecting both its Eskimo heritage and Moravian Church influence. It became a permanent settlement in 1946-47 when several older villages consolidated. Beginning in 1949, school was conducted in a church which now serves as a workshop for students. A school was established in the community in 1958-59.

Almost everyone in Manokotak participates in the commercial salmon fishery. About 95 percent of the residents leave the village during the fishing season and most of them fish near the mouth of the Igushik River. About 40 percent of the residents also trap fox, beaver, mink, otter, lynx, wolverine and muskrat. Furs are sold at the Beaver Roundup held annually in Dillingham or to furriers in Anchorage.

The entire community depends heavily on subsistence hunting and fishing. Besides salmon, species taken include sea lion, beluga whale, caribou, herring, smelt, clams, grayling, trout, pike, sheefish, grouse and ptarmigan. Bird eggs, wild celery and various berries also are harvested. Trade with Togiak and Twin Hills brings Manokotak residents seal oil and whitefish.

Birds are abundant in the Manokotak area. The bald eagle is a summer resident and can be found nesting in the tops of trees or preying on seabirds, ground squirrels and fish. The Igushik River and its wetlands provide excellent habitat for migrating waterfowl and shorebirds in spring and fall. Peak migrations usually occur during the first week of May.

Communications in Manokotak, a second-class city incorporated in 1970, include a village phone (907) 842-5978, mail plane, radio and TV. The community is served by a Moravian church and a school with grades kindergarten through 12 with enrollment of 138. There are community electric, water and sewer systems. Freight arrives by cargo plane and barge. Government address: City of Manokotak, P.O. Box 170, Manokotak, AK 99628, phone (907) 289-1027, fax (907) 289-2035. Village corporation: Manokotak Natives Ltd., P.O. Box 65, Manokotak, AK 99628, phone (907) 289-1062, fax (907) 289-1007. Village council: Manokotak Village Council, P.O. Box 169, Manokotak, AK 99628, phone (907) 289-2067, fax (907) 289-1235. e-mail: Manokotak@aitc.org.

Marshall

GPS: N61°53' W162°05'

(Also known as Fortuna Ledge.) Located on Poltes Slough, north of Arbor Island on the east bank of the Yukon River in the Yukon-Kuskokwim Delta, 75 miles north of Bethel, 400 miles west-northwest of Anchorage. **Transportation**: Boat; scheduled or charter air service from Bethel. **Population**: 340. **Zip code**: 99585. **Emergency Services**: Village Public Safety Officer; Alaska State Troopers, Bethel; Marshall Health Clinic, phone (907) 679-6226; Volunteer Fire Department.

Climate: Temperatures range between -54°F and 86°F. Rainfall measures 16 inches a year; the growing season lasts 100 days.

Private Aircraft: Airstrip 1 mile southeast; elev. 90 feet; length 1,940 feet; grav-el; no fuel; unattended. Runway condition not monitored; visual inspection recommended prior to using. No airport facilities. Transportation to town for scheduled flights.

NOTE: Marshall prohibits possession of alcoholic beverages.

Visitor Facilities: Accommodations available at Hunter's Sales Room & Board, (907) 679-6111. No restaurant, banking services or laundromat. Groceries, clothing, firstaid supplies, hardware, film and sporting goods available at Hunter's Sales and Fortuna Ledge Co-op, (907) 679-6427. Arts and crafts available for purchase include fur and beadwork. Fishing/hunting licenses available. No guide service. Marine engine repair available. Arrangements can be made to rent boats or off-road vehicles. Fuel available includes marine gas, diesel, propane and regular gasoline. No moorage facilities.

This community has been known by several names since it was first recorded in 1880. After gold was discovered on a nearby creek in 1913, the settlement quickly became a placer mining camp and riverboat landing known as Fortuna Ledge, named after Fortuna Hunter, the first child born in the camp. Later the village was named Marshall's Landing for Thomas Riley Marshall, vice president of the United States under Woodrow Wilson from 1913-21. It was incorporated as a second-class city named Fortuna Ledge in 1970, but also was commonly referred to as Marshall. The community officially became Marshall in 1984.

Marshall residents work primarily during the summer salmon season, either in fishing or processing. Other seasonal employment includes fire fighting for the Bureau of Land Management. A few year-round jobs are available through the local government, school, village corporation and businesses. Income is supplemented by subsistence activities. Residents hunt black and brown bear, moose, rabbit, waterfowl and ptarmigan, and fish for salmon, whitefish, blackfish, sheefish, lush (burbot) and pike. In the fall, families harvest blueberries, blackberries, cranberries and salmonberries. Some residents also trap beaver, lynx, mink, otter and red fox.

Marshall is located at the northeastern boundary of Yukon Delta National Wildlife Refuge.

There are 2 gold mines in the area, which are reached by all-terrain vehicles.

The community is perhaps best described by resident Darcy Kameroff: "There is an uptown and downtown and it has 2 main roads. It is quite pretty when all the flowers and plants bloom. There are 2 big buildings, the school and Hunter's Sales. Marshall is special because of the history and the people. The people are special because they cooperate and care about each other. Marshall's attractions are the old gold mine, Soda Springs, and the trout in Wilson Creek."

Communications include phones, mail plane, radio and TV. The community is served by Russian Orthodox and Roman Catholic churches. The school enrollment is 100. There are community electricity, water and sewer systems. Freight arrives by cargo plane and barge. Government address: City of Marshall, General Delivery, Marshall, AK 99585, phone (907) 679-6215, fax (907) 679-6220. Village corporation: Maserculiq Inc., P.O. Box 90, Marshall, AK 99585, phone (907) 679-6512, fax (907) 679-6740. Village council: Native Village of Marshall, P.O. Box 110, Marshall, AK 99585, phone (907) 679-6302, fax (907) 679-6187, e-mail: Marshall@aitc.org.

Mekoryuk

GPS: N60°23' W166°11'

(Ma-KOR-ee-yuk) Located at the mouth of Shoal Bay on the north shore of Nunivak Island in the Bering Sea, 149 miles west of Bethel and 553 miles west of Anchorage. **Transportation**: Scheduled and charter air service from Bethel. **Population**: 191. **Zip code**: 99630. **Emergency Services**: Village Public Safety Officer, phone (907) 827-8315; Alaska State Troopers, Bethel; Mekoryuk Health Clinic, phone (907) 827-8111; Volunteer Fire Department.

Elevation: 40 feet. **Climate**: Summer weather cool and rainy, with temperatures averaging 48°F to 54°F. Winter temperature averages 17°F to 20°F, but can get down to -30°F. Wind chill can force the temperature to -100°F. Mean annual precipitation 15 inches with majority falling as rain July to October; mean annual snowfall 57 inches.

Private Aircraft: Airstrip 3 miles west; elev. 48 feet; length 3,070 feet; gravel; no fuel; unattended. Runway condition not monitored; visual inspection recommended prior to using. Runway soft during heavy rains or spring breakup. Animals occasionally on runway. No airport facilities. Public transportation into village available.

NOTE: Mekoryuk prohibits possession of alcoholic beverages.

Visitor Facilities: Lodging is available at Bering Sea Reindeer Products, (907) 827-8940. Food is available at the Mekoryuk Coffee Shop, (907) 827-8227, and at Olrun's Rec Room. Groceries, clothing, first-aid supplies, hardware, film and sporting goods available at NIMA Store, (907) 827-8313, and David's General Store. Laundromat available. Arts and crafts available for purchase include carved ivory, grass baskets, masks, beadwork, knitted items and fur garments. Fishing/ hunting licenses available. Guide services, including lodging and meals, available. Private boats available for charter. Fuel available includes marine gas, propane, unleaded and regular gasoline. No moorage facilities. Residents rely on snow machines and 3- or 4-wheelers for local transportation.

Mekoryuk is the only community on Nunivak Island which is part of Yukon Delta National Wildlife Refuge. Approximately half the island is classified as wilderness. Nunivak, third largest island in Alaska, measures 60 miles long by 40 miles wide. The federal government built a school at Mekoryuk because its well-protected bay made it an easy place to unload goods.

The residents of Mekoryuk are socially and culturally distinct from the Yup'ik Eskimos of the Yukon-Kuskokwim Delta. They speak a separate dialect of Yup'ik, termed Cup'ik, and do not participate in many of the intervillage social activities of the mainland.

The people here live mostly off the

land and sea, although there are a few federal government jobs. Many of the residents go to fish camps around the island during the summer. According to one resident, villagers hunt birds, walrus, seal, and red and arctic fox. The island has many rivers offering excellent fishing for salmon, trout, char and grayling, including the Mekoryuk River, which runs by the village. Halibut and cod are caught in the Bering Sea. Many of the people also are involved in reindeer herding and the roundups that take place usually in July. Approximately 3,000 head of reindeer roam the island, along with 400 head of musk-oxen, which were introduced in the 1930s. People come from all over the world to hunt musk-oxen during annual permit hunts.

Some of the finest ivory carving in the world is done here. Villagers also make unique wooden masks and knit qiviut wool from musk-oxen into lacy garments which are sold in Anchorage.

The island supports many species of birds, including ducks, geese, swans, murres, puffins, cormorants, several varieties of loon, ptarmigan and arctic tern.

Attractions for visitors include wilderness trips to see and photograph musk-oxen, reindeer, seal, walrus and birds. Advance arrangements should be made for lodging and meals.

Communications in Mekoryuk, a second-class city incorporated in 1969, include phones, mail plane, year-round plane service on Alaska/ERA airlines, 2 radio stations, TV and cable. The community is served by a Covenant church and a school with grades preschool through 12 with enrollment of 56. There are community electricity and water. Sewage system is honey buckets. Mekoryuk has a 2 percent city sales tax. Freight arrives in the community by cargo plane and barge. Government address: City of Mekoryuk, P.O. Box 29, Mekoryuk, AK 99630, phone (907) 827-8314, fax (907) 827-8626. Village corporation: Nima Corp., P.O. Box 52, Mekoryuk, AK 99630, phone (907) 827-8313. Village council: Native Village of Mekoryuk, P.O. Box 66, Mekoryuk, AK 99630, phone (907) 827-8828, fax (907) 827-8514. e-mail: Mekoryuk@aitc.org.

Mountain Village

GPS: N62°05′ W163°43′

Located on the Yukon River, 20 miles west of St. Marys, 470 miles westnorthwest of Anchorage. **Transportation:** Scheduled or charter air service from Nome or Bethel, and direct air service from Anchorage. **Population:** 757. **Zip code:** 99632. **Emergency Services:** Village Public Safety Officer; Alaska State Troopers, St. Marys, phone (907) 438-2018; Mountain Village Health Clinic, phone (907) 591-2926; Volunteer Fire Department.

Elevation: 40 feet. **Climate:** Both maritime and continental influences. Winters long and cold; summers short and cool, often cloudy but with little rainfall. Mean annual precipitation 17 inches; mean annual snowfall 45 inches.

Private Aircraft: Airstrip adjacent northeast; elev. 165 feet; length 2,520 feet; gravel; no fuel; unattended. Runway condition not monitored; visual inspection recommended prior to using. No airport facilities or public transportation into village.

NOTE: Mountain Village prohibits the sale and importation of alcoholic beverages.

Visitor Facilities: Food, groceries, clothing, first-aid supplies, hardware, film and sporting goods available in the community. No laundromat or banking services. Arts and crafts available for purchase include grass baskets and Eskimo clothing. Fishing/hunting licenses available. No guide service. Marine engine repair available. Autos and charter aircraft can be rented. Fuel available includes marine gas, propane and regular gasoline. There is a village marina.

Mountain Village was named because of its location at the foot of the first "mountain" encountered by those traveling up the Yukon River. Mountain Village was a summer fish camp site until the opening of a general store in the village in 1908 prompted immigration by the residents of 2 small upriver settlements. A salmon saltery was built in 1956 and a cannery in 1964. Mountain Village became a regional educational center after it was selected as headquarters for the Lower Yukon School District in 1976. It is a second-class city, incorporated in 1967.

The town's economy is expanding due to its relative accessibility, growing fishing industry and function as a regional education center. The school district, village corporation, government and local business provide year-round employment for about 70 people. This income is supplemented by subsistence hunting and fishing for moose, swan, geese, ducks, salmon, blackfish, sheefish, whitefish, burbot, grayling and pike. Income also is obtained from trapping beaver, muskrat, otter, mink and fox.

Mountain Village is located within Yukon Delta National Wildlife Refuge. A 17.7-mile road links Mountain Village with the communities of Pitka's Point, St. Marys and Andreafsky. Communications at Mountain Village include phones, mail plane, radio and TV. The community is served by 3 churches and a school with grades kindergarten through 12 with enrollment of 230. There are community electric, water and sewer systems. Freight arrives by cargo plane and barge. Government address: City of Mountain Village, P.O. Box 32027, Mountain Village, AK 99632 , phone (907) 591-2929, fax (907) 591-2920. Village corporation: Azachorak Inc., P.O. Box 32213, Mountain Village, AK 99632, phone (907) 591-2527, fax (907) 591-2127. Village council: Asa'carsarmiut Tribal Council, P.O. Box 32249, Mountain Village, AK 99632, phone (907) 591-2814, fax (907) 591-2811, e-mail: MountainVillage@aitc.org.

Napaimute

(Na-PAI-mute) Located on the Kuskokwim River in the Kilbuck-Kuskokwim Mountains, 28 miles east of Aniak, 120 miles northeast of Bethel and 285 miles west of Anchorage. **Transportation**: Charter air service from Aniak or Bethel; riverboats; snow machines or dogsleds. **Population**: 2 permanent; 30 part time. **Zip code**: 99557. **Emergency Services**: Alaska State Troopers, Aniak.

Elevation: 200 feet. **Climate**: Napaimute's climate is continental. Annual precipitation averages 20 inches, with 85 inches of snow.

Private Aircraft: No airstrip; floatplanes land on river.

Visitor Facilities: None. *NOTE: Land use permits are required to use lands owned by the Kuskokwim Corp. Uses include fishing, temporary camping, seasonal campsite, land crossing and research. There is a $100 administration fee. Big game hunting fee is $400. Seasonal campsite permits $50, annual use fee $250. For further information, contact The Kuskokwim Corp., 62000 W. International Airport Road, Suite C-9, Anchorage, AK 99502, phone (907) 243-2944, or in Aniak phone (907) 675-4275.*

Napaimute, which reportedly means "forest people," was once called Hoffmans after George W. Hoffman, an Englishman who established a trading post at the site in 1906. The modern-day village grew around the trading post and was primarily occupied by non-Natives, although a significant number of Eskimo residents also lived here. Hoffman built a territorial school in the village in 1920. In 1942 the village had 47 residents. By the early 1950s, most residents had moved to nearby settlements, particularly Aniak. Reportedly there are only 2 permanent residents at Napaimute, although there are a few other permanent residents a few miles upriver, and as many as 30 part-time residents arrive during the summer fishing season. Napaimute is unincorporated.

Communication is by a single-sideband radio; there are no phones. There is no school. Electricity is provided by private generators; rain water is collected or river water is hauled; sewage system is honey buckets or the community privy. Village corporation: Kuskokwim Corp., 645 G St., Suite 305, Anchorage, AK 99501, phone (907) 276-2101, or in Aniak phone (907) 675-4275. Village council: Native Village of Napaimute, P.O. Box 1301, Bethel, AK 99559, phone (907) 543-7310, fax (907) 543-3369, e-mail: Napaimute@aitc.org.

Napakiak

GPS: N60°42' W161°58'

(Na-PAK-ee-ack) Located at the head of Kuskokwim Bay, 10 miles southwest of Bethel, 410 miles west of Anchorage.

Transportation: Scheduled air service from Bethel. Population: 357. Zip code: 99634. Emergency Services: Police, phone (907) 589-2920; Napakiak Health Clinic, phone (907) 589-2711; Volunteer Fire Department.

Private Aircraft: Airstrip adjacent west; elev. 20 feet; length 2,150 feet; gravel; fuel information unavailable; unattended. Runway condition not monitored; visual inspection recommended prior to using. Unmarked poles located 200 feet west and 260 feet east of approach for runway 16.

NOTE: Napakiak prohibits possession of alcoholic beverages.

Visitor Facilities: Arrangements may be made for accommodations at the school, (907) 589-2420, and Napakiak Washeteria, contact city offices, (907) 589-2611, 10 A.M. to 5 P.M. Groceries and supplies available at Jung's Trading Post and Naparyalruar, (907) 589-2227. Breakfast and lunch are available at the school on school days only. Fishing/ hunting licenses available. Boats may be rented. Information on repair service and fuel at Mott's Marina, (907) 589-2281), and 2 other outlets.

This Eskimo community reportedly was established around 1890 by residents of an older village that had been located at the mouth of the Johnson River and also was known as Napakiak. A Moravian chapel was dedicated in 1930. An airport was completed in 1973. Napakiak was incorporated as a second-class city in 1970. It is located within Yukon Delta National Wildlife Refuge. Most of the people in Napakiak speak Yup'ik as their primary language. Many residents may be gone to fish camps during the summer.

There is year-round fishing, including salmon, pike, whitefish, sheefish and lush. In winter, Tri-Cab, (907) 589-2715; and McCann's, (907) 589-2026, offer winter drives on the ice road between Napakiak and Bethel, and tours of other villages. In summer, boat tours are available, (907) 589-2715.

Napakiak's school has grades kindergarten through 12 with enrollment of 101. There are community electricity and water systems. Sewage system is honey buckets. Freight arrives by plane and barge. Government address: City of Napakiak, General Delivery, Napakiak, AK 99634, phone and fax (907) 589-2611. Village corporation: Napakiak Corp., P.O. Box 34030, Napakiak, AK 99634, phone and fax (907) 589-2227. Village council: Native Village of Napakiak, P.O. Box 2, Napakiak, AK 99634, phone (907) 589-2227, fax (907) 589-2412. e-mail: Napakiak@aitc.org.

Napaskiak

GPS: N60°42' W161°47'

(Na-PASS-key-ack) Located on the Kuskokwim River 8 miles southwest of Bethel, 400 miles west of Anchorage. Transportation: Scheduled air service from Bethel and winter air and river taxi service. Population: 395. Zip code: 99559. Emergency Services: Police, phone (907) 737-7639; Alaska State Troopers, Bethel, phone (907) 543-3494; Napaskiak Health Clinic, phone (907) 737-7329; Volunteer Fire Department.

Private Aircraft: Airstrip adjacent south; elev. 24 feet; length 3,000 feet; gravel; no fuel; unattended. Runway condition not monitored; visual inspection recommended prior to using. Center of runway is 20 feet of gravel. Runway rough due to dips and ruts, and it floods in spring.

NOTE: Napaskiak prohibits the sale and importation of alcoholic beverages.

Visitor Facilities: Accommodations at city building (907) 737-7626. Supplies available at Napaskiak, Inc., (907) 737-7413. Fishing/hunting licenses not available. Fuel available for snow machines, boat motors, and 3- and 4-wheelers. Information on other visitor services and facilities not available.

This Eskimo community may have been established around 1800 by residents of another village forced to move because of erosion. The population in 1880 was 196. Many people died in the influenza and measles epidemics of 1900 and the village was abandoned for a time. In 1905 the first Russian Orthodox priest arrived and baptized the entire village. St. Jacob's Chapel, listed on the National Register of

Historic Places, was built in 1931; a new church was constructed in 1978.

A Bureau of Indian Affairs school opened in 1939 and an airport was completed in 1974. Napaskiak, which is located within Yukon Delta National Wildlife Refuge, was incorporated as a second-class city in 1971. Many residents leave town during the summer season to go to fish camps.

The community is served by 2 schools with grades kindergarten through 12 with enrollment of 128. There is a community electric system and water supply. Sewage system is honey buckets. Freight arrives by plane and barge. Government address: City of Napaskiak, P.O. Box 6109, Napaskiak, AK 99559, phone (907) 737-7626, fax (907) 737-7412. Village corporation: Napaskiak Inc., P.O. Box 6069, Napaskiak, AK 99559, phone (907) 737-7433, fax (907) 737-2919. Village council: Native Village of Napaskiak, P.O. Box 6009, Napaskiak, AK 99559, phone (907) 737-7364, fax (907) 737-7039, e-mail: Napaskiak@aitc.org.

New Stuyahok

GPS: N59°29' W157°20'

(New STU-ya-hock) Located on the Nushagak River, 51 miles northeast of Dillingham, 290 miles southwest of Anchorage. **Transportation**: Boat; snow machine; scheduled or charter air service from Dillingham. **Population**: 468. **Zip code**: 99636. **Emergency Services**: Village Public Safety Officer, phone (907) 693-3170; Alaska State Troopers, Dillingham, phone (907) 842-5641; New Stuyahok Health Clinic, (907) phone 693-3131; New Stuyahok First Responders, phone (907) 693-3173; Kanakanak Hospital, Dillingham, phone (907) 842-5101 or 842-5202; Health Aide, phone 693-3102 or 693-3133.

Elevation: 125 feet. **Climate**: Transitional zone; primary influence maritime. Because the village is inland the continental climate significantly affects local weather. Cloudy skies, mild temperatures and moderately heavy precipitation. There often are strong winds. Average summer temperatures from 37°F to 66°F; average winter tem-

peratures from 4°F to 30°F. Annual precipitation 20 to 35 inches, with most of it occurring in August and September.

Private Aircraft: Airstrip 1 mile west; elev. 325 feet; length 1,800 feet; gravel; no fuel; unattended. Runway condition not monitored; visual inspection recommended prior to landing. Access road to parking apron not maintained; takeoffs and landings on road prohibited. No facilities at airport or public transportation into town.

Visitor Facilities: There is a roadhouse. Arrangements for accommodations in private homes also may be made. There is no restaurant, laundromat or banking facility. Groceries, clothing, first-aid supplies, hardware, film and sporting goods available in the community. Arts and crafts available for purchase include hand-sewn fur items. Fishing/hunting licenses not available. No guide or repair services, rental transportation, or moorage facilities. Fuel available: diesel and regular gasoline.

This Eskimo village was relocated several times because of flooding and has been at its present site since 1942. Stuyahok is an Eskimo word meaning "going downriver place." New Stuyahok got its first school, a log building, in 1961, and incorporated as a second-class city in 1972.

The community's economic base is the commercial salmon fishery, although about 30 people trap commercially and several are employed full time by the government or school district. Beaver, lynx, fox and mink are the primary species trapped for fur; and muskrat, otter, wolverine, bobcat, marten and weasel also are taken. Furs are sold to buyers who pass through the village, at the Beaver Roundup in Dillingham, or at the annual New Stuyahok Beaver Festival.

The entire community depends heavily on subsistence activities for food. Many residents go to fish camps during the summer season. Moose, caribou, rabbit and beaver are the primary game animals. Fishing is for salmon, pike, grayling, smelt, whitefish, sucker, rainbow trout, lingcod and Dolly Varden. In the fall, blackberries, red berries, cranberries and some blueberries are gathered.

Communications include phones and

radio. The community is served by a Russian Orthodox church and a school with grades kindergarten through 12 with enrollment of 163. There are community electric, water and sewer systems. Freight generally arrives by plane. Government address: City of New Stuyahok, P.O. Box 10, New Stuyahok, AK 99636, phone (907) 693-3171, fax (907) 693-3176. Village corporation address: Stuyahok Ltd., P.O. Box 50, Stuyahok, AK 99636, phone (907) 693-3122, fax (907) 693-3148. Village council: New Stuyahok Village, P.O. Box 49, New Stuyahok, AK 99636, phone (907) 693-3173, e-mail: NewStuyahok@aitc.org.

Newhalen

GPS: N59°43' W154°54'

Located in the Western Cook Inlet area on the north shore of Iliamna Lake at the mouth of the Newhalen River, 4.5 miles southwest of Iliamna and 230 miles south-southwest of Anchorage. **Transportation**: Scheduled air service to Iliamna, then by road to Newhalen. **Population**: 183. **Zip code**: 99606. **Emergency Services**: Village Public Safety Officer, phone (907) 571-1461; Newhalen Health Clinic; Iliamna/Newhalen Rescue Squad, phone (907) 571-1248/1631; Volunteer Fire Department, phone (907) 571-1231.

Elevation: 190 feet. **Climate**: Transitional zone. Average summer temperatures from 42°F to 62°F; average winter temperatures from 6°F to 30°F. Annual precipitation averages 24 inches, with 50 inches of snow.

Private Aircraft: There is an old airstrip at Newhalen, but it has been out of use for years. Residents use the Iliamna airport.

Visitor Facilities: Accommodations and meals by advance reservation at several wilderness lodges in the Iliamna area. There is a washeteria with showers. Groceries and some camping and fishing supplies available at local stores. Fishing/hunting licenses available in Iliamna. No marine facilities or repair services. Fuel available: diesel and gasoline. *NOTE: Hiking, berry picking, camping and fishing are permitted on lands owned by the Alaska Peninsula Corp. upon payment of a $100-per-person fee. Hunting and woodcutting on corporation lands is not permitted. Contact the corporation for more information.*

The 1890 census listed the Eskimo name of Noghelingamiut, meaning "people of Noghelin," at this location. The present name is an anglicized version of the original. The village was established in the late 1800s to take advantage of the plentiful fish and game in the area. Today, it remains a fishing village. Newhalen was incorporated as a second-class city in 1971. It is connected by a 9-mile-long road to Iliamna and the airport.

During the red salmon season most residents leave Newhalen to fish in Bristol Bay; many return at the end of the red season, although a few stay to fish the smaller pink and silver salmon runs later in the summer and fall. Other employment is in the public sector, such as with the school district or seasonal firefighting for the Bureau of Land Management. Income from these enterprises is supplemented by subsistence hunting and fishing. Freshwater fish, rabbit and porcupine are taken year-round. Moose, caribou, bear, ptarmigan, ducks and geese are hunted in season and seals are occasionally taken from Lake Iliamna. In the summer and fall, residents pick blackberries, blueberries, cranberries, salmonberries and raspberries. Wild celery and spinach are gathered in early spring.

Communications in Newhalen include phones, radio and TV. The community is served by a Russian Orthodox church and 2 schools with grades preschool through 12 with enrollment of 68. There is a community electricity system. Most homes now have wells and bathrooms, and there are 15 HUD homes. Freight arrives primarily by air cargo. Government address: City of Newhalen, P.O. Box 165, Newhalen, AK 99606, phone (907) 571-1226, fax (907) 571-1540. Village corporation: Alaska Peninsula Corp, 800 Cordova St., Anchorage, AK 99501, phone (907) 274-2433. Village council: Newhalen Village, P.O. Box 207, Newhalen, AK 99606, phone (907) 571-1410, fax (907) 571-1537, e-mail: Newhalen@aitc.org, web: http://arctic.net~newhalen/index.html.

Newtok

GPS: N60°56' W164°38'

Located north of Nelson Island on the Kealavik River, 90 miles west-northwest of Bethel, 500 miles west of Anchorage. **Transportation**: Scheduled air service from Bethel. **Population**: 284. **Zip code**: 99559. **Emergency Services**: Alaska State Troopers, Bethel, phone (907) 543-3494; Newtok Health Clinic, phone (907) 237-2111; Volunteer Fire Department.

Private Aircraft: Airstrip 1 mile west; elev. 25 feet; length 2,180 feet; gravel; no fuel; unattended. Runway condition not monitored; visual inspection recommended prior to using.

NOTE: Newtok prohibits the sale and importation of alcoholic beverages.

Visitor Facilities: Lodging and meals are available at the high school, (907) 237-2126. Supplies are available at Newtok Corp. Store, (907) 237-2413, or Nick Tom Sr. Store, (907) 237-2114. Fishing/hunting licenses not available. Information on other visitor services and facilities unavailable.

Newtok, located within Yukon Delta National Wildlife Refuge, is a relatively new village established around 1949. It was incorporated as a second-class city in 1976. Many residents go to fish camps during the summer.

Newtok has a Roman Catholic church and 2 schools with grades 1 through 12 with enrollment of 99. There is a community electric system. Water is hauled from a central watering point or ponds, and rain water is collected. Sewage system is honey buckets. Freight arrives by mail plane and barge.

Government address: Newtok Village, Box WWT, Newtok, AK 99559, phone (907) 237-2314, e-mail: Newtok@aitc.org. Village corporation: Newtok Corp., General Delivery, Newtok, AK 99559, phone (907) 237-2413.

Nightmute

GPS: N60°28' W164°44'

Located on the Toksook River on Nelson Island in the Bering Sea, 105 miles west of Bethel, 510 miles west of Anchorage. **Transportation**: Scheduled and charter air service from Bethel. **Population**: 214.: 99690 **Zip code**. **Emergency Services**: Village Public Safety Officer, Toksook Bay; Alaska State Troopers, Bethel; Nightmute Health Clinic, phone (907) 647-6312; Volunteer Fire Department.

Private Aircraft: Airstrip 2 miles north; elev. 14 feet; length 1,600 feet; gravel; no fuel; unattended. Runway condition not monitored; visual inspection recommended prior to using.

Visitor Facilities: Arrangements may be made for accommodations in private homes; contact the city of Nightmute, (907) 647-6426. Lodging also may be available at the school, (907) 647-6313. Meals available at the high school in winter. No banking services or laundromat. Groceries, clothing, first-aid supplies, hardware and film available in the community. Arts and crafts available for purchase include carved ivory, grass baskets and fur garments. Fishing/hunting licenses not available. Guide service available. No repair services or rental transportation. Fuel available includes marine gas, diesel and regular gasoline. Moorage facilities available.

According to local residents, the village grew as Native people gradually moved to Nelson Island. The Bureau of Indian Affairs established a school in the 1950s. Nightmute lost population in 1964 when many residents moved to Toksook Bay, 15 miles to the northwest, but the community was incorporated as a second-class city in 1974.

Nightmute is located within Yukon Delta National Wildlife Refuge. Residents work at seasonal jobs and engage in subsistence hunting for geese, ducks, rabbits, cranes, swans, ptarmigan, fox, beaver, muskrat, otter and mink. Fishing is for herring, king, silver, red and pink salmon, halibut, devil fish and pike. Most of the residents go to fish camp at Umkumute, 18 miles from Nightmute, during the summer.

Communications at Nightmute include phones, mail plane and TV. The community is served by a church and 2 schools with grades kindergarten through 12 with total enrollment of 65. There is a community electric system. Water is hauled from a central watering point. Sewage system is honey buckets. Freight arrives by cargo plane and barge. Government address: City of Nightmute, P.O. Box 90010, Nightmute, AK 99690, phone (907) 647-6426, fax (907) 647-6427. Village corporation: Chinuruk Inc., P.O. Box 90009, Nightmute, AK 99690, phone (907) 647-6213. e-mail: Nightmute@aitc.org.

Nome

GPS: N64°30' W164°25'

Located on the south coast of the Seward Peninsula, 550 air miles northwest of Anchorage. **Transportation**: Daily jet service from Anchorage available year-round. Charter air service to and from village; in winter, snow machines, dogsleds. **Population**: 3,620. **Zip code**: 99762. **Emergency Services**: Norton Sound Regional Hospital, phone (907) 443-3311; Nome Volunteer Ambulance Dept., phone (907) 443-3240/3311; Norton Sound Health Corp. Medivac, phone (907) 443-3311. Police and Fire, phone 911.

Elevation: 13 to 44 feet. **Climate**: Average temperature in January from -3°F to 12°F; average temperature in July from 45°F to 60°F. Mean annual precipitation 15.5 inches; mean annual snowfall 55 inches. Snow usually starts falling in early October; last snowfall in late April. If you want to take a look at the current weather in downtown Nome, visit the NomeCam at www.nome.net/nome cam.html.

Private Aircraft: Nome airport 2 miles west; elev. 36 feet; 2 intersecting runways: length 6,001 and 5576 feet; asphalt; fuel 80, 100, jet A, Al. Three cab companies available for transportation to town. Nome city aerodrome 0.9 mile north; elev. 59 feet; length 1,950 feet; gravel; closed Nov.-May.

Visitor Facilities: Accommodations available at 7 hotels and 1 bed and breakfast. There are a number of restaurants, 1 bank, laundry and shower facilities. Groceries, clothing, first-aid supplies, hardware, film and sporting goods available at local stores. Native arts and crafts available at several excellent gift shops. Fishing/hunting licenses available, as well as guide service. Public moorage facilities available. Truck and van rentals available.

For detailed information on visitor services and local attractions and current events, contact the Nome Convention and Visitors Bureau, P.O. Box 240, Nome, AK 99762, phone (907) 443-6624, fax (907) 443-5832, web www.nomealaska.org.

Nome owes its name to a misinterpretation of "? name" annotated on a manuscript chart prepared aboard the HMS Herald about 1850. The question mark was taken as a C (for cape) and the A in "name" was read as 0.

Gold was found in the Nome area in September 1898, and the town got its start that winter when 6 miners met at the mouth of Snake River and formed the Cape Nome Mining District. Originally the settlement was called Anvil City, after Anvil Creek where the first major gold strike was found. During the following summer gold was found on the beaches of Nome. News of the gold strike set off a major rush in the summer of 1900 when the news reached Seattle. By August 1900, there were some 20,000 people in Nome. The Seward Peninsula is believed to hold 100 gold dredges from bygone days; 44 dredges lie in the immediate Nome area. Gold mining continues today as an important economic activity. Reactivated gold dredges operate near the main Nome airport and north of town.

Incorporated in 1901, Nome is the oldest first-class city in Alaska and has the state's oldest first-class school district.

Nome is the transportation and commerce center for northwestern Alaska. Alaska's reindeer industry is centered in the Nome vicinity. Almost half of all wage and salary jobs are with federal, state and local governments. Nome also is a major stopover on arctic tours and a jumping-off point for tours to surrounding Eskimo villages. It is also a jumping-off point for visits to Russia: Provideniya is only a 60-minute flight from Nome.

Nome is the location of Northwest College. The city's only parking meter stands in front of the newspaper office.

The Bering Sea is only a stone's throw from Front Street. The granite sea wall protecting Nome from the sea was built between 1949 and 1951 by the U.S. Army Corps of Engineers. The 3,350-foot-long seawall is 65 feet wide at its base, 16 feet wide at its top, and stands 18 feet above mean low water.

Carrie McLain Memorial Museum, P.O. Box 53, Nome, AK 99762, (907) 443-2566, is located in the basement of the building containing the Kegoayah Kozga Library on Front Street. This history museum has a fascinating collection of some 6,000 photographs of the gold rush and early Eskimo life. Copies of the photographs can be purchased on request. Permanent exhibits include the Bering Land Bridge; natural history; Eskimo lifestyles and art; contemporary art; the Nome gold rush; and dogmushing history. Special exhibitions and demonstrations take place throughout the year. Hours vary according to season. No admission charge; donations accepted.

Nome's city hall, with turn-of-the-century decor, is on Front Street. A massive wood-burl arch sits in the lot next to city hall until March each year, when it is raised over Front Street for the Month of Iditarod festival celebrating the 1,049-mile Iditarod Trail Sled Dog Race from Anchorage to Nome. Hundreds of visitors come to Nome to take part in the various activities that include a statewide basketball tournament, the 200-mile Nome-to-Golovin snowmobile race and a snowshoe softball tournament. Another event that attracts national attention and participants is the Bering Sea Ice Golf Classic, a golf tournament played on the frozen Bering Sea in March. The highlight of the month comes with completion of the Iditarod Trail Sled Dog Race. The townspeople turn out en masse to welcome each tired musher and team at the finish line.

In June Nome celebrations include the annual Midnight Sun Festival, sponsored by the chamber of commerce. The highlight of the festival is a raft race on the Nome River, in which many unusual homemade craft take part. Winner of the raft race is traditionally awarded a fur-lined honey bucket.

Nome has what you SEEK!

Nome Visitor Bureau
P.O. Box 240WG
(907) 443-6624
www.nomealaska.org

The Anvil Mountain Run is scheduled for the Fourth of July. This 12.5-mile race follows a very rugged course from city hall to the top of 1,977-foot Anvil Mountain, so named because of the anvil-shaped rock on its peak, and down again via the face of the mountain. Other events in the community are the Memorial Day Polar Bear Swim and the Labor Day Bathtub Race.

Three roads, maintained only in summer (mid-June through early October), extend east, north and west from the city: the 72-mile Nome–Teller Road, the 72-mile Nome–Council Road, and the 86-mile Nome–Taylor Road. Travelers can spot many varieties of wildflowers and birds along these roads. More than 184 species of birds have been identified in the Nome area. Moose, bear and musk-oxen can be viewed. Blueberries, salmonberries and cranberries ripen all over the Seward Peninsula around August.

According to one resident, "The fall is beautiful, with the tundra in full foliage and long cool days with beautiful sunsets over the ocean and tundra. No trees to get in your way! You can see for miles."

Communications in Nome include phone; 2 radio stations (KNOM 780AM/96.1FM is on the web at www.knom.org/); TV; and the weekly *Nome Nugget* newspaper (www.nomenugget.com). There are community electric, water and sewer systems. The community is served by 15 churches, elementary and high schools with total enrollment of 761, a 19-bed hospital and port facilities for vessels up to 22 feet of draft in 30-foot depth.

Government address: City of Nome, P.O. Box 281, Nome, AK 99762, phone (907) 443-6663, fax (907) 443-5349, e-mail: admin@ci.nome.ak.us, Web: http://www. nomealaska.org. Village corporation: Sitnasuak Native Corporation, Box 905, Nome, AK 99762, phone (907) 443-2632, fax (907) 443-3063, e-mail: r.fagerstrom @snc.org. Village council: Nome Eskimo Community, P.O. Box 1090, Nome, AK 99762, phone (907) 443-2246, fax (907) 443-3539, e-mail: Nome@aitc.org. Nome Chamber of Commerce: P.O. Box 250, Nome, AK 99762, phone (907) 443-2223, fax (907) 443-2742.

Nondalton

GPS: N59°58' W154°51'

Located in the Western Cook Inlet area on the west shore of Six Mile Lake, 15 miles north of Iliamna and 200 miles southwest of Anchorage, within Lake Clark National Park. **Transportation**: Scheduled and charter air service from Anchorage and Iliamna. **Population**: 216. **Zip code**: 99640. **Emergency Services**: Police, phone (907) 294-2262; Nondalton Health Clinic, phone (907) 294-2238; Nondalton First Responders, phone (907) 294-2238/2224/2215. Volunteer Fire Department, phone (907) 294-2262.

Elevation: 250 feet. **Climate**: Transitional zone. Weather information from Iliamna indicates average summer temperatures in Nondalton from 42°F to 62°F and average winter temperatures from 6°F to 30°F. Annual precipitation averages 26 inches, with 64 inches of snow.

Private Aircraft: Airstrip I mile northwest; elev. 250 feet; length 2,800 feet; gravel; fuel unavailable; unattended. Runway condition not monitored; visual inspection recommended prior to using. Transport to town available.

NOTE: Nondalton prohibits the sale of alcoholic beverages.

Visitor Facilities: Accommodations and meals by advance reservation at several area wilderness lodges. No bank or public showers, but laundromat available. Groceries, first-aid supplies, hardware, film, sporting goods and Nondalton hats and T-shirts available. Fuel includes marine gas, regular and unleaded gasoline, diesel, propane, white gas and kerosene. Arts and crafts available for purchase include birch-bark baskets and dolls from the local doll factory. Fishing/hunting licenses, guides and repairs to marine engines, boats and autos all available. Rental transportation includes automobiles, boats, aircraft and off-road vehicles.

Nondalton is a Tanaina Indian name, first recorded in 1909 by D.C. Witherspoon of the U.S. Geological Survey. The village originally was located on the north shore of Six Mile Lake. In 1940, firewood supplies were depleted and growing mudflats made it increasingly difficult to reach the lake, so the village relocated to the west shore. Nondalton was incorporated as a second-class city in 1971.

Nondalton's St. Nicholas Russian Orthodox Chapel, originally constructed in 1896 and moved with the rest of the village, is on the National Register of Historic Places.

Nondalton residents work seasonally in the commercial salmon fishery or firefighting for BLM. A few other jobs are with governmental agencies and the village Native corporation.

Residents depend heavily on subsistence hunting and fishing for food. Red salmon are caught in the summer and freshwater fish, rabbit and porcupine are taken year-round. Moose, caribou, bear, ptarmigan, ducks and geese are hunted in season. In late summer and fall, residents pick blueberries, blackberries and cranberries. Wild onions are gathered in the summer.

Communications include phones, TV via satellite and radio. The community is served by a school with grades preschool through 12 with enrollment of 73. Nondalton has a Russian Orthodox church. There are community electric, water and sewer systems. Freight arrives by barge or small plane.

Government address: City of Nondalton, P.O. Box 089, Nondalton, AK 99640, phone (907) 294-2235, fax (907) 294-2239, e-mail: Noncity@aol.com. Village corporation: Kijik Corp., 4155 Tudor Centre Drive, Suite 104, Anchorage, AK 99508, phone (907) 561-4487, fax (907) 562-4945. Village corporation: Nondalton Native Corp., P.O. Box 47, Iliamna, AK 99606. Village council: Nondalton Tribal Council, P.O. Box 49, Nondalton, AK 99640, phone (907) 294-2220, fax (907) 294-2234, e-mail: Nondalton@aitc.org.

Nunam Iqua

GPS: N62°13' W164°50'

(Formerly Sheldon Point) Located on south bank of the Yukon River, 18 miles southwest of Emmonak, 500 miles westnorthwest of Anchorage. **Transportation**:

Boat; scheduled or charter airline from Emmonak; snow machine. **Population**: 201. **Zip code**: 99666. **Emergency services**: Village Public Safety Officer; Alaska State Troopers, St. Marys; Sheldon Point Health Clinic, phone (907) 498-4228.

Climate: Climate is maritime, averaging 60 inches of snowfall and 18 inches of precipitation per year. Temperatures range from -40°F to 79°F.

Private Aircraft: Airstrip adjacent southeast of village; length 3,015; gravel; unattended. No airport facilities or public transportation into village. Seaplane landings in river adjacent to village.

NOTE: Nunam Iqua prohibits the sale and importation of alcoholic beverages.

Visitor Facilities: Arrangements may be made for accommodations and meals in private homes, or at the school, (907) 498-4112. No banking services. Groceries, clothing, first-aid supplies, hardware, film and sporting goods at Swan Lake Store, (907) 498-4227. Arts and crafts available include Native jewelry, ivory, beadwork, wood carvings and Eskimo clothing. Fishing/hunting licenses not available. Arrangements may be made with local residents for guide services. No repair services. Fuel available: regular gasoline, fuel oil. No moorage facilities.

A relatively new Eskimo village, established in the 1940s, the community is also known as Sheldon Point, after a man who owned and operated a fish saltery at the site. It is a second-class city, incorporated in 1974.

Commercial fishing supports the economy. Fish-buying companies from the lower Yukon, Bering Sea, Fort Yukon and the Yukon Delta Fish Marketing Co-op come here to buy fish. A few other employment opportunities exist with the store, post office, clinic, airlines, local government and schools. Income is supplemented by public assistance payments and subsistence activities. Residents hunt beluga whales, seals, moose, geese, ducks, ptarmigan and hares, and fish for salmon, whitefish, blackfish, sheefish, lush (burbot) and smelt. Additional income is gained from trapping beaver, otter and mink.

Sheldon Point (Nunam Iqua) is surrounded by the Yukon Delta National Wildlife Refuge.

Communications include phones, mail plane, radio and sometimes TV. The community is served by a Roman Catholic church and a school with grades kindergarten through 12 with enrollment of 62. There is a community electric system and a water treatment plant. Sewage system is primarily honey buckets. Freight arrives by cargo plane, barge, small boat and snow machine. Government address: City of Nunam Iqua, P.O. Box 26, Nunam Iqua, AK 99666, phone (907) 498-4226. Village corporation: Swan Lake Corp., P.O. Box 25, Sheldon Point, AK 99666, phone (907) 498-4227, fax (907) 498-4242. Village council: Native Village of Nunam Iqua, P.O., Box 27, Sheldon Point, AK 99666, phone (907) 498-4394, fax (907) 498-4185, e-mail: SheldonPoint@aitc.org.

Nunapitchuk

GPS: N60°53' W162°29'

(Nu-NA-pit-CHUCK) Located on Johnson River 30 miles northwest of Bethel and 425 miles west of Anchorage. **Transportation**: Scheduled air service from Bethel. **Population**: 480. **Zip code**: 99641. **Emergency Services**: Police, phone (907) 527-5718; Nunapitchuk Health Clinic, phone (907) 527-5329; Volunteer Fire Department.

Climate: Transitional zone. Mean July maximum temperature 62°F; mean January minimum temperature 13°F. The village endures lots of wind and blowing snow in the winter, according to one resident.

Private Aircraft: Airstrip east of village; elev. 12 feet; length 2,040 feet; gravel; unattended. Runway condition not monitored; recommend visual inspection prior to using. There is a freight terminal and public transportation from airport. Seaplane base with small float on the river. NOTE: *Nunapitchuk prohibits possession of alcoholic beverages.*

Visitor Facilities: Three rooms with kitchen area available at IRA Council building; contact the city office, (907) 527-5327, to make arrangements. No restaurant or banking services. Washeteria

available. Groceries, clothing, first-aid supplies, hardware, film and sporting goods available in the community. Arts and crafts available for purchase include otter parkas, beaver hats, mukluks, knitted gloves and earrings. Fishing/ hunting licenses available at the city office. Marine engine repair available. No guide service. Private off-road vehicles and boats may be rented. Fuel available: propane, regular gasoline. No moorage facilities.

In the 1930s, there were 5 or 6 families in the settlement. More families moved to the area after the federal government built a school in the 1940s. Nunapitchuk has an IRA (Indian Reorganization Act) Council that was established in the 1940s. It also had a second-class city status and was then incorporated with Kasigluk in 1969 as the city of Akolmiut. In October 1982 they split and went back to their individual status as second-class cities.

Residents depend on commercial fishing and subsistence activities. They hunt for moose, caribou and small game and fish for salmon and pike. They also trap for mink, muskrat, fox and land otters.

Communications include phones, mail plane, radio and TV. The community is served by Russian Orthodox, Moravian and Pentecostal churches, and a school with grades preschool through 12 with enrollment of 154. There is an AVEC electric system. Water is hauled from wells or the washeteria, or rain water is collected. Sewage system is honey buckets. Freight arrives by air transport and barge.

Government address: City of Nunapitchuk, c/o City Clerk, P.O. Box 190, Nunapitchuk, AK 99641, phone (907) 527-5327, fax (907) 527-5011, e-mail: eliwass@unicom-alaska.com. Village corporation address: Nunapitchuk Limited, P.O. Box 129, Nunapitchuk, AK 99641, phone (907) 527-5717, fax (907) 527-5229.

Nushagak

GPS: N59°07' W157°46'

(NOOSH-a-gack) Located on the east shore of Nushagak Bay, 5 air miles from Dillingham, 330 miles southwest of Anchorage. **Transportation**: Boat; charter plane from Dillingham. **Population:** Up to 100 during summer fishing season. **Zip code:** 99695. **Emergency Services:** Alaska State Troopers, Dillingham; Kanakanak Hospital, Dillingham.

Private Aircraft: No airstrip. Small planes land on the beach at low tide.

Visitor Facilities: None. Camp or sleep in one of several vacant huts (look for one with an intact roof). Supplies are airlifted from Dillingham.

Nushagak is a former Eskimo village established as a trading post about 1819. The Russians called it Aleksandrovsk. It was called Fort or Redoubt Alexander until 1899. The area is now used seasonally as a base for set-net fishermen.

The Russian Orthodox Transfiguration of Our Lord Chapel at Nushagak is on the National Register of Historic Places.

Oscarville

GPS: N60°43' W161°46'

Located on the north shore of the Kuskokwim River across from Napaskiak, 5 miles south of Bethel, 400 miles west of Anchorage. **Transportation:** Boat, snow machine and floatplane service from Bethel. **Population:** 64. **Zip code:** 99695. **Emergency Services:** Alaska State Troopers, Bethel, phone (907) 543-3949; Oscarville Health Clinic.

Visitor Facilities: Arrangements for accommodations may be made by contacting the school, (907) 737-7214. Supplies may be available at a general store. Fishing/hunting licenses are not available. Information on other facilities not available.

In about 1906, a man named Oscar Samuelson, born in Norway in 1876, and his Eskimo wife moved to Napaskiak and opened a small store. Samuelson became a mail carrier and in 1908 the Samuelsons moved across the river to what became known as Oscarville. Samuelson opened another small store that he ran until his death in 19S3. His daughter and subsequent owners have operated the store. The first school opened in 1964. Oscarville is unincorporated.

Oscarville is served by a 2-teacher school with grades kindergarten through 12 depending on demand. Electricity is from individual generators. Water is hauled from the school well and ponds or rain water is collected. Sewage system is honey buckets. Freight arrives by plane or barge. Village corporation address: Oscarville Native Corp., General Delivery, Oscarville, AK 99559, phone (907) 543-2066. Village council: Oscarville Traditional Council, Box 1554, Oscarville, AK 99559, phone (907) 737-7321, e-mail: Oscarville @aitc.org.

Pedro Bay

GPS: N59°47' W154°06'

Located in the Western Cook Inlet area at the head of Pedro Bay in Lake Iliamna, 180 miles southwest of Anchorage. **Transportation:** Scheduled or charter air service from Iliamna, Port Alsworth and Anchorage. **Population:** 50. **Zip code:** 99647. **Emergency Services:** Health Aide, phone (907) 850-2229; Pedro Bay First Responders, phone (907) 850-2225/2255; Volunteer Fire/EMS Department, phone 850-2225.

Climate: Transitional zone, with strong maritime influences. Weather data for Iliamna, 25 miles away, generally reflect conditions at Pedro Bay. Average summer temperatures from 42°F to 62°F; average winter temperatures from 6°F to 30°F.

Private Aircraft: Airstrip 1 mile west; elev. 45 feet; length 3,000 feet; crushed gravel topping; no fuel; unattended. Runway condition not monitored; visual inspection recommended prior to using. Bush taxi service into village, phone (907) 850-2202/2210, VHF Ch. 10.

Private Boats: Some public moorage available; contact Pedro Bay Village Council.

Visitor Facilities: Bed and breakfast accommodations, Triple K Services, (907) 850-2202. No banking services. Laundry, showers, drinking water at Pedro Bay Health and Office Building. Groceries and first aid supplies available in the community. Fishing/hunting licenses available, also guide service. Limited repair services. 4-wheeler and vehicle rentals available. Community library open most weekday evenings, Saturdays.

The Dena'ina Indians have occupied this area for hundreds of years. A Dena'ina village was once located at the west entrance to Pedro Bay and the Dena'ina warred with Russian fur traders over trade practices in the early 20th century. Dena'ina Indians still live in the area. Many of the traditional ways of life have changed, but Pedro Bay tribal members are proud of their subsistence heritage. Most Pedro Bay residents depend on subsistence hunting and fishing. Red salmon are caught in the summer and freshwater fish are taken year-round. Moose, rabbit, bear, ptarmigan, grouse and ducks are hunted in season. In early summer, residents gather wild celery and onions. In the fall, they pick blueberries, cranberries, blackberries and salmonberries. For more information on local history and subsistence, contact the Pedro Bay Village Council to obtain a copy of the video, *"Pedro Bay: The Changing Face of Subsistence."*

Many residents are employed by the Pedro Bay Village Council. A few are Bristol Bay fishermen, and several are North Slope workers. Others work short-term government jobs, or seasonal construction and tourism jobs. A new school facility was built in 2001 and provides several jobs.

St. Nicholas Russian Orthodox Chapel, built in 1890, is on the National Register of Historic Places.

Pedro Bay excels in scenery and is known among Alaska tribes as one of the cleanest villages in the state. During spring and summer, brown bears gather along the salmon streams near Pedro Bay. Black bears, wolves and small game are commonly seen, and moose also winter and calve in the area. Eagles, ducks and a variety of shorebirds can be seen in and around the islands of Pedro Bay, as well as a unique population of resident freshwater seals.

Pedro Bay is located within the Kvichak River system, with headwaters in Lake Clark and Lake Iliamna. This is historically the most important spawning and rearing habitat for sockeye salmon in the world. Sportfishing for rainbow trout, arctic char and Dolly Varden also is excellent.

Communications in Pedro Bay include phones, radio and TV. The community is currently served by 1 church and a school with grades kindergarten through 12 with enrollment of 13. There is a community electric utility. Water is from private wells. Sewage system is via individual septic tanks, and solid waste is handled by a transfer facility and community landfill. Freight arrives by barge and air service. Government address: Pedro Bay Village Council, P.O. Box 47020, Pedro Bay, AK 99647, phone (907) 850-2225, fax (907) 850-2221, e-mail: PedroBayVC@aol.com. Village corporation: Pedro Bay Corp., P.O. Box 47015, Pedro Bay, AK 99647, phone (907) 850-2323, fax (907) 850-2221.

Pilot Station

GPS: N61°56' W162°52'

Located on the Yukon River, 11 miles east of St. Marys and 26 miles west of Marshall in the Yukon-Kuskokwim Delta, 430 miles west of Anchorage. **Transportation**: Scheduled and charter air service from Bethel. **Population**: 582. **Zip code**: 99650. **Emergency Services**: Village Public Safety Officer, phone (907) 549-3213; Alaska State Troopers, St. Marys, phone (907) 438-2019; Pilot Station Health Clinic, phone (907) 549-3728; Volunteer Fire Department.

Climate: More maritime than continental, averaging 60 inches of snowfall and 16 inches of precipitation per year.

Private Aircraft: Airstrip 1 mile southwest; elev. 275 feet; length 2,520 feet; gravel; no fuel; unattended. Runway condition not monitored; visual inspection recommended prior to using. Heavy winds in fall and winter and crosswinds up to 50 mph year-round often limit access. No airport facilities. Transportation usually available for arriving passengers.

NOTE: Pilot Station prohibits the sale and importation of alcoholic beverages.

Visitor Facilities: Accommodations available. No restaurant, banking services or laundromat. Groceries, clothing, first-aid supplies and film available in the community. Arts and crafts available for purchase include carved ivory, wood carvings, grass and birch-bark baskets and masks. Fishing/hunting licenses available. No guide or major repair services. Rental transportation includes boats, off-road vehicles and charter aircraft. Fuel available includes propane, kerosene, marine gas and regular gasoline. No moorage facilities.

This Eskimo village was first called Ankachak, but later moved 0.3 mile upstream to another site called Potiliuk. R.H. Sargent of the U.S. Geological Survey noted that the village name was Pilot Station in 1916. Local riverboat pilots who used the village as a checkpoint were responsible for the name change.

Employment in Pilot Station is primarily related to the summer fishing season, supplemented with year-round enterprises and subsistence activities. There also is summer fire-fighting work with BLM.

Residents hunt black bear, moose, ptarmigan, waterfowl and porcupine, and fish for salmon, whitefish, blackfish, sheefish and pike. Berries are harvested in the fall. Income also is earned from trapping beaver, muskrat, marten, fox, lynx and wolverine.

Near Pilot Station is the old village site of Kurgpallermuit, designated by the Calista Regional Corp. as an historic place because it was occupied during bow-and-arrow wars between the Yukon and Coastal Eskimos.

Pilot Station is located within Yukon Delta National Wildlife Refuge. Favorite leisure activities include Eskimo dancing, square dancing, potlatches, and dog and snow machine racing.

Communications at Pilot Station, a second-class city incorporated in 1969, include phones, mail plane, radio and TV. The community is served by 2 churches and a school with grades kindergarten through 12 with enrollment of 198. There are community electric, water and sewer systems. Freight arrives by cargo plane and barge. Government address: City of Pilot Station, P.O. Box 5040, Pilot Station, AK 99650, phone (907) 549-3211, fax (907) 549-3014. Village corporation address: Pilot Station Inc., P.O. Box 5059, Pilot Station, AK 99650, phone (907) 549-3512. Village council: Pilot Station Traditional Council, P.O. Box 5040, Pilot Station, AK 99650, phone (907) 549-3512, e-mail: PilotStation@aitc.org.

Pitkas Point

GPS: N62°02' W163°17'

Located near the junction of the Yukon and Andreafsky rivers, 5 miles northwest of St. Marys and Andreafsky, 445 miles west of Anchorage. **Transportation:** Scheduled airline from Bethel to St. Marys airport. **Population:** 147. **Zip code:** 99658. **Emergency Services:** Alaska State Troopers, St. Marys, phone (907) 438-2019; Pitkas Point Health Clinic, phone (907) 438-2546.

Climate: Both maritime and continental. Temperatures range from -44°F to 83°F at St. Marys. Annual precipitation 16 inches, with 60 inches of snow.

Private Aircraft: See St. Marys airport.

Visitor Facilities: Accommodations and supplies available in St. Marys. No accommodations, restaurant or banking services in Pitkas Point. There is a laundromat with showers. No arts and crafts available for purchase. Fishing/hunting licenses available at St. Marys. No guide service available. Repair service available for marine engines and boats in St. Marys. Autos may be rented for $70 a day. Fuel available includes marine gas, diesel, propane and regular gasoline. No moorage facilities.

Eskimos who first settled here called the village Nigiklik, a Yup'ik word meaning "to the north." The settlement was first reported by the U.S. Geological Survey in 1898. It was later renamed for a trader who opened a general store there, which was a branch of the Northern Commercial Co. station at nearby Andreafsky. Pitkas Point is unincorporated.

The village economy peaks during the summer fishing season, when most residents are involved in commercial salmon fishing. Summer also provides work in construction and fire fighting for BLM. There also are a few full-time jobs held by local people.

Public assistance payments and subsistence activities supplement this income. Residents of the area hunt moose, bear, hare, duck, geese, swan and ptarmigan. In the fall, berries are harvested from the surrounding tundra. Some income also is derived from trapping beaver, fox and otter.

Pitkas Point is surrounded by Yukon

Delta National Wildlife Refuge.

The village is connected by a 17.7-mile road to St. Marys and Mountain Village. In winter, snow machines often are used for intervillage travel.

Communications in Pitkas Point include phones, mail plane and TV. The community is served by a Russian Orthodox church and a school with grades kindergarten through 12 with enrollment of 36. There is a community electric system. Water is hauled from the laundromat building. Sewage system is honey buckets. Freight arrives by cargo plane and barge. Government address: Native Village of Pitkas Point, P.O. Box 127, Saint Mary's, AK 99658, phone (907) 438-2833, fax (907) 438-2569, e-mail: PitkasPoint@aitc.org. Village corporation: Pitkas Point Native Corp., General Delivery, Pitkas Point, AK 99658, phone (907) 438-2232.

Platinum

GPS: N59°00' W161°49'

Located on Goodnews Bay, 11 miles southwest of Goodnews Bay village, 135 miles south of Bethel, 445 miles southwest of Anchorage. **Transportation**: Scheduled air service from Bethel. **Population**: 36. **Zip code**: 99651. **Emergency Services**: Platinum Health Clinic; Volunteer Fire Department.

Elevation: 20 feet. **Climate**: Summers are mild, with cool winds and some rain, according to one resident. Mean annual precipitation 22 inches; mean annual snowfall 43 inches.

Private Aircraft: Airstrip adjacent west; elev. 9 feet; 2 intersecting runways: length 3,304 and 1924 feet; gravel; no fuel; unattended. Runway condition not monitored; visual inspection recommended prior to using. Runway soft when wet.

NOTE: *Platinum prohibits the sale and importation of alcoholic beverages.*

Visitor Facilities: Arrangements may be made for accommodations at the school, (907) 979-9111. No restaurant, banking services or laundromat. Supplies available in the community. Fishing/hunting licenses available. No guide services or rental transportation. Fuel available includes diesel, propane and regular gasoline. No moorage facilities.

Platinum got its name from an important lode of platinum that was discovered nearby in 1926 by an Eskimo named Walter Smith. The community was described as a boom town with 50 residents in 1937. The population reached a high of 72 in 1950. Platinum is a second-class city, incorporated in 1975.

People in Platinum work seasonally in commercial fishing, and also in the stores, post office, school and at odd jobs. Subsistence hunting and fishing are also important.

Residents fish in Goodnews Bay or up the Goodnews River for king, red and chum salmon and Dolly Varden. Hunting is for seals, sea lions, walrus, foxes, rabbits, squirrels, otters, beavers, mink, muskrat, ptarmigan, geese, ducks and sandpipers.

A long beach at Platinum offers good beachcombing, and the community is located within Togiak National Wildlife Refuge.

Communications at Platinum include phones and mail plane. The community is served by a church and a school with grades preschool through 12 with enrollment of 9. There is a community electric system. Water is hauled from a central watering point. Sewage system is honey buckets. Freight arrives by barge or mail plane. Government address: City of Platinum, P.O. Box 2, Platinum, AK 99651, phone (907) 979-8114, fax (907) 979-8210. Village corporation address: Arviq Inc., P.O. Box 9, Platinum, AK 99651, phone (907) 979-8113, fax (907) 979-8114. Village council: Platinum Traditional Village, General Delivery, Platinum, AK 99651, phone (907) 979-8126, e-mail: Platinum@aitc.org.

Pope & Vannoy Landing

Located in the Western Cook Inlet area on Intricate Bay on Lake Iliamna, 25 miles from Iliamna. **Transportation**: Boat; air taxi from Iliamna. **Population**: 14. **Zip code**: Via Iliamna 99606. **Emergency Services**: Alaska State Troopers, Iliamna; Health Aide, Kohanok.

Private Aircraft: No airstrip. Float or

ski landings only.

Visitor Facilities: Accommodations and meals by advance reservation at Copper River Lodge, phone (907) 571-1248. Guide services available.

Pope & Vannoy Landing is a settlement primarily of Pope family members. Art Pope's son bought a cabin and moved here in 1955. He was followed by Pope's brother-in-law in 1957, Pope and his wife in 1965, and a granddaughter, Marlene DeNeut, in 1980. Another couple from Iliamna moved over in 1983. Residents of the area obtain their supplies from Anchorage.

Electricity is from individual generators. Water is hauled from the lake or a spring. Sewage system is outhouses.

Port Alsworth

GPS: N60°12' W154°19'

Located in the Western Cook Inlet area on Lake Clark, 22 miles northeast of Nondalton, 180 miles from Anchorage. **Transportation:** Boat; scheduled and charter air service from Iliamna; Lake Clark Air charter service, (907) 781-2211. **Population:** 88. **Zip code:** 99653. **Emergency Services:** Alaska State Troopers, phone (907) 571-1236; Health Aide, Iliamna, phone (907) 781-2218; Port Alsworth First Responders, phone (907) 850-2225.

Elevation: 230 feet. **Climate:** Summers are mild, according to one resident. Temperatures from 45°F to 80°F. Winters are usually mild, with temperatures from -30°F to 40°F. Mean annual precipitation 17 inches; mean annual snowfall 68 inches.

Private Aircraft: There are 2 private airstrips in the center of the community. Aviation fuel 80, 100 available from The Farm Lodge for emergencies only. Airstrip use is by prior permission only from Glen or Wayne Alsworth, phone (907) 781-2212/2204.

Visitor Facilities: Accommodations and meals at several area wilderness lodges: Alaska's Wilderness Lodge, (907) 781-2223; The Farm Lodge, (907) 781-2211; Koksetna Lodge, (907) 781-2227; Lakeside Lodge, (907) 781-2202; and Lake Country Lodge, (907) 283-5959. Meals available in the community. No banking services or laundry facilities. There are no stores; all supplies are obtained from Anchorage or Soldotna. Arts and crafts available for purchase include Indian and Eskimo hats, dolls, yo-yos, wood articles and local paintings. Fishing/hunting licenses available, as well as guide service. No major repairs available. Rental transportation includes boats and charter aircraft. No public moorage facilities.

Early Port Alsworth was a weather reporting station and stopover for airline flights to the Bristol Bay area, according to local residents. Pioneer bush pilot "Babe" Alsworth and his wife Mary, the settlement's first postmaster, were among the early settlers in the 1940s. They homesteaded on 160 acres and developed an airstrip and flying service. They also were involved in developing the Tanalian Bible Church and Camp. Port Alsworth now has several fishing lodges and is the local headquarters for Lake Clark National Park and Preserve. One resident describes it as "one of the finest places to live and visit in rural Alaska."

Most residents make their living either directly or indirectly from tourism. Employment is through the lodges, flying service, school, commercial fishing and a few local businesses.

Local attractions include 40-mile-long Lake Clark, one of the spawning grounds for the Bristol Bay red salmon run; the ruins of historic Kijik village, listed on the National Register of Historic Places; and picturesque Tanalian Falls. Activities include hiking, wildlife photography, bird watching, river rafting, fishing, cross-country skiing, sledding, snowmobiling and hunting for moose, caribou bear and small game.

From Anchorage, air access to Port Alsworth is by way of 1,000-foot Lake Clark Pass through the Aleutian Range.

Lake Clark National Park and Preserve offers a prime wilderness experience. The area boasts steaming volcanoes, rugged mountains, craggy peaks, alpine valleys, blue-green glaciers, free-flowing rivers and sparkling lakes. Its wildlife includes eagles, hawks, waterfowl and seabirds;

grayling, northern pike, trout and salmon; bear, moose, caribou and Dall sheep. For more information write: Superintendent, Lake Clark National Park and Preserve, 4230 University Dr., Suite 311, Anchorage, AK 99508.

Communications at Port Alsworth, which is unincorporated, include phones, mail plane, radio and TV. The community is served by Tanalian Bible Church and a school with grades I through 12 with enrollment of 27. Electricity is from individual generators, water from private wells. Sewage system is septic tanks. Freight arrives by cargo plane and an occasional small barge. Village corporation address: Tanalian Inc., General Delivery, Port Alsworth, AK 99653, phone (907) 781-2054, fax (907) 781-2215.

Port Clarence

GPS: N65°15' W166°30'

Located on Point Spencer on the Bering Sea coast, 80 miles northwest of Nome, 560 miles west of Fairbanks. **Transportation**: U.S. Coast Guard aircraft or charter air service from Nome. **Population**: 22. **Zip code**: 99762. **Emergency Services**: Alaska State Troopers, Nome; U.S. Coast Guard.

Elevation: 10 feet. **Climate**: Mean annual precipitation 10 inches; mean annual snowfall 47 inches. Snow starts falling in late October; last snowfall usually in late May.

Private Aircraft: Airstrip 1 mile northeast; elev. 10 feet; length 4,500 feet; asphalt; no fuel. *NOTE: Closed to the public. Available to private aircraft only in emergencies (contact 122.8 MMZ), unless prior permission is obtained from Coast Guard District 17 headquarters in Juneau, phone (907) 463-2000.*

Visitor Facilities: None.

Port Clarence is a U.S. Coast Guard loran station with no public facilities. The airfield originally was constructed for bombers in WWII. In 1961 the Coast Guard station was built to aid in navigation for ships in the Bering Sea.

Residents of nearby communities use the Point Spencer spit during the summer fishing season.

Portage Creek

GPS: N58°54' W157°43'

Located 30 miles southeast of Dillingham, 320 miles southwest of Anchor age. **Transportation**: Boat; charter air service from Dillingham. **Population**: 18. **Zip code**: 99695. **Emergency Services**: Alaska State Troopers, Dillingham; Kanakanak Hospital, Dillingham.

Climate: Transition zone, characterized by cloudy skies, mild temperatures and moderately heavy precipitation. Average summer temperatures from 30°F to 66°F; average winter temperatures from 4°F to 30°F. Annual precipitation from 20 to 35 inches. Most precipitation occurs during the summer months.

Private Aircraft: 2 airstrips east of village; elev. 137 feet; length 1,920 and 1,470 feet; gravel; no fuel; unattended. Runway condition not monitored; visual inspection recommended prior to landing. Runway surface soft and muddy during spring breakup or heavy rains; runway edges subject to erosion. Watch out for crosswind when landing.

Visitor Facilities: None.

This site was long used as an overnight camp. As the name implies, Portage Creek is part of a summer route from the head of Nushagak Bay to the mouth of the Kvichak River which avoided the open waters of Bristol Bay and a long trip around Etolin Point.

The first residence was built in 1961. At that time a few families had left Koliganek and other villages up to Nushagak River for settlement in Portage Creek. A school was established in 1963.

Portage Creek is an example of a practice once common along the Nushagak River as well as in many other areas. Before the advent of public institutions and development, villages were extremely mobile and the relocation of a few families could signal the beginning or ending of a village. Passage of the Alaska Native Claims Settlement Act and construction of schools have ended this practice except for summer fish camps.

The primary employment for Portage Creek residents is the fishing industry, but the entire population depends to some extent on subsistence hunting and fishing. Species commonly harvested include salmon, pike, whitefish, rainbow trout, moose, caribou, duck, geese, crane. There is also berry picking in season. Varieties available include salmonberries, blackberries, cranberries and blueberries.

There is superb king salmon fishing from the riverbank in front of the village in June and early July. Arrangements for guided fishing in the area are best made in Dillingham.

Land in the Portage Creek area is owned by the local Native corporation, Choggiung Ltd., which requires that a permit be obtained for any public use of its lands.

Communications in Portage Creek, which is unincorporated, include a phone in the council house , (907) 842-5966, mail plane, radio and TV. The community is served by a Russian Orthodox church and Ohgsenakale School with grades kindergarten through 12 with enrollment of 11. Electricity is from individual generators in summer and the school in winter. Water is hauled from wells. Sewage system is outhouses. Freight arrives by barge or charter plane. Government address: Portage Creek Village Council, P.O. Box PCA, Portage Creek, AK 99576, phone and fax (907) 842-2564, e-mail: PortageCreek@aitc.org. Village corporation address: Portage Creek Association, c/o Choggiung Ltd., Portage Creek, AK 99576, phone (907) 842-5218, fax (907) 842-5462.

Quinhagak

GPS: N59°45' W161°53'

(QUIN-a-hock) Located on the southeast shore of Kuskokwim Bay, 70 miles south of Bethel, 425 miles west of Anchorage. **Transportation**: Boat; scheduled and charter air service from Bethel. **Population**: 582. **Zip code**: 99655. **Emergency Services**: Police, phone (907) 556-8314; Quinhagak Health Clinic, phone (907) 556-8320; Quinhagak EMS Quick Response Team, phone (907) 556-8448. Volunteer Fire Department.

Private Aircraft: Airstrip 1 mile northeast; elev. 10 feet; length 2,600 feet; gravel; no fuel; unattended. Runway condition not monitored; visual inspection rec-

ommended prior to using. Potholes entire length of runway. Equipment occasionally on runway. No airport facilities or public transportation into village.

NOTE: Quinhagak prohibits possession of alcoholic beverages.

Visitor Facilities: Lodging is sometimes available at the high school and washeteria. Laundry and shower facilities available. Groceries, clothing, first-aid supplies, hardware, film and sporting goods available in the community. No restaurants or banking facilities. Arts and crafts available include carved ivory, grass baskets and Eskimo yoyos. Fishing/hunting licenses available, as well as guide service. The village corporation has expanded guide opportunities for fishing in the world-class Kanektok River. Marine engine repair available, also air charter service. No rental transportation. Fuel available: marine gas, diesel, propane, regular gasoline. No moorage facilities.

Private sportfishing is prohibited on all property owned by the village corporation. All sportfishing must be from a boat, on state-owned land or with a guide.

This Eskimo village was reported by Lieutenant Sarichev in 1826. In 1975, Quinhagak was incorporated as a second-class city.

The village is located within Togiak National Wildlife Refuge.

Communications in Quinhagak include phones, mail plane, radio and TV. The school has enrollment of 146. There is a community electric system. Water is hauled from the washeteria. Sewage system is honey buckets. Freight arrives by barge. Government address: City of Quinhagak, P.O. Box 90, Quinhagak, AK 99655, phone (907) 556-8202, fax (907) 556-8166, e-mail: mukkwn@aol.com. Village corporation address: Qanirtuuq Inc., P.O. Box 69, Quinhagak, AK 99655, phone (907) 556-8289, fax (907) 556-8814. Village council: Native Village of Quinhagak, P.O. Box 149, Quinhagak, AK 99655, phone (907) 556-8165, fax (907) 556-8166, e-mail: Kwinhagak@aitc.org.

Red Devil

GPS: N61°45' W157°18'

Located on the upper Kuskokwim River

at the mouth of Red Devil Creek, 8 miles west of Sleetmute, 73 miles east of Aniak, 250 miles west of Anchorage. **Transportation**: Boat; scheduled and charter air service from Bethel or Aniak. **Population**: 44. **Zip code**: 99656. **Emergency Services**: Alaska State Troopers, Aniak; Health Care at Sleetmute or Crooked Creek; Volunteer Fire Department.

Climate: Continental. At nearby Sleetmute, temperatures range between -58°F and 90°F. Annual precipitation is 20 inches, with 85 inches of snow.

Private Aircraft: Airstrip 1 mile northwest; elev. 210 feet; length 4,750 feet; gravel; no fuel; unattended. Runway condition not monitored; visual inspection recommended prior to using. No airport facilities or public transportation.

Visitor Facilities: Accommodations and meals available. No banking services or laundromat available. Groceries available at combination roadhouse/bar/store. Handsewn fur items available for purchase. Fishing/hunting licenses available. No guide or repair services. Rental transportation includes boats and charter aircraft through local air service. Fuel available: marine gas, diesel and regular gasoline. No moorage facilities.

NOTE: Land use permits are required to use lands owned by the Kuskokwim Corp. Uses include fishing, temporary camping, seasonal campsite, land crossing and research. There is a $100 administration fee. Big game hunting fee is $400. Seasonal campsite permits $50, annual use fee $250. For further information, contact the Kuskokwim Corp., 2000 W. International Airport Road, Suite C-9, Anchorage, Ak 99502, phone (907) 243-2944, or in Aniak phone 675-4275.

The village was named after the Red Devil Mine, which was established in 1933 by Hans Halverson after numerous quicksilver deposits were discovered earlier in the surrounding Kilbuck-Kuskokwim Mountains. The mine operated from 1939 to 1946 as the Kuskokwim Mining Co. and was reopened in 1952 as the DeCourcy Mountain Mining Co. Inc. The mine was last worked in 1971, when the mercury, cinnabar and antimony

reserves were depleted. By that year the mine had produced some 2.7 million pounds of mercury—Alaska's total output. By 1971 a community had developed at the mining site. A school was established in 1958. The population was 152 in 1960, but declined when the mine closed.

In the summer of 1989 access to the inactive mine was closed because of a chemical hazard. An investigation revealed stored quantities of copper sulfate, potash and sodium hydroxide. In 1988, the federal Bureau of Land Management posted signs warning of potential health hazards and later removed 2 transformers containing polychlorinated byphenyls, or PCBS.

Employment opportunities in Red Devil today are limited. A few residents work for the school district, post office, clinic, store and flying service. There also is employment through the BLM's summer fire-fighting program. This income is supplemented by public assistance payments and subsistence activities. Local residents hunt bear, moose, caribou, rabbit, ptarmigan and waterfowl, and fish for king, chum, red and silver salmon, sheefish and whitefish. Trapping for marten, beaver, mink, wolverine, fox, otter and lynx also provides income.

Communications in Red Devil, which is unincorporated, include a phone, (907) 447-9901), mail plane, radio and TV. The community has a school with grades preschool through 12, but no church. Electricity is supplied by Middle Kuskokwim Electric Corp.. Water is from private wells or the river. Sewage system is septic tanks or privies. Freight arrives by cargo plane and barge. Village corporation address: The Kuskokwim Corp., 2000 W. International Airport Rd., Suite C-9, Anchorage, AK 99502, phone (907) 243-2944, or in Aniak phone (907) 675-4275.

Russian Mission

GPS: N61°47' W161°19'

Located on the Yukon River, 70 miles north of Bethel, 225 miles westnorthwest of Anchorage. **Transportation**: Scheduled and charter air service from Bethel.

Population: 307. **Zip code**: 99657. **Emergency Services**: Village Public Safety Officer; Alaska State Troopers, St. Marys; Russian Mission Health Clinic, phone (907) 584-5529; Volunteer Fire Department. **Elevation**: 50 feet. **Climate**: Both maritime and continental, with a greater maritime influence. Annual precipitation 16 inches; annual snowfall 60 inches. **Private Aircraft**: Airstrip adjacent south; elev. 70 feet; length 2,700 feet; gravel; attended. Runway condition monitored, but visual inspection recommended prior to using. Airport has lighting system. No public transportation to village; 500 yards to village.

NOTE: Russian Mission prohibits the sale and importation of alcoholic beverages.

Visitor Facilities: Arrangements can be made for accommodations in private homes. There is 1 room available at the Russian Mission Pump House, run by the City of Russian Mission, (907) 584-5111. Lodging also may be available at the school, (907) 584-5615, and clinic, (907) 584-5529. Food is available at various locations. Laundromat available. No banking services. Groceries, limited clothing, hardware and sporting goods available at P&K Trading Post and Native Store, Russian Mission Native Corporation, A&M's Outfit and Duffy's. Arts and crafts available for purchase include birch-bark baskets, masks and many other Native arts. Fishing/hunting licenses available. No guide services or rental transportation. Marine engine and boat repairs available. Fuel available: diesel, propane and regular gasoline. Moorage facilities available. Russian Mission has been described as "a wonderful place to visit, with friendly people and you are welcome anytime to stay."

The first Russian-American Co. fur-trading post was established at this village in 1837, but the Eskimos held the outsiders responsible for the smallpox epidemic that followed in 1838-39 and massacred the post's inhabitants. The first Russian Orthodox mission in the interior of Alaska was established here in 1851 by a Russian-Aleut priest, Jacob Netzuetov.

Originally called Pokrovskaya Mission, the title Russian Mission replaced the previous name in 1900. The village was incorporated as a second-class city in 1970.

Employment opportunities in Russian Mission are concentrated in commercial fishing and public employment programs. Most residents of the community are directly or indirectly involved in commercial fishing from June through September. There are a few full-time jobs at the local stores, the post office, the school and the clinic. Summer work also includes fire fighting for BLM. This income is supplemented by subsistence activities. Residents hunt moose, black bear, ptarmigan, waterfowl, porcupine and rabbit. They fish for salmon, blackfish, whitefish, sheefish, pike and lush (burbot). Berries are harvested in the fall. Income also comes from trapping beaver, mink, lynx, marten and fox.

Communications include phones, mail plane, radio and TV. The community is served by Russian Orthodox and Roman Catholic churches and a school with grades preschool through 12 with enrollment of 95. There are community electric, water and sewage systems. Freight arrives by cargo plane and barge. Government address: City of Russian Mission, P.O. Box 49, Russian Mission, AK 99657, phone (907) 584-5111, fax (907) 584-5476. Village corporation: Russian Mission Native Corp., P.O. Box 48, Russian Mission, AK 99657, phone (907) 584-5885, fax (907) 584-5311. Village council: Russian Mission Traditional Council, P.O. Box 09, Russian Mission, AK 99657, phone (907) 584-5511, fax (907) 584-5511, e-mail: RussianMission@aitc.org.

St. Marys

GPS: N62°04' W163°18'

Located on the Andreafsky River near its confluence with the Yukon River, 37 miles northwest of Marshall, 450 miles west-northwest of Anchorage. **Transportation**: Boat up and down lower Yukon; scheduled and charter air service from Bethel and Anchorage; road from Mountain Village. **Population**: 482. **Zip code**: 99658. **Emergency Services**: Police, phone (907)

438-2911; Alaska State Troopers, phone (907) 438-2019; St. Marys Health Clinic, phone (907) 438-2347; Volunteer Fire Department, phone (907) 438-2911.

Elevation: 100 feet. **Climate**: St. Marys climate is both maritime and continental, with a greater maritime influence. Mean annual precipitation is 17 inches. Mean annual snowfall is 69 inches.

Private Aircraft: Airport 4 miles west; elev. 311 feet; 2 runways: length 6,003 and 1900 feet; gravel; fuel available; attended variable hours. Runway conditions reported only during duty hours. Airport has passenger and freight terminals, ticket counter and restrooms; no traffic control tower. Hub airport of the Lower Yukon, served by 7 airlines. Taxi service to town.

Visitor Facilities: Food and lodging available at Bays Bed & Breakfast, (907) 438-2048; and the Road House. Meals also available at Papa's Pizza, St. Marys Marina and The Kids Center. Laundry facilities available. No banking services. Groceries, clothing, first-aid supplies, hardware, film and sporting goods available in the community. Arts and crafts available for purchase include carved ivory, grass baskets, beaded jewelry and hand-sewn skin garments. Fishing/hunting licenses available. Guide service available. Marine engine, boat and aircraft repair available. Charter aircraft available. Fuel available: marine gas, propane, regular gasoline. Public moorage facilities available.

St. Marys' history actually begins some 90 miles downriver at Akulurak. In 1903, Jesuit missionaries set up a mission at Akulufak to educate and care for children orphaned by a flu epidemic in 1900-01. Akulurak is an Eskimo word meaning "in-between place," aptly describing the settlement on an island in a slough connecting 2 arms of the Yukon River. The mission school flourished and by 1915 there were 70 full-time students. Over the years, though, the slough surrounding Akulurak silted in so severely that in 1948 the mission and village moved to higher ground.

Present-day St. Marys was chosen as the new mission site. Materials from an abandoned hotel built during the gold rush were used to construct the new mission and several village homes. The mission closed in 1987.

The names St. Marys and Andreafsky are sometimes confused. Andreafsky was established in 1899 as a supply depot and winter quarters for Northern Commercial Co.'s riverboat fleet. The village took its name from the Andrea family, who settled on the river, originally called Clear River. The family built a Russian Orthodox church in the village. When St. Marys was incorporated as a first-class city in 1967, Andreafsky was not included within the new city's boundaries and remained a separate, unincorporated community until 1980.

Employment in St. Marys peaks during the summer fishing season, when 70 percent of the residents are involved in some form of commercial fishing activity. Other seasonal employment includes construction projects and fire fighting for BLM. Other jobs are with the school district, the city, airlines, state government and Native corporations. Cash income is supplemented by subsistence activities. Residents hunt for moose, bear, duck, geese, swan and ptarmigan; and fish for salmon, sheefish, blackfish, whitefish, grayling and trout. In the fall berries are harvested. Income also is earned from trapping beaver, fox, mink, otter and muskrat.

St. Marys has become a subregional center for air transportation. Its airport is capable of handling aircraft as large as a Boeing 727. St. Marys also is linked by a 17.7-mile road to Mountain Village.

St. Marys is surrounded by Yukon Delta National Wildlife Refuge. Locally, birdwatchers can see jaegers, falcons and numerous smaller passerines. There is good fishing on the Andreafsky River for Dolly Varden, grayling, pike and salmon. Favorite activities include annual potlatches, the Yukon 150 Dog Race in February and the Andreafsky 90 Sled Dog Race, held in mid-March.

In the slough opposite the dock is a burial ground for old river steamers. Rusting boilers can be seen above the water.

Communications in St. Marys include phones, mail plane, radios and TV. The community has 2 Roman Catholic churches, public schools with grades kindergarten through 12 with enrollment of 131, and a Roman Catholic high school. There are community electricity, water and sewer systems. Freight arrives in the community by cargo plane and barge. Government address: City of St. Marys, P.O. Box 209, St. Marys, AK 99658, phone (907) 438-2515, fax (907) 438-2719, e-mail: waltonksm@yahoo.com. Village corporation: St. Marys Native Corp., P.O. Box 162, St. Marys, AK 99658, phone and fax (907) 438-2315. Nerklikmute Native Corp., P.O. Box 87, St. Marys, AK 99658; phone (907) 438-2332, fax (907) 438-2919. Village council: Yupiit of Andreafsky, P.O. Box 88, St. Marys, AK 99658, phone (907) 438-2312, fax (907) 438-2512. e-mail: Andreafski@aitc.org. Algaaciq Tribal Government, P.O. Box 48, St. Marys, AK 99658, phone (907) 438-2932, fax (907) 438-2227, e-mail: Algaaciq@aol.com.

St. Michael

GPS: N63°29' W162°07'

Located on St. Michael Island, 48 miles southwest of Unalakleet, 125 miles southwest of Nome and 420 miles northwest of Anchorage. **Transportation**: Boat; snow machine; scheduled and charter air service from Unalakleet and Nome. **Population**: 368. **Zip code**: 99659. **Emergency Services**: Village Public Safety Officer; Alaska State Troopers, Unalakleet, phone (907) 624-3646; St. Michael Health Clinic, phone (907) 923-3311; Volunteer Fire Department.

Elevation: 30 feet. **Climate**: Subarctic with maritime influence in summer, when Norton Sound is ice free (usually June to November), and a cold continental influence during the winter. Summers are moist, with clouds and fog common, but annual precipitation is only 12 inches, much of which occurs in July, August and September. Annual snowfall averages 38 inches, with most of it during October and February. Winter temperatures average -4°F to 16°F; summer temperatures average 40°F to 60°F.

Private Aircraft: Airstrip adjacent

north; elev. 93 feet; length 4,000 feet; gravel; no fuel; unattended; runway condition not monitored; visual inspection recommended prior to using.

NOTE: St. Michael prohibits the sale and importation of alcoholic beverages.

Visitor Facilities: No hotel or restaurant. Arrangements for accommodations at the school or private homes can sometimes be made by contacting the school principal, (907) 923-3041, or the city office (907) 923-3211. There is a washeteria. Supplies available in the community. Fishing/hunting licenses available. Information on other visitor services and facilities unavailable.

The Russians established a stockade post there in 1833, named after a governor of the Russian-American colony. Its name soon became Michaelovski or Redoubt St. Michael, and the post was the northernmost Russian settlement in Alaska. The Eskimo village of Tachik was located to the northeast.

During the gold rush era at the end of the century, St. Michael became the major gateway to the Interior via the Yukon River. A U.S. military post, Fort St. Michael, was established in 1897, but was closed in 1922. As many as 10,000 people were said to live in St. Michael during the Nome gold rush. The village remained an important transshipment point until the Alaska Railroad was built. St. Michael also was a popular trading post for Eskimos trading for Western goods.

Remnants of St. Michael's historic past can still be seen. Three Russian-built houses, the hulks of steamboats and several old cemeteries remain. The old Russian church and most military buildings have been torn down, and an old cannon and other Russian artifacts were moved to Sitka. The sites of the old U.S. fort and the Russian redoubt are on the National Register of Historic Places.

St. Michael is the closest deep-water port to the Yukon and Kuskokwim rivers. It remains a transfer point for freight hauled from Seattle on large oceangoing barges to be placed on smaller river barges or shipped to other Norton Sound villages. St. Michael incorporated in 1969 as a second-class city.

St. Michael's economy is based on subsistence food harvest supplemented by parttime jobs. Residents harvest sea mammals, including seals and beluga whales. Moose and caribou are important winter staples. Summer fishing provides salmon, whitefish, tomcod and herring. Waterfowl, particularly ducks and geese, are hunted in nearby marshes. The tundra yields salmonberries, blackberries, blueberries, raspberries and cranberries.

St. Michael is served by Roman Catholic and Assembly of God churches, as well as a school with grades preschool through 12 with enrollment of 116. There is a community electric system. Water is hauled from a central watering point. Sewage system is honey buckets. Freight arrives by barge and plane. Government address: City of St. Michael, P.O. Box 59070, St. Michael, AK 99659, phone (907) 923-3222, fax (907) 923-2284, e-mail: vrwshngton@aol.com. Village corporation: St. Michael Native Corp., P.O. Box 59049, St. Michael, AK 99659, phone (907) 923-2304, fax (907) 923-2406, e-mail: StMichael@aitc.org. Village council: Native Village of St. Michael, P.O. Box 59050, St. Michael, AK 99659, phone (907) 923-2304, fax (907) 923-2406, e-mail: StMichael@aitc.org.

Savoonga

GPS: N63°42′ W170°29′

(Suh-VOON-guh) Located on St. Lawrence Island in the Bering Sea, 39 miles southeast of Gambell, 164 miles west of Nome and 700 miles west of Fairbanks. **Transportation**: Scheduled and charter air service from Nome. **Population**: 652. **Zip code**: 99769. **Emergency Services**: Police, phone (907) 984-6011; Savoonga Health Clinic, phone (907) 984-6513; Savoonga First Responders/Rescue Team, phone (907) 984-6513/6234/6333. Volunteer Fire Department, phone (907) 984-6234.

Climate: Cool, moist, subarctic maritime with some continental influences during winter, when the Bering Sea freezes. Mean annual precipitation 11 inches; mean annual snowfall 58 inches. Winter

temperatures average -7°F to 11°F; summer temperatures average 40°F to 51°F.

Private Aircraft: Airstrip 2 miles south; elev. 53 feet; length 4,402 feet; gravel; no fuel; unattended. Passenger terminal at airport. There is usually transportation into the village with local people.

NOTE: Savoonga prohibits the sale and importation of alcoholic beverages.

Visitor Facilities: Accommodations at Alunga Lodge, contact Ora Gologerger, (907) 984-6520, and at a city facility with kitchen, contact the City of Savoonga, phone (907) 984-6614. Washeteria with showers available. No banking services. Groceries, clothing, first-aid supplies, hardware, film and sporting goods available at Savoonga Native Store and Wayne Penaya's Grocery Store. Arts and crafts available for purchase include carved ivory, baleen baskets, hand-sewn skin garments and Eskimo artifacts. No repair services. Arrangements may be made to rent off-road vehicles. Fuel available: marine gas, diesel, kerosene, propane, unleaded and regular gasoline. Moorage on beach.

NOTE: Visitors to Gambell and Savoonga who wish to leave the city limits are required to pay a one-time fee of $25. The entire island is private property; the fee helps monitor use and serves as a registration system to make sure people don't get lost. The corporation also requires that any stories or photographs involving areas outside the towtsite be submitted for prepublication approval.

St. Lawrence Island has been inhabited for several thousand years. The Siberian Yup'ik Eskimos lived by subsistence for many years and had little contact with the rest of the world until European traders began to frequent the area. In the 18th and 19th centuries, St. Lawrence Island supported a population of about 4,000 people. A tragic famine from 1878 to 1880 decimated the population, and in 1903 only 261 people were reported on the entire island.

A herd of 70 reindeer was introduced to the island in 1900. The herd grew during the next 40 years, increasing to a peak of 10,000 animals. The reindeer tended to remain on the eastern side of the island, and managing them from Gambell became impossible. A reindeer camp was established at Savoonga, 4 miles west of the abandoned village of Kookoolik, in 1916. Good hunting and trapping in the area attracted more residents. The population of Savoonga steadily increased, and in the 1980 census it surpassed that of Gambell. The community is built on wet, soft tundra and boardwalks crisscross the village, providing dry routes to all buildings. In 1969 Savoonga was incorporated as a second-class city.

The economy of Savoonga is based largely on subsistence hunting, with some cash income. Best known for its walrus hunts, Savoonga is called the "Walrus Capital of the World." The community holds a Walrus Festival every spring. Residents also hunt bowhead and gray whales in the spring and fall. During summer, the people fish, crab, hunt birds, gather eggs and harvest various seafoods, greens and berries. Seals, fish and crabs are harvested through the winter. Arctic foxes are trapped as a source of income, but there is no other commercial hunting or fishing. Reindeer roam free on the island. There are a few jobs in the village with the city, Native corporation, school and store.

St. Lawrence Islanders are famous for their ivory carvings, which are a popular retail item. Artifacts found at some of the older village sites on the island also are sold for income.

The area is rich in wildlife: polar bears, whales, walruses, seals and seabirds. Bird watching is popular with visitors, who come to view and photograph the 2.7 million seabirds that nest on the island.

Communications in Savoonga include phones, mail plane, radio and TV. There is a community electric system. Water is hauled from 3 watering points. Sewage system is honey buckets. The community is served by Presbyterian and Seventh Day Adventist churches and 2 schools with grades kindergarten through 12 with enrollment of 178. Freight arrives by plane, barge and ship. Government address: City of Savoonga, P.O. Box 40, Savoonga, AK 99769, phone (907) 984-6614, fax (907) 984-6411. Village corporation: Savoonga Native Corp., P.O. Box 160, Savoonga, AK 99769, phone (907) 984-6613. Village council: Native Village of Savoonga, P.O. Box 120, Savoonga, AK 99769, phone (907) 984-6414, fax (907) 984-6027, e-mail: Savoonga@aitc.org.

Scammon Bay

GPS: N61°50' W165°35'

Located on the Kun River 1 mile from the Bering Sea in the Yukon-Kuskokwim Delta, 145 miles northwest of Bethel, 525 miles west of Anchorage. **Transportation**: Scheduled and charter air service from Bethel. **Population**: 501. **Zip code**: 99662. **Emergency Services**: Police, phone (907) 558-5529; Alaska State Troopers, Bethel, phone (907) 543-2294; Scammon Bay Health Clinic, phone (907) 558-5511; Volunteer Fire Department.

Elevation: 22 feet. **Climate**: Maritime. Mean January temperature 9°F; mean July temperature 49°F. Temperatures range between -25°F and 79°F. Annual precipitation 14 inches; annual snowfall 65 inches. Easterly winds during the winter cause severe wind chill.

Private Aircraft: Airstrip adjacent north; elev. 14 feet; length 3,000 feet; gravel and dirt; no fuel; unattended. Runway and seaplane conditions not monitored; visual inspection recommended prior to using. Road to river crosses runway. Runway soft during breakup, after rains and during extreme high tides. No airport facilities or public transportation into village.

NOTE: Scammon Bay prohibits possession of alcoholic beverages.

Visitor Facilities: Arrangements may be made for accommodations at the school, (907) 558-5312. No restaurant, laundromat or banking services. Groceries, clothing, first-aid supplies, hardware, film and sporting goods available at Askinuk Store, (907) 558-5211. Arts and crafts available for purchase include carved ivory, grass baskets and masks. No guide services. Marine engine repair available. Arrangements may be made to rent autos. Fuel available: marine gas, diesel, propane and regular gasoline. No moorage facilities.

The Eskimo name for this village is

Mariak. The site is believed to have been settled in the 1700s because it had high ground and good water. The village was named after the nearby bay which honors Capt. Charles M. Scammon, who served as marine chief of the Western Union Telegraph expedition in Alaska in 1865-67. Scammon Bay was incorporated as a second-class city in 1967.

Peak economic activity in Scammon Bay occurs during the summer fishing season, when most residents are involved in commercial fishing. Other employment opportunities in the summer include fire fighting for BLM and various construction projects. There are a few year-round jobs with the city, stores, school and village corporation.

This income is supplemented by subsistence activities. Residents hunt beluga whale, seal, geese, swans, cranes, ducks, loons and ptarmigan. Fishing yields salmon, whitefish, blackfish, needlefish, herring, smelt and tomcod. Berries are harvested in the fall.

Scammon Bay is located within Yukon Delta National Wildlife Refuge. Winter trails connect Scammon Bay with nearby Hooper Bay and Chevak.

Communications in Scammon Bay include phones and mail plane. The community is served by Roman Catholic and Covenant churches and a school with grades kindergarten through 12 with enrollment of 163. There are community electricity, water and sewer systems. Freight arrives by cargo plane and barge. Government address: City of Scammon Bay, P.O. Box 90, Scammon Bay, AK 99662, phone (907) 558-5529, fax (907) 558-5626, e-mail: Faguchak@aol.com. Village corporation: Askinuk Corp., P.O. Box 89, Scammon Bay, AK 99662; phone (907) 558-5628, fax (907) 558-5963. Village council: Scammon Bay Traditional Council, P.O. Box 126, Scammon Bay, AK 99662, phone (907) 558-5113, fax (907) 558-5626, e-mail: ScammonBay@aitc.org.

Shaktoolik

GPS: N64°20′ W161°09′

(Shack-TOO-lick) Located on the east shore of Norton Sound, 33 miles north of Unalakleet, 180 miles east of Nome, 410 miles northwest of Fairbanks. **Transportation**: Boat; scheduled and charter air service from Nome or Unalakleet. **Population**: 227. **Zip code**: 99771. **Emergency Services**: Village Public Safety Officer; Alaska State Troopers, Unalakleet, phone (907) 624-3646; Shaktoolik Health Clinic, Health Aide, phone (907) 955-3511; Volunteer Fire Department, phone (907) 955-3661.

Climate: Subarctic with considerable maritime influence when Norton Sound is ice-free, usually from May to October. Winters cold and relatively dry, with an average of 43 inches of snowfall. Winds from the east and northeast predominate. Summers cool, with most precipitation occurring in July, August and September. Average annual precipitation is 14 inches. Winter temperatures average between -4°F and 11°F. Summer temperatures average between 47°F and 62°F.

Private Aircraft: Airstrip 3 miles northwest; elev. 15 feet; length 2,220 feet; gravel; no fuel; unattended. Runway condition not monitored; visual inspection recommended prior to using. No airport facilities. Public transportation available to village.

NOTE: Shaktoolik prohibits the sale and importation of alcoholic beverages.

Visitor Facilities: No hotel, restaurant or banking services. Arrangements may be made to stay at 1 bed and breakfast, in private homes, or on the school floor. Laundromat with showers available. Groceries, clothing, first-aid supplies, hardware, film and sporting goods available in the community. Arts and crafts available for purchase include carved ivory, wooden berry picking buckets, wooden masks, Eskimo dolls, parkas, mukluks and beadwork. Fishing/hunting licenses available. No guide services. Residents do their own marine engine, boat and auto repairs. Arrangements may be made to rent private off-road vehicles and boats. Fuel available: diesel, white gas, propane and regular gasoline. No moorage facilities.

Shaktoolik was first mapped in 1842-44 by Lt. L.A. Zagoskin of the Imperial Russian Navy, who called it Tshaktogmyut.

The village moved from a site 6 miles up the Shaktoolik River to the river mouth in 1933, but was subject to erosion and wind damage at that location. In 1967 the village moved again to a more sheltered location 2.5 miles to the north. Shaktoolik is a second-class city, incorporated in 1969.

The economy is subsistence, supplemented by part-time earnings from jobs with the city, school, construction, store, airlines and Native corporation. About 1,500 privately owned reindeer provide meat, hides and additional income. Residents harvest moose, caribou, whales, seals, squirrels, rabbits, waterfowl and ptarmigans. They fish for salmon, arctic char, tomcod, flounder, sculpin, herring and smelt, and in the fall they harvest berries.

The Iditarod Trail passes through Shaktoolik and links the village to Unalakleet and coastal villages to the west along Norton Sound.

Cape Denbigh, 12 miles to the northeast, is the site of Iyatayat, a national historic landmark 6,000 to 8,000 years old. Another attraction is Besboro Island off the coast, site of a major seabird colony.

Communications in Shaktoolik include phones, mail plane, radio and TV. The community is served by Covenant and Assembly of God churches and a school with grades preschool through 12 with enrollment of 65. There are community electric and water systems. Sewage system is flush toilets and seepage pits. Freight arrives by cargo plane. Government address: City of Shaktoolik, P.O. Box 10, Shaktoolik, AK 99771, phone (907) 955-3441, fax (907) 955-3221. Village corporation: Shaktoolik Native Corp., P.O. Box 46, Shaktoolik, AK 99771, phone (907) 955-3241, fax (907) 955-3243. Village council: Native Village of Shaktoolik, P.O. Box 100, Shaktoolik, AK 99771-0100, phone (907) 955-3701, fax (907) 955-2352. e-mail: Shaktoolik@aitc.org.

Sheldon Point

(see Nunam Iqua)

Shishmaref

GPS: N66°15' W166°04'

Located on Sarichef Island between the Chukchi Sea and Shishmaref Inlet, 5 miles from the mainland, 100 miles southwest of Kotzebue, 120 miles north of Nome, 550 miles west of Fairbanks. **Transportation**: Scheduled and charter air service daily from Nome. **Population**: 547. **Zip code**: 99772. **Emergency Services**: Police, phone (907) 649-3411; Alaska State Troopers, Nome, phone (907) 443-2835; Katherine Miksruaq Health Clinic, phone (907) 649-3311; Volunteer Fire Department.

Elevation: 20 feet. **Climate**: Transitional zone; winters windy, cold and dry, and snowfall averaging only 33 inches. Winter temperatures average -12°F to 2°F. Spring can be foggy, with west winds prevailing and temperatures averaging 47°F to 54°F. Average annual precipitation is 8 inches.

Private Aircraft: Airstrip 1/2 mile southwest; elev. 8-10 feet; length 5,000 feet; asphalt; no fuel; unattended. Runway condition not monitored; visual inspection recommended prior to using. All air travel is "weather permitting," says one resident.

NOTE: Shishmarek prohibits the sale and importation of alcoholic beverages.

Visitor Facilities: Accommodations available in trailer owned by Nayokpuk General Store, in private homes, on school floor and at the Shishmaref city hall. Food is available at Che-Che's Snack Bar. No banking services. Washeteria available. Groceries, clothing, first-aid supplies, hardware, film and sporting goods available at Shishmaref Native Store and Nayokpuk General Store. Arts and crafts available for purchase include carved and etched ivory, fur slippers and mukluks, horn dolls and bone carvings. Fishing/hunting licenses available. No guide or repair services; no rental transportation. Fuel available: diesel, propane, white gas, kerosene and regular gasoline. No moorage facilities.

Shishmaref is just 20 miles south of the Arctic Circle and only 100 miles east of Siberia. The original Eskimo name for the island is Kigiktaq. Lieutenant Otto Von Kotzebue named the inlet Shishmarev in 1816 after Capt. Lt. Glieb Semenovich Shishmarev, who accompanied him on

his exploration. Archaeologists excavated some of the sites at Kigiktaq around 1821 and found evidence of Eskimo habitation going back several centuries. After 1900, when a supply center was established to serve gold mines in the interior of the Seward Peninsula, the village was renamed after the inlet. The site offered a fairly good harbor and proximity to mining operations. Shishmaref was incorporated as a second-class city in 1969.

Vulnerable to the ongoing threat of land erosion, the community faces the possibility of relocation to more stable ground.

The Shishmaref economy is based on subsistence and part-time employment at local stores, the school district, city and Native corporations. Shishmaref Tannery, a local business, was established in 1991. The tannery processes up to 4,000 marine mammal skins annually, and sponsors an active local crafts industry specializing in beaded sealskin slippers. (For a brochure and price list, write The Tannery, P.O. Box 135, Shishmaref, AK 99772; phone 907/649-3581.)

In the spring, residents harvest oogruk, walrus, seals, rabbits, squirrels, ptarmigans, waterfowl, eggs, various greens and plants. Summer brings the harvest of herring, smelt, salmon, whitefish, trout, grayling, greens and plants. In fall berries, waterfowl, squirrels, moose, oogruk, seals, herring, grayling and lingcod are taken. In winter residents hunt for seals, polar bears, rabbits and ptarmigans; and fish for tomcod, flounder, sculpin and smelt. Two reindeer herds totaling 7,000 head are managed from Shishmaref, and reindeer meat and skins are sometimes available at a local store.

Shishmaref is the home of respected Iditarod Trail dog musher Herbie Nayokpuk and the late Eskimo artist Melvin Olanna.

Each year, the Shishmaref Spring Carnival, highlighted by the Seward Peninsula Open-Class Championship Sled Dog Races, takes place on the third weekend in April.

Shishmaref is surrounded by the 2.6-million-acre Bering Land Bridge National Preserve, considered to be part of the land bridge over which prehistoric hunters traveled from Asia to North America. It offers a variety of arctic wildlife and plants, hot springs, lava beds and other volcanic phenomena, and archaeological sites. For more information write: Superintendent, Bering Land Bridge National Preserve, P.O. Box 220, Nome, AK 99762, phone (907) 443-2522.

Winter travel in Shishmaref consists mainly of snow machines, dogsleds and snowshoes. There are winter trails to the mainland and along the coastline.

Communications in Shishmaref include phones, mail plane and radio. There is a community electric system. The community is served by a Lutheran church and a school with grades preschool through 12 with enrollment of 180. Water is hauled from the washeteria, collected from rain water or melted from ice hauled from the mainland. Sewage system is primarily honey buckets. Freight arrives by cargo plane and barge. Government address: City of Shishmaref, P.O. Box 83, Shishmaref, AK 99772, phone (907) 649-3781, fax (907) 649-2131. Village corporation: Shishmaref Native Corp., General Delivery, Shishmaref, AK 99772, phone (907) 649-3751, fax (907) 649-3731. Village council: Native Village of Shishmaref, P.O. Box 72110, Shishmaref, AK 99772, phone (07) 649-3821, fax (907) 6489-3583, e-mail: Shishmaref@aitc.org.

Sleetmute

GPS: N61°42′ W157°10′

Located on the Kuskokwim River, 1.5 miles north of its junction with the Holitna River, 78 miles east of Aniak, 240 miles west of Anchorage. **Transportation:** Boat; scheduled and charter air service from Bethel or Aniak. **Population:** 103. **Zip code:** 99668. **Emergency Services:** Alaska State Troopers, Bethel, phone (907) 675-4398; Sleetmute Health Clinic, phone (907) 449-9901; Volunteer Fire Department.

Elevation: 290 feet. **Climate:** Continental with temperatures ranging between -58°F and 90°F. Mean annual precipitation 21.5 inches; mean annual snowfall 77 inches.

Private Aircraft: Airstrip adjacent east; elev. 178 feet; length 3,100 feet; gravel; no fuel; unattended. Runway condition not monitored; visual inspection recommended prior to using. No airport facilities or public transportation into village. High winds in the fall and winter can prevent planes from landing for days at a time.

NOTE: Sleetmute prohibits the sale and importation of alcoholic beverages.

Visitor Facilities: Accommodations may be arranged on floor of city offices, (907) 449-9901. A store carries groceries, first-aid supplies and sporting goods. Laundry facilities and public showers available. No banking services. Fishing/hunting licenses available. Guide services available. No repair services, rental transportation or moorage facilities. Fuel available: marine gas, diesel and propane.

NOTE: Land use permits are required to use lands owned by the Kuskokwim Corp. Uses include fishing, temporary camping, seasonal campsite, land crossing and research. There is a $100 administration fee. Big game

hunting fee is $400. Seasonal campsite permits $50, annual use fee $250. For further information, contact the Kuskokwim Corp., 2000 W. Internatioal Airport Rd., Suite C-9, Anchorage, AK 99502, phone (907) 243-2944, or in Aniak phone (907) 675-4275.

The Native village of Sleetmute, which means "whetstone people," was named for nearby slate deposits. The village was founded by Ingalik Indians. In the early 1830s, the Russians developed a trading post near the present village site. By 1841, however, this post had been moved from Sleetmute to another site approximately 100 miles down the Kuskokwim River. Frederick Bishop established a trading post at Sleetmute's present location in 1906. A school was opened in 1921. Saints Peter and Paul Russian Orthodox Chapel was built in 1931. Sleetmute is unincorporated.

Most income in Sleetmute is from public employment programs, the school district and summer firefighting jobs with BLM. Some residents work in canneries in other villages during the fishing season. Residents rely on subsistence hunting for moose, bear, ptarmigan, waterfowl, porcupine and rabbit; fishing for salmon, whitefish, sheefish, trout, pike, grayling, lush (burbot), char and Dolly Varden.

Communications in Sleetmute include a phone, (907) 449-9901, radio, mail plane and TV. The community is served by a Russian Orthodox church and a school with grades preschool through 12 with enrollment of 19. There are community electricity and water; sewage system is outhouses. Freight arrives by cargo plane and barge. Village corporation address: Kuskokwim Corp., 2000 W. International Airport Rd., Suite C-9, Anchorage, AK 99502, phone (907) 243-2944. Village council: Sleetmute Traditional Council, P.O. Box 21, Sleetmute, AK 99668, phone and fax (907) 449-9901, e-mail: Sleetmute@aitc.org.

Solomon

GPS: N64°34′ W164°26′

Located on the west bank of the Solomon River, 1 mile north of Norton Sound, 32 miles east of Nome, 500 miles west of Fairbanks. **Transportation:** Via

Nome-Council Road or charter air service from Nome. **Population**: 3. **Zip code**: 99762. **Emergency Services**: Alaska State Troopers and Norton Sound Regional Hospital in Nome.

Climate: Solomon's climate is both maritime and continental. Summers are short, wet and mild. Winters are cold and windy. Weather data from Nome shows annual precipitation is 16.4 inches, with 54 inches of snowfall. Temperatures range from -30°F to 56°F.

Private Aircraft: Lee's (mining) Camp is a private strip, 5 miles north of Solomon. Permission necessary from owner to use this 1,000-foot unpaved runway.

Visitor Facilities: None.

This location was called Erok on a 1900 map of Nome Peninsula by Davidson and Blakeslee. Originally established as a mining camp in 1900 on a spit between the Solomon and Bonanza rivers, the townsite was destroyed by a 1913 storm. Townspeople decided to move Solomon east across the Solomon River to the site of the abandoned southern terminus of the Council City and Solomon River railroad, which had been known as Dickson. Flooding continued to threaten the low-lying town, and in the 1930s the townsite was moved once again to the base of Jerusalem Hill on the west side of the river.

During summer 1900, a thousand or more people lived in Solomon. The community had 7 saloons, a post office, and a ferry dock, and by 1904 was the terminus of a standard-gauge railroad that ran north.

The town's boom was short-lived. Few held productive mining claims and several disasters befell the community. Besides the 1913 storm, the 1918 worldwide influenza epidemic devastated the population. Mining picked up a bit between the wars, but people moved out again during WWII to find work. In 1956 the Bureau of Indian Affairs school closed.

Rusting railroad equipment, the old school and the river ferry today offer reminders of Solomon's historic past. The Solomon Roadhouse, built in 1904 in Dickson, was nominated to the National Register of Historic Places in 1979.

The unpaved Nome-Council Road, which originated as a trail during the gold rush, runs through town. The road, maintained only in summer, brings many visitors to the area, including bird-watchers, fishermen, hunters and tourists. A section of the road is part of the Iditarod Trail from Seward to Nome, and a spur extends up the Solomon River into the Casadepaga River valley.

Communication is by radio. There is no public electricity system. Water is hauled from the Solomon River or Jerusalem Creek. The sewage system is honey buckets or outhouses.

Many Nome residents have seasonal homes or camps at Solomon. Village corporation address: Solomon Native Corp., P.O. Box 243, Nome, AK 99762, phone and fax (907) 443-2844.

Stebbins

GPS: N63°31' W162°17'

Located on the northwest coast of St. Michael Island on Norton Sound, 53 miles southwest of Unalakleet, 120 miles southeast of Nome, 300 miles northwest of Anchorage. **Transportation**: Scheduled and charter air service from Unalakleet. **Population**: 543. **Zip code**: 99671. **Emergency Services**: Village Public Safety Officer, phone (907) 934-3451; Stebbins Health Clinic, phone (907) 934-3311; Volunteer Fire Department.

Elevation: 26 feet. **Climate**: Subarctic with a maritime influence June to November when Norton Sound is ice-free, and a cold continental influence in winter. Clouds and fog common in summer. Weather data for St. Michael indicates annual precipitation at Stebbins is 12 inches, with 38 inches of snow. Winter temperatures between -1°F and 16°F, summer temperatures between 40°F and 60°F, with a record high of 77°F.

Private Aircraft: Airstrip adjacent northwest; elev. 26 feet; length 3,000 feet; gravel; no fuel; unattended. Runway condition not monitored; visual inspection recommended prior to using. No airport facilities; public transportation to village available.

NOTE: Stebbins prohibits the sale and importation of alcoholic beverages.

Visitor Facilities: Arrangements may be made for lodging at a small inn or in private homes. No restaurant or banking services. Laundry facilities and showers available. Groceries, clothing, first-aid supplies, hardware, film and sporting goods available in the community. Arts and crafts available for purchase include carved ivory, masks and grass baskets. Fishing/hunting licenses available. For guide services, contact city office. No repair services. Arrangements may be made to rent off-road vehicles and boats. Fuel available includes marine gas, propane, diesel and regular gasoline. Moorage facilities available.

The Eskimo village of Atroik or Atowak was first recorded in 1898 by the U.S. Coast and Geodetic Survey at a site on the hillside north of Stebbins. The Native name for the village is Tapraq; the name Stebbins was first published on a USCGS map in 1900. In 1950, Stebbins was described as a village of Eskimos who made their livelihood by hunting, fishing and herding reindeer. Stebbins was incorporated as a second-class city in 1969.

The Stebbins economy is still based on subsistence hunting and fishing, supplemented by part-time wage earnings. There is presently an unmaintained herd of reindeer on Stuart Island just off the coast. Subsistence harvest includes bearded, ring and spotted seals, walrus, beluga whales, ptarmigans, rabbits, wildfowl, salmon, tomcod, flounder, sculpin, herring, smelt and berries. Commercial fishing in the area is on the increase.

Stebbins is located at the northern tip of Yukon Delta National Wildlife Refuge. Birdwatching is for peregrine falcons and a myriad of migratory wildfowl.

Recreational activities in Stebbins include basketball, bingo, Eskimo dances and an annual potlatch.

Overland travel is by snow machine in the winter. A number of trails link Stebbins with St. Michael.

Communications in Stebbins include phones, mail plane, radio and TV. The community is served by a church and a school with grades kindergarten through 12 with enrollment of 195. There are community electricity and water. Sewage system is honey buckets. Freight is hauled by cargo plane, barge and ship. Government address: City of Stebbins, P.O. Box 22, Stebbins, AK 99671, phone 934-3451, fax (907) 934-3452. Village corporation: Stebbins Native Corp., P.O. Box 71110, Stebbins, AK 99671, phone (907) 934-3074, fax (907) 934-2399. Village council: Stebbins Community Assoc., P.O. Box 2, Stebbins, AK 99671, phone (907) 934-3561. fax (907) 934-3560, e-mail: Stebbins@aitc.org.

Stony River

GPS: N61°47' W156°35'

Located on Stony River Island in the Kuskokwim River near its junction with Stony River, 185 miles northeast of Bethel, 245 miles west-northwest of Anchorage. **Transportation**: Boat; snow machine; scheduled and charter air service from Aniak. **Population**: 35. **Zip code**: 99673. **Emergency Services**: Alaska State Troopers, Aniak, phone (907) 675-4398; Stony River Health Clinic, phone (907) 537-3228; Volunteer Fire Department.

Elevation: 220 feet. **Climate**: Continental. Record high was 85°F in July 1967; record low was -57°F in January 1951. Mean annual precipitation 23 inches; mean annual snowfall 93 inches.

Private Aircraft: Airstrip adjacent north; elev. 230 feet; length 2,555 feet; gravel; no fuel; unattended. Runway condition not monitored; visual inspection recommended prior to using. No airport facilities or public transportation into the village.

Visitor Facilities: Arrangements may be made for accommodations in private homes; or in the IRA Council building by contacting the Traditional Council. No restaurant, banking services or laundry facilities. Staple items, cigarettes and snacks available at local stores; most supplies are obtained from Sleetmute, Red Devil, Aniak or Anchorage. Arts and crafts available for purchase include birch-bark baskets, wooden bowls, moccasins, mukluks, beaver mittens and beaver-and-marten hats. Fishing/hunting licenses and guide service not available. Residents repair their own marine engines. No rental transportation or moorage facilities. Fuel available: marine gas, regular gasoline.

NOTE: Land use permits are required to use lands owned by the Kuskokwim Corp. Uses include fishing, temporary camping, seasonal campsite, land crossing and research. There is a $100 administration fee. Big game hunting fee is $400. Seasonal campsite permits $50, annual use fee $250. For further information, contact the Kuskokwim Corp., 62000 W. International Airport Rd., Suite C-9, Anchorage, AK 99502, phone (907) 243-2944, or in Aniak phone (907) 675-4275.

This unincorporated Eskimo and Indian village, which has been known as Moose Village and Moose Creek, began as a trading post and riverboat landing used to supply mining operations to the north. The first trading post was opened in 1930, followed by a post office in 1935. These facilities were used primarily by people who lived in one-family settlements nearby. In the early 1960s, villagers built cabins near the store. A state school opened in 1961 and work began on the airstrip the next year.

Most income in Stony River comes from public employment programs, including seasonal firefighting work with BLM. This income is supplemented by subsistence activities. Residents hunt for moose, caribou, bear, waterfowl, ptarmigan, rabbit and porcupine. They fish for salmon, whitefish, sheefish, burbot, grayling and trout. Income also is obtained from trapping beaver, marten, lynx, fox and mink.

Communications in Stony River include phones, mail plane, radio and TV. The school has enrollment of 14. There is a community electric system. Water is pumped from individual wells. Sewage system is honey buckets or outhouses. Freight arrives by barge or chartered plane. Village corporation: The Kuskokwim Corp. (see above). Village council: Village of Stony River, P.o. Box SRV, Stony River, AK 99557, phone (907) 537-3214, e-mail: StonyRiver@aitc.org.

Teller

GPS: N65°16′ W166°22′

Located on a spit between Port Clarence and Grantley Harbor on the Seward Peninsula, 72 miles north of Nome, 540 miles west of Fairbanks. **Transportation**: Via the Nome-Teller Road or by air service from Nome. **Population**: 281. **Zip code**: 99778. **Emergency Services**: Village Public Safety Officer, phone (907) 642-3401; Alaska State Troopers, Nome, phone (907) 443-2441; Teller Health Clinic, phone (907) 642-3311.

Elevation: 10 feet. **Climate**: Maritime when the Bering Sea is ice free, usually early June to mid-November. Freezing of the sea causes a change to a more continental climate with less precipitation and colder temperatures. Mean annual precipitation 11 inches; mean annual snowfall 50 inches. Winter temperatures average -9°F to 8°F; summer temperatures average 44°F to 57°F.

Private Aircraft: Airstrip 2 miles south; elev. 293 feet; length 3,000 feet; gravel; no fuel; unattended; lighted. Runway condition not monitored; visual inspection recommended prior to using. No airport facilities. Public transportation into town available. Public phone.

NOTE: Teller prohibits the sale and importation of alcoholic beverages.

Visitor Facilities: No hotel, restaurant or banking services. Accommodations may be arranged at the school, (907) 642-3041. Washeteria available. Groceries, clothing, first-aid supplies, hardware, film and sporting goods available at Teller Commercial, (907) 642-3333, Teller Native Store, (907) 642-4521, Nanook Management Store and Sherman's Transportation. Arts and crafts available include carved walrus and mastodon ivory, hand-sewn seal skin items, and Eskimo dolls. Fishing/hunting licenses available. No guide or repair services. No rental transportation or moorage facilities. Fuel available: diesel and regular gasoline.

Captain Daniel B. Libby and his party from the Western Union Telegraph expedition wintered here in 1866 and 1867; the site was then called Libbyville or Libby Station. The first permanent settlement, named for U.S. senator H.M. Teller, was established around 1900 after the

Bluestone Placer discovery 15 miles to the south. During those boom years at the turn of the century, Teller had a population estimated at 5,000 and was a major regional trading center. Although Teller's population had dropped to 125 by 1910 and continued to decrease through 1930, the number of residents has increased gradually since then. The community was incorporated as a second-class city in 1963.

The economy of Teller is based on subsistence food harvest supplemented by part-time wage earnings. Some foxes are trapped in the area and reindeer herding has been practiced since Teller's founding. Residents hunt for seals, beluga whales, moose, squirrels, rabbits, ptarmigans, wildfowl and their eggs. They fish for salmon, herring, smelt, whitefish, sculpin, tomcod and flounder.

Teller was the landing site of the *Norge*, the first dirigible to be flown over the North Pole. The craft, piloted by Roald Amundson, flew 71 hours from Spitzbergen, Norway. Its intended landing site was Nome, but bad weather forced it to land May 13, 1926, on the beach at Teller instead. Near the landing site, a plaque commemorating the event has been placed on an old 2-story falsefront building in which some of the disassembled segments and gear from the *Norge* were stored. The storage site is on the National Register of Historic Places.

From May through October a 72-mile gravel road is open from Teller to Nome. Taxis will make the trip for $45 each way. Air taxis also operate between the 2 communities, charging $55 per person one way. Local resident Allan Okpealuk recommends the drive for its beautiful scenery, fishing spots, berry picking and bird watching.

Winter trails, traveled primarily by snow machines and a few dogsled teams, radiate from Teller to Brevig Mission, Marys Igloo and Nome. Area rivers lead to summer fish camps.

Communications in Teller include phones, mail plane, radio and TV. The community has Lutheran and Roman Catholic churches served by itinerant pastors. It also has a school with grades preschool through 12 with enrollment of 74. There are community electric and water systems; sewage system is primarily honey buckets. Freight arrives by cargo plane and barge. Government address: City of Teller, P.O. Box 548, Teller, AK 99778, phone (907) 642-3401, fax (907) 642-2051. Village corporation: Teller Native Corp., P.O. Box 509, Teller, AK 99778, phone 642-4011, fax (907) 642-4014. Village council: Native Village of Teller, P.O. Box 590, Teller, AK 99778, phone (907) 642-3381, fax (907) 642-4014, e-mail: Teller@aitc.org.

Tin City

GPS: N65°33' W167°55'

Located at the mouth of Cape Creek, 7 miles southeast of Wales, 100 miles northwest of Nome, 600 miles westnorthwest of Fairbanks. **Transportation**: Boat; scheduled and charter air service from Wales. **Population**: 10 to 20. **Zip code**: 99762. **Emergency Services**: Village Public Safety Officer, Wales; Alaska State Troopers, Nome; Tin City Air Force Station Medic.

Elevation: 270 feet. **Climate**: Mean annual precipitation 12 inches; mean annual snowfall 45.5 inches. Snowfall usually starts in late September or early October; last snow in late May or early June. Temperatures in winter -10°F to 7°F. A record high of 84°F was reached in early July 1987.

Private Aircraft: Tin City Air Force Station airport 1 mile east; elev. 269 feet; length 4,700 feet; gravel. *NOTE: Closed to the public. Aircraft on official business may land only with 24-hour advance permission from airstrip supervisor, phone 552-3793. CAUTION: Turbulence on approach due to high winds. Field on high bluff.*

Visitor Facilities: For accommodations contact Richard Lee, owner of the trading post and Tin City's sole resident not connected with the military: General Delivery, Tin City, AK 99762, (907) 664-3141. Reservations should be made in advance. There is no food or lodging available to the public at the military site. No restaurant, banking services or laundry facilities available. Groceries, clothing, first-aid supplies, hardware, film and sporting goods available. Arts and crafts available for purchase include carved ivory, moccasins and other hand-sewn skin items from Diomede, Wales, Shishmaref, Brevig Mission and other villages. Fishing/hunting licenses not available. No guide or repair services. No rental transportation or moorage facilities. Fuel available includes marine gas and propane.

Tin City was established as a mining camp at the base of Cape Mountain in 1903 after tin ore was discovered on the mountain in 1902. Tin City Air Force Station was constructed in the early 1950s; military personnel have now been replaced by GE Government Services employees. The military site is closed to the public. An abandoned White Alice communications site is located on a nearby hill.

Tin is still mined in the area. Lee Mining Camp operated in the 1960s, but was sold to Lost River Mining Co. in the 1970s. Tin is mined from breakup to fall.

There are several privately owned cabins facing the beach. Tin ore, along with jade and other minerals, can be found on the beach, according to a Wales resident. Trout and salmon can be caught with rod and reel from the beach.

Communications in Tin City include mail plane, radio and TV. There is no church or school. There are community electric and water systems and flush toilets on the Air Force site. Freight arrives by cargo plane and barge.

Togiak

GPS: N59°04' W160°24'

Located at the head of Togiak Bay, 55 air miles west of Dillingham, 395 miles southwest of Anchorage. **Transportation**: Scheduled and charter air service from Dillingham. **Population**: 824. **Zip code**: 99678. **Emergency Services**: Police, phone (907) 493-5212; Alaska State Troopers, Dillingham, phone (907) 842-5351; Tokiak Health Clinic, phone (907) 493-5511; Togiak First Responders Group, (907) 493-5511/5435; Volunteer Fire Department, phone (907) 493-5212.

Elevation: 12 feet. **Climate**: Maritime; however, the arctic climate of interior Alaska also affects the Bristol Bay coastal region. Cloudy skies, mild temperatures, moderately heavy precipitation and strong winds. Average summer temperatures from 37°F to 66°F; average winter temperatures from 4°F to 30°F. Annual precipitation from 20 to 26 inches, with most of the precipitation occurring in the summer, when low clouds and rain can reduce visibility.

Private Aircraft: Airstrip adjacent southwest; elev. 21 feet; length 4,220 feet; gravel; no fuel; unattended; aircraft instructed to land. Runway condition not monitored; visual inspection recommended prior to using. No airport facilities. Public transportation into village: call city of Togiak.

NOTE: Togiak prohibits the sale, importation and possession of alcoholic beverages.

Visitor Facilities: Accommodations are available at the Round House, (907) 493-5434 after 5 P.M. Lodging may also be arranged with the City of Togiak, (907) 493-5820. Togiak Natives Limited, (907) 493-5520, operates a fishing lodge. No banking services. Food is available at Green House Restaurant and AC Store Deli. Groceries and supplies are available at Alaska Commercial, aka Our Store, (907) 493-5334, Togiak Trading, (907) 493-5828, Kohok's Reliable Goods, Togiak Lumber and Togiak Village Co-op, (907) 493-5226. Arts and crafts available for purchase include grass baskets, some carved ivory, and fur hats and mittens. Fishing/hunting licenses available. *NOTE: Permission must be obtained from Togiak Natives Ltd. to hunt or fish on Native lands.* Sportfishing guide service on Togiak River and charter boat trips to Walrus Islands State Game Sanctuary. No repair services. Moorage facilities available. Regular gasoline sometimes available.

Many residents of the Yukon-Kuskokwim region migrated south to the Togiak area after the devastating influenza epidemic in 1918-19. "Old" Togiak, or Togiagamute, located across the bay from "New" Togiak where a cannery now is located, had a population of 276 in 1880 and only 94 in 1890. Heavy winter snowfalls made wood gathering difficult at "Old" Togiak, so gradually people settled at a new site on the opposite shore, where snow tended only to make deep drifts on the beach and a trail made wood gathering easier. In addition, a slough behind the new site provided good shelter for boats. The population of Togiak is 90 to 95 percent Eskimo with Yup'ik the primary language. Togiak was incorporated as a second-class city in 1969. A local resident classifies people in Togiak as "warm and friendly."

Togiak's economy is based primarily on commercial salmon fishing. Approximately 400 residents fish commercially. A fish-processing facility is located near Togiak. The cannery across the bay from Togiak offers tours, (907) 493-5331 or 5531. The entire community also depends heavily on subsistence hunting and fishing. Species harvested include seal, sea lion, walrus, 5 species of salmon, herring, herring roe-on-kelp, smelt, clams, geese, ducks, ptarmigan and trout. Residents also gather gull and murre eggs.

Togiak is in the center of the Togiak National Wildlife Refuge and is the gateway to Walrus Island State Game Sanctuary. At Round Island, one of the Walrus Islands group, visitors can view and photograph the 12,000 to 15,000 male walruses that summer on the island. Transportation to Round Island is by boat from Togiak or by charter plane from Dillingham or King Salmon. A trip to Round Island is a true wilderness experience; visitors must bring all their own food, shelter and equipment. *NOTE: Access to the game sanctuary is only by permit from the Alaska Dept. of Fish and Game offices in Anchorage, Dillingham or King Salmon. For information about permits and other information about the sanctuary, write the Alaska Dept. of Fish and Game, Division of Game, P.O. Box 199, Dillingham, AK 99576.* (See also Walrus Island State Game Sanctuary in the Attractions section.)

Some of the other islands in the Walrus Islands group also have large populations of seabirds such as puffins, murres, cormorants, kittiwakes, terns and gulls.

The Togiak River is known worldwide for its famous trout and salmon fishing. Fishing in the Togiak River is excellent during July, August and September for 5 species of salmon, rainbow trout and Dolly Varden.

Togiak is located within Togiak National Wildlife Refuge, a breeding and resting area for waterfowl and shorebirds. Peak migrations usually occur the first week in May.

Communications in Togiak include phones, mail plane, radio and TV. The community is served by a Moravian church and a school with grades kindergarten through 12 with enrollment of 267. There are community electricity, water and sewer systems. Freight arrives by cargo plane and barge. Government address: City of Togiak, P.O. Box 99, Togiak, AK 99678, phone (907) 493-5820, fax 493-5932, e-mail: cityoftogiak@aol.com. Village corporation: Togiak Natives Corp., P.O. Box 169, Togiak, AK 99678, phone (907) 493-5520/5845, fax (907) 493-5554. Village council: Traditional Village of Togiak, P.O. Box 209, Togiak, AK 99678-0209, phone (907) 493-5920, e-mail: Togiak@aitc.org.

Toksook Bay

GPS: N60°32' W165°07'

(TOOK-sook) Located on Nelson Island 5 miles southeast of Tununak ' 100 miles west of Bethel and 505 miles west of Anchorage. **Transportation:** Scheduled and charter air service from Bethel. **Population:** 527. **Zip code:** 99637. **Emergency Services:** Alaska State Troopers, Bethel, phone (907) 543-3494; Toksook Bay Health Clinic, phone (907) 427-7712; Volunteer Fire Department.

Private Aircraft: Airstrip adjacent west; elev. 95 feet; length 1,800 feet; gravel and dirt; no fuel; unattended. Runway condition not monitored; visual inspection recommended prior to using. Runway grade uneven. Deep dip at one end.

NOTE: Toksook Bay prohibits the sale and importation of alcoholic beverages.

Visitor Facilities: Arrangements for accommodations may be made at the school , (907) 427-7815, or Nunakauiak Yupik Corp. Hotel, (907) 427-7928/7929 year-round. No restaurants, but a snack bar offers fast-food items. Groceries and supplies are available at NYC General Store and John's Store. Fishing/hunting licenses are also available.

Toksook Bay was established in 1964 when most of the population of Nightmute moved to what was considered a better village site. Toksook Bay, which is located within Yukon Delta National Wildlife Refuge, was incorporated as a second-class city in 1972.

Winter activities include occasional Eskimo dances, basketball tournaments, musk-oxen hunts sponsored by the Dept. of Fish & Wildlife, and tomcod jigging. Summers are spent at fish camps, subsistence fishing and drying fish.

Toksook Bay is served by a Roman Catholic church and 2 schools with grades kindergarten through 12 with total enrollment of 180. There are community electric, water and sewer systems. Freight arrives by barge and plane. Government address: City of Toksook Bay, P.O. Box 37008, Nelson Island, Toksook Bay, AK 99637, phone (907) 427-7613, fax (907) 427-7811, e-mail: ook99637@aol.com. Village corporation: Nunakauyak Yup'ik Corp., General Delivery, Nelson Island, Toksook Bay, AK 99637, phone (907) 427-7929, fax (907) 427-7612. Village council: Native Village of Toksook Bay, P.O. Box 37048, Nelson Island, Toksook Bay, AK 99637, phone 427-7114, fax (907) 427-7714, e-mail: ToksookBay@aitc.org.

Tuluksak

GPS: N61°05' W160°58'

(TOO-luck-sack) Located on the south bank of the Kuskokwim River near the mouth of the Tuluksak River, 45 miles northeast of Bethel and 375 miles west of Anchorage. **Transportation:** Scheduled and charter air service from Bethel. **Population:** 302. **Zip code:** 99679. **Emergency Services:** Village Public Safety Officer; Alaska State Troopers, Bethel, phone (907) 543-3494; Tuluksak Health Clinic, phone (907) 695-6115; Volunteer Fire Department.

Private Aircraft: Airstrip adjacent southwest; elev. 30 feet; length 2,500 feet; gravel; no fuel; unattended. Runway condition not monitored; visual inspection recommended prior to using. Loose gravel to 2 inches in diameter on the northeast 1,000 feet of the runway. Potholes and ruts in runway.

NOTE: *Tuluksak prohibits the sale and importation of alcoholic beverages.*

Visitor Facilities: Arrangements for accommodations may be made through the city office, (907) 695-6212. There is a washeteria. Supplies available at 2 general stores. Fishing/hunting licenses not available.

This Eskimo village reportedly was named after a species of loon called "tulik" in the Eskimo language. It has been occupied continuously since early historic times and the Moravian missionaries had an Eskimo helper stationed there in 1895. Outside interest in the surrounding area was generated in 1907 when gold was found along Bear Creek on the upper Tuluksak River. The first Moravian chapel was built in 1912; a new chapel was completed in 1925. A Bureau of Education school opened in 1930.

Tuluksak, which is located within Yukon Delta National Wildlife Refuge, was incorporated as a second-class city in 1970. Many residents may be gone to fish camps during the summer season.

The community has 2 schools with grades kindergarten through 12. There is a community electricity system. Water is hauled from the washeteria. Sewage system is honey buckets. Freight arrives by mail plane and barge. Government address: City of Tuluksak, General Delivery, Tuluksak, AK 99679, phone (907) 695-6212. Village corporation: Tulkisarmute Inc., General Delivery, Tuluksak, AK 99679.

Tuntutuliak

GPS: N60°22' W162°38'

(TOON-too-TOO-lee-ack) Located on the north bank of the Kuskokwim River, 45 miles southwest of Bethel, 440 miles west of Anchorage. **Transportation:** Scheduled and charter air service from Bethel. **Population:** 350. **Zip code:** 99680. **Emergency Services:** Village

Public Safety Officer, phone (907) 256-2512; Alaska State Troopers, Bethel, phone (907) 543-3494; Kathleen Daniel Memorial Clinic, phone (907) 256-2129; Volunteer Fire Department.

Private Aircraft: Airstrip 1 mile south; elev. 16 feet; length 1,800 feet; gravel; no fuel; unattended. Runway and seaplane conditions not monitored; visual inspection recommended prior to using. Runway has 40-foot gravel strip down the center; gravel edges may be soft.

NOTE: *Tuntutuliak prohibits possession of alcoholic beverages.*

Visitor Facilities: Arrangements for accommodations may be made with the school, (907) 256-2415. There is a washeteria. Supplies available in the community. Fishing/hunting licenses available.

Unincorporated Tuntutuliak is located within Yukon Delta National Wildlife Refuge. Many residents may leave for fish camps in the summer.

The community has a church and 2 schools with grades kindergarten through 12 with enrollment of 93. There is a community electric system. Water is hauled from the washeteria. Sewage system is honey buckets. Freight arrives by mail plane and barge. Government address: Tuntutuliak City Office, General Delivery, Tuntutuliak, AK 99680, phone (907) 256-2112. Village corporation: Tuntutuliak Land Ltd., General Delivery, Tuntutuliak, AK 99680, phone (907) 256-2315, fax (907) 256-2441. Village council: Tuntutuliak Traditional Council, P.O. Box 8145, Tuntutuliak, AK 99680, phone (907) 256-2128, fax (907) 256-2080, e-mail: Tuntutuliak@aitc.org.

Tununak

GPS: N60°35′ W165°15′

(Tu-NOO-nak) Located at Tununak Bay on the northwest coast of Nelson Island, 120 miles west of Bethel, 520 miles west of Anchorage. **Transportation**: Scheduled and charter air service from Bethel. **Population**: 331. **Zip code**: 99681. **Emergency Services**: Village Public Safety Officer, phone (907) 652-6812; Alaska State Troopers, Bethel; Tununak Health Clinic, phone (907) 652-

6829; Volunteer Fire Department.

Private Aircraft: Airstrip adjacent southwest; elev. 17 feet; length 2,010 feet; gravel; no fuel; unattended. Runway condition not monitored; visual inspection recommended prior to using. Passenger terminal at airport; no public transportation into village.

NOTE: *Tununak prohibits the sale and importation of alcoholic beverages.*

Visitor Facilities: For sleeping accommodations in the school or clinic, contact the school, (907) 652-6827. or the city office, (907) 652-6312. Food is available at the Seaside Cafe. No banking services. Washeteria available. Groceries, clothing, first-aid supplies, hardware, film and sporting goods available at TRC General Store, (907) 652-6311, Tununak Native Store, (907) 652-6813, and Charlie Sales (907) 652-6027. Arts and crafts available for purchase include carved ivory, baskets and earrings. Fishing/hunting licenses available. No guide or repair services. Arrangements may be made to rent off-road vehicles. Fuel available: marine gas, propane and regular gasoline. No moorage facilities.

This Eskimo village was visited in December 1878 by E.W. Nelson of the U.S. Signal Service and reported as Tununuk, population 6. A Roman Catholic mission was established here in 1891. Tununak was incorporated as a second-class city in 1975.

Tununak residents go to fish camps in the summer and also work on seasonal fire-fighting crews for BLM. Musk-oxen can be seen on the cliffs surrounding the village.

Communications in Tununak include phones and mail plane. The community is served by a Roman Catholic church and a school with grades kindergarten through 12 with enrollment of 110. There is a community electric system. Water is hauled from the washeteria. Sewage system is honey buckets. Freight is hauled by cargo plane and barge. Village corporation: Tununrmuit Rinit Corp., P.O. Box 89, Tununak, AK 99681, phone (907) 652-6311, fax (907) 652-6315. Village council: Native Village of Tununak, P.O. Box 77, Tununak, AK 99681, phone (907)

652-6527, fax (907) 652-6011, e-mail: Tununak@aitc.org. Tununak Traditional Council, P.O. Box 97, Tununak, AK 99681, phone (907) 652-6312, fax (907) 652-6912.

Twin Hills

GPS: N59°05' W160°13'

Located near the mouth of a branch of the Togiak River known as Twin Hills River, 2 miles north of Togiak, 395 miles southwest of Anchorage. **Transportation**: Boat from Togiak; scheduled and charter air service from Dillingham. **Population**: 76. **Zip code**: 99576. **Emergency Services**: Alaska State Troopers, Dillingham, phone (907) 842-5641; Twin Hills Health Clinic, phone (907) 525-4326; Twin Hills First Responders Group, phone (907) 525-4821.

Elevation: 20 to 30 feet. **Climate**: Transitional zone; primary influence is maritime; however, the arctic climate of interior Alaska also affects the Bristol Bay coast. Cloudy skies, mild temperatures, moderately heavy precipitation and strong winds. Average summer temperatures 37°F to 66°F. Average winter temperatures 4°F to 30°F. Annual precipitation 20 to 26 inches, with most of the precipitation occurring in summer. Fog occurs often in winter.

Private Aircraft: Airstrip adjacent east; elev. 82 feet; length 3,000 feet; gravel; no fuel; unattended. Runway condition not monitored; visual inspection recommended prior to using. Bluff at north end may cause some turbulence when landing to the south. Loose rock up to 3 inches in diameter on runway and apron. Passenger terminal at airport; no public transportation into village.

Visitor Facilities: Arrangements may be made to stay in the school or in private homes. No restaurant, banking services or laundromat. Supplies available at The Cannery (5 miles away). Arts and crafts available for purchase include carved ivory, grass baskets and fur dolls. Fishing/hunting licenses not available. No guide or repair services. No rental transportation or moorage facilities. Fuel available: diesel, propane, unleaded and regular gasoline.

Located within Togiak National Wildlife Refuge, Twin Hills is a fairly new village located at the base of 2 hills which rise to 291 feet and 427 feet, prominent features in the generally flat coastal region. The village was established in 1965 following severe flooding in the upper Togiak Bay area. Some of the current residents migrated from Quinhagak, a small community on Kuskokwim Bay. The people of Twin Hills have strong cultural ties to the Yukon-Kuskokwim region not only because they have relatives there today, but also because many of their ancestors migrated south to the Togiak area following the devastating worldwide influenza epidemic of 1918-19.

Virtually all residents of Twin Hills participate in the commercial salmon fishery. A few jobs are available with the school, post office, clinic and the state. The entire community depends heavily on subsistence hunting and fishing, and people range great distances to obtain subsistence items. Species harvested include seals, sea lion, whale and walrus, 5 species of salmon, herring, herring roe-on-kelp, smelt, clams, geese, ducks, gull and murre eggs, ptarmigan, trout and whitefish. In addition, Twin Hills residents trade food items with people from Manokotak.

There is a road leading from Twin Hills to the beach of Togiak Bay. From there it is possible to drive a car or 3-wheeler to the Togiak Fisheries cannery on the bay across from Togiak.

NOTE: Twin Hills Native Corp. lands are closed to sportfishing, hunting and hiking by nonmembers. Before traveling in the Twin Hills area, check with the corporation about the location of restricted lands.

Communications in Twin Hills include phones, mail plane, radio and TV. There is a Moravian church and a school with grades pre-school through 8 with enrollment of 17; older students attend boarding school in other communities. There are community electricity, water and sewer systems. Freight arrives by cargo plane and barge. Village corporation: Twin Hills Native Corp., General Delivery, Twin Hills, AK 99578, phone (907) 525-9324. Village council: Twin

Hills Village, General Delivery, Twin Hills, AK 99578, phone (907) 525-4820, e-mail: TwinHills @aitc.org.

Unalakleet

GPS: N63°52' W160°47'

(YOU-na-la-kleet) Located on the east shore of Norton Sound at the mouth of the Unalakleet River, 145 miles southeast of Nome, 395 miles west-northwest of Anchorage. **Transportation:** Scheduled and charter air service from Anchorage and Nome. **Population:** 802. **Zip code:** 99684. **Emergency Services:** Police, phone (907) 6243008; Unalakleet Euksavik Clinic, phone (907) 624-3535; Medical Emergencies, phone 911; Volunteer Fire Department.

Elevation: 8 to 12 feet. **Climate:** Subarctic with considerable maritime influence when Norton Sound is ice free, usually from May to October. Freezing of the sound causes a change to a colder, more continental climate. Winters cold and relatively dry, with an average of 41 inches of snowfall. Summers cool with most rainfall occurring in July, August and September. Average annual precipitation is 14 inches. Winter temperatures average -4°F to 11°F; summer temperatures average 47°F to 62°F.

Private Aircraft: Airport 1 mile north; elev. 21 feet; 2 runways: length 6,004 and 2,000 feet; gravel; fuel 80, 100; attended. Airport facilities include passenger and freight terminals, ticket counter and restrooms. Public transportation to town available.

Visitor Facilities: Accommodations and meals at Unalakleet Lodge, (907) 624-3333; food service at The Igloo, (907) 624-3640. No banking services. Laundromat. Groceries, clothing, first-aid supplies, hardware, film and sporting goods available at Alaska Commercial Co., (907) 624-3272, UNC General Store (907) 624-3322, Northwest Alaska Trading Co.. (907) 624-3711, Lowell's Hardware, (907) 624-3169, and Bill's Video, (907) 624-3084. Arts and crafts available for purchase include carved ivory, birch-bark baskets, grass baskets, masks, ulus, beadwork, mukluks and slippers, fur hats and other clothing. Fishing/hunting licenses available, as well as guide service. Marine engine, boat, auto and aircraft repair services available. Arrangements can be made to rent autos and boats, and charter aircraft. Fuel available includes marine gas, propane, diesel and regular gasoline. Moorage facilities available.

NOTE: Land surrounding Unalakleet is owned by the Unalakleet Native Corp. Trespassing laws are strictly enforced, but permits can be obtained from the corporation office in Unalakleet for camping, hunting, fishing, bird-watching, boating, sledding and photography.

The Unalakleet area has been occupied for centuries. Archaeologists have dated house pits along the old beach ridge at 200 B.C. to 300 A.D. More than 100 of these pits extend for a quarter mile near the Unalakleet airport. The name Unalakleet means "place where the east wind blows." The Eskimo name Ounakalik was recorded by Lt. L.A. Zagoskin of the Imperial Russian Navy on an 1850 map. A village site inhabited before the smallpox epidemic of 1838-39 exists along the south side of the Unalakleet River. Reindeer herders brought to Alaska from Lapland in 1898 settled at Unalakleet and quickly established sound herding practices. Descendants of a few of them still live in Unalakleet. The community was incorporated as a second-class city in 1974.

Commercial fishing and subsistence hunting and fishing form the basis of Unalakleet's economy. A fish processing plant employs up to 50 persons from May through August. Other jobs are with the Bering Strait School District, airlines, local stores, Native corporation, city and schools. For subsistence, several species of salmon, char, grayling and herring are fished and seals, caribou, moose, bears, birds and waterfowl are hunted.

Unalakleet is the takeoff point for sportfishing in Norton Sound and the Unalakleet and North rivers.

The Unalakleet River, above its junction with the Chiroskey River, has been designated a wild and scenic river and is popular for float trips. The area is administered by BLM and additional information can be obtained from BLM,

Anchorage District Office, 4700 E. 72nd Ave., Anchorage, AK 99507.

Unalakleet is the terminus of a long-used winter trail from Anvik, on the Yukon River, that forms a leg of the Iditarod Trail. Unalakleet is a checkpoint each March for the Iditarod Trail Sled Dog Race from Anchorage to Nome.

Communications in Unalakleet include phones, mail plane, radio and cable TV. The community is served by Covenant, Mormon, Assembly of God and Roman Catholic churches. Elementary and high schools have a total enrollment of 216. There are community electric, water and sewer systems. Freight arrives by cargo plane, barge and ship. Government address: City of Unalakleet, P.O. Box 28, Unalakleet, AK 99684, phone (907) 624-3531, fax (907) 624-3130, e-mail: counk@nook.net. Village corporation: Unalakleet Native Corp., P.O. Box 100, Unalakleet, AK 99684, phone (907) 624-3411, fax (907) 624-3833. Village council: Native Village of Unalakleet, P.O. Box 270, Unalakleet, AK 99684, phone (907) 624-3622, fax (907) 624-3402, e-mail: Unalakleet@aitc.org.

Upper Kalskag

GPS: N61°32' W160°20'

(Also known as Kalskag) Located on the north bank of the Kuskokwim River, about 24 miles west of Aniak. **Transportation**: Scheduled and charter air service from Aniak or Bethel. **Population**: 262. **Zip code**: 99607. **Emergency Services**: Village Public Safety Officer; Upper Kalskag Health Clinic; Volunteer Fire Department.

Elevation: 49 feet. **Climate**: Semiarctic with maritime influences from the Bering Sea. Snowfall and precipitation are 60 inches and 19 inches, respectively. Weather records at nearby Aniak indicate that temperatures at Upper Kalskag range from a low of -55°F to a high of 87°F.

Private Aircraft: Kalskag airport serves Lower Kalskag 2 miles downriver and Upper Kalskag 1 mile east; elev. 55 feet; length 3,200 feet; gravel; no fuel. Runway is maintained by the state. Kalskag also has a grader to service the runway and main road between Upper and Lower Kalskag. Runway conditions not monitored; visual inspection recommended prior to using. Transportation into village available.

Visitor Facilities: Arrangements for accommodations may be made at the school, (907) 471-2288, and Kalskag Store, (907) 471-2268. No laundromat or banking services. Groceries, clothing, first-aid supplies, hardware and sporting goods available at Ausdahl Mercantile, Betty's Gift Shop, Kalskag Store, Video Village Center and Morgan Fuel. Fishing/hunting licenses available in Lower Kalskag. No guide or repair services. No rental transportation or moorage facilities. Fuel available: marine gas, diesel, unleaded gas and propane.

NOTE: Land use permits are required to use lands owned by the Kuskokwim Corp. Uses include fishing, temporary camping, seasonal campsite, land crossing and research. There is a $100 administration fee. Big game hunting fee is $400. Seasonal campsite permits $50, annual use fee $250. For further information, contact the Kuskokwim Corp., 2000 W. International Airport Rd., Suite C-9, Anchorage, AK 99502, phone (907) 243-2944, or in Aniak phone (907) 675-4275.

Most of the inhabitants of Upper Kalskag were originally residents of the Eskimo village of Kaltkhagamute, located on a slough 4 miles southwest of Upper Kalskag. At the turn of the century, the people moved to the present site of Upper Kalskag. Paul Kameroff, Sr., is credited with founding the village of Upper Kalskag. He operated the only general store, which was established in the 1930s, and transported freight, groceries and fuel from Bethel on a barge he named for his daughter Pauline. A federal Bureau of Education school was built in 1931. At that time the community owned a herd of 2,100 reindeer. Through the years, residents of Ohagamiut, Crow Village and the Yukon River communities of Russian Mission and Paimute moved to Upper Kalskag. The community of Lower Kalskag, 2 miles to the southwest, was established during the same time period as Upper Kalskag. Upper Kalskag was incorporated as a second-class city in 1975.

Most income in Upper Kalskag comes from public employment programs. Subsistence activities account for about 70 percent of the total livelihood in the village. Some residents still go to fish camps, but most fish at or near the village. Seasonal fish catches include king, dog, silver and red salmon; grayling, whitefish, sheefish, blackfish, pike, burbot and eel. Moose are the most important meat source, supplemented by rabbit, waterfowl and game birds. Some income also is obtained from trapping and the sale of lynx, fox, wolf, otter, muskrat, mink, marten, beaver and wolverine pelts. Berries are harvested in the fall and some residents cultivate gardens.

Upper Kalskag is located within Yukon Delta National Wildlife Refuge. The setting is described by one resident as "beautiful, with the hills just behind Kalskag and the Kuskokwim River alongside."

Communications in Upper Kalskag include phones, mail plane, radio and TV. The community is served by 2 churches and 2 schools with grades 1 through 12 with enrollment of 31. There are community electric, water and sewer systems. Freight is transported by plane and barge. Government address: City of Upper Kalskag, Box 80, Upper Kalskag, AK 99607, phone (907) 471-2220, fax (907) 471-2237. Village corporation: The Kuskokwim Corp., 2000 W. International Airport Road, Suite C-9, Anchorage, AK 99502, phone (907) 243-2944. Village council: Village of Kalskag, P.O. Box 50, Kalskag, AK 99607, phone and fax (907) 471-2207, e-mail: Kalskag@aitc.org.

Wales

GPS: N65°37' W168°05'

Located on the western tip of the Seward Peninsula, on the coast of Cape Prince of Wales, 7 miles west of Tin City, 111 miles northwest of Nome, 595 miles west of Fairbanks. **Transportation**: Scheduled and charter air service from Nome. **Population**: 154. **Zip code**: 99783. **Emergency Services**: Village Public Safety Officer, phone (907) 664-3671; Alaska State Troopers, Nome; Wales Health Clinic, phone (907) 664-3691; Volunteer Fire Department.

Elevation: 25 feet. **Climate**: Maritime when Bering Sea is ice free, usually June through November. Freezing of the sea causes abrupt change to a cold continental climate. Winters cold and windy; temperatures average -10°F to 6°F. One resident says the wind chill factor pushes the temperature as low as -100°F. Summer temperatures average 40°F to 50°F. Mean annual precipitation 11 inches; mean annual snowfall 41 inches.

Private Aircraft: Airstrip 1 mile northwest; elev. 25 feet; length 4,000 feet; gravel; unattended. Easterly winds may cause severe turbulence in the vicinity of the runway. Frequent fog, wind and occasional blizzards limit access to Wales. No airport facilities; transportation available to village.

NOTE: Wales prohibits the sale and importation of alcoholic beverages.

Visitor Facilities: Accommodations may be arranged in a trailer of the Wales Native Corp., (907) 664-3641, or in a room in the City of Wales dome building, (907) 644-3501. No restaurant or banking services. Laundromat and showers available. Groceries, first-aid supplies, hardware and camera film available at Wales Native Store, (907) 664-3351. Arts and crafts available for purchase include carved walrus ivory, moccasins, Eskimo dolls, fur mukluks and knitted caps, gloves and socks. Fishing/hunting licenses are available. Informal guide service may be available. No repair service. Arrangements may be made to rent private off-road vehicles and boats. Fuel available: marine gas, diesel and propane. Moorage on beach.

Cape Prince of Wales is the farthest west point of mainland Alaska; 2,289-foot Cape Mountain which rises above Wales is the terminus of the Continental Divide separating the Arctic and Pacific watersheds. The Wales area has been inhabited for centuries; archaeological evidence dates back to 500 A.D. A burial mound of the Birnirk culture (500 A.D. to 900 A.D.) was discovered behind the present village and is now a national historic landmark.

In historical times, the villages of Eidamoo near the coast and King-a-ghe farther inland were noted in 1827 by Captain Beechy of the Imperial Russian Navy. In 1880, Capt. E.E. Smith of the U.S. Revenue Cutter Service reported Kingigamute, meaning "the high place," with a population of 400. In 1890, the American Missionary Assoc. established a mission here and in 1894 a reindeer station was organized. Wales was incorporated as a second-class city in 1964.

Wales was a major center for whale hunting due to its strategic location on the animals' migratory route until the 1918-19 influenza pandemic claimed the lives of many of Wales' finest whalers. The village retains a strong Eskimo culture; ancient songs and dances are still performed and customs practiced.

The economy of Wales is based on subsistence hunting and fishing, trapping, some mining and Native arts and crafts. Wales artisans make excellent ivory carvings, especially birds, which are sold locally or marketed in Nome, Anchorage or Fairbanks. Other crafts such as skin sewing bring additional income to the community. There is some trapping of fox and wolverine. A private reindeer herd of about 1,500 head is managed out of Wales and local residents are employed during roundup. A few jobs are provided by the city, store, clinic, airlines, school and Native corporation.

The mining potential is great in the area. Tin placers located nearby have estimated reserves of 2,000 tons of tin. Gold also is plentiful in the region.

Vast herds of walrus and whales migrate through Bering Strait and villagers hunt them from early April to the end of June. Ice cellars are used to store and preserve the meat. Polar bear, moose, waterfowl, salmon, ptarmigan, tomcod and flounder supplement local diets, along with berries and various greens.

In Wales, the visitor will get a glimpse of Eskimo life relatively unaffected by Outside contact. During the summer,

Wales is a base for residents of Little Diomede Island, and these Eskimos often can be seen traveling to and from their island in large traditional skin boats. Air service and tours to Wales are available out of Nome.

The city has established the George Otenna Museum in the community center, City of Wales, Wales, AK 99783, phone (907) 664-3671. This local history museum features contemporary arts and crafts, as well as Eskimo artifacts and the history of Wales and the surrounding area.

Activities in Wales include the annual Fourth of July celebration with games for all ages, community feasts on Thanksgiving and Christmas, and competitive indoor games for men's and women's teams from Dec. 26 to Dec. 31 each year.

Winter trails connect Wales to Tin City and the interior of the Seward Peninsula. A tractor trail also runs to Tin City.

Communications in Wales include phones, mail plane, radio and TV. The community is served by a Lutheran church and the Wales-Kingikme School with grades kindergarten through 9 with enrollment of 54; older students go to boarding schools in other communities. There is a community electric system. Water is hauled from Village and Gilbert creeks in summer and ice blocks are cut in winter. Sewage system is honey buckets. Freight arrives by ship, barge and plane. Government address: City of Wales, P.O. Box 489, Wales, AK 99783, phone (907) 664-3501, fax (907) 664-3671. Village corporation: Wales Native Corp., P.O. Box 529, Wales, AK 99783, phone and fax (907) 664-3641. Village council: Native Village of Wales, P.O. Box 549, Wales, AK 99783, phone and fax (907) 664-3062, e-mail: Wales@aitc.org.

White Mountain

GPS: N64°41' W163°24'

Located on the west bank of the Fish River near the head of Golovin Lagoon on the Seward Peninsula, 15 miles northwest of Golovin, 65 miles east of Nome, 490 miles west of Fairbanks.

Transportation: Boat; snow machine; scheduled and charter air service from Nome; Nome-Council Road open late June, early July. **Population**: 207. **Zip code**: 99784. **Emergency Services**: Village Public Safety Officer, phone (907) 638-3411/3351; Alaska State Troopers, Nome; White Mountain Health Clinic, phone (907) 638-3311; Volunteer Fire Department, phone (907) 638-3341.

Elevation: 50 feet. **Climate**: Transitional, with less extreme temperature variations than interior Alaska. Colder continental weather during the icebound winter. Mean annual precipitation 16 inches, with 57 inches of snow. Winter temperatures average -7°F to 15°F; summer temperatures average 43°F to 80°F.

Private Aircraft: Airport 1 mile north; elev. 262 feet; length 3,000 feet; gravel; no fuel; unattended. Runway condition not monitored; visual inspection recommended prior to using. Runway slopes at both ends. Passenger terminal at airport; no public transportation into village.

Visitor Facilities: Accommodations available at a local lodge, open summers and for Iditarod Trail Sled Dog Race in March (White Mountain serves as a checkpoint on the Iditarod Trail), or arrangements may be made for lodging in private homes. No restaurant or banking services. Washeteria with laundromat and showers available. Groceries, clothing and sporting goods available in the community. Arts and crafts available for purchase include knitted gloves and caps, moccasins, beaver caps, carved walrus ivory and earrings of porcupine quills, ivory and beads. Fishing/hunting licenses available, as well as sportfishing guide service. Boat repair available. Fuel available: diesel, marine gas, propane, white gas, kerosene and regular and unleaded gasoline. Moorage on beach.

The Eskimo village of Nutchirviq was located here prior to the influx of white settlers during the turn-of-the-century gold rush. Bountiful fish populations in both the Fish and Niukluk rivers supported the Native populations. In 1899, C.D. Lane erected a log warehouse as supply headquarters for his numerous gold claims in the Council district. The name White Mountain was derived from the color of the mountain located next to the village. White Mountain was incorporated as a second-class city in 1969.

"The community is located near a hill which breaks the northeast wind," writes city clerk Dorothy Barr. "It is special because it has a friendly environment, with the residents always smiling and welcoming people who come into White Mountain."

White Mountain residents rely both on subsistence hunting and fishing and on wages from seasonal work in commercial fishing, construction, fire fighting, wood cutting, trapping, some cannery work and reindeer herding. There are a few jobs locally with the school, city, store and airlines. Residents spend much of the summer at fish camps. The year-round diet includes lingcod, pike, whitefish, grayling, trout and skipjack. Assorted greens and roots, berries, wildfowl and squirrels are harvested in the fall; seals, moose, brown bears, reindeer, rabbit, ptarmigan, flounder and sculpin in the winter; rabbits, ptarmigans, oogruk, seals, wildfowl and eggs, and assorted roots and greens in the spring; and herring, smelt, salmon and beluga whales in the summer.

Communications include phones, mail plane, radio and TV. The community is served by a Covenant church, a school with grades kindergarten through 12 with enrollment of 63, and a village library. Community electricity and water. Sewage system is honey buckets. Freight arrives by barge and cargo plane. Government address: City of White Mountain, P.O. Box 130, White Mountain, AK 99784, phone (907) 638-3411, fax (907) 638-3421, e-mail: cowmo@nook.net. Village corporation: White Mountain Native Corp., P.O. Box 81, White Mountain, AK 99784, phone 638-3651. fax (907) 638-3652. Village council: Native Village of White Mountain, P.O. Box 84082, White Mountain, AK 99784, phone (907) 638-3651, fax (907) 638-3652, e-mail: WhiteMountain@aitc.org.

WESTERN • ATTRACTIONS

Wilderness recreation in Western Alaska is defined partly by geography. Recreation in the Bristol Bay area centers around its rivers. The Kvichak (which drains Lake Iliamna), Nushagak, Naknek, Tikchik, Wood and Togiak rivers offer excellent fishing and/or floating. Most of the Yukon-Kuskokwim Delta area is included in the Yukon Delta National Wildlife Refuge, where recreation centers around hiking, boating and bird watching. Bird watching is also a favorite activity in the Seward Peninsula/Norton Sound area, where serious birders can add checks to their life list with sightings of rare Asiatic species.

Index of Western Attractions

Alaska State Parks
See Wood-Tikchik State Park

Fishing
Bristol Bay Area
Norton Sound/Seward Peninsula Area
Yukon-Kuskokwim Area

Hot Springs

National Parks and Monuments
See Bering Land Bridge National Preserve; Lake Clark National Park and Preserve

River Running
Bristol Bay Area
Norton Sound/Seward Peninsula Area
Yukon-Kuskokwim Delta Area

Special Features
See Cape Denbigh; Cape Nome Roadhouse; Kigluaik Mountains; King Island

Wildlife Refuges
See Togiak National Wildlife Refuge; Walrus Islands State Game Sanctuary (Round Island); Yukon Delta National Wildlife Refuge

Bering Land Bridge National Preserve

This 2.8-million-acre preserve is located just below the Arctic Circle on the Seward Peninsula, 50 miles south of Kotzebue and 90 miles north of Nome. It is a remnant of the land bridge that connected Asia and North America 14,000 to 25,000 years ago. More than just a narrow strip across the Bering Strait, the land bridge at times was up to 1,000 miles wide. It rose as the formation of massive glaciers during the ice ages caused the water levels of the Bering and Chukchi seas to fall. Across this bridge, people, animals and plants migrated to the New World, and the preserve is considered one of the most likely regions where prehistoric hunters crossed over. An archaeological site at Trail Creek Caves has yielded evidence of human occupation 10,000 years old.

Other interesting features of the preserve are several lava flows around Imuruk Lake, some as recent as 1,000 years ago; low-rimmed volcanoes called maar craters, which have become lakes, in the northern lowlands around Devil Mountain; and Serpentine Hot Springs, long recognized by Native Alaskans for its spiritual and medicinal values. The Inupiat Eskimo name for these springs is Iyat, which means "cooking pot." Hillsides in the preserve are dotted with the remains of ancient stone cairns, their original purpose lost in the misty past. Also of interest are the more recent historical sites from early explorations and mining activities.

Today, Inupiat Eskimos from neighboring villages pursue their subsistence lifestyles and manage reindeer herds in and around the preserve. Their camps, fish nets and other equipment are critical to their livelihood and should be left undisturbed.

Climate: Temperatures in the preserve vary. On the coast, January temperatures are -10°F to -20°F, while inland, they may reach -60°F. Maximum July temperatures on the coast are in the lower 50s, while inland they are in the mid-60s. Summer is the wettest season, receiving 3 to 4 inches of the annual 10 inches of precipitation. Snowfall averages 50 to 60 inches per year. Insects are most bothersome from mid-June to early August.

During the short summer, the preserve bursts into life, and many of the 245 species of plants bloom with bright colors.

Wildlife: The preserve includes 112 species of migratory birds; marine mammals such as bearded, hair and ribbon seals, walrus, and humpback, fin and bowhead whales; grizzly bears, some wolves, caribou, some musk-oxen from transplanted herds, moose, red and arctic foxes, weasels and wolverines. Fish in preserve waters include salmon, grayling and arctic char.

Activities: Recreational opportunities in the preserve include hiking, camping, fishing, sightseeing, wildlife observation and photography.

Accommodations: Aside from the cabin at the hot springs, there are no accommodations or campgrounds in the preserve. There are hotel and restaurant facilities in Nome and Kotzebue (although during the summer, most of the rooms are booked by tour groups) and limited accommodations in Shishmaref. Visitors to the preserve must arrive self-sufficient, with food, clothing, shelter, and in some cases, fuel. There is driftwood on beaches, but wood is scarce inland. The Park Service further advises that visitors to the preserve should have good outdoor skills, including hiking, backpacking and camping experience and the stamina to survive difficult conditions.

Access: Commercial jets to Nome or Kotzebue, with connecting flights via bush plane to Deering and Shishmaref, provide access to the preserve. Visitors to the preserve usually arrive by charter plane from Nome or Kotzebue, landing on lakes, gravel bars, beaches or private mining camp airstrips just outside the preserve. There is also an airstrip at Serpentine Hot Springs, location of a public-use cabin. That strip is 1,100 feet long and 50 feet wide; the runway slopes, crosswinds are common and the surface is muddy when wet. Access is also possible by driving from Nome on the 86-mile-long Taylor Highway to the Kougarok River, about 20 miles from the preserve, and then hiking in to the preserve. You can also travel a road from Deering 25 miles along the Inmachuk River to within 5 or 10 miles of the preserve. Or it's possible to go by boat from Shishmaref to the preserve.

For more information: Contact the Superintendent, Bering Land Bridge National

Preserve, P.O. Box 220, Nome, AK 99762; phone (907) 443-2522. USGS maps: Kotzebue, Shishmaref, Bendeleben, Teller.

 Cape Denbigh

The Iyatayat archaeological site at Cape Denbigh, 12 miles west-northwest of the village of Shaktoolik on Norton Sound, is a national historic landmark. Cape Denbigh was named by English explorer Captain James Cook on September 11, 1778; its Eskimo name is Nuklit. This site, excavated by archaeologist J.L. Giddings from 1948-52, is the type site for the Norton culture and the Denbigh Flint complex and was a momentous discovery because it was older than previously known sites. The site is located on an old beach ridge and represents 3 cultural periods dating back as far as 5,000 B.C. Access is by boat from Shaktoolik, which is reached by scheduled air service from Unalakleet. Check with the city government or the village corporation about the location of private lands in the area.

 Cape Nome Roadhouse

Located just east of Cape Nome at Mile 14 on the Nome-Council Road, this historic roadhouse is listed on the National Register of Historic Places. In 1900, the original section was built of logs hauled 70 miles from Council by horse. In 1913, after a flood destroyed the log building, an abandoned government building from Safety was reportedly moved to the site and became the present roadhouse. From about 1910, it was a major stopover for dog teams traveling the Iditarod Trail. It was the only roadhouse still standing that was used in the famous 1925 "Race to Nome" to deliver serum during the diphtheria epidemic. The building also was used as a temporary orphanage. It has been converted to a private residence.

Fishing

The Alaska Department of Fish and Game recommends that anyone traveling to remote areas should plan for the worst. Take a few days' extra food and fuel if necessary, and allow for a flexible schedule since weather can delay travel.

Although many villages have hunting and fishing license vendors, officials recommend that you purchase your license and king stamps in Anchorage or another large community or from Fish and Game at www.state.ak.us/local/akpages/FISH.GAME/adfghome.htm since sometimes the local vendors themselves have "gone fishing." King salmon stamps are often in short supply in the bush.

Sport fishing is controlled by dual management. Anglers must comply with both state and federal fishing regulations, which differ between locations. Please obtain current regulations and closure information from Fish and Game.

More information about fishing in Western Alaska is available from the regional offices of the Alaska Department of Fish and Game listed below. Also visit the ADF&G sport fish home page at www.state.ak.us/local/akpages/FISH.GAME/sportf/sf_home.htm.

For the Bristol Bay, area contact: Alaska Department of Fish and Game, Sport Fish Division, 333 Raspberry Road, Anchorage, AK 99518, phone (907) 267-2220; or Alaska Department of Fish and Game, P.O. Box 230, Dillingham, AK 99576-0230; phone (907) 842-2427; or Alaska Department of Fish and Game, 460 Ridcrest Dr., Bethel, AK 99559; phone (907) 543-1677. Special Bristol Bay regulation recording (907) 842-7347. On the web visit www.sf.adfg.state.ak.us/Region2/html/r2weekly.stm.

For Norton Sound/Seward Peninsula area, contact the Alaska Department of Fish and Game, Sport Fish Division, 1300 College Road, Fairbanks, AK 99701-1599; phone (907) 459-7207. Or, Alaska Department of Fish and Game, P.O. Box 1148, Nome, AK 99762-1148; phone (907) 443-5796, fax (907) 443-5893.

For Yukon-Kuskokwim area, contact the Alaska Department of Fish and Game, Sport Fish

Division, P.O. Box 1467, Bethel, AK 99559-1467; phone (907) 543-1677, fax (907) 543-2021.

Bristol Bay Area Fishing

Except for a few roads around Dillingham, King Salmon and Iliamna, access to sport-fishing in the Bristol Bay area is primarily by floatplane. If you have the time, however, you can sometimes walk or boat to productive fishing spot. Boats can occasionally be rented or chartered at villages along the waterways. There are daily commercial flights to transportation centers such as King Salmon, Dillingham or Iliamna, where you can catch a commuter flight to a smaller village or charter a plane to a lake or river. In addition, commercial sport-fish guides will handle logistics for you on guided fishing trips.

Bristol Bay is world famous for its sportfishing, particularly for trophy-sized rainbow trout which can reach 10 pounds in some areas. These fish are at their best in early summer or fall. Special regulations in the Bristol Bay area, such as conservative bag limits, spawning season closures and special management areas for catch-and-release and fly-fishing only, are designed to perpetuate the native wild rainbow trout stocks. Other special regulations include single-hook, artificial lures only (no bait) in large portions of the area.

Throughout the Bristol Bay area, the philosophy of catch-and-release is encouraged (especially with rainbow trout), according to the Alaska Department of Fish and Game.

Tackle-breaking king salmon are at their peak from mid-June through July. These fish may reach 30 pounds or more. Chums and reds show up by July 1, pinks by mid-July, and silvers by early August. Salmon fishing is concentrated in the river systems.

Arctic char (resident in lakes) and Dolly Varden (migrate to streams annually) are found throughout this area and are most abundant in spring to midsummer and in fall in some systems. Grayling are resident in lakes and streams during the open-water season.

Farther west, rivers and their headwater lakes in Togiak National Wildlife Refuge provide excellent sportfishing for salmon, grayling, rainbow trout and arctic char. Lake trout are available in the lakes.

Alagnak River System. Wild River in upper 50 miles. Uplands managed by Katmai National Park. Native lands along river managed by individuals and Levelock Natives Limited and Iguigig Village Corporation. The 2 major lakes, Kukaklek and Nonvianuk, are spectacular, and several tributaries offer great trout and some sockeye salmon fishing in season. Fish available: good king, chum, pink, red and coho salmon runs; good grayling, char; fair to excellent rainbow trout (catch-and-release only).

Igushik River System. Located approximately 20 miles west of Dillingham. Heads in Amanka Lake in Togiak National Wildlife Refuge and flows south 50 miles to Nushagak Bay. (Nushagak Bay tides influence the lower half of the Igushik River, making boating more difficult and creating tidal flats.) Fish available include red salmon June to August; grayling best May to September; arctic char best June to September; rainbow trout best in late summer and early fall; and northern pike all year. Charter floatplanes available in Dillingham and King Salmon. No accommodations on lake or river.

Kvichak River. This river heads in Lake Iliamna and flows southwest 50 miles to Kvichak Bay at the head of Bristol Bay. Sockeye salmon, June through August, peaking in June and July; coho salmon to November; pinks in August, chums in July.

Lake Clark Area. Located approximately 30 miles north of Iliamna in Lake Clark National Park and Preserve. Excellent fishing. Fish available: lake trout, burbot, whitefish and northern pike year-round; red salmon June to August; arctic char, best June to September; grayling, best May to September. Accessible by small plane from Iliamna, Nondalton or Port Alsworth. Several private lodges in area require advance reservations. Other accommodations limited but growing; there are several bed & breakfasts in the area.

Lake Iliamna. Alaska's largest lake (1,000 square miles) helps support the largest sockeye salmon run in the world. Iliamna, along with Lake Clark and tributary rivers, provides spawning grounds for the salmon, which grow to maturity in Bristol Bay then find their way back up the Kvichak River to lay their eggs, fertilize them and die. But sockeyes are only one of the salmon species that anglers go after in Lake Iliamna. There are also runs of pinks and chums. Other fish include Dolly Varden, arctic char, lake trout and grayling.

Regulations for the Kvichak/Iliamna drainage are conservative, designed to perpetuate the high-quality wild rainbow trout fisheries while providing anglers a variety of fishing experiences. Large rainbow trout, probably the most sought-after sport fish in western Alaska, are available all season long, but most of the big ones (up to 18 pounds) are taken in late summer and early fall. During September, the rainbows will leave the lake and enter clearwater streams to feast on salmon eggs and insects feeding on decaying salmon.

In addition to the world-class fishing, anglers are treated to beautiful fall colors. Catch-and-release is practiced here, except for the occasional mortally hooked fish (kept for dinner) and the once-in-a-lifetime trophy saved for mounting. The number of waters restricted to catch-and-release for rainbows is increasing; check regulations carefully.

Climate: Summers at Lake Iliamna tend to be cool and rainy, especially in August and September. When storms brew, winds can whip the waters of the lake into high, dangerous waves. A wilderness lodge advises its visitors to bring down vests and jackets, wool shirts and good rain gear. Binoculars and, of course, a camera are also recommended.

Accommodations range from basic shelter to luxurious, first-class, world-renowned lodges. There are no established campgrounds around the lake. Some anglers prefer to stay in Iliamna itself (see Communities this section) and take day trips out via floatplane and hire a guide with a boat. Reservations at lodges should be made well in advance, but air taxi operators can usually accommodate the day angler.

The Alaska Department of Fish and Game reminds visitors that timing is critical, particularly for anglers targeting one or two species of fish. The department's Recreational Fishing Guide (available for $5 from Alaska Department of Fish and Game) provides preliminary information, and local guides and lodges can also help you plan your trip. Air taxi operators in Iliamna, King Salmon, Dillingham and some in Anchorage and the Kenai Peninsula can put you in contact with many of the sportfishing experts. The lake and its excellent fishing are accessible by scheduled and charter flights from Anchorage, Dillingham and King Salmon.

Lake Iliamna does not lie within any established park or refuge boundaries. Much of the land is owned by Native corporations. *NOTE: Iliamna Natives Limited charges fees for camping on corporation land, $25 per person, per night for 1 or 2 people; $50 per night for a group of 3 or more. Fees are payable in advance and are nonrefundable. Hiking, berry picking and fishing are also permitted on corporation lands; hunting in general is not. Wood cutting is not permitted. These and other land-use regulations are available from the corporation office, P.O. Box 245, Iliamna, AK 99606.*

Nushagak-Mulchatna River System. This river system offers hundreds of miles of river fishing from Twin and Turquoise lakes in Lake Clark National Park and Preserve downstream to Dillingham. Float trips are popular. Fish available in the system: king salmon best in late June and early July; coho salmon best August 10 to September (cohos are very erratic, and closures or restrictions are frequent—check ahead at 907/842-7347); lake trout in headwater lakes year-round; grayling best May to September; arctic char best June to September; rainbow trout best in late summer and early fall; northern pike all year. Access by floatplane from Dillingham, King Salmon, Anchorage, Kenai Peninsula (Mulchatna) or Iliamna. Private lodges on the river. Much of the lower Mulchatna and most lands along the Nushagak from upstream of Koliganek downstream to the outlet at Dillingham are managed by Choggiung Limited at (907) 842-5218. (They have an excellent camping permit system.) Facilities are increasing in Koliganek, Ekwok and Portage Creek. Villages provide gas, phones and small clinics. Guides are available in all villages upon prior arrangement.

Tikchik System. Located approximately 80 miles north of Dillingham in Wood-Tikchik State Park (park regulations may apply). Fish available: red salmon June to August; pink salmon July to August; grayling best May to September; arctic char best June to September; rainbow trout best in late summer and early fall; lake trout and northern pike year-round. Access by floatplane from Dillingham or King Salmon. Commercial lodges on lake require advance reservations; Iliamna provides other accommodations.

Togiak System. Located approximately 60 miles west of Dillingham. Togiak River heads in Togiak Lake in Togiak National Wildlife Refuge and flows southwest 58 miles to Togiak Bay, 2 miles east of Togiak village. A popular river to float. Easily accessible by floatplane (depending on water level), wheel plane and motorboat. Upper 38 miles of river is within Togiak Wilderness Area; lower 20 miles is Togiak Village Corporation land. Lakes in the system are Togiak Lake, Ongivinuk Lake, Gechiak Lake and Pungokepuk Lake. Fish available: all salmon in season; king salmon best June and July; coho salmon best August 15 to September; grayling best May to September; arctic char best June to September; rainbow trout best in late summer and early fall; northern pike year-round. Access by charter floatplane from Dillingham, Bethel or King Salmon. Private accommodations on river.

Wood River System. Located 20 to 60 miles north of Dillingham in Wood-Tikchik State Park. The lower lake, Lake Aleknagik, may be reached by road. Entire system navigable by riverboat or can be floated. Fishing best in rivers or at the river mouths. Fish available: all salmon in season, reds predominate and very few kings; grayling best May to September, largest in United States; arctic char best June to September; rainbow trout best late summer through fall; northern pike year-round. Access by boat from Dillingham or Aleknagik village or by charter floatplane from Dillingham or King Salmon. Commercial lodges located on the system require advance reservations. Choggiung manages some Native lands and may have campsites available; call (907) 842-5218.

For more information contact King Salmon Visitor Center at (907) 246-4250; Dillingham Chanber of Commerce at (907) 842-5115, fax (907) 842-4097 or Wood-Tikchik State Park at (907) 842-2370 (summer), (907) 269-8698 (winter).

Norton Sound/Seward Peninsula Area Fishing

Access to good fishing in the Seward Peninsula/Norton Sound area is primarily by aircraft or by boat from rural villages. However, Nome area fishing is unique for the region in that it has almost 200 miles of road that provide access to more than a dozen streams. There are daily commercial flights to the transportation centers of the region—Nome and Unalakleet—where you can catch a commuter flight to a smaller village or charter a plane to a lake or river. In addition, commercial outfitters will handle logistics for you on guided fishing trips.

King salmon are at their peak from mid-June through mid-July. Chums show up by July 1, pinks by mid-July and silvers by mid-August. Salmon fishing is concentrated in the river systems.

Dolly Varden are found throughout this area and are most abundant in the fall, winter and early spring. Grayling can be caught all summer. Other species that may be encountered are whitefish, burbot and northern pike.

In general, the best fishing throughout the northern half of the Bering Sea Coast region is in July and August.

Agiapuk River. Heads 8 miles northeast of Black Mountain and flows southeast 60 miles to the Imuruk Basin, 21 miles southeast of Teller. Excellent fishery. Fish available: pink, chum and coho salmon, use spoons; grayling year-round, best in late summer, use flies; Dolly Varden best in fall. Access by plane from Nome or Teller.

Bluestone River. Located at Mile 58.1 on the Nome-Teller Road. Named for the color of the stones in the river. Fish available: pink and coho salmon; Dolly Varden best in fall, use spoons or eggs; grayling year-round, best in late summer, use flies. Road access from Nome or Teller.

Cripple River. Located at Mile 20.3 on the Nome-Teller Road. Fish present include Dolly Varden, coho and pink salmon. Road access from Nome.

Feather River. Located at Mile 37.4 on the Nome-Teller Road. Fish available: pink and coho salmon; Dolly Varden best in fall; grayling year-round, best in late summer. Road access from Nome or Teller.

Fish River. Located about 70 miles east of Nome on the Nome-Council Road, downstream on the Niuklak River. Fish available: king, chum, pink and coho salmon; grayling year-round; Dolly Varden best in fall; northern pike year-round. Road access from Nome.

Grand Central River. Located 35 miles north of Nome on the Nome-Taylor (Kougarok) Road. Very small turnoff present. Fish available: grayling, Dolly Varden and whitefish. Road access from Nome.

Inglutalik River. Heads at Traverse Peak and flows 80 miles to Norton Bay north of Shaktoolik and south of Koyuk. Fish available: king, chum, pink and coho salmon, Dolly Varden, grayling. Difficult access.

Koyuk River. Flows into Koyuk Inlet at the village of Koyuk at the head of Norton Bay off Norton Sound. This is the only river in Norton Sound with sheefish. Other fish available: northern pike, chum salmon, Dolly Varden and grayling. Boats may be available for rental or charter in Koyuk.

Kuzitrin River. Located at Mile 68 on the Nome-Taylor (Kougarok) Road. Fish available: chum salmon July to August; Dolly Varden, grayling and northern pike year-round. Also whitefish. Road access from Nome.

Kwiniuk River. Flows into Norton Sound near Moses Point, northeast of Elim. Fish available: king, chum, pink and coho salmon, Dolly Varden and grayling. Access by charter air service from Nome or Unalakleet. No accommodations in Elim. The Moses Point airport is privately owned, and permission is needed to land.

Niukluk River. Nome-Council Road ends at this river (Mile 72). There is good fishing in July and August for king, chum, pink and coho salmon. Dolly Varden fishing good August and September. Other fish available: grayling, whitefish, northern pike and burbot. Road access from Nome or by small plane from Nome to Council airstrip.

Nome River. Fishing locations 4 miles east of Nome on Main Street extension at the junction of the river and the ocean, and 10 miles north of Nome on Nome–Taylor (Kougarok) Road where river parallels road. There are numerous turnoffs. Spring and fall fishery best here. Fish available at both locations: pink salmon July to August, coho salmon August to September (check for closures), and Dolly Varden. Closed to grayling and chum salmon fishing.

Penny River. Located at Mile 13.2 on the Nome-Teller Road. Old gold mining area. Turnout present. Fish available: Dolly Varden, coho and pink salmon. Road access from Nome.

Pilgrim (Kruzgamepa) River. Located north of Nome at Mile 65 on the Nome–Taylor (Kougarok) Road. Road parallels river for 19 miles from its source at Salmon Lake. Old gold mining area. Turnoffs present. No accommodations, but there are undeveloped areas suitable for camping and a BLM campground at Salmon Lake. Fish available: pink, coho, sockeye and chum salmon; grayling; Dolly Varden; and northern pike. Above bridge, mostly grayling and sockeye. Road access from Nome.

Safety Sound. Located east of Nome at Mile 17.6 on the Nome–Council Road. Bridge crosses lagoon outlet. Boat fishing recommended. Eskimo summer fishing camps throughout the area. Fish available: pink salmon July to August, use spoons; Dolly Varden and coho salmon best in fall; flounder and burbot. Road access from Nome.

Salmon Lake. Located at Miles 36 to 44 north of Nome on the Nome–Taylor (Kougarok) Road. The lake is alongside the road; numerous side roads lead to the lakeshore. BLM campground. Fish available: Graylingand occasional Dolly Varden. The lake is closed to all salmon sportfishing.

Shaktoolik River. Flows into Shaktoolik Bay on Norton Sound just north of Shaktoolik village. Fish available: king, chum, pink and coho salmon; Dolly Varden and grayling. Access by boat from Shaktoolik or by aircraft.

Sinuk River. Located at Mile 26.7 on the Nome–Teller Road. Fish available: pink and coho salmon, Dolly Varden and grayling. Road access from Nome.

Snake River. Bridge crossing at Mile 7.9 on the Nome–Teller Road. Fish available: pink and coho salmon, grayling and Dolly Varden. Road access from Nome.

Solomon River. Located from Miles 40 to 50 on the Nome–Council Road. River parallels road. Fish available: small runs of pink and coho salmon; Dolly Varden. Closed to grayling fishing. Road access from Nome.

Unalakleet River. Mouth is at Unalakleet village on Norton Sound. Commercial fishing lodge on lower river. Accommodations in Unalakleet. Boats may be available. Good fishing for king salmon. Other fish available: coho, chum and pink salmon; Dolly Varden and grayling. Access by boat from Unalakleet.

Ungalik River. Heads on Traverse Peak and flows southwest 90 miles to Norton Bay north of Shaktoolik and south of Koyuk. Fish available: king, chum, pink and coho salmon; Dolly Varden and grayling year-round. Access is by aircraft.

Yukon-Kuskokwim Area Fishing

Access to good fishing in the Yukon-Kuskokwim area is primarily by air. If you have the time, however, you can sometimes walk or go by boat to a productive fishing spot. Boats can occasionally be rented or chartered at villages along the waterways. There are daily commercial flights to the transportation centers of the region—Bethel, Aniak or St. Marys—where you can catch a commuter flight to a smaller village or charter a plane to a lake or river. In addition, commercial outfitters will handle logistics and equipment requests for guided fishing trips. Sport fish guides and outfitters are registered with Fish and Game; check out the State Fish and Game web site for additional information at www.state.ak.us/local/akpages/FISH.GAME/adfghome.htm.

Tackle-breaking king salmon are at their peak from mid-June through July (king season ends July 25). These fish commonly weigh 30 pounds and up. Chums and reds show up in the Kuskokwim by July 1, pinks by mid-July and silvers by early to mid-August. Salmon fishing is concentrated in the clear-water or nonglacial river systems. *NOTE: Check regulations very carefully before fishing; poor king and chum salmon runs in 2001 resulted in extensive restrictions to all fisheries in the Yukon and Kuskokwim drainages.*

Dolly Varden are found throughout this area and are most abundant in late summer and September. These usually weigh 1 to 3 pounds, but an occasional 9- to 12-pounder has been reported. Grayling can be caught most of the summer, but larger ones are more plentiful from August to October in the upper reaches of streams and rivers. Grayling measuring 16 inches are not uncommon, and they can reach 23 inches. Arctic char and lake trout are found in some of the area's alpine lakes. Rainbow trout are found in some tributaries of the Kuskokwim Bay and lower Kuskokwim River.

Other species that may be encountered are whitefish, which can reach 5 pounds; burbot, which can weigh 10 to 12 pounds; and northern pike, which average 5 to 8 pounds but can reach 30 pounds. Pike have very sharp teeth, so add a couple of steel leaders to your tackle box.

Andreafsky River. This is a National Wild and Scenic River located in the northeast corner of Yukon Delta National Wildlife Refuge. It joins the Yukon River just east of St. Marys. Excellent remote float trip. Fish available: king, chum, coho and pink salmon, use spoons; grayling year-round, best in late summer, use flies; Dolly Varden best June to September, use spoons or eggs. Charter air service and accommodations available in St. Marys.

Aniak River. Joins the Kuskokwim River 1 mile east of Aniak village. Excellent remote, 150-mile float trip and daily fishing at the mouth during king and coho salmon runs. Fish available: king, chum and coho salmon, use spinners and spoons; rainbow trout, use single-hook flies or lures; Dolly Varden, best in fall, use single-hook flies or lures; grayling year-round, best in late summer, use single-hook flies or spinners; northern pike year-round, use single-hook spoons or spinners; sheefish, best May to September, use single-hook spoons; arctic char and lake trout in Aniak Lake, use single-hook spoons or plugs. Accommodations guides and air charter services at Aniak.

Anvik River. This 140-mile-long river joins the Yukon 1.5 miles south of the village of Anvik. The Anvik has a good king salmon run and one of the largest chum runs in the world. The Anvik also has healthy populations of grayling and Dolly Varden. King and chum salmon, use spoons; also good runs of pink and coho; Dolly Varden, best in fall, use spoons or eggs; grayling year-round, best in late summer, use flies; northern pike excellent year-round, use spoons or spinners; sheefish good in June. Access by scheduled air service to Anvik or by boat charter upriver. Accommodations in Anvik and at Anvik River Lodge, (907) 663-6324.

Chuitna River. Flows southeast 37 miles to Cook Inlet, 2 miles north of Tyonek. Fish available: king salmon June through early July, use egg clusters, spinners, spoons; silver salmon July and August, use egg clusters, spinners, spoons; pink salmon July and August, use small spoons or spinners; rainbow trout, use flies or lures. Accessible by wheel plane (30 minutes flying time from Anchorage). *NOTE: Much of the land along the Chuitna River is owned by the Tyonek Native Corporation, and anglers must have a guide from Tyonek. Land on the north side of the Chuitna River mouth is public land.*

Goodnews River. Heads in Goodnews Lake in the Togiak National Wildlife Refuge and flows southwest 60 miles to Goodnews Bay at the village of Goodnews Bay. The river has 3 forks: the North Fork, 47 miles long; the Middle Fork, 42 miles; and the South Fork, 25 miles. The North and Middle forks are popular float trips with lake access; the South Fork has no headwater lake. The lower 22 miles of the North Fork and 15 miles of the Middle Fork are BLM and Goodnews Village Corporation lands. Excellent fishing. Fish available: 5 species of salmon, grayling, rainbow trout and Dolly Varden (good in Semptember). Arctic char and lake trout in Goodnews Lake. Access by air charter from Bethel or Dillingham. Land floatplanes below the confluence of the 3 forks (about 2.5 miles from the village). Wheel planes land at Goodnews Bay village. Air taxis and sportfish guides offer fly in accommodations, a motorboat base camp and float packages.

Hoholitna River. Heads in Whitefish Lake and flows northwest 165 miles to the Holitna River, 13 miles southeast of its junction with the Kuskokwim River near Sleetmute. Fish available: king salmon in early July, coho salmon in mid-August and chum salmon in July; northern pike year-round, use spoons or spinners; sheefish, best late June to August, use spoons; grayling, best in late summer, use flies; Dolly Varden, best June to September, use spoons or eggs. Access by air charter from Bethel, Aniak or Red Devil.

Holitna River. Joins the Kuskokwim River 1.5 miles south of Sleetmute. Fish available: 5 species of salmon in season, but especially kings, chums and coho. Other fish upstream are: northern pike year-round, use spoons or spinners; sheefish, best late June to August, use spoons; grayling year-round, best in late summer, use flies; Dolly Varden, best in fall, use spoons. Commercial lodge on river. Access by boat from Sleetmute or Red Devil, or by air charter from Aniak, Bethel or Red Devil.

Kanektok River. Heads at Kagati Lake in the Togiak National Wildlife Refuge and flows southwest 90 miles to Kuskokwim Bay, 1.5 miles west of Quinhagak. Excellent remote float trip. Single-hook waters most of the year. Fish available: king salmon late June through July 25; coho salmon in August and September; sockeye salmon in July. One of the top rainbow trout waters in the state, best in late summer and early fall; Dolly Varden, best July to September; grayling year-round, best May to September; and lake trout and arctic char in headwater lakes. Access by charter floatplane from Bethel or Dillingham. No accommodations on lake or river, but several sportfish guides have motorboat base camps in the area. There are 2 fishing guides in Quinhagak: Kanektok River Safaris, Inc. and Britton's Finest Salmon Fishing Base Camp. Not recommended for fly-in except at 1 or 2 floatplane landing locations on the river. There are 2 rooms available for rent in Quinhagak at $75 per night. The rooms are located on the second floor of the Village Water Treatment Plant. Contact the City of Quinhagak Office at (907) 556-8165 for reservations. The lower 17 miles of the river is Quinhagak Village Corporation land.

Kisaralik River. Flows into the Kuskokwim River 20 miles northeast of Bethel. Excellent float trip. Fish available: 5 species of salmon in season; rainbow trout, best in late summer and early fall, use single-hook flies; grayling year-round, best late summer, use single-hook flies; Dolly Varden, best in fall, use single-hook spoons or spinners. Rental rafts and charter planes available in Bethel and Dillingham.

Kwethluk River. Flows into the Kuskokwim River 10 miles east of Bethel. Located in Yukon Delta National Wildlife Refuge. Fish available: 5 varieties of salmon in season, kings in July and coho in August; rainbow trout, best in late summer and early fall, use single-hook flies or lures; grayling year-round, best in late summer, use single-hook flies; Dolly Varden, best in fall, use single-hook spoons and spinners. Rental rafts and charter planes available in Bethel and Dillingham.

Owhat River. Joins the Kuskokwim River 4.5 miles upriver from Aniak. Fishing best at its mouth. Fish available: king salmon in July and coho salmon in August; sheefish, best late June to August, use spoons; grayling year-round, best in late summer, use flies; whitefish, use flies or eggs. Access by boat from Aniak.

Hot Springs

Pilgrim Hot Springs. Located on the left bank of the Pilgrim River 13 miles northeast of Salmon Lake. This site of a gold rush resort and later a Catholic mission is listed on the National Register of Historic Places. In the days of gold mining on the Seward Peninsula in about 1900, the property was known as Kruzgamepa Hot Springs and was a recreation center for miners attracted by its spa baths, saloon, dance hall and roadhouse. The roadhouse and saloon burned in 1908. The property was given to Father Bellarmine Lafortune, who turned the ranch into a mission and orphanage in 1917-18 and operated it until 1941, housing up to 120 children. Ruins of the mission school and other church properties remain at the site, which is still owned by the Catholic Church. Access is by charter air service from Nome to a small airfield at Pilgrim Hot Springs or by car on an 8-mile gravel road that joins the Nome–Taylor Road at Cottonwood.

Serpentine Hot Springs. Located within Bering Land Bridge National Preserve. The waters of Serpentine Hot Springs have long been sought for their healthful properties. Eskimo shamans gathered here in earlier times. Although the influence of the shamans has passed, native healers still rely on these waters to help treat their patients for a number of ailments. Likely the most visited area of Bering Land Bridge National Preserve, Serpentine still offers a soothing break from the harsh surrounding climate, and the nearby granite tors create a dramatic landscape that lures hikers to explore. A public-use cabin is located at the springs. Winter trails from Shishmaref and other traditional villages lead to Hot Springs Creek near the tractor trail. Traversed by snow machine and dogsled in winter, it reaches the springs from the end of the Nome-Taylor (Kougarok) Road. A 1,100-foot airstrip at the hot springs allows small wheel plane or skiplane access during most of the year.

Kigluaik Mountains

These mountains are located about 50 miles north of Nome on the Seward Peninsula, 100 miles south of the Arctic Circle. The range is oriented east to west and is approximately 75 miles long and 25 miles wide. It is bordered by the Kougarok Road (Nome-Taylor Road) on the east, the Nome-Teller Road on the west and the Imuruk Basin and Kuzitrin River on the north.

Visitors will find a wide variety of recreational opportunities in the Kigluaik Mountains (pronounced KIG-tee-uk or KIG-loo-ak): hiking, dog mushing, cross-country skiing and snow machining. There is evidence of early-day gold seekers to explore as well as plenty of fish in the clear mountain streams. Access is easy, by western Alaska standards: You can rent a car in Nome and drive to either the east or west end of the range; you can arrange for an air charter to any number of potential landing sites within the range; and in the winter, snow machines can get into areas that are not accessible during the rest of the year.

One area of particular interest starts at glacial Crater Lake, a deep, still pool that discharges into the Grand Central River. The Wild Goose Pipeline starts at Crater Lake and runs down the southern side of the Grand Central Valley. Built about 1920, the pipeline carried water to early mining operations near the Nome River, 10 to 20 miles away. The 21-inch pipeline is made of redwood slats held together with iron hoops. The wood has not deteriorated, and the pipe is still intact in some places. (Please respect this historical artifact, and help preserve the region's heritage by taking nothing but pictures!) The pipeline's name comes from the Wild Goose Railroad which carried supplies north from Nome to the early mining camps near Shelton, located on the Kuzitrin River. Remnants of old cabins, possibly built for maintenance personnel, still remain along the pipeline.

Another point of interest is the Mosquito Pass area. A hike from Windy Creek to the Cobblestone River through Mosquito Pass provides access to some spectacular side canyons, with abrupt peaks reaching nearly 3,000 feet above sea level. Cirque lakes in some of the side canyons offer outstanding photo opportunities. During the summer, you can hike into the Mosquito Pass area by leaving the Nome-Taylor Road in the vicinity of the confluence of Hudson Creek and the Nome River.

Wildlife includes wolves, grizzly bear, moose, red fox, ground squirrels and hoary marmots. Reindeer that are part of domesticated herds are also present throughout the year. The varied landscape provides nesting habitat for a variety of birds during the summer. Many Asiatic species frequent this region, making it particularly interesting for ornithologists. Among the species that have long migration routes and nest here are the wheatear, arctic warbler, bluethroat, yellow wagtail and the white wagtail. Birds of prey such as the rough-legged hawk, golden eagle and gyrfalcon may also be observed soaring overhead, taking advantage of the updrafts in this mountainous region.

Facilities in the Kigluaiks are limited. There is a campground at Salmon Lake on the eastern end of the range near Mile 40 on the Kougarok Road. There is also a public shelter cabin in the Mosquito Pass area. There are no public trails in the mountains, and the Bureau of Land Management advises that visitors should be aware of the demands of the backcountry where help may be far away. USGS maps: Nome D-1, D-2, D-3; Teller A-1, A-2, A-3; Bendeleben A-6; Solomon A-6.

For more information: Contact the Bureau of Land Management, Northern Field Office, 1150 University Ave., Fairbanks, AK 99709; phone (907) 474-2200. Or the Bureau of Land Management, Nome Field Office, P.O. Box 925, Nome, AK 99762; phone (907) 443-2177.

✸ King Island

This rocky, 1,196-foot-high island located in the Bering Sea, 40 miles west of Cape Douglas on the Seward Peninsula, is the ancestral home of the King Island Eskimos, who now live in Nome. The island was named by Captain James Cook of the Royal Navy on August 6, 1778, for Lieutenant James King, a member of his party. The Eskimo name for the island and the tiny village on stilts that clings to the hillside is Ukivok. Today, the island is inhabited only by thousands of seabirds: puffins, auklets, murres, sea gulls and kittiwakes.

King Island villagers began moving away in the 1950s, attracted by job opportunities and health facilities in Nome. The Bureau of Indian Affairs (BIA) closed the school in 1959. The village was last inhabited in 1966. A group of former residents organized to keep their cultural traditions alive, and today, the King Island Inupiat Singers and Dancers perform widely before appreciative audiences. The 2-mile-wide island is isolated 8 months of the year and reached only by a 6-hour boat ride. King Islanders still return in late May or June each year to pick greens, gather bird eggs and hunt walrus.

▲ Lake Clark National Park and Preserve

This 3.6-million-acre park and preserve is located north of Lake Iliamna, 150 miles southwest of Anchorage. The park and preserve boasts an array of features including a jumble of snow-capped, glacier-carved peaks, most unclimbed and unexplored, ranging up to 10,000 feet; 2 steaming volcanoes, including 10,197-foot Mount Redoubt, which last erupted in December 1989; countless glaciers; many lakes, ranging from 40-mile-long Lake Clark to shallow tundra ponds; deep U-shaped valleys with rushing streams; open, lichen-covered uplands where streams meander languidly; 3 wild and scenic rivers (the Mulchatna, Tlikakila and Chilikadrotna); and a coastline along Cook Inlet full of tidal bays and rocky inlets. Lake Clark is fed by hundreds of mountain waterfalls and is part of an important red salmon spawning ground. Some 56 archaeological sites have been located within the park and preserve, including the Kijik village site which is on the National Register of Historic Places.

Climate: The climate on the eastern Cook Inlet side of Lake Clark differs markedly from that on the northwestern slopes and plains. A maritime climate influences the former; drier, continental patterns dominate the latter. In summer, the temperature ranges between 45°F and 65°F in the eastern portion and reaches into the 80s in the western part. Precipitation along the coast reaches 60 inches annually while the interior gets only 20 inches. March and early April are best for cross-country skiing. From mid-April to late May, thawing streams and lakes make all travel difficult. Strong winds, severe in and near mountain passes, can occur at any time.

Wildlife: Along the coast is one of the northernmost stands of Sitka spruce rain forest while inland are several varieties of tundra, including arctic tundra usually found in northern Alaska and lowland boreal forests typical of Interior Alaska. These varied ecosystems support more than 100 species of birds and nearly 40 species of mammals, including several of the state's most charismatic wildlife: black and brown bears, wolves, caribou and moose. Dall sheep reach the southern limit of their range in the Lake Clark Mountains. Wolverine, marten, mink, land otter, weasel, beaver, lynx and red fox are found in the park and preserve. Whales and seals swim offshore along the coast, and the rocky coastal cliffs serve as rookeries for multitudes of puffins, cormarants, kittiwakes and other seabirds. Waterfowl are abundant along Tuxedni Bay and in the ponds and marshes of the tundra plains. Bald eagles, peregrine falcons and numerous other birds nest in the park and preserve.

The several major river and lake systems in the area offer world-class sportfishing opportunties for all five species of Pacific salmon and rainbow trout. Grayling and northern pike can be caught throughout most of the season of open water. Sport hunting is allowed in the preserve under Alaska Deptartment of Fish and Game regulations.

Activities: Backpacking, river running and fishing are the primary activities in this predominantly wilderness area. Rangers recommend the hike to Turquoise Lake or Twin Lakes. Also highly recommended is the Chilikadrotna River float from the Twin Lakes put in. The Chilikadrotna also offers outstanding fishing.

Accommodations: Several private lodges on Lake Clark offer accommodations and services by advance reservation, and stores in Iliamna and Nondalton have limited supplies. Port Alsworth on Lake Clark's southeast shore is the park's field headquarters. There are no other public facilities in the park. Rangers are based at Twin, Telaquana and Crescent lakes in the summer.

The Park Service advises visitors to arrive self-sufficient and carry extra supplies in the event that weather delays air or boat pickup. Warm clothing, good-quality camping and rain gear and insect repellent or a head net are essential. The Park Service further cautions that this is a vast and sometimes hostile region; the animals are wild and must be respected. Also, local residents carry on subsistence hunting, fishing and other activities, and their camps and equipment are critical to their livelihood and should be left undisturbed.

Access: The region is accessible by air from Anchorage or the Kenai Peninsula. There is daily commercial air service to Iliamna, linked by road to Nondalton at the west end of Lake Clark. In addition, there are many air charter operators in Anchorage, the Kenai Peninsula, Iliamna and other communities who fly to the park or preserve. Pilots are allowed to land on any park lake, gravel bar or glacier. There are no roads or trails in the park or preserve.

For more information: Contact the Superintendent, Lake Clark National Park and Preserve, 4230 University Dr., #311, Anchorage, AK 99508; phone (907) 271-3751, fax (907) 271-3707.

USGS maps: Lime Hills, Lake Clark, Iliamna, Kenai, Seldovia, Tyonek.

 **River Running**

River runners should contact the appropriate land manager for more detailed information on rivers listed here. Also, obtain information on current river conditions from reliable local sources, such as bush pilots, park rangers and local guides. River levels can rise dramatically and quickly with meltwater on sunny days. Rainstorms can also quickly swell rivers.

Western Alaska has 5 National Wild and Scenic Rivers: the Andreafsky, managed by the U.S. Fish & Wildlife Service, Yukon Delta National Wildlife Refuge, P.O. Box 346, Bethel, AK 99559; phone (907) 543-1015, fax (907) 543-4413, www.nps.gov/rivers/andreafsky.html; the Chilikadrotna, Mulchatna and Tlikakila, managed by the National Park Service, Lake Clark National Park and Preserve, 4230 University Drive #311, Anchorage, AK 99508; phone (907) 271-3751, fax (907) 781-2119, www.nps.gov/rivers; and the Unalakleet River, managed by the BLM, phone (907) 267-1293, www.anchorage.ak.blm.gov/unkriver.html.

Bristol Bay Area River Running

Chilikadrotna River. This National Wild and Scenic River heads in Twin Lakes in Lake Clark National Park and Preserve and flows 60 miles to join the Mulchatna River 46 miles northwest of Nondalton on Lake Clark. The first 11 miles of the river are within the park and preserve. This swift (usually 5 mph) river flows through the forest west of the Alaska Range. It offers an excellent but demanding whitewater experience with many stretches of fast water and rapids for the intermediate boater. The first 4 miles are Class II, followed by about 4 miles of flat water. Then, it's 31 miles of Class II; there are many sweepers, which when combined with the swift current and twisting course require constant alertness. About midway along this stretch (approximately 5 miles below the Little Mulchatna River), there is one Class III rapid. Rafts or kayaks are recommended; canoes should be used only by very experienced paddlers. The trip generally takes 4 days from Twin Lakes to the first Mulchatna River takeout.

This trip offers fishing for grayling, rainbow trout, Dolly Varden and pike. There also is lake trout fishing at Twin Lakes. Hiking is good throughout the course of the river, and there is mountain scenery around Twin Lakes.

Access is by floatplane from Anchorage or the Lake Clark area to Twin Lakes. Exit is from the Mulchatna River, 12 miles or more below the Chilikadrotna confluence or from villages farther down on the Nushagak River. USGS maps: Lake Clark C-2 through C-7.

Copper (Iliamna) River. This fast, clearwater river heads in Meadow Lake and flows 40 river miles southwest into Intricate Bay on Lake Iliamna. The river connects Upper and Lower Copper lakes and Upper and Lower Pike lakes. From Upper Pike Lake, the river offers a 1^1/2-day-long trip with possible short portages suitable for relatively inexperienced boaters. This stretch features 6 miles of Class II consisting of 4 miles of Class I separating several larger rapids; some border on Class III. Boaters should be alert for right-angle turns. For whitewater enthusiasts, the upper river offers a 2-mile stretch of Class III-IV between Upper and Lower Copper lakes, then 3 miles of Class III before 3 falls, which must be portaged on the left bank. From Upper or Lower Copper Lake, the trip takes approximately 3 to 3^1/2 days. Rafts are recommended.

The Copper River flows through a scenic forest and offers seasonally good fishing downstream from the falls for salmon and rainbow trout. Pike can be caught in side sloughs and lakes. Wildlife that may be seen includes bears, moose, eagles and beavers.

Access is by floatplane from Iliamna to Upper Pike Lake or to Upper or Lower Copper Lake. Exit is by floatplane from Intricate Bay or Lower Pike Lake. USGS maps: Iliamna C-3, C-4, C-5.

Mulchatna River. This National Wild and Scenic River heads in Turquoise Lake in the foothills of the Chigmit Mountains in Lake Clark National Park and Preserve and flows 220 river miles to join the Nushagak River, 65 miles northeast of Dillingham. The first 24 miles of the Mulchatna are within the park and preserve. Above Bonanza Hills for the first 22 miles, the Mulchatna is shallow Class II to Class III, rocky and fast. The alpine tundra around Turquoise Lake changes to spruce and hardwood forest downriver. Below the Bonanza Hills, the Mulchatna is an easy, leisurely float, wandering through a forest, although there is a 2-to 3-foot ledge drop about midway from the Bonanza Hills to the confluence of the Chilikadrotna River. Floaters also should be alert for numerous sweepers or logjams in the many channels of this section. There are three separate logjams that require portages around in a one-mile stretch of river near the northeast corner of the Bonanza Hills. Above Keefer Creek, the river passes through low hills; below Keefer Creek, it meanders across the tundra of the Nushagak lowlands. Rafts are recommended above Bonanza Hills; rafts, canoes or kayaks are suitable for the rest of the river. This trip usually takes 2 days from Turquoise Lake to the end of the Bonanza Hills, then 4 days to the first takeout point. Thereafter, boaters average 12 to 18 miles per day.

Portions of the river valley are swampy, but many high places provide good campsites. Fishing varies from poor to good for grayling, rainbow trout, Dolly Varden and salmon, depending on water conditions and the time of year. There is beautiful scenery and good hiking around the Turquoise Lake area. Wildlife along the river includes a large beaver population.

Access is by floatplane from Anchorage or Lake Clark area communities to Turquoise Lake or to lakes along the Mulchatna below Bonanza Hills. Exit is by floatplane from the Mulchatna 12 miles or more below the Chilikadrotna River confluence or from villages on the Nushagak served by scheduled air service. USGS maps: Lake Clark B-7, B-8,C-6 to C-8, D-3 to D-6; Taylor Mountains A-1, A-2, B-1; Dillingham C-3, D-1 to D-3.

Newhalen River. This large, clear whitewater river heads in Sixmile Lake then flows south 22 miles to Lake Iliamna. This beautiful, turquoise-colored river has flat water for 8 miles from Sixmile Lake to an area called Upper Landing reached by road from Iliamna airport. Then, there is 9 miles of Class I, with a few Class II riffles. Serious white water begins about 7 miles from the mouth of the river where there is a difficult Class V rapid followed by 7 more Class IV rapids. The Class V rapid is signaled by a ledge extending nearly the width of the river at a right-hand bend. This ledge should be run on the left. Then, there is a series of narrower ledges on a long, straight stretch, which should be run midstream. Boaters then reach a left-hand bend, below which an island divides the river into 2 chutes, with a rock pillar in the left chute. There are dangerous falls in the right chute, so run the left chute or portage on the left side. Portage can start from an eddy just above the island. This route requires a sure crossover from the midstream route around the series of ledges. A longer, safer portage begins at the wide ledge at the previous right-hand bend.

This river offers very good fishing in season for all salmon, grayling, arctic char, rainbow and lake trout. *NOTE: Boaters should be aware that all of the land bordering the Newhalen has been selected by Native corporations.* Contact BLM, 222 W. 7th Ave., Anchorage, AK 99513; phone (907) 271-5960, fax (907) 271-3684, for the location of public easements.

Access is by floatplane from Iliamna, by commercial air service, to Sixmile Lake. Or put in at Upper Landing via taxi. Exit is via a trail to Iliamna airport below a series of ledges called "The Falls" or float to the village of Newhalen. USGS maps: Newhalen dam site map or Iliamna C-6, D-5, D-6.

Nushagak River. This river heads at 60°35'N, 156°06'W and flows southwest, 275 river miles to the head of Nushagak Bay, 3 miles south of Dillingham. The Nushagak was the first river in this area ascended by the Russians in the early 1800s. Much of the river is edged by scattered forests, but the tundra is never very far away. The headwaters drain the Taylor Mountains while the major tributaries—the Nuyakuk and Mulchatna rivers—carry drainage from the western lake country and glaciers to the east. The upper reaches of this river are very isolated. It is flat water all the way, but sweepers and logjams can be major obstacles. Canoes, kayaks and riverboats all are suitable for this river.

NOTE: This river passes by the villages of Koliganek, New Stuyahok and Ekwok, and boaters should be aware that there is much private property along the river corridor. Contact BLM, 4700 E. 72nd Ave., Anchorage, AK 99507 for the location of public easements.

Access is by charter plane from Dillingham to the upper reaches of the river or by scheduled air service to any of the villages. Exit can be from one of the villages or float to

Dillingham. Dillingham has all facilities for visitors; there are limited accommodations in Ekwok and New Stuyahok.

Nuyakuk River. This river heads in Tikchik Lake in Wood-Tikchik State Park and flows about 50 miles to join the Nushagak. The upper 12 miles of the river are in the park. This river traverses a relatively flat valley and offers an easy float, with the exception of 2 short sets of rapids and a portage around a falls. The Class II rapids in the first 6 miles of the river can be easily portaged. The falls at the 6-mile point can be portaged by a well-used trail on the right that is clearly visible from the river. This trip generally takes 3 to 4 days from Tikchik Lake to Koliganek, the first village encountered going down the Nushagak. Rafts, canoes and kayaks are suitable for this river.

This trip offers very good fishing in season for all 5 species of salmon, arctic char, grayling, rainbow trout and pike. Moose, bear, beaver and waterfowl may be seen along the war. Campsites are adequate on the upper three-quarters of the river but scarce on the lower quarter.

Access is by floatplane from Dillingham or King Salmon to Tikchik Lake. Exit is by scheduled air service from Koliganek, which has no visitor facilities, or one of the other villages farther down the Nushagak. Also, floatplanes can land on most of the Nuyakuk and Nushagak rivers. USGS maps: Dillingham D-4 to D-6.

Telaquana and Necons rivers. These rivers are semiclear-water tributaries to the silt-laden Stony River. The Necons heads in Two Lakes in Lake Clark National Park and Preserve and flows 16 miles to the Stony. It offers a relatively easy float on moderately swift water through an upland forest. There are 2 short (100 to 250 yards) stretches of Class II rapids on the Necons-a set near its outlet and another close to its confluence with the Stony River. Both may be lined or portaged. The Necons provides easier access to the Stony than does the Telaquana with the trip taking a day from Two Lakes to Stony River.

The Telaquana heads in Telaquana Lake, also located in Lake Clark National Park and Preserve, and flows 29 miles to the Stony. It offers more white water and better fishing for salmon than the Necons. There are 2 small falls on the Telaquana. The first is about 11 miles from its outlet and drops about 8 feet in 2 steps; the second drops 4 to 5 feet in several steps. Both may be portaged, or the second drop may be lined or run. This trip generally takes 2 days from Telaquana Lake to Stony River. Rafts, kayaks and canoes are all suitable for these rivers although canoeists on the Telaquana should be experienced.

Telaquana and Two Lakes are scenic and offer good hiking and seasonally good hunting or viewing opportunities for moose, caribou, bear and waterfowl. Fishing is fair for Dolly Varden and grayling in both rivers and seasonally good for sockeye salmon in the Telaquana River. Reportedly, there are no good campsites at the outlet of Two Lakes.

Access is by floatplane to Telaquana or Two Lakes. Exit is by floatplane from the Stony River or lower Telaquana River, by mail plane from Lime Village or by scheduled air service from Stony River village, which has limited accommodations. USGS maps: For the Necons, Lime Hills A-3; for the Telaquana, Lake Clark D-3, D-4 and Lime Hills A-4.

Tikchik River. This river heads in Nishlik Lake in the Ahklun Mountains and flows 65 river miles south to Tikchik Lake in Wood-Tikchik State Park. This is a clear, gravelly stream. It is fast and has sweepers but no rapids. Water conditions range from flat water to Class I, making this an excellent river for fishermen to float. For one of the most highly recommended trips in western Alaska, boaters can continue from Tikchik Lake down the Nuyakuk River to the Nushagak River and then to Bristol Bay. Canoes, kayaks and rubber rafts are suitable for the Tikchik.

This river has good fishing for rainbow trout, grayling and arctic char. Along its banks, boaters may see ptarmigan, migratory birds, beavers and bears.

Access is to Nishlik Lake by chartered floatplane from Dillingham. Exit is by floatplane from Tikchik Lake for those not continuing down the Nuyakuk River.

Tlikakila River. (ta-lick-a-KEEL-a) This designated National Wild and Scenic River heads in Summit Lake and flows 51 miles to Lake Clark. This is an extremely fast but small glacial river that flows through a narrow, deep valley in the Alaska Range. A short portage may be necessary from Summit Lake to the river. Most of the river is Class I, but there are several hundred yards of Class III just below the North Fork confluence which can be portaged on the left side. This trip takes about 3 days from Summit Lake to Lake Clark. Rafts or kayaks are recommended for this river although canoes are suitable for experienced paddlers.

Access to the Tlikakila is by floatplane from Iliamna or Port Alsworth to Summit Lake. Exit is by floatplane from a small bay west of the river's mouth. Or boaters can paddle to Port Alsworth or farther down Lake Clark. USGS maps: Lake Clark B-2, B-3, C-1, C-2 and Kenai C-8, D-8.

Togiak River. This river heads in 13-mile-long Togiak Lake in Togiak National Wildlife Refuge and flows 60 river miles to the village of Togiak on Togiak Bay. This river offers an easy, leisurely float ranging from flat water to Class I through tundra sparsely covered with willow, alder, cottonwood and some spruce. Low mountains flank the upper river. Boaters should use caution in crossing Togiak Bay from the mouth of the river to the village. Strong winds are possible, and shallow sandbars may preclude staying close to the shoreline. It is possible to float the 12 miles between Upper Togiak Lake and Togiak Lake, but the river is small, multichanneled, meandering and obstructed in spots by logjams and many sweepers. There are riffles, but no rapids between the lakes.

The trip from Togiak Lake to the river mouth usually takes 4 days. Canoes, rafts and kayaks are suitable.

Refuge waters attract fishermen from all over the world. The Togiak River offers very good fishing for 5 species of salmon, grayling and arctic char. Moose, brown bear and eagles may be seen along the river.

NOTE: There is private land along the river corridor. Check the location of private land holdings by contacting the Village of Togiak, phone (907) 493-5820; or the Refuge Manager, Togiak National Wildlife Refuge, P.O. Box 270, Dillingham, AK 99576, phone (907) 842-1063, fax (907) 842-5402.

Access is by floatplane from Dillingham to Togiak or Upper Togiak Lake. Exit is by scheduled airline from the village of Togiak where there are some visitor facilities, or by floatplane at numerous locations along the main river. USGS maps: Goodnews.

Wood-Tikchik Lakes. The 2 lake systems in Wood-Tikchik State Park north of Dillingham offer a combination of lake and river paddling, good fishing and beautiful mountain scenery. Many trip variations are possible. Favorite trips include floating the Tikchik River (Class I) from Nishlik Lake to Tikchik Lake; floating from Lake Kulik down the Wind River (Class II; white water, submerged boulders) and Peace River (flat water and Class I) to Lake Beverly, then the short Agulukpak River (Class I; short and swift, boulders) to Lake Nerka and the 5-mile Agulowak River (Class I) to Lake Aleknagik, from which flows the Wood River (flat water) to Dillingham. (NOTE: Nushagak Bay tides influence the lower half of the Wood River, making boating more difficult and creating tidal flats with few, if any, campsites.) Other trip variations are exploring the fjords, enjoying the alpine setting of the Nishlik or Upnuk lakes area or floating the Nuyakuk. The Allen River connecting Chikuminuk Lake with Lake Chauekuktuli should be run only by experienced, whitewater boaters (per Alaska Division of Parks and Outdoor Recreation).

Kayaks, canoes or rafts with motors are recommended. No fuel for motors is available in the area. For lake travel, estimate 10 to 12 miles per day, paddling 5 hours per day. On the lakes, the wind can quickly create whitecap conditions; be sure to have survival gear and life jackets. Seasonally, there is good fishing for 5 species of salmon, especially sockeye, and for rainbow and lake trout, grayling, arctic char and pike. Fishing is generally best in the rivers or at the river mouths. This area has beautiful mountain scenery. Hiking is generally hampered by dense brush separating lakes and alpine areas. Choose open, breezy spots to camp to avoid mosquitoes and other insects.

Access is by floatplane from Dillingham to any of the lakes. Exit is by floatplane from one of the lakes or by road from Lake Aleknagik to Dillingham. (See Wood-Tikchik State Park this section.)

Norton Sound/Seward Peninsula Area River Running

Unalakleet River. This designated National Wild and Scenic River flows southwest through the low, rugged Nulato Hills to the village of Unalakleet where it drains into Norton

Sound. The river is approximately 105 miles long, but only the lower 76 miles is deep enough to float; often, the river is floatable only from the confluence of Old Woman River. Sweepers line much of the river's banks. Canoes, kayaks or rafts all are suitable for this river.

The usual put in point is at the Unalakleet's confluence with Tenmile Creek about 29 miles from the river's source. Stream flow is relatively fast, and there are many obstructions across the river. Fishing is excellent from this point to Old Woman River. The Old Woman Mountain can be seen as boaters approach Old Woman River. Many sand and gravel bars provide camping sites. The flow slows, depth increases and the river braids. About 4 miles beyond the Old Woman River confluence, the Unalakleet flows through a flat valley where marshes and oxbows can be seen. Around Mile 51, the North Fork joins the Unalakleet. A series of braided channels flow through heavy cover, making identification of the main channel difficult. In this area, there are several private cabins that are used seasonally for fishing, trapping and hunting. Do not trespass. The river widens as it stretches toward the confluence with the Chiroskey River, the end of the wild river corridor. For the remaining 24 miles, the river crosses Native corporation land. There is also one commercial fishing lodge on this lower portion. The trip from Tenmile Creek to the river mouth generally takes 6 days.

Fish in the Unalakleet include king, silver, chum and pink salmon, Dolly Varden and grayling. Wildlife that may be seen include moose, black and brown bears, wolves, waterfowl, beavers and foxes.

Access is by scheduled air service to Unalakleet, then a local guide or boat operator may be hired to take parties to Tenmile Creek by riverboat. Exit is from Unalakleet, where there are visitor facilities. USGS maps: Norton Sound A-1, A-2, Unalakleet D-2 to D-4.

Yukon-Kuskokwim Delta Area River Running

Andreafsky River. The Andreafsky is located within Andreafsky Wilderness, which is in the northern portion of Yukon Delta National Wildlife Refuge. The wild river consists of the Main Fork and the East Fork Andreafsky, which converge approximately 5 miles north of the village of St. Marys. The river flows southwest 120 miles to the Yukon River at Pitkas Point. Both forks of the Andreafsky are scenic, and wildlife along the river includes black and brown bears, foxes, caribou, beavers, otters, bald and golden eagles, peregrine falcons, a variety of hawks, gulls and ducks, Canada geese and tundra swans. Fish include chum, king and silver salmon, grayling and Dolly Varden.

Access to the Andreafsky River is difficult and expensive. The easiest method is to fly commercially to St. Marys. From there, arrange to have a raft towed upriver by jetboat or charter a floatplane to take you up the river to a convenient drop-off point. A major problem is that there are no lakes along the rivers on which a large floatplane can land. A small floatplane is required to land along the river. A further problem is that charter and guide services either do not exist or are quite limited. A potential visitor will need to research extensively in order to set up a float trip on the river. USGS maps: Kwiglik A-2, A-3, B-1, B-2, C-1, C-2, D-1; St. Michael A-1; Unalakleet A-6; Holy Cross C-6, D-6.

Aniak River. The Aniak flows 140 river miles to the Kuskokwim River, 1 mile east of Aniak. This river has 3 distinct phases. It is clear, fast, flat water over a gravel bed from its headwaters at Aniak Lake. It drops at 10 feet per mile for 40 miles through the forest and into the tundra. In its second phase, the course disintegrates into numerous channels filled with many sweepers, logjams and uprooted trees. It continues dropping at 10 feet per mile for 20 miles to where the Salmon River joins the Aniak. Below this very difficult stretch of Class II, the water becomes tame, flat water for the remaining 80 miles to Aniak. It is recommended that this isolated river be attempted only by the most experienced wilderness travelers. Decked canoes and kayaks are recommended.

Fishing on the Aniak is excellent for king, chum and coho salmon, pike, rainbow trout, sheefish and grayling. Aniak Lake has lake trout and grayling.

Access is by chartered floatplane from Bethel or Aniak. Exit is from Aniak, where there are overnight accommodations and other facilities. USGS maps: Bethel B-1, C-1, D-1;

Russian Mission A-1, B-1, C-2.

Holitna River. This is a slow taiga river that was the Russians' first route into the Interior from Bristol Bay. Although it once saw much activity, it is seldom visited today. The Holitna flows northeast 200 river miles from its source at the confluence of Kogrukluk River and Shotgun Creek, to the Kuskokwim River across from Sleetmute village. The Holitna poses few technical problems for the boater; it is flat water all the way.

However, boaters must be alert for sweepers and logjams. The Holitna is isolated and recommended only for travelers with wilderness experience. Canoes, kayaks and riverboats all are suitable.

Five species of salmon are available in this river, but especially kings, chums and cohos, along with pike and sheefish. Grayling and arctic char can also be found upstream.

Access is by floatplane from Bethel. Exit is from Sleetmute, which has scheduled air service, but no overnight facilities. USGS maps: Taylor Mts. D-5; Sleetmute A-4, A-5, B-3, B-4, C-3.

Kanektok River. This river heads at scenic Kagati Lake in the Ahklun Mountains in Togiak National Wildlife Refuge and flows 90 miles to Kuskokwim Bay near the village of Quinhagak. The lower 17 miles of river are on Quinhagak Village Corporation land. The upper river flows through a mountain valley while the lower portion wanders through flat tundra. There are numerous gravel bars and islands along the length of the river, particularly on the coastal plain. The first 25 miles are Class I, followed by 30 miles of Class I-II and then another 30 miles of flat water. There are no rapids in the middle 30 miles, but sweepers, combined with a moderately swift current and a winding course, require frequent maneuvering. Traveling the length of this river usually takes 5 to 7 days. Canoes, rafts and kayaks all are suitable.

Seasonally, there is very good fishing for 5 species of salmon, arctic char, grayling and rainbow trout. The number of large fish in this river qualifies it as one of the premier sport-fishing rivers on the North American continent, according to the Fish and Wildlife Service.

Access is by floatplane to Kagati Lake from Bethel or Dillingham. Exit is by scheduled commercial air service from Quinhagak, which has no overnight facilities. Several commercial float guides are available for the Kanektok. There is a float outfitter in Dillingham. USGS maps: Goodnews C-5, C-6, D-3 to D-8.

Kisaralik River. This river heads in Kisaralik Lake in the Kilbuck Mountains and flows northwest 100 miles to the Kuskokwim River, 20 miles northeast of Bethel. This is considered an exciting whitewater float for boaters with intermediate skills. The river is swift with long stretches of small rocky rapids. The upper half of the river flows through a tundra-covered valley bracketed by mountains rising 2,000 to 3,000 feet. Low bluffs parallel the river. Crossing the Kuskokwim lowlands, the river meanders slowly through paper birch, aspen and spruce forest. There are 4 short (50 yards or less) Class III rapids and then 20-yard-long Upper Falls (Class IV), which can be portaged easily on either side of the river. The left side is an easier portage, but the right side has a better campsite. Quicksilver Creek, 3 miles downriver, and the ridge through which the river cuts to form the falls are recognizable landmarks. Upper Falls is followed by 12 miles of Class II, then the Class II Lower Falls, 4 miles of Class I-II and then Class III Golden Gate. The lower portion of the river consists of 35 miles of Class I and 25 miles of flat water. This trip generally takes 6 days. Rafts or kayaks are recommended, canoes for experienced paddlers.

There is superb mountain scenery and good hiking throughout the upper portion of the river. Downstream, boaters can take a break and explore tundra-covered ridges. Seasonally, there is good fishing for all varieties of salmon, rainbow trout, grayling and arctic char. Lake trout are available in Kisaralik Lake.

Access is by floatplane from Bethel to Kisaralik Lake. Exit is by floatplane from the lower portion of the Kisaralik, or pickup by riverboat can be arranged at Bethel. There are accommodations and meals at Bethel. USGS maps: Bethel.

Kuskokwim River. This 540-mile-long river is Alaska's fourth longest. Its North Fork reaches far north to the Tanana basin and once served as a watercourse for Natives and later, prospectors and trappers. Lake Minchumina is connected by a long, once well-trodden portage to the North Fork. There are few travelers today, so boaters must be prepared to rely on their own resources.

The first village reached is Medfra, located where the East Fork merges with the North Fork. From that point, the Kuskokwim is a wide river, flowing slowly through mountains southwest to the broad coastal plain and Kuskokwim Bay. The largest settlements are McGrath, Sleetmute, Chuathbaluk, Aniak and Bethel. This river is flat water all the way. Canoes, kayaks, rafts and riverboats all are suitable.

Access is by portage from Lake Minchumina or more easily by floatplane from Anchorage, Fairbanks or McGrath. Exit is by floatplane from any point on the river or by scheduled air service from most of the communities on the river. USGS maps: Kantishna River A-5, A-6, B-5; Mount McKinley D-6; Meafra A-3, A-4, A-5, B-2, B-3, C-1, C-2, D-1; McGrath B-6, C-6, D-5, D-6; Iditarod A-1, B-1; Sleetmute C-3, C-4, C-6 to C-8, D-1, D-2, D-4 to D-6; Russian Mission A-5, A-6, B-4, B-5, C-1 to C-4; Bethel C-8, D-6 to D-8; Baird Inlet A-2, B-1, B-2, C-1.

Stony River. This river heads at Stony Glacier in the Alaska Range and flows southwest and northwest 190 miles to the Kuskokwim, about 1 mile from Stony River village. This is a swift (averaging 5 mph), silty river flowing through a forest. Below its confluence with the Necons River, it flows through foothills, then passes into lowlands. Below its confluence with the Telaquana River, the Stony flows through a series of small, scenic canyons for 19 miles of Class II. Here, there are short (100 yards or less) stretches of rapids, alternating with 1 to 4 miles of swift flat water. The remaining 90 miles of the river is flat water or Class I. The trip from the Telaquana confluence takes approximately 5 to 6 days. Rafts, kayaks and canoes all are suitable.

This river offers good grayling fishing in the clear-water tributaries; the river itself is too silty for sportfishing. There are numerous gravel bars for campsites. Mountain scenery upstream from the Necons River is good. This trip is popular with hunters; travelers who want only to sightsee should plan their trips before hunting season.

Access is by wheel plane or floatplane to the upper reaches of Stony River; floatplane to Telaquana Lake, headwaters of the Telaquana River; or Two Lakes, headwaters of the Necons River. Exit is by mail plane from Lime Village on the Stony River, scheduled air service from Stony River village or floatplane pickup from the lower river. Lime Village has no visitor facilities; Stony River has limited accommodations. Boaters may also continue down the Kuskokwim River to a larger village. USGS maps: Lime Hills A-4 to A-6, B-5 to B-8; Sleetmute B-1, C-1, C-2, D-2.

 # Togiak National Wildlife Refuge

This 4.3-million-acre refuge is located about 3 miles west of Dillingham at its closest point. More than half of the refuge is an established wilderness area. Adjacent to the refuge, there are 0.7 million acres of private land: along lower river corridors this is village corporation land; property belonging to private individuals is scattered along the waterways. The refuge, 80 percent of which is in the Ahklun and Wood River mountains, offers outstanding scenery with a wide variety of terrain, including glacial valleys, tundra uplands, wetlands, sand and gravel beaches, rugged mountains and coastal cliffs. The myriad lakes range in size from tundra potholes to 13-mile-long Togiak Lake. Togiak Valley is the site of a rare geological feature: a 2-mile-long tuya, a flat-topped, steep-sided volcano formed when lava erupted under a glacier.

Climate: Summer months are usually moist and rainy with temperatures ranging between 45°F and 75°F. Snow covers the mountains by early October. Ice forms on lakes and rivers in November and will remain until June. Winter temperatures range from -30°F to 45°F. The weather is unpredictable, and it is not uncommon for a warm, sunny day to turn cold, windy and wet.

Wildlife: Togiak Refuge is a haven for resident and migratory birds. Two hundred bird species have been recorded on the refuge, and 13 additional species have been observed in the Dillingham area. As many as 250,000 waterfowl have been counted in the bays, lagoons and lakes along he coast, where waterfowl await spring breakup in the Arctic. About 50 percent of the world's population of brant use the refuge—up to 50,000 can be seen at one time in Nanvak and Chagvan bays. Emperor geese, tundra swans, mallards, northern pintails, green-winged teal, greater scaup, harlequin ducks, black scoters, red-breasted mergansers and Steller's, common and king eiders are also abundant. Red-throated, Pacific and common loons are other abundant water birds in the refuge. Twenty raptor species occur on the refuge with bald eagles, northern harriers, rough-legged hawks, merlings and short-eared owls most abundant. Thirty-nine species of shorebirds have been documented with semi-palmated plovers, greater yellowlegs, dunlin, common snipe, red-necked phalaropes and spotted, western least and rock sandpipers most common. At least 10 species of seabirds have been observed, including black-legged kittiwakes, common murres, pelagic and double-crested cormorants, glaucous-winged gulls, pigeon guillemots and horned and tufted puffins. The refuge is home to one of the largest populations of cliff-nesting seabirds in the eastern Bering Sea, supporting 1.5 million seabirds. Cape Newenham, Cape Peirce, Bird Rock and Shaiak Island support an estimated population of 1 million common murres and black-legged kittiwakes. At least 73 species of land birds are present; these include alder fly-catchers, black-billed magpies, common ravens, tree and bank swallows, black-capped chick-adees, gray-cheeked and hermit thrushes, American robins, yellow wagtails, Lapland longspurs, common redpolls, orange-crowned, yellow, arctic, blackpoll and Wilson's warblers and American tree, savannah, fox, white-crowned and golden crowned sparrows.

Brown bears have been numerous on the refuge since its establishment in 1981. Moose and caribou were scarce at that time, but populations of both species have increased so great-ly that they are regularly seen throughout the refuge. Moose are most abundant in the Togiak River drainage. The refuge caribou include both migratory groups and a resident herd on the Nushgak Peninsula at the southeast corner of the refuge. The Nushagak Peninsula herd is the result of a group of caribou that were transplanted there in 1988. Smaller mammals include the hoary marmot, beaver, wolverine, otter mink, red fox, wolf and an occasional coyote. Pacific walrus, Steller sea lions and harbor and spotted seals haul out on the shoreline. Gray whales feed close to shore on their spring migration; beluga and killer whales are sometimes seen along the coast, and 10 other marine mammal species inhabit the area.

The refuge attracts sportfishermen from around the world with major concentrations of 5 species of salmon, grayling, rainbow trout and Dolly Varden in the Togiak, Kanektok and Goodnews drainages. Other fish available are lake trout, burbot, arctic char and northern pike.

Activities: Sportfishing and hunting are the major recreational activities on the refuge. Other activities are river floating (the Togiak, Goodnews and Kanektok rivers), hiking, sight-seeing, camping and wildlife observation/photography.

One of the primary purposes of the refuge is to provide opportunities for subsistence activities: hunting, fishing and gathering. Commercial fishing occurs along the coast at near-ly every river mouth. Togiak and Goodnews bays and Security Cove support herring fisheries.

Archaeological evidence indicates that humans have occupied the area for at least 2,000 and perhaps 5,000 years. Today, the residents of 7 nearby Yup'ik Eskimo villages use the refuge for subsistence activities. Their camps, fish nets and other equipment are critical to their livelihood and should be left undisturbed. *NOTE: Much of the land around the villages of Quinhagak, Platinum, Goodnews Bay, Togiak, Twin Hills and Manokotak is private property and should be respected. To avoid trespassing, consult the refuge office in Dillingham about the location of private lands.*

The refuge office encourages anyone planning a trip to the refuge to discuss planned itineraries with the refuge staff as a safety precaution and also to allow the Fish and Wildlife Service to assess public use of the refuge. The refuge is currently in the planning stage and may require visitors to obtain permits in the future.

Accommodations: Hotel, food and medical services can be found in Dillingham and Bethel. There are limited facilities in Goodnews Bay, Togiak and Quinhagak. There are no campgrounds or established trail systems on the refuge. Camping on gravel bars below the high water mark is encouraged to reduce environmental impact and trespass on Native lands. The refuge office suggests that drinking water be boiled or chemically purified to avoid giardiasis, an intestinal disease. Several guides and outfitters operate within the refuge.

Access: The refuge can be reached by scheduled airline to Dillingham or Bethel, then a scheduled flight to one of the adjacent villages or a charter flight to the refuge.

For more information: Contact: Refuge Manager, Togiak National Wildlife Refuge, P.O. Box 270, Dillingham, AK 99576; phone (907) 842-1063, fax (907) 842-5402; www.r7.fws.gov/nwr/togiak/tognwr.html.

Walrus Islands State Game Sanctuary (Round Island)

This sanctuary in northern Bristol Bay offers an unsurpassed opportunity to view and photograph large numbers of bull walrus from May to August. There are 7 islands in the sanctuary, but Round Island 70 miles southwest of Dillingham is the most used.

Wildlife: Up to 8,000 male walruses return to the island each spring as the ice pack recedes northward. Females with young are seldom seen in Bristol Bay as they remain near the edge of the ice pack.

An estimated 250,000 seabirds arrive on Round Island in the wake of the walruses. Common murres, pelagic cormorants, parakeet auklets, tufted and horned puffins, black-legged kittiwakes, pigeon guillemots and others nest on the rocky cliffs until August. A colony of up to 200 Steller sea lions haul out on the southern shore of the island from May to September, and gray whales pass by during April and May as they migrate north. Red foxes are year-round residents of the island.

Accommodations: Round Island provides a true wilderness experience. There are no facilities or services available to visitors. Fresh water is available in the camping area, where there is also an outhouse. There is no firewood. Visitors must bring their own food, fuel, shelter and equipment. Tents should have waterproof flies and be able to withstand winds up to 60 mph. A full suit of rain gear and waterproof boots are essential. Fish and Game advises visitors to keep their schedules flexible and bring extra supplies since unpredictable weather can delay travel to or from the island.

Round Island is very rugged. The terrain is steep and the climate can be extremely inhospitable. Visitors should be experienced wilderness campers as well as in good physical condition. It is not recommended for the novice camper, the elderly, or families with children between the ages of 2 and 6, as the camping area is bordered by very steep rock cliffs. Medical facilities for emergencies are several hours to perhaps several days away, depending upon weather conditions.

Access: Travel to Round Island is difficult and regulated by permit from the Alaska Department of Fish and Game. Access is possible only by boat and is subject to weather conditions, which can quickly change for the worse at any time of year. A list of charter operators is available from the Fish and Game office in Dillingham. Don's Round Island Charter, (907) 493-5127, in Togiak provides regular service to the island.

Two wildlife technicians are stationed on the island to conduct walrus research and enforce Sanctuary regulations. They do not give tours. When you arrive at Round Island, they will assist you in getting from your boat to the shore (a short trip on an inflatable raft). All beaches are off limits to visitors except in Boat Cove during loading and unloading. Boat Cove, on the north shore of Round Island, is the only access to the island.

Up to 12 visitors are permitted to camp on the island at one time. Permits are issued on a first-come, first-served basis and are valid for a specified 5-day time period. The camping season extends from the first of May until the middle of August. (During May, most of the island is still snow-covered, and weather is usually cold and wet.) Permits are available after January 1; most prime viewing periods are booked up by April. (Walrus numbers, seabirds and wildflowers peak in July.) A maximum of 10 permits for any given time period may be issued more than 10 days in advance. Up to 3 additional camping permits may be issued for approved scientific or educational purposes.

To obtain a permit to camp on Round Island, you must fill out an application and return it to the Alaska Department of Fish and Game, Division of Wildlife Conservation Office, Dillingham, AK. A $50 application fee must accompany your completed application form. Detailed instructions are on the back of the application form.

Day-use permits are available for $10 for visitors who do not want to camp on the island. Up to 15 day-use visitors are allowed each day.

For more information: Contact Alaska Department of Fish and Game, Division of Wildlife Conservation, P.O. Box 1030, Dillingham, AK 99576; phone (907) 842-2334; web www.state.ak.us/adfg/wildlife/region2/refuge2/rnd~isl.htm.

Wood-Tikchik State Park

This 1.7-million-acre state park-largest in the system and in the country-is located about 30 miles north of Dillingham and 329 miles southwest of Anchorage. Wood-Tikchik is an undeveloped wilderness park containing 2 separate systems of large, interconnected, pristine lakes, 6 in the Tikchik River drainage and 6 in the Wood River drainage, that are spawning and rearing habitat for the Bristol Bay salmon fishery.

Rugged mountains 3,000 to 5,000 feet tall form a backdrop for some of the lakes on the western side of the park. Pinnacle peaks, high alpine valleys, hanging valleys and dramatic, V-shaped incisions contribute to this area's fjord-like appearance. The eastern edge of the lakes overlooks numerous shoals and islands, gravel beaches and the broad tundra landscape of the Nushagak flats.

Climate: The area is characterized by cloudy skies, mild temperatures and fairly heavy precipitation. In August, some precipitation occurs 27 percent of the time along the coast. Average daily July temperatures range from 46°F to 65°F. Winds are usually moderate (0-30 mph), prevailing from the southeast/southwest in the summer and the north and east in the winter. Although annual snowfall averages 60 to 70 inches at Dillingham, it may reach 160 inches at Lake Nerka. Snow and ice cover, especially on the upper lakes, is common until mid-June. Water levels in the connecting lakes drop during the summer months. By early October, the lakes start to freeze, and snow begins to fall.

Wildlife: The area supports brown and black bears, moose, wolf, wolverine, fox, lynx, marten, beaver, porcupine, marmot, muskrat and squirrel. Fishing is excellent throughout the summer for arctic char, rainbow trout, northern pike, red salmon, Dolly Varden and grayling. Sportfishing and hunting are allowed in the park in season under Alaska Department of Fish and Game regulations. Catch-and-release fly-fishing for rainbow trout is encouraged.

Activities: The park offers excellent opportunities for boating, sightseeing, fishing and photography. Flying over the park, it might appear that there are opportunities for hiking ridgelines, but getting to the ridges is not easy. Since most access to the park is via the lakes, backpackers and hikers must bushwack through the lower elevations to reach the beckoning ridges. There are no restrictions on camping in the park, and boat motors are allowed on the lakes.

Floating and fishing are by far the most popular activities at Wood-Tikchik Lakes. The Alaska Division of Parks and Outdoor Recreation cautions that winds can quickly create rough water conditions on the lakes, and whitewater conditions may exist on streams although most streams are navigable by canoe, kayak or inflatable raft. Water levels in the streams connecting the lakes drop as the summer progresses, revealing boulders which can challenge boaters. Some portages of upper streams are advised.

The trip from Lake Kulik to Aleknagik is about 140 miles of big lakes and short, fast rivers, suitable for canoeing and kayaking. From the drop off at Lake Kulik, this paddle leads down the Wind River to Mikchalk Lake, down the Peace River to Lake Beverly then down the Agulukpak River to Lake Nerka and finally, down the Agulowak River to Lake Aleknagik. (See River Running this section.)

The Alaska Division of Parks also warns those traveling by collapsible boat to be wary of porcupines. These creatures have demonstrated a taste for the coated canvas material used for many of these boats. One ranger advised anchoring boats offshore to keep porcupines from chewing on your boat and leaving you with an unseaworthy vessel. All travelers are also advised to leave a copy of their itinerary with a friend, the air charter operator or the park ranger.

Accommodations: There are hotel accommodations in Dillingham, as well as supplies and services. There are several commercial lodges in or near the park which cater only to fishing/sight-seeing clients on an advance-reservation basis; they are not equipped to accommodate drop-in visitors. In the park, there are no developed facilities, trails, shelters, cabins, campsites, waste receptacles, sanitary facilities or emergency services. Visitors should arrive self-sufficient, and the Division of Parks and Outdoor Recreation urges the pack-it-in, pack-it-out method of wilderness camping. Visitors should be prepared for cool nights, wind chill, rain and mosquitoes.

Lakeshores tend to be narrow and rocky, with willows and alders forming a barricade to whatever flat lands lie beyond the shore. The best sites for paddlers are found at stream washes that create gravel pads perfect for pitching a tent.

Access: Wood-Tikchik is accessible by scheduled air service to Dillingham, where charter air service to the park is available at about $325 an hour, depending on size of plane, party size and number of trips. Motorboats can access the Wood River Lakes system from Dillingham. The lakes are connected by shallow, swift rivers which generally require jet-equipped watercraft, according to the Alaska Divison of Parks. There is road access to Aleknagik village on Lake Aleknagik, which is adjacent to the southern end of the park. Much of the land around Aleknagik is private property and should be respected. Access to the Tikchik Lakes is primarily by aircraft. Pickup can be arranged from any of the lakes.

For more information: Contact Wood-Tikchik State Park, P.O. Box 3022, Dillingham, AK 99576; phone (907) 842-2375 (May 15 to October 1); or HC 52, Box 8999, Indian, AK 99540; phone (907) 345-5014 (October 1 to May 15). Or contact Alaska Department of Natural Resources, Division of Parks and Outdoor Recreation, Chugach/Wood-Tikchik Area, P.O. Box 107001, Anchorage, AK 99510; phone (907) 694-2108, fax (907) 762-2535. Web site is www.dnr.state.ak.us/parks/units/woodtik.htm.

Yukon Delta National Wildlife Refuge

At over 19 million acres, this is the nation's second largest wildlife refuge, and it encompasses the great deltas of the Yukon and Kuskokwim rivers, the 2 largest rivers in Alaska. This region is treeless and, apart from the Andreafsky and Kilbuck hills, is a seemingly limitless expanse of wet-lands. The Andreafsky River, in the northern section of the refuge above St. Marys, is a designat-ed wild river within an established wilderness area. The refuge also includes 1.1-million-acre Nunivak Island, 20 miles off the coast. On Nunivak, the terrain includes volcanic craters, sand dunes, sea cliffs and rolling tundra. The southern half of the island is a designated wilderness area.

Climate: Weather in the refuge is unpredictable at best. January temperatures average near 6°F although high winds often cause a wind chill factor exceeding -60°F. Winter in the delta region begins early in October. Annual snowfall may exceed 50 inches, but winter thaws prevent much accumulation. Ice breakup usually occurs in late May or early June. Summer temperatures in Bethel on the Kuskokwim River and St. Marys on the Yukon River average in the mid-50s with occasional highs in the 60s and 70s.

Wildlife: This refuge is one of the most significant waterfowl breeding areas in North America. More than 220 species of birds have been observed, and more than 140 species nest here, including more than 100,000 swans, 500,000 geese, 1 million ducks and millions of shore and water birds. More than half the continent's black brant population hatches on the refuge coast. Cackling Canada geese and 90 percent of the emperor geese are pro-duced in the coastal lowlands. Large populations of Pacific white-fronted geese nest near the coast and on the inland tundra.

Nunivak Island shelters herds of reindeer and musk-oxen. Musk-oxen vanished from Alaska in 1865 because of overhunting. The Nunivak herd, introduced from Greenland in 1935, has provided breeding stock for establishing herds elsewhere in Alaska and the Soviet

Union. The reindeer herd and fishing are major sources of food for residents of Mekoryuk, the only village on the island. Guided muskox hunting and commercial fishing are major sources of income for the village.

Other wildlife in the refuge includes moose, caribou and grizzly and black bear. Wolves are found everywhere on the refuge. Smaller mammals include beaver, muskrat, mink, river otter and fox. On Nunivak, native land animals include red and arctic foxes, weasel, mink, shrews, voles and lemmings. Coastal waters support harbor, ribbon, ringed and bearded seals, walrus and many species of whales during migrations.

Fish found in refuge waters include trout, arctic char and grayling in the mountain streams and pike, sheefish, whitefish and burbot in lowland waters. Also, king, silver, red, pink and chum salmon migrate through the delta rivers during the summer on their way to spawning grounds.

Activities: Recreational activities in the refuge include wildlife observation, photography and boating. Other activities include hiking, camping, sled dog racing, snowmobiling and cross-country skiing. Hunting and fishing are allowed in accordance with state and federal regulations. Because of the refuge's remoteness and fickle weather, careful planning is necessary to ensure a safe trip. Top-quality equipment and good insect repellent are essential, according to the Fish and Wildlife Service.

For many centuries, the abundance of wildlife has made the delta the heart of Yup'ik culture. Residents of at least 45 villages depend on this region for subsistence purposes. Their equipment and camps are essential to their livelihood and should be left undisturbed. *NOTE: Ownership of large areas within the refuge has been conveyed to Native regional and village corporations, and this private property should be respected. Anyone planning a trip to the region should consult about the location of private lands.* Contact individual village corporations or the Association of Village Council Presidents, P.O. Box 219, Bethel, AK 99559; toll free (800) 478-3521, fax (907) 543-3596, www.avcp.org.

Accommodations: Lodging may be available in some villages but should be arranged in advance. In general, travelers to the refuge should be self-sufficient. Wilderness camping is permitted in the refuge, but there are no established campgrounds or trails.

A visitor center for the Yukon Delta National Wildlife Refuge is located across from the Bethel Regional Hospital on the main road from the airport to downtown Bethel. The center features exhibits on the refuge, its wildlife and how the resources have been and are used by Eskimos in the region. Refuge staff present periodic wildlife programs for schools and the public.

Access: The refuge is accessible only by boat or airplane. There is scheduled airline service from Anchorage to Bethel, St. Marys and flights to other villages or remote areas can be arranged.

For more information: Contact Refuge Manager, Yukon Delta National Wildlife Refuge, P.O. Box 346, Bethel, AK 99559; phone (907) 543-1015, fax (907) 543-4413.

ARCTIC

This last great wilderness of mountain range and arctic coastal plain stretches for miles across the top of Alaska, beckoning visitors with the promise of beauty, solitude and grandeur. The Brooks Range and the Arctic are true wilderness, immense and almost roadless, remote and sparsely populated.

In the Brooks Range the mountains stand like sentinels protecting the fragile ecosystem of the Arctic from casual intrusion. These mountains are themselves protected in a series of national parks and preserves that stretch from the Dalton Highway (North Slope Haul Road) west almost to the Chukchi Sea. And to the east of the highway the Arctic National Wildlife Refuge preserves the north and south slopes of the Brooks Range all the way to the Canadian border.

Oil, mining and subsistence hunting and fishing provide the majority of economic support for the Arctic. The 800-mile-long oil pipeline from Prudhoe Bay to Valdez on Prince William Sound began operation in 1977. The huge industrial complex on the North Slope created jobs for many arctic residents and provided the economic stimulus for new houses, schools, hospitals and civic buildings. Further oil field development in the region has been proposed in the Arctic National Wildlife Refuge (ANWR). In the western Arctic, the Red Dog mine promises to be the largest operating zinc and lead mine in the western world.

Residents of smaller villages rely on subsistence and temporary work, usually in construction or government. Caribou are important to inland Eskimos, while coastal villagers depend on fish and marine mammals.

Location: The Arctic Circle and the southern foothills of the remote Brooks Range delineate the southern boundary of this region. The Chukchi Sea borders to the west. The Arctic Ocean with the Beaufort Sea in the northeast are the region's northern boundaries.

Geography: The Brooks Range, though not as high as Alaska's coastal mountains or the Alaska Range, rises majestically between Interior's flat expanses and the Arctic's coastal plains. Lying east to west across the width of the state, it consists of endless gentler mountains interrupted by the spectacular granite spires of Arrigetch Peaks.

The Brooks Range spawns a host of rivers running north and south, east and west. Many of these rivers have been designated wild and scenic and are among the most beautiful and remote in the world.

A taiga forest on the south side of the Brooks Range gives way to tundra that stretches north to the Arctic Ocean. While the Arctic is covered by snow and ice for much of the year and veiled in darkness for up to 3 months, there is enough sunshine in the remaining months to transform the bleak winter tundra into a summer carpet of flowering plants.

Several varieties of tundra can be found in the Arctic. Higher elevations support alpine tundra, which is characterized by lichens, grasses, sedges and some herbs. Moss campion grows on drier slopes. Cotton grass, mosses, lichens, dwarf birch and willows cover the foothills. Sedges, mosses, cotton grass and lousewort predominate on the boggy plain, and high brush vegetation, featuring willow and alder, grows along major rivers.

The treeless Arctic is interlaced with meandering rivers and dotted with thousands of shallow thaw lakes. Permafrost, beginning a few inches under the surface and extending down as far as 2,000 feet, underlies most of the Arctic. Most areas receive less than 10 inches of precipitation a year, but soggy tundra and bogs are common in summer because there is little evaporation and poor drainage.

The Kobuk River, an important highway for prehistoric and contemporary people, and the Noatak, with its pristine watershed, drain much of northwestern Alaska. On the arctic plain, the Colville and north-flowing streams in the eastern Arctic provide access to the region's interior.

Climate: Winters are long and cold in the Brooks Range, with temperatures as low as -60°F. Summers on the south slopes are considerably warmer than on the north, and precipitation is low.

Strong winds, cold temperatures and low precipitation characterize the arctic climate. The Beaufort and Chukchi seas moderate temperatures in summer, but readings drop when ice covers the sea for 9 months each year. At Barrow, July and August temperatures average between 30°F and 40°F; in January and February between 15°F and -18°F.

Wildlife: Brown bears and grizzlies, Dall sheep, wolves, and moose roam areas of the Brooks Range and the Arctic where there is suitable habitat. Two major caribou herds, the western Arctic and the Porcupine, migrate through the Brooks Range to summer calving grounds on the arctic plain.

After being hunted out of Alaska in the mid-1800s, musk-oxen were successfully reintroduced to Nunivak Island in western Alaska in the 1930s. Today several herds range the Arctic.

Wolverines, weasels, a few river otters, snowshoe hares, lynx, arctic and red foxes, shrews, lemmings and voles also inhabit the Brooks Range and the Arctic.

The frigid waters of the Beaufort and Chukchi seas support polar bears, walrus, bowhead and beluga whales, and bearded and ringed seals. In summer when ice retreats from the coast, harbor seals, harbor porpoises, and killer and gray whales feed here. Rarer species of great whales—fin, sei and little piked—have been reported in Chukchi waters. Even more unusual are the occasional spottings of narwhals.

Many bird species migrate to summer breeding grounds in the Arctic although few winter here. Summer visitors may see the conspicuous white snowy owl guarding its nest. Endangered arctic peregrine falcons nest along rocky ridges. Thousands of snow geese raise their young near the arctic coast. In the mountains look for hawks, owls, ptarmigan and migrating waterfowl.

Ambler

GPS: N67°05′ W157°52′

Located on the north bank of the Kobuk River near the confluence of the Ambler and Kobuk rivers, 125 miles east of Kotzebue, 320 miles northwest of Fairbanks. **Transportation:** Scheduled airline, air taxi from Kotzebue. **Population:** 309. **Zip code:** 99786. **Emergency Services:** Police, phone (907) 445-2180; Ambler Health Clinic, phone (907) 445-2129; Volunteer Fire Department.

Elevation: 135 feet. **Climate:** Continental climate, characterized by long, cold winters and warm summers. Average annual precipitation 16 inches, including 80 inches of snow.

Private Aircraft: 2 airstrips 1 mile north; elev. 289 feet; length 2,400 and 3,000 feet; gravel; fuel 80, 100; unattended. Runway conditions not monitored; visual inspection recommended prior to using. No facilities at airport.

NOTE: Ambler prohibits the sale and importation of alcoholic beverages.

Visitor Facilities: Accommodations and meals available at 1 lodge. No laundromat or banking services. Groceries, clothing, first-aid supplies, hardware, film and sporting goods available. Local arts and crafts available for purchase include birch-bark baskets, masks, mukluks, beaver hats and yo-yos. Fishing/hunting licenses available, as well as guide service. Aircraft mechanic for major repair service only. Rental transportation available includes autos, off-road vehicles, boats and charter aircraft. Fuel available includes marine gas, diesel, propane and regular gasoline. Boat moorage on riverbank.

This Eskimo village was settled in 1958 when people from Shungnak and Kobuk moved here because of its spruce forest and the availability of game. The second-class city was incorporated in 1971. Ambler's economy is based on arts, crafts, and subsistence hunting and fishing. In the summer, many residents go to Kotzebue for commercial fishing. Some local employment is provided by government, school and local businesses.

Ambler is some 20 miles from the archaeological dig at Onion Portage, where artifacts dating back 10,000 years have been found. Kobuk Valley National Park lies about 15 miles downriver and the Great Kobuk Sand Dunes are approximately 35 miles away. Visitors often charter aircraft out of Ambler to Walker Lake in the Brooks Range, then float back down the Kobuk River.

Fishing near Ambler includes salmon, sheefish, grayling, whitefish and trout. The western Arctic caribou herd migrates near Ambler; other game includes moose, grizzly and black bear. Jade can be found in some local streams. A ski track is maintained in winter. Bird watching, especially good around breakup time, includes swans, cranes and other waterfowl.

Communications include phones, mail plane, radio and TV. The community is served by 2 churches and a school with grades preschool through 12 with enrollment of 93. Public water, electric and sewage systems available. Freight arrives in the community by cargo plane and barge. Government address: City of Ambler, P.O. Box 9, Ambler, AK 99786, phone (907) 445-2122, fax (907) 442-2174. Village corporation: NANA Regional Corp., P.O. Box 49, Kotzebue, AK 99752. Village council: Ambler Traditional Council, P.O. Box 47, Ambler, AK 99786, phone (907) 445-2196, fax (907) 445-2181, e-mail: Ambler@aitc.org.

Anaktuvuk Pass

GPS: N68°08' W151°45'

(An-ak-TU-vuk) Located on a divide between the Anaktuvuk and John rivers in the northcentral Brooks Range, 260 miles north-northwest of Fairbanks and above the Arctic Circle. **Transportation:** Scheduled airline, air taxi from Fairbanks. **Population:** 315. **Zip code:** 99721. **Emergency Services:** North Slope Borough Public Safety Officer, phone 661-3911; Juanita Bean Health Clinic, phone (907) 661-3914; North Slope Borough Fire Department, phone (907) 661-3529; North Slope Borough Search & Rescue, phone (907) 661-3529.

Elevation: 2,200 feet. **Climate:** Due to high elevation, temperatures remain below freezing most of the year, with daily maximum temperature higher than freezing only 142 days of the year. January is the coldest month; July is the warmest month. Mean annual precipitation is 10.3 inches. Average annual snowfall is 63 inches.

Private Aircraft: Airstrip adjacent to southeast; elev. 2,100 feet; length 4,800 feet; gravel; attended. Fuel includes avgas, and jet A and B.

NOTE: Anaktuvuk Pass prohibits the importation and possession of alcoholic beverages.

Visitor Facilities: Public campground; check with National Park Service ranger station, (907) 661-3520, or Nunamiut Corp., (907) 661-3026. No banking services. Groceries available at the local Corporation Store. Public showers and laundry at the washeteria. Local arts and crafts available for purchase include caribou skin masks and carvings. Fishing/hunting licenses available. No guide service. Fuel available includes propane, diesel and regular gasoline.

This Nunamiut Eskimo village in Anaktuvuk Pass, an historic caribou migration route, is the last remaining settlement of the inland Northern Inupiat Eskimo, whose ancestors date back to 500 B.C. The original nomadic Nunamiut bands left the Brooks Range and scattered in the early 1900s, primarily due to the collapse of the caribou population in 1926 and 1927, but also because of cultural changes brought about by contact with Western civilization. By 1938, however, several Nunamiut families returned to the mountains at Killik River and Chandler Lake. In June 1949, both groups joined at broad, treeless Anaktuvuk Pass, "the place of caribou droppings," eventually to settle permanently. The community incorporated as a second-class city in 1957.

Subsistence hunting, primarily of caribou, and permanent and seasonal employment, in addition to arts and crafts, form the economic base. This is perhaps the most scenic village on the North Slope as it is surrounded by tall mountains and is near rivers and lakes. Anaktuvuk Pass is located in Gates of the Arctic National Park and Preserve. There is public access to parklands across regional and village Native corporation lands; check with a park ranger about planned routes. Wildlife is also abundant throughout the year, including caribou, moose, grizzly bears, fish (arctic char, arctic grayling)) and a variety of birds.

Simon Paneak Memorial Museum, P.O. Box 21085, Anaktuvuk Pass, AK 99721, is open all year Mon. through Fri., 8:30 A.M.-5:00 P.M.. The museum focuses on reviving and preserving the history of the Nunamiut. Exhibits present the early natural, geological and cultural history of the Anaktuvuk Pass area, including migrations of people across the Bering Land Bridge. Exhibits also feature clothing, household goods and trapping and hunting implements used by the Nunamiut Eskimos around the time of the first contact with Westerners. Admission fee $5 per person.

Communications include phones, mail plane, radio, TV and internet. The community is served by a Presbyterian church and the Nunamiut School with grades preschool through 12 with enrollment of 82. Public electricity, water and waste water systems are available. Freight arrives by air transport. Government address: City of Anaktuvuk Pass, P.O. Box 21030, Anaktukvuk Pass, AK 99721, phone (907) 661-3612, e-mail: akp@gci.net. Village corporation:

Nunamiut Corp., P.O. Box 21009, Anaktuvuk Pass, AK 99721, phone (907) 661-6026, fax (907) 661-3025. Village council: Naqsragmiut Tribal Council, P.O. Box 21065, Anaktuvuk Pass, AK 99721, phone (907) 661-2575. fax (907) 661-3613, e-mail: AnaktuvukPass@aitc.org.

Arctic Village

GPS: N68°07′ W145°35′

Located in the Brooks Range on the east bank of the East Fork Chandalar River, 100 miles north of Fort Yukon, 290 miles north of Fairbanks. **Transportation:** Scheduled air service from Fairbanks; winter trail to Venetie. **Population:** 152. **Zip code:** 99722. **Emergency Services:** Tribal Police through Native Village of Venetie Tribal Government; Arctic Village Health Clinic; Volunteer Fire Department.

Elevation: 2,250 feet. **Climate:** Mean temperature in July is 56°F; in January -29°F, **Private Aircraft:** Airstrip 1 mile southwest of village; elev. 2,086 feet; length 3,120 feet; gravel; unattended. Check for runway construction; watch for loose gravel on approach and vehicles on runway.

NOTE: Arctic Village is a dry village; the sale and importation of alcoholic beverages is prohibited.

Visitor Facilities: No accommodations or meals. No banking services. Supplies and groceries are available at Midnight Sun Native Store, (907) 587-5418; and Gilbert Store, (907) 587-5414. There is a community-owned laundromat with showers. Arctic Village is a traditional Athabascan Indian village and crafts may be available for purchase locally. Gasoline and fuel oil are available. Travelers are advised to check with village office, (907) 587-5990, before visiting.

The Neets'ik Gwich'in Indians, a once seminomadic people known for trading babiche (sinew lacings) and wolverine skins for seal oil and skins from the Barter Island Eskimos, settled Arctic Village.

Arctic Village, along with the neighboring village of Venetie, elected to retain title to the 1.8-million-acre Venetie Indian Reservation under the Alaska Native Claims Settlement Act. The reserve and Arctic Village are bounded to the north by the Arctic National Wildlife Refuge, with recreational access to the refuge primarily from Kaktovik on Barter Island and most visitors coming from the Lower 48. It is also the migration route of the Porcupine caribou berd, which sometimes winters here.

Employment in Arctic Village is limited to the National Guard amory, post office, clinic, school, village services, trapping, crafts and summer employment on village projects.

There is an Episcopal chapel in the village which replaced the old Mission Church now on the National Register of Historic Places. Under restoration, the old church, built entirely of logs with handcrafted finish and furnishings, reflects the skill of the Native artisans under Albert Tritt, who later became its pastor.

Communications include phones, mail plane, radio and TV. There is a school with grades preschool through 12 with enrollment of 43. Village services include the laundromat and showers, and electric generator. Honey buckets and outhouses are used. Freight delivery is by plane. Government address: Arctic Village Traditional Council, P.O. Box 22050, Arctic Village, AK 99722, phone (907) 587-5328, fax (907) 587-5128, e-mail: Arctic@aitc.org.

Atqasuk

GPS: N70°28′ W157°24′

(AT-ka-sook) Located on the west bank of Meade River near Imakrak Lake, 58 miles southwest of Barrow. **Transportation:** Scheduled cargo airline, air taxi from Barrow; snow machines in winter. **Population:** 230. **Zip code:** 99791. **Emergency Services:** North Slope Borough Police Dept., phone (907) 633-6911; Atqasuk Health Clinic, phone (907) 633-6711; Fire Department, phone (907) 633-6611; Search and Rescue, phone (907) 633-2007; EMTs on standby 24 hours a day; ambulance, emergency aircraft (helicopter and twin Beech) from Barrow.

Elevation: 65 feet. **Climate:** Temperatures remain below freezing for most of the year. July and August are the warmest months, with temperatures ranging from 40°F to 60°F. Many mosquitoes. January and February are the coldest, with temperatures ranging from -30°F to -35°F. Windchill factor is significant. Annual precipitation averages 5 inches, with snowfall averaging 30 inches annually.

Private Aircraft: The Meade River airstrip south of the city runs east/west; elev. 95 feet; length 4,370 feet; gravel; rotating beacon light; runway lights can be turned on by aircraft remote or upon request; radio beacon; lighted windsock; no fuel available; unattended; runway condition monitored daily; visual inspection recommended prior to using. No facilities. No fuel available. Public and private transportation available.

NOTE: Atqasuk prohibits possession of alcoholic beverages.

Visitor Facilities: Hotel and restaurant. No banking services. Public restrooms/showers at washeteria/water treatment plant building. Meade River Store, (907) 633-6120, will sometimes cash checks. Groceries, clothing, first-aid supplies, film, laundromat and hardware are available from Meade River Store. Arts and crafts available for purchase include masks, mittens, dolls, yo-yos, ulus and parkas. Fishing/hunting licenses available. No guide service. No major repair service or rental transportation. Fuel available includes propane, regular gasoline, diesel and motor oil. No moorage facilities.

Laundromat, shower facilities and lavatory available at the Borough Washeteria, (907) 633-6320, which is open 7 days a week.

The area around this Inupiat Eskimo village has traditionally been hunted and fished by the Inupiat (northern Eskimo). During WWII, coal was mined here and freighted to Barrow. The mine was operated by residents for personal use from 1978-79 and opened again in 1987 for a trial period. The coal is now used year-round by some residents as an alternative to diesel fuel.

The village had a post office from 1951 to 1957 under the name Meade River. The village was reestablished in 1977 by former Barrow, Meade River and Tikiqluk residents and incorporated into a second-class city in 1982. Abandoned sod houses, an old cellar and gravesite near the village testify to earlier settlements in the area.

Atqasuk's economy is based on subsistence caribou hunting, fishing and berry picking. Some of the hunters migrate to Barrow for whale, seal and walrus hunting. The area has many caribou, foxes (red, white and silver), wolverines, moose, wolves and lemmings. Fish in the Meade River include grayling, burbot, 3 types of whitefish and 3 species of salmon. Local hunters bag ptarmigan, ducks and geese.

Atqasuk now has a community center, which houses city offices, the recreation department and video game room; a gymnasium; a water-treatment plant; and waste disposal services.

Communications include phones, mail plane, CB radio, radio, a newspaper and TV. The community has a Presbyterian chapel and a school with grades kindergarten through 12 with enrollment of 70. Public electricity is available. Lake water is hauled by truck. Most residences have honey buckets. Freight arrives in the community by air transport or sometimes by cat-train from Barrow in winter. (After the cat-train has delivered freight and diesel a few times, residents use the tracks to drive to Barrow.) Government address: City of Atqasuk, P.O. Box 91119, Atqasuk, AK 99791, phone (907) 633-6811, fax (907) 633-6812. e-mail: hlivanoff@aol. Village corporation: Atqasuk Corp., P.O. Box 91120, Atqasuk, AK 99791, phone (907) 633-6213, fax (907) 633-6414. Village council: Atqasuk Village, General Delivery, Barrow, AK 99723, e-mail: Atqasuk@aitc.org.

Barrow

GPS: N71°17′ W156°47′

Located on the Chukchi Sea coast, 10 miles southwest of Point Barrow, 500 miles northwest of Fairbanks. **Transportation**: Scheduled airline from Anchorage via Fairbanks. **Population**: 3,500. **Zip code**: 99723. **Emergency Services**: Public Safety Officer, phone 852-6111; Alaska State Troopers, phone

852-3783; Samuel Simmonds Memorial Hospital, phone (907) 852-4611; North Slope Borough Clinic, phone (907) 852-2611; Borough Volunteer Fire Dept./EMS/Search & Rescue/Medevac, phone (907) 852-0234/6111.

Elevation: 20 feet. **Climate**: Normal daily maximum temperature in July (warmest month) is 44°F. Normal daily minimum in January (coldest month) is -24°F. The sun rises May 10 and does not set until Aug. 2. When the sun disappears at noon Nov. 18 it does not appear again until noon Jan. 24.

Private Aircraft: Wiley Post-Will Rogers Memorial Airport adjacent southeast; elev. 44 feet; length 6,500 feet; asphalt; fuel 80, 100, jet Al; attended 4 to 10:30 P.M. or upon request, phone(907) 852-7400.

NOTE: Barrow is a "damp" community, allowing the importation of alcohol; however, there are laws pertaining to importation and licenses are required to ship alcohol into Barrow. Contact the City of Barrow for this information. The sale of alcohol is prohibited in Barrow.

Visitor Facilities: Accommodations are available at Top of the World Hotel, (907) 852-3900; Airport Inn, (907) 852-2525; Arctic Hotel, (907) 852-7786; King Eider Inn, (907) 852-4700; and UIC-Narl Hotel, (907) 852-7800. Food is available at 8 restaurants and at Ilisagvik College cafeteria. There are a dry cleaners and a bank. Groceries and supplies at AC/StuaqPak, (907) 852-6711; and Arctic Grocery, (907) 852-6666. Arts and crafts available for purchase include baleen boats, etched baleen, carved ivory, masks, parkas and fur mittens. Fishing/hunting licenses available. No guide service.

Major repair services include marine engine, boat, auto and aircraft mechanics. Air taxi service available. Fuel available includes marine gas, diesel, propane, aviation fuel, unleaded, regular and supreme. No moorage. Vehicles available ($105/day; price subject to change) at UICC Vehicle. During the summer months tour operators offer package tours of the area. Contact Tundra Tours, Inc., (907) 852-3900, or Arctic Safari Tours, (907) 852-4444, to set up a tour that can include polar-bear watching, photographing snowy owls or watching Inupiat Eskimos pull bowhead whales up the beach.

Barrow is one of the largest Eskimo settlements and the seat of the 88,000-square-mile North Slope Borough, the world's largest municipal government. It

is also the farthest north frontier settlement in the United States. Traditionally, Barrow is known as Ukpeagvik, "place where owls are hunted." Barrow takes its name from Point Barrow, named for Sir John Barrow of the British Admiralty by Captain Beechey of the Royal Navy in 1825. Beechey had been assigned the task of plotting the Arctic coastline of North America in the HMS *Blossom*. Barrow was incorporated as a first-class city in 1959.

The Will Rogers and Wiley Post Monument, dedicated in 1982 to commemorate the 1935 airplane crash of the American humorist and the famous pilot, is located across from the airport. The accident happened 15 miles southwest of Barrow where the men had landed seeking directions to Barrow, a planned stop on their trip from Fairbanks to Siberia. Upon takeoff their plane rose to 50 feet, stalled and then plunged into a river below, killing both men. Two monuments, both on the National Register of Historic Places, are located where the men died. Other sites on the national register are the Cape Smythe Whaling and Trading Station in nearby Browerville and the Birnirk archaeological site approximately 2 miles north of the Barrow airfield. Cape Smythe was built as a whaling station in 1893 and is the oldest frame building in the Arctic. The Birnirk culture, which existed about 500-900 A.D., is represented by a group of 16 dwelling mounts and is considered a key link between the prehistoric cultures of Alaska and Canada.

Visitors also may see the Eskimos heading for whale camps in April and May. Despite the fact that the village is very much in step with modern times, hunting of whales, seals, walrus, caribou and ducks is still important for both traditional and economic reasons. It provides a great portion of the food for the residents. If the whalers are successful, there is a festival called "Nalukataq" when whaling season ends in May. There is a new Inupiat Heritage Museum.

Barrow residents work for the oil companies at Prudhoe Bay, for the borough, the Native corporation and various other local businesses.

Barrow has all communication services, including cable TV, a public radio station, as well as community electric, water and sewer systems. Many homes are heated by natural gas from the nearby gas fields. The community is served by 7 churches, 3 schools (Ipalook Elementary, Hopson Middle School and Barrow High School) with total enrollment of 1,118, and Ilisagvik College affiliated with the University of Alaska Fairbanks. There is also a recreation center that includes a new gymnasium, 2 racquetball courts, a weight room and saunas, as well as adult dances and sport tournaments, exercise classes and cross-country skiing. The high school has a swimming pool, weight room and gymnasium that is open to the community evenings and weekends.

Freight arrives by cargo plane and barge. Government address: City of Barrow, Box 629, Barrow, AK 99723, phone (907) 852-5211, fax (907) 852-5871, e-mail: CityClerk@barrow.com. Regional corporation: Arctic Slope Regional Corp., Box 129, Barrow, AK 99723, phone (907) 852-8633, fax (907) 852-5733, web: http://www.asrc.com/. Village corporation: Ukpeagvik Inupiat Corp., Box 427, Barrow, AK 99723, phone (907) 852-4460, fax (907) 852-4459. Village council: Inupiat Community of the Arctic Slope, P.O. Box 934, Barrow, AK 99723, phone (907) 852-4227, fax (907) 852-4246. e-mail: Inupiat@aitc.org. Native Village of Barrow Inupiat Traditional Government;, P.O. Box 1139, Barrow, AK 99723, phone (907) 852-4411, fax (907) 852-8844, e-mail: Barrow@aitc.org. Borough government: North Slope Borough, P.O. Box 69, Barrow, AK 99723, phone (907) 852-2611, fax (907) 852-0337, e-mail: gahmaogak@co.north-slope.ak.us, web: http://www.co.north-slope.ak.us.

Bettles

GPS: N66°44' W151°41'

(Includes the city of Bettles, Old Bettles, the native village of Evansville and Bettles Field post office.) Located on the south bank of the Upper Koyukuk River in the foothills of the Brooks Range, 180 miles northwest of Fairbanks. **Transportation**: Scheduled air service from Fairbanks (Frontier Flying Service and Wright's Air Service) and charter air service in Bettles: Brooks Range Aviation, (907) 692-5444; Bettles Lodge, (907) 692-5111; and Sourdough Outfitters, (907) 692-5252. Also accessible by boat in summer, snow machine in winter. Winter ice-road to Dalton Highway at Prospect Creek usually open in March (call the city for conditions). Connected by trail to Allakaket and Anaktuvuk Pass. **Population**: 43. **Zip code**: 99726. **Emergency Services**: Frank Tobuk Sr. Health Clinic, Evansville, phone (907) 692-5035; Health Aide, phone (907) 692-5141/5738; Fire Department, phone (907) 692-5244.

Elevation: 624 feet. **Climate**: Semiarid and subarctic. January temperatures average -9˚F, with winter winds making it colder. Winter temperatures range from 15˚F to -60˚F. Summer temperatures average 75˚F, with rain and sun, and frost possible. Greatest mean monthly precipitation is in August with 2.63 inches.

Private Aircraft: Bettles airstrip adjacent north; elev. 643 feet; length 5,200 feet; gravel; fuel 1OOAV, Al+, B. FAA installation, runway maintained year-round. Evansville seaplane base 1 mile north of Bettles runway; river sometimes very low; visual inspection recommended prior to using. Alternate landing sites available; fuel available at river and airport from Koyukuk Inc., (907) 692-5088, or Bettles Lodge, (907) 692-5111.

Visitor Facilities: Meals and overnight accommodations available at Bettles Lodge; bunkhouse at Sourdough Outfitters. Campground. Groceries, clothing, hardware, film, sporting goods, topographic maps and first-aid supplies may be purchased in the lodge or from outfitters. Arts and crafts available locally include furs, gloves, hats, parkas, ivory, baskets, masks and locally crafted gold jewelry. Fishing/hunting licenses available from Bettles Lodge and Bettles Trading Post. Visitor center at Gates of the Arctic National Park and Kanuti National Wildlife Refuge office. Outfitting and guiding services available, including trips by dog team, canoe, raft, snowmachine or foot. Northern lights viewing tours available. Ecological tours. Fly-out wilderness hunting and fishing trips available. Major repair available for aircraft; check locally for mechanics to work on other types of engines. Residents may lease transportation such as boats and autos. Moor boats on riverbank. Fuel available: diesel, propane, aviation and unleaded gas; Coleman fuel. Lubricating and hydraulic oils available.

Evansville, 5 miles east of Old Bettles and 1 mile north of Bettles Field, was founded by Wilfred Evans, who built the Bettles Lodge for Wien Air in 1952. Bettles began as a trading post in 1899 and was named for the proprietor, Gordon C. Bettles. It developed into a mining town and supply point for the upper Koyukuk Valley mines, and was eventually abandoned. Bettles Field, the airstrip, was built by the U.S. Navy upriver from Old Bettles in 1945. Employment here consists mainly of state and federal jobs. Bettles was incorporated in 1985.

Bettles is the gateway to Gates of the Arctic National Park and Preserve and Kanuti National Wildlife Refuge, and is generally receptive to the growing number of visitors. The community sees a number of hikers and river rafters in summer. Visitors are advised, however, not to pick up souvenirs. Camps, cabins and claims that appear to be abandoned may be privately owned and still in use. Also, Bettles is trying to preserve some of its local mining history. A museum is being planned. There is hunting and fishing in the area, but visitors should be aware of subsistence claims and rules governing park and preserve lands.

Communications include phones, mail plane, radio and TV. There is a non-denominational church in the community and a 2-classroom school with grades 1 through 12 with enrollment of 18. There is community electric service, but water is either hauled from the river or obtained from private wells, and the sewage system is flush toilets and septic tanks. Freight comes in by cargo plane or via winter ice road. Village government address: City of Bettles, Box 26023, Bettles Field, AK 99726, phone and fax (907) 692-5191.

Coldfoot

GPS: N67°15' W150°12'

Located at Mile 175 on the Dalton Highway in the southern slopes of the Brooks Range, 248 miles north of Fairbanks. **Transportation**: Dalton Highway from Fairbanks (no permit needed); charter air service from Fairbanks. **Population**: summers, approximately 35; winters, approximately 12. **Zip code**: 99701. **Emergency Services**: Alaska State Troopers, phone (907) 678-5201 and leave message.

Climate: Subarctic winters average from 15°F to -20°F or -30°F; summer temperatures average 75°F.

Private Aircraft: State-maintained airstrip adjacent west; elev. 1,050 feet; length 4,000 feet; gravel; no fuel; unattended. No airport facilities.

Visitor Facilities: Coldfoot Services/ Arctic Acres Inn, (907) 678-5201, offers motel accommodations, restaurant, lounge, general store, post office, RV park with full hookups, laundromat, shower, dump station; automotive fuels; propane. No banking services. General store has groceries, some clothing, hardware, film, sporting goods, etc. Carved ivory, Eskimo dolls, silver jewelry available for purchase at gift shops. Fishing/hunting licenses available from Fish & Wildlife officer; no guide service.

Coldfoot is the site of an historic mining camp at the mouth of Slate Creek on the east bank of the Middle Fork Koyukuk River. Originally named Slate Creek, Coldfoot reportedly got its name in 1900 when gold stampeders got as far up the Koyukuk as this point, then got cold feet, turned and departed. The old cemetery still exists. Emma Dome (elev. 5,680 feet) lies to the west.

Coldfoot's one commercial facility is open year-round. Coldfoot Services offers CB-equipped escort up and down the Dalton Highway. In summer, pipeline and wildlife presentations, flightseeing and recreational gold panning are available.

The post office at Coldfoot opened in 1986, and postal service resumed for the first time since the early 1900s. With the increase in gold mining activities in the area, it is not unusual to find a miner bartering his gold for some cool refreshment at the local lounge.

The National Park Service, Bureau of Land Management, and U.S. Fish & Wildlife Service operate a visitor center here, offering travel information and nightly presentations on the natural and cultural history of the Arctic. The visitor center sells USGS topographical maps of the area and books of interest. It is open from June 1 through September. A Fish & Wildlife officer is stationed at Coldfoot.

Locals report good fishing for grayling at nearby creeks and a couple of hike-in lakes. Because the trans-Alaska pipeline is adjacent, there is no hunting nearby. (North of the Yukon River, hunting is prohibited within 5 miles on either side of the pipeline.) Motorcycles and all-terrain vehicles provide summertime leisure activity, and winters are taken up with dog mushing and snow machining.

The unincorporated community has no public utilities. The 4 private phones, all located at the motel, are for collect and credit card calls only. Mail arrives by truck; TV via satellite.

Deadhorse

GPS: N70°12' W148°31'

Located 498 miles by road north of Fairbanks near the Arctic Ocean. **Transportation**: Scheduled jet service from Fairbanks, or via the Dalton Highway. **Population**: Deadhorse and oilfield workers, between 3,000 and 5,000, depending on level of oilfield activity. **Zip code**: 99734. **Emergency Services**: Public Safety Dept., (907) 659-2515; emergency medical and fire handled by oil field operators Phillips Alaska and BP Exploration Alaska.

Climate: Winter temperatures hover between -55°F and -60°F. For 56 days in midwinter, the sun never rises. But from mid-April to mid-August, daylight is continuous, and temperatures can reach as high as 78°F.

General Store, (907) 659-2412, sells hunting and fishing licenses, souvenirs, clothing, snacks and other items.

The Prudhoe Bay industrial complex on the Arctic Ocean is located a short distance from Deadhorse. Access to Prudhoe Bay and the Arctic Ocean is restricted to oilfield workers and to tour groups with prior permission. For security and safety reasons, unescorted visitors are not allowed on the docks or on area roads.

Communications include phones, mail plane, radio and TV. Church services are held at several camps. Freight arrives by cargo plane, by truck up the Dalton Highway, or is shipped in from the West Coast on barges to Prudhoe during the brief 6 weeks each sumnmer when the arctic icepack moves offshore. For more information, contact Phillips Alaska, P.O. Box 100360, Anchorage, AK 99510, or BP Exploration Alaska, P.O. Box 196612, Anchorage, AK 99519-6612, or visit website: www.bp.com/alaska.

Kaktovik

GPS: N70°08' W143°38'

(Kack-TOE-vik) Located on the north coast of Barter Island on the Beaufort Sea, 390 miles north of Fairbanks. **Transportation**: Scheduled airline, air taxi via Fairbanks or Barrow. **Population**: 293. **Zip code**: 99747. **Emergency Services**: Public Safety Officer, phone (907) 640-6911; Kaktovik Health Clinic, phone (907) 640-6413; Kaktovik Volunteer Fire Department, phone (907) 640-6212.

Elevation: 40 feet. **Climate**: February is the coldest month; July the warmest. Mean annual precipitation is 6.5 inches, with 39 inches of snow.

Private Aircraft: Airstrip 1 mile from village; length 4,820 feet; fuel 80, 100; control tower. Upgrading of airstrip in planning stage through North Slope Borough. Transportation to village.

Visitor Facilities: Accommodations and meals are available at Waldo Arms, (907) 640-6513; and Sim's Camp, (907) 640-6615. Laundromat available. No banking services. Groceries and supplies are available at Kikitak Store , (907) 640-6620; and Sim's Store, (907) 640-6615.

Private Aircraft: State-maintained airport; elev. 57 feet; length 6,500 feet; paved, attended most days; fuel available.

Visitor Facilities: Accommodations are available at Arctic Caribou Inn, (907) 659-2368; Arctic Oilfield Hotel, (907) 659-2614; and Prudhoe Bay Hotel. Increased oil drilling activity can result in a shortage of available rooms; reservations are advised. Motel rooms are expensive ($125 and up a night); meals are included in some prices. Prudhoe Bay

Local arts and crafts that can be purchased include etched baleen, carved ivory and masks. Fishing/hunting licenses available, as well as guide service. Major repair services include auto and aircraft mechanic. Charter aircraft is the only rental transportation. Fuel available includes marine gas, diesel, propane, unleaded and regular. No moorage.

This Inupiat Eskimo village is on the northern edge of the 20.3-million-acre Arctic National Wildlife Refuge, the most northerly unit of the national wildlife refuge system. The unofficial jumping-off point for the refuge, Kaktovik was not prepared for the influx of visitors the community has experienced. Hikers and campers in particular should note that camping is restricted. There are no public campgrounds, but arrangements may be made with private land holders. Contact Kaktovik Inupiat Corp., (907) 640-6120, or Marx Sims, (907) 640-6615/6820.

The ruins of old Kaktovik can be seen from the road into the village from the airport. Hunting in the nearby area is for Dall sheep, moose, caribou and fox.

"Kaktovik is an arctic desert," says one resident. "It is truly amazing to see such beauty evolve from the frozen tundra. Nowhere have I experienced such beauty and tranquility."

Communications in Kaktovik, which incorporated as a second-class city in 1971, include phones, mail plane, radio and TV. The community is served by a Presbyterian church and Harold Kaveolook School with grades preschool through 12 with enrollment of 78. Public water and electricity are available; sewage system is honey buckets. Freight arrives by cargo plane and barge. Government address: City of Kaktovik, P.O. Box 27, Kaktovik, AK 99747, phone (907) 640-6313, fax (907) 640-6314, e-mail: mayor27@aol.com, web: http://www.kaktovik.com. Village corporation: Kaktovik Inupiat Corp., P.O. Box 73, Kaktovik, AK 99747, phone (907) 640-6120, fax (907) 640-6217. Village council: Kaktovik Village, P.O. Box 8, Kaktovik, AK 99747, phone (907) 640-2535, fax (907) 640-6720, e-mail: Kaktovik@aitc.org.

Kiana

GPS: N66°58' W160°26'

(Ky-AN-a) Located on the north bank of the Kobuk River, 57 miles east of Kotzebue, 390 miles west of Fairbanks. **Transportation**: Boat; snow machine; scheduled airline and air taxi from Kotzebue. **Population**: 388. **Zip code**: 99749. **Emergency Services**: Police, phone (907) 475-2129; Kiana Health Clinic, phone (907) 475-2199; Volunteer Fire Department.

Elevation: 150 feet. **Climate**: Kiana is in the transitional climate zone and has long, cold winters and warm summers. Summer temperatures average 60°F. Precipitation averages more than 16 inches annually, including 60 inches of snow.

Private Aircraft: Bob Baker Memorial Airport 1 mile from village; elev. 150 feet; length 3,400 feet; gravel; no fuel available. Runway conditions monitored by airport manager. No facilities at airport. Public transportation usually available from airfield.

NOTE: Kiana prohibits the sale and importation of alcoholic beverages.

Visitor Facilities: No lodging facilities or banking services. A small restaurant and laundromat are available. Groceries, clothing, first-aid supplies, hardware, film and sporting goods can be purchased in the community. No arts and crafts available for purchase. Fishing/hunting licenses and guide service available. Outboard engine repair only. Rental transportation includes boats and charter aircraft. Fuel available includes marine gas, diesel, propane and regular gasoline. Moorage facilities available.

This Eskimo village was probably established as a seasonal camp or central village of the Kowagmiut Eskimos. Its name means "place where 3 rivers meet." The most modern of the villages in the Kobuk River area, it became a supply center for Squirrel River placer mines in 1909. It is a second-class city, incorporated in 1964.

Kiana has a subsistence economy based on moose, caribou, rabbits and various waterfowl. Fishing includes chum salmon, sheefish, whitefish, lingcod and grayling.

In summer, many men go to Kotzebue, Red Dog mine or Prudhoe Bay to work in construction or commercial fishing.

The community is downstream from Kobuk Valley National Park, where winter's dry, cold climate still approximates that of late Pleistocene times, supporting remnant flora once common on the vast arctic steppe. From Kiana, a network of old trading trails is still used for intervillage travel, hunting and fishing. All-terrain vehicles, snow machines and, occasionally, dogsleds are used in the winter.

Communications include phones, mail plane 6 times daily, radio and TV. The community is served by 2 churches and 2 schools with grades preschool through 12 with enrollment of 130. There are public electric, water and sewer systems. Freight arrives by barge and air transport. Government address: City of Kiana, P.O. Box 150, Kiana, AK 99749, phone (907) 475-2136, fax (907) 475-2174, e-mail: CITYOFKIANA@aol.com. Village corporation: NANA Regional Corp., P.O. Box 49, Kotzebue, AK 99752, phone (907) 442-3301, fax (907) 442-2866, web: http://www.nana-online.com/intro.htm. Village council: Kiana Traditional Council, P.O. Box 69, Kiana, AK 99749, phone (907) 475-2109, fax (907) 475-2180, e-mail: Kiana@aitc.org.

Kivalina

GPS: N67°43' W164°32'

(Kiv-a-LEEN-a) Located on an 8-mile-long barrier beach between the Chukchi Sea and Kivalina Lagoon, 90 miles north of Kotzebue, 465 miles west of Fairbanks. **Transportation**: Boat; snow machine; scheduled airline, air taxi from Kotzebue. **Population**: 377. **Zip code**: 99750. **Emergency Services**: Alaska State Troopers, Kotzebue, phone (907) 442-3222; Kivalina Health Clinic, phone (907) 645-2141; Volunteer Fire Department.

Elevation: 11 feet. **Climate**: Located in the transitional climate zone, Kivalina has long, cold winters and cool summers. The Chukchi Sea is ice-covered from November to June. Precipitation is light, with an annual mean of 8.6 inches, including 57 inches of snow.

Private Aircraft: Airstrip adjacent; elev. 10 feet; length 3,000 feet; no fuel. Runway condition not monitored; visual inspection recommended prior to using. Support facilities and transportation to village.

NOTE: Kivalina prohibits the sale and importation of alcoholic beverages.

Visitor Facilities: Accommodations sometimes available in private homes. No restaurant, laundromat or banking services. Groceries, clothing, first-aid supplies, hardware, film and sporting goods can be purchased in the community. Arts and crafts available for purchase include model skin kayaks, model dogsleds, whale-bone masks, ivory carvings and baskets. Fishing/hunting licenses not available. No guide or major repair services. Boats can sometimes be rented. Fuel available: marine gas, diesel, propane, regular and unleaded. No moorage.

This Eskimo village, built on a flat sand and gravel spit, has long been a stopping-off place for seasonal travelers between the Arctic coast and Kotzebue Sound. Lieutenant L.A. Zagoskin of the Imperial Russian Navy recorded the name "Kivualinagmut" in 1847. It is a second-class city, incorporated in 1969.

Kivalina has a subsistence economy based on bowhead and beluga whales, walruses, seals, moose and caribou. There is fishing for salmon, grayling and arctic char in 2 rivers near the village. The Chukchi Sea usually is open to boat traffic from about mid-June to the first of November. Winter travel is by snow machine and dogsled from late October through May.

Communications include phones, mail plane, radio and TV. The community is served by 2 churches and 2 schools with grades preschool through 12 with enrollment of 117. There are public electric and water-supply systems. Sewage system is honey buckets. Freight arrives in the community by plane, barge and ship. Government address: City of Kivalina, P.O. Box 50079, Kivalina, AK 99750, phone (907) 645-2137, fax (907) 645-2175. Village corporation: NANA Regional Corp., P.O. Box 49, Kotzebue, AK 99752, phone (907) 442-3301, fax (907) 442-2866, web: http://www.nana–

online.com/intro.htm. Village council: Native Village of Kivalina, P.O. Box 50051, Kivalina, AK 99750, phone (907) 645-2153, fax (907) 645-2193, e-mail: Kivalina@aitc.org.

Kobuk

GPS: N66°55' W156°52'

Located on the right bank of the Kobuk River, 150 miles east of Kotzebue, 300 miles west of Fairbanks. **Transportation**: Airline from Fairbanks, charter from Kotzebue. **Population**: 109. **Zip code**: 99751. **Emergency Services**: Village Public Safety Officer; Kobuk Health Clinic; Volunteer Fire Department. **Elevation**: 140 feet. **Climate**: Kobuk is located in the continental climate zone; winters are long and cold, summers relatively warm, occasionally reaching 90°F. Mean annual precipitation 16.7 inches, including 56 inches of snow.

Private Aircraft: Airstrip adjacent; elev. 145 feet; length 2,360 feet; gravel; no fuel; visual inspection recommended prior to using. No public transportation. Restroom facilities. Floatplane operation on lake. Also 4,780-foot gravel airstrip at Dahl Creek, 3 miles from Kobuk.

NOTE: *Kobuk prohibits the sale and importation of alcoholic beverages.*

Visitor Facilities: Accommodations at 1 hotel or arrangements can be made with private homes or clinic. Laundromat with showers available. No restaurant or banking services. Groceries, first-aid supplies, hardware, film and sporting goods can be purchased in the community.

Local arts and crafts available for purchase include birch-bark baskets and picture frames, mukluks, beaver hats and fur mittens. Fishing/hunting licenses available, as well as a fishing guide. No major repair services. Rental transportation includes boats and charter aircraft. Fuel available includes marine gas, diesel, propane, unleaded and regular gasoline. Moorage available.

This Eskimo community of log homes was founded in 1899 as a supply point for mining activities in the Cosmos Hills to the north and was then called Shungnak. Area residents gravitated to the trading post, school and mission. Riverbank erosion forced relocation of the village in the 1920s to present-day Shungnak, 10 miles downriver. The few people who stayed and those who returned named the old village Kobuk. The village is a second-class city, incorporated in 1973.

Kobuk has a subsistence economy largely based on fishing and hunting. Fish include sheefish (up to 60 pounds), salmon, grayling, whitefish, pike and trout. Game includes caribou, moose, black and grizzly bear, and Dall sheep. Residents also work for the local government, school district and village corporation. Firefighting provides summer work.

Kobuk is located near the headwaters of the Kobuk River. Visitors to Kobuk Valley National Park can fly into Kobuk from Nome or Kotzebue and float down the Kobuk to the national park and the Great Kobuk Sand Dunes, or fly to Walker Lake in Gates of the Arctic National Park in the Brooks Range and float the river from there. Also of interest is the jade mine, 3 miles from Kobuk by jeep, owned by Oro Stewart of Stewart's Photo in Anchorage. Visitors are welcome in June and July to watch jade mining and cutting. No charge for cabins; bring sleeping bags and food. NANA Regional Corp. also operates a jade mine at nearby Jade Mountain. Historic trails along the river are still used for intervillage travel, hunting and fishing.

Communications include phones, mail plane, radio and TV. The community is served by 3 churches and a school with grades preschool through 8 with enrollment of 33. There are public water supply, sewer and electric systems. Freight arrives by plane or barge. Government address: City of Kobuk, P.O. Box 20, Kobuk, AK 99752, phone (907) 948-2217. Village corporation: NANA Regional Corp., P.O. Box 49, Kotzebue, AK 99752, phone (907) 442-3301, fax (907) 442-2866, web: http://www.nana–online.com/intro.htm. Village council: Native Village of Kobuk, General Delivery, Kobuk, AK 99752, phone (907) 948-2214, fax (907) 948-2123, e-mail: Kobuk@aitc.org.

Kotzebue

GPS: N66°54' W162°35'

(KOT-sa-byou) Located on the northwest shore of Baldwin Peninsula in Kotzebue Sound, 26 miles above the Arctic Circle, 550 miles north of Anchorage. **Transportation:** Daily jet service from Anchorage via Nome. **Population:** 3,082. **Zip code:** 99752. **Emergency Services:** For police, fire, ambulance, phone 911; Women's Crisis Project, phone (907) 442-3969; Maniilaq Health Center, phone (907) 442-3321; Maniilaq Air Ambulance, phone (907) 442-3321.

Elevation: 10 feet. **Climate:** In summer the temperature averages between 40°F and 50°F. During winter, the average temperature is -12°F. Record low to -52°F. Mean annual precipitation is 9.5 inches, including 25 inches of snow. During summer the sun does not set for approximately 36 days.

Private Aircraft: Ralph Wien Memorial Airport, 1 mile south; elev. 11 feet; length 5,900 feet; asphalt; fuel 80, 100, jet A. Transportation to town available. Kotzebue seaplane base within city.

NOTE: Kotzebue bans the sale of alcoholic beverages.

Visitor Facilities: Accommodations at Nullagvik Hotel, (907) 442-3331; Drake's Camp, (907) 442-2736; and Budget Inn Bed & Breakfast, (907) 442-2865. There are restaurants, banking services, several stores carrying all supplies, beauty salons, a library and taxis. Among the many Eskimo arts and crafts items that can be purchased are jade items made at a local factory as well as parkas and mukluks made locally. Fishing/hunting licenses and guide service available, as well as several air charter companies. All fuel is available.

Kotzebue is the commercial center for a 48,000-square-mile area of northwestern Alaska which includes 10 villages and a population of about 7,047. It is a second-class city, incorporated in 1958, and is the largest Eskimo village in Alaska.

The town is on a spit that is about 3 miles long and 1,100 to 3,600 feet wide. The site has been occupied for some 600 years. Centuries before Europeans arrived "Kikiktagruk" was the site of ancient arctic trading routes. It acquired its present name from the adjacent sound named for German explorer Otto von Kotzebue, who sailed the brig Riurik into the area in 1816.

The population is more than 80 percent Eskimo. The economy is based on government services, commercial fishing and subsistence hunting and fishing. The wage economy of the entire region is concentrated in Kotzebue, which contains the regional offices of several state and federal agencies.

Local attractions include the NANA Museum of the Arctic, P.O. Box 49, Kotzebue, AK 99752, (907) 442-3304, which features a 2-hour program that includes a diorama show unequaled anywhere in Alaska. Shows are scheduled at 9:15 A.M. and 3 P.M. daily; tickets for the show are $20. Collections in the museum reflect the ethnology and natural history of northwestern Alaska, along with wildlife exhibits. Also included in a trip to the museum are a visit to the jade manufacturing factory, a panoramic slide show, cultural heritage demonstrations featuring skin sewing, ivory carving, Eskimo dancing and other traditional arts, and an Eskimo blanket toss. The museum is open from June to September and hours are 8:30 A.M. to 5:30 P.M. daily. Winter hours are by appointment. General admission is free. The west end of the museum building houses administrative offices of the National Park Service, phone (907) 442-3890; or write Superintendent, Northwest Alaska Areas, National Park Service, Box 287, Kotzebue, AK 99752 for information about national parks in the area. The Park Service public information center is down the street from the museum. The excellent city museum, Ootukahkuktuvik or "Place Having Old Things," City of Kotzebue, P.O. Box 46, Kotzebue, AK 99752 requires special arrangements to view; contact the city hall. Among the items to see are a raincoat made from walrus intestine and a coat fashioned from bird feathers.

Points of interest include the large cemetery, with graves lavishly decorated with artificial flowers, and spirit houses over some of the graves.

NANA Regional Corp. offers tours and viewings of native dances. Tundra tours are also available, including special trips to reindeer herds.

During the summer, tour groups are entertained with Eskimo blanket tosses and often dances and skin-sewing demonstrations. The Fourth of July celebration, followed closely by the Northwest Native Trade Fair, is the biggest event of the year in Kotzebue. The fair features traditional Native games. A muktuk-eating contest, seal-hook throwing contest and an Eskimo buggy race are among the special events. People from all over the region come to trade handicrafts and participate in traditional dances and feasts. Starting in September, the northern lights are visible. In winter, there are various dog mushing races.

Preliminaries to the Eskimo Olympics take place between Christmas and New Year's Day. Events include the knuckle hop, high-kick, blanket toss, finger-pulling contest and greased pole walk.

In April, residents gather to watch snowmachine riders begin the Willie Goodwin Sr./Archie Ferguson Memorial Snowmachine race. The race, sponsored by the Kotzebue Lions Club, takes riders across some of the most demanding terrain at speeds of more than 100 mph. The course runs from Kotzebue to Noorvik, through the Kiana Pass and on to Selawik before turning back to Noorvik. The last stretch leads across Hotham Inlet and Melvin Channel back to Kotzebue.

As spring approaches, the ice in Kotzebue Sound begins to melt and break apart, as does the ice in nearby rivers. As the ice passes the city, it begins jamming up, and pushes itself up toward shoreline streets. One resident says, "There have been times when there was a wall of ice all along Front Street." As spring becomes summer, ice floes take on the appearance of crystals and make the sound of tinkling glass. "At times, a moose or some other animal will get stranded on the moving ice," says a resident. "There isn't much that can be done except hope the ice floats or is pushed toward land so the

animal can jump off."

Kotzebue has all communications systems, as well as community water, sewer and electricity. The community is served by 8 churches, 2 schools with enrollment of 837, a community college and a technical center. Freight arrives by ship, barge and air cargo planes. Government address: City of Kotzebue, P.O. Box 46, Kotzebue, AK 99752, phone (907) 442-3401, fax (907) 442-3742, e-mail: ngalstad@otz.net, web: http://kotzpdweb.tripod.com/city/index.html. Regional Native corporation: NANA Regional Corp., P.O. Box 49, Kotzebue, AK 99752, phone (907) 442-3301, fax (907) 442-2866, web: http://www.nana-online.com/intro.htm. Village corporation: Kikiktagnik Inupiat Corp., P.O. Box 1050, Kotzebue, AK 99752, phone (907) 442-3165. Village council: Kotzebue IRA Council, P.O. Box 296, Kotzebue, AK 99752, phone (907) 442-3467, fax (907) 442-2162, e-mail: Kotzebue@aitc.org.

Kuparuk

GPS: N70°19' W149°35'

(Koo-PAH-ruk) Located on the arctic coastal plain, 40 miles west of Prudhoe Bay, 400 miles north of Fairbanks. **Transportation:** Charter plane or gravel road from Prudhoe Bay. **Population:** Approximately 600-650 oil field workers. **Emergency Services:** North Slope Borough Police, Prudhoe Bay; Phillips Alaska security officers; Phillips Alaska medical clinic.

Climate: Summer weather usually cool, windy and foggy, but temperatures can reach 70°F. Winter weather is cold, dark and very windy. Bugs can be ferocious during calm periods in June and July.

Private Aircraft: Airstrip 0.5 mile from camp is not open to private aircraft; state-operated airport at Deadhorse is available.

Visitor Facilities: The land is privately leased and there are no visitor facilities.

Kuparuk is the Phillips Alaska base camp for the second largest oil field in the United States. Communications include phones, mail plane, radio and TV. Freight arrives by cargo plane and barge, or by truck up the Dalton Highway to Prudhoe Bay.

Noatak

GPS: N67°34' W162°58'

(NO-a-tack) Located on the west bank of the Noatak River, 55 miles north of Kotzebue, 470 miles northwest of Fairbanks. **Transportation**: Boat; scheduled air service and air taxi from Kotzebue. **Population**: 428. **Zip code**: 99761. **Emergency Services**: Police, phone (907) 485-2168; Alaska State Troopers, Kotzebue, phone (907) 442-3911; Noatak Health Clinic, phone (907) 485-2162; Volunteer Fire Department.

Elevation: 60 feet. **Climate**: Noatak is on the border between the transitional and continental climate zones; winters are long and cold; summers warm. Precipitation averages 10 to 13 inches annually, including 48 inches of snow.

Private Aircraft: Noatak airstrip adjacent southwest; elev. 99 feet; length 4,000 feet; gravel; fuel 80, 100. No airport facilities or transportation to village. Floatplanes can land on river usually from second week of June to first week of October.

NOTE: Noatak prohibits the sale and importation of alcoholic beverages.

Visitor Facilities: Arrangements can be made for sleeping at the school and in private homes. No restaurant, laundromat or banking services. Groceries, some clothing, hardware and some sporting goods available. Arts and crafts available for purchase include hand-knitted gloves, mukluks and beaver caps. Fishing/hunting licenses available. No guide or major repair services. Boats can be rented. Fuel available includes marine gas, propane and regular gasoline. No moorage facilities.

Noatak, a community of log and wood-frame homes 70 miles above the Arctic Circle, is situated on a bluff overlooking the river. It was established as a fishing and hunting camp in the 19th century and developed into a permanent settlement listed in Ivan Petroff's 1880 census as "Noatagamute," which meant "Noatak [River] people." The community is unincorporated. Its economy is based primarily on subsistence hunting and fishing. Fish include chum salmon, whitefish, grayling, pike, lingcod and Dolly Varden. Game includes caribou, moose, waterfowl, rabbits and Dall sheep. There is summer employment in Kotzebue or at the nearby Red Dog zinc mine.

Noatak is the only settlement along the 396-mile-long Noatak River, eighth longest river in Alaska. The 6.6-million-acre Noatak National Preserve encompasses the major portion of the river, except the headwaters located in Gates of the Arctic National Park and Preserve. Access to the lower river is by air charter from Kotzebue; access to the upper river for float trips is generally by air charter from Bettles to a lake along the river. Many historic trails along the Noatak are still used for intervillage travel, hunting and fishing.

Communications in Noatak include phones, TV, radio and mail plane. The community is served by a church and a school with grades preschool through 12 with enrollment of 152. There are public water, electric and sewer systems. Freight arrives by cargo plane and barge. Government address: Native Village of Noatak, P.O. Box 89, Noatak, AK 99761, phone (907) 485-2173, fax (907) 485-2137, e-mail: Noatak@aitc.org. Village corporation: NANA Regional Corp., P.O. Box 49, Kotzebue, AK 99752, phone (907) 442-3301, fax (907) 442-2866, web: http://www.nana-online.com/intro.htm.

Noorvik

GPS: N66°50' W161°03'

Located on right bank of the Nazuruk Channel of the Kobuk River, 45 miles east of Kotzebue, 400 miles west of Fairbanks. **Transportation**: Boat; scheduled and charter plane from Kotzebue. **Population**: 634. **Zip code**: 99763. **Emergency Services**: Police, phone (907) 636-2173; Noorvik Health Clinic, phone (907) 636-2103; Volunteer Fire Department.

Elevation: 70 feet. **Climate**: Transitional, with long, cold winters and cool summers. Mean annual precipitation 16 inches, with 60 inches of snow.

Private Aircraft: Robert Curtis Memorial Airport 1 mile from village; elev. 63 feet; length 2,200 feet; gravel; no fuel; unattended; visual inspection recommended prior to using. Airport manager and freight terminal at airport. No transportation to village.

NOTE: Noorvik prohibits the sale and importation of alcoholic beverages.

Visitor Facilities: Accommodations at 1 hotel. There is a restaurant. No banking services. Groceries, clothing, first-aid supplies, hardware, film and sporting goods may be purchased in the community. Fishing/hunting licenses available, as well as guide service. Repair services available for marine engines and boats. Arrangements can be made to rent autos, off-road vehicles and boats. Available fuel includes marine gas, diesel, propane and regular gasoline.

This village was established by Kowagmiut Eskimo fishermen and hunters from the village of Deering in the early 1900s. The village was first called Oksik, but became known as Noorvik around 1914. Noorvik is a second-class city, incorporated in 1964.

The economy is based primarily on subsistence hunting and fishing. There is some full-time employment in the village with local government and businesses and seasonal employment in Kotzebue, Fairbanks, the Red Dog zinc mine or Prudhoe Bay. Noorvik is downstream from Kobuk Valley National Park. Many historic trails in the area are still used for intervillage travel, hunting and fishing.

Communications include phones, mail plane, radio and TV. The community has a church and 2 schools with grades preschool through 12 with enrollment of 234. There are public water, sewer and electric systems. Freight arrives by cargo plane and barge. Government address: City of Noorvik, P.O. Box 146, Noorvik, AK 99763, phone (907) 636-2100. Village corporation: NANA Regional Corp., P.O. Box 49, Kotzebue, AK 99752, phone (907) 442-3301, fax (907) 442-2866, web: http://www.nana-online.com/into.htm. Village council: Noorvik Native Community, Box 71, Noorvik, AK 99763, phone (907) 636-2144, fax (907) 636-2284, e-mail: Noorvik@aitc.org.

Nuiqsut

GPS: N70°11' W151°00'

(Noo-IK-sut) Located on the west bank of the Nechelik Channel of the Colville River Delta, about 35 miles from the Beaufort Sea coast, 60 miles west of Prudhoe Bay, 380 miles north of Fairbanks. **Transportation:** Scheduled or charter plane from Prudhoe Bay or Barrow. **Population:** 433. **Zip code:** 99789. **Emergency Services:** Public Safety Officer, phone (907) 480-6111; Nuiqsut Health Clinic, phone (907) 480-6729; Nuiqsut Volunteer Fire Department, phone (907) 480-6613.

Elevation: 50 feet. **Climate:** Temperatures remain below freezing most of the year, rising above freezing only 122 days per year. July is the warmest month; February the coldest month. Precipitation is light, measuring 5 to 6 inches per year. Total snowfall averages 20 inches.

Private Aircraft: Airstrip adjacent; elev. 50 feet; length 4,343 feet; gravel; no fuel; unattended; visual inspection recommended prior to use. Runway soft or flooded during late spring breakup. No facilities at airport. Transportation to village.

NOTE: Nuiqsut prohibits possession of alcoholic beverages.

Visitor Facilities: Kuukpik Hotel and restaurant. Laundromat available. No banking services. Groceries, clothing, first-aid supplies, hardware, film and sporting goods may be purchased in the community. Arts and crafts available for purchase include skin masks and boats, fur mittens and parkas and carved ivory. Fishing/hunting licenses available. No guide service. No major repair services, but some rental transportation from local corporation, including pickup trucks, ATVs and boats, with or without guides, are available. Inupiat Taxi Service. Fuel available includes marine gas, diesel, propane, white gas, kerosene and regular gasoline. Moorage facilities available.

The Colville River Delta has traditionally been a gathering and trading place for the Inupiat Eskimo people, and has always offered good hunting and fishing. The village was resettled in 1973 by members of the Kuupik Corporation, the local village corporation, created under the Alaska Native Claims Settlement Act of 1971. A winter overland move to Nuiqsut was made by 27 families living in Barrow but with ties to the Colville River delta area. The new residents lived in a tent city for 18 months before permanent housing was built. Nuiqsut, which encompasses 9 square miles, was incorporated as a second-class city in 1975.

The economy is based primarily on subsistence hunting and fishing, but many residents are employed in seasonal construction work. Fish include whitefish, burbot, arctic char and grayling. Game animals include bowhead and beluga whales, caribou, seals, moose and many species of waterfowl such as swans, geese, ducks and loons. Local recreation includes riding snowmobiles and 3-wheelers, night gym, teen center activities and scheduled events at the Kisik Community Center. On the Fourth of July various outdoor games take place. Traditional dances are performed at these and other celebrations.

Communications include phones, mail plane, radio, TV and e-mail. The community is served by Presbyterian and Assembly of God churches and a school with grades preschool through 12 with enrollment of 145. There is a public electric system. Water is transferred from a freshwater lagoon to holding tanks and transported to local homes and businesses. The sewage system is currently honey buckets, but construction for a water and sewer system is in progress. Freight arrives by plane and during the winter months by ice road, hauled in by 18-wheelers. Government address: City of Nuiqsut, P.O. Box 148, Nuiqsut, AK 99789, phone (907) 480-6727, fax (907) 480-6928. Village corporation: Kuukpik Corp., P.O. Box 187, Nuiqsut, AK 99789, phone (907) 480-6220, fax (907) 480-6126. Village council: Native Village of Nuiqsut, P.O. Box 89169, Nuiqsut, AK 99789, phone (907) 480-2535, fax (907) 480-2536, e-mail: Nuiqsut@aitc.org.

Point Hope

GPS: N68°21' W166°47'

Located on a triangular foreland which juts into the Chukchi Sea 275 miles north of Nome, 570 miles northwest of Fairbanks, 325 miles southwest of Barrow. **Transportation**: Scheduled airline, air charter from Kotzebue. **Population**: 757. **Zip code**: 99766. **Emergency Services**: Public Safety Officer, phone (907) 368-2911; Point Hope Health Clinic, phone (907) 368-2234; Point Hope Volunteer Fire Department, phone (907) 368-2774.

Elevation: 13 feet. **Climate**: Temperatures cool year-round but much less severe than elsewhere in the North Slope Borough. Temperatures are above freezing 162 days of the year. February is the coldest month with temperatures averaging -15°F; August is the warmest month when the mercury soars to 44°F average. Mean annual precipitation is 10 inches, including 36 inches of snow.

Private Aircraft: Airstrip 2 miles southwest; elev. 14 feet; length 4,000 feet; asphalt; emergency fuel only; unattended. Tickets and reservations through Point Hope Native Store or other agents in town. City bus available to village.

NOTE: Point Hope prohibits the sale and importation of alcoholic beverages.

Visitor Facilities: Accommodations, restaurant and laundry facilities available. Native store will cash checks. Groceries, clothing, first-aid supplies, hardware, film and sporting goods available in the community. Arts and crafts available for purchase include carved ivory, baleen baskets, carved whale bone masks and animals, caribou skin masks, ivory-tipped harpoons and bird spears, Eskimo parkas, etched baleen and oosiks. Fishing/hunting licenses available, as well as guide service. Repair services available for marine engines, boats and autos. Arrangements may be made to rent private autos, off-road vehicles or boats, including skin boats. Fuel available: marine gas, diesel, propane, unleaded, regular and supreme. Public moorage available.

The village was named in 1826 by Capt. F.W. Beechey after Englishman Sir William Johnstone Hope.

The point's favorable location for harvesting bowhead whales attracted an earlier people to settle here some 2,000 years ago after they had migrated across a land bridge from Siberia. The Point Hope peninsula is one of the longest continually occupied areas in North America. At Point Hope are the remains of the sod houses of Old Tigara Village, a prehistoric site, and an even earlier site with about 800 house pits known as Ipiutak, occupied from about 500 B.C. to 100 A.D. Ipiutak and the surrounding archaeological district are on the National Register of Historic Places.

The Point Hope people traditionally dominated an extensive area from the Utukok River to the Kivalina River and far inland. By 1848 commercial whaling activities brought an influx of Westerners, many of whom employed Point Hope villagers. By the late 1880s, the whalers established shore-based whaling stations on the peninsula, notably at nearby Jabbertown (so named because of the many languages spoken there). These disappeared with the demise of the whaling industry in the early 1900s.

Point Hope village was incorporated in 1966 and 6 years later became a second-class city. Erosion and a threat of storm flooding from the Chukchi Sea led to its relocation to higher ground in the mid-1970s.

Construction work is the main source of income in Point Hope, while capital improvement programs create new jobs in operations and maintenance. Other jobs are available with the city, school, Native corporation and local businesses.

Nearly all men in the village participate in the spring whale hunt, in which traditional skin boats still are used. A festival, Nalukataq, at which visitors are welcome, takes place after the whaling season, around June 1. There also are village-wide celebrations on the Fourth of July, Thanksgiving and Christmas.

In addition to the prehistoric village sites, there are old burial grounds in the area, including a cemetery marked by large whale bones standing on end. Beachcombing and rockhounding are available in the area and the point also is home to an abundance of tiny arctic wildflowers. Other activities include boating and bird, wildlife and whale watching, cold-dip swimming in the lagoon, egg gathering at Cape Thompson and Cape Lisburne, and bingo 6 nights a week.

Fish available include salmon, trout, grayling and whitefish. Hunting is for caribou, moose, bear, ptarmigan, ducks and geese.

Communications in Point Hope include phones, mail plane, radio and TV. There are community electric and water systems. Sewage system is honey buckets. The community is served by St. Thomas' Episcopal Church (the oldest in the region, established in 1890) and Assembly of God and Church of Christ churches. The Tikigaq school has grades preschool through 12 with enrollment of 235. Freight arrives by cargo plane and barge. Government address: City of Point Hope, P.O. Box 169, Point Hope, AK 99766, phone (907) 368-2537, fax (907) 368-2835. Village corporation: Tigara Corp., P.O. Box 9, Point Hope, AK 99766, phone (907) 368-2235, fax (907) 368-2668. Village council: Native Village of Point Hope, P.O. Box 109, Point Hope, AK 99766, phone (907) 368-2330, fax (907) 368-2332, e-mail: PointHope@aitc.org.

Point Lay

GPS: N69°45' W163°03'

Located on the Chukchi Sea, 550 miles northwest of Fairbanks, 300 miles southwest of Barrow. **Transportation**: Scheduled airline, air charter from Barrow. **Population**: 158. **Zip code**: 99759. **Emergency Services**: Public Safety Officer, phone (907) 833-2911; Point Lay Health Clinic, phone (907) 833-2526; Point Lay Volunteer Fire Department, phone (907) 833-2611. Elevation: 10 feet. Climate: The temperature averages around 40°F in summer and -35°F in winter. July is the warmest month; January is the coldest month. Mean annual precipitation is 6.73 inches, including 18.5 inches of snow.

Private Aircraft: Seldom-used sand airstrip at old village site; length 700 feet. Airstrip at DEW line station; elev. 25 feet; length 3,519 feet; gravel. Upgrading of airstrip scheduled for near future by North Slope Borough.

NOTE: *Point Lay prohibits the sale and importation of alcoholic beverages.*

Visitor Facilities: No hotel, restaurant, laundromat or banking services. There is a store. Arts and crafts available for purchase include baleen baskets, masks, carved ivory and fur parkas. Fishing/hunting licenses available. No guide service, major repair service, rental transportation or public moorage facilities. Fuel available includes propane and regular gasoline.

Kali, the Eskimo name for the village, means "mound" and refers to the elevated area on which it stands. It is probably the last remaining village of the so-called Kukpowruk people.

The deeply indented shoreline prevented effective bowhead whaling, and the village never fully participated in the whaling culture. People of the village engage in subsistence hunting including the harvesting of beluga whales and some construction work.

Recreational activities include snowmobiling, 3-wheeling, hunting, fishing and trapping. Point Lay is an unincorporated village within the North Slope Borough.

Communications include phones, mail plane, radio and TV. Water is delivered by truck from freshwater lakes. Sewage system is honey buckets. School has grades preschool through 12 with enrollment of 85. There are Baptist and Episcopal congregations. Freight arrives by air transport and barge. Village corporation address: Cully Corp., General Delivery, Point Lay, AK 99759, phone (907) 833-2520. Village council: Native Village of Point Lay, P.O. Box 101, Point Lay, AK 99759, phone (907) 833-2428, fax (907) 833-2528, e-mail: PointLay@aitc.org.

Prudhoe Bay

(See Deadhorse)

Red Dog Mine

GPS: N67°34′ W162°58′

Located in the DeLong Mountains north of Noatak, 90 miles north of Kotzebue and 55 miles inland from the Chukchi Sea. Transportation: By air. A 55-mile state-owned gravel road connects the mine site to a shallow-water port on the Chukchi Sea. Population: 32.

Climate: Winter temperatures average -21°F to 15°F, with lows to -59°F. Summer temperatures average 40°F to 60°F with highs of 75°F. Snowfall averages 48 inches; annual precipitation 10 to 13 inches.

Private Aircraft: NANA-operated lighted gravel runway, length 5,862 feet.

Visitor Facilities: None. Red Dog Mine is the world's largest zinc concentrate mine. It is operated by Canadian-based Tech Cominco, Ltd. (www.teck cominco.com/operations/reddog/red dog.htm) on lands owned by NANA Regional Corp. The mineral site was first discovered in 1953 by pilots and geologists flying over the area. U.S. Geological Survey named the site Red Dog Creek after pioneer local pilot and miner Bob Baker's company, Red Dog. (Baker had named his company after his rust-colored dog, who accompanied him on flights.)

The majority of mine employees are Eskimo, and most are also NANA shareholders. Workers live in group facilities with water, sewer and electric systems provided and operated by Tech Cominco.

Selawik

GPS: N66°36′ W160°00′

(SELL-a-wik) Located at the mouth of the Selawik River, 90 miles southeast of Kotzebue, 375 miles west of Fairbanks. **Transportation:** By air. **Population:** 772. **Zip code:** 99770. **Emergency Services:** Police, phone (907) 484-2229; Alaska State Troopers, phone 911; Selawik Health Clinic, phone (907) 484-2199; Selawik Area Volunteer Emergency Rescue, phone (907) 484-2202; Volunteer Fire Department.

Elevation: 50 feet. **Climate:** Long, cold winters and cool summers. Precipitation is 8.7 inches annually, including 35 to 40 inches of snow.

Private Aircraft: 2 intersecting runways adjacent; elev. 25 feet; length 2,670 and 3,000 feet; gravel; no fuel; unattended. No facilities at airport. No transportation to village.

NOTE: *Selawik prohibits the sale and importation of alcoholic beverages.*

Visitor Facilities: Contact city office, (907) 484-2132, to arrange for accommodations in private homes or at the school. No restaurant or banking services available. Groceries, clothing, first-aid supplies, hardware, film and sporting goods may be purchased in the community. Arts and crafts available for purchase include masks, baskets and model dogsleds fashioned from caribou jawbones. Fishing/hunting licenses available. No guide service. Repair services available for marine engines, boats and autos. Fuel available: diesel, propane and regular gasoline. No moorage facilities.

Lieutenant L.A. Zagoskin of the Imperial Russian Navy first reported Selawik's existence in the 1840s as the settlement of "Chilivik." Some traditional sod houses are still found in this Eskimo village. Selawik is a second-class city, incorporated in 1977.

The economic base is arts and crafts, and subsistence hunting and fishing. Some residents are employed as firefighters during the summer. Fish include whitefish, sheefish, grayling, northern pike and arctic char. Caribou and moose are the most important game animals.

Selawik is located near Selawik National Wildlife Refuge. The refuge includes the delta area formed by the Kobuk and Selawik rivers, an important breeding and resting spot for migratory waterfowl. The Selawik River is classified as a wild and scenic river.

Communications in Selawik include phones, mail plane, radio and cable TV. The community is served by Seventh-Day Adventist and Baptist churches and a Friends Mission. It also has 2 schools with grades preschool through 12 with enrollment of 259. There is a cooperative electric system, and parts of town have public water. The sewage system is honey buckets. Freight arrives by cargo plane and barge. Government address: City of Selawik, P.O. Box 49, Selawik, AK 99770, phone (907) 484-2132, fax (907) 484-2209, e-mail: cos1@gci.net. Village corporation: NANA Regional Corp., P.O. Box 49, Kotzebue, AK 99752, phone (907) 442-3301, fax (907) 442-2866, Web: http://www.nana-online.com/intro.htm. Village council: Selawik IRA Council, P.O. Box 59, Selawik, AK 99770, phone (907) 484-2225, fax (907) 484-2226, e-mail: Selawik@aitc.org.

Shungnak
GPS: N66°52' W160°09'

(SHUNG-nak) Located on the Kobuk River, 150 miles east of Kotzebue and 300 miles west of Fairbanks. **Transportation:** Boat; scheduled or charter airline from Kotzebue; snowmachine or dogsled in winter. **Population:** 256. **Zip code:** 99773. **Emergency Services:** Police, phone (907) 437-3222; Alaska State Troopers, Kotzebue, phone (907) 442-3222; Shungnak Health Clinic, phone (907) 437-2138; Volunteer Fire Department.

Elevation: 140 feet. **Climate:** Shungnak is in the continental climate zone and has long, cold winters and relatively warm summers. Mean precipitation is 16 inches, including 71 inches of snow.

Private Aircraft: Airstrip 0.5 mile from village; elev. 200 feet; length 4,000 feet; gravel; fuel 80, 100; unattended. No facilities at airport. No transportation available to village.

NOTE: Shungnak prohibits the sale and importation of alcoholic beverages.

Visitor Facilities: Accommodations and other services available at Commack Lodge & Store, (907) 437-2157. Laundromat available. No banking services. Groceries and supplies available at Shungnak Native Store, (907) 437-2148, and Commack Lodge & Store. Arts and crafts available for purchase include birchbark baskets, jade, beadwork, masks, mukluks, beaver hats, mittens, parkas and bone carvings. Fishing/hunting licenses available, as well as guide service for river floating, dog mushing and other activities. Some repair service available for marine engines, boats and autos. Fuel available includes marine gas, diesel, kerosene, propane and regular and unleaded gasoline. Moorage available for boats.

The original settlement of Shungnak was 10 miles upriver at the present location of Kobuk. Residents relocated in the 1920s because of riverbank erosion at the old site. Shungnak was incorporated as a second-class city in 1967.

Shungnak has a subsistence economy

based on fishing and hunting. Fish include sheefish, whitefish, salmon and grayling. Game animals are caribou, moose and bear, as well as ducks and geese. There also is trapping for marten, beaver, fox, lynx, otter, wolverine and wolf.

There also is seasonal employment in construction, fire-fighting, mining and recreation, and some year-round employment with the local government and schools.

The 347-mile-long Kobuk, a wild and scenic river and the ninth largest in Alaska, begins in Gates of the Arctic National Park and Preserve. It has become popular for float trips to Shungnak and beyond to Kobuk Valley National Park. The upper river is excellent for bird watching in spring and summer. The river is generally safe for boats from the last week of May to the first week in October. (See also River Running in the Attractions section.)

Onion Portage Archaeological District, listed on the National Register of Historic Places, is 35 miles downriver from Shungnak. First discovered by Dr. J. Louis Giddings in 1941, this site containing 30 layers of middens and old dwellings is described as the most important ever found in the Arctic.

Other recreational activities in the area include camping, hiking, canoeing, gold panning and photography, as well as observing jade mines at Dahl Creek near Kobuk and at Jade Mountain.

Communications include phones, mail plane, radio and TV. The community is served by Friends, Baptist and Seventh-Day Adventist churches, as well as a school with grades preschool to 12 with enrollment of 83. Shungnak has a strong and active elders council. There are community water, sewage disposal and electric systems. Freight arrives by cargo plane and barge. Government address: City of Shungnak, P.O. Box 59, Shungnak, AK 99773, phone (907) 437-2161, fax 437-2140. Village corporation address: NANA Regional Corp., P.O. Box 49, Kotzebue, AK 99752, phone (907) 442-3301, fax (907) 442-2866, web: http://www.nana-online.com/intro.htm. Village council: Native Village of Shungnak, P.O. Box 64, Shungnak, AK 99773, phone (907) 437-2163, fax (907) 437-2183, e-mail: Shungnak@aitc.org.

Umiat

GPS: N69°22' W152°08'

Located on the Colville River, 75 miles south of Harrison Bay and 340 miles north-northwest of Fairbanks. **Transportation:** Charter aircraft-from Prudhoe Bay. **Population:** 5. **Zip code:** 99790. **Emergency Services:** North Slope Borough Public Safety Officer, Prudhoe Bay; Small local dispensary or Prudhoe Bay Clinic.

Elevation: 340 feet. **Climate:** Cool, fairly dry summers, but it can be windy. Extremely cold winters; Umiat frequently is the coldest reporting station in Alaska. Mean annual precipitation is 6.5 inches including 34 inches of snow.

Private Aircraft: Airstrip adjacent; elev. 266 feet; length 5,400 feet; gravel; fuel 80, 100 and jet; attended regularly; visual inspection recommended prior to using. Mountain ridges north and south. Restrooms at airport.

Visitor Facilities: No visitor accommodations or services. No laundromat, banking services or stores. No arts and crafts available. Fishing/hunting licenses not available. Fly-in hunting can be arranged. Limited aircraft repair available. Charter service is the only rental transportation. Float trips starting at the Killik River floating to Umiat on the Colville River are best in the fall when moose, caribou and grizzlies may be seen. Fuel available for aircraft only. No moorage facilities.

An emergency airfield was established here and in 1945 it became a supply and operations base for oil exploration. It still is a major airfield and refueling stop between Fairbanks and Barrow.

There is excellent moose and caribou hunting along the Colville River west of the village. Caribou hunting is usually best the week before moose season opens in early September. There are good landing areas for light planes on river bars, and coal from the riverbank can be used for fires.

Communications at Umiat include phones, mail plane, radio and TV. There is no church or school. Also, no public water, sewage or electric systems. Freight arrives by cargo plane.

Wainwright

GPS: N70°38' W160°01'

Located on Chukchi Sea coast, 85 miles southwest of Point Barrow, 520 miles north-northwest of Fairbanks. **Transportation**: Scheduled airline or charter plane from Barrow. **Population**: 546 **Zip. code**: 99782. **Emergency Services**: Public Safety Officer, phone (907) 763-2911; Wainwright Health Clinic, phone (907) 763-2714; Wainwright Volunteer Fire Department, phone (907) 763-2728.

Elevation: 30 feet. **Climate**: Maximum daily temperature above freezing point only 123 days of the year. Mean annual precipitation is 5.85 inches.

Private Aircraft: Wainwright airstrip 0.3 mile south; elev. 30 feet; length 4,494 feet; gravel; no fuel; unattended; visual inspection recommended prior to using. No facilities at airport. Public transportation available to village.

NOTE: Wainwright prohibits the sale and importation of alcoholic beverages.

Visitor Facilities: Accommodations and food available at Olgoonik Corp. Hotel and Restaurant, (907) 763-2514. No banking services. Laundromat available. Groceries and other supplies at Wainwright Co-op, (907) 763-2715. Local arts and crafts available for purchase are carved ivory figurines and jewelry, baleen boats, whale bone carvings, clocks, knitted caps and gloves. Fishing/ hunting licenses available, as well as guide service. No major repair service. Arrangements can be made to rent private autos, off-road vehicles and boats. Fuel available includes marine gas, diesel, propane, unleaded, regular and supreme. No moorage facilities.

For centuries villages have stood on the land between Wainwright Inlet and the sea, the most recent one being the Inupiat Eskimo village of Wainwright. Wainwright Inlet was named in 1826 by Capt. F.W. Beechey for his officer, Lt. John Wainwright. The present village was established in 1904 when the Alaska Native Service built a school. The com-munity was incorporated as a second-class city in 1962.

Wainwright's subsistence hunting economy is based primarily on whales and caribou, but some residents work at local businesses, the borough government and seasonal construction. Village life revolves around whaling during the spring and summer months, and the taking of a bowhead or beluga whale is cause for celebration — a Nalukataq festival, which takes place usually in June. Eskimo dances also are performed occasionally by the villagers. Other recreational activities in the village include boating; riding snowmobiles and 3-wheelers; and smelt fishing on the lagoon in the spring. Bird watching on the tundra and beachcombing for shells are enjoyable activities available to everyone.

Communications in Wainwright include phones, mail plane, radio and TV. The cornmunity is served by 3 churches and a school with grades preschool through 12 with enrollment of 144. Public water and electricity is available; sewage system is primarily chemical toilets. Freight arrives in the community by cargo plane and barge. Government address: City of Wainwright, P.O. Box 9, Wainwright, AK 99782, phone (907) 763-2815, fax (907) 763-2811. Village corporation address: Olgoonik Corp., P.O. Box 27, Wainwright, AK 99782, phone (907) 763-2613, fax (907) 763-2926. Village council: Village of Wainwright, P.O. Box 184, Wainwright, AK 99782, phone (907) 763-2535, fax (907) 763-2536, e-mail: june@asna.alaska.his.gov.

ARCTIC • ATTRACTIONS

H ome to the Arctic and Selwik National Wildlife Refuges, Cape Krusensten National Monument and Gates of the Arctic National Park and Preserve, Alaska's Arctic region is a vast, secluded wilderness, unique in its habitat and wildlife. This uniqueness makes the Arctic an outstanding region for magnificent scenery, hunting, wildlife viewing and bird watching.

Index of Arctic Attractions

 Bird watching

See Arctic National Wildlife Refuge; Cape Krusenstern National Monument; Kasegaluk Lagoon; Noatak National Preserve; Selawik National Wildlife Refuge; Teshekpuk Lake

Fishing

National Parks and Monuments

See Cape Krusenstern National Monument; Gates of the Arctic National Park and Preserve; Kobuk Valley National Park; Noatak National Preserve

River Running

Special Features

See Kasegaluk Lagoon; Leffingwell Camp; Teshekpuk Lake; Tunalik

Wildlife Refuges

See Arctic National Wildlife Refuge; Selawik National Wildlife Refuge

✕ Arctic National Wildlife Refuge

The 19.3-million-acre Arctic National Wildlife Refuge (ANWR) in the northeastern corner of Alaska encompasses the unique plants, wildlife and land forms of the Arctic. Founders of the wilderness act established ANWR to preserve the "last great wilderness," a place where natural ecological and evolutionary processes continue as they have for millennia. Eight million acres of this "unique wilderness" are designated wilderness, more than any other National Wildlife Refuge.

ANWR is home to 36 species of land mammals, including musk-oxen, Dall sheep, moose, wolves and such solitary species as wolverine, polar bear and grizzly bear. A large portion of the Porcupine caribou herd's (about 130,000 animals) migration route and calving grounds also lie within the refuge. Some 180 species of birds from 4 continents can also be seen in the refuge. Thousands of ducks, geese, swans and loons breed on coastal tundra, and birds throng coastal migration routes all summer. Snowy owls, peregrine falcons, gyrfalcons, roughlegged hawks and golden eagles nest inland. ANWR also holds 36 fish species in its rivers and lakes.

The refuge extends from the Porcupine River basin near the Canadian border north through the Sheenjek River valley and across the eastern Brooks Range down to the Arctic Ocean. Much of this land is above tree line and offers rugged, snowcapped, glaciated peaks and countless streams and rivers that drain north into the Beaufort Sea and south into the Porcupine and Yukon drainages.

Climate: Winter in the refuge is long and severe; summer is brief and intense. Snow showers can occur at any time north of the Brooks Range, but days can be warm in June and July. Mountain lakes are usually ice free by mid-July; south slope lakes usually open by mid-June. Daylight is nearly continuous in summer. Frost is not uncommon in August; by early August, autumn has turned the tundra scarlet. On the north side of the Brooks Range, snow usually covers the ground 8 to 8 1/2 months of the year. Arctic plants survive even though permafrost is within 2 feet of the surface. Annual growth of trees and shrubs is slight. It may take 300 years for a white spruce at tree line to reach a diameter of 5 inches; small willow shrubs may be 50 to 100 years old.

Activities: Visitors to the refuge have rapidly increased in the last few years. Development interests, especially oil, have focused on the refuge, helping to create an unprecedented interest in recreational visits. Rivers, especially the Kongakut, Hulahula, Canning and Sheenjek, receive high numbers of visitors. Recreational activities include kayaking and rafting on rivers both north and south of the Brooks Range. Plane charters out of Fort Yukon, Deadhorse and Fairbanks land parties at access sites throughout the refuge for excellent hiking, floating and backpacking. Though not common, mountain climbing on 9,020-foot Mount Chamberlin, 8,855-foot Mount Michelson and other peaks is possible. Coastal lagoons and other areas of the refuge offer excellent wildlife observation opportunities. The refuge includes 3 wild and scenic rivers: the Ivishak, Sheenjek and Wind. (See River Running this section for more information.)

This area, possibly more than anywhere else in America, can provide a true wilderness experience in which the wild has not been taken out of the wilderness. There is little information about specific hiking areas and rivers in the refuge, and there are no established trails or campsites. Visitors planning a trip to ANWR should be prepared mentally and physically, be well-equipped and understand the risks involved.

Accommodations: There are no lodges or other commercial facilities in the refuge. Food and equipment should be purchased in Fairbanks. Some supplies may be available in Kaktovik, but travelers should come prepared and not count on being able to buy essential items there. Camping is permitted throughout the refuge; use of stoves is recommended because wood supplies are scarce. To avoid giardiasis, boil or purify drinking water. Mosquitoes are most numerous in June and July; a good insect repellent and a head net are recommended.

Access: The refuge is open to public use year-round. Ninety-five percent of the access to the refuge is by air. The Dalton Highway also accesses the western edge. Commercial air service is available from Fairbanks to Fort Yukon, Arctic Village, Deadhorse and Kaktovik on Barter Island, the usual jumping-off sites for refuge visitors. Charter air service is available at Deadhorse, Barter Island, Fairbanks and Fort Yukon and must be prearranged. Private aircraft are permitted in the refuge. Off-road vehicles are not permitted.

For more information: Contact Refuge Manager, Fish and Wildlife Service, Arctic National Wildlife Refuge, Room 266, Federal Bldg. and Courthouse, 101 12th Ave., Box 20, Fairbanks, AK 99701; phone (907) 456-0405.

Cape Krusenstern National Monument

This 660,000-acre monument, 10 miles northwest of Kotzebue, contains some of the most important prehistoric sites in the Arctic. The 114 beach ridges of Cape Krusenstern and nearby bluffs contain a chronological record of some 4,000 years of prehistoric and historic use, primarily by Native groups. The ridges were formed by shifting sea ice, ocean currents and waves, each new one being used in succession by Eskimos for their hunting camps. Eskimos still hunt seals along the cape's outermost beach. At shoreline campsites, the women trim and render the catch for the hides and the meat and seal oil that are still vital to their diet.

Climate: Cloudy skies, frequent fog, westerly winds and minor fluctuations in daily temperatures are normal in the monument. Average daily summer temperatures range from 43°F to 53°F, with the highest temperatures occurring in July. Coldest months are January until early March when average daily temperatures range between -20°F and 0°F. August is the wettest month, with a mean monthly precipitation of 2.26 inches.

Wildlife: The monument includes grizzly bears, Dall sheep, caribou, moose, wolves, lynx and an occasional musk-ox. Walrus, polar bears and several species of seals and whales can be seen offshore at various times of the year. Many species of waterfowl nest around the lagoons in summer. Fish in monument waters include whitefish, arctic char, 2 species of salmon (including chums), northern pike, burbot, Dolly Varden and herring.

Activities: Recreational activities in the monument include primitive camping, hiking, bird watching and fishing. Visitors to the monument should be self-sufficient and prepared for a variety of weather conditions. Contact the Park Service for specific information before traveling to the area; leave a copy of your planned itinerary with the regional office.

The National Park Service office maintains a list of businesses licensed to provide services within the monument. Nonlicensed businesses may provide services outside the monument boundaries only. Contact the business for information on services and prices.

Accommodations: There are no accommodations or campgrounds within the monument. A hotel is located at Kotzebue. Camping is permitted throughout most of the monument, except in archaeological zones, where it would interrupt subsistence activities or on private land holdings located primarily along river and beachfronts. There is a dilapidated shelter cabin in the monument but no National Park Service facilities, trails or services.

Access: There are daily commercial jet flights from Anchorage to Kotzebue. From Kotzebue, access to the monument is by chartered light aircraft (1-hour roundtrip) or boat. When there is adequate sea ice in winter, access by snow machine and dogsled is possible. Weather is extremely variable and can curtail travel to the monument at any time of year. Airplanes may not be used in pursuit of subsistence hunting and fishing. Helicopter landings are not permitted unless authorized by written permit from the monument superintendent.

For more information: Contact or visit the Park Service visitor information center in Kotzebue or contact: Superintendent, Cape Krusenstern National Monument, P.O. Box 1029, Kotzebue, AK 99752; phone (907) 442-3890. USGS maps: Noatak, Kotzebue, Point Hope and DeLong Mountains.

Fishing

Rivers and lakes in the Arctic are accessible for sportfishing primarily by air, although riverboats can occasionally be rented or chartered at villages along the waterways. In the far north, there is virtually no sportfishing around communities such as Barrow, Kaktovik, Wainwright or Point Lay. However, there are lakes and rivers on the Arctic Slope that contain arctic char or Dolly Varden, which average 4 to 6 pounds and can reach 12 to 15 pounds.

Lakes in the Brooks Range are popular for lake trout, which can reach 30 pounds. Anyone planning a trip to one of these mountain lakes should be aware that they may not be totally ice free until July. Some of the largest and most scenic of these lakes are listed here.

At other locations, anglers can encounter sheefish, which can reach more than 50 pounds (53 pounds is the state record) in the Selawik-Kobuk area. Other species present in arctic waters are whitefish, which can reach 5 pounds; burbot, which can weigh in at 20 pounds; northern pike, which average 4 to 8 pounds, but can attain 30 pounds; and arctic grayling, which can reach 4 pounds and which fisheries biologists say can be found "everywhere it's clear and wet."

Most sportfishing in the Arctic takes place in August and September, with anglers flying their own planes or chartering aircraft in Fairbanks, Bettles, Kaktovik or Kotzebue. A general rule from the Alaska Department of Fish and Game is to "plan for the worst" when traveling in the Arctic. Take a few days' extra food and clothing, and allow for a flexible schedule since fickle weather can play havoc with the best laid plans.

For more information contact the Alaska Department of Fish and Game, Sport Fish Division, 1300 College Road, Fairbanks, AK 99701; phone (907) 459-7207, fax (907) 456-2259.

Anaktuvuk River. Located in the Brooks Range in Gates of the Arctic National Park near Anaktuvuk Pass. Good arctic char fishery at its best in September, use spoons and eggs. Air charter available at Bettles.

Canning River. Located at the western boundary of Arctic National Wildlife Refuge. Good arctic char fishery at its best in September, use spoons and eggs. Air charter service available in Fairbanks or Kaktovik.

Chandler Lake. Fly-in lake located on the north slope of the Brooks Range 26 miles west of Anaktuvuk Pass, about 1 hour by floatplane or small wheel plane from Bettles. Short, rough airstrip at lake. Ice may be present until July. Excellent lake trout and grayling fishing. Lake trout fishing best as ice is leaving, good through the season, use spoons or plugs; grayling year-round, use flies; arctic char through the season, best in fall, use spoons, eggs; whitefish also present, use flies, eggs. Air charter available in Bettles.

Elusive Lake. Located on the north slope of the Brooks Range 80 miles northeast of Anaktuvuk Pass. A popular lake trout fishery, best just after the ice leaves, use spoons or plugs; grayling also present. Air charter available in Fairbanks or Bettles.

Fish Lake. Fly-in lake located south of the Brooks Range, about 1 hour by floatplane from Bettles. Excellent lake trout, grayling and arctic char fishing. Lake trout fishing best in spring and good through the season, use spoons or plugs; arctic char through the season, best in fall, use spoons or eggs; grayling year-round, use flies; whitefish use flies or eggs. Air charter available in Bettles.

Heipmejack Lake. Fly-in lake located south of the Brooks Range west of Bettles, about 35 minutes by floatplane. Lake trout fishing best in spring and good through the season, use spoons or plugs; northern pike year-round, best June 1 through September 15, use spoons or spinners; whitefish use flies or eggs. Air charter available in Bettles.

Iniakuk Lake. Fly-in lake located south of the Brooks Range 50 miles west of Bettles. Lake trout fishing best in spring and good through the season, use spoons or plugs; northern pike year-round, best June 1 through September 15, use spoons or spinners; whitefish use flies or eggs. Iniakuk Lake Lodge on lake. Air charter available in Bettles.

Itkillik Lake. Located on the north slope of the Brooks Range 60 miles northeast of Anaktuvuk Pass. A popular lake trout fishery, best in spring just after the ice leaves, use spoons or plugs; grayling also present. Air charter available in Fairbanks or Bettles.

Kobuk River (Upper and Lower). Flows from Walker Lake in Gates of the Arctic National Park to Kotzebue Sound. Boats may be chartered from residents of villages along the Kobuk: Kiana, Noorvik, Ambler, Shungnak and Kobuk. The Kobuk is famous for sheefish, use spoons. It also has the northernmost commercial salmon (chum) fishery in the state. Northern pike year-round, best June 1 through September 15, use spoons or spinners; grayling year-round, use flies; whitefish present in upper river, use flies or eggs. Air charter available in Kotzebue.

Kongakut River. Located within Arctic National Wildlife Refuge. Good arctic char fishery at its best in September, use spoons and eggs. Air charter service available in Fairbanks or Kaktovik.

Kurupa Lake. Located on the north slope of the Brooks Range 75 miles west of Anaktuvuk Pass. A popular lake trout fishery best in spring just after the ice leaves, use spoons or plugs; arctic char and grayling also present. Air charter available in Fairbanks or Bettles.

Nanushuk Lake. Fly-in lake located on the north slope of the Brooks Range northeast of Anaktuvuk Pass, about 1 hour by floatplane from Bettles. Lake trout fishing best as ice is leaving, good through the season, use spoons or plugs; grayling year-round, use flies; whitefish use flies or eggs. Air charter available in Bettles.

Noatak River. Fly-in river located in northwestern Alaska flows through Gates of the Arctic National Park and Noatak National Preserve to Kotzebue Sound. Arctic char fishing excellent in the fall, use spoons and eggs; grayling use flies; chum salmon July 15 through September 30, peaking in August, use spoons; some pike also present. Arrangements may be made for accommodations at Noatak village. Commercial and charter air service available from Kotzebue.

Nutuvukti Lake. Fly-in lake located south of the Brooks Range in Gates of the Arctic National Park. No camps or boats available. Good summer fishery. Lake trout through the season, use spoons or plugs; grayling year-round, use flies; northern pike year-round, best June 1 through September 15, use spoons or spinners; burbot throughout the season, best in fall and winter, use bait such as head or tail of lake trout. Charter floatplane available in Bettles or Kotzebue.

Round Lake. Fly-in lake located on the North Slope of the Brooks Range about 1 hour by floatplane from Bettles. Lake trout fishing best as ice is leaving, good through the season, use spoons or plugs; grayling good year-round, use flies; arctic char use spoons or eggs; whitefish use flies or eggs. Air charter available in Bettles.

Sagavanirktok River. Also known as "The Sag." Located on the Arctic Slope with its outlet near Prudhoe Bay. Good arctic char fishery at its best in September, use spoons and eggs. Char fishery outstanding on Ivishak River, a tributary to the Sagavanirktok. Air charter service available in Fairbanks, Prudhoe Bay or Kaktovik.

Schrader Lake. Located on the Arctic Slope 65 miles south of Barter Island. A popular lake trout fishery best in spring just after the ice leaves, use spoons or plugs; arctic char and grayling also present. Air charter available in Kaktovik or Fairbanks.

Selawik River. Fly-in river about 70 miles southeast of Kotzebue. Fishing excellent for small- to medium-sized sheefish in summer and fall, use spoons; northern pike year-round, best June 1 through September 15, use spoons or spinners. Air charter available in Kotzebue.

Selby Lake. Fly-in lake located south of the Brooks Range in Gates of the Arctic National Park. Summer fishery is excellent. Lake trout through the season, use spoons or plugs; grayling year-round, use flies; northern pike year-round, best June 1 through September 15, use spoons or spinners; burbot throughout the season, best in fall and winter use bait such as head or tail of lake trout. Charter floatplane available in Bettles or Kotzebue.

Shainin Lake. Fly-in lake located on the north slope of the Brooks Range, 22 miles northeast of Anaktuvuk Pass, about 1 hour by floatplane from Bettles. Excellent lake trout and grayling fishing. Lake trout fishing best as ice is leaving, good through the season, use spoons or plugs; grayling year-round, use flies; whitefish, use flies or eggs. Air charter available in Bettles.

Walker Lake. Fly-in lake located in the Brooks Range within Gates of the Arctic National Park, about 45 minutes northwest of Bettles by floatplane. Lake trout fishing excellent through the season, use spoons or plugs; northern pike year-round, best June 1 through September 15, use spoons or spinners; arctic char, use spoons or eggs; whitefish, use flies or eggs. Walker Lake Wilderness Lodge on lake. Air charter available in Bettles.

Wulik River. Located in northwestern Alaska near Kivalina, 90 miles northwest of Kotzebue. Excellent arctic char fishery in spring and fall, use spoons and eggs; grayling, use flies. Midnight Sun Lodge located 30 miles upriver from Kivalina. Commercial and charter air service available in Kotzebue.

 # Gates of the Arctic National Park and Preserve

The major feature of this 8-million-acre park and preserve is the Brooks Range, an extension of the Rocky Mountains that stretches across Alaska from the Canadian border almost to the Chukchi Sea. Gates of the Arctic was the name that Robert Marshall, a forester who explored the then unmapped areas north and west of Wiseman in the 1920s and 1930s, gave Boreal Mountain and Frigid Crags. Marshall named both, and they rise like sentinels on either side of the North Fork Koyukuk River.

Climate: Long, cold winters and short, mild summers are the rule. On the Brooks Range's south slopes, midsummer temperatures range from 32°F to 85°F; winter temperatures range from 32°F to -60°F. North of the Brooks Range, summer temperatures are much cooler; winter temperatures are somewhat milder, but there is more wind. Annual precipitation of 8 to 10 inches classifies the area as semiarid, but this can be hard to believe while slogging through frequent showers and boggy tundra during the summer, particularly August. Mid-May through mid-August, the area has 18 to 24 hours of daylight. North of the Continental Divide, snow may fall every month of the year, and freezing temperatures occur by early September, sometimes in mid-August.

Wildlife: Thirty-six species of mammals live in the park and preserve, ranging in size from lemmings to grizzly bears. There are moose, caribou, Dall sheep, black bears, wolves, beavers, hoary marmots, wolverines, otters, martens, mink, weasels, lynx, red foxes, porcupines and an assortment of small rodents. Eagles and many migratory birds inhabit the area. Fish include grayling in clear streams and lakes; lake trout in larger, deep lakes; char in streams on the North Slope; and sheefish and chum salmon in the Kobuk and lower Alatna rivers. The productivity of fisheries is low due to the short seasons and cold waters of the Arctic.

Activities: Six designated wild rivers flow within and out of Gates of the Arctic: Noatak, Alatna, John, Kobuk, Tinayguk and North Fork Koyukuk. The National Park Service considers these rivers, plus the Killik, floatable. (See River Running this section.) The Mount Igikpak and Arrigetch areas offer superb rock and mountain climbing, as well as impressive photographic opportunities. Hiking in the Arctic is made more difficult by tussocks and abundant wet areas. Hikers should plan on no more than 5 miles per day. Boaters and backpackers are generally dropped off and picked up by chartered aircraft. Winter activities include cross-country skiing, snowshoeing and dogsledding. Sport hunting is allowed in the 2 preserve areas in the northeast and southwest.

Gates of the Arctic is a remote wilderness. Animals are wild and unpredictable. Keep a clean camp and use common sense. Cook away from your camp. Local residents carry on subsistence activities within the park and preserve, and their camps, fishnets and other equipment should not be disturbed.

Accommodations: Bettles has a lodge, general store and canoe rentals. There are no campgrounds in the park, but wilderness camping is allowed. To minimize impact, visitors are asked to camp on gravel bars or areas with hardy heath or moss. There are no established Park Service facilities, roads or trails in the area. Some cases of giardiasis, a parasitic infection of the intestines, have been reported, and visitors should boil or purify drinking water.

Access: Most people get to the central Brooks Range via scheduled flights from Fairbanks to Bettles, where they charter small aircraft for flights into the park and preserve. Charter flights can also begin in Fairbanks, Kotzebue and Ambler, and additional scheduled flights are available from Fairbanks to Allakaket and Anaktuvuk Pass. There is overland access from the Dalton Highway at Coldfoot and Wiseman at the southeast corner of Gates of the Arctic. Ultralights or helicopters are not permitted to land in the park or preserve.

For more information: Contact Superintendent, Gates of the Arctic National Park and Preserve, 201 First Ave., Fairbanks, AK 99701; phone (907) 678-2004, fax (907) 692-5400. USGS maps: Chandler Lake, Wiseman, Survey Pass, Killik River, Hughes, Ambler River, Philip Smith Mountains, Chandalar.

✹ Kasegaluk Lagoon

Stretching southwest along the Chukchi Sea coast from just south of Wainwright to beyond Point Lay, this shallow, 120-mile-long body of water (pronounced ka-SEE-galuk) is the largest barrier island-lagoon system in North America. It offers excellent wildlife viewing, as well as kayaking in shallow (3- to 6-foot) waters protected from ocean waves by the low barrier islands. During July, August and September, half a million migrating eiders and thousands of terns, gulls, jaegers, loons, brants and oldsquaws can be seen. Many beluga whales move into the lagoon in late June. At other times of the year, it is possible to see arctic foxes, lemmings, caribou, brown bears, various types of seals and gray whales. Kasegaluk Lagoon is considered an important and productive habitat by the Alaska Deptartment of Fish and Game. South of Icy Cape, near the mouth of the Utukok River, is the abandoned village of Tolageak, marked by the remains of Eskimo sod huts.

The only access to the lagoon area is by chartered plane from Barrow or Kotzebue. There is a landing strip at an abandoned DEW line site at Icy Cape which is not maintained and may be in poor or unusable condition. Lodging is available at Barrow or Kotzebue, but it's wilderness camping only at the lagoon. Campers and kayakers should be prepared for high winds and cold weather year-round. Take a few extra days' supply of food in the event you get weathered in. Do not in any way harass nesting birds or other wildlife. And be aware that there is considerable subsistence hunting, fishing and other activity in the area at various times of the year. The village of Wainwright owns some of the land at the north end of the lagoon. For additional information contact: Arctic District Manager, Bureau of Land Management, 1541 Gaffney St., Fairbanks, AK 99703; phone (907) 356-5130.

⛰ Kobuk Valley National Park

This 1.7-million-acre park encompasses a nearly enclosed mountain basin on the middle section of the Kobuk River in northwestern Alaska, 350 miles west-northwest of Fairbanks and 75 miles east of Kotzebue. Today's cold, dry climate approximates that of the Ice Age and supports similar plants. During the Pleistocene epoch, the Kobuk Valley provided an ice-free corridor joined to the land bridge that periodically formed between Alaska and Siberia. The valley contains artifacts dating 12,500 years of human occupation. At Onion Portage, near the eastern boundary of the park, Dr. J. Louis Giddings, the same archaeologist who made the discoveries at Cape Krusenstern, found what has been described as the most important archaeological site unearthed in the Arctic. The diggings are now within a designated National Register Archaeological District. Great herds of caribou still cross the Kobuk River at Onion Portage, attracting hunters today just as they did long ago.

Covering 25 square miles south of the Kobuk River are the wind-sculpted Great Kobuk Sand Dunes, some up to 100 feet high and overrunning the nearby forest. These, along with the Little Kobuk Sand Dunes near Onion Portage and the Hunt River Dunes, are among the few dune fields found in the Arctic.

Within the park, the Salmon River has been designated a wild and scenic river. The Kobuk River is designated a wild and scenic river from where it flows out of Walker Lake to the western boundary of Gates of the Arctic National Preserve, located east of Kobuk Valley National Park.

Climate: Long, cold winters and warm, brief summers characterize the park. Summer highs in the mid-80s to 92°F have been recorded, but the mean July temperature is in the mid-50s. Winter temperatures can drop to -60°F, and -20°F is common. Freezeup usually occurs from early to mid-October and breakup in mid- to late May. Mosquitoes appear in late May, are worst in June and disappear in August, when the whitesox and gnats come on the scene until the September frosts.

Wildlife: Animals found in the park include grizzly and black bears, caribou, moose, wolves, lynx, martens, wolverines and some Dall sheep. Numerous ponds and oxbows provide excellent waterfowl habitat; more than 100 species of birds have been spotted in the area. Arctic peregrine falcons may pass through the park during migrations. Fish found in park waters include 3 species of salmon, grayling, pike and sheefish.

Activities: Most visitors float through the park on the Kobuk River. (See River Running this section.) Some start at the headwaters in Gates of the Arctic National Park while others begin their trips in Ambler, Shungnak or Kobuk. The Great Kobuk Sand Dunes can be reached by an easy hike from the river. The lower Salmon River offers good canoeing and kayaking. Other activities include backpacking in the Baird and Waring mountains, fishing and photography. Sport hunting is prohibited.

In Kobuk Valley National Park, human settlement and use of the land is part of the area's heritage. People have hunted and fished in this region for centuries and continue to do so. Please do not interfere with local subsistence activities. Private land within the park boundaries, mostly along the Kobuk River corridor, should not be used without permission.

Accommodations: No accommodations are available in the park, and none are planned. There are no established campgrounds; primitive camping is permitted throughout the park, except in archaeological zones and on private lands along the Kobuk River. There is a hotel at Kotzebue and a lodge at Ambler. Limited amounts of groceries, gasoline and other supplies can be purchased in the villages. There are no Park Service facilities, roads or trails. The only public-use facility in the park is an emergency shelter near the mouth of the Salmon River.

Access: Aircraft provide the primary access to the park although boats can be taken to the 5 villages on the Kobuk River from Kotzebue during the ice-free season. The Upper Kobuk River can be reached from Kotzebue, Ambler, Bettles or Fairbanks. There are regularly scheduled flights from Kotzebue to the villages on the Kobuk. Flights may be chartered from Kotzebue, Kiana, Ambler or Bettles to land on sand bars or beaches. Other means of travel in the region are snow machines and dogsleds during the winter.

For more information: The national park office maintains a list of businesses licensed to provide services within the park. Nonlicensed businesses may provide service outside the park boundaries only. Contact the specific business to find out information about their services and prices. For the list and other information, write Supervisor, National Park Service, Northwest Alaska Areas, P.O. Box 1029, Kotzebue, AK 99752; phone (907) 442-3760, fax (907) 442-8316.

❋ Leffingwell Camp

On southcentral Flaxman Island stand the remains of what is believed to be the camp established by explorer and geologist Ernest de Koven Leffingwell in 1907 to carry out important permafrost studies, mapping and other studies of arctic conditions. The camp is on the National Register of Historic Places.

Leffingwell spent 6 years between 1901 and 1914 in the Canning River region and compiled the first accurate maps of that part of the northern coast. A cabin at the campsite was built from the timbers of the expedition's ship, the *Duchess of Bedford*, which had been damaged by the ice pack. The camp, about 4.5 miles west of Brownlow Point located west of Kaktovik on Barter Island, also contains the remains of 3 traditional Eskimo houses, a storage shed, ice cellar and 2 large, iron ship tanks.

Noatak National Preserve

This 6.6-million-acre preserve, located 350 miles northwest of Fairbanks and 16 miles northeast of Kotzebue, protects the largest untouched mountain-ringed river basin in America. Of its area, 5.8 million acres have been designated wilderness. The 396-mile-long Noatak River is contained within a broad and gently sloping valley, which stretches more than 150 miles east to west. The river, from its source in Gates of the Arctic National Park to its confluence with the Kelly River in Noatak National Preserve, is part of the National Wild and Scenic Rivers System. This is one of the finest wilderness areas in the world, and UNESCO has designated it an International Biosphere Reserve.

The Noatak River passes through 6 regions on its way to the sea: headwaters at the base of Igikpak Mountain; the great Noatak Basin with its rounded mountains and plentiful wildlife; the 65-mile-long Grand Canyon of the Noatak and the much steeper, 7-mile Noatak Canyon; plains dotted with spruce, balsam and poplar; the rolling Igichuk Hills; and finally the flat coastal delta.

Climate: Long, cold winters and short, mild summers are the rule in this area. Temperatures during June, July and August range from 40°F to 85°F, with average midsummer daytime temperatures in the 60s and 70s; however, subfreezing temperatures can

occur on summer nights. June is generally the clearest summer month; clouds increase in July and August. Fog around Kotzebue during the summer can create transportation problems. Winter temperatures sometimes drop to -50°F, and -20°F occurs often. Strong winds produce a severe windchill. Mosquitoes appear in late May, are worst in June and disappear in August. Whitesox are present from August until September frosts. Good insect repellent and a head net are essential.

Wildlife: The western Arctic caribou herd, numbering about 200,000 animals, crosses the preserve in April and August on migrations. Other wildlife seen in the preserve are moose, Dall sheep, grizzly bears, wolves, foxes, lynx, martens, beavers and muskrats. Approximately 125 species of birds have been identified in the preserve and another 31 are thought to occur, including the arctic peregrine falcon. Fish present in preserve waters include grayling, char, salmon, lake trout, burbot, pike and whitefish.

Activities: Recreational activities in the preserve include floating down the Noatak by raft, canoe or kayak; backpacking along the river and in the foothills; wildlife observing; and photography. (For more information on floating the Noatak see River Running this section.) Sportfishing and hunting are allowed in season. The National Park Service cautions that the Noatak basin is one of the least-traveled areas in Alaska. A passing aircraft may not even be seen for days. You are truly "on your own" here. For safety, leave a copy of your itinerary with the Park Service in Kotzebue and carry a few days' extra supply of food. Local residents carry on subsistence activities within the preserve. Their camps, fishnets and other equipment should not be disturbed.

Accommodations: There are no accommodations or campgrounds within the preserve. Camping is permitted throughout the preserve, but respect private land holdings along the lower Noatak River in the preserve.

Access: The preserve can be reached by charter aircraft from Kotzebue, Ambler, Bettles or Kiana. Chartered flights usually land on gravel bars in the river. Numerous gravel bars suitable for landing most of the season are located throughout the preserve. Floatplanes may also be landed throughout the preserve and are available from some of the charter services. Other means of travel are by boat from Kotzebue in summer and by snow machine and dogsled in winter. All travel is dependent on the weather. There are no trails or roads in the preserve.

For more information: The National Park Service maintains a list of businesses licensed to provide services within the preserve. Nonlicensed businesses may not provide services inside the preserve boundaries. Contact the specific businesses for information about their services and prices. For a copy of the list and other information, write the Supervisor, National Park Service, Northwest Alaska Areas, P.O. Box 1029, Kotzebue, AK 99752; phone (907) 442-3760, fax (907) 442-8316. USGS maps: Survey Pass, Ambler River, Howard Pass, Baird Mountains, Misheguk Mountain.

River Running

River runners should contact the appropriate land manager for more detailed information on rivers listed here. Also obtain information on current river conditions from reliable local sources, such as bush pilots, park rangers and local guides. River levels can rise dramatically and quickly with meltwater on sunny days. Rainstorms can also quickly swell rivers.

The Arctic region has 11 of the 25 designated National Wild and Scenic Rivers in Alaska. The Alatna, John, Kobuk, North Fork Koyukuk, Noatak, Salmon and Tinayguk are managed by the National Park Service. The Ivishak, Selawik, Sheenjek and Wind are managed by U.S. Fish & Wildlife Service.

Rafts, canoes, kayaks and Klepper boats can all be used on the rivers; however, rafts are the most popular because of their portability on aircraft. Unless they are collapsible, canoes and kayaks are expensive to transport and are more hazardous in the whitewater sections found on many rivers, especially those found on the north slope of mountains in the Arctic

National Wildlife Refuge.

The Fish and Wildlife Service says North Slope rivers tend to be swift, rocky and icy cold. Life jackets should have pockets to carry waterproof matches, candles, insect repellent and other survival gear. Rivers on the North Slope are usually free-flowing by mid-June and remain high and silty for several weeks, depending on the weather. Low water can be a concern in August, but it is generally not a problem.

Rivers must always be evaluated and run according to current conditions. River ratings are somewhat subjective and can change slightly depending on the stage of the river at any one time. Although rivers are generally open June through September, the safest water levels and best weather occur during July and early August. Visitors should be cautious of the higher-than-average flows that can occur any time of the year, especially after localized heavy rains upstream. It is usually possible to line through or portage the most difficult sections of the rivers.

Spring breakup generally occurs on North Slope rivers during late May and early June. Water levels are often at flood stage during this time, and navigation is hazardous because of ice floes and aufeis (thick layers of ice formed by successive freezing of stream overflows during winter). During breakup, rivers carve vertical-walled canyons through aufeis fields that can be a mile or more in length. During early summer or high water later in the season, it can be dangerous to attempt travel through such areas. By mid- to late June, the channels are generally carved and melted wide enough to allow passage. However, aufeis fields can be dangerous any time during the summer if river levels rise as a result of rains upstream. Visitors should scout all ice areas prior to floating through to ensure that the river is not flowing under or through tunnels in the ice.

Aichilik River. The Aichilik begins among the high, glaciated peaks of the Romanzof Mountains and flows north to the Arctic Ocean. Steep-sided valleys of the river's upper reaches provide scenic hiking but poor access; rapids, braiding and low flows combine to discourage floating. On the coastal plain, the river is the eastern boundary between the 1002 area and designated wilderness.

Alatna River. The upper portion of this designated wild and scenic river flows in Gates of the Arctic National Park on the south slope of the Brooks Range. River trips on the Alatna start in an area famous for the dramatic granite spires of Arrigetch Peaks to the west. The Alatna then meanders through the Endicott Mountains and the Helpmejack Hills before winding through the lowlands of the Koyukuk River.

Highly advanced paddling skills are not required on this trip, but the country is a remote wilderness. Float trips start either at the headwater alpine lakes or from Arrigetch Creek, 47 miles downstream. For the first 5 miles out of the headwater lakes, lining is necessary; then, there is a short stretch of Class III rapids just above Ram Creek that is easily portaged. The next 22 miles to Arrigetch Creek are fast-flowing with sweepers present. From Arrigetch Creek, the Alatna flows slowly, offering a good float for those with moderate river experience.

There are numerous hiking and backpacking opportunities, as well as fishing for grayling, whitefish, arctic char and pike.

Access is by floatplane from Bettles or Fairbanks to the headwater lakes or to lakes near Arrigetch Creek. Exit is possible from the village of Allakaket on the Koyukuk, where there are no accommodations, but there is scheduled air service to Fairbanks. The floater can also continue down the Koyukuk. For more information, contact Gates of the Arctic National Park, 201 First Ave., Fairbanks, AK 99701; phone (907) 678-2004. Related USGS Topographic maps: Survey Pass, Hughes, Bettles.

Canning River. This is a fast, whitewater river in the Arctic National Wildlife Refuge, beginning in the Franklin Mountains and flowing 125 miles northward, emerging west of Camden Bay on the Beaufort Sea. It flows through a scenic mountain valley and then through the arctic coastal lowlands. The clear Marsh Fork, the Canning's main tributary, passes through a narrow valley between mountains that rise sharply on both sides of the river. The main stem of the Canning River leaves the mountains about halfway from its origin. Portions of the main stem below the confluence of Marsh Fork are heavily braided, and the channel must be carefully selected. Strong headwinds may impede progress on the lower river. The Marsh Fork has a couple of rocky stretches up to 4 miles long that have rapids in the upper limit of Class II. Rafts or small, whitewater kayaks may be used on the Marsh Fork or the main stem while a folding boat is suitable only on the main stem.

This river corridor offers good hiking, arctic scenery, wildlife viewing opportunities and fishing for arctic char, grayling and whitefish.

Access to the Canning is from Fairbanks, Deadhorse or Fort Yukon or by charter wheeled plane with short landing and takeoff capability to gravel bars on the Marsh Fork or the main stem. Pickup can be arranged from gravel bars in the Canning delta.

The Arctic National Wildlife Refuge is remote, weather is unpredictable and trips should be carefully planned. Information and assistance are available by writing Refuge Manager, Arctic National Wildlife Refuge, Room 266, Federal Bldg. and Courthouse, 101 12th Ave., Box 20, Fairbanks, AK 99701; phone (907) 456-0405. USGS maps: Arctic and Mount Michelson.

Coleen River. The clear, shallow Coleen, which flows south on the east side of the Arctic National Wildlife Refuge, was a traditional route for Eskimos seeking trade with the Athabascan Indians. The river's upper tributaries are braided, have poor aircraft access and flow through scenic but undramatic mountains. Although its forested middle and lower sections have good access, the Coleen is one of the refuge's less-floated rivers.

Colville River. This is Alaska's largest river north of the Continental Divide and is the seventh longest in the state at 428 miles. The Colville heads in the De Long Mountains, part of the Brooks Range, and bisects the arctic lowlands as it flows east-northeast into Harrison Bay on the Arctic Ocean.

From its headwaters to the Kiligwa River, the Colville's water levels are shallow in some sections and must be lined. From the Kiligwa confluence to Umiat, 225 miles downriver, the Colville consists of several 1- to 4-mile pools connected by shallow riffles. The Colville is not considered a difficult river to run, but this is extremely remote country, and travelers should be experienced with wilderness camping.

The North Slope of the Brooks Range has much wildlife, including large numbers of grizzly bears. Thousands of migratory birds breed and nest here. Most notable are nesting peregrine falcons (avoid disturbing these birds!), gyrfalcons and rough-legged hawks. Dall sheep, caribou, moose and fox may also be spotted. Other activities along the river include hiking and photography. Fishing is fair for whitefish, arctic char, grayling, chum salmon, pike and trout.

Access is generally by scheduled commercial air service to Bettles, Kotzebue, Barrow or Prudhoe Bay, then charter plane to the Kiligwa River confluence. Exit is at Umiat or Nuiqsut, where there is air service to Barrow, Prudhoe Bay or Fairbanks. USGS maps: Misheguk Mountain, Utukok River, Howard Pass, Ikpikpuk River, Killik River, Umiat, Harrison Bay.

East Fork Chandalar River. The Chandalar is a major Yukon River tributary. The East Fork of the river flows swiftly south from its high mountainous headwaters nearly 60 miles through a wide, mountain-rimmed valley. From there, it meanders slowly through a forested, lake-dotted valley. The river passes Arctic Village and serves as a highway to subsistence hunting, fishing and trapping areas.

Hulahula River. This river in the Arctic National Wildlife Refuge flows west and north 100 miles to Camden Bay on the Beaufort Sea about 20 miles from Barter Island. The trip generally takes 8 days from the headwaters (although this is highly variable) and gets a fair amount of use.

This river offers magnificent views of some of the highest mountains in the Brooks Range, then continues through canyons and gorges to the lowlands of the Arctic Slope.

Rapids between Class II and Class IV can be portaged or lined. Rafts and kayaks are suitable for this trip. It is recommended that anyone taking this trip be in top physical condition and an expert river runner, as this is a fast-flowing river with many boulders, drops and rapids. This river tends to carry a substantial glacial silt load in summer, and low water can be a problem in August, but generally is not a serious concern.

There are excellent hiking and photography opportunities. Wildlife viewing includes Dall sheep in the hills and vast herds of caribou on the coastal plain.

Access to the Hulahula is generally by scheduled air service from Fairbanks to Kaktovik. Charter flights are available from Kaktovik to and from the river. The river is generally accessed at a place called Grassers Strip. The river is heavily hunted and fished by Kaktovik villagers.

Arctic National Wildlife Refuge is remote, weather is unpredictable and trips should be carefully planned. Outfitters offer float trips on the Hulahula. Also, information and assistance with planning trips to the refuge are available by writing Refuge Manager, Arctic National Wildlife Refuge, Room 266, Federal Bldg. and Courthouse, 101 12th Ave., Box 20, Fairbanks, AK 99701; phone (907) 456-0405. USGS maps: Barter Island A5; Flaxman Island A-1; Mount Michelson B-1, C-1, D-1.

Ivishak River. A National Wild and Scenic River in Arctic National Wildlife Refuge, the Ivishak heads in the Philip Smith Mountains and flows northwest 95 miles through treeless arctic tundra to the Sagavanirktok River. Fed by flows from relic hanging glaciers, it is a highly braided, swift river, rated Class I white water, Class C flat water. The upper half of the Ivishak flows through tundra-covered mountains with excellent hiking terrain. Floaters can continue down the Sagavanirktok River, traversing the North Slope. The lower Ivishak and the Sagavanirktok cross a broad, open floodplain with scrub willow. Overflow ice on the floodplain can remain much of the summer, and scouting may be needed to be sure the river doesn't disappear under an ice shelf. Best time of year to float the river is July. Popular trip length is 95 to 150 miles. Although scenic, the river's shallow water, poorly defined channels and marginal access result in low use by floaters.

For more information: Contact Refuge Manager, Arctic National Wildlife Refuge, Room 266, Federal Bldg. and Courthouse, 101 12th Ave., Box 20, Fairbanks, AK 99701; phone (907) 456-0405.

John River. This designated wild and scenic river in Gates of the Arctic National Park offers a rewarding voyage for the adventuresome traveler. It is possible to paddle the length of the river by starting at the Eskimo village of Anaktuvuk Pass. A short portage and lining on the small creek near the village is necessary. Experience is essential for safe negotiation of some fast water and easy rapids above Hunt Fork.

Most float trips, however, start at Hunt Fork and continue 100 miles to the confluence with the Koyukuk. The John, a clearwater tributary to the Koyukuk, then offers an exciting but safe trip through an extremely scenic area of the Brooks Range, which has not yet been exploited by large numbers of people. Rugged mountains along the way offer excellent hiking and are home to Dall sheep. Grizzly bears, moose and wolves may also be seen. Fishing is fair for grayling, whitefish, burbot, pike in the lakes, and chum salmon.

Access to the river is by floatplane from Bettles or Fairbanks to Hunt Fork Lake or Anaktuvuk Pass. It generally takes 5 days to float from Hunt Fork to the mouth of the John, then another half a day to line 5 miles up the Koyukuk to Bettles, where there are overnight accommodations and regularly scheduled air service to Fairbanks. USGS maps: Wiseman A-4, A-5, B-4, B-5, C-5, D-5; Bettles D-4.

Killik River. This scenic river heads in Gates of the Arctic National Park at the Continental Divide and flows northward 105 miles to the Colville River. The river passes through mountainous terrain and then into the lowlands of the Arctic Slope. The trip generally takes 10 days from the usual put in point at Easter Creek to Umiat, on the Colville River about 70 miles downstream from the Killik River confluence.

The Killik offers Class I and II rapids throughout its course. About halfway to the Colville, Sunday Rapids might be Class I or Class II, depending on water levels, and should be inspected before passage is attempted. A whitewater kayak is recommended for this river.

There is good hiking in the mountainous region, where Dall sheep can be seen. Wildlife viewing also can be excellent in the river valley, where grizzly bear, moose, caribou, wolf, fox, lynx and wolverine may be spotted. Fossils can be seen in rock outcroppings below Sunday Rapids. Fishing is for grayling, arctic char and pike.

Access is generally by scheduled airline from Fairbanks to Bettles, then charter floatplane from Bettles to the Easter Creek area. Pickup from gravel bars on the Colville just upstream from the Killik River confluence can be arranged. Or there is air service out of Umiat to Prudhoe Bay and Fairbanks. USGS maps: Survey Pass, Killik River, Ikpikpuk River.

Kobuk River. From its headwaters on the southern slopes of Arrigetch Peaks, the Kobuk River flows 347 miles to the Chukchi Sea. It is the ninth longest river in Alaska and one of the most popular for float trips. The Kobuk is designated a wild and scenic river from its headwaters at Walker Lake in Gates of the Arctic National Park to the park's western boundary. Lower stretches of the Kobuk pass through Kobuk Valley National Park.

The Kobuk flows between the Baird Mountains to the north and low-lying Waring Mountains to the south, and the wide, forested valley offers sweeping views. The Kobuk winds through 2 canyons, both with rapids, before meandering serenely to the sea. The 125-mile journey to Kobuk, where most floaters stop, can be made in about 6 days by raft, kayak or canoe. Some floaters continue on to Kiana.

River floaters can fish for sheefish, northern pike, grayling, whitefish, chum salmon and, in Walker Lake, lake trout. Bears, moose, caribou and wolves may be seen along the river.

For most of its course, the Kobuk is a gentle Class I and II float. On the upper river, less than a mile below the outlet of Walker Lake, is a mile of Class IV to V rapids, with 4 major drops of several feet, boulders, haystacks, serious hydraulics and no clear path through which to steer a boat. Portaging this section is essential

Upper Kobuk Canyon, marked by a tall canyon wall on the left and a huge boulder midstream, has rocks and riffles for more than a quarter of a mile. Lower Kobuk Canyon has 3 sections of Class III-IV rapids. The first section has several large rock outcrops and standing waves. More rocks and a couple of chutes with 5-to 6-foot ledge drops are downriver. A nearly unbroken line of boulders with narrow chutes and several more drops follows a nasty hydraulic at the bottom. Most paddlers choose to line their boats on these sections of the river rather than risk wrecking a boat far from civilization.

For centuries, the Kobuk has been a major river highway for both coastal and inland Eskimos and is still used as such today. Recreational river travelers are cautioned not to interfere with any subsistence activities taking place along the Kobuk. Also, check with the National Park Service about the location of private lands.

Access to the Kobuk River is by floatplane from Bettles or Ambler to Walker Lake. All 5 villages along the river have scheduled air service to Kotzebue or Fairbanks. There are overnight accommodations in most of the villages. It's a good idea to contact the village ahead of time if you plan to spend time there. Several outfitters offer a variety of float trips down the Kobuk. USGS maps: Survey Pass, Hughes, Shungnak, Ambler River, Baird Mountains, Selawik.

Kongakut River. This is a high-use river in Arctic National Wildlife Refuge that flows through country of primeval beauty and wildness on the north slope of the Brooks Range. The Kongakut flows northeast from the Davidson Mountains, ending 100 miles away at Siku Lagoon, 8 miles northwest of Demarcation Point in the far northeast corner of Alaska. The trip generally takes 11 days from the headwaters.

Wildlife viewing can be excellent in the refuge, particularly during migrations of the Porcupine caribou herd.

Rafts or folding boats are suitable for this trip, which is suggested for the intrepid explorer in good condition. Recommended for experienced paddlers only, the river does have some Class III waters although rapids are generally Class I and II.

Access to the Kongakut is generally by scheduled air service from Fairbanks to Kaktovik on Barter Island. Charter flights are available from Kaktovik to and from the river. The river is generally accessed fairly high in the headwaters at a place called Drain Creek. Most floaters take out at Caribou Pass although some float all the way to Beaufort Sea.

Arctic National Wildlife Refuge is remote, weather is unpredictable and trips should be carefully planned. Information and assistance with planning trips to the refuge are available by writing Refuge Manager, Arctic National Wildlife Refuge, Room 266, Federal Bldg. and Courthouse, 101 12th Ave., Box 20, Fairbanks, AK 99701; phone (907) 456-0405. USGS maps: Table Mountain, Demarcation Point.

Nigu-Etivluk. Both the Nigu and Etivluk rivers are small, swift and clear tributaries to the Colville River. The Nigu's headwaters are in Gates of the Arctic National Park, and it tumbles for 70 miles before joining the Etivluk. Then, it's another 70 miles to the Colville.

The Nigu generally has shallow, Class I water with frequent Class II rapids. The Nigu is floatable by raft only until about the third week of June or by canoe or kayak until the last week of June. The Etivluk has fast, Class I water with scattered Class II rapids. Canoes or small rafts are recommended although kayaks also are used. This trip passes through majestic mountains, rolling hills and level coastal plain.

There is good hiking in the treeless valleys and on the tundra ridges and lower mountains. Fishing is good for grayling, whitefish and arctic char. Animals that may be seen are grizzly bears, Dall sheep, caribou, wolves and foxes.

Access is by floatplane from Bettles or Fairbanks to lakes at the Nigu headwaters (be prepared to portage a mile over soggy tundra from the headwaters) or to Nigtun Lake at the Etivluk headwaters. Arrange for pickup from lakes or gravel bars along the lower Etivluk or the Colville River. Or travel down the Colville to Umiat, which has air service to Prudhoe Bay and Fairbanks. USGS maps: Killik River, Howard Pass.

Noatak River. This 396-mile-long designated wild and scenic river winds through Gates of the Arctic National Park and Noatak National Preserve before flowing into Kotzebue Sound. Considered by many to be the finest wilderness river in the Arctic, the Noatak flows through forest and tundra country entirely above the Arctic Circle. The mountains along the upper river, Noatak Canyon and the run to the sea below the village of Noatak are highlights of this river. There are several stretches of Class II rapids, but the river is generally smooth flowing. The trip from the headwaters to the village of Noatak generally takes about 16 days.

The Noatak features changing scenery along with a variety of animals and birds. The Noatak basin is particularly rich in migratory birds during spring and summer, and the river traveler may also glimpse moose, caribou, wolves or grizzly bears. Fishing is good for grayling, whitefish, arctic char, pike and chum salmon. Wild berries are abundant in July and August.

Access to the Noatak generally begins with a commercial flight from Fairbanks to Bettles and a charter floatplane flight to any of several lakes along the upper river. There is scheduled air service from Noatak village to Kotzebue, or pickup can be arranged from scattered lakes, the river itself or gravel bars. For more information, contact the Supervisor, National Park Service, Northwest Alaska Areas, P.O. Box 1029, Kotzebue, AK 99752; phone (907) 442-3760, fax (907) 442-8316. USGS maps: Survey Pass, Ambler River, Howard Pass, Misheguk Mountains, Baird Mountains, Noatak.

North Fork Koyukuk. This is a designated wild and scenic river in Gates of the Arctic National Park that provides a good, family-type, wilderness boating experience.

Canoe, raft or kayak can be used. The river is not difficult, but there are some sharp turns and obstacles to watch for. The river offers good hiking and scenery—waterfalls, jagged peaks and hanging valleys. Old cabins dot the banks, silent reminders of a historic mining past. Fishing is good for grayling, pike and whitefish.

Access to the river is generally by floatplane from Bettles to Summit Lake or to lakes near the mouth of Redstar Creek. From Redstar Creek, it takes approximately 4 to 5 days to float to Bettles. Bettles is served by scheduled commercial air service from Fairbanks and has meals and lodging.

For more information and a list of guide services licensed to operate in Gates of the Arctic, contact the National Park Service, 201 First Ave., Fairbanks, AK 99701; phone (907) 678-2004, fax (907) 692-5400. USGS maps: Wiseman A-2, A-3, B-2, C-2, C-3, D-1, D-2; Bettles D-3, D-4; Chandler Lake A-1.

Redstone and Cutler rivers. These rivers in northwestern Alaska offer access from the Kobuk River to the Noatak River. The traverse crosses some extremely remote country but connects the 2 major river systems with an 8-mile portage.

Heading north from the village of Ambler to the Redstone River is recommended. The slow-flowing Redstone permits upstream paddling and easy lining.

A low valley opening shows one obvious route for the portage. A second, somewhat shorter portage is through the next valley about 6 miles upriver. The clear, shallow Cutler River, which has a string of easy rapids, is just over the divide from the Redstone.

The traverse in the opposite direction (from the Cutler to the Redstone) is possible, but involves a longer upstream paddle and more lining.

Access to Ambler, which has overnight accommodations, is by plane from Kotzebue. Before making the traverse, it's advisable to contact the village of Ambler regarding your plans. USGS map: Ambler River.

Salmon River. A National Wild and Scenic River in Kobuk Valley National Park, the Salmon heads in the Baird Mountains and flows south 60 miles to the Kobuk River near its confluence with the Tutksuk River northeast of Kiana. The Salmon descends through a poplar-spruce forest in the western Brooks Range then meanders finally into the Kobuk. In its upper navigable reaches below Anaktok and Sheep creeks, this clear, small river alternates short shallow pools and riffles. Downriver, the pools lengthen, and the river deepens. The river is also noted for its many beautiful rock outcroppings. It is rated Class I white water, Class A flat water. Best time of year to float is July to September. Popular trip length is 140 miles. For more information, contact the Supervisor, National Park Service, Northwest Alaska Areas, P.O. Box 1029, Kotzebue, AK 99752; phone (907) 442-3760, fax (907) 442-8316.

Selawik River. This National Wild and Scenic River is located in Selawik National Wildlife Refuge. The Selawik heads in the Zane Hills and flows west 140 miles to Selawik Lake, an expansive body of water only 5 to 15 feet deep. A long, low-lying river, the Selawik rises at about 600 feet in spruce forests and follows a looped, meandering pattern west through treeless, pingodotted wetlands. The upper third of the river has numerous boulders and sweepers; on the lower 25 miles, the current is slow but strong. West winds can build waves up to 3 feet high. It is rated Class I white water. Best time of year to float is July to September. Popular trip length is 230 miles. For more information, contact the Refuge Manager, Selawik National Wildlife Refuge, P.O. Box 270, Kotzebue, AK 99752; phone (907) 442-3799.

Sheenjek River. This National Wild and Scenic River flows 200 miles south to the Porcupine River. It is located in the Arctic National Wildlife Refuge. A gentle, clear-water river flowing through a broad valley, the Sheenjek drains the south slopes of the Romanzof Mountains and skirts some of the highest peaks in the Brooks Range. Providing a long, relatively easy float, it flows south from open tundra through subarctic boreal forest to the Yukon River wetlands. Since overflow ice can remain most of the summer, scout ahead to be sure the channel is open all the way through. Rated Class II white water and Class B flat water. Can be floated July to mid-September. Popular trip length is 270 miles. For more information, contact the Refuge Manager, Arctic National Wildlife Refuge, Room 266, Federal Bldg. and Courthouse, 101 12th Ave., Box 20, Fairbanks, AK 99701; phone (907) 456-0405.

Squirrel River. This is a clear-water, free-flowing stream that originates in the Baird Mountains of northwestern Alaska. It flows for about 95 miles through a broad, mountain-flanked valley before entering the Kobuk River near the village of Kiana. The valley supports a variety of vegetative systems ranging from alpine tundra to upland spruce/hardwood and bottomland spruce/poplar forest. The Squirrel River is readily accessible by light aircraft from Kotzebue (approximately 30 minutes flying time, one way). It provides a relatively safe, easy float although there is some white water in the upper few miles of the river. Sportfishing for arctic char, chum salmon and grayling is available. There is good hiking terrain in the headwaters area. Good overnight campsites are plentiful along most of the river. Additional information is available from the BLM office located in Kotzebue, Box 1049, Kotzebue, AK 99752; phone (907) 442-3430. USGS maps: Baird Mountains A-3, A-4, A-5,

B-5, B-6; Selawik D-3.

Tinayguk River. This National Wild and Scenic River rises in the Endicott Mountains and flows 44 miles south through alpine valley in the Brooks Range to the North Fork Koyukuk River. It is located in the Gates of the Arctic National Park. Rated Class II white water, the Tinayguk has extensive, rocky rapids, especially at low water. Can be floated July to September. Popular trip length is 120 miles. For more information, contact the Superintendent, Gates of the Arctic National Park and Preserve, 201 First Ave., Fairbanks, AK 99701; phone (907) 678-2004, fax (907) 692-5400.

Wild River. This clear, fast tributary of the Koyukuk flows from Wild Lake, where fishing is good for grayling, pike and lake trout, to the Koyukuk. Trips on this river generally take place only in June, before water levels drop. Floaters pass through beautiful mountain scenery then into typical arctic taiga where the river occasionally slows on its meandering course to the Koyukuk River. Brief shallow areas may be encountered.

Access is possible by chartering a plane from Bettles to Wild Lake. The trip down the Wild River generally takes 4 to 6 days. After reaching the Koyukuk River, it's only a few miles downriver to Bettles where there are overnight accommodations and regularly scheduled flights to Fairbanks. USGS maps: Bettles D-3, D-4; Wiseman A-3, B-3, B-4, C-4.

Wind River. This river heads at 68°34' N, 147°18' W in the Brooks Range and flows southeast 80 miles within Arctic National Wildlife Refuge to the East Fork Chandalar River. At moderate to high water stages, the Wind River is swift and is considered an exciting whitewater river for intermediate boaters. At these water levels, the river is Class II from the vicinity of Center Mountain for 22 miles. Then, there's a 10-mile stretch of Class I, followed by 7 miles of Class III and 25 miles of Class II. The last 6 miles are Class III. This trip generally takes 4 days. Rafts or kayaks are recommended; canoes are suitable for advanced paddlers. Below its confluence with the Wind River, the East Fork Chandalar is Class I, with some Class II rapids at low water levels. Lining through some boulder rapids may be necessary at low water.

On the Wind, there is good mountain scenery and hiking, particularly along the upper river. There is fishing for arctic grayling, pike and whitefish. Travelers can also hike into several lakes close to the river for good pike fishing.

Access is by charter air service from Fairbanks or Fort Yukon to a lake behind Center Mountain or lakes farther downriver. Gravel bars in this area, or farther upriver, may be suitable for wheel planes; consult local pilots. Exit is from a lake located 5 miles below the confluence with the East Fork Chandalar River, possibly from East Fork itself, or continue on to Venetie, which has scheduled air service but no visitor facilities. USGS maps: Christian, Arctic A-5, Philip Smith Mountains A-1, B-1.

Selawik National Wildlife Refuge

This 2.15-million-acre refuge straddles the Arctic Circle in northwestern Alaska, 360 miles northwest of Fairbanks. The northeastern part of the refuge (240,000 acres) is wilderness. The refuge's northern boundary abuts Kobuk Valley National Park, and its southeastern corner joins Koyukuk National Wildlife Refuge. Its northwestern edge lies along Hotham Inlet across from Baldwin Peninsula and Kotzebue, the region's largest town. Selawik is a showcase of estuaries, lakes, river deltas and tundra slopes. Its most prominent feature is an extensive system of tundra wetlands nestled between the Waring Mountains and Selawik Hills.

The refuge is located near the Bering Land Bridge that once connected Asia and North America. Many years ago, animals and humans migrated across here. In later years, prospectors searched for gold. The refuge contains relics of these ancient and recent migrations.

Climate: Temperatures in June and July reach 70°F and 80°F, and there is 24-hour daylight. Insects become bothersome by mid-July. Winter comes quickly and temperatures reach the -20°F mark in October. Temperatures are coldest in January and February, when it can drop to -60°F. By winter solstice, there is only 1 hour and 43 minutes of daylight each day.

Wildlife: Selawik is a vital breeding and resting area for a multitude of migratory waterbirds. Nesting ducks number nearly 100,000. Tundra swans, sandhill cranes, Canada and white-fronted geese and several species of loons are also common in the area. Thousands of caribou winter in the refuge, feeding on lichen-covered foothills. Other common mammals include moose, grizzly bears and other furbearers. Sheefish (some weighing 40 lbs.), whitefish, grayling and northern pike inhabit lakes, ponds, streams and rivers.

Activities: Recreation in the refuge includes hiking, boating, camping, wildlife viewing and photography. Portions of the Selawik River are designated as a wild river, and it provides good river rafting and sportfishing. Limited commercial guide service is available. Hunting, trapping and fishing are permitted in accordance with state and federal regulations. Main activities in the refuge are subsistence hunting, fishing and edible plant gathering by local residents. There are more than 500 Native allotments, which are private land and should not be trespassed, in the refuge. These allotments are mainly along the rivers, including the wild river portion of the Selawik River.

Access: The refuge is accessible by boat, aircraft, snowmobile, dog team, foot and cross-country skis depending on the season and weather. There are no roads. Scheduled air service is available to Kotzebue from Anchorage and to Selawik, Kiana and Noorvik from Kotzebue. Charter air service to the refuge is available at Kiana, Ambler, Galena and Kotzebue. In the summer, floatplane and boats are the only practical way of visiting refuge islands and waters.

For more information: Contact the Refuge Manager, Selawik National Wildlife Refuge, P.O. Box 270, Kotzebue, AK 99752; phone (907) 442-3799.

✵ Teshekpuk Lake

This large lake lies just a few miles from the Arctic Ocean in the wet, low tundra region southeast of Barrow. Teshekpuk Lake, which is 22 miles across, and smaller surrounding lakes are considered crucial waterfowl and caribou habitat areas. Wildlife viewing and photography are excellent. The region is home to migratory brants, greater white-fronted geese and Canada geese, which arrive in July and August from the Alaska Peninsula, Canadian Arctic and Siberia. The lake system protects these large birds from predators while they molt and regrow their wing feathers. Other birds that nest in the region include plovers, sandpipers, phalaropes, dunlins, loons, oldsquaws, jaegers, gulls and snowy owls. Caribou, arctic foxes and lemmings can also be seen.

The only access to the area is by charter plane from Barrow or Prudhoe Bay. There is lodging in Barrow, but wilderness camping only in the lake area. Special use regulations are in effect in the summer to minimize aircraft and other disturbance of wildlife. For additional information, contact: Arctic District Manager, Bureau of Land Management, 1541 Gaffney St., Fairbanks, AK 99703; phone (907) 356-5130.

✵ Tunalik

This 5,000-foot airstrip is located south of Icy Cape in the vicinity of Kasegaluk Lagoon. The Tunalik River mouth, 10 miles south of Icy Cape at 70°11′ N, 161°44′ W, is 5 to 10 miles downstream from the airstrip, which was built to supply oil exploration expeditions. The strip is reported to be still usable although it is not maintained and should be inspected before a landing is attempted. There is a gravel pad on one side of the runway for camping. This open tundra region offers a real arctic tundra wilderness experience with good opportunities for wildlife viewing and photography in the summer. There are no facilities here. You are on your own and should be prepared with adequate clothing and extra food and supplies in the event the weather changes for the worst.

INTERIOR

Alaska's Interior is a land of superlatives. Majestic Mount McKinley (Denali) crowns the region's southern border. The Yukon, Alaska longest river, carves a swath across the entire region. The Interior encompasses almost one-third of the state, most of it wilderness. Rivers are the Interior's natural highways.

Gold discoveries of the 1880s and 1890s brought the major influx of non-Natives to the Interior. Abandoned dredges and active mining claims are common sights in the Fairbanks mining district. Gold Dredge Number 8, now a tourist attraction, is 10 miles from Fairbanks. Other dredges rest near Chicken and Jack Wade camp not far from the Fortymile River, where active gold mining continues. At Healy, southwest of Fairbanks, the state's only operating coal mine produces coal that generates electricity in the Interior.

Fairbanks is Alaska's second largest city and administrative capital of the Interior. It began in 1903-04 as a gold-mining community, then grew as a service and supply point for the Interior. Fairbanks played a key role during construction of the trans-Alaska oil pipeline in the 1970s and continues to be important to Arctic industrial activities.

The 800-mile-long trans-Alaska pipeline cuts through the Interior and is visible from several highways. The 48-inch-diameter pipeline crosses the Yukon River north of Fairbanks, passes through rolling hills 10 miles east of the city, then goes south past Delta Junction to the Alaska Range before descending to the Copper River basin and the marine terminal at Valdez.

Location: Alaska's Interior encompasses the Alaska Range on the south, stretching to the southern foothills of the Brooks Range and the Arctic Circle on the north. The Canadian border is to the east. The Interior blends with the Bering Sea Coast region on the west. The state's geographic center is located near Lake Minchumina, about 60 miles northwest of Mount McKinley.

Geography: Great rivers have forged Alaska's Interior. The Yukon, Tanana, Porcupine, Koyukuk and many others provided avenues of exploration for the Athabascan Indians and later white explorers, trappers and miners. South of the Yukon, the Kuskokwim River rises in the hills of the western Interior before beginning its meandering course across the Bering Sea Coast region.

Two distinct environments, forests and tundra, characterize the Interior. Below 2,000 feet and in river valleys, forests of white spruce, birch and aspen are broken by stands of balsam poplar and tamarack. Cottonwood thrive near river lowlands, and hardy black spruce grow in bogs. Willows, alders, berries, wildflowers, grasses and sedges abound, as does reindeer moss, a type of lichen which makes up a substantial portion of the diet of caribou.

In northern and western reaches of the Interior, the forests give way to slow-growing tundra. Above 2,500 feet, most mountains are bare, except for flowering plants and rock lichens.

Climate: The climate here is largely governed by latitude. The Arctic Circle sweeps through the region. Summer's almost 24 hours a day of sunshine gives way to thin and elusive sunlight in winter. The aurora borealis illuminates many long winter nights.

Temperatures in the Interior range widely, from winter lows of -50°F to -60°F to summer highs of 80°F to 90°F. Stagnant air masses typify the semiarid continental climate, which averages about 12 inches of precipitation annually.

Wildlife: Caribou from several different herds spend all or part of the year in the Interior. Moose are common in second-growth forests, on timberline plateaus and along the rivers. Grizzly bears, black bears and wolves range throughout the region. Dall sheep are found in the high mountains. All these species may be seen at Denali National Park and Preserve. Wolverines are classed as big game but are seldom seen. An introduced bison herd ranges near Delta Junction, and a smaller, private herd grazes near Healy.

Coyotes, red fox, lynx and snowshoe hare may be hunted or trapped. Porcupine may be hunted. Beaver, marten, mink, weasel, muskrat, land otter, flying squirrel, arctic ground squirrel, red squirrel, hoary marmot and pika are protected from hunting, though all but the pika may be trapped.

Millions of birds make their homes in this region including wigeon, pintail, green-winged teal, northern shoveler, canvasback, Canada geese, several species of scoter, scaup and swans, and many other species. Endangered peregrine falcons nest in Yukon/Charley Rivers National Preserve. Minto Flats State Game Refuge is an important staging area for waterfowl from the Yukon Flats and North Slope during fall migration.

Alatna

GPS: N66°34' W152°40'

(A-LAT-na) Located on north bank of the Koyukuk River, 2 miles downriver from Allakaket, 182 miles northwest of Fairbanks. **Transportation:** Boat or snow machine from Allakaket. **Population:** 35. **Zip code:** 99790. **Emergency Services, Elevation, Climate and Private Aircraft:** See Allakaket.

The village is situated on a high open plateau where Kobuk Eskimos and the Koyukukhotana Athabascans met to trade goods. The Indians settled across the river in what is now Allakaket.

The Eskimo village of Alatna has no visitor facilities. Water is hauled from the Koyukuk River. Electric service is provided by a generator. Sewage system is outhouses. Most services and facilities are available at Allakaket.

Allakaket

GPS: N66°34' W152°38'

(Alla-KAK-it) Located on south bank of the Koyukuk River at the mouth of the Alatna River, 2 miles upriver from Alatna, 180 miles northwest of Fairbanks. **Transportation:** Scheduled air service from Fairbanks; boat or snow machine to Alatna and Hughes. **Population:** 97. **Zip code:** 99720. **Emergency Services:** Village Public Safety Officer; Allakaket Health Clinic, phone (907) 968-2210; Volunteer Fire Department.

Elevation: 600 feet. **Climate:** Warmest month is July with a mean temperature of 58°F and 2.06 inches of precipitation. Coldest month is January, averaging -18°F. Snow from late September through May.

Private Aircraft: Airstrip adjacent village beside river (river floods south end of runway in spring); elev. 350 feet; length 4,000 feet; gravel; unattended. Runway condition not monitored; visual inspection recommended prior to using (watch for children and dogs on runway). No facilities.

NOTE: Allakaket bans possession of alcoholic beverages.

Visitor Facilities: No accommodations or meals available, though arrangements can be made to sleep on the school floor. Two stores in the community carry groceries, clothing, hardware, film and sporting goods. No banking services but there is a community-owned laundromat (washeteria) which is also the village watering point. Beaded arts and crafts and fur hats available for purchase. Fishing/hunting licenses available. Diesel, white gas and gasoline are available and boats may be rented.

This area was originally a place where the Kobuk Eskimos and the Koyukukhotana Athabascans met to trade goods. The Eskimos settled on the north bank of the river (now Alatna) and the Athabascans on the south bank. The population declined with the influx of Russians in 1838. In 1906, Archdeacon Hudson Stuck established an Episcopal mission here.

"A hard subsistence life" is how one Allakaket resident describes it here. Fishing in local rivers includes sheefish, grayling and whitefish. Gates of the Arctic National Park and Preserve are located to the north of the village, and Kanuti Wildlife Refuge is adjacent. The village has first priority for subsistence hunting, but caribou and moose are scarce.

Communications include phones, mail plane, CB radios, radio and TV. There is an Episcopal church, St. John's-in-the-Wilderness, and a school with grades preschool through 10 with enrollment of 47. There are a municipal electric service and small private generators. Water is obtained from the river and the laundromat. Sewage system is outhouses. Freight comes in by plane. Government address: City of Allakaket, P.O. Box 30, Allakaket, AK 99720, phone (907) 968-2241, fax (907) 968-2251. Village council: Allakaket Village, Box 50, Allakaket, AK 99720, phone (907) 968-2237, fax (907) 968-2233, e-mail: Allakaket@aitc.org.

Anvik

GPS: N62°39' W160°12'

Located on the Anvik River at its mouth just west of the Yukon River and east of the Nulato Hills; 34 miles north of Holy Cross, 160 miles northwest of Bethel and 350 miles west-northwest of Anchorage. **Population:** 104. **Zip code:** 99558. **Emergency Services:** Police, phone (907) 663-6334; Anvik Health Clinic; Volunteer Fire Department.

Elevation: 325 feet. **Climate:** In the continental climate zone. Annual average snowfall is 110 inches; total precipitation per year is 21 inches.

Private Aircraft: Airstrip 1 mile southeast; elev. 325 feet; length 2,910 feet; gravel and dirt; unattended. Runway condition not monitored; visual inspection recommended prior to using. Runway dish-shaped; severe erosion adjacent to runway shoulder 800 feet from south end. 2,000-foot seaplane access and float in Yukon River.

Visitor Facilities: Reserved accommodations with meals at R & L's Anvik River Lodge , (907) 262-6324. Groceries, general merchandise, gifts and novelties, local arts and crafts available. There is a laundromat. Fishing/hunting licenses may be obtained locally. Major repair services, charter aircraft available. All fuels available except premium gasoline. No banking services.

Anvik, 1 of 5 villages inhabited by the Ingalik Athabascan Indians, was incorporated as a second-class city in 1969. In 1834, Russian Andrei Glazanov reported several hundred people living here. Anvik was originally located across the Yukon River at an area called the point. Spring flooding forced people to move from the

point to a higher location where, in 1887, the Episcopal Church established a mission. Anvik has been known by many names throughout the years.

Anvik has a seasonal economy which shows an upswing in summer when local construction programs get under way. Most families have fish camps and rely heavily on subsistence activities such as hunting, fishing , trapping and home gardening.

The site of Christ Church Mission with its remaining structures is on the National Register of Historic Places.

Every other year, Anvik is a checkpoint in the 1,049-mile Iditarod Trail Sled Dog Race held in March.

Communications include phones, mail plane, e-mail, radio and TV. The community is served by an Episcopal church and a school with grades preschool through 12 with enrollment of 27. Public electricity is available. Water is provided by a city well. Sewage system is privies and honey buckets. Freight arrives by air transport and barge. Government address: City of Anvik, P.O. Box 50, Anvik, AK 99558, phone (907) 663-6328. Village corporation, Deloy Geo Inc., P.O. Box 150, Anvik, AK 99558, phone (907) 663-6376. Village council: Anvik Tribal Council, P.O. Box 10, Anvik, AK 99558, phone (907) 663-6322, fax (907) 663-6357, e-mail: Anvik@aitc.org.

Arctic Village

GPS: N68°07' W145°35'

Located in the Brooks Range on the east bank of the East Fork Chandalar River, 100 miles north of Fort Yukon, 290 miles north of Fairbanks. **Transportation:** Scheduled air service from Fairbanks; winter trail to Venetie. **Population:** 152.: 99722 **Zip code. Emergency Services:** Tribal Police through Native Village of Venetie Tribal Government; Arctic Village Health Clinic; Volunteer Fire Department.

Elevation: 2,250 feet. **Climate:** Mean temperature in July is 56°F; in January -29°F.

Private Aircraft: Airstrip 1 mile southwest of village; elev. 2,086 feet; length 3,120 feet; gravel; unattended. Check for runway construction; watch for loose gravel on approach and vehicles on runway.

NOTE: Arctic Village is a dry village; the sale and importation of alcoholic beverages is prohibited.

Visitor Facilities: No accommodations or meals. No banking services. Supplies and groceries are available at Midnight Sun Native Store, (907) 587-5418; and Gilbert Store, (907) 587-5414. There is a community-owned laundromat with showers. Arctic Village is a traditional Athabascan Indian village and crafts may be available for purchase locally. Gasoline and fuel oil are available. Travelers are advised to check with village office, (907) 587-5990, before visiting.

The Neets'ik Gwich'in Indians, a once seminomadic people known for trading babiche (sinew lacings) and wolverine skins for seal oil and skins from the Barter Island Eskimos, settled Arctic Village.

Arctic Village, along with the neighboring village of Venetie, elected to retain title to the 1.8-million-acre Venetie Indian Reservation under the Alaska Native Claims Settlement Act. The reserve and Arctic Village are bounded to the north by the Arctic National Wildlife Refuge, with recreational access to the refuge promarily from Kaktovik on Barter Island and most visitors coming from the Lower 48. It is also the migration route of the Porcupine caribou herd, which sometimes winters here.

Employment in Arctic Village is limited to the National Guard armory, post office, clinic, school, village services, trapping, crafts and summer employment on village projects.

There is an Episcopal chapel in the village which replaced the old Mission Church now on the National Register of Historic Places. Under restoration, the old church, built entirely of logs with handcrafted finish and furnishings, reflects the skill of the Native artisans under Albert Tritt, who later became its pastor.

Communications include phones, mail plane, radio and TV. There is a school with grades preschool through 12 with enrollment of 43. Village services include the laundromat and showers, and electric generator. Honey buckets and outhouses are used. Freight delivery is by plane. Government address: Arctic Village Traditional Council, P.O. Box 22050, Arctic Village, AK 99722, phone (907) 587-5328, fax (907) 587-5128, e-mail: Arctic@aitc.org.

Beaver

GPS: N66°21' W147°23'

Located on the north bank of the Yukon River, 60 miles southwest of Fort Yukon, 110 miles northwest of Fairbanks. **Transportation:** Scheduled air service from Fairbanks. **Population:** 110. **Zip code:** 99724. **Emergency Services:** Beaver Health Clinic, phone (907) 628-6228; Volunteer Fire Department. **Elevation:** 365 feet.

Private Aircraft: Airstrip adjacent north; elev. 365 feet; length 3,950 feet; gravel; unattended; recommend visual inspection prior to using.

Visitor Facilities: There are no hotels, restaurants, banks or other services. Lodging may be arranged through the Beaver Tribal Office, Chief Charleen Fisher, Paul Williams Sr.; phone (907) 628-6126. Food, groceries and supplies are available at the Inuit Co-op, (907) 628-6127, or at Henry's, (907) 628-6126. There is a post office, a community laundromat with bathing facilities. Some supplies and fishing/hunting licenses are available in the community. Diesel and gasoline are available.

Beaver is an unincorporated Eskimo and Indian village. The village was founded by Frank Yasuda, whose interest in the location was two-fold. Married to an Eskimo woman, Yasuda saw Beaver as a place to relocate his Eskimo family and friends, who were facing hard times with the decline of whaling in arctic waters. Yasuda was also a partner of J.T. Marsh and Tom Carter, who had prospected for gold throughout the Arctic before settling in the Chandalar region to the north. Yasuda founded Beaver as a river landing for the Chandalar quartz mines started by Marsh and Carter in about 1909. In 1910, the Alaska Road Commission pushed through a trail from the mines south some 100 miles to Beaver, and Marsh and Carter spent the next several years trying to turn a profit from the modest amount of gold in the mines. A stamp mill was shipped in to crush the quartz for gold, although only parts of the 28-ton mill survived the rugged trail to the mines. With the Great Depression and the subsequent withdrawal of financial backing, mining ceased.

Communications include phones, mail plane, radio and TV. The 2 churches in the community are St. Matthew's Episcopal and Assembly of God. The school, with enrollment of 19, has grades preschool through 12 and also houses the health clinic and the generator for the community. Water is available at the laundromat. The sewage system is privies. Freight service is by plane or via barge service 4 times a year. Government address: Beaver Village Council, P.O. Box 24029, Beaver, AK 99724, phone (907) 628-6126, fax (907) 628-6812, e-mail: Beaver@aitc.org. Village corporation: Beaver Kwit'chin, P.O. Box 24090, Beaver, AK 99724, phone (907) 456-4183.

Birch Creek

GPS: N66°15' W145°48'

Located on Lower Birch Creek, 26 miles southwest of Fort Yukon, 152 miles northeast of Fairbanks. **Transportation:** Mail and charter plane. **Population:** 28. **Zip code:** 99790. **Emergency Services:** Birch Creek Clinic; Volunteer Fire Department; police and medical aid available from Fort Yukon or Fairbanks.

Elevation: 450 feet. **Climate:** According to a Birch Creek resident, "summers dry and warm, winters cold and lots of snow."

Private Aircraft: Airstrip 1 mile north; elev. 450 feet; length 4,000 feet; gravel; runway condition not monitored; visual inspection recommended; radio operated landing lights.

NOTE: Birch Creek bans possession of alcoholic beverages.

Visitor Facilities: Plans are under way at this community to establish a store, meal service and other visitor facilities. Currently, accommodations and meals must be arranged for ahead of time by contacting the council office, (907) 221-

9113/2212. Supplies, including fuel, are obtained from Fort Yukon and Fairbanks. Birch Creek has no restaurant, laundromat or banking services.

Birch Creek was an Athabascan Indian village in the 1800s and became a mining community with the discovery of gold. According to a local resident, the community got its start after a break with Fort Yukon. The people here hunt moose and bear, fish northern pike and trap furs for a living.

Communications include phones, radio, TV and a mail plane. There is a 2-classroom school with grades kindergarten through 12. There is an Episcopal church. There is a water plant and a community power system. Sewage disposal system is honey buckets. Freight comes in by cargo plane. Village council: Dendu Gwich'in Tribal Council, P.O. Box KBC, Birch Creek, AK 99701, phone (907) 221-9133, fax (907) 221-2312, e-mail: BirchCreek @aitc.org. Village corporation: Tiheet'Aii Inc., Birch Creek Village, via Fort Yukon, AK 99740, phone (907) 221-2212.

Chalkyitsik

GPS: N66°39' W143°43'

(Chal-KEET-sik) Located 45 miles north of Fort Yukon, 170 miles northeast of Fairbanks, on the Black River. **Transportation:** Boat; charter or scheduled air service from Fort Yukon or Fairbanks. There is a winter trail to Fort Yukon. **Population:** 83. **Zip code:** 99788. **Emergency Services:** Alaska State Troopers in Fairbanks, phone (907) 451-5100; Chalkyitsik Health Clinic, phone (907) 848-8215.

Elevation: 560 feet. **Climate:** Summers are generally hot with some cool and rainy weather; mean temperature in July is 80°F. Winters are cold, with the mean monthly temperature in January -60°F.

Private Aircraft: Airstrip adjacent southwest; elev. 560 feet; length 4,000 feet; gravel. Airport facilities include fuel, navigational aids and lighting.

NOTE: Chalkyitsik prohibits the sale and importation of alcoholic beverages.

Visitor Facilities: Lodging is available at the local school, (907) 848-8113; (907) 662-2515 in summer. Chalkyitsik Native

Corp. Store, (907) 848-8112, carries groceries, film, hardware and sporting goods. Propane and gasoline are available, but there are no other services or facilities.

Originally an Athabascan seasonal fish camp, Chalkyitsik means "fish with a hook at the mouth of the creek." James Nathaniel of the village council says Chalkyitsik is so beautiful and serene in the summer that several visitors said they'd like to move there. "Chalkyitsik is a small town with a lot of nice people. Although employment is limited, there are seasonal jobs. Subsistence plays a major role in the village." The people work for the school, clinic, post office, Native store and village council. There is fishing for jackfish, whitefish and dog salmon; trapping; and hunting for ducks, grouse and ptarmigan.

Communications include phones, mail plane, radio and cable TV. Public buildings in town include the log community hall, the health clinic, the village council office and the Native Corp. store and office. There is a school with grades preschool through 12 with enrollment of 16, and there is an Episcopal church. A community utility service provides power. Water is hauled from the river for the washeteria, and the sewage system is honey buckets. Freight arrives by cargo plane. No moorage facilities. Government address: Chalkyitsik Village Council, P.O. Box 57, Chalkyitsik, AK 99788, phone (907) 848-8117, fax (907) 848-8986, e-mail: Chalkyitsik@aitc.org. Village corporation: Chalkyitsik Native Corp., P.O. Box 53, Chalkyitsik, AK 99788, phone (907) 848-8112, fax (907) 848-8114.

Chicken

GPS: N64°04' W141°57'

Located on the Taylor Highway, 78 miles from Tok, 95 miles from Eagle. **Transportation**: Auto in summer (Taylor Highway closed in winter). **Population**: 37. **Zip code**: 99732. **Emergency Services**: Alaska State Troopers (Tok), phone(907) 883-5111; Tok Community Clinic, phone (907) 883-5855 during business hours; Tok Public Health Clinic, phone (907) 883-4101; Tok Fire

Department, phone (907) 883-2333.

Private Aircraft: Tok airstrip; elev. 1,670 feet; length 2,500 feet; paved; unattended; fuel 80, 100.

Visitor Facilities: Meals, groceries, camping, gas and repairs, souvenirs and gold panning available at 3 local businesses. There is no phone service in Chicken.

A mining camp and post office established in 1903, Chicken probably got its name from the plentiful ptarmigan in the area: in the North "chicken" is a common name for that bird. One story has it that the early-day miners wanted to name their camp "Ptarmigan" but were unable to spell it and settled for Chicken instead. Chicken was the home of the late Ann Purdy, whose autobiographical novel *Tisha* recounted her adventures as a young schoolteacher in the Alaska Bush.

Below the airstrip at Chicken is an access point for the South Fork Fortymile River, a route which avoids the more challenging waters of the North Fork. (See River Running in the Attractions section for more information on floating the Fortymile.)

NOTE: All gold-bearing ground in the Fortymile area is claimed. Do not pan in streams.

For more information about Chicken, see *The MILEPOST®*, a complete guide to communities on Alaska's road and marine highway systems.

Circle

GPS: N65°49' W144°03'

Located on the banks of the Yukon River, at Mile 162 Steese Highway, 125 miles northeast of Fairbanks. **Transportation**: Via the Steese Highway. **Population**: 100. **Zip Code**: 99733. **Emergency services**: Circle Health Clinic; Central Rescue Squad, (907) 520-5451/5228.

Elevation: 700 feet. **Climate**: Mean monthly temperature in July is 61°F; in January, -10°F. Snow from October through April.

Private Aircraft: Airstrip adjacent north, elev. 610 feet; length 3,000 feet; gravel; unattended.

Visitor Facilities: Accommodations and meals are available. Other facilities include a grocery store, gas station, post office, trading post and general store. Hunting/fishing licenses are available. A campground on the banks of the Yukon at the end of the road offers tables, toilets and a grassy parking area.

Before the Klondike gold rush of 1898, Circle was the largest gold mining town on the Yukon River. Today, Circle is a popular put in and takeout spot for Yukon River boaters.

Circle has a school with enrollment of 23. Village corporation: Danzhit Hanlaii Corp., P.O. Box 16, Circle, AK 99733, phone (907) 773-1280. Village council: Circle Village Council, P.O. Box 89, Circle, AK 99733, phone (907) 773-2822, fax (907) 773-2823, e-mail: Circle@aitc.org.

For more information see *The MILEPOST®*, a complete guide to communities on Alaska's road and marine highway systems.

Eagle

GPS: N64°47' W141°12'

Located on the banks of the Yukon River, at mile 161 Taylor Highway, near the Alaska-Yukon Territory border, about 200 miles east of Fairbanks. **Transportation**: Scheduled and charter air service year-round; drive in summer via Taylor Highway (closed in winter); tour boat downriver (100 miles) from Dawson City, YT. **Population**: 129. **Zip code**: 99738. **Emergency Services**: Eagle Village Health Clinic, phone (907) 547-2243; Eagle EMS/Ambulance, phone (907) 547-2256/2355/2211; Village Public Safety Officer, phone (907) 547-2246; Fire Department, phone (907) 547-2282.

Elevation: 820 feet. **Climate**: Mean monthly temperature in July 59.4°F, in January -13.3°F. Record high, 95°F (July 1925), record low -71°F January 1952). Mean precipitation in July, 1.94 inches; in December, 10.1 inches.

Private Aircraft: Airstrip 2 miles east; elev. 880 feet; length 3,600 feet; gravel; no fuel; unattended. Runway condition not monitored; visual inspection recommended prior to landing.

Visitor facilities: Accommodations,

gas, groceries and some hardware items available at Eagle Trading Co., (907) 547-2220, and the Village Store, (907) 547-2270. Meals at Riverside Café, (907) 547-2250. Public and private campgrounds available. There is also an automotive service center. Laundromat, showers, fishing/hunting licenses and gifts available.

Local historian Elva Scott describes Eagle as a "remote rural community on the bank of the Yukon River, surrounded by mountains. Eagle retains an atmosphere of an isolated gold mining town, steeped in history." The Eagle Historical Society conducts daily tours in summer of the community's historic buildings: the Wickersham Courthouse, Customs Building, the historic Episcopal church, and three of the original buildings of Fort Egbert. Eagle began in the early 1880s as a fur-trading post, then boomed with the 1898 gold rush. It became Alaska's first incorporated city in 1901.

Eagle is a popular jumping-off point for Yukon River travelers. Headquarters for Yukon-Charley Rivers National Preserve is located on the bank of the Yukon River at the base of Fort Egbert; phone (907) 547-2233.

The school at Eagle has enrollment of 23. Government address: City of Eagle, P.O. Box 1901, Eagle, AK 99738, phone (907) 547-2282, fax (907) 547-2338, web: http://members.aol.com/akatha/eagle.htm. Village council: Eagle Traditional Council, Box 19, Eagle, AK 99738, phone (907) 574-2271, fax (907) 574-2381.

For more information on Eagle, see *The MILEPOST®*, a complete guide to communities on Alaska's road and marine highway systems.

Fairbanks

GPS: N64°50' W147°43'

Located 246 air miles north of Anchorage and 1,358 air miles north of Seattle. **Transportation**: Several international, interstate and intrastate airlines provide scheduled service; auto and bus access via the Alaska Highway or the George Parks Highway; railroad access via the Alaska Railroad from Anchorage. **Population**: 30,224, borough 82,840. **Zip** code: 99701. **Emergency Services**: Alaska State Troopers, 1979 Peger Road, phone 911 or toll free 1-800-0911, or, for non-emergencies, phone (907) 451-5100; Fairbanks Police, 656 7th Ave., phone 911 or, for nonemergencies, (907) 459-6500; Dept. of Public Safety, phone (907) 459-6500; Fire Department and Ambulance Service (within city limits), phone 911. Hospitals: Fairbanks Memorial, 1650 Cowles St., phone (907) 452-8181; Bassett Army Hospital, Fort Wainwright, phone (907) 353-5281; Eielson Clinic, Eielson AFB, phone (907) 377-2296. Crisis Line, phone (907) 452-4357 or 1-800-SUICIDE; Civil Defense, emergency management, phone (907) 459-1481; Borough

Information, phone (907) 459-1000.

Elevation: 434 feet at Fairbanks International Airport. **Climate**: The weather changes dramatically here. A record high 99°F July 28, 1919; the record low -66°F in January 1934. The average winter high temperature is 6°F, average low -13°F; average summer high 69°F, average low 48°F. On June 21 daylight lasts 21 hours; from June 1 through July daylight lasts more than 20 hours. Annual precipitation is 10.87 inches, with an annual average snowfall of 70.8 inches. Ice fog forms over the city when the temperature is -25°F or lower.

Private Aircraft: Facilities for all types of aircraft. Consult the Alaska Supplement for information on the following airports: Eielson AFB, Fairbanks International, Fairbanks International Seaplane, Chena Marina, Wainwright AAF and Bradley's Sky Ranch, North Pole.

Visitor Facilities: Fairbanks has about 30 major hotels and motels; reservations are a must during the busy summer season. There also are 50 bed-and-breakfast operations and several hostels. The town has more than 100 restaurants with a range of prices. Banks, laundromats and a wide variety of stores are available. All major repair services are available. Many air taxi operators, guides and outfitters are based in Fairbanks. Boats also may be rented. For a free copy of the Fairbanks Visitors' Guide, contact the Fairbanks Convention and Visitors Bureau, 550 1st Ave., Fairbanks, AK 99701, phone (907) 456-5774 or 1-800-327-5774, fax (907) 452-2867. For information on Alaska's recreational lands, contact the Alaska Public Lands Information Center, 250 Cushman St., Suite 1A, phone (907) 456-0527. The center offers free exhibits, films and brochures on forests, parks and refuges in Alaska.

In 1901, Capt. E.T. Barnette set out from St. Michael by steamer up the Yukon River with supplies for a trading post he planned to establish at Tanana Crossing (Tanacross), the halfway point on the Valdez to Eagle trail. But the steamer could not navigate the fast-moving, shallow Tanana River beyond the mouth of the Chena River. The captain of the steamer finally dropped Barnette off at the mouth of the Chena where it enters the Tanana River, a site later known as the settlement of Chena. A year later, Felice Pedrona, an Italian prospector who later changed his sname to Felix Pedro, discovered gold about 15 miles north of Barnette's trading post. A monument to Pedro marks the site of this discovery at Mile 16.5 Steese Highway. The ensuing gold rush in 1903-04 established the new gold mining community, which was named at the suggestion of Barnette's friend, Judge James Wickersham, for Sen. Charles Fairbanks of Indiana, who later became vice president of the United States under Theodore Roosevelt. The town became an administrative center in 1903 when Wickersham moved the headquarters of his Third Judicial District Court from Eagle to Fairbanks.

The city's economy is linked to its role as a service and supply point for interior and arctic industrial activities, with emphasis in recent years on the operation of the trans-Alaska oil pipeline. Active mining is taking place in the Fairbanks Mining District. Fort Knox Gold Mine, near Fairbanks, is the largest gold mine in the western hemisphere, and is expected to produce more than 300,000 ounces of gold a year for 12-20 years.

Tourism also plays an important role in the Fairbanks economy. During the winter, several sled dog races are staged in Fairbanks, including the 3-day Open North American Championship in March, and the Yukon Quest International Sled Dog Race, an annual February event which starts from Fairbanks in even-numbered years. The week-long Winter Carnival takes place in early March. The Festival of Native Arts takes place on the University of Alaska campus at the end of February. During the summer, Fairbanks hosts a number of events, including the largest summertime event in Alaska, Golden Days held in July to commemorate the discovery of gold near Fairbanks in 1902. The World Eskimo-Indian Olympics attracts international attention and is held in July. Each August, Fairbanks hosts the Tanana Valley Fair and the Fairbanks Summer Arts Festival.

Creamer's Field Migratory Waterfowl Refuge, accessed from College Road between Johansen Expressway and Aurora Drive, provides opportunities for bird banding, viewing, photography and study of plants, wildlife and geological features. The refuge is best known for its spring and fall concentrations of ducks, geese and cranes that stop over on the refuge fields during migration. Visitors may also enjoy some 3 miles of self-guided nature paths, with 2 platforms along the trails to provide views of fields, forests and wildlife. The paths pass through a variety of habitats common to the Interior.

Wilderness exploration is easy from Fairbanks, either on your own or with one of the many tour operators. Mount McKinley (Denali) in the Alaska Range, the Gates of the Arctic National Park and the mighty Brooks Range are accessible from Fairbanks. Flightseeing over the forests and mountains, rafting, camping in remote areas, sportfishing, and photographic safaris are all available.

Fairbanks has all the amenities of a large city, including 12 radio stations, 6 TV channels (plus cable) and a newspaper, the *Fairbanks Daily News-Miner*. City government address: City of Fairbanks, 800 Cushman St., Fairbanks, AK 99701, phone (907) 459-6715, fax (907) 459-6710, e-mail: fbxmayor@polarnet.com, web: http://touralaska.org/fairbanks/. Borough government: Fairbanks North Star Borough, Box 71267, Fairbanks, AK 99707, phone (907) 459-1000, fax (907) 459-1102, e-mail: fnsbis@co.fairbanks.ak.us, web: http://www.co.fairbanks.ak.us.

For more information, see *The MILE-POST®*, a complete guide to communities on Alaska's road and marine highway systems.

Flat

GPS: N62°27' W157°59'

Located on Otter Creek, 8 miles southeast of Iditarod, 59 miles northeast of Holy Cross, 85 miles southwest of McGrath, 375 miles west of Anchorage. **Transportation:** Charter plane from Anchorage or Fairbanks. **Population:** 5 in winter, 30 in summer. **Zip code**: 99584. **Emergency Services**: Alaska State Troopers, Aniak; McGrath Health Center. **Elevation**: 309 feet. **Climate**: According to residents, Flat is dry during June and July. August and September are wet. Winter is cold and windy and the temperature can drop to -50°F.

Private Aircraft: Airstrip adjacent east; elev. 309 feet; length 4,045 feet; turf and gravel; state-maintained; no fuel; unattended. Runway condition not monitored; visual inspection recommended prior to using. Runway slick when wet. Both sides of runway used as road. Trees and tailings along runway edge.

Visitor Facilities: None.

This gold-mining town was reported in 1910 by A.G. Maddren of the U.S. Geological Survey. At that time, Flat was the leading settlement on Otter Creek with a population of about 400. Its population was 158 in 1920 and 124 in 1930. Flat is unincorporated.

The area around Flat is mostly private mining claims and owners carefully watch for trespassers, according to one resident.

Some of the buildings in Flat were moved from the ghost town of Iditarod. A padlocked store and bank gather dust. A tramway once connected the 2 communities; a gravel trail now parallels the old tramway route.

Today only 1 family lives in Flat year-round. Mark Kepler, a pilot and a wizard at making things run, is the postmaster, complete with zip code and flag: "I fly the flag by the rules," he told a reporter for the Associated Press in 1989. "I raise it at dawn, which here in Alaska happens in April, and I take it down at sunset, in September." Mark's wife Sherri home-schools their children by correspondence, consulting a teacher weekly by radio.

The summer population swells when miners, who scatter to warm climates in winter, return to work their claims. The sluice boxes still show color, and if nobody is getting rich, Flat's isolation and simple lifestyle still prove a draw.

Flat has no phones ("Alascom hasn't found us yet," explains Mayor Zeke Grundoon). There is no community elec-tricity system. Most homes have indoor running water and sewer systems. Supplies are obtained by plane from McGrath or Anchorage.

Fort Yukon

GPS: N66°34' W145°16'

Located at the confluence of the Porcupine and Yukon rivers, 140 miles northeast of Fairbanks and about 8 miles north of the Arctic Circle. **Transportation**: Scheduled air service from Fairbanks; charter air service available; accessible by boat. **Population**: 595. **Zip code**: 99740. **Emergency Services**: Police, phone (907) 662-2311; Alaska State Troopers, phone (907) 662-2509; Yukon Flats Health Center, phone (907) 662-2460; Volunteer Fire Department, phone (907) 662-2311.

Elevation: 420 feet. **Climate**: Dry and warm in summer, with a mean temperature of 61°F and mean precipitation of 0.94 inch in July. Winters are very dry and cold, with a mean temperature of -20°F and mean precipitation of 0.41 inch in January.

Private Aircraft: Airstrip 0.3 mile north of town; elev. 433 feet; length 5,810 feet; gravel; fuel 80, 100, Al+. Transportation to town via municipal transit, phone (907) 662-2379/2479 or by taxi.

Visitor Facilities: Accommodations available at GZ Lodge, (907) 662-3433; and Betty's bed and breakfast, (907) 662-2558. There is no bank, but there is a laundromat. Supplies are available in the community. Groceries and supplies are available at Alaska Commercial Co., (907) 662-2330; and ANICA, (907) 662-2582. Beaded moose skin accessories and clothing, furs and carved ivory jewelry are available for purchase in local trading posts. Fishing/hunting licenses are available and local fishing trips may be arranged. Major marine engine, boat and auto repair is available. Charter aircraft and boats may be rented. Fuel is available. Boat moorage on riverbank.

In 1847, Alexander Hunter Murray founded a Hudson's Bay Co. trading post near the present site of Fort Yukon. After the purchase of Alaska in 1867, it was determined that Fort Yukon was within

U.S. territory. By 1873, the Alaska Commercial Co. was operating a steamer on the Yukon and had established a post here run by trader Moses Mercier. The gold rush of 1897 dramatically increased both river traffic and the white population of Fort Yukon, while disease reduced the population of Kutchin Athabascans. Fort Yukon remained the largest settlement on the Yukon below Dawson for many years, and was headquarters for a hospital and for pioneer Episcopal missionary Hudson Stuck, who is buried here. Fort Yukon was incorporated as a second-class city in 1959.

Hub of the Yukon Flats area, Fort Yukon employment in sales and service, local, state and federal government, and also the traditional subsistence fishing (salmon, pike, etc.), hunting (moose, bear, small game) and trapping (lynx, beaver, fox). Recreation includes boating and canoeing the Yukon River, camping, softball, swimming and driving 3-wheelers in summer; cross-country skiing, dog mushing, snow machining, ice skating, ice fishing and bingo in winter. Subsistence fish wheels, traps and garden plots exist alongside utility poles and cable TV. The Old Mission House (Episcopal) is on the National Register of Historic Places.

Communications include phones, mail plane, radio and TV. The community is served by Assembly of God, Baptist and Episcopal churches. The school has grades preschool through 12 with enrollment of 123. The city has public water, power and sewage systems. Freight is delivered by cargo plane and barge. Government address: Fort Yukon, P.O. Box 269, Fort Yukon, AK 99740, phone (907) 662-2479, fax (907) 662-2717. Village corporation: Gwitchyaa Zhee Corp., P.O. Box 329, Fort Yukon, AK 9974, phone (907) 662-3056, fax (907) 662-2646.

Galena

GPS: N64°44' W156°56'

Located on the north bank of the Yukon River, 270 miles west of Fairbanks, 350 miles northwest of Anchorage. **Transportation**: Scheduled air service from Fairbanks and Anchorage; accessible by boat or barge service from Nenana, and over marked snow machine trails. **Population**: 675. **Zip code**: 99741. **Emergency Services**: Police, phone (907) 656-2177; Alaska State Troopers, phone (907) 656-1233; Galena Health Center, phone (907) 656-1266/1366; City Volunteer Fire & EMS, phone 911.

Elevation: 120 feet. **Climate**: Mean monthly temperature in January is -12°F. Warm and sunny in summer with a mean monthly temperature in July of 60°F. August is the wettest month with 2.31 inches mean precipitation. Mean snow and sleet in January is 7.2 inches.

Private Aircraft: Galena airport adjacent northwest; elev. 152 feet; length 7,254 feet; asphalt/concrete. Galena airport is the commercial air center for 6 surrounding villages and is also the forward U.S. Air Force base for F-15 jet fighters, which is now in "reduced status," with no personnel stationed here but used by the USAF on an as-needed basis, chiefly for training flights. An FAA station is located here. Fuel 100LL, Jet A. All facilities, including passenger terminal. Taxi service available.

Visitor Facilities: For accommodations through the village corporation, Gana-A'Yoo, Ltd., contact Khotol Services Inc. P.O. Box 38, Galena, AK 99741, phone (907) 656-1606, fax (907) 656-1609. Khotol also provides the only licensed and insured vehicle rentals in Galena and they take VISA and Mastercard. No banking services. Public laundromat and showers are available. Groceries and supplies are available at Interior Trading, Galena Liquor Store and Huhndorf's Inc. Local arts and crafts available for purchase include Indian headwork, birch-bark baskets, skin moccasins, fur hats and ivory work. Fishing/hunting licenses available from the local Alaska Dept. of Fish and Game officer and guide service. U.S. Fish & Wildlife Service maintains its Koyukuk, Nowitna and North Innoko Wilderness Refuge office in Galena, phone (907) 656-1231. All types of fuel and repair service are available. Autos and boats may be rented in Galena. Moorage facilities are also available.

Galena was founded as a supply point

for nearby galena (lead ore) prospects in 1919. The airstrip was built in 1940 by the U.S. Army. Galena was incorporated in 1971. Koyukon Athabascans comprise most of the town's population. The population increases in summer with firefighters. There is some construction and commercial fishing in summer, and year-round employment in government jobs, but traditional subsistence hunting and fishing support many residents. There is sportfishing for salmon, grayling, whitefish, sheefish, burbot and pike in nearby clear-water lakes and streams. Koyukuk National Wildlife Refuge lies to the north of Galena, and the northern portion of the Innoko refuge lies across the Yukon River to the south.

As transportation hub for several outlying villages, Galena sees many visitors in summer. In winter, when the Yukon is frozen solid, neighbors come in by dogsled or snow machine. The Iditarod Trail Sled Dog Race has a check-in point in Galena every even year, and the Iron Dog race stops there every year. Galena is the turnaround point for the Yukon 800 boat race from Fairbanks, held in June. The town has its own Fourth of July softball tournament, a Native arts and crafts bazaar on Thanksgiving weekend, and a Winter Carnival the last weekend in March. Communications include phone, mail plane, radio and TV. There are 2 churches: St. John Berchman Roman Catholic Church and the Galena Bible Church. The community is proud of its city schools, which include an elementary and a high school with enrollment of 190. Project Education Residential School (PERS), a vocationally based, boarding home program for grades 9-14, began serving students in 1997 with an enrollment of 80. The school district also offers the Interior Distance Education Program (IDEA), a distance-delivery based, homeschool support program serving 3,400 students throughout the state. This school provides choices in educational programs to meet individual needs. Galena is also a branch campus of the University of Alaska. There are community electric, water and a core-sewer line system. Freight arrives by air cargo plane,

Inland Barge Service and Yutana Barge Lines. Government address: City of Galena, P.O. Box 149, Galena, AK 99741, phone (907) 656-1301, fax (907) 656-1769, e-mail: MarvinY@arctic.net. Village corporation: Gana-A'Yoo, Ltd., P.O. Box 38, Galena, AK 99741, phone (907) 656-1606, fax (907) 656-1609, e-mail: ganaayoo@arctic.net. Village council: Louden Village Council, Box 244, Galena, AK 99741, phone (907 656-1711, fax (907) 656-1716, e-mail: louden@arctic.net.

Grayling
GPS: N62°57' W160°03'

Located on the west bank of the Yukon River east of the Nulato Hills, 21 miles north of Anvik, 350 miles westnorthwest of Anchorage. **Transportation:** Scheduled and charter air service from McGrath or Aniak. **Population:** 211. **Zip code:** 99590. **Emergency Services:** Alaska State Troopers, Aniak, phone (907) 675-4398; Grayling Health Clinic; Volunteer Fire Department.

Elevation: 90 feet. **Climate:** Continental; mean annual precipitation 21 inches; mean annual snowfall 110 inches.

Private Aircraft: Airstrip 1 mile south; elev. 99 feet; length 2,315 feet; gravel; unattended. Runway condition not monitored; visual inspection recommended prior to using. North end of runway and taxiway floods in spring.

NOTE: Grayling limits the sale and importation of alcoholic beverages.

Visitor Facilities: Lodging is available through Yukon Enterprises, (907) 453-5145, or arrange for rooms with the City of Grayling, (907) 453-5148. There are no restaurants. Groceries and supplies from Grayling Native Store, (907) 453-5153, Ten Little Indians Store, (907) 453-5118) and Walker's Store, (907) 453-5170. No banking services. Arts and crafts available for purchase include birch-bark baskets, grass baskets, skin boots, fur hats and headwork. Fishing/hunting licenses available. No guide service. Fuel: diesel, propane and regular gasoline available from HYL Fuel, (907) 453-5124/5133. Moorage facilities available.

When the U.S. Revenue Service steamer *Nunivak* stopped here in 1900, Lt. J.C. Cantwell reported an Indian village of approximately 75 residents. They had a large stockpile of wood to supply fuel for steamers. When gold mining in the area diminished, the village was abandoned until 1962, when residents of Holikachuk on the Innoko River moved to the site. Grayling today is a second-class city, incorporated in 1948 under the name of Holikachuk, Territory of Alaska. The name was changed to Grayling in 1964.

Grayling's economy depends on subsistence, and employment is primarily seasonal summer work in construction, road work and commercial fishing. Most families fish for salmon, whitefish, sheefish, pike and eels, and hunt for moose, black bear, small game and waterfowl. Residents also trap marten, mink, otter, beaver, wolf, lynx and wolverine, and sell the pelts.

Grayling is located across the Yukon River from Innoko National Wildlife Refuge. Every other year Grayling is a checkpoint on the 1,049-mile Iditarod Trail Sled Dog Race.

Communications in Grayling include phones, mail plane, radio and TV. The community is served by St. Paul's Episcopal Church and the Arctic Mission, as well as a school with grades kindergarten through 12 with enrollment of 58. There are community electric, water and sewer systems. Freight arrives by barge or mail plane. Government address: City of Grayling, P.O. Box 89, Grayling, AK 99590, phone or fax (907) 453-5148, e-mail: mdeacon@kgx.iasd.gcisa.net. Village corporation: Hee-Yea-Lingde Corp., Box 9, Grayling, AK 99590, phone (907) 453-5133, fax (907) 453-5151. Village council: Grayling IRA Council, Box 49, Grayling, AK 99590, phone (907) 453-5116, fax (907) 453-5146, e-mail: Grayling@aitc.org.

Holy Cross

GPS: N62°12' W159°46'

Located on the west bank of Ghost Creek Slough (on Walker Slough), off the Yukon River, 34 miles southeast of Anvik and 420 miles southwest of Fairbanks. **Population:** 227. **Zip code:** 99602.

Emergency Services: VPSO, phone (907) 476-7180; Holy Cross Health Clinic, phone (907) 476-7174; Volunteer Fire Department.

Elevation: 150 feet. **Climate:** Summer temperatures average 7°'F to 8°'F; winter temperatures -50°'F to 50°F. Annual precipitation averages 18.97 inches, with snowfall averaging 79.4 inches a year.

Private Aircraft: Runway 1 mile south; elev. 61 feet; length 4,000 feet; gravel; fuel 80, 100; unattended. Runway condition not monitored; visual inspection recommended prior to use.

NOTE: Holy Cross prohibits the sale and importation of alcoholic beverages.

Visitor Facilities: Accommodation and meals available at Holy Cross Lodge. Food, groceries and supplies available at Holy Cross Mercantile and Holy Cross Stop & Shop. Arts and crafts include beaded jewelry and skin-sewn items such as mukluks, mittens and hats. Fishing/hunting licenses available. No guide service, banking services, moorage facilities or rental transportation. Fuel available is propane and regular gasoline.

Holy Cross first had contact with Europeans in the early 1840s when Russian explorer Lt. L.A. Zagoskin sighted the village which was called Anilukhtakpak. Population increased with establishment of a Jesuit mission and school in 1886. The founder of the mission was Father Aloysius Robaut who came to Alaska across the Chilkoot Trail.

The village was incorporated in 1968 as a second-class city. The economy is seasonal with its peak in the summer fishing season. Community and construction employment is supplemented by subsistence hunting, fishing and gardening.

Communications include phones, mail plane and TV. The community has a Roman Catholic church and a school with grades kindergarten through 12 with enrollment of 60. Public electric, water and sewage systems. Most residents have flush toilets; some use honey buckets. Freight arrives by air transport and barge. Government address: City of Holy Cross, P.O. Box 203, Holy Cross, AK 99602, phone (907) 476-7139, fax 476-7141.

Village corporation: Deloycheet Inc., P.O. Box 53, Holy Cross, AK 99602, phone (907) 476-7177, fax (907) 476-7176. Village council: Holy Cross Tribal Council, Box 89, Holy Cross, AK 99602, phone (907) 476-7124, fax (907) 476-7132, e-mail: HolyCross@aitc.org.

Hughes

GPS: N66°03' W154°15'

Located on the Koyukuk River, 120 miles northeast of Galena, 215 miles northwest of Fairbanks. **Transportation:** Scheduled air service from Galena; accessible by boat; trails to Allakaket, Alatna, Huslia and Indian Mountain. **Population:** 78. **Zip code:** 99745. **Emergency Services:** Alaska State Troopers in Galena, phone (907) 656-1233; Hughes Health Clinic, phone (907) 889-2206; Volunteer Fire Department.

Elevation: 550 feet. **Climate:** Fair weather in the summer, with both hot, sunny days and cool, rainy days. It can get windy here since the community is in a valley surrounded by rolling hills and mountains. Mean temperature in July is 60°F; in January -10°F. August is the wettest month with 2.48 inches of precipitation. Mean snow and sleet in January is 6.6 inches.

Private Aircraft: Airstrip 0.9 mile southwest; elev. 289 feet; length 3,400 feet; gravel; runway condition not monitored.

Visitor Facilities: Lodging at the school ($20 per night) or visitors may arrange with local residents to stay in private homes for a fee. Meals, laundry and banking services are not available. Supplies may be purchased in the community. Native beadwork and sometimes snowshoes, baskets and baby sleds may be available for purchase. If you can catch Alfred S. Attla Sr., in town, you can purchase a fishing/hunting license from him; if he's not around, the nearest outlet is the Alaska Dept. of Fish and Game office in Galena. No major repair services are available, but visitors can rent the town pickup or local 3-wheelers, autos or boats. Regular gasoline, diesel and propane are available. Public moorage on the riverbank.

Some of the older citizens here remember when Hughes was a riverboat landing and supply point for gold mining camps in the nearby mountains about 1910. It was named for Charles Evans Hughes (1862-1948), then governor of New York. The store remained here and Hughes became a Koyukon Indian village. The post office was reestablished in 1942 and the city was incorporated in 1973. There are about 27 military personnel stationed at Indian Mountain Air Force Station, 15 miles east of Hughes. Employment in Hughes is in local services with seasonal firefighting and trapping. There is fishing for grayling, chum, sheefish and salmon.

Communications include phones, mail plane, radio and TV. An Episcopal church is here and a school with grades kindergarten through 8 with enrollment of 11. There are municipal water and electric services; sewage is individual septic tanks or honey buckets. Freight arrives by cargo plane or barge. Government address: City of Hughes, P.O. Box 45010, Hughes, AK 99745, phone (907) 889-2206, fax (907) 889-2252. Village corporation: K'oyitl'ots'ina Ltd., 1603 College Rd., Fairbanks, AK 99709, phone (907) 452-8119, fax (907) 452-8148. Village council: Hughes Village Council, P.O. Box 45029, Hughes, AK 99745, phone (907) 889-2239, fax (907) 889-2252, e-mail: Hughes@aitc.org.

Huslia

GPS: N65°41' W156°24'

(HOOS-lee-a) Located on the Koyukuk River, 70 miles north of Galena, 250 miles northwest of Fairbanks. **Transportation:** Scheduled air service from Galena; accessible by boat. **Population:** 293. **Zip code:** 99746. **Emergency Services:** Alaska State Troopers, phone (907) 656-1233; Huslia Health Clinic, phone (907) 829-2204; Volunteer Fire Department.

Elevation: 180 feet. **Climate:** Conditions at Huslia are similar to those of Galena with cold winters, hot summers and generally low precipitation. In June and July, the average maximum temperature is in the lower 70s. During the winter months below zero temperatures are common. Local residents report a record low of -65°F and a record high of above 90°F. Most precipitation occurs between July and September with a total annual precipitation of only 13 inches. Annual snowfall is about 70 inches and generally persists from October through April.

Private Aircraft: Airstrip 1 mile northeast; elev. 180 feet; length 3,000 feet; gravel. Runway condition not monitored; no facilities.

NOTE: Huslia prohibits the sale of alcoholic beverages.

Visitor Facilities: No accommodations or meals, though arrangements can be made to stay in private homes or in the school or clinic. Most supplies available in the community at R&M Mercantile, (907) 829-2209, and other local stores. There is a laundromat but no bank. Beadwork, knitted gloves and other arts and crafts may be purchased. No local guides; fishing/hunting licenses available. There is no major repair service. Rental transportation is available. Diesel, propane and regular gasoline are available.

Huslia was originally settled in the late 1940s by Koyukon Indians from Cutoff trading post. The community takes its name from a nearby stream. Huslia was incorporated in 1969. Employment here includes seasonal firefighting, construction and trapping, along with positions at the school, church and in local government. Many local residents spend the summer at fish camps. Other summer activities include softball, berry picking, camping and gardening.

Communications include phones, mail plane, air service from Fairbanks and Galena, and TV. There are Episcopal and Roman Catholic churches and a school with grades kindergarten through 12 with enrollment of 68. The community has electric, water and sewage systems as well as privies. Freight arrives by barge and cargo plane. Government address: City of Huslia, P.O. Box 10, Huslia, AK 99746, phone (907) 829-2266, fax 829-2224. Village council: Huslia Village Council, Box 70, Huslia, AK 99746, phone (907) 829-2294, fax (907) 829-2214, e-mail: Huslia@aitc.org.

Kaltag

GPS: N64°20' W158°43'

Located on the Yukon River, 90 miles southwest of Galena, 330 miles west of Fairbanks. **Transportation**: Scheduled air service from Galena; traits to Nulato and Galena; accessible by boat. **Population**: 230. **Zip code**: 99748. **Emergency Services**: Alaska State Troopers in Galena, phone (907) 656-1233; Village Public Safety Officer; Kaltag Health Clinic, phone (907) 534-2209; Kaltag Rescue, phone (907) 534-2224; Volunteer Fire Department, phone 534-9221.

Elevation: 200 feet. **Climate**: Warm summers with high temperatures in the 70s. Rainiest months are August and September. Winters are cold with average temperatures of -20°F and lows of -60°F. A resident reports up to 6 feet of snow accumulates in winter.

Private Aircraft: Airstrip 0.25 mile from village; elev. 200 feet; length 5,000 feet; gravel; unattended. Runway condition not monitored; recommend visual inspection prior to use.

Visitor Facilities: No formal accommodations or restaurants. However, the local fire hall offers beds (b.y.o. sleeping bag), and kitchen and bathroom facilities. Some supplies are available at Victor's Store, (907) 534-2231, and Kaltag Co-op, (907) 534-2235. Marine gas, diesel, propane, kerosene and regular gasoline are available. No other services available.

This is an Indian village called Kaltag by the Russians. An 1880 census listed a Lower Kaltag and Upper Kaltag here. The present village is believed to be the former Upper Kaltag, while Lower Kaltag is now referred to as the Old Kaltag site. Kaltag was incorporated in 1969. Marion Nickoli says, "Folks are always welcome, and friendliness awaits all."

One resident describes Kaltag's way of life like this: "The people still rely on subsistence for their living. They fish during the summer (for salmon and grayling) and stay out at fish camps; they sell the fish or put some away for the winter; they also go hunting for moose, bear and other animals for food. They set traps in the winter for animals such as marten, rabbits or beaver. They sell the fur or make clothing out of it for themselves. The people mostly make a living for themselves and raise their families."

There is a Roman Catholic church and a school with grades kindergarten through 12 with enrollment of 58. There is also a community water and sewer system, although some homes still haul water and have privies. A generator provides the community's power. Freight is shipped in by plane or barge. Government address: City of Kaltag, P.O. Box 9, Kaltag, AK 99748, phone (907) 534-2301, fax 534-2236, e-mail: Jackie@ptialasja,net. Village council: Village of Kaltag, Box 9, Kaltag, AK 99748, phone (907) 534-2230, e-mail: Kaltag@aitc.org.

Koyukuk

GPS: N64°53′ W157°42′

(KOY-a-kuk) Located at the confluence of the Koyukuk and Yukon rivers, 30 miles northwest of Galena, 300 miles west of Fairbanks. **Transportation**: Scheduled air service from Galena; accessible by boat. **Population**: 101. **Zip code**: 99754. **Emergency Services**: Public Safety Officer, phone (907) 927-2214; State Troopers in Galena; Koyukuk Health Clinic; Volunteer Fire Department.

Elevation: 115 feet. **Climate**: Described as typical of interior Alaska, with warm summers, and cold, dry winters, with a temperature range of -60°F to 90°F.

Private Aircraft: Airstrip adjacent west of village; elev. 115 feet; length 3,000 feet; gravel; unattended; no facilities.

Visitor Facilities: No formal accommodations or restaurants. Visitors may arrange to stay in private homes or at the school, phone (907) 656-1201. There are showers and a laundromat at the community watering facility. Some supplies available in the community. Arts and crafts include beadwork, marten hats, moose skin gloves and sleds. Fishing/hunting licenses may be purchased in the village. Propane and gasoline are available.

Originally a Koyukukhotana Indian village, a trading post was established here in the late 1800s. The village served the growing number of miners in the area and the increasing river traffic. Today, people here make their living as trappers and fishermen; in seasonal construction or in local clerical and maintenance jobs; or they commute to larger communities for work. Fishing for salmon in the Yukon and Koyukuk rivers is done both commercially and for subsistence purposes, and local summer fish camps are active. Local people do occasional guiding, but visitors should be well prepared with equipment and supplies since none are available locally. Moose hunting is good in the fall and black bear are prevalent.

Communications include mail plane, phones, radio and TV. Freight arrives by plane or by barge. Koyukuk has a school (grades kindergarten through 10 with enrollment of 17), a public library, recreation center, a community generator and a safe-water plant. Sewage system is private privies. Government address: City of Koyukuk, Box 49, Koyukuk, AK 99754, phone and fax (907) 927-2215. Village council: Koyukuk Tribal Council, Box 109, Koyukuk, AK 99754, phone (907) 927-2253, fax (907) 927-2220, e-mail: Koyukuk@aitc.org.

Lake Minchumina

GPS: N63°53′ W152°19′

(Min-CHEW-min-a) Located on the northwest shore of Lake Minchumina, 205 miles northwest of Anchorage, 150 miles southwest of Fairbanks. **Transportation**: Scheduled air service from Fairbanks. **Population**: 32. **Zip code**: 99757. **Emergency Services**: Alaska State Troopers in Fairbanks; Lake Minchumina Rescue Squad, phone (907) 674-3215.

Elevation: 640 feet. **Climate**: Summers are cool and wet with a monthly mean temperature in July of 59°F. June is the driest summer month with 1.7 inches of precipitation. Winters are cold with moderate snowfall; monthly mean temperature in January is -6°F, mean snow/sleet for January is 9.5 inches.

Private Aircraft: Airstrip adjacent southeast; elev. 684 feet; length 4,200 feet; gravel; unattended; no facilities.

Visitor Facilities: Accommodations at

Denali West Lodge, (907) 733-2630. Groceries and supplies available from Minchumina Mercantile that opens 1 day a week and upon request. Originally a Tanana Indian village until a flu epidemic wiped it out early 1900s, Lake Minchumina saw further settlement with construction of the airstrip in 1941. The lake yields some pike. There is no central utility or sewage system here. Water is hauled from the lake or obtained from wells. Communication is through a radio-phone at the lodge and a single public phone booth near the runway , (907) 939-4000, which has an answering machine. Freight is delivered by small plane.

Government address: Lake Minchumina Traditional Council, General Delivery, Lake Minchumina, AK 99623.

Manley Hot Springs

GPS: N65°00' W150°38'

Located at Mile 152 Elliott Highway, 90 miles west of Fairbanks. **Transportation**: Scheduled and charter air service from Fairbanks; road via the Elliott flighway. **Population**: 72. **Zip Code**: 99756.

Elevation: 330 feet. **Climate**: Mean monthly temperature in July is 59°F; in January, -10°F. Snow from October through April, with traces in September and May. Emergency services: Manley Hot Springs Health Clinic.

Private Aircraft: Airstrip adjacent southwest; elev. 270 feet; length 2,875 feet; gravel; fuel 80, 100; unattended. Runway condition not monitored; visual inspection recommended prior to using.

Visitor facilities: Meals and accommodations are available at the Manley Roadhouse, (907) 672-3161. Groceries, gas, gifts, liquor and post office at Manley Trading Post, (907) 672-3221. There is a public campground; fee is $5 per night. The hot springs are a short walk from the campground. Manley Hot Springs Slough offers good pike fishing, May through September.

Once a busy trading center for nearby Eureka and Tofty mining districts, today Manley Hot Springs is a quiet settlement. The school has enrollment of 15.

For more information see *The MILE-POST®*, a complete guide to communities on Alaska's road and marine highway systems.

McGrath

GPS: N62°57' W155°35'

Located on the Upper Kuskokwim River opposite the junction with the Takotna River, 220 miles northwest of Anchorage, 250 miles northeast of Bethel, and 280 miles southwest of Fairbanks. **Transportation**: Scheduled air service from Anchorage and Yukon River communities; river travel May to October; 21.8 miles of local roads. **Population**: 401. **Zip code**: 99627. **Emergency Services**: Village Public Safety Officer, phone (907) 524-3075; Alaska State Trooper/Fish and Wildlife Protection, phone (907) 524-3222; McGrath Health Center, phone (907) 524-3299; Kuskokwim Valley Rescue Squad, (907) 524-3299/9111; Emergency Fire and

Medical, phone 911.

Elevation: 337 feet. **Climate:** Average daily maximum temperatures in summer in the upper 60s, with highs in the 80s; minimum winter temperatures below zero, with lows to -60°F. More than 40 percent of the normal annual precipitation occurs between July and September. Comparatively low precipitation in winter, with accumulated snowfall averaging 86 inches.

Private Aircraft: Airport adjacent west; elev. 337 feet; length 5,435 feet; asphalt; fuel 80, 100, Al+. All facilities including flight service station and passenger and freight terminals. McGrath seaplane base on the Kuskokwim River east of east/west taxiway; fuel 80, 100.

Visitor Facilities: Accommodations and meals are available at BJ's Café & Bunkhouse, (907) 524-3445; Takusko House, (907) 524-3198; Caroline's Kitchen and Rooms, (907) 524-3466; and Hotel McGrath B&B, (907) 524-3951. Food available at hotel with reservations. Groceries, supplies and ATM available at Alaska Commercial Co., (907) 524-3588; The Shoppe (video and variety); and General Service hardware and sporting goods, (907) 524-3485. Limited arts and crafts available for purchase include birch-bark baskets, carvings and fur items. The laundromat has shower facilities. Fishing/hunting licenses are available, as well as local guides/outfitters. All types of fuel (marine, aircraft, diesel, propane, etc.) and major repair of vehicles, heavy equipment and aircraft available. Charter aircraft flights are available. Boats and off-road vehicles may be rented from private individuals.

Prospecting in the upper Kuskokwim and Innoko River valleys in the late 1800s brought increasing numbers of non-Native people into the area. In the spring of 1907, Peter McGrath, U.S. Commissioner sent from Nome, established a trading post and recording office at Old McGrath (across the Kuskokwim River from current site). Strikes on Ganes Creek and other Innoko Valley streams in 1906, and on Otter Creek and adjacent streams in 1908, made McGrath's location strategic as a supply point. Today it continues

to serve as a supply point for a number of active gold mines in the area. The town relocated to its current location on the left bank of the Kuskokwim River in 1938. In February 1924, McGrath became the first Alaska town to receive mail by air, delivered by pioneer aviator Carl Ben Eielson. An Air Force base was located in McGrath in 1942-1943, and the new runway was an alternate stop for fueling lend-lease aircraft during WWII. Since early days, McGrath has been a transportation and supply center for the region. It was incorporated as a second-class city in 1975. The majority of employment is in government jobs, the school district and local services. Many residents also rely on subsistence activities, including fishing, hunting, vegetable gardening, and harvesting berries and timber for food and fuel.

McGrath is a 1-hour jet ride from Anchorage, but as one resident has said, "It has the attitude of the bush community. The people are independent and self-reliant, yet come together in times of celebration or crisis."

The oldest celebration in McGrath is held on the Fourth of July with floats, a parade, a huge potluck picnic and games for all ages. The McGrath State Fair is in late August. The Iditarod Trail Sled Dog Race takes mushers through McGrath each year, and dog mushing is a popular winter activity in the area.

Communications include phone, daily mail, public radio station and cable TV. Internet provider: McGrathAlaska.net (subsidiary of McGrath Light & Power). Public services and organizations include the McGrath Community Library, U.S. Fish & Wildlife Service, Alaska Dept. of Fish and Game, Dept. of Natural Resources, 4 Rivers Counseling Service, the Upper Kuskokwim Mushers Assoc., McGrath Native Village Council, Tanana Chiefs Conference subregional office, University of Alaska Cooperative Extension Service and the Kuskokwim Valley Rescue Squad, VFW, Civil Air Patrol and Girl Scouts. There are 4 churches: McGrath Christian Fellowship, St. Michael's Roman Catholic Church, McGrath Community Church and

Spiritual Assembly of Baha'is. School includes grades preschool through 12 with enrollment of 103, and postsecondary classes are available through the University of Alaska Rural Education Center. Homes are heated with wood or oil stoves. Most homes have individual cesspools, and a city-owned/maintained piped water system is utilized by most homes. Electrical power is generated by McGrath Light and Power. Barge service from Bethel delivers fuel products, heavy equipment and building materials. Other freight arrives by air. Government address: City of McGrath, P.O. Box 30, McGrath, AK 99627, phone (907) 524-3825, fax (907) 524-3536, e-mail: ksnow@mcgrathalaska.com. Village council: McGrath Native Village Council, P.O. Box 134, McGrath, AK 99627, phone (907) 524-3024, fax (907) 524-3899, e-mail: McGrath@aitc.org.

Medfra

GPS: N63°06' W154°43'

Located on the Kuskokwim River 30 miles east northeast of McGrath, 210 miles northwest of Anchorage. **Transportation**: Charter air service only. **Population**: I year-round resident. Population doubles in summer. **Zip code**: 99627. Emergency services: None..

Elevation: 435 feet. **Climate**: Weather conditions are similar to those found in McGrath with warm summers and cold winters with relatively low precipitation.

Private Aircraft: Airstrip adjacent west; elev. 435 feet; length 2,000 feet; turf; unattended. No winter maintenance or snow removal. Runway is soft during spring thaw and the north end is potholed.

Visitor Facilities: None.

Perhaps a native campsite originally, modern-day Medfra began when F.C.H. Spencer operated a trading post here in the early 1900s. Travelers to the 1917 gold strike on Nixon Fork of the Takotna River found that the easier route was along the Kuskokwim River to a landing near the site of Medfra, then traveled overland to the gold fields.

Arthur Berry bought out Spencer and for a time the site was known as Berrys Landing. By 1920 Berrys Landing had become an important transfer point for upper Kuskokwim area gold fields. In 1922 a post office was established and the settlement renamed, perhaps after an early settler to the area. Arthur Berry operated a fur farm in the area and ran the store until 1937 when he sold it to Clint W. Winans, who kept the store going until he died in 1958. Winans' widow, Bertha, operated the store until 1963 when she turned it over to Jack Smith, who continued operations until sometime in the late 1970s or early 1980s when a store opened in Nikolai.

Minto

GPS: N 64°53' W149°11'

Located on the Tolovana River, II miles from the Elliott Highway on the Minto Road, adjacent to the Minto Flats State Game Refuge, 50 miles west of Fairbanks. **Transportation**: Via the Elliott Highway; charter air from Fairbanks. **Population**: 258. **Zip Code**: 99758.

Elevation: 460 feet. **Climate**: Temperatures range from 55°F to 90°F in summer and from 32°F to -50°F in winter. Snow from October through April with traces in September and May. Emergency services: Minto Health Clinic.

Private Aircraft: Airstrip 1 mile east of village; elev. 460 feet; length 2,000 feet; gravel; unattended. Runway condition not monitored; recommend visual inspection prior to using.

NOTE: Minto prohibits the sale and importation of alcoholic beverages.

Visitor Facilities: Reserved accommodations and meals available at Lakeview Lodge, (907) 798-7448, where crafts are available. Groceries and supplies are available at North Fork Store, (907) 798-7512.

The Athabascan Indian village was moved to its present location from the east bank of the Tanana River in 1970 because of flooding. The original site, Old Minto, was established in 1915. Minto is a major access point for the Minto Flats State Game Refuge, a popular duck hunting area. Most residents make their living by hunting and fishing. Some local people also work making birch-bark baskets and beaded skin and fur items. The school serves an enrollment of 84 students. Government address: Minto IRA Council, P.O. Box 26, Minto, AK 99758, phone (907) 798-7112, fax (907) 798-7627, e-mail: Minto@aitc.org. Village corporation: Seth-De-Ya-Ah Corp., P.o. Box 56, Minto, AK 99758, phone (907) 798-7181, fax (907) 798-7556.

For more information see *The MILE-POST®*, a complete guide to communities on Alaska's road and marine highway systems.

Nikolai

GPS: N62°58' W154°09'

Located 40 miles northeast of McGrath, 195 miles northwest of Anchorage. **Transportation:** Scheduled air service from McGrath and Anchorage; charter air service based in McGrath; winter trails to McGrath, Medfra and Telida; accessible by river (May to October). **Population:** 100. **Zip code:** 99691. **Emergency Services:** Nikolai Health Clinic, phone (907) 293-2328; other services in McGrath.

Elevation: 450 feet. **Climate:** Mean monthly temperature in July is 54°F; in January, -15°F. More than half of the normal annual precipitation occurs between July and September. Relatively low snowfall in winter.

Private Aircraft: Airstrip adjacent northwest; elev. 450 feet; length 2,350 feet; dirt and gravel; unattended.

Visitor Facilities: A city-owned hotel/apartment building provides limited accommodations for visitors. A coffee shop in the community center serves breakfast and lunch. A laundromat is also located in the community center. There are no banking facilities. All supplies available at the general store. Arts and crafts, such as snowshoes, moccasins, slippers and beaded items, may be available for purchase locally. Fishing/hunting licenses may be purchased in the village and there is a local guide. Villagers use 3-wheelers, snow machines and dog teams for transportation. Gasoline is available; no major repair service.

Like other communities in this region, Nikolai was an Athabascan Indian village in the late 1800s and has been relocated since its original settlement. A trading post and roadhouse here served miners during the Innoko gold rush. Nikolai was incorporated as a second-class city in 1970.

Heavily dependent on subsistence, Nikolai residents rely on hunting (moose, caribou, rabbits, ptarmigan and waterfowl) and fishing (king, chum and coho salmon, whitefish, sheefish and grayling). Some residents spend the summer at Medfra at fish camps. There is also trapping and vegetable gardening. Seasonal construction and fire fighting offers some employment.

Communications include phones, mail plane, TV and radio, with most residents tuned to McGrath's KSKO radio station. There is a school with grades preschool through 12, with enrollment of 16, housed in a building completed in 1983. The Russian Orthodox church here was built in 1927. A large community building houses the post office, clinic, a laundromat and showers, library, poolroom, coffee shop and city offices. The city provides electricity and cable TV to Nikolai residences and home heating is with wood stoves. While some homes, the school, hotel and store have indoor plumbing and running water, most residents haul water from private wells or the community center. Sewage system is primarily outdoor privies. Fuel and heavy equipment are delivered by barge; other freight is delivered by plane. Government address: City of Nikolai, P.O. Box 9145, Nikolai, AK 99691, phone (907) 293-2113, fax (907) 293-2115. Village council: Nikolai Edzeno' Village Council, P.O. Box 9105, Nikolai, AK 99691, phone (907) 293-2311, fax (907) 293-2481, e-mail: Nikolai@aitc.org.

Northway

GPS: N62°57' W141°55'

Located 7 miles south of the Alaska Highway within the Tetlin National Wildlife Refuge, about 100 miles west of the Canadian border. **Transportation:** Auto via side road from Alaska Highway 256 miles southeast of Fairbanks; charter air service from Fairbanks, Gulkana. **Population:** est. 360 in area. **Zip code:** 99764. **Emergency Services:** Alaska State

Troopers, phone (907) 778-2245; Emergency Medical Service, phone (907) 778-2211; Fire Department.

Climate: Mean monthly temperature in July, 55°F; in January, -21°F.

Private Aircraft: Northway airport, adjacent south; elev. 1,716 feet; length 5,100 feet; asphalt; fuel 80, 100, jet; customs available; FAA station.

Visitor Facilities: Northway Airport Lodge & Motel, (907) 778-2266, groceries, liquor store, bar, propane, gas stations, air taxi service. Hardware, camera film, fishing/ hunting licenses available. Wide range of Athabascan Indian crafts including headwork, birch-bark baskets, moose hide and fur items such as moccasins, mukluks, mittens and hats.

Historically occupied by Athabascan Indians, Northway was named to honor the village chief who adopted the name of a riverboat captain in the early 1900s. The rich Athabascan traditions of dancing, crafts, and hunting and trapping continue in Northway today. The community has a community hall, post office and modern school.

Northway's airport was built in the 1940s as part of the Northwest Staging Route. This cooperative project of the United States and Canada was a chain of air bases from Edmonton, AB, through Whitehorse, YT, to Fairbanks. This chain of air bases helped build up and supply Alaska defense during WWII and also was used during construction of the Alcan and the Canol projects. Lend-lease aircraft bound for Russia were flown up this route. Northway is still an important port of entry for air traffic to Alaska, and a busy one.

For more about Northway, see *The MILE-POST®*, a complete guide to communities on Alaska's road and marine highway systems.

Nulato

GPS: N64°53' W158°06'

Located on the Yukon River, 25 miles west of Galena, 310 miles west of Fairbanks. **Transportation**: Scheduled air service via Frontier Flying Service and Larry's Flying Service; local air charter; accessible by boat. **Population**: 336. **Zip code**: 99765. **Emergency Services**: Public Safety Officer,

phone (907) 898-2290; Nulato Health Clinic and EMS, phone (907) 898-2209; Volunteer Fire Department.

Elevation: 510 feet. **Climate**: Mean monthly temperature in July, 57°F; in January, -6°F. The greatest mean precipitation occurs in August, with 2.81 inches.

Private Aircraft: Airstrip 1 mile northeast; elev. 310 feet; length 4,000 feet; gravel; unattended; no facilities.

Visitor Facilities: No formal overnight accommodations or restaurants, but there is a small lodge with 3 beds, kitchenette and privy; water must be hauled. Arrangements can be made by calling (907) 898-2205. Some supplies available in the community. There is a laundromat with showers at the safe-water facility. Fishing/hunting licenses are available, but there are no registered guides (ask local people about fishing). Diesel, propane and gasoline are available, and visitors may be able to rent boats and autos from area residents. Charter aircraft is available. There are no major repair services.

Nulato is the site of one of the most chronicled events in Alaskan history, the murder of Lt. John J. Barnard by Koyukuk Indians in 1851. Barnard came to Alaska as part of the British search party sent after Sir John Franklin. While Barnard was staying with the agent in charge of the Russian American Co.'s post at Nulato, the Koyukon Indians attacked the Russian fort, killing both Barnard and the Russian (Darabin), and 53 inhabitants of the Indian village below the fort. Various reasons have been given for the Nulato massacre, among them the traditional rivalry of the Lower Koyukon and Upper Koyukon, a possible insult by the British lieutenant of the Koyukon shaman, or the assumed challenge by the British to the Koyukuk trade monopoly. Barnard's gravesite is about 0.5 mile downriver from present-day Nulato.

The village was incorporated as a second-class city in 1963. Communications include phones, mail plane and TV. The 12-classroom school has grades kindergarten through 12 with enrollment of 117. There is electric service. Water is hauled from the river or available through the village safe-water facility. Sewage system is honey buckets. Freight arrives by barge or plane. Government address: City of Nulato, P.O. Box 65009, Nulato, AK 99765, phone (907) 898-2205, fax (907) 898-2207. Village council: Nulato Tribal Council, P.O. Box 65049, Nulato, AK 99765, phone (907) 898-2339, fax (907) 898-2207, e-mail: Nulato@aitc.org.

Rampart

GPS: N65°30' W155°30'

Located on the Yukon River, 61 miles northeast of Tanana, 85 miles northwest of Fairbanks. **Transportation**: Scheduled air service from Fairbanks; charter air service; river travel except during breakup and freezeup. **Population**: 45. **Zip code**: 99767. **Emergency Services**: Rampart Health Clinic, phone (907) 358-3219; Volunteer Fire Department.

Elevation: 380 feet. **Climate**: Cold in winter and warm in summer. Mean monthly temperature in January, -11°F; in July 57°F.

Private Aircraft: Airstrip 2 miles east; elev. 275 feet; length, 3,500 feet; gravel; no fuel; unattended. Inspection recommended prior to using. Frequent crosswinds at both ends; no line of sight between runway ends.

Visitor Facilities: No accommodations or meals available. Groceries and supplies available from Rampart Trading Post, (907) 358-3113. Local arts and crafts include marten hats and slippers. The village has a laundromat. There are no banking services, rental transportation or any repair facilities. Regular gasoline, marine gas, diesel and propane are available. Fishing/hunting licenses may be purchased here, but there are no guides.

Originally an Indian village, the community grew with the influx of miners following the 1896 gold discovery on Minook Creek. Today, Rampart is an unincorporated Athabascan village where some residents trap and fish for a living. The community is friendly and accommodating to visitors. There are still gold mines in the area. Employment also includes commercial fishing and fish processing. Residents fish for salmon in the summer. Rampart's location also makes it a good stop for anyone traveling the Yukon River, although one resident warns that there are many bears in the area.

Communications include some private phones, mail plane, radio and TV. Generators provide electrical service, but water is hauled from the Yukon River or the school well. The sewage system is outhouses. Freight arrives via cargo plane and barge. Tribal government address: Rampart Village Council, Box 67029, Rampart, AK 99767, phone (907) 358-3312, fax (907) 358-3115. Village corporation: Baan o yeel Kon Corp., P.O. Box 74558, Fairbanks, AK 99707, phone (907) 456-6259, fax (907) 456-4486.

Ruby

GPS: N64°45' W155°30'

Located on the Yukon River, 50 miles east of Galena, 220 miles west of Fairbanks. **Transportation**: Scheduled air service; river travel except during breakup and freezeup; dogsled, snow machine or skis in winter. The 36-mile-long Ruby/Poorman Road is used for subsistence and wood cutting. **Population**: 188. **Zip code**: 99768. **Emergency Services**: Public Safety Officer, phone 468-4441; Fire station, phone (907) 468-4412; Ruby Health Clinic, phone (907) 468-4433.

Elevation: 710 feet. **Climate**: Fair in summer with temperatures to 80°F, lows in winter to -50°F. The mean monthly temperature in January is -2°F; in July it is 58°F.

Private Aircraft: Airstrip 1 mile southeast of community; elev. 635 feet; length, 4,000 feet; lighted; gravel. No facilities. Transportation to town available.

Visitor Facilities: Lodging available at Moose Camp bed and breakfast, (907) 468-4489. Public campground on riverbank low slip with tent platform, firepit, shelter and outhouse. No charge. There are no restaurants. Groceries and supplies are available at Ruby Trading Co. and McCarty's Services. No banking services available. There is a laundromat with showers, and most types of fuel are available. Automobiles may be rented and there are charter aircraft, but no major repair services available. Fishing/ hunting licens-

es are available as well as guide service. Public moorage available on the river. Yukon Adventure Co. LLC offers fully guided and equipped sea kayak adventures on the Yukon River and its tributaries. No white water experience is necessary. Contact Yukon Adventures Co. LLC, P.O. Box 73, Ruby, AK 99768, phone 1-888-771-4463, web: www.YukonAdventureCo.com.

Gold was discovered on Ruby Creek near the present-day townsite in 1907, but the gold rush did not take place until 1911 with a second gold discovery on Long Creek. (Ruby/Poorman road leads to Long Creek Mine to the south.) Today Ruby is a peaceful, friendly village. Its residents make a living by commercial fishing, subsistence fishing, hunting, trapping (marten, beaver, mink, fox, wolf), logging, or working for the school, city or private businesses. There are some summer jobs in construction and fire fighting.

Recreation for residents in summer includes swimming or fishing in clear pools on the Melozi River. In winter there are races by dogsled, snowshoe, snow machine or skis. Ruby is also a checkpoint for the annual Iditarod Trail Sled Dog Race in alternate years.

Communications include phones, mail, TV and Internet connection. Ruby has a Bible church and a Roman Catholic church (St. Peter In Chains), a school with grades kindergarten through 12 with enrollment of 47, and a library. There is a public electric power system and a community well. Individual residences have private wells and septic tanks or privies. Freight arrives by cargo plane and barge. Government address: City of Ruby, P.O. Box 90, Ruby, AK 99768, phone (907) 468-4401, fax (907) 468-4443. Village corporation: Dineega Corp., P.O. Box 28, Ruby, AK 99768, phone (907) 468-4405, fax (907) 468-4403, e-mail: kdozette@aol.com. Village council: Ruby Tribal Council, P.O. Box 210, Ruby, AK 99768, phone (907) 468-4479, fax (907) 468-4474. e-mail: Ruby@aitc.org.

Shageluk

GPS: N62°41' W159°34'

(SHAG-a-luck) Located on the Innoko River, 20 miles east of Anvik, 34 miles northeast of Holy Cross, 330 miles west of Anchorage. **Transportation:** Scheduled and charter air service from Bethel, Aniak, Grayling, Anvik and McGrath. **Population:** 129. **Zip code:** 99665. **Emergency Services:** State Trooper in McGrath; Shageluk Health Clinic; Volunteer Fire Department.

Elevation: 70 feet. **Climate:** Continental. Temperatures range from -60°F to 87°F. Average annual precipitation 21 inches, with 110 inches of snow. Snowfall usually starts in October and ends in April.

Private Aircraft: Airstrip 1 mile north; elev. 70 feet, length 2,300 feet; gravel; no fuel; unattended. Runway condition not monitored; visual inspection recommended prior to using. Floods during breakup, may be soft after heavy rain. Transportation to village available for $5 per person/per ride.

NOTE: Shageluk prohibits the sale and importation of alcoholic beverages.

Visitor Facilities: Accommodations available at Innoko River School, (907) 473-8233 for $25 per person/per night. There is a washeteria with showers. Groceries and supplies are available at Shageluk Native Store, The Outpost and

G&P's video. Fuel available: gasoline, propane. Information on other visitor services and facilities unavailable.

Shageluk is an old Ingalik Indian village first reported in 1850 as Tiegoshshitno by Lt. L.A. Zagoskin. In 1861, P. Tiklimenien, considered to be the chief historian of the Russian-American Co., noted 6 villages. These were collectively called the Chageluk settlements in the 1880 census. Shageluk became one of the permanent communities in the area; however, the village was relocated to its present location in the mid-1960s because of flooding. Shageluk, which is located about 10 miles south of Innoko National Wildlife Refuge, was incorporated as a second-class city in 1970.

About half of the buildings in Shageluk are built of logs, including a 6-sided kashim, a structure used for traditional social gatherings.

Although many residents own snow machines, dog teams are popular in Shageluk. Every other year the village is a checkpoint on the 1,049-mile Iditarod Trail Sled Dog Race from Anchorage to Nome. There also are trails connecting Shageluk with Anvik and Grayling.

There are a few full-time jobs with the school, city, clinic, post office, store or village corporation and some seasonal construction work on public projects or fire fighting. This income is supplemented by subsistence activities. Residents hunt moose, black bear, small game and waterfowl, and fish for salmon, whitefish, sheefish and pike. They also trap and sell the pelts of beaver, marten, mink, fox, otter, wolverine, lynx and muskrat. Vegetable gardens are common in the village, growing potatoes, cabbage, onions, carrots, turnips and lettuce

Communications in Shageluk include phones, commercial radio and TV via satellite. The community is served by St. Luke's Episcopal Church and a school with grades kindergarten through 12 with enrollment of 36. There is a community electric system. Water is hauled from the washeteria, rain water is collected in summer and fall, and ice blocks are cut in winter. Sewage system is outhouses or honey buckets. Freight arrives by barge several times each summer or by mail plane. Government address: City of Shageluk, P.O. Box 107, Shageluk, AK 99665, phone (907) 473-8221, fax (907) 473-8220, web: http://szshx.shx.iasd. gcisa.net. Village corporation: Zho-Tse Inc., P.O. Box 108, Shageluk, AK 99665, phone (907) 473-8229. Village council: Shageluk IRA Council, P.O. Box 35, Shageluk, AK 99665, phone (907) 473-8239, fax (907) 473-8295, e-mail: Shageluk@aitc.org.

Stevens Village
GPS: N66°01' W149°06'

Located on the Yukon River, 90 miles north of Fairbanks. **Transportation:** Scheduled air service from Fairbanks via Frontier Flying Service and Larry's Flying Service; river travel except during breakup and freezeup. **Population:** 87. **Zip code:** 99774. **Emergency Services:** Alaska State Troopers in Fairbanks; Stevens Village Health Clinic; Volunteer Fire Department.

Elevation: 310 feet.

Private Aircraft: Airstrip adjacent north; elev. 310 feet; length, 2,120 feet; gravel; unattended. Runway condition not monitored; visual inspection recommended prior to using. Prevailing winds from west and southwest.

NOTE: Stevens Village prohibits the sale and importation of alcoholic beverages.

Visitor Facilities: No accommodations or restaurants. Visitors may arrange with the Village Council office, (907) 478-7114, to stay in the old school. Groceries and supplies are available at Pitka's Store and George's Store. Local women may have arts and crafts (mostly beadwork) for sale. Marine gas and regular gasoline are available. Visitors may arrange to rent boats and boat repair is available. There are no banking services.

According to local tradition, this Indian village was founded by 3 brothers: Old Jacob, Old Steven and Gochonayeeya. When Old Steven was elected chief in 1902, the village was named for him.

Stevens Village is unincorporated. People here today make their living working in the post office or store, the Native corporation clinic, in maintenance, or at the school. Villagers also do some trapping and spend summers at fish camp.

There are 2 churches: Assembly of God and Episcopal. Stevens Village School has grades preschool through 12. with enrollment of 23. There is a community power supply and safe-water supply. Sewage system is privies. Most residents have phones and there is a public pay phone in the village office. Freight comes in by plane or barge. Government address: Stevens Village IRA Council, General Delivery, Stevens Village, AK 99774, phone (907) 478-7228, fax (907) 478-7229, e-mail: Stevens@aitc.org. Village corporation: Dinyea Corp., Box 71372, Fairbanks, AK 99707, phone and fax (907) 456-8224.

Takotna

GPS: N62°59' W156°04'

Located on the Takotna River, 17 miles west of McGrath, 230 miles northwest of Anchorage. **Transportation**: Scheduled passenger and mail plane from McGrath; charter plane; river travel June through September; snow machine and dogs. Takotna has more roads than most Interior communities. About 90 miles of road connect the community with Tatalina Air Force Station; Sterling Landing, on the Kuskokwim River, where the barge docks; Ophir, an old mining community with a few occupants in summer; and other mining areas. **Population**: 50. **Zip code**: 99675. **Emergency Services**: Alaska State Troopers in Bethel; Public Safety Officer in McGrath; Takotna Health Clinic, phone (907) 298-2214; Volunteer Fire Department.

Elevation: 825 feet. **Climate**: With more than 40 percent of the normal precipitation occurring between July and September, summers are "more wet than dry," as one resident puts it. Average daily maximum temperatures during summer are in the upper 60s. Winters are drier and cold, with minimum temperatures to -60°F.

Private Aircraft: Village airstrip adjacent north; elev. 825 feet; length 1,717 feet; gravel; unattended.

Visitor Facilities: There are no formal lodges, but the community hall has beds for rent. Limited groceries are available. There is a laundromat with showers. Marine gas and diesel are available. Meals, banking services, rental transportation and major repair service are not available.

Takotna started as a supply town for gold mines in the upper Innoko region. The town prospered through the 1930s, when gold mining in the region declined and McGrath replaced Takotna as the supply center. Nearby Tatalina Air Force Station was established in 1949. Community capital improvement projects have employed many village residents in construction during the summer, although as these projects slow down, some residents may have to go to Anchorage for summer work. Takotna is a checkpoint for the Iditarod Trail Sled Dog Race.

Most residents are involved in subsistence activities. Hunting for moose, the staple red meat, is fair. There is some duck hunting and local fishing for grayling, pike and trout. Local residents also grow vegetable gardens and harvest wild berries.

Communications include phones, mail plane, radio and TV. There are no churches. The 2-classroom schoolhouse has grades preschool through 12 with enrollment of 50. There is a community electric system. Most residents heat their homes with wood stoves. Water is hauled from the PHS building or from a nearby stream (referred to locally as Takotna Waterworks). Most houses have indoor plumbing with wells; the community hall and PHS building are on septic tanks and have running water. Freight arrives by plane or by barge to Sterling Landing. Takotna is unincorporated and within the unorganized borough. Village council: Takotna Village, P.O. Box TYC, Takotna, AK 99675, phone (907) 298-2212, fax (907) 298-2314, e-mail: Takotna@aitc.org. Community non-profit: Takotna Community Assoc., Inc. P.O. Box 86, Takotna, AK 99675, phone (907) 298-2211, fax (907) 298-2325.

Tanana

GPS: N65°10' W152°04'

(TAN-a-nah) Located near the confluence of the Yukon and Tanana rivers, 135 miles northwest of Fairbanks. **Transportation**: Scheduled air service from Fairbanks and local charter; river travel in summer; snow machine and dogs. **Population**: 308. **Zip code**: 99777. **Emergency Services**: City police, phone (907) 366-7158; Tanana Health Clinic, phone (907) 366-7222/7223; Tanana Volunteer Fire/EMS, phone (907) 366-7170.

Elevation: 227 feet. **Climate**: Hot and dry in June and July, cooler in August, cold October through February. One resident says September (sunny and cool) and March and April (cold and sunny) are the best months.

Private Aircraft: Ralph M. Calhoun Memorial Airport, 1 mile west; elev. 227 feet; length 4,400 feet; gravel. Runway condition not monitored; visual inspection recommended before use. Restrooms at airstrip; transportation to town available.

Visitor Facilities: Meals and accommodations available at Tanana Lodge, (907) 366-7165. Groceries and supplies are available at Terry's 1, phone (907) 366-7233, and Tanana Commercial, (907) 366-7188. All supplies available in the community. There is a laundromat. Beadwork, parkas, mukluks, birch-bark baskets and other crafts may be purchased. Fishing/hunting licenses available. There are no banking services. Charter aircraft are the only rental transportation available. Diesel, propane, unleaded gasoline are available. Charter aircraft available to rent, and other vehicles may be rented from private individuals.

Tanana is located at a historic Indian trading locality known as Nuchalawoya, meaning "place where the 2 rivers meet." A Nuchalawoya festival, with potlatch and contests, is held in Tanana every June. Arthur Harper established an Alaska Commercial Co. trading post here in 1880, and in 1891 the U.S. Army built Fort Gibbon (the fort was abandoned in 1923). Tanana was incorporated as a first-class city in 1983. The wood-plank Mission of Our Savior Church, which overlooks the Yukon and Tanana rivers, was part of an Episcopal mission established here in 1891 by the Rev. Jules L. Prevost.

Residents cite the mission, Indian fes-

tival and Tanana's sled dog races as some of its attractions. The Yukon River sled dog championships are held in early April, and several outfitters offer sled dog trips or freighting on ski trips in winter. In summer, the Yukon River is swimmable ("65°F and silty in July"), and fish wheels are operating, especially in August and September. Boating is good throughout the area, and boat races are held over Labor Day weekend. There is canoeing on tributary streams. Tanana's residents make their living trapping, fishing and in government jobs.

Communications include phones, mail plane, radio and TV. There are 3 churches: St. Aloysius Roman Catholic Church, St. James Episcopal Mission and Arctic Mission Bible Church. The school has grades kindergarten through 12 with enrollment of 80. Tanana Power provides electricity to the city. Water is from community wells and the sewage system is both outhouses and flush toilets. Freight comes in by cargo plane and by barge. Government address: City of Tanana, P.O. Box 77249, Tanana, AK 99777, phone (907) 366-7159, fax (907) 366-7169. Village corporation address: Tozitna Ltd., P.O. Box 77129, Tanana, AK 99777, phone (907) 366-7255, fax (907) 366-7122. Village council: Native Village of Tanana, Box 77093, Tanana, AK 99777, phone (907) 366-7160, fax (907) 366-7195, e-mail: Tanana@aitc.org.

Telida

GPS: N63°23' W153°16'

(Ta-LIE-da) Located 80 miles northeast of McGrath, 185 miles northwest of Anchorage. **Transportation**: Scheduled mail plane; charter plane; small riverboat; winter trail to Nikolai. **Population**: 30. **Zip code**: 99627. **Emergency Services**: Alaska State Troopers in McGrath, phone (907) 524-3222; Telida Health Clinic, phone (907) 843-8126; Volunteer Fire Department.

Elevation: 650 feet. **Climate**: Average daily maximum temperatures in summer in the 60s, with occasional highs in the 80s. Minimum temperatures in winter below zero, with lows to -60°F. More than half the normal precipitation occurs between July and September.

Private Aircraft: No public airstrip. Private airstrip adjacent south; elev. 650 feet; length 1,900 feet; turf; unattended; no facilities. Rough spots on runway.

Visitor Facilities: Rental cabin available from Steve and Olga Eluska, (907) 843-8115. No meals, restaurants or stores. Supplies are obtained from McGrath and Anchorage. Some beadwork is done in the village. Gasoline is available and boats may be rented, but there are no other visitor services.

This old Indian village has had 3 locations since white explorers first camped in the village in 1899. The village's second location, 4 or 5 miles upstream from present-day Telida, was abandoned and is now referred to as Old Telida. New Telida was settled by the Carl Sesvi family. The lifestyle here is heavily subsistence. The Athabascan residents hunt moose, bear, waterfowl and small game; fish for whitefish, sheefish, chum salmon, grayling, pike and Dolly Varden; and trap fox, lynx, wolverine, beaver, muskrat, marten and mink. There is some vegetable gardening and families harvest wild berries in late summer and fall.

Communications in Telida, which is unincorporated, include phones, mail plane and radio. There is a Russian Orthodox church in the village. The village has electricity, and each Telida home has an outhouse. Freight comes in by plane. Tribal government address: Telida Village, P.o. Box 32, McGrath, AK 99627, phone (907) 524-3550, fax (907) 524-3163, e-mail: Telida@aitc.org.

Venetie

GPS: N67°01' W146°25'

(VEEN-e-tie) Located on the Chandalar River, 140 miles north of Fairbanks. **Transportation**: Scheduled air service from Fairbanks and Fort Yukon; winter trail from Arctic Village and Fort Yukon. **Population**: 202. **Zip code**: 99781. **Emergency Services**: Tribal Police through Native Village of Venetie Tribal Government; Myra Roberts Clinic.

Elevation: 620 feet. **Climate**: Mean monthly temperature in January, -18°F.

Mean monthly temperature in July, 57°F. Greatest mean monthly precipitation is in August, with 1.5 inches.

Private Aircraft: Private airstrip adjacent northeast; elev. 550 feet; length 4,100 feet; dirt and gravel; unattended. Runway soft and muddy after rain. Some dips in runway. *NOTE: As airstrip is privately owned, landing fees may be assessed.*

NOTE: Venetie is a dry village; sale and importation of alcoholic beverages is prohibited.

Visitor Facilities: No meals or overnight accommodations available. Some supplies available in the community. Travelers are advised to check with village office, (907) 849-8165, before visiting.

An Indian village settled in 1900, Venetie is unincorporated and is part of the 1.8-million-acre Venetie Indian Reservation. Residents are employed in seasonal trapping and fire fighting. Some year-round employment in the school and store. Venetie school, established in 1938, has grades preschool through 12 with enrollment of 44. There is an Episcopal church. Electrical power is provided by a village generator. Homes are on septic tanks. Freight comes in by plane. Tribal government address: Native Village of Venetie Tribal Government, Box 29, Venetie, AK 99781, phone (907) 587-5329/5990, e-mail: Venetie@aitc.org.

INTERIOR • ATTRACTIONS

The biggest and best known attraction in the Interior is Mount McKinley/Denali. It is the highest mountain in North America, at 20,320 feet. But the forests and tundra of the Interior are also home to a large network of hiking trails, dozens of fly-in and road-accessible fishing lakes and streams, 5 national wild and scenic rivers and 6 national wildlife refuges, to name just a few attractions.

Index of Interior Attractions

Alaska State Parks
See Chena River State Recreation Area

Bird watching
See Denali National Park and Preserve; Innoko National Wildlife Refuge; Kanuti National Wildlife Refuge; Minto Flats State Game Refuge; Yukon-Charley Rivers National Preserve

Cabins
Alaska State Parks cabins
BLM cabins
National Park Service cabins

Fishing

Hiking Trails

Hot Springs

Ice Fishing Huts

Mountain Biking

Mountaineering

National Parks and Monuments
See Denali National Park and Preserve;
Yukon-Charley Rivers National Preserve

National Recreation Areas
See White Mountains National
Recreation Area

Recreational Mining
See Nome Creek Valley

River Running

Rock Climbing

Special Features
See Ghost Towns; The Kink; Steese
National Conservation Area; Tanana
Valley State Forest

State Game Refuges
See Minto Flats State Game Refuge

Wildlife Refuges
See Innoko National Wildlife Refuge;
Kanuti National Wildlife Refuge;
Koyukuk National Wildlife Refuge;
Nowitna National Wildlife Refuge;
Yukon Flats National Wildlife Refuge

Cabins

There are 21 public-use cabins available for rent and 3 trail shelters (no rental fee) in the Interior. Alaska State Parks has 10 cabins; the Bureau of Land Management (BLM) has 11 cabins and 3 trail shelters; and the National Park Service has 6 cabins.

Alaska State Parks Cabins

The Division of Parks and Outdoor Recreation maintains public-use recreation cabins in Chena River SRA and Salcha River SRS near Fairbanks, and at Quartz Lake SRA and Fielding Lake SRS near Delta Junction; see descriptions following.

The cabins sleep 3 to 9 people and are equipped with plywood sleeping platforms, a wood stove for heating only, a table, benches and a nearby latrine. A water source is usually nearby, but water should be purified before drinking. (See list of cabin essentials on page 155.) Wood may be scarce, so gather dead and downed wood on the way to cabin.

A permit is required to use these cabins, and cabins must be reserved in advance. Cabin availability is posted at www.alaskastateparks.org. Cabin reservations may NOT be made electronically although the application form is available on the Internet site. When a cabin reservation is accepted, a combined receipt and permit to use the cabin is issued. The permit-day begins at noon on the assigned day and ends at noon on the following day. Full payment must accompany reservations. Fees range from $25 to $35 per night, depending on the cabin. Cabins can be reserved up to 6 months in advance of the first day of intended use.

Cabin reservations for the Interior may be made by mail or in person at the following offices:

Department of Natural Resources Public Information Center, 550 W. 7th Ave., Suite 1260, Anchorage, AK 99501-3557; phone (907) 269-8400, fax (907) 269-8901, TDD (907) 269-8411, email pic@dnr.state.ak.us, www.dnr.state.ak.us/pic/index.htm.

Department of Natural Resources Information Center, 3700 Airport Way, Fairbanks, AK 99709; phone (907) 451-2705.

Chena River Cabin. Located east of Fairbanks within Chena River SRA at Milepost 32.2 Chena Hot Springs Road. Sleeps 9. Accessible by road or river.

Colorado Creek Cabin. Winter-use cabin located east of Fairbanks within Chena River SRA. Sleeps 4. Accessible by snow machine, dogsled, skis or snowshoes via 5.8-mile Colorado Creek Cabin Trail from Milepost 31.6 Chena Hot Springs Road.

Fielding Lake Cabin. Located 66 miles south of Delta Junction at Milepost V 200.5 Richardson Highway in Fielding Lake State campground. Sleeps 6; 3-night maximum. Accessible by road spring through fall. Access in winter by snow machine, dogsled or 1-1/2-mile ski or snowshoe trail.

Glatfleder Cabin. Located 84 miles southeast of Fairbanks at Milepost V 277.9 in Quartz Lake SRA. Sleeps 4; 3-night maximum. Accessible year-round via a 1/2-mile walk from campground.

Lower Angel Creek Cabin. Located east of Fairbanks within Chena River SRA. Sleeps 6. Accessible in winter by snow machine, dog team, skis or snowshoes via 3.6-mile Angel Creek/Upper Chena Dome Trail from Milepost 50.5 Chena Hot Springs Road; follow yellow trail markers 3.6 miles to cabin. Summer access by ATV or on foot via Lower Chena Dome Trail from Milepost 49.1 Chena Hot Springs Road may be difficult due to wet trail.

North Fork Cabin. Located east of Fairbanks within Chena River SRA. Sleeps 7. Access at Milepost 47.7 Chena Hot Springs Road.

Quartz Lake Cabin. Located 84 miles southeast of Fairbanks at Milepost V 277.9 in Quartz Lake SRA. Sleeps 3; 3-night maximum. Available for public-use from October to April.

Salcha River Cabin. Located 39 miles southeast of Fairbanks at Milepost V 323.1 Richardson Highway in Salcha River SRS. Sleeps 3; 3-night maximum. Available for public-use from October to April.

Stiles Creek Cabin. Located east of Fairbanks within Chena River SRA. Sleeps 6.

Accessible year-round by trail; follow red trail markers for Stiles Creek Trail from trailhead at either Milepost 31.6 or 36.4 Chena Hot Springs Road to midway point on 15-mile loop ridge trail.

Upper Angel Creek Cabin. Located east of Fairbanks within Chena River SRA. Sleeps 5. Accessible in winter by snowmachine, dog team, skis or snowshoes via Angel Creek/Upper Chena Dome Trail from Milepost 50.5 Chena Hot Springs Road; follow yellow trail markers 6.7 miles to cabin. Summer access by ATV or foot via Lower Chena Dome Trail from Milepost 49.1 Chena Hot Springs Road may be difficult due to wet trail. Hikers can also access cabin from Chena Dome Trail in summer.

BLM Cabins

The Bureau of Land Management (BLM) has 10 recreational cabins and 1 shelter cabin located along the trail system, 1 road-accessible cabin in the White Mountains NRA and 2 trail shelters on the Pinnell Mountain National Recreation Trail in the Steese National Conservation Area. Many of the cabins are most easily accessed during the winter although several cabins may be reached by trail in summer. Cabin locations and GPS coordinates are given below. (See Hiking Trails this section for details on trail access.)

The cabins are either 10x12 or 12x16 feet and sleep between 4 and 8 people. Cabins are equipped with bunk beds, a table and benches, cook stove, lantern, fire extinguisher, saw, ax, broom and wood stove, with an outhouse nearby. Bring white gas for lanterns and cook stoves as well as extra lantern mantles and candles. Cut firewood is often available, but be prepared to cut wood (only dead or downed wood), and restock woodpile before leaving. Carry out garbage. Contact the BLM for a map of areas open to motorized vehicles.

Cabin reservations are required and accepted up to 30 days in advance with payment. The fee for all recreational cabins is $25/night on Friday and Saturday and $20/night Sunday to Thursday, with a 3-night limit. No reservations are required, and no fee is charged for any of the trail shelters. For cabin reservations by credit card, phone (907) 474-2251 or (907) 474-2252 in Fairbanks, or (800) 437-7021 outside the Fairbanks area. Or apply in person at the BLM office in Fairbanks.

For more information: Bureau of Land Management, Northern Field Office, 1150 University Ave., Fairbanks, AK 99709; phone (907) 474-2200, http://aurora.ak.blm.gov/.

Borealis-LeFevre Cabin. Located on a bluff on the north side of Beaver Creek, 4 miles upstream from the Big Bend. Sleeps 6 to 8. Access via Wickersham Creek Trail (20 miles of winter trail), the Summit Trail (20 miles of hiking trail), by plane or by floating Beaver Creek. N65°23' W147°44'.

Cache Mountain Cabin. Located 3 miles up O'Brien Creek from Beaver Creek. Sleeps 6 to 8. Access via Trail Creek Trail (33 miles), McKay Creek Trail (20 miles), Cache Mountain Loop Trail (26 miles from Windy Gap Cabin) or by hiking up O'Brien Creek from Beaver Creek. N65°25' W147°14'.

Caribou Bluff Cabin. Located on a ridge top overlooking Fossil Creek valley. Spectacular views of the White Mountains and Limestone Gulch. Sleeps 4 to 6. Access via Wickersham Creek and Fossil Creek trails (31 miles) or via trails from Wolf Run and Windy Gap cabin. N65°28' W147°34'.

Colorado Creek Cabin. Located on a small lake at the headwaters of Colorado Creek near the western boundary of the White Mountains NRA. Sleeps 4 to 6. Winter access via Colorado Creek Trail (15 miles). N65°29' W147°54'.

Crowberry Cabin. Located on ridge top overlooking Beaver Creek drainage. Sleeps 4 to 6. Access via Trail Creek Trail (27 mils) or from Cache Mountain Cabin (12 miles). N65°19' W147°27'.

Fred Blixt Cabin. Located in a small clearing in the forest, 0.3-mile from the Elliott Highway. Sleeps 6 to 8. Access is via a short gravel drive from Milepost 62.3 Elliott Highway.

Lee's Cabin. Located 7 miles from Wickersham Dome Trailhead via Wickersham Creek and Trail Creek trails. Sleeps 4 to 6. Access is by foot, mountain bike or ATV in summer; snowmachine, dog sled or skis in winter. N65°12' W147°37'.

Moose Creek Cabin. Located on a ridge at the edge of a large meadow. Sleeps 6-8. Access is via Trail Creek Trail (16 miles). N65°13' W147°37'.

Richard's Cabin. Located in tall white spruce trees near Bear Creek. Largest cabin in the White Mountains NRA system (16x25). Sleeps 6 to 8. Access via Bear Creek Trail. N65°25' W146°58'.

Wickersham Creek Trail Shelter. Located at Mile 11 on the Wickersham Creek Trail. 8x10 log cabin; sleeps 2. N65°16' W147°50'.

Windy Gap Cabin. Located on Fossil Creek at foot of White Mountains Range; spectacular views of limestone cliffs and peaks. Sleeps 4 to 6. Access from Wickersham Dome Trailhead via Wickersham Creek and Fossil Creek trails (43 miles); from Colorado Creek Trailhead via Colorado Creek and Windy Creek trails (33 miles); and from Cache Mountain Cabin via Cache Mountain Loop Trail (26 miles). N65°33' W147°27'.

Wolf Run Cabin. Located 1.5 miles east of Beaver Creek at base of hill in Windy Creek Valley; spectacular views of limestone cliffs and peaks of White Mountains. Sleeps 4 to 6. Access from Colorado Creek Trailhead via Colorado Creek Trail (23 miles), or from Windy Gap Cabin via Windy Creek Trail (10 miles) N65°33' W147°39'.

National Park Service Cabins

The National Park Service maintains 6 cabins within Yukon-Charley Rivers National Preserve. Five of these cabins are located near historic sites along the Yukon River, and all of them are available for no cost on a first-come, first-served basis.

For more information, contact the National Park Service, 201 First Ave., Fairbanks, AK 99701; phone (907) 456-0281, fax (907) 547-2247, www.nps.gov/yuch; or P.O. Box 167, Eagle, AK 99738; phone (907) 547-2233, email YUCH_Eagle_Office@nps.gov.

Coal Creek Cabin. Located near Coal Creek Dredge, a processing plant that was constructed in California, moved down the valley and eventually owned by Gold Placers Inc.

Glenn Creek Cabin. Located approximately 1/4 mile downstream from confluence of Glenn Creek and Yukon River, on south bank of Yukon River. Cabin is behind an island and is visible from the river. It was built in 1950 and used as a hunting base camp. N65°17' W142°05'.

Kandik River Cabin. Also known as Kandik Mouth or Ricketts-Trainor cabin. Located at mouth of Kandik River on north bank of Yukon River. Cabin was built in 1981 by Larry Ricketts and Jean Trainor for trapping, hunting, fishing and gathering. N65°22' W142°30'.

Nation Bluff Cabin. Located approximately 1 mile downstream from mouth of Nation River on north bank of Yukon River. Cabin is believed to have been built in 1934 to support a coal mining venture up the Nation River. It sits at base of Nation Bluff. N65°12' W141°44'.

Slaven's Cabin. A short distance west of Slaven's Roadhouse, a roadhouse built in 1932 and serving as an unofficial checkpoint for the Yukon Quest International Sled Dog Race. Cabin was built in 1994 and is just downstream from the mouth of Coal Creek.

Washington Creek Cabin. Located near site of Washington Creek Steam Tractor, which was brought in by a San Francisco physician for coal mining. The tractor is visible from the River.

Chena River State Recreation Area

This 254,080-acre recreation area straddles the Chena River, taking in the river valley and adjoining ridges, 30 miles east of Fairbanks between Mileposts 26.1 and 50.7 Chena Hot Springs Road.

Wildlife: The recreation area offers opportunities to view many species, including beaver, snowshoe hare, red squirrel, weasel, mink, muskrat, porcupine and marten. Wolves, wolverines and lynx are present but rarely seen. Waterfowl and shorebirds can be seen along the river. Black bears are occasionally observed along the river during salmon migrations and in berry patches on hillsides in August and September. Grizzly bears periodically wander through the area. Hunting in the recreation area is allowed in season, except within 1/4 mile of developed facilities.

According to a former Park Ranger, "The area boasts one of the highest road-accessible moose concentrations in the state. From late June until September, watch for moose along the highway, feeding in old river channels and ponds. Drive carefully; moose are often crossing the roadway."

The Chena River catch-and-release arctic grayling fishery is one of the most popular in the state. Grayling can be caught from May to October on a variety of small flies and lures. Check with the Alaska Department of Fish and Game for current regulations. The Chena also has small runs of king and chum salmon that migrate up from the Yukon and Tanana rivers in July and August although regulations prohibit fishing for salmon upstream from the Chena flood control dam, which is well below the recreation area.

Activities: The recreation area offers a full range of outdoor activities associated with the river, adjacent spruce and birch forests, alpine ridges and historic trails. Summer activities include fishing, camping, hiking, canoeing, bicycling, berry picking, target shooting, hunting, ATV use, sightseeing and horseback riding.

Winter activities include dog mushing, snowmobiling, snowshoeing, trapping, hunting and cross-country skiing. Several sled dog races cross the recreation area, including the Yukon Quest.

The road paralleling the clear-water Chena River offers several access points for float trips. Popular launch sites are at Mileposts 44.1, 39.5 and 37.9. Easy takeout points are Mileposts 39.5, 37.9 and 27. Float times vary according to stream flow, type of craft and ability of the paddlers. (See River Running this section.)

There are many backcountry routes for summer hiking along the river and on hillsides and 3 established hiking trails: the Angel Rocks Trail, Chena Dome Trail and the Granite Tors Trail. (See Hiking Trails this section.) Mosquitoes can be a nuisance, so bring repellent. Water sources on the trails are unreliable in dry weather; carry enough drinking water for the trip.

Accommodations: There are 2 developed campgrounds in the state recreation area, Rosehip Campground at Milepost 27 and Tors Trail Campground at Milepost 39.5. There are 6 public-use cabins. (See Cabins this section for details.)

Twin Bears Camp, located at Milepost 30 Chena Hot Springs Road, is available for rent by any individual or group year-round. The camp features 12 rustic cabins, each sleeping 6 to 8 people, and 2 buildings with heat, lights, showers, laundry and cooking facilities. There is also a volleyball court, horseshoe pit, basketball hoop, baseball field and group fire ring with picnic tables. For more information and reservations, contact Twin Bears Outdoor Education Association, Inc., P.O. Box 82953, Fairbanks, AK 99708; phone (907) 451-2753.

For more information: Alaska State Parks, 3700 Airport Way, Fairbanks, AK 99709; phone (907) 451-2695, http://alaskastateparks.org.

For details on access and accommodations, see The MILEPOST®, a complete guide to Alaska's road system.

Denali National Park and Preserve

Denali National Park and Preserve lies on the north flank of the Alaska Range, 120 miles south of Fairbanks and 240 miles north of Anchorage. It was first designated a national park in February 1917 and named for its best known feature—Mount McKinley—the tallest peak on the North American continent. The south summit reaches a height of 20,320 feet; the north summit is 19,470 feet. In 1980, the original park was enlarged from 3.2 million acres to more than 6 million acres, renamed Denali and designated a national park and preserve.

While the park is universally referred to as Denali National Park now, the mountain is still called McKinley by some, Denali by others. The Athabascan Indian name for the mountain was Denali, "the High One," until a prospector and Princeton graduate named William Dickey renamed the mountain McKinley in 1896, in honor of presidential nominee and gold-standard champion, William McKinley. Protests that the mountain be returned to its original name, Denali, ensued almost at once, but it was not until 1980, when the park changed its name from Mount McKinley National Park to Denali National Park, that the Alaska Board of Geographic Names changed the mountain's name back to Denali. However, the U.S. Board of Geographic Names still shows the mountain as McKinley.

Mt. McKinley/Denali remains the park's most outstanding feature and visitor attraction. It is located in the Alaska Range, which includes Mounts Foraker and Hunter, 2 of Alaska's 19 highest mountains.

Denali's sub-arctic ecosystem helped gain it International Biosphere Reserve status in 1976. Interesting features of the park include the Outer Range, Savage River Canyon, Wonder Lake, Sanctuary River, Muldrow Glacier and the Kantishna Hills. The Outer Range is located just north of the central Alaska Range and is composed of some of Alaska's oldest rocks, called Birch Creek Schist, which can be seen most clearly in the Savage River Canyon. Caribou calving grounds are located near the headwaters of the Sanctuary River, which passes through the Outer Range between Mount Wright and Primrose Ridge. Muldrow Glacier, the largest glacier on the north side of the Alaska Range, is 32 miles long and descends 16,000 feet from near Mt. McKinley/Denali's summit. Wonder Lake, 4 miles long and 280 feet deep, is a summer home for loons, grebes, and many migrating species. It also provides a wonderful reflection of Mount McKinley. The Kantishna Hills were first mined in 1906 when the town of Eureka boomed with gold seekers. The Kantishna area was included in the park in 1980. From the main entrance to Denali National Park at Milepost 237.3 Parks Highway, the 92-mile Park Road traverses the national park to private land holdings in Kantishna.

Climate: Typical summer weather in the park is cool, wet and windy. Visitors should bring clothing for temperatures that range from 40°F to 80°F. Rain gear, a light coat, sturdy walking shoes or boots and insect repellent are essential. Mount McKinley is clouded more often than not. (From June through August, the chances of seeing the summit on any given day run about 35 to 40 percent.) Winter weather is cold and clear, with temperatures sometimes dropping to -50°F at park headquarters. In the lowlands, snow seldom accumulates to more than 3 feet.

There are more than 450 species of trees, shrubs, herbs and flowering plants growing in the taiga and tundra of Denali National Park and Preserve. The major species of the taiga are white spruce in dry areas and black spruce where it's wet, intermingled with aspen, paper birch and balsam poplar. Wet tundra features willow and dwarf birch, often with horsetails, sedges and grasses along pothole ponds. Dry tundra covers the upper ridges and rocky slopes above the tree line from about 3,500 feet to 7,500 feet.

Wildlife: Wildlife viewing is probably second only to mountain viewing as a major pastime in Denali. There are 37 species of mammals in the park, including caribou, grizzly bear, wolf, wolverine, moose, Dall sheep, red fox, lynx, ground squirrel, snowshoe hare and voles.

About 155 species of birds inhabit the park. Year-round residents include the great horned owl, raven and white-tailed, rock and willow ptarmigan. The majority, however, visit the park only during summer. Some of these birds are sandhill cranes, oldsquaws, sandpipers, plovers, gulls, buffleheads and goldeneyes.

Activities: Wildlife viewing and photography, mountaineering, hiking and camping are the major wilderness activities in the park. For visitors staying close to the visitor center or campgrounds, there are ranger-led nature walks, slide programs, sled dog demonstrations and bus and flightseeing tours.

More than a thousand people attempt to climb Mount McKinley each year between April and June, most flying into base camp at 7,200 feet. The National Park Service maintains a ranger station in Talkeetna that is staffed full time, year-round. (See Mountaineering this section for more information on climbing Mt. McKinley/Denali.)

Hiking in Denali National Park is cross-country: there are no established trails in the backcountry. According to the Park Service, "Realizing trails become travel corridors that bring hikers and concentrate their impacts, traillessness helps us to disperse use and lessen impacts on the landscape." Backpackers must obtain a free backcountry permit and bear-resistant food container at the Visitor Center. Camping gear should include a gasoline or propane stove, a tent or waterproof shelter because of frequent rains and rain gear. Water should be boiled or treated. Pets are not allowed in the backcountry.

For the day hiker or the visitor with only a short amount of time, there are 7 unmaintained trails along the Park Road (between Milepost 1 and Milepost 15 at Savage River). These trails range from easy to strenuous and provide the visitor with an opportunity to experience the wilderness and grandeur of Denali without going on an extended backcountry hike.

Free park shuttle buses pick up and drop off hikers along the Park Road as well as provide scenic and wildlife viewing opportunities for those visitors not interested in hiking. A round-trip between the Visitor Center and Eielson Visitor Center takes approximately 8 hours. Denali Park Resorts offers 2 narrated interpretive tours that include either a lunch or snack. The Tundra Wildlife Tour is 6 to 8 hours round-trip and costs $71 per person ages 13 and up; for children 12 and under, the tour is $38. The Denali Natural History Tour is 3 hours round-trip and costs $37 per person ages 13 and older and $22 per person ages 12 and under.

Accommodations: The old Denali Park Hotel is closed, but there are 4 wilderness lodges located in the Kantishna area of the park.

A commercial district lies about a mile north of the park entrance on the Parks Highway. There are numerous hotels, a gas station, small convenience store, one-hour photo shop, gift shops, a bookstore, saloon and a coffee house that offers public internet access. There is a mercantile in Riley Creek Campground that carries a limited selection of groceries. Showers are also available at minimal cost. There are no public laundry facilities inside the park, and there is no food/drink service past Mile 0.5.

Backcountry Permits: Overnight stays in the backcountry of Denali National Park require a free backcountry permit. During summer months, visitors can obtain these permits from the Visitor Center. In the winter, permits can be obtained at park headquarters. Backcountry permits are issued one day in advance, and reservations are not accepted. (Day hikers do not need a special permit.)

Before obtaining backcountry permits, backpackers must do the following: 1) Watch the Backcountry Simulator program available from the Backcountry Desk. This program gives information on bear safety, minimum-impact camping, river crossing tips, wildlife and safety and emergencies. 2) Check the Quota Board at the Backcountry Desk for unit availability. Denali's backcountry consists of 43 units, in which a limited number of visitors are allowed per night; backpackers must confirm that their desired unit is not closed. *NOTE: Large groups may be separated if units are too full.* 3) Read Backcountry Description Guides available from the Backcountry Desk or the Visitor Center bookstore. These guides describe the park units and give useful information on backcountry camping and hiking. 4) Consult topographic maps to plan your trip and routes through the park. 5) Consult the backcountry gear checklist provided by the park service. Backpackers and hikers must be self-sufficient in the backcountry, so make sure you are prepared.

Campers must also obtain Bear Resistant Food Containers (BRFCs). All areas of the park require that visitors use BRFCs; they are free and are issued when you acquire your backcountry permit. Return them to the Visitor Center or park headquarters at the end of your trip. These containers can also be purchased at the Visitor Center bookstore.

Season: The park is open year-round to visitors. However, most campgrounds and food and shuttle bus services within the park are available only from late May to early September. Opening dates for facilities and activities for the summer season are announced in the spring by the Park Service and depend mainly on snow conditions in May. Closing dates for facilities and activities at the park are announced in the fall. Most park campgrounds close for the season in early September.

Visitor access to the park shifts with the change of seasons. From May to September, the public can travel the park road via the Visitor Transportation System (buses). From October through April, the Denali Park Road is open to Milepost 3. Beyond this point, the road is unplowed, and access to the park is by snowshoes, skis or dog sleds.

Access: Denali National Park and Preserve is accessible by road from Anchorage or Fairbanks via the Parks Highway. The park entrance is 237 miles north of Anchorage and 125 miles south of Fairbanks. It can also be reached by train from either Anchorage or Fairbanks via the Alaska Railroad.

There is no policy restricting access by bicycle on the Park Road although cyclists must stay on the road. Bicyclists wishing to camp in the park must either camp in one of the campgrounds, or if they are camping in the backcountry, cyclists must park their bikes in one of the campgrounds.

Each year, the park issues permits to a limited number of individuals, selected by lottery, to drive their vehicles through the park for a few days in early September. It is not unusual for these late-season visitors to have their tour curtailed because of early snows within the park. Road Lottery applications are accepted by mail during the month of July; phone (907) 683-2294 for details.

Special permits are also granted to professional photographers. Contact the park directly for details.

The park does not charge an entrance fee as most national parks do.

Parking space is limited at the Visitor Center. Day parking is available at Riley Creek Campground (walk or take the mini-shuttle to Visitor Center).

Park shuttle bus tickets and park campsites may be reserved by phoning toll free 1-800-622-7275 (PARK) or (907) 272-7275 in Anchorage.

For more information: Denali National Park and Preserve, Box 9, Denali Park, AK 99755; headquarters phone (907) 683-2294, fax (907) 683-9617, www.nps.gov/dena, email: denali_info@nps.gov. USGS maps: McKinley, Talkeetna, Healy.

For details on access and accommodations, see The MILEPOST®, a complete guide to Alaska's road system.

 Fishing

Access to sport fishing in the Interior is by road, boat and small plane. Air taxi and fishing guide services are available in many communities. It is recommended that fishing licenses be purchased before departing for the Bush, since rural vendors may be out hunting or fishing themselves.

Fish found in the Interior are whitefish, which average 1 to 2 pounds; burbot, which average 2 to 5 pounds but can attain 20 pounds; and arctic grayling. Grayling like clear, cold water and are found throughout much of the state; any grayling over 3 pounds is considered trophy size.

Interior fish species also include pike and sheefish. Northern pike average 2 to 5 pounds and occasionally attain trophy status of 15 pounds. Some lucky anglers have even caught 25- to 30-pound pike. Use a wire leader, and carry pliers for unhooking your catch.

The sheefish is another enthusiastic fighter commonly found in Interior waters, particularly Yukon River tributaries, the Minto Flats and the lower Chena River. Sheefish average 7 to 12 pounds in these waters but occasionally attain 30 pounds.

For more information about fishing in the Interior, contact the Alaska Department of Fish and Game, Sport Fish Division, 1300 College Road, Fairbanks, AK 99701; phone (907) 459-7207, fax (907) 456-2259, http://www.state.ak.us/adfg/sportf/region3/rgn3home.htm.

Big Lake. Fly-in lake located 35 miles from Cantwell by floatplane, according to Atkins Guiding and Flying Service in Cantwell. Fishing for lake trout and grayling.

Birch Creek. Located 70 miles northeast of Fairbanks, Birch Creek is accessible from the Steese Highway. Grayling up to 12 inches may be caught in this stream from June to October. Northern pike and whitefish also available.

Birch Lake. Public fishing access from Milepost V 306 Richardson Highway. Fish from shore in spring, from boat in summer, for arctic char, artic grayling, rainbow trout and silver salmon. Public-use ice fishing huts are available in winter; see Ice Fishing Huts this section.

Black River. Located about 17 miles northeast of Fort Yukon; accessible by floatplane from Fort Yukon. Fair fishing (depending upon water conditions) for grayling, Dolly Varden, northern pike, whitefish and sheefish.

Bull Lakes. Fly-in lake located 20 minutes by plane from Cantwell, according to Atkins Guiding and Flying Service in Cantwell. Fishing for lake trout and Dolly Varden.

Caribou Lake. Fly-in lake located 20 minutes by small plane from Cantwell, according to Atkins Guiding and Flying Service in Cantwell. Fishing for lake trout and grayling.

Charley River. The Charley River is considered good to excellent for grayling fishing. Northern pike are found as far as 16 miles upstream. Sheefish and king, chum and coho salmon are occasionally found in the river. Access is by aircraft.

Chena River. The Chena River flows southwest 100 miles to the Tanana River near Fairbanks. It has the most popular arctic grayling fishery in the state (catch-and-release only). Access to the river within Chena River State Recreation Area is via Chena Hot Springs Road, 30 miles east of Fairbanks. Grayling from May to October on a variety of small flies and lures. The Chena also has a small run of king and chum salmon. Check current regulations concerning the Chena River grayling and salmon fisheries.

Deadman Lake. Fly-in lake located 35 miles from Cantwell by floatplane, according to Atkins Guiding and Flying Service in Cantwell. Fishing for lake trout and grayling.

Delta-Clearwater River. A spring-fed stream near Delta junction shown as Clearwater Creek on USGS topographic maps; tributary of the Tanana River. Access from Milepost DC 1414.8 Alaska Highway. Tops for grayling May 1 to September 30, use flies or lures; whitefish in spring and summer, use flies; burbot also available; silver salmon spawn here in October.

East Twin Lake. Fly-in lake located in the Tanana Lowlands approximately 85 air miles southwest of Fairbanks, 40 miles east of the Bitzshtini Mountains. Trophy-sized pike, use spoons, spinners. Air charter service available in Fairbanks.

Goat Lake. Fly-in lake located 45 miles from Cantwell by floatplane, according to Atkins Guiding and Flying Service in Cantwell. Fishing for Dolly Varden.

Goodpaster River. Located northeast of Delta Junction. Accessible by boat via the Delta-Clearwater and Tanana rivers. Excellent grayling fishing April 1 to September 30, use flies or lures.

Koyukuk River. This river joins the Yukon River 22 miles northeast of Nulato. Boats may be available for rental at communities on the river. Pike and sheefish available at Huslia. Sheefish in late September and pike year-round at Hughes. Sheefish in September; grayling and pike year-round at Allakaket.

Lake Minchumina. Fly-in lake located 66 miles northwest of Mount McKinley, 150 miles southwest of Fairbanks, 205 miles northwest of Anchorage. Pike averaging 5 to 15 pounds, use spoons or spinners. Lodge on lake. Scheduled air service from Fairbanks to Lake Minchumina village. Charter air service available in Fairbanks or Anchorage.

Mansfield Lake. Fly-in lake located 7 miles north of Tanacross on the Alaska Highway. Fish available: northern pike year-round, use spoons or spinners; burbot year-round, use bait. Air charter service available in Tanacross or Tok.

Melozitna River. Tributary of the Yukon River; mouth located 2 miles upstream from Ruby. Good sheefish fishery upriver in July, use spoons. Boat accessible from Ruby.

Minto Lakes. Located in Minto Flats about 40 miles northwest of Fairbanks and southeast of the village of Minto. Good spring, summer and fall fisheries. Pike up to 20 to 25 pounds can be caught here. Other fish available: sheefish in midsummer, use spoons; white-fish year-round, use flies or eggs; burbot year-round, use bait. Accessible by small plane from Fairbanks; boat from Minto village, which is reached via the Elliott Highway; or via the Murphy Dome Extension Road from the top of Murphy Dome down to the Chatanika River.

Mystic Lake. Located in the foothills of the Alaska Range near the upper Tonzona River, 48 miles west of Mount McKinley, 158 miles northwest of Anchorage. Fish available: lake trout to 4 to 5 pounds, use spoons or plugs; northern pike to 4 feet, use spoons or spinners. Access by floatplane from Anchorage.

Nowitna River. Located within Nowitna NWR and designated a wild river. Flows into the Yukon River 38 miles northeast of Ruby. Fish available: northern pike year-round, use spoons or spinners; sheefish in late summer, use spoons; grayling in abundance, use flies. Salmon also spawn in this river.

Nulato River. Flows into the Yukon River 1 mile southwest of Nulato. Fish available: arctic char in late summer, use spoons and eggs; grayling May to October, use flies or lures; king and chum salmon arrive in July, use spoons. Access by boat from Nulato.

Porcupine River. Heads in Canada at N65°28', W139°32' and flows 460 miles west to join the Yukon River 2 miles northwest of Fort Yukon. Fish available: arctic grayling May to October, use flies; sheefish July to October, use spoons; northern pike year-round, use spoons. Access by boat or air charter service from Fort Yukon.

Quartz Lake. Excellent fishing for rainbow and silver salmon near Delta junction. Camping at Quartz Lake SRA campground. Public-use ice fishing huts available in winter (see Ice Fishing Huts this section).

Rainbow Lake. Located approximately 8 air miles across the Tanana River from Big Delta. Excellent rainbow trout fishing, use flies or lures. Access by floatplane during summer or by winter trail.

Salcha River. Fishing for king and chum salmon, grayling, northern pike and burbot. Access by boat from Salcha River SRS boat launch at Milepost V 323.1 Richardson Highway.

Siksik Lake. Fly-in lake located 35 minutes from Cantwell by small plane, according to Atkins Guiding and Flying Service in Cantwell. Fishing for lake trout.

Soule Lake. Fly-in lake located 20 minutes by small plane from Cantwell, according to Atkins Guiding and Flying Service in Cantwell. Fishing for lake trout and grayling.

Tetlin Lake. Located 16 miles southeast of Tok. Excellent northern pike fishery, use spoons or spinners. Access by riverboat up the Tetlin River from the Tanana River, or by floatplane from Tok, Tanacross, Northway or Fortymile on the Alaska Highway.

Tozitna River. Flows into the Yukon River 6 miles downstream from Tanana. Fish available: northern pike year-round, use spoons or spinners; sheefish July to October, use spoons. Access by boat or small plane from Tanana.

Wien Lake. Fly-in lake located 60 miles south of the Yukon River between the Nowitna and Kantishna rivers. Good fishing for northern pike up to 18 pounds. Lodge on lake. Access by floatplane from Fairbanks.

✴ Ghost Towns

Gold seekers came to the Interior before the turn of the century and built their towns and camps along its rivers. Some, like Fairbanks, flourished. Others died when the miners' luck ran out. We've listed a few of the old camps here. *NOTE: Respect private property. State and federal laws prohibit removing or destroying relics. Take only photographs.*

Caro. Located on the north bank of the Chandalar River at the mouth of Flat Creek, 26 miles south-southeast of Chandalar, 45 miles north of the Arctic Circle. This settlement was named for Caro Kingsland Clum, the daughter of Fairbanks postmaster John P. Clum, in 1907 when the Caro post office opened. The post office was discontinued in 1912. A wagon trail known as the Government Road, now overgrown with brush, once led to Caro from Beaver on the Yukon River.

Chandalar. Located on the east shore of Chandalar Lake at Rosalie Creek about 75 miles north of the Arctic Circle. This mining camp was established in 1906-07 and named after John Chandalar, who operated a Hudson's Bay Company trading post there. Chandalar had a post office from 1908 to 1944.

Diamond (or Diamond City). Located at the junction of Moose Creek and Bearpaw River, which flows out of Denali National Park and Preserve into the Kantishna River. This mining camp was the head of small-boat navigation on the Bearpaw and was probably a supply point for miners working farther upriver. Several buildings are still standing. Check with the Park Service about any restrictions.

Fortymile. Located at the junction of Bullion Creek and North Fork Fortymile River, 37 miles southwest of Eagle. The U.S. Army Signal Corps established a telegraph station called North Fork here in 1903. Prospectors later called the place Fortymile. A few cabins remain standing.

Franklin (or Franklin Gulch). Located at the junction of Franklin Creek and the South Fork Fortymile River, 48 miles southwest of Eagle. A post office was established at this mining camp in 1902; it was discontinued in 1945. A few buildings remain.

Glacier (or Glacier City). Located at the junction of Glacier Creek and Bearpaw River within Denali National Park and Preserve. Dozens of old homes, warehouses and the like remain from this mining community that thrived from about 1908 until the 1920s, when it was abandoned. This ghost town is virtually invisible from the air when leaves are on the trees; it's easiest to visit in winter when overland access is possible. Check with the Park Service about any restrictions.

Kemperville (also known as Buckholtz Roadhouse). Located on the right bank of the Tanana River at the mouth of Hot Springs Slough, approximately 6 miles downstream from Manley Hot Springs. A trading post was established here in 1909 in one of the log cabins still standing. The camp, reportedly named for prospector George Kemper, was active until 1911.

Mastodon. Located on Mastodon Creek, south of the Yukon River, 40 miles southwest of Circle. The first gold strike was made in this area in 1894. The creek, and subsequently the camp, were named by miners after they found mastodon bones and tusks at their diggings. This camp was active from 1902 to 1906.

Nation (or Nation City). Located on the south bank of the Yukon River, 2.2 miles below the mouth of the Nation River. This was a mining camp and supply point for the Fourth of July placer mining area from 1908 to 1924. Several foundations, 2 cabins and a few remaining logs from a roadhouse remain on this site. Nation is within the boundaries of Yukon-Charley Rivers National Preserve.

Rooseveldt (or Roosevelt). Located on the Kantishna River near the confluence with the Bearpaw River. This town was a regular stop for stern-wheelers in the early days. Cargo was unloaded here and placed in smaller craft for shipment to Diamond, Glacier and points farther upriver. The river has washed most of the buildings away, but a few still stand. There are many old sod doghouses behind the existing buildings.

Woodchopper Creek. Located on Woodchopper Creek at the mouth of Iron Creek, 19 miles west of the junction of the Charley and Yukon rivers, within the boundaries of Yukon-Charley Rivers National Preserve. This mining camp was established about 1907 and was active between 1919 and 1936.

🚶 Hiking Trails

Weather is always a factor when hiking in the Interior. Be prepared for rain and cool, windy weather or sun. On warm, sunny, summer days in the Interior, you can feel like you're baking. Take plenty of sunscreen along with bug repellent (mosquitoes and black flies are also a factor!).

The BLM also maintains over 200 miles of winter trails that access recreation cabins. The trails are groomed for both motorized and nonmotorized users. Winter trail activities include skiing, skijoring and dogsledding, and most of these trails are open to snow machines.

Check with the appropriate government agency and local sources for current trail conditions. For more information on White Mountains NRA trails listed here, contact the Bureau of Land Management, 1150 University Ave., Fairbanks, AK 99709; phone (907) 474-2350, http://aurora.ak.blm.gov/WhiteMtns. For trails within Chena River SRA, contact Alaska State Parks, 3700 Airport Way, Fairbanks, AK 99709; phone (907) 451-2695.

Angel Rocks Trail. Trailhead at Milepost 48.9 Chena Hot Springs Road in Chena River SRA. This is a short, 3-1/2-mile, relatively easy hike. It is less than 2 miles to the spectacular rock outcropping. At the top, there are 3 alternatives: return on the same improved trail, continue up to the end of the tor formations for beautiful views of the Alaska Range, Chena Dome and Far Mountain or continue on the loop trail. Approximate hiking time is 3 to 4 hours. USGS maps: Big Delta D-5; Circle A-5.

Bear Creek Trail. A White Mountains NRA trail, this 5-mile trail begins at Mile 10 Lower Nome Creek Road and ends at Richard's Cabin. It is used by snowmobilers, dog mushers and skiers November through late April. Trail is wet and muddy during the summer and is not recommended for summer use of motorized vehicles.

Bear Creek Trail climbs steeply from Nome Creek Road for 1 1/2 miles through black spruce and crests near Table Top Mountain before it drops down and crosses Champion Creek. Follow tripods and trail markers 2 1/2 miles, and cross Bear Creek. Turn left at the trail junction, and follow the trail 1/2 mile to Richard's Cabin. Rated moderate. USGS maps: Livengood B-1; Circle B-6.

Big Bend Trail. A White Mountains NRA trail, this 13-mile trail begins at Mile 14 Colorado Creek Trail and ends at Mile 19 on Wickersham Creek Trail. It is rated moderate with an elevation change of 1,325 feet. Wet and boggy trail conditions in summer, but ridgeline is suitable for summer hiking and ATV use. Moderate use in winter (November through early April) by snowmobiles, dog mushers and skiers. Beaver Creek corridor is closed to summer use of motorized vehicles. From the Colorado Creek Trail junction, the trail passes Colorado Creek Cabin and continues through a large open meadow for 3 miles, then climbs steeply for 1 mile to the top of the ridge. The trail follows the ridgeline south for 3 miles over its highest elevation of 2,675 feet. It then descends for 3 miles to a bridge near the "Big Bend" on Beaver Creek, then continues 5 miles through open meadows and black spruce forests to join with the Wickersham Creek Trail. USGS map: Livengood B-2.

Cache Mountain Loop Trail. A White Mountains NRA trail, this 26-mile trail begins at Windy Gap Cabin on Fossil Creek Trail and ends at Cache Mountain Cabin, 6 miles north of Beaver Creek. It is rated moderate to difficult with an elevation change of 1,775 feet. Not recommended for summer use due to wet, boggy trail conditions. Used in winter (December through March) by snowmobilers, dog mushers and skiers. The trail is closed to summer use of motorized vehicles. The trail goes through open meadows and black spruce forests. Although the trail follows creek drainages, there are few creek crossings. Spectacular views of White Mountains and limestone jags on open hillsides. USGS maps: Livengood B-1, C-1.

Chena Dome Trail. Trailhead at Milepost 50.5 Chena Hot Springs Road in Chena River SRA. (Also trailhead for Angel Creek Cabin ATV Trail.) This 30-mile loop trail circles Angel Creek Valley and rejoins Chena Hot Springs Road at Milepost 49.1. The trail crosses Chena Dome at its highest point (4,421 feet) and offers scenic alpine views not seen elsewhere in the recreation area. At each end of the loop, a 3-mile section of trail has been cut through the forest to tree line. The rest of the trail traverses tundra ridges marked by rock cairns and blanketed with wildflowers in late May, June and July. The loop provides a good 3- to 4-day trip for backpackers. Some portions of the trail are steep; wear suitable foot gear. Water may be a problem in late summer. Additional information about this hike is available on bulletin boards at the trailheads. USGS maps: Big Delta D-5; Circle A-5, A-6.

Colorado Creek Trail. A White Mountains NRA trail, this 24-mile trail begins at Milepost

57 Elliott Highway and ends at Wolf Run Cabin approximately 1.5 miles from Beaver Creek on the north side of the Windy Creek Trail. It is rated as moderate with an elevation change of 1,015 feet. Not recommended for summer use due to wet and boggy trail conditions. Used in winter (November through early April) by snowmobilers, dog mushers and skiers. From the Elliott Highway trailhead, the trail climbs gently for about 10 miles through open meadows and mixed spruce and birch, increasing in steepness for the next 3 miles to the top of the ridgeline at 1,625 feet. About 1/2 mile beyond the ridge there is a trail junction: the right trail goes 1/2 mile to Colorado Creek Cabin; the left trail continues 9 miles to Beaver Creek. The 9-mile stretch to Beaver Creek goes through an old burn area then through forested sections of spruce, occasionally breaking into open meadows which provide good views of the White Mountains. In the forested areas, the cut trail is visible and marked, but high winds may drift snow across open sections of trail, making it difficult to follow. This may also happen on the last 2 miles before Beaver Creek when the trail passes through open meadow. Once across the meadow, the trail crosses Beaver Creek and connects with the Windy Creek Trail. USGS maps: Livengood B-2, B-3, C-2, C-3.

Fossil Creek Trail. This White Mountains NRA trail is 22 miles long, rated moderate, with a 550-foot elevation change. It begins at the Borealis-LeFevre Cabin, located on Beaver Creek at Mile 20 of the Wickersham Creek Trail, and ends at Windy Gap Cabin on the Cache Mountain Loop Trail. It is closed to motorized vehicles during the summer due to wet and boggy trail conditions. Used by snowmobilers, dog mushers and skiers.

From Beaver Creek, the trail heads north through open valley and black spruce forests for the first 4 miles. The trail passes through a 1987 burn area for 2 miles then climbs 1/2 mile before dropping down to the Fossil Creek drainage. At Mile 10, the Fossil Creek Trail joins with the Fossil Gap Trail, then continues another 12 miles along the Fossil Creek drainage to trail end at the Windy Gap Cabin. This portion of the trail offers spectacular views of the White Mountains. USGS maps: Livengood B-1, B-2, C-1.

Fossil Gap Trail. This 8-1/2-mile-long trail in the White Mountains NRA accesses the Caribou Bluff Cabin and connects Fossil Creek and Colorado Creek trails. It is recommended for winter use only (November through March) due to wet, boggy trail conditions in summer. Used by snowmobilers, dog mushers and skiers. Rated moderate with an elevation change of 825 feet. The Fossil Gap Trail begins at Mile 10 Fossil Creek Trail, crossing open meadow for a short distance until it reaches Fossil Creek, where it joins a short spur trail that leads 1 1/2 miles up to Caribou Bluff Cabin. From the junction with the spur trail, Fossil Gap Trail follows Fossil Creek downstream 1.5 miles then heads back into the woods, paralleling the creek through the Gap. The trail passes through open meadows then crosses Beaver Creek and continues 1.5 miles along Beaver Creek, across a slough and then through black spruce forest to a bridge at Montana Creek and through open meadows marked with tripods to end at Mile 22 Colorado Creek Trail. Use extreme cautions crossing open water sections. USGS maps: Livengood B-2, C-2.

Granite Tors Trail. Trailhead at Tors Trail Campground, Milepost 39.5 Chena Hot Springs Road in Chena River SRA. Tors are high, isolated pinnacles of jointed granite jutting up from the tundra. Follow the dike (levee) on west side upstream 0.3 mile from campground to trail sign. It is 6 miles to the nearest tors, 8 miles to the main grouping. The upper portion of the trail is rocky, and suitable foot gear should be worn. A trail guide is available at the bulletin board in the campground. USGS map: Big Delta D-5.

Lower Nome Creek Trail. This 7.5-mile-long White Mountains NRA trail begins at Mile 8 McKay Creek Trail and ends at Mile 10 Nome Creek Road. Used in winter (November to early April) by snowmobiles, dog mushers and skiers, and in summer by ATVs. Rated moderate with an 800-foot elevation change. The trail follows a forested ridgeline north from the McKay Creek Trail for 5 miles before dropping down to Nome Creek. Follow tripods and trails markers across open areas. After crossing Nome Creek, the trail connects with Nome Creek Road (not maintained in winter) and also Bear Creek Trail. USGS maps: Livengood B-1.

McKay Creek Trail. This 17-1/2-mile-long trail begins at Milepost 42.5 Steese Highway and connects with the Trail Creek Trail near Cache Mountain Cabin. It is used in winter (November to early April) by snowmobiles. The first 8 miles of the trail are suitable for summer use. Rated moderate with a 1,025-foot elevation change. From the Steese Highway, the trail climbs steeply 5 1/2 miles to a ridge and the boundary of the White Mountain NRA. The trail follows the open ridgeline for 2 miles, then descends through spruce forests and meadows to Ophir Creek. After crossing Ophir Creek, the trail climbs steeply to another ridge and crosses an open area (follow tripods and trail markers). Trail then traverses a hillside for 4 miles before dropping down to cross Beaver Creek then O'Brien Creek, before connecting with the Trail Creek Trail. USGS maps: Livengood A-1, B-1.

Moose Creek Trail. This White Mountains NRA trail is 9 miles long, rated moderate, with a 275-foot elevation change. The trail starts at the Wickersham Creek Trail Shelter and ends at Moose Creek Cabin. It is recommended for winter use only because of wet and muddy sections of trail in summer. The trail passes through spruce forests and open burn and meadow areas and follows several creek drainages. The Moose Creek Cabin is just beyond the junction with the Trail Creek Trail at the eastern end of the meadow. USGS maps: Livengood A-2, B-2.

Pinnell Mountain National Recreation Trail. Pinnell Mountain Trail is the first national recreation trail to be established in Alaska. It is also the only trail in the Steese National Conservation Area. The 27.3-mile trail is accessible from the Steese Highway at Twelvemile Summit Wayside (Milepost 85.5) or Eagle Summit Wayside (Milepost 107.1). Day hikes or overnight stays can be enjoyed from either trailhead. Allow at least 3 days to travel the entire trail. The trail is clearly marked by rock cairns and mile markers. The trail is steep and rugged, traversing talus slopes and alpine tundra above tree line. There are 2 8x10-foot trail shelters along the trail.

This is one of the most accessible northern alpine tundra areas in the Interior. The trail winds along mountain ridges and through high passes mostly above 3,500 feet; the highest point reached is 4,721 feet. Along the trail are vantage points with views of the White Mountains, Tanana Hills and Alaska Range. Between June 18 and 25, hikers can see the midnight sun from many high points along the trail, including the Eagle Summit Wayside trailhead parking area.

Wildlife occasionally spotted from the trail includes wolves, grizzly bears and wolverines. Small groups of caribou can sometimes be seen from the trail. More frequently seen is the hoary marmot and the small pika or "rock rabbit." Birdlife includes rock ptarmigan, gyrfalcons, ravens, northern harriers, golden eagles, northern wheatears, lapland longspurs and various surf birds. Wildflowers bloom in profusion along some sections. Look for moss campion, alpine azalea, oxytrope, frigid shooting star, arctic forget-me-not, lousewort and mountain avens. Some of the oldest rocks in Alaska are found along this trail. These rocks are made up from sediments first deposited over a billion years ago.

No horses or motorized vehicles are allowed on the trail. Water is scarce; carry

Emergency and Survival Gear

- **dry matches and fire starters**
- **metal cup for boiling water**
- **extra food**
- **sleeping bag, ground pad and space blanket**
- **tent**
- **spare socks, gloves, hat and face mask**
- **first-aid kit**
- **trail maps and compass; GPS**
- **ax or handsaw and sharp knife**
- **equipment repair items and spare parts**
- **white gas for cookstoves and lanterns**
- **spare lantern mantles and candles**
- **snowshoes in winter**

your own supply, and boil or treat any water from streams. The 2 shelter cabins have water catchment systems. Backcountry camping is allowed along the trail, and 8x2-foot shelter cabins are located near Mile 10 (Ptarmigan Creek Trail Shelter) and Mile 18 (North Fork Trail Shelter) from Eagle Summit Wayside trailhead. USGS maps: Circle B-3, B-4, C-3, C-4.

Ski Loop Trail. Access to this White Mountains NRA trail is from the Wickersham Dome trailhead at Milepost 27.7 Elliott Highway. This trail can be used year-round by skiers in winter and hikers in summer although there are wet and muddy sections. Ski Loop Trail is closed to motorized vehicles year-round. This trail is an easy 5-mile loop from the highway trailhead following 1.5 miles of the Wickersham Creek Trail and 2 miles of the Summit Trail. Both trails begin at the same trailhead, so one can follow the loop in either direction. Starting with the Summit Trail, the route climbs for 1 mile to an overlook at 2,660 feet, with views of the Alaska Range on a clear day. The trail then descends into a forested saddle for 1 mile. At the trail junction, follow right trail for 1.5 miles to connect with the Wickersham Creek Trail, which leads 1.5 miles back to the parking area on the Elliott Highway. USGS map: Livengood A-3.

Summit Trail. Access to this White Mountains NRA trail is from the Wickersham Dome trailhead at Milepost 27.7 Elliott Highway. The 20-mile trail has been designed for summer use, with boardwalk installed over most wet areas. It is closed to motorized vehicles year-round. Rated moderate with an elevation change of 1,775 feet. From the highway trailhead, the trail gently climbs and descends Wickersham Dome for the first 7 miles. After 2 miles of spruce forest, it climbs to 3,100 feet near Mile 10, then descends for 2 miles before climbing to 2,505 feet at Mile 13. The final 7 miles of trail descends to 1,325 feet at Beaver Creek. The last 2 miles to Beaver Creek are along the Wickersham Creek Trail. The Borealis-LeFevre Cabin is located on the north side of Beaver Creek. Use caution crossing Beaver Creek at high water. Carry plenty of water along this trail. USGS maps: Livengood A-3, B-2, B-3.

Trail Creek Trail. This 33-mile White Mountains NRA trail is rated moderate with an elevation change of 825 feet. Recommended for winter use only because of wet, muddy sections of trail in summer. The Trail Creek Trail begins at Mile 6 of the Wickersham Creek Trail and ends at Cache Mountain Cabin. From the Wickersham Creek Trail junction, the trail follows a forested ridgeline for 4 miles, then climbs 2 miles to 2,245 feet before dropping into a saddle. After 2 miles, it enters an old burn area then descends 1 mile and opens into a large, open meadow, where the trail can be obscured by drifting snow in winter. It junctions with the Moose Creek Trail 1 1/4 miles farther, and the Moose Creek Cabin 1/4 miles beyond that, before climbing 1 1/2 miles to its highest point at 2,387 feet. The trail follows the ridgeline north then gently climbs and descends the next 9.5 miles to Crowberry Cabin (Mile 21). Trail continues along forested ridge to a meadow then descends to the Beaver Creek drainage. The trail drops steeply for 3 miles to Beaver Creek before it traverses another 6 miles to Cache Mountain Cabin. Use caution while traveling on Beaver Creek as the overflow ice may be thin. USGS maps: Livengood A-2, B-1, B-2.

Wickersham Creek Trail. This White Mountains NRA trail is 20 miles in length, rated easy to moderate with a 1,150-foot elevation change. The trail begins at the Wickersham Dome trailhead at Milepost 27.7 Elliott Highway and ends at the Borealis-LeFevre Cabin. Used in winter by snowmobiles, dog mushers and skiers. Used in summer by hikers and ATVs; watch for wet and muddy conditions. From the trailhead, the trail follows a forested ridgeline 5 miles east to a 2,545-foot peak; good view from top of Alaska Range and White Mountains. The Wickersham Creek Trail junctions with Trail Creek Trail at Mile 6 and with Moose Creek Trail at Mile 11. The Wickersham Creek Trail Shelter (sleeps 2, reservations not required) is at Mile 11.2. From the shelter, the trail descends through spruce forest for 4 miles, then climbs the next 3 miles, breaking into open forest. The trail drops steeply the last 2 miles to Beaver Creek. The Borealis-LeFevre Cabin is visible through the trees on the north side of Beaver Creek. Use caution crossing Beaver Creek. USGS maps: Livengood A-2, A-3, B-2.

Windy Creek Trail. This White Mountains NRA trail is 9 miles in length, rated moderate to difficult with a 1,000-foot elevation change. It connects Wolf Run Cabin on the Colorado Creek Trail to Fossil Creek Trail at Mile 22. Recommended for winter use (November to early April) because of wet, muddy sections of trail in summer. Beyond Wolf Run Cabin, the trail parallels Windy Creek and follows the creek drainage 5 miles up the valley, winding through black spruce forests and open meadows. The trail climbs steeply for 2 miles through Windy Gap and emerges on top of a plateau overlooking the Fossil Creek drainage with views of the White Mountains, Limestone Gulch and Windy Arch. The trail then descends into forest and drops steeply 1 mile to Fossil Creek and the Windy Gap Cabin. USGS maps: Livengood C-1, C-2.

 Hot Springs

Chena Hot Springs. Located 50 miles by air or about 60 miles by road from Fairbanks at the end of Chena Hot Springs Road. Chena Hot Springs were first reported in 1907 by U.S. Geological Survey field teams. The resort offers food, lodging, camping and swimming year-round. For more information: Chena Hot Springs, P.O. Box 58740, Fairbanks, AK 99711; phone (907) 452-7867, toll free (800) 478-4681 (U.S), fax (907) 456-3122, www.chenahotsprings.com. USGS map: Circle A-5.

Circle Hot Springs. About 100 miles northeast of Fairbanks, the springs are 8 miles off Mile 127.8 Steese Highway. Circle Hot Springs Resort offers year-round swimming, lodging, food and RV parking; phone (907) 520-5113.

Manley Hot Springs. Located 152 miles from Fairbanks via the Elliott Highway, the springs are on a hillside just outside the community of the same name. The private hot springs are contained in 3 concrete baths inside a greenhouse. Check in at the house on the hill, or phone (907) 672-3171 for reservations. A fee is charged.

Melozi (Melozitna) Hot Springs. Located on Hot Springs Creek, 30 miles northeast of Ruby. There is a group of 20 or so springs along the creek. USGS map: Melozitna A-4.

Tolovana Hot Springs. Located approximately 50 air miles northwest of Fairbanks on the southeast slope of Tolovana Hot Springs Dome. The hot springs are accessible by trail or bush plane. Primary access is via the 11-mile, year-round trail from Milepost 93 Elliott Highway. The privately-owned hot springs has 2 wood tubs and 2 cabins for rent. Tolovana provides a wilderness adventure, and facilities are rustic. Phone (907) 455-6706 for reservations (required) and directions (necessary). Or write Tolovana Hot Springs, P.O. Box 83058, Fairbanks, AK 99708; e-mail tolovana@mosquitonet.com, www.mosquitonet/~tolovana/. USGS map: Livengood B-4.

 Ice Fishing Huts

Alaska State Parks offers day-use ice fishing huts for rent at Quartz Lake SRA located at Milepost V 277.9 Richardson Highway, about 10 miles north of Delta Junction, and at Birch Lake SRS, Milepost V 306 Richardson Highway, 56 miles southeast of Fairbanks. Constructed by the Alaska Deparment of Fish and Game as part of the Federal Aid in Sport Fish Restoration Program, the huts have wood-burning stoves and 4 fishing holes each. All other equipment and supplies, including firewood, must be provided by the user. The huts are for fishing only; check-out time is midnight. Latrines are located on shore.

For rental information, contact Alaska State Parks, 3700 Airport Way, Fairbanks, AK 99709; phone (907) 451-2705, https://nutmeg.state.ak.us/ixpress/dnr/parks/icehuts.dml.

 Innoko National Wildlife Refuge

This refuge is located about 300 miles northwest of Anchorage in the central Yukon River valley. Its 2 units encompass approximately 4 million acres. The northern unit is administered by the Koyukuk National Wildlife Refuge office in Galena. The southern or main unit of approximately 3.85 million acres includes the middle portion of the Innoko River and its drainage. The Yukon River borders on the west, the Kaiyuh Mountains on the north, the Kuskokwim Mountains on the east and the Beaver Mountains on the south.

About half of the refuge consists of black spruce muskeg, wet meadow, and sedge or horsetail marsh. The other half is mostly white spruce and birch-covered hills, most of which do not exceed 1,000 feet in elevation. The rivers are lined with a combination of alder, birch and white spruce, as well as extensive willow bars. Thousands of lakes and ponds dot the wetlands area. Approximately 1.24 million acres are designated Wilderness Area, with restrictions on the use of certain motorized equipment and vehicles other than boats, snow-mobiles and floatplanes.

Climate: Summer temperatures may exceed 80°F although 60s and 70s are more common. Visitors should anticipate rain at any time during the spring, summer or fall and should carry rain gear. Also, a surprise freeze can happen even in the summer, particularly in June or August, so visitors should prepare accordingly. During the fall, it is wise to expect cold, wet weather. Winters are cold; the temperature may drop to -60°F.

Wildlife: This refuge was established to protect waterfowl nesting and breeding habitat. More than 300,000 waterfowl and shorebirds use the wetlands, which encompass nearly 80 percent of the refuge lands. This is an important nesting area for white-fronted and less-er Canada geese, pintail, wigeon, shoveler, scaup, scoter, red-necked grebe, lesser yellow-leg and Hudsonian godwit.

The refuge is home to moose, black and grizzly bears and wolves. Caribou use the refuge in winter when deep snow drives them down from the mountains. This area is also renowned for its beaver population. Other furbearers include muskrat, marten, wolverine, lynx, river otter and red fox.

Fish found in refuge waters include salmon, sheefish, grayling, blackfish, whitefish and northern pike.

Activities: Recreational opportunities include moose hunting, trapping, floating the Innoko and Iditarod rivers, hunting black bear, fishing, wildlife observation and photography. The refuge staff will assist in planning trips.

Access and Accommodations: Chartered aircraft from Anchorage, McGrath or Galena provide access to the refuge. Supplies and commercial lodging are available in McGrath and Galena; some supplies and limited lodging in Grayling; and limited supplies in Shageluk.

There are no facilities in the refuge; wilderness camping only. No roads or trails exist. Campers should be prepared for a wet environment and be sure to bring waterproof boots, a tent and warm sleeping bag. Drinking water should be boiled or purified. A first-aid kit and plenty of mosquito repellent are recommended. The Fish and Wildlife Service also recommends that anyone planning to enter the refuge check in with the refuge manager in McGrath for safety purposes.

For more information: Refuge Manager, Innoko National Wildlife Refuge, P.O. Box 69, McGrath, AK 99627; phone (907) 524-3251, fax (907) 524-2141, e-mail fw7_innoko_comment@fws.gov, www.r7.fws.gov/nwr/innoko/innwr.html.

USGS maps: Ophir, Holy Cross, Iditarod and Unalakleet for the lower unit and Nulato for the upper unit.

Kanuti National Wildlife Refuge

This 1.6-million-acre refuge straddles the Arctic Circle approximately 150 miles north-west of Fairbanks and south of Bettles. It extends westward to the villages of Allakaket and Alatna. The refuge encompasses a portion of the Koyukuk River basin and the Kanuti flats near the southern foothills of the Brooks Range. It is characterized by lakes and marshes dotting the broad, rolling plain of the Kanuti and Koyukuk river valleys.

Climate: Kanuti's climate is typically continental. The long summer days are mild, with maximum temperatures mostly in the high 60s and low 70s. The sun does not set from June 2 through July 9. From November through March, minimum temperatures average below zero and readings of -45°F to -55°F are common. Annual precipitation averages approximately 14 inches. Snow has occurred during all months but July. Winds prevail from the north 10 months of the year, but are seldom strong.

Wildlife: Some 105 species of birds have been observed on the Kanuti, which provides important nesting habitat for waterfowl, particularly white-fronted geese, Canada geese, pintail, wigeon, scaup and scoters.

Portions of the large western Arctic caribou herd winter within the refuge. Black bears, grizzly bears, wolves, wolverines and moose are found there, along with numerous smaller mammals. Fish in refuge waters include 4 species of salmon, arctic char, grayling, whitefish, sheefish, lake trout, burbot and northern pike.

Activities: Fishing, hunting, trapping, wildlife observation, photography, camping and boating are the main activities in Kanuti. Backpacking is good in only a few areas due to the terrain.

Access and Accommodations: The refuge is accessible by charter air service from Bettles and by boat down the Koyukuk River from Bettles to Allakaket. Commercial and charter air service is available in Fairbanks to Bettles and in Allakaket. Overnight accommodations are available in Bettles but not Allakaket. On the refuge, there are no facilities; wilderness camping only. Visitors should arrive self-sufficient. As a safety precaution, visitors should leave a copy of their itinerary with a friend.

For more information: Contact Refuge Manager, Kanuti National Wildlife Refuge, Federal Bldg. and Courthouse, 101 12th Ave., Box 20, Fairbanks, AK 99701; phone (907) 456-0329, fax (907) 456-0506, email r7_kanwr@fws.gov, www.r7.fws.gov/nwr/kanuti/kan-nwr.html.

✺ The Kink

Originally the name of a sharp bend in the North Fork Fortymile River, it came to mean the 15-foot-wide channel (eroded to 50 feet by the 1970s) that was blasted 100 feet through a ridge that formed the neck in the bend.

In 1904, miners blasted through the channel to divert the flow of the river and leave approximately 2.8 miles of riverbed open for mining. It was abandoned in 1905 when prospects turned out to be unprofitable. Now on the National Register of Historic Places, The Kink was a major engineering feat at its time and place and is considered a permanent monument to man's undertakings in the pursuit of gold at the turn of the century.

The Kink is located 40 miles southwest of Eagle on the east side of the North Fork Fortymile River, about 1 mile south of the confluence of Hutchinson Creek.

Koyukuk National Wildlife Refuge

This 3-1/2-million-acre refuge is located 270 miles west of Fairbanks. Lying in the circular floodplain formed by the lower Koyukuk River, the refuge is heavily forested and contains much wetland. Fourteen rivers and hundreds of creeks meander throughout the refuge, providing habitat for salmon, beaver and waterfowl. More than 15,000 lakes are also found in the refuge. The topography is relatively gentle. Lowland forests gradually merge with tundra vegetation at the 3,000-foot elevation.

The refuge has a 400,000-acre wilderness area surrounding the 10,000-acre Nogahabara Sand Dunes. These, along with the Great Kobuk Sand Dunes, are the only large, active dune fields in interior Alaska. Both were formed some 10,000 years ago by windblown deposits during the mid- to late Pleistocene period.

Wildlife: Moose frequent the area and are important to the subsistence economy of villages in the area. The entire region is part of the winter range of the western Arctic caribou and Galena Mountain herds. With the presence of both moose and caribou, wolves also are common. Black bears are abundant in the forests, and grizzly bears inhabit the open tundra at higher elevations and more frequently along river corridors. The refuge is productive beaver country and excellent habitat for other furbearers.

Fish available in the refuge include king and chum salmon. Whitefish and northern pike are abundant in lowlands, and arctic grayling are found in colder headwater streams.

Access and Accommodations: Access to the refuge is by boat, snowmobile or charter plane from Fairbanks or Galena. There are some groceries and accomodations in area villages; wilderness camping is permitted.

For more information: Koyukuk/Nowitna Refuge Complex Manager, P.O. Box 287, Galena, AK 99741-0287; phone (907) 656-1231, fax (907) 656-1708, email koyukuk@fws.gov, www.r7.fws.gov/nwr/koyukuk/kynwr.html.

Minto Flats State Game Refuge

Created in 1988, this state refuge encompasses more than 500,000 acres 35 miles west of Fairbanks and straddles the Tanana River. An enormous, low-lying wetlands north of the Tanana, Minto Flats is dotted with numerous lakes, oxbows and potholes. One of the highest quality waterfowl habitats in Alaska and probably in all of North America, Minto Flats is the third most popular duck hunting area in the state. The wetland is also an important year-round hunting, fishing and trapping area for local villagers and others, and archaeological evidence suggests use of the area by Athabascans predates historic contact.

Wildlife: The flats produce as many as 25,000 ducks annually and support a breeding population averaging 213 ducks per square mile. Trumpeter swans nest on numerous lakes dotting the area, and white-fronted geese, sandhill cranes, common and arctic loons nest on the flats. The flats are also an important staging area for waterfowl from the Yukon Flats and the North Slope during the fall migration. Predominant species are tundra swan, mallard, pintail, scaup, green-winged teal, redhead, bufflehead and gadwall.

Also found in the refuge are moose, black bear, a large beaver population, river otter, lynx, wolverine, wolf, coyote, red fox, ermine, mink, muskrat and marten.

Activities: The Alaska Department of Fish and Game reports more than 5,000 hunter days are logged each year, and more than 5,000 ducks and 350 geese are taken. Fishing for northern pike, burbot, sheefish, humpback whitefish, grayling and king, coho and chum salmon is also popular. Tolovana Lodge offers float trips throughout Minto Flats.

Accommodations: There are no developed public-use facilities in the refuge. A general store is located in Minto, a village adjacent to the flats. Accommodations are available by advanced reservation at Tolovana Lodge, located at the confluence of the Tanana and Tolovana rivers, 55 miles west of Nenana. (The lodge is accessed from Nenana; phone 907/832-5569.) Generally, those using the flats camp on one of the islands in the flats. Fresh water should be carried, and anyone headed for the area during the fall hunting season should be prepared for any type of weather, from 70°F to rain to snow. Hip boots are a must, and a boat or inflatable raft is also recommended.

Access: The flats can be reached by floatplane from Fairbanks; by boat from Minto, which can be reached from Fairbanks via the Elliott Highway; by boat from Nenana down the Tanana River, then up Swanneck Slough into the flats; or by the Murphy Dome Road. In winter, snow machines and skiplanes can be used.

For more information: Alaska Department of Fish and Game, 1300 College Road, Fairbanks, AK 99701; phone (907) 452-1531, fax (907) 452-6410.

Mountain Biking

Interior has many great opportunities for mountain biking, from trails to hundreds of miles of gravel road.

The BLM maintains several trails for bikes, hikers and off-road vehicles (ORVs) along the Denali Highway. These include Maclaren River Road, Maclaren Summit Trail, Osar Lake and Landmark Gap. For more information, contact the Bureau of Land Management, Northern Field Office, 1150 University Ave., Fairbanks, AK 99709; phone (907) 474-2200, http://aurora.ak.blm.gov/.

Dalton Highway. The Dalton Highway is 414 miles long from the Elliott Highway to Deadhorse. The route is ideal for cyclists seeking solitude and a challenging ride. The Dalton provides unique and beautiful scenery, wildlife viewing and other recreational activities. Conditions vary on this gravel road, and during some seasons, the surface is very rough. Watch for ruts, rocks, soft shoulders, trucks and road maintenance equipment. Calcium chloride is also used on the road to control dust. There are several 10- to 12-percent grades. Services along the highway are limited.

Denali Highway. Biking on the Denali Highway is popular and is one of the best ways to enjoy the sensational scenery in the area. The ride is rugged once the pavement ends 21 miles from Paxson. From this point, the road is improved gravel but has long stretches of washboard and large potholes. The highest point, Mclaren Summit, is 4,086 feet. This summit is the second highest pass on an Alaskan road. There are many opportunities for camping, hiking, fishing and other activities on the Denali Highway. There are also limited facilities along the way. Cyclists should use caution on this route, as there is plenty of motor vehicle traffic on the road.

Stampede Road. Stampede Road is a gravel road that accesses beautiful highland country on the north side of Denali. The road ends about 8 miles from the Parks Highway. Aside from scenic cycling, there is also wildlife viewing in the area. Camping, hunting and shooting are prohibited. There are limited accommodations along the scenic and historic road.

For detailed road logs of the Dalton Highway, Denali Highway and other Interior gravel roads, see *The MILEPOST®*, a complete guide to Alaska's road system.

🏃 Mountaineering

While Southcentral boasts the Chugach Range, with 21 peaks topping 7,000-feet, the Interior has the Alaska Range and the highest mountain in North America, Denali/Mt. McKinley's South Peak at 20,320 feet. McKinley's North Peak, at 19,470 feet, is the second highest peak in Alaska. The Alaska Range offers dozens of other mountaineering opportunities including nearby Mt. Foraker (17,400 feet) and Mt. Hunter (14,573 feet).

Snow and weather conditions for climbing major Alaska Range peaks are usually best from May through July. April is an excellent month for many of the lower peaks with conditions often cold and clear while winter extremes still linger on the high peaks like Denali and Foraker.

The Alaska Range is heavily glaciated, and extensive networks of crevasses exist throughout the range. Climbers should be experienced in glacier travel and consider being roped at all times when traversing glaciers. Most of the glaciers have icefall zones, and icefall activity can be unpredictable and fatal. Avalanches are also common in the Alaska Range. Good judgement and a careful approach to route-finding are the key elements in avoiding avalanches, according to the National Park Service. Carry avalanche transceivers, shovels and probe poles.

Registration is mandatory for climbs on Mt. McKinley and Mt. Foraker. Both peaks are within Denali National Park and Preserve and managed by the National Park Service. Information and registration forms are available from the Talkeetna Ranger Station, Denali National Park and Preserve, P.O. Box 588, Talkeetna, AK 99676; phone (907) 733-2231, fax (907) 733-1465, www.nps.gov/dena/mountaineering/.

The Talkeetna Ranger Station is staffed year-round by mountaineering rangers who have extensive experience in the Alaska Range. They can provide invaluable information and assistance to anyone planning a climb on Denali/Mt. McKinley and other area peaks, including the Ruth, Kitchatnas and Little Switzerland. The station maintains a reference library that includes more than 150 photographs of the Central Alaska Range by Bradford Washburn; a complete set of American Alpine Journals; a map collection; and specific route information for numerous peaks. Climbers are welcome to use all of these resources while in Talkeetna.

Denali/Mt. McKinley

Whether you call it Denali or McKinley, climbing the mountain requires planning. The National Park Service addresses everything from search and rescue to equipment and supplies at www.nps.gov/dena/mountain/talkeet.htm. The following information is excerpted from their web site.

Search and Rescue. Rescue is not automatic. Search and Rescue operations are conducted on a discretionary basis. The level of response is determined by field personnel based on their evaluation of the situation. Park users are expected to exhibit a degree of self-reliance and responsibility for their own safety commensurate with the degree of difficulty of the activities they undertake.

Mandatory Requirements (for Mt. McKinley and Mt. Foraker). Each expedition member must register with the Talkeetna Ranger Station at least 60 days in advance. Registration forms are available from the Talkeetna Ranger Station.

All of the group's forms should be sent in together. Since the rangers deal with over 300 expeditions each year, each party must have a distinct name that is used on all correspondence.

All climbers must stop by the Talkeetna Ranger Station for an orientation and briefing prior to their expedition's departure. Climbers must check out with the Talkeetna Ranger Station immediately upon their return from the mountain.

Everything taken into the park and backcountry must be brought out. Do not leave any permanent caches on the mountain. Abandoning surplus food, fuel, wands, and other equipment in caches or disposing of it in crevasses is prohibited. Follow the instructions provided by rangers on proper human waste disposal. Citations are given for improper disposal of garbage and human waste.

If you plan to climb with a guide, make sure your guide is authorized to operate within Denali National Park and Preserve. There are 6 authorized guide services; call the Talkeetna Ranger Station for names. Unauthorized guiding is illegal, and your climb could be cancelled at any time.

Climbing Clean. Everything MUST be carried off the mountain. Sleds or haul bags make excellent descent towing bags.

Temporary caches should be buried under large snow blocks or loose snow at a minimum of 3 feet deep. When relaying loads, be careful to bury your food caches to protect them from ravens. More than one expedition has come to grief from the depredations of these birds. At lower altitudes, wolverines and bears have been known to destroy caches near the edge of glaciers. It is not permitted to leave permanent caches in the park.

All drinking water is obtained from melted snow. Drinking water contaminated by human waste can cause intestinal disorders, and the resulting dehydration may become a serious problem at high altitude. Use pit toilets where provided. Elsewhere, biodegradable bags are used for latrines. Plan on bringing additional bags for this use. Detailed instructions on disposal of human waste are available from the Talkeetna Ranger Station.

Expeditions must remove their own fixed lines and make an effort to remove old lines. Several lines are managed by the Park Service seasonally on the West Buttress headwall between 15,500 and 16,200 feet. Other than these, all other fixed ropes must be removed on descent. Old fixed lines are often in bad condition and should be considered a hazard. One climber was killed when he relied on an old fixed line.

The Expedition. The expedition should consist of at least 2 to 4 members. A larger expedition of 4 or more provides greater inherent strength and self-rescue capability. Expeditions should not exceed 12 members. Each member should have solid mountaineering skills, glacier travel knowledge, stamina, conditioning, excellent equipment and the mental fortitude to survive in severe arctic conditions.

Solo Climbing. A solo climber has virtually no self-rescue ability in the event of a serious accident or illness, and he/she creates undue risks to the search and rescue party. The Park Service strongly recommends against solo travel.

Climbing Season. The highest success rates occur in June. Colder minimum temperatures and strong northwest winds commonly occur in May. It is not uncommon to find it -50°F at the 17,200-foot camp in early May. Late June and July are warmer but more unsettled. By late July, travel on the lower glaciers is made difficult by melting snow bridges over crevasses and by more inclement weather with heavier snowfall and increased avalanche danger. Winter climbing in Denali borders on the ridiculous. Average temperatures range from -30°F to -70°F at the 19,000-foot level. The jet stream (100mph plus winds) often descends over the mountain's upper flanks in winter. Combine this wind with the venturi effect that doubles wind velocity in such areas as Denali Pass, and you have wind chill off the charts and one of the most hostile environments on this planet. Some of the world's best climbers have either disappeared or perished in winter.

Routes. With over 30 routes on Denali, the West Buttress, West Rib, Cassin Ridge and Muldrow are the most frequently climbed. The West Buttress and the Muldrow are the easiest ascent routes; the primary climbing difficulties being crevasses, steep ice and exposed, ice-covered ridges. Denali is attempted by approximately 1,200 climbers each season with more than 80 percent attempting the West Buttress. With this many climbers in such a short season, climbers can expect to encounter several hundred others.

Approaches. From the south, the usual approach is by ski plane from Talkeetna to the Southeast Fork of the Kahiltna Glacier or to the Ruth Glacier in the Don Sheldon Amphitheater.

Specific route information can be obtained from the Talkeetna Ranger Station. Talkeetna is also the base of operations for the air services. Helicopters are not allowed to land in the park unless there is an emergency.

Acclimatization. Depending on the individual, it requires 1 to 2 weeks to become well acclimatized to a given altitude on Denali. Talkeetna is close to sea level, which is a major disadvantage for someone who has established some acclimatization and is waiting to fly in. The mountaineering booklet available at the Talkeetna Ranger Station gives a day-by-day schedule for the fastest recommended rate of ascent of the West Buttress.

Medical Problems. The lack of oxygen (hypoxia) associated with high altitude climbing and the extreme cold of Denali can cause the following medical problems: mental impairment and poor judgement; dehydration; fatigue; lassitude; hypothermia; frostbite; acute mountain sickness (AMS); high altitude pulmonary edema (HAPE); cerebral edema (CE); and retinal hemorrhages. Another potentially fatal hazard is carbon monoxide poisoning from cooking in poorly ventilated tents.

Equipment and Supplies. For a complete and detailed list of equipment and supplies, contact the Talkeetna Ranger Station, or visit www.nps.gov/dena/mountain/talkeet.htm.

Nome Creek Valley

Nome Creek Valley is located north of the Steese Highway in White Mountains National Recreation Area. Since the 1890s, miners and trappers have been living a subsistence lifestyle in this valley. And today, visitors can camp, hike, fish and gold pan just as the early sourdoughs did.

Access is via a gravel road from Mile 57 Steese Highway, then 6 miles on U.S. Creek Road to Nome Creek Road.

The Nome Creek Valley offers 2 hiking trails (Quartz Creek and Table Top Mountain), 2 campgrounds (Mt. Prindle and Ophir), catch-and-release fishing for arctic grayling in Nome Creek and access for floating Beaver Creek.

The most popular attraction in Nome Creek Valley is the Nome Creek Gold Panning Area. This is a section of Nome Creek that has been set aside and designated for recreational gold panning. Visitors can pan for gold using only hand tools and light equipment, including gold pans, rocker boxes, sluice boxes, picks and shovels. The site offers travelers a chance to travel back in time and experience the activity that brought so many to Alaska during the Gold Rush. Please use caution when panning; use back eddies and side pools to reduce silt entering the main channel, and pan only in stream channels or on gravel bars to reduce erosion and protect vegetation.

For more information: Bureau of Land Management, Northern Field Office, 1150 University Ave., Fairbanks, AK 99709; phone (907) 474-2200, http://aurora. ak.blm.gov/WhiteMtns/html/nomecr.html#goldpan.

Nowitna National Wildlife Refuge

This 2.1-million-acre refuge is located approximately 200 miles west of Fairbanks in the central Yukon River valley. It protects a lowland basin bordering the Nowitna and Yukon rivers and encompasses forested lowlands, hills, lakes, marshes, ponds and streams. The dominant feature is the Nowitna River. Over 220 miles of its nearly 300 total miles runs through the refuge, and the entire river is a nationally designated wild river. This river is considered outstanding for float trips and also provides spawning grounds for salmon, northern pike and sheefish. The primary purpose of the refuge is to conserve fish and wildlife populations, including moose, furbearers and waterfowl, and habitats in their natural diverse states.

Nowitna is 1 of 4 refuges (the others are Innoko, Kanuti and Koyukuk) encompassed by solar basins, which are characterized by encircling hills, light winds, low rainfall, severe winters and short, warm summers.

Wildlife: The forested lowlands of Nowitna Refuge provide excellent wetland habitats that support abundant populations of fish and waterfowl. Up to 20,000 waterfowl, including trumpeter swans, are annually produced on the refuge. Other wildlife found here include moose, black and grizzly bears and wolves.

Activities: Moose hunting is a major activity on the refuge. Marten, mink, wolverine, lynx, beaver and muskrat are important furbearers that provide income, food and recreation for local residents. Fishing for northern pike and sheefish is excellent. Other fish found in refuge waters include salmon, whitefish and arctic grayling.

Access and Accommodations: Access to Nowitna is by boat or charter air service, primarily from Fairbanks. The nearest community to the refuge is Ruby, situated just west of the western boundary of the refuge.

For more information: Complex Manager, Koyukuk/Nowitna Refuge Complex, P.O. Box 287, Galena, AK 99741-0287; phone (907) 656-1231, fax (907) 656-1708, email nowitna@fws.gov, www.r7.fws.gov/nwr/nowitna/nownwr.html.

River Running

The boating season generally begins in June in the Interior, with maximum stream flow occurring late May to early June. There is usually sufficient flow for small boats on most rivers through August although low water can mean "boat dragging" for rafters on some rivers during July. Rapid runoff from rainstorms during July and August can cause the river to rise as much as several feet within hours, posing a hazard for floaters. This is remote country, and you are a long way from help. Plan accordingly.

The Interior region has 5 National Wild and Scenic Rivers: Birch Creek and the Fortymile River, managed by the BLM; Beaver Creek, managed by the BLM and U.S. Fish and Wildlife Service; the Charley River, managed by the National Park Service; and the Nowitna, managed by U.S. Fish and Wildlife Service.

River runners should contact the appropriate land manager for more detailed information on rivers listed here. Special recreation permits are required for river guides to operate commercial activities on public lands. Check with the appropriate land agency for a list of authorized guides. For BLM-managed rivers, contact the Bureau of Land Management, Northern Field Office, 1150 University Avenue, Fairbanks, AK 99709; phone (907) 474-2250, www.aurora.ak.blm.gov.

For additional information about the Charley River and the Yukon River within the preserve, contact Yukon-Charley Rivers National Preserve, P.O. Box 167, Eagle, AK 99738;

phone (907) 547-2233, email YUCH_Eagle_Office@nps.gov, www.nps.gov/yuch.

Also obtain information on current river conditions from reliable local sources, such as bush pilots, park rangers and local guides. The local club, Fairbanks Paddlers, posts river reports on their web site at www.fairbankspaddlers.org/.

Beaver Creek. Beaver Creek originates within White Mountains NRA northeast of Fairbanks and then flows in a northerly direction through the Yukon Flats National Wildlife Refuge into the Yukon River. The entire 127 miles are designated National Wild and Scenic River. This clear-water stream is described as moderately swift and shallow, classified as Class I overall by the BLM. Watch for sweepers. Canoes, kayaks and rafts are suitable to Victoria Creek. Rafts are not recommended for the slow water through Yukon Flats. Good grayling fishing. Other fish available in Beaver Creek are burbot, whitefish and northern pike. Wildlife includes moose, Dall sheep, beaver, bears, eagles, owls and ducks. This is considered a very scenic float through the rolling hills and past the limestone peaks of the White Mountains.

From its headwaters, the river drops 9 feet per mile to the end of the wild river corridor, 16 miles below Victoria Creek, 127 miles away. The trip to this takeout point usually takes 5 to 7 days. Exit is by floatplane or gravel bar landing approximately 2 miles downstream from Victoria Creek. It is possible to continue on from this takeout point, as the river meanders north through Yukon Flats National Wildlife Refuge to the Yukon River, and exit at the Yukon River Bridge on the Dalton Highway. This segment is another 268 miles, which takes approximately 8 to 14 days.

The Beaver Creek put in point is at the lower end of Nome Creek Road, 19 miles from Milepost F 57.3 Steese Highway via U.S. Creek Road. Arrange for air charter pickup from Victoria Creek or vehicle pickup from Yukon River Bridge at 56 Mile on the Dalton Highway. USGS maps: Circle B-6, C-6, D-5, D-6; Livengood B-1, B-2, C-1, C-2, D-1.

Birch Creek. A National Wild and Scenic River, Birch Creek originates about 70 miles northeast of Fairbanks and flows generally east then north into the Yukon River. Most of the 126 miles of Birch Creek designated wild and scenic river is within the Steese National Conservation Area. The river continues for another 218 miles to the Yukon.

This river is accessible by vehicle at both ends from the Steese Highway. The put in is at the upper Birch Creek Wayside at Twelvemile Creek at Milepost F 94 Steese Highway, where there is a parking area and canoe launch. The takeout point is at the Lower Birch Creek Wayside at Milepost F 140.4 Steese Highway. It is 126 miles between these points; the trip generally takes 5 to 10 days.

Birch Creek is classified as Class I and II, with some Class III rapids. Canoes, kayaks or rafts all are suitable although paddlers have pointed out that rafts are better only if the river is high. The upper 10 miles may be shallow and require lining through riffles. The relatively short stretches of white water occur between Clums Fork and South Fork, with a stretch of Class II "rock garden" rapids just below Clums Fork, followed by the Class III "Shotgun" rapids. During high water, also watch for standing waves and hydraulics. Fishing for grayling, northern pike and whitefish. Watch for peregrine falcons in the cliffs. Good camping on gravel bars except during high water. The river corridor is closed to the summer use of motorized vehicles. USGS maps: Circle A-3, A-4, B-1 to B-4, C-1.

Black River. This slow, meandering stream flows some 200 miles to join the Porcupine River, about 17 miles northeast of Fort Yukon. Much of the river is within Yukon Flats National Wildlife Refuge. The section above the confluence of the Salmon Fork flows moderately fast (3 to 4 mph) through forested lowlands of white spruce and willow. Below the Salmon Fork confluence, the river slows to 2 to 3 mph as it widens and passes along numerous bluffs. Below Chalkyitsik, the river slows further to 1 to 2 mph as the meanders increase in size.

This trip takes approximately 13 to 16 days from the vicinity of Birch Lake to Fort Yukon or 9 to 10 days from Birch Lake to Chalkyitsik. Canoes or kayaks are suitable for this trip.

Above the Salmon Fork, and again upstream from Chalkyitsik, sand or gravel bars are infrequent or not suitable for campsites. Upstream winds on the lower river can create whitecaps in a short time. There is low water after July 1, and the river is not usually floatable above Chalkyitsik. Views are generally limited to the river corridor because of high banks although bluffs below Salmon Fork add variety.

Fishing varies from poor to fair depending on water conditions and season for grayling, Dolly Varden, northern pike, whitefish and sheefish. Moose, bear and other wildlife inhabit the area, but high vegetation limits viewing. Waterfowl is abundant.

Access is by floatplane from Fort Yukon to the river or to adjacent lakes between Salmon and Grayling forks. Exit is by floatplane from the Black or Porcupine rivers, by scheduled air service from Chalkyitsik, or float to Fort Yukon. To reach Fort Yukon, paddle 3 miles up the Sucker River from its confluence with the Porcupine River to a road-accessible landing. USGS maps: Black River A-3, B-3, B-4, C-4 to C-6; Fort Yukon C-1 to C-3.

Chandalar River. Both main forks head in the Brooks Range and flow south to become the Chandalar River, which empties into the Yukon River south of Venetie. Below the confluence of the North and East Fork Chandalar rivers, it is quite fast and never dull. The Junjik River, which joins the east fork above Arctic Village, offers whitewater challenges. The upper East Fork Chandalar is very fast but not spiked with rapids. The more difficult North Fork flows through Chandalar Lake.

From the usual put in on the East Fork Chandalar, there are 72 miles of fast, flat water to Arctic Village. For those trying the Junjik, it's Class II, descending at 6 feet per mile, to the East Fork Chandalar, then on to Arctic Village for a total of 40 river miles. From Arctic Village, the East Fork Chandalar is Class II, dropping at 7 feet per mile for 160 river miles, to its confluence with the North Fork. From the usual put in at Chandalar Lake, the North Fork offers 120 miles of Class II and III, dropping at 15 feet per mile. Below the confluence of the North and East forks, the Chandalar is 90 river miles of flat water, dropping at 5 feet per mile, to the Yukon.

The East Fork Chandalar is bounded on the east by the Venetie Reservation, owned by the people of Venetie and Arctic Village, and by Arctic National Wildlife Refuge to the north and west. The Chandalar River is bounded to the northeast by the reservation and to the southwest by Yukon Flats National Wildlife Refuge. Camping is permitted on wildlife refuge lands; do not use reservation lands without permission.

Access is by charter air service from Fairbanks or Fort Yukon to the rivers. Exit is by scheduled air service from Arctic Village or Venetie.

Charley River. All 106 miles of this National Wild and Scenic River flow within Yukon-Charley Rivers National Preserve. The Charley originates at the 4,000-foot level and flows northeast to join the Yukon River. From the put in point at Copper Creek, it is a 4-day float to the Yukon, then another 2 days to Circle. Access is by charter aircraft from Fairbanks, Circle, Eagle or Tok. There are 3 landing strips: Joseph, Three Finger Rapids and Gelvin's.

The Charley is rated Class II, with a few areas rated Class III. Paddlers should be experienced. Inflatable rafts are most commonly used on the river. The Charley flows from its headwaters with an average gradient of 31 feet per mile and an average current of 6 to 8 mph. During high water, the upper two-thirds of the river provide a good whitewater experience. As the water level lowers, maneuvering becomes a constant necessity, and some rapids must be scouted to determine the best channel. The Charley is considered good to excellent for grayling fishing.

Exit the Charley at the Yukon River confluence by floatplane or by riverboat to Eagle, or continue on to Circle. Most paddlers go on to Circle. USGS maps: Charley River A-4, A-5, B-4 to B-6; Circle D-1; Eagle C-6, D-5, D-6.

Chena River. A tributary of the Tanana River, the Chena is the focal point for the Chena River SRA. There are several launch points along Chena Hot Springs Road. Local paddlers suggest a float from Milepost 39.5 to 37.9 for easy paddling; Milepost 44.1 to 37.9 for a longer float; and Milepost 52.3 to 47.3 for paddlers with more skill. Allow about 1 hour on the river for each road mile traveled. The Chena should not be underestimated. The river is cold and the current very strong. Watch for river-wide logjams and sweepers. Access to the Chena is from Fairbanks via the Steese Highway to Chena Hot Springs Road. USGS maps: Fairbanks D-1, D-2.

Fortymile River. This clear-water stream located in east-central Alaska is fed by numerous creeks and streams and flows eastward into the Yukon River at Fortymile in Canada. It is over 392 miles long, of which 392 miles is designated a National Wild and Scenic River. Mining claims cover several stretches of the Fortymile, and virtually all of the bed of the South Fork is claimed. (Although the Fortymile River is a national wild and scenic river, the riverbed belongs to the state, which allows underwater mining claims.) *NOTE: Mining claims are posted. Please avoid these areas!*

There are 2 major options for float trips on the Fortymile: the Middle Fork or South Fork. Between these there are numerous access points, both road and fly-in, and a variety of trips of varying lengths. For the Middle Fork trip, charter out from Tok to the airstrip at an abandoned mining settlement at the confluence of Joseph Creek and the Middle Fork Fortymile. Access to the river is by a 50-yard trail from the east end of the airstrip. There are takeouts at the Fortymile Bridge, Milepost 113.2 on the Taylor Highway, and at the Clinton Creek bridge at Clinton, YT, Canada. If floating the Fortymile to the Yukon River, travelers will cross into Canada on the Fortymile and then back into the United States on the Yukon. Upon arriving in Clinton, YT, travelers must report to Canadian customs at the Top of the World Highway. (After reentering the United States on the Yukon River, check in again with U.S. customs at Eagle.) If leaving the river at the Fortymile Bridge, land just downstream from the bridge on the right bank.

The 90-mile trip from Joseph to the Fortymile Bridge usually takes 4 to 5 days; the 182 miles from Joseph to Eagle via the Yukon River takes about 7 to 9 days.

The Middle Fork is classified by BLM as Class I overall. However, there are several Class II rapids, as well as a Class V rapid. In late July and August, the river may be low, making for a safer if slower voyage. In general, the rapids become progressively more difficult downstream, but all can be checked out on foot first and easily portaged. The Class III rapids, known as "The Chute" is on the North Fork Fortymile just below its confluence with the Middle Fork. Exercise extreme care at the first right turn after the confluence. Canoes can be lined on the right bank. Rafts should stay close to the right bank. A few miles farther is the Class V rapids known as "The Kink." A few miles downriver from O'Brien Creek is the Class III rapids known as "Deadman Riffle," which is hazardous for canoes. This area is not far from the Canadian border. Shortly before reaching Clinton, there is a Class IV rapids called "The Canyon." Line from either bank depending on water level. This rapid is in 2 sections separated by a quarter mile of calm water; it is very dangerous during high water. There is road access once again at the Clinton Creek Bridge, or floaters can continue on to the Yukon River and float the 57 miles to Eagle. At Eagle, there are 2 boat landings. The upstream landing is generally preferred because vehicles can be driven very close to the water. The downstream landing requires a 2-story climb up a steep stairway to reach downtown Eagle.

Floating the clear-water South Fork Fortymile will avoid The Chute and The Kink. This fork is Class I overall, with some Class II and III rapids.

Access points to the Fortymile National Wild and Scenic River system from the Taylor Highway are: the bridge over the West Fork of the Dennison Fork of the Fortymile River, Milepost TJ 49.3; the BLM Mosquito Fork Bridge River Access at Milepost TJ 64.3; from Airport Road below Chicken airstrip; and at the BLM South Fork River Access at Milepost TJ 75.3.

The trip is 72 miles from the West Fork of the Dennison Fork to Fortymile Bridge and takes 3 to 4 days; from Fortymile Bridge to Eagle via the Yukon River, it is 92 miles and takes 4 to 5 days. A few miles above the confluence of the South and North forks, floaters will pass by the site of Franklin, a small mining community established about 1887. It was the hub of mining activity for the southern portion of the Fortymile mining district.

For additional information about the Fortymile River system, contact the Bureau of Land Management in Fairbanks, or the BLM Field Office in Tok, P.O. Box 307, Tok, AK 99780; phone (907) 883-5121. USGS maps: Eagle B-3 to B-5, C-3. Canadian Maps: 40-Mile 116-C7, Cassiar Cis. 116-C8, Shell Creek 116-C9, Mount Gladman 116-ClO.

Innoko River. The Innoko River heads south of Cloudy Mountain in the Kuskokwim

Mountains, northwest of McGrath, and flows northeast and southwest 500 miles to junction with the Yukon River. The middle portion of the river flows through Innoko National Wildlife Refuge and is accessible for an easy Class I to Class II float for experienced wilderness paddlers.

The river, from put in at Ophir to Cripple Landing, is very scenic with wildflowers along the hillsides and abundant wildlife, including grizzly and black bear, moose, wolf, otter, marten, beaver, porcupine and a variety of waterfowl. Fishing for grayling and pike. Numerous small waterfalls tumble into the Innoko along the way.

Historic sites along the upper river include the site of Folger, near the mouth of Folger Creek, and Cripple Landing, just above the North Fork. Little evidence of a town remains at Folger, once a thriving community that supplied mines to the northeast. At Cripple Landing, there is an old trading post/post office building (privately owned) and 3 abandoned cabins. Like Folger, Cripple Landing was a supply point for area mines during the early 1900s.

Closer to the junction of the Innoko and Dishna rivers is Rennie's Landing, where 2 buildings and a warehouse remain. Privately owned, this site serves as a fall and winter trapping headquarters. The site of Simel's trading post, also known as Fairview, is 2.6 miles above the confluence and is marked only by a few foundation outlines on the rapidly eroding river bank. Across the river at Simel's, hidden by willow and cottonwood trees, are the boiler and paddle-wheel from one of the old steamers that plied the river during the gold rush days.

Eighteen miles below the mouth of the Dishna River is the site of Diskaket, an Athabascan winter village that became a crossroads on the gold rush trails. Remains of three buildings and a cemetery are all that's left of the old village, which has been nominated as a National Historic Site. From Diskaket to the abandoned village of Holigachuk (privately owned), just upriver from Shageluk, only occasional cabin sites show evidence of man's presence.

Watch for sweepers. Wind and rain can slow progress, and paddling will be necessary as the river slows. Best time for a river trip is usually in July. Normally clear, the Innoko may be muddy during mining season.

Recommended float is from Ophir to Shageluk, near the mouth of the Innoko. Takeout point during low water is by wheel aircraft at Cripple Landing or by float-equipped aircraft from the Dishna River down (upriver below North Fork only during high water). Arrange with air taxi operators in Galena, McGrath, Bethel or Aniak. Ophir is accessed by road from Takotna.

For more information: Refuge Manager, Innoko National Wildlife Refuge, P.O. Box 69, McGrath, AK 99627; phone (907) 524-3251. USGS maps: Ophir A-2, B-2, C-1, C-2, C-3, D-1, D-2.

Kantishna River. The Kantishna is an ancient route between the Tanana and the Kuskokwim (via the Lake Minchumina portage). In later years, many prospectors and trappers traveled up the river, summer and winter, to work their claims or traplines along the foothills of Mount McKinley.

This river is not difficult. It meanders and flows slowly. More skillful paddlers may wish to try an alternate route on the tributary stream, Moose Creek, which has some rapids and shallow stretches in dry seasons. Canoes, kayaks and riverboats are suitable.

Access is by air charter service from Anchorage to Lake Minchumina or by scheduled air service to the community of Lake Minchumina. Float the Muddy River, which drains Lake Minchumina, east 25 miles to Birch Creek, which joins shortly thereafter with the McKinley River to become the Kantishna. From the outlet of Lake Minchumina to the confluence of the Kantishna and the Tanana River is 220 miles of flat water. USGS maps: Mount McKinley D-3, D-4, C-4, B-4, B-3, A-3; Kantishna River B-1, B-2, C-1.

Nabesna River. This river heads at Nabesna Glacier and flows northeast to join with the Chisana River to form the Tanana River near Northway Junction on the Alaska Highway. The river begins in Wrangell-St. Elias National Park and Preserve and flows through Tetlin National Wildlife Refuge.

This cold stream is in a wide, graveled valley and is braided and quite fast at the start. Eventually, it slows to meander through the foothills and taiga forest east of the Wrangell

Mountains. The first 10 miles from the put in point are rated Class I to II, with a gradient of 20 feet per mile. The gradient for the next 15 miles of flat water is 13 feet per mile, and the gradient for the last 40 miles is 5 feet per mile. Canoes, kayaks or rafts are suitable.

The river can be reached from the 45-mile-long Nabesna Road, which leaves the Glenn Highway (Tok Cutoff) at Milepost 65.2 from Tok. This gravel road becomes very rough after Milepost 28.5; check on road conditions at the Slana Ranger Station. There are several creeks that must be forded. A trail approximately 5 miles long leads to the Nabesna River from Milepost 41. Exit the river at Northway or at the Alaska Highway at the confluence of the Chisana River. USGS maps: Nabesna B-4, C-4, C-3, D-3, D-2; Tanacross A-2.

Nenana River. The Nenana River heads at Nenana Glacier in the Alaska Range and flows north 140 miles to the Tanana River at the town of Nenana. This river is easily accessible at several locations on the Denali and Parks highways and the Alaska Railroad. A popular put in is at Mile 16 (from Cantwell) on the Denali Highway. Put ins on the Parks Highway are: McKinley Village Resort, Milepost A 231.1; Riley Creek Bridge, Milepost A 237.2; Nenana River Bridge No. 3, Milepost A 238; Healy, Milepost 248.8; Rex Bridge over Nenana, Milepost A 275.8. Put ins along the Alaska Railroad: Windy Station; Denali Park Station; Riley Creek Bridge; Healy and Nenana.

From the Mile 16 put in on the Denali Highway, the Nenana River is Class I to II for the 38 miles to McKinley Village. From this point for the next 32 miles to below Healy, heavy water and very difficult rapids rated at Class IV to V through a narrow canyon make the river suitable only for expert paddlers. Others should skirt this section via the Parks Highway. (Organized raft tours are offered down this part of the river by outfitters based near the entrance to Denali National Park and Preserve.) Below this canyon area, the Nenana's course to the Tanana has braided channels, but no difficult rapids. Canoes, kayaks and rafts are suitable for the upper and lower river. Kayaks or rafts only on the middle river.

The Upper Nenana River float runs approximately 18 river miles from the Mile 16 put in on the Denali Highway to the takeout at Nenana River Bridge No. 1 at Milepost A 215.7 Parks Highway. The river along this stretch is rated Class I to II. Below the bridge, the river rating changes to Class II, III and IV white water. USGS maps: Fairbanks A-5, B-5, C-5; Healy B-3, B-4, C-4, D-4, D-5.

Nowitna River. This river is 283 miles long, with 225 miles of the river located within Nowitna National Wildlife Refuge. It is designated a National Wild and Scenic River. The Nowitna heads in the forested uplands of the Kuskokwim Mountains and flows northeast to the Yukon River. With the exception of a 15-mile-long stretch through a canyon surrounded by high peaks, the river flows through terrain that is generally flat or low, rolling hills.

Broad, clear and deep, it is rated Class I white water and Class C flat water. High water and ice dams can back up the river in spring. The river is used by trappers in winter, and there are 9 trapline cabins within the river corridor. The Nowitna is also used by moose hunters during September.

The Nowitna River is approximately 200 miles from the nearest road and population center. Access is by riverboat or floatplane. For more information, contact the Refuge Manager, Nowitna National Wildlife Refuge, P.O. Box 287, Galena, AK 99741; phone (907) 656-1231.

Porcupine River. This river heads in Canada at N65°28', W139°32' and flows 460 miles to the Yukon River, 2 miles north of Fort Yukon. Difficulties along the river are minor, so the trip is considered suitable for families with older children. Canoes or kayaks are recommended for the trip; rafts are also suitable, but progress may be slower due to upstream, mid-afternoon winds.

The Porcupine is generally slow moving (2 to 4 mph) flat water to Class I with somewhat swifter current (4 to 6 mph) through multi-hued, steep-walled canyons beginning a few miles upstream from New Rampart House, in Yukon Territory. From the border to Fort Yukon, the river flows within the Yukon Flats National Wildlife Refuge. Downstream from Canyon Village, AK, the canyons give way to low rolling hills on either side of the river. Farther downstream, the river meanders across the wetlands of the Yukon Flats. To reach Fort Yukon, paddle 3 miles up the Sucker River from its confluence with the Porcupine River to a road-accessible landing.

The most common put in is at Old Crow, YT. From there, it generally takes 6 to 10 days to float the 250 miles to Fort Yukon. It is also possible to charter a plane to the upper Porcupine or to Summit Lake on the Bell River, a tributary of the Porcupine, and extend the trip some 250 additional miles.

Grayling, whitefish, northern pike, sheefish and burbot are present in the Porcupine. Coho, king and chum salmon from the Bering Sea migrate up this system, one of the longest fish migrations in North America.

Old Crow is served by scheduled commercial air service from Whitehorse or Dawson City, YT. Fort Yukon, where travelers can clear customs upon reentering the United States, is served by scheduled commercial air service from Fairbanks. USGS maps: Coleen A-1 to A-4, B-1, B-2; Black River D-4 to D-6; Fort Yukon C-1 to C-3, D-1.

Yukon River. The Yukon River originates in the coastal mountains of Canada and flows 2,300 miles in a great, wide arc to the Bering Sea. Popular put ins for the Yukon River are at Dawson City in the Yukon; Eagle, at the end of the Taylor Highway; Circle, at the end of the Steese Highway; and about 1/2 mile upstream from the Yukon River Bridge on the Dalton Highway (Milepost 56). Exit points are at Eagle, Circle, Fort Yukon, the Dalton Highway or Tanana. Or pickup by charter air service can be arranged from the river. Floaters can also continue from Tanana down the broad, flat-water Yukon to the Bering Sea. Some communities along the way have overnight accommodations, and most of the larger ones have scheduled air service. The Yukon River is suitable for canoes, kayaks and rafts.

If starting your float trip in Canada, be sure to check in with U.S. customs upon arrival at Eagle. Between Eagle and Circle, the Yukon flows for 128 miles through Yukon-Charley Rivers National Preserve and, shortly after Circle, into Yukon Flats National Wildlife Refuge for 300 miles. According to the National Park Service, "The segment of the Yukon beginning at Dawson and continuing downstream through [Yukon-Charley] preserve comprises one of the most scenic yet safely traversable stretches of any large river in North America."

Floaters generally take 4 to 10 days to travel from Eagle to Circle, depending on whether they take any side trips up tributaries or day hikes. Most camp on open beaches or river bars where winds keep the insects at bay.

Downriver from Eagle, the vivid black-and-white limestones of Calico Bluff form one of the most striking attractions on the river. NOTE: Land on both sides of the Yukon River from Calico Bluff to Woody Island is privately owned.

The river enters Yukon-Charley Preserve 12 miles north of Eagle and leaves the preserve 14 miles south of Circle. There are numerous historic sites along the Yukon within Yukon-Charley Rivers Preserve, many dating from the gold rush: Nation City, Washington Creek Steam Tractor, Charley Village, Frank Slaven's Roadhouse and Coal Creek Dredge. There are 6 public-use cabins along the river; see Cabins this section.

Through the preserve, the river drops 230 feet for an average gradient of 1.5 feet per mile, producing a 6- to 8-mph current. Flows of 10 to 11 mph occur during and just after breakup, which usually takes place in early May. Width of the river along this stretch varies from less than 1/2 mile to several miles near Circle, where the stream becomes braided, making it difficult to pick out the main channel. There are no rapids on this section, but reef-formed riffles may be encountered in the low water of late summer, and debris may be encountered in early summer. Beware of the occasional whirlpool. In any season, strong winds may develop, building waves of 2 or 3 feet over exposed stretches; small boats should head for shore at such times.

The Yukon River enters Yukon Flats National Wildlife Refuge along its southern boundary approximately 10 miles downstream from Circle. Then, it flows northwesterly in a braided channel for some 60 miles to Fort Yukon, where it bends and flows southwesterly for another 240 miles in a meandering course with many sloughs before leaving the refuge in a narrow valley between the Ray and White mountains.

Fort Yukon is the primary community along this stretch of the river. Floaters generally take 4 to 7 days to pass through the refuge.

Downstream from the wildlife refuge is the Rampart section, from the Dalton Highway to Tanana. This 128-mile section of the river classified as Class I has broad vistas, mile-wide river channels, high rock bluffs and hills covered with spruce and paper birch. From the Dalton Highway, it generally takes 5 days to float to Tanana. After the village of Rampart, the river passes between the high walls of Rampart Canyon.

USGS maps: (From Eagle to Circle) Charley River A-1, A-2, B-2 to B-6, C-6, D-6; Circle C-1, D-1; Eagle C-1, D-1. (From Circle to Dalton Highway) Fort Yukon, Beaver. (From Dalton Highway to Tanana) Livengood C-6, D-6; Tanana A-3 to A-5, B-1 to B-3, C-1, D-1.

Rock Climbing

Rock climbing in the Interior provides a unique wilderness adventure. There are several areas for good climbing in the region, but the most popular are Angel Creek Rocks, Granite Tors and Grapefruit Rocks.

Mosquitoes are abundant in these areas; head nets and/or bug repellent is highly recommended. Also, bring water because there are few sources at the rocks. Obtain all supplies before departing Fairbanks. You will need, at bare minimum, a climbing harness, rock shoes, locking carabiners, a belay/rappel device, a climbing rope and webbing.

If you are an inexperienced climber, the University of Alaska Fairbanks offers a rock climbing class (www.uaf.edu).

Angel Creek Rocks. Angel Creek Rocks are a series of granite outcroppings at Milepost 49 Chena Hot Springs Road. There is a 3.5-mile loop trail to the rocks (see Hiking Trails this section). In some places, the rock sloughs off, but there are other places where the rock is solid and rough; choose routes carefully. The rocks are also covered with lichen and moss. This is primarily a top-rope climbing area.

Granite Tors. The tors are located northeast of Fairbanks at Milepost 39 Chena Hot Springs Road. There is parking at the campground. Access is by a 15-mile loop trail up the south bank of the Chena River (see Hiking Trails this section). The trail forks as it leaves the river, and the right fork of loop trail takes you 5 miles to first rocks, which are the most developed. The left fork leads to the North Tor and East Tor Island Group. There are day climbs at Granite Tors, but the more distant tors are usually overnight trips. Water may be a problem after June, and foggy weather can make navigation on the trails difficult. There are many game trails in the area, so be sure to stay on the main trails.

Grapefruit Rocks. Grapefruit is a group of limestone crags located 40 miles north of Fairbanks on the Elliott Highway. Just past small bridge that crosses Globe Creek, Upper Grapefruit can be seen on the hillside. There is a large pullout for parking just past the road cut. The hike to the rocks is 15 minutes. Lower Grapefruit is accessible from another large turnout about 100 yards up the road and a 10-minute walk down a jeep trail to the rocks.

Steese National Conservation Area

The Steese National Conservation Area is managed by the BLM and encompasses 1.2 million acres of public land which are divided into the North and South units. It is located 70 miles northeast of Fairbanks along the Steese Highway. Congress established the area in 1980 as part of the Alaska National Interest Lands Conservation Act (ANILCA) for the "immediate and future protection" and conservation of scenic, scientific, cultural and other area resources.

Steese is home to Birch Creek National Wild and Scenic River, Pinnell Mountain National Recreation Trail and crucial wildlife habitat, including caribou calving grounds and home range and Dall sheep habitat. Steese is one of the 9 national conservation areas in the U.S.

Activities in Steese Conservation Area include canoeing and rafting on Birch Creek, hiking, backpacking, hunting, fishing, trapping, climbing, camping, cross-country skiing, snowshoeing, snowmobiling and bird watching. Hovercraft and airboats are prohibited, and off-road vehicles are restricted in some areas. Camping at one site for longer than 10 days in a calendar year is also prohibited.

For more information: Bureau of Land Management, Northern Field Office, 1150 University Ave., Fairbanks, AK 99709; phone (907) 474-2200, http://aurora.ak.blm.gov/Steese/GenInfo.htm.

 Tanana Valley State Forest

Created in 1983, this 1.81-million-acre state forest is located almost entirely within the Tanana River basin and includes 200 miles of the Tanana River. It extends from near the Canadian border approximately 265 miles northwest to Manley Hot Springs and encompasses areas as far south as Tok. The forest is interspersed with private and other state lands throughout the basin. The elevation varies from 275 feet along the Tanana River below its confluence with the Kantishna River to more than 5,000 feet in the Alaska Range, south of Tok. The Bonanza Creek Experimental Forest west of Fairbanks is located within the State Forest.

Almost 90 percent of the land base is forested by spruce and hardwoods. Seven percent is shrubland. The major tree species are paper birch, quaking aspen, balsam poplar, black spruce, white spruce and tamarack. Over 60 percent of the forest, about 1.1 million acres, is suitable for timber production. Forty-four rivers, streams and lakes within the forest have significant fish, wildlife, recreation and water values and will receive additional protection. Nearly all of the land will remain open for mineral development.

Climate: The Tanana basin includes some of the warmest and coldest areas of the state. The continental climate is characterized by cold, dry winters and warm but relatively moist summers. The mean July daytime high temperature in Fairbanks is 72°F, while the mean January daytime low in Tok is -30°F. Precipitation averages about 12 inches each year for the entire region; however, variations in altitude influence the amount of precipitation.

Wildlife: The Tanana River valley provides habitat for moose, caribou, bears and bison. A large population of beaver is found in the region, especially in the Chena River drainage. Other furbearers include muskrat, mink, red fox, lynx, marten, land otter, weasel and wolverine. Three species of salmon—king, chum and coho—are found in the Tanana River drainage. Arctic grayling and northern pike are found throughout the clear-water streams and lakes of the area. Waterfowl nest on the lakes, sloughs and ponds scattered throughout the lowlands. Spruce grouse are found in the forested regions; peregrine falcons have been reported in the bluffs along the Tanana River; and bald eagles are known to overwinter in the southeastern section near the Delta-Clearwater rivers.

Activities: Fishing, hunting, hiking, boating, cross-country skiing, dog mushing, snow-machining and some ATV use are pursued throughout the forest. Some 250 miles of trails have been identified in the forest, some of which are maintained. The Tanana Basin Trails Management Plan, which is not complete, inventories trails in the borough, several of which are located within the State Forest, and will provide more detailed information on existing trails and plans for their management. Many rivers, lakes and streams within the forest offer sportfishing and boating opportunities.

Accommodations: The Eagle Trail State Recreation Site is the only developed facility within the State Forest and has 40 campsites. Additional campgrounds, public use cabins, boat launches and waysides are planned. Eighteen communities are located near the forest, including Fairbanks, the second largest city in Alaska. Supplies, lodging, charter transportation, rentals and guides are available in Fairbanks or may be found in some of the smaller communities.

Access: Approximately 85 percent of the forest is located within 20 miles of a highway, making it one of the more accessible public lands in the Interior. Rivers and trails throughout the river basin provide additional access to areas within the forest.

For more information: Department of Natural Resources, Northern Region, Division of Forestry, 3700 Airport Way, Fairbanks, AK 99709-4699; phone (907) 451-2660, fax (907)

451-2690. Other sources of information include: Alaska Department of Fish and Game, 1300 College Road, Fairbanks, AK 99709, phone (907) 452-1531; Department of Natural Resources, Division of Parks and Outdoor Recreation, 3700 Airport Way, Fairbanks, AK 99709, phone (907) 451-2695; or the Fairbanks North Star Borough, P.O. Box 71267 (809 Pioneer Rd.), Fairbanks, AK 99707, phone (907) 459-1000, www.co.fairbanks.ak.us.

White Mountains National Recreation Area

The one-million-acre White Mountains National Recreation Area, managed by the Bureau of Land Management, is located between the Elliott and Steese highways, approximately 30 miles north of Fairbanks in the Yukon-Tanana Highlands. It is the largest NRA in the U.S.; the only NRA in the nation managed by the BLM; and the only NRA in Alaska. It was established in 1980 as part of the Alaska National Interest Lands Conservation Act (ANILCA).

Composed of white limestone and named for their color by early prospectors in the area, the White Mountains peak at 5,200 feet elevation and extend 70 miles from Preacher Creek on the east to Beaver Creek on the west. The area is notable for its scenery and for its year-round recreation, with camping, fishing, hiking, gold panning and river floating in summer, and snowmobiling, skiing, skijoring and dog sledding in winter.

Climate: From May to September, temperatures may range from 20°F to 80°F, with snow possible at any time at higher elevations. Wind can become a problem in areas with little shelter, such as treeless ridges on the summer trails. Winter temperatures may dip as low as -70°F. Any wind will drop the chill factor to a critical level, so adequate protection from the cold and wind is necessary at all times.

Activities: The BLM maintains more than 200 miles of winter trails and 40 miles of summer hiking trails within the recreation area. Snowmachiners, dog mushers, cross-country skiers, skijorers and snowshoers use the winter trails. (See "Rules of the Road" this section for winter travel etiquette.) The BLM uses snow machines to maintain the winter trails although the trails are not always packed early in the season; check with the BLM office in Fairbanks for current trail conditions. Also check with the BLM for information on summer use of off-highway vehicles within the recreation area.

Winter trails in the recreation area follow: Bear Creek, Big Bend, Cache Mountain Loop, Colorado Creek, Fossil Creek, Fossil Gap, Lower Nome Creek, McKay Creek, Moose Creek, Ski Loop, Trail Creek, Wickersham Creek and Windy Creek. Summer hiking trails are: Summit, Fossil Gap (to Caribou Bluff Cabin), Lower Nome Creek, McKay Creek, Quartz Creek, Trail Creek (to Lee's cabin), Wickersham Creek (to the trail shelter) and Windy Creek (to Wolf Run Cabin). (See individual trail descriptions under Hiking Trails this section.) The trails connect with 10 recreation cabins and 1 trail shelter managed by the BLM. Fred Blixt Cabin is accessible via the

Rules of the Road

1. When snowmachines meet skiers and mushers head-on, the snowmachines should pull off the trail, turn their engines off, and let dog teams, skijorers and skiers pass.

2. When approaching other trail users from behind, snowmachines should slow down and wait until the traveler in front signals he is ready for you to pass.

3. Skiers and skijorers should get off the trail and restrain their dogs when dog teams pass.

4. Dog mushers should pull off the trail to allow faster dog teams to pass.

5. Operating a snowmachine or ATV while intoxicated is prohibited.

Elliott Highway. (See descriptions under Cabins this section.)

White Mountains NRA also includes major portions of Beaver Creek, a national wild and scenic river that flows through the heart of the White Mountains. Called the longest "road-to-road" float trip in North America, it is more than 360 river miles between road put in and takeout points on this Class I river. It can take up to 3 weeks to complete this float. (See description of Beaver Creek in the River Running section for more details.)

Nome Creek Valley is also included in White Mountains NRA (see Nome Creek Valley this section).

Access: The Elliott and Steese highways access White Mountains National Recreation Area. Wickersham Dome Trailhead at Milepost 28 Elliott Highway is the start of the Wickerhsam Creek and Summit trails, which connect with the network of trails within the recreation area. Colorado Creek Trailhead is at Milepost 57 Elliott Highway. And Fred Blixt Cabin is at Milepost 62.3 Elliott Highway. McKay Creek Trail, Lower Nome Creek Trail and the Davidson Ditch Trailhead are located along the Steese Highway. Access to the Nome Creek Valley area is also from the Steese Highway at Milepost 57.3.

For more information: Bureau of Land Management, 1150 University Ave., Fairbanks, AK 99709; phone (907) 474-2250, http://aurora.ak.blm.gov/WhiteMtns/.

For details on access and accommodations, see The MILEPOST®, a complete guide to Alaska's road system.

Yukon-Charley Rivers National Preserve

Designated a preserve in December 1980, the 2.5-million-acre Yukon-Charley Rivers National Preserve is located along the Canadian border in east-central Alaska. The preserve protects a 115-mile stretch of the Yukon River and the entire 106 miles of the wild and scenic Charley River. The preserve also protects numerous historic sites along the Yukon River that date from the 1898 gold rush.

The Yukon flows by old cabins and the remains of old mining camps. The Park Service is preserving a dredge, camp buildings and equipment as a clue to the region's mining history. Gold was discovered on Coal Creek in the early 1900s by miner Frank Slaven. His claims were later sold, and the company that bought them had a dredge shipped up from San Francisco. It was the first gold dredge to operate in Yukon-Charley and continued operation until the early 1960s. A roadhouse named for Slaven is on the National Register of Historic Places. It opened about 1930, taking advantage of the traffic along the Yukon River and up Coal Creek. The main mining camp on Coal Creek is also part of the donation. The camp includes 10 cabins that served a variety of uses. They were built on skids, so they could be moved along with the floating gold dredge. Some gold discoveries at Circle and other eastern Yukon localities preceded the Klondike gold rush.

By contrast, the Charley River watershed is virtually untouched by modern man. It flows crystal clear and is considered to be one of Alaska's finest recreational streams. The 2 rivers merge between the early-day boom towns of Eagle and Circle.

The preserve also protects paleontological and archeological sites in the Yukon-Charley Rivers basin, where people have been present for at least 10,000 years. Much of the preserve was unglaciated during the last ice age, and researchers expect to find sites older than 10,000 years. Because it was in the ice-free corridor, the area also contains a diverse cross section of vegetation.

Climate: The preserve is located in a subarctic climate zone, characterized by exceptionally cold winters, relatively warm summers, low annual precipitation and generally light winds. Summer highs average in the low 70s and lows in the mid-40s. However, freezing at night can occur any month of the year at higher elevations. Winter lows can reach -40°F and lower for extended periods. Normal winter temperatures range from -5°F to -25°F. Precipitation is light, about 8 to 10 inches annually, mostly falling as rain in summer. Thunderstorms are common in summer. Snow cover is light but continues for about 7 months of the year. Breakup of the Yukon River ice usually occurs in early May. In mid-May, 24-hour daylight begins. The transition from summer to winter is rapid; peak fall colors occur in the high country in late August and by mid-September most aspens and birches at lower elevations have turned golden. Ice begins flowing in the Yukon in October, with freezeup usually by mid-November.

Wildlife: The preserve includes caribou from the Fortymile herd which migrate to Canada and back. A moderate number of moose browse along streams and lowland areas, while Dall sheep occupy heights above the Charley River. Other wildlife includes grizzly and black bears, wolves and many small mammals.

More than 200 species of birds have been reported to occur in the preserve, including bald and golden eagles, rough-legged hawks and gyrfalcons. Endangered Peregrine falcons nest in the high bluffs along the Yukon River. The preserve also contains some of North America's finest habitat for peregrine falcons, which nest in cliffs and rocks. Yukon-Charley lies along a major flyway for waterfowl that breed on the Yukon Flats and winter in the continental United States.

Fish in preserve waters include king salmon in July and chum salmon in September or October. A few coho salmon are also taken. Other species include sheefish, whitefish, northern pike and burbot. Sportfishing centers primarily on arctic grayling, found at the mouths of tributary streams early in the season and farther upstream as the summer progresses. Northern pike are found in the lower reaches of most tributary strearyis and in the back-water sloughs of the Yukon. Dolly Varden are found in one nameless tributary of the upper Charley River.

Activities: The river corridors make rafting the most popular recreational activity in the preserve.

Floating the 154 miles of the Yukon River from Eagle to Circle is the most popular means of visiting the preserve. Most travelers spend about 4 days on this section. July and August are the most popular months for floaters. (See also River Running this section.)

Most people prefer to float the Charley River in late June to mid-July. No fees or permits are required to use any of the rivers. Inflatable raft rentals, charter boat service and fixed-wing and helicopter charters are available in nearby communities.

The float on the Yukon River from Eagle to Circle is a great trip for a 1- or 2-week family vacation. Both Eagle and Circle are accessible by road. Besides river floating and camping, recreational opportunities in the preserve include hiking, fishing, wildlife observation and photography, cross-country skiing, dogsledding, snowmobiling and snowshoeing. Sport hunting is permitted in season.

The Park Service cautions that the preserve is a vast and sometimes hostile environment. The preserve's small staff can provide only minimal patrol or rescue services. Self-sufficiency is the rule; visitors are completely on their own once they leave the well-traveled Yukon River corridor. Weather conditions or equipment failure can often cause schedules to go awry; visitors should bring extra supplies to be prepared. As a safety precaution, visitors may leave a copy of their planned itinerary with the rangers at the Park Service office in Eagle. Also, local residents carry on subsistence activities within the preserve. Their camps and equipment are crucial to their livelihood and should be left undisturbed.

Accommodations: There are 6 public-use cabins along the Yukon River within the preserve (see Cabins this section). Food, gas, lodging and groceries are available in Eagle and Circle. Both communities also have campgrounds and public boat landings. There are no formal campgrounds in the preserve, but camping is permitted on any federally owned land. Campsites on river bars are recommended because there is usually a breeze to keep the insects at bay.

NOTE: Private land is located on both sides of the Yukon River from Calico Bluff near Eagle to Wood Island.

Access: The preserve is accessible primarily by small plane or boat from Eagle, 12 river miles south of the preserve on the Taylor Highway, or Circle, 14 river miles to the north on the Steese Highway. Both Eagle and Circle are easily accessible by auto or plane from Fairbanks. There are no roads or maintained trails within the preserve.

For more information: Stop by the headquarters for Yukon-Charley Rivers National Preserve, located in Eagle on the bank of the Yukon River at the end of the parade ground at Fort Egbert. Books and USGS maps are sold there, and a library of reference material is available. Or contact the Superintendent, Yukon-Charley Rivers National Preserve, P.O. Box 167, Eagle, AK 99738; phone (907) 547-2233, email YUCH_Eagle_Office@nps.gov, www.nps.gov/yuch/.

USGS maps: Eagle, Charley River, Big Delta, Circle.

Yukon Flats National Wildlife Refuge

This refuge, about 100 miles north of Fairbanks, encompasses more than 11 million acres in east-central Alaska. The area is primarily a complex of wetlands, more than 40,000 lakes, ponds and sloughs.

The refuge is bisected by the Yukon River, America's fifth largest river, which meanders for 300 miles through the refuge. Here, the river breaks free from canyon walls and spreads out through a vast floodplain. In the spring, millions of migrating birds converge on the flats before the ice moves from the river. The refuge has one of the highest densities of nesting waterfowl in North America and contributes more than 2 million ducks and geese to the continent's flyways.

The Porcupine River is the major tributary of the Yukon River within the refuge, joining the Yukon just downstream from Fort Yukon. Other tributaries include the Chandalar, Christian, Hadwenzic, Hodzana, Sheenjek and Dall rivers and Birch and Beaver creeks. Several of these rivers provide important spawning habitat for salmon.

Climate: Yukon Flats has a continental subarctic climate characterized by great seasonal extremes of temperature and daylight. Summer temperatures regularly top 90°F, and Fort Yukon holds the record high for the state of Alaska at 100°F. Winter minimums to -60°F and lows in excess of -70°F have been recorded. Precipitation is low, averaging about 6.5 inches annually at Fort Yukon. July and August are the wettest months. Freezeup usually occurs in October. Breakup occurs at Fort Yukon around May 15; larger lakes are not free of ice until later.

Wildlife: Mammals on the refuge include a substantial population of moose, as well as caribou, wolves, grizzly and black bear, marten, lynx, snowshoe hare, beaver, muskrat, some red fox and wolverine and Dall sheep in the White Mountains.

Chinook, coho and chum salmon from the Bering Sea pass through and spawn in the Flats each summer—the longest salmon run in the United States. Other fish found in refuge waters include Dolly Varden, arctic grayling, several species of whitefish, sheefish, burbot and northern pike.

Activities: Residents of Beaver, Birch Creek, Chalkyitsik, Circle, Fort Yukon, Stevens Village and Venetie use the refuge for subsistence activities, accounting for 90 percent of the public use of the refuge. Sport hunting and river floating account for visitor use of the refuge. There are considerable private holdings within the refuge, particularly along river corridors; contact the refuge office for the location of these lands to avoid trespassing.

Accommodations: There are no accommodations within the refuge. There are commercial visitor facilities at Fort Yukon and Circle but not at the other villages in the area.

Access: Yukon Flats Refuge can be reached by air and water. Scheduled commercial air service is available to all communities in the refuge. Charter air service to remote areas of the refuge is available in Fairbanks, Fort Yukon and Circle. A few bush airstrips, numerous lakes, and sand or gravel bars make most areas of the refuge accessible by light aircraft. Local residents use riverboats, canoes, kayaks and rafts for river floating and other recreational activities. There is no road access to the refuge although the Dalton Highway runs adjacent to the refuge's southwestern boundary.

For more information and assistance in planning a trip to the refuge: Refuge Manager, Yukon Flats National Wildlife Refuge, 101 12th Avenue, Room 264, Fairbanks, AK 99701; phone (907) 456-0440, toll free (800) 531-0676, fax (907) 456-0447; e-mail YukonFlats@fws.gov, http://YukonFlats.fws.gov.

ARCTIC

Air Charters
Ambler Air Service, Box 7, Ambler 99786; (907) 445-2121.
Arctic Air Guides Flying Service, Box 94, Kotzebue 99752; (907) 442-3030.
Brooks Range Aviation, Box 10, Bettles 99726; (907) 692-5444, www.brooksrange.com.
Cape Smythe Air; (907) 659-2743.
Coyote Air, Box 9053, Colfoot 99701; (907) 678-5995, (800) 252-0603, www.flycoyote.com.
Inuit Air, Box 285, Kotzebue 99752-0285; (907) 442-2505.
Northwestern Aivation, Box 741, Kotzebue 99752; (907) 442-3525, www.alaskaonyourown.com.
Wright Air Service, 3842 University Ave. S., Fairbanks 99709; (907) 474-0502.

River Running
Alaska Wilderness Canoe Trips, Box 82293, Fairbanks 99708; (907) 455-7331.
Equinox Wilderness Expeditions, 618 West 14th Ave., Anchorage 99501; (907) 274-9087.
Kobuk River Charters, Box 47, Kiana 99749; (907) 475-2140.

Wilderness Lodges
Bettles Lodge, Box 27, Bettles 99726; (907) 692-5111, www.bettleslodge.com.
Iniakuk Lake Wilderness Lodge, Box 80424, Fairbanks 99708; (907) 479-6354, www.gofarnorth.com.
Kiana Lodge, Box 89, Kiana 99749; (907) 333-5866, www.alaskaoutdoors.com/kiana/.
Peace of Selby Wilderness; (907) 672-3206, www.alaskawilderness.net.

INTERIOR

Air Charters
Atkins Guiding & Flying Service, Box 22, Cantwell 99729; (907) 768-2143.
Circle Air, Box 35, Central 99730; (907) 520-5223, www.circleair.com.
Denali Air, Box 82, Denali Park 99755; (907) 683-2261, www.denaliair.com.
Denali Flying Service, Box 1017, Willow 99688; (907) 495-5899, www.denaliflying.com.
Doug Geeting Aviation, Box 42, Talkeetna 99676; (907) 733-2366, (800) 770-2366, www.alaskaairtours.com.

ERA Helicopters; (800) 843-1947, www.eraaviation.com.
40-Mile Air, Box 539, Tok 99780; (907) 883-5191.
K2 aviation, Box 545, Talkeetna 99676; (907) 733-2291, (800) 764-2291, www.flyk2.com.
Larry's Flying Service, Box 72348, Fairbanks 99707; (907) 474-9169, www.larrysflying.com.
McKinley Air Service, Talkeetna; (800) 564-1765, www.alaska.net/~mckair.
Pere Air; (907) 683-6033, (877) 683-6033, www.pereair.com.
Talkeetna Aero Services, Box 433, Talkeetna 99676; (907) 733-2899, (800) 660-2688, www.talkeetnaaero.com.
Talkeetna Air Taxi, Box 73, Talkeetna 99676; (800) 533-2219, www.alaska.net/~flytat.
Tanana Air Service, 3730 S. University Ave., Fairbanks; (907) 474-0301.
Warbelow's Air Ventures, 3758 University Ave. S., Fairbanks 99709; (907) 474-4683, www.warbelows.com.
Wright Air Service, 3842 University Ave. S., Fairbanks 99709; (907) 474-0502.

Fishing
Alaska Fishing & Raft Adventures, 269 Topside Rd., Fairbanks 99712; (907) 455-7238, (800) 890-3229, www.aktours.net.
Arctic Grayling Guide Service, Box 83707, Fairbanks 99708; (907) 479-0479, www.wildernessfishing.com.
Deltana Outfitters, Box 1538, Delta Junction 99737; (907) 895-5006, www.deltana.com
Easy Does It Charters, Box 482, Delta Junction 99737; (907) 895-5260, www.easydoesitcharters.com.
Li'L Fox Charters, 2343 Steese Hwy., Fox 99712; (907) 460-6566.
Marina Air, 1195 Shypoke, Fairbanks 99709; (907) 479-5684, www.akpub.com/fhwag/marina.html.
Tozitna River Huskies, Box 169, Tanana 99777; (907) 366-7245, email tozriver@adl.com.
Wilderness Enterprises, Chena Hot Springs Road; (907) 488-7517.

Horseback
Bald Eagle Ranch Bed and Breakfast, Delta Junction; (907) 895-5270, www.baldeagleranchbb.com.
D & S Alaskan Trail Rides, Mile 132.9 Parks Hwy.; (907) 733-2205, www.alaskantrailrides.com.

Denali Saddle Safaris, Box 435, Healy 99743; (907) 683-1200.

Mountaineering
Alaska Denali Guiding, Box 566, Talkeetna 99676; (907) 733-2649, www.denaliexpeditions.com.
Alaska Mountaineering School, Box 13, Talkeetna 99676; (907) 733-1016, www.climbalaska.org.
Alpine Guides Alaska, HC 31 Box 5118, Wasilla 99654-9703; (907) 373-3051, www.alaska.net/~alpineak.

River Running
Alaska Wilderness Canoe Trips, Box 82293, Fairbanks 99708; (907) 455-7331.
Borealis River Guides, 2417 Fantail Circle, Anchorage 99515; (907) 783-2518, www.alaskariverrafting.com.
Denali Outdoor Center, Box 170, Denali Park 99755; (907) 683-1925, (888) 303-1925, www.denalioutdoorcenter.com.
Denali Raft Adventures, Draw 190 MP, Denali Park 99755; (907) 683-2234, (888) 683-2234, www.denaliraft.com.
Raft Denali, Box 500, Healy 99743-0500; (907) 683-7238, (800) 789-7238,www.raftdenali.com.
Too-Loo'Uk River Guides, Box 106, Denali Park 99755; (907) 683-1542,www.akrivers.com.
Water Walkers Rafting, Box 82862, Fairbanks 99708; (907) 452-4594, www.waterwalkersrafting.com.

Wilderness Lodges
Anvik River Lodge, Box 109, Anvik 99558; (907) 663-6324, www.anviklodge.com.
Camp Denali, Denali Park; (907) 683-2290.
Denali Backcountry Lodge, Kantishna; (800) 8841-0692, www.denalilodge.com/mp.
Denali Wilderness Lodge, Denali Park; www.denaliwildernesslodge.com/mp.
North Face Lodge, Denali Park; (907) 683-2290.
Kantishna Roadhouse, Kantishna; (800) 942-7420, www.KantishnaRoadhouse.com.
Salcha River Guest Camp, 2376 Nugget Loop, Fairbanks 99709; (907) 455-6244, www.salchariver.com.

SOUTHCENTRAL

Air Charters
Bald Mountain Air Service, Homer; (800 478-7969, www.baldmountainair.com.
Bear Lake Air & Guide Service, Box 1802, Seward 99664; (907) 224-5985, www.seward-alaska.com/bearlakeair.
Beluga Lake Float Plane Service, Box 2072,

Homer 99603; (907) 235-8256.
Copper Valley Air Service, Box 234, Glennallen 99588; (907) 822-4200, www.coppervalleyair.com.
Cordova Air Srvice, Box 528, Cordova 99574; (907) 424-3289.
Denali Flying Service, Box 1017, Willow 99688; (907) 495-5899, www.denaliflying.com.
Doug Geeting Aviation, Box 42, Talkeetna 99676; (907) 733-2366, (800) 770-2366, www.alaskaairtours.com.
Ellis Air Taxi, Box 106, Glennallen 99588; (907) 822-3368, www.ellisair.com.
Era; (800) 866-8394, www.eraaviation.com.
Kachemak Bay Flying Service, Inc., Box 1769, Homer 99603; (907) 235-8924, www.alaskaseaplanes.com.
Ketchum Air Service, Inc., 4261 Floatplane Dr., Anchorage 99502; (907) 243-5525.
K2 aviation, Box 545, Talkeetna 99676; (907) 733-2291, (800) 764-2291, www.flyk2.com.
Lee's Air Taxi, HC01 Bo 2660, Glennallen 99588; (907) 822-3343,
McCarthy Air, McCarthy; (907) 554-4440.
McKinley Air Service, Talkeetna; (800) 564-1765, www.alaska.net/~mckair.
Rust's Flying Service, Box 190325, Anchorage 99519; (907) 243-1595, www.flyrusts.com.
Smokey Bay Air, Box 457, Homer; (907) 235-1511.
Talkeetna Aero Services, Box 433, Talkeetna 99676; (907) 733-2899, (800) 660-2688, www.talkeetnaaero.com.
Talkeetna Air Taxi, Box 73, Talkeetna 99676; (800) 533-2219, www.alaska.net/~flytat.
Talon Air Service, Inc. Box 1109, Soldotna 99669; (907) 262-8899.
Trail Ridge Air, Inc., Box 111377, Anchorage 99511; (907) 248-0838, www.trailridgeair.com.
Willow Air Service, Mile 70 Parks Hwy.; (800) 478-6370.
Wrangell Mountain Air, McCarthy; (907) 554-4411, (800) 478-1160, www.WrangellMountainAir.com.

Fishing
Afishunt Charters, Box 39388, Ninilchik 99639; (800) 347-4114, www.afishunt.com.
Alaska Sunrise Fishing Adventures, Box 205, Sterling 99672; (800) 818-1250, www.alaskasunrisefishing.com.
Aurora Charters, Box 241, Seward 99664; (907) 224-3968, (888) 586-8420, www.auroracharters.com.
Backlash Charters, Seward; (800) 295-4396, www.seward.net/~backlash.
Bear Paw Charters, Box 694, Anchor Point 99556; (907) 235-5399, email bearpaw@xyz.net.

Big Sky Charter & Fish Camp, Mile 82.5
Sterling Hwy.; (907) 252-9496, (877) 536-2425,
www.kenaiguide.com.
The Bookie, Box 195, Homer 99603;
(907) 235-1581, (888) 335-1581,
www.alaskabookie.com.
Bread 'N Butter Charters, Whittier; (888) 472-2396, www.alaska.net/~junebbak.
Bruce Nelson's Float Fishing Service, Box
545, Cooper Landing 99572; (907) 595-1313.
Capt. Bob's Charters, Seard; (907) 242-4102,
www.alaskafishing.com/captbobs/.
Cap'n George's Charters, Box 2842, Homer
99603; (907) 235-4801, (800) 593-8110,
www.capngeorge.com.
Captain Pete's, Box 3353, Homer 99603; (907)
235-2911, www.captpete.com.
Central Charters Booking Agency, Homer;
(907) 235-7847, (800) 478-7847,
www.centralcharter.com.
Che'nai Charters, Seward: (907) 224-8766,
www.chenai.com.
Chihuly's Charters, Box 39294, Ninilchik
99639; (907) 567-3374,
www.ptialaska.net/~chihuly/.
Clive's Fishing Guide Service, Mile 156.8
Sterling Hwy., Anchor Point; (907) 235-1236,
http://puffin.ptialaska.net/~clives.
Cook Inlet Charters, Box 39292, Ninilchik
99639; (907) 567-7335,
www.cookinletcharters.com.
Deep Creek Fishing Club, Box 410, Ninilchik
99639; (907) 567-7373,
http://alaskafishinglodge.com.
Denali Anglers, Box 77, Talkeetna 99676;
(907) 733-1505, www.denalianglers.com.
EZ Limit Guide Service, Box 4278, Soldotna
99669; (907) 262-6169,
www.alaskafishing.com/ezlimit.
The Fish House Fishing Charters, Box 1209,
Seward 99664; (907) 224-3674.
The Fish Hut Charters & Lodging, Kenai;
(877) 827-2675, www.fishhut.net.
Fisherman's Choice Charters, Box 940276,
Houston 99694; (800) 989-8707,
www.akfishermanschoice.com.
Fishtale Charters, Box 101, Anchor Point
99556; (907) 235-6944,
www.fishtalecharters.com.
Great Alaska Fish Camp, 3381 Sterling Hwy.,
Sterling 99672; (800) 544-2261,
www.greatalaska.com.
Grove's Klutina River King Salmon Charters,
(907) 833-5822, (800) 770-5822,
www.alaskan.com/groves.
Harry Gaines Kenai River Fishing Guide, Box
624, Kleani 99611; (888) 262-5097,
www.harrygaines.com.
Heavenly Sights Charters, Box 2545,

Soldotna 99669; (800) 479-7371,
www.heavenlysights.com.
Hi-Lo Charters & Riverside Lodge, Kenai;
(800) 757-9333, www.hilofishing.com.
Ingram's Sport Fishing Cabins, Box 748,
Cooper landing 99572; (866) 595-1213,
www.kenairiverlodging.com.
Inlet Charters, Box 2082, HOmer 99603; (800)
770-6126, www.halibutcharters.com.
Irish Lord Charters, Box 545, Kasilof 99610;
(907) 262-9512, (800) 515-2055.
Johnson Bros. Guides & Outfitters, 44526
Sterling Hwy., Soldotna 99669; (907) 262-5357.
J & J Smart Charters, Box 23, Ninilchik
99639; (907) 567-3320, (888) 425-4288,
www.alaskaoutdoors.com/Smart.
Jeff King's Budget Charters, Box 2711,
Soldotna 99669; (907) 262-4564, (888) 578-5333, www.alaska.net/~lakerfsh.
Kenai Cache Tackle L& Guiding, Box 533,
Cooper Landing 99572; (907) 595-1401,
www.kenaicache.com.
Klutina Salmon Charters, Box 78, Copper
Center 99573; (907) 822-3991,
www.klutinacharters.com.
Leisure Time Charters, Box 155, Ninilchik
99639; (907) 567-3407.
Luck of the Irish Charters, Valdez;
(907) 835-4338.
Mahay's Riverboat Service, Box 705,
Talkeetna 99676; (800) 736-2210.
Ninilchik Charters, Box 39538-MP, Ninilchik
99639-0638; (907) 567-7321, (888) 290-3507,
www.ninilchik.com.
Ninilchik Salt-Water Charters; (800) 382-3611, www.alaskabigfish.com.
North Country Halibut Charters, Box 889,
Homer 99603; (907) 235-7620, (800) 770-7620,
www.northcountrycharters.com.
Northern Comfort Charters, Valdez; (907)
835-3070, (800) 478-9884,
www.northerncomfortcharter.com.
O'Fish'ial Charters, Ninilchik; (907) 567-7314,
(888) 697-3474, www.ofishial.com.
R & D Charters, Box 1972 Soldotna 99669;
(907) 262-6601.
**Rod 'N Real Alaskan Sportfishing Guides &
Outfitters**, 266 Redwood Court, Soldotna
99669; (907) 262-6064,
www.alaska.net/~rodnreal.
Roe's Charter Service, Box 401, Ninilchik
99639; (907) 567-3496, (888) 567-3496,
www.alaskafishingcharter.com.
Sablefish Charters, Box 1588, Seward 99664;
(907) 224-3283, (800) 357-2253.
Sea Mist Charters, Prince William Sound;
(877) 688-2166.
Silver Fox Charters, Box 402, Homer 99603;
(907) 235-8792, www.silverfoxcharters.com.

Tacklebuster Charters, Homer; (800) 789-5155, www.tacklebuster.com.
Talkeetna River Guides, Box 563, Talkeetna 99676; (800) 353-2677, www.alaska.net/~trg/trg_dir/.
Talkeetna Riverboat Service, Box 622, Talkeetna 99676; (907) 733-3336.
Tim Berg's Alaskan Fishing Adventures, Kenai Peninsula; (800) 548-3474, www.alaskanfishing.com.
Tom's Cabins & Guide Service, Box 2102, Soldotna 99669; (907) 262-3107, www.fishkenai.com.
Trophy Charters, Box 1775, Homer 99603; (800) 770-6400, www.bobstrophycharters.com.
Vader Charters, Ninilchik; (877) 303-7466, www.Vader-Charters.com
Willow Creek Outfitters, Mile 71.4 Parks Hwy.; (907) 495-3474, (800) 478-6370.

Horseback
Alaska Horsemen Trail Adventures, Kenai Peninsula; (907) 595-1806, www.arctic.net/~horses.
Grizzly Lake Ranch, Box 340, Gakona 99586; (907) 822-5214.
Hicks Creek Roadhouse, HC 3 Box 8410, Palmer 99645; (907) 745-8213.
Tak Outfitters, Box 66, Moose Pass 99631; (907) 288-3640, www.HorsebackAlaska.com.

Mountaineering
Alpine Guides Alaska, HC 31, Box 5118, Wasilla 99654-9703; (907) 373-3051, www.alaska.net/~alpineak.
Mica Guides, Mile 102 Glenn Highway; (800) 956-6422, www.micaguides.com.
St. Elias Alpine Guides, McCarthy; (907) 554-4445, www.steliasguides.com.

River Running
Alaska River Adventures, Box 725, Cooper Landing 99572; (907) 595-2000, www.alaskariveradventures.com.
Copper Oar, McCarthy; (907) 566-0771.
Chugach Outdoor Center; (907) 277-7238, (866) 277-7238, www.alaskaraft.com.
Class V Whitewater Inc., Girdwood; (907) 783-2004, www.alaskanrafting.com.
Denali Floats, Box 330, Talkeetna 99676; (907) 733-2384.
Equinox Wilderness Expeditions, 618 West 14th Ave., Anchorage 99501; (907) 274-9087.
Nova; (800) 746-5753, www.novalaska.com.
Osprey Expeditions, HC 60 Box 246Z, Copper Center 99573; (907) 822-5422, www.ospreyexpeditions.com.
Ouzel Expeditions, Box 935, Girdwood 99587; (907) 783-2216, www.ouzel.com.

River Wrangellers, Box 146, Gakona 99586; (907) 822-3967, www.alaskariverwrangellers.com

Sea Kayaking
Alaska Canoe Base & Kayak, Box 3547, Homer 99603; (907) 235-2090, www.alaskapaddler.com.
Alaska Kayak Camping Company, Box 1101, Seward 99664; (907) 224-6056, www.seward.net/kayakcamp.
Alaska Sea Kayakers, Box 770, Whittier 99693; (907) 472-2534, (877) 472-2534, email alaskaseakayakers@yahoo.com.
Anadyr Adventures, Box 1821, Valdez 99686; (907) 835-2814, (800) 865-2925, www.anadyradventures.com.
Kayak & Custom Adventures Worldwide, Box 2249, Seward 99664; (907) 258-3866, (800) 288-3134, www.kayakAK.com.
Keystone Outfitters, Box 1486, Valdez 99686; (907) 835-2606, www.alaskawhitewater.com.
Panagea Adventures, Valdez; (907) 835-8442, (800) 660-9637, www.alaskasummer.com.
Sunny Cove Sea Kayaking Co., Box 3332, Seward 99664; (907) 224-8810, (800) 770-9119, www.sunnycove.com.

Wilderness Lodges
Great Alaska Adventure Lodge; (800) 544-2261, www.greatalaska.com.
Kenai Fjords Wilderness Lodge, Box 1889, Seward 99664; (800) 478-8068, www.kenaifjords.com.
Kenai River Drifters Lodge, Box 141551, Anchoage 99514; (907) 595-5555, www.drifterslodge.com.
Kenai River Sportfishing Lodge, Cooper landing; (800) 478-4100, www.alaskawildland.com/mp.
Kennicott Glacier Lodge, Box 103940, Anchorage 99510; (800) 582-5128, www.KennicottLodge.com.
Otter Cove Resort; (907) 235-7770, www.ottercoveresort.com.
Quiet Place Lodge, Box 6474, Halibut Cove 99603; (907) 296-2212, www.quietplace.com.

SOUTHEAST

Air Charters
Air Excursions, Box 16, Gustavus 99826; (907) 697-2375.
Alaska Fly N' Fish Charters, 9604 Kelly Court, Juneau 99801; (907) 790-2120, www. alaskabyair.com.
Alaska Seaplanes, 1873 Shell Simmons Drive, Juneau 99801; (907) 789-3331, (800) 478-3360, www.akseaplanes.com

Gulf Air Taxi, Box 367, Yakutat 99689; (907) 784-3240.

Haines Airways Inc., Box 470, Haines 99827; (907) 766-2646, (877) 359-2467, www.hainesairways.com.

L.A.B. Flying Service Inc., Box 272, Haines 99827; (907) 766-2222, (800) 426-0543, www.haines.ak.us/lab.

Mountain Flying Service, Box 1404, Haines 99827; (907) 766-3007, www.flyglacierbay.com.

Skagway Air Service, Box 357, Skagway; (907) 983-2218, www.skagwayair.com.

Temsco Helicopters, Inc.; (877) 789-9501, www.temscoair.com.

Ward Air, Juneau Airport; (907) 789-9150.

Wings of Alaska, 8421 Livingston Way, Juneau 99801; (907) 789-0790, www.wingsofalaska.com.

Fishing

Alaska Angling, Box 1142, Petersburg 99833; (907) 772-4499.

Alaska Best Fishing, Inc., Box 1312, Craig 99921; (888) 826-8500, www.alaskabestfishing.com.

Fairweather Fishing and Guide Service, Box 164, Gustavus 99826; (907) 235-3844.

Howard Charters, Box 54, Pelican 99832; (907) 735-2207, (877) 254-8433, www.HowardCharters.com.

Inlet Cafe Charters, Box 93, Pelican 99832; (907) 735-2282.

John Latham Guide & Outfitter, Box 245, Yakutut 99689; (907) 784-3287, www.johnlathum.com.

Ketchikan Plum Tree Inn & Charter, (907) 247-6500.

Northern Lights Charters, Box 793, Ward Cove 99928; (907) 247-8488, www.ktn.net/nick.

Northern Star Charters & Lodge, Box 24, Elfin Cove 99825; (907) 239-2250.

Pelican Charters, Box 98, Pelican 99832; (907) 735-2460, www.Pelicancharters.com.

River Running

Chilkat Guides, Ltd., Box 170, Haines 99827; (907) 766-2491, www.raftalaska.com.

Skagway Float Tours, Box 1321, Skagway 99840; (907) 9893-3688, www.skagwayfloat.com

Sea Kayaking

Alaska Discovery Wilderness Adventures, 5310 Glacier Hwy, Juneau 99801; (800) 586-1911, www.akdiscovery.com.

Auk Ta Shaa Discovery, 76 Egan Drive, Juneau 99801; phone (907) 586-8687.

(Auke Bay Kayak Rentals, Auke Bay Harbor, Box 21734, Juneau 99801; (907) 790-6545, www.Kayaktour.com .

Coastal Island charters, Box 1897, Wrangell 99929; (907) 874-2014, www.alaskacic.com.

Deishu Expeditions, Box 1406, Haines 99827; (907) 766-2427, www.seakayaks.com.

Glacier Bay Sea Kayaks, Box 26, Gustavus 99826; (907) 697-2414

Sea Otter Kayak Glacier Bay, Box 228, Gustavus 99826; (907) 697-3007, www.he.net/seaotter.

Sea Tours Alaska, Box 992, Craig 99921; (907) 826-2210, www.seatoursalaska.com.

Sitka Sound Ocean Adventures, Box 1242, Sitka 99835; (907) 747-6375.

South Passage Outfitters, Box 1967, Port Townsend, WA 98368; (360) 385-3417, www.icystrait.com.

Southeast Exposure, Box 9143, Ketchikan 99901; (907) 225-8829, www.southeastexposure.com.

Southeast Sea Kayaks, 5 Salmon Landing, Ketchikan 99901; (800) 471-1262.

Spirit Walker Expeditions, Box 240, Gustavus 99826; (907) 697-2266, www.seakayakalaska.com.

Tongass Kayak Adventures, Box 2169, Petersburg 99833; (907) 772-4600, tongasskayak.com.

Wilderness Lodges

Admiralty Island Wilderness Homestead, Four Crab Cove, Funter Bay 99850; (907) 789-4786, www.ptialaska.net/~nwart.

Alaska King Lodge, Prince of Wales Island; (877) 471-0684, www. safariworldadv.com.

Annie Mae Lodge, Box 55, Gustavus 99826; (907) 697-2346, (800) 478-2356, www.anniemae.com.

The Cove Lodge, Box 17, Elfin Cove 99825; (907) 239-2205.

Coffman Cove Cabins, Prince of Wales Island; (907) 329-2251.

El Capitan Lodge, Box 9817, Ketchikan 99950; (800) 770-5464, www.elcapitanlodge.com

Elfin Cove Sportfishing Lodge, Box 44, Elfin Cove 99825; (907) 239-2212, www.elfincove.com.

Fireweed Lodge, Box 116, Klawock 99924; (907) 755-2930.

F.I.S.H.E.S, Box 245, Hoonah 99829; (907) 945-3327, www.fishes@hoonah.net.

Glacier Bay Country Inn, Box 5, Gustavus 99826; (800) 628-0912, www.glacierbayalaska.com.

Fishermen's Inn, Box 8092, Port Alexander 99836; (907) 568-2399,

www.fishermensinn.com.
George Inlet Lodge, 11728 So. Tongass Hwy., Ketchikan 99901; (888) 550-6077, www.georgeinletlodge.com.
Glacier Bay Bear Track Inn, Box 255, Gustavus 99826; (907) 697-2284, www.beartrackinn.com.
Gold Coast Lodge, Box 9629, Ketchikan 99901; (907) 225-8375, (800) 333-5992, www.goldcoastlodge.com.
Good River Bed and Breakfast, Box 37, Gustavus 99826; (907) 697-2241, www.goodriver.com.
Gustavus Inn at Glacier Bay, Box 60, Gustavus 99826; (800) 649-5220, www.gustavusinn.com.
Haida Way Lodge, Box 690, Craig 99921; (800) 347-4625.
The Hobbit Hole, Box 13, Elfin Cove 99825; (907) 723-8514, www.hobbitholealaska.com.
Humpback Lake Chalet in Misty Fjords, Box 6000, Ketchikan 99901; (907) 225-6684.
Inner Harbor Lodge, Box 38, Elfin Cove 99825; (907) 239-2245, www.innerharborlodge.com.
Johnny's East River Lodge, Box 433, Yakutat 99689; (907) 784-3287, www.johnnyeastriverlodge.com.
Laughing Raven Lodge, Box 8115, Port Alexander 94836; (907) 568-2266, wwwportAlexander.com.
Ravenswood Retreat Lodge, Box 22, Meyers Chuck 99903; (907) 946-8204, www.ravenswoodlodge.com.
Shearwater Lodge & Charters, Box 57, Elfin Cove 99825; (907) 239-2223.
Shelter Cove Lodge, Box 798, Craig 99921; (907) 826-2939, (888) 826-3474.
Snows Cove Lodge & Fishing Charters, 700 Water Street, Ketchikan 99901; (907) 225-5529.
Sportsmans Cove Lodge, Ketchikan 99901; (9800) 962-7889.
Sunnahae Lodge, Box 690 155, Craig 99921; (907) 826-4000.
Tanaku Lodge, Box 74, Elfin Cove 99825; (907) 239-2205.
Waterfall Resort, Box 6440, Ketchikan 99901; (907) 225-8530, (800) 544-5125, http://waterfallresort.com.
Weeping Trout Sports Resort, Box 129, Haines 99827; (907) 766-2827, www.weepingtrout.com.
Whales Cove Lodge, Box 101, Angoon 99820; (907) 788-3123.
Wooden Wheel Lodge, Box 118, Point Baker 99927; (888) 489-9288, www.woodenwheellodge.com.
Yes Bay Lodge, Box 8660, Ketchikan 99901; (907) 225-7906, (800) 999-0784.

SOUTHWESTERN

Air Charters
Branch River Air Service, 4540 Edingburgh Dr., Anchorage 99515; (907) 248-3539, www.branchriverair.com.
C-Air, Box 82, King Salmon 99613-0082; (907) 246-6318.
Chignik Airways, Box 13, Chignik Lagoon 99656; (907) 840-2212, email jamoore@gci.net.
Egli Air Haul, Inc., Box 169, King Salmon 99613; (907) 246-3554.
Harvey Flying Service, Box 3062, Kodiak 99615; (907) 487-2621.
Highline Air Service, 1829 Mill Bay Rd., Kodiak 99615; (907) 486-5155, www.highlineair.com.
Katmai Adventures, Inc., 2015 Merril Field Dr, Anchorage 99502; (907) 246-3000.
Katmai Air, 4125 Aircraft Dr., Anchorage 99502; (907) 243-5448, www.katmailand.com.
Kodiak Air Service, 415 Mill Bay Rd., Kodiak 99615; (907) 486-4446.
Lake Clark Air., Box 1, Port Alsworth 99653; (800) 662-7661, (907) 781-2211.
Lake Country Air, Inc., 48590 KSRM Ct., Kenai 99611; (907) 283-9432.
Peninsula Airways, Inc., 6100 Boeing Ave., Anchorage 99502; (907) 243-2485, www.penair.com.
Rick's Charter Service, Box 11, King Cove 99612; (907) 497-2343.
Sea Hawk Air, Inc., Box 3561, Kodiak 99615; (907) 486-8282, www.seahawkair.com.

Fishing/ Hunting
Alaska Trophy Adventures, Box 31, King Salmon 99613; (907) 246-8280.
Angler's Alibi, Box 271, King Salmon 99613; (907) 246-1510.
Chilaska, Box 47039, Pedro Bay 99647; (907) 571-1502, www.chilaska.com.
Katmai Fishing Adventures, Box 221, King Salmon 99613; (907) 246-8322, www.katmaifishing.com.
Ten Bears, Inc., Box 4123, Kodiak 99615; (907) 486-2200, www.tenbears.com.

Wilderness Lodges
Afognak Wilderness Lodge, General Delivery, Seal Bay 99697; (907) 486-6442, www.afognaklodge.com.
Alagnak Lodge, Box 351, King Salmon 99613; (907) 246-1505, www.alagnaklodge.com.
Alaska Rainbow Lodge, Box 39, King Salmon 99613; (907) 246-1504, www.alaskarainbowlodge.com.
Alaska's Enchanted Lake Lodge, Box 97, King

Salmon 99613; (907) 246-6878, www.enchantedlakelodge.com.

Bear Trail Lodge, Box 316, King Salmon 99613; (907) 246-2327, www.beartraillodge.com.

Bearfoot Alaska Resort and Lodge, Box 457, Dillingham 99576; (888) 684-0177, (907) 842-3440, www.bearfootalaska.com.

Branch River Lodge, Box 513, King Salmon 99613; (907) 246-7452, www.branchriverlodge.com.

Eagle Bluff Lodge, Box 11, King Salmon 99613-0011; (907) 246-4464, www.eagleblufflodge.com.

Fox Bay Lodge, Box 13, King Salmon 99613; (907) 246-6234, www.foxbaylodge.com.

Katmai Lodge., 1515 Pacific, Suite 201, Everett, WA 98201; (907) 439-3082, www.katmai.com.

Katmai Wilderness Lodge, Box 4332, Kodiak 99615; (907) 486-8767.

Ketok Lodge, Box 5014, Koliganek 99576; (907) 596-3408, www.home.gci.net/~ketoklodge.

Lodge at Hidden Basin-Kodiak Island, 2700 Nugget Lane, Anchorage 99516, (907) 345-7017, www.hiddenbasinalaska.com.

Mike Cusack's King Salmon Lodge, 3601 C St., Suite 1350, Anchorage 99503; (907) 277-3033, www.kingsalmonlodge.com.

Newhalen Lodge, Inc., 3851 Chiniak Bay Dr., Anchorage 99515; (907) 522-3355.

No See Um Lodge, Inc., Box 382, King Salmon 99613; (907) 246-3070, www.noseeumlodge.com.

Rapids Camp Lodge., #1 Rainbow Run, King Salmon 99613; (800) 624-6843, www.rapidscamplodge.com.

Rohrer Bear Camp., Box 2219, Kodiak 99615; (907) 486-5835, www.home.gci.net/~sportfishkodiak.

Royal Wolf Lodge, Box 299, King Salmon 99613; (907) 533-1507.

Whale Pass Lodge, Box 32, Port Lions 99550; (800) 456-3425, (907) 454-2500, www.whalepasslodge.com.

Wildman Lake Lodge., 2024 Stonegate Circle, Anchorage 99515; (907) 522-1164.

WESTERN

Air Charters

Andrew Airways, Inc., Box 1037, Kodiak 99615; (907) 487-2566, www.andrewairways.com.

Bay Air, Box 714, Dillingham 99576; (907) 842-2570, email bayair@nushtel.com.

Branch River Air Service, Box 545, King Salmon 99613; (907) 246-3437, www.branchriverair.com.

Iliamna Air Guides, Box 162, Iliamna 99606; (907) 571-1251.

Iliamna Air Taxi, Inc., Box 109, Iliamna 99606; (907) 571-1248.

Lake & Peninsula Airlines, 3323 Dry Creek, Port Alsworth 99653; (907) 781-2228.

Lake Clark Air, Box 1, Port Alsworth 99653; (907) 781-2211.

Peninsula Airways, Inc., 6100 Boeing Ave., Anchorage 99502; (907) 243-2485, www.penair.com.

Sea Hawk Air, Inc., Box 3561, Kodiak 99615; (907) 486-8282, www.seahawkair.com.

Tikchik Airventures, Box 71, Dillingham 99576; (907) 842-5841.

Wilderness Lodges

Alaska's Fishing Unlimited Lodge, Box 190301, Anchorage 99519; (907) 243-5899, www.alaskalodge.com.

Alaska's Lake Clark Inn, 1 Lang Lane, General Delivery, Port Alsworth 99563-9999; (907) 781-2224.

Alaska's Wilderness Lodge, Inc., 1 Wilderness Point, Port Alsworth 99653; (800) 835-8032, www.fishawl.com.

Bearfoot Alaska Resort and Lodge, Box 457, Dillingham 99576; (888) 684-0177, (907) 842-3440, www.bearfootalaska.com.

Iliaska Lodge, Inc., Box 228, Iliamna 99606; (907) 571-1221, www.iliaska.com.

Island Lodge, General Delivery, Port Alsworth 99653; (907) 349-3195, www.islandlodge.com.

Koksetna Wilderness Lodge, General Delivery. Port Alsworth 99653; (907) 781-2227.

Mission Lodge at Aleknagik, Inc., Box 165, Aleknagik 99555; (907) 842-2250, www.missionlodge.com.

Rainbow King Lodge, Box 106, Iliamna 99606; (907) 571-1277,www.rainbowking.com.

Rainbow River Lodge, Box 330, Iliamna 99606; (907) 571-1210, www.alaskarainbowriverlodge.com.

Redoubt Mountain Lodge, LLC, Box 56, Skwentna 99667; (907) 733-3034.

Sliver Salmon Creek Lodge, Box 3234, Soldotna 99669; (907) 252-5504, www.silversalmoncreek.com.

Stoney River Lodge, Inc., General Delivery, Stoney River 99577; (907) 526-5211, www.stoneyriverlodge.com.

Valhalla Lodge, Box 190583, Anchorage 99519; (907) 294-2250, www.valhallalodge.com.

Index

INDEX

INDEX

INDEX